MUNICH
THE PRICE OF PEACE

MUNICH
THE PRICE OF PEACE

by TELFORD TAYLOR

VINTAGE BOOKS
A DIVISION OF RANDOM HOUSE
NEW YORK

To the memory of
JOE BARNES
1907–1970

LIBRARY OF CONGRESS CATALOGING IN PUBLICATION DATA

Taylor, Telford.
Munich: the price of peace.

Reprint of the 1979 ed. published by Doubleday, Garden
City, N.Y.
1.   Munich four-power agreement, 1938.   2.   World War,
1939–1945—Causes.   I.   Title.
[D727.T37 1980]   940.53′12   80-11732
ISBN 0-394-74482-9 (pbk.)

Manufactured in the United States of America

ACKNOWLEDGMENTS

Crown copyright documents in the Public Record Office appear by permission of the Controller of H.M. Stationary Office.

From *For the President: Personal and Secret—Correspondence Between Franklin D. Roosevelt and William C. Bullitt,* edited by Orville H. Bullitt. Copyright© 1972 by Orville H. Bullitt. Reproduced by permission of Houghton Mifflin Company and Andre Deutsch, Ltd.

From *The Diaries of Sir Alexander Cadogan,* edited by David Dilks. Copyright © 1971 by the Executors of the Estate of the Late Sir Alexander Cadogan. Reprinted by permission of David Higham Associates, Ltd.

From *Old Men Forget: The Autobiography of Duff Cooper.* Copyright © 1954 by E. P. Dutton & Company. Reprinted by permission of E. P. Dutton & Company and Viscount Norwich.

From *The Life of Neville Chamberlain, by Keith Feiling.* Copyright © 1946, 1970 by Sir Keith Feiling. Reprinted by permission of Macmillan Publishers, Ltd., of London and Basingstoke, and Archon Books of Hamden, Connecticut.

From *Servir,* by General Maurice Gustave Gamelin. Paris: Librairie Plon, S.A., 1946. Translated by Telford Taylor. used by permission of Librairie Plon, S.A.

From *The Strategy of Appeasement,* by Keith Middlemas. Copyright © 1972 by Keith Middlemas. Reprinted by permission of George Weidenfeld & Nicholson, Ltd., and Times Books, a division of Quadrangle/The New York Times Book Co. From the unpublished diary of Sir Thomas Inskip. Used by permission of Viscount Caldecott.

From *Chief of Staff: The Diaries of Lieutenant–General Sir Henry Pownall,* Vol. I, 1933–40, edited by Brian Bond. Copyright © 1972, 1973 by Willoughby Gray and Brian Bond. Reprinted by permission of Leo Cooper, Ltd., of London, and Archon Books of Hamden, Connecticut.

From the unpublished papers of Colonel Truman Smith. Air Intelligence Activities: Office of the American Military Attaché, American Embassy, Berlin, Germany. Courtesy of the Manuscripts and Archives Department of Yale University Library.

From *Austrian Requiem,* by Kurt von Schuschnigg, translated by Franz von Hildebrand. Copyright © 1946 by G. P. Putnam's Sons. Reprinted by permission of G. P. Putnam's Sons.

From *Témoignages a l'histoire,* by Captain Paul Stehlin. Paris: Editions Robert Laffont, 1964. Translated by Telford Taylor. Used by permission of Editions Robert Laffont.

From *Diary, 1937–38,* by Galeazzo Ciano. London: Methuen, 1952. Reprinted by permission of Edda Ciano.

From *Baldwin,* by Keith Middlemas and John Barnes. Copyright © 1969 by Keith Middlemas and John Barnes. Reprinted by permission of George Weidenfeld & Nicolson, Ltd., and Macmillan Publishing Company, Inc.

Contents

INTRODUCTION   xi

Part I — MUNICH: SEPTEMBER 1938

1 Invitation to the Quadrille   1
2 En Route   14
3 Ring Around the Table in Munich   24
4 Euphoria   58

Part II — THE MISE EN SCÈNE: 1918–1936

5 The Dead Hand of Versailles   69
6 The Rise of the Third Reich   78
7 The Decline of the Third Republic   103
8 Sawdust Caesar   143
9 The Eastern Arena   170
10 For King and Country?   197

Part III — THE GERMAN SWORD UNSHEATHED: 1936–1938

11 Nazi Respectability and the Anti-Comintern Pact   255
12 The Spanish Civil War and the Condor Legion   272
13 November 5, 1937: The "Hossbach" Conference   294
14 The Fuehrer Takes Command   308
15 The Annexation of Austria   331
16 The Plan for the Conquest of Czechoslovakia   377

Part IV — HOW THE ISSUE WAS DRAWN: 1936–1938

17 Among Bohemia's Meadows and Forests   397
18 Among the Eastern Neighbors   411

19   The Road from Moscow to Prague Runs through Paris   430
20   The Road from Paris to Prague Runs through London   457
21   Edouard Daladier: Man of Indecision   504
22   Neville Chamberlain As Diplomat   535
23   Neville Chamberlain As Armorer   588
24   Neville Chamberlain: Man of Decision   617

Part V — THE CONFRONTATION: 1938

25   The Wehrmacht: On the March but Out of Step   681
26   Chamberlain At the Berghof   732
27   The Lone Eagle, the Voice of America, and the Voice of Empire   754
28   The Hard Sell   776
29   The Godesberg Ultimatum   795
30   If at First You Don't Succeed   831

Part VI — POSTLUDE AND RETROSPECT

31   Peace With Honor   899
32   Peace For Our Time   926
33   An Assessment of Munich   978

Who Was Who at Munich   26–27

Agreement Reached on September 29, 1938, between
Germany, the United Kingdom, France, and Italy   50

Order of Battle, German Air and Ground Forces, September 1938   1006

Notes   1008

Sources and Acknowledgments   1031

Bibliography   1034

Maps

Spain and its approaches, 1937   278–79

Deployment and destination of major German Army units for occupation of Austria in March 1938   364

Deployment of major German Army and Air Force headquarters for the attack on Czechoslovakia   708

Deployment of German Army and Air Force headquarters for "Green," location of Czech fortifications, and general location of Czech forces   710–11

Illustrations following pages 246, 438, 630, and 822

Index   1044

PRE-MUNICH
EUROPE
▭▭▭▭▭
Germany west of the Rhine
(the Rhineland), remilitarized by
Germany in March, 1936, and
Austria annexed by Germany
in March, 1938.

NORWAY

SCOTLAND
Glasgow
Edinburgh

NORTH
SEA

NORTHERN
IRELAND

IRELAND

Dublin

York

Liverpool

Birmingham

ENGLAND

Amsterdam

NETHERLANDS

ESS

London

Bristol

Dover

Calais

Antwerp
Brussels
BELGIUM

Liège

Godesberg

Brighton

Cherbourg

RHIN

ATLANTIC

OCEAN

Brest

SEINE

Paris

MARNE

Metz

Nancy
Strasbourg

MOSELLE

Nantes

Tours

LOIRE

F R A N C E

SAÔNE

SWITZ

BAY OF

BISCAY

Bordeaux

GARONNE

Geneva

Lyon

G

RHÔNE

Santander

Bilbao

Nice

Marseille

Oporto

DUERO

Burgos

EBRO

Perpignan

CORSIC

PORTUGAL

S P A I N

Madrid

Barcelona

Ajacc

TAGUS

Lisbon

Toledo

GUADIANA

Valencia

BALEARIC
ISLANDS

Seville

Cartagena

Cag

Gibraltar

MEDITERRANEAN

Tangier

SPANISH MOROCCO

Melilla

Algiers

TL

MOROCCO

A L G E R I A

Introduction

During the early morning hours of September 30, 1938, the political leaders of Britain, France, Germany, and Italy signed an agreement known to history by the name of the city where their meeting took place: Munich.

In itself, the Munich Agreement covered only the procedures by which the territorial claims against Czechoslovakia of Germany primarily, and of Poland and Hungary secondarily, should be determined. But the scope and significance of the Munich crisis far transcended the document's bare provisions. The meeting was the product of a diplomatic earthquake that shattered the pre-existing power structure of Europe, and the culmination of an international crisis that brought the great powers to the verge of war. Its material and symbolic consequences alike were enormous, and today the Munich episode appears in retrospect as a nodal point in the course of modern history.

Thus the word "Munich" acquired a meaning quite apart from its designation of the capital of Bavaria—a city beloved by generations of travelers for its architecture, museums, music, lovely environs, and excellent beer. In the world of international affairs, "Munich" has come to describe a conciliatory, yielding approach to the resolution of conflicts, and in this sense "Munich" is commonly coupled with a policy of avoiding confrontations of force by giving way to the demanding party, a policy to which the term "appeasement" is attached.

Household words of yesteryear such as "Quisling" and "fifth columnist" have faded from the vocabulary of international politics, but "Munich" and "appeasement" have endured, and their end is not in sight. Both are pejorative. "Adlai wanted another Munich," said a hostile observer of the late Adlai Stevenson's attitude during the Cuban missile crisis. A decade earlier, during the presidential campaign of 1952, Stevenson had accused Eisenhower of appeasing the Republican "Old Guard" by describing Ike's meeting with Robert Taft as the "Munich of Morningside Heights." While Secretary of State, Dean Rusk frequently used "Munich" to describe the disastrous consequences that he thought would follow if opponents of American policy in Vietnam were to have their way.

At the time it was signed, however, the Munich agreement was generally applauded everywhere except in Czechoslovakia and the Soviet Union. The four men of Munich—Neville Chamberlain, Edouard Daladier, Adolf Hitler, and Benito Mussolini—returned to their respective capitals to be received as heroes. To be sure, dissenting voices were soon heard: Winston Churchill described the settlement as a "disaster of the first magnitude," and in the United States, Rabbi

Stephen Wise, reversing Chamberlain's proud claim of "peace with honour," called it "dishonour without peace."

Despite these Cassandras, the people of the Western Hemisphere felt great joy that the threat of war had been averted. Munich got its bad name because it seemingly failed the pragmatic test. Within less than six months Czechoslovakia was no more, and within less than a year the war that became the Second World War began. But despite that tragic sequence and the generally adverse verdict of historians, the Munich settlement has not lacked for able and articulate defenders. Given the unhappy military circumstances in which Britain found herself in 1938, "I feel that Munich was inevitable," wrote the young John Fitzgerald Kennedy in 1940. Britain and France were "completely justified" in yielding to Hitler's demands, declared the Lord Chancellor, Viscount Maugham, in a 1944 postmortem. And the English historian A. J. P. Taylor, not content to defend Munich as a necessary expedient born of weakness, acclaims it as "a triumph for British policy. . . . a triumph for all that was best and most enlightened in British life."

Many factors and many men shaped and had a hand in the Munich episode. But in this drama there were, beyond question, two leading actors—Neville Chamberlain and Adolf Hitler. In that sense this is a book about those two men.

Hitler was the individual *sine qua non* of the Munich crisis. There is no need to speculate on how much the subsequent course of history would have been changed if Corporal Adolf Hitler had been one of the millions of First World War dead. No doubt the natural strength of Germany would have reasserted itself one way or another, and sooner or later the Versailles-begotten structure of Europe would have been shattered, or crumbled from obsolescence. But it was Hitler who gave direction and timing to the exercise of Germany's renascent power. It was to his decisions and initiatives that the other governments were reacting, and it was he who forced the confrontation of which Munich was the result.

If the confrontation was of Hitler's making and would have occurred whoever had been Prime Minister in London, the resolution of the crisis was the work of Neville Chamberlain. To be sure, it was Hitler who hosted the Munich meeting, and the agreement itself was initially drafted in Berlin. But it was Chamberlain who decided that Czechoslovakia could not and therefore should not be protected against the German threat, and who undermined the Czechs' will to resist, shattered the Czech-Franco-Russian defensive alliances, rang down the curtain on the Europe of Versailles, and gave effect to his chosen policy of appeasement.

The character and motives of Neville Chamberlain, I believe, have been much distorted in the mirror of historical literature, in which his image is that of a timorous, bumbling, and naïve old gentleman, waving an umbrella as a signal of cringing subservience to a bully. Nothing could be further from the truth. Chamberlain did what he did at Munich not because he thought he had to, but because he thought it right. For him, appeasement was a policy not of fear but of common and moral sense. In public life he was a dominant and often domineering man, profoundly convinced of the rightness of his own judgments, and skilled in bending others to his will. Sadly mistaken he may have been; cowardly or indecisive he was not, and for him Munich was no surrender, but a passionately moral act.

There were, however, many others of high station, in Britain and France especially, who applauded Chamberlain's policies but did not share his motives. Some were strongly moved by fear of communism, and recoiled at a war in alliance with the Soviet Union, which would draw the Red legions westward into Central Europe. Others saw Munich as a temporary retreat, dictated by a realistic appraisal of comparative armed strength. In the latter sense, Munich was a German military triumph—bloodless, but of enormous dimension—and the prime instrument of that triumph was the German Air Force: the *Luftwaffe*.

It is a remarkable fact that Munich was the only victory of strategic proportions that the Luftwaffe ever won. During the war it furnished invaluable tactical support to the German Army, but was turned loose on its own only at Dunkirk, over Britain, and against Malta, and on each occasion it failed.

But at the time of Munich, the Luftwaffe was the psychological spearhead of German power. Colonel Charles A. Lindbergh, the famed "Lone Eagle" of the first nonstop New York-to-Paris flight, spread reports of the Luftwaffe's invincibility in the highest circles of London and Paris. It was the fear of carnage and panic in those cities, more than any other one factor, which caused the French and British air staffs to advise that war should be avoided at almost any cost.

In fact, the victory would have been beyond the capacity of the Luftwaffe if put to the test. By an even greater irony, it was a victory which the victors were virtually unconscious of having achieved. The German air arm was not designed for long-range strategic bombardment. Its Commander-in-Chief, Hermann Goering, assisted by an inflated notion of its power, may have had a glimmering sense of the fear his forces had spread. But the professional German airmen, who made a much more accurate assessment of the range and strength of their weapons, were quite unaware that their opposite numbers in Britain and France were so deeply affected by fear of a Wellsian holocaust.

Another odd feature of Munich is that Hitler, the ostensible beneficiary, was as much displeased with the outcome as Winston Churchill and Rabbi Wise. For Hitler, the Sudetenland and the grievances of its German-speaking inhabitants were the excuse but not the reason for the crisis he provoked. What he really wanted was a military invasion that would carry him into Prague as conqueror and subjugator of the Czech nation, just as he later used Danzig and the Corridor as an excuse to destroy Poland.

The reason that Munich failed the pragmatic test so soon was that Hitler's goal was unchanged, and in March of 1939 he took what he had meant to take in the fall of 1938. Thus what Chamberlain regarded as a farsighted act of appeasement on his part actually infuriated Hitler by denying him the conqueror's laurels and complete dominion.

The ultimate paradox of the Munich crisis is that nothing of great importance was decided at the Munich conference. The big decisions about Czechoslovakia were made earlier, at Berchtesgaden, and later, in Berlin.

Munich symbolized the death of the old Europe and was a harbinger of what was to come—a "prologue to tragedy," as the late Sir John Wheeler-Bennett called it. Once the conference had been called the outcome was inevitable. Thus, although there are much color and human interest, there is no suspense in an account of the conference itself. This circumstance explains why I have put it at the beginning rather than the end of the book, since the significance and impact of the story lie not in what transpired on the day of Munich, but in the why and how of the crisis as a whole.

While Adolf Hitler's initial image as a bizarre demagogue grew and darkened into that of a powerful despot bent on conquest, many highly placed Europeans, like Georges Bonnet of France, were willing to pay any price for peace. Others, like Winston Churchill, thought that peace could not be bought at any price— that Hitler had no peace for sale.

Neville Chamberlain was in neither of those camps. He believed that Hitler could be appeased, and peace purchased. He paid a terribly high price and got very little peace in return. Although Chamberlain himself was bitterly disappointed in the results of his bargain, there were those then, and are those now, for whom the price was not too high.

In this book I have sought to provide not only a narrative of the circumstances and events leading to the Munich crisis, but also, and with the aid of newly available source material, to make a fresh assessment of the men and methods by which the crisis was "resolved." Munich has become a standard weapon in the dialectic of politics, and today, after the lapse of forty years, it is especially pertinent to inquire whether this episode, dramatic and historically significant as it was, really teaches the lesson commonly attributed to it, or other lessons, or none at all.

MUNICH
THE PRICE OF PEACE

Part I

MUNICH: SEPTEMBER 1938

CHAPTER 1

Invitation to the Quadrille

1

On the morning of September 29, 1938, the leaders of the four major powers of Western Europe were converging on the lovely old city of Munich, in southern Bavaria. Two were coming together from the south by rail, and two separately from the west by air.

The host, Adolf Hitler, and his guest of honor, Benito Mussolini, had met on the old Austro-German border at Kiefersfelden, and were on their way to Munich in the Fuehrer's special train. Neville Chamberlain, Prime Minister in Britain, and Edouard Daladier, Premier in France, were both airborne before nine o'clock, respectively from London and Paris. Lesser officials and journalists streamed into Munich from all directions, for the expected dénouement of a prolonged international crisis during which Europe had been teetering on the brink of war.

The borderlands of Bohemia and Moravia—the so-called Sudetenland—were the immediate cause of this confrontation of arms and wills. But that morning no one was coming to Munich from Czechoslovakia. Not until the afternoon, when the conference was well under way, was Prague permitted to send representatives, and then not to participate in the discussions but only to be informed of their country's fate.

Nor did anyone come from Moscow. Maxim Litvinov and other Soviet spokesmen rumbled ominously about Russia's exclusion from the meeting, but everyone knew that Hitler would never have agreed to give them a seat at the table. Indeed, it had been difficult enough to persuade the Fuehrer to hold any conference at all, and only a last-minute appeal from his friend and fellow-dictator Mussolini had deflected him from a military solution.

The idea of such a meeting had not, however, originated with the Duce. The problem of the Sudetenland had been red hot since late May 1938, when reports of menacing German troop movements had led to a partial mobilization of the Czech Army. During the four months that had elapsed since then, resolution of the crisis by means of an international conference had been suggested by a wide variety of persons, including the United States Ambassador to France (William C. Bullitt), the French and British ambassadors to Germany (respectively André François-Poncet and Sir Nevile Henderson), the German and Italian military attachés in Prague (Colonels Rudolf Toussaint and Count Valfre di Bonzo), and President Franklin D. Roosevelt.

Adolf Hitler, however, had never shown any sign of interest in such a project. Furthermore, the several proponents were not of one mind concerning the number and identity of the participants. Anyone could propose a conference, but it was not so simple a matter to decide who should be seated at the table. Franklin Roosevelt had fudged the issue in his last-minute appeal to Hitler by proposing a "conference of all the nations directly interested in the present controversy." Which countries could fairly be described as "directly interested"?

On the face of the matter, surely, if any country could be so described it was Czechoslovakia. The Sudetenland lay within and along her borders, as drawn by the Treaty of Versailles. It was the demand for greater cultural and political autonomy on the part of its German-speaking inhabitants—the *Sudetendeutsche*—which was the ostensible and, in many minds, the actual cause of the crisis. Protracted negotiations between Sudeten German leaders and the Czech Government had been broken off in mid-September, and now the demand was for severance of the Sudetenland from Czechoslovakia and its annexation by Germany —by Adolf Hitler's Third Reich.

For several years the German Government had been giving the Sudeten leaders covert support, and in February 1938, Hitler, in a speech to the Reichstag, openly announced his determination to protect the rights of Germans in adjoining nations. From then on the tone of Nazi government and German press references to Czechoslovakia grew ever more bellicose. On September 12, at the annual Nazi Party rally in Nuremberg, Hitler proclaimed the right of the Sudeten Germans to "self-determination." This brought the issue to white heat, and set in train the events which led directly to the gathering in Munich at the end of the month. Germany, as precipitator of the international crisis, was thus the major power most "directly interested."

Both Germany and Czechoslovakia had allies, under varying degrees of obligation to render them assistance in the event of war. The nation most tightly bound by alliance was France. Poland and Czechoslovakia were the eastern bastions of her post-First World War system of European alliances, and in the case of Czechoslovakia, French obligations were embodied in the 1925 Treaty of Mutual Assistance, under which the two countries reciprocally agreed to lend "aid and assistance" in the event that either was attacked "without provocation."

Ten years later the Soviet Union became associated with this defensive alliance, but under more complicated and ambiguous treaty arrangements. On May 2, 1935, France and the Soviet Union signed a Treaty of Mutual Assistance against unprovoked attacks upon either of them, but this, of course, did not apply in the event that France entered upon a war in fulfillment of her treaty obligations to Czechoslovakia.

That contingency was covered by the Soviet-Czechoslovak treaty signed two weeks later. This provided for a defensive alliance, but the reciprocal obligation was explicitly made conditional on France's having commenced to lend assistance to the attacked nation, whichever one it might be. What was not so clear was whether the duty to assist would then attach at once, or only after proceedings under Article 16 of the Covenant of the League of Nations, to obtain from the Council of the League a declaration that an act of aggression had occurred.

Britain too was bound by treaty (the Locarno Pact) to defend France against unprovoked aggression, but she had no commitments to Czechoslovakia beyond her general obligations under the League of Nations Covenant. The Anglo-French entente, however, was not limited to the letter of Locarno. Both countries had been bled white by Germany in the First World War, and under Britain's traditional balance-of-power strategy in Europe, the defeat of France by Germany could not be tolerated. As a practical matter, accordingly, France's obligations to Czechoslovakia were of great concern to Britain, and indeed the British Government had involved itself far more deeply than the French in seeking a peaceful solution of the Sudeten question.

Fascist Italy was tied to Nazi Germany by strong ideological affinity and strategic community of interest and purpose. But there was no formal military alliance. Protocols signed secretly in the fall of 1936 were concerned with issues (Ethiopia, Austria, and Spain) which by 1938 were obsolete, or only remotely related to the Czech crisis. In November 1937, Italy joined in the "Anti-Comintern Pact," which Germany and Japan had inaugurated a year earlier for the ostensible purpose of combatting communist activities. Thus Mussolini was under no treaty obligation to come to the aid of his fellow-dictator. But Duce and Fuehrer found it advantageous to accept a posture of fraternal solidarity under the name of the "Rome-Berlin Axis," and Mussolini had made it plain and public that, so far as the Sudeten issue was concerned, Italy was firmly aligned with Germany.

Totting up the immediate disputants and their allies, accordingly, there were six nations—Czechoslovakia, Germany, France, Russia, Britain, and Italy—that were "directly interested" under any reasonable interpretation of that phrase. In addition there were three Eastern European countries that were, in various ways, closely concerned. Like Czechoslovakia, Poland was linked in defensive alliance with France. On the other hand Poland, and Hungary too, nurtured territorial claims against Czechoslovakia because of the inclusion of Polish and Hungarian minorities within her Versailles-drawn borders. If German claims at the western end were to be satisfied, Polish and Hungarian claims at the eastern end would surely be pressed. Finally, Poland and Rumania lay between Russia and Czechoslovakia, and thus would at once be involved should the Russians seek to furnish the Czechs with direct military support.

However, there was nothing to be gained from an international conference without German participation. With whom might the Fuehrer deign to sit down? Bolshevist Russians were almost interchangeable with Jews as the devils of Nazi dogma, and Hitler had often pointed to the Ukraine as a choice portion of the future German *Lebensraum*. A year later, announcement of the Nazi-Soviet pact would hit the world with stunning impact, but in the fall of 1938 it was widely assumed that Hitler would reject out of hand any proposal that the Soviet Union be seated at a conference on the Sudeten question.

Common sense would also suggest that Hitler was most unlikely to countenance a conference at which his "side" would be outnumbered. As a practical matter, this meant that, if France and Britain were both represented, Italy must also be. But what then of the Czechs themselves? Their inclusion would again put the Axis countries in the minority, and their physical presence must inevitably stiffen, with shame if nothing else, the spines of their French allies. Furthermore, Czechoslovakia was not a "great power," and her President, Eduard Beneš, was a continuing target of Nazi abuse. At the Nuremberg Party festivities the number-two Nazi, Hermann Goering, had derided the Czechs as a "miserable, pygmy race" and their country as a "petty segment of Europe." It was hardly to be expected that Adolf Hitler would tolerate them as equal participants at any conference graced with his own presence.

All of this strongly indicated that, if there were to be a conference with German participation, it would be a four-party meeting of Germany, France, Italy, and Britain. Satisfactory as this selection might be to the Axis dictators, it would put Britain and France, especially the latter, in an unlovely posture. Czechoslovakia was France's ally, and it was Czechoslovakia's territorial integrity and future as a nation that were threatened by Germany. How could France as ally and protector negotiate a settlement in a meeting from which her ally and protégé was excluded? How could England as mediator seek a fair solution in a forum open to only one of the litigants?

Opinion in most "neutral" countries, and especially in the United States, was strongly anti-German and pro-Czech. It is indeed ironic, therefore, that the idea of a four-party conference, from which Czechoslovakia would be excluded, was first broached, albeit privately, by the American Ambassador in Paris. In a personal letter to President Roosevelt, written at the time (May 20, 1938) of the Czech mobilization in reaction to rumored German troop movements, William Bullitt declared that it would be an unspeakable tragedy "if France, in support of Czechoslovakia, should attack" Germany. The continent of Europe would be "devastated," and therefore "we should attempt to find some way which will let the French out of their moral commitment." To accomplish this, Bullitt proposed that the President should:

> Call to the White House the Ambassadors of England, France, Germany and Italy. Ask them to transmit to Chamberlain, Daladier, Hitler, and Mussolini your urgent invitation to send representatives at once to The Hague to attempt to work out a peaceful settlement of the dispute between Germany and Czechoslovakia. Add that if the four Governments desire, a representative of the United States will sit with them. You should also make a personal appeal of the sort that you know best how to make referring to the fact

that we are the children of all the nations of Europe, that our civilization is a composite of all the civilizations of Europe, that just as we are grateful for Shakespeare so are we grateful for Beethoven, that just as we are grateful for Molière so are we grateful for Leonardo da Vinci et cetera, that we cannot stand by and watch the beginning of the end of European civilization without making one last effort to stop its destruction; that you are convinced that the only result of general European war today would be an Asiatic depotism established on fields of dead.

Wise or unwise in his recommendations, Bullitt was alive to the probable consequences, and ready to face them:

The conference at The Hague would probably have to recommend that a plebiscite be held in Czechoslovakia to determine the will of the different peoples of that country. If the Czechs should refuse to hold such a plebiscite the French would have an escape from their desperate moral dilemma and general European war would be avoided.

You would be accused, or the man sent to The Hague as your representative would be, of selling out a small nation in order to produce another Hitler triumph. I should not hesitate to take that brick on my head and I don't think you should either if thereby you could avoid a general European war.

Bullitt wrote his letter a few days after a long talk with the French Foreign Minister, Georges Bonnet, who had expressed "with the greatest vehemence and emotion" his belief that "a French declaration of war on Germany today in order to protect Czechoslovakia would mean the defeat and dismemberment of France." Other diplomatic conversations had convinced Bullitt that "the Czechs prefer to see their nation succumb in a conflagration which will destroy all Europe rather than make the large concessions which alone would satisfy Hitler and the Sudeten." However one may assess the recommendations, there is no denying that Bullitt's letter was, in some respects, a remarkably prescient analysis, and it is fascinating to discover the four men of Munich named so far in advance of their meeting, even though Bullitt was wide of the future mark in specifying The Hague as the conference site.

There appears to be no record of Roosevelt's reply or other reaction to his ambassador's proposals, nor of any further efforts at that time by Bullitt to gain their acceptance. But the conference idea was simultaneously occurring to others. In May 1938 exaggerated reports of German troop movements had aroused the British Foreign Office to a livelier sense of the dangers in the situation, and an experienced counselor, William Strang, was dispatched to visit and exchange impressions with the British embassy staffs in Prague and Berlin. A week after Bullitt wrote his letter, Strang was in Prague canvassing various methods of resolving the German-Czech issues with the minister, Basil Newton, and two of his aides.

Several alternatives were discussed, and then the conferees comtemplated the possibility that "no accommodation between the Sudeten Germans and the [Czech] Government is possible." In that event "there may be a case for calling an international conference on Czechoslovakia, attended by the powers chiefly concerned, with a view to the despatch of an international commission, under the auspices of the conference, to recommend a solution." Which powers were "chiefly concerned" was left unspecified, perhaps because it was agreed that the German Government "would be unlikely to assent, and if they did not, the Italian government would probably take the same line."

Thus far the conference idea had been submerged in the private reflections of American and British diplomats. It was left to the French Ambassador to Germany, André François-Poncet, to bring the notion to the surface of international discussion. Early in June, while in Paris, François-Poncet obtained from his superiors at the Quai d'Orsay authority to propose to the Germans a tripartite conference of France, England, and Germany to reach a "fair solution" which would then be recommended to the Czech Government, with the inducement of a triple guarantee and a neutralization comparable to that of Switzerland.

In its disregard of the Italians, this was a characteristically French proposition. François-Poncet privately described his plan to Bullitt and to the British Ambassador in Paris, Sir Eric Phipps, neither of whom gave him any encouragement. The British Foreign Office registered strong distaste and instructed their ambassador in Berlin, Sir Nevile Henderson, to try to talk François-Poncet out of his notion. When François-Poncet returned to Berlin, Henderson did his best; he told the Frenchman that the Germans would never agree, that Britain would not guarantee Czechoslovakia, and that the issue ought to be resolved directly by the Czech Government and the Sudeten German leaders.

Nothing daunted, François-Poncet obtained an interview (on June 23) with the German Foreign Minister, Joachim von Ribbentrop, and opened the conversation by proposing a conference of the "Great Powers" from which there might emerge a Czechoslovakia "similar to Switzerland, so that there would be, as it were, two great poles of neutrality in Europe." Ribbentrop's reaction was uncompromisingly hostile: an international discussion was "the wrong course"; no "genuine pacification" could be effectuated that way; Czechoslovakia herself was a product of international consultation at Versailles, and that experience "should not be forgotten." The two men did not have a high personal regard for each other, and the meeting ended on a sour note.

For many weeks thereafter, the conference idea was relegated to the diplomatic attic, where it slumbered but stirred and muttered fitfully. Public attention was focused on the doings of Lord Runciman, whom the British sent to Prague as "investigator and mediator" of the Sudeten issues. Even before Runciman's arrival in Czechoslovakia, however, Sir Nevile Henderson broached a four-party conference proposal to his superiors in London. He received no encouragement, but the notion continued to turn up in back-room meetings in London, Berlin, and Prague during late July and most of August.

Apparently the thought was also finding some favor in certain Axis military circles, according to reports from the British military attaché in Prague, Lieutenant Colonel H. C. T. Strong. On August 17 his German opposite number, Colonel Rudolf Toussaint, in the course of a gloomy survey of the international outlook, told Strong that the only hope of avoiding a European war lay in a four-power ruling that the Sudeten region should be annexed to Germany. Five days later Stronge was treated to the same advice by the Italian military attaché, Colonel Count Valfre di Bonzo.

2

Came the annual Nazi Party Rally at Nuremberg, and with Hitler's speech on September 12 the international tension reached crisis pitch. The next day Edouard Daladier bestirred himself to the extent of endeavoring to telephone Chamberlain, in order to propose that the British and French governments invite Hitler to confer and work out a Sudeten settlement. It was the same proposal that François-Poncet had put to Ribbentrop in June, and was diplomatically unseaworthy because Hitler's bold, black ally Mussolini would be excluded, and Germany outnumbered at the green table. Perhaps not unaware of this drawback, Daladier sought to rationalize the tripartite feature on the theory that France would represent the Czechs, Germany the *Sudetendeutsche,* and Britain Lord Runciman. Surely only a Frenchman could have conceived such wonderful reverse logic; since Britain had sent Runciman to Prague, Runciman should now send Britain to the conference!

Daladier's effort to speak directly with Chamberlain was blocked by Sir Alexander Cadogan, Permanent Under-Secretary of the Foreign Office, who thought such a conversation would be "hopeless," and told Paris that any message from the French Premier must be sent through the British Ambassador, Sir Eric Phipps. Chamberlain had little French and Daladier less English, but the real difficulty was not linguistic. In June, François-Poncet's plan had fallen on deaf British ears because Chamberlain had already settled on the Runciman mission as his next move. On September 13 he was equally uninterested in any French proposals because he had already decided to go to Germany himself and seek a settlement by personal negotiation with Adolf Hitler. Odd numbers would not work, and Chamberlain preferred two to four. International the meeting would be, but a tête-à-tête could hardly be called a "conference" in the sense up to then envisaged.

Chamberlain's intended method was to ascertain Hitler's price for peace, return to London to secure French acceptance, and then, by joint Anglo-French pressure, impose the settlement on Czechoslovakia. When he met with Hitler at Berchtesgaden on September 15, the Fuehrer demanded cession to Germany of the preponderantly *Sudetendeutsch* districts of Czechoslovakia. The French agreed, the pressure was laid on Prague, and on September 21 the Czech Government agreed to the cession of German-majority districts, subject to final adjustment of the new frontiers by an international commission.

On the next day, well satisfied with these arrangements, Chamberlain flew to Germany for a second meeting with the Fuehrer, at Godesberg. To the Englishman's astonishment and chagrin, Hitler at once condemned these accomplishments as wholly inadequate. In the course of two days and as the outcome of two long conferences and an interchange of letters between the two leaders, Hitler embodied his new demands in a memorandum and map, pursuant to which marked areas would be occupied by German troops no later than October 1, and other areas would be subjected to a subsequent plebiscite. The discussions were often acrimonious, and were concluded with nothing more than Chamberlain's undertaking to present the new demands to the Czech Government.

Chamberlain returned to London on September 24, to begin a round of gloomy deliberations with the Cabinet and, on the next two days, with the French Premier, Edouard Daladier, the Army Chief of Staff General Maurice Gamelin, and other French representatives. Hitler's Godesberg memorandum was put to Prague, and was categorically rejected on September 25. Mobilization of the Czech Army had been ordered during the Godesberg meeting, and along the borders of Bohemia and Moravia, German troops were deployed and ready to attack. French reserve units were dispatched to man the Maginot defenses, the British Navy was ordered mobilized, and slit trenches were dug in Hyde Park.

In the Berlin Sportspalast, Adolf Hitler roared denunciation of the Czechs and defiance of the world: at No. 10 Downing Street, Neville Chamberlain sat before a radio microphone and spoke wearily and desperately of the horrors of war, incredibly looming because of "a quarrel in a far away country between people of whom we know nothing." On September 26, Franklin Roosevelt sent a public telegram to Hitler, Beneš, Chamberlain, and Daladier declaring that "the fabric of peace on the continent of Europe, if not throughout the rest of the world, is in immediate danger," and appealing "for the sake of humanity everywhere" that the recipients not "break off negotiations looking to a peaceful, fair, and constructive settlement of the questions at issue."

It was during this period of the greatest tension that the idea of settlement by means of an international conference, dead since Daladier's proposal of September 13, was reborn. Now the parent was none other than Neville Chamberlain, who had twice previously smothered the infant aborning. But the Runciman mission had come to nothing, personal diplomacy at Berchtesgaden and Godesberg had left Europe on the brink of war, and something—or anything—else had to be tried.

Apparently Chamberlain first broached the conference idea on the afternoon of September 25 to Jan Masaryk, the Czech Ambassador in London, when the latter came in with his government's rejection of the Germans' Godesberg demands. Assuming that Hitler could be persuaded to settle the Sudeten question peacefully "by means of an international conference attended by Germany, Czechoslovakia and other powers," would the Czech Government be willing "to take part in this new effort of saving the peace"? The inquiry elicited a qualified affirmative reply from Prague.

Before Chamberlain took occasion to act on this basis, however, Franklin Roosevelt spoke loudly from the sidelines. Ambassador Bullitt, the original proponent of the conference idea, had been agitating for it again with his chiefs in Washington, and now with greater success. On the evening of September 27, Roosevelt sent a second open message to Hitler, exhorting him to continue negotiations and avoid a resort to force, and adding the suggestion that the talks be widened into "a conference of all the nations directly interested in the present controversy" which should be "held immediately—in some neutral spot in Europe."

This was the first public espousal of a multiparty conference, and the President was at pains to give his message maximum exposure. But it was all pretty vague; Roosevelt rejected Bullitt's recommendation that the parties to the conference be named, and resorted to the ambiguity of "nations directly interested." Furthermore, the President was proposing a party at which he would be neither host nor guest: "The government of the United States has no political involvements in Europe, and will assume no obligations in the conduct of the present negotiations."

While the message was being drafted in Washington, in Paris Bullitt was routing Daladier out of bed to apprise him of its coming and get his reaction. The French Premier professed hearty approval of a conference to which "France would of course be glad to send a representative." Then, according to Bullitt:

> I asked him what states should be included and he gave the list, France, England, Germany, Poland, and Czechoslovakia. I asked him if he would object to the inclusion of Hungary. He said that he would object most emphatically because he had absolute information that the Poles, Germans, and Hungarians had agreed that Poland and Hungary should divide the whole of Slovakia. He would never permit this and would prefer to go to war rather than accept it . . .

Was Daladier serious, or building up a bargaining position, or pulling Bullitt's leg? It is scarcely conceivable that Daladier really thought that Hitler would allow himself to be found in such company, comprising, as it would have, the pillars of Versailles and the French postwar system of alliances. Again and in accordance with what was becoming an old French custom, the very existence of Italy was ignored.

Meanwhile discussions—calm but desperate on the British side, strident and well nigh hysterical on the German—had been held in Berlin between Hitler and Chamberlain's personal emissary, Sir Horace Wilson. In consequence of these, on September 27, Hitler dispatched a letter to Chamberlain which, while conceding nothing from the Godesberg terms, professed "regret" at "the idea of any attack on Czechoslovak territory" and closed with a backhanded suggestion that Chamberlain continue his efforts as a peacemaker.

It was in response to this letter that Chamberlain, on the morning of September 28, finally made a formal proposal to Hitler for a settlement by international conference and treaty:

> After reading your letter I feel certain that you can get all essentials without war and without delay.
> I am ready to come to Berlin myself at once to discuss arrangements for transfer [of the Sudeten areas] with you and representatives of Czech Government, together with representatives of France and Italy if you desire.

Nevile Henderson delivered the message to Hitler shortly after noon. The Fuehrer commented that it would probably be unnecessary for Chamberlain to come again to Germany, but excused himself from a definite reply on the ground that he was in the course of discussion with the Italian Government, and "no final answer can be given until he has concerted with them."

Benito Mussolini, up to this time, had had no direct contact with Hitler on the

Czech issue; indeed, early in September the Duce had complained to Galeazzo Ciano, his Foreign Minister and son-in-law, that "the Germans are letting us know almost nothing of their programs with regard to Czechoslovakia." By late September, however, a better liaison had been established, and the Italian dictator was supporting the German position in speeches, newspaper articles, and diplomatic press releases. He had not, however, given any sign of enthusiasm for Italian involvement in a military way.

On September 27 the British Ambassador in Rome, the Earl of Perth, requested and received authority from London to ask Mussolini to "use his influence to induce Herr Hitler" to accept Chamberlain's proposals. The following morning (September 28) the Earl waited upon Ciano with what amounted to an official British request that Mussolini intervene as a mediator. Ciano at once laid the request before his chief, who, nothing loath to assume the role of international peacemaker, telephoned the Italian Ambassador in Berlin, Bernardo Attolico, and instructed him to go to Hitler and ask that no military action be taken for another twenty-four hours, so that there might be further consideration of Chamberlain's proposition.

Attolico saw Hitler shortly before noon, and the latter, with only slight hesitation, agreed to stay his hand for the moment and consult further with Mussolini via Attolico. After receiving Henderson and hearing Chamberlain's offer to come to Berlin, Hitler told Attolico that he would "only talk to Chamberlain again provided not only that Italy was represented but that Italy was represented by Mussolini in person." The Duce at once agreed to come, and by midafternoon Hitler had decided to play the host to a four-party conference at Munich.

The Fuehrer's invitation was extended to Daladier by a telephone call from Goering to François-Poncet, who subsequently wrote in his memoirs:

> I forwarded the invitation without comment; an hour later it was accepted. I immediately informed Goering. *"Gott sei Dank,* thank God!" he cried. "Bravo!"

Shortly after three o'clock, Nevile Henderson received a message of similar purport from the Foreign Ministry, which he communicated by a telephone call to Sir Alexander Cadogan at the Foreign Office. Neville Chamberlain, at that moment, was at the dispatch box in the House of Commons (which had been in recess since the end of July), reporting on the crisis and the events of the last two months. Cadogan wrote the news on two sheets of paper and made all speed to the House, where the message was passed along the Government bench to Sir John Simon, who was seated next to Chamberlain.

The House was packed, tense, and hanging on the Prime Minister's every word and inflection; the Queen Mother and other royalty, and high clergy, ambassadors, and other notables filled the galleries. When the message from Berlin reached Simon, Chamberlain had brought the account nearly up to the present moment. He told the House of his conversation with Jan Masaryk, and of the Czech Government's agreement to join in a settlement conference. He read to the House his letter to Hitler, proposing a five-party meeting, and his contemporaneous letter to Mussolini, requesting the Duce's support for that project. He reported that Mussolini had asked Hitler to postpone "action" for twenty-four hours, to assist in finding the way to a peaceful settlement.

At this point, and after several previous failures, Sir John Simon drew Chamberlain's attention to the contents of the message. "Shall I tell them now?" asked Chamberlain in a whisper. Simon replied affirmatively, whereupon Chamberlain turned back to the House with evident relief and joy, saying:

> "That is not all. I have something further to say to the House yet. I have now been informed by Herr Hitler that he invites me to meet him at Munich to-morrow morning. He has also invited Signor Mussolini and M. Daladier. Signor Mussolini has accepted and I have no doubt M. Daladier will also accept. I need not say what my answer will be. [An Hon. Member: "Thank God for the Prime Minister!"] We are all patriots, and there can be no hon. Member of this House who did not feel his heart leap that the crisis has been once more postponed to give us once more an opportunity to try what reason and good will and discussion will do to settle a problem which is already within sight of settlement. Mr. Speaker, I cannot say any more. I am sure that the House will be ready to release me now to go and see what I can make of this last effort. Perhaps they may think it will be well, in view of this new development, that this Debate shall stand adjourned for a few days, when perhaps we may meet in happier circumstances."

The Prime Minister did not draw the attention of the House to the circumstance that he had asked for a five-party meeting but had been invited to a gathering of four, from which Czechoslovakia would be excluded. Instead, he treated it as taken for granted that the invitation should not only be accepted, but acclaimed by a leaping of the heart.

No one else in the House commented on the discrepancy between what had been asked and what received from Berlin. Instead, there was the cry of "Thank God for the Prime Minister!" and—with a few notable exceptions, including Anthony Eden and Harold Nicolson—the House rose in a body and engaged in a fervid demonstration of relief, approval, and praise.

3

If Neville Chamberlain was at first unaware that he had agreed to join a conference from which the nation primarily affected—and whose participation he had solicited less than a week before—was to be excluded, he did not long remain so. "The only discordant note," Ambassador Joseph P. Kennedy informed Washington, "was that Masaryk riding back with me from Parliament said 'I hope this does not mean they are going to cut us up and sell us out.'" Soon after Parliament adjourned, Masaryk was at the Foreign Office, where he was told that public opinion would not tolerate a disruption of the conference over the issue of Czech representation.

Later that evening, Chamberlain wired his minister in Prague, directing him to assure President Beneš that "I shall have the interests of Czechoslovakia in mind and I go . . . with the intention of trying to find accommodation between the position of German and Czechoslovak governments by which arrangement may be made for an orderly and equitable application of the principle of cession to which he has already agreed." But this message crossed an anguished plea from Beneš that "nothing may be done in Munich without Czechoslovakia being heard," and that provision should be made for a "representative of Czechoslovakia to be at hand to plead the Czech cause." In reply, that evening, Chamberlain could say only that he would "bear this point in mind."

The following morning the British Foreign Secretary, Lord Halifax, invited to his office the Soviet Ambassador Ivan Maisky, in order to explain that Russia's exclusion from the conference was not to be laid at Britain's door, but was necessary because: "We all had to face facts and one of those facts was, as he very well knew, that the heads of the German Government and of the Italian Government would not be willing in present circumstances to sit in conference with Soviet representatives." Maisky then pressed Halifax on the question of Czech representation at Munich, to which the Foreign Secretary replied "that this matter was one of those that the Prime Minister had very clearly before him, and in regard to which he would do his best."

It is altogether probable that Chamberlain was pleased by the exclusion of the Russians and Czechs. In February 1938, during the debate in the Commons on Anthony Eden's resignation as Foreign Secretary, Chamberlain had declared: "The peace of Europe must depend upon the attitude of the four major Powers —Germany, Italy, France, and ourselves." Later that day he had defended the exclusion of the Soviet Union from his listing by describing "Russia" as "partly European but partly Asiatic." As for Czechoslovakia, surely the Prime Minister was secretly, if not openly, relieved that the precise and articulate Beneš would not be there to raise sticky questions and make it more difficult to accommodate the outcome to Hitler's demands.

Even had he felt otherwise, there was nothing that Chamberlain could do. He had begged Hitler to be invited to Germany a third time, and had pleaded with Mussolini to intercede in his behalf to the same end. Having cast himself in the role of suppliant, Chamberlain was in no position to complain about his host's guest-list.

Given the idea of a conference settlement, the result was inevitable. Adolf Hitler was not disposed to join meetings called by others, to attend at places picked by others, or to sit at table on equal terms with the representatives of second-class powers like Czechoslovakia. Nor was he likely to grace an international gathering with his own presence unless he could control the agenda and ensure a favorable outcome. All this Hitler achieved when Chamberlain enabled him to play the magnanimous host.

And so it came about that the four-party idea, privately broached by Bullitt in May, became the pattern of Munich in September. The official press release from the Wilhelmstrasse informed the world that the Fuehrer had invited Mussolini, Chamberlain, and Daladier to Munich for a "conference." But little of importance remained open for decision; the substance of the deal was already settled, and it was only a matter of packaging.

Despite the breaking-point tension of which it was the focus, the Munich meeting was essentially a ritual dance. Hitler had invited his guests not so much to a conference as to a quadrille.

CHAPTER 2

En Route

1

At the time of Munich, Neville Chamberlain was in his seventieth year and looked every bit of that. Quite unaccustomed to flying, he had in the past two weeks made two round trips to Germany by air, at a time when aircraft were far slower and less comfortable than they are today, and he now faced the prospect of a third. Since his flight to Berchtesgaden, Chamberlain had presided over a series of continuous and sometimes agonizing conferences with his ministers, and with the French representatives. He had addressed his nation by radio, reported his doings to the House of Commons, and handled a multitude of diplomatic problems.

Furthermore, he faced an uncertain and perhaps unpleasant confrontation at Munich. Himself, he "didn't care two hoots whether the Sudetens were in the Reich, or out of it, according to their wishes," but he cared greatly about the appearance of things, and at Godesberg, Hitler had seemed bent on making them look their worst, and now there was this awkward business of excluding the Czechs. How would the Fuehrer behave at Munich? Would he seat the British and French leaders on the world stage only to humiliate them further?

All in all, Chamberlain had ample excuse for fatigue and apprehension, and might have been expected to put a grim face on things. But the old man was tough, and parliamentary and public reaction to his acceptance of Hitler's invitation had given him a great lift. The ovation on the floor and in the galleries of the House of Commons had been quite unprecedented and almost pathetically sincere. From across the Atlantic came a congratulatory and characteristic message from Franklin Roosevelt: "Good man" was all it said. That evening Downing Street was crowded with worshipful well-wishers shouting: "Good old Neville!" He came to the window and spoke as if to children excited and up past their bedtime: "I think you can all go to bed and sleep quietly tonight. It will be all right now."

Thus buoyed, Chamberlain was in a positively jaunty mood when he arrived at Heston Airport early in the morning, and found his cabinet assembled there to bid him Godspeed. Contrary to legend, on this occasion the Prime Minister was not carrying an umbrella, and he faced the cameras smiling and waving his black fedora, flanked by the diminutive Kingsley Wood and the towering Halifax, with Hore-Belisha's moonface beaming over his left shoulder.

With homely whimsey, Chamberlain remarked the repetitious feature of his aerial departures to Germany: "When I was a boy, I used to repeat 'if at first you don't succeed, try, try, try, again.' That is what I am doing." And he added, seeking a higher literary level: "When I come back, I hope I may be able to say, as Hotspur says in Henry IV, 'Out of this nettle, danger, we pluck this flower, safety.'" The quotation was an apt reflection of his own state of mind but, alas, the nettle long survived the flower.

Lord Halifax had not accompanied his chief either to Berchtesgaden or Godesberg, and now once more he was left behind to watch the home front. In the plane with the Prime Minister went six other men, of whom the most senior was Sir Horace Wilson, nominally Chief Industrial Adviser to the government but actually the Prime Minister's closest consultant and agent. Wilson had just spent two highly unpleasant days in Berlin desperately trying to convey Chamberlain's messages to a Fuehrer whose torrent of invective made it hard to get a word in edgewise. The five others were Sir William Malkin, Legal Adviser to the Foreign Office; William Strang, head of the Central European Department of the Foreign Office; Frank Ashton-Gwatkin, a Foreign Office counselor who had been a member of Lord Runciman's mission; the Prime Minister's parliamentary private secretary Lord Dunglass, better known in later years as Sir Alec Douglas-Home, Foreign Minister and Prime Minister during the early sixties; and Chamberlain's personal secretary, Oscar S. Cleverly.

Perhaps before or during this trip to Munich the Prime Minister conferred with his chosen advisers in order to develop a plan for the incipient negotiations, but if so, no record has come to light. There was no consultation between London and Paris. In flight, Chamberlain told Lord Dunglass that the trip was "a last throw," but that "he could not see how it could pay Hitler to push things to the point of war."

At about noon the British Airways plane carrying the delegation settled on the Munich airport. A guard of honor was drawn up, and Joachim von Ribbentrop was on hand to receive the visitors. Chamberlain was the last of the principals to arrive, and he and his companions were taken by car to the Fuehrerbau on the Königsplatz, where the conference was to be held.

2

Edouard Daladier had none of Chamberlain's grounds for self-congratulation, and rather more for self-doubt. It was not Britain but France that was Czechoslovakia's ally, bound to give aid against attack. It was not Britain but France that could put a hundred divisions into the field, and would bear the brunt of the fighting, should war come. In terms of both responsibility and military power, the center of gravity was in Paris, not London.

Despite all this, Daladier had allowed Chamberlain to take the initiative and call every turn. The Runciman mission, Berchtesgaden, Godesberg—all were made in London; France had been pulled along in the British wake, and plainly, if things came to scratch at Munich, the French would be in Chamberlain's hands.

Furthermore, in London Chamberlain ruled the roost, as Daladier did not in

Paris. French premiers rarely dominate their governments, and Daladier, for all his sobriquet "Bull of Vaucluse," had plenty of trouble with a cabinet that comprised a spectrum from the peace-at-any-price Foreign Minister, Georges Bonnet, to the intransigent Minister of the Colonies, Georges Mandel.

Finally, there was the matter of conscience and individual responsibility. At no point does Neville Chamberlain appear to have doubted the wisdom of his own course, while Edouard Daladier was a chronic victim of the pangs of ambivalence. If Hitler were once again to get his way, where would it all end? Would not the *tricolore* be forever stained if the pledge to Prague were not redeemed? On the other hand, should the flower of young France be sacrificed, and Paris laid in ruins by the Luftwaffe, just on account of those obstinate Czechs? Was not Bonnet right that war with Germany would be suicide for France?

These agonies of doubt may have been temporarily assuaged by the almost hysterical demonstrations of relief that greeted the announcement of the Munich meeting. Paris rejoiced no less than London: "The feeling of relief in Paris tonight," Bullitt cabled to the Secretary of State, Cordell Hull, "is comparable to the feeling of relief when the news came that the armistice had been signed." With few exceptions, politicians and press vied with each other in exultation. "Hope is reborn!" cried Georges Bidault in *L'Aube,* while in *Le Populaire* the former Socialist Premier, Léon Blum, wrote that:

> The announcement of the Munich meeting has raised a great wave of faith and hope. It would have been a crime against humanity to break off negotiations or render them impossible. The Munich conference is an armful of wood thrown on the sacred hearth at the moment when the flame fell and was about to die out.

Daladier had previously scheduled a radio address to the nation for the evening of September 28, and now his task was greatly eased:

> I had announced that I would speak to the country this evening on the international situation; but at the beginning of the afternoon I was told of a German invitation to meet Chancellor Hitler, Mr. Chamberlain, and Signor Mussolini at Munich tomorrow. I have accepted this invitation.
>
> You will understand that the day before such important negotiations it is my duty to postpone the explanations that I wanted to give you. But before I depart I should like to thank the French people for their attitude, an attitude filled with courage and dignity.
>
> Above all I wish to thank the Frenchmen who have been recalled to the colours for the fresh proof of calm and resolve that they have given.
>
> My task is hard. Since the beginning of the difficulties that we are now experiencing I have never for a single day ceased to work with all my strength to safeguard peace and France's vital interests. Tomorrow I shall continue this effort with the thought that I am in full agreement with the nation in its entirety.

No more than Chamberlain did Daladier draw attention to the exclusion of the Czechs from the gathering. No more than the English did the French take note of the omission. On what point was the entire nation in "full agreement"?

The Premier did not say, but between the lines one could read the words "Peace! At any—or almost any—price!"

General Gamelin, according to his own account, was not prepared to bid so high. At a conference with Daladier on the morning of September 28, the Premier had asked the general what was most essential to be preserved, in the event that a transfer of territory could not be avoided. Gamelin replied that, unless the fortifications remained in Czech hands, their country would no longer have any "effective military value."

This was sound military advice, but events had long since outstripped such ideas, inasmuch as the territorial cessions which the Czechs had already been forced to accept included most of the fortifications. It is interesting to speculate on the consequences had Daladier appeared at Munich with Gamelin at his side, but no such notion seems to have crossed the mind of either the general or the Premier. Furthermore, later that day General Vuillemin, Chief of the Air Staff, told Daladier that the French Air Force was in no condition for war.

Who would accompany the Premier to Munich? According to Bonnet, it was known in Paris that the two Axis foreign ministers, Ribbentrop and Ciano, would be present. Bonnet had uniformly accompanied Daladier to the Anglo-French discussions in London, but on this occasion: "I let it be known that I would prefer to remain in Paris, and I asked M. Léger to take my place."

Alexis Léger, the senior civil servant, with the title of Secretary-General at the Quai d'Orsay, gives a very different account. Hitler, says Léger, did not want the foreign ministers (except for Galeazzo Ciano, who was the Duce's son-in-law) present, so that the four chiefs could settle the matter summarily. This cut across the French tradition of *collective* cabinet responsibility, pursuant to which the Foreign Minister generally was present with the Premier at important diplomatic conferences. But this time the Cabinet decided to yield to Hitler's preference, and Léger, despite his objections, was instructed to accompany Daladier.

Léger, as a nonpolitical official, then asked for Cabinet instructions regarding the positions he should take on the issues likely to arise at Munich. Bonnet told him that the Cabinet had made no such decisions,* whereupon Léger procured a memorandum from the General Staff advising that the new Czech borders should lie outside the Czech fortifications, and should cause no disruption of the country's east-west communications or narrowing of the "waist" between Moravia and Slovakia. These instructions were in line with what Gamelin had told Daladier that morning, and were similarly beyond hope of realization in view of concessions already made by the Prague government.

It was foggy but not too thick for a take-off when the French delegation arrived at Le Bourget the following morning. Léger was accompanied by Charles Rochat, an experienced diplomat and chief of the Foreign Ministry's European

---

* However, Bonnet subsequently wrote that he provided Léger with a memorandum stating that only territories "predominantly German" should be ceded, and that the new frontiers should be guaranteed by the four powers. Furthermore, the Munich conference should be enlarged so as to include the United States, the Soviet Union, Poland, and the other Balkan states, and proceed to study and dispose of all the controversial European problems.

section, and Daladier brought along his faithful *chef de cabinet* and fellow *Vauclusien,* Marcel Clapier.

Daladier's departure drew a large crowd of officialdom; in addition to most of the Cabinet there were prefects, air transport bigwigs, press, and many diplomats prominent among whom were the British Ambassador, Sir Eric Phipps, and the German chargé d'affaires, Dr. Curt Braeuer.

Waiting to carry the Premier and his party was a silver twin-engined aircraft, the *Poitou.* It took off shortly before nine o'clock, and reached Munich at quarter-past eleven. Ribbentrop was at the airport; he escorted Daladier past a guard of honor and to an automobile for the drive to the famous Vier Jahreszeiten (Four Seasons) Hotel, where the French were to be accommodated. As the cortège of cars approached the center of Munich, the crowds thickened, and loudly acclaimed the French Premier.

Despite the honorific and enthusiastic reception, Daladier seemed ill at ease: "Broad-backed, sunburned, his head buried deep between his shoulders, his brow deeply furrowed with wrinkles, Daladier appeared gloomy and preoccupied. Léger seemed even more so." Such was the impression made on Ambassador François-Poncet, who had come from Berlin by the overnight train and was on hand at the airport to greet his chief.

Arrived at the Four Seasons, Daladier assembled his party in his suite and listened to a briefing by François-Poncet. The Premier himself then said a few words, of which one sentence in particular stuck in the mind of Captain Paul Stehlin, the assistant air attaché, who had come from Berlin with the ambassador. "Everything depends on the English," said Daladier, "we can do nothing but follow them."

Stehlin heard this with surprise, but in fact there was little cause for astonishment. The *Poitou* was a French aircraft, but Daladier had been carried, or sucked, to Munich in the wake of British initiative, and now he had no cards of his own to play.

The telephone rang. Stehlin picked up the receiver and reported that Hermann Goering was waiting on Edouard Daladier, to escort him to the Fuehrerbau.

3

Of the four principals making their ways to Munich, beyond doubt the happiest was Benito Mussolini. The Duce was about to take the center of the stage, a prospect naturally gratifying, and especially so because he had been chafing under a growing awareness that the Germans were prone to relegate him to the wings.

Earlier that year, during the events leading up to the German annexation of Austria, Mussolini had been exceedingly irritated by Hitler's failure to give any notice of what was being planned. *Anschluss* itself, much as Mussolini tried to put a good face on it, had been a real blow, in that Italy's Central European policy, since the First World War, had been based on the preservation of Austrian independence. Then, no sooner had Austria been absorbed than the Germans in the Italian Tyrol raised a clamor for annexation of part of that troubled area to the German Fatherland. In April, Mussolini had been incensed by an article in a Leipzig publication "in which the South Tyrol question is agitated again, and offensive language is used about the Italian mountain population." The indignant Duce confided to Galeazzo Ciano that "these Germans will compel me to swallow the bitterest pill of my life; I mean the French pill." And Ciano, for his part, was worried lest "imprudent" German behavior in the South Tyrol might "blow the Axis sky high."

Came September, and it was the same story all over again. A crisis was developing, and Mussolini was exasperated by the lack of news from Berlin. What was Hitler's program? Did he expect any help from Italy? Consultation there was none, and urgent requests for information produced only vague rejoinders. Nuremberg, Berchtesgaden, and Godesberg came and passed, with no direct word from Hitler until September 25, when he finally vouchsafed to his Italian allies the information, already known to them through other channels, that, if the Czechs had not yielded by October 1, Germany would attack.

But three days later, things were much brighter in Rome. The ambassadors of Britain, France, and the United States were stumbling over each other's heels in haste to reach the Duce and beg him to intervene with Hitler to save the peace of the world. It was Mussolini's telephone message to Hitler that clinched the postponement of hostilities and led Hitler to propose the conference in Munich, on condition that the Duce be present in person. For once, the voice of Rome counted for something in the German counsels! And now Benito Mussolini could go to Munich as the Great Peacemaker, and cut the leading figure! Furthermore, it was a role in which Mussolini was confident he could excel. His experience and temper were cosmopolitan, and he was by far the best linguist of the four. Hitler spoke nothing but German; Daladier had a bit of Italian and Chamberlain a touch of French; Mussolini was thoroughly at home in French, and competent if not altogether fluent in both English and German.

Talking to Ciano, just before their departure, Mussolini pretended to be only "moderately happy" at the way things were turning out, because "though perhaps at a heavy price, we could have liquidated France and Great Britain forever; we now have overwhelming proof of this." The "proof," presumably, was the weakness suggested by British and French anxiety for peace.

However that may be, Mussolini's boast was nothing but the play-acting in which he indulged even with his closest associates. Comfortably ensconced in his private train, the Duce was in fine humor, and at dinner regaled Ciano "with great vivacity on every subject":

> He criticizes Britain and British policy severely. "In a country where animals are adored to the point of making cemeteries and hospitals and houses for them, and legacies are bequeathed to parrots, you can be sure that decadence has set in. Besides, other reasons apart, it is also a consequence of the composition of the English people. Four million surplus women. Four million sexually unsatisfied women, artificially creating a host of problems in order to excite or appease their senses. Not being able to embrace one man, they embrace humanity."

Having thus delivered himself, the Duce retired, while Ciano stayed up to play the Great Man to the newspapermen and government aides who were making the trip. Early next morning the travelers reached the old Austro-German border, where they found Adolf Hitler in his more sumptuous train. Mussolini and Ciano finished the journey to Munich in the Fuehrer's carriage, while the other Italians followed in their own train.

4

Munich was Adolf Hitler's meeting, and it was in Berlin that the only purposeful work in preparation for the conference had been done. Basically, this consisted of drafting a rather sketchy agenda and a statement of the German demands.

The work was done by a somewhat oddly assorted trio; Hermann Goering, Baron Constantin von Neurath, and Ernst von Weizsaecker. During the hurly-burly on the morning of September 28, with François-Poncet and Nevile Henderson pressing new concessions on Hitler, and Attolico, the Italian Ambassdor, rushing in and out of the Chancellery with messages from Mussolini, Goering had weighed in heavily with arguments for a settlement by conference. In this he had been strongly supported by Ribbentrop's predecessor as Foreign Minister, Neurath, who had been relegated to virtual retirement six months earlier, but now made a brief reappearance in the Fuehrer's councils. Between them, and with the aid of Mussolini's intervention, Goering and Neurath succeeded in overriding the influence of Ribbentrop, who was catering to Hitler's itch for military conquest.

Soon after Hitler decided in favor of the conference, Goering and Neurath got together with Ernst von Weizsaecker, the number-two man in the Foreign Office, who shared their views on the matter in hand. With Weizsaecker doing most of the drafting, a scenario for the conference was speedily blocked out in a short memorandum.

Their program envisaged a three-step meeting. First the four principals would agree on the answers to a number of basic questions: What parts of the Sudetenland would be ceded to Germany outright? What parts would be dealt with by plebiscite? When would German military occupation begin, and when be completed? How would the new frontier be formally determined? After these matters were resolved, a protocol embodying the results would be prepared by a drafting committee. Then, as the third and final step, the four principals would sign the documents and set up the necessary commissions to carry out their provisions. Together with this agenda was a specification of the German demands, which called for an initial occupation of four border districts between October 1 and 7 and for the subsequent cession of other areas and the holding of plebiscites in accordance with an attached map.

By-passing Ribbentrop, for whom he had little use, Goering took the draft directly to Hitler, who examined it rather cursorily but indicated that it was acceptable. Weizsaecker then buttonholed the Foreign Ministry interpreter, Paul Otto Schmidt, to have a translation prepared for the Italian Ambassador, who spoke no German. Knowing that Schmidt was not competent in Italian, Weizsaecker asked him to put it into French, a language which Attolico could handle.

Attolico at once had had the memorandum repeated by telephone to Rome for the benefit of Mussolini and Ciano. In this there appears to have been no "force-feeding"; the Duce did not like to improvise, and had previously asked the Germans for a statement of Hitler's position.

And so, as Mussolini and Ciano journeyed northward, they were fortified by the knowledge that these terms would be acceptable to Hitler. Nor was there much cause for concern about British and French acquiescence; had not Chamberlain already assured Hitler that he could "get all the essentials without war and without delay"? There would be some dickering to save face, some drafting to be done, and a pageant to be performed of which the Duce, if all went well, would be the hero . . .

5

Lawyers and psychologists especially have long been aware of the fallibility of human perception and recollection, particularly under stress. In the sudden confrontation of alarming circumstances, men see and hear what never happened and are blind to salient features of the actual situation. But there was nothing in Hitler's reception of Mussolini to affright the onlooker, and it was certainly not an unexpected event.

Thus, it is more than a little surprising that the four recorded accounts of the meeting by professed eyewitnesses differ sharply about the circumstances of the encounter. Paul Otto Schmidt, official interpreter for the Foreign Ministry and Hitler's personal interpreter, tells us that he and Hitler drove by automobile from Munich to Kufstein and boarded Mussolini's train for the journey to Munich. Galeazzo Ciano's diary entry for September 29 also specifies Kufstein as the meeting place but states that he and Mussolini moved into Hitler's railway carriage, where maps of the Sudetenland and Germany's western fortifications were spread on a table. Ciano's *chef de cabinet,* Filippo Anfuso, on the other hand, declares that the meeting took place not at Kufstein but some twenty-five miles into Bavaria and closer to Munich, at Rosenheim.

These discrepancies, intrinsically unimportant, are valuable reminders that the reader should not credit everything that he finds in the memoirs. And the contradictions are rendered much more understandable by realization that Schmidt's "eyewitness" account is wholly, and Anfuso's partly, fabricated.

For Schmidt was not competent in Italian, and it would have made little sense to send him to meet Mussolini's party when his excellent command of English and French would be much more useful for the arrival of Chamberlain and Daladier in Munich. Furthermore, his story of Hitler driving to Munich and climbing with a roll of maps into the Duce's railway carriage is inherently incredible; what sort of hospitality would that have been? Finally, and fortunately for historical accuracy, there was another and more reliable recording witness, who states that Schmidt did indeed leave the train from Berlin at Munich.

Lieutenant Colonel Peterpaul von Donat, of the Luftwaffe General Staff, was fluent in Italian and, from time to time, was asked by Hitler, Goering, or other bigwigs to act as an interpreter. Late in the afternoon of the twenty-eighth he had been ordered to board the Fuehrer's special train in Berlin, in order to serve in this capacity at the meeting with Mussolini. His account of what transpired is more complete and plausible than any of the others.

At Munich (according to Donat) Goering, Ribbentrop, and Schmidt detrained in order to receive the British and French delegations coming by air from London and Paris. Hitler, with the Chief of the High Command, General Wilhelm Keitel, and a number of lesser lights including Donat, went on to Kiefersfelden, the last railway stop on the German side of the former border, opposite Kufstein in Austria, by now the Ostmark. A few moments after their arrival, Mussolini's train pulled in and, after a short greeting on the platform, the Duce and Ciano climbed into Hitler's private car, leaving Anfuso and the rest of the Italian delegation in their own train.*

Hitler, who appeared serene and determined, declared it very fortunate that "we two revolutionaries" were changing the face of Europe and restoring their two nations to positions of power and respect. He then asked Keitel to present the military situation, and the general displayed on a map of Czechoslovakia the locations of the planned German attacks from Austria, Bavaria, Saxony, and Silesia. Mussolini could follow the discourse in German, but Ciano, though fluent in English and French, had to rely on Donat's whispered translation. Mussolini occasionally interjected questions, especially about the strength of the Czech fortifications.

Hitler then made a clean breast of the fact that the western front was "completely exposed" (*völlig entblösst*). There had been some fortification between the Rhine and the Moselle, but only weak forces were deployed there. On the Belgian and Dutch frontiers there was virtually nothing, and the situation on the Upper Rhine was "not much better."†

Mussolini reacted with a thoughtful countenance, and Hitler hastened to reassure him that the Czechs would be overrun in a three-to-four-day *Blitzkrieg,* before the west could mobilize. England and France were not well armed and would not face the risk of war. General Vuillemin, Chief of Staff of the French Air Force, had just been given an impressive picture of the Luftwaffe's strength.‡ The appearance of Chamberlain and Daladier in Munich was the best evidence that they would shun any danger of war.

* In view of Mussolini's sensitivity about the German annexation of Austria, it was more tactful for Hitler to receive him on historically German soil at Kiefersfelden than at Kufstein. Although Donat's account was not published until June 1971 (*Deutsches Adelsblatt,* Nr. 6, p. 126), he states that it was written directly after the occasion. I am indebted to David Irving for bringing it to my attention. Donat was aware of Anfuso's published account (1950) and its inconsistency with his own.

† Completely to the contrary, Anfuso wrote that Hitler described the western fortifications as "finished and perfected," and declared that he would launch an attack near Aachen that would defeat "the democracies" before they had mobilized. It is possible that Donat was mistaken in stating that Anfuso was in the Italian train. But Anfuso is a garrulous and unreliable witness (he erroneously wrote that Ribbentrop was present), and the statements Anfuso attributes to Hitler are militarily preposterous. It seems probable that Anfuso has given us an embellished version of what he was told by Ciano.

‡ At this point in his account Donat inserted a comment that he himself had been part of Vuillemin's escort during the French general's visit to Germany, and that the guest had been deluded by "Potemkin masterpieces" contrived by flying German aircraft from one field to another ahead of the French party's arrivals, so that in fact they unknowingly saw the same planes several times.

In response to Mussolini's inquiry, he was then shown an ethnographic map of Czechoslovakia, and Hitler pointed out the areas to be ceded, adding that they laid no claim to any Czech-populated districts. But what he had marked for cession he was determined to get.

According to Donat, the two dictators made no plans for the negotiations in which they were about to engage, and no reference was made to the German settlement memorandum which had been transmitted to Mussolini: "During the whole time, except for Keitel's presentation and the questions by Mussolini, only Hitler spoke: he was the giver, the others were the receivers. Ciano did not get into the discussion."

Whatever Mussolini may have thought of all the Hitlerian bellicosity, Ciano sensed it as *ignis fatuus.* An "atmosphere of agreement" surrounded the occasion: "Even the people waving as the train passes make one realize their joy at the event which is in the air."

At about eleven o'clock the train pulled into the Munich station, where the dictators were greeted by Goering, General Franz Ritter von Epp (the *Reichsstatthalter* of Bavaria), and other Nazi dignitaries. The children had been let out of school for the great day, and through cheering crowds Mussolini and Ciano were driven to their guest rooms in the Prince Charles Palace on the Königinstrasse.

6

Other special trains to Munich were also on the move. Hermann Goering, having made a strong pitch for peace in Berlin, was determined to be part of the Munich circle: "I asked the Fuehrer, or rather, I told him, that under all circumstances I would go along," Goering related in his testimony at the Nuremberg trials: "He agreed. Then I suggested that I could also take Herr von Neurath with me in my train. He agreed to that also."

Still another special train from Berlin was laid on for Foreign Ministry officials and diplomatic representatives of the three powers. The passengers included Weizsaecker and Erich Kordt (Ribbentrop's *chef de cabinet*) from the Foreign Ministry; Nevile Henderson and his first secretary, Sir Ivone Kirkpatrick; François-Poncet and two junior colleagues, Jean Leroy and the air attaché, Captain Paul Stehlin; the Italian Ambassador, Dr. Bernardo Attolico. The last was escorted to the station by his attractive and linguistically gifted wife, who embraced François-Poncet and tearfully begged him to "save the peace for us other Italians who love France."

Meanwhile, journalists and others observers were converging on Munich from all over Europe. Since the conference had been called on less than twenty-four hours' notice, there was a great pushing and clawing for transportation, accommodations, and communications facilities. William L. Shirer, then representing the Columbia radio network in Berlin, finished his evening broadcast and dashed for the train to Munich. If the morrow promised interest, the upshot did not appear uncertain to Shirer, who forecast in his diary that "Mussolini, Chamberlain, and Daladier . . . will rescue Hitler from his limb and he will get his Sudetenland without war, if a couple of days later than he boasted."

There was no special train from Prague.

CHAPTER 3

Ring Around the Table in Munich

1

According to Baedeker, the Königsplatz in Munich is a "masterly creation of neo-classic architecture." Masterly or not, it is assuredly neoclassic and, like many other of the city's buildings and monuments, is largely the product of the dreams of King Ludwig I and the designs of his favorite architect, Leo von Klenze.

The square is bisected east-west by the Briennerstrasse, and at the western entrance stands the Propyläen, adapted by Klenze from the famous ruin on the Acropolis, and erected by Ludwig in honor of his son Otto, the first King of Greece in modern times. The Propyläen's dates are not auspicious, for it was commenced in 1848, the year in which Ludwig thought it wise to abdicate because of unpopularity largely aroused by his relations with the dancer Lola Montez, and was completed in 1862, just as Otto himself was driven from the throne of Greece.

On the north side of the square stands Klenze's Greek-style Glyptothek (sculpture gallery), and on the south side another neoclassic structure of similar vintage by Ziebland, the State Gallery of Modern Art. The east side is bounded by the Arcisstrasse, crossed by the Briennerstrasse. As one stands in the Königsplatz looking eastward along the Briennerstrasse, a quarter of a mile distant at the Karolinenplatz rises the shaft of a bronze obelisk, again the work of Ludwig I and Klenze. The Briennerstrasse takes its name from Brienne-le-Château, a town in northeastern France where Bavarians fought with the allies *against* Napoleon in 1814. With fine impartiality, Ludwig dedicated the obelisk to the thousands of Bavarians who perished in Russia while fighting *for* Napoleon in 1812.

It was among these relics of the royal Wittelsbachs that Adolf Hitler, nearly a century later, established the national headquarters of the Nazi Party.* At first blush the architectural atmosphere may not appear congenial to a professedly revolutionary movement, and it is probable that his decision owed much to chance. In 1930, before the Nazi seizure of power and when Hitler still had to watch his pennies, the Party had managed to acquire an 1828 Biedermeier-style building called the "Barlow-Palais," on the Briennerstrasse just east of the

---

* Officially called the National Sozialistische Deutsche Arbeiter Partei (National Socialist German Workers Party), or NSDAP.

Königsplatz. It was altered for use as the main Party headquarters, and in 1931 Hitler named it the Brown House.

A few years later he was Chancellor and Chief of State, and the NSDAP was the only political party in Germany. There was no lack of funds, and the Party headquarters needed more office space. In 1935 construction was begun on two huge buildings on the Arcisstrasse, one on either side of the Briennerstrasse, facing the Königsplatz. The Fuehrer, artist *manqué* that he was, lavished much personal attention on the two-year project, which was carried out by the official Party *Baumeister*, Paul Ludwig Troost.

Whatever one's feelings about the neoclassic style, it would be hard to deny that Ludwig I and Klenze builded better than Hitler and Troost. A hundred yards long, fifty deep, and only three stories high, with evenly spaced window rows, the identical buildings look like a pair of casernes to which a few heavy porticos have been glued. Between them, opposite the Propyläen, two "temples of honor" were erected in memory of the sixteen Nazis who were killed in the 1923 "Beer Hall Putsch."

Today nothing remains of the temples or the Brown House, but the two big buildings on the Arcisstrasse still stand. The northern edifice, used now by the Amerikahaus and the Bavarian State Archives, was built as the working quarters for the Fuehrer and his personal Party staff, and was called the Fuehrerbau.

It was to the Fuehrerbau that the participants in the Munich conference were brought shortly after noon on September 29, 1938, and it was in Hitler's private office—his *Arbeitszimmer*—that the principals conferred.

2

Of the guests, Neville Chamberlain and his party were the first to arrive at the Fuehrerbau. Over the portico was a large bronze eagle, and inside they passed through a grandiose central hall and up a stone staircase to a lobby or salon, where a buffet lunch was served by liveried footmen. Inside and out were swarms of black-uniformed SS men, every one the image of stiff, heel-clicking punctilio.

Daladier and François-Poncet, meanwhile, were en route in an open automobile with Goering, resplendent in a white uniform which, the Premier thought, "accentuated his curves." *Unser Hermann* was exuberantly hospitable, oozing charm at every one of his many pores in his anxiety to please the Frenchman. At first Daladier sniffed suspiciously at his gargantuan and effusive escort, but the cheers of the crowds lining the streets through which they passed soon drove the clouds from his brow. As they approached the Fuehrerbau, host and guest were waving and smiling like the politicians they both were.

Goering swept the Frenchmen inside and up the stairs; François-Poncet thought the interior resembled "some modern mammoth hotel furnished by a professional interior decorator." In the salon they encountered Chamberlain, Wilson, and Strang, all clad in black. François-Poncet did not find the Prime Minister very appetizing: "Chamberlain, grizzled, bowed, with bushy eyebrows and prominent teeth, his face blotchy, his hands reddened by rheumatism."

Whatever his faults, Benito Mussolini was not one to be caught standing

WHO WAS WHO AT MUNICH

Participants in the Opening Conference in Hitler's Office

1. Adolf Hitler
2. Joachim von Ribbentrop*
3. Neville Chamberlain
4. Sir Horace Wilson
5. Benito Mussolini
6. Galeazzo Ciano
7. Edouard Daladier
8. Alexis Léger

9. Paul Otto Schmidt

Later Participants and Extras

German

10. Hermann Goering
11. Ernst von Weizsaecker
12. Constantin von Neurath
13. Otto Abetz
14. Erich Kordt
15. Heinrich Himmler
16. Fritz Wiedemann
17. Rudolf Hess
18. Hans von Mackensen
19. General Wilhelm Keitel

20. Major Rudolf Schmundt

British

21. Sir Nevile Henderson
22. William Strang
23. Sir William Malkin
24. Frank Ashton-Gwatkin
25. Sir Ivone Kirkpatrick
26. Lord Dunglass

Italian

27. Bernardo Attolico
28. Filippo Anfuso

29. Dino Alfieri

French

30. André François-Poncet
31. Charles Rochat
32. Jean Leroy
33. Marcel Clapier

34. Captain Paul Stehlin

Czechoslovakian†

35. Hubert Masařík
36. Vojtech Mastny

*As described in the text, the participation of Ribbentrop in the opening meeting is questioned but probable; Weizsaecker is listed by Wilson as present at the first meeting, but this is improbable.

† The Czech representatives were required to remain in their hotel rooms throughout the discussions at the Fuehrerbau, and only after the agreement was signed were they officially informed of its contents.

WHO WAS WHO AT MUNICH

Identity of the Participants

1. Fuehrer and Reichskanzler
2. Foreign Minister
3. Prime Minister
4. Chief Industrial Adviser, and Chamberlain's personal consultant
5. Duce and Prime Minister
6. Foreign Minister
7. Premier
8. Secretary-General of the French Foreign Ministry
9. Official Interpreter for the German Foreign Ministry
10. Second man in the Third Reich, Luftwaffe Commander
11. State Secretary of the German Foreign Ministry
12. Former Foreign Minister
13. Ribbentrop's personal representative in Paris
14. Ribbentrop's *chef de cabinet*
15. Leader of the SS (*Schutzstaffel*)
16. Hitler's civilian aide
17. Third man in the Third Reich and Deputy Fuehrer
18. Ambassador to Italy
19. Chief of the Armed Forces High Command
20. Hitler's military aide
21. Ambassador to Germany
22. Chief, Central European Department, Foreign Office
23. Legal Adviser to the Foreign Office
24. Counselor, Foreign Office
25. First Secretary of the British Embassy in Berlin
26. Chamberlain's personal parliamentary secretary
27. Italian Ambassador to Germany
28. Ciano's *chef de cabinet*
29. Minister of Propaganda
30. French Ambassador to Germany
31. Chief, European Section, Foreign Ministry
32. On François-Poncet's staff, at Munich handling encoded messages
33. Daladier's *chef de cabinet*
34. Assistant Air Attaché, Berlin
35. Counselor, Foreign Ministry
36. Czech Minister to Germany

around and waiting for anyone else, and he knew how to make an entrance. So, too, trains can carry more people than can planes, and now the Duce and Ciano entered the Fuehrerbau at the head of a troupe of followers, all in black-shirt uniform and covered with braid and medals. Hitler emerged from wherever he had been awaiting the moment, and went down the grand staircase to greet him. After such special treatment Mussolini knew better than to be seen fraternizing with the enemy. He vouchsafed brief handshakes to Chamberlain and Daladier, and went to a corner of the salon where he and a number of the Germans staged a friendly reunion.

A step behind the Duce came the Fuehrer, apparently ill at ease, and seeming rather to cling to his fellow-dictator for moral support against this alien invasion of the Nazi sanctum sanctorum. He saluted Chamberlain mechanically and Daladier, whom he had never met, rather less so. The Frenchman's first impression of Hitler at this, their only encounter, was mixed:

> Now, behind all these gaudy visitors, Hitler, pale and tense, came in alone. I remarked his brown hair, with a heavy lock falling over his forehead. His dull blue eyes, shifting rapidly during the brief greetings, gave him a hard and remote expression.
>
> He was dressed very simply, like a man of the people, in a khaki jacket, with a swastika armband on the right sleeve,* and long trousers falling on scuffed black shoes. Such was the way this man appeared to me—the man who by trick, force, and violence had made himself supreme dictator of Germany.
>
> I had said, and repeated in London, that his aim was to dominate Europe. Seeing him now, I thought that I had not been mistaken.

The tiny British and French delegations, in sober mufti, were lost in a swirl of Nazi and Fascist uniforms; there were linguistic difficulties and the atmosphere was uneasy. Kirkpatrick managed brief conversations with the Italian and French parties, some of whom he knew from his earlier postings to Paris and Rome. Chamberlain moved over to thank Mussolini for making the occasion possible. Seeking to relax the atmosphere with small talk, the Prime Minister, an incorrigible Izaak Walton, asked Mussolini whether he liked angling. But the Duce was not to be drawn; a blank stare rebuffed the fishing ploy, and the conversation petered out.

Hitler had no personal use for the buffet and was impatient to get going. There was a slight delay because Daladier had lost track of Léger and Hitler tried to get the Premier to go it alone. But Daladier was quite unwilling: "I can't begin without him. Léger knows all the details, I know nothing." Léger, in turn, had to hunt for a lady secretary who had all the papers. Finally the French got organized, and shortly before one o'clock the principals proceeded to Hitler's office.

Who were they? It is certain that at least eight persons were present from the outset: Hitler and Paul Otto Schmidt, the senior German Foreign Ministry interpreter; Chamberlain and Sir Horace Wilson; Daladier and Léger; Mussolini and Ciano.

* In fact, as pictures show, the armband was on the left sleeve.

Beyond these eight, the testimony of eyewitnesses—just as in connection with the Hitler-Mussolini meeting at Kiefersfelden—is in conflict. Léger, interrogated on the point thirty years later, insisted that no one else was there; that Hitler was initially accompanied by no one but Schmidt, whose responsibilities were limited to interpretation, and that Ribbentrop was excluded, in line with Hitler's desire to keep the foreign ministers out. The Frenchman's recollection is corroborated by Sir Alec Douglas-Home (then Lord Dunglass), who recalled seeing Ribbentrop in the corridors during most of the opening conference. Sir Horace Wilson, however, insists that Ribbentrop was present from the beginning, and his contemporaneous notes also list Ribbentrop's deputy, Ernst von Weizsaecker, as one of the initial conferees. Schmidt agrees that Ribbentrop was present, but recalls Weizsaecker as coming to only the later sessions. Ciano and Schmidt both report Ribbentrop's, but not Weizsaecker's, attendance.

These discrepancies are less surprising considering that there were three distinct sessions of the conference, and that during the second and third the principals were no longer *in camera,* but rather the focus of an increasing group of secondary participants and kibitzers. It was easy to remember mistakenly someone as present at the outset who, in fact, appeared only at the later sessions. Despite Léger's firm belief, it is difficult to conceive that Hitler would have excluded Ribbentrop from a meeting to which the much junior Ciano was admitted. It is also unlikely that he would have outnumbered the others by bringing in Weizsaecker, who probably joined the group only after the first sitting.

Whether eight, nine, or ten in number, Hitler led the chosen into his office and the doors were closed. The conferees found themselves in a large rectangular room with a fireplace at one end, a heavy chandelier, and a large desk near the fireplace. Over the mantel hung one of the painter Lenbach's many portraits of Bismarck, and on the other walls were the works of several German artists—Böcklin, Feuerbach, Menzel.

None of the usual trappings of summit conferences was at hand; no long green table, only a small round one; no name cards, pads, or freshly sharpened pencils were provided, whether because of haste, oversight, or Hitler's desire thus to manifest the summary nature of the anticipated proceedings. The orderly British civil servants were shocked: Strang recalls Munich as a "huggermugger* affair," and Sir Horace Wilson primly noted that "the organization of the conference was very imperfect, and there appeared to be no arrangements for the taking of notes."

The seating arrangements were completely impromptu. Nobody took the chair; there was no agenda; the conversation followed no fixed plan but jumped back and forth from one subject to another. According to Daladier, Hitler ensconced himself in an armchair at the left of the entrance, with Schmidt on his right, and left it to the others to seat themselves—Chamberlain and Wilson next to Schmidt, Mussolini and Ciano on a sofa in the center, and the two Frenchmen completing the ring around the central table.

* A word of obscure, probably Celtic origin, used by Strang in his memoirs as denoting a state of utter confusion.

3

The files of the German Foreign Ministry contain an unsigned memorandum purporting to have been prepared in Munich at seven in the evening of September 29, and presumably dictated by Paul Otto Schmidt from the notes he made as interpreter in the course of the discussion. The memorandum covers only part of the first meeting, which lasted a bit over two hours, until about three in the afternoon. This document is the most complete and objective record of the opening session that we possess, but it is flat and neutral and undertakes no expression of the tone and temper of the proceedings.

Upon his return to London, Horace Wilson dictated a brief memoir on the conference, "written from memory." Outside of the Schmidt and Wilson accounts, the participants have left us only a few scraps of recollection: a passage in Chamberlain's letter written three days later to his sister Hilda; a couple of paragraphs in Ciano's diary; Daladier's oral account to Ambassador Bullitt on October 3, and his articles on Munich written for a French newspaper (*Candide*) many years later, in 1961. Neither Hitler nor Mussolini, nor any of the other participants in the first meeting, left any useful record of what transpired.

From these sources, primarily from Schmidt's memorandum, the course of discussion, in outline, emerges clearly enough:

(1) Hitler opened the meeting with a statement the gist of which was that German occupation of the Sudetenland must commence without delay, and the ultimate boundaries be settled by plebiscite;

(2) During or following the comments in reply by Chamberlain and Daladier, Mussolini produced the draft of German demands which had been telephoned to him from Berlin the previous day, and put them forward as his own proposed settlement;

(3) Daladier and Chamberlain at once accepted the draft as the basis of discussion;

(4) Chamberlain expressed unwillingness to guarantee fulfillment of the German demands without their prior acceptance by the Czech Government;

(5) Chamberlain's point led to a prolonged dispute with Hitler, in the course of which the Prime Minister unsuccessfully urged that a Czech representative attend the conference;

(6) On Chamberlain's suggestion, the meeting was adjourned temporarily so that the "Mussolini" proposal might be distributed and studied.

But what did all this really look and sound like? Consider Horace Wilson's cool and compendious description of the discussion leading up to Mussolini's production of the draft: "This meeting . . . began by a brief statement by Herr Hitler thanking those present for their acceptances of his invitation and pointing out the need for speedy decisions. Mr. Chamberlain replied suitably, as did M. Daladier and Signor Mussolini. Towards the close of his remarks Signor Mussolini said that he thought the best way of making progress was for someone to produce a basis for discussion, and he therefore read the Memorandum. . . ." In like vein, Chamberlain wrote to his sister that Hitler's "opening sentences, when we gathered around for our conference, were so moderate and reasonable that I felt instant relief."

Daladier's version of the same colloquy is almost totally dissimilar. Hitler opened the meeting, he told Bullitt, with a "tremendous discourse," to which Daladier responded by observing that "all four countries represented were prepared to make war at once; the question was whether Czechoslovakia was to be attacked and invaded and destroyed, or whether there was to be a reasonable settlement." Whereupon, the Premier declared, Hitler "calmed down," and an orderly discussion ensued.

Twenty-three years later, Daladier painted the picture in equally vivid colors and greater detail:

> Hitler arose and delivered a diatribe against the Czechs. It was a real explosion. Spreading his arms or clenching his fists, he accused the Czechs of a frightful tyranny over the [Sudeten] Germans, with torture, and the expulsion of thousands in panic-stricken herds.

Daladier claims that he then asked whether it was Hitler's intention to destroy Czechoslovakia and annex it to Germany. If so, there was nothing for him to do but return to France. Greatly agitated, Mussolini cried that it was all a misunderstanding, and Hitler then, in calmer tones, assured Daladier that he had no wish to annex any Czechs, and only wanted to bring all the Germans into a common national community. Mussolini then pulled a sheet of paper from the outer pocket of his tunic, and said it was a sketch of a compromise proposal. Daladier asked that the text be made available for study, and the conference adjourned for that purpose.

So was borne the "French" version of how the conference began, in which Daladier looms large. It is also to be found in the memoirs of François-Poncet and Stehlin, who, since they were not present, must have relied on what Daladier told them. In view of how things soon turned out, this chest-thumping is more than a little pathetic, and very little of what Daladier says he said appears in Schmidt's notes of the discussion. But if the Frenchman's imagination was working to assuage his conscience, equally the British were straining out of their memories the unseemly moments. The settlement would soon have to be sold to Parliament and the people, and the more reasonable Hitler could be made to appear, the easier that would be.

All things considered, it is likely that Ciano captured the opening scene most accurately in recording that "The Fuehrer . . . speaks calmly, but from time to time he gets excited and then he raises his voice and beats his fist against the palm of his other hand." Daladier's version of what he himself said may have been wishful thinking, but his description of Hitler's opening statements is apparently far more accurate than those of Chamberlain and Wilson. Such is the conclusion compelled by Schmidt's contemporaneous notes, which would not be expected to contain any derogatory comments on Hitler's behavior, and which show quite clearly that Hitler spoke at considerable length, and in words heavy with menace:

. The existence of Czechoslovakia in her present form threatened the peace of Europe. . . . Germany could no longer contemplate the distress and misery of the Sudeten German population. Reports of the destruction of property were coming in in increasing numbers. The population was exposed to a barbaric persecution. Since he, the Fuehrer, had last spoken to Mr. Chamberlain, the number of refugees had risen to 240,000 and there seemed to be no end to the flood. . . . This tension made it necessary to settle the problem in a few days as it was no longer possible to wait weeks. At the wish of Mussolini he, the Fuehrer, had declared himself ready to postpone mobilization* in Germany for 24 hours. Further delay would be a crime. . . . However, in order to ascertain exactly what territory was involved, it could not be left to a commission to decide. It was much rather a plebiscite that was necessary, especially as for 20 years no free election had taken place in Czechoslovakia. He had declared in his speech in the Sportspalast that he would in any case march in on October 1. He had received the answer that this action would have the character of an act of violence. Hence the task arose to absolve this action from such a character. Action must, however, be taken at once. . . . From the military aspect the occupation represented no problem, for the depths on all fronts were comparatively small. With a little good will it must consequently be possible to evacuate the territory in 10 days; indeed, he was convinced, from 6 to 7 days. . . . The conditions governing the transfer could be discussed, but action must soon be taken. . . .

All this amounted to nothing more pacific than an indication that, if the British and French could ensure that the Czechs would evacuate the lands Hitler wanted, there need be no hostilities; the action would thus be "absolved" of violence. The brutal cynicism of such an absolution was lost upon the British if not the French, and, when Mussolini pulled out the draft, this was precisely the solution which was presented. The first clause stipulated that evacuation begin October 1, and the second that "the guarantor Powers, England, France, and Italy, will guarantee to Germany that the evacuation will be completed by 10th October, without any existing installations having been destroyed."

Mussolini's production of the Weizsaecker-Neurath-Goering memorandum, which had been put into Italian since its transmittal to Rome the previous afternoon, caused Herr Schmidt a moment of uneasiness, since he knew no Italian. As it was read, however, the interpreter soon recognized it for what it was, and remembered the French text he had made twenty-four hours earlier well enough to translate the Italian text back into the other languages.

The British and French were, of course, ignorant of the document's provenance, but it is doubtful that they would have reacted differently had they known. As they listened, Chamberlain and Wilson found it a "reasonable restatement of much that had been discussed" previously, and were ready to accept it as a basis for discussion. They were worried that the French might be less receptive, but "to our relief" (as Wilson noted) Daladier "at once said he was prepared to adopt Signor Mussolini's document as a basis for discussion." Chamberlain then agreed outright to the first clause, specifying October 1 for

---

* In fact the German forces were already deployed for war, though no formal mobilization order had been issued. It was the attack itself, as well as open mobilization, which Hitler had agreed to postpone.

commencement of the evacuation, but said that "he wanted to discuss carefully Clause 2." Apparently Chamberlain saw in the provision for a guarantee that the Czechs would complete the evacuation by October 10, without destruction of "existing installations," an opportunity to raise the matter which was most troubling to him: the exclusion of Czechoslovakia from the conference. How, Chamberlain asked, could Britain give such a guarantee when "there had been no opportunity to ascertain how far, if at all, the Czech government were or would be disposed to consent"?

The Prime Minister's *démarche* was not at all to Hitler's liking, and led to the first angry outburst—Wilson described it as a "tirade"—from the Fuehrer. He was not interested in assurances from the Czechs; they were already "carrying out demolition work" in the areas to be ceded. He had been asked to stay his hand; if those who had done the asking were not prepared to take the responsibility for Czechoslovakia's compliance, then perhaps he had best resume his previous methods!

Chamberlain and Daladier both hastened to reassure Hitler that they fully agreed with his demand for an immediate settlement, and the Fuehrer appeared to be measurably "soothed," as Wilson put it. But the problem was not so easily settled. Chamberlain asserted that the word "guarantee" meant a great deal in the English language, and that before he would set his name to such a document "he must know whether he could honor it." He did not insist that a Czech representative participate in the discussions, but reiterated his desire for "the presence of a Prague representative in the next room, in order that assurances could be obtained from him."

Hitler replied that no Czech representative was in fact "available," and that "if the Czech government's consent had first to be sought on every detail, a solution could not be expected before a fortnight had passed." Meanwhile the Czechs busily were destroying bridges and buildings. Under the Duce's proposal, details of the transfer would be handled by an International Commission on which Czechoslovakia would be represented. What he wanted was that the great powers would "throw their authority into the scales and accept the responsibility for correct completion of the transfer."

So the argument swayed back and forth among the four leaders. Mussolini agreed with Hitler that it was "not possible to await a Czech representative" and that "the great Powers must undertake moral guarantees as regards evacuation and prevention of destruction." Daladier at first supported Chamberlain's insistence on the presence of a Czech representative, and then backed water: "If the inclusion of a Prague representative would cause difficulties he was ready to forego this, for it was important that the question should be settled speedily."

Chamberlain did not explicitly withdraw his request for a Czech presence, but turned the discussion to points of detail. As Wilson recorded: "The conclusion was reached that the heads of the four Powers must accept responsibility for deciding—in the circumstances—how the situation should be dealt with." The ritual dance would remain a quadrille.

At the conclusion of this discussion, on Chamberlain's suggestion, the meeting was temporarily adjourned so that the draft produced by Mussolini could be studied and amendments prepared. The suspension turned into a luncheon recess, and shortly after three o'clock the delegations left the Fuehrerbau, the British and French for their respective hotels, and Mussolini, as honored guest, to Hitler's private dwelling.

4

While the principals had been conferring, the others were enduring that most nerve-racking of occupations in critical circumstances: waiting. Some of the British and French, such as Strang and Dunglass, remained in the rooms assigned to the visiting delegations, while others roamed the corridors and anterooms, where Goering, Keitel, and other German bigwigs, the Italian visitors, and black-uniformed SS officers were much in evidence. There was abundant rumor, and desultory gossip; Donat interpreted a conversation between Hitler's personal physician (Dr. Theodor Morell) and his Italian opposite number, in which the former disclosed the Fuehrer's chronic insomnia and dependence on medications, and the latter boasted of the Duce's iron constitution: *"mens sana in corpore sano."*

When the meeting adjourned, Hitler's appearance strongly suggested that he had not been enjoying himself. The whole idea of a conference at which his was not automatically the last word was alien and irksome to him, and as he left the scene he appeared, to Kirkpatrick, in a very dark mood: "Hitler accompanies Mussolini. I can see him now walking along the gallery on the first floor. He is talking very fast to Mussolini. The Duce's face is impassive, but Hitler's is black as thunder and he is emphasizing his remarks with short, angry movements of his hands."

A French journalist in the crowd gathered outside the Fuehrerbau saw Hitler emerge from the building and "plunge directly into his car." He was followed by Chamberlain and then by Daladier, shambling absent-mindedly toward Mussolini's vehicle: "A black guard pointed out his mistake, and the French Premier, with an imperceptible shrug, moved aside for Mussolini." Lighting a cigarette, Daladier entered his own vehicle, closely followed by Goering, who viewed the little contretemps as a huge joke and was laughing heartily: "The crowd was amused and clapped loudly. No doubt the fact that the marshal and the French Premier were sitting side by side appeared as a good omen."

Hitler and Mussolini lunched together in the former's private apartment on the Prinzregentenstrasse. Ciano, who (as well as Himmler) was of their company, was surprised to find the Fuehrer living in "a modest apartment in a large building full of other residents," but was impressed by the "many very valuable pictures" on the walls. Here Donat took over the interpretation duties, and he has left us a detailed account of the Hitlerian monologue, broken by occasional questions from Mussolini, which accompanied the meal. "In contrast to his serenity that morning," Donat writes, "Hitler now was aroused and full of rage, to which he gave free rein, at Chamberlain." Then, quoting the Fuehrer:

Daladier is a lawyer,* who understands the particulars and consequences;

* No lawyer, Daladier had a fine academic background in classics and history.

with him one can negotiate clearly and satisfactorily. But this Chamberlain is like a haggling shop-keeper who wrangles over every village and small detail; he's worse than the Czechs themselves. What has he lost in Bohemia? Nothing at all!

The Fuehrer went on to discuss the Godesberg encounter, where Chamberlain had impressed him as an "insignificant" man whose dearest wish was to go fishing on a weekend: "I know no weekends and I don't fish!" It was high time for England to stop playing the role of "Governess of Europe." Repeating his morning description of himself and the Duce as "revolutionaries," he spoke of a future struggle against England which would give "men in their time of full strength their years at the summit."

Hitler then asked Mussolini whether the Italian royal house was not an obstacle to his objectives, and whether it was true that the royal family remained "pro-English." Mussolini replied that during the Italo-Ethiopian War, Crown Prince Umberto had spoken "wrongly." Thereupon Mussolini had told him that the House of Savoy had survived only thanks to the Duce, and that Fascism was so firmly anchored in Italy that the monarchy must cleave to it through thick and thin. The Crown Prince had then promised to conduct himself loyally.

Mussolini turned the issue back on Hitler, asking about Germany's internal security. Hitler answered that he had the entire working class behind him, and the only opposition came from reactionaries in clerical circles and among the landowning nobility. The Duce shrewdly inquired whether domestic tranquillity might suffer from a pardon for Pastor Niemöller*; "everywhere one had heard his name, and after so long an imprisonment might not his release be a good thing?" But Hitler was "all iron": "No! The man is too dangerous. . . . He has great freedom in the concentration camp and is well treated, but he won't be let out!" And the Fuehrer called on Himmler to confirm the pastor's good circumstances.

After these edifying interchanges, late in the afternoon Hitler, still irritable and impatient with the whole scene, escorted his guest back to the Fuehrerbau.

5

The Fuehrer was not the only one displeased by the course of events. Back in his suite at the Four Seasons, Daladier was calling Hitler's demands "inacceptable" and growling about returning to Paris. Goering, who seemed bound to dance attendance at every possible moment, telephoned to suggest that they lunch together, but Stehlin, still handling the telephone for the French, was instructed to decline: "Tell Goering I must work with my colleagues." Stehlin phrased the refusal as best he could, but Goering's disappointment was manifest, and he held Stehlin on the phone for a bit of psychological warfare: "What did Daladier need to discuss? Had the conference changed things?"

* The Reverend Martin Niemöller, a submarine commander in the First World War who became a prominent Protestant clergyman in Berlin, and at first supported the Nazis. Disillusioned and opposed to Hitler's efforts to dominate the church, he was arrested in 1937 and was held in "protective custody" in the concentration camps Sachsenhansen and Dachau until freed by Allied troops in 1945.

Stehlin said he thought not, but Goering nevertheless urged him to emphasize to Daladier the difficulty of getting Hitler to accept the "Mussolini proposition."

According to Stehlin "neither Daladier nor François-Poncet was duped," but neither was anyone fooled by Daladier's own discontented mutterings. There was nothing the French could do but get it over with. Nor were his comments to an inquiring journalist a model of French lucidity; asked for his "impressions," the Premier replied: "I have no impression . . . when I say that I have no impression, it must be understood that I do not say that I have a bad impression. On the contrary, the mere fact that we are all four here is in itself a good sign, as I see it."

At their quarters in the Regina Palace Hotel on the Maximiliansplatz, the British were the only delegation that was trying to put the luncheon recess to some use. As Chamberlain and Wilson saw it, the right thing was being done, and all that was now necessary was to do it tidily. But on this occasion the usually systematic Germans were being most untidy, and in addition to the organizational defects bemoaned by Sir Horace Wilson, communications between the Fuehrerbau, the Regina Palace, and London were poor. Kirkpatrick observed: "The burden thrown on the telephone system . . . was so great that it was quicker to send a car with a message to our office in the hotel than to attempt to telephone."

For the British, the major stumbling block revealed at the opening session was the matter of the guarantee. By the end of the session it had become clear that, if an agreement were to be reached, it would be by the four, without hearing from the Czechs. And so during the recess the British sought to improve the shining hour by drafting some amendments to the Mussolini draft, to save their own position in a manner likewise acceptable to Hitler.

To this end, they prepared a preamble reciting that the four powers "have agreed on the following terms and conditions governing the cession of the Sudeten-German territory" and that "they each hold themselves responsible for the steps necessary to secure its fulfillment"; by this means Germany was involved as a party to the agreement rather than only as its beneficiary. In addition, the second clause was modified by removing the troublesome words "guarantor" and "guarantee" and stipulating instead that England, France, and Italy "agree" that the evacuation, with no destruction, be completed by October 10, and that "the Czech government will be held responsible for carrying out the evacuation without damage as aforesaid."

Of course, as a practical matter it made not the slightest difference whether the three powers "guaranteed" Czech compliance or "agreed" to hold Czechoslovakia "responsible" for compliance. But elimination of the naughty word "guarantee" was a neat little face-saver and, once the linguistic problems were surmounted, the changes might prove acceptable to the other delegations.

During the luncheon discussion, Sir Horace Wilson drew up a list of "points to be settled" at the second session.* The first two related to the boundaries of the areas to be occupied by the Germans between the first and tenth of October. The third asked: "What is to be position of Czechs and other non-Germans in

---

* Only the first of two pages of this list appears to have survived.

transitional period?"—i.e., during the initial German occupation and before the final settlement of the new border. As a proposed solution, Wilson noted: "Presumably the right of option which the Chancellor had already accepted is to hold good. Those who stay to receive fair treatment. Transfers to be encouraged." The fourth point related to the "preservation of order" in the areas not yet definitely allocated to either country, and it was tentatively proposed to use the British Legion of ex-servicemen. The fifth point concerned "Property" in the areas to be ceded, none of which was to be "destroyed"; an International Commission would settle the compensation to be paid by the Germans for state and private property transferred to them.

Sir Horace Wilson thought he had an understanding that the French would stop at the Regina Palace on their way back to the Fuehrerbau, but for whatever reason, they did not show up. Thus the British and French returned to the conference without contact or consultation with each other or the Czechs.

Outside the Regina Palace, large crowds were demonstrating great enthusiasm for Mr. Chamberlain. A band was playing "The Lambeth Walk"—a then popular English dance tune punctuated by shouts of "Oy!"—heard on this occasion in Bavarian instead of Cockney accents. Neville Chamberlain was getting more and more popular almost everywhere except in Czechoslovakia, and he drove back to his afternoon's work midst loud and indubitably sincere acclamations— the "Hero of Munich Crowds," according to the Associated Press.

6

While the conference participants were reassembling at the Fuehrerbau, an airplane from Prague was en route to Munich carrying two Czech representatives, or, more accurately, "observers." Beneš' anguished plea that his country's voice should be heard to plead its cause had resulted only in brusque "advice" from Halifax, during the evening of the twenty-eighth, that Prague should "have suitable representative, authorized to speak in their behalf, available to go to Munich at short notice tomorrow."

Just how the arrangements for the Czechs were made is not clear from the records. At about nine in the morning of the twenty-ninth, the Czech Foreign Minister, Kamil Krofta, informed his *chef de cabinet,* Hubert Masařík, that he and the Czech Minister to Germany, Vojtech Mastny, had been designated as "observers" attached to the British delegation at Munich. Early that afternoon Jan Masaryk informed Halifax that Mastny and Karel Lisicky, the Czech counselor in London, were "proceeding to Munich to be at disposal of British and French delegations for information only, as suggested by Mr. Chamberlain." Beneš explicitly stipulated that Czechoslovakia was not taking part in the Munich conference, but his government was willing to participate in a subsequent "international conference where Germany and Czechoslovakia, among other nations, would be represented"—the plain implication being that a meeting at a place and with participants specified by Hitler was not such a meeting.

The news of Munich had been a bitter blow to Beneš and Jan Masaryk, whose hopes had been raised by the apparent impasse after Godesberg. Their despair was matched by anger and chagrin among the Czech generals. The Chief of Staff, General Ludwik Krejcí, returned from his headquarters in Moravia to Prague, and waited upon the President, in company with General Jan Syrový (Inspector General of the Army and newly designated Premier) and the three principal field commanders, Generals Vojcechovsky, Luza, and Prchala, and General Blaha, chief of the President's Military Cabinet. The military men pleaded with Beneš to make no more concessions; things had reached the point at which the country must fight. The Army was ready to do its duty, and the western powers would be shamed into giving support.

Wearily, Beneš replied that he must look at a bigger picture. Britain and France, he declared, would not come into the fray, but rather would say that Czechoslovakia was guilty of having started the war. The soldiers departed, bitter and dejected.

Mastny and Masařík, accompanied by a code clerk and a member of the Czech Press Bureau,* took off from Prague at three in the afternoon and arrived at Munich at about half-past four. How the Germans had been informed of their coming is unclear. No French or British were on hand to meet the Czechs at the airport, and, as Masařík related in his subsequent report, the German greeting was chilly:

> The reception we met with at the aerodrome was like that for police suspects. We were taken in a police car, accompanied by members of the Gestapo, to the *Regina,* where the British delegation was also staying. We were forbidden to leave our rooms, which were guarded by policemen. The conference was already in progress, and only with difficulty did I get first Rochat and then Ashton-Gwatkin on the telephone. The latter told me he wished to speak to me immediately at the hotel.
>
> At 7 P.M. I had my first conversation with Mr. Ashton-Gwatkin. He was nervous and very reserved. From certain cautious remarks, I gathered that a plan, the details of which Mr. Gwatkin could not then give me, was already completed in its main outlines and that it was much harsher than the Anglo-French proposals. On our red map, I explained to him all our really vital interests. Mr. Gwatkin showed a certain understanding of the question of the Moravian corridor, though he completely ignored all the other elements of the problem . . . I drew Mr. Gwatkin's attention to the consequences of such a plan from the internal political, economic and financial aspect. He answered that I did not seem to realise how difficult the situation was for the Western Powers or how awkward it was to negotiate with Hitler. On which, Mr. Gwatkin returned to the Conference, promising that we should be called at the first interval.

The Czechs had come as "observers," but it had already been made clear that they would have little opportunity to observe anything that could not be seen from the rooms of the Regina Palace.

Shortly after four-thirty the several parties returned to the Fuehrerbau with the British and French, as previously, preceding the dictators. Before the meet-

---

* Lisicky was not with them, and how he got to Munich does not appear in the records; Masaryk asked Halifax to bring him back to London on one of the British planes. There seems to be no doubt about his presence in Munich, but according to Masařík he was not present at any of the Anglo-Czech meetings.

ing was resumed, Chamberlain and Daladier fell into a conversation which persisted after Hitler's arrival. The Fuehrer's irritation at their inattention was manifest to Kirkpatrick, who observed his "gestures of impatience" and angry look as he dispatched Ribbentrop "to summon the two statesmen to the table."

Despite this inauspicious beginning, the participants, other than Hitler, were more relaxed than they had been. Likewise, the composition and character of the meeting were now greatly changed, though no less confused. The circle of participants was at once enlarged by the addition of the Berlin ambassadors—Attolico, Henderson, and François-Poncet. The last-named has described the scene as the second meeting began:

> The delegates were grouped in a semi-circle around a vast fireplace, the British on the left, the Italians and Germans in the center, the French on the right. Within the British group there was scant conversation; within the German and Italian groups there was much. Mussolini was deeply ensconced in his armchair. His extraordinary mobile features were never at rest for a moment; his mouth would part for a wide smile or contrast in a pout; his brows rose in surprise or were knit threateningly; his eyes, generally curious and amused in expression, would suddenly dart lightning.

After some general discussion, specific issues and proposals emerged which required drafting and translation, and these things could not be accomplished without the assistance of others. The subordinate members of the delegations had been accommodated in nearby rooms, and there began a constant to-ing and fro-ing, as documents were sent out of the conference room for redrafting or translation, and then brought back for consideration by the principals. Hitler himself was accustomed to functioning in a shifting group of aides and advisers, and now no effort was made to confine the circle; as Schmidt remembers, "legal advisers, secretaries and adjutants came into the room and formed a tense audience around the heads of governments who sat in the middle."

Since many more were present, for at least part of the time, than at the opening session, additional firsthand recollections are available, including those of François-Poncet, Stehlin, Kirkpatrick, Kordt, and Goering. Erich Kordt, in fact, is the signatory of the German Foreign Ministry's record memorandum of the afternoon meeting, but this is probably based in large part on Schmidt's translation notes. However that may be, the Kordt memorandum and Sir Horace Wilson's notes are the only documents that attempt a chronological account, and both are admittedly incomplete and reflect the confusion of the occasion.

At the outset, Chamberlain sought to move matters along by settling the limits of the "predominantly German territory" to be occupied by German troops within ten days. To his annoyance, Daladier at once broadened the discussion by raising a question concerning the methods and concepts by which disposition of the more doubtful territories would be determined, and suggested international occupation forces and exchanges of population, as well as the plebiscites called for in the German-Italian proposal.

In addition, Daladier argued that the new boundaries should not be drawn exclusively on the basis of language, but rather that "geographical, economic, and political realities must be taken into consideration." Hitler disagreed sharply, characterizing the suggestion as "dangerous, for it was to this very idea that the Czechoslovak State owed its creation in 1918," and adding: "At that time a structure economically, but not nationally, viable had been created. Moreover, economic difficulties were more easily overcome than national difficulties, all the more so as Czechoslovakia, which was not an old cultural nation, could not assimilate German elements."

In retrospect, it seems apparent that Daladier was trying to lay the basis for some horse-trading on the location of the new frontiers, probably to preserve to the Czechs some of their fortifications, in line with Gamelin's advice the previous day. One of the four "predominantly German" areas designated for immediate occupation was the heavily fortified neck north of Olomouc (Olmütz), on the frontier of German Silesia, south of Breslau. Other territory to be subject to disposition by plebiscite lay opposite on the old Austrian border, around Brno (Brünn). Cession of these two areas would have nearly pinched the country in two, leaving a Moravian "waist" less than forty miles wide between Brno and Olomouc. To avoid this and, as he put it, not only to save the fortifications but also "on grounds of communication policy and for psychological reasons," Daladier proposed that these areas not be ceded, and that in exchange Germany take "a corresponding strip of Czech territory in the Böhmerwald."

Hitler would have none of this exchange, but—whether because he had taken a sort of liking to Daladier or in order to move things along—he was willing to yield the appearance of a compromise. After "lengthy negotiations" he accepted the addition of language (eventually embodied in Paragraph 6 of the final agreement) which authorized the International Commission, which was to administer the treaty, to "recommend to the four Powers" that "in certain exceptional cases, minor modifications in the strictly ethnographical determination of the zones which are to be transferred without plebiscite" might be made.

Daladier proceeded to make a big thing of this, declaring that "acceptance of this formula would considerably ease the position in France" and that "He would report in France that the Fuehrer had made this personal gesture to him." But this was all face-saving chatter, for Hitler had made no real concession. The Commission had only the power to "recommend," Germany and Italy could vote to reject any change favorable to Czechoslovakia, and it was out of the question that France or England, once the crisis was past, would make a new major issue over the borders of Moravia.

The technique of resolving difficult problems by leaving them for later disposition via the International Commission proved very useful, and most of the "points" on Wilson's list were settled in this manner. The property-minded Chamberlain was still worried about British responsibility for German claims of Czech damage to "installations" in the areas to be ceded, and put forward the proposal of charging off any such claims against "compensation due from Germany to Czechoslovakia, for state property." Hitler replied that these state properties had been paid for by taxes levied on the Sudeten Germans, "and so there can be no question of indemnification." Chamberlain persisted, to the vast annoyance of Hitler, who, according to Schmidt, "finally exploded" by shouting: "Our time is too valuable to be wasted on such trivialities." Hours later the matter was disposed of by a "Supplementary Declaration" that "all questions which may arise out of the transfer of territory shall be considered as coming within the terms of reference of the international commission."

The discussion of these questions, in which some of the participants were more interested than others, in conjunction with the delays for drafting and translating, soon fragmented the meeting. "The conference . . . virtually breaks up into little groups which try to work out the various formulas," wrote Ciano, with evident approval. "This permits us to talk with greater confidence, and the ice is broken." From time to time plenary talks would be resumed, as a new draft or proposal appeared likely to command general agreement.

Hanging over the meeting was the matter of the Polish and Hungarian territorial claims, and the Italians endeavored to deal with this problem. Indeed, according to Ciano, Mussolini virtually forced the question on the meeting: "The others, without exception, would gladly have said nothing about it. In fact, they try to evade its discussion. But where there is a strong will, the strong will always predominates and others coalesce around it. The problem is discussed and solved by means of a formula which I do not hesitate to describe as very brilliant."

Ciano's diary does not tell us whether the "brilliant formula" was his own or his father-in-law's. However that may be, it consisted of a proposed annex to the basic agreement, in which the four powers would declare "that the same principles which have permitted the solution of the problems of the Sudeten Germans should be adopted also for the analogous problems of the Polish and Hungarian minorities within . . . one month," and that this might be accomplished either through "the usual diplomatic channels" or at another four-power conference.

"Brilliant" or not, the Italian formula was unacceptable to the British because, as Wilson recorded, "It seemed to imply, by the use of the words 'the same principles,' that we were agreeing to the display of force for the transfer to Poland and to Hungary of the 'Polish' and 'Magyar' areas." A sound point it was, and interestingly revelatory of the British delegation's awareness that the Sudeten cession, whatever ribbons might be tied around it, was a yielding to the threat of force. As for the Poles and Hungarians, the British succeeded in erasing the uncomfortable implication from the Italian draft by a substitute, eventually adopted, which simply provided that, if within three months the Czechs, Poles, and Hungarians had failed to settle the matter by agreement, there would be another four-power meeting to resolve the conflict.

The only other major question was that of an international guarantee of Czechoslovakia's new borders, as had been previously proposed by France and Britain, in order to provide the "rump" nation with a measure of security despite the loss of her fortifications. On this the French, with Alexis Léger as spokesman, took the lead. Hitler and Mussolini declined to be associated in any guarantee until the Polish and Hungarian claims were settled, and Léger's persistence provoked yet another angry outburst from Hitler. The British did not approve the draftsmanship of the French proposal, and Sir William Malkin proposed a substitute, eventually accepted by all parties, which recited that the British and French governments stood by their prior offer to join in "an international guarantee of the new boundaries of the Czech State against unprovoked aggression," and that Germany and Italy undertook to do the same once "the question of the Polish and Hungarian minorities has been settled."

The draftsmen then turned to the task of putting into proper shape in four languages the amended draft agreement and the several supplements and annexes. For this purpose a drafting committee had been set up, and its members were hard at work. The principals, meanwhile, had once again recessed, this time for dinner.

7

It should not be thought that the discussions and decisions of the second session took place in the order in which I have described them, for it is quite impossible to determine their exact sequence from the surviving records and recollections. But it is not really necessary to construct a chronologically accurate play-by-play account; those were the issues and those were the decisions, and it is more important to recapture something of the atmosphere in which these things took place.

"Atmosphere," however, is a highly subjective thing, and, naturally enough, the various participants sensed it in different ways. To the Germans, no doubt, the ambiance was familiar and supportive, and perhaps it was hardly less so to the Italians. But to William Strang it was alien and "intimidating":

> While the conference was sitting, I spent the time with the Prime Minister's Private Secretary in the room allotted to our delegation. Through the open door we could watch the comings and goings. Field Marshal Goering in his white uniform walking to and fro in the upper gallery. Flocks of spruce young S.S. subalterns in their black uniforms, haughty and punctilious, as though life were a drill, acting as A.D.C.'s and orderly officers, one or other of whom would from time to time come to us, click his heels, and ask if we required anything. Down in the basement there was a kind of beer-hall where life was less intimidating.

In no respect are these subjective differences more striking than in connection with Mussolini's image at the meeting, and especially the apparent relation between Mussolini and Hitler. Here is the way Chamberlain saw it, in a contemporaneous letter to his sister:

> Mussolini's attitude all through was extremely quiet and reserved. He seemed to be cowed by Hitler, but undoubtedly he was most anxious for a peaceful settlement, and he played an indispensable part in attaining it.

But this was not at all the way matters appeared to François-Poncet:

> Standing at his [Mussolini's] side, Hitler gazed intently upon him, subject to his charm and as though fascinated and hypnotized. Did the Duce laugh, the Fuehrer laughed too; did Mussolini scowl, so scowled Hitler. Here was a study in mimicry. It was to leave me with a lasting and erroneous impression that Mussolini exercised a firmly established ascendancy over the Fuehrer. At any rate that day he did.

In this description, the French Ambassador may have overlooked that, in consequence of his linguistic attributes, Mussolini understood what the others were saying. Hitler did not, and it would have been only natural for him to follow Mussolini's reactions as the French and British spoke. Nevertheless, Chamberlain's impression that Mussolini was "cowed" must have been mistaken; the Duce's vanity would hardly have allowed him to appear such, and he was a good actor. Schmidt, perhaps the most dispassionate observer present, has written: "Mussolini was in good form in Munich. . . . He combined the parliamentary methods of debate with a dictatorial manner of expressing himself." Hitler, in contrast, "had not yet freed himself from Mussolini's influence; he seemed to follow the latter's lead willingly, and needed his support." In any event, Mussolini remained a hero to his son-in-law, who solemnly recorded in his diary:

The Duce, slightly annoyed by the vaguely parliamentary atmosphere which conferences always produce, moves around the room with his hands in his pockets and a rather distracted air. Every now and then he joins in the search for a formula. His great spirit, always ahead of events and men, has already absorbed the idea of agreement and, while the others are still wasting their breath over more or less formal problems, he has almost ceased to take any interest. He has already passed on and is meditating other things.

If Mussolini was perhaps the most contented principal and the best adjusted to the occasion, Daladier was unquestionably the most unstable and shaken. With his own colleagues, the Premier was gloomy and bitter; he "shook his head, muttered, and cursed circumstances," François-Poncet recalls, and Stehlin describes him as "unhappy and crushed." It must have been a very painful conscience that stimulated him to invent spurious tales of his own derring-do, for subsequent dispensation to those who had not been present. Ambassador Bullitt was the audience for some of these, and reported the conversation to Washington:

Daladier . . . announced that certain terms of the German ultimatum were entirely unacceptable to him and that he was prepared to make war rather than accept them. I gathered that these terms concerned the demand that the Czechs should leave in the Sudeten regions foodstuffs, cattle, et cetera, et cetera. He said that Hitler began to explode at this point and that he, Daladier, left the room and walked up and down in an anteroom smoking cigarettes until about an hour later when Hitler appeared and said to him "what you ask is entirely unjust and unfair; nevertheless in the interests of peace in Europe I shall concede it."

Daladier said that after this the conversations were relatively amicable and that Goering especially had devoted a great deal of attention and personal flattery to him saying that he had given France her old warlike spirit. Goering had invited him to spend an extra two days in Munich to visit the "sausage sociology" which amused him intensely. Goering had embarrassed him by saying that he would like to make an immediate trip to Paris which he had never visited. Daladier said that this had been the only moment of embarrassment that he had had during the negotiations and that he had replied that he hoped to invite Goering later.

The only thing in the first paragraph that rings true is that Daladier was, indeed, a heavy cigarette smoker. It was Chamberlain, not Daladier, who had raised questions about the livestock, and neither Schmidt's nor Wilson's notes, nor any of the other accounts, mention any such belligerent *démarche* as Daladier claims to have made. In any event, and with all respect to the Czech farmers in the Sudetenland, it is simply not to be believed that Daladier would have agreed to carve up Czechoslovakia, at a conference from which that country was excluded, and then make a *casus belli* of the cattle.

And yet, as the second paragraph indicates, for all the wishful fantasy and guilt feeling in which Daladier was enveloped, he got along with the Germans and Italians rather better than did Chamberlain, who insisted on behaving as if they were all doing the Lord's work when everyone else knew that it was highway robbery. Daladier, in contrast, assumed an attitude of *"Merde!"* mixed with *"Tant pis,"* which was at least more pragmatic and certainly less sanctimonious. Having fought at Verdun, he was also able to play the role of the old soldier, to which Hitler was always susceptible, and Schmidt overhead the Fuehrer telling the Duce: "I can get on very well with Daladier; he's been at the front as we have, and so one can talk sense with him." Alas for the dignity of France, Daladier did not confine himself to reminiscences of the trenches, and went on to lay the blame on the ally to whom the pledge was broken and whose voice was unheard. Ciano wrote:

> Daladier, particularly, is loquacious in personal conversation. He says that what is happening today is due solely to the pig-headedness of Benes. In the last few months he has repeatedly suggested to Benes that the Sudetens should be given autonomy. That would at least have deferred the present crisis. He grumbles about the French war-mongers, who would have liked to push the country into an absurd and impossible war—for France and England would never have been able to do anything really useful for Czechoslovakia once she was attacked by the forces of the Reich.

Hardly surprising, then, that Daladier's attitude toward the work of the conference was slack, and that Weizsaecker observed him "go off into a neighboring room after a long and desultory debate and sit down on a sofa and ask for Munich beer." Not so Chamberlain, who was pressing not only to get things neatly buttoned, but also to exploit the gathering for helpful tête-à-têtes. Between him and Daladier there was little that had not already been said or was best left unspoken; during one of the many pauses the two took a turn together in the corridor and dropped into the French room, where Stehlin and Leroy were hard at work, but not so hard that Stehlin could not tell that they were talking not about Czechoslovakia but—of course, fishing!

With Hitler and Mussolini, the Prime Minister had weighty matters to raise, especially with the Duce, for whose favor Chamberlain had long set his cap. They had a long and inconclusive discussion of the Spanish Civil War, and Chamberlain hinted at a disposition to stay over for a fuller talk on the morrow, but

Mussolini decided against this, for fear of offending German sensibilities. Chamberlain was pleased to find that "His manner to me was more than friendly; he listened with the utmost attention to all I said, and expressed the strong hope that I would visit him early in Italy, where I should receive a very warm welcome."

As night fell, the scene in the Fuehrerbau was one of increasing disorder. At times Schmidt, as interpreter, was at his wit's end:

> From my long experience of conferences I knew that it produces great confusion if, as the result of interrupted translations, some of the delegates can no longer follow the argument. Friends who were watching the Big Four session through some glass doors told me that when I demanded that my translations should be heard I looked like a schoolmaster trying to keep an unruly class in order.

As for Hitler himself, the passage of time did nothing to allay his irritation and impatience. Daladier found him silent, tense, and pallid. Weizsaecker says that for a time Hitler "sat with his watch in his hand and appeared to be playing, so to speak, with the idea of giving an order for mobilization." Kordt declares that at one point Hitler ostentatiously summoned his military aide, Colonel Rudolf Schmundt, and instructed him to cancel the order for mobilization—a gesture lost on the intended audience, who did not understand what he was saying.

Another source of annoyance may have been that the delays were threatening Hitler's plans for a grandiose state dinner, for the accommodation of which an enormous table had been laid in the banquet hall of the Fuehrerbau. As the time approached, however, it became apparent that dinner would be a recess and not a finale—the major issues had been dealt with, but there were still points of detail and draftsmanship to be resolved, and a third session would be necessary before there would be anything to sign.

Furthermore, not all of the invitations to the banquet were accepted. The British and French delegations both declined, pleading the need for consultation with their respective capitals. No doubt there were other and sufficient reasons; a gala meal *à quatre* would have lent itself too readily to political cartoons in which the *pièce de résistance,* under the carving knife, would be labeled "Czechoslovakia."

So the Germans and Italians dined together, and probably with greater camaraderie than the presence of the "democrats" would have allowed. Hitler, however, was still fuming over the events of the day; Léger, in particular, had exasperated him with arguments about the prospective guarantee. He denounced Léger as "A Martiniquer, a negro,* who ought not to be permitted to be involved in European affairs." After letting off steam in this wise, the Fuehrer reminisced about his wartime experiences. Mussolini, for his part, discussed the Italo-Ethiopian War, and called the western allies fools for not having imposed oil sanctions, which, he said, would have brought Italy to the verge of catastrophe within a week.

In the course of the meal the lighting failed for a moment or two. A

---

* Léger's early years were spent in Guadeloupe. He was not Black.

uniformed adjutant bearing a candle appeared at once, saluted, and announced: *"Mein Fuehrer! Ein Kurzschluss!"* Anfuso recalls the episode with the observation that the short circuit was proclaimed "in the same manner as a declaration of war." The sly Italians in their black shirts did well to poke fun at their hosts while they still could, for this was about the last occasion at which they would meet the Germans on equal terms.

8

Once again the British had a "business dinner," during which they prepared and sent to the drafting committee a proposal to resolve the vexed question of compensation for state properties, by referring all financial aid questions to a "German-Czech Commission with a neutral chairman." This proved unacceptable to the Germans—a result which Wilson blamed on Ribbentrop, who was everyone's pet hate—and so it was agreed in the drafting committee (on which Sir William Malkin represented the British) that the proposal would be brought back before the conference. But when the principals reassembled, the British draft was missing, and Wilson was told that it "had been lost." This was too much and, as Wilson put it: "We took a stand on this, pointing out that there must be a number of questions—property, currency, outstanding loans, etc.—of the kind contemplated by the draft clause." The matter was resolved by an annex committing all such matters to the International Commission.

Before rejoining the conference, however, Wilson found time to see the Czechs. Dr. Masařík's official report relates:

> At 10 p.m. Mr. Gwatkin brought Dr. Mastny and myself to Sir Horace Wilson. In accordance with Mr. Chamberlain's wish, Sir Horace told us in the presence of Mr. Gwatkin the main lines of the new plan, and handed us a map on which were marked the areas which were to be occupied at once. To my objections he replied twice with absolute finality that he had nothing to add to his statements. He paid no attention whatever to what we said concerning places and areas of the greatest importance to us. Finally he returned to the conference and we remained alone with Mr. Gwatkin. We did what we could to convince him of the necessity of revising the plan. His most important reply was that the English delegation favored the German plan. When he began to speak again of the difficulties of negotiating with Hitler, I said that, in fact, everything depended on the firmness of the two western Great Powers. Mr. Gwatkin answered, in a very serious tone, "if you do not accept you will have to settle your affairs with the Germans absolutely alone. Perhaps the French may tell you this more gently but you can believe me that they share our views. They are disinterested."

Meanwhile in the *Arbeitszimmer,* time was hanging heavy while the final drafts were duplicated and translated, subject to what Wilson called "very long delays due to inefficient organization and lack of control." Goering had joined the gathering around the fireplace in order, as he later said, "to create a friendly atmosphere on all sides." Chamberlain took advantage of the lull to propose to Hitler that the two of them might meet again in the morning: "He jumped at the idea, and asked me to come to his private flat. . . ."

Daladier could not stand the situation any longer and fled back to the Four Seasons, taking Stehlin with him and leaving instructions that he was not to be recalled until the documents were ready for signature. Stehlin found him "tired and sad"; his comments on the scene he had just departed were "brief and bitter," and he soon changed the subject:

"You are an aviator. I had a talk with your chief, General Vuillemin, who was very disturbed. What is your opinion?"

For fifteen minutes I talked to him about the Luftwaffe, its strength, its function, its relations with the army, and everything which distinguished it from our own aviation. He listened with great attention:

"I am grateful to you for speaking with such frankness. Do you believe, with Vuillemin, that after a few days of fighting we would no longer have any aircraft?"

It would have embarrassed me to answer, for I had no right to pass judgment on my chiefs. Daladier did not insist, and pursued his own thoughts:

"Now the game has been played, and perhaps there was nothing else to do. One must think of the future. We must make up for lost time, especially with your branch of the service, which is at once the most important and the worst prepared. Come and see me in Paris."

A little after midnight the telephone rang. It was François-Poncet calling to say that it was time to return to the conference. . . .

Whatever his other failures, Daladier certainly succeeded in charming Captain Stehlin, an Alsatian of strong religious and patriotic convictions who had, in common with many French officers, nourished strong prejudices against Radical Socialist politicians such as the two Edouards—Daladier and Herriot. But now "after hours passed, the prejudices inherited from my upbringing and officer's training were overborne by a feeling of sympathy and respect, and a glow of friendship." By the end of the day Stehlin had acquired "a great respect for this man, *si malheureux et accablé.*"

The young officer's "respect" might have been slightly tarnished had he overheard Daladier, after his return to the Fuehrerbau, telling Ciano that the French and "even the Czechs" were "satisfied" with the agreement. The signing itself was a scene of mixed and, no doubt, contrived emotional displays. Goering and Mussolini, enjoying the double satisfactions of playing on the winning team and being the two chief peacemakers, were openly jubilant. The British put a good face on things, but at least for Kirkpatrick it was a matter of the stiff upper lip: "The Munich Conference was in every way a sad affair. I can remember no redeeming feature."

Daladier, despite his shameful remark to Ciano, looked anything but "satisfied," and Mussolini sought to cheer him up: "You will be acclaimed on your return to France." Daladier remarked that the French would be glad that peace had been preserved, but would be aware of the sacrifices entailed. *"Vous verrez, vous verrez,"* replied Mussolini, and moved on to converse with Chamberlain. Daladier separated himself from the others and sought refuge in an armchair. Ciano sat down next to him; Stehlin observed them in discussion for a few moments, but the conversation soon flagged, and they sat silent, each "look-ing straight ahead with the same disillusioned and resigned air."

As the final preparations for signing were made, Hitler remained aloof and sulky. Kirkpatrick has described the scene:

> In the closing stages Goering and other Nazi leaders came into the room. Goering is the centre of a conversation and there is some laughter. . . . But Hitler sits moodily apart. He wiggles on the sofa, he crosses and recrosses his legs, he folds his arms and glares around the room. At intervals with obvious effort he joins in a conversation, only to relapse into silence. At last the agreement is ready for signature. The four statesmen sign. Three look satisfied that they have done the right thing. But Hitler scratches his signature as if he were being asked to sign away his birthright.

Hitler and the others had to sign the documents in four languages, and there were five annexes to the main agreement, so that twenty signatures were neces-sary. There was additional delay because of insufficient ink. When Stehlin put the French version before Hitler, Schmidt was summoned to check the transla-tion before the Fuehrer, wearing the spectacles in which he hated to be photo-graphed, would sign. He then forced himself to say a few words of thanks to his guests "for their efforts to achieve the happy result of the negotiations." Cham-berlain, no doubt sincerely pleased with the day's work, made an appropriate re-sponse: he "associated himself with the Fuehrer's remarks on the satisfaction of the peoples concerned with the outcome of Munich" and "stressed the impor-tance of the agreement for the future development of European politics." Much less content was André François-Poncet, overheard by Ciano to remark, as he was collating the several documents embodying the agreement: "See how France treats the only allies who remained faithful to her."

9

"Then arose the question, what to do about the Czechs?" wrote Sir Horace Wilson, in a sentence that fairly screamed for the adjective "awkward" before either "question" or "Czechs," depending on the point of view. A British sug-gestion that Daladier in person should "take the Agreement to Prague" found no favor with that gentleman, and it was then arranged that the news should be broken by Chamberlain and Daladier, jointly and immediately, by giving Mastny and Masařík a copy of the agreement.

The meeting with them took place at about quarter past two in the morning, in Chamberlain's rooms at the Regina Palace. Sir Horace Wilson's description of the event is brief and dispassionate:

> I gave M. Daladier the prepared copy (with map) so that he might hand it to M. Mastny. M. Mastny read it and asked a number of questions. He was given a pretty broad hint that—having regard to the seriousness of the alter-native—the best course was for his Government to accept what was clearly a considerable improvement upon the German Memorandum. He and his col-leagues said they would fly to Prague and at once place the documents before their Government. We agreed with the French the instructions to go to our re-spective Ministers at Prague. We sent Mr. Ashton-Gwatkin to Prague with the

two Czechs so that he could both carry the instructions to Mr. Newton [the British Minister in Prague] and add the necessary background. . . .

Masařík's account of the confrontation is much more graphic:

At 1:30 A.M. we were taken into the hall where the Conference had been held.* There were present Mr. Neville Chamberlain, M. Daladier, Sir Horace Wilson, M. Léger, Mr. Ashton-Gwatkin, Dr. Mastny and myself. The atmosphere was oppressive; sentence was about to be passed. The French, obviously "embarrassed," appeared to be aware of the consequences for French prestige. Mr. Chamberlain, in a short introduction, referred to the agreement which had just been concluded and gave the text to Dr. Mastny to read out. During the reading of the text, we asked the precise meaning of certain passages. Thus, for example, I asked M. Léger and Wilson to be so kind as to explain the words "preponderantly German character" in Article 4. M. Léger, without mentioning a percentage, merely remarked that it was a question of majorities calculated according to the proposals we had already accepted. Mr. Chamberlain also confirmed that there was no question except of applying a plan which we had already accepted. When we came to Article 6, I asked M. Léger whether we were to consider it as a clause assuring the protection of our vital interests as had been promised in the original proposals. M. Léger said, "Yes," but that it was only possible to a very moderate degree, and that the question would come under the International Commission. Dr. Mastny asked Mr. Chamberlain whether the Czechoslovak member of the Commission would have the same right to vote as the other members, to which Mr. Chamberlain agreed. In answer to the question whether international troops or British forces would be sent to the plebiscite areas, we were told that that was under consideration, but that Italian and Belgian troops might also participate.

While M. Mastny was speaking with Mr. Chamberlain about matters of perhaps secondary importance (Mr. Chamberlain yawned without ceasing and with no show of embarrassment), I asked MM. Daladier and Léger whether they expected a declaration or answer to the agreement for our Government. M. Daladier, obviously embarrassed, did not reply. M. Léger replied that the four statesmen had not much time. He added positively that they no longer expected an answer from us: they regarded the plan as accepted and that our Government had that very day, at latest by 5 P.M. to send its representative to Berlin to the meeting of the International Commission and finally Czechoslovak official whom we sent would have to be in Berlin on Saturday, in order to fix the details of the evacuation of the first zone. The atmosphere was becoming oppressive for everyone present.

It had been explained to us in a sufficiently brutal manner, and that by a Frenchman, that this was a sentence without right of appeal and without possibility of modification.

Mr. Chamberlain did not conceal his fatigue. After the text had been read, we were given a second slightly corrected map. We said "Good-bye" and left. The Czechoslovak Republic as fixed by the frontiers of 1918 had ceased to

---

* This statement is erroneous, as Mr. Masařík acknowledged in a letter (March 26, 1974) to the author. Beyond doubt, the meeting took place in Chamberlain's hotel rooms at the Regina Palace.

September 29, 1938.

AGREEMENT
REACHED ON SEPTEMBER 29, 1938,
BETWEEN GERMANY, THE UNITED KINGDOM,
FRANCE, AND ITALY

Germany, the United Kingdom, France, and Italy, taking into consideration the agreement, which has been already reached in principle for the cession to Germany of the Sudeten German territory, have agreed on the following terms and conditions governing the said cession and the measures consequent thereon, and by this agreement they each hold themselves responsible for the steps necessary to secure its fulfillment.

1) The evacuation will begin on October 1st.

2) The United Kingdom, France, and Italy agree that the evacuation of the territory shall be completed by October 10th, without any existing installations having been destroyed, and that the Czechoslovak Government will be held responsible for carrying out the evacuation without damage to the said installations.

3) The conditions governing the evacuation will be laid down in detail by an international commission composed of representatives of Germany, the United Kingdom, France, Italy, and Czechoslovakia.

4) The occupation by stages of the predominantly German territory by German troops will begin on October 1st. The four territories marked on the attached map will be occupied by German troops in the following order: the territory marked number I on the 1st and 2d of October, the territory marked number II on the 2d and 3d of October, the territory marked number III on the 3d, 4th, and 5th of October, the territory marked number IV on the 6th and 7th of October. The remaining territory of preponderantly German character will be ascertained by the aforesaid international commission forthwith and be occupied by German troops by the 10th of October.

5) The international commission, referred to in paragraph 3) will determine the territories in which a plebiscite is to be held. These territories will be occupied by international bodies until the plebiscite has been completed. The same commission will fix the conditions in which the plebiscite is to be held, taking as a basis the conditions of the Saar plebiscite. The commission will also fix a date, not later than the end of November, on which the plebiscite will be held.

6) The final determination of the frontiers will be carried out by the international commission. This commission will also be entitled to recommend to the four Powers, Germany, the United Kingdom, France, and Italy, in certain exceptional cases, minor modifications in the strictly ethnographical determination of the zones which are to be transferred without plebiscite.

7) There will be a right of option into and out of the transferred territories, the option to be exercised within 6 months from the date of this agreement. A German-Czechoslovak commission shall determine the details of the option, consider ways of facilitating the transfer of population and settle questions of principle arising out of the said transfer.

8) The Czechoslovak Government will, within a period of 4 weeks from the date of this agreement, release from their military and police forces any Sudeten Germans who may wish to be released, and the Czechoslovak Government will within the same period release Sudeten German prisoners who are serving terms of imprisonment for political offenses.

ADOLF HITLER
ED. DALADIER
MUSSOLINI
NEVILLE CHAMBERLAIN

Munich, September 29, 1938.

ANNEX
TO THE AGREEMENT

His Majesty's Government in the United Kingdom and the French Government have entered into the above agreement on the basis that they stand by the offer, contained in paragraph 6 of the Anglo-French proposals of September 19th, relating to an international guarantee of the new boundaries of the Czechoslovak State against unprovoked aggression.

When the question of the Polish and Hungarian minorities in Czechoslovakia has been settled, Germany and Italy for their part will give a guarantee to Czechoslovakia.

ADOLF HITLER
NEVILLE CHAMBERLAIN
MUSSOLINI
ED. DALADIER

Munich, September 29, 1938.

———

ADDITIONAL
DECLARATION

The Heads of Governments of the four Powers declare that the problems of the Polish and Hungarian minorities in Czechoslovakia, if not settled within 3 months by agreement between the respective Governments, shall form the subject of another meeting of the Heads of the Governments of the four Powers here present.

ADOLF HITLER
NEVILLE CHAMBERLAIN
MUSSOLINI
ED. DALADIER

Munich, September 29, 1938.

———

SUPPLEMENTARY
DECLARATION

All questions which may arise out of the transfer of the territory shall be considered as coming within the terms of reference to the international commission.

ADOLF HITLER
NEVILLE CHAMBERLAIN
MUSSOLINI
ED. DALADIER

Munich, September 29, 1938.

COMPOSITION OF THE
INTERNATIONAL COMMISSION

The four Heads of Government here present agree that the international commission provided for in the agreement signed by them today shall consist of the Secretary of State in the German Foreign Office, the British, French and Italian Ambassadors accredited to Berlin, and a representative to be nominated by the Government of Czechoslovakia.

ADOLF HITLER
NEVILLE CHAMBERLAIN
EDOUARD DALADIER
BENITO MUSSOLINI

Munich, September 29, 1938.

exist. In the hall I met Rochat, who asked me what the reactions would be at home. I replied curtly that I did not exclude the worst and that it was necessary to be prepared for the gravest eventualities.

Kirkpatrick's recollection of this unhappy encounter is critical of Daladier for his "apparent brutality" in that he "did not mince words conveying that France expected Czechoslovakia to submit without further ado" and is partial to his chief: "Mr. Chamberlain, on the other hand, showed the greatest sympathy and understanding." But those qualities appear to have impressed Kirkpatrick rather more than the Czechs, and anyhow Daladier was simply saying what Chamberlain wanted said, in order to crush any lingering hopes in Prague and restrain the Czechs from upsetting the apple cart. Surely none of those present could have enjoyed the occasion. Mastny came to tears, and François-Poncet sought to console him by suggesting that "all this is not final" but only "one moment in a story which has just begun and which will soon bring up the issue again."

Departing the Regina, Daladier ran into a crowd of reporters, including William L. Shirer, who subsequently wrote: "Someone asked, or started to ask: 'Monsieur le Président, are you satisfied with the agreement?' He turned as if to say something, but he was too tired and defeated and the words did not come out and he stumbled out the door in silence." Back at the Four Seasons, the Premier left it to François-Poncet to tell the news to Paris:

> Returning to our hotel at 2:30 A.M., I called Bonnet by telephone to inform him of what had happened, while Daladier, still cursing and lost in gloomy thoughts, weighed the difficulties he was likely to meet on his return to Paris. Bonnet swept aside my detailed explanations. "Peace is assured," he said. "That is the main thing. Everybody will be happy."

Events were soon to vindicate Bonnet's gauge of the immediate reaction in France, but Daladier was still speculating apprehensively: "Mussolini has told me that I will be acclaimed. I expect that Paul Reynaud and Georges Mandel will resign; I will replace them. After that, we must profit by the lesson of this terrible day."

10

For some of the Munich participants, the night's work was not yet finished. Masařík was writing his report and telephoning to free the Czech pilots from their guards so that they could prepare for the return flight. Subordinates in the delegations were telephoning or encoding messages on the results of the meeting; the British telephoned the text of the agreement to London at four in the morning.*

---

* There appears to have been no important communication between the British delegation and the Foreign Office during the discussions in Munich. Halifax sent two telegrams which arrived early in the evening; one made suggestions for control of the ceded areas during the transition period, and the other reported the supposedly helpful psychological impact of the Fleet's mobilization on "German public opinion." Neither message seems to have been utilized in Munich.

In London, Cadogan recorded in his diary that September 29 was an "easy day—the calm in the middle of the typhoon." Halifax was kept busy explaining the situation to the Soviet and American ambassadors, and thanking the Italian Ambassador, Dino Grandi, for the Duce's helpful intervention.

There was no time to be lost, for the agreement had been signed in the early morning of Friday, September 30, and by its terms the German military occupation of "Zone I" was to commence on the very next day, October 1. Already the first meeting of the International Commission for execution of the agreement—composed of Weizsaecker, the French, British, and Italian ambassadors in Berlin, and a Czech to be designated—had been called for five o'clock on Friday afternoon in Berlin.

First off the mark were the Czech delegation and Mr. Ashton-Gwatkin, who left Munich by air at six in the morning to take the agreement to Prague. Despite their early start the tidings reached the Czech capital ahead of them, for the text of the treaty had already been wired to the German chargé d'affaires, Andor Hencke, who promptly roused the Czech Foreign Minister, Kamil Krofta, and put it in his hands at six-twenty in the morning. Hencke also informed Krofta of the International Commission meeting scheduled for that afternoon, and requested the dispatch of "an authorized representative and a military expert" to Berlin.

Before retiring, Chamberlain and Daladier had also sent messages to their respective ministers in Prague. Basil Newton was told that he "should at once see the President and . . . urge acceptance of plan that has been worked out today after prolonged discussion with a view to avoiding conflict. You will appreciate that there is no time for argument; it must be a plain acceptance." That was plain enough if not brutal, but somehow offends less than Daladier's message to the French Minister, Victor de Lacroix: "Please as a matter of extreme urgency approach M. Benes to satisfy for yourself that he will accept. I beg that you will tell him of all the emotion I feel in reaching the conclusion of these negotiations, in which the lack of a Czechoslovak representative did not depend on me." On whom, it might well be asked, did a Czech presence "depend" more than on the Premier of the great power bound by solemn treaty to stand at Czechoslovakia's side in the event of attack? The disclaimer was nothing but a cheap effort to saddle the British with the blame, nor was it seemly for Daladier thus to parade his "emotion" to the very victim of the French renege.

Parallel instructions were sent to the Italian Minister in Prague (Francesco Franzoni), and during the morning he, as well as Lacroix and Newton, sought opportunity to convey their governments' views to Beneš. The President, however, was already in a meeting, and the envoys were obliged to transmit their exhortations through his aides.

At half-past nine that morning, before going into conference on the terrible issue that confronted him, Beneš telephoned the Soviet Minister, Serge Alexandrovsky, and asked him to ascertain Moscow's "attitude" toward "these two possibilities . . . of further struggle or capitulation." The other great powers, Beneš declared, had "shamefully sacrificed" Czechoslovakia to Hitler "for the sake of their own interests," and it was vital that he have the Soviet answer by early evening.

Unable to establish telephonic contact with Moscow, Alexandrovsky sent off a telegram, and then betook himself to Hradčany Castle "To get a clear picture." At about noon he was informed by Beneš' secretary that it had been decided to accept the Munich terms, and that consequently there was no need for Moscow to answer the question that Beneš had put. A second telegram to Moscow, conveying this information, was apparently received and deciphered simultaneously with the first; however that may be, Beneš' question was not answered.

Prudently, Beneš assembled a large group to share responsibility for so painful a decision—the members of General Syrový's cabinet and Dr. Hodža's preceding cabinet, leaders of the principal political parties, and Generals Krejcí (the Army Chief of Staff) and Husárek. During the previous day, while the Munich conference was in process, a number of the participants had urged Beneš that the country should fight even if left in the lurch by the French; these included Ladislav Rasin, leader of the right-wing National Democrats, Klement Gottwald, secretary-general of the Communist Party in Czechoslovakia, and several of the principal generals. Apparently Beneš' decision to accept the Munich terms rather than fight, alone or with the Soviet Union as the sole ally, was due primarily to unwillingness to bring down on his country the rain of death and destruction which war with Germany would have entailed, and suspicion that, if the Soviet Union joined the fray: "the West would have believed that we were an instrument of Bolshevisation in Central Europe" and "would have washed its hands of a German-Soviet war."

The wisdom of the Czech capitulation has since been questioned, but under the circumstances of that morning it would have required a very bold if not rash group of men to lead their country to war. The decision to yield is the more understandable in that the basic concession—to cede to Germany a large part of the Sudetenland—had already been made after Chamberlain's trip to Berchtesgaden. To the Czech leaders, it all appeared as a matter of Scylla and Charybdis or, as General Syrový is said to have put it, a choice between being murdered or committing suicide.

And so, shortly after noon, Dr. Krofta received Newton, Lacroix, and Franzoni in a group, and announced: "The President and the Government submit to the conditions of the Munich Agreement, which has come into being without us and against us. Our view of them will be expressed later in writing." Newton and Lacroix attempted to express sentiments of condolence, but were cut short by Krofta's observation that Munich was "a disaster which we have not merited," and his prediction that "tomorrow it will be the turn of others." Franzoni, who remained silent, later reported that Krofta was "a completely broken man" who "intimated only one wish, that the three Ministers should quickly leave his room."

For the weary Dr. Mastny, there was no rest or time for quiet sorrow. In accordance with the jointly expressed wishes of Henderson, Attolico, and François-Poncet, he was designated as the Czech representative on the International Commission, and soon he was on his way back to Berlin for the meeting scheduled for that same afternoon. With him went General Husárek, who was to head the military delegation. Masařík was also asked to go but declined, saying that he had "done enough work as a grave-digger."

While the Czech representatives were flying to Berlin, a fifty-member committee of the majority coalition met in the House of Parliament, to hear and discuss the decisions that had been taken. The Government's public announcement of its acceptance of the Munich terms concluded with a declaration "before the whole world" of its "protest against the decisions which were taken unilaterally and without our participation."

As Premier, General Syrový, the one-eyed hero of the Czech Legion which fought with the Allies during the First World War, addressed the nation by radio late in the afternoon, to announce and justify his government's conclusion that "if we must choose between the diminution of our territories and the death of our whole nation, it is our sacred duty to preserve the lives of our people, in order that . . . we may not be obliged to abandon our belief that our nation will rise again, as it has done so often in the past." As Chief of Staff, General Krejcí issued an order to the troops calling for "unconditional obedience" to the government's decision, and assuring them that: "Our Army was not defeated. It has preserved unblemished its good repute. . . . The Republic will have need of us." A popular Czech poet, Josef Hora, spoke the mood and pride of the people: "In the days of our sorrow when others, more powerful, have decided to beggar our ancient country, lift up your heads, all of you, in pride and calmness. It is not we who should be ashamed."

CHAPTER 4

Euphoria

1

While these sad and bitter meetings were being held and pronouncements made in Prague, elsewhere there was great rejoicing. At the Four Seasons in Munich, the French delegation was awakened early by a large crowd calling for Daladier. François-Poncet's appearance elicited loud cheers, which he disavowed: "I am only the Ambassador." From the throng came prompt reply: "All right, so long live the Ambassador!" Daladier himself assumed that it was a staged demonstration, but was reassured by the secretary of the French Consulate—*"charmante jeune fille qui connaissait admirablement l'allemand"*—who informed the Premier that the crowd was composed of people on their way to work who had been in "great fear" and now had but one thought: there would be no fighting.

From the hotel balcony Daladier acknowledged the acclaim. Goering appeared on the scene, apparently astounded at these goings-on: "He is annoyed because the cheers are not for him," whispered the pretty secretary to the Premier, with obvious satisfaction. Thus Daladier finally won victory of a sort at Munich, and he recovered his spirits enough to tell the German press that "war has been avoided, and a peace with honor assured for all nations."

At about noon Ribbentrop arrived to escort the French to the airport. Cheering crowds lined the route, and at the field there was a guard of honor to be reviewed and a band to play the *Marseillaise*. Shortly after one o'clock the *Poitou* took off on its return flight.

What the Germans applaud does not always please the French, and Daladier himself remained wrapped in a gloom which turned to surprised concern when the *Poitou* arrived over Le Bourget. Enormous crowds were visible from the air, and it is said that Daladier thought they had come to boo him, and ordered the pilot to circle for a few moments so that he could prepare for the ordeal. But Mussolini's prediction of the previous evening proved accurate. No more than the *Müncheners* did the *Parisiens* care about the terms of the accord; they wanted only peace, and peace it appeared to be.

And so when the apprehensive Premier appeared at the door of the *Poitou*, he looked out over a veritable sea of acclamation, from which rose a steady chant: *"La paix! La paix!"* Women detached themselves from the crowd and ran toward him, holding out their babies. Cabinet ministers were on hand to congratulate him, and Bonnet climbed into Daladier's automobile for a triumphal drive into Paris. The French radio had announced the route, and there were great crowds and crashing cheers all the way. On the Boulevard Haussmann the British journalist Alexander Werth found himself an observer of the scene:

> And then . . . came a small open car, with Daladier standing up in it and looking rather red and bewildered. Next to him, with a self-satisfied smirk on his face, sat M. Bonnet. *"Vive Daladier!" "Vive la Paix!" "Vive la France!"* And the girls on the balcony of the Galeries Lafayette waved their little flags.

There were, to be sure, a few *grognons*. *"Vive la France malgré tout,"* muttered a man standing by Werth. Daladier himself remained withdrawn and skeptical, and is said to have *sotto voce* castigated "the fools" who did not know "what they were cheering." But on October 4 the Chamber of Deputies, with only the Communists and two of the extreme right dissenting, approved the Munich Agreement by a vote of 535 to 75.

2

Benito Mussolini had an even more triumphal homecoming, untroubled by the doubts that nagged at Daladier. He was up betimes for a seven-thirty departure; Hitler, for once breaking his slugabed habits, escorted his guest to the station through crowds chanting: "Fuehrer!" and "Duce!" but most insistently *"Friede!"*

The special train crossed the Brenner Pass into Italy, and "from the Brenner to Rome, from the King down to the peasants, the Duce receives welcomes such as I have never seen," Ciano recorded: "He says himself that this enthusiasm was only equalled on the evening when the Empire was proclaimed." But Anfuso observed that the cheers "were not for the Duce as founder of the Empire but as the angel of peace." At Verona and even at Bologna, the "stronghold of bellicose Fascism," it was plain that "the Italians prefer the olive branch to the laurel, and the dove to the eagle."

At Florence, the Duce was met by King Victor Emmanuel, who had motored there from his estate at San Rossore. In Rome, someone (Achille Starace, secretary-general of the Fascist Party, according to Anfuso's surmise) had erected a facsimile of the Arch of Constantine, bearing the legend "Rome tames" (*Roma doma*). Anfuso thought this absurd; who indeed had Rome "tamed"? The Duce himself showed displeasure: "Who had this arch built? Who had this absurd idea? Who organized this carnival?"

But the questions went unanswered and were forgotten as Mussolini was called to the window by the crowds outside the Palazzo Venezia. "Comrades, you have lived through memorable times," cried the Duce. "In Munich we worked for peace according to justice. Isn't this the ideal of the Italian people?" And the multitudes roared their answer: *"Sì! Sì!"* In Italy, as in Germany and France, Munich was hailed as a Pact of Peace.

3

Weary from his labors of the previous day, William Strang had had but a few hours of early morning sleep when he was awakened by a telephone message from the Prime Minister. Would Strang be good enough to prepare "a short statement on the future of Anglo-German relations" to which Hitler might agree, and bring it to the Prime Minister as soon as possible? Drafting while he dressed and breakfasted, Strang produced a three-paragraph statement and took it into Chamberlain, who "rewrote the second paragraph and made some other minor changes."

The rewriting involved the insertion of a favorable reference to the Anglo-German Naval Agreement of 1935. Strang, who thought that treaty "not a matter to be proud of," tried to dissuade his chief but was rebuffed by the assertion that "it was the type of agreement which we should now try to reach with Germany." An effort to have Daladier informed of the Prime Minister's intention to deal unilaterally with Hitler brought Strang another put-down: Chamberlain "saw no reason whatever for saying anything to the French."

At breakfast with Dunglass, Chamberlain made it clear that he intended, if Hitler signed the document, to give it "maximum publicity" on his return to England, so that:

> . . . if Hitler signed it and kept the bargain, well and good; alternatively . . . if he broke it, he would demonstrate to all the world that he was totally cynical and untrustworthy, and . . . this would have its value in mobilising public opinion against him, particularly in America.

As usual, Chamberlain was sure of his own judgment, and now his *élan* was reinforced by the first plaudits of a day of such acclamation as few other men have ever enjoyed:

> As he was about to leave for his interview, he asked: "What is that noise?" I [Strang] said: "The street is full of people. They want to see you." I suggested that he should step on to the balcony. He did so, and received an ovation astonishing in its warmth. As he went down the stairs and through the hall, he had to press through a gay and radiant crowd, bronzed and still in their summer clothing.

Lord Dunglass accompanied Chamberlain to Hitler's apartment, which the Prime Minister subsequently described (in a letter to his sister Hilda) as a "flat in a tenement where the other floors are occupied by ordinary citizens." The sadly overworked Schmidt had been summoned to interpret, and made a record of what was said. Chamberlain thought the occasion "friendly and pleasant," but Dunglass found Hitler "sullen" and "unresponsive," and Schmidt described him as "pale and moody"—a condition Schmidt laid to the Fuehrer's displeasure at the German people's "aversion from war and joy at the maintenance of peace," as manifested in their vociferous acclaim for Chamberlain and Daladier. Whatever Hitler's inner feelings may have been, it is clear that he left the initiative strictly to Chamberlain, volunteering nothing but responding rather freely to the several matters raised by the Prime Minister.

At the time of the meeting there had as yet been no news from Prague. After reciprocal congratulations on the past evening's achievements, Chamberlain's first concern was the possibility that the Czechs might reject the agreement. If they were "mad enough" to do this, he hoped that Hitler would do nothing "which would diminish the high opinion of him which would be held throughout the world in consequence of yesterday's proceedings," and, in particular, he "trusted that there would be no bombardment of Prague or killing of women and children by attacks from the air." Hitler replied that "as a matter of principle" he intended to "limit air action to front line zones"; that he would "always try to spare the civilian population and to confine himself to military objectives; he hated the thought of little babies being killed by gas bombs."

Granting Chamberlain and even Hitler the charity of judgment that their concern for little babies was sincere, it is still difficult to read these words without a touch of nausea. Already under development were the Halifax and Lancaster heavy bombers that were intended as Britain's prime offensive weapon in the event of a continental war. Guernica had been ravaged by German planes and pilots only a year before; Warsaw and the London Blitz came within the next two years. It is hard to suppress the suspicion that in raising the matter Chamberlain was chiefly worried about his own public image, in the event that the man he had tried so hard to propitiate was at once to lay Prague in smoking ruins.

There ensued inconclusive discussion of three subjects consecutively raised by Chamberlain: the Spanish Civil War, abolition of bomber aircraft by international agreement, and economic relations between Germany and southeastern Europe. He had suggested to Mussolini the previous evening that the four powers of Munich should call both sides in Spain to observe an armistice, pending a four-power-sponsored settlement. Hitler "laughed heartily" at Chamberlain's report that Mussolini had described himself as "tired of Spain"; he promised to give Chamberlain's proposal his personal attention, but nothing ever came of the idea.

In the light of subsequent events, the discussion of Chamberlain's "ban-the-bomber" notion is especially interesting and curious. Arguing by analogy from the limitations on warship tonnage and naval gun calibers under the Washington Conference, Chamberlain opined that "the qualitative method of restricting armaments was the one which had the most practical results." Hitherto it had been thought that abolishing bomber aircraft would be futile "because bombs could still be dropped from civilian machines." But now bombing had become a "highly specialized affair" requiring much special equipment: "Therefore abolition of bombing aircraft seemed to him to be the practical thing to agree on." Anticipating Hitler's objection that the Soviet Union would never agree to such a thing, Chamberlain remarked "the perfection which had been reached by the modern fighting machine and also the pitch of efficiency to which Herr Hitler had brought his anti-aircraft defences" and asked him to bear in mind "that in future he need no longer regard Czechoslovakia as a starting-off place for Russian aggression. . . ." In view of these circumstances, could not the Fuehrer "feel that Russia could be left out of account"?

It is idle, but nonetheless intriguing to speculate on the reaction of the British and German air staffs had Hitler given an affirmative reply, and thus made possible a joint communiqué that the two leaders would promote an international agreement to scrap the bomber. The airmen were spared that puzzlement, for

Hitler politely but definitively declined to treat the Soviet Air Force as irrelevant. The Czechs, he said, could easily "prepare a few landing grounds and it would be possible for Russia to land from 2000 to 4000 machines in a space of from two to three hours."* Furthermore, one ought not "to overestimate the effectiveness of anti-aircraft defences." Worldwide agreement was the only possible basis for such a proposition.

In retrospect, these diffuse and even desultory exchanges are interesting chiefly as possible indicators of Chamberlain's intentions and aspirations at Munich. Did he really hope to initiate fruitful negotiations on these matters? Did he regard Munich as the foundation for a general European settlement? Or was he merely trying, under more relaxed circumstances, to probe the mind of a man with whom his repeated and protracted interchanges had thus far been confined to the Czech crisis?

It is quite possible that the Prime Minister's immediate purpose was even more limited and mainly tactical—that his prime or sole objective was to get Hitler to sign the document in his pocket, and that the long palaver was simply intended to create a friendly atmosphere, and to conceal from Hitler that Chamberlain had requested the meeting only to that end. There is an uncharacteristic lack of follow-through in Chamberlain's presentation of the preceding matters, suggesting his impatience to reach the main thing, which he did after a brief and vacuous interchange on German trade with southeastern Europe. As he described the scene to his sister:

> At the end I pulled out the declaration, which I had prepared beforehand, and asked if he would sign it. As the interpreter translated the words into German, Hitler frequently ejaculated *"ja, ja"*, and at the end he said "yes, I will certainly sign it; when shall we do it?" I said "now", and we went at once to the writing-table, and put our signatures to the two copies which I had brought with me.

The famous paper, which never won a public display case and now rests obscurely in a file at the Imperial War Museum in London, reads as follows:

> We, the German Führer and Chancellor and the British Prime Minister, have had a further meeting today and are agreed in recognizing that the question of Anglo-German relations is of the first importance for the two countries and for Europe.
>
> We regard the agreement signed last night and the Anglo-German Naval Agreement as symbolic of the desire of our two peoples never to go to war with one another again.
>
> We are resolved that the method of consultation shall be the method adopted to deal with any other questions that may concern our two countries, and we are determined to continue our efforts to remove possible sources of difference and thus to contribute to assure the peace of Europe.

Neither Schmidt nor Dunglass shared Chamberlain's impression that Hitler was delighted to sign the document. Dunglass thought he signed "perfunctorily,"

---

* At the rate of one aircraft per minute, this would require twelve to twenty-four airfields equipped to receive and service heavy aircraft coming in from a long flight over Rumania.

and Schmidt later wrote: "My own feeling was that he agreed to the wording with a certain reluctance, and I believe he appended his signature only to please Chamberlain, without promising himself any too much from the effects of the declaration."

Contemporary journalistic opinion was sharply divided on its significance: in Germany, Frederick Birchall of The New York *Times* declared that "never has a simpler document been issued in history with consequences more far-reaching or more pregnant with hope," while his colleague in London, Ferdinand Kuhn, called it an "unexpected footnote"—a "gesture . . . which settles nothing." John Gunther thought it a "complete victory" for Hitler because it gave him "what he had always wanted—a friendship pact with England," but William L. Shirer dismissed it as "a very clever face-saving stunt" on the part of Chamberlain.

The other two Munich principals were not impressed or, at least in Daladier's case, much pleased. At lunch with Bullitt in Paris two days later the French Premier, misinformed on the genesis of the meeting, declared that "Chamberlain had been taken in a bit by Hitler who had persuaded him to remain after the others had left and had convinced Chamberlain that Germany was ready for peace. . . . Chamberlain was an admirable old gentleman, like a high-minded Quaker who had fallen among bandits, and . . . Chamberlain's last conversations with Hitler had not been helpful."

In Rome, Hitler's personal emissary, the Prince of Hesse, visited Ciano to explain what had happened. The Prince's account was not wholly accurate, and reflected a certain sheepishness on the German side. The reactions of Ciano and Mussolini were dry and scornful:

> Chamberlain asked the Fuehrer for an interview and talked to him about the possibility of a conference on Spain and also about an extraordinary proposal to abolish the bomber aircraft of the Four Powers [*sic!*].* Finally he took a piece of paper out of his pocket and put before the Fuehrer a draft of the communiqué, which he declared to be necessary to him for his parliamentary position. The Fuehrer did not think he could refuse. And the Duce, to whom I [Ciano] related this story said to me: "Explanations are superfluous. You do not refuse a glass of lemonade to a thirsty man."

Others might scoff, but Chamberlain was hugely pleased with his morning's work. Schmidt rode back with him to the Regina Palace, as "people shouted their greetings and pressed around our car, many trying to shake his hand." At the hotel, as he sat down to lunch with Strang, "the Prime Minister complacently patted his breast pocket and said, 'I've got it!'" Over coffee and cigars Chamberlain held a press conference and announced:

> I have always been of the opinion that if we could find a peaceful solution of the Czechoslovakia question it would open the way generally to appeasement of Europe. This morning I had a further talk with the Fuehrer and we both signed this declaration.

Then the British went off to the airport and a foul weather afternoon take-off

* The "sic!" is Ciano's.

to London. En route, Sir Horace Wilson asked Strang "to set out in summary form all the points on which the Munich Agreement was an improvement, from the Czech point of view, on the Godesberg memorandum." The result, Strang noted, was impressive "on paper," but within the next ten days the apparent gains proved worthless.

Within the homing aircraft, however, Neville Chamberlain, though tired, was "pleasantly tired." And now his cup of praise was to be filled and refilled a thousand times to overflowing. Awaiting him at Heston Airport was a command invitation from His Majesty George VI:

> I am sending this letter by my Lord Chamberlain, to ask you if you will come straight to Buckingham Palace, so that I can express to you personally my most heartfelt congratulations on the success of your visit to Munich.
>
> In the meantime, this letter brings the warmest of welcomes to one who, by his patience and determination, has earned the lasting gratitude of his fellow-countrymen throughout the Empire.

Once again on hand at Heston was the faithful Halifax, who joined his chief in the car for the drive to Buckingham Palace. The enthusiasm—almost the ecstasy—of the London crowds was pictured by the hero of the occasion to his sister:

> Even the descriptions of the papers give no idea of the scenes in the streets as I drove from Heston to the Palace. They were lined from one end to the other with people of every class, shouting themselves hoarse, leaping on the running board, hanging on the windows, and thrusting their hands into the car to be shaken.

At the palace, Chamberlain appeared on the balcony with Their Majesties; for the King it was a "great day," and he told his mother, Queen Mary: "The Prime Minister was delighted with the result of his mission, as we all are, and he had a great ovation when he came here." Then he was off to an early evening Cabinet meeting, where he put Strang's memorandum on the differences between Godesberg and Munich to good use. Even the First Lord of the Admiralty, Alfred Duff Cooper, found the gains "really considerably greater than I had understood," but this did not prevent him from resigning, on the ground that the Munich settlement was a national disaster.

It was the first dissenting voice, as yet well nigh inaudible against the thundering roar of general approval. At the Prime Minister's official residence, No. 10 Downing Street, enthusiasm reached its highest pitch: "The scenes culminated in Downing St.," he told his sister, "when I spoke to the multitudes below from the same window, I believe, as that from which Dizzy announced peace with honour 60 years ago."* Dunglass, in his later incarnation as Sir Alec Douglas-Home, recalled that:

> I was with Chamberlain as we approached the foot of the staircase in No. 10, where Cabinet colleagues and others were assembled. Out of the crowd

---

* In July 1878, after signing (with Bismarck and the representatives of Russia, Turkey, and Austria-Hungary) the Treaty of Berlin, which concluded the Russo-Turkish War, "Dizzy" (Benjamin Disraeli, Lord Beaconsfield) returned triumphantly to London, bringing what he called "peace with honour."

someone said, "Neville, go up to the window and repeat history by saying Peace in our time." I could not identify the voice but Chamberlain turned rather icily towards the speaker, and said "No, I do not do that kind of thing."

Despite this rebuff, the Prime Minister proceeded to do just "that kind of thing." Waving over his head the paper that he and Adolf Hitler had signed that morning, he told the crowd:

My good friends, this is the second time in our history that there has come back from Germany to Downing Street, peace with honour. I believe it is peace for our time.

The street below rang with shouts of "Good old Neville!" and the strains of "For he's a jolly good fellow!" Turning paternal, as he had in the same spot two nights earlier, he admonished his worshipers to "go home and get a nice quiet sleep."

Sleep was what the Prime Minister himself needed more than anyone else, for he was falling victim to autointoxication. Actually, his feet were not so far off the ground as these frabjous words suggest. On the way to Buckingham Palace, he had remarked to Halifax that the popular enthusiasm would be "over in three months," and soon he publicly repudiated the "peace with honour" theme, asking the House of Commons not to take literally words that he had "used in a moment of some emotion, after a long and exhausting day, after I had driven through miles of excited, enthusiastic, cheering people."

For the moment there was little need for such restraint as the encomiums poured in—from political friend and foe, from German officers and professors, from General Jan Smuts, the King of the Belgians, and the Archbishop of Canterbury, from the old nursemaid of his childhood, who, bless her heart, trustingly congratulated "dear Mr. Neville" because "it fell to you to face that German, and talk as you must have done. . . ." A "National Fund of Thanksgiving" was proposed in his honor (which he rejected), and in France the newspaper *Paris-Soir* sponsored a public subscription to present a villa to *"le Seigneur de la Paix,"* to be located near a stream where he could fish.

But when the House of Commons met on October 3 to debate the settlement, discordant voices were heard. For the Labor Opposition, Mr. Herbert Morrison declared that the Czechs had been "lost and betrayed." More significant were the defections within the Prime Minister's own party. In his speech of resignation, Duff Cooper declared that the "deep difference" between himself and his chief had been that Chamberlain "has believed in addressing Herr Hitler through the language of sweet reasonableness," whereas "I have believed that he was more open to the language of the mailed fist." With gloomy and foreboding eloquence, Winston Churchill described the settlement as "a disaster of the first magnitude," which was "only the beginning of the reckoning . . . the first foretaste of a bitter cup which will be proffered to us year by year unless, by a supreme recovery of moral health and martial vigour, we arise again and take our stand for freedom as in the olden times."

On the division, Chamberlain carried the House by 366 to 144 votes, but there were some thirty Conservative abstentions, including Churchill, Eden, Duff Cooper, Leopold Amery, Harold Macmillan, and Harold Nicolson. Chamberlain was troubled but unshaken in his faith that he had done the right thing. To the Archbishop of Canterbury he wrote that "some day the Czechs will see that what we did was to save them for a happier future," and that Munich had "at last opened the way to that general appeasement which alone can save the world from chaos."

If the general public did not see the matter in these large dimensions, that did not diminish their joy that there was to be no war. Perhaps their feelings of impatience with the dissenters were best expressed by the Queen Mother, in a letter to her son, the King: "I am sure you feel as angry as I do at people croaking as they do at the P.M.'s action, for once I agree with Ly. Oxford* who is said to have exclaimed as she left the House of Commons yesterday, 'He brought home Peace, why can't they be grateful'. . . ."

4

The many who were deeply grateful were, with few exceptions, soon disillusioned. In the upshot, as we will see, none of the Munich provisions that had been inserted for the benefit of Czechoslovakia was fulfilled. The clause in Article 6 authorizing departure from a strictly ethnographic basis, for which Daladier had thanked Hitler so effusively, was applied only for the advantage of Germany. The new boundary was determined by the International Commission only in empty form, and actually by Berlin's *Diktat*. The territorial cessions to Poland and Hungary were settled neither by mutual agreement nor four-party decision, but by Poland's ultimatum, in the first case, and in the second by the Ribbentrop-Ciano "award." The guarantees promised in the first annex were never given.

So much for "peace with honour."

Nor did Munich, as Neville Chamberlain glowingly predicted to the Archbishop of Canterbury, bring about "that general appeasement which alone can save the world from chaos." Within ten days Hitler, in a public speech in Saarbrücken, sharply admonished Britain to "drop certain airs inherited from the Versailles epoch." Soon the German press and radio were full of condemnation of British and French rearmament and warnings of the war that would surely come if madmen like Churchill and Duff Cooper should come to power.

Early in November, the shooting of a German diplomat in Paris by a Jewish refugee was made the occasion for an officially fomented outburst of anti-Semitic barbarities by which the Nazis showed their utter contempt for the good will of other countries. These atrocities did not stop the French Government from inviting Ribbentrop to Paris early in December to sign a "good neighbor" agreement to parallel the Hitler-Chamberlain declaration of September 30. This hollow ceremony was held against the background of belligerent shouts in the

---

* Presumably Lady Margot Oxford, a strong rooter for the Prime Minister. On the day of Munich she had ticked off Harold Nicolson for rejecting her opinion that Chamberlain was "the greatest Englishman that ever lived."

Italian Chamber of Deputies, demanding the annexation of Savoy, Nice, Tunis, and Djibouti.

In mid-March 1939, German troops overran Bohemia and Moravia, and from the Hradschin, Hitler proclaimed a Reich Protectorate. Slovakia remained autonomous, under German military and diplomatic domination. A week later the Baltic port of Memel, then part of Lithuania, was forcibly annexed to East Prussia. On April 7, Italian troops overran Albania. On September 1, Germany attacked Poland, and the war which was to become the Second World War began, eleven months after Munich.

So much for "peace for our time."

How and why did all this come to pass?

Was German military power sufficient to sustain the challenge that Hitler flung in the face of Europe in 1938? Did the generals and admirals of the Wehrmacht support him in this venture?

Why, after Chamberlain's trip to Berchtesgaden and Czechoslovakia's capitulation on the "big transaction," did Hitler escalate the crisis almost to the point of war? If France, with the probability of British and Russian support, had stood firmly behind her treaty obligations to Czechoslovakia, would the Nazi regime have survived the test?

Who were the men and what were the beliefs and motives that governed the decisions of the British and French governments? What were their estimates of comparative military strength, and were they accurate? Did Chamberlain truly believe that he was following the road to European stability and peace? Why did Daladier surrender the initiative to Chamberlain? Did the British leaders think that they were "buying time"? Would the western allies have fought at longer or shorter odds in 1938 than in 1939? How much, if at all, were their decisions affected by anti-communist feelings, and the purpose of turning Hitler eastward?

Is there any "lesson of Munich" to be learned from studying the crisis and attendant questions such as those I have suggested?

Part II

THE MISE EN SCÈNE
1918-1936

CHAPTER 5

The Dead Hand of Versailles

1

The formal end of the First World War is commonly marked by the signing of the Treaty of Versailles on June 28, 1919, whereby the state of war between Germany and the Allied powers was terminated. Good, bad, or indifferent, the treaty was a fact with a future. For the next twenty years, Versailles was the keystone of Europe's diplomatic structure, and the what and why of Munich cannot be examined outside the context of the treaty and its aftermath.

Little more than eight months earlier, Woodrow Wilson had announced the Armistice to the people of the United States, with the triumphant assertion that: "Everything for which America fought has been accomplished." Alas, it was not so simple as all that:

> *I don't know what the war's about*
> *But you bet, by gosh, we'll soon find out!*

sang the American doughboy on his way to France. But it is doubtful that many of them ever did, and the question was hardly clarified by their country's repudiation of the treaty and refusal to join the League of Nations—the kernel of Wilson's program to "make the world safe for democracy."

Indeed, the United States Government bore a large share of responsibility for the natal infirmities of Versailles. Germany had accepted the Armistice on the basis of the "Fourteen Points" formulated by Wilson early in 1918. But the treaty that emerged from the Paris Peace Conference—deliberations from which Germany was excluded—undeniably diverged in many ways from the idealistic principles of the Fourteen Points, and thus the belief took root in Germany that the Fatherland had been trapped into laying down her arms on false pretenses, and that Versailles was not a treaty but a *Diktat*.

The outcome was almost equally unsatisfactory to the French, whose leaders had little faith in Wilson's efforts to raise the level of international morality. Twice in half a century France had been invaded by Germany, and Premier Georges Clemenceau and Marshal Ferdinand Foch sought future security for France in a plan to detach from Germany her lands west of the Rhine (the "Rhineland") and establish a long-term French military occupation of the left bank of the Rhine. Both Wilson and the British Prime Minister, David Lloyd George, strongly opposed this proposal, and eventually the French agreed to settle for a fifteen-year occupation and permanent "demilitarization" of the Rhineland, in reliance on a pledge that the United States and Britain would defend France against any future German attack. But the United States Senate refused to ratify the Versailles Treaty, and in so doing it killed the Anglo-American guarantee on which the French Government had counted. Thus deserted, and confronting a Germany decisively superior in population and economic resources, France put her faith in her own military power and continental alliances, and gave no support to the program of general disarmament and security for all through the Covenant of the League of Nations, which the Versailles settlement envisaged.

Thus Wilson appeared to the Germans as the man who proved unable or unwilling to fulfill the representations on the basis of which they had sued for peace, and to the French as the man who failed to provide the guarantees he had pledged, and in reliance on which they had yielded in the Rhineland. The result was a peace which Germany saw as dishonorable, vengeful, and oppressive, but which France viewed as inadequate to ensure her future security.

2

The Fourteen Points fell considerably short of furnishing a precise outline of the peace for which they were supposed to constitute the foundation. Many of them were couched in hortatory, evangelical terms, and some were general to the point of abstraction. "Open covenants of peace openly arrived at"—the famous First Point—might or might not be a viable method of diplomatic intercourse, but it was certainly not a blueprint of territorial readjustment. "A free, open-minded and absolutely impartial adjustment of all colonial claims . . ." (Fifth Point) bespoke a laudable attitude, but how was it to be applied in particular?

Other points, to be sure, were straightforward and readily susceptible of consummation. In accordance with the Seventh and Eighth Points, Belgium, which had lain under German occupation throughout the war, was evacuated and restored to sovereignty, and Alsace and Lorraine were reannexed to France. The Fourteenth Point called for the formation of a "general association of nations" under "specific covenants" which would guarantee the "political independence and territorial integrity" of all nations "great and small." This program was substantially fulfilled by the establishment of the League of Nations under a Covenant within which Article 10 embodied just such a guarantee. The treaty itself could hardly be criticized for America's refusal to join* and virtual withdrawal from the European scene.

Still other points were plain enough in purpose but exceedingly difficult of execution. The Ninth Point, for example, called for "a readjustment of the frontiers of Italy . . . along clearly recognizable lines of nationality." To this day the Austro-Italian Tyrol defies the identification of such lines. More important for present purposes was the Thirteenth Point, under which an independent Polish state was to be created "which should include the territories inhabited by indisputably Polish populations" and which would likewise have "a free and secure access to the sea." Were these two stipulations compatible? Was there *any* way to give Poland such access without sowing the dragon's teeth of German irredentism?

Unhappily for the prospect of a peaceful and happy Europe, some of the points, vague as they were, had enough specific content so that invidious comparisons could plausibly be made between the points and the treaty provisions that purported to implement them. Distribution of all the German colonies among the victor nations, even though done under mandate from the League of Nations, could hardly be called an "absolutely impartial adjustment" of colonial matters. The "equality of trade conditions among all nations" invoked by Point Three did not square with the treaty requirement that Germany grant "most-favored nation" terms to her conquerors for five years without reciprocity. Point Four, perhaps the most significant for the future, envisaged "adequate guarantees given and taken that national armaments will be reduced to the lowest point consistent with domestic safety." But the treaty provided for the disarmament of Germany alone, and while this was said to be done "in order to render possible the initiation of a general limitation of the armaments of all nations," there were surely no "adequate guarantees given" to this effect. The one-sidedness of the military aspects of the treaty was underscored by Germany's exclusion from the League of Nations, and thus from the benefits of the guarantees of territorial integrity in Article Ten.

The Treaty of Versailles was a long and complicated document which dealt with many matters in addition to those already mentioned, some of major importance—reparations in cash and kind from Germany, based on the famous "war guilt" clause; international control of international rivers; the establishment of an "International Labour Organization"; provision for the punishment of war criminals, including the former Kaiser, Wilhelm II. All of these were factors in the shaping of "Europe Between the Wars"—the Europe which produced and experienced the Munich crisis of 1938.

But for present purposes there are two portions of the treaty that are of cardinal importance, and the details of which must be brought to mind. These are

* Those old enough to recall the presidential campaign of 1920 may remember the Democratic slogan:

Now is the time for all good men
To come to the aid of Article Ten.

the territorial dispositions, embodied in Parts II and III of the Versailles Treaty, and the related Treaties of St. Germain (with Austria) and Trianon (with Hungary), and the military, naval, and air clauses of Part V, which imposed drastic restrictions on Germany's armed forces.

3

In Western Europe, the territorial provisions of the treaty raised virtually no problems relevant to the story of Munich. To be sure, the loss of Alsace and Lorraine deprived Germany of important industrial and mineral resources, but the Weimar politicians and Hitler alike were vehement in disclaiming any purpose to recapture those lands. Neither the minor alterations of the Ardennes frontier in favor of Belgium nor the cession (after a plebiscite) of northern Schleswig to Denmark was of much moment. The annexation to Italy, pursuant to the Treaty of St. Germain, of the Austrian Tyrol south of the Brenner Pass aroused deep resentment among the 250,000 German-speaking inhabitants, but no serious issue among the major powers.

It was in Central and Eastern Europe that the train of powder was laid. The essence of the problem that confronted the peace conferees at Paris can be very briefly stated: *What was to be done about the national aspirations of the many millions of non-Russian Slavs in Germany, western Russia, and the Austro-Hungarian "empire"?*

Much the largest of these subject Slav nationalities were the twenty million Poles who, in consequence of the eighteenth-century partitions of Poland, inhabited Russia, Germany (Silesia and West Prussia), and the Austrian "crownland" of Galicia. Next in size were, north of the Danube, the closely related Czechs (Bohemians and Moravians) in Austria and Slovaks in Hungary, and, mostly south of the Danube, the Serbs, Montenegrins, Croats, and Slovenes in Hungary and in Bosnia and Herzegovina (annexed to the empire in 1908), and in the kingdoms of Serbia and Montenegro, which had been overrun and occupied by empire forces during the war. In Hungary there were also many Ruthenians and Rumanians.

A Polish nation could be geographically reconstituted without doing mortal injury to the three "host" countries. But for the other aspirant Slav nationalities, the great question was the future, if any, of the "Dual Monarchy"—the Austro-Hungarian Empire of over fifty million dominant Germans and Hungarians and dominated Slav peoples. If this polyglot entity were to endure, plainly it would have to be on a "federalized" basis, with political and cultural autonomy for the major nationalities.

Such, in fact, was the hope of many who thought that the survival of Austria-Hungary, rickety as it was, offered the best foundation for "stability" in Central Europe. This was Woodrow Wilson's initial view, and his Tenth Point specified "the freest opportunity of autonomous development" for "the peoples of Austria-Hungary, whose place among the nations we wish to see safeguarded."

But the Tenth Point was as good as dead even before the end of the war, and Wilson was among those who finished it off. The Czech nationalists Thomas

Masaryk* and Eduard Beneš had promoted their cause with great skill in Western Europe and the United States; the French Government publicly endorsed the project of an independent Czechoslovakia in June 1918, the British followed suit in August, and early in September, Wilson approved an announcement recognizing the Czecho-Slovak National Council as a "*de facto* belligerent government." Meanwhile the Serbian government-in-exile at Corfu and a "Yugoslav Committee" had made a public affirmation of the independence and unity of the Serb, Croat, and Slovene peoples, and in May 1918 the United States Government publicly endorsed independence for Yugoslavia. As for the Poles, the prime ministers of Britain, France, and Italy had declared themselves for Polish independence in June 1918, and as we have seen, an "independent Polish state" was Wilson's Thirteenth Point.

The consequence of all this was that, as the First World War drew to a close, the Austro-Hungarian Empire simply disintegrated. In vain the Austrian Government in Vienna appealed to Wilson and his Tenth Point, for on October 19 the State Department replied that any peace discussions must be on the basis of independence for Yugo-Slavs and Czecho-Slovaks. This news hastened the death of the old regime, and by the time of the Armistice (November 11, 1918) a "National Committee" in Prague had proclaimed an "independent Czechoslovak state," the leaders of the Galician Poles had declared themselves "subjects and citizens of a free and reunited Polish State," and "national councils" had taken power in Croatia.

And so, when the Paris Peace Conference assembled in 1919, the independence of newly constituted Poland, Yugoslavia, and Czechoslovakia was taken for granted, as was the cession of a large part of Transylvania by Hungary to Rumania, which had entered the war on the "right" side. Austria was reduced to its Germanic nucleus and Hungary to its Magyar; the two rump states had little affinity for each other, and the old "empire" was extinguished.

The task that still faced the peace conference—difficult enough, to be sure—was how to fix the frontiers of the new states. Insofar as these were common borders with Germany, Austria, or Hungary, they were determined by the Treaties of Versailles, St. Germain, and Trianon respectively. Thus it was under the Versailles Treaty that Poland was given access to the Baltic Sea via the former German lands in West Prussia and Poznań—the famous "Polish Corridor," which was to furnish Adolf Hitler with his excuse for war in 1939.

For present purposes, the Czechoslovak borders are of the greatest interest. At the western end the solution was simple—probably too simple: by the Treaty of Versailles, the former Austro-German border was adopted as the new Czech-German line, and the Treaty of St. Germain established the old administrative boundary between Bohemia and Austria proper as the new Austro-Czech frontier. This looked like preservation of the *status quo* but in fact was nothing of the sort, for some three million Germans—the *Sudetendeutsche,* whose grievances were the ostensible focus of Munich—thus became inhabitants of the new nation. Under the empire they had been numbered among the dominant Ger-

* Masaryk was in fact born of a Slovak father and a Moravian mother.

man-Austrians who ruled the empire from Vienna; now they were a sub-dominant racial minority in a new land governed by Czechs in Prague.

Drawing the eastern boundaries presented different but equally difficult problems. The Slovaks had lived in Hungary, but not in a politically organized way. "Slovakia" was not an administrative entity and there was no previously established Slovak-Hungarian boundary. Slovaks and Hungarians were intermingled in a fashion that defied ethnic line-drawing. On the northern side of the new country, relations with Poland were deeply troubled by a dispute over the tiny but economically significant (coal, manufacturing, a railroad junction) duchy of Teschen, which had been part of old Bohemia but had a predominantly Polish population. Before the frontiers in these areas were resolved, there were brisk and unseemly military fisticuffs between Czech and Polish and between Czech and Hungarian troops.

Thus Czechoslovakia was born into an angry, hungry neighborhood. For the time being Germany pressed no claim to the Sudetenland, but the Sudeten Germans clamored for autonomy and a bigger share of state perquisites. Hungary eyed Slovakia coldly and bided her time. Poland and Czechoslovakia shared a strong mutual interest in safeguarding the Versailles dispensations to which they both owed so much, but the Teschen dispute left a bad taste in Warsaw, and there was no rapport. For diplomatic and military support, Czechoslovakia would have to cast her nets far from her own borders.

4

Thus were the defeated powers cut down and the map of Europe redrawn. Part V of the Versailles Treaty, containing the "military, naval, and air clauses," was to ensure that Germany would respect the new frontiers. The spirit of the Fourteen Points was paid lip service by a preliminary protestation of purpose to achieve "a general limitation of the armaments of all nations," but the operative clauses disarmed only Germany.* This was to be accomplished by five types of limitation, on (1) manpower, (2) quantity and types of weapons, (3) structure and method of armed forces organization and training, (4) armaments manufacture, and (5) geographical location of military installations.

At first blush the manpower restrictions appeared to be the most drastic. The German Army—the Army of Moltke and Schlieffen that had made Germany a great power, the Army of Hindenburg and Ludendorff, whose millions had overrun half of Europe and knocked at the gates of Paris—was reduced to an over-all strength of one hundred thousand men, and the Navy to fifteen thousand.

For the future of German arms, however, the prohibition of weapon categories was the most damaging. The four great new weapon types of the First World War were aircraft, submarines, tanks, and poison gases. All four were prohibited to the Germans by the treaty.

Army and Navy alike were subjected to detailed and crippling limits on the

---

* Austria, Hungary, and Bulgaria were subjected to comparable armament restrictions by the Treaties of St. Germain, Trianon, and Neuilly.

number and size of armaments of permissible types. Precise schedules fixed the number and specified the calibers of guns and small arms which the Army might utilize. The Navy, which had scuttled its High Seas Fleet at Scapa Flow rather than turn the ships over to their conquerors, was barred from renewed effort to rival Britain. For the future there would be no more than six each of battleships and light cruisers, and a dozen each of destroyers and torpedo boats. Furthermore, the "battleships" would be little more than heavy cruisers, for their displacement was not to exceed ten thousand tons.

The draftsmen of this portion of the treaty had studied their military history, and knew that a century earlier, when Napoleon by the Treaty of Tilsit had forced a reduction of the Prussian Army to forty-two thousand men, the treaty's teeth had been drawn by the fathers of the modern army—Gerhard von Scharnhorst and August von Gneisenau—who used a short period of intensive training, with rapid turnover, to produce a large "shadow army" of reserves. To forestall a repetition of this stratagem, the hundred-thousand-man Army was to be composed of men recruited for twelve-year enlistments, and officers engaged to serve for twenty-five years.

Nor were the Army's brain and nervous system overlooked by the surgeons of Versailles. The "Great General Staff" of the Army—symbol of the proud traditions of the past, and directly responsible to the Kaiser—was to be dissolved and not "reconstituted in any form." Veterans' associations were forbidden to "occupy themselves with any military matters," and all military academies, including the great Berlin Kriegsakademie, founded by Scharnhorst, and the principal school for officer cadets, had to be shut down.

The treaty provided for the establishment of a "Military Inter-Allied Commission of Control" to supervise execution of the military clauses. Importation of foreign arms and their manufacture for export were alike forbidden. The Germans were to inform the commission of the location and contents of all munitions depots, to facilitate the confiscation or destruction of everything in excess of treaty limits. For the future, German domestic armament manufacturing could be conducted only at plants approved and licensed by the Allied powers. The great Krupp firm, for example, was restricted to making only large guns; smaller guns and other weapons were licensed to Rheinmetall and other companies.

The treaty declared that the purpose of the military forces permitted to Germany was "the maintenance of order within the territory and the control of the frontiers." The key word was "control" rather than "defense," and the treaty contained various limits on the location of military installations which were intended to make it difficult for Germany to defend herself against attack, especially in the west. Naval works and fortifications could not be located within fifty kilometers of the coast, and those on the North Sea island of Helgoland had to be demolished. Most important of all these provisions, perhaps, were those relating to the Rhineland, which Clemenceau and Foch had wished to put under permanent French occupation. Under the territorial clauses all German territory west of the Rhine, and a strip fifty kilometers wide east of the river, were to be demilitarized—stripped of fortifications and barred from use for maneuver or mobilization.

5

If the arms limitations thus imposed on Germany had actually been used in accordance with their declared purpose to bring about a "general limitation of the armaments of all nations," conceivably even the Germans might ultimately have found them palatable. But German and French generals were in complete agreement that disarmament was visionary folly, and so, as we have seen, the treaty was viewed in Germany as unjust and in France as inadequate.

Nor was this condemnation from both Germans and French taken elsewhere as a sign of the treaty's intrinsic fairness. On the contrary, and especially in Britain, Versailles had a bad press from the very beginning.

In large measure, this early disrepute was brought on by one of the "bright young men" at Paris: the English economist John Maynard Keynes, whose book *The Economic Consequences of the Peace,* published in 1919 a few months after the treaty was signed, vividly explicated its shortcomings. It is true that Keynes focused his analysis on the economic provisions, especially those dealing with "reparations." But his wrath ranged more broadly, and the integrity and wisdom of the treaty as a whole were effectively impugned by the label "Carthaginian Peace" which he fastened on it.

In later years a few anti-Keynesian historians raised their voices to declare that Versailles was not all that bad, and today, of course, the frame of reference is quite different. It is difficult to weep over the iniquities of reparations, or seizure of the German colonies, or the Polish Corridor when, thirty years later, many of us are not displeased by the division of Germany into two ideologically antithetical states, and have taken calmly the absorption of Eastern Germany into Poland and Russia, with Stettin rechristened Szczecin, and Immanuel Kant's Königsberg mapped as Kaliningrad.

Fortunately there is no need, in these pages, to decide whether Versailles should be entered in the black or the red ink of the historical ledger. The important point is that during the twenties and thirties it was widely regarded among historians, economists, politicians, and policy-makers as an unjust peace, and that these guilt feelings effectively obstructed action to enforce its terms when the Germany known to history as the Third Reich started casting off the treaty restrictions. Some, indeed, went so far as to declare that Versailles was responsible for Nazism itself, and that the Allies had only themselves to blame for the advent of Adolf Hitler.

Right or wrong in his evaluation of the treaty, Keynes put his finger on the crucial question of its future: would it prove susceptible of modification to meet new circumstances? Article XIX of the League Covenant empowered the Assembly to "advise the reconsideration . . . of treaties which have become inapplicable and the consideration of international conditions whose continuance might endanger the peace of the world." One of the leading men at Versailles and Geneva, General Jan Smuts of South Africa, when signing the treaty spoke of the looming need for its revision through League action to "pass the sponge of oblivion" over provisions "out of harmony with the new peaceful temper and unarmed state of our former enemies."

In the economic field, these hopes were measurably fulfilled over the course of a decade by the scaling down of reparations payments and their eventual cancellation. But the military and territorial provisions remained unchanged until Hitler, by unilateral action, repudiated them. Fearful of the consequences of relaxing them, France gradually lost the will and eventually the strength to enforce them.

So Versailles lost its vitality and withered—a dead hand heavy enough to block a healthy evolution of Franco-British policy toward Germany, but impotent to check the mood and muscle of the Third Reich. Adolf Hitler had only to shrug, and the hand fell off.

CHAPTER 6

The Rise of the Third Reich

1

The Kaiser abdicated and fled to Holland, and the last of his chancellors resigned and dumped governmental responsibility on the leaders of the Social Democrats. Under their aegis, a National Assembly was elected early in 1919 which met at Weimar and chose a former saddler, Friedrich Ebert, as President. In August the Assembly promulgated a constitution, and thus the Weimar Republic was born.

Its early years were tempestuous. Revolutionary socialist and communist groups seized power in parts of Berlin, Munich, and elsewhere and contested the Government's authority. Some of the demobilized soldiers joined "Soldiers' and Workers' Councils" comparable to the Russian soviets; others were recruited into vigilante military formations—the so-called *Freikorps*—that divided their time between the suppression of left-wing groups, fighting the Poles in Silesia and Soviet troops in the Baltic, and nihilistic freebootery.

Challenge from the left was followed by challenge from the right. The Versailles terms aroused violent opposition in military and nationalist circles, and in 1920 the treaty-required reductions in the size of the Army and Navy triggered an attempted *coup d'état,* led by General Walther von Lüttwitz,* in the course of which Ebert and his government were temporarily driven from Berlin. But most of Lüttwitz's brother officers did not support his attempt, and a general strike, called by the Social Democrats, isolated and paralyzed Berlin and put an end to the affair within a few days.

Armed revolt was not the only threat to the new republican government's stability. Germany's economic situation was precarious, and the Allied demands for reparations were onerous. The French were not disposed to be forgiving, and in 1920 and 1921, after charging Germany with defaulting her obligations under the treaty, they occupied a number of West German cities, including Frankfurt and Düsseldorf. A violent inflation gripped the country; by the fall of 1923 a dollar exchanged for over two billion marks. Earlier that year France

---

* Lüttwitz was associated with a fanatically nationalist Prussian bureaucrat named Wolfgang Kapp, and the revolt has gone down in the history books as the "Kapp-Lüttwitz Putsch." The troops that occupied Berlin were a *Freikorps* naval formation called (after its commander) the "Ehrhardt Brigade."

had occupied the entire Ruhr industrial area in a largely futile effort to squeeze out more reparations.

Meanwhile, a small but growing nationalist party—the National Socialist German Workers' Party, later to be known all over the world as the "Nazi" Party— had found energetic leadership in the person of a young Austrian ex-corporal, Adolf Hitler. In November 1923, in collaboration with the retired General Erich Ludendorff and with the tacit support of a number of army officers, Hitler made an attempt to seize power in Munich. The so-called "Beer Hall Putsch" collapsed under the fire of a handful of Bavarian police when Hitler led his followers in a march on the Feldherrnhalle, but the affair revealed a possible community of interest, between the professional officer corps and the Nazis, which bore deep significance for the future of Germany.

For the time being, however, the German generals remained faithful, in their fashion, to the Republic. Indeed, the Weimar regime survived these early crises primarily because of a loose but effective understanding between the civilian politicians and the leaders of the Reichswehr. It had begun at the time of the Armistice on the western front, when Hindenburg had agreed to retain command of the Army after the Kaiser's abdication, in return for Ebert's commitment to "co-operate in the suppression of Bolshevism" and respect the integrity and discipline of the Army under the High Command. What this meant in practical effect was that the civilian government would not attempt to "republicanize" or "radicalize" the Army, which would remain under the command of its old leaders and preserve its imperial traditions, while the Government and Army alike would co-operate in preserving "law and order" and suppressing revolutionary groups.

2

During Ebert's presidency, German chancellors came and went as fast as French premiers, and most of their names—Scheidemann, Bauer, Müller, Fehrenbach, Wirth, Cuno, Marx, Luther—echo but faintly in the corridors of history. On the military side, however, there was one name only, and that was one to conjure with—Hans von Seeckt, who took command of the Reichswehr in 1920, immediately after the failure of the Lüttwitz coup.*

A monocled Prussian nobleman whose icy, impassive bearing and countenance won him the sobriquet "Sphinx," Seeckt seemed to epitomize the old regime, but in both intellectual breadth and political grasp he far outstripped most of his colleagues. As Chief of Staff to various commanders, Seeckt had been the architect of several notable victories in the 1914–18 war, and his service as military adviser to the Turks and as a member of the German mission at Versailles had expanded and sophisticated his perception of men and trends.

After the Armistice and demilitarization of most of the Army, Seeckt saw clearly enough that open resistance to the treaty terms was quite impossible, that revolution from the left would destroy the Army as he had known and

* Hindenburg resigned his command and went into retirement after the Versailles Treaty was signed. His immediate successor, General Walter Reinhardt, gave way to Seeckt after the Kapp-Lüttwitz Putsch.

wished to preserve it, and that revolution from the right would, in all probability, bring French troops thundering across the Rhine. For the time being there was no alternative to support for the Republic, as a regime in which the Army as an autonomous entity—a "state within a state"—could preserve its traditions and expertise. The disarmament provisions of the Versailles Treaty would have to be outwardly respected, but only in order to give the Army a breathing spell for recuperation, and the laying of plans to frustrate and eventually repudiate the treaty and re-create a formidable German military machine.

And so the "General Staff" was abolished in name only and its functions taken over by a "Troops Office." The staff training formerly imparted at the War Academy was decentralized and carried out in the field, and a secret "flying group" was set up in the Defense Ministry to keep abreast of developments in aerial warfare. In the private sector, the Krupp firm was encouraged to set up a dummy company in Holland to develop and build submarines, and to use the Swedish firm of Bofors for artillery design. Meanwhile, making a virtue of necessity, the long service required by the treaty was exploited to make of the small Army a true military elite, in which every man was trained so that "he would be capable of the next higher step in case of war."

Conservative and communist-hater that he was, Seeckt did not allow his domestic political predilections to govern his assessment of foreign affairs. Germany would remain at the mercy of the victors unless she found allies; Austria-Hungary was gone, and the new Versailles-born states were natural enemies. There was nowhere to look but toward the east, and as early as 1920 discreet talks were held between Reichswehr representatives and Soviet agents, and a secret office for Russian affairs was set up in the Defense Ministry.

In the spring of 1922, this bizarre liaison was strengthened by the Treaty of Rapallo, whereby Germany and the Soviet Union canceled their war damage claims, re-established diplomatic and consular relations, and agreed to foster economic interchange "with mutual feelings of good will." Thereafter Seeckt pressed harder than ever for a policy of alignment with Russia, the prime object of which would be "the obliteration of Poland" and re-establishment of the old German-Russian border. The immediate fruits of such a strategy would be the establishment of an armaments base in Russia beyond the pale of the Versailles Treaty; the long-term gains, undermining that treaty and the hegemony of France by destroying Poland, thus gathering strength which would eventually draw Britain to the German side, in order to preserve a balance of French and German power in Europe.

Seeckt did not retain power long enough to pursue the more distant goals, but was able to exploit the Russian relation extensively for Versailles-forbidden rearmament. There were exchanges of Russian and German officers for staff training; shells for the Reichswehr were manufactured in Russian plants; the production of poison gas was undertaken near Samara, and a tank training school was constructed near Kazan, both subsidized by Germany; most important of all, a German school of military aviation was established at Lipetsk, near Voronezh.

President Ebert and a number of his ministers took a dim view of these goings-on, fearing that they would be discovered by the Allies, with punitive consequences. But the politicians knew little of the details and were beholden to Seeckt, who, throughout his tenure as Chief of the Army Command, came to the support of the Republic against threats from right and left alike—against Hitler in Munich, against communists in the Ruhr.

In all this, there was more than a touch of *noblesse oblige*, as if Seeckt were protecting a vassal rather than rendering service to a sovereign. "No one but I can make a Putsch, and I assure you I shall make none," he told the Cabinet on one occasion. When Ebert, alarmed at the prospect of Bavarian separatism, asked Seeckt whether the Army would "stick to us," the general replied that the Army would "stick to me." When the combination of inflation and the French occupation of the Ruhr brought about a near-revolutionary condition, it was Seeckt who exercised emergency powers to pull the Government through the crisis.

For a time it seemed that Seeckt might grasp the formalities as well as the actualities of power, but he was not of that metal, and his days were numbered. Strangely enough it was the death in 1925 of Ebert, whose presidency Seeckt had both protected and dominated, that was the prelude to his own downfall.

3

Friedrich Ebert died suddenly of appendicitis. Seeckt would have liked to succeed him, but had long held himself outside of and above party affiliation, and he had no organization support. On the first ballot seven candidates divided the vote, and a second election was called. And then, from the shadows of retirement, unwillingly and persuaded only by the blandishments of his onetime naval collaborator, Grand Admiral von Tirpitz, there emerged the square and venerable figure of Field Marshal Paul von Beneckendorff und von Hindenburg, hero of Tannenberg, Chief of Staff to the Kaiser, and ranking officer of the old Army. Running an above-the-battle campaign and backed by a nationalist-conservative coalition, Hindenburg narrowly defeated Wilhelm Marx, candidate of the left and center, and became the second and last President of the German Republic.

What Seeckt and Ebert had accomplished in collaboration Hindenburg embodied in his own ample person. He had been chosen by popular election, and his picture hung in millions of German parlors. He was seventy-seven years old and the doyen of the officer corps; to him, Seeckt was a clever junior. Too clever by half, for in 1926 Seeckt incautiously and in violation of the Versailles Treaty* allowed the Kaiser's grandson, August Wilhelm, to put on a uniform and take part in Army maneuvers. There were screams of protest from the Social Democrats, whispers of criticism from his rivals in high places, and Hindenburg required him to resign.

It was the end of Seeckt as a force in German politics. After his retirement he contributed to military literature, went to China as adviser to Chiang Kai-shek, and died in 1936. It was also the end of effective personal leadership of the

* In violation because the treaty required all officers to serve for twenty-five years, while Prince August Wilhelm (familiarly known as "Auwi") was an officer only for the period of the maneuvers.

German Army, for Seeckt had no successor in that role. Hindenburg himself was too old and wooden, while his presence and enormous prestige overshadowed the serving generals and effectively shut out any who might have aspired to independent power or national stature.

Indeed, Hindenburg's influence was, if anything, bad for the cohesion and integrity of the officer corps. Lead he could not; interfere he could, especially in personnel matters—promotions, retirements, and assignments. Seeckt's successor as commander of the Army, Wilhelm Heye, was a decent man and good soldier, but he was no politician and was never really master in his own house. Many of the Army's senior officers had served under Hindenburg in times past. He liked some better than others, and was not above favoritism. Furthermore, the old man was lonely; he had been a widower since 1921, and enjoyed the company of younger men who could amuse and charm him with anecdote and flattery.

Hindenburg had been originally commissioned in 1866 as a lieutenant in the Third Regiment of Foot Guards, and his son Oskar had served in the same unit —the *Dritte Garde,* as it was known in the Army. By 1925 a major, Oskar was assigned in Berlin and acted as an adjutant to his father. Friendship with Oskar often meant access to the Old Gentleman, and these circumstances were now exploited by a fellow alumnus of the *Dritte Garde*—Lieutenant Colonel Kurt von Schleicher, who was then serving on Seeckt's staff, and had been a close friend of the Hindenburgs for several years. Schleicher was an exceedingly able staff officer, but his talents were by no means limited to military affairs. His work on legislative and budgetary matters, and performance as a spokesman of the Army to the Cabinet and the Reichstag were so impressive that in 1926 he became a sort of chief of staff to the Minister of Defense, Otto Gessler. Highly political, with a taste for intrigue and a shrewd touch in using other men for his own ends, Schleicher now became the leading figure in military affairs of state.

Because of his age, unfamiliarity with and indifference to the customs of politics, and ingrained habit of relying heavily on his immediate staff, Hindenburg's presidency was peculiarly susceptible to manipulation by a close and closed circle of advisers. He kept on Ebert's ministerial assistant Otto Meissner, an assiduous and able bureaucrat who maintained his position under chiefs as diverse as Ebert, Hindenburg, and Adolf Hitler. Meissner quickly saw the value of close collaboration with the President's son Oskar and his favorite Schleicher, and thus was formed the nucleus of a camarilla that influenced and came to dominate Hindenburg's exercise of his powers as President and Commander-in-Chief.

As Hindenburg returned to and Seeckt faded from the scene, Germany was starting to pull out of the morass of inflation and insurrection, and the Republic enjoyed a period—brief as it was to prove—of economic and political stability. The chief architect of this happy interlude was the best-remembered German politician of those years, Gustav Stresemann, who served briefly as Chancellor in 1923, and thereafter as Foreign Minister until his death in 1929.

Because of his association with the Locarno agreements of 1925, Stresemann is commonly recalled as a peace-minded idealist. In fact he was a thoroughgoing conservative and nationalist. Like Seeckt, however, he was a realist and gradualist. Unlike Seeckt, he was western-oriented, and pursued a policy of reconciliation with Germany's former enemies through fulfillment of the Versailles terms. Reparations payments were resumed under the so-called "Dawes Plan" of 1924, and in 1925 the French pulled out of the Ruhr. A year later, at Locarno, the German-French and German-Belgian borders were guaranteed by the Locarno security pact among those three countries, Britain, and Italy. The use of force to change the frontiers was mutually renounced, and Britain and Italy agreed to come to the aid of France or Germany if either was wrongfully attacked by the other.

Locarno was widely hailed as marking the dawn of a new and peaceful era in Europe, and its chief sponsors—Stresemann, Austen Chamberlain, and Aristide Briand—won great acclaim. It also marked Germany's return to international respectability. In 1926 she was admitted to the League of Nations, and part of the Rhineland was evacuated. By 1930 the Rhineland was free of occupation troops, and the Allied disarmament commissions were withdrawn from Germany.

But while these hated marks of the Versailles *Diktat* were being erased, the clouds gathered again, and soon they were nearly as dark as they had been during the black years of inflation and the Ruhr occupation. In 1929, a general economic depression began to settle over Europe. Germany had borrowed heavily in America to meet the reparations payments; now there were no more credits to be had. The Young Plan of 1930 called for a reduced schedule of payments, but the German nationalists violently opposed its acceptance, and Hindenburg lost support among the conservative parties. Early in 1930, as the depression gripped Germany with the freezing fingers of winter and unemployment, the Socialist-dominated coalition government of Chancellor Hermann Müller tottered, and the crisis became political as well as economic.

Meanwhile Schleicher (promoted brigadier general in 1929) had expanded his influence in many directions. In 1929, when Otto Gessler was forced out of the Ministry of Defense because of disclosures of clandestine naval rearmament, Schleicher engineered the selection of his old chief, Wilhelm Groener, who at the end of the war had succeeded Ludendorff as Hindenburg's chief of operations. The following year Heye retired, and Schleicher successfully urged the appointment in his place of General Kurt von Hammerstein-Equord, who had served with Schleicher and Oskar von Hindenburg in the Third Foot Guards.

Thus having installed old patrons and friends as Minister of Defense and commander of the Army, and high in presidential favor, Schleicher set about chancellor-making, as Müller's departure grew imminent. His selection was Heinrich Brüning, a wartime front-line officer who, as a member of the Reichstag since 1929, had ingratiated himself with Schleicher by his strong support for the military budgets. In 1929 Brüning became parliamentary leader of the Catholic Center Party, and in March 1930, when Müller's political position became untenable, Hindenburg asked Brüning to form a cabinet.

For the next two years these four men—Brüning, Groener, Hammerstein, and Schleicher—formed a quadrumvirate within which Schleicher, the least in rank, had the closest access to the levers of power. It was an able group, but they were fighting tides they could not stem. The economic depression deepened, and the reparations payments under the Young Plan could not be met. In June 1931 the "Hoover moratorium" was arranged, and payments were never resumed, but with unemployment spreading and an empty treasury, popular disenchantment with the policy of "fulfillment" was intensified. Germans of all shades of opinion were exasperated by the continuing failure to carry out the general disarmament commitments of the Versailles Treaty—conservative nationalists because Germany remained under the treaty restrictions, liberal idealists because the League of Nations disarmament commission was moving so slowly. Not until January 1931 did the League council get around to authorizing an international conference on disarmament, to begin in February 1932. By then it was too late to have much effect on the course of German politics.

Concurrently with and largely in consequence of these sharpening dissatisfactions, the shadow of Adolf Hitler lengthened. Imprisoned for little more than a year after his unsuccessful Munich coup in 1923, Hitler had put his enforced leisure to good use by writing that disjointed and repetitive but strangely gripping book *Mein Kampf*. Upon his release he re-established the Nazi Party, which grew but slowly during the next few years, which were fat for Germany, and correspondingly lean for malcontents.

In the 1928 elections, the Nazis polled only 810,000 votes and took twelve seats in the Reichstag. Two years later nearly six and a half million pro-Nazi votes put 107 Party candidates into the 577-member Reichstag. Social Democratic, Catholic Center, and non-Nazi nationalist strength declined, while the Communists gained spectacularly and seated 77 deputies. The right and left extremists thus comprised nearly a third of the entire assemblage, and the Nazi delegation was the second largest—proportions which made it even more difficult for any cabinet to command a majority, and pushed Brüning inevitably toward government by presidential decree, under Article 48 of the Weimar Constitution, which vested emergency powers in the President.

The Nazis were making converts in the Army as well as gains in the electorate. As Minister of Defense, Groener was determined, as he had been ten years earlier, to protect the Republic against extremists whether of the left or the right, and in January 1930 he issued a general order coupling the Nazis with the Communists, and reminding the troops of their duty to eschew party politics and serve only the State. But times had changed, and the old phrases had spent their force. There was little room at the top in a 100,000-man Army and a 15,000-man Navy; promotion was slow, and the young subalterns chafed at the bit. The Versailles restrictions were hated, and Hitler was the man who vowed loudest to shake them off.

Barely six weeks after Groener's decree, three young lieutenants of the artillery regiment garrisoned at Ulm were arrested and charged with spreading Nazi propaganda in the Army. Groener at first tried to dispose of the case by a routine court-martial, but the intransigent attitude of the accused officers, one of whom succeeded in reaching the press with a violent attack on the Republic and an assertion of their right "to fight with all means for our freedom," forced the issue to a higher level. In September 1930, ten days after the election in which the Nazis had achieved their enormous gains, the three subalterns were arraigned before the Supreme Court of Germany in Leipzig, on charges of high treason.

The officers were convicted and sentenced, but the trial became a political *cause célèbre* far transcending the fate of the defendants,* and a divisive affair for the Army. The regimental colonel at Ulm—Ludwig Beck, later Chief of the General Staff and still later a leader of the anti-Hitler conspirators—testified as a character witness for one of the defendants. Hitler, sensing the explosive political possibilities of the occasion, appeared as a defense witness and skillfully swept his fingers over the harp strings of history, comparing his own crusade against Versailles to that of Gneisenau and Scharnhorst against the Napoleonic yoke. From his retirement, Seeckt accused Groener of "weakening the spirit of comradeship and solidarity within the officers' corps." General Heye, who retired as commander of the Army during the episode, publicly expressed regret that the trial had occurred, and his deep fears about its aftereffects.

4

General Heye's apprehensions were well founded, though on the face of things the Government looked well able to face challenge from the right. Hindenburg and the Brüning-Groener-Schleicher-Hammerstein quadrumvirate, embodying as they did the last hope for survival of republican Germany, were by no means liberal democrats. It was an authoritarian, military, and military-minded group; at its head was the visible and venerable symbol of the old regime, and Brüning's cabinet included six holders of the Iron Cross.

Not unnaturally, these men hoped to provide a rallying point for conservative and nationalistic Germans of high and low degree. Nor were they unaware that, given Germany's desperate economic plight and political neuroses, symbols were not enough. With calculation and vigor, Brüning embarked on a program of domestic belt-tightening to restore the economy, and a diplomatic campaign to persuade the Versailles victors to ease the burden of reparations, relax the armament restrictions, return the Saarland to Germany, and otherwise move toward a readjustment that would heal the festering sores left by the hated *Diktat*.

It was a brave effort but it did not succeed, and Brüning's failure sounded the death knell of the Weimar Republic. The depression worsened, and he was dubbed the "Hunger Chancellor." His foreign policies made progress, but it was not fast enough to shore up his domestic political position. The old methods did not seem to be working, and the result was a wave of extremism, reflected on the left by notable Communist gains at the expense of the Social Democrats, and on the right by far larger Nazi election victories which reduced the old-line conservative parties to mere splinters.

As Brüning's popularity waned, other nationalist groups joined the Nazis in

---

* They were sentenced to eighteen month's imprisonment, during which one of them was converted by fellow-prisoners to communism! One of the others, Hans Ludin, later became a storm-troop leader, and in 1940 was appointed Ambassador to Slovakia, where he was executed at the end of the war.

opposition. In the fall of 1931, a right-wing rally was held at Harzburg, where the veterans' organization Stahlhelm paraded together with Nazi storm-troopers, and Hitler was flanked not only by the Nationalist leader Alfred Hugenberg, but by pillars of the conservative establishment such as the banker Hjalmar Schacht, and Seeckt himself. Such portents made a deep impression on the volatile, intrigue-prone Schleicher, who had begun a sequence of clandestine meetings and negotiations with Hitler and his henchmen. The quadrumvirate was beginning to lose cohesion, though as yet the cracks were not apparent.

Hindenburg's seven-year term as President expired in the spring of 1932, during his eighty-fifth year. With great difficulty he was persuaded to stand for re-election, but the efforts of Brüning and Schleicher to avoid a contest were unsuccessful, as Hitler and Hugenberg, as well as the Communists, declined to stand aside. There ensued a most extraordinary campaign, in which the monarchist, Protestant field marshal was supported by Jews, Catholics, and virtually all the moderate and liberal groups, while the Austrian-born ex-corporal won the backing not only of the disgruntled lower middle class, but also of the conservative agrarians, the Ruhr and Rhineland industrialists, the former Crown Prince, and General von Seeckt!

The main burden of Hindenburg's campaign fell on Brüning, who labored indefatigably and, in the end, successfully. On the first ballot in February, Hindenburg outpolled Hitler by over three to two, but barely missed the necessary absolute majority; in the April runoff ballot he was returned to office by a majority of 53 per cent, with over 19 million votes to 13.5 million for Hitler.

It was an impressive victory for Brüning, and should have produced a grateful President and a new lease on life for the Government. It did neither; the Old Gentleman was not prone to gratitude, and no sooner was he embarked on his second term than everything started to go wrong and the quadrumvirate disintegrated, a victim of Hindenburg's senility and Schleicher's intrigues.

Groener was the first to go. Immediately after the election he had presented to Hindenburg a decree suppressing the Nazi storm troopers, on the grounds of treasonable activities to the State. Harassed provincial officials had for some time been pressing Groener for this measure, and when he first proposed it to his colleagues, it was warmly approved by both Schleicher and Hammerstein. Soon, however, their attitudes changed, and although the President signed and promulgated the decree, it became clear that Schleicher, far from supporting his chief, was whipping up opposition to the decree and to him personally, among the senior Army commanders.

The right-wing press and conservative public figures joined the Nazis in heaping abuse on Groener, and his standing with the President was badly undermined by son Oskar, at Schleicher's instigation. On May 10 there was a tumultuous debate in the Reichstag, where Groener was subjected to a murderous heckling from the right-wing benches. Schleicher and Hammerstein informed Groener that he no longer enjoyed the confidence of the Army leadership, and on May 13 Hindenburg accepted his resignation.

Brüning's chancellorship did not survive the month. He had been the architect of the President's re-election; now he was blamed for subjecting the field marshal to public abuse and making him look foolish as the hero of liberals and democrats. Egged on by Schleicher and Oskar, Hindenburg's Prussian Junker friends poured poison into the presidential ear; Brüning was a dangerous "internationalist" with "Bolshevik policies." On May 30 he was coldly dismissed.

5

Schleicher's machinations had now carried him to the top of the heap—an exposed position for which he had little stomach, as his forte was wire-pulling from behind the scenes. Now that the main responsibility for governance of the Reich had fallen on his shoulders, his shallowness and instability of purpose soon betrayed him into fatal errors of judgment.

The first and worst of them lay in his selection of the man whom he now proposed to Hindenburg as Brüning's successor. Franz von Papen was a political lightweight, a gentleman rider and dabbler in politics whom no one took seriously, and wholly unfit by experience, connections, or ability for the office of Chancellor. Schleicher thought he could control him, and that Papen's cavalry-officer dash and social graces would please Hindenburg. He was wrong on the first count and only too right on the second, for Papen became the President's "Fränzchen" and soon supplanted Schleicher in the Old Gentleman's affections.

Seven of the nine ministers in the Papen cabinet were of the old nobility. All were of the right, and there was no representative of labor. The new Government was strictly a presidential creature with no substantial support in the Reichstag. Communists, Social Democrats, and Catholic Center were in solid opposition. The Nazis gave equivocal "toleration," bought by Schleicher's commitment to Hitler that the decree banning the storm-troopers would be rescinded, and that the Reichstag would be dissolved and a general election held.

Schleicher himself had been obliged to resign from the Army and take over Groener's former post as Minister of Defense. He was the "strong man" of the Government, but had virtually no following in the Reichstag. His strength lay only in the favor of Hindenburg and the loyalty of Hammerstein and other generals. In the Army as a whole his standing was much less secure, for he had always been regarded as a "desk general," and his long career of wheeling and dealing had won him not only the sobriquet "Creeper" (the literal meaning of his surname), but likewise the enmity of some of his colleagues, such as the commander in East Prussia, General Werner von Blomberg.

The promised election was held at the end of July, after a campaign of unprecedented violence. In the Hamburg suburb of Altona, a Communist-storm-trooper clash took fifteen lives. The outcome was a total repudiation of Papen's "Cabinet of Barons," as the conservative parties took but 44 seats of 608 in all. The Nazis more than doubled their representation, and with 230 seats became the largest party. The Communists also gained, while the moderate parties— Social Democrats and Center—retained a combined strength of 230, just equal to the Nazis.

Who could govern? It was difficult to find a workable majority coalition, and without one presidential government by decree would have to continue; but who would be Chancellor? As leader of the largest party, Hitler claimed the prize, and Schleicher, deluded like so many others by the notion that he could "tame" the Nazis, met with Hitler early in August and discussed the formation of a cabinet with Hitler as Chancellor and himself as Vice-Chancellor or Minister of Defense.

But when Schleicher repaired to the Reichschancellery to put across his plan, he soon discovered that Papen had no intention, despite the election results, of giving up the plums of office that he so enjoyed, and that Hindenburg had equally little disposition to offer the chancellorship to the "Bohemian corporal." Schleicher made no headway, and began to sense that it was "Fränzchen" and not himself who now had the inside track with Hindenburg and the camarilla.

Unaware that Schleicher's plans had misfired, Hitler came to Berlin at Hindenburg's request in mid-August, confident that the next day would see him Chancellor. To his chagrin and astonishment, Papen offered him the vice-chancellorship, while Hindenburg stated in no uncertain terms his unwillingness to give full power to the Nazis, and read Hitler a stiff lecture on his followers' bad behavior during the election campaign. Hitler angrily refused the second place and went off in a fury of frustration.

Since it was plain that the Reichstag would reject the Papen government at the first opportunity, Hindenburg armed his favorite with a dissolution decree, prepared even before it met. The sitting, in mid-September, was tumultuous but brief, and after presentation of the dissolution decree there was an adjournment to await new elections, scheduled for November 6.

No one had much stomach for another campaign, and there was little reason to expect results which would make the formation of a majority government any easier. In the upshot the moderate parties lost slightly, the conservatives gained but remained little more than splinters, and the Communists gained once again, returning 100 out of 584 members. Most significant were the Nazi losses: 2 million votes and 34 seats. With 196 members they remained much the largest party, but Hitler's chances of finding a majority, and his political bargaining position, were both significantly weakened. In the ensuing local elections the Nazis lost more ground. Hitler had still other troubles, for the stream of contributions was drying up, and his party was in dire financial straits.

This second overwhelming popular rejection of his government left the jaunty Chancellor quite undaunted. At his suggestion Hindenburg offered Hitler the vice-chancellorship, or the chancellorship if majority support in the Reichstag were secured. As Papen fully expected, Hitler declined the first and could not meet the condition of the second alternative, and once again left the scene in a huff.

On December 1, Papen made his big move. At a meeting with Hindenburg and Schleicher he proposed that the Reichstag be indefinitely prorogued, that political parties, trade unions, and other large associations be suppressed, and that he continue as Chancellor of a presidential cabinet that would govern by decrees to be enforced by the police and the Reichswehr. This was, in essence, a proposal for the destruction of the Republic, and substitution of a military dictatorship under a civilian Chancellor.

Hindenburg might have accepted Papen's plan, but the Chancellor had reckoned without Schleicher. Next day, when Papen presented his proposal to the Cabinet, Schleicher was ready with strong counterarguments, and armed with a report from his Ministry of Defense on the results of a *Kriegsspiel* (war game), which had demonstrated the Army's inability to secure public order and safety if faced by a general strike and terroristic rioting by both Communists and Nazis.

Schleicher thus persuaded the Cabinet to reject Papen's proposals, and Hindenburg was informed that his Chancellor no longer enjoyed the confidence of the Cabinet or the Army. The old President sadly let his Fränzchen go, and had nowhere to turn for a successor except to Schleicher, who, on the evening of December 2, became the last Chancellor of the Weimar Republic.

6

It is hard to tell how far the Army's dismal report on its own peace-keeping capacities was a genuine military assessment, and how far a contrived device produced by Schleicher to frustrate Papen. By the end of 1932, the internal unity of the Reichswehr might not have survived prolonged and violent civil strife. The name of Hindenburg was still potent, at least among the older officers, but many must have been aware that he was a closeted relic, easily led by the nose. Certainly the soldiers would not have fought gladly for Franz von Papen, and even Schleicher was too much the "Creeper." Hammerstein was acknowledged as able and courageous, but he was notoriously lazy, and a "Schleicher man" on political matters. Among the younger and some of the senior officers, sympathy with the Nazis' announced aims, and admiration for their success in attracting the youth of the nation, was widespread.

However all that might be, Schleicher, having ousted Papen on the basis that a military solution was too hazardous, could hardly prescribe the same medicine. He had told Hindenburg and the Cabinet that a parliamentary majority might be found by bringing in the Nazis, either through a deal with Hitler or by splitting the party, which was in bad shape and, said Schleicher, riddled with dissension. That was the basis upon which he had been appointed, and Hindenburg refused him the protective dissolution decree with which Papen had been armed. The Reichstag would meet again at the end of January, so Schleicher had just two months in which to work his promised magic.

But it wouldn't do, and the scheme fell through. Hitler was no more willing to serve as Vice-Chancellor under Schleicher than under Papen. Seeking to conquer by dividing, Schleicher then offered the vice-chancellorship to Gregor Strasser, leader of the Berlin Nazis and sometimes a dissenter from Hitler's decisions. But Hitler knew that game much too well, and within less than a week Strasser was read out of his Party offices, and soon left Germany. Desperately, Schleicher sought alliances with the trade unions, the Social Democrats, and the Nationalists, but nowhere met with success.

And now Papen showed the man who had both made and unmade him that two could play such tricks. On January 4 he met with Hitler at the Cologne house of the banker Baron Kurt von Schröder, and opened the negotiations which produced the combination of Nazis and Nationalist conservatives that brought Hitler to power. On January 22 there was another Hitler-Papen conference hosted by Joachim von Ribbentrop in Berlin, attended by Hermann Goering, and, more importantly, by the President's chamber confidants, son Oskar and Otto Meissner. Meanwhile the Nazis' financial worries were being eased by substantial contributions from the West German industrial magnates, led by Gustav Krupp.

Late in January, Schleicher confessed to Hindenburg his inability to find a majority, and requested a decree of dissolution so that his government could continue despite a hostile Reichstag. Hindenburg curtly refused, and Schleicher found himself an interim Chancellor, cut off from the President's confidence, and virtually without influence on the course of events.

The significance of Oskar von Hindenburg's presence at the Hitler-Papen meeting in Berlin was that the old man was still averse to accepting the "Bohemian corporal" as Chancellor, and wanted his Fränzchen back again. Probably from a mixture of ambition and the need to cover the contingency of Hindenburg's absolute refusal to countenance Hitler, Papen began to explore the alternative of a combination with the Hugenberg Nationalists, excluding the Nazis—virtually his old plan scotched by Schleicher in December. These maneuvers filled Schleicher and Hammerstein with apprehension, for the last thing they wanted was to find themselves at the head of an Army called in to defend a government of so narrow a base and slender prestige. Anything, even Hitler, would be preferable.

And so the last week of January witnessed the extraordinary spectacle of the Army leaders pulling every available string to block a Papen and ensure a Hitler chancellorship. Hammerstein went so far as to assure Hitler that the Army would, if necessary, take further steps to "influence the position" against Papen.

Before the end there was another bitter pill for Schleicher, who might have expected that at least he would stay in office as Minister of Defense. On January 29 he learned that Hindenburg had summoned to Berlin General von Blomberg, no friend to Schleicher, then on temporary duty in Geneva as military delegate to the Disarmament Conference. Blomberg arrived at the Anhalter railroad station early on the morning of January 30, and was confronted by Hammerstein's adjutant with orders to report forthwith to the Defense Ministry, and by Oskar von Hindenburg, ready to take him directly to the President. The general went with Oskar.

Whether it was the coming of Blomberg, whom he liked, or other circumstances that finally swayed Hindenburg remains as cloudy as his mind must by then have been. Later that morning Adolf Hitler took the oath as Chancellor, in a cabinet that comprised Papen as Vice-Chancellor, Blomberg as Minister of Defense, Hugenberg as Minister of Agriculture and Economics, Franz Seldte of the *Stahlhelm* as Minister of Labor, two Nazis (Goering and Wilhelm Frick) as Ministers respectively without Portfolio and of the Interior, and five holdovers from the "Barons' Cabinet." Schleicher thus became a retired general without a job.

There were only three Nazis in the Cabinet, but everyone seemed to know who was boss. That night Berlin was in the hands of the Brownshirts, and a great torchlight parade down the Wilhelmstrasse acclaimed Hitler at his window in the Reichschancellery. All over Germany, there were wild demonstrations of enthusiasm. In Bamberg the procession was led by a cavalry lieutenant in uniform. He was Claus von Stauffenberg, who in 1944 placed a bomb under the Fuehrer's map table at Rastenburg in an unsuccessful effort to kill Hitler and overthrow the Nazi regime.*

7

The advent of Adolf Hitler as the leader of Germany spelled, almost immediately, the destruction of the Weimar Republic and, eventually, the holocaust of the Second World War and the virtual extinction of Jewry in a large part of Europe. Coming closer to the core of our present inquiries, it also spelled the doom of the Versailles system, and the dismemberment of Czechoslovakia at Munich.

Because of the terrible course and consequences of the Third Reich, the question of responsibility for Hitler's coming to power is still much debated, and those in positions of authority and influence in Germany at the time are generally saddled with most of the blame. That is fair enough as far as it goes, for it is undeniable that Krupp, Thyssen, Schacht, and other financial moguls backed Hitler and came to his aid with cash at a critical point in his fortunes, and that Schleicher and Hammerstein, and in quite a different way Blomberg, were party to Hindenburg's selection of Hitler as Chancellor.

But it is quite wrong to regard Hitler as the creation of the magnates and generals. They supported him not because they were in all respects pleased by his methods, but because his program, vague as it was, had ingredients of persuasive appeal to them and to Germans of every station; because of his demagogic skill and remarkable ability to lead and inspire; because, to use an expression borrowed from quite another time and place, he and he alone showed the ability to get the country moving again.

Furthermore, it is at best difficult to specify an alternative choice that would have been viable in January 1933. Hitler's designation was the consequence of earlier mistakes, and of them the Germans were not the only perpetrators. Given the economic and political situation of Europe in the early thirties, the reparations requirements and armament restrictions on Germany were unjustifiable and counterproductive. A speedier willingness on the part of the Versailles victors to revise the treaty terms might have enabled Brüning to maintain majority government, govern without recourse to the dangerous emergency powers, and taken much of the wind out of Hitler's sails. Flexibility on outdated provisions

* It is a remarkable circumstance that several leaders of the anti-Hitler conspiracy of later years were among his earliest and most enthusiastic supporters. The plot's elder statesman, General Beck, as a regimental colonel in 1930 celebrated Hitler's election success with festivities in the officers' mess. General Henning von Tresckow, the conspiracy's principal agent on the eastern front, as a lieutenant in 1929 gave a pro-Nazi speech to a meeting of his brother officers in Potsdam. After the Leipzig trial of the Ulm subalterns, Lieutenant Helmut Stieff, later a general and one of the principal conspirators at Hitler's headquarters, told his wife that he and his colleagues kept their commissions only in the hope that "this whole clique of Schleicher & Co." would be swept away by "the true national movement which no one can stop."

might thus have been a preservative of other treaty terms, such as the boundaries of Czechoslovakia.

Brüning's own decision to run Hindenburg for the presidency in 1932 was, of
course, based on his belief that no one else could beat Hitler, and that was an
understandable and perhaps an accurate assessment. But surely it was a sign of
political bankruptcy that an octogenarian field marshal, with his mind sunk in
the imperial past, should have been the candidate of the moderate forces, and
his age and mental infirmities were built-in hazards which might be expected, as
they did, to undermine the republican edifice. These hazards were greatly increased by Schleicher's lethal combination of abilities and disabilities, which
worked the destruction of solid men like Brüning and Groener, led him to pull
up Papen like a rabbit out of a hat and as quickly disown him, and eventually
left Schleicher painted into a corner, desperately backing the very man who
would throw him out of power.

If there were misjudgments by those who should have known better before
Hitler became Chancellor, there was worse to follow. The chancellorship was
not *ipso facto* dictatorship; the Nazis could be outvoted in both Cabinet and
Reichstag, and it was Papen, not Hitler, who had the President's ear and favor.
Indeed, as viewed by Hindenburg and Papen, the whole idea was to give Hitler
responsibility under the presidential checkrein, in a Cabinet dominated by non-
Nazi nationalists.

Singly or collectively, these men were no match for the shrewd and ruthless
Hitler, who played his hand with great skill. Three days after taking office he
met the military leaders at Hammerstein's home, and made an excellent impression by his moderation of manner, and a promise of unstinting support for enlargement of the Reichswehr. Blomberg soon became a most admiring supporter. Again in need of funds for the Reichstag elections scheduled for early
March, Hitler made an equally effective appeal to the Rhine industrialists, assembled at Goering's home under the aegis of Krupp and Schacht.

At the March elections the Nazi vote rose by over 20 per cent, and the Party
took 288 of 647 seats; with the 52 Nationalist votes the coalition had a slender
majority. A few weeks later, under extreme Nazi pressure, the Reichstag committed virtual suicide by passing an Enabling Act which authorized the Cabinet
to govern by decree. The real Nazi seizure of power—the so-called *Macht-
ergreifung*—followed at once, with the suppression of all other political parties,
the Nazification of all important organizations, the extensive use of concentration camps, and total control of the press and radio by that master of propaganda, Dr. Joseph Goebbels.

Changes in the composition of the Army and governmental leadership
reflected these Nazi successes. The police came under the control first of Hermann Goering, and then Heinrich Himmler. More Nazis were added to the Cabinet, including Rudolf Hess and the chief of the storm troopers, Ernst Roehm.
Schleicher's friends were cleaned out of the Ministry of Defense; Hammerstein
himself held on for a year, and then was replaced by the apolitical General
Werner von Fritsch. The non-Nazi Cabinet members were isolated and intimi-
dated. Hindenburg still doted on his Fränzchen, but he was receiving good re-

ports of Hitler from Blomberg, and the old man was now failing to the point that Papen could rarely turn his personal favor to any practical account.

By the end of his first year in office, accordingly, Hitler had pretty well disposed of political opposition to the Nazi regime and, despite its excesses, he had retained the support of the Army and big business. But now there arose *within* the Party a challenge and a problem that seriously threatened that support. Among the storm troopers, a large radical wing* took seriously the word "Socialist" in the Party title, and began to call for a "second round" of revolution that would curb the privileges and powers of the Junker landlords, industrial barons, and officers—the conservative establishment that had long dominated Germany, and from whose support Hitler had benefited decisively. Roehm himself cherished ambitions to absorb the regular Army into the storm troops, and subordinate the Army commanders to an over-all ministry of which he would be the head. In February 1934 he laid just such a plan before the Cabinet.

Hitler thus confronted a sharp issue between one of his ablest and most powerful lieutenants and the Army leadership, whose support he did not yet feel strong enough to forgo. In fact, Hitler apparently had little use for Roehm's program on the merits, as he soon made plain. But Roehm was far more confident in his dealings with Hitler than the other Nazi chieftains (he used the familiar *du* in personal address), and among the storm-troop leaders many were primarily loyal to Roehm rather than Hitler.

These issues were resolved, as is well known, by the murderous "Night of the Long Knives" or "Blood Purge" of June 30, 1934. There is much in the background of this massacre that remains obscure, and many of the published accounts include matter that is unconfirmed by documents or trustworthy testimony. It is clear, however, that the storm-trooper crisis coincided with a general awareness that Hindenburg's end was rapidly approaching, and that his death would, of course, confront Hitler and the nation with the problem of succession. In the light of what actually happened, it seems more than probable that some sort of understanding was reached between Hitler and the generals, the burden of which was that Hitler would put an end to the storm trooper's rivalry of the Army, and that the generals would not oppose Hitler's assumption of Hindenburg's powers as President.

And so it came about, beginning early in the morning of June 30. By the end of the day Roehm and many of his lieutenants were dead, and the occasion was exploited for paying off old political scores as well. Papen was spared, but several of his staff were killed. The victims included Schleicher and his wife, shot down in their home, as well as his erstwhile deputy, General Ferdinand von Bredow.

There was a wave of horror and revulsion, but from Blomberg there came only praise for Hitler's "soldierly decision and exemplary courage" in wiping out "mutineers and traitors." Hindenburg, with what degree of awareness one cannot say, telegraphed to Hitler his "profound thanks and appreciation" for saving Germany "from serious danger." Hitler himself informed the Reichstag that he

* Known as "Beefsteak": outside brown, inside red.

had been "responsible for the fate of the German people" and had therefore constituted himself "Supreme Judge."

A month later Hindenburg died, and Hitler at once proclaimed amalgamation of the two offices in himself, with the title "Füehrer and Reich Chancellor," in which capacity he was also Supreme Commander of the Reichswehr. The generals had paid a high price for what they got—far too high, and payable only at the expense of the Army's honor, by condoning lawless massacre and swallowing the assassination of two fellow-officers. In May the swastika badge had been added to all military uniforms and now, on August 2, 1934, all officers and men were required to take a new oath of allegiance—not to the Reich or the office of the Chief of State, but to Adolf Hitler by name, as Fuehrer and Supreme Commander.

8

Historians of the prewar years have often delighted in excoriating the failure of the European democracies to strangle the Third Reich at its birth. Had Hitler not set forth in *Mein Kampf* just what he proposed to do? Was it not plain as plain could be that he would embark on a march of conquest and plunge the world into a devastating war? How could the ministers of England, France, and other concerned countries have been so blind as not to perceive the danger, and take steps to prevent the disasters that so soon followed?

In fact it was not so simple; Hitler's course of conduct was not then so easy to foretell or forestall. What a political adventurer writes in a book is not necessarily what he will do if he attains high office. Hitler as Chancellor was, at first, far less bellicose than Hitler the leader of an extremist splinter party. Furthermore, actions are often thought to speak louder than words, and Hitler's foreign policies, during his first two years of office, gave little cause for alarm.

To be sure, Hitler's rise to power was largely due to his effective exploitation of nationalist sentiment, especially by his denunciation of the Versailles Treaty. By no means did he abandon these themes, but his speeches during his early years of office were notably devoid of threats of warlike action; on the contrary, he portrayed himself as an apostle of reason and peace. Indeed, it was this very posture which he struck to justify his first major foreign policy move, in October 1933: withdrawal from the League of Nations and the Geneva Disarmament Conference. Germany alone of the great powers had been disarmed by the Versailles Treaty, he observed, and Germany would stay disarmed and even scrap what little she had if the other powers would do likewise. But despite her patience, no progress had been made. Germany was still denied equal rights in the international community, and in these circumstances, it would be an "intolerble humiliation" to remain a member of these international bodies. National honor required an end to these conditions, Hitler declared, seemingly more in sorrow than anger, and he was thus able to vent popular feelings of hostility toward the Versailles victors, without running any substantial risk of reprisal.

In private and semiprivate meetings with "responsible" Germans whose support he sought, Hitler was less hypocritical but very prudent. He did, indeed, stress the importance of rearming, and rejected the Stresemann policies of "fulfillment" and the Brüning tactics of negotiation: "The restoration of the Wehrmacht will not be decided at Geneva but in Germany, when we have gained internal strength," he had told the tycoons at Goering's home in February 1933. But these and other contemporaneous talks to the industrialists were devoid of reckless military adventurism. Even a private letter that Hitler wrote in December 1932 to (the then) Colonel Walter von Reichenau, Blomberg's chief of staff in East Prussia, said nothing of *Lebensraum* and was primarily concerned with the need for internal "regeneration" before Germany could think of wielding military power.

With his confidants and others that he considered "safe," Hitler was not so circumspect, and often enlarged on the "eastern space" theme of *Mein Kampf*. With the generals and admirals he might lift a corner of the veil, but remained relatively discreet for the first several years. At Hammerstein's home, for his initial encounter with the military leaders, Hitler specified repudiation of the Versailles Treaty and reconstruction of the Wehrmacht as his primary goal. And then? He was not sure; "perhaps" a conquest of *Lebensraum* in the east. But for the moment there should be no such talk, because rearmament itself involved grave danger: "We shall see whether or not the French have real statesmen; if so they will not give us time, and will fall upon us." A year later, addressing a mixed gathering of storm-trooper and Army leaders, Hitler spoke of the eventual necessity of military action in order to obtain "living space for the surplus population," and declared that a militia like the storm troops could never accomplish such a task, which must be left to the Army. But his projected schedule for these adventures was not rapid; five years for adequate defense, and eight years for an attacking force. This timetable postponed any thought of aggressive action until 1942; by that time most of his listeners would be in retirement, and no doubt this helps to explain the failure of these remarks to generate much excitement in military circles.

Hitler's coming to power did, however, lead to a major shift in Germany's strategic posture in the east. Ever since the early days of Seeckt, the Reichswehr and the Red Army had maintained a close relation which the Germans had exploited to keep abreast of developments with tanks and military aircraft, weapons denied to Germany by the Versailles Treaty. In Seeckt's mind, the Soviet connection was coupled with a strategy looking to the eventual destruction of Poland, and the absorption of her territory by Germany and Russia. Even if their thinking did not go that far, most German officers regarded the Polish Corridor as an outrage, and believed that the frontier must eventually be altered in Germany's favor, by force if necessary.

Like Seeckt, Hitler had marked down Poland as a future victim, but he was violently opposed to the entente with the hated Bolsheviks. Furthermore, it was Poland and not Russia that lay along Germany's eastern borders; the Poles had a large if antiquated army, and the Germans a small one with neither tanks nor aircraft. Nervous as he was over the risks of rearmament, Hitler especially feared that the Poles might, perhaps at French instigation, use some pretext to invade Silesia or East Prussia, and bring about hostilities for which Germany was quite unprepared. Meanwhile the Russians, apparently because of Hitler's advent, became disenchanted with the German connection and terminated the Red Army-Reichswehr contacts. In January 1934, to general surprise in other

European capitals, Germany and Poland signed a treaty of mutual nonagression.

During these early years, Hitler's only foreign adventure was political rather than military, and involved Austria, whose independence and separation from Germany were guaranteed by the Versailles Treaty. Hitler was Austrian, neighboring Bavaria was the cradle of Nazism, and Nazis soon flourished in Austria, encouraged by their success in Germany. The amalgamation of Germany and Austria—the *Anschluss*—was a cardinal point of the Nazi program on both sides of the border, and the Austrian Nazis received financial and other support from their German counterparts.

The Austrian problem was an especially sticky one for Hitler, since her independence was not only stipulated at Versailles, but was a basic desideratum in the foreign policy of Benito Mussolini, no friend of Versailles but much happier with a weak Austrian than a strong German neighbor on his northern frontier, especially in view of the obstinate irredentism of the German-speaking inhabitants of the Italian Tyrol. In *Mein Kampf* and later writings, Hitler had bracketed Italy with England as Germany's two most eligible European allies, and had disavowed support for alteration of the Austro-Italian border. Furthermore, he genuinely admired Mussolini, and hoped to exploit the authoritarian common denominator of Fascism and Nazism.

But Fuehrer and Duce were at cross-purposes in Austria, and the divergence had not been adjusted when, late in July of 1934, the Austrian Nazis staged a violent but unsuccessful *Putsch,* in the course of which the Chancellor, Engelbert Dollfuss, was assassinated. How deeply Hitler was involved is uncertain, but he had been strongly backing the Austrian Nazi movement, and his responsibility was plausible if not actual. Mussolini was outraged, and coupled a telegram of support for Austrian independence with a military demonstration on the Austrian frontier. From the German standpoint the affair was a dismal fiasco, and Hitler was obliged to cool his ardor for *Anschluss* and adopt a more gradual Austrian strategy, the execution of which he now entrusted to a new ambassador, none other than Franz von Papen, who had resigned as Vice-Chancellor after his narrow escape from death in the Roehm purge a few weeks earlier.

During his first two years of power, as this record shows, Hitler made no overt moves in contravention of treaty provisions, or that would be likely to provoke any kind of military reply. Certainly the Versailles victors could hardly criticize a nonagression pact with Poland or the cutting of connections with Soviet Russia, a pariah government. Withdrawal from Geneva and the League was not reassuring, but violated no obligations. The Dollfuss murder was an Austrian affair, at least officially. None of these things offered any justification for international action against the Reich.

9

Had the Versailles victors been looking for a legal basis for intervention, however, they could have found it in the German rearmament program which Hitler had made the first order of business. Violations of the Versailles arms limitations had in fact occurred fairly frequently under the Weimar Republic, but were not of sufficient magnitude to cause much alarm. With the advent of Hitler, prohibited military activity mushroomed. The generals were given the green light for a threefold expansion of the Army and formation of armored units; the Navy more than doubled its strength and commenced the construction of two large battle cruisers; Goering established an ostensibly civil Air Ministry and began laying the groundwork for a third branch of the armed services, soon to be known as the *Luftwaffe*.

All this was done covertly, but on such a scale that much of it became known in other countries. It was, as we have seen, this initial phase of rearmament that Hitler thought the most dangerous. But if one accepts his definition of a French statesman as one who would immediately "fall upon" Germany, there were no French statesmen in power in Paris.

As rearmament proceeded and its concealment became increasingly difficult, Hitler and the generals concluded that by the spring of 1935 the curtain of secrecy would have worn too thin, and the time would be ripe for open acknowledgment. Under the Versailles territorial provisions a plebiscite was due to be held in January 1935 to determine the future national affiliation of the Saarland, and it was thought unwise to risk upsetting the applecart before that time. The result, as expected, was an overwhelming vote for reunion with Germany. Meanwhile, the new blue-gray uniforms of the Luftwaffe began to be seen in the streets, and bombers and fighters maneuvered in the skies. Secrecy had been stretched to the breaking point, and on March 10, 1935, Goering utilized an interview with Ward Price, Berlin correspondent of the London *Daily Mail* and in high favor with top Nazis, to announce publicly that the Luftwaffe did indeed exist.

A week later, Hitler issued a formal proclamation in which he denounced the arms limitations of Versailles, announced the reinstitution of compulsory military service, and fixed the future size of the Army at thirty-six divisions grouped in twelve corps. The French protested to the League of Nations, and the League Council duly censured Germany for its unilateral repudiation of obligations. At Stresa, in April, the French, British, and Italian governments condemned the German action.

But the international disapproval was only verbal, and within a few weeks the moral force of the frown was dissipated by one of the frowners. During the spring there had been a confidential exchange of views between the British and German governments on the possibility of a naval treaty, and in pursuance of this project Hitler sent Joachim von Ribbentrop as a special emissary to London. On June 18, 1835, the two governments adopted the Anglo-German Naval Agreement, permitting German naval construction up to 35 per cent of the tonnage of the British Fleet, with the understanding that the German quota might include submarine tonnage equal to that of the British Commonwealth. These stipulations envisaged gross violations of the naval clauses of the Versailles Treaty. Britain had, in fact, joined with Germany in a bilateral repudiation of the treaty, and the French and Italian governments, closely affected as they were, sharply criticized what had been done.

Meanwhile, with the shackles of secrecy cast off, the new German military machine was taking shape. New defense laws enacted in May 1935 laid the organizational basis. The old "Reichswehr" became the "Wehrmacht," and the "Ministry of Defense" the "Ministry of War" (*Reichkriegsministerium,* or RKM). Blomberg, as Minister, was also the Commander-in-Chief of the Wehrmacht* under Hitler as "Supreme Commander." Under Blomberg, in turn, were the Commanders-in-Chief of the three services: Goering, Fritsch, and Raeder, of the air, ground, and sea forces respectively. The title "Chief of the General Staff" (naïvely prohibited by the Versailles Treaty) was revived and assumed, for the Army, by General Beck. In the autumn, the War Academy in Berlin was formally reopened on the hundred twenty-fifth anniversary of its founding, in the presence of Hitler, Seeckt, and Mackensen, and with speeches by Blomberg, Fritsch, Beck, and the new commandant of the Academy, General Curt Liebmann. With one voice they extolled both the "spirit of the Old Army" and the greatness of the Fuehrer, who had freed Germany from the vengeful *Diktat* of Versailles and thus laid the basis for a new and greater Reich.

10

These actions in 1935 swept away the Versailles limitations on the size, organization, and weaponry of the German armed forces, but left untouched what was perhaps the most important treaty restriction of a military nature: the prohibition of troops and military installations in the Rhineland, including the east side of the river to a depth of fifty kilometers. As long as this requirement remained in effect, the French could strike into Germany's prime industrial area without encountering significant resistance.

Unquestionably Hitler and the generals shared the desire to throw off this restriction and remilitarize the Rhineland as soon as possible, and by the summer of 1935 clandestine preparations were already under way. But the risks seemed great; demilitarization of the Rhineland was stipulated by Locarno as well as Versailles, and was France's only remaining Treaty-built-in safeguard against Germany. The question for Germany, therefore, was not so much "whether" as "when," and on the issue of timing the generals were very cautious. Hitler was less so, and other international developments now combined to give him two things he needed for the move: a friend and a pretext, albeit the first was uncertain and the second flimsy.

Mussolini's nose had been put out of joint by the Dollfuss affair, and in April 1935 he had joined with England and France in denouncing Hitler's repudiation of the Versailles arms limitations. A few months later, however, he undertook the conquest of Ethiopia and at once became embroiled with the League of Nations and subjected to the threat of sanctions, largely on British initiative. While the Duce's feelings toward France and especially England underwent a pronounced chill, Germany, no longer a League member, assumed an attitude of

---

* Blomberg was the only military man ever to hold the position of Commander-in-Chief of all the German armed forces. Previously the Emperor or President had command authority over the services, and after Blomberg's retirement in 1938, his title lapsed and Hitler, as "Supreme Commander," took direct command of the Wehrmacht.

neutrality, benevolent toward Italy. Early in 1936, discreet diplomatic feelers produced fairly satisfactory though private assurances that Italy would not, in the event of a German move, honor her obligations under the Locarno Pact.

Meanwhile the French, concerned over the revival of German power and the German-Polish *rapprochement,* had initiated a partial revival of the pre-First World War alliance with Russia. The Franco-Soviet and the Czech-Soviet mutual assistance pacts were both signed in May 1935; the Czech Government ratified their treaty in June, but in France the matter became politically controversial and did not come before the legislature until February 1936.

On May 21, 1935, a week after the Franco-Soviet treaty was signed, Hitler made a long speech in the Reichstag in which he declared that by the new alliance "an element of legal insecurity had been brought into the Locarno Pact." Germany would, to be sure, "uphold and fulfill" all her Locarno obligations, but this undertaking was importantly qualified by the phrase "so long as the other partners are on their side ready to stand by that pact." This amounted to a thinly veiled threat that French ratification of the Soviet alliance would be treated as a violation of Locarno, and release Germany from her obligations thereunder.

The bearing of all this on the Rhineland situation was plain enough, and in November 1935 the French Ambassador in Berlin, François-Poncet, informed his government that Hitler might well use the Franco-Soviet pact as a pretext for remilitarization of the Rhineland. His premonition was accurate; it is not clear just when Hitler decided to make the move, but in January it was announced in Paris that the Russian pact would soon be brought before the Chamber of Deputies for ratification, and this news may well have provided the immediate stimulus.

The debate in the French Chamber opened on February 11, 1936, and on the next day Hitler went to Berlin and then to Munich for discussions of the project with Blomberg, Fritsch, and the German Ambassador to Italy, Ulrich von Hassell. The Chamber ratified the Russian pact on February 27th and similar action by the Senate was generally expected to follow shortly. On March 2, Blomberg issued secret military orders for the troop movements to the three service commanders, but with no date specified for their execution. Two days later the Foreign Affairs Committee of the French Senate approved the alliance, and the next day, March 5,* Blomberg ordered that the operation be carried out on the seventh, as indeed it was, initially by three battalions of infantry and two squadrons of fighter aircraft.

While the troops were marching in, Hitler was in Berlin making another long speech in the Reichstag, in the course of which he read a memorandum, justifying the action, which was presented to the other Locarno powers. He reiterated and amplified the argument that the Russo-French alliance was a breach of Locarno, in that it was directed against Germany, and might obligate France to join Russia in a war against Germany irrespective of the attitudes of the other

* Instructions were also sent this day to German diplomatic representatives abroad, and the datebook of Hitler's activities kept by Martin Bormann (Hitler's private secretary and close associate) contains an entry for March 5 which indicates strongly, though not conclusively, that this was the day of final decision.

Locarno nations and outside the framework of the League of Nations. Accordingly, Hitler declared, France had "destroyed the political system of the Rhine Pact, not only in theory but in fact," and Germany was therefore restoring "full and unrestricted sovereignty in the demilitarized zone of the Rhineland."

The next few days were very tense. The three German service attachés in London sent Blomberg a jointly signed telegram the gist of which was that the situation was grave, and the chances of peace or war evenly balanced. At one point Blomberg appears to have wavered and proposed that the troops be withdrawn, but Hitler stood firm, and events vindicated his judgment. Italy was silent, France divided, and the British, though badly jarred, proved unwilling to go to war when, as it was remarked, Hitler had merely "walked into his own backyard." In a few days the likelihood of military counteraction disappeared; Hitler had done it again.

The notion that he had simply gone out the back door to water his garden was homely and comforting but dangerously shallow. In fact, Hitler had fatally undermined the foundation of the entire French system of eastern security, especially the treaties of mutual assistance with Poland and Czechoslovakia.

As long as the Rhineland lay undefended, France could, in the event of a German attack against her eastern allies, inflict an immediate and grievous if not fatal blow, and this capacity was not only a very strong deterrent against such an attack, but carried the prospect of prompt and effective aid if it were nonetheless made. The consequence of remilitarization was that the French lost that capacity. With German troops in the Rhineland and the border fortified, as it soon would be, France could accomplish nothing except by breaking through the defenses. This would become increasingly difficult as German rearmament proceeded, and would in any event take time, during which the Poles or Czechs might bear the brunt of the attack and be overrun before the French could do them any good.

Furthermore, the credibility of the French security system was badly shaken. If France would not go to war when she had both ample justification and overwhelming superiority, in order to preserve the factor of greatest value to her smaller allies, what reason was there to think that she would do so later and under much less favorable circumstances?

By the Anglo-German Naval Agreement, Britain had become Hitler's accomplice in tearing up the Treaty of Versailles. Now, by their inaction, Britain and France had allowed Germany to tear up Locarno, and put the Eastern European countries in great jeopardy. Hitler had survived the period of greatest danger to his designs, during which he lacked the means of military defense, and had to rely on a series of judgments that the Versailles victors would not do what they could so easily do to stop him. Now the road was clear for ultimate advancement of his cherished "eastern space" aspirations, and the countries that lay immediately athwart the road were Austria, Czechoslovakia, and Poland.

11

There is little evidence that until 1936, Czechoslovakia played much of a part in Hitler's thinking. The people of that country were predominantly Slavic, and were lumped in his mind with the other Slavs as an inferior race, inhabiting areas that Germany would one day dominate as part of the "eastern space" policy. The Germans in Czechoslovakia should eventually be part of Greater Germany. Discoursing on the future in close circles, Hitler would describe Austria and Bohemia-Moravia as part of the "nucleus" of Greater Germany, and declare that the Czechs must be gotten out of Europe.

But this was all very vague and futuristic, and nowhere in *Mein Kampf*, or his later writings and speeches, does Czechoslovakia emerge as a focus of special interest until the time of the French and Czech treaties with the Soviet Union and of the Rhineland remilitarization. Nor do the generals appear to have entertained any aggressive designs in that direction.*

Russia's new relationship to France and Czechoslovakia, however, was reflected in changing attitudes in Berlin. Blomberg and Fritsch had both been adherents to Seeckt's view that Russia was a desirable ally; they regretted the breaking of their contacts with the Red Army, and were doubly concerned when, in the spring of 1935, it had become apparent that the Soviet Union was about to join France and Czechoslovakia in alliances primarily intended to furnish mutual security against Germany,

Late in April of 1935, Fritsch remarked on the dangers to Germany inherent in the new combination, and it was probably these circumstances that caused Blomberg to issue, on May 2, 1935, a highly secret order (under the cover name *Schulung*) to the three service commanders, ordering operational planning for an attack against Czechoslovakia, with a defensive deployment on the French frontier. Quite possibly the request was made at Hitler's direction; however that may be, the German forces were so far from ready for any such undertaking that General Beck (*de facto* and soon-to-be officially the Army Chief of Staff) reacted with utter horror. Beck declared that if the inquiry were anything more than theoretical he would resign his position, and denounced the projected operation as "an act of desperation" which would lead to an "inglorious end" and bring down on the military leaders "the severest condemnation, not only of its own age, but also of history."

For the time being nothing more was done about Czechoslovakia in German military circles, but in less than a year it became apparent that the Czech-Soviet pact had altered, for the worse, Hitler's diplomatic posture vis-à-vis Czechoslovakia. In his speech to the Reichstag announcing the Rhineland remilitarization, Hitler not only denounced the Franco-Soviet treaty as a violation of Locarno, but added the charge that it "introduces the threatening military power of a mighty

* Much has been made, in several books on the period, of a memorandum of March 30, 1935, by General von Reichenau, at that time Blomberg's principal subordinate in the Ministry of Defense, requesting the three service chiefs to respond to his inquiry, in which a "surprise attack" on Czechoslovakia was mentioned. The hypothesis of the inquiry, however, was that France and Italy had attacked Germany, that Russia had come in with them and was using Czechoslovakian airfields, and that Czechoslovakia herself had taken aggressive military action against Germany. In that posture of events, the service chiefs were asked to consider the possibility of a "surprise attack against Czechoslovakia to seize Russian-Czech airbases." Given the circumstances assumed by the inquiry, it can hardly be said to reflect aggressive planning on Germany's part.

empire into the center of Europe by the roundabout way of Czechoslovakia, the latter country having signed an agreement with Russia."

So far from being accompanied by threats, these accusations were made the occasion for declarations of Germany's willingness to conclude "new agreements for the creation of a system of peaceful security for Europe." But despite these soothing protestations, it was apparent that the Czech-Soviet treaty had injected a new and disquieting factor into Czech-German relations. The presence of three million Sudeten Germans in Czechoslovakia was no longer the sole potential issue between the two countries. Czechoslovakia was now portrayed as the spearhead of Soviet penetration into Central Europe—a threat not only to German security but to European civilization. It was a theme that Hitler could play with feeling, and that was bound to strike responsive chords in many quarters, not only in Germany.

From Prague in 1936, the German cloud seemed no more menacing than the proverbial one no bigger than a man's hand. Hitler had not yet ventured any action to extend Germany's frontiers. But he had removed the two main external obstacles to future expansion, by throwing off the Versailles armament restrictions and sending troops into the Rhineland. Fingers had been shaken in disapproval, but no move was made to stop him. If he could get away with these things when Germany was virtually defenseless, what could he not put across once she had recovered military strength?

By 1936 that time was not far off, and in 1937 larger and darker clouds began to gather.

CHAPTER 7

The Decline of the Third Republic

1

The treaty was signed, the presidents and premiers departed Versailles, and the French confronted the task of repairing the ravages of their victory. Clear across northern France ran the terrible belt of devastation—ruined towns and shattered factories, fields and forests mutilated almost beyond salvage and sown with the debris of war. The costs of restoring lands and buildings would be astronomical, and where would the money come from? For the average Frenchman, be he peasant, worker, or bourgeois, there could be but one answer: the Germans will pay! It was a cry that was to dominate French politics and policy for the next decade.

Some of the damage could not be repaired. A million and a half young Frenchmen had been killed. Genetically, the war years had been a desert, and there would be another period of weakness—the so-called "white years"—during the thirties. With the aid of powerful allies France had "won" this war, but could she ever win another? As D. W. Brogan put it, France "was a victor but she had in many respects the psychology of a defeated power."

To be sure, the victors' prizes were more than laurel wreaths. The enlargment of the French colonial empire, and especially the recovery of Alsace and Lorraine, were both psychologically and materially rewarding. Germany could certainly be forced to pay some, and perhaps a lot. Despite the disappearance of the hoped-for Anglo-American guarantee, the restrictions on German arms and the Rhineland demilitarization gave France a wide margin of security, for the time being.

Small wonder, then, that France clutched the fruits of victory so closely. England and the United States had let her down at the peace table, and her old ally Russia had gone Bolshevik. For the future, France must rely on her own strength, augmented as it was by the "head start" of the Versailles arms provisions, and supplemented by alliance with the other beneficiaries of the treaty— Poland, Czechoslovakia, Rumania, and Yugoslavia. Internationally, France sought above all to preserve the *status quo;* she was a satisfied power but an exhausted nation.

Down with the Reds, soak the Boches! It was a time for conservative nationalism. Like Winston Churchill in 1945, Georges Clemenceau—the "Tiger of

France" and architect of victory—promptly suffered political defeat. Partly because he was the principal author of Versailles and had not secured the Rhineland, he was denied the presidency and retired from public life. His successor as Premier was Alexandre Millerand, leader of the right-wing Bloc National. A strong anti-Bolshevik, Millerand sent General Maxime Weygand to Warsaw in 1920 to help stem the Red advance into Poland, and gave his blessing to Baron Wrangel's futile counterrevolutionary campaign against the Soviet Government.

Meanwhile the newly elected President, Paul Deschanel, had gone mad, and Millerand was chosen in his place. He was succeeded as Premier, for a brief period, by the perennial Aristide Briand, and then by the new leader of the nationalists, former President Raymond Poincaré. During the twenties these two men—Poincaré and Briand—were the leading figures of French politics.

The immediate postwar years were a period of domestic reconstruction, financed largely by government loans. They were called "recoverable expenditure," or "advances on account of reparations," and were made in the expectation that they would be covered by payments from Germany. These, however, were not immediately forthcoming, and the result was a series of unbalanced budgets, inflationary pressures, and increasing weakness of the franc.

Germany's total obligation was fixed by the Reparations Commission in April 1921 at 33 billion dollars,* of which France was to have 58 per cent. The amount was intrinsically fantastic, and Germany, deep in the throes of civil unrest and monetary problems of her own, was in no shape to make substantial cash payments. At the time of the commission's decision, indeed, the payments so far made had barely covered the costs of the Allied occupation forces in the Rhineland.

Soon France and Britain fell to squabbling over the methods by which reparations were to be exacted. Many Englishmen were inclined to attribute Germany's economic distress to exorbitant French demands, while the French regarded Britain as indifferent to restoration of the war-devastated regions, and concerned only for the revival of her own trade. As months passed with no substantial yield from the reparations claims, French attitudes toward both England and Germany grew increasingly bitter. France would have to fend for herself financially as well as militarily, and the man to implement the new policy was Poincaré, who became Premier in January 1922 and held office for over two years.

The Poincaré medicine was, in concept, simplicity itself. If nothing of value was coming out of Germany, why then France must go in and take what was owed her. The new Premier was a lawyer whose deep conservatism was matched by his integrity, and he insisted on a legal basis for the resort to force. Over British dissent, the Reparations Commission determined that Germany was in default, and Belgian troops and Italian engineers were part of the predominantly French force that occupied the Ruhr in January 1923.

But the fruits of occupation were slow to ripen. The German Government or-

---

* The amount was fixed in gold marks at 132 billion, the equivalent of 33 billion dollars or over six and a half billion pounds, at the current rate of exchange.

ganized a campaign of passive resistance—a virtual sitdown strike of both labor and management—in consequence of which nearly all commerce in the Ruhr came to a halt. As a punitive measure, to be sure, the occupation was a considerable success, for Germany was cut off from her most productive industrial region, and the mark was dealt a final blow that produced an astronomical and ruinous inflation.

The strain proved too great for the Germans, and in September 1923 the Government abandoned passive resistance. The occupation began to pay its way and even show a small surplus. But the yield was much less than had been hoped for, and the occupation grew increasingly unpopular in France. Poincaré's military handling of the reparations question had failed—or appeared to have failed—and in May 1924 he resigned, following the national election in which the parties of the left were triumphant.

2

With this sharp leftward swing of the pendulum, power was taken by what became known as the "Cartel des Gauches," in which the leading figures were Briand and Edouard Herriot. New political winds were blowing in London and Berlin as well as Paris; Britain had her first Labour government under Ramsay MacDonald and, in Germany, Stresemann took the helm at the Wilhelmstrasse and launched his policy of "fulfillment."

Western Europe was ready for a détente, and everyone wanted to liquidate the Ruhr occupation. An international committee was set up to rescue Germany from her economic predicament, and establish a basis on which she could start to pay something on the reparations account. The outcome was the so-called "Dawes Plan" (after the American committee chairman, General Charles G. Dawes, subsequently Vice-President of the United States), under which Germany was to make annual payments on an ascending scale, reaching 652 million dollars in five years; how long the payments would continue was left unspecified. In 1925 the occupation forces were withdrawn from the Ruhr, and Germany began to make payments which, though far below original expectations, yielded more than France had previously received. For the moment, the reparations issue receded into the background.

In addition to his numerous, though generally brief, periods of service as Premier, Briand served as Foreign Minister, virtually without interruption, from 1925 to 1932. With Herriot, he had been returned to office on a wave of disillusionment with Poincaré's "get tough" tactics on reparations, and he now turned to a policy of *rapprochement* with Germany, and of support for collective security, whether through the League of Nations or regional pacts of mutual assistance. His German opposite number, Stresemann, was not at heart a kindred spirit of the idealistic Briand, but was steering a parallel course. Reconciliation of Germany and France was highly congenial to the temper of the times in Britain, and Austen Chamberlain, the Conservative but internationally minded Foreign Minister, was eager to co-operate in the new dispensation.

The outcome of this triple collaboration was the Locarno Pact of 1925, with its interlocking mutual guarantees of the Franco-German-Belgian frontiers. At last France had part of what she had lost in 1919, when the stipulated Anglo-American guarantee went up in the smoke of Senate isolationism in Washington, for now she had a firm guarantee of British aid against German aggression. Germany and Belgium had comparable security, and in the warmer international atmosphere of 1926, Briand and Stresemann shared the Nobel Prize for Peace.

In domestic affairs, however, things did not go so well. By 1925, some 80 billion francs* had been spent on reconstruction, most of it financed by short-term government loans. In the spring of that year the Bank of France, under directors hostile to the Cartel des Gauches, refused further loans to the government, and a Senate vote of no confidence overthrew Herriot.

There ensued what William L. Shirer has called a "cascade of cabinets," with six governments in fourteen months. One "expert" after another was called to the Ministry of Finance, but they worked no magic. By July 1926 the Treasury was empty, short-term loans could not be met, and the franc fell to fifty to the dollar. Herriot's new government was voted down on the first day of its existence, and angry mobs were gathering around the Palais-Bourbon.

In these extremities, President Doumergue recalled Poincaré, who succeeded in forming a government of all parties except the Communists and left-wing Socialists—a so-called government of "National Union" that included Herriot, Briand, and three other former premiers. As a solid man of the right, Poincaré was in good odor with the bankers, who tided over his government until he could put forward his legislative program. In this there was nothing very novel; the great change was that Poincaré, enjoying the trust of the propertied classes, could persuade the legislators, scared as they were by the recent near-disaster, to enact taxes and other measures which they would have, and indeed had, refused his predecessors. So government revenues soared, there was a healthy budget surplus, and the franc doubled in value by the end of 1926.

In France as in Germany, the late twenties were politically stable, prosperous, and reasonably contented years. The period of compulsory military service was reduced to one year. Paris was truly the City of Light, and the mecca of the postwar literati. Poincaré had pulled the country out of a nasty mess, and in the elections of 1928 the conservative and center parties profited by his success and took control of the Chamber.

A few months later the radicals withdrew from the coalition cabinet, and the "National Union" gave way to a government of the right. Briand, however, stayed on at the Quai d'Orsay, and in 1928 won acceptance of the document with which his name remains associated—the Kellogg†-Briand Pact renouncing war as an instrument of national policy. The conciliatory posture toward Germany was maintained despite the distrust still felt by many, no doubt including Poincaré, the "Man of the Ruhr." Nevertheless, in 1929 Germany's reparation obligations were further reduced under the Young Plan (named for the American participant, Owen D. Young of the General Elec-

---

* Because of fluctuating international franc values, it is difficult to translate this amount into dollars or pounds, and the estimates vary greatly; D. W. Brogan puts the equivalent at 700 million pounds.

† After Frank B. Kellogg, then American Secretary of State.

tric Company), and the following year the last troops left the Rhineland, bringing the Allied occupation to an end.

If there was peace abroad and relative plenty at home, still there were rifts in the lute. The financial crisis of 1925–26 had left an ugly mark; the implacable hostility of the wealthy to any measures that threatened their deeply entrenched privileges manifested an increasing alienation from the rest of the country, and foreshadowed a disposition to sacrifice the Republic to their own interests, and a growing affinity for a more authoritarian governmental system. The Poincaré recovery had not been an unmixed blessing for the lower income groups, who had shouldered the bulk of the increase in indirect taxes, while the income tax rate was reduced in the upper brackets. While prosperity lasted, these cracks in the social structure did not widen, but they boded ill for times of greater stress.

And those times lay not far ahead, as the post-First World War twenties gave way to the pre-Second World War thirties. The old men were passing from the scene. Clemenceau and Marshal Ferdinand Foch, the Allied supreme commander of the First World War, both died in 1929, and in July of that year Poincaré fell ill and had to resign and retire from public life. André Tardieu tried to carry on the Poincaré tradition, but he was not by half the same impressive figure, and there was another "cascade" of cabinets, with five governments in seventeen months.

Briand stayed on at the Foreign Ministry; he had become a fixture—a sort of trademark of the peace that all the French hoped would endure, and they loved to hear the old man say: *"Tant que je serai là il n'y aura pas de guerre. Arrière les canons!"* But the international world was getting much less tractable to his high-minded pursuits, and economic depression was shaking all Europe to its heels. Briand aged and grew disheartened; in January 1932 he was let out of his beloved Quai d'Orsay, and a few weeks later he died. The Premier who sacked him was Pierre Laval, the first of the new men—Laval, Daladier, Flandin, and Blum—who were destined to lead France during the prewar years.

3

"The French Army is the finest in the world!" How often one heard that comforting cliché, as Hitler's shadow grew. There is no need to test the proposition with reference to the distant Soviet and Japanese armies. In Europe to the Russian border, the French Army, if not the "finest," was certainly the strongest army, at least until the mid-thirties. Except for the Italian Army, to which it was definitely superior, however, the French pre-eminence was not achieved intrinsically but by default, since German arms were narrowly limited by the Versailles Treaty, the British dismantled their army almost completely, and the other countries were too small or weak to count as possible rivals.

The prime purpose of the French Army, after Versailles, was to protect France against a rearmed or rearming Germany. It is in terms of that mission, accordingly, that the efficacy of French arms in the between-war years must be judged.

In the postwar organization of the French Army, at the highest level of the military establishment was the War Council (*Conseil Supérieur de la Guerre*), of which the Minister of War was *ex officio* President. The Army had no commander-in-chief; command authority was divided between the Inspector General, who was also Vice-President of the War Council, and the Chief of the General Staff. The Council itself included all the marshals, and those generals who had commanded an army or group of armies during the war. "This method of selection," wrote General Maxime Weygand in 1947, "was a guaranty of competence." In fact it was a guarantee of mental ossification if not senility, and Weygand's opinion proves only that he had learned nothing from the French military catastrophe of which he was a part.

The three great French military figures of the First World War were Joffre, Foch, and Pétain, all made Marshals of France. After the war Joffre served briefly as President of the Commission for the Study of Fortified Areas, but he resigned this post in 1922. Foch became President of the Allied Military Committee, charged with enforcement of the military provisions of the Versailles Treaty. This important task was his main responsibility; he attended meetings of the War Council but had no special authority in its deliberations. Foch and Joffre were both in their seventies, and their influence on French military organization and policy soon dwindled.

Not so Pétain, who was five years younger and retained extraordinary physical vitality. Throughout the twenties and until February 1931 he was Inspector General and Vice-President of the War Council, and when he relinquished these appointments he was seventy-five, but by no means finished.* His effect on French military doctrine was disastrous, as he admitted after the war: "My military mind was closed. When I saw the introduction of other tools, other instruments, other methods, I must say they didn't interest me." Alas for France, this self-scrutiny came many years too late.

Joffre had been an adherent of the "attack" school, and in the final report for his commission he recommended the construction of a series of fortified areas along the frontier from the Channel to Switzerland, behind and between which a mobile army could maneuver for defense and attack. Pétain would have none of this. He was the hero of Verdun, and he won his accolades under the motto: "They shall not pass!" His mind was imbedded in the defensive techniques of the slogging, inching warfare of the western front, and he absorbed nothing from the more open tactics used in Russia and the Balkans. Under his aegis, French military theory adopted as its gospel the continuous fortified front, which, it was thought, could perhaps be bent but not broken by the German thrust, and behind which France could muster her resources while allies were coming to her aid, and thus repeat the victory of 1918.

In combat thus envisaged, infantry and artillery would still be the queens of battle, and armor and aircraft mere handmaidens. The Manual of Instructions approved by Pétain in 1921 described the mission of the tank as being "to augment the offensive power of the infantry," and mentioned airplanes only *en passant:* "By day it scouts, by night it bombards."

To be sure, there were a few who saw the shape of things to come. General

. * Pétain was Minister of War in 1934, subsequently Ambassador to Spain, and in 1940, at the age of eighty-four he became Chief of State of "Vichy" France.

J. B. E. Estienne, the leading wartime tank commander, predicted as early as 1920 that "the tank will soon shake to the very foundations not only the tactics but also the strategy and organization of modern armies," and described future mechanized forces that would pierce far behind the enemy's lines and destroy his capacity—views later amplified by a young officer named Charles de Gaulle. Estienne continued to press his recommendations for large armored units, but unsuccessfully; the Manual of Instructions for the Employment of Tanks issued in 1930 still preached the doctrine that: "Combat tanks are machines to accompany the infantry . . . Tanks are only supplementary means, put temporarily at the disposition of the infantry. They strengthen considerably the action of the latter but they do not replace it."

To indulge mythological analogy, the French high command was for all the world like Wagner's dragon Fafner, sleepily guarding his *Rheingold*—the Treaty-conferred assurances that there would be no German Army to fear. While the German generals snatched desperately to make the best of what little they had, the French slumbered on a full stomach. Why stretch? France had other needs for her limited resources, and so the army pay stayed low and recruiting was difficult, weapons and other wartime equipment were kept in use long past the point of obsolescence in order to economize, left-wing hostility to "militarism" kept appropriations down, and staff training degenerated as initiative and imagination were stifled under a combination of psychological surfeit and financial starvation.

4

France's single and enormous new military investment during the between-war years was the Maginot Line—an enterprise which has been covered with ridicule, mostly based on profound misapprehension of its purpose and potential. It is more than a little ironical that those most vociferous in their condemnation have seldom been heard to criticize the opposing German fortifications—the West Wall, Siegfried Line, or *Limes,* as they were variously called—although when war came the Maginot Line fulfilled its limited purpose admirably, while the Germans never reaped any substantial military benefit from their West Wall.

The Maginot Line was named for its principal but by no means solitary sponsor André Maginot, described by William L. Shirer as "a mutilated war veteran who served as Minister of War until his sudden death in 1932 from poisoning occasioned by eating bad oysters at a New Year's banquet"—a most inadequate biography. A lawyer and member of the Chamber of Deputies, Maginot in his mid-thirties was appointed Under-Secretary for War in 1913. When the war came he enlisted as a private, and within a few months suffered a severe leg wound and was invalided out of service. Thereafter he was Minister of Colonies during the war, Minister of Pensions for many years after 1920, Minister of War in Poincaré's cabinet of the early twenties, Minister of Colonies again in 1928, and in 1929 once again Minister of War.

A man of gigantic physique and, despite his crippled leg, of great energy and initiative, Maginot was deeply convinced that the Versailles guarantees were in-

sufficient, and determined above all to protect his ancestral Lorraine against future German invasion. When in 1922 he became Minister of War, he naturally
took great interest in the work of the Commission on Fortifications, then headed
by General Adolphe Guillaumat. The generals were in disagreement. Pétain favored a network of concrete-lined trenches, supplemented by reinforced observation posts and underground communications. Others, including the Chief of
Staff, General Debeney, thought these inadequate, and proposed concrete
fortifications mounting heavy artillery, with elaborate underground storage and
garrison facilities.

Seeking to break the impasse, Maginot suggested the construction of experi-
mental sectors of both types. In 1924 he was replaced as Minister of War by
Paul Painlevé, but the two men formed an effective working partnership, and
construction of the experimental sites was begun in 1928. By that time the
Army leaders had settled upon a compromise plan closer to Debeney's than
Pétain's views, in that it envisaged a chain of great underground forts as the
basis of the defense line. These were to be constructed all along the Franco-
German border from Switzerland to Luxembourg. Nothing similar was planned
for the Franco-Belgian frontier; here the Army let itself be ruled by Pétain's
pronouncement that "The northern frontier can only be defended by advancing
into Belgium."

In November 1929, Maginot once more became Minister of War, and early in
1930 finally won legislative approval and the appropriation of over 3 billion
francs, to commence construction in good earnest. A year later he obtained another 2.5 billion, and by the time of his death, in January 1932, the work was
well under way.

"The trouble with the Maginot Line," William L. Shirer has written, "was that
it was in the wrong place." He should have said that it was not in enough
places, for to serve its purposes it had to be where it was, but certainly it would
have served them better had it been extended further westward. Mr. Shirer's critique continues:

> The classical invasion route to France which the Germans had taken since
> the earliest tribal days . . . lay through Belgium. This was the shortest way
> and the easiest, for it lay through level land with few rivers of any conse-
> quence to cross. It was the route the Germans had taken again in 1914.

Whatever lesson might be drawn from the early tribal paths, during the nineteenth century Belgium had not been the military road to Paris. In 1814 against
Napoleon, and again during the Franco-Prussian War of 1871, the invaders
came in through Lorraine, just where the Maginot Line was to be strongest.
And in 1914 the Germans went through Belgium precisely because they feared
delay before the fortifications of Toul and Verdun. The Belgian route was not
the shortest way from Germany to the heart of France, and required crossing
the Meuse River, while the entire border between Lorraine and Germany—
from Luxembourg to the northeast corner of France opposite Karlsruhe—was
devoid of sizable rivers or other natural defenses.

Beyond question, therefore, the Maginot Line had to be where it was, and if it would have been still more useful if extended along the Belgain border, it never-theless gave France a very considerable measure of security. The immediate stimulus to its construction was awareness that the Versailles-authorized occu-pation of the Rhineland would soon be coming to an end (as it did in 1930), and that the "hollow" or "white" years (*années creuses*) of reduced conscrip-tion, in consequences of the reduced birthrate from 1914 to 1918, would begin about 1935. But more basic motivations were apprehension that Germany could not indefinitely be kept disarmed, and desire for a shield against sudden attack by superior forces.

The Maginot Line provided such a shield. Once constructed, the German ground forces could get into France only by forcing the line or going through Belgium. Either way would take time, and if they went through Belgium, that would reinsure British participation. The line could be manned rapidly by reservists living in its neighborhood—the so-called *frontaliers*—and inde-pendently of general mobilization. Furthermore, the line represented a great saving in manpower as well as time, for it could be defended with far fewer men than such a length of front would otherwise require, and older men could do the job. These economies would correspondingly enlarge and improve the quality of the maneuvering field army, and partly compensate for France's physical in-feriority to Germany.

5

In its conception, accordingly, the Maginot Line was valid.* But it did not eliminate the necessity of a field army and an air force designed for the situation France confronted, and those needs were not met. What the Army most needed, apart from the large trained reserve which conscription in a measure gave it, was a mobile, ready striking force near the Rhineland, and an air force that might deter, and could at least blunt, an attack by a renascent German air force. Her leaders gave France neither one nor the other.

Deprived of the anticipated Anglo-American guarantee, in 1921 France en-tered into a mutual defense pact with Poland, supplemented by a secret military convention explicitly limited to the contingency of German aggression, and in 1924 she signed a generally comparable alliance with Czechoslovakia. In 1926, France and Rumania and in 1927 France and Yugoslavia signed indentical polit-ical agreements of mutual assistance, less valuable to France than the Polish and Czech alliances in that neither Rumania nor Yugoslavia was contiguous with Germany or militarily as strong as Poland or Czechoslovakia.† By the Locarno agreement Britain guaranteed France against German aggression but did not commit herself to aid a France which attacked Germany pursuant to the eastern mutual assistance pacts. In fulfillment of these pacts, accordingly, France could not reckon with certainty on British assistance.

---

* In 1971 the French government offered the Maginot fortifications at public auction. The fortress at Hastroff was purchased for 15,000 francs by M. Georges Stephanian, a hairdresser, "as a protest against what he considers the futilities of modern life."

† Furthermore, the Rumanian and Yugoslav agreements were operative only "within the framework of the League of Nations," while the Polish and Czech alliances were inde-pendent of League action and self-operative.

As long as Germany's forces remained within the Versailles limits, she could not contemplate aggression against Poland or Czechoslovakia and would, indeed, be hard pressed to defend herself against an attack by either of the smaller countries. But the whole point of the defensive alliances was to furnish mutual security against a rearming Germany and, given her population and industrial resources, it would not require a great deal of German rearmament to put France's eastern allies in peril.

How could France come to their aid? The Maginot Line was an immovable shield, quite useless for this purpose. France's professional army was not much larger than the Reichswehr, and many of the active-duty reservists would be new trainees. Mobilization of the trained reserve and deployment of the main army would take time—so much time that Germany might finish off her smaller eastern enemies before French strength could be brought to bear.

The key to the situation was the demilitarized Rhineland, but in the event of war it would not stay demilitarized very long. The enormous but temporary advantage of the demilitarization could be exploited only by a ready striking force —not large, but mobile and powerful enough to reach and hold the west bank of the Rhine until reinforcements could be brought up, and thus write finis to Germany's ability to wage war for more than a few weeks. Had such a force been stationed near the Rhineland in 1936, it is certain that Hitler would not have dared the gamble he took. Lacking such a force, France's eastern allies might still hope for eventual rescue, but must reckon with the possibility that they would have to take the brunt of Germany's initial onslaught and be overrun.

Apart from all the foregoing, the Maginot Line was of no use against air attack, and the only reasonable assumption was that a rearming Germany would have air as well as ground forces. Unless France were to equip herself with adequate defenses against air bombardment, Paris and other treasured cities would be in peril of grievous damage, and the country would be rendered vulnerable to "aerial blackmail." A strong striking air force might deter the Germans from testing the doctrine of Giulio Douhet* and discourage them from attacking France's eastern allies. In the event of such attack, it would enable the French to provide them some immediate assistance from the air, even if they could give only little or late help on the ground.

If it seems strange that France would spend billions on the Maginot Line while starving the air arm, perhaps the explanation is that, until after Hitler came to power, Germany had no organized air force. Lulled by a false sense of security, the French allowed their air arm to age and dwindle. In 1928 the Air Force was established as an independent service, with an Air Ministry and General Staff, but this organizational change accomplished nothing of consequence.

The antiaircraft ground defenses were in even worse condition; in 1930 there was nothing but a few hundred batteries dating from the First World War. The following year, a new post of Inspector General of Aerial Defense was created. The first incumbent was none other than the seventy-five-year-old Pétain, who

---

*Italian airman, famous as the author of *The Command of the Air,* first published in Italian in 1931, embodying the doctrine of the military supremacy of air power.

had just resigned as Inspector General of the Army. Pétain held this position until 1934, when he became the Minister of War, and for several years thereafter remained influential in aviation policy. The extraordinary narrowness of his conceptions is reflected in a letter which he sent to the War Council in 1932:

> The day when we will have, for defense, 200 fighter aircraft to meet enemy attacks, and 200 powerful bombers for retaliation, each capable of carrying two tons of bombs 1000 kilometers, that day peace will be assured.

As the late British general and military writer J. F. C. Fuller put it, the Maginot Line "was a shield, it wanted a sword," whereas "the French field army was a broomstick." The Air Force was an even less adequate tool. The verdict is harshly spoken, but it is a fair description of the army which for many years was, to be sure, the strongest in Europe, but nonetheless quite inadequate to meet France's military needs.

6

The thirties were the seventh and last decade in the life of the Third Republic —in Leonard Woolf's phrase, a decade that was "down hill all the way." The years that were to end in military disaster began with economic depression, as France succumbed to the epidemic that gripped most of the Western World.

Economic misery likewise stopped the flow of reparations payments from Germany. The "Hoover moratorium" of 1931 on reparations payments was followed in July 1932 by the Lausanne Conference, at which reparations, but not war debts, were finally buried. Washington politicians were capable of rising above party on at least one issue, and that was Europe's obligation to pay back the money which, as Calvin Coolidge put it, they had "hired." But if the United States refused to recognize any connection between reparations and war debts, most of Europe was not so blind. In December 1932, Edouard Herriot was thrown out of office by a Chamber angered by his insistence that the installment then due should be met. British payments dwindled to tokens and soon ceased. It was left to Finland to uphold Europe's financial honor, while Uncle Shylock replaced Uncle Sam as America's image.

French politics were as unstable as economics. From November 1929 to November 1933 there were twelve governments headed by eight different premiers. None of them seemed able to cope with the depression; parliamentary government lost popular respect, and politicians their self-respect. As the golden glow of the late twenties faded, France grew rancorous. Once again, as in similar circumstances ten years earlier, the gulf between rich and poor, capital and labor, widened ominously. France seemed to be losing the denominators of national unity.

In 1933, these tensions approached danger pitch. Edouard Daladier began his first term as Premier on January 31, one day after Adolf Hitler took the oath of office as Chancellor.* Success breeds imitation, and in France quasi-Nazi and

* The early weeks of 1933 were a watershed of political leadership. Franklin D. Roosevelt was sworn in as President of the United States on March 4, 1933; as he and Hitler died within a few weeks of each other, their periods of leadership were virtually identical.

Fascist organizations sprouted—*Solidarité Française* of the wealthy perfumer François Coty, and *Le Francisme* of Maurice Bucard. The established right-wing groups, such as the royalist *Action Française* and the *Jeunesse Patriotes,* grew larger and more active. Most important was a war veterans' league called *Croix de Feu,* converted by its new leader, Colonel François de la Rocque, into a semimilitary, authoritarian organization whose gangs could mobilize street demonstrations and disrupt liberal and left-wing meetings.

Revelations of extensive corruption in high official circles strengthened the hand of these antidemocratic forces, especially the scandalous affair of Serge Stavisky, whose many fraudulent operations were strangely overlooked by the authorities, and whose ostensible suicide early in January 1934 was widely viewed as a police murder to close his mouth. Ministers in the government then headed by Camille Chautemps appeared to be implicated in the Stavisky mess, and on January 27 Chautemps resigned, not for lack of a majority in the Chamber but from fear of the mounting street violence largely generated by the right-wing groups.

The Stavisky scandal had not touched Daladier, who had been Premier through most of 1933, and he now endeavored to form a broadly based government that might regain popular confidence. But he failed; his cabinet had to be largely drawn from his own party, and his clumsy efforts to clean up the administration by kicking upstairs some of those compromised turned comical when he sought to transfer the head of the secret police (Sûreté Générale) to be head of the state theater, the Comédie Française.

On February 6, 1934, when the Chamber of Deputies met to vote on the new Cabinet, utter chaos ensued. The Chamber itself was virtually unable to do business, what with shouting and singing on right and left alike, and fisticuffs on the floor. The press organs of the far right leagues summoned their members to mass demonstrations, and by evening the Place de la Concorde was jammed with their adherents, fighting the police and struggling to get across the Pont de la Concorde to the Palais-Bourbon, where the Chamber was meeting. The police were barely able to hold the mob on the other side of the Seine, and it was a bruising, bloody evening that ended with sixteen dead rioters, a dead policeman, and many hundreds of injured.

While all this was going on, the Chamber had punctuated its own pandemonium with a vote of confidence for the new Daladier government and then adjourned, or rather disintegrated in panic not without excuse, as shouts of "hang the Deputies!" were plainly audible. A number were threatened on their way home, and Herriot was assaulted and escaped being thrown into the Seine only by dint of *sang-froid et esprit.** But Daladier and his colleagues were not displaying these qualities; they were psychologically overborne by the terror and bloodshed, and on the afternoon of the next day the Government resigned because, as stated in the public communiqué, they were unwilling to "use soldiers against the demonstrators" or resort to other "exceptional measures susceptible

---

* Herriot was Mayor of Lyons, at the confluence of the Rhône and Saône rivers, and he put off his assailants, until rescued from them by the police, by protesting against the insult of the threatened immersion in the Seine.

of causing a . . . new effusion of blood." Thus, within less than ten days, two governments supported by a majority of the deputies were ousted by the street mobs of the far right.

February 7, 1934 was a fine day for the Paris underworld, which exploited the fatigue and disorganization of the police to rob and loot all over Paris. Two days later the Communists had their turn, with an "anti-Fascist" demonstration in the Place de la République which took six more lives and resulted in hundreds of injuries. Finally, on February 12, the Socialists and trade unionists staged a massive but generally peaceful one-day strike.

These February dates soon acquired a deep political significance. "In the years that followed," wrote the late Alexander Werth, "France was split into two parts—the Right following 'the men of the 6th February', and the Radicals . . . 'the men of the 9th and 12th of February' who had come to symbolize not communism, but the first anti-Fascist reaction." And indeed on February 12, almost for the first time, the Communists joined in the Socialist general strike, foreshadowing the "Popular Front," which emerged later.

For the moment, however, the right was on top. When Herriot had been so speedily dispatched in July 1926, President Gaston Doumergue had called for Poincaré. By 1934, Poincaré was at death's door, and it was none other than ex-President Doumergue, a not too well preserved seventy-one, whom President Lebrun asked to form another government of "national unity." The new Cabinet was heavy with years and ex-premiers—Herriot, Tardieu, Barthou, Sarraut, Laval, and the venerable Pétain as Minister of War.

Doumergue, however, was not a man of unity, or even of the center. He was in close and secret touch with Colonel de la Rocque, whose *Croix de Feu* was taking on the dimensions of a popular mass movement. The Premier soon called for constitutional changes, an increase in the executive power, and pressed his recommendations in an unprecedented series of radio broadcasts, possibly suggested by President Roosevelt's "fireside chats," but far more paternal, and eventually almost monarchical, in tone. By November 1934 the situation became intolerable to the Radicals, who resigned and brought down his government. Rumors of a rightist coup proved empty, and Doumergue vanished from the political scene.

After his passing the outlook of the French Government remained conservative but shifted perceptibly toward the center. The new Cabinet was headed by Pierre-Etienne Flandin, a man of impressive physical stature and moderate competence, friendly to Britain and, despite his later wooing of Hitler, at this time a firm supporter of the Republic against the rightist leagues.

Flandin at once disavowed Doumergue's authoritarian proposals, and formed another "national unity" government, which lasted until June 1935. It was a "bankers' government," wedded to upholding the franc in a deflationary economy, and these policies were continued by Laval when he took over from Flandin (who had been painfully injured in a motorcar crash) and headed a similar government through the second half of 1935. In December, disaffection on the left grew steadily, and early in 1936 the Radicals deserted Laval as they had

Doumergue in 1934, and a sort of caretaker government under Albert Sarraut held on pending the general elections scheduled for May.

The year and a half of Flandin, Laval, and Sarraut witnessed the waning of the rightist leagues and the rise of the left coalition known at first as the *Rassemblement Populaire,* and later, adopting a phrase of the Communist leader Maurice Thorez, as the *Front Populaire.* The near-success of the far right in February 1934 had given the Communists in Moscow as well as Paris a bad scare, and in May, *Pravda* published an appeal for Socialist-Communist cooperation in a "united front" against the Fascists.

Real or not, the Fascist danger seemed so in the summer of 1935. Unlike Flandin, Laval was basically friendly to the *Croix de Feu,* which now began a series of "lightning rallies" all over France, including one at Algiers featured by a display of thirty aircraft belonging to the organization. De la Rocque's utterances grew more and more incendiary; in July he declared that he "no longer cared a hang for legality," and in September it was announced that the *Croix de Feu* would use force to prevent a government of the left from taking office.

The louder the Fascist voices, the stronger grew the links joining Communists, Socialists, and Radicals. Bastille Day of 1935 symbolized the issue that was being drawn. The *Croix de Feu,* 30,000 strong, marched up the Champs-Elysées to the Arc de Triomphe, where a solemn de la Rocque lighted the Unknown Warrior's flame as the sidewalk crowds shouted: *"La France pour les Français."* Meanwhile Daladier, Blum, and Thorez were side by side at the Bastille, giving the anti-Fascist clenched fist salute to crowds demanding *"Les Soviets partout!"* and *"De la Rocque à la lanterne!"*

For all the pageantry and discipline of the *Croix de Feu* parade, the two most significant features of the day were that the police were able to keep the two demonstrations separated, so that there was little or no disorder, and that at least three times as many people turned out at the Bastille as on the Champs-Elysées.

There were, however, uglier components, and in November 1935 an armed *Croix de Feu* group in Limoges opened fire on anti-Fascist counterdemonstrators, inflicting serious wounds. The result was a ban, surprisingly agreed to by right as well as left, on the carrying of arms at public demonstrations, together with other legislation, most unwelcome on the right, giving the Government authority to dissolve organizations that fomented disorder or maintained private militia.

So the *Croix de Feu* had its sting drawn, and faded into a conservative political league, largely ineffective because it did not run candidates and its purposes were clouded by de la Rocque's increasingly obscure pronouncements. As the election approached, the right sensed defeat, and its case was greatly worsened when, in February 1936, a gang of *Action Française* fanatics dragged the Socialist leader Léon Blum from his car and beat him savagely.*

Now the Socialists had a martyr and leader all in one, and in the spring elec-

---

* In consequence, the leader of *Action Française,* Charles Maurras, was convicted of incitement to murder under the 1935 "Anti-Fascist" law, for writing that Blum was "a man who must be shot—but in the back."

tions they became, for the first time, France's strongest party, with 20 per cent of the popular vote and 25 per cent of the seats in the Chamber. Communist gains were equally spectacular, while the Radical-Socialists, theretofore the largest party, lost heavily. Overall, the Popular Front candidates outpolled the conservatives decisively though not overwhelmingly, and emerged with a strong majority in the Chamber of Deputies.*

And so in June 1936, at a time when in Germany the popularity of Hitler and the Nazi regime was reaching its highest level, in France the pendulum swung sharply to the left. Léon Blum, a Jew, became Premier in a cabinet of Socialists and Radicals; the Communists declined to participate in order to preserve freedom of action. From the right there were howls of anguish and predictions of national doom.

Like Adlai Stevenson accepting the nomination for the presidency of the United States in 1952, Blum on taking office referred to the biblical passage about the cup that did not pass from Jesus' lips. Unlike Stevenson, Blum disavowed reluctance to drink the cup, and declared that he "did ask for it." Perhaps, if he could have foreseen what lay ahead, he would have chosen otherwise. His premiership lasted a full and turbulent year and ended unhappily, and Blum, like Stanley Baldwin in England, was to bear more than his fair share of blame for the disaster that befell France in 1940.

7

For about fifteen years after the First World War, French foreign policy was largely a function of internal politics and economics. It was inner-directed and was shaped in accordance with France's own felt needs, which were largely the exploitation and preservation of the fruits of victory, and dictated a comparatively static foreign outlook.

Even after Hitler's advent the old attitudes persisted, and in 1933 the Quai d'Orsay was still heavily concerned with disarmament, interallied war debts, and other mementos of 1918. But it was beginning to come clear that there was more cause for concern about the next than the last war. Stresemann was dead and Brüning had fled; the man who had written *Mein Kampf* ruled Germany, and instead of worrying about Germany's "equal rights" to arms, it was high time to consider how to cope with the uncomfortable actuality of rapid German rearmament. In Italy, Benito Mussolini was beginning his second decade as Duce, and was building a fleet and an air force which, sooner or later, he might put to some use. In Asia, the Japanese were on the warpath and turning up their noses at remonstrances from the devotees of collective security.

In this new and uglier world, static policies were no longer suitable; things were happening to which France must react, and contingencies looming for which she must plan. The political importance of the Quai d'Orsay was thus much enhanced. In the past, cabinets had risen and fallen on domestic issues, but now foreign problems were beginning to dominate the scene, and both

* The popular vote was 5,628,921 for the Popular Front and 4,218,345 for their opponents, which yielded the former 378 and the latter 220 Chamber seats.

Laval and Blum were soon to fall victim to what appeared as failures of foreign policy.

Who would take the lead in dealing with these new questions? Briand, who had ruled the Quai d'Orsay since 1925, died in 1932, but one of his erstwhile protégés stayed on as head of the permanent staff—Alexis Léger, in his other personality one of the greatest French poets, St.-John Perse. Born in Guadeloupe to a French family long settled there, Léger entered the diplomatic service and was sent to China. After the war he was attached as Far Eastern adviser to the French delegation at the Washington Naval Conference, where he attracted Briand's favorable attention. In 1925, Léger was named Ambassador to Turkey, but on Briand's insistence* the appointment was canceled, and Léger remained at the Ministry of Foreign Affairs for the next fifteen years, first as chief of the political and commercial affairs division, and after 1932 as Secretary-General. A shrewd realist, Léger early reached the conclusion that France was overextended in her eastern treaty commitments—that her obligations to come to the aid of Poland, Czechoslovakia, Rumania, and Yugoslavia could not be adequately fulfilled, and that she should exchange her shaky military preeminence for a more limited and practical role of moral leadership.

If Léger was able to preserve a measure of continuity in the staff and administration of the Foreign Ministry, the same could hardly be said of the ministers who headed it, of whom there were three in 1932 alone. There followed Joseph Paul-Boncour in 1933, Louis Barthou under Doumergue, Laval in both Flandin's cabinet and his own, Flandin during the first half of 1936, Yvon Delbos from the summer of 1936 until the spring of 1938 (the longest period of consecutive service since Briand), and Georges Bonnet thereafter until the war. These were six men of strongly contrasting temperaments and viewpoints, and the course of French foreign policy was correspondingly tortuous.

There were likewise new faces, though not so numerous, at the Ministry of War, referred to by the knowing as the "Rue St. Dominique."† New they were but hardly fresh, for both Maxime Weygand and Gustave Gamelin were sexagenarians who, during the First World War, had been chiefs of staff respectively to Foch and Joffre. They came to the War Ministry simultaneously at the beginning of 1930, Weygand, then sixty-three, as Chief of Staff, and Gamelin, five years younger, as his deputy (*premier sous-chef*). In accordance with prior understanding when, in 1931, Pétain finally quit as Inspector General, he was succeeded by Weygand, and Gamelin became Chief of Staff. When Weygand retired in January 1935, the two posts were merged under Gamelin, who, in 1938, was given the additional position of Chief of Staff for National Defense. It was

---

* Georges Bonnet tells a story (*Dans la tourmente, p. 19*) that the Briand-Léger relation had its origin during a cruise on the Potomac River during the Washington Conference of 1925. Briand, regaling the company with anecdotes, was urged to write it all down in a book. He asked Léger, then a junior secretary, whether or not he should, and Léger replied: "A book is the death of a tree." ("*Un livre c'est la mort d'un arbre.*") Briand was so charmed that he kept Léger with him when they returned to France.

† The Ministry of War was located at No. 3 Rue St. Dominique.

Gamelin, accordingly, who bore primary responsibility for military advice to the Government during the several diplomatic crises of the immediate prewar years.

8

Hitler was the New Man and the Great Unknown of the 1933 diplomatic scene, but it was Mussolini who gave the European chancelleries something unexpected to chew on by proposing a "pact of collaboration" among the four major powers of Western Europe—Britain, France, Germany, and Italy, the four-to-be of Munich. Because of its exclusively western membership, the project was viewed with great suspicion by France's eastern allies as well as by Russia. On its face, the treaty appeared to constitute a détente between Germany and the Versailles victors. But whatever it signified to the participants when they signed the so-called "Four Power Pact" at Rome in July, Hitler pulled the plug and drained out the meaning when Germany quit the League and the Geneva disarmament confernce in October. The pact was never ratified.

By this time, the French Ministries of War and Foreign Affairs were fairly inundated with reports of German rearmament, and it was apparent that the Versailles restrictions would soon be dead letters. In this situation, and in immediate consequence of the domestic political crisis of February 1934, there now occurred an abrupt shift in the direction of French policy, and a brief but remarkable period of aggressive diplomacy under the aegis of Louis Barthou, Foreign Minister in the Doumergue cabinet. Like Doumergue, Barthou was in his early seventies; he had been a cabinet minister as far back as 1894, and as Premier in 1913 had put through a three-year military service law over fierce leftist opposition. He was a conservative nationalist of Poincaré's complexion, and equally believed in the efficacy of old-fashioned medicine.

To Barthou, the Four Power Pact was anathema and, with Germany sowing dragon's teeth in every field, disarmament seemed to him a bad joke. On April 17, 1934, France notified the British Government that she "refused to legalize German rearmament" and would henceforth "assure her security by her own means."

By this announcement, Barthou did not at all mean that France would rely solely on her own military strength. On the contrary, he at once embarked on a policy—promoted by personal visits to the capitals of the "Little Entente" countries (Czechoslovakia, Yugoslavia, and Rumania)—of cementing France's eastern alliances, while also preserving France's ties with Britain and Italy, and needling the English into greater awareness of the German menace, so that they would look to their own armaments. The eastern program presented great difficulties, as the alliance with the Poles had been allowed to stagnate, Poland was still resentful of Czechoslovakia for the seizure of Teschen, and there was considerable strain between Yugoslavia and Italy.

To cut through these difficulties, Barthou proposed a so-called "eastern Locarno," comprising Germany, Russia, Poland, Czechoslovakia, and Rumania, to guarantee the borders of those countries with the backing of France and, if willing, of Britain and Italy as well. But neither Germany nor Poland warmed to the idea; Hitler did not want to bind himself to the *status quo,* and Poland feared Russian aid against Germany more than she feared Germany, with whom she had recently signed a ten-year treaty of nonaggression.

Neither daunted nor surprised by the German and Polish attitudes, Barthou pressed ahead with plans for a revival of the prewar Franco-Russian alliance. In view of France's internal political situation, with the mutual hostility of right and left and the deep-seated bourgeois fear of communism, this was a project of some delicacy. The Army, too, gave Barthou cause for concern, especially since Weygand was deeply conservative, a devout Catholic, and reputed to harbor royalist sympathies. But both Weygand and Gamelin reacted favorably, on the ground that "Russia represented the last great eastern counterweight against Germany."

During the summer of 1934 Barthou and Gamelin proceeded to Geneva, where they conferred with the Soviet foreign minister, Maxim Litvinov. A first step toward alliance was the admission of the Soviet Union to the League of Nations, and this was accomplished in September, largely by dint of Herriot's able efforts in support of Barthou's policy.

Three weeks later, on October 9, 1934, King Alexander of Yugoslavia arrived at Marseilles to begin a state visit to France. He was met by Barthou, and a few minutes later both were shot dead by Croatian terrorists. Had Barthou survived and remained in power, certainly the course of French diplomacy would have been quite different. However that might have been, by the time of his death the negotiations with the Russians were well advanced, and early in December, Litvinoff and Barthou's successor at the Quai d'Orsay, Pierre Laval, signed a preliminary "protocol" of the projected treaty.

While putting the ancient but vigorous Barthou at the Quai d'Orsay, Doumergue had installed the even older Pétain at the Rue St. Dominique. The combination was disastrous, for if France, as Barthou proclaimed, was turning its back on disarmament and seeking "security through her own means," certainly that called for a military revival to support the new diplomacy. Instead, Pétain cut the military budget by 20 per cent during the very month of Barthou's announcement. The appointment of Pétain as Minister of War thus made a fatal gulf between the military and diplomatic limbs of French policy—a gulf which should have been foreseen. Two years earlier, Weygand and Gamelin had proposed an extension of the fortifications at crucial places along the northern border, and had been blocked largely in consequence of a memorandum by Pétain opposing the project and reiterating his view that the north must be defended by moving into Belgium.

As Minister of War, Pétain exerted a catastrophic influence. The "hollow years" were beginning, and both Weygand and Gamelin saw clearly enough that the only suitable compensatory measure was extension of the term of compulsory service to two years. The old marshal frustrated them again; appearing before the army committees of the Chamber and Senate, he condemned the extension as unnecessary, and as politically impossible because "the people would not stand for it."

Pétain's testimony was otherwise remarkable for its opacity. Anxious inquiries about the defenses along the Belgian border were brushed aside with a wild assortment of conflicting observations. The front was "uniformly garrisoned and defended all the way to the Escaut River"; the northern border could not be defended by fortifications because the areas needing protection (chiefly coal mines) lay too close to the frontier; anyhow the border need not be fortified because it would be defended by moving into Belgium. Especially sad, in the light of what actually happened in 1940, was Pétain's categorical pronouncement that the area of the Ardennes was, because of its topography, "not dangerous."

In his memoirs, Gamelin described Pétain's conduct as reflecting the shortcomings of old age, and was especially critical of the marshal's acceptance of a cut from 600 to 400 million francs in the armaments budget. But Weygand and Gamelin were themselves far from young, and lacked the spirit and vision to achieve a sufficiently enlarged and modernized army. When, at the end of 1934, General J.-L.-M. Maurin succeeded Pétain as Minister of War, Gamelin's first move was to have Pétain made a permanent member of the Council of National Defense. And in 1936, while Goering's Luftwaffe was burgeoning and Guderian was laying the basis of the German panzer divisions, the new French Manual of Instructions laid it down as basic military doctrine that the "technical progress" in weapons did not modify "the essential rules hitherto established in the domain of tactics." Consequently:

. . . the doctrine objectively fixed at the end of the war (1918) by the eminent chiefs who had held high commands must remain the charter for the tactical employment of large units.

9

Barthou's diplomatic legacy bore fruit when the Franco-Soviet Treaty of Mutual Assistance was signed at Paris on May 2, 1935. Laval then went to Moscow to celebrate the event, in the course of which Stalin announced, in the official communiqué covering the visit, that he "understood and fully approved the policy of national defense, drawn up by France to maintain armed forces at the level necessary for security." This was good "popular front" talk and strengthened the French Government's hand for a rearmament program, but it was ironical that Laval, no popular fronter and fast moving toward the right, should have been the recipient, and the communiqué was highly misleading in its assumption that any such program was being effectively prosecuted, or that French arms were at a level "necessary for security."

Of France's other eastern allies, only Czechoslovakia showed an enthusiastic disposition to follow the Barthou line. During the autumn of 1934 Gamelin visited the country to observe Army maneuvers and discuss additional defense measures, and the following year work was begun on a system of fortifications, modeled on the Maginot Line and placed along the German frontier. In May 1935, a few weeks after the signing of the Franco-Soviet Treaty, Czechoslovakia signed her own pact with the Russians.

But the rest of Barthou's grand design for Eastern Europe was unrealized, and Laval was not the man to complete it. He deeply distrusted the Russians, and sought rather to bolster France's position by strengthening her ties with Italy. So Russian proposals for a military convention were cold-shouldered, and throughout 1935 Laval even refused to bring the mutual assistance pact before the French Parliament for ratification.

Laval's bid for *rapprochement* with Italy got off to a promising start, for France had something to sell which Mussolini was eager to buy: support for Austrian independence of Germany. The first meeting between Duce and Fuehrer (at Venice, in June of 1934) had not gone well, and the following month the abortive Austrian Nazi coup, in the course of which Chancellor Dollfuss was assassinated, left Mussolini resentful, and fearful of future German efforts to achieve an *Anschluss*. Mussolini's fear was heightened by the circumstance that he was already preparing for the conquest of Ethiopia, which would draw major elements of the Italian Army into Africa, and deplete the forces available for the support of Austria.

With these strong cards in his hand, Laval went to Rome early in January 1935, and signed an accord which settled some long-standing African colonial issues between the two countries and, more importantly, committed France to consult with Italy in the event of any threat to Austria's independence. In furtherance of this undertaking, and after prolonged examination of the political aspects with Léger, Gamelin went to Rome the following June to work out a program of military collaboration with the Italian Chief of Staff, Marshal Pietro Badoglio. The two soldiers were old personal friends and found little difficulty in developing an over-all plan of campaign, covering France, Italy, and the Little Entente countries (Czechoslovakia, Yugoslavia, and Rumania), for defending Austria against a German attack.

The principal features of this program were the sending of a French army corps to eastern Italy in order to form a common front with the Italians on the left and the Yugoslavs on the right (thus avoiding direct military contact between those two nations, which were still on poor terms), and the reciprocal dispatch of an Italian corps to the Belfort area, where it would act as the allied right wing on the Franco-German front and protect Italian air units to be stationed behind the corps for operations over southern Germany. Direct support for Austria would take the form of an advance to Vienna from the south and east by an allied force comprising, from left to right, the main Italian Army, the detached French corps, the Yugoslavs, and the Czechs backed by the Rumanians. After his return to Paris, Gamelin organized a big "war game" to which the chiefs of staff of the Little Entente countries were invited, and in the course of which the Gamelin-Badoglio plan was disclosed and analyzed.

Meanwhile, in March, Germany had formally denounced the Versailles arms limitations, through Goering's unveiling of the Luftwaffe and Hitler's orders for the reinstitution of military conscription and establishment of a thirty-six-division army. If these events aroused only mild alarm in France, it was because they came as no surprise. German circumvention of the Versailles restrictions was already an old story when Hitler came to power, and although he greatly accelerated the pace of rearmament, he kept it under cover so that no issue was publicly drawn. The March proclamations enabled the newspapers to print what was already widely known. They gave rise to no serious suggestions that military force or other sanctions should be brought to bear on Germany to make her again disarm.

Nevertheless, the Germans had admitted—had even boasted about—a unilateral repudiation of the Versailles Treaty, and France could not afford to ignore the matter. On her initiative, a three-power conference—Britain, France, and Italy—was held at Stresa early in April. The heads of the three governments (Ramsay MacDonald, Flandin, and Mussolini) reaffirmed their support of Austria's independence and agreed that they would "oppose by all appropriate means any unilateral repudiation of treaties which may endanger the peace of Europe." A few days later, at Geneva, the Council of the League of Nations likewise condemned Germany's violation of the Versailles arms limitations.

So was born the so-called "Stresa Front," which at first seemed to vindicate Laval's policy of Franco-Italian solidarity. Hitler's wooing of Mussolini had been in vain, and François-Poncet observed great discouragement among the German diplomats in Berlin. But the "Front's" apparent health was a delusion, for it was congenitally defective—well-nigh stillborn—as Britain and Italy were already set on courses which would pull them apart, wreck the Front, and leave France holding an empty bag.

The British, it soon appeared, were tired of Versailles and futile disarmament conferences, and wished to make their own settlement with Hitler. The upshot, barely two months after Stresa, was the Anglo-German Naval Treaty. The Italians were annoyed, the French were furious, and the Stresa Front was badly fractured.

Much worse was soon to come from the Italians. Largely preoccupied with internal problems during the first decade of his rule, by 1933 Benito Mussolini was restive and gazing longingly down the road of military adventurism. Most of Ethiopia (then commonly called Abyssinia) lay within what France and Britain had long recognized as an Italian "sphere of influence," and in 1934 General Emilio de Bono, an aging war hawk and Minister of Colonies, persuaded the Duce to lay plans for the conquest of Haile Selassie's ancient but primitive land.

Seeking a *casus belli,* the Italians provoked an armed clash near the ill-defined Ethiopia-Somaliland border, followed by demands to which Haile Selassie replied by referring the dispute to the League Council. Then, on December 30, 1934, Mussolini personally prepared a secret directive for resolution of the conflict by "destruction of the Abyssinian armed forces and the total conquest of Ethiopia."

Such was the situation when Pierre Laval arrived in Rome just after the turn of the year. The published text of the Rome accord did not mention Ethiopia, but, in a secret letter to Mussolini, Laval renounced all French economic interests in that country, except for the railroad from Djibouti (in French Somaliland) to Addis Ababa. Even more important than the letter were Laval's oral assurances to Mussolini, the precise scope of which remains uncertain; they may well have been deliberately vague. Some months later Laval, at a meeting of the Supreme Military Council, declared that he had made a "secret treaty" with Mussolini, and in 1940 he told the French Senate, at a secret session, that he had given the Italians a "free hand," but only for peaceful action.* Badoglio, however, told Gamelin that Laval had given the Duce a "free hand" without qualification,

* According to Laval, he told Mussolini: *Désormais, vous avez les mains libres, mais les mains libres sur le plan pacifique.*

while Flandin, who was Premier at the time, vigorously denied (in his memoirs, published in 1947) that any such blanket assurances were given.

Under all the circumstances, it is unlikely that Laval gave explicit approval to an Italian military adventure, but highly probable that he conveyed to Mussolini, by tone or gesture, that France would interpose no obstacles to the fulfillment of his aims in Ethiopia. In any event, General de Bono departed for Eritrea on the very day that the Rome accord was signed, and the Italian military buildup in her East African colonies was promptly begun. Troops and equipment were dispatched by way of the Suez Canal, so that the British had full knowledge of what was going on. But neither at Stresa in April nor on any other occasion that spring did Britain give Mussolini any reason to think that she would stand in his way.

Whether Mussolini would have persisted in his plan of conquest even in the face of convincing warnings of grave consequences is a matter of speculation. British naval power dominated the Mediterranean, and by closing the Suez Canal the Italian forces in East Africa could be cut off from their homeland. But no such warning was given, and compromises proposed by France and Britain during the summer were angrily rejected by Mussolini. On October 3, 1935, De Bono's forces crossed the Eritrean frontier into Ethiopia, and the war began —a war of bad consequences not only for the participants, but for Britain, France, and the League of Nations as well.

For France especially, the war posed a cruel dilemma. Close relations with Italy, for mutual support against Germany, had become a cardinal point of French diplomacy, symbolized at Stresa. Was this bond to be sacrificed on the altar of international morality and in the protection of Ethiopia, a distant and semibarbaric land where France had no essential interests? On the other hand, France had been the principal sponsor of Ethiopia's admission to the League of Nations in 1923, and Article 16 of the League Covenant explicitly envisaged the application of sanctions against any member nation resorting to aggressive militarism. A week after the Italian attack, the League Assembly condemned the invasion as a violation of Article 16 and voted for sanctions. If the notion of collective security had any value for France, now was the time to put the principle into practice. Furthermore, at Geneva, Britain had given the appearance of strong support for the League and the application of economic sanctions against Italy. For France, good relations with Italy were indeed desirable, but the continued friendship of Britain was the linchpin of French foreign policy.

So Pierre Laval's diplomatic sins in Rome recoiled on his own head. He had become Premier in June while retaining the portfolio of foreign affairs, and now he found himself in a desperate straddle, giving lip service to collective security and striving to stay in line with Britain without mortally offending Mussolini and destroying the newborn Franco-Italian entente.

In this tortuous course, Laval found a willing English collaborator in Sir Samuel Hoare, who had succeeded Sir John Simon as Foreign Secretary. When they met at the League Assembly in Geneva just before the outbreak of war, the two men agreed that, whatever action might be voted on sanctions, they would rule out a naval blockade, closure of the Suez Canal, or any other measures that might lead to war with Italy. Three months later they met again in Paris and concluded the famous, or as many thought, infamous "Hoare-Laval Plan" to end the war by a settlement under which Italy would annex a large part of Ethiopia.

Once again Laval had been too clever by half. Whatever pragmatic arguments might be advanced in favor of the plan, it was a gross betrayal of the collective security principle to resolve the conflict by authorizing the aggressor to swallow half of the victim. British opinion was outraged, the Government disowned the plan, and Anthony Eden replaced Hoare as Foreign Secretary. Laval's own government fell six weeks later; he left the Quai d'Orsay an embittered man and held no further office until 1940, in the Vichy regime of Pétain.

Laval and Hoare had succeeded in preventing the application of any sanctions that would seriously harm Italy's economy or impede her military operations, and it was the old story of half measures being worse than none. Mussolini was not to be propitiated, and in December he repudiated the Rome accord. The conquest of Ethiopia took the Italians seven months; early in May of 1936, Haile Selassie fled his country, and a few days later all of Ethiopia was proclaimed part of the Italian "Empire." In July the League abandoned sanctions, which had degenerated to an empty gesture.

The consequences for France of Laval's Italian adventures had been utterly disastrous. The Stresa Front was destroyed, and the Italians alienated and thrown toward Germany. The League of Nations was badly discredited, and the prospects of genuine collective security fatally undermined. The bond between France and Britain was badly strained, while at the same time the loss of Italy's friendship made France more than ever dependent on Britain, and seriously limited her future freedom of action. Henceforth, French foreign policy was to be largely determined in London.

10

Pierre Laval had been wooing Hitler as well as Mussolini. Interviewed by Alexander Werth (then writing for the *Manchester Guardian*) shortly after he became Foreign Minister, Laval pointed to Germany on the map of Europe, and asked Werth if he could "really imagine that we can have peace and collective security in Europe so long as we haven't brought *this* into our peace system." That was well enough as a proposition of geopolitics, but overlooked the question whether Hitler was interested in collective security or would support a European "peace" other than under German domination.

Like Chamberlain in his later turn, Laval thought that if Hitler were cleverly wooed he might be won. Soon Laval was sending unofficial and very right-wing emissaries to Berlin, and Joachim von Ribbentrop, Otto Abetz, and other Nazi agents were invited to Paris. On November 21, 1935, Laval called a meeting of the Military High Commission* for a general foreign policy overview, and gave expression to his thinking on Germany:

* The Haut Comité Militaire, composed of the three service ministers and three chiefs of staff, the Minister of Colonies, the Secretary-General of the Foreign Ministry, and Marshal Pétain.

François-Poncet is seeing Hitler today.* I have also conveyed my point of view by a special emissary.

Hitler has on several occasions shown desire for an *entente* with France. At Marshal Pilsudski's funeral, Marshal Petain had a long conversation with Goering. . . .

Now we want to live in peace with Germany, if she will declare herself contented with her present frontiers. But Hitler has already said that. Hitler must also explain that *Mein Kampf* was written at the time we occupied the Ruhr. There might be a joint declaration of desire to live as good neighbors, and then we might reopen discussions with Germany on limitation of armaments. . . . We must not seem to be making demands on Germany. I should add that, since the Abyssinian affair, Germany seems less anxious. . . . Anyhow, we can never keep up with Germany in terms of rearmament. And I am of the opinion that rearmament leads to war. . . .

General Gamelin was so upset by the occasion that, early the following morning, he wept "for the first time since the death of my mother, and for the fate of my country," and poured his feelings into a private memorandum, reproduced in his memoirs a decade later. For what reason was Laval bypassing his ambassador in Berlin? Why should France ratify a treaty with Russia and simultaneously nullify it by an entente with Germany? What would the Czechs and Poles make of such a move? And why should one count on any German promise about frontiers? Léger had been visibly embarrassed by Laval's presentation, but Pétain and others had seemed in agreement. "My poor country, where are your leaders?"

There remains some mystery about the specific content of Laval's report; we do not know who was the "special emissary" to Hitler, nor what Pétain and Goering said to each other at Pilsudski's funeral. The two had met in the fall of 1934 when they represented their respective countries at the obsequies for King Alexander of Yugoslavia. On both occasions, Pétain's ostentatious courting of Goering was remarked by the famous publicist "Pertinax" (André Géraud of the *Echo de Paris*). In Poland they were joined by Laval, returning from his trip to Moscow—hardly an auspicious avenue to an encounter with Goering. Nevertheless, on May 18, 1935, in Cracow, Laval and Goering had a long talk† in the course of which the former was at great pains to play down the importance of the Franco-Soviet treaty, and urged that Germany renounce territorial ambitions in Eastern Europe, while Goering proposed a "truce" in order to lay the basis for a Hitler-Laval meeting and the formulation of a Franco-German agreement.

Laval and Pétain are also reported (by Pertinax) to have communed at length while in Poland, and to have discovered a mutual antipathy to parliamentary democracy and formed a mutual admiration society. In any event, the

* Ambassador François-Poncet did in fact see Hitler that day in order to inform him that the Chamber would soon start to debate ratification of the Franco-Soviet pact, and assure him that it was "defensive" and "in no sense directed against Germany."

† The transcript of this interview survived, and appears to be the work of Charles Rochat, head of the political section of the Foreign Office staff, who had accompanied Laval to Moscow.

growing closeness of the two men was widely remarked at the time—a harbinger of their collaboration in the Vichy regime five years later.

More immediately, however, the Pétain-Laval link and their eagerness for a Franco-German tie was symptomatic of a profound change in the political complexion of France, a change that had enormous consequences during the final years of the Third Republic. This was the switch of most of the political right wing from an anti-German to a pro-Hitler point of view.

Traditionally, it was the right which had been the voice of French militaristic nationalism and, Cato-like, preached eternal distrust of *les Boches*. The world was a jungle; collective security, disarmament, and the League of Nations were for the birds; strong allies were highly desirable, but above all France herself must be strong.

These attitudes were, of course, especially marked in the aftermath of Versailles, and were widely shared on the left as well. But as postwar tensions eased, the internationalist and collectivist bases of socialism reasserted themselves, and the French left gave strong support to the League and disarmament. The right, whether royalist, neo-Fascist, or conservative republican, remained skeptical of such airy idealism. Thus the Socialist Briand's name is linked with that of Stresemann for Locarno and Kellogg in the outlawry of war, while the conservative nationalists Poincaré and Barthou are remembered for the occupation of the Ruhr and the "encirclement" of Germany.

And so it was for two years after the advent of Hitler; for the right condemned the Nazis both because they called themselves socialists and because they appeared to be dangerous German nationalists. Despite the right's contempt for the League, they criticized Germany for quitting it. They were outraged by Hitler's repudiation of Versailles, and pleased by the Stresa Front.

But that same year saw the beginnings of what was to prove a fatal shift, in that the right began to assess foreign policy primarily in terms of domestic political issues. The right-left polarization, symbolized by February 6 and 12 of 1934, distorted the lens through which the right looked eastward, whether toward Germany, Russia, or Italy. During the Flandin and Laval governments the last two were in the foreground, and it was the Franco-Soviet pact and the Italo-Ethiopian War that precipitated the shift.

The change began in the spring of 1935, marked by the raising of the military service requirement to two years, which the right supported and the left opposed; the Stresa Front, supported by both; and the signing of the treaty with the Soviet Union, which the left supported and which split the right. As Alexander Werth put it, the treaty was supported by the left on grounds of collective security, and the right on grounds of national security. But for the extreme right, ideology was more important than security, and its adherents denounced entering into alliance with godless Communists.

While the debate over ratification of the treaty raged, the issue of sanctions against Italy arose at Geneva. The moderate right approved Laval's efforts to straddle the question and stay in the good graces of both Britain and Italy. The more militant right, however, found numerous grounds of opposition to the sanctions: contempt for the League and for notions of collective security, ancient distrust of "perfidious Albion," admiration for Mussolini and Fascist authoritarianism.

The failure of sanctions, Mussolini's victory in Ethiopia, and the growing political strength of the French left, all worked to strengthen the hand of the militant right. By the beginning of 1936, confronting the strong possibility of a popular front victory in the spring elections, the right was virtually united* in opposition to ratification of the Soviet alliance.

These objections were variously expressed, but at their root was a particular fear—fear that France would become a liberal-socialist country closely linked with communist Russia. What would be the consequences of a French victory over Germany, won in alliance with the Soviet Union? Would not France be pushed permanently to the far left, perhaps even to communism?

As these fears spread among conservatives, their image of Adolf Hitler was correspondingly reshaped. It was comforting to view Hitler's Germany not as France's ancient foe springing once more to arms, but rather as civilization's bastion against the red barbarism looming in the east. And now voices that in the past had sung songs of *gloire* and *victoire* were raised in praise of peace. "Sanctions mean war!" was the cry from the right. Let Mussolini have his colonial empire, and let Hitler find his *Lebensraum* in the east. Then Mussolini will be our friend, Hitler will not come in our direction, the red menace will be contained or crushed, France will be at peace, and we shall prosper.

So the French right moved toward what later was called "appeasement," while the left continued to rest its faith in general disarmament and collective security. And it is these trends and attitudes that largely determined the French response when, on March 7, 1936, small contingents of the Wehrmacht crossed the Rhine into land theretofore forbidden to them.

11

Whatever else might be said about the German remilitarization of the Rhineland, it came as no surprise to the French Government. As early as the summer of 1932, six months before Hitler took power, the Ministry of War had informed the Foreign Ministry of continuing violations of the Rhineland restrictions. Probably in reaction to these infractions, in October 1932 the French General Staff had drawn up a retaliatory "Plan D," which envisaged a French reoccupation of the Saar region,† and a further penetration into the Rhineland to a line from Trier on the Moselle River through Kaiserslautern and Landau to the Rhine.

Hitler's early protestations that he would respect the Locarno Pact, including the Rhineland restrictions, began to ring hollow soon after his repudiation of the Versailles armament restrictions. On March 22, 1935, the diligent French

---

* There were a few notable exceptions, including Paul Reynaud, Georges Mandel, and the writer Pertinax.

† In 1932 the Saar was still under French control, so this part of the plan must have been based on the sound assumption that the Saar would be returned to Germany by the 1935 plebiscite envisaged in the Treaty of Versailles.

consul general in Cologne, Jean Dobler, reported to his superiors in Paris the secret construction of barracks, utilization of Rhineland airfields by military aircraft, and establishment of an army regional headquarters in Cologne.

During the next twelve months Dobler was the source of a steady stream of reports confirming clandestine preparations for the open return of German troops to the Rhineland. The local police forces were augmented and militarized; stocks of munitions were accumulated in the old Cologne forts; ground and training crews arrived at the airfields; army camps and maneuver areas were laid out here and there. Dobler supplemented these physical observations with reports of speeches by visiting Nazi bigwigs such as Goebbels, and talks with local officials, on the basis of which he predicted open remilitarization in the spring of 1936. Confirmatory on-the-spot reports reached Paris from the consul general in Düsseldorf.

Meanwhile, similar information was coming from the embassy in Berlin. François-Poncet's November interview with Hitler led to his report that the Fuehrer's violent denunciation of the Franco-Soviet pact presaged "the denunciation of Locarno and the occupation of the demilitarized zone." In January 1936 the military attaché, General Renondeau, advised the Minister of War that he had "no doubt" that remilitarization was in prospect; the date was uncertain, but he feared that it was not far off.

Apprehension of a German move into the Rhineland was by no means confined to the French. Early in 1936 it was manifest in Poland, Czechoslovakia, and Greece. In none of these countries was there much confidence that France would act decisively to forestall the action or to throw back the Germans if confronted with a *fait accompli*.

Thus in January the French Minister in Prague, Paul-Emile Naggiar, informed Paris that the Czech Government was anxious about the Rhineland's future status, and questioned whether the French were ready to use force, in view of "a sort of crystallization of opinion in France in favor of a policy of neutrality." Some weeks later the Greek Minister in Paris was complaining about a "pacifist depression" in France and a widespread desire for "peace at any price." On February 1, the French Embassy in Warsaw reported that the Polish Foreign Minister, Colonel Jozef Beck, had shown "the greatest skepticism about the possibility of maintaining the demilitarized zone." At the end of the month Naggiar transmitted the gist of a conversation with Beneš, in which the President put his finger squarely on the significance of the Rhineland to France's eastern allies:

> Benes thinks that, in embarking on any aggression toward the east or south-east, Germany would not want to leave her western frontiers, which today are vulnerable because of the demilitarized Rhineland, without protection. In the eyes of the Army that risk is too great, despite the work accomplished among certain sections of the public to favor the view that Germany should be given a free hand in any direction except the west.
>
> One can rest assured, according to the President, that the day the Third Reich calls in question the Rhineland restrictions, it will be to enable her to protect the western frontier, in order to attack toward the east or southeast.

Dobler, the consul general, complained, with some cause, that his reports went unacknowledged and that he was seldom consulted by the resident staff of the Quai d'Orsay—the *sédentaires,* in the apt and acrid French designation. But it is clear that his dispatches were read, and he had unofficial direct access to Georges Mandel, then the Minister of Posts and Telegraph. At least by mid-January, the French political chiefs were well aware that the Germans might move at any time. On January 25 the Sarraut cabinet took office with Flandin at the Quai d'Orsay, and the Rhineland question at once became his prime concern.

The French General Staff was equally well informed. In October 1935, reports from the military intelligence service prompted Gamelin to advise the Foreign Ministry that a repudiation of the Rhineland restrictions might be expected "before the autumn of 1936 at the latest." The warning was reiterated on the day after Christmas, and on February 25, in a War Ministry memorandum, it was concluded that ratification of the Franco-Soviet treaty would result in an immediate and total reoccupation of the Rhineland by German troops. Hitler would once more confront France with a *fait accompli,* in consequence of which she would lose "her last guarantee of security."

But if the French Government was thus abundantly forewarned, it was certainly not forearmed. France's record in the Rhineland episode is one of military and political paltering and prevaricating; of paralysis of will; of errors of assessment and judgment so gross that it is hard to believe some were not deliberate; of avoiding today the small risk, only to confront the greater risk tomorrow. The Rhineland militarization was, as Beneš foresaw, more than a harbinger of Munich; it was, in very large measure, a determinant.

In the spring of 1935, Pierre Laval, then both Premier and Foreign Minister, passed through Cologne en route to Moscow, and Dobler boarded his train to report. After describing a recent foray of German troops into the forbidden zone, Dobler suggested a confidential but strong démarche in Berlin to the effect that further violations would cause the French to march in. "So that's your opinion," said Laval, "but it isn't mine." No protests were made as the reports of violations and preparations for reoccupation mounted, and no preventive political action was taken throughout Laval's period of office. The military leaders were equally inactive.

The government of Albert Sarraut took office late in January 1936, barely six weeks before the Germans made their move, and what little the French did by way of preparing for the anticipated blow was done in that short time. Sarraut's government was regarded as a stopgap, intended mostly to keep the administrative wheels turning until the spring elections. The Premier himself was an old sixty-four and, if not of heroic mold, was a decent man, once a bit to the right and now a touch to the left of center, who had been in and out of office for thirty years. Flandin was given the Quai d'Orsay not so much for any proven capacity in foreign affairs as to provide political party balance. The Minister of War, General Joseph-Léon-Marie Maurin, was a friend and contemporary of Gamelin, initially picked for ministerial office by Flandin, with Pétain's approval. He was, if such is possible, even more defense-minded than Pétain. In the Chamber of Deputies, replying to Paul Reynaud's plea in 1935 for the creation of an offensive armored force, Maurin expressed horror at the idea:

> How can anyone believe that we are still thinking of the offensive when we have spent so many billions to establish a fortified frontier! Should we be mad enough to advance beyond this barrier—on I don't know what sort of adventure?

It was on these three ministers—Sarraut, Flandin, and Maurin—plus Gamelin that the main burden of decision and action rested. With the retirement of Pétain and Weygand, Gamelin had become the dominant French military figure. In mid-January 1936 he prepared a memorandum on the growing German military menace, which was considered on January 18 by the Military High Commission, composing the ministers and chiefs of staff of the naval, air, and ground forces. Both the memorandum and the resulting discussion reflected the extreme caution, to describe the attitude most charitably, with which the Rhineland problem was being met.

Estimating Germany's effective ground strength at 790,000 men, Gamelin included 200,000 labor service (*Arbeitsdienst*) and 40,000 SS men, though in fact neither group had significant military value. Warned three days earlier by his intelligence service that the Rhineland would be remilitarized "in the near future," Gamelin recommended nothing to counter the threat, even as he pointed out with great lucidity that loss of the Rhineland guarantee would put France's eastern allies at Germany's mercy. The only action taken at the meeting was an agreement to ask the Chamber for additional military appropriations.

On the diplomatic side, the situation that Flandin confronted on taking over the Quai d'Orsay was not altogether encouraging. Of the Locarno powers other than France and Germany, Italy was herself under League sanctions generated by the Ethiopian affair, and could hardly be expected to leap into action against the Germans, who had not joined in the sanctions. Belgium, as Flandin soon found out, was disposed "to be prudent, and leave to France and England the task of handling the Rhineland problem."

Much, then, depended on the reaction in England, a country which Flandin greatly admired, and the manners and dress of which he assiduously cultivated. Two days after taking office he was in London for the funeral of King George V, and took occasion to discuss the Rhineland with both Prime Minister Stanley Baldwin and Anthony Eden, himself a newly appointed Foreign Secretary. Flandin found both Englishmen very circumspect. Baldwin chiefly wished to avoid any risk of war, and Eden threw the question right back as "a matter for the judgment of the French government":

> How much importance did they attach to the demilitarized zone? Did they wish . . . to maintain it at all costs, or . . . prefer to bargain with the German government while the existence of the zone still had value in German eyes. . . . If they wished to negotiate with Hitler, they should do so; if they intended to repel a German invasion of the zone, they should lay their military plans.

The French did neither one nor the other. With regard to the possibility of negotiations Gamelin did, at Flandin's request, examine the possibility of agreeing to a "restricted" remilitarization, under which, for example, no fortifications or new airfields would be built. But Maurin was strongly opposed to opening any discussion on relaxing the Rhineland terms, and the Germans were not approached.

Indeed, until the latter part of February the French did not do much of anything about the danger that was staring them in the face. In his postwar memoirs, Gamelin declared that he instructed the generals on the German frontier to study "certain operations involving a series of local, rapid advances into German territory . . . especially an advance to the Saar River between Saarbrücken and Merzig." If in fact such studies were made (and there is no trace of them in the French archives so far released), certainly nothing was done to make possible their execution.

Nor are they mentioned in letters interchanged by Maurin and Flandin between February 12 and 17, in which the two ministers discussed political and military steps to be taken if and when the Germans moved into the Rhineland. On the national level, they agreed that there should be immediate complaint made at Geneva for violation of both Versailles and Locarno. The military measures envisaged by Maurin were purely defensive and, indeed, he gave it as his opinion that it would be "contrary to France's interests to use our right to occupy the demilitarized zone," as this might make France appear as the aggressor, in which event "we would find ourselves alone confronting Germany." No such operation should be contemplated "without the full agreement of the British government."

On February 14, the British military attaché, Lieutenant Colonel Beaumont-Nesbitt, put to a French general staff officer the blunt query: "What do you propose to do, alone or with us, if the Germans occupy the left bank of the Rhine?" The question was discussed five days later at a meeting of the air, sea, and ground chiefs of staff. Like Maurin, Gamelin scouted the idea that France alone could occupy the demilitarized zone. He indulged in some wishful thinking about stationing small British Army contingents on the Franco-German border—a curious forerunner of the "plate-glass window" strategy invoked years later to justify the continuing presence of American forces in Western Europe. Furthermore, Gamelin thought that it would be impossible "to prevent Germany indefinitely from doing what she wants within her own frontiers"; the best one could hope for was to preserve the demilitarized zone until after 1940, when the "hollow years" would be over.

None of this went very far to answer Beaumont-Nesbitt's question. The next day Gamelin and Maurin took off on a two-day tour of the Lorraine fortifications. On his return, Gamelin received information leading him to believe that the Germans would seize on the imminent ratification of the Franco-Soviet treaty as a pretext for immediate entry into the Rhineland. Maurin's panicky reaction was to send a note to the Quai d'Orsay, suggesting that ratification be postponed, and that the question whether the treaty was in conflict with Locarno be submitted to the International Court of Justice at The Hague!*

On February 27 the Chamber of Deputies ratified the Soviet pact, and that same day, *for the first time,* the French Cabinet met to consider what action should be taken when the Germans make the expected move. No record of the proceedings has survived; the postwar memoirs of Gamelin and testimony of Sarraut are the only available sources. According to these, Sarraut questioned Maurin on the military plans, and was informed that the nature of the French peacetime Army was such that it could only take defensive measures. If any offensive action were to be taken, the *frontaliers* would have to be called to man the Maginot Line, and a partial mobilization (the *"couverture"*) of the ready reserve would be necessary, so that there would be "a defensive base for the forward move." An "industrial mobilization" was also an essential preliminary. Informed the following day of what had been said, Gamelin fully agreed, the more in that the immediately available French ground forces were by his count, less than half as numerous as those of the Germans, including the police and Nazi Party formations.†

The Cabinet decided that France should not act alone, but in conjunction with the other Locarno powers and in the framework of the League of Nations. According to Sarraut, the factors that weighed most heavily in so deciding were France's long-standing commitment to the principles of collective security, strong indications that Britain would insist on the Geneva route, and equally strong indications that France's own military chiefs had no stomach for single-handed military action. The official formulation of France's position, which was passed on confidentially to the Belgian Ambassador that same day and to Eden on March 3,‡ was as follows:

> The French government will not take any isolated action. It will act only in accord with the cosignatories of Locarno.
>
> In case of a flagrant and incontestable violation of . . . [the Rhineland restrictions] the French government will immediately consult with the British, Belgian and Italian governments with a view to taking common action in execution of the League of Nations pact and the Locarno agreements.
>
> While awaiting the opinion of the guarantor powers, the French government reserves the right to take all measures, including those of a military character, preparatory to such collective action as may be decided upon by the Council of the League of Nations and the Locarno guarantors.

Prudent as the statement appears to be, it was in fact recklessly cautious, and

---

* Two days later, Léger told Gamelin that such a gesture would be ineffective, and Premier Sarraut rejected the proposal on the ground that it would be a retreat and might precipitate a dangerous ministerial crisis.

† The inclusion of these so-called "paramilitary" formations accounted in large part for the supposed German numerical superiority. As already observed, these were substantially useless for immediate military purposes.

‡ Flandin told the Belgian Ambassador that the statement would not, for the time being, be disclosed to the Germans, and the available documents contain no indication that the Italians were informed.

at bottom nothing but a procrastination. The French already knew that Italy was disaffected, that Britain was reluctant to become involved, and that Belgium would simply follow the lead of her protectors. Collective security was an appealing concept, but in Ethiopia its fruits had already turned sour. The Geneva machinery was cumbersome and time-consuming, whereas the essential characteristic of the Rhineland restrictions was that their military value would dwindle very rapidly after the first large-scale violation.

The Cabinet decision of February 27 took no account of these circumstances, crucial as they were to a wise decision. Nor did it settle the question which France would most probably confront. It was one thing to prefer joint action with allies to going it alone; it was quite another to renounce individual action if one's allies should fall away. If collective action through the League to force a German withdrawal could not be had, should France then submit to the *fait accompli?* Even if the Locarno powers should let her down, would not France's eastern allies, who had so much to lose, rally to her side?

These questions, which the Cabinet did not decide and apparently did not discuss, were in fact those with which the events of March 7 would confront them.

12

At seven o'clock in the morning of Saturday, March 7, in Cologne, the indefatigable Dobler was abroad in his automobile, investigating reports that German troops had appeared in the fifty-kilometer demilitarized strip on the east bank of the Rhine. He found a German antiaircraft unit assembled at the Hohenzollern Bridge, ready to cross the Rhine into Cologne at noon, in synchronization with Hitler's speech in the Reichstag announcing the move. After telephoning his observations to the Quai d'Orsay, Dobler scouted the Rhine as far north as Essen, and that evening was able to inform Paris that "the reoccupation, north of the Moselle, has been accomplished with very few troops."

When the news reached Paris that morning, Premier Sarraut summoned to his office a group comprising Flandin, Maurin, Paul-Boncour, and Mandel of the Cabinet, and Generals Gamelin and Colson. For Sarraut, it was "now or never" that the generals should put forward some definite proposals. Mandel and Paul-Boncour urged immediate military action to drive the Germans back. "For my part," Gamelin later wrote, "I asked above all that we first take precautionary measures"—canceling military leaves, calling up the *frontaliers,* and so forth. "I would like to see you in Mainz as soon as possible," said Paul-Boncour. "Ah, that is another affair," Gamelin replied. "I would like nothing better, but I must be given the means." Sarraut asked what would be the situation "if we were alone, without allies, confronting Germany." Gamelin answered that at the outset France would have "the preponderance" but that in a long war Germany's greater population and resources would count heavily.

That was all. No basic decision was reached and, except for the preliminary "precautionary measures," no military decisions were made. After the meeting Flandin received the press and announced that France was appealing to the League of Nations.

Meanwhile the diplomatic world was spinning frantically. In Paris, Ambassador Sir George Clerk hurried to the Quai d'Orsay to urge, on behalf of his government, that France "take no action tending to commit the future" before consulting with Britain. In London, Anthony Eden summoned the French Ambassador, Charles Corbin, to make a similar plea. Nothing could be decided in London, said Eden, before the Cabinet meeting the following Monday (March 9). Corbin did not find his attitude very encouraging:

> Without drawing definite conclusions, I could not help noting that, even though he formally disapproved the [German] denunciation of a treaty, this aroused no emotion, but rather the unexpressed relief that follows a misfortune long feared. His attitude was that of a man who looks for the advantages that can be drawn from a new situation, rather than for the barriers that can be raised against a dangerous threat.

From Brussels came the expected word that Belgium would take the "same attitude as France and England," with no indication of what she would do if her two big friends found themselves at odds. The Locarno powers were running true to form, but what would they do if France went ahead on her own? Alexis Léger, whom Gamelin saw late in the afternoon and found eager "to act and act energetically," thought they would be drawn in by force of circumstance: "The British and Belgians are inclined to bow before the *fait accompli*," said Léger, "but they will have to follow us."*

In the eastern capitals, the reaction was quite different. In Warsaw, Colonel Beck received Ambassador Léon Noël with the observation: "This time it is serious," and went on to confirm Poland's fidelity to her alliance with France and invite an "exchange of views." In Prague, Foreign Minister Krofta told the French chargé d'affaires that Czechoslovakia "would adopt exactly the same attitude as France." From Bucharest came word that the Foreign Minister, Nicholas Titulescu, favored economic sanctions against Germany. Even in Austria, bound in no way to France, a high official told the French Minister that "next time it will be our turn," and warned that "Austrian confidence in us depends on the vigor and promptness of our counteraction."

Such was the state of affairs the following morning, Sunday, March 8, when the French Cabinet was convened.† No transcript of the proceedings has been unearthed, but from the accounts of a few of those present—Paul-Boncour, Maurin, and Jean Zay (the Minister of Education)—it is clear that Maurin threw a wet blanket on the discussions. Someone suggested that France do what Mussolini had done at the time of the Dollfuss affair in Austria, when the dispatch of Italian troops to the Brenner Pass had caused Hitler to back-pedal. Maurin saw no parallel. Wittingly or not, he gave the impression that the Army

---

* On March 23, talking with the American Ambassador, Jesse I. Straus, Léger declared that France should have mobilized immediately, in order to avoid the "shilly-shallying" in London and present the British with a *fait accompli*.

† There is a curious conflict of testimony about the date, in that both Paul-Boncour and Maurin put the meeting on Monday the ninth, whereas Gamelin (who was not present but had report of the meeting from Maurin) puts it on Sunday the eighth, as does the Report of the Parliamentary Commission of Inquiry. France's formal protest to the League of Nations was sent in the evening of the eighth, and it is unlikely that this could have been done without Cabinet approval.

could do nothing without full mobilization.* Rightly enough he warned his fellow-members that military intervention carried the risk of war, but he is also reported to have declared that "the present state of the French army does not permit us to run these risks."

Few of those present were prepared to face a war, and even the bolder ones were appalled by the prospect of full mobilization, which would disrupt the country politically and economically on the verge of an election, which might make France appear to be using Germany's treaty violation as a pretext for full-scale war, and which was characterized as "using a hammer to kill a fly." Sarraut, Flandin, Paul-Boncour, and Mandel pressed for military action, but in the face of Maurin's negativism and the other ministers' reluctance, Flandin finally threw in the sponge: "I see, Mr. President, there is no use insisting."

And so on Sunday as on Saturday, the only decision was not to decide. That evening Flandin transmitted to the League France's formal complaint against Germany for violation of the Versailles and Locarno stipulations, and Premier Sarraut made a nationwide radio broadcast. In its course, Sarraut made a statement, ill-considered in that it did not accurately reflect his or the Cabinet's viewpoint: "We are not disposed to let Strasbourg lie within the range of German cannon." Those who itched to see France give Germany a bloody nose were delighted, others were horrified, but in context it is clear that Sarraut meant only that, in order to prevent Strasbourg from being thus imperiled, France was appealing to the League Council and the Locarno signatories. If anyone was frightened, it was not the Germans.

Meanwhile, the three chiefs of staff and their deputies were meeting at Gamelin's home. This conference is not mentioned in his memoirs, and the omission is highly significant, for the record of the discussion† draws a thick line of doubt across Gamelin's postwar writing and testimony, in which he denied that he had insisted on general mobilization as a necessary first step, and claimed to have favored a move into the zone.

Gamelin began by reporting that the government had asked him: "Are you in a position to act?"‡ He had answered that, if the conflict were limited to the Franco-German border, both sides had forces large enough to "saturate" the area, and the front would soon become "stabilized." The Chief of the Naval Staff, Admiral Durand-Viel, reminded Gamelin that the Government's question was whether his troops could drive the Germans out of the zone. Gamelin did not answer directly, but predicted that "As soon as we enter the zone, there will be war." Such action, therefore, would require "general mobilization"; furthermore, it could be undertaken only in conjunction with the troops of the other Locarno powers. This last fantasy was too much for Durand-Viel, who pointed

* The question whether Maurin and Gamelin had demanded full mobilization or partial mobilization (*couverture*) was hotly debated in the *postmortems*. The contemporary documentation indicates that the generals were anything but consistent on this point in their presentations, and could well have given the civilian ministers the impression that full mobilization would probably be necessary.

† The transcript is in the handwriting of Vice Admiral Jean Abrial, Deputy Chief of the Naval Staff.

‡ "*Êtes-vous en état de tenir?*"

out that England and Italy were at swords' points over Ethiopia, and that England had nothing to offer but "moral support." Nevertheless, Gamelin continued to harp on the notion of bringing British and Italian troops to France, and then going into Germany via Belgium.

Far from thinking of sending troops to France, the British did not even want to send Anthony Eden to Paris. Desperately, Flandin wired Corbin that the British were not taking the situation seriously enough, and directed him to procure Eden's attendance at a Locarno conference in Paris on Monday. But Eden was not to be rushed; he would have to be in the House of Commons on Monday, and anyhow he was dubious of the wisdom of a Locarno meeting before the League Council had considered the matter. Finally, he was persuaded to come to Paris on Tuesday morning.

Monday the ninth was another day of inaction and of gloomy waiting. In the morning Gamelin met with his field commanders for a briefing which a young staff officer* found utterly depressing. The units on the frontier were not self-sufficient and therefore could not move forward; therefore nothing could be done without general mobilization, etc. The afternoon brought word of Eden's speech in the Commons, which did little to lighten the atmosphere in Paris. In a sort of maiden-aunt way Eden scolded the Germans for naughtiness in breaking treaties, but assured his listeners that there was "no reason to suppose that the present German action implies a threat of hostilities," and went on to promise Hitler that his new peace proposals would be considered "seriously and objectively."

The Locarno convocation in Paris on the morning of Tuesday the tenth lived up, or rather down, to the expectations generated by the participants' previous behavior. Flandin made a strong pitch for economic and military sanctions, and went far beyond the Cabinet's warranty in declaring that France was quite prepared to go alone into the Rhineland and clear the Germans out; all she wanted was her co-signatories' "moral support."

If this was largely bluff it was not called, for no one was willing to give Flandin what he demanded. The Italian delegate sat silent; he had declared himself only an observer, as his country was already under sanctions. Eden was accompanied by Lord Halifax (then the Lord Privy Seal), and they joined in discouraging all thought of military action. By negotiations, the Englishmen declared, Hitler might be persuaded to refrain from fortifying the Rhineland, and even to rejoin the League of Nations! The Belgian Prime Minister, Paul van Zeeland, echoed the British views. It was a conference with a very low coefficient of credibility, and it broke up with no other result than an agreement to foregather in London two days later, in preparation for the League Council meeting scheduled for March 14, also in London.

The Chamber of Deputies also convened on Tuesday, and, as they were leaving the session, Flandin asked Maurin to study the possibility of a *"prise de*

---

* Tony Albord, later a general, who attended in place of his chief, General Héring, commandant of Strasbourg, who was unable to be present. Albord's postwar writings raise some confusion about the date, but comparison with Gamelin's memoirs establishes it with reasonable certainty as the morning of March 9.

gages" (taking as security) of German cities in the Rhineland—Saarbrücken
and Kehl were mentioned—in order to put the Germans under pressure to
withdraw, or at least increase France's leverage in negotiations. Gamelin conferred with his deputy, Alphonse Georges, and the two generals agreed that the
idea was good in principle, but only if a partial mobilization were first undertaken. Shortly thereafter Gamelin was summoned to an evening meeting of the
service ministers and chiefs of staff at Premier Sarraut's home on the Avenue
Victor Hugo.*

According to his own account, Gamelin began by addressing himself to Flandin's *prise de gages* proposal. There would have to be a partial mobilization,
and the Germans might resist, which would immediately require general mobilization. Cities were "veritable fortresses," so there could be no thought of taking
Saarbrücken "until after we have won the battle." Kehl lay across the Rhine, and
the Germans were already there. The best route into the Rhineland lay through
Belgium; would she let us pass? Would Italy be with us or against us or neutral?
What would Russia, Poland, and Czechoslovakia do to hold German forces in
the east? Maurin supported Gamelin's analysis, and the ministers of the air and
naval services (Marcel Deàt and François Pietri) declared themselves opposed
to any operation except with the approval of the League of Nations—a condition which, if experience was any guide, foreclosed any action for weeks at least.
Sarraut, who still nurtured hopes of a positive military program, was sadly disappointed.

Gamelin and Maurin embodied their views on the *prise de gages* in a formal
"note" submitted to Sarraut the following morning. It was an extraordinary document. As a *gage,* it was proposed to occupy the left bank of the Saar River
from Saarbrücken to Merzig—a strip about twenty-five miles long and ten miles
wide, and a *gage* of dimensions so minuscule as to be absurd. It was also proposed to occupy the independent principality of Luxembourg, which the Germans had not threatened, in order "to shelter it from German invasion." These
two "operations," if such they could be called, would require the mobilization of
1,200,000 men, the expenditure of 30 million francs per day, and could not be
commenced until eight days after decisions taken. Full naval and air mobilization would be immediately necessary. The strength of the German forces in
the Rhineland was estimated at 90,000 army and 205,000 auxiliary troops, with
a "value" of twenty-seven to twenty-nine divisions.

The "note" did not analyze the value of a *prise de gages,* although it was at
best dubious, since it would not expel the Germans from the zone and would
appear as an invasion, but without decisive consequences. The Luxembourg idea
was especially preposterous, even though her prior consent was stipulated; the
world is cynical, and it surely would have been charged that the consent was
forced. It would have been France, not Germany, that sent troops into the territory of a small, helpless neutral. The 90,000 German "army" troops included

---

* Once again there is confusion about the date, as Sarraut puts the meeting on Monday,
March 9. But Gamelin and Maurin both put it on March 10, and the former's account
contains reference to a meeting that day of the Chamber of Deputies, which in fact occurred
not on the ninth but on the tenth. There is no transcript of the proceedings; Gamelin's,
Maurin's, and Sarraut's postwar recollections are the only available sources.

30,000 police of limited military value and 30,000 *Arbeitsdienst* of none. The 205,000 "auxiliaries" were once again the SS, SA, and Nazi Party motor corps members, none of whom were trained, armed, or organized for military service. The possibility that Poland and Czechoslovakia might join in the action was ignored. Even forty years later, the mind boggles that two officers of the supposed ability and integrity of Maurin and Gamelin could have put their names to so grossly inept and misleading a document.

Meanwhile the French Naval Staff were mulling over another question from Flandin, who had gone to London for the Locarno and Council meetings: "What naval measures of coercion, short of striking a blow, could be taken in conjunction with England and Italy, such as a *prise de gages,* blocking a port, occupying Helgoland, or seizing ships?" The inquiry was the subject of a long letter from Vice-Admiral Abrial in Paris to Vice-Admiral Robert, chief of the French delegation at the London Naval Conference.

Abrial was a bit scornful of Flandin's maritime naïveté, and described his question as offering "original themes for the students at the Naval College." But he was not wholly averse to the idea of collective action to check the Germans, and in this direction he had been somewhat encouraged by a talk that day with Léger, who told him that France had "a good chance not only to upset Hitler's triumph of bluff, with all its dangerous future consequences, but also, perhaps by honorable compromise, to strike a blow at Germany's strength and prestige, with good results for our future security."

But the idea of naval sanctions found no support either in Paris or London. Pietri solemnly warned Sarraut that they would amount to "naval warfare." Flandin found Stanley Baldwin unalterably opposed to any action that would involve "even one chance in a hundred that war would follow." England, he said, "is simply not in a state to go to war." Léger's advice to the admirals was a last flicker of the fire that Sarraut, Paul-Boncour, and Mandel had tried to keep burning under the generals.

By the time the Council of the League met in London, German troops had been in the Rhineland for a week, and the idea of a military riposte was dead. Both militarily and psychologically it was already too late; after staying her hand and invoking the Council, France could hardly resort to force once the deliberations had begun.

So the diplomatic charade in London played itself out. Germany was invited to state its case, and Ribbentrop, all injured innocence, denounced the Franco-Soviet treaty as "directed exclusively against Germany," and declared that Russia, "so far distant from Germany that she could not possibly be attacked by that country, has indirectly advanced to the German frontier by means of a similar military alliance with Czechoslovakia." Eventually, as often happens in courts of law, the plaintiff got the verdict but the defendant won the case. On March 19 the Council duly condemned Germany for her violations of Versailles and Locarno and requested her not to fortify the zone or increase her forces there, and to permit the Locarno powers to occupy a twenty-kilometer-wide strip on the German side of her French and Belgian frontiers. Hitler promptly rejected these proposals, and France came away from London with nothing but a letter by which the British Government agreed to consult about the "new situation," to hold military staff talks, and to come to France's aid in the event of "unprovoked aggression."

Flandin tried to use the last point to put a good face on things, but it was painfully apparent that it did not substantially broaden Britain's pre-existing commitments. In France the elections were only six weeks off, and the Rhineland question was soon consumed in the heat of the struggle between right and left.

13

If democratic governments should always conform to the dictates of "instant public opinion," Gamelin and Maurin and their like-minded colleagues of the sea and air should not be too much blamed for the débacle of March 7, 1936. From one end to the other of the political spectrum the cry for peace was unanimous; no important voice was raised in support of Sarraut's call, if such it was, to push the Germans back from Strasbourg.

For the right, by now violently opposed to the Franco-Soviet pact, the answer was simple: it was this scandalous treaty that had forced Hitler to do what he did, and to oppose him would be to join with the communists against the one man who was fending them off. "We do not have to march against Hitler with the Soviets," wrote Charles Maurras in the royalist *Action Française.* "Above all we do not want war!" And the same theme was echoed by *Gringoire, Le Jour,* Henri de Kerillis of *Epoque,* and the rest of the right-wing press. The conservative Paris daily *Le Matin* headlined Hitler's denunciation of communism rather than France's loss of the Rhineland guaranty. Daladier and the Radical-Socialists endorsed the Government's handling of the situation, as did the labor unions and veterans' organizations.

Farther to the left the German action was denounced, but counteraction was held to be desirable only through the League and the mechanisms of collective security; seemingly nothing had been learned from the Ethiopian sanctions fiasco. "Hitler has torn up a treaty and broken all his promises, but at the same time he speaks of peace and Geneva," declared the socialist organ *Le Populaire:* "We must take him at his word." Léon Blum, recovering from a brutal physical attack by right-wing goons, wrote that Hitler's act was a violation of international law, which it was the province of the League to handle. The communist *L'Humanité* carried articles by Jacques Duclos, Maurice Thorez, and others, calling for collective economic sanctions while denouncing "those who wish to foment war and massacre."

Thus, on the right, fear of communism devoured fear of Nazi Germany and made Adolf Hitler into a *defensor fidei,* while on the left internationalism and pacifism blinded its adherents to the weakness of the League and caused them to forget the intrinsic nature and purpose of the Rhineland guarantee. It is the function of political leaders to illumine the issues and to exploit their access to facts, and France was not wholly lacking in men able to do that. Sarraut and Flandin made an effort—they were not great men and it was a feeble one—to make their fellow-countrymen, and their British allies, aware of what was at stake, and take action with the speed and resolution that the situation required. One may criticize them for yielding too readily, but at least they tried.

The record of the French military leaders in this affair is lamentable. At the height of the crisis, Gamelin told the Army General Staff: "At all costs we must make sure that none can say that Army did not dare to march." In retrospect, it is hard to see how one can say anything else.

Their fears, to be sure, were largely the consequence of their own earlier blunders. They failed to give France a mobile striking force; they burdened her with a system that deprived even the infantry divisions on the frontier of the ability to move until their complement of men and equipment was filled out by a partial mobilization—the sacred *couverture*—that would take eight days. The Rhineland stipulations, however, were of no value to an army that was purely defensive; of what use was it to forbid the Germans to fortify their frontier if the French had no thought of crossing it? And how could France's treaties with Poland and Czechoslovakia be justified or fulfilled without the arms to make them meaningful? The French generals gave their country a shield, and then struck from her hands the sword she needed to honor her commitments and even to defend herself.

More than any one man, Pétain was to blame, but of course the responsibility for keeping him so long in office was widely shared. Furthermore, Weygand had succeeded him in 1931, and Gamelin became Army Chief of Staff five years before Hitler sent those few battalions across the Rhine bridges. They had ample time to cure the worst of these ills, but lacked the will and wit to do so.

When the day came, badly prepared as they were, the stakes were so high, and Germany's weakness so manifest, that the French commanders should, if nothing better offered, have loaded their men into trucks and sent them across the border. They would have had no difficulty in driving out the small German contingents, and, as we now know, they probably would not even have had to do that; the German troops were not in combat deployment, and would surely have been ordered to retreat if the French moved in.

But Gamelin did not dare to improvise, and it was fear that the Cabinet might ask him to move, by any means available, which probably explains the woeful inaccuracy and superficiality of his reports, alarmist and discouraging as they were. Thus in picturing the risks of war he pointed to Germany's greater industrial capacity, without mentioning that, with the Rhineland under French occupation and much of the Ruhr within the range of French guns, this advantage would be greatly diminished—that this consequence, indeed, was one of the prime purposes of the remilitarization stipulations.

Gamelin's estimates of comparative French and German military strength never took account of the Polish and Czechoslovakian forces, whose weight, especially in 1936, when the German panzer units were not yet ready, would have been very considerable.* In presenting the strength of the German Army,

* In his memoirs (*Servir,* vol. II., p. 213) Gamelin wrote "it is curious that I was not informed at the time of Poland's support." The statement itself is more "curious" than the circumstance it alleges. Especially since Poland and France had been linked since 1921 by both political and military conventions, one would suppose that France's responsible mili-

Gamelin contented himself with numerical at the expense of qualitative data, and thus made no reference to the fact that, in 1936, the trained components of the old Reichswehr had been broken up for use as cadres for the new units of the expanding Army, so that the German forces were in a state of training and transition, and in very poor shape for immediate combat.

Finally, Gamelin's inclusion of the Nazi Party "auxiliaries" in his calculation of German military strength was indefensible, and must have been disingenuous.* His own *couverture* might take eight days, but it would have taken months to equip and train the German labor corps, and most of the storm troop and motor corps members would have required a trip to Florida to drink at Ponce de Leon's fountain of youth before they would ever have been fit for combat.

In short, Gamelin in his advice to the Cabinet painted a picture far darker than reality, and held out as a *gage* only the left bank of the Saar River—a useless prize, and one which could not be taken for eight days. Small wonder the Cabinet did not buy, and Gamelin's attempt in his memoirs to saddle Sarraut with the blame is, to put it mildly, very unseemly.

However the blame he apportioned, the consequences of inaction were disastrous for France and her eastern allies alike. Gamelin himself saw this clearly enough at the time; at a meeting of the chiefs of staff on April 30 he observed that, as soon as the Germans had fortified the Rhineland, they would be able "to contain the French Army with reduced strength, and thus to attack Czechoslovakia and Poland." There were equal awareness and deeper concern in Eastern Europe. The day after the Germans crossed the Rhine, Ambassador Noël was warning Paris that, if nothing were done, "Poland, after having shown her fidelity to the alliance, will find in these events an occasion and a pretext for new political combinations and maneuvers." After it became clear that the French would let the matter pass and that the German coup had succeeded, there were messages of consternation from Warsaw, Bucharest, Belgrade, Prague, and Vienna.

It was a sorry legacy, foreign and domestic, military and political, that Laval, Flandin, and Maurin left to the government of Léon Blum, which took office early in June, following the triumph of the left in the May elections. And as if the old problems were not difficult enough, Blum had barely six weeks in office before he and his colleagues were confronted by the new and wrenching issues posed to France by the Spanish Civil War—an event which would once again illustrate France's dependence on Britain, and which further accelerated the decline of the Third Republic.

---

tary leaders could and would keep themselves well informed of Poland's military capacity and intentions. Furthermore, Gamelin was in constant touch with Léger at the Foreign Ministry, a man who surely was well informed and, by Gamelin's own account, was strongly in favor of military action.

  * It is noteworthy that, in their estimate of Germany's effective military strength on January 18, the Army General Staff included neither the storm troopers nor the motor transport port "corps" and showed a total "auxiliary" strength in all Germany of 240,000. By including those two components in the estimate of March 11, Gamelin showed 205,000 "auxiliaries" in the Rhineland alone.

CHAPTER 8

Sawdust Caesar

1

History is a tale that has neither beginning nor end; historians seek in vain the perfect point of departure. On a longish cast, one might do worse than pick the secret Treaty of London, signed April 26, 1915, as the first link in the chain of events leading directly to the Rome-Berlin "Axis" and Italy's alignment with Germany at the time of Munich.

When the First World War began, Italy was bound in the Triple Alliance with Germany and Austria-Hungary. But Italy had never regarded the alliance as requiring her to make war against England; in those days Britain really ruled the waves, and Italy had a coastline of some 2,500 miles, more than four times the length of her land frontiers. Furthermore, the Triple Alliance was for mutual defense, while the Austrian ultimatum to and declaration of war against Serbia were very arguably aggressive and therefore put Italy under no obligation. As the guns of August began to thunder, the Italian Government declared neutrality.

But Italy had territorial claims against Austria, and ambitions in the eastern Mediterranean lands and in Africa. Before the war was six months old, Italian representatives were chaffering like Arabs in a bazaar, in Vienna for the price of continued neutrality, and in London for the price of joining the Allied cause. Since most of what Italy wanted would be given at Austria's expense, the Allies did not find it hard to better the offers from Vienna and Berlin. Four weeks after the Treaty of London was signed, Italy declared war against Austria-Hungary.

Although the treaty was not published during the course of the war, its general outlines soon became known in European diplomatic circles. It was in fact an Italian memorandum accepted by the three Entente powers (Britain, France, and Russia),* and it provided that for Italy the fruits of victory should include the Trentino, the Italian Tyrol, Trieste and the Istrian Peninsula, the province of Dalmatia, the Albanian city of Valona and a virtual protectorate over Albania, and the Dodecanese Islands. Furthermore, Italy was to share "equitably"

---

* The document, comprising sixteen articles and accompanied by separate declarations of mutual undertaking not to conclude peace separately, was signed by the British Foreign Secretary, Sir Edward Grey, and the French, Italian, and Russian ambassadors in London.

in any spoils of war in Turkey and in parceling out Germany's African colonies among the victors.

If the Treaty of London had been respected at the Paris Peace Conference, there might well never have been a Duce, and even had there been one he surely would have acted otherwise than he did, for Italy would have been, like France, a "satisfied" power. But by the time the war ended, tsarist Russia was no more, the Austro-Hungarian Empire was disintegrating and the succession states were placing their claims to her former lands, the United States (in no way bound by the treaty) had entered the war, and Woodrow Wilson had projected the Fourteen Points and other principles of peacemaking that had little in common with the old-fashioned *Realpolitik* of which the treaty was a part.

Wilson did, to be sure, support Italy's claims to the Trentino and Tyrol, and the Italo-Austrian border was shifted north to the Brenner Pass, later to be celebrated as the site of Fuehrer-Duce meetings. But Italy got little else at Paris. Dalmatia was an integral part of newborn Yugoslavia, and it was by direct negotiations between Rome and Belgrade that their conflicting claims were eventually and very grudgingly adjusted. The Istrian Peninsula, including Trieste and adjacent Fiume, together with a few islands and the city of Zara, was annexed to Italy; they were welcome additions, but it was pretty small beer compared to the great expectations raised by the Treaty of London.

Perhaps less intrinsically important, but much more exasperating, was the lack of regard shown by Britain and France for Italy's aspirations in the eastern Mediterranean and in Africa. Italy was able to retain possession of the Dodecanese Islands, but got nothing on the mainland of Asia Minor, while her allies came off with League of Nations mandates in Syria and Palestine. In Africa, not one of the former German colonies was mandated to Italy. Nor was much sympathy shown for Italy's postwar economic distress; Wilson not only scotched her claims under the Treaty of London, but also turned a deaf ear to her pleas for a 50-million-dollar loan.

So Italy won victory but little glory on the battlefield, and suffered humiliating defeat at the green table. The war left her a legacy of resentment against her erstwhile allies, and of suspicion and antagonism toward her neighbors across the Adriatic. For France, the Treaty of Versailles was the keystone of security, and for the succession states it was the source of independence. But for Italy, Versailles was a bitter memory; that was where she had been cheated of the fruits of victory and treated like a second-class power. And thus were planted the seeds of "revisionism," which would come to flower in Ethiopia in 1935 and thereafter in the Rome-Berlin Axis, with all that followed from that fateful alignment.

2

Diplomatic defeat and the consequent territorial disappointments were not the only difficulties that beset postwar Italy. She was a poor country with few natural resources, and her chronic economic ills were greatly aggravated by the war-caused rise in the public debt, the diminution of normal markets in Germany and Austria, the drying-up of traditional emigration outlets, and the return of millions of soldiers to communities unable to employ them. Military service conditions were bad, and mutinies in a number of garrisons forced the government to evacuate the troops from Albania and give up the idea of annexation. In the cities there was deep industrial unrest, and in 1920 a wave of violent strikes, featured in northern Italy by the occupation of factories by the workers. In the countryside, there were bloody clashes between farm laborers and vigilante bands supported by the landowners. These bands were already called *Fascisti,* a name originally derived innocently enough from the word *fascio,* meaning a bound-together group.

Such were the circumstances and forces that Benito Mussolini exploited for his rise to power in the fall of 1922, just over a decade earlier than that of Hitler. They were two very different men with very different political methods, but there is an interesting parallel in that in both cases a situation developed in which the Chief of State—President Hindenburg in Germany, King Victor Emmanuel III in Italy—could see no feasible alternative to selecting as Premier the chief of a quasi-revolutionary minority party, one who had no prior cabinet experience.

Much more than Hitler, Mussolini fitted the classic mold of the European political agitator. His father Alessandro, an unschooled blacksmith, was an active and literate international socialist, and the future Duce was named for the Mexican revolutionary Benito Juárez. He was a violent, rebellious boy, and in 1902, at the age of eighteen, he threw over the teaching career for which he had qualified, and emigrated to Switzerland, where he lived hand to mouth, heard a few lectures by the economist Vilfredo Pareto, came under the tutelage of the Russian Marxist proselytizer Angelica Balabanoff, and picked up a bit of German and more than that of French. Upon his return to Italy a few years later he taught school, drifted into journalism, became a Socialist Party functionary, and served a short prison term for fomenting riots in Forlì. This won him the laurels of a Socialist martyr-hero and, upon his release, flowering oratorical talents moved him rapidly upward in the Socialist hierarchy. In December of 1912 he became editor of the party organ *Avanti,* in Milan.

When the First World War began, Mussolini at first assumed the general Socialist attitude of neutrality. Very soon, however, he shifted toward intervention on the Allied side. With the aid of French-provided funds he founded a new journal, the *Popolo d'Italia,* and joined with other interventionist leftists in creating *"Fasci"* of young men who demonstrated for war against Austria. In consequence, Mussolini was denounced by his Socialist colleagues and then expelled from the party. After Italy's declaration of war in the spring of 1915 he was called for military service, which he rendered creditably but without distinction until 1917, when he was wounded and discharged.

Back in his editor's chair in Milan, Mussolini used his paper to support the war effort and combat defeatism after the Italian disaster at Caporetto. When the war ended, he aligned himself with the returning veterans, some of whom were forming black-uniformed bands of so-called *Arditi* ("bold ones") who, rather like the German *Freikorps* of the same period, roamed the country in an adventuristic, freebooting way, often fighting with communist, socialist, and other proletarian groups. And it was with the aid of the *Arditi* that, in March of

1919, Mussolini founded what he then called the *Fasci di Combattimento* in Milan, as a new political movement.

The new organization had virtually no program, and its positions on the issues of the times followed no consistent pattern. It was against the Socialist Party from which Mussolini had been expelled, but not against socialist doctrine. The nationalist sentiments of the *Arditi* were reflected in Mussolini's denunciation of the French and English "plutocracies" and demands for the annexation of Dalmatia and the city of Fiume. The temper of the movement was one of activism for its own sake; as Mussolini himself wrote ten years later: "My own doctrine . . . had always been a doctrine of action."

Electorally, the Fascists were a flop. In the elections of November 1919 they failed to elect a single member of the Chamber of Deputies; Mussolini himself polled only 4,000 votes in Milan, against 180,000 for his Socialist opponent.

From this débacle Mussolini was rescued, albeit inadvertently, by the spectacular poet and *haut aventurier* Gabriele D'Annunzio. With the disposition of Fiume still unresolved by the great powers, in September 1919 D'Annunzio, at the head of about a thousand "troops"—a mixed bag of *Arditi* and regular army officers who had rallied to the poet's cause—marched across the Istrian border and occupied the city. D'Annunzio succeeded in holding it for fifteen months, as a self-appointed trustee for Italy, under an anomalous and highly eccentric "Regency."

The Italian Government repudiated D'Annunzio's action, but it was the sort of coup that appealed to the Italian sense of drama, and served well as a release for Italy's resentment against her treatment at Paris. Mussolini acclaimed D'Annunzio as a national hero, and declared that "the government of Italy is not in Rome but in Fiume." He flew there for talks which were of no intrinsic consequence, but which enabled the future Duce to see, absorb, and soon to emulate the extraordinary rituals of power with which D'Annunzio had invested his regime. There were banners galore, parades and rallies of *Arditi* in black shirts and fezzes, and daily speeches from the balcony of the government palace to excited throngs, with antiphony between the poet-orator and the audience: "To whom Fiume?" from the balcony, and the response "To us!" in a roar from the crowd, followed by the *Arditi* "war cry" *"Ayah! Ayah! Alala!"* There was also the forcible administration of castor oil to "purge" dissidents of wrong ideas.

In November 1920, Italy and Yugoslavia signed a treaty under which Fiume was to be an independent state, and the following month Italian forces blockaded and shelled the city. D'Annunzio departed into retirement on Lake Garda; he stayed in contact with Mussolini and the Fascist movement, but was gravely injured a few months later when he fell from a window of his villa and suffered a skull fracture, from which he never fully recovered. As D'Annunzio faded into obscurity, Mussolini was left the undisputed leader of the Fascist movement, and inherited many of the *Arditi* and "legionaries" of the Fiume venture.

Other developments were now playing into Mussolini's hands and contributing to the strength of the Fascist *squadre*. Continuing strikes and disturbances led to a general outcry for law and order, and landowners and industrialists alike were glad to subsidize Fascist assaults on farm and industrial labor unions and on left-wing political groups. As was later the case in Germany, many of the military were attracted by rightist activism, and the old-line conservative politicians were not sorry to see the Socialists thus beset. In the elections of May 1921, Mussolini polled 125,000 votes in Milan, and he and thirty-four other Fascists were elected to the Chamber.

If the electoral success was modest, the growth of the movement, especially in the north, was highly impressive. The "Fascist Revolution" now entered its most violent phase. Italo Balbo in Ferrara, Dino Grandi in Bologna, and Roberto Farinacci in Cremona were among the leading regional Fascist chieftains, and under them the Fascist *squadre* began to acquire a paramilitary organization that made larger operations possible. In May 1922, Balbo issued an ultimatum to the Italian Government to initiate a public works program to diminish unemployment in Ferrara, and then assembled over 60,000 armed Fascists who occupied the city and kept it in a state of total paralysis until, after some hours, the Government capitulated to Balbo's demands. It was the prototype of other such ventures in the northern cities, some successful and some less so, which rapidly established the Fascists as a *de facto* rival of the Government, some of whose officials sympathized more or less openly with the insurrectionists, while others lacked the will to take firm measures against a militant organization with growing popular support.

In July 1922, the government of Luigi Facta fell on a heavy adverse vote in the Chamber of Deputies. King Victor Emmanuel failed in his effort to find a successor who could put together a majority, and his redesignation of the uninspiring Facta was a confession of the bankruptcy of the parliamentary system. There was increasing public sentiment for a "strong man," and Mussolini now sensed that the time was ripe to seize power by force.

On October 16, 1922, he summoned Balbo and other Fascist luminaries to Milan to plan what was envisaged as a "March on Rome," at a secret conference attended also by two army generals (Fara and Ceccharini) on active duty, and a recently retired corps commander, General Emilio de Bono. The plan was to concentrate the Fascist militia at three points close to Rome—Civitavecchia for the forces from northwestern Italy, Monterodondo for those from the northeast, and Tivoli for those from the center and south. It was decided to postpone action until after the Fascist Party congress to be held on October 24 at Naples.

Perhaps as a hedge, perhaps to allay the suspicions and fears that rumors of these plans were generating, Mussolini now embarked on a course of bargaining in Rome for Fascist portfolios in a new cabinet to replace the Facta government. At the same time, he maintained the pressure by menacing speeches; in Naples he reviewed a march-past of 40,000 Fascist militia, and then told them that "the hour has struck" and that: "Either they will give us the government, or we shall take it, by falling on Rome." In his hotel room Mussolini held another meeting of his leading associates, at which a timetable was drawn up calling for mobilization at the three designated cities on October 27, and an advance toward Rome the next day.

By that date the Fascist mobilization was well under way, but Mussolini was convinced that he would not have to use force, and the timetable was extended by twenty-four hours. Facta and other old-line aspirants to his office were dickering frantically with Mussolini and each other. On October 28 Facta submitted to the King a proclamation that Rome was under siege, and drafted orders to the Army commanders to resist any Fascist moves toward the capital. But the King, advised of extensive military involvement in the Fascists' plans, refused to sign, and on October 29 the King's aide-de-camp sent word to Mussolini in Milan that he should come at once to Rome for appointment as President of the Council of Ministers. He departed that evening by train, and on his arrival in Rome the following morning, October 30, presented himself, clad in his black shirt, to King Victor Emmanuel at the Quirinal.

That evening he was back at the royal palace in a borrowed frock coat, to present his proposed cabinet. Of the fourteen ministers, only four were Fascists, and the King was well pleased with his new Premier, in whom he discerned "the will to act, and act well."

Meanwhile, the Fascist mobilization had been troubled by heavy rains, which caused numerous defections. Not more than 14,000 in all had reached the three assembly points; the Army would have had no difficulty in putting them to rout had its leaders wished to do so. Now the time had come to reward the faithful, and on October 31 they were brought into Rome and reviewed by King and Duce together, after which they were packed into trains and sent home.

3

When Benito Mussolini took office as Premier, he was but thirty-nine years old, and very short on political and administrative experience. He had been a member of the Chamber of Deputies for eighteen months, and leader of his party for three and a half years. As a journalist and orator he had of course dealt extensively with political questions, usually in a polemical or declamatory way. But he knew nothing of the machinery of government and, indeed, was virtually unknown to the official world in Rome.

He was equally a stranger to the world of diplomacy and, except for his prewar Swiss sojourn and a short visit to Berlin in 1922, he was untraveled. The Fascist proclamation of the March on Rome spoke of the "mutilated victory" of 1918, but the Party had no considered foreign policy. Nevertheless, Mussolini also took over the Ministry of Foreign Affairs, which he held until 1929.*

Ignorant as he was of diplomatic techniques and usages, Mussolini knew, perhaps better than the professional diplomats at the Palazzo Chigi, what style of foreign policy the Italian people wanted. Essentially, it was a question of style more than of substance, for although there was a general belief that Italy had been cheated of her just reward, there was no specific focus of territorial ambition other than Fiume. The great thing was to re-establish Italy in a proud posture, and see to it that her representatives behaved with dignity and were treated with the deference accorded to emissaries of the great powers.

* Mussolini also took the Ministry of the Interior, which he turned over to Luigi Federzoni in 1924 at the time of the Matteotti murder.

The Duce's personal style was remarkably—almost inordinately—suited to these ends. His magnificent brow, incandescent eyes, and prognathous facial structure bespoke the man of decision and iron will. With stern mien, head thrown back, and imperious walk and gesture, he was the very model of a Latinate dictator. He played with lions, took his horses over the jumps, swam in the waves, piloted airplanes, reviewed the troops, appeared with his handsome sons, received visitors in the largest imaginable office in the Palazzo Venezia, harangued the crowds from balconies à la D'Annunzio, and with great skill fostered the image of the protean superman who would revive the ancient Roman glories.

In keeping with these attitudes was Mussolini's behavior as he set out, a few weeks after becoming Premier, for the international conference on Turkey at Lausanne in Switzerland. En route he telegraphed to his distinguished seniors, Poincaré and Lord Curzon, a request that they meet with him the day before the conference was to open. They complied, and Mussolini emerged from the meeting with a communiqué stating that Italy would be treated as an equal—an "achievement" which pleased the Italian public as much as it exasperated the Italian diplomatic experts trailing after the Duce.

A year later, while an international commission was fixing the Greco-Albanian border, the Italian members were assassinated, apparently by Albanians but on Greek soil. At once Mussolini dispatched an ultimatum to the Greek Government, demanding humiliating apologies and an indemnity of 50 million lire. When the Greeks denied their responsibility and gave only partial acquiescence, the Italian Navy shelled and marines occupied the Greek island of Corfu. Once again the Italians were mightily pleased and, although the action was sharply criticized in the League Council, the Greeks were soon persuaded by the great powers to make apology and pay the indemnity, whereupon the Italians evacuated Corfu.

Meanwhile, the Italo-Yugoslav negotiations for establishment of the free city of Fiume had become deadlocked over boundary questions. In July 1923 Mussolini proposed that the city proper be annexed to Italy, and part of the port area be ceded to Yugoslavia. Soon thereafter he declared that unless the Yugoslavs should accept the office by September 15, he would act unilaterally. He was as good as his word; when the day came an Italian general took over the administration of Fiume. In January of 1924, by the Pact of Rome, Yugoslavia accepted the apportionment stipulated by Mussolini, and thus he finally put the seal of success on D'Annunzio's venture.

But none of these deeds was as bold as Mussolini made it appear to be, and at bottom his foreign policy was a cautious one, based on his awareness of Italy's economic and military weakness. He accepted without protest the 1923 Treaty of Lausanne, which confirmed Italy's sovereignty over the Dodecanese Islands, but gave no recognition to her claims, based on the 1915 Treaty of London, on the Asiatic mainland of Turkey. Italy's African claims, asserted under the same treaty, were adjusted with Britain on a very modest basis, involving the cession to Italy of Jubaland* and a favorable adjustment of the Libyan-

---

* The northeast province of Kenya, adjoining Italian Somaliland. The cession substantially enlarged the Italian colony and bettered its port facilities.

Egyptian border. Far from maintaining the bellicose attitude toward England that he had articulated in the immediate postwar period, Mussolini now proclaimed the "profound" friendship between the two countries. He had been so charmed at Lausanne by Lord and Lady Curzon that he undertook to learn English, and soon developed unusually warm personal relations with both Austen Chamberlain and the British Ambassador in Rome, Sir Ronald Graham.

Italy's African claims vis-à-vis France were not so readily adjusted, and Franco-Italian relations remained bedeviled by these and other questions until the brief honeymoon with Laval in 1935. But there were no major crises, and the two countries' common participation in the Locarno agreements manifested a general parallelism of outlook in Western Europe.

All in all, it would be fair to say that during Fascism's first ten years, Italian foreign policy, if not wholly passive, was far from aggressive. There were much sound and the semblance of fury, but little action. Perhaps the storm over the Corfu incident threw a scare into Mussolini, for not until twelve years later, when he launched the Ethiopian venture, did he risk a major European confrontation, and even then, in all probability, he did not expect the opposition that developed.

But the calm of this period was the product of prudence rather than disposition. The resentments and jealousies born at Paris and symbolized by the phrase "mutilated victory" (*vittoria mutilata*), the antidemocratic ideology of Fascism, and the Duce's yearning to play the Roman conqueror, all generated impatience with the *status quo* and sympathy with revisionism in principle, if not in all particulars.

The play of these factors may be seen in the Treaty of Friendship with Hungary, signed in 1927 and celebrated with a gala dinner in honor of the Hungarian President-Foreign Minister, Count Bethlen. The Duce admired the authoritarian, semifeudal regime of Admiral Horthy as much as he, the renegade Marxist, despised the socialist workers of Vienna who exposed the fact that Italy was secretly sending armaments to Hungary, in violation of the peace treaties. Furthermore, Hungary was the focal point of revisionism in Eastern Europe, because of the surgery inflicted upon her at Paris for the benefit of Yugoslavia, Czechoslovakia, and Rumania. The treaty with Hungary thus aggravated Italy's uneasy relations with Yugoslavia, as well as with France, champion and protector of the succession states.

It is hard to see what benefit Italy derived from the Hungarian alignment, much as it may have given Mussolini the childish pleasure of thumbing his nose at the French. Furthermore, there was no consistent thrust in Italian revisionism, for, as regards Germany and Austria, Italy was almost as much dedicated to the *status quo* as France herself. The extension of Italy's northern frontier to the Brenner Pass had brought within her borders some 200,000 German-speaking South Tyrolese. Fascism was not solicitous of cultural minority rights, and Tyrolese irredentism flourished in Bavaria as well as Austria. In common with the succession states, therefore, Italy stood categorically opposed to a restoration of the Hapsburg dynasty, signalizing as it would have the prospect of reviving the Austro-Hungarian imperium. And just as strongly Italy shared France's hostility to the union of Austria and Germany, for this would bring a greatly strengthened Germany instead of an impotent vestigial Austria to the other side of the Brenner Pass.

This extraordinary ambivalence in Italian policy was clearly reflected in Mussolini's speech to the Italian Senate in June of 1928, in which he openly espoused the general principle of treaty revision—"No treaty has ever been eternal, because the world moves on"—while at the same time emphasizing that: "There are, in the Peace Treaties, certain great accomplished facts which correspond to the highest reasons of justice, accomplished facts which remain such and which no one of us thinks of revoking or even of discussing." This was as much as to say that the *status quo* was sacred for what Italy had received at Paris, but not for things of which she had been cheated. To be sure, this was not an unnatural indication of self-interest, but it hardly provided a stable basis for friendship with any other European power.* And, indeed, Mussolini's foreign policy during these years was very much that of the lone wolf that he was in his personal life; Italy had no real friends. With Britain there was cordial acquaintance, but no working alliance in pursuit of common aims.

Internally, however, Mussolini had greatly strengthened his position. He had survived the scandal of the murder, by high-ranking Fascists in 1924, of the Socialist deputy Giacomo Matteotti. Thereafter, the slogans and other paraphernalia of Fascism sprouted and proliferated—the Fascist youth organization (*Balilla*), the workers' leisure program (*Dopolavoro*), the "Battle of Grain" to reduce imports and strengthen the currency, the banning of strikes pursuant to a spurious "Charter of Labor," the establishment of a Special Tribunal for political trials and the security police (*Ovra*), the incarceration of a lengthening list of political prisoners, the reclamation of the Pontine Marshes, and the fabrication of the rather creaky machinery of the Corporative State. In February of 1929, Mussolini and Cardinal Piero Gasparri signed the Lateran Agreements, ending the sixty-year impasse between the Church and the kingdom by the establishment of Vatican City and confirmation of Roman Catholicism as the state religion of Italy. It was a solid triumph for Mussolini, and marked the beginning of his time of greatest prestige.

In September 1929, Mussolini relinquished the Ministry of Foreign Affairs to his longtime Fascist associate Dino Grandi, who had been the Under-Secretary since 1925. Apparently the purpose of the change was to mitigate the incongruity of saber-rattling speeches for home consumption and an unadventurous, generally conciliatory foreign policy. At all events, the following year Grandi was assuring the London Naval Conference that Italy wished a tranquil world and a pacified Europe, and two years later at Geneva he put forward a comprehensive plan for the abolition of tanks, submarines, and bomber aircraft. Meanwhile, at home the Duce was telling the crowds in Leghorn and Florence that Italy "would form a compact mass that could be hurled against the rest of the world," and that "words are beautiful things, but rifles, guns, ships, and air-

---

* Mussolini did, however, display a curious and perhaps spurious prescience in predicting that "between 1935 and 1940 Europe would find herself at a very interesting and delicate point in her history."

planes are still more beautiful" and would "reveal to the world the calm and warlike countenance of Fascist Italy."

In fact, Italy was much richer in words than in arms, though naval construction was beginning, and the Air Force had had a face-lifting under the aegis of another early Fascist, Italo Balbo. Spectacular transatlantic flights by Balbo and attention-catching speeches at Geneva were making Balbo and Grandi too popular for the Duce's taste; in 1932 he took back the Foreign Ministry and sent Grandi off to London as Ambassador. The following year Balbo was put off the home stage by being appointed Governor General of Libya, and Mussolini took title to the Ministries of War and Air, with regular generals as Under-Secretaries.

And so the Duce's brow and jaw became Italy's physiognomy, on a head held high in a rapidly changing world. Across the Atlantic, Franklin D. Roosevelt was inaugurated President of the United States, but Mussolini was not impressed. "There are times when the masses must be told hard truths," he declared, banging his fist on the table, but Roosevelt "does not understand the psychology of the masses." In Berlin, a few hundred miles to the north, Adolf Hitler was the new Chancellor of the Reich. The Duce was pleased by his "imitator's" success, but condescending to the *nouvel arrivé:* "A man with Hitler's past must have a certain personal force," he told the Hungarian Foreign Minister, but nevertheless, judging by the radio speeches to which Mussolini had listened, the German "has a good style, but his ideas are a little commonplace."

4

On the record, Mussolini's condescension was not unwarranted. He was six years older than Hitler, and had become Prime Minister over a year before the dismal failure of the Munich "Beer Hall Putsch." When Hitler became Chancellor, Mussolini had been *Capo del Governo* for more than a decade. There is no evidence that Mussolini took any notice of the Nazis until their notable success in the 1930 elections, or any sustained interest in Hitler until 1932, when his accession to power began to appear possible.

Meanwhile, however, the Fuehrer-to-be had been burning incense to "the great man south of the Alps, who," as was written in *Mein Kampf,* "made no pacts with the enemies of Italy, but strove for their annihilation by all ways and means." Mussolini was to be ranked "among the great men of this earth," and the German "would-be statesmen" of the Weimar Republic were, in comparison, "miserable and dwarfish."

This admiration, furthermore, was redeemable in solid political currency. In the diplomacy of *Mein Kampf* and Hitler's later writings and speeches, Italy and Britain were Germany's two natural allies. Despite Nazism's pan-Germanism, the Brenner Pass was its southern limit, with no irredentism for the South Tyrol.

The Italo-German affinity was not, however, so perfect as Hitler liked to proclaim. In the very first paragraph of *Mein Kampf,* Hitler declared the reunion of Austria and Germany to be the "lifework" of his generation. It was in Eastern Europe that the Fatherland would conquer its *Lebensraum,* and this spelled the likelihood of conflict with Italy in the Balkans. The course of the Danube was the rift in the lute.

And so, as Hitler the Chancellor rapidly established himself as Hitler the Fuehrer of Germany, his fellow-dictator south of the Alps viewed these developments with very mixed feelings. Like Fascism, Nazism was antidemocratic, and that was good; the new Germany would be a counterpoise to the western democracies and Italy might more easily break away from the leading strings in which she was held by the French Army and the British Navy. Hitler had vowed that he would smash the Versailles *Diktat,* and that paralleled Mussolini's revisionist aims. But revisionism was a good thing of which there could be too much, and one had best keep a weather eye on the Austrian situation, where French and Italian interests were identical.

In Geneva, the disarmament talks were going badly. France and Germany were as much at loggerheads as ever, and British efforts at compromise were getting nowhere. No one knew just what Hitler's advent spelled in diplomatic terms, and everyone was casting about for some way to break the impasse. The time was ripe, thought Mussolini, for Italy to take the center of the stage, and for him to launch his first major diplomatic initiative in the councils of Europe.

5

When Mussolini sent Grandi to London and took back the reins at the Foreign Ministry, he brought to the Palazzo Chigi two men—Fulvio Suvich and Pompeo Aloisi—who were to be his chief assistants on foreign affairs for the next four years. Suvich, a Fascist deputy from Trieste with experience as a delegate to the League of Nations, was made Under-Secretary. Aloisi, a patrician Roman and career diplomat who had served as Ambassador to Japan, became *chef de cabinet* and chief of the Italian delegation to the League.

Early in March of 1933, Mussolini retired to his mountain retreat at Rocca della Caminate for a weekend of winter sports, and upon his return proudly handed to Suvich the draft of a "Political Pact of Understanding and Collaboration between the Four Western Powers." Invoking the spirit of the League Covenant and the Kellogg-Briand Pact, the significant provisions of the Duce's brainchild affirmed "the principle of revision of peace treaties" in order to avoid war, recognized Germany's claim to equal rights in the implementation of disarmament, and pledged the four powers (Britain, France, Germany, and Italy) to seek common policies, political and nonpolitical, in and outside of Europe.

From the Italian standpoint, the attractions of such a treaty were numerous. It would commit Britain and France in principle to the idea of revisionism, which Mussolini had long been advocating, and which was the principal aim of Hungarian and—far more important—of German foreign policy. The establishment of a concert of the four western powers would tend to downgrade the League of Nations, where the smaller nations could speak and act to some effect, and diminish the influence of France and the Little Entente and other lesser powers allied with her. At the same time, the Pact might better enable Italy to engage with France in preserving Austrian independence.

Mussolini's original intention was to send the draft first to Berlin for Hitler's

approval, and then bring the British and French prime ministers (Ramsay Mac-
Donald and Edouard Daladier) to Turin to sign the accord. The first part of the
program began well enough, for revisionism and German "equality" of armaments were congenial themes in Berlin. But they were much less so in Paris, and
of course the coupling of revisionism with a concert of four *western* powers, including Germany, sent a shudder of apprehension through the eastern capitals
—an anxiety no whit allayed by the circumstance that the Duce was telling his
visitors that Germany ought to be given a coastal corridor to connect West and
East Prussia, and Hungary should be ceded the contiguous areas with a
"Magyar" majority.

Confronted with resurgent German nationalism, the French had no desire to
rebuff Mussolini. They played it cool, and instead of rejecting the draft out of
hand, set about extracting the poison by eliminating the explicit references to
"revision" and German "parity," and turning the document into little more than
an undertaking of mutual consultation.

Of course, the more the revisionist sting was drawn, the less attractive the
pact appeared in Berlin. Hitler was increasingly disenchanted, and on the eve of
the scheduled initialing of the treaty it was touch and go whether he would
agree. In the upshot he did, and the pact was initialed on June 7 and signed on
July 15, 1933, by Mussolini and the British, French, and German ambassadors
in Rome. The signatories undertook to "consult together" for a period of ten
years "within the framework of" and "without prejudice to decisions which can
only be taken by" the League of Nations, and to "re-examine" questions left
unresolved by the Disarmament Conference. The Duce was denied his hoped-
for conclave of prime ministers, but put a good face on things by a speech to the
Italian Senate in which he contended valiantly if unconvincingly that the amendments had not destroyed the revisionist thrust of the agreement as originally
drafted.

However stunted his brainchild, Mussolini was undeniably the author of a
pact signed by the four major western powers, and that, for him, was the main
thing. But it still had to be ratified and, while that was a routine matter in Rome
and Berlin, it was far from such in London and Paris. Within a few weeks the
Quai d'Orsay was warning the French Ambassador in Rome, Count Charles de
Chambrun, that, failing some plain evidence of Italo-French co-operation,
ratification would be difficult.

Ratification was soon proved not only difficult but impossible. Mussolini had
hoped that the four-power concert would be able to break the disarmament impasse, but in the event disarmament was the rock on which the pact foundered,
and it was Adolf Hitler who did the steering. For him, Geneva was primarily
important as a forum in which to expose French unwillingness to disarm and
thus lay the basis for denouncing the Versailles arms restrictions. By the fall of
1933 he had concluded that Geneva and the League itself had outlived their
usefulness for this purpose, and on October 14, Germany withdrew from both
the Conference and the League of Nations.

It was a deathblow to disarmament, and it killed off the Four-Power Pact as
well, for its preamble and articles were replete with references to the "respon-

sibilities" and "obligations" assumed by the parties under the Covenant of the League, from which Germany had now withdrawn. Apart from the juridical aspect it could hardly be expected that France would remain in any mood to "consult" with Germany on disarmament or other burning issues of the moment.

The Duce's cherished handiwork lay in ruins, and he was furious. To make matters worse, because of bungling at the Wilhelmstrasse, Ambassador von Hassell gave Mussolini advance warning only of the withdrawal from the Disarmament Conference and not from the League, and when the full news reached him, the belief that he had been deceived put him in a rage. Aloisi described Hitler's action as "stupefying," and Suvich, on Mussolini's instructions, read Hassell a stern lecture, the burden of which was that Hitler's "absurd gesture" had shattered all existing bases of negotiation among the great powers. On October 21, Sir Ronald Graham, who had enjoyed the best of relations with Mussolini, had a "farewell interview" at which Germany was still the focus of the Duce's wrath:*

. . . when we came to talk of Germany I have rarely seen His Excellency show more annoyance and disgust. He said Germans by their precipitate action had broken three windows, those of the Conference, the League of Nations and the Four-Power Pact. They now expected him to pick up the pieces but he refused to do anything of the kind. Von Papen had said to the Italian Ambassador at Berlin that now was the moment to operate the Pact. Signor Mussolini entirely disagreed, he refused to take any initiative whatever and intended to maintain an attitude of complete reserve. He had designed the Pact within the ambit of the League. . . .

His Excellency said that . . . he had stretched every point to help Germany, and the only thanks he got were a series of German actions calculated to injure Italian interests and susceptibilities. . . . He added that Italian sympathies, which had at one time been attracted to Germany, were cooling down and would become more and more frigid. . . .

6

Mussolini's efforts to launch the Four-Power Pact led to his first experience with the business end of the Nazi regime. It was a painful episode, and he had made this abundantly plain to Hassell for the benefit of his superiors in Berlin.

A few weeks later a messenger of peace appeared in Rome in the person of Hermann Goering, bearing a personal letter from the Fuehrer to the Duce—the first of many such during their time of power. Thanks for Italy's "valuable support for the German nation" were coupled with apologetic explanations of the failure to inform Mussolini of the decision to quit the League; justification of this step was the principal content of the letter. Goering's two meetings with Mussolini on this occasion were at best "correct," and the records of what was said embody the contradictions of wishful thinking, for Suvich described as a "triumph for Mussolini" Goering's statement that Germany would disavow in

---

* Sir Ronald was being replaced by Sir Eric Drummond (soon, by inheritance, to become the Earl of Perth), who had been Secretary-General of the League of Nations since its birth in 1919.

writing all desire to annex Austria, while on his return to Berlin, Goering reported that he had told Mussolini that "ultimately the union of Germany and Austria could not be prevented."

In December, Suvich repaid Goering's visit with a quick trip to Berlin. He was treated with great courtesy, but the ubiquitous brown and black SA and SS uniforms left him with the impression of Germany as an "armed camp," and Austria remained a bone of contention in his talk with Hitler. No rapport was achieved. Goering had asked Mussolini to recall his ambassador in Berlin, Vittorio Cerruti, who had become *persona non grata,* but no change was made. In February 1934, Cerruti told Neurath that German-Italian relations were "worse than they had been in many years," and the two men had an unpleasant exchange with mutual threats of altered policies unless there were a "change of attitude." The following month Cerruti's warning was given substance by the signature of a pact of economic and political co-operation among Italy, Austria, and Hungary.

At the end of March, Vice-Chancellor Franz von Papen passed through Rome en route to a spring vacation in southern Italy. A chance encounter with Mussolini at the opera led to discussions the next day in the course of which Papen proposed a personal meeting between the two dictators, to establish direct contact and explore troublesome questions such as Austria and disarmament. Mussolini reacted favorably, and after considerable arranging and rearranging, agreement was reached for a meeting near Venice in mid-June.

Since long before he came to power Hitler had been hoping for such an occasion; Filippo Anfuso, vice-consul in Munich in 1927, recalled Hitler's vain angling for an invitation at that time. The Duce had turned a deaf ear until Hitler became Chancellor, and then Germany's scuttling of the Four-Power Pact dampened his enthusiasm for the idea. But he still nurtured hope of reviving the four-power concert, and by the spring of 1934 was at least curious enough to welcome the opportunity for a closer look at the *nouvel arrivé.*

Hitler, for his part, was now ambivalent, and finally agreed to the meeting on the basis of "guidelines" which stipulated that the purpose of the encounter was to be "personal acquaintance and contact," that disagreements about Austria could not be adjusted "as long as a regime is at the helm in Austria which suppresses the National Socialist system," and that there were to be "no ovations of any sort" in the course of the visit.

Hitler and Neurath apparently anticipated a very informal if not casual reception, for they arrived at the Venice airport in mufti—the Fuehrer himself in a belted raincoat and carrying an unimpressive gray fedora. He cut a very poor figure beside the Duce, resplendent in his honorary Fascist corporal's uniform, and Hitler's experience in international ceremonial likewise put him at a disadvantage in comparison to Mussolini, who by now was an old hand at receiving foreign dignitaries.

Things were off to an awkward start, and they were not improved by the site of the opening luncheon and conference—the eighteenth-century Villa Pisani at Stra, a few miles east of Padua. The Tiepolo frescoes were admired, but the old villa was rundown and infested with mosquitoes—"as big as quail," according to Anfuso—who showed the distinguished visitors no respect, and forced transfer of the next day's proceedings to Venice, where Hitler was put up at the Grand Hotel.

Mussolini later told Suvich that at his initial reception Hitler's eyes were full of tears, and remarked "that is his weakness." But in taking the tears, if tears they were, as a sign of softness, Mussolini was sadly misled, for beyond question Hitler was the harder of the two. Mussolini was a ruthless, treacherous egomaniac, but he was not, as Hitler was, demonic. If the Duce had a mistress, he also had a wife and children, and was susceptible to nepotism. He could strike Caesarian poses, but offstage he was an insecure and lonely man. His ambition, though colossal, worked within established bounds. Thus he accepted and, indeed, was faithful to the monarchy, and he thought the Nazis' hostility to the Jews and the Christian churches both rash and reprehensible.

Hitler deliberately eschewed the family and friendly amenities, and saw great institutions like the church not as immutable limiting factors, but as antiquated nuisances, to be rendered impotent or destroyed. He took himself and his own ideas far more seriously than did Mussolini, about whom there always hung a suspicion of play-acting. The Duce had marvelous panache, but his mastery of the techniques of gaining and holding power was not matched with purposefulness in its exercise. As a dictator he was a bit of a dilettante, while Hitler, had he been a medieval monarch, would surely be remembered as "Adolf the Terrible."

Mussolini prided himself on his linguistic accomplishments, so interpreters were dispensed with and the two leaders talked privately in German. Hitler had no such petty vanity, and no doubt was well pleased to deal in a language which he used far more proficiently than his host. For historians the unhappy consequence is that we know only what the two principals later told the subordinates about the conversations.

Despite some discrepancies, however, it is clear that during their first conversation—at the Villa Pisani in the afternoon of June 14, 1934—Hitler did most of the talking, the conversation centered on Austria, and disagreement was obvious and left unresolved. Hitler did concede that no question of *Anschluss* was ripe for discussion, but he insisted that Dollfuss must go, and that the Austrian Nazis be given participation in the Government*—demands which Mussolini "took note of" but to which he did not agree.

The following day the two men had another afternoon tête-à-tête at the Alberoni Golf Club on the Lido. Mussolini was more talkative, and the subjects—disarmament, the League of Nations, shortcomings of the British, French, and Russians—less controversial. Hitler gave a strong hint of things to come in declaring that disarmament was not worth discussing, because "in seven or eight months the question would no longer trouble him." Later that afternoon there was a huge reception at the Doges' Palace. The Piazza San Marco was "stuffed like an egg," and the Fuehrer had a chance to view the Duce's magic with the

---

* According to Neurath's memorandum in the Wilhelmstrasse files, Hitler also asked that Mussolini "withdraw the protecting hand he had held over Austria," but this bold if not insulting request is not mentioned in other accounts.

crowd and hear him declare, rather condescendingly, that his meeting with
Hitler "was not destined to redraw the map of Europe"—an oblique reference
to Austria, the significance of which could hardly have been lost on his auditors.

That evening Hitler gave Mussolini a dinner at the Grand Hotel, which Aloisi
thought "very cold" because of Hitler's lack of personality, and the next day the
Fuehrer flew off to Munich and a sea of domestic troubles. Anfuso describes his
visit to Venice as a "disaster"; perhaps that is an overstatement, but there can
be no quarrel with Aloisi's verdict that "none of the current problems had received even the beginning of a solution." The official circulars stressed the two
leaders' mutual agreement that "the Austrian question must not be allowed to
hinder the development of German-Italian relations," but this was only wishful
thinking, as events were soon to prove.

7

Two weeks after the Venice meeting, Adolf Hitler had his bloody rendezvous
with Ernst Roehm at Bad Wiessee, and the "Night of the Long Knives" began.
As news of the massacre and of Hitler's personal part in it reached Rome,
Mussolini appears to have been genuinely shocked; according to his sister Ed-
vige, he declared Hitler "a cruel and ferocious character who calls . . . Attila to
mind," adding: "Those men he killed were his closest collaborators, who
hoisted him to power. It is as if I came to kill with my own hands Balbo,
Grandi, Bottai!" The pederastic proclivities of Roehm and his associates and
the summary executions without trial especially offended Aloisi, and after making his diplomatic rounds Hassell was obliged to report to Berlin that "the
events of June 30 cast what I would call a shadow over the days at Venice."

The shadow turned pitch black on July 25, 1934, when Austrian Nazis, in the
course of an unsuccessful *Putsch,* killed Chancellor Dollfuss. His assassination
was the outcome of the Nazi terror in Austria for which Mussolini believed
Hitler to be responsible, and his rage was all the greater in that Dollfuss had
been expected to visit Italy that very week, and his wife was already Mussolini's
guest, to whom he himself had to break the news.

The Italian Government promptly issued a communiqué stating that "movements of land and air forces were ordered towards the Brenner and Carinthia
frontier districts"—a statement which exaggerated the military actualities* but
nonetheless gave point to Italy's determination to protect the Austrian Government against forceful overthrow, whether the force came from inside or outside
the Austrian borders. Mussolini, who had muzzled the newspapers at the time of
the Roehm purge, now gave them free rein. Sir Eric Drummond reported to
London that never in his experience had the press been so violently anti-German, and Hassell visited the Palazzo Chigi to make a sharp, but futile, protest.

The proximate consequence of the Italo-German estrangement was that Italy

---

* Biographers of Mussolini and other writers on the period have generally taken the Italian *communiqué* at face value, and have even stated that the Italians "mobilized." But Sir
Eric Drummond's dispatches, based on information from Italian military sources, indicate
clearly that there were already a number of Alpine divisions on training maneuvers near
the Austrian frontier, and that the military significance of routine movements was inflated
in the *communiqué* for political reasons.

drew closer to Britain and France, and especially the latter. At Venice, Mussolini and Hitler had agreed that to admit the Soviet Union to the League would simply give the Russians a new platform for communist propaganda, but a few months later, when Barthou began his campaign to bring Russia into the League, Mussolini directed Aloisi to support the move. In September, Britain, France, and Italy joined in reaffirming an earlier joint declaration in support of "the independence and integrity of Austria." Toward the end of the year, French and Italian diplomats began negotiations looking to an accord which would settle Italy's long-standing African claims and lay the basis for stable and friendly relations between the two countries. In January 1935 these efforts were crowned with success when Pierre Laval came to the Italian capital and reached an accord with Mussolini.

Meanwhile, relations between Italy and Germany were going from bad to worse. Hassell saw Mussolini in October and again in December; each time his reports to Berlin were gloomy. The Duce "greatly distrusted Germany's policy in southeast Europe," accused the Nazi Party organization of whipping up anti-Italian sentiment, and went so far as to voice fear that German rearmament might lead to an attack against Italy.

In such an atmosphere of distrust, it was hardly surprising that Italy joined with Britain and France in condemning Hitler's repudiation of the Versailles arms restrictions by his pronouncement of March 16, 1935, on the reinstitution of military conscription and the program for a thirty-six division army. On March 21 the Italian Government transmitted to Berlin a formal note making "the most comprehensive reservations with regard to the German government's decision and its probable consequences," and characterizing the action as "particularly grave . . . in view of the state of uncertainty which it is arousing in all countries."

Indeed, it was on Italian soil—at Stresa, near the Swiss border—that Mac-Donald, Simon, Laval, and Flandin met with Mussolini to condemn "unilateral repudiation of treaties which may endanger the peace of Europe," and reaffirm their joint resolve to support Austria's independence. Three days later, on April 17, 1935, the three nations pointed the finger of blame directly toward Berlin when the Council of the League met at Geneva. France, Britain, and Italy jointly submitted a resolution declaring that Germany's reintroduction of conscription was contrary to her international obligations and must be regarded as a threat to European security.

Thus was born the "Stresa Front," which momentarily completed Germany's diplomatic isolation. From Rome, Hassell sent his superiors a bleak appraisal:

> The deterioration of German-Italian relations, which has been apparent for about a year, has recently reached a climax. Italy . . . today sees in German armaments an overt threat and is campaigning against the German action almost as energetically as in France. Fascism, which longed for National Socialism to come to power and greeted its advent with joy, now generally views it with criticism and hostility. Mussolini, who raised the claim for revision of treaties, now seems to have gone over to the conservative camp of the defenders of Versailles.

It was a fair appreciation of Mussolini's attitude.* Early in May he was telling his subordinates that the bridges between Italy and Germany were all down; that if Germany wished to co-operate for the peace of Europe, so much the better, but otherwise we will crush her, for from now on we are completely on the side of the western powers."

In the spring of 1935, nothing could have seemed a more remote possibility than the imminent collapse of the Stresa Front and the establishment, eighteen months later, of the "Rome-Berlin Axis."

8

Soon after he came to power, in all probability, Mussolini began to contemplate the conquest of Ethiopia.† For him as for all Italian nationalists, the defeat inflicted by Emperor Menelik at Adowa in 1896 was an enduring humiliation. With most of northern Africa in French or British hands, Ethiopia was the only area available for new colonial adventures, and its annexation would give Italy an African empire of contiguous units and considerable dimensions.

By January 1933, if not sooner, Mussolini began to transmute dreams into plans. A secret committee, headed by the Minister of Colonies, General Emilio de Bono, had been studying the military situation. A new minister, Count Luigi Vinci-Gigliucci, was being sent to Addis Ababa, and the Duce gave him his instructions in the presence of Suvich and Aloisi. Count Vinci's task would be to allay all suspicions and by an open policy of friendship to mask the plans that would be laid in Rome. Mussolini did not fully share the optimism in military circles, but expressed his belief that a war with Ethiopia would be successful "on condition that we are completely free in Europe."

These last few words are crucial to an understanding of Italian foreign policy during the next few years, and demonstrate the close connection, in Mussolini's mind, between his Ethiopian ambitions, on the one hand, and on the other the Four-Power Pact, the Rome accord with France, and the Stresa Front. Mussolini wanted peace in Europe not only for its own sake, but also so that he could make war in Africa. If a large part of the Italian armed forces were to be committed in Ethiopia, Mussolini would have to cover his rear, especially on the Austrian and Yugoslav frontiers, and the Four-Power Pact was intended to accomplish just that.

When Hitler tore up the pact by quitting Geneva and the League, and compounded the evil by fomenting disorders that threatened the survival of Austria, Mussolini had nowhere to turn for the security he needed except to France. Faced with a rearming Germany, the Quai d'Orsay was eager enough to patch things up, but negotiations were interrupted by the assassination of Barthou, and it was not until the late fall of 1934 that the project was taken up in ear-

---

* It is noteworthy that, throughout this period of general hostility between the two governments, Mussolini remained on good terms with the German diplomatic and military representatives in Rome, especially the latter. Like many others, he hoped that the Reichswehr leaders would exercise a restraining influence on Hitler and, despite his growing anxiety over German rearmament, he allowed Italian airfields to be used for clandestine training of the nascent Luftwaffe.

† In a speech to the Italian Chamber in 1935, Mussolini declared that it was in 1925 that he "began to examine the [Ethiopian] problem."

nest. Then several difficulties arose, especially Laval's insistence on the improvement of Italy's relations with Yugoslavia, and participation of the Little Entente in the protection of Austria. As late as December 14, 1934, Mussolini was unwilling to agree on either point.

That very day, however, Emperor Haile Selassie, frustrated by Italy's refusal to submit to arbitration the issue of responsibility for the border clash at Wal Wal earlier in December, brought the dispute before the Council of the League of Nations. Then, on December 20, Mussolini drew up his secret directive for "the total conquest of Ethiopia." These developments underscored Mussolini's need for French support, and on Christmas Day he advised Aloisi that "this Abyssinian affair will ripen when we have concluded the agreement with France," and directed him to speed up the negotiations.

As 1934 drew to a close, Mussolini grew almost frantic in his anxiety for a treaty—almost any treaty, it seemed. On December 29 he gave way on a cardinal point by agreeing that both the League and the Little Entente should participate in the agreement for the protection of Austrian independence. On this last day of the year, there still were stubborn questions; Aloisi feared a rupture, but Mussolini told Suvich that he wanted an accord "at any price." The basis was finally settled on January 2, and two days later Laval arrived in Rome to conduct the final negotiations.

The Rome agreements reached on January 7 were, as has already been seen, an apparent diplomatic triumph for the French. Mussolini settled for a song Italy's colonial claims from the First World War: a piece of worthless desert for Libya, a bit of coastline for Eritrea, other odds and ends. The only rational explanation, and one that is borne out by subsequent events, is that Laval gave informal assurance with respect to Italy's expanding influence in Ethiopia—assurances which were not very explicit,* and the intended scope of which it is now impossible to determine.

Whatever actually passed between Laval and Mussolini in private, Mussolini concluded that he had what he needed to proceed, and General de Bono left for Eritrea at once. In February the transportation of troops and matériel began, and General Rodolfo Graziani was sent to Italian Somaliland to take command of the southern front. Early in May, Mussolini wrote to De Bono that five regular and five Black Shirt divisions would be sent to Eritrea and that the attack should be made in September or October.

From Italy to East Africa the water route was through the Mediterranean and the Suez Canal, and the air flight line crossed Egypt; Britain controlled Egypt and the canal and the Royal Navy dominated the Mediterranean. What would her attitude be, as Mussolini's intentions unfolded? Dino Grandi's early soundings in London were discouraging; Britain was a pillar of the League of Nations, and the British public would be outraged by Italian aggression in the old imperialist manner that had won Britain her own empire.

---

* Aloisi, who participated extensively in the negotiations, wrote nothing about any general understanding on Ethiopia in his diary, which contains many entries on highly secret matters. The Hoare-Laval fiasco precipitated a lively exchange of private letters between Mussolini and Laval, the texts of which are given in Lagardelle, *Mission à Rome Mussolini* (1955), pp. 275-87.

An opportunity to probe if not persuade the British official mind had been presented at Stresa. Although Germany's denunciation of the Versailles arms limitations was the *raison d'être* of the meeting, the Italian delegation was prepared to discuss Ethiopia if the British so desired. When no such desire was shown, Mussolini himself raised the issue inferentially by reading the draft declaration that the three powers would oppose "any unilateral repudiation of treaties which may endanger the peace," and proposing to add the limiting words "of Europe." The British—MacDonald, Simon, and Sir Robert Vansittart—sat silent; Mussolini wrote the words in, as they appeared in final published declaration, and drew the conclusion that the British had tacitly indicated their lack of concern for the fate of Ethiopia. Both surprised and pleased, he chided Grandi for having wrongly gauged the British attitudes: "You told me that on Austria the English answer would be 'yes' and on Africa 'no.' As it happens, their answer on Austria was 'no,'* and on Africa 'yes.'"

But the Duce was wrong, understandably misled by the British silence. The very next day at Geneva, where the Council was discussing the Ethiopian complaint, Aloisi had to "defend himself sharply against a surreptitious intervention by Simon, hardly a friendly act after Stresa." It soon became clear that Britain, far from tolerating or winking at Italy's venture, was the principal source of trouble. Late in May, Aloisi remarked that "the duel is not Italian-Ethiopian but English-Italian, and the entire League Council is behind England."

Not surprisingly, Mussolini was outraged. Militarily and psychologically, he had gone beyond the point of no return. The Fascist militia had been incorporated into the Army, and Mussolini had proclaimed his intention to create "a nation of workers and soldiers," since "the relations between nations are based on armed force." A massive deployment of Italy's forces in her East African colonies was under way, and the Duce was telling his visitors that "to remain healthy, a nation must go to war every twenty-five years." When he realized that the British were opposing his designs, he put his head down and charged like a bull, telling Aloisi that he would mobilize three more divisions, that he would quit the League, that he scorned world opinion, and that he would go the limit and "set fire to Europe." The courtly but subservient Baron persuaded his chief not to leave the League, but was sent back to Geneva with instructions to concede nothing, and to delay and obstruct League action at every turn.

In June, Anthony Eden went to Rome with proposals for a settlement which would give Abyssinia an outlet to the sea, and Italy the province of Ogaden. Mussolini rejected the offer as totally inadequate, and turned a deaf ear to Eden's vigorous argument against a military adventurism which would stultify the principles of the League. Subsequent "compromise" proposals put forward at Paris in August and Geneva in September were equally unacceptable to Mussolini, who told Aloisi that "even if they offer me everything, I would prefer to avenge Adowa."

In fact, the would-be Caesar was a badly frightened and unstable man; a few weeks later, on the eve of war, he remarked that an offer of the so-called "vassal

---

* The British had declined to join in a guaranty of Austrian independence, and pledged only "consultation" should it be threatened.

regions" of Ethiopia, leaving Haile Selassie as sovereign of the old Amharic provinces, would have "yielded a solution." But no such proposal was forthcoming at that time, and the Duce's vanity overcame his fear. He had gone too far to draw back, and by his own speeches and pageantry had whipped up a belligerent public attitude, so that when in September the British reinforced their Mediterranean fleet, there was a violently hostile popular reaction throughout Italy.

On October 3, 1935, De Bono's forces in Eritrea crossed the Ethiopian frontier and the war began. Two days later Aloisi, in Geneva, told the League Council that Italy had marched only to defend her colonies against Ethiopian aggression. Adowa fell on October 6, and a month later De Bono took Makale, some eighty miles in from the border.

From a military standpoint, the Italians' principal enemy was not the ill-equipped Ethiopian Army, but the combination of distance, terrain, and climate. The logistic problems were enormous; De Bono had advanced to Makale against his own better judgment, on orders from Rome,* and once there he had to halt and organize his supply lines. At this point he was recalled and replaced by the Army Chief of Staff, Marshal Pietro Badoglio, who devoted the next two months to logistic preparations before resuming the offensive in mid-January of 1936.

Meanwhile, the international reaction to the Italian attack had been almost universally hostile. Within a week, and with but three dissenting votes,† the Council and Assembly of the League had both declared Italy the aggressor, and a few days later, with the same measure of agreement, it was determined to subject Italy to financial and economic sanctions, including an embargo on war materials, but not on oil or coal. Anti-Italian feeling was sharpened by reports that the Italian Army was using poison gas and that the Air Force was attacking buildings and vehicles marked with the Red Cross. Mussolini's son Vittorio made matters worse by a book of his adventures as a pilot in which he called bombing a "magnificent sport" and described an attack on defenseless Ethiopian cavalry who "gave me the impression of a budding rose as the bomb fell in their midst and blew them up."

Early in December, Sir Samuel Hoare (who had succeeded Simon as Foreign Secretary) came to Paris and initialed the "Hoare-Laval deal," under which the province of Tigré and various other parts of Ethiopia would be ceded to Italy. In general, the plan was not unlike a proposal outlined by Mussolini to Aloisi some weeks earlier, and discussed between Grandi and Vansittart just before Hoare left for Paris. The Italian offensive was temporarily stilled, and Mussolini was living in daily fear that the League would put an embargo on oil, or that the British might refuse him use of the Suez Canal, or take some other decisive measure. The Hoare-Laval plan did not give him all he wanted, but it did offer more than the Army had as yet conquered, and Mussolini was about to accept it

---

* The orders came from Mussolini, but partly on the advice of Suvich and Aloisi, who were expecting a French offer of mediation, and pointed out the desirability of occupying as much territory as possible before the mediation took place.

† Albania, Austria, and Hungary. Denmark abstained.

as a basis of negotiations when Hoare resigned, in consequence of the strongly adverse popular reaction when the content of the plan was made public.

The collapse of the "deal" tumbled Laval as well as Hoare from the seats of power, and ended the possibilities of settlement. At Geneva there was more talk of an oil embargo, but the will was lacking, and soon it became apparent that Badoglio and Graziani, who had renewed their advance in mid-January, would complete the conquest before sanctions could take effect. Early in May, Haile Selassie fled his country and Badoglio entered Addis Ababa. Mussolini announced annexation of the entire country, and on May 9, 1936, King Victor Emmanuel was proclaimed Emperor of Ethiopia. Seized with the futility of it all, the League lifted the sanctions and put the seal on Mussolini's victory, the tawdriness of which was equalled only by its evanescence.*

9

As Italy became ever more deeply embroiled militarily in Africa and diplomatically in London, Paris, and Geneva, Mussolini from time to time threw a glance over his shoulder toward Berlin and his estranged fellow-dictator. Germany had left the League and was under no obligations with respect to sanctions; in a strongly disapproving world, neutrality was comforting. Early in May of 1935—barely two weeks after Stresa—Ambassador Cerruti called on Neurath and requested "that both in the press and elsewhere Germany should adopt as reserved an attitude as possible concerning the Italo-Abyssinian conflict." Later in the month Mussolini received Hassell and, indicating that "for Italy the sensitive point at the moment was Abyssinia," proposed that Germany and Italy "conclude a mutual press truce."

Hitler, for his part, was observing closely and with increasing satisfaction the growing estrangement between Italy and her erstwhile western allies, and the consequent cracking of the Stresa Front. At first quietly, he began to exploit the breach and give Mussolini a bit of support by agreeing to a reciprocal cessation of the press war, and putting an embargo on the shipment of aircraft to Ethiopia. By the end of May, Hassell was able to report so "marked" a tendency toward "improving relations with Germany" that "one might almost speak of a reversal of Italy's attitude."

During the rest of 1935, Italo-German relations remained in this condition of circumspect détente. In August, Ambassador Cerruti, whose removal Hitler had requested many months earlier, was finally transferred to Paris and replaced by Bernardo Attolico, whom, it was hoped, the Nazi leaders would find more congenial.† When the fighting in Ethiopia began, Germany maintained her policy of neutrality, disregarded the League sanctions, and continued to supply Italy with much-needed coal. But the arm's-length quality of the relation persisted, as the

---

* Haile Selassie returned to Addis Ababa on May 5, 1941, five years to the day after Badoglio captured the city.

† Cerruti, who had been in Berlin since 1932, appears to have adopted a somewhat tutorial attitude toward the Nazis, as neophytes in the art of totalitarian government. Attolico had been Ambassador to Moscow since 1930. Although he spoke no German, he was selected for the post in Berlin in the expectation that he would conduct himself so as to "improve the atmosphere."

two countries' differences over Austria were no closer to solution, and the Germans were well aware that Mussolini was still relying heavily on France to protect her against Britain's dangerous enthusiasm for sanctions.

The Hoare-Laval affair, however, undermined the Franco-Italian entente and gave Mussolini another push in the direction of Germany. Shortly after the turn of the year Mussolini was characterizing Germany's attitude as "benevolent neutrality" and proposing a settlement of the Austrian problem by means of an Austro-German nonaggression pact, under which Austria would remain "formally independent" but "in practice a German satellite," while simultaneously assuring Hassell that Stresa was "dead and buried once and for all." Informed of these observations, Hitler instructed Hassell to "continue our policy of benevolent neutrality toward Italy." "Germany," the Fuehrer declared, "was at present as good as completely isolated" with "no really reliable friends," and therefore "he could only welcome it if relations of mutual trust between Italy and Germany were restored."

So Nazi Germany helped Fascist Italy weather the European crisis precipitated by the Ethiopian war, and soon it came time for Italy to pick up the check. Early in 1936, Hitler was making ready to denounce Locarno and remilitarize the Rhineland, and on February 14 he called Hassell to Munich to discuss the advisability of informing Mussolini and inviting his toleration if not approval of the move. On Febuary 22, Hassell, received by Mussolini, extracted from the Duce the representation that, in the event of French ratification of the Franco-Soviet pact and a consequent German denunciation of Locarno, Italy "would not co-operate with France and Britain insofar as they might declare that . . . they were compelled to take action."

On March 3, 1936, Suvich, on Mussolini's instructions, prepared and showed Hassell a memorandum recapitulating the main points of discussion with Mussolini. For Hitler, the crucial sentence embodied Mussolini's undertaking that Italy "would not participate in any counterreaction which might be called forth by a German reaction to the ratification" of the Franco-Soviet treaty.

Four days later German troops moved into the demilitarized zone and crossed to the west bank of the Rhine. At the ensuing Locarno and League Council meetings, Cerruti in Paris and Grandi in London declared that, since Italy was herself under sanctions, they would act only as "observers." Mussolini assured Hassell that Italy would refuse to join in any action against Germany, and instructed Grandi accordingly. In the end, Italy joined with the other Locarno powers in declaring that Germany's unilateral act had violated the Versailles and Locarno treaties, but refused to participate in general staff talks with the other Locarno powers or to support any form of counteraction.

In 1935, Mussolini's Ethiopian venture had helped Germany by deflecting international attention from Hitler's denunciation of Versailles, and Germany's neutrality and economic support had given Mussolini comfort and support in carrying through his program in the face of sanctions. In 1936 the German march into the Rhineland helped Italy by putting the Ethiopian war into the shade, and Mussolini's refusal to support the French helped Hitler to survive the initial crisis and turn the Rhineland occupation into a *fait accompli*.

It was tit for tat, but Hitler had had much the better of these tacit bargains, as the parallelism of expediency rapidly developed into a *rapprochement*.

10

By the summer of 1936 it had become apparent, even to Mussolini himself, that his efforts to pursue an independent European policy had failed. In 1934, Hitler, by his crudely overt support of the Austrian Nazis, had thrown Mussolini into the arms of France. In 1935, Britain, by her hostile but indecisive sanctions policy, pitched him right across the Rhine to Hitler.

The parallelism of Berlin and Rome was, however, the product of unforeseen circumstance rather than design, and its benefits were not equally divided. Whether Ethiopia remained independent or became an Italian domain was of small moment to the Germans. But the remilitarization of the Rhineland greatly lessened French capacity for effective military aid to Germany's potential victims, including Austria. Thus France's value as an ally in defense of Austrian independence was seriously undermined, and the military plans laid jointly by Gamelin and Badoglio in June 1935 became so much waste paper.

It has been said that Mussolini pressed his campaign in Ethiopia in 1935 so that he could complete the conquest and bring his troops back home before Germany's rearmament had progressed so far that she might dare to threaten Austria. If such was his plan, it was overtaken by events. By the time Addis Ababa had fallen, his friend Laval was out of power and France was in the throes of the election that brought in Blum and the Popular Front, Britain was the motive force behind the League sanctions, and German troops were streaming into the Rhineland.

In these circumstances, Mussolini must have concluded that the road via Stresa was a dead end, and that he would do better to foster a community of interest with Germany. For this purpose he was prepared, if reluctantly, to write off his Austrian policy, at least to the extent of giving Germany a much freer hand there. Even before the German move into the Rhineland, in January 1936 Mussolini had told Hassell that he recognized Austria's character as a "German state," and would not oppose her becoming a "satellite" of the Reich.* In May, discussing Austria's internal troubles with Aloisi, the Duce remarked that Italy was "about to lose Austria completely" and that "the policy followed by Suvich for four years was ending in complete failure"—a charge which the latter hardly deserved, since it was Mussolini's Ethiopian adventure, and the consequent rupture of the Stresa Front, that was chiefly responsible for undermining Italy's support of Austria against German pressures.

However the blame might be divided, the reorientation of policy was basic. During the spring of 1936, Mussolini was urging the Austrian Chancellor, Kurt von Schuschnigg, to move toward a *rapprochement* with Germany, and the new attitudes bore fruit on July 11, when a joint communiqué was published, in

---

* Mussolini's determination to protect Austria's independence had not been at all times firm. On September 1, 1934, in the presence of Aloisi and the Italian Ambassador to Yugoslavia (Galli), he observed that there was little hope of preventing *Anschluss*, but only of delaying it.

which Germany recognized "the full sovereignty of the Federal State of Austria," while Austria agreed to "maintain a policy based on the principle that Austria acknowledges herself to be a German State." Simultaneously, Schuschnigg and Papen initialed a secret "Gentlemen's Agreement" for the regulation of specific matters—such as a press truce and an Austrian amnesty for political prisoners—most of which would work to the benefit of Germany. Mussolini registered "lively satisfaction" with the new dispensation, which, he said, would "remove the last mortgage on German-Italian relations."

New policies in Rome brought new faces. In June 1936, Suvich and Aloisi both left the Palazzo Chigi, the former as Ambassador to the United States, while the Baron was put to pasture, with fatal consequences to the continuation of his historically invaluable diary. Suvich's successor as Under-Secretary was Giuseppe Bastianini, a Fascist Party functionary who turned to diplomacy in 1928, and had been Ambassador to Poland since 1932. But the big change was that Mussolini formally relinquished the ministerial portfolio of Foreign Affairs, which he had held since Dino Grandi's departure to London in 1932. The "replacement," if such a word is permissible in this context, was the Duce's own son-in-law,* the thirty-four-year-old Count Galeazzo Ciano, who had been serving as Minister of Press and Propaganda since 1932, and now became his father-in-law's immediate subordinate and closest adviser in the shaping of Italy's foreign policy.

The changing of the guard at the Palazzo Chigi was the signal for renewed efforts on Hitler's part to propitiate the Duce and turn the marriage of convenience into one of inclination. To conduct the courtship, Hitler, as he often did, stepped outside of regular diplomatic channels. His first emissary was Hans Frank, at that time† President of the Academy of German Law and Hitler's principal legal adviser, who fancied himself as an Italophile. Frank came to Rome in April and again in September on "legal-cultural" missions, and on each occasion saw Mussolini. At the second interview Frank transmitted Hitler's view that "contacts between the Nazi and Fascist hierarchies are necessary over and above diplomatic channels," and his wish to receive the Duce in Germany "at the earliest possible moment," as well as to "make personal contact" with Ciano, to whom an immediate invitation was extended. Mussolini expressed pleasure at the invitation, but observed that his visit would "cause a great stir" and must be "well prepared so as to produce concrete results." Ciano, however, could go at once, and his visit might appropriately be made the occasion for German recognition of Ethiopia's incorporation in the Italian Empire.

Meanwhile another unofficial emissary was carrying on the courtship at a lower level of the Fascist hierarchy. Prince Philip of Hesse, a Nazi and friend of Goering, by marrying Princess Mafalda had become King Victor Emmanuel's son-in-law. In September of 1936 he extended an invitation, for a visit to his

---

* Ciano's father, Count Costanzo Ciano, was a naval war hero and early convert to Fascism. Galeazzo entered the foreign service, and was a vice-consul in China at the time of his marriage to Edda Mussolini in 1930.

† Hans Frank was Governor-General of German-occupied Poland during the war, and for his actions in that capacity was convicted and executed at the Nuremberg war crimes trials.

ancestral *Schloss* in Kassel, to Filippo Anfuso, a young diplomat whom Ciano had brought to the Palazzo Chigi as his personal assistant. With his chief's approval, Anfuso went to Kassel to reconnoiter. He found his host uncommunicative, but several days later was flown to Nuremberg, where, at the Grand Hotel, he quite unexpectedly found himself in the presence of Adolf Hitler. The Fuehrer made no mention of state visits and said very little about Austria. He began by professing his "reverence" for Mussolini as the first European to have conquered Marxism. The main theme of Hitler's discourse was the desirability of Italo-German collaboration. Both countries, he said, had ample reason to distrust Britain, and Italy was Germany's "only possible ally in Europe." Germany's natural sphere of interest was in Central Europe, while Italy's lay in the Mediterranean; in such a division lay their common destiny of greatness.

Following these feelers, a formal invitation was issued to Ciano for a visit during the third week of October. In preparation, drafts of a communiqué and a secret protocol were worked over, and an agenda settled upon which would involve "working sessions" with Neurath in Berlin and a visit to Hitler at Berchtesgaden, as well as a reception and performance of *Don Giovanni* in Munich. In Berlin, the two foreign ministers had no difficulty in agreeing on the protocol, which indeed consisted largely of very general commitments to "proceed in close contact," to "come to an understanding," and to "examine jointly," in connection with a wide variety of matters including membership in the League of Nations, commercial policies in the Danube region, and the protection of Europe against communism. Both countries had become involved in the Spanish Civil War, and it was agreed that they would recognize the Nationalist (Franco) government "as soon as possible." Italy agreed to "give diplomatic support" to German colonial claims and to protect German interests in Ethiopia, the incorporation of which into the Italian Empire was recognized by Germany in a separate and public announcement.

On October 24, Ciano was received by Hitler at Berchtesgaden, and exposed for the first time to one of Hitler's famous monologues. "His way of expressing himself was slow and somewhat verbose," Ciano recorded. "Each question was the subject of a long exposition and each concept was repeated by him several times in different words." The principal "concepts" of the discourse were "Bolshevism" and "British encirclement," and the thrust was much the same as it had been with Anfuso the previous month: the natural parallelism of Italian and German foreign policy, and the role of the two countries as leaders of a "common front" of nations, united "under the banner of Anti-Bolshevism," to break the power of the democratic "bloc" led by Britain and France.

With fresh memories of the Anglo-German Naval Agreement, and aware of the stream of British visitors who had been enjoying the Fuehrer's hospitality, the Italians were chiefly interested in preventing Hitler from leaving them in the lurch by trading Rome for London. As an extra bit of insurance, Ciano had brought with him "as a special dispatch from the Duce," a collection of British diplomatic documents obtained by Grandi, including pessimistic and biting comments by Eden and others on events in Nazi Germany. Ostensibly they served their purpose, for Ciano observed that upon reading them Hitler "reacted violently" and launched into a diatribe against the "incompetents" who governed England, and who must be opposed by "active" measures "led and guided by our two countries."

At the conclusion of the private talk, there was a general gathering of the faithful on the Berghof terrace, where tea and cakes were served. The view was magnificent; Hitler pointed out the landmarks to Ciano, including, in the distance, the Austrian city of Salzburg, remarking: "And so I am obliged to look at my German homeland through binoculars!" It was the only mention that he made of Austria, but the episode lost nothing in the telling a few days later, when Ciano made report of the occasion to his father-in-law.

The Ciano visit and the Berlin protocols laid the foundation for the Italo-German collaboration that was to endure until the Italian surrender and the collapse of the Fascist regime in 1943. All that the new relation lacked was a name, and within a few days of Ciano's return, on November 1, 1936, Mussolini, perhaps inadvertently, gave it one in the course of a speech at the Piazza del Duomo in Milan. "One great country has recently gathered a vast amount of sympathy among the masses of the Italian people; I speak of Germany," declared the Duce: "The Berlin conversations have resulted in an understanding between our two countries over certain problems which had been particularly acute. But . . . this Berlin-Rome line is not a diaphragm but rather an axis* around which can revolve all those European states with a will to collaboration and peace."

The word stuck, and the "Rome-Berlin Axis" thus became part of the diplomatic vocabulary. It was not an alliance; it was not even a nonaggression pact, and indeed contained nothing with respect to the settlement of disputes between the two countries. Essentially it was little more than a declaration of common interests in foreign policy. Despite its formal limitations, however, it greatly strengthened the hands of both dictators during the remaining prewar years, and it was as parties to the Axis that Hitler and Mussolini met at Kiefersfelden on the way to Munich in 1938.

* The word did not come fresh to Mussolini's mind in 1936. In 1923 he had written that "the axis of European history" ran through Berlin, and in June 1934, just after his meeting with Hitler at Venice, the Hungarian Premier, Gyula de Gömbös, wrote that "Berlin and Rome form the two ends of an axis which, if it should find a state of equilibrium, could provide a basis for peaceful evolution of European affairs."

CHAPTER 9

The Eastern Arena

1

Ravished of her borderlands by military defeat, torn by revolution, harassed by foreign intervention, and stricken by famine, Soviet Russia licked her wounds and eyed the future hungrily. It harbored many dangers to the newborn regime, but Karl Marx had bequeathed the Bolsheviks a crystal ball. Lenin, Trotsky, and their followers gazed therein and thought they saw revolution in many lands as the natural product of the First World War.

And so, as the power that had fallen from palsied czarist hands was accumulated among the Soviets, many of the Bolshevik leaders thought of Petrograd as the headquarters of world revolution rather than the capital of Russia. Along the eastern front, where huge armies still confronted each other at the end of 1917, fighting was to give way to fraternization, to open the German soldier's eyes to the Socialist vision and send him home a good revolutionary.

The new Government's first diplomatic act—the "Decree on Peace" of November 8, 1917—called for "an immediate peace without annexation and without indemnities." When the negotiations between Russia and the Central Powers (Germany, Austria-Hungary, Bulgaria, and Turkey) opened the following month at Brest-Litovsk, the Germans took the wind out of the Russians' sails by first accepting the formula, and then pointing out that the areas occupied by the German and Austrian armies were not ethnically Russian, and that their disposition should be settled according to the principle of nation self-determination.

Beneath the Bolshevik breast there beat the Russian heart. The German proposals to carve out of eastern Russia a set of "buffer" satellites broke up the conference, and the Soviet delegation departed under cover of Leon Trotsky's extraordinary formula "neither peace nor war." But if the German delegation was momentarily baffled* by this pronouncement, they were not slow to reply by resuming the offensive. As they approached Petrograd, Trotsky resigned as Commissar for Foreign Affairs, and Lenin read his colleagues an ultimatum: the German terms were to be accepted or he would resign. On March 3, 1918, the Soviet delegates signed the Treaty of Brest-Litovsk, by which Russia was stripped of Finland, the Baltic and Polish lands, the Ukraine, and part of the Caucasus.

* *"Unerhört"* (unheard of) exclaimed the German General Max Hoffman, when he heard Trotsky's famous phrase.

For the first year of its existence, Soviet Russia's foreign policy was to appease Germany and stave off a total conquest that would have destroyed the Russian state. Brest-Litovsk was the embodiment of that policy, but if it was a draconic peace it was a short-lived one, as it was formally repudiated by the Germans when they signed the Armistice at Compiègne, France, in November 1918.

The German collapse ended the greatest single threat to the Soviet state, but not all fighting between Germans and Russians. Under the terms of the Armistice the Germans were to withdraw at once from Russia proper, but not from the Ukraine, Poland, or the Baltic provinces. Meanwhile these same areas were collecting forces to establish and defend their independence of Russia. Counterrevolutionary bands of "White" Russians were assembling in the east under Admiral Alexander Kolchak, and in the west under Generals Anton Denikin and Nikolai Yudenitch. Furthermore, Russia's erstwhile allies were intervening, at first in the hope of keeping Russia in the war but, after the Armistice, on ideological grounds, to aid the "Whites" against a regime now regarded as the source of insidious social and political poison. At various times from 1918 to 1920 there were British forces in Transcaucasia and French in Odessa; French, British, and American units in Archangel and Murmansk; and Americans, British, French, and many Japanese in and near Vladivostok.

Thus beleaguered, and at times almost despairing of maintaining themselves in Russia, the Bolshevik leaders continued to rest their deepest faith in the spread of revolution abroad, and especially in Germany. Early in 1919 the Spartacist uprising in Berlin and the Communist-Socialist domination of Munich, as well as Béla Kun's short-lived Communist regime in Hungary, lent apparent substance to these hopes. But none of these ventures survived the summer of 1919, by which time the White forces were posing their greatest threat. Had the White leaders been shrewd enough to make common cause with the Finns, Balts, Poles, Ukrainians, and other nationalities seeking independence or at least autonomy, the Bolsheviks might have been overthrown and the course of history greatly changed. But Kolchak, Denikin, and their cohorts were oldfashioned nationalists intent on restoring the imperial borders if not the empire itself. Such a program was, of course, anathema to the Poles, Finns, and other border nationalities.

By the spring of 1920, the worst of the civil war was over. Exhausted by four years of war, France and Britain had no stomach for prolonged military involvement in Russia's internecine struggles, and had withdrawn most of their forces. The last of the White generals, Baron Piotr Wrangel, was bottled up in the Crimea.

And now, while and because the White star was fading, Russia was attacked by Poland, her traditional western foe. Reborn as an independent nation, the Poles sought to exploit Ukrainian separatism, and joined with the troops of the Ataman Semyon Petlura in a drive to Kiev, which they took early in May. Like other invaders before and after, they then fell victim to the Russian counterpunch, and by August the Red armies had reached the Polish ethnic frontier. Lenin himself was intoxicated by success and the prospect of communizing

Poland and spreading the flames of revolution to Germany. New stars were discovered in the Russian military firmament, as the young Semyon Budenny and
younger Mikhail Tukachevsky led their forces to the gates of Warsaw.

But the Russians were now as badly overextended as the Poles had been at
Kiev, and were soon routed by Polish counterattacks. Both sides had had
enough; an armistice was signed in October, and in March 1921, by the Treaty
of Riga, the Russo-Polish frontier was fixed where it was to stay until 1939.

Meanwhile Wrangel had been forced to evacuate the Crimea, and in 1921
Georgia and the rest of Transcaucasian Russia came into the Soviet fold. In
1922 the Japanese, under combined Russian and American pressure, finally
pulled out of Vladivostok. Except for Finland, the three Baltic states (Estonia,
Latvia, and Lithuania), Poland, and Bessarabia, the Soviets had established their
control over the former empire of the Czars, vast and varied as it was.

2

Even before the last units of White generals were driven from Russian soil,
Lenin had been stricken by the illness which rapidly impaired his capacities and from which he died in January 1924. There ensued a struggle for supremacy in which Leon Trotsky was soon worsted by Josef Stalin. But for some
years Stalin's power was based on shrewdly contrived alliances with other
influential Communist Party figures, and it was not until about 1930 that he
emerged as the virtual dictator of the Soviet Union.

Throughout the twenties, the struggle for power was waged chiefly in the context of domestic economic and social problems. "When the fighting ended in
1921," wrote Louis Fischer, "the Communist regime turned inward to nurse its
wounds, rebuild its ruined body, and wrestle with baffling problems of political
administration." Foreign trade had declined to a trickle, the transport system
was a wreck, and famine swept large parts of the country. Shortage of consumer
goods and agricultural requisitions alienated workers and peasants, and forced
the famous compromise of Marxist economic principle called the New Economic Policy, under which small-scale private trade was tolerated, and foreign
capital and skills solicited. As hopes of foreign revolution faded, the Bolsheviks
turned to the task of "building a self-sufficient socialist society in one country."

If Russia's main energies were then turned inward, her leaders were acutely
aware and indeed fearful of the capitalist world beyond her borders. As managers of the one nation where socialism had triumphed, the Bolsheviks were ex
officio the high priests of communism the world over. This duality of responsibility was sharply reflected in Soviet foreign policy, the primary aim of which
was defense against foreign attack, and the secondary aim, domination of the
world Communist movement.

These two horses did not always run smoothly in harness. The Soviet attitude
toward war itself was ambivalent. War among the capitalist countries "creates
favorable fighting conditions for the forces of social revolution" and was therefore to be welcomed and exploited for revolutionary ends. But there was likewise great danger that the capitalist countries would see in the success of

communism in Russia the seed of their own destruction, and would gang up on the Soviet Union before turning on each other.

Preservation of their own regime, therefore, suggested a cautious and even a propitiatory foreign policy, in order to minimize the risk of attack until Russia should have regained her economic health and means of self-defense. How could this be done if Russia were at the same time the fountainhead of revolutionary doctrine and the main source of support for the Communist parties in France, Germany, and elsewhere that were openly seeking to overthrow the capitalist governments in those lands?

The Bolsheviks resolved the problem by means of a capitalist device familiar to every business lawyer: a "dummy corporation" ostensibly separate from the Soviet Government, and called the Third Communist International, or "Comintern." Its headquarters were in Moscow, and between 1919 and 1935 it held seven "Congresses" attended by Communist leaders from all over the world, at which Communist Party doctrine and tactics were expounded in militant resolutions and declarations formulated by the Russians.

Not surprisingly, the "official" foreign policies of the Soviet Government and the revolutionary activities and attitudes of the Comintern were often at odds, and in 1924 *Pravda* still had enough sense of humor to publish a cartoon showing the Foreign Commissar, Georgi Chicherin, tearing his hair in dismay while the head of the Comintern, Grigori Zinoviev, made a fiery speech. In fact of course, Foreign Ministry and Comintern alike were ruled by the Politburo, and the fiction that the Soviet Government was not responsible for the Comitern was transparent from the outset—not so much a mask as a figleaf. Abroad nobody was fooled, and indeed it was the subversive activities sponsored by the Comintern, together with the Soviet Government's refusal to assume the financial obligations contracted by the Czarist regime, that most obstructed re-establishment of normal diplomatic relations with other countries.

In Western Europe, the conduct of foreign policy was in the hands of leading political figures—Austen Chamberlain in Britain, Briand in France, Stresemann in Germany, the Duce himself in Italy. But in Moscow, the Commissariat for Foreign Affairs (*Narkomindel*) was managed by men of little or no importance in the Soviet political hierarchy. Chicherin was Foreign Commissar from 1918 to 1930; he had been in the imperial diplomatic service, and was a man of broad culture, high polish, and great skill in negotiation. For twelve years he was the voice of the Soviet Union at the green table, but for all the respect in which he was held in the international diplomatic fraternity, at home he was a valued technician rather than a trusted counselor, and in 1930 he was thrown on the scrap heap.

Chicherin was succeeded by his longtime deputy, Maxim Litvinov, who headed *Narkomindel* during a more open period of Soviet diplomacy and became an even more prominent figure in Washington as well as the European capitals. He came to the fore just as Stalin's grip on the levers of power became unshakable and, for all his British wife and Western ways, the rotund, engaging Litvinov, as much as his predecessor, was a guest and mouthpiece of the Politburo.

As for the substance of Soviet foreign policy, from the end of the Polish war in 1920 until 1932 it was largely defensive and devoid of important initiatives. The two exceptions were Russia's deep involvement in China and her relations with Germany; the former is of only collateral relevance to the story of Munich, while the latter is of crucial importance.

"Misery loves company" is a fair explanation of the genesis of the Russo-German understandings reached in the early twenties. To the Germans, Versailles was a *Diktat;* to the Russians, an imperialist swindle. Both were pariahs in international society, excluded from the clubby respectability of membership in the League of Nations. Both were temporarily weak and potentially powerful, and both wished to break through the web of isolation in which they were enmeshed by Versailles and the French system of European alliances. Russia needed German industrial and military skills, while Germany needed a secure and secret proving-ground for weapons and techniques forbidden her by the Versailles arms provisions. The natural results of these neatly fitted needs were the 1922 Treaty of Rapallo, the military and trade agreements based on the common interests which it symbolized, and the nonaggression pact embodied in the 1926 Treaty of Berlin.

A marriage based on mutual weakness was bound to suffer strain as the parties to it gathered strength. After Stresemann and Locarno, Germany's gaze was generally westward, and focused on reparations, rearmament, and other features of revisionism. In Moscow, meanwhile, Stalin and his colleagues were preoccupied with internal matters; collaboration between Red Army and Reichswehr was tolerated because it strengthened the Red Army, just as foreign concessionaires were welcomed if their activities bolstered the Soviet economy.

Close as they were in a technical way, the Russo-German relations remained furtive. It was as if the two countries were leaning against each other back to back, rather than linked side by side, and even before Hitler came to power the connection was showing signs of wear.

3

Until 1932, Germany was the only major European power with which the Soviet Union enjoyed relations which were not only friendly but so certified by treaty.* That year witnessed a sudden burst of Soviet diplomatic initiative, and may be said to mark the end of Russia's diplomatic isolation, as nonaggression treaties were concluded with Finland, Latvia, and Estonia in the early months, with Poland in July, and with France in November.

Soviet historiography being what it is, the motivation for this change of posture remains a matter of inference. Reporting to his government in June 1931, the British Ambassador in Moscow, Sir Edmond Ovey, remarked a "new tendency in Soviet foreign policy," which he described as a "tendency to co-operate with foreign countries" and ascribed to the Soviet leaders' gradual loss of faith "in the imminence of a world revolution" and the growing influence of Western-minded officials such as Litvinov and Anatoli Lunacharsky. These may well have

---

* Russia had also entered into nonaggression pacts with Turkey (1925), Lithuania and Afghanistan (1926), and Iran (1927).

been contributing factors, but if one is to seek for circumstances that might have moved Josef Stalin, they are more likely to be found in the Far East—in the rise of Japanese nationalism, and the looming Sino-Japanese conflict which burst into open warfare with the Manchurian "incident" of September 18, 1931. The combination of a rapacious Japan and a fragmented China spelled bad trouble for Russia's eastern interest and aims, and would naturally have stimulated a search for greater security in Europe.

Except as indicating a belief that Germany alone was insufficient as a European point of support, there is no reason to think that the 1932 nonaggression pacts were "directed against" that country. But from the German viewpoint, the shift in Soviet posture was distinctly unwelcome. Hostility to Poland, both defensive and offensive, had provided much of the original impetus for the Rapallo policies, across which the Soviet pact with Poland now cast a shadow. Condemnation of Versailles and opposition to the French system of alliances was the foundation of Russo-German friendship, and was bound to be shaken by both the Franco-Soviet and the Polish-Soviet treaties. In March 1933 the German Ambassador in Moscow, Herbert von Dirksen, told Litvinov quite plainly that these pacts "had caused a strain in our relations."

But the strain was not yet sharp enough to affect the economic and military relations between the two countries. Dirksen, a wealthy Prussian aristocrat with extensive personal contacts in the German business world, strongly supported the Rapallo policies. In public speeches and private consultation he urged "a greater initiative on the part of Germany in her economic policy toward Russia." In March 1931 a delegation headed by the Ruhr steel magnate Peter Klöckner, and including representatives of Krupp, Siemens, and other giant concerns, visited Russia and concluded trade agreements that put Germany far ahead of all other countries as both supplier and customer of Russia. Over five-thousand German engineers and skilled workmen were employed in Russian industries.

The good relations between the Red Army and Reichswehr generals continued. In September 1932, General Mikhail Tukachevsky, the Deputy Commissar of War, headed a party of Russian officers as guests at the German Army maneuvers. At his invitation, the following spring General Alfred von Vollard Bockelberg, chief of the German Army ordnance department, paid a return visit in the course of which plans for joint research in chemical warfare were discussed.

Despite all this, Russian doubts of Germany's reliability became manifest in 1932, at the same time that the Germans were distressed by the Polish and French nonaggression pacts. The worldwide economic depression was especially severe in Germany, and the extensive unemployment, financial dislocation, and political unrest betokened an instability which made the future course of German foreign policy highly unpredictable. The Russians' worries were aggravated by the rapid shifts in political leadership, with Papen and Schleicher first collaborating and then fighting, while Hitler's shadow darkened.

Curiously enough in retrospect, the Russians were at first much more frightened of Papen than of Hitler. The Nazi leader was, of course, a Fascist and political villain of deepest dye, who had frankly revealed in *Mein Kampf* his desire to carve up and feast on Russia. But the Kremlin persisted in regarding Hitler as a capitalist tool, and the success of his party as a symptom of the Weimar regime's disintegration; this was welcome as an essential preliminary to a workers' revolt under Communist leadership.

Papen, however, was a member of the class for whom Hitler was a stooge. A Catholic Rhinelander with affinities for France, a nobleman, former cavalry officer, and wealthy Communist-hater, Papen was just the man, in Russian eyes, to bring about a coalition of the imperialist powers against the Soviet Union. Their fears in this regard were not unwarranted; during the summer of 1932 at the Lausanne Conference on reparations, Papen (then Chancellor) and the Under-Secretary of the German Foreign Office, Bernhard von Bülow, had several private talks with the French delegate, Lefebvre Laboulaye, in which the Germans characterized their Russian treaties as "a necessity imposed by circumstances, and not freely chosen by Germany," and extolled the merits of a Franco-German *rapprochement,* including general staff contacts. Since Papen was notable for his indiscretions and the French were surely not above throwing the apple of discord, it is not suprising that the Russians got wind of these goings-on.

If Schleicher's brief emergence as Chancellor gave the Kremlin any comfort it was very short-lived, and the Hitler-Papen government was, from the Russian viewpoint, just about the worse possible combination. At first the Soviet press reaction was exceedingly cautious, but the day after Hitler became Chancellor, Litvinov expressed grave concern to Dirksen. Throughout the spring of 1933, Dirksen was frequently in conference with Litvinov and the Deputy Commissar, Nikolai Krestinsky, whose Party credentials were stronger than his chief's. Each side assured the other that there was no intention of changing the Rapallo policies, and each side proclaimed its deep anxiety about the loyalty of the other, with accusations and counteraccusations of lust for *la belle France*. Dirksen strove manfully to keep things on an even keel, but events soon set his efforts at naught, and he was obliged to report a "serious deterioration" in relations. In Germany, the storm troopers were indifferent to international niceties, and Soviet trade and consular representations were arrested, beaten, and otherwise harassed. The Nazi press poured out quantities of anti-Soviet vitriol, and in April the Soviet papers opened a counterbarrage. At the London Economic Conference in June, the German Minister of Economics, Alfred Hugenberg, delivered an anti-Russian diatribe with plain implications that the Soviet Union should be dismembered and the Ukraine opened up for foreign exploration.

Sometime in May or June 1933, the Bolshevik leaders must have decided that Hitler was there to stay for some time, that his anti-Communism was not purely domestic, and that continuation of the Rapallo policies was more hazardous than advantageous. In the pages of *Pravda,* Karl Radek (its editor) declared that, whatever the Versailles Treaty's faults, the "program of seeking revision" was "the foreign policy program of German fascism" and was "simply another name for a new world war." This, of course, was an open and explicit disavowal of the very essence of Rapallo, especially emphatic because Radek was one of its architects.

Even more significant, though unknown except to those directly involved, was the Russians' decision to put an end to the collaboration between the Red Army and the Reichswehr. Within a few days after Bockelberg's departure, a termination notice was given in what Dirksen described as a "sudden and unfriendly manner"; all the joint military installations in Russia were to be closed, and the Russian officers canceled their scheduled visit to the German maneuvers. In August, General Oswald Lutz, chief of the mechanized warfare section of the German Army General Staff, came to Russia to supervise closing the joint tank-training station at Kazan and make official farewells. The German Embassy reported sadly to Berlin that "The chapter of co-operation on the basis of strong mutual confidence must be regarded as closed." By the end of September the last German officers had departed, and contacts between the two armies were limited to the military attachés.

Krestinsky explained these decisions to Dirksen on the hardly credible ground that the Western European powers were talking of disarmament and peace, and that Russia wished "to reduce [military] co-operation so as to forestall possible criticism." In September the German military attaché, Colonel Otto Hartmann, was told by the Russian officer who had been in charge of the collaboration program (one Smagin) that the visit to the maneuvers had been cancelled for fear that Russian officers might be subjected to indignities in public places. But surely the true reason for the Soviet decision was given by Tukachevsky at a farewell dinner for Dirksen, when the Soviet marshal told the retiring ambassador that termination and cancellation alike were the consequences of an appraisal of German foreign policy as having become anti-Soviet.*

The ending of military collaboration was, it is now clear, a Soviet political decision based on their reaction to Hitler's posture and apparent intentions. The termination was not welcomed by the German generals, and probably no more by their Russian colleagues. Repeatedly, through 1933 and 1934, Tukachevsky, Yegorov (Chief of the Red Army General Staff), and Marshal Klimenti Voroshilov (Commissar for War) told Hartmann or one of the German diplomats, with every appearance of sincerity, that they had greatly valued their collaboration with the Reichswehr, and hoped that it might be resumed—subject always to the caution that this could happen only if there were a betterment in general relations between the two countries.

But events took the opposite course, and in March 1935 an article over Tukachevsky's signature appeared in *Pravda,* in which the author described "Hitler's imperialist plans" against not only the Soviet Union but Belgium, France, Austria, and Czechoslovakia as well, and declared that in a few months Germany would have an army of some 850,000 men. With Berlin's approval, Colonel Hartmann made strong protest to Gekker, the Red Army officer charged with liaison with the Germans. With typical Teutonic passion for detail, Hartmann was particularly outraged by Tukachevsky's exaggeration of German military strength. Gekker, whatever his subsequent fate,† was sharp enough to see an

---

* Much of the German documentation of this affair has disappeared (or perhaps never existed), and the Soviet archives, of course, remain closed.

† Gekker "disappeared" in the spring of 1937 just before the execution of Tukachevsky and others.

opening, and observed that "the best way of correcting the picture drawn by Tukachevsky would be for him to be provided with the requisite data from official German sources." "Naturally," reported the discomfited Hartmann, "I did not follow up this suggestion."

Meanwhile, Soviet enthusiasm for German engineers had also cooled, and unmistakable indications of displeasure caused them to leave in droves. Change of faces on the diplomatic stage did nothing to check the downward trend, as Ambassador Dirksen (transferred to Tokyo) was replaced briefly by Rudolph Nadolny (who displeased his superiors) and, in October 1934, by Count Werner von Schulenburg, who held his post until the German attack in 1941.* During the same month the new Soviet Ambassador in Berlin, Jakob Surits, presented his credentials and staff to Adolf Hitler in a ceremony which Bülow described as "short and cool," adding that "It was strange that the personnel subsequently presented were all Jews." From then on the intensity of the verbal warfare between the two countries mounted steadily.

Beyond question the distrust and animosity were genuine on both sides—in the Kremlin, fear of an eventual German attack; in Germany, fear of a Franco-Russian "encirclement" and, in Hitler's mind, a determination to shatter the Soviet state and make the Ukraine and other eastern lands part of a greater Germany. But these fears and plans were of the future, and in the present, beneath the noisy diatribes in the controlled press of the two countries, there remained a layer of cold-blooded co-operation. On April 9, 1935, only ten days after Tukachevsky's *Pravda* article, a trade agreement was signed in Berlin by which the Germans granted Moscow a 200-million-mark credit to finance Soviet purchases in Germany. To be sure, Russian efforts to use the credit for the purchase of submarines were too much of a good thing, and in January 1936, Hitler forbade all transactions in war matériel. But commercial relations, and continuing negotiations for credits, continued right through the period of deepest political hostility, with raw materials moving westward to Germany, and industrial machinery and other capital goods eastward to Russia.

From 1935 on, in short, Nazi-Soviet relations were at their very worst, with unending torrents of reciprocal abuse, but Russo-German relations were cool and calculated, and continued to countenance a mutually beneficial economic co-operation. In Moscow, Ambassador Schulenburg managed to maintain minimal amenities and keep open the channels of diplomatic intercourse. From time to time the Russians put out feelers to test the prospects of bettering the over-all relation, the ambivalence of which was a considerable factor in the approaching reckoning at Munich.

4

If it was the Japanese who triggered the Kremlin's decision to broaden the base of Soviet foreign policy, manifested in the nonaggression pacts of 1932, the death of Rapallo and the rapid deterioration of relations with Germany gave the Russians a much stronger push in the same direction. In May 1933, Soviet Rus-

---

* In the fall of 1935, Hartmann was replaced as military attaché by General Ernst Koestring, who likewise remained until 1941.

sia and Fascist Italy signed a trade and credit agreement which was heralded in *Izvestia* as "a new proof that the Soviet Union sincerely desires to establish peaceful relations with the capitalist countries and will gladly meet any of them halfway if they seriously wish to establish normal and close relations." At international conferences in Geneva and London, Litvinov emerged as a leading international figure in disarmament and economic discussions. In November 1933 he was in Washington to negotiate a settlement under which the United States at long last granted diplomatic recognition to the Land of the Bolsheviks. The following year, largely on French initiative, the Soviet Union was accepted as a member of the League of Nations with a permanent seat in the Council.

No longer the Ishmael of the international community, the Soviet Government now moved to strengthen its ties with France, and joined in Barthou's efforts to establish an "eastern Locarno." These came to nothing, and Barthou's assassination and replacement by Laval chilled the prospects of a Franco-Soviet military alliance, but the mutual defense pacts with France and Czechoslovakia brought Russia into closer relations with the Anglo-French power structure—an affiliation signalized by Anthony Eden's and Pierre Laval's visits to Moscow in the spring of 1935.

While Litvinov and the *Narkomindel* were thus multiplying their countries' points of contact and support, the Comintern was going through a parallel policy evolution, which eventually led to what became known as the "United Front." As initially used in the Comintern's proclamations and publications, however, it meant something different from and narrower than the broad, left-liberal, anti-Fascist "front" of later years.

Renegade friends are always more hated than acknowledged enemies, and until the early thirties the Comintern's attitude toward the Social Democrats was in line with this generalization. At the Sixth Congress of the Comintern, in 1928, the Socialist parties of Austria and Germany were declared "a particularly dangerous enemy of the proletariat, more dangerous than the avowed adherents of predatory social imperialism." As late as September 1932, a speaker at the Comintern's "Twelfth Plenum" declared that not Fascism itself, but "social-fascism"—i.e., the social democrats—was "our chief enemy in the workers' movement." And six months later, when the Comintern called for a "United Front of struggle against the fascist offensive," it was made explicit that the front was not to comprehend the bourgeoisie or the social-democratic parties," but was to be a proletarian front of Communist and social democratic workers. In the jargon of the Comintern, this was called "the United Front from below."

In December 1934 the concept was broadened in recognition of the changed political situation in many countries, where Fascist forces were growing rapidly and threatening the very existence of social democracy. Accordingly, the time had come to tolerate "the United Front from above"—i.e., collaboration with the social democratic organizations themselves—in order to prevent communism and the Soviet Union itself from being engulfed by the on-rushing tide of "Fascist imperialism."

With Russian participation in the League of Nations and conclusion of the defensive alliances with France and Czechoslovakia, Communist collaborationism continued to spread. In France, the Communist leader Maurice Thorez was calling for a "Popular Front of work, liberty and peace" based on a program designed to attract middle-class liberals to a broad alliance of the left against Fascism, which soon flowered at the great demonstration in Paris on Bastille Day in 1935. Communist doctrine appeared to have turned leftist-ecumenical, and the new Popular Front was duly certified at the Seventh (and last) Congress of the Comintern at Moscow during the summer of 1935.

5

Thus the Soviet Union, with Litvinov as its mouthpiece, outshouted all others in denouncing Fascism and Nazism and calling for international action to halt their ravages, at the same time that Hitler began to assume a posture as the defender of European civilization against the Communist barbarism looming in the east. In both cases, credibility was seriously impaired by domestic policies. For the libertarian democrat, what was there to choose between the tyrannies of Hitler and Stalin? In Germany were concentration camps, anti-Semitism, political murder contrived and condoned by the Chancellor and Fuehrer himself, and a regime based on the ideas and predictions of *Mein Kampf*—a most unlovely setting for the jewel of civilization. In Russia the agricultural collectivization program, executed with utmost ruthlessness, had brought famine, and death or the miseries of transportation to the far reaches of Siberia, to millions of peasants. Soon the Moscow purge trials, in consequence of which many figures of the Rapallo era (Krestinsky, Tukachevsky and Yegorov among others) met their end, were adding a weird and frightening dimension to the Soviet image. Such events were a source of acute embarrassment to the liberal democrats of the Popular Front.

How genuine was Soviet allegiance to the anti-Fascist cause, and what were the Kremlin's real purposes in sponsoring the United Front? The Soviet leaders were not all alike and, despite Stalin's dominance, there may well have been diverse viewpoints. Documentary or other direct evidence is lacking and may never become available. Given the past record of Soviet diplomacy and the nature of Communist doctrine, however, it is safe to say that Russia's participation in the United Front was tactically rather than ideologically motivated. There is no reason to think that Stalin and his colleagues regarded capitalist democracy, however libertarian, as intrinsically "better" than Fascism. Nor had they any basic objection to war, unless it involved a threat to the Soviet Union; lacking any such threat, wars were even welcome as providing the necessary conditions for successful social revolution.

Accordingly, the distance the Soviet Government would go in support of the United Front would be determined, in large measure, by the actions of its other members and of the western democracies. Soon it became apparent that the other governments were not prepared to go very far. The Soviet Union had been a member of the League but a few months when there came, in rapid succession, Germany's denunciation of the Versailles arms restrictions, Italy's invasion of Ethiopia, and Germany's military reoccupation of the Rhineland. Whether or not the Russian leaders had expected the League or the Locarno powers to react decisively to these events is hard to say; in November 1935 Schulenburg reported a conversation with Litvinov in which the Russian declared that Mussolini had made a bad mistake, and that Britain "not only intended to drive Italy out of Ethiopia but, over and beyond, was striving to weaken Italy in general and to humiliate Mussolini."* If Litvinov seriously entertained these great expectations, the subsequent record of Britain and the League must have severely shaken him. Whatever his inner feelings, it was Litvinov who delivered the most eloquent epitaph, during the League session of July 1936 at which the sanctions against Italy were lifted: "We are gathered here," he declared, "to close a page in the history of international life which it will be impossible to read without a feeling of bitterness." Nevertheless, there should be no defeatism: "As for myself, I would rather have a League of Nations that tries to render at least some assistance, even if it proves ineffective . . . than a League that closes its eyes to aggression and lets it pass, unperturbed. . . ."

Litvinov contrived to make it his chief business to ensure that neither eyes nor ears could remain closed to aggression and threats of aggression. The Soviet Government duly and dutifully joined in the sanctions against Italy, and in condemning Germany's unilateral denunciation of the Versailles restrictions. After the Rhineland reoccupation Litvinov told the League Council that, unless effective counteraction were taken, the League might become a harmful rather than a beneficial institution, as "it may lull the vigilance of the nations and give rise to illusions." Meanwhile the Soviet Ambassador in London, Ivan Maisky, was denouncing the notion that aggression in the east might be tolerated without endangering peace in the west, and vice versa: "This is the greatest of delusions. . . . Peace is indivisible."

These were all brave words, and it may be that Litvinov and Maisky believed in what they said. Nevertheless, at the very same time Vyacheslav Molotov (then Chairman of the Council of People's Commissars) was telling a French journalist: "There is a tendency among certain sections of the Soviet public toward an attitude of thoroughgoing irreconcilability to the present rulers of Germany, particularly because of the ever-repeated hostile speeches of German leaders against the Soviet Union. But the chief tendency, and the one determining the Soviet Government's policy, thinks an improvement in Soviet-German relations is possible."

This avowal, open and to a Frenchman, was a powerful reminder that, for the Soviet leaders, destruction of the Nazi regime was not the purpose of the United Front. Superficially, it is incongruous to describe Russia's foreign policy as insular, and in that sense comparable to Britain's, but the parallel is not altogether mistaken. Protected by the waters of the Channel, England feared hostile combinations led by a Spain or a France grown too strong. Guarded by the vast reaches of Eastern Europe, Russia too played the balance of power game. Alarmed by the outburst of militant energy in Nazi Germany, the Kremlin viewed the League, and the French and Czech treaties, as something of a counterweight.

* Schulenburg's report and the marginal notes indicate agreement with Litvinov's assessment on the part of Schulenburg and Hans Dieckhoff, a department chief in the German Foreign Ministry.

But it was no part of Soviet policy to lead a bloody crusade against the Nazis; that would have been "pulling the chestnuts out of the fire" for the capitalists of the western democracies. No more would the Soviet leaders have welcomed the prospect of Germany overrun by the French and Poles, and thus swept into the western powerstructure. The United Front was no crusade, but rather a tactical tool of the moment, which was to be discarded without compunction if, under shifting circumstances, some other implement should appear more useful.

6

Between Russia and Central Europe, from the Baltic to the Balkans, lay six nations of Eastern Europe—Lithuania, Poland, and Rumania adjacent to Russia, and in a second layer west of these, Czechoslovakia, Hungary, and Yugoslavia. Their total population was close to one hundred million, of which the greater portion were non-Russian Slavs. Most of this vast area was economically primitive and poverty-ridden, divided by numerous regional feuds and antagonisms, and it defied the occasional efforts of the two strongest countries—Poland and Czechoslovakia—to form an effective power bloc in Eastern Europe.

These quarrels were the product in part of the post-First World War territorial settlements, and in part of location and tradition. The latter factors were most significantly revealed in the differing attitudes toward Soviet Russia. Neither the bourgeois-democratic regime in Prague nor the reactionary King Alexander I in Belgrade had any ideological affinity for Bolsheviks, but in both Czechoslovakia and Yugoslavia the people looked eastward and saw not the Soviet Union but Slavic Russia. Neither country had a common border or territorial dispute with Russia, and the fears of both lay to the west—immediate fears of Germany and Italy, lingering fears of a Hapsburg restoration in Austria or Hungary. Red or White, Russia remained the older brother, protecting all good little Slavs against Turks and Teutons.

Quite opposite were the feelings in Hungary and the three countries bordering on the land of the Soviets. Hungary was the land of the Magyars, who had no love for Slavs, great or small, and extensive territorial claims against all three of their Slav neighbors. Rumania and Russia were at odds over Bessarabia, which Rumania had seized during the Revolution. Modern Lithuania was carved out of imperial Russia's Baltic provinces. Poles and Russians were ancestral enemies, and the border between the two nations was little more than a compromise made possible by mutual fatigue following their bitter and bloody war in 1920.

Poland, Czechoslovakia, and Yugoslavia were born of, and Rumania was greatly aggrandized by, the postwar treaty settlements. All four were allied with France, and shared her interest in preserving the Versailles "system." One might have expected that these shared objectives would have produced a strong military and diplomatic cohesion among the four. Three of them, to be sure, were joined in the Little Entente, the prime purpose of which was mutual protection against Hungary's revisionist aspirations; there were half a million Magyars in northern Yugoslavia, three quarters of a million in Slovakia, and one and a half million in Rumania.

But Poland was not a member of the Little Entente. Much the largest and most populous of the Eastern European countries, Poland was the weakest link in the chain of common interests, and the weakness was primarily due to her less than friendly attitude toward Czechoslovakia.

7

Poland's diplomacy between the wars was largely governed by her unenviable location between Germany and Russia, and the history of her relations with her two powerful neighbors. She had long common borders with both Germany and Russia; neither was a natural frontier, and both were disputed. In 1920, Poland was strong enough to fight the Red Army to a standstill, and until the thirties her forces outmatched the Reichswehr, limited as it was by the Versailles restrictions. But she could not hope to hold off an assault by either a rearmed Germany or a Russia recovered from the scourge of revolution.

Furthermore, alliance offered only limited protection. None of the eastern countries was strong enough to give decisive help against a Germany or Russia at full strength. France was temporarily the military mistress of Western Europe and could offer security against Germany as long as the Rhineland remained demilitarized. But France was distant and could be of little immediate help against Russia, or against Germany protected by Western fortifications. The prospect of benefiting from a long-term French rescue operation was better than nothing, but intrinsically it was highly unattractive. Far better it would be to construct a diplomacy that would minimize the possibility of attack by either Germany or Russia, and this was the gist of Polish foreign policy as the two colossi regained strength.

But what sort of diplomacy would achieve this end? It was not an easy problem, and perhaps insoluble. If Germany and Russia were working in tandem, they might make a deal and divide Poland between them, as Frederick and Catherine had done in the eighteenth century. If the two giants were to come to blows, Poland was bound to be the battlefield, and, even if she were to join the winning side, would come out at best a satellite of the victor.

The roots of the dilemma reached back to prewar times, and were visible in the disagreements among the leaders of the Polish independence movement. The National Democratic Party, bourgeois and anti-Semitic, regarded Germany as the principal enemy, and sought autonomy within a pan-Slavic Russian Empire. Polish Socialists, in contrast, were strongly anti-Russian, though in the last prewar years the left-wing Socialists increasingly subordinated nationalist aims to international class solidarity.

When the First World War came, the National Democrats proclaimed their support for the Entente powers including Russia, and their leader, Roman Dmowski, went first to Petrograd and then via London to Paris, where, in 1917, he became chairman of the "Polish National Committee," which claimed to speak for the Poland-to-be. In Poland, meanwhile, Jozef Pilsudski, leader of the Socialists, had formed "Polish Legions" which were fighting beside the Central Powers on the Russian front.

Locked in mortal combat, Germans and Russians both were glad of Poles for cannon fodder, but neither country was willing to pay much of a price, and their attempts to enlist wide Polish support were about equally maladroit. The Russian Revolution and the looming defeat of the Central Powers greatly enhanced the prospects of Polish independence, and in July of 1917, Pilsudski openly broke with the Germans and was imprisoned by them until the end of the war.

In the fall of 1918, the disintegration of the Austro-Hungarian Empire and the defeat of Germany removed the last obstacles to Polish independence. Released from prison, Pilsudski won support from the right as well as from his old Socialist comrades, and was designated Supreme Commander and Chief of State. The famous pianist Ignace Jan Paderewski succeeded in adjusting relations between Pilsudski and Dmowski's Committee in Paris; Paderewski himself became Premier and Foreign Minister, while Dmowski remained in Paris as Poland's chief representative at the Peace Conference. Elections were held in January 1919, and sovereign power was then vested in the elected legislative body, the Sejm, which immediately confirmed Pilsudski in both his offices.

Three days before the elections, Czech troops attacked the Polish garrisons in the Silesian province of Teschen, and planted the seeds of a dispute that soured Polish-Czech relations from then until the time of Munich. Small in area but rich in minerals and industries, Teschen was claimed by Czechoslovakia as a part of what had been Austrian Silesia, but the mixed population included many Poles. The Czech action was prompted by French support for their claims, and in 1920 the Interallied Commission awarded the bulk of the Teschen district, including 140,000 Polish-speaking inhabitants, to Czechoslovakia. Bowing to the Allied award, Paderewski wrote that the decision "had dug an abyss between the two nations."

Independence did not end the divergence between Dmowski's National Democrats, who sought to push Poland's boundaries westward at the expense of Germany, and the Socialists, who still saw Russia as the great danger and wanted to roll back the Soviet frontier and make common cause with the Belorussians and Ukrainians. Pilsudski was of the latter persuasion but, powerful as he was, thought it wise to compromise with Dmowski, especially since the National Democrats were the strongest single party in the Sejm. The result was that Poland pursued an expansionist policy in both directions, and came into possession of territories coveted by both Germany and Russia. In the west she was less successful, as Allied decisions and plebiscites left most of Silesia and East and West Prussia to Germany, but the Polish corridor to the Baltic was a sure guarantee of German envy and ultimate enmity.

In the east Pilsudski had a much freer hand, as the Versailles Treaty postponed the fixing of Poland's eastern frontiers, and Russia was in the throes of civil war. Correctly anticipating that, in the upshot, possession would be nine points of the law, and shrewdly refusing to support White Russian generals like Denikin, who wanted to revive the Russian Empire, Pilsudski put his formidable energies into the creation of a Polish Army. By April 1919 it was 200,000 strong; a few months later it had doubled in size, and by the spring of 1920 it numbered all of 700,000 men, and Pilsudski felt strong enough to open a major offensive against the Red Army, in collaboration with Petlura. Kiev soon fell to them, the dreams of a great federation led by Poland seemed on the verge of realization, and Pilsudski (now field marshal) was idolized as the greatest military hero in Polish history, as well as the father of her reborn independence.

But the Poles had overreached themselves. The Ukrainian people failed to rise en masse behind Petlura. The Red Army was no longer preoccupied with revolutionary fighting, and by midsummer the Russian counterattack had reached Warsaw.

Pilsudski rallied his forces, split the Russian front, and recaptured Minsk. The exhausted and war-weary antagonists struck an armistice in October, and Poland's eastern border was finally determined by the Treaty of Riga, signed in March of 1921. It was a victory for Poland insofar as it ran well over a hundred miles to the east of the line previously proposed as a compromise by the British Foreign Secretary, Lord Curzon. On the Polish side of the frontier dwelt a million Belorussians and four million Ukrainians—too few to furnish the basis for a federated state, but quite enough to constitute a grave minority problem, and to promise future Russian efforts to push the boundary westward, as indeed was done in 1939 and again in 1945.

As for her two small neighbors on the north, Poland's relations with Latvia were good enough, but with Lithuania were worst of all. The bone of contention was the city of Vilna, claimed by the Lithuanians as the capital of their ancient duchy, but predominantly Polish in culture and population. Pilsudski himself was a native of the Vilna region, and cherished dreams of re-establishing the old union of Poland and Lithuania. In October 1920, soon after the Red Army had been driven out of Vilna, Pilsudski instigated a coup whereby a Polish army general, Lucian Zeligowski (also a Vilna native), occupied the city in somewhat the fashion that D'Annunzio took Fiume. An election early in 1922 furnished the basis for the annexation of the Vilna area to Poland, confirmed by the Allies the following year. Lithuania repudiated the decision, and maintained a theoretical state of war with Poland until 1926. Diplomatic relations were not established until March of 1938.

With her last remaining neighbor, Rumania, Poland's relations could be described as reasonably satisfactory. There was no boundary dispute between the two countries, and both had reason to fear the Soviets—Rumania because of her annexation of Bessarabia, Poland for her land-grabbing in Belorussia and the Ukraine. In March 1921 they signed a defensive alliance, providing for mutual assistance in the event of a Russian attack on either, which endured until Poland's destruction in 1939.

Thus, when Poland's borders were finally settled in 1923, she found herself on basically hostile terms with four of her six immediate neighbors. The issues with Germany and Russia were perhaps insoluble, but those with Lithuania and Czechoslovakia were not. The lack of rapport with Czechoslovakia was especially unfortunate, for a solidarity between the two would have greatly reinforced the barriers to Germany's eastward expansion. Furthermore, the disputed Teschen boundary was neither the sole nor the basic cause of disharmony; rather it was Poland's distrust of Czechoslovakia because of the latter's affinity for Russia.

There was good ground for Polish resentment, inasmuch as during the summer of 1920, when the Red Army was approaching Warsaw, the Prague government had refused to allow Hungary to send troops across their country to reinforce the Poles, The anomalous result was that Poland, whose very existence was based on the Versailles settlement, remained on the best of terms with Hungary, against whose revisionist aspirations the Little Entente was directed. Linked by mutual anti-Bolshevism, Poland and Hungary yearned for a common border, to be established at the expense of the Czechs by annexing Ruthenia and parts of Slovakia. For quite different reasons, German and Polish leaders shared the view that polyglot Czechoslovakia was not a "viable" nation.

8

Despite his age, illness, and death in 1935, the history of Poland between the great wars is dominated by Józef Pilsudski. To those who still remember, he looms out of the past as an imperious, white-mustachioed old man in uniform. Despite his wartime exploits and marshal's rank he was not a military man by training, but rather a university intellectual, a revolutionary jounalist, and a Socialist politician. Charismatic, highly articulate, politically resourceful, and patriarchal, he bore more than a touch of resemblance to "le grand Charles" De Gaulle, of more recent memory.

Not the least of these similarities was the seemingly casual yet artful manner in which both men could assume and relinquish power and position. Under the 1921 Constitution, the office of the President was purely formal, and Pilsudski disclaimed all interest in it. After relinquishing his title as Chief of State to the President, Pilsudski carried on as Commander-in-Chief for a few months, but in May 1923 he resigned, and retired to his country estate. Despite or because of his military-revolutionary life style, he was impatient of parliamentary maneuvering, and saw little promise in a government devoid of executive authority and controlled by a party-ridden legislature. Observing the course of events with increasing disenchantment, Pilsudski retained the support of both the Socialists and important groups of Army officers. Using this curious combination of forces, in May 1926 the marshal brought off a successful *coup d'état* with the aid of a general strike called by the Socialist Party and the railway labor unions, and a body of troops collected for him by his close friend General Zeligowski, the Minister of War.

When Pilsudski took power he was in the sixtieth year of an exceedingly arduous life, and his physique and personality alike were ravaged by the strains to which he had subjected himself. Disgust with the corruption and inefficiency of politicians caused him to resort to dictatorial measures and lean increasingly on trusted Army friends and protégés—the members of what soon became known as the "government of colonels." For only two short intervals in the nine years of his rule did Pilsudski himself assume the premiership; the rest of the time he was Minister of War, and exerted his power through unofficial channels. The presidency he entrusted to an old Socialist acquaintance, Professor Ignacy Mościcki, who remained in office until the German conquest of Poland in 1939.

Under the aegis of the marshal and his colonels Poland retained the parliamentary forms, but in reality the regime grew increasingly dictatorial, especially after 1930. Pilsudski himself remained personally incorruptible, simple in his habits, and intensely patriotic in his aims. But despite his unquestioned integrity in these respects, the old man became increasingly bitter, cynical, and suspicious, and his political morality degenerated. Extensive police surveillance, unlawful arrests and imprisonments, and even political murder marked and marred his rule. Meanwhile the power of the President, Pilsudski's creature, was strengthened by the Enabling Act of 1933, which authorized the President to issue decrees with the force of law,* and by a new constitution adopted in April 1935, a few weeks before Pilsudski's death.

In the field of foreign relations, the first five years of the "Pilsudski era" were uneventful. Poland's diplomatic situation did not improve during the twenties. Her two archenemies were bound by the Rapallo Treaty and the clandestine but close military relations sponsored by Seeckt. The Locarno agreements weakened the Franco-Polish alliance by raising the question whether French military aid to Poland should be automatic and immediate in the event of an attack, or subject to League of Nations procedures, while Germany's international position was greatly improved by her admission to League membership with a permanent seat in the Council, which she at once utilized to attack Poland's treatment of the German minority in Polish Silesia. The growing strength of the Nazis and other German nationalist groups, and their strident demands for revision of the Polish-German border, gave Pilsudski increasing cause for alarm, and brought about a gradual shift in his appraisal of the foreign scene, in which Russia had always been the main enemy. The sharpening Japanese threat to Soviet power in the east and the advent of Litvinov combined to facilitate a détente between Russia and Poland, and in July 1932 the two countries signed a nonaggression pact.

In December 1930, Pilsudski installed one of his most devoted young colonels as second man in the Foreign Ministry. Jozef Beck was a Galician who had fought in Pilsudski's legion during the First World War, and thereafter made a career in the Army intelligence service, including a tour of duty as military attaché in Paris. Two years later Pilsudski made him Foreign Minister, a post which Beck was to hold until the débacle in September 1939.

Beck's appointment coincided with the death of the Weimar Republic and the advent of Hitler and the Nazi regime. Although Pilsudski seems at first to have thought that an Austrian plebeian would be less likely than a Prussian Junker to press for a revision of the Polish-German borders, he was soon alarmed by reports of German rearmament.† Secret soundings in France convinced the marshal that France would not act decisively to prevent German military resur-

---

* Enacted on March 26, 1933, the Polish Enabling Act was similar to and comtemporaneous with the notorious Enabling Law approved by the Reichstag on March 23, 1933, which was a crucial step on the road to Hitler's dictatorship in Germany.

† According to Beneš, early in 1933 he was approached by Beck with a proposal for a Polish-Czech alliance against Germany, which Beneš rejected "because he thought it would be very dangerous to give Germany clear cause for fearing encirclement."

gence, and he concluded that Poland's security would profit from improved relations with Berlin, to match those already achieved with Moscow. Hitler, playing his cards close to his chest in the early stages of rearmament, was only too glad to talk peace and friendship, and the easing of tension was signalized in April 1933 by simultaneous meetings between the Fuehrer and the Polish minister in Berlin, and Pilsudski and the German military attaché in Warsaw. The following January a ten-year nonaggression declaration was signed, matching the comparable treaty already consummated with Russia.*

It was hardly surprising, therefore, that when Louis Barthou came to Warsaw in April 1934 to promote his "eastern Locarno" ideas, he found the marshal not only disinterested but even scornful of France's determination to check German ambitions. "You will yield again and again," he predicted, and, in reply to Barthou's expostulations, reminded the Frenchman of an episode when the two of them, under Pétain's guidance, had visited the battlefields of northern France. Barthou had narrowly escaped tumbling into a crater, and upon regaining his equilibrium had remarked: "I am accustomed to falling; I have been a French cabinet minister thirteen times."

At least on the surface, the relations between Berlin and Warsaw sweetened far beyond the requirements of the nonaggression pact. Both regimes were militaristic and authoritarian, and shared ideological antipathy to communism. Joseph Goebbels, Hans Frank, and especially Hermann Goering visited Poland frequently, and in Berlin, Ambassador Lipski had ready access to an uncommonly agreeable Fuehrer, whose every public reference to Poland was conciliatory, and who touted Pilsudski as one of the truly great men of the era.

In March 1935, Poland joined the other Versailles signatories in formally condemning Hitler's repudiation of the treaty's arms restrictions, but the event caused no stir in Warsaw, where the actuality and extent of German rearmament were already well known. The following month Anthony Eden was in Poland preaching the dangers of a resurgent Germany, but all he got for his pains was a lecture from a contrary-minded Pilsudski, who told Eden that Britain's low assessment of Russian military power was quite erroneous, and that the Nazi regime in Germany was "good for Poland."

It was the old marshal's last meeting with a foreign diplomat. Mortally ill from stomach cancer, he was unable to see Pierre Laval when, on May 10, the latter stopped in Warsaw enroute to Moscow, and he died two days later. There was no one man upon whom the hero's mantle could gracefully fall. The

---

* Jules Laroche, an insightful diplomat who had been the French Ambassador since 1926 and well knew Poland and its language, thought that still other motives prompted the swing to Hitler. As Pilsudski viewed matters, Mussolini's abortive Four-Power Pact had been intended to divert Hitler toward the east, and Pilsudski countered it with an agreement which might deflect him southward. Both the old marshal and Beck, Laroche thought, were "ulcerated" by the exclusion of Poland from the *Directoire Européen,* and wished to show France that they could act independently of her, as indeed they did on this occasion, for Paris was given no advance warning of the pact with Germany. Furthermore, while Pilsudski valued the French alliance, he was not particularly *sympathique* to them; after all, during the first three years of the First World War he had led the Polish fight against France's ally, czarist Russia.

authoritarian regime of the "colonels" continued, with President Mościcki and General Edward Smigly-Rydz* taking respectively political and military leadership, and Colonel Beck in virtually complete control of foreign affairs.

Beck's talk with Laval, just before Pilsudski's death, ominously reflected the former's animosity toward Czechoslovakia and a general decay in Franco-Polish relations. Twice Laval stated that Beneš had asked him to put "special questions" in Warsaw, and twice Beck repulsed him by observing that Beneš was at liberty to communicate directly. Laval then observed that the questions were of interest to France as well, and asked whether, if German aggression against Czechoslovakia should oblige France to intervene, Poland would attack Czechoslovakia. "Tell M. Beneš that I refuse to answer the question," Beck replied. "That is the categorical and official attitude of the Polish government." He then launched into a long diatribe against the Czechs, listing many grievances, after which Laval inquired whether France could be of any assistance in alleviating the situation. Beck answered in the negative, and on that cold note the meeting ended.

It was a performance reflecting both Beck's consummate self-assurance and his capacity for giving offense. Both physically and intellectually he cut a fine figure, but his colleagues in the diplomatic world found him arrogant, devious, and unpredictable, and a mordant Frenchman observed that "when Beck started to speak truthfully, it was immediately apparent." The French Ambassador, Léon Noël, suspected that Beck's ill-concealed antipathy to France had its origin in a mysterious incident which had led to his recall from Paris when he was military attaché there. However that might have been, his conduct as Foreign Minister was harmful to Franco-Polish relations, and Noël went so far as to record that "throughout his ministry, his diplomacy at all times ran counter to French ideas and initiatives."

Some of these differences surfaced soon after Noël's arrival in Warsaw, in the course of an exploratory discussion with Beck's immediate subordinate Count Jean Szembek, the Under-Secretary for Foreign Affairs. The Ambassador, while acknowledging Poland's need for stable and peaceful relations with Germany, complained of the "incomprehensible" manifestations of "collaboration," including especially the frequent interchange of official visits. Szembek, for his part, complained of the French penchant for great-power conferences from which Poland was excluded, and observed acidly that it was French statesmen such as Barthou whom Poland had to thank for "bringing the Soviets into Europe." Time did little to assuage these wounds, which rather were aggravated by Beck's chip-on-the-shoulder attitude toward several of the French diplomats, including Noël and, especially, Léger.†

Such was the unhappy state of affairs when, on March 7, 1936, Hitler sent his

---

* His natal surname was Rydz; "Smigly" was a revolutionary pseudonym meaning "the quick one." Known almost indifferently as Smigly-Rydz or Rydz-Smigly, he was Pilsudski's chosen successor as Inspector General of the Army.

† At Geneva in January of 1936, Beck sought to bring about the appointment of a Pole as League of Nations High Commissioner in Danzig. The French opposed the idea, and, when Léger pointed out the bad impression such a selection might make in Germany, Beck retorted that he had "no need for instruction on how Poland should conduct herself toward Germany."

handful of troops into the Rhineland. On the surface, the Polish reaction was impeccably loyal; that very afternoon Beck received Noël and asked him to inform his government that "Poland will be faithful to the undertakings that tie her to your country." Noël, for his part, took this assurance at face value, and there is little doubt but that some at least of the Polish leaders expected and even hoped that France would react decisively, or that Poland would have fulfilled her commitments had matters come to scratch.

Beck himself, however, was convinced that France would not resort to force, so that he could safely make promises which he would never be called on to make good. Furthermore, he had no stomach for such a fray. On two occasions, during the month preceding the German move, he told Szembek that remilitarization of the Rhineland was not covered by the Franco-Polish treaty, and that Poland therefore would *not* be obliged to assist France. Beck repeated these views on March 7; Germany's action did not constitute a *casus foederis** under the treaty with France, and anyhow France would not move without the support of the British, whose fleet was tied up in the Mediterranean by the Ethiopian crisis, and whose defenses were in no condition to risk a war with Germany.

So little regard had Beck for French feelings that he wholly neglected to exploit his assurances, empty as they were, so as at least to win a measure of gratitude. The official Polish news agency (*Iskra*) took the German line, and informed Polish newspaper readers that the French, by allying themselves with Moscow, were responsible for the turn of affairs. At the League Council meeting in London, Beck clashed sharply with Flandin, and his relations with the Quai d'Orsay were strained anew. On May 9, Poland, without prior notice, denounced her commercial treaty with France, and later that month, in conference with a group of subordinates, Beck described France as "an instrument in the hands of the Comintern."

By the summer of 1936, Noël had concluded that Beck's attitude was so pernicious that the French should seek his removal. Opportunity was not lacking, for the Polish Government was actively soliciting a large French loan for military and industrial expansion. The May elections in France had swept the Popular Front to power, with Léon Blum as premier and Yvon Delbos at the Quai d'Orsay, free from the entanglements of the Laval-Flandin era. General Gamelin visited Poland early in August, and General Smigly-Rydz was then invited to return the visit and negotiate the loan. It was an open secret that between the general and Beck no love was lost. Noël's proposal was that his government should condition the loan on the removal of Beck, and an intensified collaboration between the Polish and French general staffs, which would also involve a bettering of Warsaw's relations with Prague, so that plans for common defense against Germany could be made on the basis of Polish-Czech military collaboration.

Although Noël's program won his superiors' initial approval, it was not carried through. On August 30, 1936, Smigly-Rydz was received in Paris with

---

* A legal expression meaning literally "case of the treaty," and signifying an event which requires performance of a treaty obligation. The political and military accords of 1921 between Poland and France plainly covered a German military entry into the Rhineland.

great ceremony. He attended maneuvers in Rheims and Nancy, received the grand cordon of the Legion of Honor, and, with the assistance of the newly appointed Ambassador, Juliusz Lukasiewicz (Beck's close friend), the general quite outbargained his hosts. The French had contemplated extending a credit of 2 billion francs against the purchase of war materials, under strict controls. Smigly-Rydz categorically rejected this offer the day before his scheduled departure; the French, as he had expected, yielded to his demands that half the loan be in cash and available for industrial expansion. Tentative efforts on separate occasions by Blum and Gamelin to raise the issue of Polish-Czech relations were deflected by Smigly-Rydz and rebuffed by Lukasiewicz. Gamelin and Delbos probed the general's attitude toward Beck, and found the terrain unpromising for further action. Apparently the French were even more eager to make the loan than the Poles were to receive it; the agreement was signed at Rambouillet on September 17, and Smigly-Rydz returned to Warsaw in triumph. A few weeks later he was made a Marshal of Poland, and his success in procuring the loan unconditionally served, much to Noël's chagrin, to strengthen Beck's position likewise.

But it was a costly victory, for Poland and Czechoslovakia needed each other, and their hostility greatly weakened the French system of alliances. Soon after Pilsudski's death, Beck told Szembek that "there are two European political entities which are condemned, sooner or later, to disappear: Austria and Czechoslovakia." It was characteristic of the bright but flighty colonel to be so alert to proximate dangers and blind to those ensuing, so that he could clearly perceive the hazards to other countries without projecting the consequences for Poland. His intimates and advisers appear to have been no wiser. When Smigly-Rydz warned Szembek that Germany rearmed might be dangerous, the latter discounted such fears by remarking "the Third Reich's tendency to direct its expansion in a southerly direction." Lukasiewicz went so far as to declare that it would be "useful for Poland that Germany should lay hands on Czechoslovakia."

The result of the Pilsudski-Beck diplomacy was that, in effect, there were two "Little Ententes" in Eastern Europe—the announced entente of Yugoslavia, Rumania, and Czechoslovakia aligned against Hungary's revisionist aims, and the tacit entente of Poland and Hungary against Czechoslovakia. Perhaps misled by Hitler's Austrian lineage, Beck apparently concluded that the Nazis could be deflected to the southeast and might forget or tolerate the Corridor. Hungering for revenge at Teschen, and imagining that a common Polish-Hungarian frontier in Slovakia and Ruthenia would give added security against Russia, the men of Warsaw were pleased by the thought of Czechoslovakian disintegration. As long as France stood as the protecting power, a direct attack against Czechoslovakia was out of the question; the solution lay in a German assault, diplomatic or military. Thus, vis-à-vis Czechoslovakia, France and Poland were in opposing camps.

Brave, benighted, quixotic Poland—anti-Russian, anti-German, and anti-Semitic; born of Versailles but in league with those who wish to murder her parent; culturally Francophile, friendless among the great powers other than

France, yet scornful of her own protector; spurning her neighbors with whom she might have made common cause against the German peril—was off and running on the road to suicide.

9

Under the twentieth century's professed standards of international wisdom and morality, the Czechoslovakia of Thomas Masaryk and Eduard Beneš was by far the best boy in the school. Both Masaryk and Beneš were of humble birth, but excelled at their studies and became professors. Masaryk blossomed into the philosopher-statesman and father of his country, with Beneš as his good right hand and eventual successor. Their regime was almost ostentatiously dedicated to democratic liberalism, internationalism, and peace through collective security. Beneš dominated his country's foreign policy from its birth and until Munich, and was the only small-power diplomat who was able to hold center stage at Geneva, and raise his voice in the League councils in concert or competition with the spokesmen of the Big Four. Czechoslovakia was the showpiece of the Versailles system—a stable, peaceful, prosperous democracy and a pillar of the League of Nations.

But, as is too often the case, virtue was its own and only reward. Czechoslovakia was a bit too much the teacher's pet; some of the smaller nations' representatives were jealous, and "realists" like Pilsudski, who put a low value on collective security and the League system, were inclined to sneer. Beneš was a dull and prolix speaker, and his very omnipresence at Geneva made him a bit of a bore. Far more important, of course, was the failure of collective security itself in the crises provoked by Japan, Italy, and then Germany. In the upshot, the diplomacy of Beneš failed to give his country the great-power support she needed against her hostile neighbors: Germany, Hungary, and Poland.

Only by spurious use of hindsight, however, is it possible to fault Beneš for the policies he initially prescribed for his newborn nation. It was the death of the Austro-Hungarian Empire that had breathed life into Czechoslovakia; consequently, reappearance of the Hapsburgs in either Vienna or Budapest was the greatest peril, and to be opposed at all costs. Of the great powers, Germany was the only one from which Czechoslovakia had much to fear. The Versailles Treaty was the instrument that killed the empire and forbade German military resurgence. The French Army and the League of Nations, by the might of arms and the right of collective security, were the means by which Versailles was to be enforced. Czechoslovakia was a small but satisfied power, and preservation of the *status quo* was almost if not quite her *summum bonum*.

Given these circumstances, what diplomacy could have appeared more promising than to cleave to the League and to France? So at Geneva, Beneš put his tongue and brain behind the several efforts, all abortive, to strengthen the Covenant and put teeth into the idea of collective security. And so Marshal Foch came to play godfather to the fledgling Czechoslovak Army and a permanent French military mission remained in Prague. In January 1924 the military relation was certified by a formal alliance, calling for mutual assistance in case of any breach of the Treaty of St. Germain, or of aggression against either of the partners.

But France was distant, and Beneš wanted more immediate allies against Hapsburg or Hungarian adventurism. As early as 1920 he was in Belgrade and Bucharest, laying the foundations of the Little Entente. Dedicated primarily to preservation of the Treaty of the Trianon, and the Hungarian boundaries it established, the Little Entente was also Beneš' attempt to exploit the common denominators of foreign policy among Czechoslovakia, Yugoslavia, and Rumania, and enable them to speak with one voice, as loud as that of a great power—a natural strategy, but not likely to please Italy, just within, or Poland, just without, the great-power category.

Committed as he was to the Versailles system, Beneš was shrewd enough to adopt a conciliatory attitude toward the Germanic nations that virtually surrounded Bohemia. He was anxious not only to keep the Hapsburgs out of Vienna, but also to keep Vienna and Berlin apart. The best preventive of an *Anschluss,* he thought, was an Austria in good health, economic and political. So Czechoslovakia joined in loans to the financially fragile Austrian Government, and with England, France, and Italy in the 1922 treaty supporting Austria's political independence and territorial integrity. As for Germany, a commercial treaty in 1920 was followed by the Locarno arbitration treaty in 1925, and in 1926, Beneš strongly supported Germany's admission to the League of Nations with a permanent seat in the Council.

Meanwhile Czechoslovakia had thrived economically, and achieved a level of prosperity both unequaled and envied by her neighbors. The country was governed by shifting coalitions of Agrarians, Social Democrats, and bourgeois nationalist parties. Regardless of the composition of the cabinet, Beneš remained Foreign Minister, while domestic politics were dominated throughout the twenties by the Agrarian leader Antonín Svehla.

Not surprisingly, the principal internal problems grew out of the nation's polyglot composition. Slovakia was economically and culturally backward compared to Bohemia-Moravia, and jealous of Czech dominance of the bureaucracy and professions. Slovak autonomists and separatists found leaders in the priests Andrej Hlinka and Josef Tiso. The more than three million Sudeten Germans, on the other hand, had been on top of the heap in imperial times and looked down on the Czechs, their new masters. There was an indigenous Sudeten German "Nazi" Party, even before Hitler appeared on the scene—anti-Semitic, antidemocratic, racialist, and dedicated to the annexation of the Sudeten areas to Germany—which was able to elect five members of the Czech parliament in 1920, six in 1925, and eight in 1929.*

Czechoslovakia rode out the economic depression of the early thirties better than most of her neighbors, but the industrialized Sudetenland was badly hit and, as in Germany, poverty fed the Nazi flame. So did Hitler's rise to power;

* Founded in Vienna in May of 1918, the Sudeten group called itself the Deutsche National-Sozialistische Arbeiterpartei (D.N.S.A.P.). Hitler's organization reversed the first two words, resulting in the initials "N.S.D.A.P.," which lent themselves to the contraction "Nazi."

Czech Nazism proliferated and grew more belligerent, and in the fall of 1933 the Prague government dissolved the D.N.S.A.P. and suppressed the movement. Simultaneously a Sudeten German gymnasium instructor, Konrad Henlein, announced the formation of the "Sudeten German Home Front" (*Sudetendeutsche Heimatfront,* of S.H.F.), which was to be "above all parties and estates."

At the outset the Front publicly repudiated separatism and endorsed "the fundamental requirements of democracy." But there was an ominous ambiguity about its real nature, for it welcomed the outlawed Nazis as well as more moderate Sudeten Germans, and Henlein's avowed position as *Fuehrer* of the Front hardly matched his public praise of "liberalism" and "respect for individual rights." The front was phenomenally successful as a political vehicle for Sudeten nationalism, and in the elections of May 1935 it garnered 1,250,000 votes (three fifths of the entire German electorate), and emerged suddenly as the second largest party in the national parliament—slightly smaller than the Agrarians and larger than the Social Democrats.

10

At the end of 1935, Thomas Masaryk, laden with years (he was eighty-five) and honors, retired from the presidency and two years later he died. Beneš became President but retained close control of foreign policy, with his friend and follower Kamil Krofta as Foreign Minister. The Premier of the coalition cabinet was Dr. Milan Hodža, a Slovak and leader of the Agrarian Party.

As Beneš moved to his new offices in the Hradschin, there were clouds all around the international horizon. Viewed from Prague, one of the darkest was the decline of the Little Entente. In 1933, in happy co-operation with King Alexander of Yugoslavia and the Foreign Minister of Rumania, Nicholas Titulescu, Beneš had turned the Little Entente from a mere defensive alliance against Hungary into an international organization, with a secretariat and an economic council. But in 1934, King Alexander was assassinated, while in Rumania Titulescu's position was becoming shaky, and in 1936, King Carol gave him his walking papers.

To be sure, Hungary remained the three countries' common enemy, but there was no rapport or common front on other issues. It was plain that Hungary could achieve none of her revisionist aims without the aid of a great power, and by 1936 it was equally plain that Germany was the only country that might be able and willing to give sufficient backing. As German power waxed and broke through the Versailles restrictions, the French alliance system started to disintegrate. Nazism in Germany was echoed, more or less clearly, by authoritarian tendencies in virtually every Central European country except Czechoslovakia. Instead of relying on their own combined strength supported by France, Rumania and Yugoslavia started down the road already taken by Poland—the Pilsudski-Beck diplomacy of staving off the German threat by wooing the Nazi leaders.

In Yugoslavia, the new policies were primarily the work of the Regent, Prince Paul, and of Dr. Milan Stoyadinovitch, a banker-politician who became Premier in the spring of 1935. Alexander's son Peter was only eleven in 1934; his cousin

Paul, named as Regent in the King's will, was an apolitical, art-collecting, English-educated snob, with a horror of communism, distaste for democracy, and an affinity for rightist authoritarians. Stoyadinovitch, who prided himself on his realism and lack of sentiment, at once set about improving his country's relations with the nearby great powers, Italy and Germany. He had little use for the French and no intention of allowing Yugoslavia to be pulled into war in France's wake, in the event of a German invasion of Austria or Czechoslovakia. In March 1937, when signing a nonaggression and economic agreement with Italy, Stoyadinovitch told Ciano that, while the Little Entente would undergo no "formal transformation" and Yugoslavia and Rumania would remain in close contact, "the relations between those two countries and Czechoslovakia will be reduced to an empty formality."

Rumania's drift away from parliamentary democracy was largely the product of economic instability and royal ambition. In 1928, when King Ferdinand died, his playboy son Carol was in exile, and the throne passed to Carol's son Michael, aged six. But the ensuing regency was weak and unpopular, and in 1930, with the approval of all major parties, Carol returned from exile in Paris and was proclaimed King; the regency was dissolved and Michael became Crown Prince. Immediately there was a falling-out between King Carol and the Prime Minister, Iuliu Maniu, who claimed that the King's return had been predicated on his agreement to put aside his mistress, Magda Lupescu, with whom he had been living in Paris. But Carol, faithful in his fashion, brought the lady to Bucharest, whereupon Maniu resigned in a dudgeon of propriety. Others were less shocked, and Carol not only kept his mistress but also succeeded in isolating Maniu, wrecking the party structure, and laying the basis for a personal regime which eventually enabled him to exercise dictatorial powers.

Authoritarian as he was, Carol was pro-French and anti-German, and until 1936 he continued to support Titulescu, whose diplomacy generally paralleled that of Beneš. During the early thirties, however, economic depression and pervasive anti-Semitism precipitated a Fascist-type organization called the "Iron Guard," which opposed Titulescu's policies of support for France and the League of Nations and conciliation with Russia, and favored co-operation with Fascist Italy and Nazi Germany. By a combination of terrorism, nationalist appeal, and exploitation of peasant unrest the Iron Guard made considerable political headway. During the Italo-Ethiopian war, Titulescu overplayed his hand in supporting sanctions, and in August of 1936, Carol replaced him with the less international-minded Victor Antonescu. It was the first sign of Carol's shift to a more neutral attitude as between France and Germany, and a concomitant loosening of Rumania's ties with Czechoslovakia.

Sensing the unfavorable trends among his neighbors, Beneš moved energetically to shore up his country's own defenses. Two-year compulsory military service was established in 1934, and plans, strongly influenced by the Maginot Line, were made for a fortifications system along the German frontier. A Czech military mission was sent to France, and General Belhague, a French engineer, came to Czechoslovakia. In 1936, Parliament enacted a State Defense Law, establishing a Supreme Defense Council and authorizing special security restrictions in the border areas.

In the diplomatic sphere Beneš followed the French lead to a defensive alliance with Russia. This step was not without domestic political complications. In 1922, at Rapallo, Beneš had negotiated a trade treaty with Chicherin, and from then on worked for *de jure* recognition of the Soviet Government. Bourgeois nationalists and the Agrarians, however, were strongly anticommunist, and it was not until 1934 that full diplomatic relations were established. In May of 1935, two weeks after signature of the Franco-Soviet treaty, Beneš and the Soviet Ambassador signed the Czechoslovak-Russian treaty of defensive alliance, mutually conditioned on France's fulfillment of her obligations.

Impressed by the Henleinists' success in the 1935 elections, Beneš belatedly began a drive for better treatment of the Sudeten Germans. There is no doubt of the sincerity of those efforts, but events conspired against their success. The treaty with Russia had given the Nazis an excuse for open and violent criticism of the Beneš government, and German military power was increasing day by day. The new fortifications lay mostly in the border areas inhabited by Sudeten Germans, and the security restrictions bore most onerously on them. The Front relied increasingly on Nazi support, and Henlein sought to make his followers' grievances a matter of international concern, whereas Beneš had always insisted that his country's minorities problems were a strictly internal affair.

In June 1936, Henlein delivered a speech at Eger* in which he declared that "every people and its responsible leaders must be acknowledged to be solely responsible for the adjustment of their own national status," and that "we would rather be hated with Germany than derive any benefit from the hate against Germany." This open acknowledgment of the Nazi character of his movement, and the implied demand that the Czech Government deal with Henlein as the local leader of a "people," foreshadowed the Sudeten intransigency that would emerge in 1938.

Despite the Russian alliance, the new fortifications, and the growing military strength behind them, 1935 and 1936 were bad years for the Czechoslovakia of Masaryk and Beneš. At home, the Sudeten problem had turned from an annoyance into a threat. Abroad, remilitarization of the Rhineland had deprived France of the ability to give immediately effective aid against Germany, and the Little Entente was but the ghost of its old self. Mussolini had made a laughing-stock of the League and collective security. Of Czechoslovakia's contiguous neighbors, Germany and Hungary were openly hostile, Poland nursed treacherous designs, Austria was indifferent, and Rumania unreliable.

Until 1935, Prague might safely assume that France, in the interest of her own security, would never tolerate a German attack against Czechoslovakia. By the summer of 1936 it should have been, if it was not in fact, clear to Beneš that he himself might be forced to make the decision for peace or war, and that there would be few foreign friends encouraging him to take the latter course.

---

* Cheb in Czech. Since most of the literature on the Sudeten crisis uses the German placenames, I have followed suit.

CHAPTER 10

For King and Country?

1

Young Kenelm Digby of St. John's College, descended from a line of Irish peers, was standing before the Oxford Union to open the debate on his motion: "That this House will in no circumstances fight for its King and Country." It was the ninth of February, 1933. In Germany, less than two weeks earlier, Adolf Hitler had become Chancellor, but neither Digby nor those who spoke after him had much to say about the Nazis. Remarking Digby's "tub-thumping" style, *Isis* quoted his opening charge that "our armistice celebrations have become a bad and bitter joke" and his praise for the Soviet Union as "the only country fighting for the cause of peace . . . that had rid itself of the war-mongering clique." This tribute drew a caustic rejoinder from K.R.F. Steel-Maitland of Balliol, leading for the opposition, who observed that it was not in Britain but in the Soviet Union that there were a million men under arms.

The issue for debate had been proposed to the Standing Committee of the Union by its librarian, David Graham of Balliol. The wording caused no alarm; on the contrary, it was thought highly appropriate because it could be supported by those who would go to war for some things but not for "King and Country" (such as communists, or dedicated internationalists who would fight only for collective security under the League of Nations), as well as by outright pacifists. The meeting drew an attendance of about five hundred, and a record number of fifty-seven students asked to be heard. The President of the Union, Frank Hardie of Christ Church, thought it a suitable occasion for outside speakers—at that time an uncommon practice in the Union—and Quintin Hogg, a rising young Conservative and former President of the Union, readily agreed to speak against the motion. Obtaining a proponent was not so easy, and Hardie unsuccessfully approached Norman Angell and John Strachey before he secured an acceptance from the well-known writer and lecturer C. E. M. Joad.*

Hogg's theme, a familiar one then as now, was that the pacifists and those

---

* Joad, best known for his philosophical writings and head of that department at Birkbeck College of the University of London, died in 1953. Hogg was a member of Parliament from 1938 to 1950, when by inheritance he became Viscount Hailsham, a title which he resigned in 1963 and returned to the House of Commons. In 1970 he returned to the peerage as Lord Chancellor. Dr. Frank Hardie, author of *The Political Influence of the British Monarchy 1868–1952* and other works, wrote an account of the "King and Country" debate and its aftermath, which is deposited in the Bodleian Library.

who supported unilateral disarmament were not "true friends of peace." Intervention in world affairs without the force to back it up was the surest road to war, while a strong Britain was "a necessary factor for peace." Incautiously he resorted to the classic challenge to pacifists about their conduct if they saw their wives being raped, and this gave Joad opportunity to quote Lytton Strachey's reply to a comparable question: "I should interpose my body!"

Next, Joad declared that the issue was "anachronistic" and should have read: "That this House would never commit murder on a large scale whenever the Government decided that it should do so." He painted a terrible picture of aerial warfare: "Within 20 minutes of the declaration of war with a western European power" there would be bombers over Britain, and of what use would be antiaircraft defenses when "a single bomb can poison every living thing in an area of three quarters of a square mile"? Then, in the peroration of what the *Oxford Magazine* called a "magnificently serious speech," he denounced the victory in 1918 as utterly futile. The war fought to make the world safe for democracy had led to widespread military dictatorship. "We fought to make a new world, with the result that the old one is in the throes of economic collapse. We fought to make England a fit land for heroes to live in, with the result that these heroes can now secure from the State the miserable pittance it gives them for a dole." Therefore, even in the event of an actual invasion of an unarmed England, "only at most a policy of passive resistance should be adopted."

There were ten additional student speakers on each side, including some who became well known—for the motion A. W. J. (Tony) Greenwood, Member of Parliament and Minister of Housing, and Max Beloff, Gladstone Professor of Government at Oxford; against it Angus Maude, Member of Parliament and writer on economics, and J. R. D. Crichton, Judge of the High Court. Among the opponents was a German Rhodes scholar, A. F. K. Schlepegrell. David W. S. Hunt of Wadham College, who in 1933 was among those proclaiming unwillingness to fight for King and Country, in 1940 was a subaltern in the Welsh Guards. He ended the war as a colonel on the staff of the Allied headquarters in Italy, and in later life, as Sir David Hunt, K.C.M.G., he was private secretary to both Winston Churchill and Clement Atlee, and then High Commissioner in Nigeria.

In the upshot, the motion carried by 275 ayes to 153 noes. Given the times, this was hardly surprising; in 1927 the Cambridge Union had voted 213 to 138 for "uncompromising pacifism." Furthermore, irreverently stated issues were not unusual in English academic dialectics. A few years later the Oxford Union voted preference for the Red Flag over the Union Jack.

Accordingly, Hardie and his colleagues had little reason to anticipate the storm that soon broke about their ears. A letter published in the London *Daily Telegraph* referred ominously to "communist cells in the Oxford colleges."* Another published letter accused the Standing Committee of putting the motion "in a form obviously intended as a jibe on loyalty and patriotism." The *Daily*

---

* On this point the *Oxford Magazine* commented editorially that the Oxford communists were at an unemployment rally, and had been notably absent from the Union when the "King and Country" motion was debated.

Express, with diction worthy of Spiro Agnew, ascribed the vote to "practical jokers, woozy-minded Communists and sexual indeterminates."

At this point, a circular letter initiated by Randolph Churchill and signed by Hogg, Lord Stanley of Alderley, and others, was sent to all Life Members of the Union asking support for Churchill's motion that the vote on the "King and Country" motion be expunged from the minutes. On February 16, at the Union's next weekly meeting, the hall was invaded by a score of unidentified intruders (thought by the *Oxford Times* to have been supporters of the English neo-Fascist, Oswald Mosley) who tore the offending pages out of the minutes book.

But the critical reaction was overwhelmed by the counterreaction. When Randolph Churchill's motion* was called up at the meeting on March 2, it was defeated 750 to 138, as the student members of the Union, irked by this interference on the part of the oldsters, turned out in unprecedented numbers. In Nottingham and Sheffield similar debates were banned, but in Manchester, Leicester, Edinburgh, and about twenty other universities, comparable resolutions were adopted. Defeated in Belfast, the motion was carried in Capetown. In the United States, a 21,000-vote poll taken by the Student Union showed 8,000 pacifists and 7,000 who would fight only if their country were invaded.

Adolf Hitler's name first entered the discussion at the Union meeting on March 2, when Lord Stanley of Alderley began his speech for the Churchill motion with the words "I am not Hitler . . ." His sentence was cut short by the explosion of a stink bomb, but it was Churchill and Stanley, not Hitler, at whom the bomb was directed.

2

The "King and Country" debate was a colorful reflection of the British temper between the two great wars. Exhausted and disgusted by the prolonged bloodbath in Flanders' fields, wracked by internal economic strains, and already tiring of the burdens of empire, neither the people nor their leaders were in any mood to embark on new crusades.

Indeed, there was question enough whether the country still had the means and the will to maintain its centuries-old foreign policy. In a classic memorandum composed in 1907, Eyre Crowe, who had just completed his great reform of the Foreign Service, described "the general character of England's foreign policy" as based on "the possession of preponderant sea power" and prevention of the rise of a hostile "general combination" of powers. Therefore England "must be the natural enemy of any country threatening the independence of others and the natural protector of the weaker communities" against any neighboring country "ambitious to extend its frontiers." In short, England's security depended upon an international equilibrium "technically known as the balance of power." Thus "the opposition into which England must inevitably be driven to any country aspiring to . . . dictatorship assumes almost the form of a law of

---

* Rumblings of Churchillian indignation were still audible fifteen years later in *The Gathering Storm*, in which the author refers (page 85) to the "ever-shameful" resolution of the Oxford Union.

nature." Seven years later, fearing that Wilhelm II entertained just such aspirations, Britain went to war, but so much blood had to be poured into the scales that, when it was all over, many Britains were ready to question whether the "balance" was worth preserving at so frightful a cost.

Furthermore the victory, if such it might be called, brought few laurels. Returning soldiers did not boast of their deeds of valor. The generals had been bumblers, and the end was the product not of brilliant maneuver, but of attrition from the insensate slaughter of trench warfare. Maybe Jutland had saved the nation from defeat, but it was hardly a jewel of the first water in the crown of Britannia, ruler of the waves, and it was the Germans, with their U-boats, who had taken the initiative at sea and come perilously close to closing the trade routes. Far from extolling the heroics of combat, the postwar literature was a stream of antiwar books that revived memories of horror and ridiculed the class nature of the Army.

The war had been an awful folly, and the peace not much better. Tarnished by analyses such as Keynes's *Economic Consequences of the Peace,* Versailles soon became a symbol not of glory but of guilt. It was not that the English loved the Germans. Of course the Huns were beastly, but that was no excuse for being beastly to them; it wasn't gentlemanly, and anyhow it didn't seem to be good business. The collapse of the mark and the French occupation of the Ruhr reinforced Keynes's warnings that it was idle to expect that Germany could "pay for" the war. If the twin pillars of the League Covenant were collective security and general disarmament, it was quite unreasonable that France should keep her arms and Germany have none. By the end of the twenties, according to the liberal editor of the *New Statesman and Nation,* Kingsley Martin: "Almost everyone, Conservatives, Liberals and Labour alike, regarded the French notion of keeping Germany permanently as a second-class power as absurd, and agreed that the Versailles Treaty must be revised in Germany's favor."

But this France would not do, and Germany was impotent to force the issue. If general disarmament was unattainable, perhaps collective security was not so remote a hope, and might be a cheap means of preserving the European "balance" on which England's safety still depended. But the United States was a renegade and Russia and Germany outcasts from Geneva, while France was a skeptical and Italy a resentful participant. At Downing Street and Whitehall, English statesmen were of two minds about the merits of the League, but without British support it certainly was not going to amount to much, and support was given. If Czechoslovakia was the star pupil of the Geneva school, Britain was its acknowledged, albeit reserved and sometimes condescending, leader in the persons, during the twenties, of Lord Robert Cecil and Neville Chamberlain's half-brother, Austen. And so it came about that Austen Chamberlain was the principal architect of the 1925 Locarno Pact, which provided a security structure for Western Europe and brought Germany into the League and an end to Allied occupation of the Rhineland.

The treaties were signed on Austen Chamberlain's sixty-second birthday, and he soon became Sir Austen with the Star of the Garter on his breast. Locarno was the climax of his career, and for the next ten years the "spirit of Locarno" was regularly invoked as a diplomatic solvent. But its terms reflected the narrow English concept of security. The Polish Corridor, Chamberlain declared, was not worth "the bones of a British grenadier," and Britain assumed no responsibilities east of the Rhine. Furthermore, although the pact was made part of the League framework, it seemed to foreshadow a Europe dominated by the four western powers, and in Geneva there was jealous talk of a "Locarno cabal." And indeed, from the British standpoint the pact's main attraction was that it established a *modus vivendi* between France and Germany.

Meanwhile, Britain's primary political concerns of the twenties were domestic and imperial. At home there were unemployment, tariffs, the coal mines, and the general strike to worry about; in Ireland there were de Valera and the Sinn Fein, and in India there was Gandhi. Foreign relations with the more distant great powers were rather a nuisance. The Anglo-Japanese alliance of 1902 was terminated in 1923, and the two countries drew apart. The Russians were unreliable and forever stirring up trouble in the ranks of Labour, and in 1924 the famous "Zinoviev letter" put a damper on Anglo-Russian relations that lasted several years. Across the Atlantic, the United States was being very stuffy about war debts.

Despite these unpleasantnesses, it appeared that for the time being, Britain had nothing to fear in a military sense. With the possible exception of France, no power was capable of attacking the island homeland, and the French were governed so completely by fear of Germany that it seemed quite impossible that they would turn on the ally they would most need should the *Boches* march again. For reasons of economy at least, disarmament was highly desirable, and in August of 1919, Prime Minister David Lloyd George, primarily to put a brake on the military estimates, had the War Cabinet lay down a guiding rule that planning was to proceed on the basis that Britain would not be involved in a major war during the next ten years.

This was the famous, or infamous, "Ten-Year Rule," which looms so large in the military history of Britain between the wars. As a prediction in 1919 it was sound and borne out by events, for war did not come to Britain for ten or, indeed, for nearly twenty years. Furthermore, when first announced it seems to have been not wholly unwelcome in military circles, and the Chief of the Air Staff, Hugh "Boom" Trenchard, used it to justify the investment of his newborn service's funds in badly needed buildings, airfields, and other basic facilities rather than in combat aircraft.

Still, it was a question-begging rule, conducive to the postponement of awkward problems. That war would not come for ten years did not mean that preparations could be delayed that long, and the preparations for a war against Japan would be quite different from those needed if Russia were to be the foe. Furthermore, it was one thing to say in 1919 that there would be no major war until 1929; it was quite another to keep moving the entire ten-year period with the advance of the calendar. In fact the Ten-Year Rule remained in effect until 1932, by which time it was a very bad forecast indeed.

3

The politics of Britain between the wars were dominated by Stanley Baldwin. From May 1923, when he succeeded the mortally ill Bonar Law as Prime Minister, to May 1937, when he resigned his third prime ministership and retired from politics, Baldwin was the leader of the Conservative Party—the largest party in the House of Commons throughout those years except from 1929 to 1931, and the majority party most of that time. Baldwin was Prime Minister from May 1923 to January 1924, from November 1924 to June 1929, and from June 1935 to May 1937. From 1931 to 1935, as Lord President of the Council and Conservative leader, he was the strong man of the national government headed by Ramsay MacDonald. As his successor, Baldwin chose Neville Chamberlain.

In tune with the mood of the country, Baldwin was not deeply interested in diplomatic or military matters. But as the King's First Minister, he had the ultimate responsibility for the conduct of foreign as well as domestic affairs, and for the state of Britain's defenses when he gave up the seals of office less than a year before the German annexation of Austria.

On the whole, the judgments of historians have been harsh—sometimes harsher than those rendered on Neville Chamberlain. Writing in 1940 as a Harvard undergraduate, John F. Kennedy thought that Chamberlain had no alternatives at Munich, because the Baldwin government had failed to give Britain the arms necessary to a firmer policy. Sound or unsound, this analysis, so far from being original, was right in line with contemporary British opinion. On laying down his high office in 1937, Baldwin was made an earl and loaded with honors; by the end of 1940 Chamberlain was dead, and Baldwin's name was the focus of condemnation and even execration: "An Enemy of the People" is the title of his biographers' last chapter. In 1942 things reached such a pitch that there even was public controversy over the requisitioning for scrap of the gates at the entrance to Baldwin's estate. At question time in the House of Commons a Conservative MP added the crowning insult: "Is the honourable Member aware that it is very necessary to leave Lord Baldwin his gates in order to protect him from the just indignation of the mob?"

Winston Churchill, by both his speeches in the House of Commons in 1936 and his postwar writings, put the great weight of his prestige and opinion behind a negative assessment of Baldwin's leadership. The latter had "gathered and carefully maintained . . . a wide authority," Churchill wrote in 1948, but "had used as little as possible" of it. Baldwin was "detached from foreign and military affairs," he "knew little of Europe and disliked what he knew," and he "represented in a broad way some of the strengths and many of the infirmities of our island race."

Indeed, Stanley Baldwin had much to answer for before the bar of British history. But a fair judgment calls for closer scrutiny than has generally been afforded of his record in comparison with those of his critics, and it may be enlightening to begin with Winston Churchill himself, generally acclaimed as the statesman who most clearly perceived and eloquently portrayed his country's looming perils.

Churchill was Chancellor of the Exchequer in Baldwin's second government, from 1924 to 1929. Throughout this period the Ten-Year Rule was in force and, so far from questioning its wisdom, Churchill constantly invoked it as a basis for his attacks on the naval budgetary estimates. He had conceived a program of social reform comprising reduced income taxes, expansion of old-age insurance, and provision for widows' pensions and cheap housing. To finance these measures, he sought to reduce defense expenditures, and the Royal Navy was by far the biggest spender.

Shortly after taking office, Churchill submitted a memorandum to Baldwin arguing that approval of the Admiralty's estimates would blot out any schemes for social reform, and "sterilize and paralyse the whole policy of the Government." Vigorously he questioned the Admiralty's fear of Japan as a possible enemy: "A war with Japan! But why should there be a war with Japan? I do not believe there is the slightest chance of it in our lifetime." For the former and future First Lord of the Admiralty, even the Ten-Year Rule was not good enough as a basis for cutting the naval estimates; the Admiralty should be told:

> that they are not expected to be in a position to encounter Japan in the Pacific Ocean and they are not to prepare for such a contingency . . . They should be made to recast all the plans and scales and standards on the basis that no naval war against a first class Navy is likely to take place in the next twenty years. They should be told that the lives of all their ships are to be prolonged; that the replacements in the programme are to be spread over at least three times the period specified . . .

With the support of Austen Chamberlain and over the vigorous objections of William Bridgeman (the First Lord, and a close friend of Baldwin's) and Admiral Lord Beatty of Jutland fame (Chief of the Naval Staff), Churchill persuaded the Cabinet to approve a £10-million cut in the naval estimates.

Soon Churchill was urging that the Cabinet-approved policy of basing a fleet at Singapore should be abandoned, arguing with magnificent inconsistency first that Japan was not so strong that Britain needed to build in competition with her, and then that her superiority in the Pacific was bound to be so overwhelming that competition would be futile.

In March 1925, Churchill turned his attention to the cruiser replacement program, and sought to bar any new construction that year and limit future replacement to one cruiser each year. The ensuing struggle lasted until July and was finally resolved on the basis of a compromise proposed by Baldwin, under which the Admiralty's program was to be fulfilled, but at a slower pace. In February 1928, Churchill made another, but unsuccessful, effort to suspend cruiser construction.

Churchill's attitude has been explained as "characteristic" of his tendency "to throw himself wholeheartedly into the immediate, perhaps exclusive, duties of whatever office he occupied at the time."* This diagnosis raises interesting if ac-

* The words are those of Baldwin's biographers, Middlemas and Barnes, *Baldwin* (1969), p. 326. In his own account, Churchill says only that as one of Baldwin's "leading colleagues" during the years 1924 to 1929, "I take my share of responsibility for all that happened." Churchill, *The Gathering Storm* (1948), p. 25. See also Churchill's speech in the House of Commons on March 8, 1934, in which he declared himself ready to offer a "detailed" and "vigorous" justification of "those years."

ademic speculations: what would Churchill's attitude toward defense spending have been in the pre-Munich period if Baldwin, on returning to power, had recalled Churchill to the Exchequer, instead of replacing him with Neville Chamberlain? Would the pressure for economies from 1934 to 1935 have blinded Churchill's eyes as Chancellor to the dangers he discerned so clearly when out of office?

These questions are worth pondering as an aid to better understanding of Stanley Baldwin and the temper of the British people, whose moods and views he so closely sensed and accurately reflected, at the time Hitler came to power. The Oxford Union may have phrased its "King and Country" issue provocatively, but it was the students, rather than their critics, who were in tune with the times. This was dramatically demonstrated at a series of by-elections, beginning in the fall of 1934 at East Fulham in London. The Labour candidate, John Wilmot, was a Navy veteran of the First World War and no pacifist, but he campaigned on a platform of collective security through the League of Nations, and succeeded in portraying his opponent, who supported the maintenance of British defensive strength, as a warmonger. And if Wilmot's position was moderate, that was hardly true of the support given him by the Labour Party leader, George Lansbury, who informed the constituency that he would "close every recruiting station, disband the Army and disarm the Air Force" and "abolish the whole dreadful equipment of war and say to the world 'do your worst.'" In the upshot, Wilmot turned a previous Conservative majority of over 14,000 into a Labour victory by a 5,000-vote margin, a swing of over 26 per cent.

East Fulham was no fluke. During the next four months, at by-elections in seven other geographically and economically diverse constituencies, the swing to Labour ranged from 20 to 25 per cent. Conservative fortunes improved a bit during the summer of 1934, but in the fall the anti-Government trend was renewed; no need for the political genius of a Baldwin to perceive that the British public would not easily be awakened to the nascent Nazi danger, or converted to the cause of rearmament.

4

At the end of the First World War, the British had an Army of over 3 million men, a Navy of over 4,000 craft including some 60 battleships and battle cruisers, and an air strength of 3,300 first-line aircraft and nearly 300,000 men. Five years later the Army and Air Force were at no more than one tenth of their wartime strength. In the early 1930s, before Hitler came to power, the effective strength of the RAF was some 700 aircraft, far inferior to the French and Italian air arms, and certainly no stronger than those of Russia, Japan, and the United States. The Army was a miserable shadow of its former self, and could have mobilized but one infantry division and one cavalry brigade.

The Navy was not so shrunken; the tradition of Rule Britannia and the practical need of means for protecting Britain's far-ranging seaborne trade enabled the Admiralty to preserve the core of the fleet. The Washington Treaty of 1922, with its various limitations on naval armaments and its agreed 5-5-3-1.75-1.75 capital-ship ratios respectively for Britain, the United States, Japan, France, and

Italy, gave Britain protection against the emergence of a superior naval power and at the same time spared her from hopeless competition against America's greater resources.

But if substantially intact, the British Navy of the thirties was sadly down-at-the-heels. Except for the *Nelson* and *Rodney* (commissioned in 1927) no new capital ships were commissioned from one war to the next. Churchill's pressure from the Exchequer slowed the replacement program, and the cruiser fleet fell far below the size which the Admiralty deemed necessary for the protection of trade. When the Labour Government took office in 1929, cruiser replacement sustained further cuts, and work on the Singapore naval base was postponed.

This grave decline in Britain's military power—largely the product of psychological and economic factors—was neither inadvertent nor haphazard, but rather governed by specific official assumptions with respect to the dangers which might in the future confront the empire. For advice, the Government relied directly on the Committee of Imperial Defence (CID), a Cabinet committee with a permanent secretariat headed by Sir Maurice Hankey and, after 1925, chaired by the Prime Minister himself. Interservice consultation was assured by the establishment, in 1923, of a Chiefs of Staff Committee (COS), through which the three service chiefs were charged with "an individual and collective responsibility for advising on Defence policy as a whole."

What dangers to the empire did these ministers and military men discern? Germany was disarmed, Russia in the throes of revolution, and the chances of hostilities with France or America seemed remote indeed. Only small forces were needed to keep India and the Near East under control. The ten-year rule was the symbol of the British Government's conclusion that nothing much needed to be done. Nothing much, but not quite nothing at all, for there were two areas of mild concern. One was in the Far East, where the end of the Anglo-Japanese alliance had weakened Britain's naval posture in the Indian and Pacific oceans. The other was in the sky over the home islands, where memories of Zeppelins and Gothas and the predictions of Giulio Douhet gave rise to an uncomfortable feeling that the United Kingdom should not be left defenseless against air attack, improbable as such an event appeared in the early twenties.

The Navy was the "Senior Service" and much the largest, and its preoccupation with events on the other side of the globe decisively influenced Britain's over-all strategy. It was not that the Government was forgetful of their stake in the Franco-German balance; in 1925 a Foreign Office memorandum remarked that "the true strategic frontier of Britain is the Rhine. . . . Any policy which permitted Germany first to swallow up France, and then to deal with Great Britain would be fatal strategically." But 1925 was the year of Locarno, and Austen Chamberlain's diplomacy seemed to be dealing adequately with the European situation. In the Far East, however, there was no Locarno, and what good would it do to send the fleet to the Pacific if it had no base of operations? So concern about Japan came to dominate British strategy in the twenties, and construction of a huge naval base at Singapore was the principal item of military expansion in the service budget estimates, despite Winston Churchill's vehement protests in behalf of the Treasury.

The modest revival of British air strength during the twenties was the outcome of a clash of strategic opinion between the Navy and the newborn Air Ministry and independent Royal Air Force. From 1919 to the end of 1929 the voice of the Air Force was that of its Chief of Staff, Sir Hugh Trenchard—a man whose vocal powers won him the nickname "Boom." Soon after taking office, Trenchard weighed in with a plan for an air arm of forty standing and forty-two reserve squadrons, coupled with a recommendation that the Air Force be given primary responsibility for defending the home islands against direct assault, and a prediction that the air arm would "grow larger and larger and become more and more the predominating factor in all types of warfare."

Trenchard's vocal level was high in decibels, but not as influential as that of Earl Beatty, the First Sea Lord, and the idea that air power should replace sea power as Britain's main rampart was soon scuttled. But the Cabinet was sufficiently impressed by the awful potential of the bomber to authorize, in 1922, the establishment of a home air force, modestly fixed at twenty-three squadrons with about 250 aircraft. This was less than half the size of the French Air Force, and, in a bid for "parity" that was a harbinger of later years, in June of 1923 the Baldwin government authorized a metropolitan air force of fifty-two squadrons, with a first-line establishment of 394 bombers and 204 fighters, to be completed by 1928. Defending the program in the House of Commons, Baldwin declared that "British air power must include a home defence force of sufficient strength adequately to protect us against air attack by the strongest air force in striking distance of this country."

Home air force and Singapore base both wilted badly in the piping peaceful years. Especially after Locarno it was difficult to treat seriously the putative necessity of air parity with France. In 1925, completion of the fifty-two-squadron program was postponed from 1928 to 1936. Appropriations for the armed services declined from £116 million in 1926–27 to £110 million in 1930–31. In 1930, with thirty-nine of the fifty-two squadrons in being or authorized, completion of the remainder was postponed once again, this time to 1938. Furthermore, the economic depression was now making itself felt as a limiting factor on armaments, and the air estimates for 1932 and 1933 contained no provision for additional aircraft for home defense, although the RAF was still ten squadrons short of the fifty-two that had been projected ten years earlier. Total armament appropriations dropped to their nadir—£102.7 million—in 1932–33, as the Nazi era began.

A year earlier, when the pinch of financial distress was at its sharpest, there had occurred the first in the long sequence of events that would ultimately rouse the British leaders to the dangers facing the empire. As the Navy had feared, Japan was the disturbing agent. Nipponese nationalism had been mounting, signalized by political assassinations and military defiance of civilian control. In September 1931, under color of their right to operate and police the South Manchuria railway, Japanese forces occupied Mukden. A few months later, following anti-Japanese incidents in Shanghai, the Tokyo government sent a naval force which used the Japanese sector of the International Settlement as a base for attacking Chinese forces in the Chapei district of Shanghai. Meanwhile in the north, the Japanese Kwantung army had been overrunning Manchuria, and in September of 1932 the puppet state of Manchukuo was established under Pu Yi, the former child emperor of China.

The Chinese had appealed to the League of Nations immediately after the occupation of Mukden, but the "China incident," as the Japanese insisted in describing the affair, presented the international community with a very knotty problem. Neither the United States nor the Soviet Union—the only two powers in a position to take direct military action against Japan—was a member of the League. Especially without an adequate base at Singapore or elsewhere in the Far East, the British could hardly challenge the Japanese fleet in its home waters, and they prudently concluded to act only through the League.

In Shanghai, Britain and America were able to co-ordinate their actions by reinforcement of their ships and garrisons, and a disengagement of the Chinese and Japanese forces was soon accomplished. But the larger issue of Manchuria proved insoluble. In Washington, Secretary of State Henry L. Stimson was primarily interested in preserving the Chinese "open door" principle, and in January 1932 he dispatched a public note informing the Chinese and Japanese governments that the United States would recognize no settlement that impaired American treaty rights, infringed Chinese sovereignty, or deprived China of territory by means that violated the 1928 Kellogg-Briand Pact. He invited London to take the same position, but the Japanese had already promised to maintain the "open door," and the Foreign Office took the view that questions of Chinese sovereignty were in the hands of the League. That body, for its part, appointed an international commission of investigation, headed by Lord Lytton.

Generally praised for its objectivity and thoroughness, the Lytton Report was discussed by the League Assembly during the winter of 1932–33. It concluded that Japan had genuine and serious grievances against China for nonobservance of the former's treaty rights in Manchuria, but condemned the establishment of the puppet regime and recommended that all armed forces other than police be withdrawn. In February the League Assembly accepted the Lytton Report; Japan's reaction was to announce her resignation from the League, and send her army into the Chinese province of Jehol, lying between Manchuria and the Great Wall. Helpless to stem the Japanese advance, in May 1933 the Chinese accepted the Tangku truce, which provided for a demilitarized zone north of the Great Wall, and produced four years of uneasy peace.

For the British Government, there were at least two important conclusions to be drawn from the Manchurian affair: that the United States could not be relied on to support British or League efforts to use international pressure to keep the peace, and that Britain was virtually powerless to resist Japan in the Far East.

On the first score, the Shanghai settlement in the spring of 1932 had shown that, at the local level, Americans and Englishmen could co-operate effectively. But what was possible for the consuls in Shanghai was too difficult for Stimson in Washington and the Foreign Secretary, Sir John Simon, in London. The root of the difficulty was America's nonmembership in the League, and the national attitudes which limited Stimson's range of action. London could hardly give full support to the League and its procedures and at the same time work closely with the United States outside the League. The result was mutual recrimi-nations* and a wave of anti-Americanism in British governmental circles. Stanley Baldwin privately declared on February 27, 1932: "With Russia and America out of the League, sanctions are a mistake. . . . If you enforce an eco-nomic boycott you will have war declared by Japan and she will seize Singapore and Hong Kong and we cannot, as we are placed, stop her. You will get nothing out of Washington but words, big words, but only words." A year and a half later Neville Chamberlain noted in his diary: "S.B. [Baldwin] says he has got to loathe the Americans† so much that he hates meeting them and he actually re-fused an invitation to dine with Ramsay [Macdonald] to meet the James Roosevelts (the President's son). I myself am going—to look at the creature."

Baldwin's pessimistic assessment of British power in the Far East was shared in the Foreign Office and the military services. In February 1932, Sir Robert Vansittart, Permanent Under-Secretary at the Foreign Office, observed:

1. If Japan continues unchecked . . . our position and vast interests in the Far East will never recover. This may well spread to the Mid East.
2. *We* are incapable of checking Japan in any way if she really means busi-ness and has sized us up. . . .
3. Therefore, we must be done for in the Far East unless
4. The United States are eventually prepared to use force. . . .
5. By ourselves, we must eventually swallow any and every humiliation in the Far East. . . .

The immediate consequence of these attitudes was the death of the Ten-Year Rule. A year earlier (March 9, 1931), at a meeting of the COS committee, the Deputy Chief of Naval Staff, Admiral Sir Frederick Dreyer, had raised ques-tions concerning perpetuation of the rule, by inquiring whether the Foreign Office fully appreciated the "grave responsibility" so incurred. The Secretary of the Cabinet and CID, Lord Hankey, replied that the COS would be fully justified in calling for a re-examination of the rule. The matter was then referred to a subcommittee of the CID, where Sir Austen Chamberlain argued for the rule's abolition, but in June the CID continued it subject to reconsideration in 1932.

---

* A good illustration is the correspondence between Baldwin's close friend Thomas Jones (Deputy Secretary to the Cabinet from 1916 to 1930) and the American educator Abraham Flexner. On February 27, 1932, following a talk that day with Baldwin, Jones wrote Flexner a letter strongly critical of American "weakness" in the preceding September, when Mukden was occupied: "I think the official view roughly is that we can do nothing without you, and that you do not mean action which might lead to war." On March 17 Flexner replied, complaining that the British should have backed Stimson more strongly in connection with his "nonrecognition" note in January. See Jones, *A Diary with Letters 1931–1950* (1954), pp. 27–28 and 35.

† Baldwin's low opinion of Americans dated back at least to 1923, when he told the edi-tor of the *Manchester Guardian* (C. P. Scott) that Anglo-American co-operation was espe-cially difficult because of "the total lack of men of commanding ability." Charles Evans Hughes was "perhaps the best of them," but what had "struck" Baldwin was "the extraor-dinary ignorance of the mass of people of anything outside their own country and generally the low intellectual level." Baldwin was highly literate, but neither he nor Neville Cham-berlain had academic records of any distinction, nor could either be called well versed in foreign matters.

On February 4, 1932, just after the Shanghai crisis had erupted, the Chief of the Imperial General Staff (CIGS), General Sir George Milne, revived the issue at a COS meeting, commenting that the "futility" of the Ten-Year Rule had been demonstrated by events in the Far East "during the last week." He was supported by the First Sea Lord, Admiral Field, who observed that the Foreign Office itself had "proved conclusively that the ten year rule was untenable."

Six days later the First Lord of the Admiralty, Sir Bolton Eyres-Monsell, raised the matter in the CID. Neville Chamberlain, then Chancellor of the Exchequer, replied that the state of British economy forbade the rule's abolition. Baldwin, playing for time, declared that he had already asked the COS to prepare a comprehensive memorandum for submission to the whole Cabinet. The paper was submitted on March 22, describing the Ten-Year Rule as an "insurmountable barrier" to imperial defense policy, and recommending that a start be made on meeting Britain's defensive commitments, especially in the Far East. On the following day, despite a note of disapproval from the Treasury, the Cabinet noted "no dissent" from these recommendations, but cautioned that arms expenditures should not be increased without taking economic conditions into account.

Thus, on March 23, 1932, the Ten-Year Rule was, as a practical matter,* erased. But this action was not the creation of a policy, but merely the removal of a limitation. What guidelines were to replace the rule?

5

The Japanese invasion of Manchuria in September 1931 came at a time when the British Government was in the throes of reorganization. Just three weeks earlier, the Labour Government had collapsed in disagreement over the handling of the financial crisis and had been replaced by a three-party National Emergency Government, with Ramsay MacDonald remaining as Prime Minister, Baldwin as Lord President, and Sir Herbert Samuel (the Liberal leader) as Home Secretary. After the Conservative sweep in the October elections, Neville Chamberlain came in as Chancellor of the Exchequer, Sir John Simon as Foreign Secretary, and new Conservative appointees at all three service ministries.

The most significant appointment was Chamberlain's. Winston Churchill, at the Exchequer in the Baldwin 1924–1929 Cabinet, had split from his party colleagues over the India policy and resigned from the Conservative "shadow cabinet" some months earlier. Neville Chamberlain had been Chancellor during Baldwin's short-lived first government in 1923,† and his reappointment in 1931 enabled him to assume increasing leadership in the Government and soon emerge as heir-apparent to Baldwin.

As Lord President of the Council, Baldwin had no departmental respon-

* Apart from the "no dissent" notation, the Cabinet appears never to have formally rescinded the Ten-Year Rule, but from other documents it is clear that Hankey, and the ministers directly concerned, ceased to treat it as effective after this date.

† It is a curiosity of Cabinet history that Chamberlain was succeeded by Philip Snowden (Labour) in 1924, while Snowden gave way to Churchill later that year, replaced him in 1929, and was in turn replaced by Chamberlain in 1931.

sibilities, but as leader of the majority party, overwhelmingly victorious at the polls, he held the reins of power, and he has been much criticized for holding them too loosely. For these strictures there is considerable basis. Baldwin had no natural affinity for foreign problems and left them largely to MacDonald and Simon, neither of whom had the perception or touch for high diplomacy. Intuition Baldwin had aplenty, but concentration and analysis were increasingly uncongenial to him as he aged; in 1932, when Baldwin was sixty-five, his close friend and adviser Tom Jones remarked that "His powers of resisting the close discussion of a problem are enormous."

In part, however, Baldwin's apparent lassitude was due to his awareness that power can be dissipated by misuse as well as nonuse, and to his extraordinarily acute sense of political timing. Manchuria had jolted the inner circle, but to the British public as a whole the world of 1932 and 1933 was a peaceful one. Given the poor state of the economy, a rearmament program would have seemed more than perverse. Ending the ten-year rule, significant as it was psychologically, had scant immediate consequence. In October 1932 the Cabinet finally approved resumption of work on the Singapore base, but the general level of arms expenditures remained at rock bottom through 1933.

There were other, less political, reasons for this reluctance to take the path of rearmament. The years 1932 to 1934 were those of peak activity, albeit fruitless, in the field of international disarmament. For Britain, disarmament had been not a façade but a cornerstone of foreign policy, espoused in the hope that the budget, already stretched, could be spared the additional strain of rearmament. Lord Robert Cecil was one of the chief architects of the Geneva Disarmament Conference, which, after more than a decade of preparation, met at Geneva early in 1932 under the presidency of the former Foreign Secretary, Arthur Henderson. Disarmament was an article of faith which transcended party lines; in 1931, sharing a platform with MacDonald and Lloyd George, Baldwin declared that Britain was "bound by treaty and by honour to international disarmament" and predicted, accurately enough, that failure to achieve it would soon create a situation "fraught with immense danger to Europe, with danger to the world."

Despite the warning of Manchuria, the credibility of Britain's support of disarmament could hardly survive a sudden increase in her arms budget. Nor could the British afford early discouragement in the quest. When it became apparent that German demands for equality and French for security were irreconcilable, and the German representatives absented themselves from the conference in October 1932, the British came forward with a five-year disarmament plan which was circulated to the members on January 30, 1933, the very day that Hitler became Chancellor. In March, MacDonald appeared at Geneva to present the plan in person. Even after Germany, in October 1933, quit the conference for good, Sir John Simon felt able to advise King George V: "It would be reckless to declare that Germany's withdrawal has destroyed all prospect of a Disarmament Convention." But that was precisely what Hitler had accomplished, and in 1934 the conference petered out.

Armament and disarmament are two faces of the same coin, and it was impossible to shape a policy with respect to quantity, quality, ratio, and other kinds of arms limitations without deciding what arms should be kept and improved. It was therefore natural, if superficially paradoxical, that the Disarmament Conference led to the first careful studies, since the First World War, of the state and future of British arms, through a special Disarmament Committee of the Cabinet.

Baldwin's participation in the work of this committee gave him a horror of the consequences of air warfare which led him to propose radical limitations on air armaments as the only realistic approach to disarmament as a whole. In June 1932 he won Cabinet support for the abolition of military bombing, and the following November, in an emotion-charged speech, he told the House of Commons:

I think it is well also for the man in the street to realize that there is no power on earth that can protect him from being bombed. Whatever people may tell him, the bomber will always get through. The only defence is offence, which means that you have to kill more women and children more quickly than the enemy if you want to save yourselves.

This was not only a ghoulish harbinger of things to come, but also the initial exposure of a strategic issue which was soon to split the Air Staff and bedevil all planning for the defense of Britain. If the bomber would indeed "always get through," what was the value of fighter aircraft and other air defenses? These were the plain implications of Baldwin's pronouncement, and its echoes were still reverberating strongly at the time of Munich.

In the upshot, the British projection of Baldwin's plan was heavily qualified. At the outposts of empire—Iraq, Somaliland, the North-West Frontier of India —it had been found that aircraft and a few bombs could sometimes subdue rebellious tribesmen much more quickly and economically than could the Army. Mussolini's use of bombs against the Ethiopians was not without British precedent, and the Air Minister, Lord Londonderry, put up a strong case for the retention of air bombing "for police purposes." This exception became part of the British position at Geneva, but the entire air proposal died, along with the rest of the disarmament plans, after Germany withdrew from the conference in October 1933.

At about this time, Baldwin and some of his Cabinet colleagues concluded that the prospects of disarmament were too remote to be relied upon, and that the time had come to start shoring up Britain's own defenses. For several years the Chiefs of Staff, in their annual reports, had been warning the Cabinet that things had deteriorated past the point of safety even under the Ten-Year Rule, and in 1930 they added the specific admonition that the armed forces were "not in a state of readiness to fulfill our guarantee" under the Locarno agreements.

The month of November 1933 was a turning point. Nazi militancy and militarism were beginning to make an impression, and on November 7, in the House of Commons, Winston Churchill, who had not joined in the chorus of support for disarmament, pointed to "the great dominant fact . . . that Germany has already begun to rearm," and called upon the Government "to assure us that adequate provision is made for our safety, and for having the power and the time, if necessary, to realize the whole latent strength of our country."

It was the first of the long series of Churchillian warnings, and even as he spoke the CID had under consideration the annual review from the Chiefs of Staff, in which they expressed "our opinion that Germany is not only starting to rearm but that she will continue this process until within a few years she will again have to be reckoned with as a formidable military power." On the basis of this forecast the COS warned that increases in the service budgets "over a number of years" must be anticipated and, since their responsibilities were no longer covered by the Ten-Year Rule, asked the CID to formulate new guiding principles for imperial defense. In that connection, the COS recommended that first priority be given to "the defense of our Possessions and interests in the Far East," second to "European commitments," and third to the defense of India against "Soviet aggression."

Meeting on November 9 with the Prime Minister in the Chair, the CID approved the recommended priorities. Chamberlain proposed as a substitute for the old Ten-Year Rule a new one: "that in considering defence questions account need not be taken of any likelihood of war with the U.S., France or Italy, say for the next ten years." This was wisely rejected, but the CID gave Chamberlain's thought some projection by agreeing that: "No expenditure should for the present be incurred on measures of defence . . . to provide exclusively against attack by the U.S., France or Italy." More important, the CID recommended appointing a special committee to "prepare a program for meeting our worst deficiencies."

All of this was promptly approved by the Cabinet, and the last recommendation was implemented by creation of the Defence Requirements Committee (DRC), comprising the three service chiefs and representatives of the Foreign Office and the Treasury, with Hankey as chairman. On February 28, 1934, the DRC submitted its report—a document which might well be called the seedling of British rearmament—and its contents remained a major Cabinet question until mid-July.

The salient feature of this report was the replacement of Japan by Germany as the focal point of concern. True, Japan was already strongly armed and the peril in the orient greater, in the light of "our total inability to defend our interests in the Far East." But there did not appear to be "any immediate danger" there, and it was to be hoped that friendly relations with Japan could be restored. In Europe, on the other hand, the failure of Germany and France to come to terms, and the quickening pace of German rearmament, dictated the conclusion that "we take Germany as the ultimate potential enemy against whom our 'long range' defence policy must be directed." Fortunately, since Germany was not yet fully armed, "we have time, though not much time, to make defensive preparations"—about five years, it was thought.

Essentially, these preparations should comprise an enlarged home air force to defend the islands against air attack, and a small expeditionary force to bolster the defenses of Belgium and Holland against a German invasion. The two elements were interrelated, since if Germany succeeded in overrunning the Low

Countries her capacity for an air assault against Britain would be greatly increased, while British air bases on the Continent would comparably increase the RAF's effectiveness against the German homeland.

The recommended program called for the expenditure of some 82 million pounds (over and above the regular sustaining military budget) during the next five years. Nearly half was to go to the Army, for an expeditionary force of approximately six divisions. The fifty-two squadron home air force was to be completed at once, and the RAF's over-all strength increased by thirty-six squadrons. The Navy and the Far East were not to be forgotten; there would be a substantial ship construction program, and Britain would "show a tooth" in the Pacific by completing the Singapore defenses in 1938.

Considering what was actually brewing in Germany and Japan, these proposals were modest indeed. But for the Britain of 1934 they were strong medicine, and throughout the spring, in both the full Cabinet and its Disarmament Committee, a secret but intense war of words was waged. The Prime Minister's health was failing, and Baldwin assumed primary responsibility for national defense matters.

In March, shortly after the report had been submitted, he rose in the Commons to defend the 1934 air estimates, which, for the first time in several years, provided for four new squadrons and a slightly larger budget. From Clement Attlee, as Labour leader, came loud disapproval—"we on our side are for total disarmament because we are realists." From Winston Churchill came a warning that "Germany is arming fast" and an admonition to Baldwin: "He alone has the power . . . and the responsibility" to guide the nation "wisely and safely in this dangerous question." To Attlee, Baldwin replied gently that he, too, would "try to be a realist," and that he had not abandoned all hope of disarmament. To Churchill, he answered with an old promise—the promise of parity:

> If all our efforts for an agreement fail, and if it is not possible to obtain this equality in such matters . . . then any Government of this country—a National Government more than any other, and *this* Government—will see to it that in air strength and air power this country shall no longer be inferior to any country within striking distance of our shores.

It was, almost verbatim, the same promise Baldwin had made in 1923, when the fifty-two squadron program was first authorized—unfulfilled in the decade that had since elapsed, and destined to remain so for the greater part of another.

In June, Neville Chamberlain moved to inflict on the DRC report the same radical surgery that Churchill, ten years earlier, had administered to the naval and air estimates. Now Chamberlain, after three months of intensive discussion of the report, roundly declared that "we are presented with proposals impossible to carry out." His solution was to cut the five-year costs from 82 to about 50 million pounds, chiefly at the expense of the Army and Navy. On the newly accepted basis that Germany was the most likely enemy, he advocated a redistribution of the appropriations so as to provide for a larger home air force than the DRC had proposed. But if that were to be done, "we certainly can't afford at the same time to rebuild our battle fleet." Singapore would have to be postponed again, and the Army's expeditionary force put off indefinitely.

These proposals involved not only diminution of the scale, but also a basic change in the strategic concept, of the DRC recommendations. Scrapped was the prospect of a balanced three-service force and of participation in the defense of the Low Countries—the latter despite a well-reasoned COS analysis which argued that limiting British operations to the sea and the air would cause France and her Continental allies to conclude that England was "abandoning them to their fate," whereas "the arrival of even small forces which we propose to provide will have an incalculable moral effect out of all proportion to the size of these forces." Instead, almost total reliance would be rested on the home air force, in the hope that Germany might be deterred from an aerial arms race.

In effect, if not in theory, Chamberlain's views prevailed. Politically speaking, Baldwin had little with which to fight. The 1931 election had been fought on domestic economic issues; the Government had no popular mandate for increased arms expenditures, and the by-elections since East Fulham had shown that the voters would, in all probability, decisively reject an avowed rearmament policy. In the crucial discussions in July, Baldwin was able to salvage the Singapore base, and keep the question of an expeditionary force open for annual review. But the Cabinet's final decision, taken July 18, 1934, was much closer to the Chamberlain than the DRC proposals.

Nothing was said publicly about the Army and Navy features of rearmament, and Baldwin's statement to the Commons on July 19 was largely confined to an exposition of the Government's recommendation that forty-one squadrons be added to the RAF over the course of the next five years.* There was a violent attack from the Labour and Liberal opposition, to which Baldwin replied in the debate on July 30, with memorable words:

> The greatest crime to our own people is to be afraid to tell them the truth. . . . The old frontiers are gone. When you think of the defence of England you no longer think of the chalk cliffs of Dover; you think of the Rhine. That is where our frontier lies.

The reference to the Rhine was not original; the Foreign Office had used the same figure of speech in 1923. But it was quite another thing for the Prime Minister to say this in the Commons, and, as Winston Churchill observed at the time, Baldwin's phrase "traveled from one end of the world to the other."

Churchill himself thought the plan quite inadequate, and declared that Germany already had an air force two thirds as strong as Britain's home force, that by the end of 1935 the Germans would achieve parity, and a year later would outstrip Britain in the air. The Government's proposal carried the Commons by an overwhelming vote, but the exchange between Churchill and Baldwin was a foretaste of sharper ones soon to come.

6

Recognition of Nazi Germany as the "ultimate potential enemy" did not mean acceptance of the inevitability of war. Indeed, the limited rearmament au-

---

* The plan, described in the records as "Scheme A," would have given Britain in 1939 a home force of some 84 squadrons (43 bomber, 28 fighter, and 13 reconnaissance) with 960 aircraft, and 27 overseas squadrons with 292 aircraft. The whole front-line strength of the RAF would thus have comprised 1,252 aircraft in 111 squadrons.

thorized in 1934 was intended by some of its sponsors primarily as a deterrent to German adventurism. In the minds of the British leaders the diplomatic rather than the military field of action was still primary. If general disarmament were unobtainable, then peace must be sought by reaching an understanding with Germany. This would certainly involve concessions or, as the process was soon described, appeasement. What sort of a "creature"—to use Neville Chamberlain's favorite word for exotic and unprepossessing individuals—was this Hitler, and what did he really want?

And so, soon after Hitler became Chancellor, there began a long sequence of visits, official and unofficial, by prominent Britishers anxious to assess him as a person and explore the possibilities of "understanding." In general, Hitler welcomed these interviews, an attitude in which he was encouraged by some of his entourage, notably Goering and Ribbentrop. It should be remarked, however, that the way between London and Berlin was pretty much a one-way street; the Nazi dictatorship could assure visiting foreigners an untroubled reception, but Nazis did not fare so well in England, as Alfred Rosenberg, the Party "philosopher," discovered when he visited London as the Fuehrer's personal emissary in 1933. Ribbentrop fared somewhat better at first but later gave offense, and the Wilhelmstrasse soon realized that prominent Nazi personalities were simply not welcome to the British public.

It is a measure of Ramsay MacDonald's loss of touch with reality that in November of 1933, encountering the German Ambassador, Leopold von Hoesch, at a public function, the Prime Minister suggested that Hitler visit London and assured Hoesch that the Fuehrer "would receive a most friendly reception in England from the people and the Government." Neurath promptly and rightly characterized the idea as "absurd," and a few months later Hoesch, an old-school diplomat and no Nazi, was treated to a lecture by no less a personage than King George V, who informed him that "Germany was the peril of the world, and that, if she went on at the present rate, there was bound to be a war within ten years."

The new German Chancellor, in contrast, was all milk and honey to his early British visitors. Arthur Henderson, out of office but President of the Geneva Disarmament Conference, saw Hitler in the summer of 1933 and was assured that Germany would "accept any control the others accept." The first official visitor from London, however, was thirty-six-year-old Anthony Eden, whom Baldwin had installed as Under-Secretary of the Foreign Office in 1931, and in the Cabinet as Lord Privy Seal in January of 1934. Through Ribbentrop as a private representative, Hitler appeared to be angling for a Baldwin visit to Berlin. For this Baldwin had little stomach, but he concluded that it would indeed be desirable "to get into touch with Herr Hitler," and to this end Eden, accompanied by the British Ambassador, Sir Eric Phipps, was received by Hitler on February 20, 1934. Eden's impressions were certainly not unfavorable; Hitler was no dilettante and had done his homework. Next day the Fuehrer, with Hess, Goebbels, and Neurath, came to the British Embassy for lunch and further disarmament talks. Eden reported to London that, while Hitler was pessimistic about the outcome of the Geneva Conference, he was modest in his claims for German rearmament in relation to France, and appeared sincerely to support the Locarno agreements.

But if Hitler's claims were "modest," the intelligence reports on the pace of German rearmament were not. In October 1934 the Air Ministry had information that the Germans were planning a front-line strength of 1,300 aircraft within two years, a goal which the British had set for 1939. In November the CID reported that Germany already had an army of 300,000 men—treble the size permitted by the Versailles Treaty—and that aircraft production was going forward with "feverish haste."

Could not Hitler, who in person had seemed so reasonable, be convinced of the dangers Germany was creating? Early in November, MacDonald told Hoesch that the pace of German air rearmament was likely to lead to a race like that between the British and German navies before 1914. Then, on November 27, the British Government made a *démarche* in the form of a statement, read in London by Simon to Hoesch and in Berlin by Ambassador Phipps to Neurath and later to Hitler, in which the Government expressed its "grave concern" over the rapid progress of German rearmament, and warned Berlin that the subject would be discussed in the Commons on the following day by both Baldwin and Churchill. Neurath and Hitler justified their country's policy by the failure of disarmament talks, and Hitler professed surprise at Baldwin's remark that the Rhine was Britain's frontier: "What would people say in Britain if he, the Fuehrer, declared that the frontiers of German air defense lay on the Thames?"

On the next day (November 28) Winston Churchill, in the House of Commons, advanced the view that "the strength of our national defences, and especially of our air defence, is no longer adequate to secure . . . peace, safety and freedom. . . ." He asserted that Germany's "illegal air force is rapidly approaching equality with our own," that next year it would be "at least as strong," by the end of 1936 "nearly 50 per cent stronger," and "in 1937 nearly double." Baldwin's reply was a flat contradiction:

> It is not the case that Germany is rapidly approaching equality with us. . . . Even if we confine the comparison to the German air strength and the strength of the Royal Air Force immediately available in Europe . . . her real strength is not 50 per cent of our strength in Europe today. As for the position this time next year, if she continues to execute her air program without acceleration . . . we estimate that we shall still have a margin in Europe alone of nearly 50 per cent. I cannot look further forward than the next two years. Mr. Churchill speaks of what may happen in 1937. Such investigations as I have been able to make lead me to believe that his figures are considerably exaggerated.

Churchill and others read this as a "sweeping assurance," but in fact Baldwin's predictions were carefully—even artfully—qualified by the phrase "if she [Germany] continues to execute her air program without acceleration." But would she? The Air Ministry's intelligence already indicated that Germany's first-line strength would surpass Britain's by the fall of 1936, and Baldwin's reply to Churchill had skipped over that year, whether inadvertently or disingenuously.

Efforts to probe Hitler's intentions continued; in January of 1935 two British peers—Lord Allen of Hurtwood, a confidant of MacDonald's, and Lord Lothian, a friend of Baldwin's—had ostensibly cordial but desultory and inconclusive discussions with the Fuehrer on the possibility of arms limitation agreements. Lothian's report was hopeful, and early in March arrangements were made for Sir John Simon and Anthony Eden to go together to Berlin and explore the treaty possibilities. But the visit was postponed in consequence of Hitlerian wrath, aroused by the British White Paper on Defence, issued March 4, which acknowledged "minor deficiencies in all the Defence Services" and deplored the pace of German rearmament and the mood of the German public as contributing to a general "feeling of insecurity." A few days later Goering publicly acknowledged the existence of the "illegal" Luftwaffe and, on March 16, Hitler denounced the Versailles arms limitations and proclaimed the resumption of military conscription and plans for a thirty-six-division Army.

It was a bitter pill for the British, but the Government took it calmly, and Simon and Eden proceeded to Berlin for meetings with Hitler on March 25 and 26, 1935. Eden found the Fuehrer much more truculent than the previous year, and, after the first day's talk, noted in his diary: "Results bad . . . whole tone and temper very different to a year ago, rearmed and rearming with the old Prussian spirit very much in evidence." Hitler was willing to sign a naval pact with Britain at a 35:100 ratio, but in the air he claimed parity with the French Air Force, entailing a first-line strength of 1,500 aircraft. Simon then asked what was the Luftwaffe's present strength, and Hitler replied matter-of-factly that Germany had already achieved parity with Britain—a claim which at once became a main topic of discussion in Government circles.*

Even before Hitler dropped his verbal bomb, it had been realized in those circles that the July 1934 program for expansion of the RAF was inadequate in the light of the German plans. In the spring of 1935, consequently, the Government came forward with a new prospectus—called Scheme C—for a home air force of 123 squadrons comprising 1,512 aircraft, to be completed by 1937 instead of 1939. Scheme C was short-lived, and in retrospect is memorable only because its presentation instigated the third in the series of Baldwin-Churchill confrontations in Commons. In March and again early in May, Churchill squarely challenged the accuracy of what Baldwin had said the previous November, fortified on the second occasion by reports of Hitler's statement to Simon and Eden. Baldwin replied on May 22:

> First of all, with regard to the figure I gave in November of German aeroplanes, nothing has come to my knowledge since that makes me think that that figure was wrong. I believed at that time it was right. Where I was wrong was in my estimate of the future. There I was completely wrong. I tell the House so, frankly, because neither I nor my advisers . . . had any idea of the rate at which production . . . was being speeded up in Germany in the six months between November and now. We were completely misled on that subject. . . . There was a great deal of hearsay, but we could get no facts, and the only facts at this moment that I could put before the House, are those

---

* Sir John Simon's impression of Hitler was not as pessimistic as Eden's. Met on his way home at the Amsterdam airport by the Dutch Foreign Minister, Simon described Hitler as not at all arrogant, but "rather retiring and bashful and of a certain mystic temperament," principally focused on Russia and "unconcerned with affairs in Western Europe." He later told King George V much the same story, picturing Hitler as "an Austrian Joan of Arc with a moustache." It is hard to say what all this tells us about Hitler; Eden thought Sir John's "antennae were weak"—a view shared by many others—and Simon himself once confessed to Eden that he "never knew what people were thinking."

which I have from Herr Hitler himself, and until I have reason to doubt them, which I have not at present, I put these figures* before the House.

This was a handsome confession of error, but it was part of Baldwin's charm that he could be more frank in appearance than in fact, and it is doubtful that he had actually been so badly informed about the probable pace of German air rearmament. So far as concerns 1934 and 1935, however, it is now known that both Churchill and Hitler grossly overstated the existing strength of the Luftwaffe. An air force does not take so long to build as a fleet, but it cannot be done overnight, and in the spring of 1935 the combat strength of the Luftwaffe was virtually nil. Training, design, and production were proceeding apace and expanding rapidly, but the formation of operational units had only begun, and when Hitler met with Simon and Eden the Luftwaffe could hardly have put more than a dozen *Staffeln* of ten aircraft each into combat.† But the base was rapidly broadening, and by 1936 the threat of German air power would become reality.

Although neither of them realized it at the time, the entire argument between Churchill and Baldwin about the comparative strength of the RAF and Luftwaffe in 1934 and 1935 was of little practical moment. Both in Germany and Britain the fighters and bombers then being produced were largely wooden biplanes, destined for rapid obsolescence. The real battlefield of these years lay in the fields of design and industrial expansion, and here the British were making great strides in 1934 and 1935, little as this was known at the time.

On May 17, 1935, in a secret report by the DRC Subcommittee on Air Parity, it was stated: "The firms of Hawker and Supermarine are, we are informed, designing low wing monoplanes with retractable undercarriages, flaps for slow landing, and estimated speed of 300 m.p.h. Prototypes may be expected in July and October 1935 respectively." The Air Ministry expected trouble with the unfamiliar design, and these aircraft were not to be counted on for the Scheme C program.

The designs so mentioned were for aircraft (designed by R. T. Mitchell and Sidney Camm) that became known respectively as the Hawker Hurricane and the Supermarine Spitfire, the two British fighters of the Battle of Britain. The first Hurricane flew in November 1935, and the Spitfire six months later.‡

Perhaps even more important to the defense of Britain were remarkable developments in the secret chambers of science—what Churchill was later to call

* The "figures" were 1,500 first-line aircraft, estimated to be the strength of the French Air Force, which Hitler had said Germany would match. Under Scheme C, the British home defense air base would comprise seventy bomber and thirty-five fighter squadrons, with about 1,250 front-line aircraft.

† This was known to the British Air Staff, if not to Hitler or Churchill. On May 28, 1935, the Chief of the Air Staff, Sir Edward Ellington, transmitted to the Air Minister (Lord Londonderry) a letter from the British air attaché in Berlin, with the comment: "I have no doubt that in March when the Hitler conversation took place, the German Air Force had practically no first-line strength as defined by us. Even now I doubt that it is more than 250 to 300."

‡ The standard German fighter of the Second World War, the highly successful Messerschmitt 109, was designed at about the same time as the Hurricane and Spitfire, but the Germans moved faster on mass production, and the aircraft was already in use in Spain in 1937.

the "wizard war." Baldwin's fatalistic prediction that "the bomber will always get through" was widely but not unanimously accepted in knowledgeable circles, and in the fall of 1934 there were stirrings among the scientists in which both Baldwin and Churchill were involved. The latter's close friend and personal scientific adviser, Professor F. A. Lindemann, rightly and publicly attacked the lack of results in air defense research, and in September 1935, Churchill and Lindemann visited Baldwin at his vacation retreat at Aix-en-Provence to present "the Prof's" ideas concerning aerial mines and infrared rays.

The Air Ministry did not find these promising, but in December, with Baldwin's approval, it established a Committee for Scientific Study of Air Defence, headed by Sir Henry Tizard. Under the aegis of this group, and based on the original proposals of Robert A. Watson-Watt, the Air Ministry developed the system of detecting approaching aircraft by reflected radio waves, first called "RDF" but soon and since known as radar. Its principle was first successfully demonstrated on February 26, 1935, and within two years a start was made on the chain of coastal radar stations which were to play so vital a part in the Battle of Britain.

The conjunction of Lindemann and Tizard led to one of the most remarkable scientific confrontations of the century, and when Churchill became Prime Minister, Tizard was put on the shelf and Lindemann took the seat of scientific power and later became Lord Cherwell. The controversy is colorfully described, from Tizard's viewpoint, in C. P. Snow's *Science and Government,* wherein the author raises the question whether, if Churchill had become Prime Minister in 1935 and Lindemann had then replaced Tizard, the Battle of Britain might have been lost for want of adequate aircraft detection equipment. It is a good question but, happily, it need not be answered.

7

King George V celebrated his silver jubilee on May 6, 1935, and a few weeks later Ramsay MacDonald, whose health had continued to fail, resigned as Prime Minister. It is said that he expected Baldwin to follow suit, but in the upshot they simply changed places, and the National Government continued, with Baldwin as Prime Minister for the third time. Across the Atlantic, Walter Lippmann wrote that "no other man in the United Kingdom could begin to command the confidence which Stanley Baldwin inspires at home and abroad."

Thus Baldwin assumed formal as well as practical control of the Government, and in fact his responsibilities were broadened since MacDonald, though increasingly incapacitated, had not been a figurehead, and Baldwin had left the conduct of foreign affairs largely to him and Simon, hoping that the very junior Eden would help keep things straight. Baldwin now had a much freer hand with Cabinet appointments, and immediately upon taking full charge he made two important changes: at the Air Ministry, where Lord Londonderry was replaced by Sir Philip Cunliffe-Lister (soon to become Lord Swinton), and the Foreign Office, which Sir John Simon voluntarily quit to take the Home Office. As his successor, Baldwin was torn between Eden and Sir Samuel Hoare, then at the India Office, and he resolved the dilemma by the rather curious expedient of giving Hoare the Foreign Office and Eden a newly created Cabinet position as Minister for League of Nations Affairs. These appointments were especially important because there were two major matters—one involving Germany and the other Italy—hanging over from the MacDonald-Simon regime, and for the balance of 1935, as rearmament continued, diplomacy took the center of the stage.

Hitler had broken up Geneva, refused to entertain the Barthou "eastern Locarno" ideas, and the prospects of an air pact faded with his denunciation of the Versailles limitations. From all the discussions with him, he had given just one firm and positive indication: he was willing to sign a naval treaty with Britain at a 35:100 ratio.

According to the German naval chief, Admiral Erich Raeder, Hitler had suggested such a pact in private conversation soon after he became Chancellor.* Rightly sensing that he would get nowhere as long as the British were seriously engaged at Geneva, nothing was said until November 1934, when Raeder, following Hitler's instructions, broached the idea of an Anglo-German naval agreement to the British naval attaché. The previous day, when Sir Eric Phipps had come to complain about German rearmament, Hitler took advantage of the occasion to inform the ambassador that Germany would agree to a 35 per cent ratio. In January he gave the same assurances to Lord Allen of Hurtwood and Lord Lothian and in March to Simon and Eden. On this last occasion his overtures bore fruit in the form of an invitation extended by Simon to send a naval delegation to London.

At this stage, the British appear to have assessed Hitler's proposal primarily as one of many factors in the international naval situation. The Washington Treaty was to expire in 1936, and Japan, unwilling now to accept any status inferior to those of Britain and the United States, had announced her abandonment of the ratio system. Wishing to stave off an all-out naval race, the British hoped to substitute limitations on ship displacement, gun calibers, and other elements of naval construction for consideration at the conference to be held in London at the end of 1935. A bilateral pact with Germany, it was thought, might eliminate uncertainty about her plans and win her support for the British proposals. A stipulated Anglo-German ratio was collateral to and, indeed, superficially inconsistent with England's broader aim to win general agreement on other kinds of limitation.

For Hitler, however, the ratio was crucial, and immediately after Simon and Eden had departed Berlin he told Raeder that it had been made clear to Simon that the 35 per cent figure was nonnegotiable. He took the coming negotiations out of the Foreign Ministry and designated Ribbentrop as a special envoy to lead the German delegation. Before his departure, Ribbentrop was carefully briefed by Hitler, Raeder, Neurath, and Blomberg, and specifically instructed to make no concession and divulge no information until the ratio point had been

---

* According to Raeder, Hitler suggested a German naval limitation to one third of Britain's strength, and Raeder "for practical reasons" suggested a 35 per cent ratio instead—"a suggestion which he [Hitler] promptly accepted." Raeder did not explain the "practical reasons," but it should be noted that 35 per cent was the exact equivalent of the ratios permitted to France and Italy under the 5-5-3-1.75-1.75 Washington Naval Treaty provisions for capital ships.

accepted. Then on May 21, in a major speech to the Reichstag, Hitler publicly committed himself to the 35 per cent limitation, and disavowed all thought of naval rivalry with Britain.

Accordingly, there was little excuse for British surprise at German insistence on the 35 per cent ratio as the basis of discussion. Nevertheless, when Sir John Simon—in his last appearance as Foreign Secretary—opened the discussions on June 4, he delivered a sort of lecture on the unwisdom of ratios in general and, when Ribbentrop replied that acceptance of ratios in general and 35 per cent in particular was an essential preliminary to any further discussion, Simon betrayed his anger and left the room. Sir Robert Craigie, the remaining Foreign Office representative,* endeavored to continue the discussion, but Ribbentrop was adamant, and the meeting broke up so that the British might get further instructions.

At Baldwin's request, MacDonald called a small group of ministers to the Cabinet room that afternoon and, according to a naval eyewitness,† Baldwin informed his listeners that the Admiralty and the Foreign Office were both in favor of acceding to the German proposal. He declared that "there was no question of being rushed into a formal acceptance," which was more than a bit disingenuous, since if Ribbentrop were told that his demand would be met, the British would, as a practical matter, be bound. Baldwin then asked if anyone objected. None did, though Eden voiced some reservations about the probable French reaction. Baldwin then observed that, for him, the crucial reason for accepting the ratio was that, since clandestine violation would be virtually impossible, Germany would have to comply with or openly abrogate it, and "If this is so, then this agreement is tantamount to erecting a danger signal on the road ahead."

The Cabinet duly approved the ratio, but directed that the treaty not be signed until the other naval powers had been consulted. Japan and the United States made no objection, but the Italian reply was noncommittal and the French protested tardily but sharply. Meanwhile the drafting of the agreement was concluded,‡ and on June 18, 1935, it was consummated by an exchange of notes between the two governments. It provided for a "permanent relationship" between the navies of Germany and the British Commonwealth, over-all and by ship categories, at the 35:100 ratio. An important exception was made for submarines, which (as long as the 35 per cent over-all limitation was not exceeded) Germany could build to parity with the British, although she undertook not to

* Craigie was head of the American department of the Foreign Office and had been deeply involved in naval disarmament questions for several years. Vice-Admiral Sir Charles Little was the senior British naval representative. The German delegation, in addition to Ribbentrop, comprised Erich Kordt and Ernst Woermann of the Foreign Ministry, Rear Admiral Karlgeorg Schuster, and Lieutenant Commander Heinz Kiderlen.

† The account in this paragraph is taken from Middlemas and Barnes's *Baldwin* (pp. 827–28) and, according to the authors, is based on information given subsequently by Vice-Admiral Hughes-Hallett, who was then one of the naval staff participating in the negotiations.

‡ The British made a last-minute effort to avoid an open breach with the Versailles Treaty by proposing to sign subject to subsequent approval by the Versailles powers, but Ribbentrop would have none of it and, once again, the British gave way.

exceed 45 per cent except in circumstances of "necessity" as she might determine. The Germans also made a statement, not incorporated in the written
agreement, that they would abide by the London agreement of 1930 with respect to the conduct of submarine warfare, the provisions of which forbade the
sinking of merchant ships unless passengers and crew were first put into boats
under safe circumstances.*

Presenting the matter in the Cabinet on the day after signature, Hoare declared that it put Britain in control of instead of in competition with the German
Navy. "A better agreement," he said, "could not be obtained," and "it was essential to seize the present opportunity. . . . Everything possible had been done
to obtain the goodwill of France and Italy. Nevertheless, the French Government had sent a note. . . ." The First Lord of the Admiralty, Sir Bolton Eyre-
Monsell, reported that the Navy was very happy with the agreement. He anticipated some criticism of the submarine provisions, but "the Admiralty were
rather less apprehensive of submarines today than they had been during the
War." The Cabinet then approved the agreement and decided that Eden should
go to Paris to mollify the French. There was debate in the Commons a few
weeks later in which both Churchill and Lloyd George voiced strong opposition,
but in the vote the agreement was approved by a large majority.

From the German standpoint, the motivation for the agreement was plain
enough. Not only could naval rearmament now proceed quite openly and without regard to the Versailles restrictions, but, much more important, the bases,
both practical and moral, of all these restrictions were swept away by British
participation in a bilateral agreement that violated their terms. As Raeder subsequently wrote:

> This naval agreement was a political success for Germany in that Britain's
> willingness to substitute a voluntary agreement in place of the rigid Versailles
> Treaty conditions not only broke up the so-called "Stresa front" but also
> sanctioned Germany's right thereafter to rearm. Now, at last, Germany could
> no longer be justly accused of violating the disarmament conditions of the
> Treaty of Versailles.

The treaty likewise ended the diplomatic isolation into which Germany had
fallen by quitting the League and denouncing Versailles. Furthermore, all this
was gained by a step which Germany could picture as a generous concession on
her part to the cause of peace. Had she not voluntarily consented to a permanent position of naval inferiority? Even the old hero of Jutland, Lord Beatty,
saw the matter in this light: "I am of the opinion," he told the House of Lords,
"that we owe thanks to the Germans. They came to us with outstretched hands
and voluntarily proposed to accept a 35 to 100 ratio in fleet strength. If they
had made different proposals, we would not have been able to stop them." But
the noble lord was being had, for the treaty imposed no significant limitations on
German naval rearmament. Given the size of the British Navy in 1935, the 35
per cent limitation would have authorized a German Navy of 425,000 tons, as

* The London Agreement was not yet in force, as France and Italy had not ratified it.
The submarine provisions later became binding under the London Submarine Agreement of
November 6, 1936, which Germany signed.

compared to 86,000 tons of German ships then afloat. Even if the British fleet remained static, it would have taken years for the Germans to build up to the permitted limit and, given manpower and material shortages, this could only have been done at the expense of the Army and Luftwaffe.*

The British ledger balances very differently. The pact with Germany in no substantial way strengthened the British hand at the naval conference, from which Japan withdrew in January of 1936 when her demand for parity (5-5-5) was not met. Baldwin's desire for a "danger sign" is hard to appreciate, considering the numerous other red flags that German air and ground rearmament and aggressive diplomacy would be bound to wave.

The bad French reaction was foreseen, albeit dimly. It may have been true, as Eden told Léger, that the Versailles restrictions were no longer worth much, but it was Hitler's open repudiation of Versailles that had pulled together the Stresa Front, and it should have been apparent that for the British to countenance a reborn German Navy, including U-boats, would deeply wound French and Italian feelings, especially in naval circles. Russia and the small Baltic countries were also directly affected. Perhaps the British thought that the value of a friendly gesture toward Germany outweighed the hurt to France and Italy; if so, it was a singularly ill-timed assessment, with the Ethiopian problem already approaching the boiling point.

On a personal basis neither Simon nor Hoare† is to be severely judged, since the former opposed the ratio and the latter took office after the Cabinet had in substance accepted the German proposition. Indeed, the Foreign Office as a whole is perhaps not greatly to be blamed, since the diplomatic drawbacks could be overborne or mitigated by compelling naval considerations. The Admiralty insisted that there were such reasons, and it is on Eyres-Monsell and Admiral Ernle Chatfield, the Chief of the Naval Staff, that the principal blame must be visited.

For blame there assuredly is, as it is impossible to make an intelligible case for the treaty from Britain's standpoint. The admirals must have been mesmerized by memories of the naval race preceding the First World War. The German Navy in 1935 was so small that the 35 per cent limitation would have no practical effect for some years. By that time the circumstances favoring compliance with the treaty might well have changed, and who could assume that Germany would not then denounce the treaty, as she had just denounced Versailles?

The Admiralty's professions of satisfaction with the German promise to

---

* In his memoirs, Lord Templewood (né Hoare) claims that the agreement "slowed down German naval construction." There is not the slightest evidence for this conclusion. It is true that Germany had not nearly reached the treaty ratios in 1939 except in submarines, but this was not due to treaty limitations, since they had not been approached, but to strategic decisions to invest available resources primarily in the two other services.

† Hoare's *apologia* in his book, however, is replete with inaccuracies and *non sequiturs*, such as the erroneous statement that Hitler had entered into the agreement "on his own initiative and against the advice of his experts," when in fact Raeder had favored the proposal from the very beginning, and the contentions that the argument slowed down German naval construction, which it did not, and that it "guaranteed the French Navy a decisive superiority over the German Navy," when in fact it only left them the right to maintain superiority by construction sufficient to meet any enlargement of the British and, consequently, German fleets.

comply with the still untested rules of submarine warfare can only be described as either disingenuous or, in Churchill's words, the "acme of gullibility." The limits of the German submarine strength, on the other hand, might, if observed, have been of some benefit. In a war against Germany, submarines would be of only minor importance to Britain, while they would probably be Germany's major naval offensive weapon. Under the terms of the agreement, Britain could limit Germany's strength by limiting her own, and the advantage would be all her way. But this point seems never to have been made and was, in any event, of only short-term value since submarines, unlike the larger surface warships, can rapidly be produced in quantity once the basic designs and tooling are accomplished.

Perhaps the most dangerous feature of the agreement, however, was that it took no account of Britain's naval requirements in other parts of the world. A 100:35 superiority over the Germans was reassuring as long as the main British fleet was in the North Sea, but what if it were in the Mediterranean or, much worse, at Singapore? Churchill made this point very strongly in the Commons:

> What a windfall this has been to Japan! Observe what the consequences are. . . . The British Fleet, when this program is completed, will be largely anchored in the North Sea . . . and the whole advantage of our having a great naval base at Singapore upon which a battle fleet can be based, if necessary, to protect us in the Indian Ocean and to maintain the connection with Australia and New Zealand . . . is greatly affected by the fact that when this German fleet is built we shall not be able to keep any appreciable portion of the British Fleet so far from home.

In Moscow, Maxim Litvinov had already come to the same conclusion, which he expressed even more sharply to the American Ambassador, William C. Bullitt. Litvinov referred to the British as "blacklegs,"* predicted that the treaty "will be disastrous not only in Europe but also in the Far East," since Britain "will have to retain the greater part of her naval forces in the North Sea . . . diminish her forces in the Mediterranean," and would find it "absolutely impossible to send a fleet to Singapore." Bullitt added that he had recently encountered "Mr. Wheeler Bennett, who for many years has been connected with the British Secret Service" and who had remarked that "he and all the British diplomatists he has seen since the conclusion of the Anglo-German agreement, believe that henceforth Singapore will be totally useless."

8

The second piece of diplomatic business which Baldwin, Hoare, and Eden inherited from MacDonald and Simon was the growing Italian threat to Ethiopia. Once again a large part of the damage had been done before the new foreign affairs team was fairly settled in office. Beginning in February 1935, a few weeks after the Laval-Mussolini agreements were reached, Italian troops and matériel bound for Somaliland and Eritrea started pouring through the Suez Canal, right under British noses. These preparations did not pass unnoticed in

---

* For the benefit of those whose English is not equal to Mr. Litvinov's, a "blackleg" is Albion's idiom for a scab.

Whitehall, and by the time of the Stresa conference, in April, the Cabinet and Foreign Office were alive to the dangers of the situation.

It had been originally planned that Baldwin, Simon, and Eden would go to Stresa, but when the time came Eden was ill, and MacDonald decided to make the trip. Since it was thought unwise for the two senior ministers to leave the country, Baldwin stayed at home. Accordingly the delegation comprised Mac-Donald, Simon, and Sir Robert Vansittart. It has often been surmised that things would have gone better had Baldwin or Eden been of the party; however that may be, it is clear that those who went wholly failed to expose or clarify the issue that Mussolini's imperial designs had raised. MacDonald, nearing the end of his tenure as Prime Minister, was foggy and inarticulate, while neither Simon nor Vansittart was much concerned about Ethiopia's plight, and both were intent on keeping Italy as part of the common front against the looming German menace. And so, when Mussolini added the significant qualification "of Europe" to the official communiqué condemning actions "which may endanger the peace," everyone silently acquiesced.* The Duce concluded that the path to conquest in Ethiopia was open, and subsequent warnings, through diplomatic channels, fell on deaf ears in Rome.

The seriousness of the situation finally dawned on the British Cabinet on June 19 in the course of a long discussion of this "most inconvenient dilemma." The British Ambassador in Rome, Sir Eric Drummond, was a former Secretary-General of the League of Nations, and might have been expected to champion collective security through the League to protect Ethiopia against aggression. But now it was reported to the Cabinet that Sir Eric thought that abolition of Ethiopian sovereignty might be countenanced, since Britain in 1923 had opposed Ethiopia's admission to the League on grounds of general unfitness. Neither Hoare nor Eden supported Drummond's recommendation, but the Cabinet was sharply divided on what should be done, and Hoare's report that the French "were showing every sign that they would be on the side of Italy" underlined the difficulty of the problem. A compromise seemed to be in order, and finally it was decided to put to the Duce a proposal (previously agreed upon by Hoare, Eden, and Vansittart) that Ethiopia cede the region of Ogaden, adjoining Italian Somaliland, for which the British would provide compensation by giving Ethiopia a bit of British Somaliland, including the port of Zeila on the Red Sea.

So armed, Anthony Eden set out for Rome, and met with Mussolini on June 24. They found common ground in the French language, but nowhere else. The Duce took a prompt and strong dislike to the young British diplomat, and simply brushed aside Eden's warnings of unfavorable British reaction to a breach of the peace. He insisted that Laval had given him a free hand, and his coun-

---

*Laval and Flandin represented France at Stresa. Vansittart later wrote that he had personally warned the Italian professional diplomats that military action against Ethiopia would have serious consequences, and justified MacDonald's silence on the ground that Laval would not have supported an objection to Mussolini's addition to the communiqué. MacDonald's awareness of the issue is questionable. At his departure from Stresa a journalist asked him whether he had discussed Ethiopia with the Duce, to which MacDonald replied: "My friend, your question is irrelevant."

terproposals for a peaceful settlement were so far from the British proposition that there was no possibility of negotiation.

Early in July the Foreign Office informed the Cabinet that Eden's trip had removed "all doubt as to Mussolini's attitude," and that Italy's program of action would violate the Covenant of the League of Nations and the Kellogg-Briand Pact. There was to be a meeting of the League Council in September, at about the time Mussolini might be expected to attack, and Hoare reminded his listeners that, if Britain failed to fulfill her commitments under the Covenant, that "would amount to an admission that the attempt to give the League coercive powers was a mistake." At the same time, however, the Cabinet's discussion reflected a gloomy consensus that, if the League were to impose economic sanctions against Italy, they would be "almost bound to lead to hostilities." Laval's reluctance to take the situation seriously was making a bad situation much worse.

Eden returned to London on the same day that Lord Robert Cecil, President of the League of Nations Union, announced the results of a nationwide "Peace Ballot" conducted under his aegis. Over eleven million Britishers participated, casting their votes with virtual unanimity for continued membership in the League and general disarmament, and by an overwhelming majority for abolishing military aircraft and prohibiting the private manufacture and sale of arms. Closely touching the Italo-Ethiopian situation was the fifth and last question:

Do you consider that, if a nation insists on attacking another, the other nations should combine to compel it to stop by
  (a) Economic and non-military measures?
  (b) If necessary, military measures?

Economic sanctions were generally approved, but over 2,350,000 people, a quarter of the total, voted against military sanctions. Despite the oversimplified nature of the questions, the result was an impressive demonstration of support for collective security, but the split on military sanctions reflected misunderstandings and doubts that afflicted Cabinet Ministers no less than the voters.

It was, to be sure, a vexing problem for the British Government. For fifteen years British policy had been to support the League, and disarmament under the mantle of collective security. The Manchurian affair had shaken but not broken the League as a peace-keeping force, and the idea of collective security underlay Locarno as well as the Covenant. No doubt all members of the Cabinet recognized the danger, if not the impossibility, of letting Ethiopia go by default, but they differed widely in the value they put on the League machinery, and in their assessment of the consequences of sanctions, should the League use them against Italy. Almost obsessed with concern for the Far East, and distrustful of the French Navy, the Admiralty was strongly opposed to anything that might endanger good relations with Italy and the safety of the Mediterranean sea lanes. Eden's advocacy of League action against Italy, a course favored also by Neville Chamberlain, they viewed as illusory and dangerous.

Samuel Hoare, forceful and rather cold, was no enthusiast for the League or for semibarbaric Ethiopia, and no crusader for democracy. As an "old Conservative," Hoare told the German Ambassador, he had "no antipathy at all toward foreign totalitarian governments." But as a practical politician he had no wish to destroy the League and undermine the foundations of British policy, and he tended to view the problem as a "technical" one: to find a formula that would preserve the integrity of the League and at the same time avoid a rupture with Italy.

In this quest he was strongly supported by the two senior British civil servants —Sir Robert Vansittart, and Sir Warren Fisher, Permanent Under-Secretary of the Treasury. Vansittart and Fisher were both members of the Defence Requirements Committee and influential far beyond the usual reach of even very senior career officials. Both were impressed, if not obsessed, with the German danger,* and both favored compromise with Italy at the expense, if necessary, of Ethiopia, in order to preserve Italy as an ally and guarantor of Austrian independence. Hoare himself had testified that he soon came under the compelling influence of Vansittart, and that the two men entered upon a close collaboration in developing and "selling" to the Cabinet a policy of compromise to avoid an outcome that would pit the League, and hence Britain, against the Duce.

Perhaps even stronger than these attitudes, as a deterrent to decisive British action against Italy, was the desire, especially deep in service circles, to avoid war until rearmament was much further advanced. This is strikingly reflected in a report submitted on July 1, 1935, by a newly established subcommittee of the CID called the Defence Policy and Requirements Committee (DPRC)†—a body presided over by Baldwin himself and including the Lord President, Chancellor of the Exchequer, Foreign Secretary, the three service ministers, and the President of the Board of Trade. Perhaps no single document goes so far to explain British foreign policy during the international crises that preceded the Second World War as this little-noticed report, written under pressure of the German Air Force expansion and warning that:

> . . . it is of the utmost importance that this country should not become involved in war within the next few years. We cannot urge too strongly . . . that no opportunity should be lost to avoid the risk of war, whether in the Far East or Europe, as long as possible.

The report was signed by the subcommittee's secretary (the ubiquitous Hankey), but unquestionably this passage accurately reflected Baldwin's own views. "Keep us out of war," he told Hoare: "We are not ready for it." And George V's counsel was the same. According to Hoare, who had several audiences with him during the summer of 1935, the King had a "consuming desire" for some compromise that would avoid war: "I have been through one world war," he lamented. "How can I go through another? If I am to go on, you must keep us out of one." From the Dominion High Commissioners, Hoare heard the

* Vansittart regarded Sir Eyre Crowe as "the greatest public servant of his age" and described him as "the moving spirit of antipathy to German designs."

† Not to be confused with the Defence Requirements Committee (DRC) established in November 1933. Although both were subcommittees of the CID, each was called "Committee."

same message and drew the conclusion that the Dominion governments "were not prepared to go to war on the Ethiopian issue."

If French zeal for collective security had not been dampened by Laval's understanding with Mussolini, the upshot might have been different. But even so staunch a pillar of the League as Edouard Beneš warned Hoare against any action that would endanger Anglo-French solidarity, and the Rumanian Foreign Minister Titulescu sounded the same note of caution. Seeking to reinforce himself at home, Hoare consulted not only his own Conservative colleagues, but opposition leaders and outstanding backbenchers such as Churchill and Austen Chamberlain. All favored "collective action" through the League, but all stressed the necessity of French participation. "Go as far as the French will go," Churchill advised Hoare, adding a caution against putting Laval under any pressure that would "weaken the anti-German front."

From this mélange of fears and values—collective security, Anglo-French solidarity, fear of Japan and Germany—Hoare developed what he himself has described as a "double policy . . . . of negotiation with Italy and respect for our collective obligations under the Covenant, based on Anglo-French cooperation." But the trouble was that the "collective obligations" could be fulfilled neither by deals with Mussolini which would stultify the Covenant, nor in cooperation with a French Government which was unwilling to co-operate in any meaningful way. It was a policy unsound in principle and disastrous in application.

Baldwin and the other ministers failed to foresee the contradictions into which Hoare's policy was leading them, and continued through July and early August to pin their hopes on "a fair settlement within the League." To this end, in mid-August Eden and Vansittart (Hoare being temporarily disabled by arthritis) went to Paris for discussions with Laval and the Italian Ambassador, Vittorio Cerruti. Various compromise proposals were put to the Italians, but Mussolini rejected them all and demanded extensive annexation and an Italian mandate from the League over the entire country. This was far more than the British could stomach, and Eden left Paris convinced that a crisis was inevitable and that the French would be of little help in its resolution. Baldwin returned from vacationing in France for an emergency meeting of the Cabinet on August 22 and authorized the Admiralty to make such disposition of the Navy as was necessary to meet the possibility of war with Italy.

The Chief of the Naval Staff, Admiral Ernle Chatfield, at once moved the Mediterranean fleet from Malta to Alexandria, so as to lessen the danger of an Italian air attack. He had no doubt that the Navy was strong enough to deal with the Italians, but warned the ministers that it would sustain losses—perhaps as high as four battleships—which would seriously weaken it vis-à-vis Japan.

The Cabinet's decision was in essence an endorsement of Hoare's "double policy." Britain would publicly reaffirm her loyalty to League obligations, but would take no lead in proposing sanctions and do nothing in which the French would not join.

These qualifications, of course, were not part of the public announcement that League obligations would be fulfilled, and the Government now proceeded to handle the matter in a manner which gave a misleading impression of the lengths to which it was prepared to go. With the full approval of both Baldwin and Neville Chamberlain, Hoare prepared a speech for delivery at the September session of the Assembly of the League, the content and purposes of which he later described as follows:

> The success of the speech seemed to me to depend upon whether or not I could give the League some kind of future programme. . . . There might still, I thought, be a chance of putting new life into its crippled body. I accordingly determined to make a revivalist appeal to the Assembly. At best, it might start a new chapter of League recovery, at worst, it might deter Mussolini by a display of League fervor. If there was any element of bluff in it, it was a moment when bluff was not only legitimate but inescapable.

So disposed, Hoare left for Geneva on September 9, and, during the next two days, had lengthy private discussions with Laval, in the course of which it was agreed that, come what might, the idea of war with Italy was to be totally excluded "as too dangerous and double-edged for the future of Europe." The two likewise agreed that any sanctions which might be invoked should not be of such a type as to "provoke Mussolini into open hostility"; closing the Suez Canal was accordingly ruled out, as well as military or naval sanctions, such as a blockade of Italian ports.

Then, with these limits on action privately settled with Laval, on September 12 Hoare mounted the tribune of the Assembly and delivered himself of a pro-League speech, so categorically and even stirringly phrased that it was indeed "heard round the world":

> On behalf of His Majesty's Government in the United Kingdom I can say that . . . they will be second to none to fulfill, within the measure of their capacity, the obligations which the Covenant lays upon them. . . . In conformity with its precise and explicit obligations, the League stands, and my country stands with it, for the collective maintenance of the Covenant in its entirety, and particularly for steady and collective resistance to all acts of unprovoked aggression.

Brave words indeed, but they were a bluff, and failed to fool the intended target. Unawed, Mussolini rejected the compromise proposals put forward by the League, and a few weeks later launched the invasion of Ethiopia. But Hoare had succeeded admirably in fooling not only the League but his own countrymen as well. In Geneva, the Dutch delegate excitedly proclaimed: "The British have decided to stop Mussolini, even if that means using force." Vacationing on the Riviera, Winston Churchill was "stirred" as he read Hoare's speech, and thought it had "united all those forces in Britain which stood for a fearless combination of righteousness and strength." In London, Baldwin authorized the Navy to send the giant battle cruisers *Hood* and *Renown*, with numerous smaller warships, to Gibraltar. And when De Bono's troops crossed the Ethiopian frontier, the League promptly branded Italy as an aggressor who had violated the Covenant, and resolved to take collective action against her by way of sanctions.

Now all eyes turned toward London and, given Laval's attitude and their own determination to avoid war, the Baldwin government was on the spot. Indulging the hope that mild economic sanctions might check the Duce, the Cabinet sent Eden to Geneva with instructions to take no initiative, but to co-operate with the League Committee charged with the shaping and administration of sanctions. The committee shortly adopted a program comprising various financial and trade restrictions which became effective in November.

For two months the hollowness of the British policy was not apparent, and Baldwin rode to a smashing victory at the November elections, on a platform of fidelity to the League, rearmament, and collective security. But the sanctions had no visible effect on Mussolini's belligerency in Ethiopia, though the Italian advance soon ground to a halt. Meanwhile, some members of the League were growing restive over the ineffectiveness of the sanctions so far declared. The Canadian delegate proposed an embargo on oil shipments to Italy,* and a meeting of the League Committee, to consider the matter, was scheduled for mid-December.

At this crucial juncture, the Chiefs of Staff, and especially Admiral Chatfield, again raised their voices to counsel caution. Their views were reinforced by a Defence Requirements Committee report, adopted November 21 which casts light on the services' distrust of collective security as a basis for British policy. In pre-League days, it was pointed out, Britain could choose for herself when and where to bring her military power to bear. Under no circumstances would she have contemplated confrontations with friendly Japan or Italy over their behavior in Manchuria or Ethiopia, remote as these lands were from vital British interests. Now, however, under the regime of collective security, Covenant obligations might, at any moment and unexpectedly, pull Britain into conflicts in which she had little direct interest and for which no military preparations had been previously thought necessary. Rather drily, the Cabinet was reminded that in November 1933 it had approved a CID recommendation that no money be spent on defensive measures useful only against France, the United States, or Italy. Now, only two years later, defensive measures against Italy had to be hastily improvised, to meet the contingency that collective security, operating through sanctions, might provoke Italy to the point of war. And this was happening, they stressed, at a time when Japan was stirring ominously and Germany was rearming feverishly. The specter of simultaneous hostilities with two, let alone all three, of these countries was simply not to be contemplated in military terms, and must surely be avoided.

On December 2, the Cabinet met to decide what should be done. Neville Chamberlain and Eden were ready to see the oil sanctions put into effect; Hoare, Runciman, and the service representatives were unhappy at the prospect. As Foreign Secretary, Hoare took the lead in the discussions and expressed fear that oil sanctions would be *too* effective and might force Mussolini into a "mad dog" act. However, the League Committee strongly favored oil sanctions, and

---

* In so doing the delegate, Walter Riddell, was badly out of step with the cautious views of Prime Minister Mackenzie King, and Riddell's proposals were in substance disowned by Ottawa.

Britain, having pledged full support of the League, could not afford to appear obstructive. The best thing to do would be to "press on with the peace negotiations as rapidly as possible" and to hope that they might go well enough to warrant postponing the oil sanctions. Hoare then revealed that, for reasons of health, he was going to Zuoz in Switzerland for a rest and that he proposed en route to stop in Paris "to see M. Laval and to try and press on his talks with him." All this the Cabinet approved and so laid the scene for the ill-fated Hoare-Laval agreement.

Historians of the period have often attributed the fiasco to Hoare's illness and Laval's overreaching. To be sure, Hoare was far from well, but he was not seriously disabled, and indeed was planning to recoup his health at Zuoz by figure skating, at which he was expert. Hoare had made it plain, both in Cabinet and in the House, that he hoped to achieve a negotiated settlement that would obviate the need for further sanctions, and that is precisely what he tried to do. In Paris he was supported by Vansittart, who, so far from "happening" to be in Paris, or being "drawn into the affair" (as Winston Churchill put it in *The Gathering Storm*), had gone there (as Vansittart himself informed the French Ambassador in London, on the morning of his departure) "to take part in the conversations with M. Laval which the Secretary of State was about to initiate."*

As Vansittart viewed the prospects in his talk with the French Ambassador, Charles Corbin, the problem "was one of finding reasonable and even generous terms to Italy, bearing in mind that it was only possible owing to the special nature of the case and that Italy was, in fact, an aggressor." All this was duly reported by Vansittart to his colleagues in a Cabinet memorandum, with the further observation: "There must therefore be an obvious limit to appetite on the one side and connivance on the other"—and connivance was a very good word to describe the program which he and Hoare now framed with Laval, to cajole the Duce into laying down his arms.

And so Hoare went on to Switzerland "well satisfied" with the agreement which he and Laval initialed on December 8, proposing a settlement involving large territorial cessions and economic concessions to Italy, and a corridor to the sea for Ethiopia. Eden and Baldwin, when they learned the terms, thought them far too generous to Italy, but what Hoare had done was generally in line with the policy approved by the Cabinet on December 2, and on the ninth the Cabinet approved the proposals in principle and directed that the British Ambassador in Addis Ababa be instructed to urge Haile Selassie to accept them.

As a piece of *Realpolitik,* there was much to be said for the Hoare-Laval proposals, and their weakness was that no one but Hoare and Laval had been thinking in those terms. Hoare's own speech in September, and Baldwin's election campaign in November, had been based on the Covenant and collective security, and the League members, the British people, and indeed most of the interested world public had come to view the matter from that standpoint. It was an impossible basis for a settlement under which the nation condemned as an

---

* Before leaving for Paris, Hoare informed both the Dominion High Commissioners and the King's private secretary that he hoped to reach agreement with Laval on a basis for peace proposals, and that he was taking Vansittart with him because of the importance of the talks with Laval.

aggressor was to be substantially rewarded for its aggressions. Baldwin and his colleagues failed to perceive the inevitable and disastrous consequences of the imbalance. In this failure there is great blame, and it is unfair to visit the bulk of it on Hoare.

That unhappy man had blacked out while skating and broken his nose on the ice. By the time of his return to London on December 16, his plan was dead, and he and Laval were widely regarded as a pair of swindlers. The enormously influential editor of the *Times,* Geoffrey Dawson, who had strongly backed Hoare for the foreign affairs portfolio, now urged him to resign and wrote an editorial ridiculing the proposed Ethiopian corridor to the sea as a "corridor for camels," since Laval had inserted a stipulation that no railroad should be put through the corridor, in order to protect the French-controlled railway from Addis Ababa to Djibouti. And on December 18 the same Cabinet that had approved his plan on the ninth in substance demanded that Hoare resign.

He did so at once and was replaced by Eden, who had consistently favored a much tougher policy toward Italy. But .the Hoare-Laval proposals had effectively undermined Britain's leadership at Geneva, and it was too late to retrieve the situation. American participation in an oil embargo was more than doubtful, and this factor, coupled with French delaying tactics, caused the League Committee to refer the oil sanctions proposals to a committee of experts, who reported in February that, if rigorously observed and if the United States did not increase its exports to Italy, sanctions might be effective in three months' time. On February 26, 1936, Baldwin and Eden were able to persuade the Cabinet, over the dissents of Eyres-Monsell and Runciman, that Britain should support the application of oil sanctions.

But when the League Committee met early in March, Pierre Flandin (Laval's successor as Foreign Minister) succeeded, with Eden's reluctant acquiescence, in obtaining a week's postponement to make another attempt at conciliation. Before the week was out, the Germans marched into the Rhineland, and the question of oil sanctions was drowned in a sea of other troubles. On April 22, Eden reported to the Cabinet that at Geneva "hardly anyone had been thinking of Abyssinia," and gave voice to his own doubts that it "was possible to make collective security work in Europe so long as the two dictators, Mussolini and Hitler, dominated the situation." Less than three weeks later, Badoglio was in Addis Ababa and the Italian Empire was proclaimed.

Until early June, Eden succeeded, over the objections of several of his colleagues, in keeping the existing sanctions in effect, hoping that Mussolini could be induced to give public promises about his future policies in Ethiopia that might save Britain and the League a bit of face. But the Duce was not disposed to be co-operative, and on June 10, Neville Chamberlain, who in the past had supported Eden, made a public speech describing the continuance of sanctions as "the very midsummer of madness." A week later, on Eden's own recommendation, the Cabinet agreed that "the policy of the Government should be to take the initiative at the League of Nations in proposing the raising of sanctions against Italy." On July 6, after hearing a dramatic plea by Emperor Haile Selassie, now a fugitive from the Italian presence in his country, the Assembly of the League voted to lift the sanctions.

So ended one of the most disastrous passages in the history of British statecraft.* In retrospect, it seems plain that the wisest course, if bold, would have been to play the game of collective security to the hilt and bring Mussolini down, even if it meant a war, in which Italy would have had no allies. But benefit might also have been derived from a more cautious, if cynical, policy of keeping the Duce on the side of the angels in Europe by allowing him a bit of deviltry in Africa.

The vice of the British policy was that it was a little of both and not enough of either. It should have been realized from the outset that ineffective sanctions would be far worse than none at all. The error was compounded by marshaling world opinion behind the banner of the Covenant and then proposing deals that flaunted the principles Britain had herself invoked. In the upshot, Britain got the worst of all possible worlds—an arrogant, resentful Mussolini thrown into ominous combination with an increasingly confident and acquisitive Hitler, a League of Nations damaged beyond repair as an engine of collective security, and a national image badly tarnished at home and abroad. "I have never before heard a British Minister . . . come down to the House of Commons and say that Britain was beaten . . . and that we must abandon an enterprise we had taken in hand," declared David Lloyd George in the House debate on lifting the sanctions, adding, as he pointed to the Government front bench: "Tonight we have had the cowardly surrender, and *there* are the cowards."

9

The looming and then very real confrontation with a previously friendly Fascist Italy had a healthy effect on the pace of British rearmament. Mussolini's bad behavior reinforced the fears aroused by the continuing flow of ominous reports on German rearmament. During the last week of May 1935, these fears were articulated in a remarkable exchange of memoranda among the three most prestigious British civil servants—Hankey, Warren Fisher, and Vansittart, all of whom were members of the Defence Requirements Committee. These documents outlined the policy toward Germany that the British Government pursued from then until the spring of 1939.

The exchange was initiated on May 22 by Vansittart, in a memorandum to his two compeers, stimulated by both diplomatic and unofficial information which led him to conclude that "authoritative Germans" had no fear of France or Italy, were aware of Britain's "present weakness," and believed that their country would soon "be in a position to dictate" to Britain. Warren Fisher replied the next day that Vansittart had set forth the "views which gradually

---

* In his later writings, Vansittart defended Britain's "no risk of war" policy on the grounds that she would have been inadequately supported by other countries and the Dominions, that Germany might have allied herself with Italy, and that naval losses in the Mediterranean might have caused Britain to lose "the next war." The first ground is probably valid but insufficient, and the two others fanciful. In any event, these arguments do not meet the criticism that Hoare's "double policy" visited on Britain the worst consequences of both alternatives.

over the past few years I myself have quite independently formed," and that Britain's only hope of preventing "a successful German outbreak" lay in "full rearmament" and a diplomacy which would re-establish good relations with Japan and thus enable Britain to concentrate all her resources against Germany. Hankey, however, wrote to Vansittart on May 24 that he was "rather disturbed" by the "tone" of the latter's memorandum. He referred favorably to Hitler's speech in the Reichstag on May 21, in which the Fuehrer had promised continuing support for Locarno, and Hankey admonished Vansittart that "you will be making a profound mistake if you do not throw every possible energy you possess into trying to secure a deal with Germany out of Hitler's speech." Britain desperately needed time "to recondition our own defense," Hankey went on, and therefore "we should, in the most cordial and generous spirit, follow up Hitler's overtures" and "really must cast suspicion from our minds."

Vansittart answered, courteously but a bit testily, that of course the Foreign Office would pursue "any genuine opening," as indeed it had been doing. But, he wrote, the German "bellicose spirit" was even "more dangerous than the rapidity of rearmament," and Germany was not to be trusted to keep her agreements. He closed by advising Hankey not to "try to hurry up my conversion," since "you may be glad one day that I kept my finger on the spot." In a more conciliatory vein, Hankey replied on May 28 that "we are evidently closer in thought than your first letter led me to believe," and the same day Fisher wrote soothingly to "Van dear" that "as between Maurice, you, and myself there is the common ground that we must equip ourselves thoroughly" and that "we are all agreed that we must do all we can to secure anything that may be possible out of the German attitude"; the only difference among them was that while "you and I have . . . no belief in German professions of peace, Maurice may be a shade more optimist."

So ended the correspondence, and the measure of agreement among the three embodied the two elements of British policy toward Germany: rearm, and simultaneously seek what Hankey, perhaps unaware of his own cynicism, described as "a deal with Germany." Rearmament was reflected immediately in the reorganization and expansion of the program which Baldwin was about to initiate upon his return as Prime Minister, and the "deal" in the Anglo-German Naval Agreement, signed a few weeks later. In the longer run, rearmament was vindicated by Britain's ability to stand alone in 1940, and the "deal" found consummation at Munich in 1938.

While the three senior civil servants were debating high policy, at the Air Ministry the staff was ruefully contemplating the implications of the latest reports on the German Air Force, indicating that operational units were being rapidly formed and that, by October of 1935, they would have fifty squadrons, comprising 600 aircraft, on station. Winston Churchill had sent a memorandum to the ministry in late April, containing detailed comparisons of the two air forces and concluding that the Government's promise of maintaining air parity was not being fulfilled and that Britain was entering a time of "perilous weakness." Churchill's memorandum was scrutinized within the Air Staff by Wing Commander C. E. H. Medhurst of the operations and intelligence branch, who informed the Chief of the Air Staff (Ellington) that Churchill's "statements are substantially correct looked at from a broad aspect, but incorrect in relatively unimportant detail."

It was, apparently, these renewed fears of German air power, together with emerging worries about Italy, that prompted Baldwin to create the new ministerial defense committee which issued the report of July 1, 1935, urging that war should be avoided "as long as possible." The Defence Requirements Committee, comprised as it was of the three service chiefs and three senior civil servants, was not politically responsible, and no doubt it was to enable close and informed analysis at the ministerial level that Baldwin, in the late spring of 1935, established the Defence Policy and Requirements (DPR) Subcommittee of the CID. The DPR Report of July 1 recommended a re-examination of the scale and distribution of defense expenditures in the light of current developments, and a week later the DRC was directed to do the groundwork.

That body made an interim report on July 24, estimating that Germany would not attain her intended naval strength until 1942, that her army would closely approach the French in size by 1939 and considerably exceed it by 1942, and that the air force would be formidable by 1938. On these bases it was considered unlikely that the Germans would "deliberately" launch an aggression before 1942, but that "it is not safe to postpone the date at which we should aim at a reasonable state of preparedness beyond January 1939—which only gives us three budget years." The DRC warned that this would require a greatly accelerated program of military expenditure and asked for authority to develop detailed plans on that basis. Five days later the DPR generally approved the request, and the DRC returned to its labors.

These bore fruit in the DRC's next Report, completed November 21, 1935, in forty-eight pages supported by sixty pages of schedules tabulating the estimated requirements for the three services. The committee's dim view of collective security has already been remarked, and bitter experience with the impact of that concept on Britain's relations with Italy and Japan now led the DRC to declare "it to be a cardinal requirement of our national and imperial security that our foreign policy should be so conducted as to avoid the possible development of a situation in which we might be confronted simultaneously with the hostility, open or veiled, of Japan in the Far East, Germany in the West, and any Power on the main line of communication between the two." And this, of course, was precisely the outcome, when Britain found herself at war with Germany in 1939, Italy in 1940, and Japan in 1941.

To forestall these hazards if possible and confront them if necessary, the DRC recommended four major enlargements of Britain's military capacity: (1) a two-ocean Navy, strong enough to deal with Germany, and at the same time maintain a Far Eastern fleet "adequate to act on the defensive and to serve as a strong deterrent against any threat to our interests in that part of the globe"; (2) restoration of the Army's capacity to provide antiaircraft and coastal defense; (3) creation of an Army field force available for employment on the Continent, especially to protect the Low Countries against German occupation; and (4) provision of large aircraft and pilot reserves, so that the 123 squadrons envisaged under Scheme C could be maintained with replacements for combat losses. It was recognized that this program would require not only a great increase in the service estimates, but also the creation of a so-called "shadow armament industry" subsidized by the Government and consisting of reserve industrial capacity available for the immediate expansion of production in the event of war.

The DRC report was discussed in Cabinet on December 4 and was referred for ministerial analysis to the DPRC, to which, at Hoare's suggestion, Baldwin now added, as industrial consultant, a prestigious Scottish manufacturer in whom he had great confidence, William Douglas Weir, who had served as Director General of Aircraft Production and, briefly, as Air Minister at the end of the First World War, and who had been serving since May as an adviser to the Air Ministry. During January of 1936 the DPRC held nine meetings, at most of which Baldwin presided, to review the DRC report in detail.

At the first meeting on January 16, 1936, the DPRC had before it a memorandum from Lord Weir, raising two basic and pointed questions about the DRC's recommendations. The first related to the air proposals and arose from the DRC's recognition of "a possibility of [air] attack from Germany, so continuous and concentrated and on such a scale that a few weeks of such an experience might so undermine the morale of any civilian population as to make it difficult for the Government to continue the war."* Reminding his readers that Baldwin had "repeatedly pointed out that immunity from air attack is almost impossible to achieve" (". . . the bomber will always get through," Baldwin had told the Commons in 1932), Weir criticized the air proposals as laying too much stress on defense and too little on the deterrent effect of a large striking force. Should not the air estimates be both modified in composition and enlarged in quantity, asked Weir, so that the home air force would be "a striking and offensive air weapon of such strength . . . as would represent the most effective possible deterrent to any European enemy, a weapon so powerful as to compel the most wholesome respect from both friend and foe?"†

Weir's other target was the Army proposal for a field force for use on the Continent: German resources in manpower were far greater, ground forces could not be brought to bear as rapidly as air and naval power, and the expense would be enormous. It thus appeared "probable that on the face of it there appears no more difficult or costly method of making our contribution to our Allies in

* The reality of this possibility depended in considerable part on whether the Luftwaffe would be designed primarily for co-operation with the Army or for independent strategic operations. In May of 1934, the British Chiefs of Staff were of the opinion, based on intelligence reports, that the Germans themselves had not decided this question. Two months later, however, the British air attaché in Berlin reported that "the main aim of Germany's air strategy is the continuous day and night bombing of the enemy's vital centres with a standard type of large multi-engined comparatively invulnerable day and night bomber . . . she considers air attack will be the decisive factor in future war." The first Chief of the Luftwaffe General Staff, General Walther Wever, was indeed thinking along those lines, but in fact the issue was still unresolved in January of 1936. Wever was killed in an air crash in June of that year, and thereafter, the "strategic bombing" advocates lost ground, and the Luftwaffe developed as a primarily tactical air force, poorly equipped for the heavy bombardment of distant targets.

† Weir had for some years been an advocate of strategic bombing as a means of defense.

Europe than through increased British Army strength." For Weir, accordingly, the question was whether the increase in the Air Force which he proposed would not justify dispensing with the Army field force, thus achieving both financial economy and a more potent deterrent factor.

Needless to say, these ideas put the Army's nose badly out of joint, and the Chief of the Imperial General Staff, Field Marshal Sir Archibald Montgomery-Massingberd, immediately counterattacked, pointing out that Germany was as superior in industrial potential as in manpower and would never "allow us to build an air force of greater strength than her own"; that no superiority in bombers could "compensate for the situation of London," combining as it did "objectives that in Germany are spread over Berlin, Hamburg, and the Ruhr"; and observing that Lord Weir's denigration of the Army field force had been written in ignorance of Chiefs of Staff studies made two years earlier, which had conclusively shown that the Low Countries must be protected against German occupation primarily to guard Britain from air attacks at such close quarters, against which the difficulties of defense would be greatly increased.

But Lord Weir had the heavier artillery. At the DPRC's initial meeting he informed its members that, in view of the shortage of skilled labor, fulfillment of the DRC proposals would require considerable interference with normal business and conversion to a "semi-war organization." Supported by the President of the Board of Trade, Walter Runciman, Weir gave a discouraging survey of the industrial shortages and bottlenecks that loomed and reminded the Air Minister, Viscount Swinton, that his "shadow factory" projects, however they might increase plant capacity, would not cure the labor shortage.*

Confronted with this dilemma—interference with normal business or a cut in the program—the DPRC, as Weir had hoped, took the latter course. At the second meeting, on January 14, the Chancellor of the Exchequer joined forces with Weir. If Germany were to move in Eastern Europe, said Neville Chamberlain, a British expeditionary force would not be needed in the west; if she attacked in the west, British ground forces might not reach the Continent quickly enough to be of help. By this marvelous logic the need for a field force appeared to be entirely eliminated, and Chamberlain drove on to Weir's conclusion that an air offensive would provide "more effective protection than defensive action on the part of the land forces," and that the committee ought therefore to consider expanding the air program and contracting the Army estimates, which likewise were the root of the industrial and labor difficulties raised by the DRC recommendations. Chamberlain's position was, essentially, the same as the one he had adopted in 1934 with respect to the DRC's first report.

By the third meeting, the Weir-Chamberlain view had already so far prevailed that the DPRC gave the Air Ministry "a free hand to reconsider the composition of the Royal Air Force with a view to providing the most effective offensive and defensive force vis-à-vis Germany." Warned by Hankey that the Weir-Chamberlain program would mean an Army incapable even of helping to defend the Low Countries, at the fourth meeting (January 16) Baldwin intervened with a compromise proposal, under which the first contingent (four

---

* Weir had close personal and professional ties with both Runciman and Swinton.

regular infantry divisions and one mechanized division with a brigade of tanks) of the proposed Army field force would be provided for, and the funding of the remainder (twelve divisions of territorial troops, to be ready within four to eight months after the outbreak of war) be postponed for further consideration in three years' time.

Weir's reaction was cautious; it was "difficult," he said, "to appreciate, exactly, the effect on industrial questions which the Prime Minister's proposal involved." But Baldwin's suggestion prevailed, and was embodied in the DPRC's recommendations to the Cabinet, transmitted early in February, together with a memorandum from the Air Ministry setting forth the modifications in the air estimates proposed in responses to the DPRC's offer of a "free hand" to strengthen the offensive power of the home air force. These comprised primarily the substitution of medium for light bombers in thirty of the projected squadrons—a change which, according to the Air Ministry, would make a "great improvement in the offensive and deterrent power" of the RAF, inasmuch as the medium bombers (unlike the light bombers, which were eliminated altogether) would have greater range and load and be able "under certain circumstances" to reach Berlin.

On February 25, 1936, the DPRC's recommendations were approved by the Cabinet "generally and provisionally, on the understanding that the programmes contained therein were liable to modification in the light of new conditions such as . . . developments in the range and offensive power of aircraft." *In toto*, they envisaged the expenditure for expansion of some 400 million pounds over the next five years. The Cabinet was very sensitive to the possibility of adverse public reaction, and Neville Chamberlain observed that "it would probably be advisable to avoid figures which could be added up to a larger amount than public opinion was anticipating."

In line with this warning, the Cabinet's public statement, embodied in the "Defence White Paper" submitted to Parliament on March 3, declared that "any attempt to estimate the total cost" would be "premature," and merely warned that the funds required would be larger than theretofore. No mention was made of the two-ocean naval standard or the plan to lay down seven new capital ships in the next four years; the White Paper disclosed only that two would be laid down in 1937, and that the cruiser total would eventually be raised to seventy, with five new ships scheduled for 1936. No details were given concerning the Army field force, and the immediate increase in the Regular Army was set at only four battalions. The description of the RAF program was equally vague.

As a factor in the determination of British foreign policy during the next three years, the Air Force program was the most important of the three and, unlike the two others, was intended to achieve a reasonably satisfactory level of strength by 1939. Scheme C, adopted a year earlier, was now replaced by Scheme F,* destined to remain the basis of RAF expansion until after the German annexation of Austria in March 1938. In first-line aircraft the increase was modest; the home air force was to rise from 1,512 to 1,736 aircraft, and ten

---

* Schemes D and E were almost at once revealed to their air staff authors as inadequate, and were never presented to the Cabinet.

squadrons each were added to the Fleet Air Arm and the overseas units. But 50 million pounds was earmarked for additional aircraft and factory capacity so that a reserve of 225 per cent could be maintained behind the first-line squadrons. And, in line with Lord Weir's stress on offensive power, the eighteen medium and thirty light bomber squadrons of Scheme C became forty-eight medium bomber squadrons in Scheme F.

The White Paper contained an additional item, reflecting the growing demand, in the Commons and the editorial pages of *The Times,* for an over-all Ministry of Defence. Opposition from the three existing service ministries killed off the idea of a full-fledged ministry over them, but in February, Baldwin persuaded the Cabinet to approve the appointment of a Minister for the Coordination of Defence, who would serve as his deputy in presiding over the CID and its subordinate committees, and generally ride herd on the services and make recommendations for improved defense organization. Hoare, the two Chamberlains, Halifax, and Churchill were all considered for the job, and the last-named very much wanted it. It came as a "heavy blow" to him when Baldwin, to general surprise, picked the Attorney General, Sir Thomas Inskip, who had little political stature and less familiarity with defense problems; in the Commons lobbies it was covertly joked that it was the most remarkable appointment since the Emperor Caligula had made his horse a consul. Subsequent judgments on Inskip's discharge of his duties were more charitable, but the selection was not calculated to stimulate popular concern for defense or galvanize the bureaucracy into speedier action.

Certainly there were organizational and technical problems galore for Inskip and the service ministries to weigh. But the Army was starved and friendless, and the War Office seemed to be mired in red tape and sunk in dreams of the past. The Navy was better led and had first call at the Treasury, but its outlook was imperial rather than European.

The RAF, confronted as it was with the threat of immediate assault on the homeland, was the most responsive to changing times and techniques. The Hurricanes and Spitfires designed in 1934 and 1935 took to the air, in prototype, in 1935 and 1936. Specifications were drawn in 1936 for the heavy four-engined bombers—the Stirlings, Halifaxes, and Lancasters—that were to wreak havoc on the German cities during the second half of the war. The experimental basis for the radar defense chain was laid in the same years. And in the summer of 1936 the disparate roles of the home air force were recognized by breaking up the unitary headquarters—Air Defence of Great Britain—and establishing the commands that would endure throughout the war years: Bomber Command, Fighter Command, and Coastal Command.

The command separation of fighters and bombers, and the simultaneous prospective availability of radar, and of bombers of capacity and range and fighters of speed and firepower theretofore unknown, threw into bold relief a basic question that had not yet been fully confronted: was Britain to be defended primarily by the deterrent threat of heavy bombers, or by the ability of radar, fighters, and ground defenses to shield the homeland against German bombers? It was an issue which Lord Weir had touched but not resolved in the DPRC meetings. The much-maligned Inskip was to speak cogently and effectively on this question in 1937, but it was not to be definitely answered until dangerously close to the zero hour.

All in all, however, there is no gainsaying that 1935 and 1936 witnessed substantial progress in the reorganization, modernization, and expansion of Britain's military power. But if substantial, it was far from sufficient, in view of the sorry state into which British arms had fallen during the era of the Ten-Year Rule, the speed at which German rearmament was progressing, and the evidence of the Nazis' belligerent intentions which kept pouring in.

The reason the British did not do more is that their leaders were not yet ready to do anything that would "hurt." Lord Weir had only to declare that the DRC program could not be carried out without interference with normal business, and at once a ministerial consensus to cut back the program developed. "What we have to do," Parliament was informed by the White Paper, "is to carry through, in a limited period of time, measures which will make exceptionally heavy demands upon certain branches of industry and upon certain classes of skilled labour, without impeding the course of normal trade." Even though the sky was darkening rapidly, Merrie England would still do "business as usual."

10

The Germans marched into the demilitarized Rhineland on March 7, 1936, four days after publication of the White Paper and six days before Inskip's appointment. The event fundamentally altered the balance of power in Europe, to the maintenance of which British rearmament was dedicated. Nevertheless, the news that was a bomb-burst in Paris was a dud in London.

To be sure, the appearance of German troops west of the Rhine came as no surprise to the British. Throughout the last half of 1935 the British Ambassador in Berlin, Sir Eric Phipps, bombarded Whitehall with ominous reports, some of which were circulated to the Cabinet by Hoare on November 25, with a note warning that there was "no time to lose in the preparation and completion of our air defensive arrangements." Phipps met with Hitler and Neurath on December 13, at which time the Fuehrer "struck a cynical note of regret at having failed to reoccupy the [demilitarized] zone on March 16th last"—i.e., when he denounced the Versailles armament restrictions. "Whenever a favorable opportunity presented itself," Phipps reported, Hitler "will proceed to that reoccupation."

When Eden took over the Foreign Office from Hoare, he continued the circulation of Phipps's dispatches, adding his own notes of alarm. More to the point, on January 10, 1936, he directed an inquiry to the CID for evaluation of the military consequences of a German march-in, attaching the reports indicating its increasing likelihood. The replies were not gems of strategic analysis. The Air Staff parochially remarked that militarization of the Rhineland would be of negligible importance in air warfare, while the Army, in a correct but narrow response, pointed out that German defense was hampered by the zone, and the French derived a corresponding advantage, because the German Army would have to concentrate behind an unfortified line miles back of the likewise unfortified frontier.

Eden articulated the strategic significance of the Rhineland more clearly than the military chiefs, and advised his cabinet colleagues, in a mid-February memorandum, that "the disappearance of the demilitarized zone will not merely change local military values but is likely to lead to far-reaching political repercussions of a kind which will further weaken France's influence in Eastern and Central Europe, leaving a gap which may eventually be filled either by Germany or by Russia." But he was singularly unperturbed by this prospect and concluded: "Taking one thing with another, it seems unadvisable to adopt an attitude where we would either have to fight for the zone or abandon it in the face of German reoccupation. It would be preferable for Great Britain and France to enter betimes into negotiations with the German Government for the surrender on conditions of our rights in the zone while such surrender still has a bargaining value." What "conditions" Hitler might agree to that would come close to balancing the enormous strategic gain to Germany, Eden did not say.

Meanwhile Eden had discussed the situation with both the German and French foreign ministers, who were in London late in January for George V's funeral. Neurath gave smooth assurance that Germany would respect Locarno, coupled with denunciation of the Franco-Soviet pact, then pending ratification. Flandin was greatly worried but vague about French intentions in the event the Germans should walk in. When Eden and Flandin met again in Geneva early in March, after the Chamber of Deputies had ratified the pact, the Frenchman was even more apprehensive but no more decisive. If the Germans should move in, he told Eden, France would report the violation to the League Council, concert common action with Britain, Belgium, and Italy, and reserve the right to take independent military action.

Eden returned to London on March 5, 1936, and reported to the Cabinet that evening. The ministers had before them not only Eden's memorandum on the military importance of the Rhineland, but also the Phipps dispatches, a long study of the Anglo-German-French situation by Vansittart, and comments on them by Eden. The thrust of all these papers was that Germany was rearming for a purpose and that the risk of war was great; that France was unreliable on collective security unless her own borders were threatened, but that she was likewise unwilling to make concessions to Germany; that Britain must push her own rearmament, but simultaneously strive for an understanding with Germany that might avert war. Vansittart's memorandum was ghoulishly prescient, envisaging, in probably chronological order, German annexation of Memel and Danzig, Austria and the German district of Czechoslovakia, and then the Baltic states and the Polish Corridor. But even the Germanophobe Vansittart failed to draw the inference that the Rhineland was the key to all of this, and observed fatalistically that the "zone must go anyway."

In the Cabinet discussion the Rhineland problem was closely intertwined with that of oil sanctions against Italy. At Geneva, Flandin had succeeded in putting off a decision on sanctions, and had put to Eden the question whether Britain would support France in the event that Germany should breach Locarno in the Rhineland, and particularly would she do so if Italy, as was not unlikely under the circumstances, should repudiate her Locarno commitments.

It was a question the Cabinet was loath to answer, and the discussion was distinctly pusillanimous. Eden, Simon, and the Lord Chancellor (Hailsham) thought Italy's defection would not absolve Britain of her Locarno obligations, and Eden pointed out that, in the original negotiations, the British Government had intended to sign without Italy, since the Italians had only come in at the last moment. But Simon then asked rhetorically whether, if Italy reneged, was Britain "expected to support the whole edifice?" MacDonald won general approval of his observation that the matter should be handled diplomatically so "as to avoid our stating our position," and hope was expressed that "we could stall on giving an answer until diplomatic action put the matter out of date." But Eden was realist enough to remind his colleagues that Flandin was stalling on the oil sanctions issue pending the British reply on Locarno, and exposed the unpleasant truth that both governments were defaulting on the obligations which each found distasteful. The Cabinet finally agreed to seek advice on the "nature and extent of our obligations," and meanwhile to tell Flandin that, in the event Italy pulled out, "the proper course was for the signatories to confer together as to what to do in the changed situation."

This less than bold conclusion would have been important if Italy's co-operation had really been a crucial factor. But of course it was not, and Baldwin made the decisive judgment when he declared that "the reality of the position was that neither France nor England was really in a position to take effective military action against Germany" and that "M. Flandin ought to be put up against this reality."

If this was so, the problem was how to get Germany into the Rhineland legitimately rather than in violation of Locarno, and whether a *quid pro quo* could be extracted from Hitler. To these ends, it was agreed that Eden would open negotiations with Germany, looking toward a treaty for the limitation of air armaments, and then seek to draw in the French and settle Rhineland and air pact together. This amounted, it is apparent, to sacrificing the Rhineland and with it a large part of France's military power in return for an air agreement which, if observed by Hitler, would certainly be advantageous to France but of much greater benefit to Britain, immediately vulnerable as she was only to air attack.

Eden lost no time in broaching the project to the German Ambassador, who, at the end of the conversation, told Eden that Berlin had warned him that an important diplomatic declaration would be coming the next day. And at ten in the morning on Saturday, March 7, Hoesch read to Eden the announcement of the military reoccupation of the Rhineland, couched in soothing words about the possibility of nonaggression pacts and Germany's rejoining the League.

Eden's first move was to summon the French Ambassador and request that his country do nothing "to make the situation more difficult"; the Cabinet would meet on Monday, and then the two governments should confer. He then consulted Vansittart and other senior Foreign Office staff and asked the news officer, Sir Reginald Leeper, what the British press would say next day. "I think they will say that Germany is on her own territory" was the answer. "I was afraid that would be your answer," Eden remarked, and departed for Chequers to inform the Prime Minister of the situation. He found Baldwin "clear in his mind that there would be no support in Britain for military action by the French"—a judgment in line both with Leeper's prediction and Baldwin's own opinion, expressed in Cabinet but two days earlier, that neither France nor England "was really in a position to take effective military action against Germany."

Eden returned to London and spent the rest of the weekend preparing a memorandum for the Cabinet. He advised against any military action or any demand that Germany withdraw. Acknowledging that German's action had "deprived us of a useful bargaining counter," he nevertheless concluded that Hitler's offer to negotiate new treaties should be taken up, since "it is in our interest to conclude with her as far-reaching and enduring a settlement as is possible whilst Herr Hitler is in the mood to do so." On Sunday, Eden showed the fruits of his labor to Vansittart, who approved "enthusiastically." His reaction would have been more surprising, given his attitude toward Germany, if he had not so recently and strongly opposed sanctions against Italy that he could hardly urge otherwise for Germany.

Meanwhile Hitler's move was also under discussion at Blickling Hall in Norfolk, where Lord Lothian was host to a party comprising Baldwin's close friend and adviser Thomas Jones, Lord and Lady Astor, Sir Thomas and Lady Inskip, Sir Walter Layton of the *Economist* and *News Chronicle,* and Arnold Toynbee. On Saturday evening, after hearing the news on the BBC, the company constituted themselves a "shadow cabinet" to formulate the position that the Government should take. As telephoned by Jones to Baldwin the next morning, the counsel from this prestigious assembly was to "welcome Hitler's declaration wholeheartedly," to condemn the German entry but treat it "as relatively *de minimis* and not to be taken tragically in view of the peace proposals which accompany it," to "accept Hitler's declaration as made in good faith and put his bona fides to the test by trying it out," and to "follow our own initiative" and not be "dragged at the tail of France."

Toynbee had just returned from Germany, where he had met Hitler and been treated to a two-hour lecture delivered "with masterly coherence and lucidity." The noted historian was "convinced of the Fuehrer's sincerity in desiring peace in Europe and close friendship with England," and Jones asked Toynbee to put his impressions in writing for immediate dispatch to Baldwin. Jones's purpose in all this he described as follows:

> What I am trying to secure is that S.B. should have his mind made up on the big major issue of accepting Hitler at his face value and trying him out fairly now that the last trace of humiliation has been removed. One wants S.B.'s mind firmly made up *before* he enters the Cabinet where he will encounter all sorts of contradictory advice, Simon's legalities, and Ramsay's tortuosities and ambiguities. It is a day for the quite simple and direct Lincoln touch.

Leading press organs, as anticipated, were playing much the same tune. The *Observer* editorial came close to approving the German move, and *The Times,* in a leader entitled "A Chance to Rebuild," saluted Hitler's proposals as offering the "best hope" of European stabilization. On his way to the Cabinet Monday morning, Eden probed his taxi driver's reaction and drew the reply "I suppose Jerry can do what he likes in his own back garden, can't he?"*

The Cabinet approved Eden's plan to go to Paris with Halifax (the Lord Privy Seal) for a meeting of the Locarno powers other than Germany, and made minor revisions in the statement Eden would make in the Commons that afternoon. The statement amounted only to a description of Eden's two interviews with Hoesch, a condemnation of Germany's unilateral action and a promise to come to the aid of France or Belgium if Germany should attack—an eventuality which, of course, no one expected. Harold Nicolson, then a Member, noted in his diary: "General mood of the House is one of fear. Anything to keep out of war." The following morning Nicolson had a long talk with Ramsay MacDonald, following which he recorded that: "The country will not stand for anything that makes for war. On all sides one hears sympathy for Germany. It is all very tragic and sad."

In Paris, Eden and Halifax encountered a Flandin talking boldly of sanctions economic and, if necessary, military, in a way that bore little resemblance to the cautious views of most of the other French ministers, or of Gamelin. The British, of course, did not know this and, although they suspected that Flandin was exaggerating the lengths to which France would go, they returned to London greatly concerned that the French attitude might make it impossible to proceed with any negotiations based on Hitler's peace proposals. In Paris it had been arranged that further Locarno talks, as well as the meeting of the League Council which France had convoked, would be held in London within a very few days, and Eden's next task was to formulate, to the satisfaction of his colleagues, the position Britain would take.

The Cabinet met in the late afternoon of March 11; German troops had already been in the Rhineland four and a half days. Eden reported himself impressed by the gravity of the situation and the unanimity of the French and Belgians: "Both nations felt that, if the German challenge was not taken up now, a much more formidable situation would arise . . . war in two years' time was a certainty and would be fought under very unfavorable conditions." If Germany got away with this move, collective security would be a ludicrous doctrine, and the French would put the blame on Britain "due to our failure to implement our Locarno obligations."

Nevertheless, Eden and Halifax remained of the opinion that it would do no good to force the Germans out of the Rhineland, and that a settlement by negotiation was in order. If Britain did nothing, Eden warned, France and Belgium would probably invoke the Locarno guarantees while Italy remained aloof, and the Cabinet would be confronted with the very problem it wanted to avoid. Accordingly, he proposed to request Hitler to withdraw all except "symbolic" forces from the Rhineland while new pacts to replace Locarno were negotiated. This approach should be made on Britain's sole initiative, without consulting

* According to Churchill, Lord Lothian was the originator of this phrase, minus the reference to Jerry. Halifax and Geoffrey Dawson of *The Times* also used it. Eden's taxi driver was mindful of the First World War, in which British soldiers ("Tommies") referred to the Germans as "Jerries."

the French, a procedure which Halifax supported with the observation that if the French were told it would be in the press next day.

Although Eden acknowledged that the French, if they discovered this gambit, "might suggest that we had betrayed them behind their back," the only Cabinet member who seemed disturbed by this was Ramsay MacDonald. He was "reluctant to go back on a friend before agreement was reached as to how the problem was to be handled," and feared that revelation of a secret British proposal to Hitler "would create a situation worse than the present one, since it would arouse an indignation that would besmirch us."

But Baldwin rallied strongly to the Eden-Halifax program. The sanctions proposed by the French, he predicted, "would not result only in letting loose another great war in Europe. They might succeed in crushing Germany with the aid of Russia, but it would probably only result in Germany going Bolshevik." And then, in a statement that reflected all of the Prime Minister's worst failings —procrastination, provincialism, and resentment at sharp confrontation—he declared that:

> . . . at the time when Locarno was signed the Government had felt that commitments could be accepted without undue risk owing to the strength of the French forces and the fact that Germany was totally disarmed. When the Disarmament Conference failed and Germany started to re-arm, the Government here started to do the same. In a democratic country, however, a good deal of time was taken to educate public opinion and get a plan accepted, and consequently we were now caught at a disadvantage. All that was perfectly well known to the French Government, and it seemed very unfriendly of them to put us in the present dilemma. People would take a long time to forget it. He himself had said at the Election that he was never going into sanctions again until our armaments were sufficient. He felt that the French ought to welcome our coming re-armament rather than expose us to the present embarrassments.

To be sure, in part this diatribe reflected resentments against the French aroused by their lack of co-operation in the Ethiopian affair, and the distressing state of French arms partially disclosed by the recent Anglo-French staff talks. But it overlooked the crucial question whether "present embarrassments" were not preferable to future dangers, and the Franco-Belgian prediction that a war two or three years later was much more to be feared than an immediate confrontation. Duff Cooper, for the War Office, was the only member to address himself to this, pointing out "that in three years' time we should have reconditioned at any rate to some extent our small forces, yet by that time Germany would have 100 divisions and a powerful fleet. We should not relatively, therefore, be in a better position."

But this view, however reasonable, was not in accordance with the advice from the Chiefs of Staff, who envisaged war with Germany as "a disaster for which the Services with their existing commitments in the Mediterranean are totally unprepared." Neither of the two other service ministers supported Duff Cooper, and Neville Chamberlain closed out the argument by recalling that Baldwin "had said in Parliament that it was the task of this country to try and bring France and Germany together." There was prevalent distrust of the French and skepticism of the Franco-Belgian prediction that Hitler would not fight if confronted with force. In conclusion the Cabinet approved Eden's recommendation, adding that "he should send for the German Ambassador that very night," make it clear that "this was our own spontaneous suggestion and that it had not been discussed in Paris," and emphasize "that if Herr Hitler adopted the suggestion at all, he should do it well."

It is understandable to say that the French deserved the treatment they were getting, but it was hardly the right moment for the two governments to play tit for tat. Despite MacDonald's and Duff Cooper's warnings, the Cabinet decision was naïve and duplicitous; the members had learned nothing from the Hoare-Laval debacle, and were saved from another public humiliation only because Flandin's brave words had not reflected his government's true position. Eden put the proposition to Hoesch that evening, Hitler immediately replied that he would not increase the troops in the Rhineland but made no commitment to reduce the number sent in or to refrain from building fortifications. The news of the British offer leaked to the press, and the French were ashamed to be insulted because they did not really mean business. Flandin arrived in London on March 12 for the Locarno talks with little of his former belligerence, asking that Germany withdraw the units she had sent in pending the negotiation of new pacts that would legalize the presence of German troops in the zone, but prohibit its fortification.

At the German Embassy, meanwhile, the three service attachés were in a state of high tension, and on March 13 sent a joint cable direct to Blomberg describing the situation as "exceptionally grave," with the chance of "an extremely unfavorable development . . . in the next few days." In view of the British Government's determination to avoid war this was, of course, a gross exaggeration. But after the Eden-Halifax visit to Paris there were a few days during which in London it was feared, quite wrongly, that the French might take independent military action that would eventually pull Britain into the fray. The British Chiefs of Staff had already described the prospect of war with Germany as a "disaster," and on March 12 they advised the Cabinet that, if the risk was real, all three services should be mobilized, and the forces previously sent to the Mediterranean to cope with the Ethiopian crisis brought home.

In view of the political decisions already taken, the discussions within the three services were virtually academic, and wholly so after it became clear that the French would not move independently. But they are revealing of the extraordinary and, at least in retrospect, excessive timidity with which the British military leaders reacted.

The Chiefs of Staff met on March 12 for an initial assessment of the military situation that would confront Britain if called upon to honor the Locarno commitments. Admiral Chatfield thought that the naval forces immediately available in home waters were inadequate, and that the best solution would be to abandon Malta and the central Mediterranean and hold on at the Gibraltar and Alexandria bases at each end. This would make it possible to bring the *Hood* and *Renown* back home, where they were badly needed as the only ships both

1. Munich, September 29,
1938: The Cast. Left to right,
front row: Chamberlain,
Daladier, Hitler, Mussolini,
Ciano. Back row: Schmidt,
Wilson, Ribbentrop,
Weizsaecker, Léger.
Deutsche Presse-Agentur.

2. Hitler greeting Mussolini
at Kiefersfelden on the
German-Austrian border,
September 29, 1938.
Bundesarchiv.

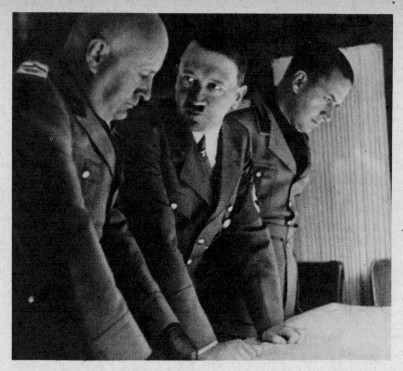

3. Mussolini, Hitler, and Ciano in Hitler's railway carriage en route from Kiefersfelden to Munich, September 29, 1938. *Bundesarchiv*.

4. The Fuehrerbau in Munich, where the conference was held. *Bundesarchiv*.

5. Hitler's office in the Fuehrerbau, prepared for the conference. Above the mantel is a Lenbach portrait of Bismarck. Apparently seats were provided for nine participants. *Bundesarchiv*.

6. The conference in process. At Hitler's left is the interpreter, Paul Otto Schmidt, and beyond him (half hidden by Hitler's head) Chamberlain. Mussolini and Ciano are seated on the sofa. On the right Weizsaecker (under the lamp), Ribbentrop, and Daladier. Not shown: Wilson and Léger. *Bundesarchiv*.

7. Chamberlain and
Mussolini at Munich.
Bundesarchiv.

8. Daladier signs the
agreement, as Goering and
Hitler watch. *Bundesarchiv.*

9. Chamberlain, Hitler, and Schmidt in Hitler's Munich apartment on the morning of September 30, 1938, shortly before signature of the Anglo-German declaration. *Bundesarchiv.*

10. André Maginot, Minister of War 1922–24 and 1929–32, promoter and planner of the French fortifications which bore his name. *Imperial War Museum.*

11. Sir Winston Churchill in 1937. *National Archives.*

12. André François-Poncet, French Ambassador in Berlin 1931–38 and in Rome 1938–40, with Joseph Goebbels, German Minister of Propaganda. *National Archives*.

13. Léon Blum, French Premier 1936–37 and March–April 1938. *National Archives*.

14. Pierre Laval, French Foreign Minister 1934–36 and Premier 1935–36, with Maxim Litvinov, Soviet Commissar for Foreign Affairs 1930–39. *National Archives*.

large enough and fast enough to catch and cope with the three German pocket battle cruisers—the *Deutschland, Admiral Graf Spee,* and *Admiral Scheer*.

From the air and army chiefs the reports were doleful indeed. Field Marshal Montgomery-Massingberd described the Army's position as "thoroughly unsatisfactory," whether for coastal or antiaircraft defense. As for an expeditionary force, he could put two divisions into France within a few weeks, but they would have no tanks, antitank guns, or other modern field weapons. The RAF, said Air Vice-Marshal Courtney (Deputy Chief of the Air Staff, substituting for Ellington), could spare nothing for the Continent; even a "token force" would leave Britain exposed to enemy air attack.

After this somber interchange, the Joint Planning Subcommittee* was asked for a formal report on "the present position of our Defence Forces at Home," and the betterment which would accrue from mobilization and the withdrawal of forces from the Mediterranean. Two days later the planners reported that Britain's home defenses were denuded "to an extent almost unparalleled in the past." For all three services, the Ethiopian conflict was at least partly responsible. For the Air Force, an additional factor was the dispersal of first-line squadrons to train new units. In consequence, for immediate purposes the RAF "could produce no offensive or defensive effort whatever." Within a short time a few squadrons could be reassembled, but they would be "utterly inadequate for Home Defence in a war against Germany even at the present stage of the latter's armament program." Withdrawal of forces from the Mediterranean would enable the Army in two or three months to equip its field force with tanks, but would not significantly strengthen the home air defenses.

There was nothing objectively inaccurate about the service estimates of their own resources, and painful awareness of inadequacies is generally preferable to blind optimism. But in their over-all assessments, the Chiefs of Staff both overestimated Germany's ability to wage strategic air warfare, and underestimated the pace of German rearmament, thus failing to perceive that, for the next few years, time would be on the side of the Germans. The Air Staff calculated that, with 320 bombers available for attacking England, the Germans would be able to deliver between 100 and 150 tons of bombs per raid. Considering the types of plane then in use, the distance the German bombers would have to cover, and the greater need to use their bombers to support the Army against the French, this was a gross overestimate.†

The British Army was, to be sure, a negligible factor, but the last thing the French at that time needed was more divisions. The Chiefs' description of war

* This subcommittee was composed of the staff officers in charge of plans in each of the services. At the time its members were Colonel R. Forbes Adams, Captain T. S. V. Phillips (drowned when the *Prince of Wales* was sunk by the Japanese early in 1942), and Group Captain Arthur Harris, better known in later years, when he led Bomber Command, as "Bomber Harris."

† During the first seven weeks of the night Blitz attacks on London (September 7 to November 13, 1940). The Germans put an average of 163 bombers per night over the city, which dropped an average of 201 tons of high explosives and 182 incendiary canisters. These aircraft (including many more modern than those available in 1936) took off from bases in France and the Low Countries, which of course were not available in 1936, and were used at a time when there was no ground fighting that required air support.

with Germany as a "disaster" was given against a background of strength comparisons that showed overwhelming naval superiority, and a total of seventy-six French and twenty-one Belgian divisions against thirty-two German divisions, many of which were not battle-worthy because of the dispersal of trained cadres to newly formed units. In the air, it was believed that the Germans outnumbered the combined British and French in bombers but not in fighters, and it was well known to the air staffs that the Luftwaffe was still largely in the training stage. At the end of 1935, following a "war game," the German Air Staff had reported that the Luftwaffe's strength in the spring of 1936 would be insufficient to cope with a war against France and Czechoslovakia "with the slightest chance of success."

But even if the military advice had been much more optimistic, the decision in London would have been the same. Duff Cooper in London, Léger and a few others in Paris perceived that whatever the present risk it was far less than the dangers two or three years hence, but few, whether highly or lowly placed, would listen. And so Baldwin told Flandin that "if there is one chance in a hundred that war will result from your police operation, I have not the right to involve England because Britain is not in a state to go to war." But warfare is not a matter of absolutes but of comparatives, and in 1936 Britain and France were in a far better state to go to war with Germany than they were thereafter.

The conclusion is inescapable that a great deal of the British military pessimism in the spring of 1936 was a product of their distrust of the French. Chatfield and Ellington had not wanted to be embroiled with the Italians, but once committed in the Mediterranean they were bitterly resentful of French failure to co-operate, and the staff talks in the winter of 1935–36 were a dismal failure. Now Flandin came begging for support, and there was at least a measure of *Schadenfreude* in telling him that there was none to be had.

This contemptuous attitude toward the French lasted well past the crisis days of the Rhineland. Once the idea of a military response had faded away, the Locarno deliberations turned into an effort—futile, as it was soon proved—to extract concessions from Germany that would save face and reassure France and Belgium. On March 19, the three aggrieved Locarno powers issued a declaration reaffirming their obligations and instructing their general staffs to hold discussions looking to their fulfillment, coupled with proposals that the German borders with France and Belgium be patrolled by an international force, and that the Germans not increase their troops in the demilitarized zone or build fortifications pending discussion of Hitler's offers.

Ribbentrop's reaction to the declaration was to reject everything and protest violently against the projected Anglo-Franco-Belgian general staff talks. He was not alone in his objections. On April 1, 1936, the British Chiefs of Staff sent a memorandum to the CID opposing the talks because the French might, in consequence, rely on Britain and pull her into continental conflicts. Two days later the CID approved only "limited" staff conversations, and when they took place (in London, from April 15 to 17), they amounted only to a narrow exchange of information. Air Vice-Marshal Courtney announced at the outset that he could make no promises, gave the visitors some sketchy figures on British air strength, and asked what airfields the French and Belgians could make available. Since, however, Courtney would not say whether the RAF would actually use any, the French were obliged to point out the difficulties of planning on so contingent a basis, although they and the Belgians did list fields that could be turned over. The outcome of the talks may most charitably be described as inconclusive.

Hostility to the staff talks had not been confined to the military advisers. Eden had had some difficulty in getting the Cabinet to approve them, Baldwin was worried about opposition from Conservative backbenchers, and the Labour members were vehemently opposed.

If, in retrospect, illusion and myopia appear to have deeply infected the British Government's handling of the Rhineland crisis, it must be borne in mind that the ministers, military leaders, and members were accurately reflecting the prevailing attitudes of the British public. It is ironical that the press and public reacted so positively to collective security measures as applied to Ethiopia, where Britain's interests were only slightly involved, and altogether negatively to the prospect of applying them to Germany, whose move raised grave menace to Britain's very survival. But, though ironic, it is explicable: their leaders had communicated effectively the significance of Italy's aggression, but had never made plain the purposes of the demilitarized zone or the consequences of its abolition, or clothed the Locarno commitments in the shining raiments of the League Covenant.

But the failings of the Baldwin government were not confined to lack of leadership and effective public education. No doubt the ministers would have communicated better had they themselves understood more clearly. It was a strategic blunder of the first magnitude to assume that Britain would be in a better military posture a few years later. Men who could make so timid and blindered a decision in 1936 were unlikely to make a bolder or wiser one in 1938.

11

"I assure the House that it is the appeasement of Europe as a whole that we have constantly before us," said Anthony Eden in the Commons on March 26, 1936, defending his handling of the Rhineland violation. It was not until well after Stanley Baldwin retired from public life that the word became a symbol of weak and myopic yielding when resistance would be both bolder and, in the long run, safer. But the despised word turned on Baldwin as much as on Neville Chamberlain and, in many minds, Baldwin was the greater appeaser of the two —indifferent to the Nazi menace, slow and apathetic in his handling of British rearmament. Baldwin "had the trust of the people as it has been given to few politicians in our history," wrote the author of a book entitled *Appeasement: A Study in Political Decline,* but he "exploited it to the last limit, and in the end betrayed it."*

In retrospect, however, the record of the Baldwin years strongly suggests that, while there is abundant ground for severe criticism, much of what has been written is misdirected. If by "appeasement" is meant a foolish faith in the pacifying effect of concessions to a foe bent on aggression, or a gullible reliance on

---

* The author was A. L. Rowse, an historian and Fellow of All Souls College, Oxford.

promises from a source already established as untrustworthy—the charge to which Neville Chamberlain has been commonly subjected—there is scant basis for convicting Baldwin. It is true that Baldwin was under a constant barrage of reports and counsel from his friend Tom Jones, certifying to Hitler's peaceful intentions and the desirability of taking the Fuehrer at his word. But while he listened, it is not apparent that Baldwin succumbed to these advices. He would have welcomed an understanding with Germany, but made no treaties with her that left Britain in jeopardy of deceit. After the Rhineland he described Hitler and Mussolini to Jones as "lunatics" with whom "you can never be sure of anything," and his support of the Anglo-German Naval Agreement was based in part on his belief that Germany's compliance or noncompliance would offer a better gauge than words of her true intentions.

The other and more frequent criticism of Baldwin is that he did not set a faster pace of rearmament. The late President Kennedy, in his student study of prewar England, wrote that Baldwin "made the mistake of misjudging Germany's potentialities and the Nazi psychology," and that this failure led to a two-year delay (1934 to 1936) in commencing rearmament, and to inadequate effort in 1936.

Undeniably British rearmament was both slow and insufficient, but in assessing Baldwin's responsibility it is necessary to take account of the obstacles he confronted, in both the official and the public domains—obstacles created by his political friends and foes alike and by the electorate. Neville Chamberlain was not speaking just for himself but for the dominant opinion of the Conservative Party when, as Chancellor of the Exchequer, he slashed away at the financial estimates in the DRC's 1935 and 1936 reports. From the opposition benches, Baldwin could count on nothing but bitter hostility to the military budgets. By-elections, the press, and many other indicators of public opinion all showed the enormous distaste for military preparations in every part of the country.

Despite this Baldwin, as Conservative Party leader and, after June of 1935, as Prime Minister, was able to establish the administrative machinery for a systematic survey of his country's military needs, make a good start on bringing the Navy back to strength, and greatly expand the Air Force. If British aircraft production lagged behind the German, aircraft design of fighters (Spitfires and Hurricanes) was at least as good, and of bombers (Lancasters and Halifaxes) much better. In radar and other aspects of the "wizard war" the British were soon far in the lead.

It is all very well to say that these things, substantial as they were, still were not enough, and of course that is true. But in retrospect it is difficult to see who both could and would have done more. Winston Churchill as a Cabinet member would not have made the speeches that he delivered as a backbencher during those years. Churchill himself accused Baldwin of playing politics with the national safety, basing his condemnation on Baldwin's well-known speech in the Commons on November 12, 1936, in which he said:

I put before the house my own views with an appalling frankness. . . . I am speaking of 1933 and 1934. You will remember the election at Fulham in the autumn of 1933, when a seat which the National Government held was lost by about 7000 votes on no issue but the pacifist. . . .

That was the feeling of the country in 1933. My position as the leader of a great party was not altogether a comfortable one. I asked myself what chance was there—when that feeling that was given expression at Fulham was common throughout the country—what chance was there within the next year or two of that feeling being so changed that the country would give a mandate for rearmament? Supposing I had gone to the country and said that Germany was rearming and that we must rearm, does anybody think that this pacific democracy would have rallied to that cry at that moment? I cannot think of anything that would have made the loss of the Election from my point of view more certain. . . .

Churchill interpreted this speech as an avowal by Baldwin "that he had not done his duty in regard to national safety because he was afraid of losing the election," and described it as "an incident without parallel in our parliamentary history."* But it is plain from the context of the speech, and the repeated references to 1933 and 1934, that Baldwin was not speaking of the 1935 election, but rather of an election which he might have precipitated, but did not, by going to the country in 1933 or 1934. Baldwin's point was, of course, that the electorate could not have been persuaded in the earlier years to give the Government a mandate for rearmament, and that an effort to do so would simply have brought in a Labour government openly opposed to rearmament. In 1935, after Hitler's denunciation of the Versailles armament restrictions and Mussolini's assault on Ethiopia, the voters were more receptive and did in fact support Baldwin's program of rearmament "to make the Empire and the country safe and to fulfill our obligations to the League."

But if Baldwin was neither taken in by Hitler's fair words nor remiss in his insistence on rearmament to meet the dangers he clearly perceived, still that does not free him from grave blame for Britain's plight in later years. In the words of A. L. Rowse, ". . . on the fundamental test, the safety of his country and the lives committed to him, he was tried and found wanting." And where he failed was in his handling of the strategic and diplomatic questions and crises that Britain confronted in 1935 and 1936—the Anglo-German Naval Agreement, the Italo-Ethiopian conflict, and the Rhineland. The evil consequences of the first two were chiefly diplomatic, in that they rent the fabric of collective security and plunged London and Paris into a fog of mutual mistrust;† the third undermined the European security system, put Eastern Europe at Germany's mercy, and doomed France to military inferiority.

It is, of course, no answer to this indictment that Baldwin's ministerial col-

---

* In *The Gathering Storm* (1948) at p. 216. He first made the charge in a "fortnightly letter" of December 11, 1936, reprinted in his *Step by Step 1936–1939* (1939) at pp. 68–70.

In distorted form, Baldwin's speech has been received into contemporary fiction. See Agatha Christie, *Passenger to Frankfurt* (1970), p. 56: "It's not really so very long since Mr. Baldwin made his famous remark—'If I had spoken the truth, I should have lost the election.'"

† It should also be remarked that the imposition of oil sanctions against Italy might well have brought down Mussolini, as the Duce himself disclosed to Hitler at the Munich conference in 1938.

leagues and military advisers saw these matters much as he did, for these were
the men with whom he surrounded himself, and for whose continuance in office
he was politically responsible. But it is a sharper question whether he would
have gotten better guidance elsewhere. Certainly not from the political opposition, nor from *The Times* or the press generally.

Nor, on these matters, was Winston Churchill's record much better than Baldwin's, except on the naval agreement with Germany. He sat out the time and aftermath of the Hoare-Laval crisis vacationing in Barcelona and Morocco, on
the advice of friends who "said that I should only do myself harm if I were
mixed up with this violent conflict." He spoke in the Commons on the Defence
White Paper on March 10, three days after the German entry into the
Rhineland, and made only a glancing reference to the matter, perhaps because
he was hoping for appointment as Minister for the Coordination of Defence,
and did not wish to antagonize Baldwin. Not until after Inskip's appointment
did Churchill publicly explore and deplore the significance of what had occurred.

But Churchill was not the responsible First Minister; Baldwin was. Why did
this superbly gifted politician fail? It is enlightening to look at his closest
colleagues and friends. In Cabinet he leaned not on Eden or Duff Cooper, but
on Neville Chamberlain and Halifax; in the Civil Service not on Vansittart but
on Sir Horace Wilson; outside the Government on Tom Jones, and Geoffrey
Dawson of *The Times,* the editorial page of which was heavily colored by lingering Versailles guilt feelings. Despite Hoare's blunders at Geneva and Paris,
he was back in the Cabinet as First Lord of the Admiralty by May 1936.

If these associations reflected Baldwin's personal predilections, his strengths
as a politician and weaknesses as a diplomatist and strategist were in tune with
the times. To use a musical analogy, he was like an Aeolian harp, through
which the breezes of England blew and found resonance. Hear the rhythm of his
speech to the Peace Society in October of 1935, just before the election:

> We live under the shadow of the last War, and its memories still sicken us.
> We remember what modern warfare is, with no glory in it but the heroism of
> man. Have you thought what it has meant to the world to have had that swath
> of death cut through the loveliest and best of our contemporaries, how public
> life has suffered because those who would have been ready to take over from
> our tired and disillusioned generation are not there?
> Perhaps we avert our thoughts from these terrors, and send them roaming
> over this "dear, dear land" of ours. . . . We think, perhaps, of the level eve-
> ning sun over an English meadow, with the rooks tumbling noisily home into
> the elms, of the plowman "with his team on the world's rim, creeping like the
> hands of a clock," one of those garnered memories of the long peace of the
> countryside that a wise man takes about with him as a viaticum. To what
> risks do we expose our treasures—irreplaceable treasures, for you cannot
> build up beauty like that in a few years of mass-production? Make no mis-
> take; every piece of all the life that we and our fathers have made in this land,
> everything that we have and hold and cherish, is in jeopardy of this great
> issue.

Harold Laski, no easy critic, thought this "the greatest speech a Prime Minister has ever made." However that may be, this was an eloquence that sang not of arms and the man, but of the beauty that war would threaten. And it goes far to explain why Baldwin was too easily swayed by the perils of the moment, too little governed by the dangers of the future.

Part III

THE GERMAN SWORD UNSHEATHED
1936-1938

CHAPTER 11

Nazi Respectability and the
Anti-Comintern Pact

1

Whatever the reaction abroad to Hitler's remilitarization of the Rhineland, there was no doubt that the German people heartily approved. Simultaneously with the march-in the Reichstag was dissolved, and three weeks later an election was held to pass judgment on the Fuehrer's policies, by a *"ja"* or *"nein"* vote. Ninety-nine per cent of the qualified electors voted, and of them 98.8 per cent —45 million to 540 thousand—said, *"Ja!"* Of course, it was hardly a free ballot, but contemporary and unfriendly observers such as William L. Shirer found no reason to "doubt that the vote of approval for Hitler's coup was overwhelming."

In the stormy history of the Third Reich, the two years that followed the Rhineland remilitarization appear as a period of comparative calm and stability. The rough compromises worked out among business, military, bureaucratic, and Party interests reached an equilibrium, temporary and precarious as it was. Rearmament and public works had sopped up unemployment, while *Wehrfreiheit* in 1935 and 1936 had restored national pride. Memories of the "Night of the Long Knives" were fading, and new conflicts were buried under a blanket of official silence, unsensed by the uninitiated. An atmosphere of celebration, especially in 1936, isolated the doubters and questioners.

On April 20, 1936, Adolf Hitler's forty-seventh birthday was the occasion for widespread and largely genuine rejoicing among the many, and preferment for a chosen few among the military. As the *Voelkischer Beobachter* put it, the anniversary was a day of "festival for the whole German people . . . and, above all, for the soldiers of the young German *Wehrmacht*." Hitler used the occasion to

announce promotions for Blomberg and the three service chiefs—Blomberg to
the top rank of field marshal (*Generalfeldmarschall*), and Fritsch, Goering, and
Raeder to the next highest grade (*Generaloberst* for the Army and Luftwaffe
and *Generaladmiral* for the Navy). By special decree, the title of "National
Hero" was bestowed on the retired General von Seeckt and the long-dead Prince
Eugene of Savoy.

These honors ushered in the period of most rapid increase in the Wehrmacht's effective strength. In 1935 the military budget accounted for 15.8 per
cent of the Government's total expenditures; in 1937 the percentage was nearly
doubled, and in 1938 it reached 42.7 per cent. Teething troubles eased greatly
in 1936, and by 1937 new operational units, sufficiently trained to be considered battle-worthy, were being formed with great rapidity. In August 1936,
Hitler laid the basis for a great rise in the Wehrmacht's peacetime size and level
of training by ordering extension of the term of compulsory military service
from one to two years.

When he denounced the Versailles arms restrictions in May 1935, Hitler had
fixed the future size of the peacetime Army at thirty-six divisions under twelve
corps headquarters. By the end of 1936 this order of battle had already been attained, though of course the equipment and training of the newer units still left
much to be desired. Early in 1937, however, it became apparent that the thirty-
six-division dimension had been an immediate but not an ultimate objective, as
a thirteenth corps headquarters was added to the establishment. More importantly, new formations of motorized and armored troops were making their appearance, and by the winter of 1937–38 the Army order of battle included three
panzer, four motorized infantry, and three "light" (motorized infantry with a
battalion of tanks) divisions under three additional corps headquarters.

Under General von Fritsch, the leadership elements of the Army functioned
efficiently and, on the whole, harmoniously. Hitler did not interfere in operational matters, and there was little cause for internal political dissension. Professional disagreements there were; as Chief of Staff, General Beck was cautious
and conservative—far too much so for the proponents of new and revolutionary
panzer tactics, envisaging the use of tanks in large, independent formations
rather than as infantry support weapons. In the end the "tank men"—General
Oswald Lutz and his famous subordinate and successor, General Heinz Guderian—carried the day, and shaped the panzer *Blitzkrieg* tactics on which the
Wehrmacht's future victories were chiefly based. In the fall of 1937 there were
large army training maneuvers in which, for the first time, tanks were employed
in divisional units.

The Navy was the Wehrmacht's Cinderella, but on so small a base even a few
big ships made a substantial accretion in percentage terms. The future battleships *Bismarck* and *Tirpitz* were laid down in 1936; the large battle cruisers
Scharnhorst and *Gneisenau* were launched later that year, and the heavy
cruisers *Admiral Hipper* and *Blücher* in 1937.

Except on a long-term basis, however, Germany could not hope to approach
the British in surface strength, and for immediate purposes it was the submarine
program that was most significant. In 1935 and 1936 the shipyards delivered

thirty-five U-boats to the German Navy. Captain Karl Doenitz, the Commander of Submarines, was developing new tactics involving operations in groups or "wolf packs," for which medium-sized, maneuverable craft were most suitable. But a number of senior staff officers opposed these novel ideas and forecast a repetition of First World War tactics, with large submarines operating alone and at great distances from their bases. Because he felt that the issue had not been satisfactorily resolved, and relying on Hitler's personal assurance that there would be no war before 1944, Raeder in 1936 put a virtual stop to new construction, with the result that only one U-boat was delivered in 1937 and nine in 1938.*

Of the three services it was the Luftwaffe which chiefly caused the fear of Germany which spread and deepened over Europe from 1935 on, and is most important in the story of Munich. From its birth, the Luftwaffe led a stormy life, for both political and professional reasons. Its Commander-in-Chief, Hermann Goering, was second only to Hitler in the hierarchy of the Third Reich, and he constantly threw his weight around in a way that aroused much jealousy and resentment in the Army and Navy. There was considerable opinion in German military circles that there was no reason for an independent air force, and that rather—as was then the case in the United States—the Army and Navy should each have an air component.

Thus the partnership of Goering with the professional soldiers was at best an uneasy one. Nevertheless, there was mutual interdependence. Little as they liked him, the generals and admirals were bound to support Goering's developmental task, for it was too plain for argument that, in any future war, effective air power over Europe and its adjacent waters would be vital to Germany's military success. Goering, for his part, was largely dependent upon the Army and, to a lesser extent, the Navy to staff and officer his new service. To be sure, Goering was able to recruit some of his associates from the German civil air line, the Deutsche Lufthansa, and from old comrades of his First World War days, some of whom had made careers as test pilots or flying instructors. His deputy, Erhard Milch, came from the Lufthansa; his technical director was the famous racing pilot Ernst Udet, and there were many other "Old Eagles," as they were called, who were glad to get back into uniform. But upwards of three quarters of the top-ranking leaders of the Luftwaffe were transferred from the officer corps of the Army and Navy, of whom some had flying experience, but more did not.

What was to be the Luftwaffe's principal mission in time of war? For England, vulnerable to air attack and with a comparatively small army, the answer had seemed clear: the RAF would defend its own homeland and bomb the enemy's—strategic defense and strategic attack. For Germany, a continental power relying primarily on a large army, it was plain that tactical support of the ground forces must be a basic and probably the major mission of the Luftwaffe,

---

* At the time of Munich, accordingly, forty-odd submarines were in commission, but some of the crews were still in the early training stage. Only eighteen more were delivered in 1939, and the lag in construction thus proved very costly to the Germans when the war came.

and the remaining question was whether or not it should also be equipped for long-range strategic employment.

Largely staffed as the Luftwaffe was with former Army officers who naturally tended to think of aircraft as aerial field artillery and overlook their strategic potential, it is not surprising that the Army viewpoint prevailed. The leading advocate of strategic capability was the first Luftwaffe Chief of Staff, General Walther Wever, and under his aegis the Junkers and Dornier aircraft companies started developmental work on a long-range heavy bomber. But Wever was killed in an airplane crash in June 1936, and in April 1937 his successor, General Albert Kesselring, ordered the work stopped.*

In the tactical field, however, the Germans made rapid advance in the techniques of air support. In contrast to the French, who scattered tanks and planes among the ground troops in comparatively small units, the Germans concentrated both for use en masse. The young French assistant air attaché, Captain Paul Stehlin, was allowed to view maneuvers in which the excellent results of the new air tactics made a deep impression, but Stehlin's voluminous and precise reports had no visible results in France.

Meanwhile, the Luftwaffe was both growing physically and maturing organizationally. Aircraft alone do not an air force make, and the Luftwaffe was useless for combat purposes until airfields and communications were built and developed, schools and headquarters established, and trainees graduated and assembled in operational units. With the benefit of clandestine training in Russia until 1933, and in Italy from 1933 to 1935, the first combat-ready formations were established in 1936. By the end of the year there were over a hundred operational squadrons of about ten aircraft each, and by the end of 1937 these numbers had more than doubled. During these same two years, the German aircraft manufacturers developed the basic types which were to constitute the Luftwaffe's backbone throughout the war—the Heinkel 111 and Dornier 17 level bombers, the Junkers 87 dive bomber (Stuka), and the Messerschmitt 109 fighter.

And so from the mines and mills and industrial laboratories of the Ruhr and the Rhine, from the Fatherland's farmlands and teeming cities, and from the martial skills and traditions of two centuries, the Wehrmacht of the Third Reich drew the breath of life and gathered strength. For the professional soldier, these were halcyon days, as recruits, weapons, new and interesting tactical problems, and promotions all came ever faster. Testifying at the Nuremberg trials, senior generals such as Johannes Blaskowitz and Hans Reinhardt agreed that during these years before 1938 there was hardly "a single officer who did not back up Hitler in his extraordinary success," and that "there was no reason to oppose Hitler, since he produced the results which they desired." Perhaps the most comprehensive and articulate summary of the military attitude toward Hitler

---

* The decision reflected more than narrow tactical thinking. Germany's resources were large but not unlimited, and construction of an air force sufficiently equipped for both tactical and strategic use would have taxed the available supplies of rubber, oil, and other crucial materials to a point that would have seriously cut down on Army armament requirements.

was written a decade later at Nuremberg by the man who commanded the Wehrmacht during those years, Werner von Blomberg:

In the early years of his regime, Hitler stressed his adherence to the historical tradition. . . . During these years we soldiers had no cause to complain of Hitler. He fulfilled hopes which were dear to all of us. If the generals no longer choose to remember this, it is obviously a case of deliberate forgetfulness. No thinking soldier could shut his eyes to the fact that after 1933 rearmament commensurate with the greatness of Germany could only be carried out with Hitler's help. . . . The German people agreed with the Hitler of those days. The masses obtained tangible advantages in the matter of social justice, the labour market, and above all an increasing importance of Germany as a political body. How could we soldiers, who had continually to deal with the masses, think otherwise! Whoever asserts the contrary now is betrayed by his memory. . . . Until Hitler entered upon the period of aggressive politics, whether one dates it from 1938 or 1939, the German people had no decisive reason for hostility to Hitler, we soldiers least of all. He had not only given us back a position of respect in the life of the German people, and had freed all Germans from what we considered to be the shame of the Treaty of Versailles, but by the rearmament of Germany, which only Hitler could achieve, he had given the soldiers a larger sphere of influence, promotion and increased respect.

No general raised any objection then, or offered any resistance. That would have appeared absurd to us all then, even to those who now think otherwise. The approval of the younger officers may well have been more lively and more convincing than that of the older ones, but what now appears in retrospect, to some generals, as a refusal to accept Hitler was, I am convinced, merely the traditional resistance to anything new.

. . . To sum up I would say that Hitler in the first period which lasted at least up to 1938 strove to obtain the trust of us soldiers, with complete success. . . .

. . . One should not repudiate that to which one formerly gave approval in the main. Hitler proved fatal for the German people, but there were years, at first, when we believed that in a positive sense he was Germany's man of destiny.

2

A "man of destiny" Hitler truly was, and though the generals failed to discern the shape that destiny would take, they were not much more shortsighted than many who were looking in upon Nazi Germany from the seats of power in other countries. If Hitler the Fuehrer was not idolized outside the German borders, Hitler the Chancellor was increasingly feared and, in many quarters, admired.

This growing respect for the Third Reich was strikingly demonstrated when the Olympic Games were held in Berlin during the first two weeks of August 1936. Thousands of foreign visitors crowded the capital, and the opportunity was used with great skill to show the Nazi regime to best advantage. The Fuehrer himself was frequently present,* and he and his entourage and guests—

* Hitler's manifest glee at German victories and gloom at defeats, and his ill-concealed aversion for America's black athletes such as Jesse Owens and Ralph Metcalfe, were highlighted in Westbrook Pegler's memorable press coverage of the Games.

Goering, Goebbels, Hess, Himmler, the King of Bulgaria, Italian, Greek, and Swedish princes—were the cynosure of all eyes. Almost every evening there were gala receptions and concerts for the select few, and bands and fireworks for the many. Captain Stehlin was mightily impressed, and William L. Shirer sadly confessed to his diary that "the Nazis have succeeded with their propaganda." Visiting Americans, Shirer noted, were "favorably impressed with the Nazi set-up," and inclined to believe Goering's complaints that the American newspaper correspondents were "unfair."

In foreign relations, too, Hitler appeared to be achieving his chosen ends. These were not the ends of Weimar days, for the ties with Soviet Russia, born of Rapallo and the Reichswehr-Red Army collaboration, had been broken in 1933, and now the link with Chiang Kai-shek—so carefully forged by Seeckt, Falkenhausen, and others in the long line of German military consultants in China—was weakening, as Nazi Germany and imperial Japan found themselves in parallel course.

This new affinity was first openly manifested in June of 1936, when Hitler received the Japanese Ambassador, Count Kintomo Mushakoji. Japan had "changed inwardly" and "become authoritarian," the ambassador avowed, and now "regarded Bolshevism and the Communist idea as her great enemies." Accordingly, Japan "was in the fullest sympathy with Germany and her Fuehrer, and desired the closest collaboration with Germany." Hitler expressed hearty approval of these sentiments, and declared himself "prepared for this cooperation."

Instead of conducting the ensuing negotiations through normal Foreign Ministry channels, Hitler entrusted them to Ribbentrop, who had handled the Anglo-German Naval Agreement and the Rhineland-Locarno crisis effectively and was about to be appointed Ambassador in London.* On August 16, Ribbentrop informed Hitler that the Japanese had approved "in principle" the conclusion of an "anti-Comintern" agreement between the two countries, and on October 23 the "German-Japanese Agreement against the Communist International" and various secret supplementary agreements, annexes, and notes were initialed by Ribbentrop and Mushakoji.

The published provisions of the agreement were largely hortatory, calling for nothing more than exchange of information on Comintern activities and cooperation in preventive and deterrent measures against Communist agents. But there was also a "Secret Additional Agreement" pursuant to which each signatory agreed that neither would conclude any "political" treaty† with the Soviet Union "contrary to the spirit of" the Anti-Comintern Pact and that, in the event of "an unprovoked attack or threat of attack" by Russia against either signatory, the

* His predecessor, Hoesch, had died of a heart attack in the spring of 1936. Ribbentrop was appointed on August 11, and arrived in London late in October 1936, after the initialing of the Anti-Comintern Pact.

† The word "political" was intended, as evidenced by notes simultaneously exchanged between the two countries and annexed to the secret agreement, to exclude fishery, commercial, and boundary treaties between Japan or Manchukuo and the Soviet Union. In another note, it was declared that the Treaty of Rapallo of 1922 and the Neutrality Treaty of 1926 between Germany and Russia, "insofar as they have not become null and void under the conditions" now existing, were not regarded as contrary to the spirit of the pact.

other would "take no measures which would tend to ease the situation" of the Soviets, and would immediately consult on what measures to take "to safeguard their
common interests."

The various documents comprising the pact were formally signed on November 25, 1936. Ribbentrop returned from London, and he and Mushakoji signed
as "Extraordinary and Plenipotentiary Ambassadors." There was a press conference, at which William L. Shirer's risibilities were tickled by Ribbentrop's announcement that Germany and Japan had joined together to defend "Western
civilization." The secrecy of the "Secret Additional Agreement" could not have
been very closely held, for Shirer recorded the same day that "it seems obvious
that Japan and Germany have drawn up at the same time a secret military treaty
calling for joint action against Russia should one of them get involved in war
with the Soviets."

If the notion of Japan as a defender of Western civilization was bemusing,
there was no lack of serious purpose in the pact, vague as its language was.
Hitler himself did not attend the signing, but he had struck the same note in a
speech at Munich a few weeks earlier, predicting that the time would soon come
when "Europe will no longer regard with resentment the founding of a National
Socialist German Reich, but will rejoice that this dam was raised against the
Bolshevik flood." And Ribbentrop, in his statement at the signing, pointed the
direction that German diplomacy was taking:

> Japan will never permit any dissemination of Bolshevism in the Far East.
> Germany is creating a bulwark against this pestilence in Central Europe. Fi-
> nally, Italy, as the Duce informs the world, will hoist the anti-Bolshevist ban-
> ner in the south.

There, for propaganda purposes tricked out in anti-Communist garb, was the
triple relationship which, four years later, took final form as the Tripartite Pact.
Actually, Italy did not formally adhere to the Anti-Comintern Pact until a year
later. October 23, 1936, however, had witnessed not only the initialing of that
document, but also signature of the Neurath-Ciano Protocol, clause 3 of which
recorded their two governments' recognition "that Communism is the greatest
danger threatening the peace and security of Europe," and intention "to combat
Communist propaganda with all their strength and to direct their own actions in
this sense."

There were many other evidences of the growing Italo-German affinity which
had been touched off by mutual forbearance during the Ethiopian and Rhineland crises. In April 1936, Captain Stehlin was surprised and chagrined to encounter in Berlin, in the bar of the Eden Hotel, the same Italian delegation that
he had helped to entertain in Paris the previous year. A few weeks later,
Mussolini's daughter Edda, married to Ciano, was received in Germany with
great éclat, and in June the chief of the Italian Air Staff, General Valle, appeared on the Berlin scene. Two months later, a German Army delegation,
headed by General Wilhelm Adam and including such famous-to-be officers as
Manstein and Paulus, attended Italian maneuvers at Avellino. The Germans
were not much impressed by the military demonstration, but greatly enjoyed

hobnobbing with the Duce and meeting King Victor Emmanuel and the Crown Prince.

3

Italians were by no means the only VIP visitors during these piping times. Charles Lindbergh, hero of the first nonstop transatlantic flight, came to Berlin late in July, to be feted by Goering and the Luftwaffe. Shortly after the Olympics ended, the Regent of Hungary, Admiral Nicholas Horthy, came to Munich for a meeting with the Fuehrer, from which Horthy came away with the impression that, as soon as Germany had rearmed, Hitler proposed to "show his enmity to Czechoslovakia by some concrete action." Six weeks later another regent—Paul of Yugoslavia—was the first chief of state to be received at the Berghof, Hitler's recently completed retreat on the Obersalzberg, overlooking Berchtesgaden in Germany and Salzburg in his native Austria.

The Fuehrer's most numerous and most-sought-after guests, however, were British. During the spring of 1936, Ribbentrop angled desperately for a visit by Baldwin himself, using the Prime Minister's confidant, Tom Jones, as an intermediary. In mid-May, Jones went to Berlin to confer with Ribbentrop, and the next day, May 17, the two flew to Munich for a meeting in Hitler's private apartment on the Prinzregentenstrasse. The Fuehrer was agreeable and conciliatory, and expressed a "great desire" to meet Baldwin, whom Jones described as "a shy and modest statesman who had never gotten over his astonishment at finding himself Prime Minister." This was at least a more truthful ploy than Hitler's unctuously smiling response: "And I too."

Jones reported back to Baldwin three days later. The Prime Minister was gripped by his account; it was "like an Oppenheimer story." For several weeks he toyed with the idea of meeting Hitler at a "mountain rendezvous" in August, but in mid-June, Eden and Vansittart persuaded him to drop the project. Apparently it stayed in his mind, for in November he told Jones that a visit to Hitler was "not outside the bounds of possibility." But by this time he was absorbed in the royal crisis that culminated in Edward VIII's abdication, and the plan was not revived thereafter.

With other great or noble names Hitler had better luck, partly through the good offices of T. P. Conwell-Evans, a Welshman who had lectured at Königsberg and was Honorary Secretary of the Anglo-German Fellowship. Early in September 1936, he escorted to the Berghof the greatest living Welshman, David Lloyd George. By way of making it an all-Welsh occasion, and probably to ensure that the meeting would be reported to Baldwin, Conwell-Evans summoned Jones,* who was on vacation in nearby Switzerland.

The victorious Prime Minister and the defeated corporal of the First World War hit it off famously. Hitler greeted his white-maned guest as "the man whom we in Germany have always regarded as the actual victor of the World War," and in reply the old "Welsh Wizard" saluted his host as "the man who, after defeat, has united the whole German people behind him and led them to re-

---

* Jones had been Secretary to the Cabinet during and after the First World War, and was as close to Lloyd George as he became to Baldwin.

covery" and, marching over to the enormous picture window, congratulated Hitler on the "splendid place you have found up here."*

In close harmony, they reminisced about the war, discussed international politics, and then turned to domestic social problems. Lloyd George was surprisingly well informed on German health insurance and social welfare, and Hitler gave what his visitor described as a "brilliant exposition" of Nazi public works, such as the famous *Autobahnen*. They talked for three hours, and Lloyd George was invited back the next day for tea, with his children Megan and Gwilym.

On returning to Britain, Lloyd George spread far and wide his views that Hitler was "a man of supreme quality" with no warlike plans. Hitler, too, was well pleased, and in later years spoke of Lloyd George as "the Briton who made the deepest impression on me" and who, had he had the "necessary power," would "certainly have been the architect of a German-English understanding."

Joining Lloyd George in praise of Hitler's ability and pacific intentions† were two noble lords, one Irish and the other a Scot. The Irishman was Lord Londonderry, whom Baldwin had dropped from the Cabinet after the November 1935 elections. He saw Hitler three times in 1936 and used the interviews as the focus of his pro-German book *Ourselves and Germany,* published in 1938. The Scot was the rich and influential‡ Philip Kerr, since 1930 the Marquess of Lothian, who first met Hitler in 1935 through Conwell-Evans, and came again to Berlin in May 1937. On this second occasion, Lord Lothian saw Goering and Schacht as well as Hitler, and at these meetings the issues which were to lead to Munich and the Second World War were articulated more sharply than theretofore.

Lothian met first with Goering on the morning of May 4 and at once opened up the question of colonies. Adjustments were possible, but not any great territorial changes, and he counseled Goering that Germany should follow the policies of Bismarck rather than Wilhelm II. Goering immediately dismissed the notion that small colonial adjustments would meet the needs of the times; Europe, he said, was far more important, and German aims embraced Austria, Danzig,

---

* Hitler had moved in only a few weeks earlier; the Berghof was "dedicated" on July 8, 1936.

† One visitor whose distrust of Hitler was not set at rest by a personal interview was Sir Robert Vansittart, who came to the Olympic Games at Ribbentrop's invitation. Vansittart and the British Ambassador in Berlin, Sir Eric Phipps, had married sisters and, as Lady Phipps was not well, Lady Vansittart took over as hostess at the embassy functions that accompanied the Games. It was Lady Vansittart who introduced the Marquess of Clydesdale (captain of the British Olympic boxing team and later the Duke of Hamilton) to Rudolf Hess, and it was the Duke of Hamilton whom Hess sought to contact when he parachuted into Scotland in 1941.

In retrospect, Ribbentrop described his impression of his Berlin luncheon with Vansittart as "addressing a wall." At the meeting with Hitler, Vansittart, who was fluent in German, advised the Fuehrer not to pay much attention to "visiting lightweights and busybodies"— no doubt having Londonderry, Lothian, and Jones in mind.

‡ His country estate, Blickling Hall, was almost as frequent a weekend rendezvous for the "establishment" set as the better-known Astor estate, Cliveden. In the late summer of 1936, Lothian made Blickling available to Baldwin, who was suffering from nervous fatigue, as a quiet haven for rest and recuperation. In 1939, Lothian was appointed Ambassador to the United States, where he died the following year.

autonomy for the Sudeten Germans in Czechoslovakia, and the end of Russian influence in that country. Lothian did not challenge any item on this list; England he declared, recognized that Eastern Europe was a German "sphere," as long as the "political independence" of the small countries was respected, and Germany's dominance was established by detaching them from dependence on France and Russia.

That afternoon, at the Chancellory, Lothian found the Fuehrer "grave," at times "bitter," and highly critical of British policy as insufficiently anti-Communist, especially with regard to the Italo-Ethiopian conflict and the Spanish Civil War.* Furthermore, when Britain, the United States, France, Belgium, Holland, and Portugal had colonies, it was "intolerable" (*unerträglich*) that Germany should have none. But the colonial theme was not pursued, and Hitler passed rapidly to the same items that Goering had put on the counter: Czechoslovakia (a "sector" of Russia, and an oppressor of German minorities) and Austria. Lothian observed that it was not England, but "Mussolini and the Pope" who were the obstacles to German policies vis-à-vis Austria. When Hitler replied, "The Pope, certainly," Lothian was sharp enough to point out that, since the Pope was supporting Franco, as was Germany, Hitler ought not to be too critical of him, and this led to "smiles all around" and general relaxation. The next day, at the Reichsbank, Schacht echoed the Fuehrer's views, adding that, if sores like Austria and Czechoslovakia were salved, abnormalities like anti-Semitism might disappear.

To Hitler, as to Goering, Lothian disclaimed for Britain any "primary interests in Eastern Europe." Indeed, his expressions throughout his visit to Berlin could hardly fail to convey a view that French influence in that area was an obstacle to peaceful readjustment, and that Germany could rightfully take charge, as long as the "independence" of the existing governments was respected. The American Ambassador, William E. Dodd, who had known Lothian for some years, on this occasion found him open in his "hatred" of France, annoyed by criticism of German bombings in Spain, and "more Fascist than any other Englishman I have met."† Dodd was a choleric anti-Nazi and given to overstatement, but it is true that Lothian held France largely responsible for the failure to do "justice" to Germany at and after Versailles, and attributed the Nazi brutalities, of which he was well aware, to "the reflex of the external persecution to which Germans have been subjected since the war."

Thus were Hitler's next targets—Austria and Czechoslovakia—disclosed to a man whose report would be heard and weighed in the highest British circles, and whose own reaction, unofficial as it was, would not pass unnoticed in Berlin. There were other highly placed British visitors in these months who likewise spoke fair words to the Fuehrer. The pacifist Labour leader George Lansbury came in April and exhorted Hitler to propose an international peace con-

---

* To Lord Lothian's inquiry about the relation between Ethiopia and communism, Hitler replied that, if Mussolini had been defeated there, Italy would have succumbed to communism, and Europe would have thus lost a leading protector against that political disease.

† In 1935, Lothian had written Dodd a letter suggesting that the Western democracies should unite to block any German move westward and deflect Hitler to the east. A Russo-German war was not undesirable, and it was essential that Germany and Japan attain a stronger place in world affairs.

ference under President Roosevelt's aegis. Mistaking the Fuehrer's non-committal boredom for agreement, Lansbury jubilantly proclaimd, via the BBC, that a peaceful solution would be found and "the catastrophe of war will be avoided." In October came to the Berghof a particularly ardent Hitler admirer, the fabulously rich Aga Khan, and, a few days later, no less a person than ex-king Edward VIII, now the Duke of Windsor, with his American-born duchess. The Duke praised German social welfare, while Hitler played up to his noble guests, and after the parting remarked that Mrs. Simpson "would have made a good Queen."

All of these visits, to be sure, were private and unofficial. But at the end of April 1937 a new British face appeared on the diplomatic scene in Berlin. Sir Eric Phipps, ambassador since 1933, wanted to be transferred to Paris, and the time to grant his wish was ripe. He had no rapport with the Nazi leaders, and his dispatches to London had long been full of caustic comment and ominous predictions. Tom Jones, after his visit to Hitler in 1936, had urged Baldwin to replace Phipps with someone "unhampered by diplomatic tradition, able to enter with sympathetic interest into Hitler's aspirations."

By a strange irony it was Sir Robert Vansittart, no friend of German appeasement, who appointed just such a man as Jones had in mind.* In January 1937, Sir Nevile Henderson, then serving in Buenos Aires, received a telegram from Eden offering him the Berlin appointment. Henderson accepted, by his own account, convinced that he "had been specially selected by Providence . . . to preserve the peace of the world," and in April he set out to Berlin under instructions from Baldwin and Chamberlain to "do my utmost to work with Hitler and the Nazi Party as the existing government in Germany." On his arrival in the German capital, Henderson publicly deprecated the emphasis on "Nazi dictatorship" and recommended a focus on "the great social experiment which is being tried out in this country." He told Ambassador Dodd that France was "a back number and unworthy of support," that Germany "must dominate the Danube-Balkan zone," and that "England and Germany must come into close relations, economic and political, and control the world." Dodd's daughter Martha sized up Henderson as the "parody of the facetious and suave diplomat," intent on ingratiating himself with the Nazis.

Such were the British who were personally exposed to Hitler's observation during those times, and such was the temper of His Majesty's diplomatic representative in Berlin as the Fuehrer laid his plans and dreamed his dreams.

4

While the British visitors were coming wide-eyed to Berlin and the Berghof, events were steadily strengthening Germany's ties with Italy. Common policy in Spain, and Ciano's visit on October 1936, led to Mussolini's announcement of the "Axis" in November. In January 1937, Hermann Goering came to Italy for

---

* Vansittart and Eden appear to have had no idea of the tack Henderson would take. Henderson was not personally known to Eden, and Vansittart, on whose recommendation Eden acted, appears to have made his choice incredibly casually, on the basis that Henderson was "a good shot" and should "have his reward" for doing his "stint in South America."

a ten-day visit which took him to Naples and Capri as well as Rome, and brought him into contact with the Italian royal family and military leaders as well as the Duce and his entourage.

Goering met with Mussolini on his arrival and again on January 23, at the end of his stay. At the first meeting, the ebullient Goering's patent assumption that Austria must inevitably become part of Germany sat very poorly with Mussolini. Perhaps advised of his host's displeasure, Goering was at pains, during the second talk, to assure Mussolini "that there will be no surprises so far as Austria is concerned." Mussolini, for his part, declared that he believed in "evolution in political forces" and that Italy would no longer maintain a "watch on the Brenner" in behalf of the Versailles powers—thus indicating that Italy's Austrian politics would not be shaped in concert with England and France, and that some, though unspecified, changes in Austria's status would be permissible.

Apart from Austria, the conversation touched on the Spanish Civil War, formulation of parallel attitudes toward Britain and France, and general military matters. Goering also asked "why Italy had not left the League of Nations," to which Mussolini replied that *"de facto* Italy has left the League," but that he wished to continue formal membership until the League had recognized his Ethiopian conquest—"a dose of castor oil which the League will have to swallow sooner or later." Toward the end of the talk, Goering declared that "the Fuehrer would be extraordinarily happy if the Duce would care to pay a visit to Germany" so as to "underline the common policy of the two countries." Mussolini neither accepted nor rejected the invitation, but replied, rather circumspectly, that such a visit "is within the bounds of possibility."

Alarmed by the Goering visit and various manifestations of German hostility, the Austrian Chancellor, Kurt von Schuschnigg, came to Venice on April 22 to cement his support from Mussolini. The Duce was equivocal; Italy would hope to maintain Austrian independence by "bringing it into harmony with the Rome-Berlin Axis." Three days later Goering was again in Rome, immensely curious about the Schuschnigg meeting, and renewing the invitation to Mussolini for a visit to Germany. On May 3, Neurath appeared in Rome for general policy consultations and found Mussolini still concerned for Austria's nominal independence. The Duce told the German Foreign Minister that "at bottom the Austrians have no other wish than to live in the shadow of mighty Germany while maintaining their independence" and counseled against trying to impose an anti-Catholic or anti-Semitic regime on Austria.

Meanwhile the invitation to Germany went unanswered. It was not a good time for Mussolini to parade himself; in March the Italian divisions supporting Franco in Spain had suffered a humiliating reverse at Guadalajara. Toward the end of August, however, Italian forces participated in overrunning the loyalist stronghold at Santander. On August 27, Ciano ordered the Italian commander in Spain, General Ettore Bastico, to send home "flags and guns captured from the Basques" (to allay his envy of the French for the Invalides and the Germans for their Military Museum—"A flag taken from the enemy is worth more than any picture," he wrote), and on the same day the Count noted in his diary that he was "personally making arrangements for the Duce's visit to Germany" and had that day "approved the first draft of the program" and admonished his assistants* to: "Pay attention to the uniforms. We must look more Prussian than the Prussians." Within a few days, Mussolini had personally approved the schedule and completed the speech which he planned to deliver in Berlin.

The Third Reich meanwhile was climbing to new heights of international respectability, manifested at the annual Nazi Party anniversary—the Nuremberg *Reichsparteitag*—which was held during the second week of September. Theretofore the representatives of the great powers had stayed away from Nuremberg on the basis that it was a Party rather than an official celebration. In 1937, however, Nevile Henderson decided to go and drew with him in his wake François-Poncet and the American chargé, Prentiss Gilbert, who went despite the strong remonstrance of Ambassador Dodd, who was at home on leave. Three special trains brought the diplomatic representatives of many other countries from Berlin to Nuremberg for the great occasion.

Accordingly, when Benito Mussolini, on September 25, arrived at Munich, he found his host approaching a peak of international acceptance, not unmixed with admiration. On the German side, the principal purposes of the visit were to impress upon Mussolini the Reich's growing strength, and upon the other powers the two dictators' closeness. But the Austrian question brooded over the occasion. A few days before the Duce's arrival, Neurath and Papen agreed that, in view of Mussolini's repeated admonitions, "The façade of Austrian independence is to be maintained," but that his visit should be exploited so as to ensure "Italian noninterference in plans for gradual economic and military *rapprochement* with Austria," and that this process might include the removal of Schuschnigg as an obstacle to German plans.

In the end, however, politics was subordinated to display. Upon his arrival in Munich, Mussolini was driven to Hitler's private flat, and an hour of private talk—their first since the uncomfortable confrontation at Venice in 1934. They spoke of friendship with Japan, support for Franco, and the decline of the western democracies; nothing decisive was said about Austria.

After that the stage managers took over and, as Anfuso put it, the two dictators were like an engaged Spanish couple, forever chaperoned. Each traveled in his own special train, and that evening they departed Munich for Mecklenburg, and a day of military maneuvers. The Luftwaffe's new Messerchmitt fighters were displayed, and Ernst Udet landed a few yards from Mussolini in a Storch—the courier plane that did yeoman service during the war and in which Mussolini himself was rescued from imprisonment on the Gran Sasso, after his deposition and the Italian surrender in 1943.

On September 27, the Reich's industrial potential was on show, with a trip through the Ruhr and a visit to the Krupp works in Essen. At the end of the day, the two trains drove side by side on parallel tracks into the Berlin Heerstrasse station, and the great men and their retinues were driven in open cars— to the great discomfort of the warm-blooded Italians—through the Tiergarten

---

* These included Achille Starace, Secretary-General of the Fascist Party; Dino Alfieri, Minister of Propaganda; Mussolini's private secretary, Osvaldo Sebastiani; and Ciano's brother-in-law, Count Massimo Magistrati, counsellor at the Italian Embassy in Berlin.

and to the eighteenth-century palace on the Wilhelmstrasse, formerly occupied by Hindenburg, where Mussolini was lodged. The agenda for the next two days included Frederick the Great's tomb and the Sans Souci palace in Potdsam, and a visit to Goering's Karinhall, where Anfuso was nipped by one of the host's lion cubs. Staggered by the luxury of the surroundings, Mussolini asked whether Goering "governed" some province or other area, and, on being answered in the negative, frowned disapprovingly and opined that such extravagant living would give his own subordinates dangerous dreams.

In the evening of September 28, there was an immense public gathering at the Olympic Stadium, the Maifeld. After military exhibitions, Hitler acclaimed his guest as "one of those lonely men of the ages on whom history is not tested, but who themselves are the makers of history." Mussolini responded in German, which he spoke fluently, but with a south German accent which the Berlin audience found a bit quaint. In the midst of his speech a terrific thunderstorm broke, with no respect for dignitaries. Shielding his manuscript against wind and rain, Mussolini bravely finished, but German efficiency for once was lacking, and, in the ensuing pandemonium, the Duce was jostled and separated from his bodyguard and drenched to the skin before he reached the haven of the Wilhelmstrasse Palast. Hitler advised him to have a hot bath and some camomile tea, but the ancient palace plumbing was slow in yielding hot water, and the Duce had to go to the nearby Adlon Hotel for his bath, to Hitler's deep chagrin.

Despite this discomfiture, Mussolini was in good spirits the next day upon his departure. From the German standpoint, the visit had been a huge success. At times Mussolini had found Hitler puzzling,* but on the whole, the bad taste of the Venice visit had been washed away, and the impression of German strength firmly implanted. Ciano noted in his diary that "the Rome-Berlin Axis is today a formidable and extremely useful reality," and, upon his return to Rome, assured the German Ambassador, Hassell, that Mussolini had "the firm intention to continue German-Italian cooperation." The Germans sensed the receptive attitude in Rome, and soon took steps to turn it to account in practical and formal fashion.

5

Quitting Germany well content with the Axis, Ciano recorded that he would now "try to draw a line from Rome to Tokyo, and the system will be complete." Negotiations for an Italo-Japanese anti-Comintern pact, to complement the existing German-Japanese agreement, had in fact been under way for some time, but had stalled early in September of 1937 because Mussolini wished also to conclude a general political agreement providing for mutual "benevolent neutrality" in the event not only of war with Russia but also with any other power. In view of Anglo-Italian tensions, the Japanese, not unnaturally, feared that Mussolini was seeking "to commit Japan against England"—an obligation which, given their deep involvement with China,† the Japanese were loath to as-

---

* The Duce found the Fuehrer's long and ogling handshakes embarrassing, and was jarred when Hitler described himself as a "pagan." Mussolini subsequently commented to Anfuso that, in modern times, one could be *like* a pagan, but could not *be* one.

† The famous incident at the Marco Polo Bridge outside Peking had occurred on July 7, 1937, and by the end of the month the Japanese had occupied Peking and Tientsin, and the Sino-Japanese War was under way.

sume. Furthermore, Mussolini wished to secure Japanese recognition of Italy's Ethiopian "empire" as part of the package.

On September 22, in reply to Neurath's inquiry about the progress of the negotiations with Italy, the Japanese Ambassador in Berlin, Count Kintomo Mushakoji, was evasive, and then "began to speak about a joint German-Italian-Japanese agreement." Perhaps the Japanese hoped that, by substituting a procedure for Italian adherence to the existing German-Japanese treaty, it would be easier to move to one side the additional matters that Mussolini was seeking to inject, or perhaps they wished to push Germany and Italy closer together. However that may be, Neurath's reaction was prompt and negative: "I told him that we did not desire such an agreement. We already had the Anti-Comintern Pact with Japan. We had also made agreements with Italy, as he knew. It was now for Rome and Tokyo to decide whether they wished to make similar direct agreements."

More than formalities lurked under the seemingly trivial issue. Italy had few ties with China,* Italy and Japan were the two powers that had defied the League's attempt to check their conquests, and the Fascist government, virtually from the outset, made no secret of its benevolence toward the Japanese in their war with the Chinese. The German Army, on the other hand, had been deeply involved in the fortunes of Chiang-Kai-shek since 1927. The great Hans von Seeckt, after his retirement, had served as Chiang's military adviser, and since 1935, General Alexander von Falkenhausen had been head of the German military mission to Chiang, which in 1937 comprised some thirty officers and specialists.† Blomberg and Fritsch, and Neurath at the Foreign Office, were partisans of the Chinese relationship (as they had been of the Soviet ties) and not inclined to put a high value on Italy as a military ally. At Nuremberg, Neurath described the "so-called Berlin-Rome-Tokyo policy" as "detrimental and in some ways fantastic."

The Sino-Japanese War, accordingly, was an awkward development for the Reich government, linked as it was to China in a military way and to Japan through the anti-Comintern treaty. In the light of Italy's known preference for Japan, a three-way pact would link Germany more closely with Japan, vis-à-vis China than would an Italo-Japanese agreement, so the reason for Neurath's preference for the latter procedure is evident.

But Neurath's influence with Hitler was steadily weakening, and his veto of the tripartite plan was soon overridden, as the Japanese and Ribbentrop, who had negotiated the German-Japanese treaty a year earlier, made common cause. On October 20, Ciano received successively the Japanese Ambassador, Masaaki Hotta, and Hassell, accompanied by Ribbentrop's emissary, Dr. Hermann von Raumer. Ciano was then informed for the first time that the two other governments were now favoring a triple agreement instead of the previously projected

---

* Some Italian officers were attached as instructors or consultants to the Chinese Air Force.

† There were two other generals, twenty-one other officers, and nine engineers and technicians. The officers were all put on the German Army's retired list when they went to China, but most of those who returned to Germany were reactivated during the Second World War.

Italo-Japanese treaty. Ciano declared that he had "no objections in principle," but noted in his diary his suspicion that "something was not quite right,"* and that he suspected a Neurath-Ribbentrop rift. His suspicions were soon borne out by the news from Berlin that Neurath was trying to persuade the Italian Ambassador there, Bernardo Attolico, that Italy should not agree to the new proposal, and by the arrival in Rome, on October 22, of Ribbentrop himself.

This was highly irregular diplomacy; Ribbentrop was the Ambassador to Britain and had no proper status in Italy. Furthermore, in putting forward the tripartite plan, he was flouting his own superior's wishes. Nevertheless, Mussolini and Ciano received him warmly and readily consented to the new plan, which contemplated a ceremonial signing in Munich within the next few days. Ciano, however, took the precaution of sending the Prince of Hesse, who was still functioning as an unofficial courier between Duce and Fuehrer, to visit the latter and "find out what he thinks about the Tripartite Pact." The Prince reported back a week later with Hitler's personal approval of the plan, which he "claims to have originated himself."

Meanwhile, it had been decided to solemnize the treaty in Rome instead of Munich, and on November 6, 1937, the ceremony was held at the Palazzo Chigi, with Ribbentrop, Ciano, and Hotta the signatories. The document, entitled "Protocol," referred to the German-Japanese agreements signed the previous year, and recited that Italy "accedes" to it and "shall be considered as an original signatory." For the Italians, at least, it was a very great occasion, as is revealed by Ciano's excited diary entry:

> November 6. We signed the Pact this morning. One was conscious of an atmosphere definitely unlike that of the usual diplomatic ceremony. Three nations are embarking together upon a path which may perhaps lead them to war. A war necessary in order to break through the crust which is stifling the energy and the aspirations of the young nations. After the signature we went to see the Duce. I have seldom seen him so happy. The situation of 1935 has been transformed. Italy has broken out of her isolation: she is in the centre of the most formidable political and military combination which has ever existed.
>
> In the afternoon there was a conversation à trois—Duce-Ciano-Ribbentrop. . . .
>
> In the evening there was a grand dinner at the Palazzo Venezia. The two Japanese Military Attachés, both good Fascists, were radiant. They are in favour of a military pact. They were delighted when I said to them, in the Duce's presence, that they ought to occupy Vladivostok, that pistol pointed at Japan.

It remained for Italy to join Japan and Germany as seceders from the League of Nations. That body had not swallowed the castor oil prescribed by Mussolini during his interview with Goering in January, and soon after the tripartite signing, Mussolini decided to quit the League as soon as circumstances were propitious. The final move was delayed by a visit from the Yugoslav Prime Minister, Milan Stoyadinovitch, with whom the Fascist leaders were on good terms, and

---

* Ciano used French for the comment: *"Mais il y a quelque chose qui cloche."*

whom they did not wish to embarrass. Shortly after his departure, at a meeting of the Fascist Grand Council on December 11, Italy's resignation from the League was approved by acclamation. In a speech from the balcony of the Palazzo Venezia, the Duce informed the populace: "We are leaving without regret the tottering temple where they do not work for peace but prepare for war." Hitler had already let it be known in Rome that Germany would "heartily welcome the withdrawal," and shortly declared that the Reich had given up any thought of returning to the League.

6

Thus Hitler succeeded, with the aid of Ribbentrop, in breaking out of the diplomatic isolation in which Germany found herself in 1934, in spite of her subsequent repudiations of both Versailles and Locarno through open rearmament and remilitarization of the Rhineland. Nothing succeeds like success. Britain was impressed and wanted a *modus vivendi,* and leading Britons were queuing at Hitler's door; Poland, Yugoslavia, Hungary, and Bulgaria were all courting his favor; Italy and Japan were linked with the Reich in the Anti-Comintern Pact; the Wehrmacht was growing like the infant Hercules.

But in July of 1936, the infant started to put away childish things. It was, indeed, during this very time of comparative harmony at home and respectability abroad that the cutting edge of the new Wehrmacht first drew blood.

CHAPTER 12

The Spanish Civil War and the
Condor Legion

1

On July 24, 1936, a motley trio arrived in Berlin by air, bearers of a letter to Hitler from General Francisco Franco in Spanish Morocco, asking help for the insurrection against the Spanish Government on which Franco had just embarked. Through the good offices of Ernst Bohle, head of the Foreign Department (*Auslandsorganisation*) of the Nazi Party, they were soon escorted to Bayreuth, where the Fuehrer was enjoying the Wagner opera festival.

The arrival of these oddly assorted emissaries—Captain Francisco Arranz, a Spanish Air Force captain; Adolf Langenheim, leader of the Nazis in the German community in Tetuán (the capital of Spanish Morooco); and Johannes Bernhardt, a German salesman involved in trade with the Spanish garrison at Tetuán—was a surprise in Berlin. The German Embassy in Madrid had reported extensive unrest and rioting, but as late as June 27, the chargé d'affaires had discounted the likelihood of a *coup de main* from the right.

This skepticism of the imminence of revolution was surprising in view of the turbulent state of Spain since the establishment of republican government in 1930, following the fall of the dictator Don Miguel Primo de Rivera and the subsequent flight into exile of King Alphonso XIII. Parliamentary government did not bring political stability, and cabinets rapidly came and went. In the elections of February 1936, the leftist "popular front" coalition triumphed, but it was a virtually unmanageable assortment of republicans, trade unionists, socialists, syndicalists, anarchists, and communists, with little by way of common denominator except anticlericalism. Strikes and riots plagued civil life and fostered rightist counteragitation; a domestic brand of Fascism—the Falange, led by Primo de Rivera's son José—was organized in 1934 and won many adherents in nationalist and military circles.

The leftist victories in the 1936 elections added fuel to the flames. July 13 the monarchist spokesman José Calvo Sotelo was abducted and murdered by government police, and this touched off the rightist uprising. It began on July 17 in Spanish Morocco and the Canary Islands, where Franco was in semiexile, and spread the next day to southern Spain, and then over the entire country.

Initially the leadership of the revolt was scattered among several insurgent generals in addition to Franco—Manuel Goded in Barcelona, Emilio Mola in

Pamplona, Gonzalo Queipo de Llano in Seville, and Sacanell Sanjurjo, who had led an unsuccessful revolt in 1932 and was living in Portugal. Sanjurjo was expected to be Chief of State if the coup succeeded, but he was killed in an air crash on takeoff at Lisbon,* while Goded was captured, and soon executed, as the uprisings in Barcelona and Madrid failed, and eastern Spain remained in government hands.

In northwestern Spain, however, the generals were more successful, and on July 24, Mola established a revolutionary junta at Burgos. Meanwhile, Queipo de Llano had prevailed in Seville and Cádiz, but mostly by bluff. To cement the rebels' hold on southern Spain, reinforcements were desperately needed, and across the Strait of Gibraltar, in Spanish Morocco, the rebel colonels Blanco Yagüe and Juan Beigbeder were in full control by July 19, with the cream of the Spanish forces—the Army of Africa, some 30,000 strong, comprising the Foreign Legion and regular Moorish units.

Such was the situation on the morning of July 19, when Franco arrived at Tetuán in a DeHavilland *Dragon Rapide* provided by a Monarchist newspaper.† It was urgently necessary to get a substantial part of the Army of Africa across the strait in order to establish a secure basis in southern Spain and then drive north to link up with Mola. The difficulty was that on July 18 and 19 the crews of most of the Spanish warships had overcome their officers and proclaimed loyalty to the Government. By the evening of the nineteenth, a fleet of some twenty warships, weirdly commanded by committees of their crews, was off Gibraltar. Before it assembled, the rebels in Morocco succeeded in getting a few hundred Moors across the water to Cádiz, but thereafter the Government blockade precluded any large-scale movement by sea, and only a handful of aircraft, mostly obsolete, were available.

Franco promptly decided to seek foreign assistance, and thought first of Italy. The *Dragon Rapide* was again called upon, and Luis Bolín, the journalist who had procured the plane for Franco, flew off to Biarritz, where he picked up his editor, Marqués Luca di Tena, and then to Marseilles, where the two took commercial passage to Rome. They arrived there on July 21 and obtained audience with Ciano and Anfuso, but no promises of support were forthcoming until after the appearance on the twenty-fourth, of an emissary from General Mola, the monarchist Antonio Goicoechia, to whom Mussolini had secretly given financial aid in 1934. A day or two later, Mussolini agreed to help the rebels, and on July 30 twelve Savoia-Marchetti aircraft took off from Sardinia, headed for Spanish Morocco.

Meanwhile, on July 22, Franco had turned his attention toward Germany. Colonel Beigbeder had been military attaché in Berlin, and that evening he

---

* The accident occurred in a light plane, said to have been overloaded with Sanjurjo's baggage, stuffed with the dress uniforms he insisted on carrying to adorn his person as the new Spanish Chief of State.

† The arrangements were made by Colonel Alfredo Kindelán of the Spanish Air Force, and subsequently commander of Franco's air force. The editor of the Spanish journal *ABC* instructed his London correspondent, Luis Bolín, to charter the aircraft in England and fly to the Canaries to pick up Franco. The plane was piloted by a Captain Bebb, apparently ignorant of the flight's purpose. Bolín flew with Franco to Tetuán and subsequently became Franco's press chief.

prevailed on the German Consulate in Tetuán to send a telegram to Major General Erich Kühlenthal, the German military attaché accredited to both Paris and Lisbon, as follows:

> General Franco and Lieutenant Colonel Beigbeder send greetings to their friend, the honorable General Kühlenthal, to inform him of the new Nationalist Spanish Government, and request that he send ten troop-transport planes with maximum seating capacity through private German firms.
>
> Transfer by air with German crews to any airfield in Spanish Morocco. The contract will be signed later.
>
> Very urgent! On the word of General Franco and Spain.

It is hard to believe that Franco and Beigbeder thought that Kühlenthal could grant so portentous a request on his own authority. However that may be, it is doubtful that the telegram ever reached its destination. The Tetuán consulate sent it via the Foreign Ministry in Berlin, and upon its receipt there the head of the Political Department, Dr. Hans Dieckhoff, at once informed the War Ministry: "In the view of the Foreign Ministry compliance with the Spanish request is out of the question at this time."

There were many Germans in Spain, and the Foreign Ministry was naturally worried that open intervention on the rebel side would provoke reprisals. Two days before Franco's messengers reached Berlin, Raeder had ordered the fleet commander, Vice-Admiral Rolf Carls, to sail for Spain with the pocket battle cruisers *Deutschland* and *Admiral Scheer* to protect and, if necessary, to evacuate Germans. In this there was nothing intrinsically unneutral; British, French, Italian, American, and other naval units were soon in Spanish waters on comparable missions. And in view of the Foreign Ministry's cautious attitude, it is not surprising that the Franco emissaries who reached Berlin on July 24 were not received by any military or diplomatic officials, or that Dieckhoff counseled the absolute necessity "that at this stage German government and Party authorities continue to refrain from any contact" with the visitors.

The "Party authorities," however, took quite another attitude. Bohle and Hitler's deputy Rudolf Hess lent willing ears to the Spaniards' story, and soon the guests were whisked off to Bayreuth and a late evening audience with the Fuehrer, who had just returned to *Wahnfried* (the Wagner home, where he was a guest) from a performance of *Die Walküre*.

No record or reliable account of this meeting has come to light. It would have been natural for Hitler to greet the Spaniards sympathetically, for the insurrection was pictured as an anti-Communist crusade, and in Berlin the anti-Comintern pact with Japan was already being hatched. Furthermore, there had been earlier contacts between Nazi and Spanish military circles, and it is credibly reported that General Sanjurjo had been cordially received by Hitler in the spring of 1936.

But while sympathy was cheap, German military intervention in the Spanish Civil War was a serious and risky proposition, involving, as it did, hazards to the Germans resident in Spain, incurring the ill-will of governments friendly to the Spanish Republic, and the dispatch of troops hundreds of miles from Germany to a noncontiguous country in which they might be cut off by hostile action. In the German Army as well as diplomatic circles there was opposition to such adventurism with a Wehrmacht that was still beset by growing pains.

Hitler, however, lost no time in coming to an affirmative conclusion. He does not appear to have even consulted the Foreign Ministry, which, two days later, was still discouraging the dispatch of aircraft to the rebels.

After his meeting with the Spaniards, Hitler summoned Blomberg and Goering as well "as an admiral who was present in Bayreuth"—quite possibly Admiral Wilhelm Canaris, head of the Wehrmacht intelligence service, who had extensive Spanish contacts and a strong affinity for the generals who were leading the revolt. Goering, according to his testimony ten years later at Nuremberg, urged Hitler "to give support under all circumstances, firstly in order to prevent the further spread of communism in that theatre and, secondly, to test my young Luftwaffe at this opportunity in this or that technical respect."

It was on this basis, so far as we know, that Hitler reached his decision to aid the insurgents. The next day he told Ribbentrop, who was also in Bayreuth and took the view that "we would do well to keep out of Spanish affairs," that he had already decided otherwise because "Germany could in no circumstances tolerate a Communist Spain. . . . If Spain really goes Communist, France will also be Bolshevised and then Germany is finished." This fear that the Reich could not survive between Communist blocs on both east and west, if stated in exaggerated form, was undoubtedly genuine, and in later years Hitler gave the same reasons for his action.*

Hitler and Mussolini had reached their decision to aid the Spanish revolt almost simultaneously but quite independently of each other. Indeed, throughout the first few weeks of the Civil War there was little or no consultation, let alone co-ordination, between Berlin and Rome.† But there was no mistaking the superior speed and efficacy of the German response to the rebels' pleas.

Bolín and Luca di Tena had arrived in Rome on July 21, and nine days elapsed before the twelve Savoia-Marchetti trimotors took off from Sardinia for Melilla, in Spanish Morocco. Bolín was a passenger, as well as General Giuseppe Valle, Under-Secretary for Air, and Ettore Muti, an officer of the Fascist Militia—the "Black Shirts." One plane crashed in the sea, and two others in French Morocco, where the French easily discerned the incompletely erased markings of the Italian Air Force. When the nine surviving aircraft reached Melilla, there was no gasoline for the remainder of the trip; they managed to get one plane, with Bolín, to Tetuán on the thirty-first, and gasoline was then sent to Melilla by boat. While in Melilla, the Italian crews were mustered into the Spanish

---

* In February 1942, soliloquizing at table with subordinates at his military headquarters in East Prussia, Hitler attributed his intervention to "the danger of the Red Peril's overwhelming Europe," adding that, but for this fear, he would have let events take their own course, so that the Church would have been destroyed.

† On July 25, Ciano and Hassell had expressed to each other mutual concern that communism not establish itself in Spain. But it was merely agreed that each country would keep the other informed, and that Italy, pending the arrival of German naval forces in Spanish waters, would undertake the protection of German nationals in Spain. On August 4 at Bolzano, Canaris met with his Italian opposite number, General Mario Roatta, and was informed that Mussolini had decided to give "unofficial" support to Franco.

Foreign Legion. Not until early August were the planes available to Franco, and little more Italian help reached him for many weeks thereafter.

The Franco emissaries to Germany reached Berlin on July 24, three days after their compatriots' arrival in Rome, and Hitler made his decision in Bayreuth two days later. The following morning, twenty Junkers 52 trimotored transport aircraft took off from Tempelhof airport in Berlin, refueled at Stuttgart, and went on to Tetuán. They were flown by Lufthansa pilots, experienced in long international flights, and seconded for emergency military service. At Tetuán no time was spent on formalities. The leader, Lufthansa Captain Henke, put down in Seville that evening (July 27) with twenty-two Moroccan soldiers. Subsequently, the German pilots achieved an average of four flights each day between Tetuán and either Seville or Jerez de la Frontera, generally carrying about double the normal seventeen-passenger load of a Ju-52.

While the German planes were en route to Spain, Goering's staff was already putting together another party of volunteers to go by sea. On July 31, eighty-five Luftwaffe volunteers who had been assembled at the Döberitz air base were given parting instructions by General Milch and entrained for Hamburg, where they embarked on the freighter *Usaramo*. They comprised pilots, ground crews, radio technicians, and other specialists, and were commanded by Major Alexander von Scheele, recently recalled to active duty, and fluent in Spanish after many years in South America. With a cargo that included six Heinkel 51 fighter aircraft, twenty light antiaircraft guns, and signals equipment, the *Usaramo* made port in Cádiz on August 5, and the next day freight and passengers were landed and sent to Seville.

Meanwhile, with the aid of the reinforcements brought by air from Morocco, Queipo de Llano gained control over the southern tip of Spain, from Seville to Huelva, Cádiz, and Gibraltar. On August 5, Franco was able to put a convoy, carrying 2,500 soldiers, across the strait from Ceuta to Algeciras. He himself flew to Seville the next day to take command of the Army of Africa in Spain. The German party from the *Usaramo* arrived at about the same time, and, thus strengthened in the air, Franco's forces commenced their march toward Mérida and a junction with Mola's forces in the north.

2

Like Franco and Mola, the Spanish Republican leaders in Madrid had foreign friends to whom they cried for help. On July 19, the newly chosen Prime Minister, José Giral, sent a telegram to Léon Blum, who had been Premier in France barely six weeks:

> Are surprised by dangerous military *coup*. Beg of you to help us immediately with arms and aeroplanes. Fraternally yours. Giral.

In terms of protocol, it was as remarkable a message as Beigbeder's to General Kühlenthal, for Giral had completely by-passed normal diplomatic channels; no doubt he hoped to profit by the circumstance that both he and Blum were heads of Popular Front governments.

Giral's plea presented Blum and his colleagues with a vexing dilemma. They were liberal democrats who wished their Spanish comrades well, and the initial reaction was to respond generously. But in the longer run their own pacifist inclinations, British coolness, and French rightist opposition swung the Blum government to the "nonintervention" fiction which all the major European countries endorsed and which Germany, Italy, Portugal, and the Soviet Union so brazenly violated.

On July 30, however, Blum's interventionist hand had been momentarily strengthened when the two Italian aircraft, enroute to Melilla, crashed in French Morocco. This plain proof of Italian intervention enabled Blum and his supporters, at a Cabinet meeting on August 2, to obtain authorization for supplying the Spanish Government with some sixty military aircraft and an irregular flow of technicians, combat volunteers, and equipment. It was not much but it was timely, and greatly assisted the Spanish Government in slowing the rebel advance.

On August 8, however, the French Government announced that all shipments of war material to Spain were embargoed as of the next day. But as official French aid dwindled, a stream of volunteers, largely recruited and organized by the Comintern, poured into loyalist Spain, across the French border and into the ports held by the Government, to form the International Brigades. In October the first Soviet ships, bringing arms, arrived at Cartagena and Alicante.

During the early fall a shifting but ascertainable front between loyalist and insurgent Spain emerged, with the rebels in control of Andalusia in the south and most of the northern provinces, while Government forces held Barcelona, Madrid, most of eastern Spain, and Asturias and Santander on the Bay of Biscay. And so, except for the rebels' conquest of the Biscay provinces in the fall of 1937, the division was to remain until the spring of 1938.

As the prospects of speedy victory for either side dwindled, "nonintervention" emerged as the diplomatic formula for preventing the conflict from spreading beyond Spanish borders. As originally proposed by the French Government on August 2, 1936, it contemplated an agreement among the three major Mediterranean powers—Britain, France, and Italy—to ban the export of arms or other munitions of war to Spanish territory. Soon Germany, Portugal, and Russia were added to the list of invitees. By the end of the month, all except Portugal had accepted the French proposals. When the Non-Intervention Committee held its first meeting, on September 9 in London, twenty-six European countries were represented, and Portugal joined a fortnight later.*

The reasons why the countries chiefly interested joined in the Non-Intervention Agreement were different in each case. The English political leaders had no great love for the Spanish Republican government, and were primarily concerned with confining the war to Spain. Blum and his colleagues, in contrast, were strongly pro-Republican, but were acutely aware that the French parties of

---

* Portugal was probably the most reluctant adherent to nonintervention. The dictatorial, arch-conservative Salazar regime was badly frightened by the emergence of liberal democracy and socialism in Spain and correspondingly sympathetic to the Spanish nationalists. But pressure from Britain, Portugal's long-standing ally and protector, and awareness that Portugal could not safely stand apart from the policy that the other European countries were at least nominally accepting, finally resulted in Portuguese attendance at the Non-Intervention Committee meeting of September 28, 1936.

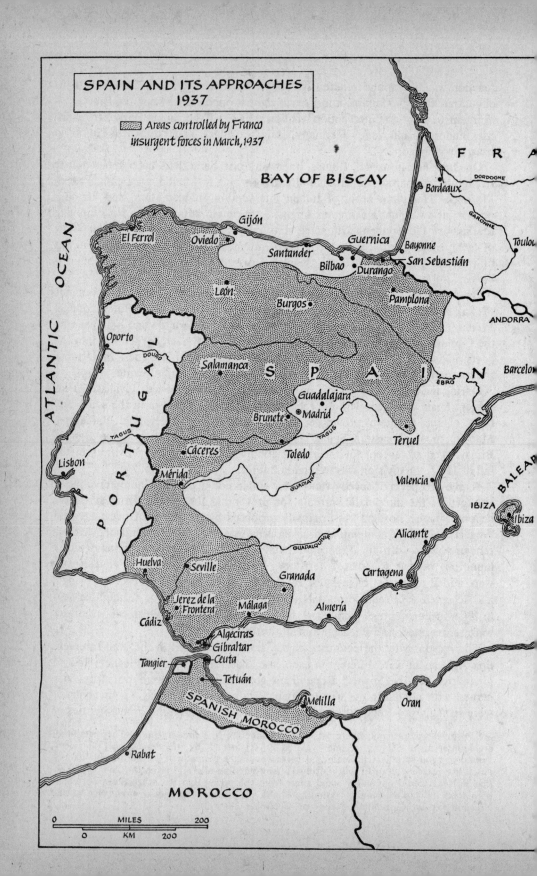

SPAIN AND ITS APPROACHES
1937

Areas controlled by Franco
insurgent forces in March, 1937

BAY OF BISCAY

ATLANTIC OCEAN

FRA

Bordeaux

DORDOGNE

GARONNE

Toulou

ANDORRA

Gijón

El Ferrol   Oviedo

Guernica

Santander   Bayonne

Bilbao   Durango   San Sebastián

León   Burgos   Pamplona

Oporto

DOURO

Salamanca   S   P   A   I   N

Barcelo

EBRO

Guadalajara

Brunete   Madrid

Teruel

TAGUS   TAGUS

Cáceres   Toledo

P   O   R   T   U   G   A   L

Lisbon

Mérida   Valencia   BALEAR

GUADIANA

IBIZA   Ibiza

Alicante

Huelva

Seville   Granada   Cartagena

GUADALQUIVIR

Jerez de la   Málaga   Almería
Frontera

Cádiz

Algeciras
Gibraltar

Tangier   Ceuta

Tetuán

Melilla   Oran

SPANISH   MOROCCO

Rabat

MOROCCO

0   MILES   200

0   KM   200

the right and center were fearful of communism in Spain, and that outright aid to the Republicans, tainted with leftism as they were, would endanger France's own political stability. "Nonintervention" enabled Blum to quiet his supporters by telling them that it would stop the flow of German and Italian arms to the rebels.

The Soviet Union, emerging from diplomatic isolation and newly allied with France, was probably moved to accept the French proposals in order to maintain her still rickety status as an acknowledged European power. Germany and Italy saw the plan as advantageous because it would cut off the material aid which Blum would otherwise feel obligated to extend to the Spanish Government.* But for Russia, Germany, and Italy alike their adherence to nonintervention was purely a diplomatic device, unaccompanied by any intention of giving the policy more than lip service.

Reporting Italy's acceptance of the French proposals, the German chargé d'affaires in Rome, Baron Johann von Plessen, informed Berlin that it was "obvious" that the Italian Government "does not intend to abide by the declaration anyway." And if German diplomats were not quite so openly contemptuous of their own undertakings, Berlin made no real effort to preserve a credible neutrality.

On August 3, with the Junkers airlift already in full swing, the *Deutschland* arrived off Ceuta. Admiral Carls came ashore to pay Franco what amounted to a state visit, replete with troop inspections, bands, and toasts—a gesture which the local population naturally regarded as open German support for the Nationalist cause.

On August 14, a week after Scheele's party reached Seville, the German consul informed Berlin that the men had appeared in the streets "in their uniforms and white Olympic caps" and were at once recognized and acclaimed as Germans, so that "it has long since been impossible to keep the enterprise secret." And by August 27, three days after the German Government announced its adherence to the nonintervention declaration, the German chargé in Madrid reported that Junkers aircraft had just bombed the local airfields, and plaintively requested Berlin to keep German warplanes away from the city "at least as long as Lufthansa traffic is maintained."

3

In Berlin, the chief organizer of the Franco military assistance program was Hermann Goering, who, as he put the matter at Nuremberg, "sent a large part of my transport fleet and a number of experimental fighter units, bombers, and anti-aircraft guns, and in that way had an opportunity to ascertain, under combat conditions, whether the material was equal to the task." Within the Air Ministry, a special staff—*Sonderstab "W"*—was set up under General Helmuth Wilberg to administer the undertaking. For purposes of camouflage, two dummy

* The Italians and Germans, indeed, urged the French to broaden the nonintervention declaration so as to cover volunteers as well as war materials, no doubt hoping thereby to stem the flow of volunteers through France to the loyalist side. The declaration was not modified, as the French thought such a ban could not be enforced, but the issue remained alive for many months.

corporations were used: ROWAK in Germany and HISMA in Spain,* where the incoming supplies were handled by Johannes Bernhardt, who had exploited his prestige as one of the original Franco emissaries to Germany through designation as HISMA's director. The *Usaramo* was soon followed by the *Kamerun* and *Wigbert,* freighters which, thanks to Salazar's personal authorization, were unloaded at Lisbon, and their cargoes sent across Portugal to Franco.† A military air transport service, with four flights weekly, was established between Germany and rebel-held Spain.

The principal purpose of Scheele's party was to train the Spaniards in the use of modern military equipment, and, for some time, the only Germans who engaged in combat were the air crews. After the need for air transport from Morocco diminished, the Junkers 52s were converted for use as bombers, under the command of Lieutenant Rudolf Freiherr von Moreau. On August 13, Moreau and another plane flown by Henke and Lieutenant Max Graf Hoyos attacked the Republican armored cruiser *Jaime I* in Málaga harbor. It was the infant Wehrmacht's first combat mission. Hoyos scored a hit which caused many casualties and disabled the ship for some weeks, thus relieving pressure on the rebels' sea traffic between Morocco and Spain. Meanwhile, the Heinkel fighters that had been brought by the *Usaramo* were assembled and put into service.‡

But, while the Junkers transports had been of enormous and perhaps decisive help during the first weeks of the revolt, stabilization of the front brought a new situation. There is no evidence that either Hitler or Mussolini anticipated a long war, and one can only guess whether or not they would have become involved had they foreseen the temporal dimensions of the encounter. For Germany, the issue was sharply drawn in a memorandum by Admiral Raeder, submitted to Hitler on August 22, 1936, which declared it "absolutely necessary to achieve clarity as to German political aims in Spain in order to take the proper military and political measures and to protect ourselves against surprises for which we are not prepared or organized at present." Raeder's judgment was that, in view of the Spanish Government's broad base of popular support, the Franco government could not hold out for long "without large-scale support from the outside." Accordingly, if German support for the rebels were to continue, Franco would have to be provided with "the considerable forces needed to assure his victory." From Raeder's standpoint a prompt decision was vital, "since almost the whole German fleet is at present in Spanish waters."

Two days later Germany signed the Non-Intervention Agreement, and the next day—August 25—Blomberg dispatched two officers to Rome to work out with the Italians a joint program of aid to the rebels. They were the War Minis-

---

* The initials stood for *Rohstof- und Wareneinkaufsgesellschaft* (Raw Materials and Merchandise Marketing Company) and *Compañia Hispano-Marroquí de Transportes* (Spanish-Moroccan Transportation Company).

† This convenient state of affairs lasted only a few weeks. Under British pressure Salazar closed Lisbon to German military shipments early in September, and thereafter the German vessels docked in Cádiz or rebel-held ports on Spain's Biscay coast.

‡ Among the fighter pilots in the first group was Lieutenant Hannes Trautloft, a leading fighter commander in the Second World War, and subsequently Commander of the West German Air Force.

try intelligence chief, Admiral Wilhelm Canaris, and a staff lieutenant colonel, Walter Warlimont. Mussolini soon agreed to join in the plan, and an Italian cruiser took the two Germans, accompanied by Canaris' opposite number, General Mario Roatta, to Tetuán, from where they were flown to Spain for conferences with Queipo de Llano at Seville, and Franco at his headquarters in Cáceres. With the title "Plenipotentiary Representative of the German Armed Forces" Warlimont remained as the unofficial but ranking German representative in rebel Spain, while Canaris returned to Berlin to advise his superiors on Franco's crucial needs, and division of the burden of assistance between Germany and Italy.

"Nonintervention" did less than nothing to reduce the scale or intensity of the fighting. In Toledo, the loyalists drove a rebel force into the famous Alcázar, and Moreau's Junkers dropped supplies to the besieged garrison. On September 27, Moors of the Army of Africa lifted the siege, opening the way to Madrid, and on October 1, Franco assumed supreme command of all the rebel forces and was installed at Burgos as Head of State. His telegrams to Hitler and Mussolini announcing his assumption of power drew no official replies, but it was agreed between Berlin and Rome that the Franco regime would be formally recognized after the expected taking of Madrid.

But Madrid did not fall, and when Hitler received Ciano at the Berghof late in October, it was decided that both countries would give Franco more help. In November, rebel military pressure on Madrid caused the Spanish Government to move to Valencia, and shortly thereafter it announced a naval blockade of rebel ports. These circumstances furnished excuse for recognition of the Franco government; it was extended by Germany and Italy on November 18, and simultaneously their representatives to the Republic were recalled.

As "Diplomatic Representative to the Spanish Nationalist Government," Hitler appointed Wilhelm Faupel, an Army general staff officer who had left the service after the First World War and sought his fortune first in Argentina and then in Peru, where he had been appointed Inspector-General of the Army, with the rank of lieutenant general. Faupel had returned to Germany in 1931 as head of the Ibero-American Institute, and no doubt his combination of military and linguistic attributes commended him as a suitable emissary to Franco.

Meanwhile Blomberg and Goering had made plans for increased aid to Franco, the outlines of which were embodied in the former's memorandum of October 30, 1936. Canaris had already returned to Spain, and he was now directed to admonish Franco that "the combat tactics hitherto employed" by him were not "promising of success"; they had been "hesitant and routine," and the rebel leaders had "failed to exploit the present favorable ground and air situation" so as to accomplish the occupation of Madrid, which was of "decisive political importance." Additional German military aid must therefore be conditional upon the integration of all German units under a German commander responsible directly and only to Franco himself.

The Luftwaffe would continue to provide the greater part of the assistance and, since Warlimont was an Army artillery officer with no air experience and lacked sufficient seniority, he was recalled and replaced by General Hugo

Sperrle of the Luftwaffe. Fighter, bomber, and reconnaissance aircraft, together with signals companies and antiaircraft batteries, would comprise the Luftwaffe's contribution, while the Army would provide two light tank companies, and a few antitank, signals, and transport troops. Two able Army lieutenant colonels, Hans Ritter von Funck and Wilhelm Ritter von Thoma, were sent to Spain, the former as military attaché and the latter as commander of the armored units in the field.

The new German forces were assembled in Seville early in November. They were dubbed the "Condor Legion,"* and Sperrle took command under the *nom de guerre* "General Sander." Since, from the German standpoint, training under combat conditions was one of the primary values of the venture, their personnel turnover was high, but the Legion's strength at any one time never much exceeded six thousand men. According to General von Thoma,† only about 10 per cent of these were ground troops; they were mostly junior officers and noncommissioned specialists whose principal mission was to train the Spaniards in using the tanks and antitank weapons supplied by the Germans.

The Condor Legion was initially committed in support of Franco's efforts to take Madrid. Scheele's men were already there, and, according to Lieutenant Hoyos, the Germans sustained their first casualties on November 4, 1936, when a Junkers 52 was brought down. It was an ominous event for the Germans; Russian I-15 and I-16 fighters were appearing, and showing clear superiority over the Heinkel 51 biplanes. The first Soviet ships bringing military aid had reached Spain late in October, just as the heavy bombing of Madrid began, and on November 12 two German fighters were shot down by the Russians.‡

Berlin was so alarmed by the comparative inadequacy of the Heinkels that three experimental prototypes of the Messerschmitt 109 were sent to Spain during the winter of 1936–37 for combat testing. The future basic German fighter plane of the Second World War soon proved its worth, and in the spring and summer of 1937, after regular production commenced, about forty were sent to Spain,* where they established a clear superiority over the Russian fighters. Si-

---

* The source of the name is obscure. The German accounts of the Spanish involvement date it from November 1936, but the entry for July 23, 1936, in the diary of Bella Fromm (see the Bibliography), possibly written later, refers to the "Condor Regiment." Until November, the Germans used the cover name *Zauberfeuer* (Magic Fire) for the over-all Spanish undertaking, while Scheele's party was called *Reisegesellschaft Union* (Union Travel Company), and a small German naval training contingent was *Gruppe Nordsee* (North Sea Group).

† As told to Liddell Hart after the end of the Second World War. Thoma, commanding the Afrika Korps under Rommel, was captured by the British at El Alamein in November 1942. He was an early arrival in Spain, but his statement to Liddell Hart (*The German Generals Talk,* at p. 92) that he departed Germany "on the night that General Franco's revolt was due to begin" and met Franco at Mérida is wholly mistaken. There is no evidence of any German aid until July 25, and the rebel forces did not take Mérida until August 10, three weeks after the start of the Civil War. Unlike most of his colleagues, Thoma remained in Spain until the end of the war.

‡ However, German casualties in Spain were light. By January 12, 1937 (according to an entry in General Alfred Jodl's diary), the Legion had suffered only twenty-one fatal casualties.

* Although generally known as the Me-109, after its designer Willy Messerschmitt, the official designation was the Bf-109, after the manufacturing company, the Bayrische Flugzeugwerke.

multaneously, early models of one of the Luftwaffe's new bombers, the Heinkel 111, appeared in the Spanish skies.

The men of the Condor Legion wore Spanish-type uniforms, but their insignia of rank were raised one level, so that German sergeants appeared as lieutenants, and lieutenants as captains. The units were identified by the number "88," so that the bomber group* was K/88, the fighter group J/88, and so forth. The Legion retained its integrated command structure, and Sperrle and his chief of staff, Colonel Wolfram von Richthofen, dealt directly with Franco and the chief of his air force, General Alfredo Kindelán.

4

Late in October 1936, the first Italian infantry volunteers began trickling into Spain, as Mussolini, jealous of his Mediterranean prerogatives, sought to outdo the Germans in supporting the rebel cause. On November 27, Ciano told Hassell that "a whole division of Black Shirts" (Fascist Militia) would be sent to Spain, subject to "certain guaranties as to the future course of Spanish policy." The very next day, and without further notice to Berlin, the Italian and rebel governments entered into a secret agreement under which the former undertook to continue to assist the "Spanish Nationalist Government," and both agreed to pursue policies of mutual support, military and economic. On reading the text, Neurath expressed displeasure that Berlin had not been consulted; he acknowledged a "greater Italian interest" in Spain, but drew the conclusion that, if Italy wished thus to assert priority, she must then furnish the greater part of the necessary aid.

Meanwhile Faupel had arrived at Franco's headquarters at Salamanca. He had been instructed "not to concern himself with military matters," but on December 8 he advised Berlin "in agreement with Sperrle and Funck" that, if a Franco victory were to be ensured, "one strong German and one strong Italian division would be required." Both Blomberg and Neurath took a dim view of this proposal and, at a military conference in Rome on December 6, at which Mussolini presided and Blomberg was represented by Admiral Canaris, it was made clear that the Germans would not send any large Army units to Spain.†

On December 17, however, Mussolini told Hassell that "in view of the unsatisfactory situation" in Spain "he had decided to send 3,000 Black Shirts with their equipment tomorrow from Gaeta to Cádiz by a large ship of the South American service." They arrived in Cádiz on December 22, and the next day Ciano told Hassell that another 3,000 would go "during the next few days."

Many more soon followed. When Goering visited Rome on January 23, 1937, Mussolini told him that "the number of Italian volunteers has reached 44,000."

---

* The German unit designations are confusing if literally translated, since in the Royal Air Force the basic "squadron" (a dozen aircraft) corresponded to the German *Staffel,* and the "wing" (some thirty planes) to the German *Gruppe,* while the British called their largest unit the "Group," and the Germans the *Geschwader*—literally a "squadron."

† According to a Foreign Ministry memorandum by Dieckhoff, the Italians agreed with the Germans not to send "complete units" to Spain.

This may at the time have been an exaggeration,* but approximates the number of Italian ground troops ultimately sent to Franco. These men assembled under the designation *Corpo Truppe Volontarie* under the command of General Mario Roatta, known in Spain as "Mancini," and initially comprised chiefly Black Shirt Militia. They were first committed to battle early in February, when nine Italian battalions assisted Queipo de Llano in taking Málaga.

Encouraged by this modest success, Roatta moved his troops to the Madrid front, and launched an offensive toward Guadalajara, some fifty miles northeast of the Spanish capital. With 30,000 Italians grouped in four divisions, and in conjunction with 20,000 Spanish Nationalist troops under General Moscardo, the attack was launched on March 8, 1937. At first good progress was made, but a combination of bad weather, Russian local air superiority, fierce resistance by the International Brigades,† and the Fascist Militia's poor training soon checked the Italian advance. By March 13 things were turning dark for the Fascists, and on the eighteenth they were driven into precipitate retreat.

The Guadalajara offensive moved the Nationalist front in that area about twelve miles closer to Madrid, but at the cost to the Italians of some 6,000 casualties and heavy losses of equipment. Far more important than the military balance sheet were the psychological consequences; the loyalists gained a clear-cut and badly needed propaganda victory, and Italian prestige suffered a disaster. On March 25, Hassell found the Duce in a state of "great agitation on account of events in Spain" and "ill-concealed dissatisfaction with Italian achievements." But he snatched eagerly at Hassell's observation that "the psychological effect would readily be dissipated by a new victory," and told Hassell that he had warned the Italian commanders "that none of them would return home alive unless they achieved victory." After such a warning, it was unlikely that the Italian forces would be committed to battle except under circumstances that virtually guaranteed success.

5

Frustrated before Madrid, Franco turned his attention to the Government-held strip along the Biscay coast, in which the three major ports were, from east to west, Bilbao, Santander, and Gijón. General Mola's Army of the North, supported by the Condor Legion and an Italian division, attacked toward Bilbao on March 31, to the tune of Mola's threat to "raze all Vizcaya‡ to the ground."

The bombers of the Condor Legion at once gave point to the threat by bombing the town of Durango, fifteen miles southeast of Bilbao. It was a road and

---

* Italian Air Ministry figures for the same dates showed some 16,500 ground troops in Spain. Mussolini's figure may have included volunteers available but not yet sent to Spain. In December 1937, Ciano told Hassell that there were "40,000 Italians in Spain." In Thomas, *The Spanish Civil War*, it is stated (p. 634): "The Italian forces in Spain at their maximum, in mid-1937, numbered about 50,000."

† By appropriate irony, the Fascist "Black Flames" Division encountered the Garibaldi Battalion, in which Pietro Nenni, leader of the Socialists in postwar Italy, commanded a company. Also on the scene as "inspectors" of the International Brigades were Luigi Longo and Vittorio Vidali, prominent in later years as leaders of the Italian Communist Party.

‡ The Basque province of which Bilbao is the capital.

railway junction but defenseless; 250 civilians were killed, but little or no military damage was inflicted. Mola's forces netted a small advance but were halted by heavy rains, and the front was quiet for several weeks.

When the offensive was resumed, Sperrle's bombers struck again, this time at Guernica y Luno, some twelve miles east of Bilbao on the Mundaca River estuary. A farm and market community of only a few thousand inhabitants, for the Basques Guernica was a shrine of liberty, as it was by the famous "Tree of Gernika" that the Spanish monarchs swore to respect Basque rights. The town lay between Mola's forces and Bilbao, but otherwise had no military importance.

Late in the afternoon of April 27, successive waves of aircraft, including Heinkel 111s and Junkers 52s, bombed Guernica for nearly three hours. The dead numbered 1,654, the wounded 889, and the center of the town was destroyed. The extent of the destruction and its cause were widely observed and confirmed by newspaper correspondents as well as the inhabitants. In those more innocent days such an action was both surprising and outrageous, and Guernica, already a symbol of ancient values, now became a byword for the horrors of war, and the subject of Pablo Picasso's famous painting.

There was extensive comment and condemnation in world press and political circles, and discussion in the British Parliament. The observed participation of German aircraft naturally pointed the finger of blame toward the Condor Legion, but the Nationalist government denied all responsibility and accused the Basques of destroying their own town. From London, Ribbentrop wired Berlin that Franco ought to "issue an immediate and energetic denial," and from Salamanca, Faupel sent in an extract from the Nationalist press bureau's release which stated: "Guernica was destroyed with fire and gasoline. It was set afire and reduced to ruins by the Red hordes . . . with the devilish intention of laying the blame before the enemy's door and producing a storm of indignation among the . . . Basques." Eden asked Ribbentrop whether Germany would agree to an international investigation of the incident, but this proposal was summarily rejected, by Hitler personally, as "entirely outside the bounds of possibility."

If these German denials gained any credence in the world at large, they found none within the Condor Legion itself. Lieutenant Adolf Galland, destined for fame as a fighter pilot and commander during the Second World War, joined the Condor Legion early in May 1937, about two weeks after Guernica, and found "great depression among the members of the Legion," who "did not like discussing Guernica" because "one of our first principles was to destroy the enemy ruthlessly but if possible spare civilians." Galland states that the target of the attack was a nearby road bridge over the Mundaca, and attributes destruction of the town to the poor aim of inexperienced crews. Perhaps so, but Mola's earlier threat to "raze all Vizcaya to the ground," the preceding attack on Durango, the duration of the Guernica bombing, the false denials of German responsibility, and the later German raids on Barcelona do little to support the apologia. The Luftwaffe was sent to Spain to be blooded, and Guernica was part of the process.*

Bilbao fell to the Nationalists on June 19, but Mola did not live to relish the fruits of victory; he had been killed in an air crash on June 3, ending a rivalry which Franco found irksome. Roatta, too, was no longer on the scene, having been replaced by General Ettore Bastico, of Italo-Ethiopian War fame. Italian troops participated in the campaign but gained little glory. The "Black Arrow" Division had captured the pretty little fishing port of Bermeo, but then was surrounded and had to be rescued by Spanish troops.

The Nationalist offensive in the north was now interrupted by a Republican attack on the Madrid front, launched on July 6 toward Brunete. The Condor Legion moved south to support Franco's defense, and Galland's pilots used their old Heinkel 51s to good effect for ground attack. The Italians, meanwhile, spent large sums to publicize their valor and indispensability, but did little actual fighting. On July 9, Faupel reported that "the bulk of the Italian troops remained inactive in reserve during the entire fighting around Bilbao," and on July 31 a German Foreign Ministry official noted that "the Italian volunteers have been standing at ease for weeks and cannot be persuaded to launch even the smallest attack."

The Brunete offensive was checked during the last week of July, and on August 14 the Nationalists resumed their northern campaign with an attack toward Santander, supported by the ubiquitous Condor Legion. The odds overwhelmingly favored the Nationalists, and Bastico threw in three of his divisions. This time the Italians' victory hunger was gratified, and the fall of Santander on August 25 was the signal for Fascist rejoicing in Rome and, as we have seen, laid the necessary psychological basis for Mussolini's trip to Germany the following month.

On the Biscay coast, the Republicans still held a small pocket around Gijón. The Nationalists reduced it in a seven weeks' campaign ending October 21, when Gijón fell. The Condor Legion's aircraft were again on hand, but not the Italians.

There now came a lull in the fighting which was to last until December 15, when it was broken by the Republican attack at Teruel. The Government still held the Mediterranean coast from the French border to beyond Almería, and inland to a front that protected all of Catalonia, most of New Castile, and much of Aragón. Both Republican and Nationalist regimes seemed reasonably stable, and the situation gave every appearance of a stalemate.

6

In contrast to the indecisive military developments during 1937, the diplo-

---

* In *The Day Guernica Died* (1976), by Max Morgan-Witts and Gordon Thomas, the authors re-examined the question of personal responsibility for Guernica in the light of new sources, including the diary of Sperrle's Chief of Staff, Richthofen. The authors established that neither Mola nor Sperrle was on hand when the decision to carry out the attack was made. Accordingly, the authors put primary blame on the Chiefs of Staff, respectively Colonel Juan Vigón and Richthofen.

matic repercussions of the Spanish fighting were of great significance. The continuing deep involvement of Germany, Italy, and Russia, despite the efforts of Britain and France to localize the conflict, led to irritations and confrontations which—just as with Ethiopia in 1935 and 1936—pushed Mussolini closer to Hitler, despite desperate efforts in London to re-establish good relations with once-friendly Italy.

The Non-Intervention Committee had come into being in September 1936, just before Germany, Italy, and Russia started pouring men and matériel into Spain in quantity. Despite the semblance of camouflage, these gross violations of the Non-Intervention Agreement were soon observed and remarked in the public prints. The Committee's deliberations soon took on an unreal quality, inasmuch as three of the chief participants were the worst miscreants.

In an effort to give the Committee a little more bite, on November 12 (just as the Condor Legion was arriving in Spain), the British representative, Lord Plymouth,* submitted a plan to discover breaches of the agreement by posting observers at Spanish ports and border points. After much discussion and delay, agreement was reached in March 1937, under which an international board was established to administer some five hundred border and port observers, and Britain, France, Germany, and Italy provided a naval patrol off the Spanish coasts. The control system officially began on April 20; Germany and Italy were given responsibility for patrolling the Republican-held Mediterranean coast.

Thieves may be set to catch other thieves, but not to catch themselves. The German and Italian patrol vessels might be expected to do their best to spot Russian ships headed for Loyalist ports, but hardly to report their own bootleggers headed for Franco territory. The system was especially mad inasmuch as both Germany and Italy had recognized the Franco regime and withdrawn their representatives from Madrid. In February of 1937, Faupel was raised to the rank of ambassador. Italy had signed what amounted to a mutual assistance pact with Franco in November, and on March 20, 1937, while the control system was in process of organization, Franco and Faupel signed a comparable secret agreement on behalf of their respective governments. At the same time, Guadalajara revealed the presence of large Italian troop units on the Nationalist side.

Under such circumstances, it was hardly surprising that the Spanish Government took a dim view of the German and Italian naval patrols, or that "incidents" soon occurred. During the last week of May the Loyalist air force carried out several raids in the Balearics, where German, Italian, and British patrol ships were lying. The Italian naval auxiliary *Barletta* was hit by a bomb on May 29, but, although six officers were killed, the Italians did no more than report the incident to the Non-Intervention Committee.

Then, on May 29, two Government aircraft bombed the German battle cruiser *Deutschland,* anchored in the harbor of Ibiza. Thirty-one seamen were killed and seventy-eight wounded, but the ship was not seriously damaged and at once sailed to Gibralter, where the wounded men were put ashore. Neurath at once directed Ribbentrop to inform the Non-Intervention Committee that Ger-

* Ivor Windsor-Clive, Earl of Plymouth, was Parliamentary Under-Secretary of the Foreign Office, and chairman of the Non-Intervention Committee.

many would withdraw her ships from the naval patrol and would cease to participate in the Committee's deliberations, pending "a positive guarantee against a
repetition of such attacks." The Italians gave similar notice.

But these remonstrances were far from enough to satisfy an outraged
Fuehrer. It was a fine thing for Hoyos and Henke to bomb the *Jaime I*, but
quite another for the filthy Reds to touch the *Deutschland*. By way of reprisal,
Hitler ordered the Navy to bombard the Government-held seaport of Almería,
and on May 31 the *Deutschland*'s sister ship, *Admiral Scheer*, and four destroyers fired some two hundred rounds into the city, destroying many buildings
and killing nineteen inhabitants. In the scales of war this was not a heavy toll, but,
compared to the *Deutschland*, the streets of Almería seemed an unworthy target,
and the reaction in other countries, already conditioned by Guernica, was highly
critical. Still sensitive to foreign opinion, Hitler was greatly agitated by the adverse judgments, and months later was still defensive and prickly on these subjects.

After much wheedling, the Germans and Italians agreed to rejoin the naval
patrol, but on June 19, Berlin charged that the cruiser *Leipzig* had been the target
of two unsuccessful torpedo attacks by "Spanish-Bolshevist submarine pirates."
The Spanish Government denied the charge, and the facts still remain obscure.
But it was the end of the naval patrol, for the French and British declined the German demand for a joint naval demonstration off the Republican coast, and the
Germans and Italians then withdrew from the patrol though not from the Committee.

Whether or not torpedoes were actually fired at the *Leipzig*, the example
shortly found favor in other quarters. On August 3, Franco sent an urgent message to Rome, relaying a report that large shipments of tanks, guns, and airplanes
were en route from Russia to Spain, and asking for Italy's aid in blocking the
transports, either "by providing Spain with the necessary number of ships, or
through intervention by the Italian fleet itself." The Caudillo (as Franco was now
called) dispatched his brother, Nicolás Franco, to Rome, where he arrived on August 5 and was soon closeted with Mussolini.

Ciano, on the same day, informed Hassell that Mussolini would seek to stop
the Russian vessels, "not with surface vessels, but only with submarines, in
Sicilian waters," and might also transfer several "older warships" to Franco, "if
necessary changing the silhouette." If the submarines were obliged to surface, they
would display the Spanish flag.

Using Nationalist aircraft as well as Italian submarines, this pretty plan was at
once put into operation. The difficulty was, as the Italians well knew, that Russian
aid was being carried not only in Soviet and Spanish bottoms, but British, Mexican, French, and Greek as well. In consequence, many neutral vessels were targets of these attacks, which began on August 6 and lasted for about four weeks.
On August 16 Ciano told Plessen (the Germans chargé d'affaires) that "the Italian
'blockade' of the Spanish coast was functioning excellently; in the last few days
seven transport vessels had been sunk, and he assumed that shipments would soon
cease." Ciano was prone to exaggerate, but in fact at least ten ships had been attacked and four sunk by that time, and during the last week of August there was

more of the same. On August 31, Ciano recorded in his diary that "the naval blockade is producing striking results: four Russian or Red steamers sunk, one Greek captured, one Spanish shelled and obliged to take refuge in a French port."

It was all splendid fun, but, as Ciano noted two days later, "international opinion is getting very worked up." Especially exercised was Britannia, ruler of the waves, when her destroyer *Havock* was attacked on August 31 by a submarine, while on patrol off Alicante. The unsuccessful assailant was the Italian submarine *Iride*, but the British did not know this at the time. Two days later the British tanker *Woodford* was torpedoed and sunk off Valencia.

The lives of British sailors were values more readily comprehensible in London than Ethiopian independence or the Locarno guarantees, and the government reacted with what, at least to the Italians, was surprising vigor. On September 5 the British and French governments issued invitations, addressed to all the powers concerned, to a conference on the general subject of submarine piracy in the Mediterranean, to be held at Nyon (near Geneva) beginning five days thence.

Meanwhile France and Britain had both increased their naval forces available for escort duty, and the Italians were already getting cold feet. Mussolini, according to Ciano, was "very calm" and "doesn't believe the English want a collision with us," but on September 4, faced with the brewing international storm, he ordered the Italian Navy to suspend the blockade "until further orders." Germany and Italy stayed away from Nyon, and the conferees rapidly adopted a plan for patrolling the entire Mediterranean with warships ready to sink on sight any submarine attacking a non-Spanish ship. Thirty-five British and twenty-eight French destroyers were made available for the task.

Mussolini and Ciano professed indignation at Italy's exclusion from the plan produced at a conference in which they had declined to participate, and as a face-saving gesture the agreement was subsequently altered to provide for Italian participation in the patrol. To his diary, Ciano crowed with pride: "From suspected pirates to policemen of the Mediterranean—and the Russians, whose ships we were sinking, excluded!" But, confronted with the destroyer patrols, the "pirates" vanished as quickly as they had appeared, and in October, Russian shipments were once again reaching Republican ports.*

7

And so, as 1937 drew to a close, and after over a year of fighting with the support of both Condor Legion and *Corpo Truppe Volontarie*, the Nationalist forces were still a long way from victory. And, although at the outset of the Civil War the motives of Hitler and Mussolini in sending aid to Franco were approximately parallel, in the course of time and events it had become apparent that the Italian involvement was much the deeper. Italy's closer proximity to Spain was by no means the only reason for these developments; jealousy of British and French influence in the Mediterranean and domestic political factors

---

* None of this inhibited Mussolini, during his visit to Germany in late September, from boasting to the German Chief of Protocol, Vicco von Bülow-Schwante, that "he had already sunk 200,000 tons, and he would continue." In fact, there were no further sinkings except a few in January and early February 1938, at a time when the Nyon patrol was temporarily relaxed.

were also at work, goading Mussolini to increase his investment in a Franco victory.

The peculiar nature of the Hitler-Mussolini relation was also important. Proud of his seniority as dictator, yet aware of Germany's vastly superior military and economic resources, Mussolini was immediately attracted to enterprises in which he could take the lead and thus "keep ahead of the Joneses."

After Guadalajara, Mussolini was "stuck" in Spain for prestige reasons; he needed—or thought he needed—military triumphs to bolster his regime domestically and enhance the Italian image abroad. The longer and larger the Italian investment in Spain, the greater Mussolini's need for a triumph, so that in the end he became almost as dependent on a Nationalist victory as Franco himself. When in Germany, he told Bülow-Schwante: "The war in Spain had to be won under any circumstances, and there was no doubt he would persevere until it was successfully concluded."

True to this determination, on October 17, 1937, Mussolini told Hassell that, despite his "pained astonishment" at the request, he had agreed to send still another division to Franco. And when Ribbentrop came to Rome a few weeks later for the Tripartite Pact signing, the Duce revealed that he had "handed over to Franco six submarines and four surface vessels," and declared that "if the attainment of victory required a further effort, he was willing to make it, even if it meant sending new regular forces." Of course, it would not be charity; "we wish to be paid and must be paid."

Financial reimbursement, however, was not by any means the entire *quid pro quo*. "We want Nationalist Spain, which has been saved by all manner of Italian and German aid, to remain closely associated with our maneuvres," Mussolini told Ribbentrop, adding that Franco "must necessarily remain attached to our political system." When Ribbentrop asked about Italian intentions in Majorca, the Duce replied that "we have established at Palma a naval and an air base . . . and intend to remain in that situation as long as possible." Furthermore, "Franco must come to understand that, even after our eventual evacuation, Majorca must remain an Italian base in the event of a war with France. . . We intend to keep all the installations there so as to be able in a few hours to bring Majorca into effective play as one of our Mediterranean bases." With both Majorca and Pantelleria in operation as bases, Mussolini predicted that "not one negro will be able to cross from Africa to France by the Mediterranean route."

For all this fine talk, the Italian-Spanish partnership was no love feast. After the defeat at Guadalajara, Franco wished to use the Italians in easy assignments until they had shown ability for heavy combat, while the Italian generals, mindful of the Duce's threats, wanted "decisive action which promised great success." These disagreements led to much unpleasantness between Franco and General Bastico. After the Santander campaign Franco officially demanded Bastico's recall, and early in October he was replaced by General Francesco Berti. On October 17, Anfuso returned from a visit to Spain with the impression that "our troops are tired and Franco can hardly wait for them to clear out"—an attitude which Ciano characteristically attributed to the Caudillo's jealousy "of our successes."

The Germans had their troubles too, largely because of the personalities of Faupel and Sperrle. Neither of them was in the least charming, and neither had the slightest use for the other. When appointed, Faupel had been told that military matters were not his concern, but as a former general staff officer and trainer of South American troops, he could not resist sticking his nose into Sperrle's business. For his part Sperrle, a huge man with a perpetual scowl, antagonized the Spanish Air Force officers with his harsh criticism of their proficiency, and was openly hostile to Bernhardt and the other civilian officials of HISMA, the German-Spanish supply organization.

In the spring of 1937, Faupel complained to Hitler about Sperrle's conduct, but Blomberg supported Sperrle and Hitler refused to interfere. In July things reached the breaking point when Sperrle refused to see Faupel when the ambassador called on the general at his quarters. Faupel reported the impossible state of affairs to the Foreign Ministry, only to discover that his own tenure was coming to an end. Habituated as he was to South American political intrigue, and persuaded by his experience that aristocrats did not make good Fascist revolutionaries, Faupel most undiplomatically showed his preference for the working-class radical wing of the Falange. Soon he was *persona non grata* with Franco, who quietly asked Berlin to recall him.

Faupel was replaced by a career diplomat, Eberhard von Stohrer, who as a junior official had served in the German Embassy in Madrid during the First World War. Meanwhile Admiral Canaris had recommended that Sperrle should also be replaced; his successor, on November 1, was General Helmuth Volkmann.

On October 25, Stohrer reported his "preliminary impressions" in Nationalist Spain, advising Berlin that, while the military situation was "very favorable," the war was far from won and would surely continue well into 1938. Unlike Mussolini, however, Hitler showed no inclination to augment the Condor Legion so as to ensure a Nationalist victory. Although the war was taken seriously, the attitude in Berlin was much more relaxed than in Rome. Hitler's objectives had remained the same as they were at the beginning: to prevent Communist domination of Spain and exploit the opportunity to test the Wehrmacht under combat conditions.

Furthermore, the German operation in Spain continued to be conducted on a very low key. Hitler was not ready for war, and was almost as anxious as the British to prevent the conflict from spreading. Nor did he feel the need of military triumph to bolster the Nazi regime at home. Consequently there was no chest-thumping in the press, and no celebrations, as there were in Italy after Santander.

But as Mussolini's involvement in Spain deepened and Italy's relations with Britain and France worsened, Berlin's attitude toward the conflict began to change. In a memorandum dated July 4, 1937, Ernst von Weizsaecker, Director of the Political Department of the Foreign Ministry, took note of the increasing diplomatic tensions resulting from Italy's open and massive support of the Nationalists, and declared that Germany's "goal now should be rather the prevention of general conflict than the unconditional and complete victory of the Franco party in the Spanish Civil War."

Weizsaecker was a conservative, professional diplomat and no Hitler-idolator, and it may be assumed that his purpose in writing was to warn against the risk of a war for which Germany was ill-prepared. But his disparagement of the importance to Germany of a "complete" Franco victory is suggestive. Would Nazi interests be better served by a continuation of the Spanish Civil War than by a speedy Nationalist triumph? The war was increasing Italy's dependence on Germany, and shifting the focus of international tensions to the Mediterranean. Would not this tend to enlarge Germany's freedom of action in Central Europe —in Austria, at least, and perhaps elsewhere?

On September 30, 1937, the day after Mussolini left Berlin to return to Italy, the German Foreign Ministry sent a confidential telegram to all the German diplomatic missions in Europe describing the Duce's visit. The two dictators were said to have agreed that "an early end of the Spanish Civil War and the reconstruction of Spain is urgently desired by both parties," and to have refrained from any discussions "which Austria could consider dangerous or impinging upon her independence." But these unexceptionable sentiments were coupled with mutual acknowledgments that reflected the realities of their relation: in Spain, "the interests and potentialities of Italy will have due preference and, quite generally, Italy will not be impeded by Germany in the Mediterranean"; whereas "on the other hand, the special German interests in Austria will not be impaired by Italy."

For the immediate development of German diplomatic and military policy, accordingly, there was a close relation between the Spanish Civil War and the Austrian question. An Italy mired in Spain and at odds with Britain and France would be most unlikely to reassert the role of defender of Austrian independence which she had played in 1934 at the time of Dollfuss' assassination. And Britain and France, disturbed by Mussolini's threat to their sea lanes in the Mediterranean, would be far from eager to go to war for Austria without Italian help.

Whether or not Hitler ever consciously drew precisely these inferences, it is certain that by November 1937 he had come to view the Spanish Civil War not primarily as an anti-Communist crusade or a handy military proving ground, but as a feature of the European scene which could be turned to Germany's strategic advantage. This is made plain by the record of the famous and much-debated "Hossbach" conference of November 5, 1937, to the substance and significance of which we now turn.

CHAPTER 13

November 5, 1937:
The "Hossbach" Conference

1

On January 30, 1937, Adolf Hitler marked the completion of four years as Chancellor with a long speech to the Reichstag. He formally repudiated Germany's signature with respect to the clause of the Versailles Treaty that laid on her the burden of guilt for causing the First World War, and gave thanks to "Providence, whose grace has enabled me, once an unknown soldier in the war, to bring to a successful issue the struggle for our honor and rights as a nation." He spoke, too, of the lost German colonies and the Germans abroad, "forced to live as a minority within other nations." But the speech as a whole was pacific in tone and the Fuehrer dramatically reassured the world: "The epoch of surprises is over! Peace is our highest aim!"

Throughout 1937, Hitler was as good as his word, and in any chronology of European events it looks like an uneventful year compared to 1935 (Versailles), 1936 (Rhineland), and 1938 (Austria and Sudetenland). But, as the two preceding chapters should have made clear, 1937 was a year of great military and diplomatic significance. Indeed, Germany's immediately effective military power probably grew more rapidly in 1937 than in any other year.

It was also the year in which awareness of the pace and scale of German rearmament, and awareness that in all likelihood war would ultimately ensue, began to spread beyond a handful of high officials and Hitler's personal entourage. In December 1936, at the time Mussolini was sending and Faupel was urging massive military aid to Franco, Hermann Goering—newly in the saddle as boss of the German war economy, displacing Schacht—delivered himself of two speeches to highly select audiences, plainly intended to create an atmosphere of war emergency. Addressing his principal Luftwaffe staff officers on December 2, Goering (according to the telegraph-style notes kept by Goering's aide, General Karl Bodenschatz) declared:

> World press aroused over landing of 5000 German volunteers in Spain. Official complaint by England in association with France. . . .
> The general situation is very serious. . . . Accordingly, the order is: from today, highest state of operational preparedness, regardless of financial difficulties. . . .
> We are already at war, it's only that as yet there is no shooting. . . .

Two weeks later, Goering was addressing an assemblage of some one hundred tycoons of German industry, and preaching the same sermon with the same conclusion:

> The battle we are approaching demands a colossal measure of productive capacity. No end of rearmament can be visualized. The only alternatives are victory or destruction. . . . Our whole nation is at stake. We live at a time when the final battle is in sight. We are already on the threshold of mobilization and are at war. All that is lacking is the shooting.

With few exceptions, the German industrialists responded to these exhortations with energy, ingenuity, and enthusiasm. The steel plants of the Ruhr poured out guns and tanks, making extensive use of designs developed by the Krupp firm years earlier. Scientists of the great I. G. Farben Chemicals combine had developed during the late twenties the techniques for producing gasoline from low-grade coals, and under the Nazi regime their production facilities were greatly expanded. Gasoline and rubber from natural sources would not be readily available to Germany in the event of war and both commodities were, of course, essential to the Air Force and to the Army's mobile units. By 1935, Farben had devised a process for the synthesization of "buna" rubber of good quality from coal and grain alcohol, and in 1936 it began construction of a huge synthetic rubber plant at Schkopau.

It is virtually impossible to overstate the military importance of the Farben processes for synthetic gasoline and rubber, and it was in 1936 and 1937 that the hopes for effective exploitation of these inventions became reality and alleviated German fears of blockade. Naturally, Farben executives and other industrial leaders were increasingly drawn into close contact with the armed services and government economic planning agencies. Many took official positions, for example Carl Krauch of I. G. Farben, who took charge of research and development on Goering's Four Year Plan staff. In March 1937, Blomberg as War Minister established a "leadership corps" of industrialists, to each of whom he gave the title "Defense Economy Leader" (*Wehrwirtschaftsführer*) and whose role he described as follows:

> The war economy leaders shall be the responsible collaborators of the Wehrmacht in preparing and carrying out the mobilization of the armament industry in the conduct of the war. Their significance, their tasks and duties in connection with rearmament place them in a position corresponding approximately to that of reserve officers on active duty.

Goering and Blomberg were Hitler's two principal deputies for all matters pertaining to war—the former as Plenipotentiary for War Economy and Air Minister, and the latter as War Minister and Commander-in-Chief of the Wehrmacht. We may safely assume, therefore, that these bellicose speeches and screeds accurately reflected the temper with which the Fuehrer wished the military and industrial leaders of the country to be infused.

Up to this time, however, there had been no sign of any official program of

military action, other than the small Spanish involvement, which could be characterized as aggressive or anything but defensive. Indeed, Blomberg's directives
as Commander-in-Chief quite explicitly renounced any aggressive designs.

Blomberg's "Directive 1937/38" is worth careful scrutiny, especially since it
was his last, and covers the period during which he was dismissed and Hitler assumed direct command of the Wehrmacht. Classified secret, and with copies distributed only to the three service chiefs and Blomberg's own deputy, General
Keitel, it was dated June 24, 1937, and was entitled "Directive for the unified
preparation of the armed forces for war." It bore a statement that it would be
in effect from July 1, 1937, until "probably" September 30, 1938.*

The directive was in three parts, the first of which was entitled "General
Guiding Principles," and began as follows:

> The *general political situation* justifies the presumption that Germany need
> not anticipate an attack from any quarter. Indications of this are, primarily,
> the lack of desire for war in almost all nations, particularly the Western
> powers, and also the unpreparedness for war of a number of states, and of
> Russia in particular.
>
> The intention to unleash a European War is entertained just as little by
> Germany.
>
> Nevertheless the politically fluid world situation, which does not preclude
> surprising incidents, demands constant preparedness for war on the part of
> the German Wehrmacht:
> (a) to counter-attack at any time,
> (b) and to make possible the military exploitation of favorable circum-
> stances should they arise.
>
> The Wehrmacht's preparations for a possible war during the mobilization-
> period 1937/38 must be made with these possibilities in mind. . . .

Part 2 of the directive was entitled "Probable War Contingencies," and
comprised two such eventualities, each based on the hypothesis of simultaneous
attacks on Germany from both east and west. The first assumed a surprise
French attack, in which case the Wehrmacht would deploy its principal strength
in the west and go on the defensive in the east; the plan to meet this attack was
given the cover name "Red," and was known in German staff circles as *"Fall
Rot"* (Eventuality Red). The second plan—*"Fall Gruen"* (Eventuality Green)
—envisaged "a surprise German operation against Czechoslovakia in order to
parry the imminent attack of a superior enemy coalition," presumably including
France, Russia, and Czechoslovakia. For this purpose, only a light screen of
troops would be left in the west to hold against a French attack, while the
bulk of the German forces would speedily overrun Bohemia and Moravia, thus

---

* This is the day that the Munich Agreement was signed; the coincidence is enticing but
meaningless. The qualification "probably" indicated the possibility that events might require
an earlier replacement of the directive.
The covering letter shows that there had been a like directive issued on June 26, 1936,
superseded by the new one. I have not seen the 1936 version. There had been earlier Wehrmacht directives for special situations: the *"Schulung"* directive of May 2, 1935 (see p.
101), a "Directive for the Armed Forces in case of Sanctions," issued October 25, 1935, at
the time when the League was in the process of imposing sanctions on Italy, and the directive of March 2, 1936, for the entry of Army and Air Force units into the Rhineland.

depriving Russia of air bases and eliminating "for the duration of the war" any "threat by Czechoslovakia to the rear of operations in the west."

The third and final part was called "Special Preparations," and embraced three separate contingencies, of which only the first* is presently interesting. It dealt with Austria. Otto, the Hapsburg Pretender, was growing up and getting his name in the papers. The thought of a renascent Hapsburg Empire was as unwelcome to Hitler and the generals as it would have been to any German nationalist regime. Otto's name was now used as a cover word for "armed intervention" in order "to compel Austria by force to give up a restoration." Such a contingency, the directive warned, might arise either separately, or in conjunction with "Red," or as a prelude to "Green."

If Blomberg's directive was not precisely a platform for world federalism, neither did it project any imminent threat to world peace. To be sure, the opening reference to "military exploitation of favorable opportunities" manifested a willingness to use the Wehrmacht for aggrandizement if the circumstances were propitious for gain without too much risk. In its entirety, however, the directive was defensive rather than aggressive in tone, and proposed no adventures for the fifteen-month period which it covered.

This document had, however, a significance quite independent of its content, relating to a fundamental issue on which there was deep division of opinion between Blomberg and Fritsch. Germany was confronting the same problems of command that were facing the military establishments of other countries, in most of which army and navy had remained separate entities, fiercely independent of each other, and responsible only to a higher civilian authority, whether ministerial, royal, or presidential. But with the advent of air power during the First World War, the need for interservice co-ordination grew much more acute and provoked endless debate about the wisdom of establishing a *military* command and general staff over the three services.

In Germany the Army was and always had been the dominant military service; the Navy was a poor relation, and the Luftwaffe an upstart. For all Goering's brashness, his air force was designed primarily for tactical support of the Army rather than independent strategic employment. Under these circumstances, it was natural that the Army leaders should assert the right to leadership in the event of war, and bitterly oppose the creation of any superior military authority.

Accordingly, Blomberg's unprecedented designation in 1935 as Commander-in-Chief of the Armed Forces was exceedingly unwelcome to the Army leadership. Fritsch and his chief of staff, General Ludwig Beck, were strongly of the opinion that Blomberg's role should be restricted to that of a civilian minister of war; the idea of a "General Staff of the Wehrmacht" was anathema to them, and they bitterly opposed Blomberg's efforts to use his title, and the staff of RKM, so as to assert command authority over the Army.

During 1937, these differences led to several explosive situations. In January,

---

* The second, called "Richard," was the possibility of war with "Red Spain," and no doubt was stimulated by the recent *Deutschland* and *Leipzig* episodes. The third was entitled "Extension Red/Green," and dealt with the possibility that England, Poland, and Lithuania might be part of the hostile coalition.

Fritsch, enraged because he was not consulted with regard to the selection of a wartime supreme commander, threatened to resign, and was dissuaded only by promises of better treatment in the future. Two months later Blomberg proposed to hold maneuvers involving all three services under his supervision, and once again Fritsch flared with resentment against the use of RKM for operational purposes.

The directive of June 1937, as another assertion of Blomberg's authority, was bound to rekindle the fire at OKH. Keitel, whom Blomberg had assigned to draft the directive, had been on good terms with both Fritsch and Beck and now, in an effort to placate them, he took his draft to OKH and submitted it for Beck's review. His propitiatory gesture went for nothing; Beck told Keitel that the Army had no intention of undertaking any "preparations" for the various contingencies described in the directive. When it was finally issued, according to Keitel, "the Army General Staff proceeded to bury the directive in a safe somewhere, and took *no* action whatsoever."

In August, Fritsch renewed the battle with a long memorandum on "Organization of the Wehrmacht High Command and Leadership of the Wehrmacht in Wartime," prepared by the OKH chief of operations, General Erich von Manstein. When Blomberg read it, he covered his copy with marginal question marks and exclamation points. On September 1 in private conference with Fritsch, he rejected the latter's proposed limitations on his authority.*

Within the higher circles of the Army, there was general approval of Fritsch's views, while Blomberg and his small circle of supporters at the War Ministry were widely regarded as apostates from the true Army doctrine. But if Fritsch spoke for the generals, Blomberg spoke in the name and with the authority of the Fuehrer and Supreme Commander. Up to this time, Hitler had not involved himself in these organizational and command issues, and had been cautious about openly challenging the generals. But the winds of change were blowing with increasing strength, and on November 5, 1937, Hitler—the Hitler of *Mein Kampf*—finally spoke.

2

The combined forces maneuvers so distasteful to OKH were held late in September, and were viewed by Hitler, Mussolini, and numerous other distinguished invitees. During October, Hitler spent much of his time at the Berghof, where he received visits from the Aga Khan and the Duke of Windsor. He returned to Berlin during the last week of October to find a number of matters pressing for his attention, including Italy's adherence to the Anti-Comintern Pact, increasing awkwardness resulting from the new affinity with Japan while a German military mission remained with Chiang Kai-shek, and finalization of a treaty with Poland for the protection of national minorities. Ribbentrop was sent to Rome, where he signed the new Anti-Comintern Pact on November 6,

---

* On this copy of the Fritsch memorandum, Blomberg wrote a short note summarizing the conference. Despite the depth of the conceptual disagreement, the conference was apparently amicable. Blomberg gave assurance that he would not use his authority to "go over Fritsch's head," and both agreed on the desirability of more frequent meetings—an intention which events soon rendered academic.

1937, Blomberg was admonished on November 4 that "the War Ministry should undertake to rid itself of the reputation of having a pro-China attitude," and the treaty with Poland was signed on the morning of November 5, with Hitler's personal assurances to the Polish Ambassador, Jozef Lipski, that Danzig would remain inviolate and Polish rights there would be respected.

That afternoon, at a meeting in the Reich Chancellery which lasted more than four hours, Hitler first addressed and then engaged in discussion a group consisting of the Foreign Minister, Neurath, and the four military commanders-in-chief: Blomberg, Fritsch, Goering, and Raeder. Also present was Hitler's military adjutant, Colonel Friedrich Hossbach; he took notes on the proceedings, and a few days later used them as the basis of a memorandum on the conference.

This is the only surviving record of the meeting which, accordingly, is commonly referred to by Hossbach's name.* However, the German records also contain a copy of a note dated November 5 from Blomberg to Fritsch, Raeder, and Goering, confirming the meeting with the Fuehrer for four o'clock that afternoon, and directing each of them to have available in the Chancellery at half-past five an officer "informed in detail on the armament situation and raw materials requirements of his particular branch." In accordance with these instructions General Liese and Admiral Witzell (the Army and Navy chiefs of ordnance) and General Udet from the Luftwaffe, each accompanied by several juniors, were at the Chancellery during the later part of the meeting.

Hitler first explained that the subject for discussion was so important that he had decided against bringing it before the full Cabinet. What he had to say should "be regarded, in case of his death, as his last will and testament."

He launched at once into a favorite subject: *Lebensraum.* German economic and demographic problems, Hitler reasoned, could not be solved either by autarky, since there were only limited possibilities of self-sufficiency in raw materials and none at all in foodstuffs, or by increased international trade, because of market fluctuations and British domination of the sea lanes. Therefore, the only solution "lay in the acquisition of greater living space." Overseas colonies would not do; "areas producing raw materials can more usefully be sought in proximity to the Reich than overseas." There was an echo of Haushoferian geopolitics:† "The German people with its strong racial core would find the most favorable prerequisites for . . . achievement in the heart of the European continent."

The question for Germany, accordingly, was "where could she achieve the greatest gain at the lowest cost." German policy would have to reckon with "two hate-inspired antagonists, Britain and France, to whom a German colossus in central Europe was a thorn in the flesh." But the British Empire was not

---

* The document itself is often called the "Hossbach protocol." This is a misnomer, as the memorandum had no official authority, and was never signed or approved by any of those present other than Hossbach, who actually entitled the document *"Niederschrift,"* perhaps best translated as "notes."

† Hitler had in fact known Karl Haushofer and his theories since the early Nazi days in Munich.

"unshakable," and France was confronting "internal political difficulties." In any event:

> Germany's problem could only be solved by means of force and this was never without attendant risk. The campaigns of Frederick the Great for Silesia and Bismarck's war against Austria and France had involved unheard of risk, and it was the swiftness of Prussian action in 1870 which had kept Austria out of the war. If one accepts as basic . . . the resort to force with its attendant risks, then there remains to be answered the questions "when" and "how."

As guides to the answer, Hitler postulated three possible situations. The first assumed that no unusual opportunities for military action would arise during the next several years, in which case Germany should act at the time when her military strength would be at maximum. By 1943–45, her rearmament would be at peak efficiency; thereafter, weapons presently being produced in quantity would become obsolescent, and the secrecy of "special weapons" would be comprised.* Furthermore, the economic strain of supporting a large army would lower both the standard of living and the birthrate, and the Nazi movement and its leaders would age. If he lived so long, said Hitler, it would be "his unalterable resolve to solve the German space problem no later than 1943–45."

But opportunity might knock much sooner. The second possible situation was that "internal strife in France might develop into such a domestic crisis as to absorb the French Army completely and render it incapable of use for war against Germany." In that event, the time for action against Czechoslovakia would have come. The third situation also involved France, and the possibility that she might become "so embroiled in war with another state that she cannot proceed against Germany."

In these circumstances, whether imminent or after 1943, who were the intended victims of German power? On this score Hitler left no room for doubt:

> For the improvement of our politico-military position our first objective, in the event of our being embroiled in war, must be to overthrow Czechoslovakia and Austria simultaneously in order to remove the threat to our flank. . . . If the Czechs were overthrown and a common German-Hungarian frontier achieved, a neutral attitude on the part of Poland could be more certainly counted on in the event of a Franco-German conflict. . . . The incorporation of these two states with Germany meant, from the politico-military point of view, a substantial advantage because it would mean shorter and better frontiers, the freeing of forces for other purposes, and the possibility of creating new troops up to 12 divisions, that is, one division per million inhabitants.

---

* Probably this is a reference to forerunners of the V-2 rockets used against London in 1944. With the support of both Army and Luftwaffe, the experimental rocket station at Peenemünde, on the Baltic Sea, was established in 1936 and 1937. The late General Franz Halder informed me that he had witnessed experiments with the propellant fuel for V-2s in 1938, and his diary entry for September 26, 1939, refers to long-range rockets, with a one-ton explosive charge, under development at Peenemünde and probably ready for use in three to four years.

As for the risk of intervention by the other great powers, if a planned attack were carried out in 1943–45, Hitler thought that in all probability England, and perhaps France as well, "had already tacitly written off the Czechs." Italy would not object to eliminating the Czechs, but "it was impossible at the moment to estimate what her attitude on the Austrian question would be, as that depended on whether the Duce were still alive." Russia moved slowly, and Japan's attitude would make her intervention "more than doubtful."

But Hitler was laying great store by his third possibility, and hoping that the Spanish Civil War and the resultant tensions in the Mediterranean might lead to hostilities among Italy, France, and Britain. And at this point he enlarged on the views expressed by Weizsaecker the preceding July:

> From the German standpoint, a 100 per cent victory for Franco was not desirable; rather we were interested in a continuance of the war and in keeping up the tension in the Mediterranean. Franco in undisputed possession of the Spanish peninsula precluded the possibility of . . . the Italians' . . . continued occupation of the Balearic Islands. But the permanent establishment of the Italians on the Balearics . . . might lead to a war of France and England against Italy.

On the basis of speculations which his military auditors must have thought fanciful, Hitler declared that the possibility of Italy's defeat in a war with Britain and France was slight. If, in its course, Germany undertook to settle the Czech and Austrian questions, the likelihood of interference from the western powers could be heavily discounted. In the event of such a war, Hitler "was resolved to take advantage of it whenever it happened, even as early as 1938" in order to "carry through the campaign against the Czechs . . . with lightning speed."

A general discussion ensued to which, so far as appears from Hossbach's record, Admiral Raeder did not contribute. None of the others raised objections to Hitler's exposition of the need for *Lebensraum* or his specification of 1943–45 as the ultimate time for action, but his third possibility—of a Franco-British war with Italy, to be exploited by Germany in the near future—came under sharp criticism from Blomberg, Fritsch, and Neurath. The two Army men "stated that the French Army would not be so committed by the war with Italy that France could not simultaneously enter the field with forces superior to ours on our western frontier." Fritsch thought France would need only twenty divisions on her Alpine frontier with Italy, leaving her enough other strength to invade the Rhineland. Blomberg stressed the weakness of the German fortifications in the west, contrasted with the "strength of the Czech fortifications which had now acquired a structure like a Maginot Line which would gravely hamper our attack." Both stressed the necessity that Germany not find herself at war with both Britain and France, whereat Hitler repeated his earlier predictions that Britain would not interfere and that France could not fight without British support. Neurath objected that "an Anglo-French-Italian conflict was not so proximate as Hitler appeared to assume," to which Hitler replied that the summer of 1938 seemed to him a possible time.

However, none of the objectors refused to go along with Hitler's program.

Fritsch disclosed that he had ordered his staff (apparently in pursuance of the "Green" contingency in Blomberg's June directive) "to examine the possibility of conducting operations against the Czechs with special reference to overcoming the Czech fortification system." He also "expressed the opinion that under existing circumstances he must give up his plan to go abroad on his leave, which was due to begin on November 10," but Hitler "dismissed this idea on the ground that the possibility of a conflict need not yet be regarded as so imminent." Goering suggested that "in view of the Fuehrer's statement we should consider terminating our military undertakings in Spain," and with this Hitler agreed in principle, but reserved decision until "the appropriate moment."

The final sentence of Hossbach's memorandum states: "The second part of the conference dealt with specific questions of armament." A decade later he explained his failure to record this part on the ground that it was an unexpected expansion of the discussion into a technical area not usually brought up at the Reich Chancellery. Perhaps some or all of the lesser figures summoned in accordance with Blomberg's memorandum were called in.

Quite likely it was during this "second part" of the meeting that, according to Hossbach's later recollection, a sharp altercation took place between Blomberg and Fritsch on one side and Goering on the other, with Hitler as an "attentive listener," in the course of which Blomberg mercilessly criticized Goering's administration of the Four Year Plan. At the end of the meeting, Hitler grabbed his own notes and departed before Hossbach could ask to use them as the basis for his memorandum, and subsequently, despite repeated urgings, refused to find time to review his adjutant's memorandum.

3

The conference of November 5, 1937, was the first of several, of which records have survived, at which Hitler disclosed to a group of his executants his intention to use military force for specified conquests. Hossbach's memorandum was introduced in evidence at the first Nuremberg trial, and the Tribunal relied on it heavily to support its conclusion that the German leaders planned aggressive wars, and that those present "knew that Austria and Czechoslovakia would be annexed by Germany at the first opportunity."

Others have attributed to the meeting an even deeper and more ominous significance. To William L. Shirer this was a "fateful" meeting at which Hitler "communicated his irrevocable decision to go to war." Sir John Wheeler-Bennett has called Hitler's statements "a blue-print for aggression," while the German historian Walter Görlitz interprets them as plainly indicating "his wish for another war."

These interpretations have not gone unchallenged, and those who have pronounced the conference a much less significant affair include not only historians but some of the participants as well. Furthermore, the reliability of Hossbach's memorandum has been critically viewed.

The provenance of the document is, to be sure, less than fully satisfactory. Hossbach's original memorandum has not come to light; the document produced at Nuremberg purports to be a copy typed several years later, and when Hossbach was shown it during the Nuremberg trial he was unable to swear that it was a true copy of his original. But he also expressed the opinion, based on the document's organization, style, and other details, that it is indeed a reproduction of his original memorandum. There is little reason to doubt that the Nuremberg document is at least an approximately accurate copy of what Hossbach wrote.

But there remains the question, how accurate a rendition of the proceedings is Hossbach's memorandum?* It makes no pretense of being a verbatim record, and is obviously incomplete. "As I had no stenographic skill," Hossbach later wrote, "I could not make a literal or complete rendition of the conference. In the nature of the case, the memorandum was primarily intended to have the fullest possible account of Hitler's remarks, while the discussion was treated more briefly, and, because of the excitement aroused by statements and contradictions, I was unable to use the key-words on which later to base a truthful reproduction."

On the face of the memorandum it appears that the portion devoted to Hitler's exposition is well organized and full, while the description of what must, considering the length of the document compared to the duration of the meeting, have been a long discussion is very sketchy. It is, in any event, reassuring that none of the five participants in the conference who survived the war and saw the Nuremberg document challenged its general accuracy, even though the three who were defendants at the trial, accused of complicity in aggressive warmaking, might well have been moved to do so.†

But at Nuremberg two of the three—Goering and Raeder—did indeed attack, not the validity of the document, but the significance of the conference itself. Goering, after pointing to the possibility of error in Hossbach's rendition, testified that Hitler told him, just before the meeting, that its purpose was "to put pressure on General von Fritsch, since he [Hitler] was dissatisfied with the rearmament of the Army," and that "it would not do any harm if Herr von Blomberg would also exercise a certain amount of pressure on von Fritsch." Neurath was to be present because Hitler "did not want things to look too military." Raeder testified that the conference did not alarm him, partly because he was accustomed to Hitler's manner of exaggerated speech, and also because Goering and Blomberg both told him that Hitler's purpose was to "spur on the

---

* The memorandum is dated November 10, and it has been wrongly assumed that this establishes a five-day gap between the meeting and Hossbach's writing. Hossbach himself could not remember whether he wrote the memorandum on the sixth or later. Since, as he tells us, he was unsuccessfully attempting to persuade Hitler to review the document, it is not surprising that the date was not put on until later, when Hossbach finally delivered the paper to Blomberg.

† Fritsch died in Poland in 1939, and Hitler in his Berlin bunker in April 1945. Blomberg died early in 1946; at Nuremberg he was questioned about the meeting, and the bulk of the Hossbach memorandum was read to him. He stated that he had heard Hitler express like ideas on earlier occasions, but "not connected up like this," that the "other officers present" thought the presentation "rather fantastic," and that the only reason for taking the matter seriously was that Hitler spoke of the probability of war in 1943–45, which he had not done before.

Army to carry out its rearmament somewhat faster," and that the occasion "was not to be judged so seriously."

The third Nuremberg defendant-participant gave a diametrically opposite account. Neurath testified that he was "extremely upset" by Hitler's speech because he realized for the first time that "the whole tendency of his plans was of an aggressive nature."* Two days later he conferred with Fritsch and Beck, and it was agreed that Fritsch, "who was due to report to Hitler in the next few days, should explain to him all the military considerations which made his policy inadvisable," and that Neurath would subsequently "explain the political reasons to him." However, Neurath had no opportunity to do this until mid-January, and then met with no success, whereupon he insisted on resigning as Foreign Minister, and "on 4 February he granted my release without further comment."

Of course, none of the three statements was disinterested. It was very much to Neurath's advantage to convey the impression that, as soon he became aware of Hitler's warlike plans, he resigned. For Goering and Raeder, who did not resign, on the other hand, it was desirable to play down the significance of the episode, so as to explain why they were not alerted to the Fuehrer's aggressive intentions. Furthermore, assuming (as may well be the fact) that Goering and Blomberg sought to quiet Raeder's fears, that too is very understandable, since Raeder's fear of war with England was well known to both of them, and the Navy would not need to prepare for hostilities limited to landlocked Austria and Czechoslovakia.

However, the historical significance of the Hossbach conference has also had its detractors among historians. Hitler's biographer Alan Bullock concludes that the Fuehrer's purpose was not "to announce some newly conceived decision to commit Germany to a course deliberately aimed at war," but only "to override the doubts about the pace of rearmament expressed by General Fritsch, and earlier by Schacht." A. J. P. Taylor's disparagement is more pungent:†

Hitler aimed to isolate Schacht from the other Conservatives; and he had therefore to win them for a program of increased armaments. His geopolitical exposition had no other purpose. The Hossbach memorandum itself provides evidence of this. Its last paragraph reads: "The second part of the conference was concerned with questions of armament." This, no doubt, was why it had been called.

If this is an accurate exegesis, it is more than strange that Dr. Schacht is nowhere mentioned in the memorandum, and that Hossbach made no effort to record the only important part of the meeting. It is an implausible interpretation, and Taylor's supporting analysis is so marred by misconceptions, er-

---

* Neurath's counsel submitted an affidavit from Neurath's "distant relative" Baroness Ritter of Munich, stating that, as a result of the meeting, Neurath "was so severely shaken that he suffered several heart attacks." Neurath himself did not so testify, but his counsel obviously hoped that the Tribunal would credit the Baroness' story.

† Bullock appears to have been influenced by Taylor, as the first edition of his Hitler biography, published in 1952, contains no such, or any comparable, passage (pp. 338–39). In this particular, it appears to me that the first edition is the closer to the truth.

rors, and omissions* that it cannot be taken seriously, which perhaps he never intended that it should be. By the time of the meeting Schacht had lost his struggle with Goering, and it was quite unnecessary and would have been quite out of character for Hitler to spend four hours with this group merely to show that Schacht was wrong.

Because Hitler's second and third "eventualities"—civil strife in France or a Franco-British-Italian war—did not come to pass, Taylor describes Hitler's exposition as "in large part day-dreaming." Speculators who misjudge the future course of the stock market are mistaken, but not on that account dreamers. Given the domestic tensions in France, and Italy's submarine operations in the Mediterranean, in the fall of 1937 these possibilities were not absurdly remote. Anyhow, in projecting these two hypotheses, Hitler certainly did not mean to exclude other favorable contingencies, not yet forseeable, which might arise. The burden of his song was that the Wehrmacht must be made ready to strike quickly should opportunity knock.

Of course, the import of the Hossbach meeting has been overstated.† Hitler offered nothing so precise as a "blueprint for aggression," but rather a general strategic orientation. Nor was there a decision "to go to war," as Shirer and Görlitz put it, since war might be avoided. But there was, indisputably, a decision to go to war *if necessary* and at the most propitious moment—a decision to use military force, or the threat of military force, for the annexation of Austria and Czechoslovakia, by 1943–45 at the latest, and sooner if it could be done without serious risk of war with Britain and France.

Certainly that is the way Hitler's auditors viewed the meeting, as its immediate aftermath shows. Nothing that had been decided called for any immediate action by the Navy or the Foreign Ministry, but elsewhere there was instant activity, and considerable disagreement on what course to follow. Some of this is reflected in Jodl's diary entry for November 5, which must have been written

---

* Taylor describes the gathering as a "curious" one because, except for Goering, the participants were not "Nazis" and Hitler "knew that all except Goering were his opponents, and he did not trust Goering much." This is a wholly mistaken characterization. Blomberg dared to differ with Hitler in private but never opposed his decisions and, by his own confession, was completely under Hitler's spell—so much so that scornful fellow-officers called him "the rubber lion" and "Hitler Boy Quex." Raeder's relations with Hitler at that time were excellent. Hitler was not a trusting soul, but in 1937 he certainly trusted Goering with wider responsibilities than anyone else. He had less rapport with Fritsch and Neurath than with the others, but neither could be called an opponent of his regime.

In any event, if a high level discussion of the military outlook was to be held, these were the responsible individuals. At Nuremberg, Goering disclosed that the same group had met on several prior occasions: when Germany left the League of Nations, when rearmament was publicly announced, and when the Rhineland was remilitarized.

† In his book (at p. 134) A. J. P. Taylor decries "the view that there is nothing to be discovered about the origins of the Second World War," since "Hitler . . . decided on war, and planned it in detail on 5 November, 1937." He does not tell us who holds such a view, and I am aware of no such farfetched claims in print.

The jump from the late Thomas Reed Powell, of the Harvard Law School, to A. J. P. Taylor, of Magdalen College, Oxford, is long, but anyone who makes it must be struck by the extraordinary resemblance between their literary styles. It is a crisp, effective, and often amusing style. Powell was meticulously accurate and a rigorous analyst.

after Blomberg had returned from the Chancellery and discussed what had transpired with Keitel and perhaps others:

> The Fuehrer unfolds to the Commanders-in-Chief of the Wehrmacht, Army, Navy, and Luftwaffe, as well as the Foreign Minister, his thoughts on the future development, purposes and leadership of state policy.
> There is a divergence in the reporting of his ideas between what the *Chef WA* [Keitel] was told by Blomberg and what Goering told the Chief of the Luftwaffe General Staff (no protocol was made).
> My intention is to put some thoughts on paper and submit them to the branches of the Wehrmacht and also to work on deployment orders.

But at OKH headquarters on the Bendlerstrasse there was no such alacrity to put the Fuehrer's designs into execution. It may be, as Neurath testified, that Fritsch reopened the discussion with Hitler prior to Fritsch's departure for a vacation in Egypt, but this is uncertain. General Beck, however, was greatly alarmed when he read Hossbach's memorandum, and by November 12 had written a lengthy critique of Hitler's presentation. Major territorial changes in Europe, he declared, could not be accomplished without great upset and the probability of war with Britain and France, and Hitler had insufficiently reckoned with Russia as a power factor. The notion that war must be resorted to no later than 1943-45 Beck characterized as "superficial," and the possibility of France's internal collapse "wishful thinking." As for a Franco-Italian war, that would not divert French strength sufficiently to justify a German adventure, and annexing Austria and Czechoslovakia would not greatly augment German strength.

What, if any, distribution Beck gave to his memorandum is not known. During Fritsch's absence he was reporting directly to Blomberg, but there is no record or recollection that Beck pressed his views there, and Hitler had gone to the Berghof. At the War Ministry, however, the work continued,* and in mid-December, Blomberg issued a supplement to his directive of June 24, giving effect to the conclusions at the Hossbach conference.

The new directive† stated that the foreign situation had developed in such a way that "Case Green" (the plan for a lightning invasion of Austria and Czechoslovakia) was now much more important than "Red," since, according

---

* The seriousness with which Blomberg regarded the discussions at the Hossbach conference is reflected in a memorandum which he sent to the three service commanders-in-chief on November 18, 1937, telling them that Ambassador François-Poncet had learned of it the next day and transmitted the news to Paris. Blomberg appended a list of all the some fifteen Army, Navy, and Air Force officers who had been waiting in the Reich Chancellery while the conference was in progress, and requested inquiry and report by November 24. The replies from the Navy indicated that many military and civilian officials, mostly connected with budget and procurement matters, had been waiting in the "smoking-room," and could have well been told or overheard details of the conference when the participants departed. Raeder added that François-Poncet and Goering had both been at an international gathering of the Hunting Exposition later that evening. François-Poncet's memoirs do not mention the episode.

† The supplemental directive is dated December 7, 1937, and Jodl's diary entry for December 12 states that the Fuehrer had approved it. On December 21, 1937, Keitel distributed two appendices, the first of which dealt with the possibility of a two-front war against France and Czechoslovakia.

to the Fuehrer's orders, the objectives of such a war had expanded. The three services were admonished to make no assumption that there would in fact be a war in 1938, but were instructed to abandon all undertakings that would interfere with the enlargement or mobilization of the Wehrmacht, and that "the main focus of all mobilization and deployment exercises should now be 'Eventuality Green.'"

Three months after the conference of November 5 Blomberg, Fritsch, and Neurath were all out of office. It would be easy to infer that their opposition at the meeting was the direct cause of their downfall. Especially in the case of Blomberg, this may well be an oversimplification. Beyond question, however, the impressions that Hitler gathered at this meeting were a powerful contributing factor in the political convulsion which was about to grip the Third Reich.

CHAPTER 14

The Fuehrer Takes Command

1

Soon after the Hossbach conference Hitler returned to the Berghof, where he remained for some days. Here, on November 19, 1937, came Edward Lord Halifax, Lord President of the Council in the British Cabinet, and close friend and adviser to Neville Chamberlain, for luncheon and a long talk with the Fuehrer.

Although many prominent Britishers had made the pilgrimage to Hitler during the past two years, no Cabinet minister had visited him since Simon and Eden in March 1935. Halifax, however, was not Foreign Secretary and did not come in an official capacity. The lordly Yorkshireman was a fanatical devotee of the chase, and as Master of the Middleton Hounds had received an invitation from Hermann Goering as *Reichsjägermeister,* to attend the International Hunting Exposition to be held in Berlin during the first three weeks of November.

The invitation reached Halifax early in October, together with informal assurances that an interview with Hitler could be arranged. It was productive of some friction in London. Eden, from his own account, "was not eager, but saw no sufficient reason to oppose it," since "I was sure that Lord Halifax wanted to go and thought it probable that the Prime Minister would have the same sentiments." Neville Chamberlain, indeed, was delighted with the project, and Ambassador Henderson was instructed to arrange the schedule so as to include a meeting with Hitler in Berlin during the Hunting Exposition.

It now developed, however, that the Fuehrer had no intention of returning to Berlin during the Exposition—he loathed hunting—and that if Halifax wished to see him, it would be necessary to go to Berchtesgaden. This further dampened Eden's enthusiasm, and the situation was further complicated when the *Evening Standard* in London broke the news of the coming trip, before any official anouncement in Berlin and before Paris had been informed, to the vast displeasure of Germans and French alike. But Chamberlain was insistent on going ahead with the plan, and on November 17, Halifax flew to Berlin. He spent two days attending the Hunting Exposition, where he was mightily impressed and acquired from the Berliners the nickname "Halalifax" ("*Halali*" being the German equivalent of "Tally-ho"). Then, with Neurath, the interpreter Schmidt, and Ivone Kirkpatrick from the British Embassy, he proceeded by train to Berchtesgaden.

Upon arrival the party was driven directly to the Berghof, where Halifax, emerging from the car, mistook Hitler's "black trousered legs, finishing up in silk socks and pumps" for those of a footman until warned by "Neurath or somebody throwing a hoarse whisper at my ear of *'der Fuehrer, der Fuehrer.'"* Once seated in the study, Hitler invited his guest to open the discussion. According to Schmidt, it began badly when Halifax stated that he had brought no new proposals, and had come to ascertain the German Government's views on the political situation—an opening gambit which apparently gave Hitler the impression that his intentions were being scrutinized to see if they were honorable. The result, in any case, was a long Hitlerian monologue, verging on diatribe, the burden of which was that it was useless for him to try to reach agreements with democracies because, with the exception of the Anglo-German Naval Agreement, they had rejected all of his "reasonable solutions" as a result of the demagogic and obstructionist attitudes of the political parties and the press. Hitler was particularly disgruntled over British newspaper reports on German activities in Spain, including Guernica and Almería.

Halifax replied that if this was really Hitler's view, both of them were wasting their time, since Britain was unlikely to change her form of government. Hitler wriggled out by saying that he had in mind France rather than Britain, and then stated: "Between England and Germany there was only one difference, namely the colonial question." Halifax had already remarked that "no English government could deal with the colonial question by direct negotiation with Germany alone" but only "as a part of a genuine settlement by means of which quiet and security might be established in Europe." Now, seeking to lead the discussion to more general matters, he asked Hitler's attitude with regard to the "possibility of leading Germany back to a closer cooperation with other nations in the League," and to Germany's joining in disarmament discussions. Then, in a manner which gave Eden pain when he subsequently saw the record, Halifax stated that:

All other questions fall into the category of possible alterations in the European order which might be destined to come with the passage of time. Amongst these questions were Danzig, Austria, and Czechoslovakia. England was interested to see that any alterations should come through the course of peaceful evolution and that methods should be avoided which might cause far-reaching disturbances, which neither the chancellor nor other countries desired.

Hitler pooh-poohed the importance of the League question; it could not be an Anglo-German problem, since the United States was not a member, and "no one could maintain that on this ground there were profound differences between England and America." Disarmament was a more difficult question now than it had been, since "England herself was rearming to a degree which had no parallel in British history. Was England ready to abandon her rearmament?" Then there was Russia, recently "brought into Europe not only as a moral but as a very weighty material factor, particularly in view of her alliance with Czechoslovakia." In view of all this, Hitler "had no idea how the disarmament question should be brought within the realm of practical possibilities," and "he was a fanatical enemy of conferences which were doomed to failure from the start."

After these rather telling counterpunches, Hitler, ignoring Halifax's reference to Danzig, blandly observed:

As far as Czechoslovakia and Austria were concerned, a settlement could be reached given a reasonable attitude. The Agreement of July 11 [1936] had been made with Austria and it was to be hoped that it would lead to the removal of all difficulties. Czechoslovakia was herself in a position to clear away existing difficulties. She only needed to treat the Germans living within her borders well and they would be entirely happy. Germany set great store by good relations with all her neighbours.

In reply to Halifax's request that Hitler outline a solution to the colonial question, the Fuehrer took the position that, since the whole idea of Germany's war guilt should be repudiated, she was entitled to the return of all her prewar colonies; if in any particular case Britain or France found this intolerable, it was up to them to propose substitutes. Germany did not want colonies "in a region where the danger of international complications was great," or in the Sahara.

Neurath then had the gall to cite "Germany's collaboration in the Spanish Non-Intervention question" as an example of her "international cooperation," and Hitler once again expressed a hope "that a reasonable solution could be found with Czechoslovakia." Halifax, who had not been scoring many hits, remonstrated mildly "that he did not entirely agree with the Chancellor on one or two points, though he did not intend to pursue the matter since it was a question of points which were not essential to the present conversation." He then made a frank bid for "further conversations between representatives of the two Governments." The only result was another rebuff. Hitler replied that "for the present he had in mind the diplomatic channel," and that there was no purpose in a conference until its base had been laid by successful prior negotiations. That meant that England and France must first "make up their minds whether they wanted to meet the German demand [for colonies] at all and if so in which direction."

The conferees then went to lunch, which was enlivened by Hitler's advice to Halifax—recently Viceroy—on how to deal with Britain's troubles in India: "All you have to do is to shoot Gandhi. If necessary shoot some more Congress leaders. You will be surprised how quickly the trouble will die down." After lunch the conference was resumed only briefly; Hitler for a second time rejected Halifax's plea for "direct negotiations," and renewed his onslaught against the press: "A first condition of the calming of international relations was the cooperation of all people to make an end of journalistic free-booting." Then, after some correct but rather cool amenities, Halifax and his party took their leave.

That evening in Munich, Halifax was shown the Nazi shrines—the site of the 1923 Beer Hall Putsch, the old Brown House on the Briennerstrasse, and the new one on the Königsplatz, including Hitler's office,* where the Munich con-

---

* In the office Halifax observed a death mask of Frederick the Great "who," as the noble guest naïvely recorded, "is evidently a hero."

ference would take place ten months later. The next day he took lunch at Karinhall, where he was greeted by a Hermann Goering "dressed in brown breeches and boots all in one, green leather jerkin surrounded with a green leather belt, on which was hung a dagger in a red leather sheath." Halifax was "immensely entertained at meeting the man," despite wondering "how many people he had been responsible for getting killed." Politically, the meeting brought out nothing new, as Goering followed closely in the verbal footsteps of his master. According to Schmidt, who was again present, Goering spoke "with infinitely more diplomacy," and certainly the atmosphere was much less frosty.

A new note was injected that evening, however, at a dinner party given by Nevile Henderson. Among the guests was Field Marshal von Blomberg, who advised Halifax that the colonial question was of only secondary importance; the real problem lay in Central and Eastern Europe. The Germans "knew Czechoslovakia," counseled Blomberg, "and he could assure me most solemnly that the country was an outpost of Russia, and that nobody—not even the French—liked the Czechs!" Germany's population growth made expansion vital, and, as Blomberg later warned Kirkpatrick, Britain would be well advised "not to sit on the safety valve." This viewpoint was, of course, precisely in line with what Blomberg had heard from Hitler's own lips at the Hossbach conference, and was a far cry from the Halifax talk at the Berghof, with its emphasis on colonies and low-keyed references to Austria and Czechoslovakia.

On Sunday, November 21, the deeply religious Halifax (Hitler subsequently referred to him as the "English Parson") went to church, and later received Joseph Goebbels and wife at an Embassy tea. The little *Doktor* leveled a new attack on the British press, coupled with a request that steps be taken to prevent it from printing personal criticism of Hitler. "I had expected to dislike him intensely," Halifax recorded, "but am ashamed to say that I did not."

The next day he took the train to Calais and London, making notes as he rode on the impressions he had gathered. The notes remarked but did not resolve the contrast between the Hitler and Blomberg presentations. "What we want is assurance that Germany is *not out for war*," he wrote. "We want an understanding, we will have to pay, and colonies are our only money." He opined comfortingly that Hitler was "sincere" in denying any intention of going to war over Austria and Czechoslovakia, and envisioned a possible mutual agreement to abstain from the use of force.

Despite the generally optimistic nature of these reflections, Halifax was aware that the visit to Hitler had not produced a meeting of the minds: "One had a feeling all the time that we had a totally different sense of values and were speaking a different language."* Certainly Halifax's subsequent description of the Fuehrer as "like Gandhi in Prussian boots" shows little awareness of the kind of man he was talking to. At the time, Halifax thought that "it was all to the good making contact," but in retrospect the best that he could say was that his visit did no harm.

Eden thought otherwise and was especially disturbed by Halifax's handling of

---

* It is interesting that Hitler also used the phrase "speaking a different language" to describe to Schmidt his impression of the conference.

the Austrian and Czechoslovakian questions. He "wished that Halifax had warned Hitler more strongly against intervention in Central Europe" and remarked that the words "alterations through the course of peaceful evolution" might well mean something quite different to Hitler than to Halifax. How right Eden was clearly appears from the secret telegram which Neurath sent to the German embassies in Rome, London, Paris, and Washington, in which this part of the talk was summarized as follows:

> Halifax admitted of his own accord that certain changes in the European system could probably not be avoided in the long run. The British did not believe that the *status quo* had to be maintained under all circumstances. Among the questions in which changes would probably be made sooner or later were Danzig, Austria, and Czechoslovakia. England was only interested in seeing that such changes were brought about by peaceful development.

All in all, Halifax had said nothing likely to change Hitler's opinion, expressed during the Hossbach conference, that "Britain had already tacitly written off the Czechs." And Hitler, for his part, had strongly implied to Halifax that Austria and Czechoslovakia were questions between those states and Germany in which Britain had no basis for interference—an implication explicitly confirmed on November 24 by the Reich press chief, Otto Dietrich, at a conference of Berlin newspaper editors.

The success and *éclat* of the last two years, together with Germany's growing strength, were now being reflected in Hitler's tactics and increasing truculence. He was feeling his oats. If Halifax wished to come to the Berghof, well and good, and Hitler would receive him. But he confuted and contradicted Halifax without compunction and gave not an inch on any point. Anthony Eden noted that Hitler, although demanding colonial restoration, had given no guarantees about his policy in Central Europe; Britain was asked to make all the concessions with no *quid pro quo*. "If we do not get, we shall not give," he informed his ministerial colleagues. But that was not the way Neville Chamberlain saw these matters, and three months later Eden was out of office.

2

During the closing weeks of 1937, Hitler was confronted with administrative problems, which he detested, arising out of Dr. Hjalmar H. G. Schacht's resignation from his offices as Minister of Economics and Plenipotentiary for War Economy. Already President of the Reichsbank, he had been appointed to the former position in 1934 and the latter in May 1935, and for the following year he and Blomberg were the major authorities in the rearmament program. But the banker was stiff-necked, self-righteous, and self-confident, did not get along well with the Nazi panjandrums, and in April 1936 the seeds of conflict were sown when Hitler appointed Goering as Co-ordinator of Raw Materials and Foreign Exchange. The Fat One was no economist but he knew Hitler's mind, and he pressed for public borrowing and economic self-sufficiency, while Schacht insisted on the necessity of maintaining the German export market and keeping rearmament within the limits of Germany's financial capacity. The decisive vote in this debate was Hitler's, and Goering won it decisively by his appointment, in October 1936, as Plenipotentiary for the Four Year Plan.

The result was an impossible overlap of conflicting authority, in which Hitler supported Goering at every turn, while at the same time desiring Schacht to carry on, in order to avoid the public embarrassment of his resignation. But early in 1937, Schacht virtually went on strike, despite Blomberg's desperate efforts to keep the peace. In July there was a temporary truce, soon broken by Goering, and in August, Schacht went to the Berghof and put his resignation in Hitler's hands. He was persuaded to stay on for two months, but a last meeting with Goering on November 1 produced another impasse, and on November 26, 1937, his resignations as Minister and Plenipotentiary for War Economy were accepted but not publicly announced.

On the understanding that Goering would continue as the focus of authority in the economic field, Hitler appointed as Minister of Economics Walther Funk, a journalist with a smattering of economics who had been editor of the *Berliner Börsenzeitung* in Weimar days, and since 1933 Goebbels' deputy in the Propaganda Ministry. Schacht remained President of the Reichsbank and, on Hitler's insistence, took the empty title of Minister without Portfolio. For some reason the effective date of Funk's new appointment was first set for January 15,* and on December 10 for January 31, 1938; by that time it was submerged in much bigger doings, and was finally announced on February 4 as part of the general upheaval to which we will shortly turn.

The Goering-Schacht conflict was one of several among Hitler's principal subordinates which had been building up beneath the apparently calm surface of German internal politics in 1936 and 1937, and which involved primarily Goering and Heinrich Himmler as the hunters, and Blomberg and Fritsch as the quarry. These duels were waged much more covertly than the one between Goering and Schacht, and at the end of 1937 the issues had not yet been drawn but were rapidly coming to a head.

Between Goering and Blomberg the problem was the former's vanity and jealousy of Blomberg's higher military rank, especially after his promotion to field marshal in April of 1936. As Blomberg put it in his memoirs, Goering "resented the fact that he was not the first soldier of the Reich, but shared second rank with two others." Furthermore, by 1937 Blomberg was much in the public eye, giving orations on state occasions such as Seeckt's funeral, and addressing workers in munitions plants. Goering had wanted to represent Germany at the coronation of George VI in May of 1937, but Blomberg was sent instead. To add to Goering's irritation, Blomberg was not overawed and did not hesitate to differ with or contradict him, sometimes in public. At the Italian maneuvers in

---

* This greatly disturbed Blomberg, who on November 29 urged Hitler and Goering that Funk should at once be appointed Plenipotentiary for War Economy, as "the urgency of unified further work on preparations for the conduct of the war does not admit of this office being paralyzed until 15.1.38." The result was that Goering himself took over temporarily the Ministry of Economics, and on entering his new office at once telephoned his predecessor to announce: "Herr Schacht, I am now sitting in your chair!" When Funk took office as Minister, he also was given the title Plenipotentiary for Economy (*not* War Economy), and in essence he functioned as Goering's deputy for administrative matters.

the fall of 1937, in the presence of Mussolini and in the course of discussing Russia's military potential, Blomberg, who had been in Russia during the days of Reichswehr-Red Army collaboration, declared that Goering grossly underestimated the strength of the Soviet regime. At the Hossbach conference, as we have seen, Blomberg sharply attacked Goering's administration of the Four Year Plan. *Unser Hermann* eyed the incautious field marshal ever more narrowly and bided his time.

Himmler's motivations were much less personal, and his goal was not rank, but power. With great skill, he had utilized the Roehm affair not only to eliminate his superior and most dangerous rival, but also to push Goering out of the police and internal security fields and into the military arena, which the Fuehrer regarded as his own preserve, and where Goering could at best hope to be second man. Thus a sort of power vacuum opened in the internal management of the Reich, and this Himmler started to fill with his chosen engine, the SS.

This was the man who now turned his formidable energies to the destruction of the officer corps. He did not repeat Roehm's mistake of attacking too soon, or seek to accomplish his end with one blow. Roehm had risked too much by stepping faster than Hitler's tempo and had forced the Fuehrer to choose between him and the Reichswehr before Hitler was ready to challenge the generals. Himmler was ready to gear himself to Hitler's pace, and to strike with him, rather than striving to force his hand.

The immediate issue between Himmler and the Army related to the size and role of the armed SS units, later to be known as the Waffen SS. The establishment of these avowedly military SS formations threatened, just as had the SA under Roehm, the Wehrmacht's prerogatives as "sole arms bearer of the Reich." Nevertheless, Hitler supported Himmler in this regard, partly because it was a cardinal, and politically sound, point of principle with him that the Wehrmacht should under no circumstances be used to put down internal disturbances. In Hitler's words:

> It is necessary to maintain . . . a state military police capable of representing and imposing the authority of the Reich within the country in any situation.
>
> This task can be carried out only by a state police which has within its ranks men of the best German blood and which identifies itself unreservedly with the ideology at the base of the Great German Reich. . . .
>
> We must never again tolerate that the German Wehrmacht based on universal conscription should be used against its own compatriots, arms in hand, when critical situations arise in the interior. Such a step is the beginning of the end. . . . Our history contains sad examples of this. The Wehrmacht in the future is intended for all time for use solely against the Reich's foreign enemies.

Nevertheless, Blomberg and Fritsch succeeded in keeping Himmler's military forces within reasonable bounds. By the end of 1936 the entire armed strength of the Waffen SS amounted only to the equivalent of one Army division. It was not enough to satisfy Himmler, and in March of 1937 he began to press Blomberg and Fritsch for an increase, especially for the purpose of policing the borders of the Reich against "penetration by communists, saboteurs and adventurers." A discussion early in March between Fritsch and Himmler led to "no positive results." Fritsch was firmly opposed to any enlargement of the armed SS units, and Blomberg supported his objections. On March 22, at a conference in which Goering also participated, the Army categorically rejected Himmler's request to establish an SS "border protection corps." But Himmler was obviously ill-disposed to let the matter rest, and in May, Blomberg expressed grave misgivings to Keitel concerning the constant development of the SS.

Sharp as was this disagreement over the SS border units, the fundamental source of the hostility lay far deeper. At bottom, the conflict between Fritsch and Himmler was a struggle for the allegiance of German youth.

For throughout modern German history the Army not only had been the core of the Reich in terms of power politics, but had become a basic social institution and a major educational force as well. The indoctrination to which all German conscripts were exposed during their period of military service was the foundation of the national outlook to which Beck referred in his 1935 speech before the War Academy, in describing Germany as a "military-minded nation." The officer corps and the ranking military leaders were the objects of the veneration so inculcated and the beneficiaries of the scale of values thus established.

The resumption of compulsory military service in 1935 threw into bold relief the issue whether the Army should continue to exert the dominant influence over the hearts and minds of young Germans. The crucial and all-important question was whether they should learn to worship the old, established gods or the new deities of Nazism.

The battlefield on which Fritsch and Himmler met was, in short, an ideological one. Prussianism or neopaganism; emperors and field marshals or the Fuehrer of the Thousand-Year Reich and his attendant archangels—this was the symbolic paraphernalia of the struggle for power between the Party and the officer corps. And in this struggle it was Himmler rather than Goering who was the Army's chief antagonist.

3

In December 1937, Field Marshal von Blomberg's comings and goings took an erratic turn, not unnoticed by his subordinates Keitel and Jodl. Several times he drove alone in civilian clothes to the village of Oberhof in the Thuringian Forest and, on December 15, in a state which Jodl thought "highly excited," he secluded himself there for a full week. This behavior especially aroused the concern of Keitel, whose son Karl-Heinz was courting Blomberg's daughter Dorothea.

Then, on December 20, General Erich Ludendorff, of First World War and Beer Hall Putsch fame, died in Munich. Hitler decreed a state funeral at the Feldherrnhalle for December 22, with Blomberg as orator-eulogizer. Keitel ordered a special train, to which a salon coach recently given Blomberg by Hitler was hitched, and then discovered that the train would have to pick up Blomberg at Oberhof and leave him there after the ceremony. Came Christmas, and Blomberg's daughters spent it with the Keitels, while their father celebrated the Nativity at Oberhof. Inquiries to Blomberg's adjutant elicited only the information that the field marshal was "visiting a lady who had broken her ankle skiing."

The lady in question turned out to be a Fräulein Erna Gruhn, a stenotypist at the Reich Egg Board, and not of suitable lineage or status to be the bride of a noble Prussian field marshal. Sensible that his brother officers, from whom he was already somewhat estranged, would look upon such a marriage as a *mésalliance* discreditable to the officer corps, Blomberg sought support from less stuffy circles by taking his troubles to—Hermann Goering.

How much the listener foresaw when he heard Blomberg's story is speculative;[*] probably he realized only that it would be advantageous to have the field marshal under obligation to him. However that may be, he advised Blomberg not to let social considerations stand in the way, and that he and the Fuehrer himself would be marriage witnesses, so as to nullify the effect of any criticism. With this support, Blomberg disclosed his intentions to Hitler at the Ludendorff funeral and, on January 12, 1938, Jodl noted in his diary: "Field marshal surprisingly marries Frl. Gruhn." It was a quiet civil ceremony in the War Ministry building and, although Hitler and Goering were witnesses, there was little attendant publicity.

The newlyweds' honeymoon was soon interrupted by the death of Blomberg's mother in Eberswalde (a few miles north of Berlin), and her funeral and the settlement of her estate kept Blomberg away from his desk most of the time until January 24. Meanwhile, the scandalmongers had been having a field day with the name and reputation of the new *Frau Feldmarschall*. Mocking telephone messages from anonymous callers were received at both the War Ministry and OKH, and rumors that the lady's past was not merely plebeian began to circulate. These came to the ears of both Fritsch and Hossbach, who took counsel together and decided that it was a personal affair of Blomberg's and the Army should stand back of him.

Meanwhile, the Berlin police had noticed that the erstwhile Fräulein Gruhn had moved to Blomberg's flat in the War Ministry, and on January 21 the Police President of Berlin, Count von Helldorf, appeared in Keitel's office with her dossier, which showed that in times past her mother had made a massage salon into a very interesting place, with criminal consequences for both mother and daughter.

Aware that they were handling dynamite, Keitel and Helldorf sought to verify that the subject of the dossier and Blomberg's new wife were one and the same person. Keitel was unable either to reach Blomberg, who was at Eberswalde, or to identify the photograph in the dossier. Whereupon, with incredible stupidity or real treachery (of both of which Keitel was quite capable), he sent Helldorf to Goering, who, as a witness to the wedding, could presumably answer the question.

Probably it was stupidity. By this time Keitel's son and Blomberg's daughter

[*] There are many uncorroborated stories of the Blomberg and Fritsch cases in the literature. The account in the text is limited to what is reasonably certain. Hermann Förtsch, then a lieutenant colonel and instructor at the War Academy, utilized his own correspondence with surviving officers and relatives of the participants in these episodes in his *Schuld und Verhängnis* (1951), from which I have taken a few apparently reliable details.

had become engaged, and Keitel's professional future appeared closely tied to Blomberg's favor. Keitel had had very little direct contact with Hitler, and there is no reason to suspect that he foresaw his own advancement through Blomberg's fall. However that may be, the fat was now in the fire, for Blomberg's only chance of emerging unscathed lay in judicious and confidential handling of the dossier, if not its complete suppression, which friendly authorities could surely have secured.

By January 24, Goering had put the dossier into Hitler's hands. The Fuehrer spent most of the next day pondering the problem in consultation with Goering and Hossbach. He was annoyed at Blomberg for having led him to witness the marriage without full knowledge of the circumstances (Blomberg apparently told Hitler and Goering only that his intended bride had "a certain past," and may have known no more himself), but he regarded the field marshal as a loyal supporter. Goering went to confront Blomberg with the dossier, reported back that he had "admitted all," and Hitler finally summoned the unhappy field marshal and told him that he must resign.

The parting was not unfriendly. Hitler consulted Blomberg at length about the selection of his successor, and ultimately adopted the latter's suggestion that Hitler himself take over direct command of the Wehrmacht. Blomberg was given the impression that he was merely being given a year's vacation to allow the scandal to subside, that he would remain on the Army list as a field marshal, and that he "would take over the supreme command in war-time."

Lulled by Hitler's honeyed words, Blomberg and his new bride hied themselves to Capri and relaxed in the warm Italian sun. His tragicomedy was nearly finished, but a moment of burlesque was interjected before the final curtain. A young naval officer assigned to RKM, Lieutenant von Wangenheim, became fired with officious zeal and took off for Capri in hot pursuit of the bride and groom. Raeder had asked him to convey to Blomberg the advice that he divorce "this woman," but Wangenheim had in mind a more definite solution. He reached Capri on January 31, and promptly appeared before Blomberg and "tried to put a pistol into his hand." For this idea the honeymooning *Feldmarschall* had no stomach, and rejected the proffered weapon with the observation that Wangenheim "apparently held entirely different opinions and a different standard of life."

Raeder's advice to get a divorce was symptomatic of the wave of criticism rising from the officers corps. Beck thought Blomberg had disgraced his profession, and admonished Keitel that Blomberg "should be forced to divorce that woman or else be taken off the list of officers." But Blomberg refused to abandon her, and was shortly stricken from the Army rolls. He dropped from sight and sound in the affairs of the Third Reich as suddenly and totally as a stone dropped into a millpond.

The great expectations with which Hitler had infused him were never fulfilled. Upon his return to Germany in 1939, he was met with "a curtain of silence drawn around my person and activities," and informed that the promises made to him "could no longer be realized." He offered his services when the war broke out, but they were refused. And so Blomberg lived quietly and in complete obscurity in a small Bavarian village near the Tegernsee throughout the war, the end of which he survived by less than a year.

4

General von Fritsch returned to Berlin on January 2, 1938, and resumed his usual duties. The rumors about Blomberg's wife distressed him, but apparently he did not intervene for or against the field marshal with Hitler,* and remained unaware until January 25 that his own situation was in jeopardy. That evening Hossbach appeared at his quarters and told him that during the day Hitler, in the presence of Goering, had exhibited a police dossier of evidence that Fritsch had engaged in homosexual acts in violation of the German penal code. Hossbach had been explicitly ordered by Hitler not to inform Fritsch of the accusation, but the adjutant, after an internal battle between "order and conscience," had decided that the latter had the stronger claim. Fritsch categorically denied the charge, and the following morning Hossbach reported this to Hitler, who, for the moment, took calmly the disclosure that his adjutant had disobeyed his order.

Hossbach also insisted, on Fritsch's behalf, that the Army Commander-in-Chief be given the opportunity to appear before Hitler and refute the accusation in person. The opportunity was extended late in the evening of the same day, but in a manner hardly calculated to advance Fritsch's cause. Himmler and Goering were also present, as well as an odoriferous and theretofore obscure individual named Schmidt. As Fritsch was in the course of denying the accusation, Schmidt was introduced into the room and identified Fritsch as the person whom he had observed commit a homosexual offense some years earlier.

Hitler suspended Fritsch from his position as Army Commander-in-Chief, and Fritsch, humiliated and apparently too stunned for a convincing display of righteous anger, returned to his apartment at the Bendlerstrasse. Goering appeared in the room where Hossbach had been waiting and dramatically declared that Fritsch's guilt had been established beyond question. Hossbach continued to insist that Fritsch be given a chance to clear himself, and succeeded in having Beck summoned to the Chancellery despite the late hour. After conferences both with Hitler and with Fritsch at the latter's apartment, Beck put forward a demand for a trial of the charges before a military court of honor, but Hitler did not immediately give his consent, and this issue was not resolved that evening.

Circumstances now conspired to Hitler's advantage. Fritsch was a lifelong bachelor who was not known to have ever had much to do with the opposite sex and he was a very reserved man. He was thus especially vulnerable to accusations of this type, and his situation was greatly worsened by the fact that the gossip about Frau Blomberg had turned out to be not unfounded. Finally, he did not help his own cause by revealing to Hossbach that he had been in the habit of giving food to one or two boys of the Hitlerjugend at his Bendlerstrasse apartment. Although this was not an uncommon practice at the time, and Fritsch's behavior was later proved to have been wholly innocent, at the outset

---

* I know of no basis for Bullock's statement in his *Hitler* (p. 417) that Fritsch took the initiative in urging Hitler to dismiss Blomberg.

it lent color to the charges and caused even Hossbach some anxiety. And the entire concatenation of circumstances gave others pause, even within the officer corps. Beck was at first inclined to believe the charges, and Blomberg commented just before his departure for Capri that Fritsch was not a "woman's man."

The result of all this was that, even if Fritsch had been the type of man to rally the generals behind him to meet Hitler's attack (which he was not), his personal situation was so beclouded as to make such a move very difficult. Fritsch himself was slow to realize that anything more was at stake than a ghastly mistake about his own person. Furthermore, he was inept at political infighting, and most of his colleagues in the higher levels of the officer corps were no better equipped. Thus Hitler was able to deflect the attention and energies of Fritsch and his supporters to the proposition that Fritsch be accorded opportunity to clear his name before a court of honor; in the meantime Hitler proceeded almost unopposed with a sweeping reorganization of the Wehrmacht's leadership. The officer corps was defeated before its members realized that they, and not Fritsch alone, were the real targets of Hitler's assault.

Like Blomberg's dismissal, the news of Fritsch's suspension was held *in camera* for nearly ten days, while rumors flew thick and fast.* Meanwhile the Minister of Justice, Franz Guertner, and military lawyers from the War Ministry's legal division considered the procedural problems, and Fritsch retained Count Rüdiger von der Goltz as his defense counsel. Ultimately an extraordinary court-martial, comprising the three service commanders-in-chief (Goering, Raeder, and Fritsch's successor, General Walther von Brauchitsch) and two judges of the Supreme War Tribunal, was convened to hear the charges.

As soon as a systematic investigation was undertaken, the case against Fritsch exploded. The accusing dossier was found to be the work of the SS, and Himmler's men had not contrived their charge well enough to stand judicial scrutiny. It was discovered that Schmidt was a sordid and convicted blackmailer, who had stuffed the Gestapo files with accusations of sexual perversion against numerous prominent persons. Among them were Funk (soon to be appointed Minister of Economics), a former ambassador, the SS police president of Potsdam, and the famous international tennis star Baron Gottfried von Cramm.

Some of the charges were apparently true, others highly questionable or totally unfounded. The opening of these files had, at all events, disastrous consequences for the unhappy Cramm. Upon his return to Germany from Italy after a six-month tournament tour abroad, the scheduled triumphant reception was suddenly canceled, and he was arrested a few days before the opening of Fritsch's trial. In all probability, the purpose was to establish the "truth" of at least one of Schmidt's charges.†

* A torchlight parade of storm troopers was scheduled for January 30, the anniversary of Hitler's appointment as Chancellor, and some 130 prominent persons were on a list to receive invitations to watch the parade from the windows of the Chancellery. The records of Hitler's *Adjutantur* for January 29 show that Fritsch and Schacht and his wife were among a few whose names were stricken from the list.

† Cramm was arrested on March 5 and convicted under Section 175 on May 14. He was sentenced to one year's imprisonment but was paroled on October 16, 1938.

Schmidt's accusation against Fritsch was that he had seen the Army Commander-in-Chief commit an offense with a *Lustknabe* near the Potsdam railroad station in November 1934. Thereafter, Schmidt declared, he had successfully blackmailed the general, who paid him a substantial sum of hush money at a rendezvous in the Lichterfelde quarter of Berlin. But numerous items in Schmidt's story in the Gestapo files did not fit Fritsch, and the pretrial investigators were eventually able to unearth a retired Rittmeister von Frisch living in Lichterfelde, who admitted that he had been the actual culprit and victim of Schmidt's extortion.

While the investigation was in process, however, Fritsch, despite the contrary urgings of Beck and Hossbach, had yielded to Hitler's demand that he submit his resignation. By the time the court-martial assembled in mid-March 1938, Brauchitsch was already ensconced as Commander-in-Chief of the Army, and Fritsch had no post. The court-martial soon found the accusations to be groundless, and Fritsch was completely vindicated, but he did not get his old job back or, indeed, any other.

In effect, Fritsch had been turned into a ghost of his former self; for a few months the ghost gibbered indignantly and fruitlessly, and then subsided into silence. Beck, Hossbach, and a few others pressed for Fritsch's return to active duty in an appropriate capacity, but Hitler turned a deaf ear to all such pleas, and Fritsch had few strong cards to play. The Luftwaffe was under Goering's thumb, Raeder had no stomach to make an issue of the matter, and Brauchitsch was in no mood to jeopardize his own appointment.

Fritsch rightly gauged the prospects of further resistance as well-nigh hopeless and settled back into embittered retirement. In June, Hitler exculpated him in a speech before an assemblage of the leading troop commanders, acknowledging that an unfortunate mistake had been made, but explaining that reinstatement was out of the question, as the public had been told that Fritsch's health had failed—a lame excuse, but sufficient unto the occasion, as many of the generals had benefited from promotions following the shake-up, and German officers are as aware as those of other nationalities that military advancement does not often come to those who "make waves."

A more public rehabilitation took place on August 11, 1938, when Fritsch was given the honorary title of *Chef* of Artillery Regiment 12, which he had once commanded. This was an honor seldom bestowed, but for Fritsch it was more funeral than triumph.

Fritsch's last year was a weird and pathetic sort of half-life. Regiments are commanded by colonels, not senior generals, and Fritsch's designation as *chef* of an artillery regiment was supposed to be strictly honorary. Fritsch would not have it so. He watched his regiment's training maneuvers, and reported to it during the Czech crisis in the autumn of 1938. And in August 1939, as war loomed, he rejoined his regiment, by then already stationed in East Prussia. A few weeks later, he met his death from a Polish machine-gun bullet in a field on the outskirts of Warsaw.

5

The simultaneous removal of Blomberg and Fritsch presented Hitler with broad opportunities for reorganization of the Wehrmacht's leadership, but also with difficult problems of choice and selection. From the extent and duration of his consultations on these questions, it appears that the crisis came upon him unexpectedly and that he had no preconceived plan for filling the high-level vacancies thus created. In the early stages of the affair he leaned most heavily for advice on Goering, Hossbach, and Blomberg himself. But with Blomberg's departure, his place was taken by his principal subordinate, General Wilhelm Keitel, and thereafter it was Goering and Keitel who were most often in attendance as the decisions were made.

The alacrity with which Hitler took Keitel into his confidence is surprising, for the general had been in his presence only a few times, and always in a subordinate role. Only once had he spoken in Hitler's presence, and so little impression had he made that, when Blomberg first brought up his name, Hitler, indulging the common presumption that all German generals are "vons," referred to him as "von Keitel." Probably his elevation at this time was largely due to assurances given Hitler by Blomberg and Goering that Keitel was completely responsive to the wishes of his superiors, and a reasonably good administrator, well qualified for the role, common in European governments, of *chef de cabinet*.

Actually, however, Keitel's elevation was the consequence not only of his own characteristics, but of Hitler's decision that he himself would take over Blomberg's post. Hitler did not come to this conclusion immediately; he knew that Goering coveted the position and the rank that it carried, and both Blomberg and Keitel recommended that he be selected. But Hitler rejected the proposal, telling Blomberg that Goering lacked patience and diligence and was too self-indulgent, and Keitel that Goering had more than enough to do already, with both the Luftwaffe and the Four Year Plan on his plate.

But if not Goering, who?* Fritsch was disqualified by his own troubles, and anyhow it was clear that Goering would bitterly resent being once again subordinated to an army general. Indeed, the only person to whom Goering would gladly yield was Adolf Hitler, and so Blomberg's proposal that Hitler assume direct command perfectly suited that aspect of the situation. By January 27, Hitler had decided to follow this course and informed Keitel that "the unified and concentrated leadership of the Wehrmacht is sacred and untouchable to me, and I will take it over with your help."

This decision eliminated the need for, and indeed the possibility of, any command position between Hitler and the three services. All that was needed was someone to head the interservice staff to assist the Fuehrer in his role as Commander-in-Chief, and that was the post into which Keitel now stepped. Well

---

* Hossbach had unsuccessfully suggested Generals Beck or von Rundstedt, or as an interim solution, the retired General Friedrich Graf von der Schulenburg, who had become an ardent Nazi, with honorary rank in the SS, and for whom Hitler had a liking. Hitler warmed to the idea, but the seventy-two-year-old Schulenburg, contacted by telephone, declined the post for reasons of health.

aware of Goering's weakness for the trappings rather than the essence of power, Hitler made him a field marshal, so that he became the ranking officer of the Wehrmacht, though with command over only the Luftwaffe.

The first order that Hitler gave Keitel was to find a new adjutant, "who will be a confidant to me and to you, and not to the services," to replace Hossbach,* whose primary fealty to the Army and to Fritsch had been carried to the point of disobedience. Keitel at once selected Major Rudolf Schmundt, who had once been his regimental adjutant, and whose new duties were destined to last until the bomb exploded at Hitler's headquarters on July 20, 1944; Schmundt was one of the few who perished from the blast.

6

The selection of a successor to Fritsch was a much more difficult problem, and a touchy one, since Beck and some others thought there should be only a temporary replacement pending the outcome of the court-martial. On January 27, Hilter discussed the question with both Blomberg and Keitel. The former recommended either his former deputy, General von Reichenau, by then commander of the Munich military district, or General von Brauchitsch, who had recently been given command of the new armored group headquarters at Leipzig.

Keitel first proposed General Gerd von Rundstedt, the oldest general on active duty and, next to Fritsch, the senior in rank. He was a soldier of real ability and impressive bearing, and Hitler had a good opinion of him, but thought him too old for the job. Keitel then† suggested Brauchitsch, to which Hitler responded with a question: "Why not Reichenau?" Keitel replied that he was superficial and impulsive, did not work hard enough, and was generally disliked by his brother officers and regarded as more interested in politics than in his profession. Hitler acknowledged the last point but was not altogether persuaded, and postponed a decision pending further consultation with others, including Runstedt and Beck, both of whom were strongly opposed to Reichenau.

For a full week the choice hung between Reichenau and Brauchitsch. The former learned what was in the wind and came to Berlin, but was cold-shouldered by his colleagues and apparently did not succeed in seeing Hitler. Keitel brought Brauchitsch to Berlin, but Hitler would not receive him immediately, and his prospects were shadowed when it developed that he, like Blomberg, was having woman trouble: he wished to divorce his wife and marry another.‡

However, the marital obstacles were soon disposed of through the good offices of Hitler, Goering, and Keitel. The last-named induced Brauchitsch's son to persuade his mother to consent to a divorce. Goering, as a self-appointed judge of domestic relations, examined the situation and reported to Hitler that

---

* Hossbach returned to OKH briefly and then was given command of a regiment. By the end of the war he was the general commanding the Fourth Army.

† Hitler and Keitel also discussed Joachim von Stülpnagel, a leading general of the Reichswehr who had retired in 1931 and become the manager of the *Berliner Börsenzeitung*. According to Jodl's diary, he was dropped from consideration as "not loyal."

‡ According to the calendar kept by Keitel's adjutant, Eberhard, Brauchitsch arrived in Berlin late on January 28. Keitel spent most of the twenty-ninth with Hitler, and upon his return at the end of the day, Eberhard recorded: "Project Brauchitsch falls through, Keitel says (family not in order)."

there was nothing therein to condemn. The Fuehrer, for his part, made available to Brauchitsch the necessary and "not inconsiderable" funds to make a settlement with his first wife. It was all perfectly respectable, not at all like Blomberg's *déclassé* affair that had so outraged his colleagues.

However, a last-minute hitch of a quite different kind threatened Brauchitsch's elevation. At some point in the discussion he had been asked to consent to certain transfers and mandatory retirements among the senior Army generals. On February 2, Jodl learned that Brauchitsch was insisting on an opportunity to reflect on these personnel changes: "This again makes his appointment as Commander-in-Chief of the Army insecure, because personnel changes above all are a *sine qua non*. The Fuehrer has always desired them. . . . Therefore, Brauchitsch has been asked to come to Berlin again. . . . If Brauchitsch does not agree, then the Fuehrer will take Reichenau after all."

The situation became increasingly delicate. Jodl advised Keitel "to be extremely careful when effecting any change in personnel, in order to avoid irreparable damage. . . . We cannot afford to lose our best leaders . . . only what is absolutely necessary may be changed." Nevertheless, upon his return to Berlin for another meeting with Goering (who "asked that this discussion should take place in his presence") and Keitel, Brauchitsch agreed "to nearly all of the important changes, the greatest part . . . he would have effected on his own initiative." Apparently this was not good enough for Hitler and Goering. The following morning (February 3) Jodl found Keitel "greatly depressed" because:

> The Fuehrer and Goering dislike increasingly the idea of appointing Brauchitsch and are more in favour of Reichenau. General Keitel does not see how he can bear all this. He is thoroughly convinced that this appointment would lead to the third, and most intolerable, shock to the Army.
>
> General Keitel would have to bear the responsibility, and it would be said that he chose this solution, or at least that he did not prevent it, and he would have to keep silent and be unable to say how hard he fought against the decision.
>
> I support this opinion; everything must be attempted to prevent this disaster.
>
> A great number of the old elite group will leave; General Beck will not stay, and General Halder will not agree to be Chief of the General Staff under Reichenau, as they would not be able to cooperate.

After further explication by Brauchitsch of his views on National Socialism, the Church, and Army personnel matters, Hitler's doubts were finally overcome. And so, on February 4, 1938, Walther von Brauchitsch, newly promoted to the rank of *Generaloberst*, became Commander-in-Chief of the German Army. As a consolation prize, Reichenau was given the post as commander of the armored group which Brauchitsch thus vacated.

7

The departure of Blomberg and Fritsch, and their replacement by Hitler and Brauchitsch, was now made the occasion for a reorganization of the German military command structure. The Ministry of War (RKM) was abolished, and its components were reassembled under the title High Command of the Armed Forces (*Oberkommando der Wehrmacht*), commonly referred to by the initials "OKW." Hitler alone, as Supreme Commander (*Oberster Befehlshaber*) of the Armed Forces, had authority to issue commands to the Army, Navy, and Air Force. Keitel was given the title of *Chef* of OKW, but he had command authority only over the small OKW staff, and he actually functioned as chief of staff to Hitler.

Simultaneously, in the civil area, another important change was made as Hitler replaced Neurath with Ribbentrop in the Foreign Ministry. The shift had been foreshadowed by Hitler's increasing reliance on Ribbentrop, who had handled the negotiations both for the Anglo-German Naval Agreement and the Anti-Comintern Pact. Unlike Blomberg and Fritsch, however, Neurath was given a dignified avenue of retreat; he remained a minister and was designated president of a newly appointed "Secret Cabinet Council," the other members of which included Goering, Hess, Ribbentrop, Goebbels, Lammers, Keitel, Brauchitsch, and Raeder. On paper it looked very impressive, but it was only a cover operation for Neurath's benefit, and the "Secret Cabinet Council" never held a single meeting.

These portentous changes were embodied in two Hitler decrees dated February 4, 1938, one signed by Keitel as chief of OKW, and the other by Lammers as chief of the State Chancellery. "From now on I personally take over direct command of the entire Wehrmacht," the OKW decree announced, and both were given front-page publicity the following day. *"Strongest Concentration of all Powers in the Fuehrer's Hands"* screamed the headlines of the Party newspaper, the *Völkischer Beobachter*. The news of Blomberg's and Fritsch's retirements "for reasons of health" was half buried in the welter of announcements, and their pictures were not used, though letters to each from Hitler—the one to Blomberg much the warmer—were printed. Major display was given to photographs of Brauchitsch, Keitel, Ribbentrop, Neurath, Goering as field marshal, and, of course, the Fuehrer himself.

Other appointments and retirements were announced with much less fanfare. Three ambassadors—Hassell in Rome, Dirksen in Tokyo, and Papen in Vienna —were recalled from their posts. It was the end of his official career for the first, who was cordially disliked by both Ribbentrop and Ciano, and whose replacement the Italians had been urging.* Dirksen, however, was sent to London to replace Ribbentrop, and the indestructible Papen was soon up and doing again as ambassador to Turkey.

A reorganization of the Ministry of Economics was announced by Goering, acting under authority given him by Hitler on November 26, 1937, the effective date of Schacht's resignation. Schacht was not mentioned, but Goering announced that he would install Funk as Minister of Economics at noon on the following Tuesday. Goering also promulgated, in his capacity as Minister of

---

* Hassell subsequently joined the conspiracy to overthrow Hitler and was executed after the unsuccessful attempt on Hitler's life in July of 1944.

Aviation, a reorganization of the Luftwaffe, with concomitant appointments and promotions.

Much the most significant of the less publicized changes were those in the upper reaches of the Army, which Hitler had insisted upon as a condition of Brauchitsch's appointment. The better to understand these, it should be recalled that, until the death of Hindenburg, Hitler had no command relation to the Reichswehr. Fritsch had been appointed to the top Army position in February 1934 by Hindenburg, over the objections of Hitler and Blomberg, who had wanted Reichenau. Throughout his presidency, Hindenburg had regarded personnel questions in the Army as his own preserve, and after his death Fritsch and Beck managed to keep control within the Army, exercised through the chief of the Army Personnel Office, General Viktor von Schwedler.

It was this office which Hitler wished to get under his control, and it was made clear to Brauchitsch that the transfer of Schwedler and two of his section chiefs was "*a conditio sine qua non*" of his appointment. Brauchitsch somewhat hesitantly agreed, and on February 4 it was announced that Schwedler and his two subordinates were transferred to field commands. Schwedler's replacement, chosen by Brauchitsch on Keitel's urging, was the latter's younger brother Bodewin.* This gave Hitler full information concerning and control over all appointments and promotions.

The Fuehrer had other changes in mind. The first questions Keitel put to Brauchitsch upon the latter's arrival in Berlin were whether he would bring the Army closer to the Nazi ideology, and take a chief of the General Staff with the same outlook. Hitler had no fondness for Beck, who strongly opposed Blomberg's attempts to subject the Army to his operational command, and who was forever condemning any suggestions of military adventurism. Brauchitsch at first indicated willingness to replace Beck, whom he greatly admired, but subsequently changed his mind. Keitel and Jodl, for all their disagreements with Beck, also supported him, and in the upshot Hitler gave way and Beck stayed. However, Beck's principal subordinate, General Erich von Manstein, who had prepared much of the material in support of the Army's case for command supremacy in wartime, was transferred from OKH to a divisional command. He was replaced by General Franz Halder, but only after Hitler's mistrust of Halder's Roman Catholicism had been allayed.

For some time General von der Schulenburg, whose judgment Hitler valued, had been recommending that General Max von Viebahn, a member of Schulenburg's staff in the First World War and now commander of a division in Koblenz, be brought to Berlin for a high staff position. This, too, was done as part of the general shake-up, by bringing Viebahn into OKW as head of the operations staff, immediately subordinate to Keitel and superior to Jodl. Keitel, who knew but never could "make head or tail of this mysterious man," took him on with considerable misgivings, which soon proved well founded.

* A note in Jodl's diary for February 4 indicates that Keitel was able, by going to Hitler, to block the appointment of Colonel Friedrich-Karl Cranz (a section chief in the Personnel Office) to Schwedler's post, but it is not clear whether this means that Hitler had wanted Cranz and Keitel talked him out of it, or that Keitel used Hitler's authority to prevent Brauchitsch from appointing Cranz.

Finally, the announcements of February 4 included a list of seven Army and six Luftwaffe generals who were retired from active duty.* The seven Army generals were Wilhelm Ritter von Leeb (commander of the army group at Kassel and next in seniority to Rundstedt), Ewald von Kleist (corps commander at Breslau), Franz Kress von Kressenstein (corps commander at Wiesbaden), Oswald Lutz (chief of the OKH office for motorized troops), Günther von Pogrell (Inspector of Cavalry), Kurt Liese (chief of Army ordnance), and Günther von Niebelschütz (Inspector of Army Schools).

The selection of these seven officers has never been fully explained; Hossbach thought it unlikely that they were named by Hitler, who hardly knew most of them, and that they were settled on by Goering, Keitel, and Brauchitsch, in response to Hitler's general wish to open up some of the top commands to younger men. But Hitler and Goering certainly had reports from Party circles about the behavior and personalities of the generals in field commands where they were thrown in contact with the local authorities. It is probable that these reports, no doubt reflecting unfavorably on the more aristocratic, religious, monarchist, or outspokenly anti-Nazi generals, who stood in the way of Himmler's "educational" ideas, played a part in the selections,† and Leeb, Kleist, Kressenstein, Pogrell, and Niebelschütz all fitted this pattern.

A curious feature of the episode is how differently the retired generals were subsequently treated. Leeb was recalled to active duty within a few months to take one of the major commands for the assault on Czechoslovakia, and during the Second World War both Leeb and Kleist had leading roles and became field marshals. Kressenstein and Liese, on the other hand, were not recalled during the war, and the remaining three served only in secondary assignments. At least in some cases, accordingly, these retirements were not a purge of dissidents; perhaps it was believed that the social and religious predilections of a commander were less important when leading troops in combat than in peacetime training.

---

* It is noteworthy that the Army appointments and retirements were announced by Hitler, while those of the Luftwaffe were announced by Goering's Ministry of Aviation, although Hitler now had direct command of both services. Presumably the intention was to underline Hitler's control of the Army and nurse Goering's vanity. The Luftwaffe generals who were retired were all former Army officers who had been taken into the Luftwaffe in its formative years to help with organizational, administrative, and training problems. They included General Wilberg, whose leading role in German military aid to Franco has been described.

† An extraordinary amount of misinformation about these retirements has been published, even by distinguished historians. The original culprit appears to be the late Sir John Wheeler-Bennett, who, in his *The Nemesis of Power* (p. 373), wrote that sixteen "high-ranking generals" were ousted, including Rundstedt, Leeb, Kressenstein, Kuchler, Kluge, Weichs, and Witzleben. In fact, only Leeb and Kressenstein were correctly included; none of the others was retired at that time, and the correct number of victims is thirteen, of whom six were Luftwaffe officers. But the number sixteen and the erroneous listings were then repeated by Gordon Craig in *The Politics of the Prussian Army 1640–1945* (p. 495) and by William L. Shirer in *The Rise and Fall of the Third Reich* (pp. 318–19). These errors are especially bemusing since the list of officers retired was published in the German press, and six of the Army generals (omitting Liese) had been correctly listed in Görlitz, *Der Deutsche Generalstab* (p. 456), as well as (including Liese) in my *Sword and Swastika* (p. 170 and Appendix 2, "Apocrypha of the Blomberg-Fritsch Crisis," pp. 377–78).

Unquestionably, however, the vacancies thus created were filled by generals friendly to the Nazis, or at least to Hitler. Of the two who obtained top field commands, Reichenau was well known as the leading Nazi supporter in the officer corps, and List (who replaced Leeb) was also of that persuasion. So, too, were Busch, Schroth, Guderian, and Schobert, who replaced respectively Kleist, Kressenstein, Lutz, and Reichenau in his former post at Munich.

8

In a continental nation where the Army had always been the dominant service, an airman was now the only field marshal, outranking all the Army generals. In a country whose military machine was rapidly becoming the most powerful in the world, the Commander-in-Chief was a former corporal who had been out of uniform for nearly two decades. These were two of the more curious items in the capacious grab bag of February 4, 1938, along with promotions and transfers for many, and retirements for a few. What did it all mean?

Hitler spent the afternoon and evening of February 5 justifying his actions, first before a hastily summoned gathering at the Reich Chancellery of senior generals and admirals, from both Berlin and the field and sea commands, and then at a meeting of the Cabinet. Hitler introduced Brauchitsch and Keitel to that body (which apparently never met again), and Lammers read the decree establishing the Secret Cabinet Council (which never met at all). To the generals, however, Hitler held forth at some length and, although no minutes were kept, several in the audience subsequently recorded their recollections, which, on the whole, are mutually consistent.

Hitler appeared flanked by Goering, with his new field marshal's baton, and Brauchitsch. The burden of his address was that the military shake-up was entirely the consequence of Blomberg's *mésalliance* and circumstantial corroboration of the charges against Fritsch. Blomberg had imposed on him and Goering by inducing them to be witnesses at his marriage to a woman with a criminal past. Furthermore, he had a weak character; he had lost his nerve at the time of the Rhineland remilitarization, and had had a delaying influence on rearmament. As for Fritsch, Hitler had had the accusing dossier for two years past, but had taken no action for fear of its negative effect, if disclosed, on Germany's image abroad. But with the departure of Blomberg, and Fritsch's consequent emergence as the ranking Army officer, these questions had to be cleared up. Fritsch had himself disclosed his feeding of the boys from the *Hitlerjugend,* and upon confrontation the accuser had identified Fritsch as the culprit. Guertner, the Minister of Justice, had examined the situation and recommended a judicial inquiry; under these circumstances Fritsch must step down, and Brauchitsch would take over the Army command. These blows to the Wehrmacht required unified and strong leadership to repair the damage, and he, the Fuehrer, would undertake that himself.

After Hitler had departed, Brauchitsch laid his fellow-generals under strict orders not to discuss the Fritsch case and to draw no conclusions pending the decision of the military court. This injunction, of course, ruled out for the time being **any** collective action in support of Fritsch.

Most of what Hitler told the generals was true as far as it went, but of course there was far more to the episode than the accusations in the two dossiers. There is much about Hitler's motivation, however, that remains obscure.* Perhaps Hitler, as he said, had known of the Fritsch dossier for several years, but the possibility cannot be excluded that he was a party to its concoction. Indeed the broad question of how far the events of February 4 were the consequences of a preconceived plot, involving Himmler, Goering, and perhaps Hitler, or were rather Hitler's exploitation of opportunities that came to him unexpectedly, remains murky.

If Blomberg had not married Erna Grühn, would Hitler have found other reasons to dismiss him? If Blomberg had not fallen on his face, would Hitler have brought the charges against Fritsch? And what part, if any, did the conduct of Blomberg, Fritsch, and Neurath at the Hossbach conference play in Hitler's decision to sack all three of them? None of these questions can be answered with assurance, but the likelihood is that Blomberg would have survived as long as he co-operated with Hitler's plans, that before long Fritsch and Neurath would have been supplanted in any event, and that the Hossbach conference was one of a sequence of episodes that convinced Hitler of the necessity of bringing in a new team.

One thing that is quite clear is that the Blomberg and Fritsch cases were, from Hitler's standpoint, quite distinct. Blomberg was Minister of War—a political and not a career position from which Hitler could have at any time removed him for any reason or no reason, just as he removed Neurath. Blomberg's status as Commander-in-Chief of the Wehrmacht was unprecedented, and unwelcome to all three of the services, whose commanders-in-chief stood to gain direct access to Hitler by Blomberg's elimination. If it be added that Blomberg had lost touch with his fellow-generals and drew no support from the officer corps, it becomes plain that Hitler needed no Erna Grühn to get rid of him. But Blomberg had given Hitler strong support when it was badly needed and, though he argued, he obeyed orders and was both ostentatiously and sincerely loyal. Hitler disliked unfamiliar faces and probably would have kept on with Blomberg indefinitely unless some future event had brought them into sharper disagreement.

Fritsch, though of lower rank, was bigger game. He embodied the traditions

---

* The obscurity is certainly not lessened by A. J. P. Taylor's pronouncement (in *The Origins of the Second World War*, p. 141) that "of course the object of the whole operation" was to produce a "stir" so that "the resignation of Schacht could now be smuggled quietly in among the other changes." No such idea occurred to any of the numerous participants in the crisis who have left records of their thoughts and acts during the critical period. No such idea occurred to Schacht himself, as appears from his three accounts of the Blomberg and Fritsch dismissals, in *Account Settled*, pp. 111–14; *Confessions of "The Old Wizard,"* pp. 353–54; and *My First Seventy-Six Years*, pp. 386–94. According to Jodl's diary entry for February 3, 1938, Schacht send word to General Georg Thomas, Chief of the Economic Division of the War Ministry, that "the SS would use all means to cast suspicion on the Wehrmacht and push it to the wall," and that "such methods were visible in the accusations against the Commander-in-Chief of the Army." Furthermore, although Schacht had resigned as Minister of Economics, he remained President of the Reichsbank until 1939, and a *Reichsminister* without portfolio until 1943.

of the Army—of Hindenburg and Seeckt—and, with the support of Beck and Manstein, was forcefully opposing Hitler's efforts, through Blomberg, to focus operational control of the Wehrmacht outside of and above the Army instead of in the Army's own General Staff. He stood athwart Hitler's wish for control of appointments and promotions, and Himmler's drive to "politicize" the Army and infuse it with Nazi ideology. Hindenburg had foisted him on Hitler, who had wanted Reichenau, and there was no rapport between them. And, unlike Blomberg, Fritsch was held in high esteem by his brother officers and, were he so minded, could have made things very difficult for Hitler.

It is fair to conclude that, in all probability, Hitler was looking for a way to get rid of Fritsch and, had he been sure that the Himmler dossier was solid, would have moved against him sooner. But it was at best suspect, and one can but marvel at the infernal skill in timing and handling that Hitler displayed in exploiting a libelous falsehood so successfully. Fräulein Grühn was a disaster for Fritsch as well as for Blomberg, for one proven scandal tends to corroborate others, and dismissing Blomberg made it easier to deal with Fritsch. Beck and his sanctimonious colleagues simply played into Hitler's hands by trumpeting their outrage at Blomberg's "whore" (as Beck called her), for it enabled Hitler to escalate Blomberg's *faux pas* and the unproven Himmler dossier on Fritsch into an apparent state of crisis, amply justifying the strongest measures on his own part to preserve the image and unity of the Wehrmacht.

So far as concerns Fritsch, accordingly, Hitler would have had ample reason to eliminate him had there never been a Hossbach conference. But after Ethiopia, the Rhineland, Manchuria, and Spain, Hitler sensed the quickening tide of events and the likelihood that opportunities to move against Austria or Czechoslovakia might soon arise. Blomberg, Fritsch, and Neurath had all made plain their misgivings about his analysis and intentions. It was time for a change.*

Whatever his motives, Hitler had gained an enormous increment of power, and loosened the brakes on his own strategic decision-making. True, there was still need for a measure of self-restraint in his dealings with the Army. He preferred Reichenau to Brauchitsch, but settled for his second choice rather than face the wave of resentment and resignations which Reichenau's appointment would have entailed. He wanted Beck out of the way, but decided not to force the issue, and it was Beck who was to prove the major obstacle to Hitler's designs, as they unfolded during the coming months.

But the Army's leadership was both crippled and corrupted, and no longer in a position to offer effective resistance to the Fuehrer. Brauchitsch had been obliged to mortgage his personal and professional soul as the price of office. A dozen or more other senior generals were indebted for their promotions to these

---

* A few weeks later, Goering told Sir Nevile Henderson that Fritsch had been dismissed because he disagreed with Hitler's foreign policy. Blomberg, on a visit to Berlin during the war, asked a nephew who worked with the Propaganda Ministry whether he had heard anything about the dismissals of himself and Fritsch, and was told that Goebbels had quoted Hitler to the effect that "I couldn't use two men who were running about preaching against the war."

unsavory events. The Army had suffered the murder of Schleicher and Bredow in 1934, and now witnessed the destruction of Fritsch on trumped-up charges without lifting a finger to save him. Outwitted, demoralized, and bribed, the officer corps now faced the terrible issues of Europe on the eve of war, with no voice strong enough to speak effectively for the Army.

CHAPTER 15

The Annexation of Austria

1

Conferring with Keitel on January 31, 1938 about the Blomberg-Fritsch problems, Hitler remarked that he wanted to "take the spotlight off the Wehrmacht," and make "Europe catch its breath" at the spectacle of a governmental reorganization which would give an "impression not of instability but concentrated strength." Then he added: "This will not embolden Schuschnigg, rather it will make him quake." For all the turbulent and bizarre events of the moment, Austria and its chancellor, Kurt von Schuschnigg, were very much on Hitler's mind.

The unification of Germany and Austria, as is well known, had been a cardinal objective of Hitler's statecraft since its initial formulation. But his efforts in this direction during the first years of his chancellorship had misfired when the Austrian Nazi coup of July 1934 failed and saddled Hitler, in general opinion, with responsibility for the murder of Chancellor Engelbert Dollfuss. The consequence was the Stresa Front against Germany, the alienation of Mussolini, and a period of diplomatic isolation.

Whatever the extent of Hitler's personal involvement in the abortive July *Putsch,* he was unquestionably alarmed by its consequences and at once decided to draw in his horns. In these straits, on the very night of Dollfuss' death, Hitler, who was at the Bayreuth Festival, spoke on the telephone with Franz von Papen in Berlin and begged him to accept an appointment as Minister to Austria.

For most onlookers, it was a surprising offer and an astonishing acceptance. Less than a month had elapsed since the Roehm purge, in which Papen had been kept under house arrest and several of his close associates murdered. Papen nevertheless accepted the appointment, by his own account, because "my conscience told me that I must do everything to restore order," and "if the situation was to be saved, it would have to be someone who was at least in a position to influence Hitler and . . . like myself, was independent and had his own political line." On Hitler's part, Papen's selection appeared desirable because, as a Catholic non-Nazi and friend of Dollfuss, the ex-Vice-Chancellor would be well qualified to pour oil on the troubled waters and at the same time promote the policy of bringing Austria into the German orbit.

Hitler's letter of July 26, 1934, recommending Papen's appointment to Hin-

denburg, who was in the last week of his long life,* condemned the assassination
of Dollfuss, proclaimed a desire for better relations with Austria, and specified
that Papen would be Minister "on special mission for a limited period of time" and
directly subordinated to Hitler rather than Neurath. Papen subsequently asserted
that Hitler also agreed that the German Nazi Party would "be forbidden to interfere in internal Austrian affairs," and that "Austrian union with Germany must
never be resolved by force, but only by evolutionary methods."

It was a sadly torn little country, and an unstable regime, that Papen found
upon his arrival in Vienna in August of 1934. Parliamentary democracy had
perished in March 1933, largely as a result of the seemingly unbridgeable gulf between the Social Democratic majority in the industrialized Vienna region (with
about a quarter of the country's less than seven million inhabitants), and the conservative, Catholic rural areas. The authoritarian, clerical Dolfuss had dissolved
the Parliament in March 1933 and governed thereafter by emergency decree.
Socialist resistance erupted into civil war on February 12, 1934; the workers made
their stand in the big low-cost housing developments of Vienna but were routed
out, with heavy loss of life, by government artillery. The Social Democratic Party
was declared illegal, and Dollfuss' creation, the "Fatherland Front," was made the
sole lawful political organization.

Kurt von Schuschnigg, who succeeded Dollfuss as Chancellor, was a Jesuit-
educated lawyer with monarchist leanings who had been Minister of Justice and
shared Dollfuss' outlook. The young Chancellor (he was only thirty-seven) had to
walk a thin and swaying political tightrope, with Social Democrats and Nazis both
driven underground, and much feuding between rival groups within the Fatherland Front. Many of the Nazis involved in the July revolt had fled to Germany,
where they formed an "Austrian Legion," which maintained clandestine contact
with the militant Nazi elements in Austria, led by Captain Josef Leopold. For internal support against its opponents, the Government relied chiefly on the *Heimwehr,* a paramilitary "home defense" movement in which Prince Ernst von Starhemberg was the leading figure. The Prince became Vice-Chancellor in
Schuschnigg's new government, but soon developed Fascist leanings and ambitions to become Regent. He was not the man to bring it off; by 1936 Schuschnigg
felt strong enough to disarm the *Heimwehr* units, and Starhemberg resigned and
soon faded from the scene.

As part of his new low-keyed policy toward Austria, Hitler, in his speech to
the Reichstag on May 21, 1935, declared that "Germany neither intends nor
wishes to interfere in the internal affairs of Austria, to annex Austria or to conclude an *Anschluss.*" The protestation, however, was part of Hitler's effort to
quiet the fears aroused by his denunciation, two months earlier, of the Versailles
armament restrictions, and it was included in the speech at Papen's request in

* Hindenburg's letter appointing Papen was signed July 28, 1934, four days before his
death; apparently it was the Old Gentleman's last official signature. According to Papen, the
famous Dr. Ferdinand Sauerbruch, Hindenburg's physician, later said that the President,
before signing, remarked doubtfully: "Is this what Papen really wants?" Sauerbruch's published account makes no mention of this, but relates that Hindenburg insisted on getting out
of bed and putting on his frock coat, declaring that official functions could not be performed in a nightgown.

order to facilitate his task of normalizing relations between the two countries. It was entirely disingenuous, for *Anschluss*—the unification of Germany and Austria—remained Hitler's cherished goal. The détente was only a matter of tactics, as Papen well knew. He kept in close though not always harmonious contact with the Austrian Nazis and was alert to detect and if possible block political developments inimical to Hitler's ultimate aim.

Within Austria, attitudes toward *Anschluss* were mixed and fluctuating. During the early years of the Weimar Republic, when the German Social Democrats were still a potent force, their Austrian counterparts would have welcomed unification, but after the advent of Hitler, of course, they saw the matter quite otherwise. Conservative non-Nazi circles were divided but on the whole were opposed to *Anschluss*. Some were monarchists who would have been glad to see the Hapsburgs, in the person of Otto, again on the throne, and many others, as devout Catholics, were repelled by Nazi attitudes toward the Church. The Schuschnigg regime reflected these sentiments and was dedicated to the preservation of Austrian independence.

For external support against German pressures, Schuschnigg relied primarily on Mussolini. This was more than a little anomalous, since Austria had been the main obstacle to Italian unification and independence in the previous century. Italians and Austrians had fought each other savagely during the First World War, and for many Austrians the Trentino was *irredenta*. Much was made of Mussolini's military demonstration on the Austrian border at the time of Dollfuss' assassination, but in fact Italian troops in Austria would have been about as unwelcome as Russians in Poland. The matter came up in conversation between the Duce and the Chancellor during the latter's first official visit to Italy, in August of 1934:

MUSSOLINI: Tell me frankly, your Excellency, would you, politically speaking, have been in a position to accept military help from Italy against Hitler? That is, if, for instance, our divisions had actually entered Austria one month ago, instead of merely staging a display of power on the borders?

SCHUSCHNIGG: We were most grateful for the Italian assistance as it was offered to us then. . . . But actual military assistance within our borders would have been quite frankly—out of the question. The presence of Italian troops on our soil would have rendered the position of the Austrian Government untenable. . . .

An entry by an allied force that included French, Yugoslav, and Czech as well as Italian troops, as planned by Gamelin and Badoglio the following year, might have been another matter. But the Laval-Mussolini understanding and the Stresa Front collapsed under the pressures of the Italo-Ethiopian War, and, as Germany and Italy drew closer together, it became painfully apparent in Vienna that Italian support would no longer be based on Versailles and Locarno or in concert with the western democracies against Germany. Italian policy would be shaped within the framework of the nascent Axis, as Mussolini indicated to Schuschnigg during the latter's visit in the spring of 1936, by urging him to take prompt and energetic measures for improved relations with Germany. "Apart from that," the Duce added, "you will enjoy much greater security than before when Italy in turn has a friendship treaty with Germany. Such an agreement depends, of course, on the elimination of the dispute about Austria."

Papen had, in fact, submitted a draft proposal for an Austro-German treaty in July 1935, which Mussolini and Schuschnigg now reviewed in detail. Mussolini's attitude left the Austrians little choice except to proceed, and the result was the Austro-German Agreement, part public and part secret, signed by Schuschnigg and Papen on July 11, 1936.*

Schuschnigg and his colleagues were well aware that the agreement was worth no more than the respect Hitler would pay it. "No one thought that it would cause Hitler to desist from further pressure for the incorporation of Austria," Schuschnigg later wrote. "We estimated the validity of the agreement at two years; it was hoped that, during this time, the Powers would not give way to further illusions about the dangerous nature of Berlin's policy and would once more coalesce in the Stresa front." But these hopes were not to be realized, and two years proved an overestimate.

2

After authorizing Papen to sign the agreement, Hitler had second thoughts, and when Papen telephoned the news of its consummation, the Fuehrer "broke into a flood of abuse" and declared that he had been trapped "into making exaggerated concessions in return for purely platonic undertakings by the Austrian Government, which they would probably never fulfill." But the international press reaction was favorable, and his attitude soon changed again; Papen was invited to Bayreuth as Hitler's guest and given the rank of ambassador.

For a time, the agreement appeared to work tolerably well. On July 23, Papen was able to report that amnesty benefits had been extended to over 17,000 political prisoners, many of whom were Nazis or supporters of *Anschluss*. In deference to Hitler's demand that pro-Germans be taken into the government, Edmund von Glaise-Horstenau, who though not a Nazi was a strong pan-Germanist, was brought into the government and, a few months later, became Minister of the Interior. Hitler, for his part, called Captain Leopold to Berchtesgaden and told him that, for the time being, the Austrian Nazis should stay within the law and do nothing to upset the applecart. German restrictions on trade with Austria were lifted, to the considerable benefit of the Austrian economy.

As part of the Cabinet reshuffle incident to the agreement, Schuschnigg appointed as Secretary of State for Foreign Affairs a young civil servant, Guido Schmidt, whose ability had impressed both himself and the President, Wilhelm Miklas. In November 1936, Papen shepherded Schmidt on a visit to Berlin, in the course of which there were official dinners and festivities, and interviews with Blomberg, Neurath, Goering, and Hitler. A "Protocol," elaborating some of the provisions of the July agreement, was signed by Schmidt and Neurath; it proclaimed the two countries' mutual hostility to communism,† envisaged closer economic and cultural relations, and recognized the right of German citizens

---

* The contents are described on pp. 166–67.
† This was in line with the German-Japanese Anti-Comintern Pact, signed in Berlin just four days later.

staying in Austria to display the Nazi flag and other Party insignia. Schmidt returned to Vienna highly pleased with his reception and laudatory of his German hosts, to such an extent that Schuschnigg told Glaise-Horstenau (who promptly reported to Papen) that "Berlin's domestic demands were not so great as he had feared," and that "Papen was much more National Socialist than Hitler and Goering."

But that was the end of the honeymoon, such as it was. Papen's reaction to Schmidt's euphoria was a decision to "disturb these rosy dreams" by reminding Schuschnigg that Germany would expect speedier fulfillment of her demands respecting amnesty and the appointment of "National Opposition" elements—i.e., others who, like Glaise-Horstenau, sympathized with the German viewpoint. The turning point came a few days later, in immediate consequence of Schuschnigg's speech to the Fatherland Front at Klagenfurt, in which the Chancellor specified Austria's three main enemies as communism, the domestic Nazi movement, and internal defeatism. Neurath at once instructed Papen to express "astonishment" and advise Schuschnigg that his remarks had ruled out any possibility of Neurath's visiting Austria "for the time being." Papen carried out his mission on December 2, coupling the scolding with a denunciation of the Fatherland Front's "black clericalism" and unwillingness "to adjust itself to the new situation" created by the July agreement.

From here on, the Austro-German relation was downhill all the way. In January 1937, Hitler saluted the New Year with a rebuke to Schuschnigg for failing to grant amnesty to the Nazis who had seized the Chancellery in Vienna at the time of the Dollfuss murder. When Neurath came to Vienna, his route from the railway station to the German legation was lined with Nazi sympathizers shouting: "Heil Hitler!" The next day, on the return trip to the station, Neurath was driven through a mass of counterdemonstrators crying: "Hail Austria!" and "Down with Hitler!" His conversations with Schuschnigg were courteous enough but brought out the sharp conflict between the ways that the two governments were treating the provisions of the July agreement regarding Nazi Party activities in Austria. For Schuschnigg, the stipulation that "Austrian National Socialism" was "an internal affair" which Germany agreed not to "influence directly or indirectly" meant that Austria was free to proscribe the Nazi Party and punish its members when they violated the laws. For Neurath, the clause calling for "internal pacification of the National Opposition and its participation in shaping the political will in Austria" required a drastic change in the official attitude toward the Austrian Nazis, and he bluntly informed Schuschnigg that better relations could not be achieved "as long as the persecution of National Socialism continued in Austria."

On April 22, Schuschnigg went to Venice for what proved to be his last meeting with Mussolini. The Duce was friendly and assured his guest that his "attitude towards the Austrian problem was unchanged, being based, as always, on the necessity for Austrian independence." But there were signs of erosion of this policy: Mussolini reported Goering's expressions of dissatisfaction with Austria's implementation of the July agreement, stressed the need for "bringing Austrian independence into harmony with the Rome-Berlin Axis," and remarked pointedly that "Italy's intervention in Spain made considerable demands on her resources." He interrupted his attentions to Schuschnigg in order to inspect a German "Strength-through-Joy" ship that was flying the swastika and had arrived in the harbor, and then he departed Venice suddenly, leaving it to Ciano to bid the Austrian farewell.

Upon Schuschnigg's return, events took another turn for the worse. Under the July agreement, German citizens in Austria were allowed to fly the swastika flag on May 1, a German national holiday. In the Styrian town of Pinkafeld, a young Austrian lieutenant erroneously ordered a German flag taken down. The incident caused an explosion of indignation among the Germans and their partisans, and Hitler ordered Papen to Berlin. The Fuehrer was loud and abusive, and Papen only with difficulty persuaded him to continue the "evolutionary" policy.

Back in Vienna, Papen sought to impress upon Schuschnigg "the extraordinary gravity of the situation existing between our two countries." The flag incident had stretched Hitler's patience close to the breaking point, and he "could not tolerate an anti-German minority in Austria pouring ridicule on everything sacred to Germandom." The July agreement, Papen asserted, "was being sabotaged" by the Austrian Government, which had done nothing to bring the "National Opposition" into the political picture.

Schuschnigg responded that Germany had not lived up to her agreement to refrain from interference in Austria's internal affairs, to which Papen answered that Hitler "could not be held responsible," since he "had instructed me to declare that any violation of the July Agreement was contrary to his wishes." It was a lame and specious retort; Papen himself had secretly countenanced continued German financial support for the Austrian Nazis, and early in May the Austrian police raided the Nazi Party headquarters in Vienna and seized what Papen described as "very incriminating papers regarding the connection between the German and Austrian N.S.D.A.P. . . . such as memoranda of conversations of Austrian National Socialist leaders with the Fuehrer and other leading German personages; evidence of funds made available from the Reich for organizational purposes of the Austrian N.S.D.A.P.; material for political propaganda against Austrian Government officials, emanating principally from Austrian exiles in the Reich . . . and other correspondence of the Austrian *SS* with German *SS* offices."

Despite these wholesale violations of the July agreement, the façade of its observance was maintained during the summer of 1937. Another member of the National Opposition, the Vienna lawyer and Nazi supporter Artur Seyss-Inquart, who also had the personal confidence of Schuschnigg and President Miklas, was appointed a state councilor. Early in July a German Foreign Ministry delegation, headed by Weizsaecker, came to Vienna to negotiate further implementation of the agreement, and secured concessions from the Austrians on a number of relatively minor matters, including the sale in Austria of Hitler's *Mein Kampf,* and the quashing of criminal proceedings against a number of Austrian Nazis who had fled to Germany and wished to return.

It now became apparent that Papen was beginning to lose his primacy as

Hitler's adviser and executant on Austrian policy. Earlier in the year he had fallen at odds with Captain Leopold; the official journal of the Austrian Nazis printed a sharp attack against Papen in May, and in June he ordered the members of the Legation staff "to break off all relations with Captain Leopold and his agents." Nevertheless, when the Weizsaecker delegation came to Vienna a few weeks later, Leopold was called into conference with the Germans in Papen's presence. Furthermore, there was a new face in the German delegation; Wilhelm Keppler, an industrial engineer who had attached himself to Hitler in 1927, and had since functioned as a personal economic adviser to the Fuehrer. At the conclusion of the July negotiations, Keppler betook himself promptly to the Berghof and made a personal report in which he no doubt described the Papen-Leopold feud. The result was a personal directive from Hitler, extending to Keppler "basic authority to handle questions connected with Austria in relation to the Party." This meant that the matters of greatest importance to Hitler were removed from Papen's sphere of authority, and Seyss-Inquart, newly chosen as the German observer-representative in the Austrian Government, sent his informational reports to Keppler rather than Papen.

Neurath, too, asserted his authority more forcefully at this time. Early in August, while weekending in western Austria, he was visited by Guido Schmidt, seeking to justify his government's policies. Neurath was much sharper than he had been with Schuschnigg six months earlier; the Schuschnigg regime "was opposed to the policy desired by the majority of the Austrian people," and the July agreement "had been very imperfectly carried out by Austria." Neurath reported the conversation to Hitler, sending a copy to Papen, with the conclusion that "the will to carry out the Agreement of July 11, 1936 is not present on the part of the Austrian Government, and we shall hardly succeed in regulating German-Austrian relations by this method."

This, of course, was a direct attack on the Papen policy of working things out through Schuschnigg and Schmidt. Neurath was an "old line" diplomat but spoke his master's mind. Papen realized that his own stock was in decline, and the old fox started to lay the groundwork for new initiatives on his own part. On August 21, in a long letter to Neurath, he declared that Guido Schmidt had lost his influence over Schuschnigg and should "from now on be considered merely as a pawn." In a second letter, dated September 1, he raised a doubt that German policy could be effectively implemented through Schuschnigg, and the question whether "we ought not, with the cooperation of external and internal factors, to consider bringing about a change of chancellors." The question was discussed during Mussolini's visit to Germany later that month; the Duce's attitude toward Schusschnigg was ambivalent, and a decision was postponed on the basis that "we should not overthrow Schuschnigg without the certainty of a suitable successor."

Hermann Goering now began to loom larger in the Austrian picture. Hitler himself had previously summoned Captain Leopold and other leaders of the Austrian Nazis and personally laid down their guidelines. But Keppler, to whom Hitler had delegated Austrian Party matters, was on Goering's staff at the Office of the Four Year Plan, and, when Leopold refused to recognize Keppler's authority and denounced Seyss-Inquart as well, Goering called in Leopold and, in Keppler's presence, made the captain promise "to maintain strict discipline" and cease to interfere with Seyss-Inquart's activities. Henceforth there were two lines of authority emanating from Hitler on Austrian matters: through Goering and Keppler to Leopold's illegal Nazis and the National Socialist "moderates" such as Glaise-Horstenau and Seyss-Inquart, and through Neurath and Papen to the Austrian Government. Not surprisingly, the consequence was constant friction between the Austrian ends of the two channels, especially between Papen and Leopold.

Aware of Goering's growing impatience and seriously disturbed by Berlin's hostility and an escalation of violent demonstrations by Leopold's adherents, in November Schuschnigg and Schmidt sought to prevail on the *Reichsjägermeister* to pay a hunting visit to the Austrian Tyrol,* hoping thus to establish a helpful personal contact. But Goering replied that such a trip would serve no purpose unless some major step toward unification, such as a customs and currency union, could be announced, and this the Austrians were not willing to concede.

In December, Papen returned to Vienna after an absence of some weeks. Schuschnigg asked him to call, and expressed his distress at the course of events. Papen seized the opportunity for a round condemnation of Schuschnigg's failure to bring Austria into line with German policies and goals:

> The German Reich was now embarked on a movement of the greatest historical significance. By exerting the best and strongest energies of the Reich and utilizing the present international situation, the Fuehrer was trying to restore the world position of the Reich. In this process Germany had to demand more than more passive assistance from Austria; she had to demand that Austria, with heart and soul . . . support this struggle of the German world for its existence. . . . This passive attitude was itself a negation. . . . Both in the Spanish affair and in the fight against Bolshevism through the Anti-Comintern Pact, and also in her attitude toward the problem of the League of Nations, Austria had gone her own way.† Instead of creating a closer cordial relationship by means of evolutionary development in this sphere of culture, defense, and economics, she could not go a fraction of an inch too far for fear of displeasing the Western powers.

Moved by this and the numerous other manifestations of German displeasure, Schuschnigg reopened discussions with Seyss-Inquart for a larger participation by the National Socialists. At first these talks were unproductive, and early in January, Seyss-Inquart informed Keppler that he wished to resign "because various suggestions made by him have recently been rejected" by Schuschnigg. He

---

* Schmidt had been Goering's guest at Karinhall in September 1937; his host had shown him a map which omitted the boundary between Austria and Germany, remarking that huntsmen know only one boundary, the game preserve, and only one law, "Don't poach."

† The Austrian Government had not officially taken a pro-Franco position, though the Catholic population was heavily pro-Franco and Germany's aid to the rebels had increased Hitler's popularity. Austria had remained a member of the League, although Hitler had suggested to Guido Schmidt, during the latter's visit to Berlin November 1936, that Austria should follow Germany's example and withdraw.

was at once admonished by Goering to "remain at his post" and, if necessary, "to come to Berlin and report."

Later that month, however, an event occurred that measurably spurred the negotiations. On January 22, 1938, Dr. Leopold Tavs, director of the Austrian Nazis' Vienna headquarters, gave a newspaper interview in which he declared that the relation of the Austrian to the German Nazis was "one of complete trust and one hundred per cent obedience." He was arrested and charged with high treason, and a search of his offices and home yielded a document embodying an "action program," envisaging a German demand for Schuschnigg's resignation, the designation of Captain Leopold as Hitler's deputy for Austria, and the deployment of German armed forces on the Austrian border to enforce those terms.

Although there was no proof that such a program had German approval, Schuschnigg and his colleagues were greatly alarmed and began to negotiate with Seyss-Inquart in earnest. On February 1, the latter was able to report to Keppler that Schuschnigg had agreed to an eight-point program, to include the release of all of the July 1934 rebels who were still in jail, extensive appointment of National Socialists to governmental and civic positions, and greatly broadened personal authority for Seyss-Inquart. Keppler passed the information on to Ribbentrop (newly designated Foreign Minister) and Goering, who on February 6 "approved the efforts and the progress made so far by Councillor Seyss-Inquart" and directed that the negotiations "continue in order to obtain as comprehensive promises as possible from Schuschnigg." Goering did not, however, "desire any kind of direct written agreement between Schuschnigg and Seyss-Inquart, but wishes that the groundwork be laid for negotiations on a different basis and between other persons."

The blind reference in the last clause indicated that a shift in the scene of the negotiations was imminent—a shift which set in train the short course of events leading directly to *Anschluss*.

3

The proposal that Schuschnigg should meet Hitler in Germany in order to iron out their differences was first broached by Papen at the December conversation when he upbraided the Chancellor for not following Germany's lead closely enough.* Schuschnigg did not rise to the bait, but Papen, back in Germany over the New Year, repeated his idea to Hitler with more success, and on January 7 was able to convey to Schuschnigg the Fuehrer's invitation to a meeting at Berchtesgaden a few weeks hence. Schuschnigg accepted in principle, but by the end of January the Blomberg-Fritsch crisis had enveloped Berlin, and on January 26, Papen passed on Hitler's suggestion that the meeting be held on February 15. The next day he reported that the Tavs document had made Schuschnigg "conscious of the impossibility of letting the present state of affairs continue," and that he was "most eager for the personal meeting and, in Glaise-Horstenau's opinion, would also be prepared to change his attitude fundamentally."

* The proposal is not mentioned in Papen's report of the conversation, but both Papen and Schuschnigg recalled that the former raised the subject on that occasion.

Papen then took off for Garmisch-Partenkirchen and the German-Austrian ski-ing competition, and then went on to Berlin, where he again saw Hitler, whom he found "sullen and touchy." Small wonder that he did, considering all that the Fuehrer had on his mind, including unpleasant news soon to be given Papen. From Vienna on February 4, that gentleman cheerily wired Hitler: "On my return from Berlin I found a situation here which in every respect seems favora-ble for the conversations contemplated with Schuschnigg. . . . State Councillor Seyss-Inquart, in particular, was urged to accept a ministerial post in the Cabi-net. I asked him to abstain for the time being from making any promises, since, if the conference at the Obersalzberg can be arranged, we shall raise a number of demands which will have to be agreed upon in advance. . . . But it strikes me as urgent . . . that I be summoned as soon as possible for a personal report, so that the details of the contemplated conversations with Schuschnigg may be settled." It is apparent that, although the Schuschnigg-Hitler meeting was "con-templated," the arrangements were still inconclusive.*

Instead of being "summoned for a personal report," within a few hours Papen received a telephone call from Lammers in Berlin, who told him that "the Fuehrer wishes me to inform you that your mission in Vienna has ended." Lammers gave no explanation other than that Neurath had been let out of the Foreign Ministry, and that Hassell and Dirksen were also being recalled. The following day came the published news of the governmental shake-up conse-quent upon the Blomberg and Fritsch dismissals.

The baffled and crestfallen Papen bade farewell to Schuschnigg and Schmidt, and then presented himself to Hitler, who had gone to the Berghof on February 6, leaving Berlin reeling from the previous day's announcements. According to Papen's account, the Fuehrer was "exhausted and distrait," offered no coherent explanation of Papen's dismissal, and came alive only when reminded of the pending discussion of a Schuschnigg visit. Reacting with enthusiasm, and with a fine disregard of diplomatic sensitivities, Hitler begged Papen to go back to Vienna and complete the arrangements for Schuschnigg's visit.

And so, to the astonishment of all concerned, Papen reappeared in Vienna on February 7, and at once got in touch with the Chancellor. Schuschnigg was as-sured that the ambit of the conversation would be enforcement of the July 1936 treaty, that no German demands prejudicial to Austrian independence and sov-ereignty would be made, and that there would be a joint Austro-German press communiqué after the meeting, the date of which was fixed for February 12.†

Why did Hitler dismiss Papen on February 4? Why did he send him back to Vienna two days later? These questions have puzzled many, and there is no firsthand evidence of his motives. But his actions, though bizarre, are not inex-plicable. Except for Fritsch, most of those dismissed on February 4 were not

* An editor's note to the "Documents on German Foreign Policy" (D-I p. 499) states: "Despite a diligent search of the files of the German Foreign Ministry, the material found on the Obersalzberg Conference is scanty."

† By an unhappy irony, the date chosen was the fourth anniversary of the Socialist workers' revolt in Vienna, the suppression of which had marked the death of democracy in Austria.

personally obnoxious to Hitler—witness the highly successful wartime careers of Leeb and Kleist, Neurath's appointment as Reich Protector of Bohemia and Moravia upon the occupation of those lands in March of 1939, and the designation of Papen himself, a month later, as Ambassador to Turkey. It is hardly strange that, in the welter of personnel problems facing him, Hitler overlooked Papen's role in arranging for the Schuschnigg interview or that, once reminded and impatient of protocol, he asked Papen to finish that particular job.

As for Papen's recall, that was an expectable by-product of Hitler's decision to accelerate the march toward *Anschluss*. By the end of 1937, Hitler was virtually certain that Mussolini would no longer stand in his way and that, with the Duce on the sidelines, France and Britain were most unlikely to intervene. All that was necessary was to set the stage so that the Austrians would appear to welcome the takeover. Papen had been useful in arranging the scenery, but now the time had come for harder tactics, for which Goering and Keppler were better suited than Papen and Neurath, and in the use of which Hitler himself was now ready to take a hand.

4

On the evening of February 10, the Fatherland Front gave a huge official ball at the Hofburg. All Vienna was there—diplomats, bureaucrats, officers—and Guido Zernatto, Secretary-General of the Front and one of Schuschnigg's closest allies, was well pleased with the scene, as he and the Chancellor discussed the coming trip. The following afternoon Schuschnigg called in Seyss-Inquart to tell him of the project, and discovered that he was already informed—a development which should have put Schuschnigg on his guard.

A few hours later, Zernatto accompanied Schuschnigg and Schmidt to the railway station. The Chancellor appeared unsure of himself; Zernatto encouraged him to bring back "a clear success," but Schuschnigg shrugged and said that he could guarantee no such thing, while remarking to Schmidt that, for dealing with Hitler, it might have been better to send Dr. Wagner-Jauregg, the famous Viennese psychiatrist.

The trip was made in Schuschnigg's private car, which was attached to the night train to Innsbruck and put off on a siding at Salzburg. The Chancellor was accompanied only by Guido Schmidt and two aides. The following morning the party was driven to the German frontier, where they were met by Papen, and then on to Berchtesgaden. Papen said that they were expected at the Berghof at eleven o'clock, and added that three German generals would also be on the scene: Keitel, Reichenau, and Sperrle.* The midwinter roads were so icy that, at Berchtesgaden, the party had to use half-track reconnaissance cars for the ride up the Obersalzberg to the Berghof.

Hitler greeted his visitors courteously and then took Schuschnigg into his study for a private discussion, while the others waited outside. Schuschnigg en-

* The selection was logical, since Keitel was the newly appointed chief of OKW, while Reichenau, though designated to succeed Brauchitsch at Leipzig, was still commanding the Munich Military District VII, which bordered Austria. Sperrle, recently returned from Spain, had been named to command Air Fleet 3, with headquarters at Munich and its airfields in south Germany.

deavored to get the conversation off to a pleasant start, but Hitler at once set a harsh and comtemptuous tone:*

SCHUSCHNIGG: This room with its wonderful view has doubtless been the scene of many a decisive conference, Herr Reichskanzler.

HITLER: Yes, in this room my thoughts ripen. But we did not get together to speak of the fine view or of the weather.

SCHUSCHNIGG: First of all, Herr Reichskanzler, I would like to thank you that you have given me the opportunity for this meeting. I would like to assure you that we take the treaty between our two countries, which we signed in July, 1936, very seriously, and that we are most anxious to remove all the remaining misunderstandings and difficulties. In any case, we have done everything to prove that we intend to follow a policy friendly towards Germany in accordance with our mutual agreement.

HITLER: So you call this a friendly policy, Herr Schuschnigg? On the contrary, you have done everything to avoid a friendly policy. For instance, you quite complacently remained a member of the League of Nations, in spite of the fact that the Reich withdrew from the League. And you call that a friendly policy?

SCHUSCHNIGG: Nobody asked Austria to withdraw from the League of Nations. We could not assume that such a step was expected of us, for at the time of our agreement, in July, 1936, Germany had long since left the League without ever stipulating that Austria should do the same. . . .

HITLER: Anyway, it is self-evident that you had to leave the League. Besides, Austria has never done anything that would be of any help to Germany. The whole history of Austria is just one uninterrupted act of high treason. . . .

SCHUSCHNIGG: All the same, Herr Reichskanzler, many an Austrian contribution cannot possibly be separated from the general picture of German culture. Take, for instance, a man like Beethoven . . .

HITLER: Oh—Beethoven? Let me tell you that Beethoven came from the lower Rhineland.

SCHUSCHNIGG: Yet Austria was the country of his choice, as it was for so many others. Nobody would, for instance, refer to Metternich as a German from the Rhineland.

HITLER: That's as may be. I am telling you once more that things cannot go on in this way. . . .

The dialogue continued in this vein, rather like Samuel Goldenberg and Schmuyle in Moussorgsky's *Pictures at an Exhibition* (a comparison that neither Chancellor would have relished). With heavy sarcasm, and unwitting irony in the light of subsequent events, Hitler challenged Schuschnigg to "a plebiscite in Austria in which we two run against each other." He berated Schuschnigg for fortifying the Austrian border:

* No interpreter was needed, and neither participant made notes. Schuschnigg subsequently recorded the dialogue from memory, and set it forth *in extenso* in his *Austrian Requiem* (pp. 20–32). Guido Zernatto heard Schuschnigg's and Schmidt's report when they arrived in Vienna the next morning and recounted what he heard in *Die Wahrheit "über" Österreich*, pp. 209 *et seq.*

HITLER: . . . You don't seriously believe that you can stop me, or even delay me for half an hour, do you? Who knows? Perhaps you will wake up one morning in Vienna to find us there—just like a spring storm. And then you'll see something. I would very much like to save Austria from such a fate, because such an action would mean blood. After the army, my S.A. and the Austrian Legion would move in, and nobody can stop their just revenge—not even I. Do you want to make another Spain of Austria? I would like to avoid all that—if possible.

SCHUSCHNIGG: I shall investigate the matter and will have any defence work on the German border stopped. I am fully aware that you can invade Austria; but Herr Reichskanzler, whether we like it or not, that would mean bloodshed. We are not alone in this world, and such a step would probably mean war.

HITLER: It is easy enough to talk of war while we are sitting here in our comfortable easy-chairs. But war means endless misery for millions. Do you want to take this responsibility upon yourself, Herr Schuschnigg? Don't think for one moment that anybody on earth is going to thwart my decisions. Italy? I see eye to eye with Mussolini, the closest ties of friendship bind me to Italy. And England? England will not move one finger for Austria. . . .

After another diatribe about "the persecution of National Socialists in Austria," Hitler declared that he was giving Schuschnigg a last opportunity "to come to terms."* He would have to address the Reichstag next week, and "the German people must know what the situation is." Accordingly, "I can only wait until this afternoon." But when Schuschnigg asked: "What exactly are your wishes?" Hitler put him off with a curt "That we can discuss this afternoon." The two men had been talking for two hours, but there had been no terms or negotiations, only psychological warfare.

At luncheon, Schuschnigg found present the newly appointed German Foreign Minister, Joachim von Ribbentrop. The three generals appeared, but only Sperrle had much to say, recounting the activities of the Condor Legion—a clever touch, since the Austrians strongly favored Franco. The pressure was relaxed, but the Austrians were not asked to sing their country's praises. Hitler delivered a long and vainglorious monologue, touching on the esteem in which he was held by his people, the bridges he would build in Hamburg, larger than any in America, and the purity of his personal finances. He described a German warship then under construction and proposed to name it the *Tegetthoff* (after the nineteenth-century Austrian naval hero Wilhelm von Tegetthoff)† and invite Schuschnigg and Admiral Horthy to the launching. Then, as coffee was served, he excused himself without explanation.

The Austrians were left for a long time in desultory chat with the generals and the press chief, Otto Dietrich. The Fuehrer's party was considerably larger

---

* According to Zernatto's account, Hitler told Schuschnigg that he had previously planned to invade Austria on February 26, but had then decided to attempt once more a peaceful solution.

† The ship, a heavy cruiser, was subsequently christened the *Prinz Eugen,* so that Austria was honored in the sense that Prince Eugene of Savoy spent his life in the service of the Austrian Empire, although he was born French or Italian.

than Schuschnigg had been led to anticipate. In addition to Ribbentrop, Dietrich, and the generals, Keppler was on the scene, as well as an Austrian art critic and minor Nazi figure, Dr. Kajetan Mühlmann, who appears to have been sent by Seyss-Inquart. The last-named had been keeping Keppler informed of his negotiations with Schuschnigg and Zernatto, and Mühlmann had been sent primarily as a messenger with the latest information.

Thus, in drawing up the demands to be presented to Schuschnigg, Hitler and his aides had full knowledge of how far Schuschnigg had already agreed to go in the discussions with Seyss-Inquart, and no doubt this information assisted them greatly in gauging how much more to ask for. Formulation of the new demands appears to have been accomplished after lunch by Hitler and Ribbentrop, perhaps with Keppler's assistance.

At any rate, later in the afternoon Schuschnigg and Schmidt were presented by Ribbentrop and Papen with a draft protocol under which Schuschnigg, as Federal Chancellor, agreed to carry out, by February 18, ten specified measures. These included the appointment of Seyss-Inquart as Minister of the Interior "with authority over security"; a general amnesty "for all persons punished by the courts or police because of their National Socialist activities"; removal of all economic, social, and military discrimination against National Socialists; preparations for the "assimilation of the Austrian to the German economic system," with the appointment of Dr. Hans Fischböck (a Nazi economist) as Minister of Finance; and a linking of the German and Austrian armed forces through general staff conferences, the exchange of officers, and the appointment of Glaise-Horstenau as Minister of the Armed Forces. In addition, there was a vaguely phrased but crucial item in which the Austrian Government recognized "that National Socialism is compatible with Austrian conditions," provided that its ideas were carried out in harmony with the Austrian Constitution. To implement this concept, Schuschnigg was to agree that his government would "take no steps which would in effect outlaw the National Socialist movement," while the German Government would agree "to prevent interference in the internal affairs of Austria" by German Nazi Party agencies, and to recognize Seyss-Inquart as the only person authorized to carry out this part of the program.

Schuschnigg immediately taxed Papen with a gross violation of the conditions under which he had agreed to come to the Berghof, inasmuch as the draft went far beyond the scope of the July 1936 agreement, and contained provisions clearly incompatible with Austrian sovereignty. Papen claimed to be equally disturbed at the turn of events. Ribbentrop, newly in office, knew little about the background of the situation and could only say that Hitler wanted it signed without alteration. Both of the Austrians criticized the vagueness of the provision on Nazi activities, and neither Papen nor Ribbentrop could make adequate explanation.

At this point Schuschnigg was told that Hitler wished to see him again. Leaving Schmidt to work out amendments with Ribbentrop and Papen, the Chancellor returned to Hitler's study, where he found the Fuehrer "pacing excitedly up and down" and heard him deliver an ultimatum:

Herr Schuschnigg, I have decided to make one last attempt. Here is the draft of the document. There is nothing to be discussed about it. You will either sign it as it stands, or our meeting has been useless. In that case I will decide during the night what will be done next.

Schuschnigg replied his signature would be of no value, since the protocol called for Seyss-Inquart's appointment to the Cabinet, and "according to our Constitution, Cabinet members are appointed by the President, just as it is only the President who can grant an amnesty." All that he could indicate by his signature was willingness to recommend these measures to the President, with no guarantee that he would approve. Hitler angrily insisted on a guarantee and, when Schuschnigg again protested his incapacity, Hitler flung open the door, bellowed for General Keitel, and told the Chancellor that he "would be called later."

It was all theatrics; when Keitel came in, ready for orders, Hitler told him there was none, and that he should just sit down and wait a few minutes. Papen came in and pointed out the counterproductive consequences of the threats, and pretty soon Schuschnigg was recalled. With a great show of false magnanimity, the Fuehrer announced: "For the first time in my life I have changed my mind," and that Schuschnigg would be given three days to obtain President Miklas' approval.

Meanwhile Schmidt had succeeded in working out some changes with Ribbentrop and Papen. As finally signed, the document declared that the "Federal Chancellor holds out the prospect of the following measures, concerning which he will send a binding reply by Tuesday, February 15, 1938." The specific items were still ten in number, but there were a number of softening changes: Austrian Nazi émigrés were excepted from the amnesty, the stipulation that Glaise-Horstenau be made Minister of the Armed Forces was abandoned in favor of an agreement to substitute General Franz Boehme* for Lieutenant-Field Marshal Alfred Jansa as Chief of the General Staff, and Dr. Fischböck was to be given a "leading post" instead of a ministerial appointment. The vague paragraph on legalization of the National Socialist movement was amended to provide that its members "shall in principle have opportunity for legal activity within the framework of the Fatherland Front and all other Austrian organizations . . . on an equal footing with all other groups, and in accordance with the Constitution." Subject to the "binding reply" safeguard, the clauses relating to the Austrian Nazis, and the appointment of Seyss-Inquart, were to be carried out by February 18. The final drafting of the protocol took some time, and it was not until late in the evening that the document was ready for signature by the two chancellors and the two foreign ministers.

There was a laconic press communiqué which merely announced that the meeting had taken place, and that it "was the result of a mutual desire to talk over all questions pertaining to relations between the German Reich and Austria." Schuschnigg and Schmidt declined Hitler's invitation to stay for dinner, and were joined by Papen for the auto trip back to Salzburg, where they boarded the train to Vienna.

* How Boehme's name got into the final protocol is a mystery. Jansa had been notified in January that he would soon be retired for age, and that his sucessor would be Lieutenant-Field Marshal Eugen Beyer. This change was made on February 16, 1938.

To Zernatto, who met them the next morning at the station, Schuschnigg declared that he might as well have been talking to a Hindu; Hitler was "a man from another world." Glaise-Horstenau, who had met Hitler at the time of the July 1936 agreement, had described the Fuehrer as "more of a prophet than a politician." Schuschnigg began his report to Zernatto with the observation: "Now at last, I know what Glaise meant!" However great the difficulties Schuschnigg found in communicating with the "Hindu," the "Prophet" had succeeded in communicating most impressively to Schuschnigg.

5

Before Keitel left the Berghof to return to Berlin, Hitler ordered him to put military pressure on the Austrian Government by staged German Army maneuvers and other deceptive measures. As organized by Keitel, Jodl, and Admiral Canaris, these included airplane flights and mountain troop exercises near the Austrian border, synthetic radio traffic between Berlin and Munich, and the spreading of rumors, such as the suspension of troop furloughs, the assemblage of rolling stock in southern Germany, and the recall of the German military attaché in Vienna, General Wolfgang Muff.

Hitler's order had specified continuance of these measures until February 15, the date on which Schuschnigg's "binding reply" was due. Whether they had any effect on the Austrian Government is doubtful* but irrelevant, as they were unnecessary; after Schuschnigg had put his signature to the Berchtesgaden agreement, its rejection in Vienna would have meant both a repudiation of the Chancellor and a direct confrontation with Hitler under most unfavorable circumstances. President Miklas did indeed object strongly and with reason to the appointment of Seyss-Inquart, but Schuschnigg's counsel at length prevailed, and on the fifteenth he was able to advise Papen that the agreement would be carried out.

And so, during the next few days,† the amnesty was announced, Beyer succeeded Jansa as Chief of the General Staff, Dr. Fischböck was given an economic appointment, and Seyss-Inquart was named Minister of Interior with control of security matters. Schuschnigg made a number of other Cabinet changes, bringing in Zernatto as Minister without Portfolio and promoting Guido Schmidt to Minister for Foreign Affairs. Seyss-Inquart, the key to the program for bringing the Austrian Nazis into the Fatherland Front and the mainstream of Austrian political life, was not altogether pleased with his appointment, since he rightly detected incompatibility between allowing Nazi activities and insignia while still prohibiting Nazi Party organization. With Schuschnigg's approval, he at once proceeded to Berlin and a long discussion with Hitler on February 17. This did nothing to resolve his dilemma but he did obtain from the Fuehrer approval of a general policy of gradualism. "One can-

---

* After *Anschluss*, Canaris found evidence that the Austrian military intelligence service had recognized the German measures as synthetic deceptions.

† American readers with long memories may be interested to be reminded that three of the State Department documents alleged to have been given by Alger Hiss to Whittaker Chambers were dispatches from Vienna and Paris relating to the Austrian developments of mid-February 1938.

not proclaim a dogma," he was told, "one must proceed from a pan-German and national German conception to a Nationalist Socialist one."

For the time being, Hitler thought it prudent to maintain the façade of the "evolutionary" policy, accelerated by the additional inroads on Austrian sovereignty accomplished at Berchtesgaden. In accordance with the obligation not to interfere in Austria's domestic problems, on February 16, Rudolf Hess distributed an order forbidding "Reich-Germans to meddle in the internal affairs of Austria, to carry on National Socialist propaganda across the border, or to issue instructions to Austrian National Socialists." At Berchtesgaden, Hitler had promised Schuschnigg that the Reichstag speech would include "some favorable commentary for Austria," and from Rome,* Ciano had sent word by the Prince of Hesse that he "hoped the independence of Austria would be explicitly mentioned." These hopes were not realized; Hitler's speech of February 20 bore on independence only to the extent that might be implied from the following passage near its end:

> In recent days a further agreement has been reached with that country which for various reasons is particularly close to us. It is not only that we are the same people, but above all it is a long common history and culture which unite the Reich and German Austria. The difficulties which arose when attempting to execute the agreements of July 11th [1936] obliged us to attempt to clear away for ever the obstacles to a final reconciliation. . . . I am happy to state that this opinion was also shared by the Austrian Chancellor who asked to pay me a visit. . . . All this is a finishing touch to the agreements of July 11th. At this point I should like to express before the German people my sincere thanks to the Austrian Chancellor for the great understanding and the ready warmth with which he accepted my invitation and strove with me to find a way which is as much in the interests of both countries as it is in the interests of the whole German people whose sons we all are, whatever our birthplace. I believe that we have thereby made a contribution to European peace.

Whatever comfort the Austrians might otherwise have derived from these words was, however, dissipated by an earlier reference to "ten million Germans" across the Reich's borders who were "subjected to continuous suffering because of their sympathy and solidarity with the whole German race and its ideology," and whose "right of racial self-determination" Hitler vowed to protect. The ten million could only comprise the three million Sudeten Germans in Czechoslovakia and the seven million Austrians, and the passage thus constituted a thinly veiled attack against the Austrian state itself.

Schuschnigg, meanwhile, had been playing his cards very close to his chest or, as his detractors might argue, not at all. Except in Rome, soothing descriptions of Berchtesgaden had been circulated to Austrian diplomatic missions abroad, and no effort had been made to alert friendly powers to the gravity of Austria's

---

* The Italians were not pleased by the news of Berchtesgaden. Attolico complained to Ribbentrop, and Ciano to the Prince of Hesse, that the Italian Government should have been informed and consulted in advance. And, as Mussolini and Ciano became more fully informed about Hitler's abusive behavior on February 12, their disenchantment increased.

plight. But Hitler's speech, and other news from Berlin, persuaded Schuschnigg that the time had come for a dramatic reaffirmation of Austrian sovereignty, and the occasion he selected was a convocation on February 24 of the federal legislature—the Bundestag—at which his new cabinet was officially presented.

"The one and only point on the agenda today is: Austria," the Chancellor announced, and went on to list the famous fighters for Austrian independence, from Maria Theresa to Engelbert Dollfuss. There were harsh words for those Austrians who failed to realize that "it is not Nationalism or Socialism which is the watchword in Austria, but patriotism." There would be no concessions beyond the terms of the Berchtesgaden agreement: "We knew that we were able to go, and we did go, up to that boundary beyond which clearly appear the words, 'Thus far and no farther!'" Austria was German and was resolved to be at peace with Germany, but would "remain a free and independent state." For the future, the watchword was the immortality of Austria and her national colors: "True German and red-white-red to the death!"*

The speech had a mixed reception both at home and abroad. In Vienna the response was enthusiastic, while in Graz—the Styrian capital in southeastern Austria near the Hungarian and Yugoslav borders, where the Nazis were strong —an SA mob stormed the city square where Schuschnigg's speech was being broadcast, turned off the loudspeakers, and hoisted the swastika flag over the town hall. Mussolini's initial reaction to the speech was highly favorable, and he declared that "Austrian patriotism had been reawakened after languishing for twenty years." In Paris, the speech was much remarked during a foreign policy debate in the Chamber of Deputies, during which Foreign Minister Delbos described Austrian independence as an essential factor in the European balance of power.

In Germany, the controlled press took no notice of the speech, and there was no official reaction. Papen, however, took the opportunity of his farewell visit to Schuschnigg to lecture the Chancellor for his unnecessarily "dramatic defense of Austrian independence," by which his "cordial words for Austria's German mission had been all but drowned out." The debate in the French Chamber had been an unfortunate consequence, for "Austrian independence supported by French and Czech crutches was unbearable for Germany," and Schuschnigg should not "delude himself into believing that Austria could ever maintain her position with the aid of non-German European alliances." The worried Chancellor, according to Papen, disavowed any responsibility for the French reaction and agreed that it was "most disturbing."

Meanwhile, Hitler was giving a personal demonstration of how seriously the commitment of noninterference in Austrian domestic affairs should be taken. At Berchtesgaden he had agreed that Leopold, Tavs and several of their most uninhibited Nazi colleagues, whose dismissal was desired by both Schuschnigg and Seyss-Inquart, would be removed to Germany. On February 21 in Berlin, Hitler, flanked by Goering and Keppler, called in Leopold, criticized his conduct

---

* In German, the phrase is a rhyme of *rot* (red) and *tot* (dead): *"Rot-weiss-rot bis in den Tod!"*

as "insane" for allowing records of incriminating conversations and plans to fall into the hands of the police, and ordered him "to keep aloof from Austrian politics," while reassuring him that he would be given "other employment."

So far this was all in accordance with the Berchtesgaden agreement, but Hitler next summoned a former Austrian Army major, Hubert Klausner, who had just been released from prison under the amnesty, designated him as Leopold's successor, and "gave him a lengthy explanation of the way in which the Party in Austria was to be led." Keppler was to be Klausner's "contact man" with the Reich, and Klausner was given permission to come directly to Hitler, "at any time." Hitler also directed that "good working arrangements had to be created with Dr. Seyss-Inquart, who had no ambitions of any kind to lead the Party," and who "had assumed a very hard task and had to be supported by the Party in every way."

To be sure, the import was cautionary, but by naming Klausner as leader, and giving him guidelines, Hitler was flagrantly violating both the Berchtesgaden protocol and his own directive, through Hess, to all Reich Germans. Furthermore, after the Klausner-Leopold matters were disposed of, Hitler instructed Keppler that the "Austrian Legion" in Germany was to be maintained "since the need for intervention by force might yet arise."

The following day Hitler went to Berchtesgaden, where, on February 26, he summoned Ribbentrop and Keppler to a meeting with Leopold, Tavs, and the three other Austrian Nazis who had been, in substance, exiled to Germany. Hitler put the five expellees in Keppler's charge, and directed that they should "be paid well" and remain available as a source of information "particularly with regard to personalities." With Ribbentrop's approval, Keppler was given primary responsibility for Austrian questions, and Hitler instructed him to visit Vienna about once a month "in order to guarantee the execution of the Berchtesgaden agreement." The Fuehrer then delivered himself of a general statement on the strategy to be pursued. As summarized by Keppler:

> . . . the Austrian question could never be solved by a revolution. He had had to abandon this course for Germany after 1923 and saw no possibility of a solution by this method. Furthermore, German efforts to this end would necessarily plunge him into the most painful situations, since it would not be possible to choose the time for action. There remain only two possibilities:
> 1. Force,
> 2. Evolutionary means,
> and he wanted the evolutionary course to be taken, whether or not the possibility of success could today be foreseen. The Protocol signed by Schuschnigg was so far reaching that if completely carried out the Austrian problem would be automatically solved. He did not desire a solution by violent means, if it could be avoided, since the danger to us in the field of foreign policy became less each year and our military power greater each year. He mentioned military measures—a line of fortifications in the west, air force, the annual increment of half a million trained troops, etc.

There is no reason to question the accuracy of this as a representation of Hitler's attitude toward his Austrian problem at the end of February 1938. It is in harmony with what Hitler had said at the Hössbach conference, in its reliance on the march of time to offer favorable opportunities. There is nothing in the Hossbach record which suggests that Hitler then contemplated dealing with Austria *before* Czechoslovakia—rather the contrary, partly because Mussolini had no interest in Czechoslovakia's survival, while Austria was still a touchy question with him.

On the other hand, there was a great difference between the Czech and Austrian problems in that the former would probably yield only to force, while Austria might be absorbed by a combination of external pressure and internal political evolution—as Hitler put it, the concessions already given in the Berchtesgaden protocol might lead to an automatic solution.

Keppler was now the chosen agent to exert the pressure and assess progress, and early in March he appeared in Vienna for the first of the visitations which Hitler had told him to undertake. Things got off to a rough start, as Keppler did not hit it off with Guido Schmidt, and was able to see Schuschnigg only after threatening to make so unsatisfactory a report to Hitler that "special steps would follow." Keppler finally saw the Chancellor late in the afternoon of March 15, but from the subsequent accounts of the two participants one would hardly think that they had been in the same room. According to Schuschnigg, Keppler "now demanded everything which had been laboriously eliminated from the original list at Berchtesgaden," including "the formal legalization of National-Socialism." These demands, Schuschnigg writes, he "flatly rejected" and at the end of the interview he "had the definite impression that the boats were now burnt."

Some details are common to both accounts, but Keppler recalled chiefly Schuschnigg's avowal of support both for "National Socialist ideas" and, at some future time, for *Anschluss*. "The conversation began tempestuously," he minuted, "but concluded in an entirely conciliatory manner." Summing up, Keppler "had the impression that Schuschnigg will by no means submit to force but that if treated sensibly he will come along to a great extent, if this is made possible for him without loss of prestige. We can rely on his loyalty as regards the Berchtesgaden Agreements."

Upon his return to Berlin, on March 8, Ribbentrop took Keppler to Hitler, who "was very satisfied with my report." On the spot Keppler was appointed a State Secretary in the Foreign Ministry, and instructed "not to press Schuschnigg" and "not to discuss the *Anschluss* at all," but to "get on good terms with him personally and to smooth the way for him so that later on he might find it easier to adjust to the intended new conditions."

As of March 8, 1938, accordingly, it is clear that Hitler, though envisaging progress toward *Anschluss,* had no intention or expectation of bringing it about in the immediate future.* Five days later it was all over, and Austria became the Ostmark, a province of the German Reich.

* On March 7 Keppler wrote a note to Seyss-Inquart informing him that in May Hitler intended to travel through Austria to Italy in order to visit Mussolini, and that Heinrich Himmler wished to discuss security measures for the journey with Seyss-Inquart's staff.

6

Hitler and Keppler may have been satisfied with the tempo of events in Austria, but Schuschnigg was not. Seyss-Inquart had been right in doubting the viability of a system in which National Socialism as a political party remained outlawed, while National Socialist insignia, publications, and demonstrations were permitted. Keppler reported on March 6 that "in Austria the Party is now in fine shape" and "ready for action as a disciplined body in the political game," and that the demand for brown cloth had exhausted the supply; furthermore, in Graz "extensive fraternization has taken place with the military and the police," so that "it is to be hoped that, after further fraternizing . . . the use of the military and the police against the Party will no longer be possible." Whether or not Seyss-Inquart sincerely endeavored to enforce the Berchtesgaden limitations, by the end of February he had substantially given up the effort, and declared that he could do nothing in the face of the "dynamic of the Party." Indeed, he himself in Graz and Linz reviewed parades of uniformed Nazis and told mass meetings that "The National-German Reich is already a fact in the minds of men."

It was plain which way the wind was blowing, and a general disintegration set in. Jews who could afford to were fleeing to other lands, there were runs on banks and cancellations of contracts, and Arturo Toscanini cabled his refusal to conduct at the coming Salzburg Festival "because of the political developments in Austria."

In these straits Schuschnigg and his colleagues, late in February, had begun to consider holding a plebiscite on the question of Austrian independence, hoping than an overwhelming affirmative vote would reverse the trend, unite all but the extreme Nazis behind the regime, and make plain to the world that the Austrian people were determined to maintain their national identity. Schuschnigg by now had good reason to fear that continued clashes between the Austrian military or police forces and the Nazis might be seized upon by Hitler as a pretext for intervention to "restore order" and "protect Nationalist Socialist Germans from persecution." A resounding popular vote for independence might both dampen Nazi ardor and deprive Hitler of plausible excuses for interference.*

Serious consideration of the plebiscite began at the end of February, and was confined to a small circle of Schuschnigg's trusted associates. There were many administrative problems to be worked out, the more difficult in that Austria had held no election since 1930. According to Schuschnigg, the decision to proceed was taken "irrevocably" on March 4, in consequence of the new demands presented that day by Keppler. President Miklas approved the project, and on March 6 and 7 the plan was unfolded to closed meetings of Fatherland Front officials. The wording agreed upon—to which the voter would respond with "Yes" or "No"—was:

* The constitutional basis for a plebiscite was somewhat questionable. Schuschnigg justified it under Article 93, giving the Chancellor the right to lay down broad lines of national policy, from which he derived the subsidiary power to consult the popular will by means of a plebiscite.

For a free and German Austria, an independent and social Austria, a Christian and united Austria; for peace and employment and for the equality of all who stand for their people and their nation.

Other than Austrian colleagues, Schuschnigg consulted Mussolini and no one else.* Francesco Salata, the Italian Minister to Austria, was told about the project as early as March 1, and shortly thereafter the Austrian military attaché in Rome, Colonel Emil Liebitzky, was fully briefed on the Berchtesgaden conference, the fulfillment steps taken in Austria, and the plebiscite plan, for a report to Mussolini.† The Duce, who now thought Schuschnigg's speech of February 24 "wanting in tact towards Germany and the Fuehrer," approved of all the concessions Schuschnigg had made, but counseled sharply against the plebiscite. It was the last message Schuschnigg received from his "protector" in Rome and he disregarded the negative advice, believing he had no alternative.

Schuschnigg realized full well that he was making a risky move, as is evidenced by the secrecy of the initial consultations and the short time which was to intervene between the public announcement and the taking of the vote. The Cabinet was not informed, since Seyss-Inquart and Glaise-Horstenau were both members and were constant informants of the German authorities. Schuschnigg scheduled the announcement for Wednesday, March 9, and the vote for the following Sunday, March 13, no doubt hoping to get the count before Hitler could move. Perhaps he hoped that Hitler, having baited him at Berchtesgaden with the notion of a plebiscite in which the two chancellors would run against each other, would feel shame at blocking a test, albeit a different one.

However that may be, Schuschnigg pressed on, aware that "the decision to hold a plebiscite was an act of desperation, under extreme pressure, and in a situation which we had always tried to avoid." On March 8, Seyss-Inquart was finally told what was in the wind (Glaise-Horstenau had gone to Germany), and the next day Schuschnigg went to Innsbruck and, in the course of addressing a mass meeting and radio audience, announced the plebiscite. Dressed in the Tyrolean fashion, the Chancellor exhorted his listeners to say "Yes" to Tyrol, "Yes" to Austria, and ended his speech with the war cry of the Tyrolean hero Andreas Hofer: *"Mannder, es isch Zeit!"* (Men, the time has come!)

7

Schuschnigg's efforts to maintain secrecy were not completely successful. Stenographic notes of a confidential planning conference at the Fatherland Front offices on March 6 somehow fell into the hands of Himmler's SS the following day. The Austrian Minister of Commerce, Fritz Stockinger, incautiously told a business friend about an earlier high-level plebiscite conference, and this information reached General Muff on March 8.

From one source or another, Keppler in Berlin received information of the

---

* The story that the French Minister to Austria, Gabriel Puaux, instigated the plebiscite, to which Papen and others have given credence, was categorically denied by both Schuschnigg and Puaux.

† By a quirk of protocol, Colonel Liebitzky had direct access to Mussolini in his capacity as Minister of War, while Pellegrino Ghigi, the Austrian Minister in Rome, had to go through Ciano as Foreign Minister.

planned plebiscite on the morning of Wednesday, March 9. A telephone call to Seyss-Inquart elicited no information about the plebiscite (Schuschnigg had asked him to say nothing prior to the public announcement), but a warning that "the situation has suddenly gotten quite serious." Keppler at once sought audience with Hitler, to whom he had reported optimistically only the previous day. The Fuehrer reacted with utter astonishment: "It is out of the question for Schuschnigg, three weeks after Berchtesgaden, to break the agreement. It is utterly incredible." But he was sufficiently impressed to call for an aircraft to take Keppler back to Vienna to find out what was going on.* He arrived there just in time to hear Schuschnigg's Innsbruck speech on the radio, and promptly passed the news to Hitler by telephone.

The Fuehrer's incredulity was now transmuted into anger but not yet into decision. It was plain that, given the circumstances under which the plebiscite was to be taken and the phrasing of the question, a heavy "yes" majority was to be expected and this would surely slow the progress toward *Anschluss*. Hitler "was determined not to tolerate it," but how was it to be stopped?

That evening Goering was contacted for consultation on countermeasures. General von Reichenau, who, as a prominent sportsman, had gone to Cairo for a meeting of the Olympic Games Committee, was recalled, and his successor as commander of the Munich Military District, General Eugen von Schobert, was also summoned. Then Hitler learned that Glaise-Horstenau was in Germany† and he, too, was at once brought to Berlin. He conferred with Hitler for over two hours late in the evening of March 9, but by his account the meeting "led to no concrete decision."

Glaise-Horstenau had been told to expect a call from Hitler early the next day, but it did not come; the Fuehrer was conferring with his generals. Sometime during the night of March 9, Hitler must have started to comtemplate seriously the use of German armed force to forestall the plebiscite, and the following morning both the Reich Chancellery and the Bendlerstrasse started buzzing with the toings and froings of excited generals.

Responding to a summons for ten o'clock—an unusually early hour for the Fuehrer—Keitel and Viebahn appeared at the Chancellery, where, to their dismay, Hitler demanded an operational plan for a military entry into Austria. Recalling that Blomberg's directive of June 24, 1937, had included a section entitled "Otto," which envisaged the possibility of armed intervention in Austria to block a Hapsburg restoration, Viebahn called Jodl at the Bendlerstrasse and told him to bring the document to the Chancellery.

But "Otto" in Blomberg's directive was no plan of operations; it stated only

---

* According to a message on March 9 from Weizsaecker to Ribbentrop, who was in London making farewells, Keppler was instructed to prevent the plebiscite or, if this was not possible, to have added to it a question on *Anschluss*. If indeed these were his orders, Keppler apparently did nothing to carry them out, probably because Schuschnigg's speech appeared to have committed him beyond the possibility of retreat. After he reported Schuschnigg's speech to Hitler, he was told to return to Berlin, and he flew back the following mornirg.

† Glaise-Horstenau, after retiring from the Austrian Army, had become an archivist and historian. He had gone to Stuttgart to give a lecture on "Central Europe in the Year 1000 A.D.," and then visited relatives at Landau in the Palatinate.

that "political conflicts among the Austrian people" should be utilized for an Army "drive in the general direction of Vienna and the suppression of all resistance," with the support of unspecified units of the Luftwaffe. The document was intended only to alert the Army and Luftwaffe to the necessity of preparing plans.

Accordingly, Keitel soon returned to the Bendlerstrasse to see whether the Army staff had done anything to implement the directive. Brauchitsch was sitting on the Fritsch trial tribunal,* which had convened that same morning, and Beck was in charge at OKH. He held out empty hands: "We have prepared nothing, nothing has been done, nothing at all," he told Keitel. Everything would have to be improvised and, since the plesbiscite was set for Sunday the thirteenth, the OKH had barely forty-eight hours to draw the orders and deploy the troops along the Austrian border. Taking with him his principal subordinate, General von Manstein,† Beck hurried over to the Chancellery, where Hitler described the nature of the Austrian crisis, and discussed at some length the possibility that other powers might intervene in the event of a German march-in. England and France, he thought, were preoccupied with other problems. Russia had no common border with either Austria or Germany, and Poland would never let Russian troops cross her territory. He would give Czechoslovakia soothing assurances. But Italy, for all of the bonds of the Axis, was still a source of worry to the Fuehrer; how would the Duce react to the news of a military entry into Austria?

After this exposition, Hitler renewed his request for an operational plan, to be put in motion early on Saturday, March 12. Beck consulted Manstein, and then advised that, if the operation were to be carried out at all, it should be done with substantial forces, even if no resistance from the Austrians were to be expected; a merely symbolic entry might invite similar moves from Italy or Czechoslovakia, to support their demands for a voice in the settlement. The generals proposed, accordingly, to mobilize the five infantry divisions of the Munich and Nuremberg military districts, as well as a new armored division that was training in nearby Würzburg, and put them all under the command of an *ad hoc* army headquarters. In order to get these forces assembled on the Austrian border by the morning of the twelfth, they told Hitler, mobilization orders would have to be issued by four o'clock that afternoon. Hitler approved the troop selections

---

* At Nuremberg, Brauchitsch testified that he was not at the Fritsch trial but "away on official business," and Keitel in his *Memoirs* (p. 58) wrote that Brauchitsch was "away on an official journey." The OKH records (N.A.T-78 R. 24) show that Brauchitsch on March 4 had planned to go to Breslau on the morning of March 10 for a V Corps celebration at which he was to speak, but the script of the speech bears a pencil notation: "Trip fell through. General von Rundstedt substituted." Graf Kielmansegg, in his book on the Fritsch trial, describes its opening on March 10, listing Brauchitsch present with the other members of the tribunal.

Whether Brauchitsch was at the trial or commenced his journey to Breslau and then was recalled, it is clear that he was not available for the Austrian consultations on the morning of March 10. According to Bock's final report on the Austrian operation, Brauchitsch was present and participating in the planning at half-past four that afternoon.

† Manstein had been transferred to a divisional command as part of the reshuffle in February, but had not yet taken up his new post. Manstein's statement in his memoirs that all this took place on March 7 is in error.

but was worried about the political consequences of a mobilization order, and promised a final decision before the specified deadline.

The exceptionally gifted Manstein* now took the lead in drafting the necessary orders, in collaboration with Colonel Otto Stapf, who headed the General Staff section responsible for mobilization. Hitler's authorization to send the orders out did not arrive until seven o'clock in the evening, but the mobilization was commenced and proceeded reasonably smoothly notwithstanding the delay —an impressive piece of staff work, especially considering that there had been no mobilization in Germany since the First World War.

Military District Commands VII and XIII were both subordinated to Group Command 3 at Dresden, led by General Fedor von Bock, second only to Rundstedt in seniority on the Army's active list. Not devoid of amiability and humor in casual social intercourse, once in uniform and on duty Bock was the epitome of lean, hard Prussian militarism. The old Frederickan *Geist* was deeply ingrained in his character; he was a stern disciplinarian, enormously energetic, and physically courageous, but as a professional soldier he was distinguished more by industry and determination than brilliance. He and his Dresden staff were now designated as the headquarters of a newly established "Eighth Army," and all troops taking part in the operation were put under his command.

And so, late in the afternoon of March 10, in response to urgent summons, Bock and the other commanders and chiefs of staff of the major units selected for "Otto" came hurrying to Berlin and the Bendlerstrasse for their orders and guidelines. General von Schobert of Military District VII was already in the city. General Maximilian von Weichs, of District XIII, sent his chief of staff, Colonel Wilhelm Stemmermann. In February, General Heinz Guderian had replaced General Lutz in command of the XVI Armored Corps headquarters in Berlin, and now he was summoned to Beck's office and told to go to Würsburg and take over the 2nd Panzer Division. Thinking it unwise and unnecessary to replace the able divisional commander, Rudolf Veiel, Guderian proposed that his XVI Corps headquarters be sent in and given control of the 2nd Panzer Division and some additional formations. Beck at once agreed, and gave him the SS motorized regiment *Leibstandarte Adolf Hitler,* from which the Fuehrer's military bodyguard was drawn, and which Hitler wished to be given a share in the venture.

Various other SS and police units, and a few squadrons of reconnaissance and carrier aircraft, were also attached to the Eighth Army, giving it a total strength of a little over 100,000 men. The Luftwaffe assembled in Bavaria, under Sperrle's command, one fighter group and three of bombers, as well as a large number of transport aircraft, some to be used to carry staff and special troops into Austria and some for dropping propaganda leaflets.

While Beck and his staff had been busying themselves with the deployment and mobilization orders, at OKW Jodl had been drafting Hitler's first directive

---

* During the early months of the Second World War, Manstein served as chief of staff at General von Rundstedt's army group, and was the principal architect of the plan of campaign for the Battle of France. Thereafter he commanded successively at corps, army, and army group levels, and was regarded by many as Germany's ablest field commander.

as Commander-in-chief of the Wehrmacht. It was distributed at two o'clock in the morning* of Friday, March 11:

1. If other measures fail, I intend to enter Austria with armed force to establish constitutional conditions and to prevent further outrages against the German-minded people.
2. The whole operation will be led by me. According to my instructions:
 The Commander-in-Chief of the Army will direct the land operations with the 8th Army in the formation and strength suggested to me, and with attached units of the Luftwaffe, SS and police,
 The Commander-in-Chief of the Luftwaffe will direct the air operations with the forces suggested to me.
3. Missions:
 a) Army—the march-in must be carried out in the manner described to me. The Army's first objective is the occupation of Upper Austria, Salzburg, Lower Austria, Tyrol, the speedy taking of Vienna and the securing of the Austro-Czech frontier.
 b) Luftwaffe—must demonstrate and drop propaganda material, occupy Austrian airports for bringing in reinforcements, support the Army upon request as may be necessary and hold bomber units in readiness for special tasks.
4. The forces of the Army and Luftwaffe assigned to this operation must be ready for the march-in on March 12th at the latest by noon.
 I reserve the authority to give permission to cross or over-fly the frontier and to fix the time for this.
5. The behavior of the troops must give the impression that we do not wish to wage war against our brother-people. It is in our interest that the whole operation be carried out without any violence and as a peaceful entry welcomed by the population. Therefore, any provocation is to be avoided. But if resistance is offered, it must be broken ruthlessly by force of arms.
6. On the German frontiers with the other nations, no security measures are to be taken for the time being.

At no point during the events and discussions leading to this order does Hitler appear to have encountered any opposition from the officers with whom he dealt. This is not surprising; *Anschluss* was in line with the prevailing nationalist aspirations and the Army generally welcomed the opportunity. For some, indeed, the operation was a relief from the conscience-nagging course of the Fritsch case. Manstein thought Hitler's analysis of the situation logical and convincing. Even General Beck, who a few months earlier had written so strong a critique of Hitler's exposition at the Hossbach conference, co-operated promptly and effectively in bringing off the coup. When Guderian came to his office for marching orders, Beck remarked: "If the *Anschluss* is to be carried out, this is probably the best moment to do it."

But although Hitler had talked of *Anschluss* to the generals, he may well have meant something short of outright annexation. In any event, he was still waver-

---

* Hitler did not actually sign the order until early afternoon on the 11th.

ing and, indeed, had not finally decided to send in the troops. Directive No. 1 commenced with the statement that they would go in "If other measures fail . . ." His position all along had been that the Austrians *wanted Anschluss*, and that would hardly be reinforced by a bloody encounter between German and Austrian troops. It was, therefore, vital that Schuschnigg and his plebiscite be upended from the inside, and that the German march-in at least *appear* to take place on invitation and be unopposed.

Accordingly, the generals were not the only visitors to Hitler's office that busy Thursday. Early in the afternoon he received one Odilo Globocznik, an Austrian Nazi who had come to Berlin the previous day with the latest Party intelligence from Vienna. Hitler declared that he was determined to block the plebiscite, and sent Globocznik back to Vienna with a letter taking the wraps off the Austrian Nazis and a message for Seyss-Inquart, telling him to await written instructions which would be forthcoming on the morrow.

Then, at the end of the day, Hitler finally sent for Glaise-Horstenau, and tried to press into his hands, for delivery to Seyss-Inquart, drafts of a letter of resignation from Schuschnigg's cabinet and a radio speech in which Seyss-Inquart would explain the reasons for his resignation. Glaise-Horstenau, who had some sense of the dignity of his office as an Austrian minister, declined to take the documents, and suggested that Hitler send them by courier. Leaving Hitler's office, he encountered Goering, who tried to give him a draft of a telegram to be sent from Vienna, asking Hitler to send in troops to restore order. Once again the Austrian refused, despite abusive remonstrances from Goering. The following morning he flew back to Vienna empty-handed, but the documents had already arrived there by courier, and Glaise-Horstenau lost little time before informing his fellow ministers that, unless the plebiscite were canceled, German troops would soon be streaming across the frontier.

Meanwhile, in Vienna, Kurt von Schuschnigg's Thursday had been reassuring. Arriving that morning on the train from Innsbruck, he had been saluted at the station by a guard of honor and a reception committee of government and Fatherland Front officials. The publicity campaign for a "yes" vote in the plebiscite was in full swing, with posters and sound trucks all over the city. Nazi demonstrators were outnumbered and outshouted by Fatherland Front and trades union adherents. Socialists, monarchists, and Jews had pledged full support for the plebiscite and "Ja," as well as the Catholics, speaking through the strong, stern voice of Theodor Cardinal Innitzer.

To be sure, Schuschnigg and Zernatto both received that morning complaining letters which Seyss-Inquart had written the day before. They did not know that Seyss-Inquart had already sent a copy of his letter to Schuschnigg, via Globocznik, to Berlin, and neither of them found the contents particularly alarming, since their burden was a request for changes in the plebiscite procedures, and increased political representation for the Nationalist Socialists as the price of their "yes" vote. Schuschnigg sent a dignified reply, defending the constitutionality of the plebiscite and pointing out that Hitler himself, during the Berchtesgaden meeting, had invited such a test. That evening, the Chancellor and Schmidt had a meeting with Seyss-Inquart, at which the procedural reforms were accepted, and it was agreed that the Nazis' participation in both the federal and provincial governments would be increased, and that they would vote "yes" in the plebiscite.

Schuschnigg went to bed that night well pleased with the support that he had developed during the day. Seyss-Inquart, however, had gone from the Chancellor's office to a nocturnal Party gathering, where Globocznik was reporting on his visit to Berlin. No one was at all interested in the concessions Seyss-Inquart had wrung from Schuschnigg, because, as Globocznik informed them, the plebiscite was to be blocked and, for the Party, the lid was off.

8

Friday, March 11 was the crucial day. Schuschnigg's rude awakening was a five-o'clock telephone call from the police, informing him that the German customs office at Salzburg had just been closed, and all railroad and highway travel across the border had been stopped. The Chancellor dressed and drove to St. Stephen's to pray, and then to the Chancellery, where even more ominous news awaited him: "Leo is ready to travel," the signal of an imminent German invasion.

Seyss-Inquart also rose early that morning, to meet Glaise-Horstenau at the Vienna airport and pick up the documents which the courier had brought from Berlin, one of which set a noon deadline for a postponement of the plebiscite. The two ministers reached the Chancellery at about ten o'clock, and confronted Schuschnigg with Hitler's ultimatum. They then went off to a meeting with the Party leaders, and the Chancellor summoned Zernatto and other close advisers. Various compromises were discussed but were categorically rejected by Seyss-Inquart when he and Glaise-Horstenau returned to the Chancellery early in the afternoon. Finally, after consulting President Miklas, Schuschnigg gave way, and at about half-past two he told Seyss-Inquart that the plebiscite would be canceled.

Meanwhile, at the Reich Chancellery in Berlin, a motley throng of dignitaries was gathered outside Hitler's office, where the Fuehrer was awaiting the results of his ultimatum. Papen, who had returned to Vienna to pack his belongings, was urgently summoned Thursday evening; when he arrived at the Chancellery the following morning he found Goering, Goebbels, Himmler, Brauchitsch, Keitel, and a host of lesser lights dancing attendance. Ribbentrop was in London making his farewells, and Neurath was acting for the Foreign Ministry. From time to time one or more of the group were called in to the Presence, to consult or listen to Hitler's excited monologues.

Uncertainty about Mussolini's reaction was still Hitler's main worry, and at about noon he completed a letter to the Duce, called for his customary personal courier to Rome, Prince Philip of Hesse, and dispatched him by air with instructions to present the document immediately upon arrival. It was a long, turgid, overwrought, and utterly preposterous missive, intended both to justify and to propitiate:

> EXCELLENCY: In a fateful hour I am turning to Your Excellency to inform you of a decision which appears necessary under the circumstances and has already become irrevocable.

In recent months I have seen, with increasing preoccupation, how a relationship was gradually developing between Austria and Czechoslovakia which, while difficult for us to endure in peacetime, was bound, in case of a war imposed upon Germany, to become a most serious threat to the security of the Reich.

In the course of these understandings, the Austrian State began gradually to arm all its frontiers with barriers and fortifications. Its purpose could be none other than:

1. to effect the restoration at a specified time;
2. to throw the weight of a mass of at least 20 million men against Germany if necessary. . . .

For years the Germans in Austria have been oppressed and mistreated by a regime which lacks any legal basis. The sufferings of innumerable tormented people know no bounds.

Germany alone has so far received 40,000 refugees who had to leave their homeland, although the overwhelming majority of the people of Austria entirely share their ideology and their political views.

With a view to eliminating a tension which was becoming increasingly unbearable, I decided to make a last attempt to reach an agreement with Herr Schuschnigg and definitely establish full equality for all under the law. . . .

Herr Schuschnigg made me a solemn promise and concluded an agreement to this effect.

From the very beginning he failed to keep this agreement.

But now he has gone so far as to deal a new blow against the spirit of this agreement by scheduling a so-called plebiscite which actually is a mockery. . . .

Since the day before yesterday the country has been approaching closer and closer to a state of anarchy. . . .

I am now determined to restore law and order in my homeland and enable the people to decide their own fate according to their judgment in an unmistakable, clear, and open manner.

May the Austrian people itself, therefore, forge its own destiny. Whatever the manner may be in which this plebiscite is to be carried out, I now wish solemnly to assure Your Excellency, as the Duce of Fascist Italy:

1. Consider this step only as one of national self-defense and therefore as an act that any man of character would do in the same way, were he in my position. You too, Excellency, could not act differently if the fate of Italians were at stake, and I as Führer and National Socialist cannot act differently.
2. In a critical hour for Italy I proved to you the steadfastness of my sympathy. Do not doubt that in the future there will be no change in this respect.
3. Whatever the consequences of the coming events may be, I have drawn a definite boundary between Germany and France and now draw one just as definite between Italy and us. It is the Brenner.

   This decision will never be questioned or changed. I did not make this decision in 1938, but immediately after the end of the World War, and I never made a secret of it.

I hope that Your Excellency will pardon especially the haste of this letter and the form of this communication. These events occurred unexpectedly for all of us. Nobody had any inkling of the latest step of Herr Schuschnigg, not even his colleagues in the Government, and until now I had always hoped that perhaps at the last moment a different solution might be possible.

I deeply regret not being able to talk to you personally at this time to tell you everything I feel.

Always in friendship,

Yours,

ADOLF HITLER

The charges of armed conspiracy between Austria and Czechoslovaki were, of course, sheer fabrication, so improbable that it is hard to believe that Hitler expected Mussolini to take them seriously.* Nor was there anything in the concluding assurances that was not already understood between the two dictators. The implicit theme was "one good turn deserves another," and perhaps Hitler also thought the letter might be helpful to Mussolini for face-saving.

With Prince Philip on his way, the Fuehrer turned his attention back to Vienna, from where there was still no word of Schuschnigg's answer to the ultimatum. At quarter to three, only a few minutes after Schuschnigg's capitulation on the plebiscite (of which Berlin still had no news), Goering put through a telephone call to Seyss-Inquart,† and opened the conversation by inquiring whether there was "any news." Seyss-Inquart replied that Schuschnigg had canceled the plebiscite, but if he expected that this information would satisfy his interlocutor, he was immediately undeceived. Goering replied that "the measures taken by Chancellor Schuschnigg were not satisfactory in any respect," as they involved no "change in the present situation, which had been brought about by Schuschnigg's conduct in breaking the Berchtesgaden agreement."

Goering broke off the call to consult Hitler. A quarter of an hour later he telephoned Seyss-Inquart again and presented a new and much more drastic set of demands. Schuschnigg had broken the agreement and Berlin "had no further confidence in his actions." Accordingly: (1) Seyss-Inquart and Glaise-Horstenau were to hand in their resignations and demand that Schuschnigg do the same;‡ (2) Seyss-Inquart must be designated Chancellor; and (3) Seyss-Inquart should then send the telegram to Hitler asking that German troops be sent in to help the new government restore order.

* They were also diplomatically most incautious—so much so that the German Foreign Ministry insisted on the suppression of these portions in the subsequently published version of the letter.

† The German Air Ministry recorded this and other telephone calls on March 12 and 13, and the transcripts survived and were put in evidence at the first Nuremberg trial.

‡ Expecting Schuschnigg to refuse to call off the plebiscite, Seyss-Inquart and Glaise-Horstenau had gone to the Chancellery, after the Party meeting, with their resignations from the Cabinet, in order to precipitate a governmental crisis. Schuschnigg's decision to cancel the vote met the terms of the Berlin ultimatum and removed the basis for the resignations or for any revolutionary Party activity. Glaise-Horstenau, and perhaps Seyss-Inquart and Schuschnigg himself, thought the cancellation would resolve the crisis, and Seyss-Inquart's telephone conversation with Goering was the first indication that it would not.

What explains this sudden hardening of attitude in Berlin? According to Goering's testimony at Nuremberg, it was all his own doing:

> Then . . . the answer came that the plebiscite had been called off and that Schuschnigg had agreed to that. At this moment I had the instinctive feeling that the situation was now mobile and that finally we had the opportunity we had long and ardently awaited—the possibility of bringing about a complete solution. And from this moment on I must take 100 percent responsibility for all further happenings, because it was not the Führer so much as I myself who set the pace and, even overruling the Führer's misgivings, brought everything to its conclusion. . . . My telephone conversations have been read here. I demanded spontaneously, without first having spoken to the Führer about it, the immediate retirement of Chancellor Schuschnigg. When this was granted, I put my next demand, that now everything was ripe for the Anschluss. And that took place. . . .

It is true that Goering took the initiative in moving beyond the first ultimatum. It is also true that his was the dominant voice among Hitler's henchmen that day, and that he threw his considerable weight behind the "complete solution." Nonetheless, his testimony at Nuremberg is of a piece with his inveterate self-inflation. Hitler, not Goering, made the final decisions. Hitler allowed Goering to handle the telephone to Vienna, but Goering did not venture to give final instructions without the Fuehrer's prior approval. Nor was *Anschluss* finally determined upon at this stage of things; indeed, it is uncertain what the course of events would have been had Vienna immediately agreed to the second ultimatum.

But it was accepted only in part, and the roadblock was not Schuschnigg but President Miklas. The former took only a short time to decide that the time had come to step down, and laid the resignations of himself and his entire cabinet before Miklas, who remarked bitterly: "I see that everyone deserts me now." The President accepted the resignations with the stipulation that the ministers remain in office pending the appointment of a new Chancellor, but he flatly refused to appoint Seyss-Inquart, roundly declaring that Austria was a sovereign state, and that Berlin had no business undertaking to dictate his cabinet selections.

At about four o'clock Seyss-Inquart telephoned Goering and told him that Schuschnigg "was on his way to President Miklas in order to hand in his resignation, as well as that of the whole cabinet," and Goering promptly inquired whether or not his caller had taken over the chancellorship. Seyss-Inquart promised to inform Goering on this point by five-thirty, and Goering emphasized "that this, beside the resignation of Schuschnigg, was an absolutely firm demand."

But Miklas was not yielding; instead, he was casting about for some trusted figure to take Schuschnigg's place. At about five o'clock Seyss-Inquart told Globocznik to call Goering and give him some information about Austrian Nazi activities. Goering was very brusque on the telephone, and threw Globocznik into such a state of frightened confusion that he quite erroneously told Goering that Seyss-Inquart was already in office as Chancellor. Thus misled, Goering proceeded to give Globocznik a number of names of those to be included in Seyss-

Inquart's cabinet, including his own brother-in-law, Dr. Franz Hueber, as Minister of Justice.

When Goering came back from the telephone with the false news of Seyss-Inquart's appointment, Papen and others at once urged Hitler to give up the plan to send in troops, on the ground that this was no longer necessary. It is indicative of Hitler's uncertainty of aim at this late time that he agreed, and instructed Keitel and Brauchitsch to hold up the orders.* But within half an hour, when Seyss-Inquart again took the telephone, Goering learned that he had been misled and that Miklas was still adamant. Highly indignant, Goering instructed Seyss-Inquart to fetch General Muff and with him confront Miklas with a peremptory demand for Seyss-Inquart's appointment, and the threat that, if this were not done within two hours, "the troops who are already at and advancing toward the frontier will march in tonight and Austria will cease to exist."

At about this time a familiar face reappeared in Vienna. Keppler, whom Hitler had dispatched at midafternoon, arrived while Muff was carrying out his delectable assignment. He went first to the German Legation and then to the Chancellery, where he found both Seyss-Inquart, who brought him up to date, and General Muff, who had just had a very unsuccessful encounter with Miklas. Keppler then went to see Miklas, with equally negative results.

The stubborn old President would yield neither to Muff's threats nor Keppler's blandishments, and once again it was Schuschnigg who gave way and broke the impasse. He had been unable to reach Mussolini by telephone, and his last-minute appeals for support had elicited from Rome only a cold refusal to give him aid or counsel, and from other capitals no more than weak expressions of concern. The Austrian Army was quite incapable of offering sustained resistance to a German invasion, and the seven-thirty time limit, which Goering had fixed for compliance with the ultimatum delivered by Muff, would soon expire. Schuschnigg was still the caretaker Chancellor, and his last executive action was to tell the Austrian commander, General Sigmund Schilhausky, to withdraw his troops from the frontier to a line behind the Enns River, and offer no resistance to the Germans. Shortly after the appointed time there came a report, later discovered to be false, that the invasion had already begun, and this appears to have been the circumstance which prompted Schuschnigg to address the nation by radio and announce his resignation.

The Chancellor went on the air at about seven-fifty:

> Men and women of Austria, today has faced us with a difficult situation. . . . The Government of Germany has presented to the Federal President an ultimatum, with a time limit, demanding that the President nominate as Federal Chancellor the candidate specified to him, and to appoint a cabinet in accordance with the German government's proposals. Otherwise, an invasion by German troops will take place at the appointed time. . . .

* This is established not only by Papen's recollection, but also by the transcript of Goering's subsequent telephone conversation with Seyss-Inquart, and by Jodl's diary entry for March 11 at six o'clock in the evening: "Border will not be crossed for now," and at eight-thirty: "General Viebahn informs me that the situation has changed again, and the march-in will take place."

The President has instructed me to inform the Austrian nation that we are yielding to force. Because we are resolved on no account, even at this grave hour, to spill German blood, we have ordered our armed forces, in the event of an invasion, to withdraw without resistance, and to await the decisions of the next few hours. . . .

And so I take my leave of the Austrian people at this hour with a German word and a heartfelt wish: May God protect Austria!

No sooner had Schuschnigg finished speaking than Seyss-Inquart was again on the telephone, reporting to Goering, who had already had word of the speech, and was chiefly concerned about Miklas' continuing refusal to appoint Seyss-Inquart. Schuschnigg's broadcast had left the governmental situation in Austria hopelessly muddled, for now the Schuschnigg cabinet had abdicated even its caretaker authority, and Miklas had not nominated a new one. In Vienna, Seyss-Inquart told Goering, the President and other officials were simply waiting for the march-in, and assuming that the Germans would take over the executive power. "Very good," replied Goering. "I will give the order to march in, and you make sure that you get the power. Notify the leading people that anyone who offers resistance will be subject to court-martial by our troops. That includes leading personalities. . . . The President refused to appoint you, and that also can be considered resistance."

Duly impressed, Seyss-Inquart now took to the radio and announced that he, as the sole member of the Cabinet still in office (which in fact he was not, since Miklas had accepted the resignation of the entire Cabinet), would assume the executive power. But Miklas did not recognize his authority, the Nazi leaders paid him little mind, and the scene at the Chancellery remained one of utter confusion.

In Berlin, however, Miklas' obduracy, Schuschnigg's speech, and the news that the Vienna leaders were simply waiting for the expected invasion to resolve the situation, all combined to trigger issuance of the order for the march-in which, two hours earlier, Hitler had ordered withheld. Outside Hitler's office, observers saw him and Goering emerge from a telephone booth in deep conversation, ended by the Fuehrer's slapping his thigh and exclaiming: *"Jetzt geht's los!"** A little later, at eight forty-five, Hitler as Commander-in-Chief signed Directive No. 2:

1. The demands in the German ultimatum to the Austrian Government have not been fulfilled.
2. The Austrian Wehrmacht has ordered its troops to withdraw before the entering German troops and to avoid combat.
   The Austrian Government has ceased to function.
3. To avoid further bloodshed in Austrian towns, the German entrance into Austria will begin, in accordance with Directive No. 1, at daybreak on March 12th.
   I expect the specified objectives to be reached, by the fullest efforts, as quickly as possible.

* Roughly translatable as "Here we go!" or "Now for it!" The observer was Wilhelm von Grolmann, an old Hitler supporter who had participated in both the Kapp and Beer Hall revolts, and at this date was a high police official in the Ministry of Interior.

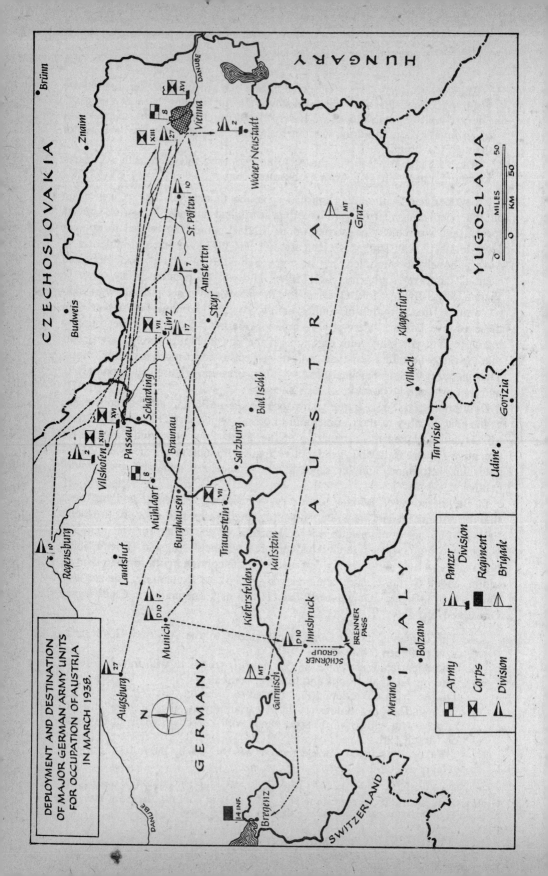

DEPLOYMENT AND DESTINATION
OF MAJOR GERMAN ARMY UNITS
FOR OCCUPATION OF AUSTRIA
IN MARCH 1938.

CZECHOSLOVAKIA

Brünn

Znaim

Budweis

HUNGARY

DANUBE

Vienna

Wiener Neustadt

St. Pölten

Amstetten

Steyr

Linz

Schärding

Braunau

Bad Ischl

Passau

Vilshofen

Salzburg

Mühldorf

Burghausen

Traunstein

Kufstein

Kieferstelden

AUSTRIA

Graz

Klagenfurt

Villach

Tarvisio

Gorizia

Udine

YUGOSLAVIA

MILES
KM
0   50
0   50

Regensburg

Landshut

Munich

Augsburg

N

GERMANY

Innsbruck

SCHÖRNER GROUP

BRENNER PASS

Garmisch

Bregenz

SWITZERLAND

ITALY

Bolzano

Merano

Panzer
Division

Regiment

Brigade

Army

Corps

Division

Assured as they now were that the march-in would not be resisted, Hitler and Goering renewed their efforts to wring an invitation out of Vienna. As soon as the directive was signed, Goering was again, and for the last time that day, on the telephone to Vienna, giving instructions to Keppler:

. . . Listen carefully! The following telegram should be sent here by Seyss-Inquart. Write it down: "The provisional Austrian Government which, after the resignation of the Schuschnigg government, has the task of again restoring law and order in Austria, addresses to the German Government this urgent request for support in its task, and help in preventing bloodshed. For this purpose it asks the German Government to send troops as soon as possible." . . . Please show him [Seyss-Inquart] the text of the telegram, and tell him that we are asking him—well, he does not even need to send the telegram, all he needs to do is say "agreed."

Seyss-Inquart did not send the telegram, and whether or not he authorized Keppler to "agree" to it remains a doubtful matter.* Whatever the truth of that may be, about an hour later, when Otto Dietrich (the Reich press chief) called Keppler to say that he "needed the telegram urgently," Keppler replied that Goering could now be told "that Seyss-Inquart agrees." Thereupon in Berlin a "telegram," spuriously time-stamped as sent at ten minutes after nine and received at forty minutes after nine, was prepared, and the Foreign Ministry at once sent a circular telegram to numerous German diplomatic missions informing them that the Seyss-Inquart "provisional government" had requested the dispatch of German troops, and that "in order to prevent catastrophic conditions the German Government considered it necessary to comply with this appeal." The following day, Berlin added to its own mendacity in another circular telegram, which categorically denied that any ultimatum had been presented to the Austrian Government, and declared the "truth" to be "that the question of sending military forces from the Reich was first raised in the well-known telegram of the newly formed Austrian government."

One thing remained necessary to Hitler's peace of mind. Prince Philip of Hesse had arrived in Rome and by nine o'clock was in Ciano's office with Hitler's letter. The two went to Mussolini, who could do little but put a good face on things; in his diary Ciano recorded that the Duce was "pleased" and "tells Hesse to inform the Führer that Italy is following events with absolute calm." At ten-thirty Prince Philip called Berlin, and Hitler himself, greatly relieved and almost incoherently ecstatic, took the telephone:

HESSE: I have just come back from the Palazzo Venezia. The Duce accepted the whole thing in a very friendly manner. . . .
HITLER: Then please tell Mussolini I will never forget him for this. . . . Never, never, never, whatever happens. . . . As soon as the Austrian affair has been settled, I shall be ready to go with him through thick and thin, no matter what.
HESSE: Yes, my Führer.
HITLER: Listen, I shall make any agreement—I am no longer in fear of the terrible position which would have existed militarily in case we had got-

* Keppler testified at Nuremberg that, after much discussion, Seyss-Inquart said to him, "Do what you like," which Keppler construed as reluctant agreement.

ten into a conflict. You may tell him that I do thank him ever so much, I will never, never forget him. I will never forget him.

HESSE: Yes, my Führer.

HITLER: I will never forget it, whatever happens. If he should ever need any help or be in any danger, he can be sure that I shall stick with him whatever happens, even if the whole world is against him.*

HESSE: Yes, my Führer . . .

Thus, reassured and happy, Hitler ended his day. Meanwhile in Vienna, as midnight approached, the Republic of Austria was in its death throes. Arriving in Vienna that morning, William Shirer had seen Schuschnigg's propaganda leaflets dropping from airplanes over the city and the Nazis on the streets few and frightened; by six o'clock that evening, after the news that the plebiscite was canceled, he found himself "swept along in a shouting hysterical mob . . . shouting like Holy Rollers *'Sieg Heil! Heil Hitler! Ein Volk, ein Reich, ein Führer!'"* with the police looking on approvingly. Schuschnigg's radio speech, with its confession of defeat and warning of a German invasion, was the signal for a general Nazi take-over. In some of the provinces, the local governments at once capitulated to the Party leaders. In Vienna, Shirer saw swastika armlets on the police, and Nazi toughs heaving bricks through Jewish shopwindows. Jews and others marked for the Nazi terror started to flee Austria, chiefly to Switzerland and Czechoslovakia.

Outside the Chancellery, a huge crowd gathered, and the shouts and jeers were plainly audible in the rooms where Schuschnigg, Miklas, Seyss-Inquart, and their respective supporters still remained. Seyss-Inquart was busy drawing up cabinet lists and, as reports of Nazi successes came in from all over the country, Miklas started to give way. Shortly after midnight the President finally signed the documents designating Seyss-Inquart and his chosen colleagues as the Government, and enjoined on the new Chancellor the task of preventing the German invasion.

In fact, neither Seyss-Inquart nor Keppler, at his elbow, could see any remaining need for German troops to come in. At about two o'clock, at Seyss-Inquart's request, Muff and Keppler called the German Foreign Ministry and pressed on the official at the night desk, Guenther Altenburg, strong arguments that the march-in be canceled. Others, in Berlin, were independently taking the same line; Brauchitsch, Viebahn, and perhaps other generals had been calling Keitel and Weizsaecker and urging that the troops be held behind the frontier. Rather boldly, Weizsaecker had Hitler's adjutant, Wilhelm Brückner, wake the Fuehrer and put the matter before him. In a few moments the answer came back that Hitler thought it too late to change plans, and Seyss-Inquart should be so informed.

In Vienna, few were left at the Chancellery, and the old officialdom were mostly under arrest or in flight. The shortest escape route from Vienna was due east to Bratislava in Czechoslovakia, about thirty miles away. Zernatto and a

---

* Hitler was as good as his word and rescued Mussolini from the Gran Sasso d'Italia in 1943, where after the Duce's fall from power he was imprisoned by the Badoglio government.

handful of friends and colleagues—including Dollfuss' widow, Alwine, who had just returned from Rome and a fruitless personal appeal to Mussolini—made the trip safely; others were turned back at the border.

Some made no attempt to escape, or were arrested before they had thought of leaving. At the *Rathaus,* the anti-Nazi Mayor of Vienna, Richard Schmitz, was soon in custody. So were Hornbostel of the Foreign Ministry, Hüttl of the police, and other old Canutes who had struggled to hold back the Brown Tide.

After installing the Seyss-Inquart cabinet, President Miklas drove to his home and large family; he had many offspring, and Goering, when told that Miklas refused to give way, had cynically remarked to Muff that "with fourteen children one must perhaps stay put." He was followed by SS men under Otto Skorzeny, who five years later was to be Mussolini's rescuer from imprisonment on the Gran Sasso in the Abruzzi. When Miklas reached his house an ugly confrontation between the SS and Miklas' personal bodyguard occurred, and bloodshed was averted only by the telephonic intervention of one of Seyss-Inquart's ministers. Miklas won a temporary respite; he was still President of Austria, corpse as she was, and he was needed by the conquerors for a few more hours.

Schuschnigg was advised to escape and could have, but he firmly declined. Seyss-Inquart drove him home, through lanes of yelling Nazis, and promised to visit him soon and see to his welfare. But the promise was never kept. Schuschnigg awoke the next morning to find his home encircled by storm troopers, and entered upon a confinement, first in house arrest and later in much more unpleasant circumstances, which was to last over seven years. The Nazis were never magnanimous victors.

And so ended what Gordon Brook-Shepherd aptly called "Austria's longest day."

9

Shortly before dawn on Saturday, March 12, 1938, for the first time since the First World War, German troops crossed their own frontiers to occupy another country. Bock's army was deployed along the entire German-Austrian border, the greater part of which, from Switzerland nearly to the Danube, lay within Schobert's VII Corps Military District. But the extreme northern end of the border, from Passau (where the Danube crosses from Germany to Austria) to the Czech border, was in Weichs's XIII Corps Military District, and was of special strategic importance, as it gave the most direct access both to the Austro-Czechoslovakian border and to Vienna, via the roads along the Danube through Linz and St. Pölten.

Accordingly, it was in the general area of Passau that the strongest German forces were concentrated. General Guderian established his armored corps headquarters in the city itself. Weichs was behind him at Vilshofen, a few miles further up the Danube, and Schobert at Traunstein, about twenty miles west of Salzburg. Bock's Eighth Army headquarters for command of the entire operation was set up at Mühldorf, on the Inn River about fifty miles east of Munich.

Apart from Vienna, the two most important German goals were the Italian and Czech frontiers.* Despite Mussolini's reassuring response to Hitler's letter, the OKH thought it wise to reach the Brenner Pass both speedily and delicately. Instead of a corps headquarters, a noncombat training command was to handle the occupation of the Austrian Tyrol, and the commander of a mountain infantry regiment, Lieutenant Colonel Ferdinand Schoerner (who spoke excellent Italian), was to hurry to the Brenner with friendly greetings for those across the border. As for the Czechs, Goering had sought to allay their apprehensions by giving the Czech Ambassador, Vojtech Mastny, his "personal word of honor that this is a question of *Anschluss* only, and that not a single German soldier will come anywhere near the Czechoslovak border."

Not all of the Army units were assembled and ready to move on schedule Saturday morning, and Guderian's motorized troops, which were to be the spearhead of the march to Vienna, had an especially difficult time. General Veiel's 2nd Panzer Division had to come from Würzburg, two hundred miles west of Passau, and the SS motorized regiment all the way from Berlin. Veiel did not reach Passau with the main body of his troops until Friday at midnight; he arrived with no maps and with empty gas tanks. Baedekers had to do for maps, local fuel dumps had to be commandeered, and it was not until nine o'clock the following morning—an hour past "H-hour"—that Guderian's vanguard crossed the frontier.

By the time the last troops were coming in Friday night, it had become clear in Berlin that no resistance would be encountered, and the order was sent out that "the invasion was to take place not in a warlike but in a festive manner." The infantry units sent hastily for their bands and banners, and Guderian's tanks and other vehicles were decked with flags and greenery.

Early on Saturday morning, hundreds of German planes rose from Bavarian airfields. Some circled lazily over Vienna, Linz, and other Austrian cities dropping leaflets, while others came down at Austrian airports to secure the fields and disembark high German officials. Heinrich Himmler landed at the Vienna airport at about three o'clock in the morning, to take charge of police and security matters. Had the Austrian people known of his plans for their country, the incoming German troops might have had far less warm a welcome.

From Salzburg to Passau the Salzach and Inn rivers run along the frontier, and before dawn the Germans had secured the bridgeheads and customs gates, generally with the co-operation of the Austrian officials. At eight o'clock the infantry started the march-in. Weichs moved his headquarters to the Austrian border town of Schärding, and Schobert to Adolf Hitler's birthplace, Braunau-am-Inn. To avoid provoking a Czech reaction, Weichs sent only a small screening force toward their frontier but luckily was able to use Austrian troops for reconnaissance, and they soon reported that there was no military reaction from the Czech side.

Behind an advance guard of armored reconnaissance and motorcycle troops, Guderian led in the main body of the 2nd Panzer Division, with the SS regi-

---

* On March 11, OKW had sent out a supplementary directive stating that "if Czechoslovakian troops or militia units are encountered, they are to be regarded as hostile," whereas "the Italians are everywhere to be greeted as friends."

ment, which had arrived from Berlin only that morning, bringing up the rear. By noon he had covered the forty-five miles to Linz. "The flags and decorations on the tanks proved highly successful," he later wrote. "The populace saw that we came as friends, and we were everywhere joyously received. Old soldiers from the First World War saluted us as we drove by. At every halt the tanks were decked with flowers and food was pressed on the soldiers."

The infantry made their way in more slowly, but to equal popular enthusiasm. For many Austrians the display of feeling was genuine, and others were afraid not to display satisfaction. It was the first of the "flower wars"—the *Blumenkriege,* as the Austrian and Sudetenland occupations came to be called.

10

On the morning of the march-in Hitler, taking with him Keitel, Dietrich, Martin Bormann, and a few others, flew to Munich and then drove to Bock's headquarters at Mühldorf, where he arrived shortly after noon. Greatly relieved to learn that the troops had met with no opposition and were being welcomed everywhere, Hitler lunched contentedly and then drove to Austria, the homeland that he had not seen since before the First World War. There was, of course, only one appropriate place for the historic return: Braunau-am-Inn, where he was saluted by General von Schobert a few minutes before four o'clock in the afternoon. He visited his birthplace and then continued on toward Linz, along roads lined with demonstrative admirers.

Earlier that afternoon Guderian, departing from Linz in the direction of St. Pölten, encountered a quartet of dignitaries arriving from Vienna—the new Chancellor Seyss-Inquart, the new Vice-Chancellor Glaise-Horstenau, the ubiquitous Keppler, and Heinrich Himmler. They told Guderian that Hitler was due to arrive in Linz shortly, and Himmler asked him to deploy his troops so as to close off the roads into the town. Telling his advance guard to proceed only as far as St. Pölten, Guderian turned back and made the necessary dispositions to safeguard the Fuehrer's entry. He arrived shortly before eight o'clock, and appeared on the balcony of the *Rathaus,* where the visiting bigwigs were assembled and had been seriatim addressing the huge crowd gathered in the marketplace. Seyss-Inquart now took the microphone and, saluting his "guest" as *"mein Fuehrer,"* declared:

> We Austrians declare our allegiance to this leadership, freely and openly, proudly and independently and for all time. . . . The mighty forces of the Reich are moving into our land to the delight of Austria. Austria's soldiers are going out to greet places in Germany.* . . . Our goal is the German-national Reich . . . we are standing on the threshold of its advent and Adolf Hitler is its Fuehrer!

If this was an acknowledgment of Hitler's leadership of the two countries, it was still far from being a bid for a merger. Hitler too, by addressing Seyss-Inquart as "Herr Chancellor," seemed to acknowledge Austrian sovereignty, but

---

* Seyss-Inquart had secured permission for parades of a few crack Austrian units in Germany, so that the military occupation would have the appearance of mutuality.

the rest of this speech in the city of his boyhood, though ambiguous, moved much closer to the idea of unification:

> If it was Providence that once called me from this city to the leadership of the Reich, then it must also have given me the mission to restore my homeland to the Reich. . . . And I believe that I have now fulfilled it. Everyone of you bears witness and stands surety for this! On what day you will be called upon I do not know. I hope it will not be long delayed. For on that day you must stand up and be counted. . . . The result must show the world that any future attempt to tear this nation apart will be a vain one. . . . You must look on the German soldiers, who are marching into Austria at this time, as fighting men who are ready to sacrifice themselves for the unity of the whole great German nation, for the might of the Reich, for its greatness and majesty, now and forever more. *Deutschland, Sieg Heil!*

There was stupendous applause, the audience sang *Deutschland über Alles* and the *Horst Wessel* song, and Hitler retired to his hotel in a state of frenetic ecstasy. Guderian, despite the lateness of the hour, drove to St. Pölten, from where he led his advance guard through a heavy snowstorm to Vienna. Seyss-Inquart, Keppler, and the other visitors also returned to the capital, where Nazi celebrations lasted into the early morning hours. Hitler, however, remained in Linz.

11

Sunday March 13 was to have been the day of Schuschnigg's plebiscite.* Instead, it was the day of *Anschluss.*

No doubt for some time Hitler had been contemplating the possibility of annexing Austria as part and province of the Reich, and Goering, since the beginning of the crisis, had sensed the opportunity and urged his leader to go all the way. Nevertheless, right up to the moment of his departure from Berlin, Hitler had apparently envisaged a junction of the two countries through his own person as Fuehrer of the Nazi Party and Chief of State in both of them—a weird echo of the old Dual Monarchy of Austria-Hungary. Wilhelm Stuckart, a legal officer in the Ministry of the Interior, had been assigned to draft the necessary laws and decrees for such a structure, and on March 12 he was directed to take them to Hitler at Linz.

At some point during his triumphal progression Hitler decided to annex Austria. Perhaps it was the cumulative effect of Goering's urgings.† Perhaps Hitler had seen and was swayed by a memorandum transmitted from London by Ribbentrop on March 10, following several conversations with Lord Halifax, predicting that England would not interfere with a forceful solution of "the Aus-

---

* News traveled slowly to the Tyrolean village of Tarrenz. On March 13, not having heard that the plebiscite had been canceled, the inhabitants unanimously voted *"Ja"* to Schuschnigg's question. A few weeks later, again unanimously, they voted *"Ja"* to *Anschluss.*

† Goering's deputy, Erhard Milch, flew to Vienna on March 12 to supervise the Luftwaffe's activities, enjoined by Goering to persuade Hitler to effect the *Anschluss.* But Milch did not see Hitler until the afternoon of March 13, at least several hours after Hitler had made his decision.

trian question" provided that there would be "a very quick settlement." Perhaps it was the adulation of the Austrian crowds that moved him, and probably it was a combination of all these things. His speech from the *Rathaus* balcony suggested the trend of his sentiments but, according to Keppler, who was with him for several hours that evening, at no time did Hitler mention the possibility of *Anschluss.**

On Saturday morning, however, Hitler telephoned to Keppler in Vienna, directing him to take up with the Austrian Government the project of an *Anschluss,* and sent Stuckart there to assist in drafting the necessary documents.

The process was brisk indeed. By midafternoon Keppler, Stuckart, and other German and Austrian bureaucrats had completed a draft which Seyss-Inquart placed before his cabinet. It was speedily accepted, and signed by Seyss-Inquart and Glaise-Hortenau. President Miklas made a last gesture of disapproval by refusing to sign the law, but he then transferred his functions and authority to Seyss-Inquart as Chancellor, on the basis (provided for in Article 77 of the Constitution) that he was "hindered in the exercise of his office," and resigned. The *Anschluss* law was a ridiculously perfect example of putting the cart before the horse, as the first article declared categorically: "Austria is a province of the German Reich" and the fifth article that the law would be immediately effective, while the second article directed: "On Saturday, April 10, 1938, a free and secret plebiscite . . . shall be taken on reunion with the German Reich."

As soon as the adoption of the Austrian law was reported to Berlin, a corresponding decree was prepared for Hitler's signature, under which the Austrian law was declared to have become "a German law," and it was provided that the general Austrian laws should remain in effect there until, by the Fuehrer's order, they would be superseded by German laws. That evening Seyss-Inquart flew back to Linz to report officially to Hitler that the Austrian law had been enacted, and Hitler then signed the German unification decree as well as another amalgamating the Austrian armed forces with the Wehrmacht.

And so, at about midnight at the Hotel Weinzinger in Linz, Austria became the Ostmark, a province of the Third Reich.

Preoccupied with the details of *Anschluss,* Hitler found time while in Linz to visit his parents' graves, and send Mussolini a telegram repeating once more his vow "never to forget." Brauchitsch and Manstein arrived from Berlin and conferred with Hitler briefly before going on to Vienna to supervise absorption of the Austrian Army into the German military structure. In the evening there was a dinner at which General von Weichs, one of the many guests, heard Hitler declare that it would have been very inconvenient had Schuschnigg promptly agreed to cancel the plebiscite, since it was only his obduracy which had furnished the reason to demand his resignation.

On Monday morning Hitler set out by car for Vienna. It was another triumphal passage, and he did not reach the capital until early evening. General Milch, deputizing for Goering (whom Hitler had left in charge in Berlin), rode

* It is also indicative of Hitler's continuing indecision that Goering, in a long telephone conversation early Sunday morning with Ribbentrop in London, was still assuming that the Austrian Government would remain in existence at least until a plebiscite could be held.

with Hitler from St. Pölten to Vienna, and was told that the annexation had
been a last-minute decision, prompted by the enthusiastic reception in Linz. The
cavalcade entered Vienna to the ringing of church bells, and Hitler drove to the
Hotel Imperial, where he said a few words from the balcony to the multitude assembled on the Ringstrasse, and received from Mussolini a slightly enigmatic
telegram, devoid of congratulations: "My attitude is determined by the friendship between our two countries sealed in the Axis pact."

Tuesday, March 15, was given over to celebration. Frick, Lammers, Schacht,
and other high officials had been pouring out of airplanes at the Vienna airport;
among them was Papen, rewarded for his share in the venture with the Gold
Medal of the Nazi Party. At eleven o'clock, hundreds of thousands, gathered in
the Heldenplatz and nearby streets, heard Seyss-Inquart, newly announced as
Reichstatthalter (Reich Governor), salute the Fuehrer as Chancellor and declare that "the Ostmark has come home!" After thunderous, chanted choruses
of "We thank our Fuehrer," Hitler, who had great difficulty making himself
heard over the adulatory din, proclaimed "this country's new mission":

> The most ancient Ostmark of the German people shall henceforth be the
> newest bulwark of the German nation and the German Reich. This land is
> German, it has recognized its mission, it will fulfill it and never be surpassed
> in loyalty. . . . And thus it is that I can at this time proclaim the greatest act
> of fulfillment of my life: As Führer and Reich Chancellor I now proclaim be-
> fore German history the entry of my homeland into the Reich.

There followed a two-hour parade of all available German and Austrian
troops, after which Hitler returned to his hotel to receive Cardinal Innitzer,
who, a few days earlier, had strongly supported Schuschnigg's plebiscite and
was now performing a complete political flip-flop. Then at the end of the day,
ill-disposed to linger in this city where as a young man he had lived years of
failure and poverty, Adolf Hitler flew back to Munich, the city of his rise to
fame and power.

Before leaving, Hitler signed decrees extending to Austria the Reich laws forbidding the formation of political parties other than the Nazi Party, prescribing
the oath of loyalty to Hitler, and excluding Jews from the public service. The
Nazi night was fast closing over Austria. For the first few days, to be sure, the
Jews had no unemployment problem, as they were kept busy obliterating
Schuschnigg and Fatherland Front posters, painting *"Jude"* on their storefronts,
and on their hands and knees scrubbing sidewalks.* Supplementary decrees
came thick and fast, extending to Austria Himmler's police power, the Nuremberg racial laws, and other Nazi measures. Seyss-Inquart's authority did not
long withstand the pressures of ambitious German Nazis. Josef Buerckel, who
had greatly impressed Hitler with his successful Nazification of the Saar, was
soon given charge of all Party matters in Austria, and Seyss-Inquart was forced
back into second place. Decisive power flowed more and more into Himmler's
hands.

Even for the Austrian Army, these were difficult times. On March 12, as the

---

* The harassments of Jews by the Nazi occupiers were extensively reported in the British
press, including the *News Chronicle* and *Manchester Guardian,* and especially by G. E. R.
Gedye in the *Daily Telegraph.*

march-in began, Bock had written to the Austrian Inspector-General Schilhausky a cordial note of greeting "in recognition of our ancient comradeship in arms," expressing also the hope of soon "paying my respects to you in person." Three days later Schilhausky was abruptly dismissed from the service, along with General Wilhelm Zehner (who had been Secretary of War in the Schuschnigg cabinet) and numerous other senior officers. Under the chairmanship of General Muff, a mixed commission of German and Austrian officers was set up to screen for political reliability the Austrians who wished to be taken into the Wehrmacht—a process which General von Weichs viewed as "a highly distasteful cleaning-up." In the upshot about half of the Austrian generals and colonels, and perhaps 20 per cent of those in the lower grades, were dismissed or pensioned off. Those dismissed for political unreliability found the prospects of employment very dismal, and some thirty were sent to Dachau or other concentration camps.

It was in this dark and oppressive atmosphere that the plebiscite was held on April 10. General Zehner was murdered by the Gestapo that very day, and the first group of Austrian political prisoners had arrived at Dachau ten days earlier. Goering, Goebbels, Ley, and Hess came to Austria to speak, and Hitler himself returned for the last week of the campaign, and addressed huge organized crowds in Graz, Klagenfurt, Innsbruck, Salzburg, Linz, and Vienna. And on the appointed day, in response to the question "Do you acknowledge Adolf Hitler as our Führer and the reunion of Austria with the Reich as effected on March 13," the 4,284,975 who went to the polls voted by 99.7 per cent *"Ja!"* As William L. Shirer, who was on the scene, observed at the time: "It took a brave Austrian to vote 'no,' as everyone felt the Nazis had some way of checking up on how they voted." But it is probable that, even under less frightening circumstances, *Anschluss* would have carried by a respectable margin.

12

Kurt von Schuschnigg's conduct of his office during the final crisis has been sharply criticized in retrospect, not so much for his decision to offer no armed resistance to the German march-in, but for his failure, after the Berchtesgaden meeting, to rally support from the western democracies by fully revealing to them the pressures to which his government had been subjected, and impressing on them the gravity and imminence of the peril to Austrian independence.* It is true that Guido Schmidt's circular telegram to the Austrian missions abroad not only fell far short of fully disclosing the thrust and temper of the Berchtesgaden confrontation, but also instructed the Austrian representatives to emphasize "the necessity for calm and our confidence in the normal development of our relations with the Reich which have now been clarified by the Berchtesgaden discussions." This was the opposite of a cry for help and may, indeed, have aided the Wilhelmstrasse to allay French and British worries about the portent of Berchtesgaden.

One may well doubt, however, that appeals for aid from the western democracies, no matter how loud and clear, would have produced any helpful

* The most detailed version of this critique is in Brook-Shepherd's *Anschluss*, pp. 73–77.

response. The French concept of intervention in Austria had always been based on the assumption of Italian participation, and with Mussolini on the sidelines French military aid was most improbable. Furthermore, France was still in a state of political instability, and the Chautemps cabinet fell on March 10, just as the crisis was peaking. In England, Vansittart had been kicked upstairs, and Anthony Eden was in the process of kicking himself out of the Cabinet. Neville Chamberlain, tightening his grip on foreign affairs, would surely have been deaf to the most eloquent pleas from Vienna.

Quite apart from the poor prospects of success, an overt appeal for western aid would have been wholly out of keeping with the policy Schuschnigg had been pursuing since the collapse of the Stresa Front. On Mussolini's urging Schuschnigg had signed the treaty of July 1936 and embarked on a policy of conciliation and concession toward Germany, relying on the Duce to restrain Hitler from going too far in the direction of *Anschluss*. It was in furtherance of that policy that Schuschnigg had yielded at Berchtesgaden and, having done so, after that it would have made no sense to reverse direction and infuriate Hitler, and Mussolini too, by appealing to France and Britain. Indeed, such a move would have been quite contrary to the spirit of both the 1936 and the Berchtesgaden agreements, insofar as they contemplated a co-operative parallelism of German and Austrian foreign policy.

However, these circumstances only push the locus of the issue back from 1938 to 1936, and raise the question whether the basic mistake was not made in accepting the conciliation-concession policy in the first place. When the Stresa Front was broken and the Axis loomed, might not Austria have aligned herself with Czechoslovakia, and sought protection against Germany from the League of Nations and the Versailles powers? This, of course, would have cost Schuschnigg the support of Mussolini, but how much was that likely to remain worth as the Axis hardened?

But these speculations are idle, for such an alignment was simply not in the cards. Czechoslovakia was a social democracy and, except for the Sudeten Germans, a land of peoples who had chafed under the Austrian yoke and were glad to see the empire shattered. Austria, small and weak in her reduced state, had been the core of that empire. Austrians and Germans shared more than a common language; they had been allies in the First World War, and in both countries there was considerable pro-*Anschluss* feeling and resentment against the Versailles ban. Austria was conservative and Catholic, with little affinity for a France where Léon Blum could become Premier, and none for a France allied with the unholy Soviet Union. For an Austrian government to have relied upon an unpopular provision in the very treaty that had broken up the empire, and upon the parliamentary democracies, for protection against a Germany that was linguistically and historically close kin, would have been politically impossible at home and probably unrewarding abroad.

Accordingly, it is not surprising to read Schuschnigg's later explanation of the policy he chose:

> As I stood at the grave of my predecessor, Chancellor Dollfuss, the situation was very clear to me. I knew that in order to save Austrian independence,

I had to embark on a course of appeasement. This meant that everything had to be avoided which could give Germany a pretext for intervention, and that everything had to be done to secure in some way Hitler's toleration of the *status quo*.

And that was precisely the policy which Schuschnigg pursued, with patience and forbearance, until the plebiscite, which promptly proved to be the "pretext for intervention." Essentially, Schuschnigg fell into the same trap in which Chamberlain found himself caught a year later. Both tried to do business with Hitler. To be sure, Schuschnigg was aware that "Hitler would observe the agreement only so long as it suited his own external political aims," but he woefully underestimated Hitler's impulsiveness and disregard of procedural limitations. Suspicious as he was, Schuschnigg was still astonished that his preliminary understanding with Papen about the permissible scope of the Berchtesgaden talks was, in the event, wholly ignored. Seven months later, Neville Chamberlain was to suffer an equally unpleasant surprise at Godesberg.

Far from building up a reserve of goodwill, the two years of appeasement led only to a situation where any independent initiative in Austria was a serious if not fatal risk, and so the Schuschnigg plebiscite precipitated the ultimatum. In his last book of retrospection, Schuschnigg is at pains to justify his decision, at that last moment, to order the Army and people not to offer resistance. He was a man of peace, he was German, and he could not face the prospect of an armed encounter between the kindred forces.

His decision readily evokes sympathetic understanding. But there is no gainsaying that, in ordering General Schilhausky to withdraw and lower his guns, Schuschnigg rendered great service to Hitler, for whom it was virtually a *sine qua non* of success in the Austrian operation that the German entry should not only be unopposed but at least appear to be both invited and welcomed by the inhabitants.

In Poland and Czechoslovakia, Hitler could say that German minorities were being oppressed by Slavs—inferior peoples who were fit only to be clobbered into submission by the master race. But Austrians were Germans; they were plainly not suffering at the hands of some other nationality, and Hitler's posture was, as it had to be, that it was an unrepresentative and even illegally constituted Austrian Government which was standing athwart the desires of the majority to embrace Nazism and *Anschluss* with their fellow-Germans of the Reich.

That picture of the Austrian scene would have been irreparably damaged by military resistance to the German march-in. The Austrian Army was small, but as Schuschnigg himself has written: "A fighting withdrawal, spread over two days, would have been possible even on March 11th . . . The army and gendarmerie were reliable instruments in the hands of the government." And even as little as two days of fighting would have greatly altered the visual and psychological impact of the German move. The Wehrmacht's guns would have been firing and its planes dropping bombs. The troops would have been deployed for battle instead of lined up for parade. There would have been no bands, and plenty of field ambulances. No greenery would have softened the harsh silhouettes of the tanks. There would have been no *Blumenkrieg*.

An armed encounter, even though brief, would have had a profoundly different effect in other countries, especially in Italy and the western democracies. Mussolini had not, in fact, been nearly as content with Germans on the Brenner as he had pretended to Prince Philip. To his diary Ciano confided that the "fatal event . . . has not been pleasant for us—far from it." The German chargé in Rome, Count von Plessen, reported to Berlin later in March that Mussolini's tolerant attitude was based on "political realism" and that "in his heart Mussolini is just as unenthusiastic about the developments in the Austrian situation as most Italians." The Duce had no easy time justifying his stance to his Fascist colleagues in the Grand Council, and found it necessary to make a major public speech of explanation on March 16, to calm a public which, in Ciano's words, had been "pretty severely shaken." But his task was not nearly so difficult as it would have been in the event of an armed clash on the roads from Passau and Salzburg to Vienna. To the apparent desires of the Austrian people for unification with the Reich, Mussolini could gracefully yield. On the other hand, the spectacle of the country which had looked to him for protection being overrun by force of arms would have been far more damaging to Mussolini politically and a severe if not disastrous strain on his relations with Hitler.

Still more important was the tempering effect of the "festive" entry on public opinion in France and especially in Britain. While in both of those countries there was a highly indignant reaction to the diplomatic pressures which Germany had exerted, this was greatly mitigated by the impression that the Austrians had only gotten what most of them seemed to want. After German rearmament, the Anglo-German Naval Agreement, Ethiopia, and the Rhineland there did not seem to be much left of Versailles, Locarno, or the League Covenant anyway, and after all the Austrians were "really" Germans. Such reflections dulled the British people's ability to sense the import of *Anschluss* for the future, or to grasp the full measure of Hitler's intentions, whereas if the Austrian Army had fought, the alarm bells would have rung much louder. The consequences would have been a sharper public awareness and a firmer response a few months later, when the Czech crisis erupted.

Of course, it would be quite unfair to blame Schuschnigg and his colleagues for failing to foresee all these consequences of their decision not to fight, plain though they may seem in retrospect. Nor, even if they had been gifted with such perception, could it have been asked of them that they use their country as a bloody tocsin, to awaken Europe to its peril.

Armed resistance would certainly have greatly increased the immediate adverse consequences and multiplied the victims of the German invasion, and to the little handful of men in Vienna, dangling at the end of their string of authority, it did not seem morally defensible to subject their countrymen to those dangers. After seven years of prison, and after witnessing ten years of postwar occupation of Austria as an "enemy" country, Kurt von Schuschnigg was "still thankful" that he did not do what he might have done, and there are few if any men of that time who could have said, with any show of credibility, that they would have done otherwise.

CHAPTER 16

The Plan for the Conquest of
Czechoslovakia

1

"After the annexation of Austria," Jodl's diary tells us,* "the Führer indicates that he is in no hurry to solve the Czech question. Austria must first be digested." The digestive process was to prove a very brisk one, and at the Bendlerstrasse the generals were already at work on plans for the military conquest of Czechoslovakia—plans which were given the name "Case Green" (*Fall Grün*) in accordance with the terminology of Blomberg's 1937 directive. Jodl's diary entry went on: "Nevertheless, preparations for Case Green will be energetically continued, and must be newly worked out on the basis of the changed strategic situation consequent on the annexation of Austria."

Anschluss had, indeed, greatly improved or worsened the military picture, depending from which side of the Czech-German border the question was examined. The Czechoslovakian forces were, of course, greatly inferior in numbers to the German, and would benefit from short frontiers and good natural defenses. The annexation of Austria lengthened the Czech-German border by some two hundred miles, or about 40 per cent, and only the westernmost fifty miles were really mountainous; the eastern three quarters was rolling or flat though somewhat protected by rivers. Hitler had been wont to complain that Czechoslovakia was "a dagger pointed at the heart of the Reich," but again the choice of metaphor depended on the viewer's vantage point, for, after *Anschluss,* one might equally well have seen Czechoslovakia's head as taken between the German jaws. Bohemia and Moravia now lay almost encircled by the Reich, pinched between Silesia on the north and the Ostmark only 125 miles to the south.

In Austria, the local Nazi Party had been Hitler's tool for undermining the Schuschnigg regime; in Czechoslovakia, the comparable instrument was Konrad Henlein's Sudeten German Party. Ever since that party's impressive success at the polls in May of 1935, it had received an annual subsidy of 180,000 marks from the German Foreign Ministry. The Party maintained a Berlin office,

* The entry is undated; it follows the entry for March 11, 1938, and precedes the one for May 22. Ensuing paragraphs of the undated entry refer to events on May 21 and 30, and it may be inferred that it is a catching-up entry made after a period in which the diary was not kept.

headed by one Friedrich Bürger, which maintained close touch with the German Government, and Henlein visited Berlin from time to time for consultations.*

Formally, Czech-German relations remained governed by the arbitration treaty signed at Locarno in 1925, but after the conclusion of the Czech-Russian mutual assistance pact in 1935, the tone of the Nazi-controlled press grew increasingly sharp in its references to Czechoslovakia. Under Goebbels' direction, a sustained and escalating propaganda campaign against the Czechs and their government was mounted, primarily for the purpose of publicizing grievances— some real, some contrived—based on their attitude toward the Nazi Reich and their treatment of both German nationals and Sudeten German residents in Czechoslovakia. These complaints included the expropriation of German-owned properties in connection with defense construction in the border regions, suppression of German Nazi Party activities in the Sudetenland, prohibition of the sale of *Mein Kampf,* and failure to suppress anti-Nazi publications of the German Social Democrats and other émigrés who had fled to Czechoslovakia after Hitler seized power.

Throughout the winter of 1937–38 these protests were presented, with decent restraint, through regular diplomatic channels. The German Minister in Prague, Ernst Eisenlohr, made an informal démarche to Premier Hodža early in October, and there ensued a round of meetings and negotiations among Hodža, Beneš, Eisenlohr, and Henlein and his deputy, Karl Hermann Frank. In support of the demand that the German émigré press be silenced, early in November Goebbels temporarily suspended the German press attacks against Czechoslovakia. But (as the Germans well knew) the Czech Government lacked the total control of the press which Goebbels enjoyed, and Berlin remained unsatisfied by Prague's remedial measures. In December, German discontent was increased by the expropriation, for defense purposes, of lands owned by Reich nationals near Jägerndorf in northeastern Moravia. Hitler personally approved retaliatory confiscation of Czech-owned properties in Germany and, as a further indication of displeasure, refused to receive the Czech Minister in Berlin, Dr. Vojtech Mastny, despite repeated requests.

Accordingly, relations between the two governments, though correct, were tense and worsening by the time of Schuschnigg's ordeal at Berchtesgaden and Hitler's ensuing Reichstag speech of February 20, in which he spoke of "ten million Germans"—meaning Austrians and Sudeten Germans—who were "suffering because of their sympathy and solidarity with the whole German race and its ideology," and whose "right of racial self-determination" he would protect. The implied threat did not pass unnoticed in Prague any more than in Vienna, and late in February, Hodža warned Eisenlohr that the Czech Government would have to reject publicly the idea of foreign interference in domestic affairs, while simultaneously he promised new concessions to the Sudeten Germans and regular future consultation with Henlein.

* The German officials primarily involved in dealings with the Sudeten German Party were Guenther Altenburg, chief of the Foreign Ministry desk for Austria and Czechoslovakia, and SS General Werner Lorenz, head of a bureau (*Volksdeutsche Mittelstelle*) for the repatriation of ethnic Germans, who reported both to the Foreign Ministry and to Rudolf Hess.

This game of diplomatic battledore and shuttlecock was rudely interrupted by the Austrian crisis and *Anschluss*. During the march-in, to be sure, Hitler was greatly concerned to allay Czech fears, so as to avoid any chance that the Prague government might order mobilization or otherwise interfere. At a large official reception on the evening of March 11, after reports of the impending march-in had begun to circulate in the diplomatic community, Hermann Goering gave repeated and fulsome assurance to Dr. Mastny that the Austrian operations would be "nothing more than a family affair" and that Germany wished to pursue a policy of improved relations with Czechoslovakia, provided only that the Czechs would "keep out of things altogether" in Austria. Mastny at once telephoned Prague, and then returned to Goering with confirmation of previous statements that his government would pursue a hands-off policy, whereupon the field marshal gave his "personal word of honor" (*Ehrenwort*) that "this is a question of the Anschluss of Austria only, and not a single German soldier will come anywhere near the Czech border."

On the following day Goering telephoned Mastny and reconfirmed these declarations, while Neurath, speaking "on behalf of the Führer,"* made the same points and added that Hitler "hopes that relations between Czechoslovakia and Germany will improve further, but a condition for this is that the Czech Government shows more understanding for the three and a half million Germans in Czechoslovakia." The State Secretary of the Foreign Ministry, Hans Georg von Mackensen, also received Mastny and encouraged the latter to believe that "the clarification of the Austrian situation will tend to improve German-Czechoslovak relations."

But the only truth in all this was that Hitler wished to confine the events of March to Austria. He did not hope for improved relations with Czechoslovakia —rather the reverse, as became apparent before the end of the month. Goering's words were treacherously Delphic. Eight years later, at Nuremberg, he gave his own evaluation of his word of honor: "An explanation was desired for the moment and in connection with Austrian events. I could conscientiously assure him [Mastny] on my word of honor that Czechoslovakia would not be touched then, because at that time no decisions had been made by us, as far as a definite time was concerned with respect to Czechoslovakia or the solution of the Sudeten problem."

In fact, *Anschluss* with Austria marked the end of the "correct" policy toward Czechoslovakia. Up to that time, the German Government had confined its relations with the Sudeten German Party largely to advice and financial support, and had left to its leaders the responsibility of decision-making on tactics and goals. But on March 16, the very day that Hitler returned to Berlin from Vienna, Eisenlohr reported that Henlein and Frank had now assured him that the "course of German foreign policy" as communicated to them by the German legation "is to be the sole determining factor for policy and tactical procedure of the Sudeten German Party." Eisenlohr's instructions were "to be strictly ob-

* At Nuremberg, Neurath denied that he "spoke on Hitler's instructions," but his own file memorandum of March 14, 1938, states that he spoke "on behalf of the Führer," as does the Foreign Ministry's telegram to Eisenlohr sent later that day.

served," and the minister's authority would include the right to review all Party speeches and press releases, and to summon Henlein to Prague "at any time."

Eisenlohr, however, was a mere conduit for policies determined in Berlin, and on March 28, Henlein went there and received instructions from Hitler himself, at a meeting attended also by Hess, Ribbentrop, and Lorenz. The Fuehrer certified Henlein as "the rightful leader of the Sudeten German element," and assured the former gymnastics instructor that "I will stand by you; from tomorrow you will be my Governor."* But the thrust of the strategy which Hitler proceeded to prescribe was far more significant than any title of distinction. It was "that demands should be made by the Sudeten German Party which are unacceptable to the Czech Government." Henlein was a quick learner and paraphrased his directions as being "always to demand so much that we can never be satisfied"—an interpretation which Hitler immediately approved. And the following day, at a conference which included Ribbentrop, Mackensen, Weizsaecker, Eisenlohr, Henlein, Karl Hermann Frank, and subordinate Foreign Ministry and Sudeten participants, it was agreed that the Sudeten German Party's policy should be to remain in parliamentary opposition and refrain from participation in the Government, to avoid any action which "could give the impression abroad that a solution had been found," and to formulate "a maximum program which would guarantee as its final aim total freedom for the Sudeten Germans."

Such were the aims and tactics that lay concealed beneath the soothing assurances imparted to Mastny. Meanwhile in the Sudetenland itself, news of *Anschluss* had excited and sharpened the militancy of the Germans. On Sunday, March 27, the day before Henlein's reception by Hitler, there were large enthusiastic demonstrations in Eger, Asch, Saaz, and other cities where the Germans were in a majority now becoming dominant. The Czech police behaved with restraint but reaped small credit for their exemplary conduct, which was instead regarded as an abdication of authority. There was common rumor that the Wehrmacht would move in after the April 10 plebiscite on *Anschluss*.

Soon it became plain that the turbulent course of events in the Sudetenland would make it increasingly difficult for Prague to carry through the various measures of Sudeten autonomy on which Henlein and his followers were insisting. This consequence, of course, was precisely suited to Hitler's purpose that the Henleinists continue to press unacceptable demands that would ultimately lead to confrontation and showdown.

2

On March 28, Hitler told Henlein that "he intended to settle the Sudeten German question in the not too distant future," but did not indicate how soon that would be. The reason for this failure was that Hitler did not know, any more than he had known in the case of Austria, before Schuschnigg's plebiscite announcement triggered the decision.

Furthermore, the governing factors were now substantially different. Except

* Hitler used the word *Statthalter*, the same title that he had just conferred on Seyss-Inquart for Austria.

for the fair-weather friend in Rome, Austria had no allies, while Czechoslovakia had her French and Russian treaties, and considerable deposits of goodwill in other quarters. Czechoslovakia was far more powerful militarily than Austria, and her collapse would be a much heavier blow to France and to European defenses against Germany. Hitler was certainly aware that an armed assault on Czechoslovakia entailed a substantial risk of precipitating a general European war, whereas with Austria the immediate danger had been negligible.

In Hitler's judgment, however, the degree of that risk depended principally on the length of time that would be required to overrun Czechoslovakia. If the Wehrmacht were to get stuck in the Czech defenses, sympathy for the underdog and shame for the desertion of an ally might pull in the French, with Russia and Britain in her wake. Whereas if it were all over in a week or less, those powers would confront a *fait accompli* and the uninviting prospect of a long war only in order to bring the dead back to life. This was, as events proved, a shrewd and largely accurate assessment. And *Anschluss,* by extending the German-Czech frontier, encircling Bohemia and making possible a pincer attack from both sides of the Moravian waist, had markedly improved the possibility of speedy conquest.

There was still another importantly altered factor: Italy. During the Austrian crisis, Mussolini's attitude had been the main focus of Hitler's concern. No comparable worry attached to the Sudeten problem. Although that matter had never been formally raised for discussion between Berlin and Rome, Mussolini had never shown any interest in the fate of the Prague government. In December 1937, conversing with the Yugoslav Premier, Milan Stoyadinovitch, the Duce had declared that "Italy neither can nor wishes to intervene on behalf of Prague in any way," since Czechoslovakia's "difficult situation does not interest us directly, whereas it ranges against Czechoslovakia our German and Hungarian friends." If this was not already known in Berlin, it became so by late April 1938, when Mackensen (who had succeeded Hassell as ambassador in Rome) sent word to Weizsaecker (who had followed Mackensen as State Secretary in the Foreign Ministry) that "our trusty informant" had stated that Italian diplomatic circles were expecting that "the German-Czech problem will come to a head very swiftly," and that "Italy will cause no difficulties whatsoever with respect to the solution which Germany deems most suitable."

On the face of things, therefore, it is surprising that Italy once again should loom large in Hitler's thinking on Czechoslovakia. This time, however, it was not fear of Mussolini's opposition but hope for his support which concerned Hitler. There were obstacles. Between Berlin and Rome there was an Axis but no treaty, and despite the fair words exchanged at the time of *Anschluss,* that event had strained the Axis by causing the Duce loss of face abroad and political embarrassment at home. The situation was not at all improved by excitement and false hopes raised by *Anschluss* in the South Tyrol, where the German-speaking population was increasingly infected with Nazism and, as in the Sudetenland, the radical elements were talking of annexation to the Reich. Furthermore, *Anschluss* had revived Italian interest in a *rapprochement* with Britain—a project greatly aided by Anthony Eden's resignation from the Cabinet in February 1938. Negotiations were begun in March, and on April 16 a conditional Anglo-Italian accord was signed in Rome.

Mussolini's visit to Germany in September 1937 had, expectably, led to an invitation to Hitler for a trip to Italy. This had been accepted, and the time fixed for the first week of May. Sometime earlier, probably about April 20, Hitler, in the presence of his new adjutant, Lieutenant Colonel Schmundt, indulged in some ruminations about the strategic relation between Mussolini's attitude and the timing of an attack against Czechoslovakia, plainly prompted by his forthcoming trip to Italy. Schmundt made some rough notes of Hitler's observations, which have been preserved:*

(1) Either Mussolini regards his work as finished, or not. a) If so, Czechoslovakia in distant future. Close the Western frontier, then wait and see. "Return with empty bag." b) If not, then African "Empire." Impossible without German aid. Precondition Czechoslovakia. "Return with Czechoslovakia in the bag."

(2) Mussolini, no visionary, can adequately gauge Germany's military potentialities, and fit into them the timing of his own projects.

(3) In opposition to France and England, the Czech question is soluble only in close alliance with Italy. France and Britain will not oppose (only thus can the four weeks' regrouping be overcome). Subtract the white divisions: Africa and Franco-Italian frontier. . . .

(6) No General Staff discussion by individual branches of the Wehrmacht. Permission to the Army must be withdrawn. Only through the Supreme Command. Concealment of actual intentions important. . . .

The burden of these cryptic jottings might be paraphrased thus: When I go to see Mussolini, I must find out whether or not he contemplates Italian aggrandizement. If not, Germany has little to offer him and no bargaining power. In that event I will fortify the Franco-German frontier and wait for an opportunity. If Mussolini does want more territory, he will need German help, and the Czech project is a precondition of our giving it. In the face of French and English opposition, we can go ahead in Czechoslovakia only with Italian help, for it will require four weeks for us to regroup to face west after dealing with Czechoslovakia, and we need Italy to draw off French forces to Africa and the Franco-Italian border. This must all be kept very hush-hush; the OKH should now be excluded, and only OKW do the initial planning.

Almost certainly, these reflections were prompted by the impending Anglo-Italian Agreement,† which in substance bargained British recognition of the Ethiopian conquest against Italy's promise to refrain from aggrandizement in

---

* This document is the first in a file, collected by Schmundt, comprising fifty-two documents dealing with Case Green. The second document is dated April 22, 1938. Hitler was preoccupied with the *Anschluss* plebiscite until April 10, and was at the Berghof during the third week of that month. April 20, 1938, was his forty-ninth birthday, and he was in Berlin for the official celebration. It appears most probable that his reflections on Mussolini and Czechoslovakia took place at about that time. The notes do not indicate whether or not anyone other than Schmundt was present.

† The "white" divisions referred to in the notes are presumably the French forces thus removed from the German border.

Spain, or elsewhere in the Mediterranean-Red Sea areas at the expense of Britain. If the agreement were to become effective, it would greatly narrow Italy's permissible range of action in those areas, but it was conditioned on League recognition of the Ethiopian annexation and the fulfillment of Italy's promise to withdraw from Spain without securing any privileges there. As Weizsaecker saw it, the agreement "gives both powers a breathing spell" but "leaves sufficient possibilities for declaring it void someday when it is no longer consistent with the over-all policies of the contracting powers."

And so, while he knew Italy would not oppose his Czech designs, Hitler needed, or thought he needed, to know where Mussolini would stand if matters came to scratch with Britain and France.* This was the question in the forefront of his mind on May 2, 1938, as he set out on his second visit to Italy.

3

Mussolini might be the Duce, but Italy was nevertheless a kingdom and, since Hitler was visiting Italy as Chief of State, it was little King Victor Emmanuel II, not Mussolini, who was the official host. Months before the scheduled date the King was interesting himself in the arrangements for the visit, but not with pleasurable anticipation, for he did not like Germans. Austrians had at least been "correct," he told Ciano early in January 1938, but "Berlin has always been the most treacherous of chanceries."†

Hitler arrived in Rome by train in the evening of May 3, accompanied by an enormous entourage—five hundred by interpreter Schmidt's reckoning—including Ribbentrop, Hess, Himmler, Goebbels and other ministers, Party and government officials, and wives. Ribbentrop had fitted out all his subordinates in spanking new diplomatic uniforms, and the *chef de protocole* circulated a prescribed schedule of uniforms, mufti, and tails for each hour of each day.

The visit began uneasily. After King and Duce met Fuehrer at the railway station, Mussolini disappeared and Hitler and the King were ensconced in the first of a line of horse-drawn carriages for the drive through Rome, which had been overabundantly festooned with banners and other decorations. Monarch and Fuehrer made heavy going of it conversationally; the guest gazed solemnly at the illuminated Roman ruins, and put tourist questions which the King failed or did not choose to understand. Inside the palace not one Fascist black shirt was to be seen. Hitler and his followers were surrounded by haughty royalty and nobility—a milieu highly uncongenial to the Nazi guests. Himmler audibly remarked that the "air smelled of the catacombs," to the vast displeasure of the hosts, as gossip of his remark made the rounds. If the King's account is to be credited, Hitler caused a

---

* On May 9, 1938, a "high official" of the Wilhelmstrasse told Sir Nevile Henderson that Hitler's attitude in the Czech question "will largely depend on the mood in which he returns from Rome and on the degree of support promised by Mussolini."

† Hindenburg was still alive when Hitler met Mussolini at Venice in June 1934, so Hitler did not then come as Chief of State and did not meet the King.

Hitler's agent for planning the 1938 visit was Prince Philip of Hesse (the King's son-in-law); he and an Italian committee headed by Ciano developed the program. In April the Chief of Protocol for the German Foreign Ministry, Vicco von Bülow-Schwante, came to Rome and approved the arrangements.

brief scandal by asking "for a woman," and shock gave way to derision when it appeared that all he wanted was a chambermaid to remake his bed.

During the week that Hitler remained in Italy there were military parades and demonstrations, public speeches and balcony appearances, a cruise on the battleship *Cavour* off Capri to watch naval maneuvers, an act of *Lohengrin* in the Piazza di Siena in Rome, *Aïda* at the San Carlo in Naples, and a return visit to Rome for fireworks and an official banquet. Then, to the relief of both Duce and Fuehrer, the royal presence was shaken off and the two dictators went to Florence. Hitler was utterly charmed by the city, the atmosphere was relaxed, and on May 9 he bade Mussolini farewell with every appearance of affection and trust, and regret that the visit had come to an end.

In Italy, the memory of *Anschluss* was still sour, and many Italians dislike Germans on general principles. The crowds were small and cool during the early part of the visit, but the atmosphere improved after Hitler publicly acknowledged Italian sovereignty in the South Tyrol, and proclaimed the Brenner frontier "eternally inviolate."

Considering the size and heterogeneous composition of the German delegation, the occasion was tolerably successful. There was some sniggering among the Italians—Mussolini reported to Ciano that "Hitler puts rouge on his cheeks to hide his pallor," a young Italian naval officer, not recognizing Goebbels, compared him to a cigar vendor, and the King continued to describe his guest as "some kind of a psycho-physiological degenerate." But the Italians were painfully aware that the German arm ended in the harder and bigger fist, and were at great pains to impress their guests on their own terms. They succeeded best at sea; compared to the Italian, the German Navy was puny indeed, and Mussolini had the satisfaction of seeing a look of envy cross Hitler's face as a large number of Italian submarines (including, no doubt, some that had been playing the pirate off the Spanish coast) submerged simultaneously and surfaced in beautiful synchronization.

No doubt Mussolini was irked at being put back to second place behind the King, but he kept himself under better control than did his guests. Ribbentrop complained to him that the royalty were arrogant to Hitler, but Mussolini calmly admonished him to "tell the Führer to exercise patience." Goebbels, blandly disregarding his own diminutive and misshapen physique, told Ciano to keep the throne but "put the Duce on it—that chap [the King] is too small." Himmler and Hess told Anfuso that the Quirinal was "in the world of an old-fashioned film." Despite the Fascists' ambivalence toward the House of Savoy, none of this went down very well, and Ciano was finding Ribbentrop's loquacity and disjointed exuberance a frightful bore. But there were no real disasters* and the glow of Florence finally dissipated the chill.

All in all, the Italians could congratulate themselves on bringing off the gar-

---

* There was a catastrophe for Bülow-Schwante for leaving Hitler in the white tie and tails that he had worn for *Aïda*. When the Fuehrer found himself surrounded by uniformed Italians for the drive through Naples to the railway station, he flew into a rage, denounced Bülow-Schwante for letting him leave Naples "dressed like a French minister," and fired the unfortunate *chef de protocole* on the spot.

gantuan but delicate reception without a major hitch, and with impressive display. From the German standpoint, there was less cause for gratification. On returning to Berlin, Ribbentrop circularized the German Missions abroad with the news that "the Führer's visit to Italy is to be accounted a great success," but there was little to bear out so optimistic an assessment.

In line with Hitler's desire to secure Italian support for his Czech project, he and Ribbentrop went to Rome prepared to offer Mussolini a full military alliance. There is no record of preliminary discussions between the two capitals, and it remains uncertain whether or not Mussolini and Ciano had any reason to expect such an offer. However that may be, forty-eight hours before Hitler's arrival, Ciano submitted to his father-in-law "an outline of a possible treaty with Germany," pointing out that Italy had just signed an agreement with Britain and the French were angling for one, and "unless we define our relations with Berlin as well, everyone will say that the Axis has been liquidated and we are going back to Stresa."

This was, of course, a very much narrower purpose than Hitler had in mind. Mussolini approved Ciano's outline, but when Ciano, at the beginning of the visit, handed a draft of the agreement to Ribbentrop, the German reaction was decisively negative. Weizsaecker informed Berlin that the Ciano draft was "immediately laid aside and called meaningless," and upon his return to Germany noted in his diary: "Mussolini . . . gave us a box on the ear with the—improvised—draft of a treaty, which resembled rather a peace treaty with an enemy than a pact of loyalty with a friend."

On May 5, the third day of the visit, Ribbentrop gave Ciano a draft which the latter regarded as offering "a pact of military assistance, public or secret, whichever we prefer." Ciano, who was considerably more cautious than his patron, "did not hesitate to tell the Duce I was against this, just as I have tried to delay the conclusion of a pact for political consultation and assistance." Postponement seemed to him the wiser course, especially since Chamberlain was confronting difficulties both at home and at Geneva in carrying out the conditions of the recently signed Anglo-Italian Agreement.

Mussolini's reaction was basically favorable. He told Ciano that he "had a thousand and one reasons for not trusting the western democracies" and that he intended eventually to make the pact with Hitler. In the words of the Schmundt notes, Mussolini did not "regard his work as finished." Ciano had just returned from a visit to Albania to attend King Zog's wedding, and he and Mussolini were already thinking about annexing that country, as indeed they did a year later. Hitler had no sooner departed Florence than Mussolini was warning Ciano that "a diplomatic crisis will be precipitated and France and England will inevitably be against us," and to meet the situation "it is important to secure the pact with Germany." This was the beginning of the train of thought which led to the "Pact of Steel" between the two dictatorships, formalized in May 1939.

But these inclinations were not disclosed to the Germans. Mussolini and Ciano made it plain to them that the time for an alliance was not at hand, and Weizsaecker informed Berlin that Ribbentrop was "not pressing for the conclusion of such an agreement, and the idea has now been abandoned."

The Ribbentrop and Ciano drafts thus came to nothing, and the conversations between the two principals seem to have been equally sterile. Hitler talked no politics with Ciano and, according to that diarist, was "restrained in his conversations with the Duce." Schmidt, on the other hand, recalls that he "had an easy time as an interpreter" because "Mussolini and Ciano were obviously trying to evade any serious political discussion—though Hitler, and more especially Ribbentrop, were constantly seeking it." He also recalled a "very violent argument" between Ribbentrop and Ciano because of the latter's lack of enthusiasm for the draft treaty of alliance.

No doubt the fiasco with the treaty proposals chilled exploration of the two parties' secret plans. There was considerable discussion of the South Tyrol, on the basis that territorial changes were foreclosed, and that Mussolini would allow a measure of cultural autonomy. But the Italians said nothing of Albania, and the Germans gave out the impression that little of moment was impending in Central Europe; the Polish Corridor was to be accepted "for an indefinite period," and the Czechoslovakian question was "not urgent." The conclusion drawn in Berlin was that, in the event of a conflict between Germany and Czechoslovakia, Italy would neither hinder nor support the German action. In short, that she would sit that one out.

4

In terms of Hitler's analysis as recorded by Schmundt, the Fuehrer had returned from Italy "with empty bag," and accordingly plans for attacking Czechoslovakia should be held in suspense, while the western frontier was fortified and opportunity awaited. There is no evidence that Hitler was of any different frame of mind when he returned from Italy. But now, with *Anschluss* achieved and the Italian situation clarified, he turned his attention to the military aspects of the Czech question.

He did not have to start from scratch. Case Green was one of the two major portions (the other being Case Red) of Blomberg's 1937 directive, and while OKH had ignored the part of the directive directed toward Austria (*Otto*), it had done some work on Green during the autumn of 1937. The plan, in outline, contemplated the concentration of four armies and an independent corps against Czechoslovakia, while the western front was to be covered with three weak armies, and the Polish frontier by a fourth. This deployment embodied the concept, previously adopted, that in the face of a hostile coalition, the Wehrmacht's best strategy would be to effect speedy defeat of the weaker antagonist, and then to confront the stronger.

During the ensuing months, the Bendlerstrasse generals were heavily occupied with other matters—the Blomberg and Fritsch affairs, Austria, and the continuing debate between OKH and OKW concerning their respective powers and responsibilities in the event of war. As the Army saw it, the transmutation of RKM to OKW consequent upon the Blomberg-Fritsch crisis had by no means solved the leadership problem—rather the contrary, since the Commander-in-Chief of the Wehrmacht was no longer a career officer and field marshal, but only a retired corporal. Early in March, Brauchitsch submitted a long memorandum, largely the work of Beck and Manstein, envisioning a separation between leadership of the national war effort and command of the armed forces. Hitler, with Keitel as executive agent, would direct the over-all war effort, including the war economy, propaganda, and so forth. For the conduct of military operations, however, Hitler would act through a Chief of the General Staff of the Wehrmacht who would also be the Army Commmander-in-Chief—the theory being that for continental warfare the Army was the dominant service and should have the over-all leadership.

As ranking officer of the Wehrmacht and second man in the Reich, Hermann Goering was bound to and did strongly oppose such a plan, which would have subordinated the Luftwaffe to the Army Chief. Nor was it congenial to Hitler's conception of his own role, for the Army plan echoed the command structure of the First World War, with the Kaiser as "Supreme War Lord" while the real power lay in the hands of Hindenburg and Ludendorf. And on April 19, 1938, OKW issued a reply memorandum, largely composed by Jodl, which stressed the all-embracing, total character of modern warfare, and the need for unity in its direction. In an appendix, Jodl rhapsodized on the "War of the Future":

> War in its total form is a power conflict between two or more states using all means. . . . It serves the preservation of the State and Folk and the assurance of their historical future. These high goals give war its total character and ethical justification. It lifts war above the purely political act, or a mere military duel for economic advantage. . . . Only the singleness and unity of State, Armed Forces, and People can assure success in war. . . .

Displeased with the Army's proposals, and well aware that Beck would be a vigorous opponent of military adventurism, Hitler turned to his OKW staff for assistance as his appetite for Czechoslovakian conquest grew. That meant primary reliance on Keitel and Jodl, for General von Viebahn's tenure at OKW had been very brief. His nerves had completely given way during the *Anschluss* march-in; he had prophesied disaster, prayed loudly and publicly, and finally locked himself in his rooms at the Bendlerstrasse and threatened would-be intruders with a pistol. On his return from Vienna, Keitel sent him back to OKH. He was not replaced at OKW, and Jodl once again took charge of the operations staff.*

Because of his growing distrust of the OKH generals, Hitler (as the Schmundt notes on the Italian factor show) decided to exclude them from the early stages of the planning for Czechoslovakia. His first confidants were Keitel and Schmundt, and shortly after his birthday celebration the latter made notes of the Fuehrer's exposition to Keitel of the prospects for Green:

A. Political Possibilities

1. A strategic surprise attack out of a clear sky with no cause or justification won't do. Result would be: hostile world opinion, which can lead to critical situation. . . .

---

* Formally, Jodl was chief of the plans section of the operations staff, temporarily vested with leadership of the staff itself. Warlimont, who had been Jodl's deputy, was temporarily in a field command assignment. Viebahn was hospitalized but shortly returned to active duty on the OKH staff, and later held minor commands during the war.

2. Action after a period of diplomatic clashes, which gradually come to a crisis and lead to war.
3. Lightning-swift action as the result of an incident (e.g., assassination of German ambassador in connection with an anti-German demonstration).

B. Military Conclusions

1. Preparations are to be made for political possibilities 2 and 3. Case 2 is less desirable since Green [Czechoslovakia] will have taken precautions.
2. The loss of time from transporting the bulk of the divisions by rail—which is unavoidable but must be held to a minimum—must not prevent a lightning-swift blow.
3. "Separate thrusts" are to be made immediately in order to penetrate the enemy fortified lines at numerous points and in operationally favorable directions. . . . Simultaneous attacks by Army and Air Force.
   The Air Force will support the individual columns. (E.g., dive bombers: sealing off installations at penetration points, hampering the bringing up of reserves, destroying signals communications, thereby isolating the garrisons.)
4. Politically the first four days of military action are decisive. If there are no effective military successes, a European crisis will certainly arise. Accomplished facts must show the senselessness of foreign military intervention, draw allies into the project (division of spoils!) and demoralize Green.
   Therefore, bridge the time gap between the first penetration and commitment of forces being brought to the front by a determined and ruthless thrust by a motorized army (e.g., via Pilsen and Prague). . . .

Leaving these general directives for Keitel and his staff to work on, Hitler went off to the Berghof and then to Italy. Meanwhile Henlein, in a speech at the Sudeten German Party rally in Karlsbad on April 24, had listed eight demands for action by the Prague government. Some of these were particulars, such as the appointment of German public officials in the Sudeten area and compensation for "damages suffered" by the Sudeten Germans at Czech hands, but at least two of them were fundamental and patently subversive of the Czech Government and Constitution: one was for the recognition of the Sudeten Germans as a distinct legal entity within the state, and the other "complete freedom to profess adherence to the German element and ideology." These nicely fitted Hitler's prescription of demands "unacceptable" to Prague.*

While Hitler and Ribbentrop were in Italy, the British and French ministers in Prague, at their governments' direction, made simultaneous and strong representations to the Czech Foreign Minister (Krofta) that the Sudeten question was gravely threatening European peace, the military situation for resistance to Germany was unfavorable, and Prague should go the limit in meeting the Sudeten demands. The gist of these exhortations (formally presented on May 7) was

---

* Recognizing the hazards which the new and more aggressive policies toward Czechoslovakia, would entail, on April 25 the German Foreign Ministry sent a secret circular to its missions abroad directing them to take precautionary steps to ensure when necessary the destruction of classified documents, repatriation of military-age Germans, and co-operation in the planning of a war economy.

made known at the Wilhelmstrasse, and the first secretary of the British Embassy in Berlin, Ivone Kirkpatrick, followed up with an off-the-record request for a "confidential" statement of what Berlin really wanted, so "that the British Government would bring such pressure to bear in Prague that the Czechoslovakian Government would be compelled to accede to the German wishes."

All of this information was available when Hitler returned from Italy to Berlin on May 10, and its message was that the last thing Britain wished to do was fight for Czechoslovakia. Two days later Henlein came to Berlin en route to London, and agreed with Ribbentrop that he would stress the reasonableness of the Karlsbad demands and "deny that he was acting on instructions from Berlin." On the heels of his departure came a message from Eisenlohr, informing his chiefs that the "overwhelming majority" of the Sudeten Germans, "intoxicated by the success in Austria," were expecting annexation of the Sudetenland to the Reich by a march-in of German troops.

Despite his lack of success in Italy, therefore, Hitler had much cause for encouragement in his designs as he went off for a rest at the Berghof. From Britain, France, and the Sudeten German Party, pressures in Prague were mounting which bade fair to create either or both of the desirable preconditions which he had described to Keitel. And no sooner was he ensconced in his Alpine retreat than he started a barrage of questions telegraphed to OKW by Schmundt. How many German divisions near the Czech frontier could be ready to march within twelve hours? How long would mobilization take? What were the nature and strength of the Czech fortifications? The questions were answered for OKW by Lieutenant Colonel Kurt Zeitzler, then one of Jodl's senior subordinates in the plans section, and destined to be the Army Chief of Staff four years later.*

Meanwhile the OKW offices had completed a draft of a general directive for Green, which was transmitted to Hitler under cover of a letter from Keitel dated May 20, 1938. He reminded Hitler that the Blomberg directive of June 1937 would expire and a new one be due on October 1, 1938; immediately, however, the Green section needed revision because of the incorporation of Austria "and the newly suspected intentions of the Czech general staff." The draft, Keitel noted, had not yet been discussed with the commanders-in-chief of the three services, and would not be until "its fundamental ideas have been approved by you, my Führer."

The new draft for Green, largely the work of Jodl, was divided in six sections. The first was entitled "political prerequisites":

> It is not my intention to destroy Czechoslovakia through military action in the near future without provocation. Therefore inevitable political developments *inside* Czechoslovakia must force the issue, or political events in Europe create an especially possible opportunity that may never recur.

The second and third sections merely paraphrased Hitler's instructions to Keitel a month earlier. A period of diplomatic clashes or a serious incident

---

* The questions and answers were not, in fact, very revealing of over-all plans. There were twelve ready divisions in the German garrisons circling Bohemia and Moravia. Zeitzler was Chief of the General Staff of the Army from 1942 to 1944.

(preferably the latter) would be a necessary prelude to an attack, and success during the first four days would be crucial in order to discourage hostile intervention and bring Hungary and Poland into the game.

The fourth and fifth sections outlined the Wehrmacht's operations, and were largely modeled on the plans previously sketched by OKH. The mass of ground and air strength would be concentrated against Czechoslovakia, with only light screening forces on the western and eastern fronts. Simultaneous surprise assaults on the ground and in the air were to penetrate the Czech fortifications and open the way for mechanized troops to "thrust into the heart of Czechoslovakia." For the Luftwaffe, the prime mission was destruction of the Czech Air Force, especially its fields and bases, so as to deny them to the Russians and French. Czech industrial installations were, as far as possible, to be spared so as to be available for continuing the war if necessary. A sixth section stressed the necessity of expanding the German war economy.

All in all, the OKW draft did not carry matters much beyond the point at which Hitler had left them with Keitel a month earlier. Nor is there any indication that Hitler had as yet perceived any means of accelerating the tempo. But now, as previously in the case of Austria, events occurred within the boundaries of the intended victim which set things on a quicker course which was a lead, in four months, directly to the Munich crisis.

5

On Thursday, May 19, 1938, Sir Nevile Henderson received and passed on to London a report from the British consulate in Dresden that there was "strong reason to believe that German troops are concentrating in southern Silesia and northern Austria" and that military leaves were about to be suspended. Later that day Henderson transmitted a comparable report from Bavaria, adding that "my French colleague has also heard rumors of concentration of troops on the [Czech] frontier." In Prague the following day, Krofta telephoned Eisenlohr to express alarm over reports that German troops were concentrating in Saxony.

So began what diplomats thereafter referred to as the "May crisis." If these reports were credible, Prague had ample cause to fear that German border demonstrations, or even an invasion, might be in the offing. The first of a series of Czech municipal elections was to be held on Sunday, May 22, and the Sudetenland was increasingly turbulent. The Sudeten German Party had broken off negotiations with the Czech Government when Henlein had gone off to Berlin and London, and Henlein himself, shortly after his return, went to Berchtesgaden to meet with Hitler.* *Anschluss* had shown that Hitler could act impulsively, and he had repeatedly declared that he would not tolerate oppression of the Sudeten Germans. The danger that some incident might trigger an invasion seemed very real, and on the evening of May 20 at Eger two Sudeten German motorcyclists who failed to heed a Czech policeman's challenge were shot dead. That night the Prague government, responding to the Czech General Staff's demand that five classes of reservists be called for active service, more cau-

---

* Jodl's diary entry for May 22, 1938, reports a "basic conference between the Fuehrer and K. Henlein," but there appears to be no surviving record of what was said.

tiously called up one class and a number of specialist troops, to reinforce the garrisons in the Sudetenland.

The Wilhelmstrasse, after consulting OKW, vehemently denied that any hostile concentrations, or even unusual troop movements, had taken place. Nevertheless, when Eisenlohr and his military attaché, Colonel Rudolf Toussaint, went to see the Czech Chief of Staff, General Ludvik Krejcí, they were informed that Prague had "irrefutable proof that in Saxony a concentration of from eight to ten divisions had taken place." Who was telling the truth?

When Weizsaecker, on information from Keitel, told Henderson that the reports were "absolutely nonsense," the ambassador sharply reminded his informant that similar inquiries six weeks earlier, during the Austrian crisis, had also been met with denials which soon proved false. Thus influenced by healthy suspicion, Henderson decided not to take the German story at face value, and sent the British military attaché and his assistant (Colonel Frank Mason-Macfarlane and Major Kenneth Strong) to reconnoiter the suspect areas. On May 22, "Mason-Mac" (as he was known) drove all through Silesia, and Strong through Saxony. Neither was able to detect any significant sign of troop movements or concentrations. Meanwhile the French attachés, alarmed by reports from their consuls in Dresden and Leipzig, surveyed the region between Berlin and the Czech borders, by both automobile and airplane. They saw nothing out of the way, and Captain Stehlin concluded that "our Czech friends, because of the press campaign, had deceived themselves to the extent of describing a military situation which existed only in their imagination."

Ribbentrop and Weizsaecker put the matter much more strongly and flatly accused Prague of fabricating the rumors of German military moves in order to provide an excuse for their own mobilization. But the reports did not all come from Czech sources, and with the benefit of hindsight it is now clear that there were German troop movements and concentrations that became known to the excellent Czech intelligence service and that, under the prevailing tense circumstances, were quite sufficient to justify a state of alert in Prague. It is equally plain that, at the time, Hitler had no intention of imminently taking hostile action against Czechoslovakia.

The reasons for the movements that so alarmed Prague were that the Wehrmacht was growing, forming new units, and testing new techniques, and, with the coming of spring, maneuvers and war games were the order of the day. In response to Weizsaecker's inquiry, Keitel, while denying any abnormal movements, disclosed that there was indeed an unusual number of troops at the Königsbrück training ground, about twenty miles north of Dresden, the capital of Saxony, where General Krejcí had claimed to have "irrefutable proof" of a concentration. Furthermore, during the week May 15 to 23, a combined Army and Luftwaffe war game was under way in adjacent Thuringia, where the tactics of ground-air collaboration were being explored with particular reference to the Green and Red contingencies.

It must have been events such as these, probably exaggerated or distorted in the description, which were the basis of the reports that came to Prague and to the British and French embassies in Berlin. In Prague the reports were interpreted in the light of the Czech General Staff's assessment of the probable German plan of campaign—a shrewd one which, as events later proved, was close to the mark. Badly outnumbered but with strong defenses *if manned and ready,* the Czechs most feared being overwhelmed by a sudden attack before they could mobilize. They reasoned that the Germans would try to achieve surprise "under guise of moves for training purposes" which would bring strong concentrations of troops to the border without the publicity necessarily involved in formal mobilization. What Prague heard from Saxony, and perhaps elsewhere, fitted the formula too closely for comfort, and the Czech generals decided that an alert and a partial mobilization were the least that prudence dictated.

But in fact the German preparations were not nearly so far advanced as the Czechs feared. The revised Green directive, which had not yet even been signed, opened with a renunciation of imminent action. At OKH and in the field only a bare start had been made toward developing the plans and making the preparations for such an operation. In immediate military terms, the "May crisis" was of no importance, but its diplomatic and psychological repercussions were enormous, for Hitler appeared to have had his bluff called, and that was something which he could not abide.

Casting about as he was for any stick with which to beat the Czechs, Ribbentrop had summoned Mastny, denounced his government's circulation of false reports of German troop movements, and threatened that such tactics "could have only one result with the German Government, namely, that these troop concentrations . . . would take place with lightning speed." The next day (May 21) Henderson found the German Foreign Minister "in a highly excitable and pugnacious mood," complaining that the ambassador had, without previous agreement, released to Reuters the German denials. Ribbentrop threatened as punishment to cut off the British from any further access to military information, and raged over the incident at Eger, which had just been reported to him. The Czechs were "mad," he shouted, and "if they persisted in their present attitude they would be destroyed." British efforts to bring them to their senses "had led to no result whatever."

Reports of these interviews, coupled with the continuing rumors of German military moves, naturally caused great concern in London and Paris. In the evening of May 21, Henderson was again in Ribbentrop's office, this time armed with a telegram from Lord Halifax noting with disapproval the German threats of intervention, reminding the German Government of "their responsibilities," and declaring that "His Majesty's Government could not guarantee that they would not be forced by circumstances to become involved" if German aggression should trigger French intervention in pursuance of her treaty obligations.

The next day Henderson was back at the Wilhelmstrasse with a personal message from Halifax to Ribbentrop, warning that if Germany resorted to force "it is quite impossible for me to foretell results that may follow, and I would beg him not to count upon this country being able to stand aside. . . ." Meanwhile François-Poncet had made similar representations to Weizsaecker, and in Paris, Premier Daladier invited the German Ambassador to his home in order "to speak frankly as a French ex-serviceman to his German comrade" and to warn him that if Germany attacked Czechoslovakia "the French would have to fight if they did not wish to be dishonored." The result, he declared, could be the "utter destruction of European civilization" and the triumph of "Cossack and Mongol hordes."

Now, a consequence of these reports of troop movements and diplomatic *démarches* was that Hitler and his government suffered considerable loss of face. Although in fact there had been no intention to take any kind of hostile military action, the contrary was widely believed and reported in the world press, and when nothing happened, it was made to appear that Hitler had backed down when confronted with the Czech call-up of reserves and the British and French warnings. Henderson reported to Halifax on May 28 that there was deep resentment on the part of the German Government because of "ready acceptance all over the world of the theory that Germany concentrated troops with intention of attacking Czechoslovakia and was only restrained by energetic action of England" and "general jubilation at diplomatic defeat of Germany and rebuff to Herr Hitler." Furthermore, the episode had given the Czechs welcome (though misleading) encouragement, for the call-up had gone smoothly, had had a calming effect in the Sudetenland, the elections had taken place with no major incidents, and the British and French had given strong diplomatic support.*

It may easily be imagined how little any of this was to Hitler's liking. At the height of the tension he received Keitel's draft of Green, and soon Schmundt was telegraphing more questions to OKW, some of which Zeitzler answered on May 23. Then came a telegram from Schmundt with information which Hitler wished to have conveyed to Keitel, and in part to Brauchitsch:

(1) Inform General Keitel: The Führer is going into Green in detail. Basic ideas unchanged. Surprise factor to be more emphasized. Conference with the parties concerned will take place after return at the latest. Conference here not foreclosed.

(2) Return probably beginning of next week. Inform Generals Brauchitsch and Keitel:

(A) The Führer suggested holding exercises in taking fortifications by surprise attack. I informed him that . . . Army is planning such an exercise in September. Führer thinks that too late. He himself will discuss it with Commander-in-Chief of Army.

(B) The Führer repeatedly emphasized the necessity of pushing the fortification work in the West.

As the references to Brauchitsch show, the program had reached a stage at which OKH had to be brought into the picture, to develop the tactics and techniques essential to the strategy on which the Green plan was based. So, too, the telegram reflects growing impatience, no doubt fed by the exasperating events of the past few days, to get on with the project. However, there was no ensuing

---

* A very different consequence, however, was that Sir Nevile Henderson was more than half persuaded, by his attachés' negative reports, that the Czechs had concocted the rumors to cover their own actions, and were responsible for the crisis. This no doubt reinforced Henderson's anti-Czech feelings and his inclination to give way to German demands.

conference at the Berghof. Hitler visited Fallersleben on May 26 to lay the cornerstone of the new Volkswagen factory, and then went on to Berlin, arriving in a very truculent mood.

On May 28 he called a meeting in the winter garden of the Reich Chancellery. Keitel, Brauchitsch, Beck (who took notes) and the Fuehrer's civilian aide, Fritz Wiedemann, were there, but who else we do not surely know, although the location and the nature of Hitler's speech suggest that it was a sizable gathering.*

According to Wiedemann, Hitler declared: "It is my unshakeable will that Czechoslovakia shall be wiped off the map." Such a statement does not appear in Beck's notes, but in all probability Hitler said this or something like it since, as will soon appear, he wrote it two days later. He began, however, with a rehash of the geopolitical lecture that he had delivered at the Hossbach conference six months before—*Lebensraum,* autarky, and so forth—and then passed to the political situation. France and England were incorrigibly hostile to an expanding Germany. In the event of war against them, Germany would need to extend her coasts by taking Belgium and Holland. Czechoslovakia would be an enemy in the rear, and therefore must be eliminated (*beseitigt*). France and England did not want war, Russia was not yet ready for an offensive war, Poland and Rumania feared Russian "help" more than Germany, Yugoslavia would stand aside, Italy was uninterested, and Hungary would join with Germany. England's rearmament would not be complete until 1941–42, France's not until even later. There was unusual strain between them and Italy, and that country, whose strength should not be minimized, wanted Tunis and would exploit France's weakness.

Only at the end of this mixture of punditry and pep talk did Hitler approach the military side of the matter, and then it was merely to repeat the exhortations, in his telegram from the Berghof, that the western fortifications, and techniques for breaking the Czech defenses, be given first priority. As far as Beck's notes reveal, no one else spoke; the occasion was anticipatory of the harangues later delivered to similar gatherings at the time of major military decisions.

Two days later, on May 30, Hitler finally signed the revised directive for Green. The military provisions were not significantly altered, except for the addition of a seventh section stipulating that "all preparations for sabotage and insurrection will be handled by OKW." But the opening paragraphs, dealing with the political preconditions, had undergone an ominous modification, and now read:

It is my unalterable decision to destroy Czechoslovakia by military action within the foreseeable future. It is the responsibility of the political leadership to determine or bring about the politically and militarily suitable moment.

* Erich Kordt, a Foreign Ministry official, later wrote that "prominent leaders from the Party and State" were present. At Nuremberg, Keitel testified that he and Brauchitsch were there, and Beck's notes survived the war. Wiedemann, in a postwar affidavit, named Neurath, Ribbentrop, Goering, and Raeder as also present, Neurath testified that he was not in Berlin at the time, and none of the three others appears to have mentioned it in later testimony or writing. Neurath's testimony may well be inaccurate, as he was in Berlin and conferred with Sir Nevile Henderson on the evening of May 26.

An inevitable development of conditions in Czechoslovakia or other political events in Europe creating an unexpectedly favorable opportunity, which
may perhaps not recur, may cause me to take early action.

The proper choice and decisive and full use of a favorable moment is the
surest guarantee of success. Accordingly the preparations are to be made at
once.

A covering letter signed by Keitel directed that execution of the plan "must be
assured as final October 1, 1938, at the latest." To be sure, one cannot say that
but for the May crisis there would have been no Munich. Hitler was looking for
provocation; he soon would have found it somewhere, and the timetable might
have been the same. But certainly the Czech call-up, and the diplomatic and
press reaction, were the immediate causes of this change of tempo. In his diary,
Jodl recorded: *

The intention of the Führer not to stir the Czech problem as yet is changed
because of the Czech troop concentrations of May 21st, which occurs without
any German threat or apparent cause.

German inaction causes the Führer a loss of prestige, which he is unwilling
to accept. Therefore on May 30th the new directive "Green" is issued.

Six weeks earlier, when Schuschnigg announced his plebiscite, Hitler could
crush Austria by merely clenching his fist. When Prague ordered the call-up,
however, he had no such easy road to conquest. A sword would be wanted; the
German sword needed to be tempered and sharpened, and that would take time.
But from the end of May, Adolf Hitler was determined that it would take as little
time as possible.

* See the parallel comment of Weizsaecker, in his *Memoirs,* pp. 135–36: "The world
press . . . by spreading the story that Hitler had yielded to foreign pressure . . . really set
Hitler going. From then on he was emphatically in favor of settling the Czech question by
force of arms . . ."

Part IV

HOW THE ISSUE WAS DRAWN
1936–1938

CHAPTER 17

Among Bohemia's Meadows and Forests

1

If Hermann Goering's word of honor, given so ostentatiously on the eve of
Anschluss, was intended to lull Eduard Beneš into a false sense of security, the
attempt was a failure. Ten years earlier Beneš had told Stresemann that if Austria were ever annexed by Germany "within six months there would be a great
European crisis out of which would come a new European war." He had several
times repeated this prediction and, now that the feared event was actual, it
seemed to him "virtually certain" that there would be war. The dead Masaryk's
son Jan, now Minister in London, was equally scornful of the Fat Man's *Ehrenwort,* and told Lord Halifax that it would be observed only "as long as it suits
them, and not a minute longer."

Such skepticism was wholesome, but what was to be done? In determining national strategy, the strongest voice was still that of the President—in Elizabeth
Wiskemann's apt phrase, the "admirably energetic little schoolmaster"—who,
with his friend and follower Kamil Krofta as Foreign Minister, dominated
Czech diplomacy. But on domestic questions Beneš was no dictator, and his
influence, though considerable, was shared uneasily with Premier Hodža and
other party leaders in the coalition cabinet.

For nearly two decades, Masaryk and Beneš had based their country's security on Versailles, the League of Nations, and the French alliance. Now Versailles was dead, and the League was mortally ill from Ethiopian and Spanish
infections, while the Rhineland reoccupation had undermined the French guarantee. Beneš own creation, the Little Entente, was paralyzed by reactionary
royalism and fear of Germany. Collective security, as the basis of national pol-

icy, seemed to be leading the country into a cul-de-sac. Was there no more promising road?

Czechoslovakia might have relaxed or even cast off her ties with France and Russia and sought a bilateral understanding with Germany, following the Polish example. There were some Czechs, chiefly in financial and agrarian circles, who favored this. Indeed, a few months after the Rhineland remilitarization Hitler had sent unofficial emissaries to Prague to propose such an arrangement.* This was, of course, an attempt to accomplish with Czechoslovakia what had already been secured from Austria by the July 1936 treaty. It took but eighteen months to show where that road might lead and, while Colonel Beck in Poland was still smugly balanced on his tightrope, Beneš was rightly distrustful of such arrangements between small countries and large ones obviously bent on aggrandizement, and was sure that Poland, too, would soon crash.

Deeply convinced that reliance on Nazi Germany's good faith would be the shortest route to national suicide, Beneš concluded that the old roads were less hazardous, and that the best hope lay in their improvement. Accordingly, he and the other leaders of the Prague government continued to pursue a set of policies in quintuplicate, embracing (1) reinsurance of support from Czechoslovakia's formal allies, France and Russia, and France's ally across the Channel; (2) propitiation of Germany by avoiding provocation; (3) strengthening internal unity by concessions to the Sudeten and other minority nationalities; (4) seeking diplomatic and, if possible, military support among Czechoslovakia's neighbors in Eastern Europe; and (5) strengthening her own military defenses. None of these was new, but after *Anschluss* all were more urgent.

On the military side, construction of the newly planned fortifications was the major undertaking. Despite the natural obstacles provided by the mountains along the northern Czech-German frontier, the country's elongated configuration made effective fixed defenses enormously expensive in both money and manpower. The German border alone extended for nearly 700 miles, to which *Anschluss* added 250 more. The unfriendly Polish and Hungarian frontiers comprised another 775 miles. To fortify such a stretch was far beyond the capacities of a polyglot nation of 15 million, prosperous as it was compared to its neighbors.

In June 1936 the Chief of Staff submitted an ambitious plan, to be fulfilled within ten to fifteen years. Priorities were therefore crucial. The narrow neck between Moravia and Slovakia offered the Germans the best geographical opportunity to cut the country in two, and first priority was therefore given to the northern frontier from the Oder River westward to Trautenau.† After *Anschluss* the area of immediate concern was, of course, the former Austro-

---

* According to Beneš (Memoirs, pp. 14–20) these were the geopolitician Albrecht Haushofer and an Austrian aristocrat, Count Ferdinand Trautmannsdorf. The negotiations came to nothing, as Beneš concluded that Hitler's purpose was to detach Czechoslovakia from the League and her French and Russian connections, and undermine her independence.

† See map on pp. 710–11. Second priority was accorded westward extension of the fortifications to the Elbe river, southeast of Dresden.

Czech border, and on March 29, 1938, the British military attaché in Prague (Colonel Stronge) reported that the Czechs were "working day and night" there to strengthen the fortifications.

The fixed fortifications were of four main types. For frontal fire near the front there were small concretized emplacements for machine guns, manned by four or five soldiers, and offering protection only against rifle fire and grenade splinters. Farther back were "medium" emplacements manned by a noncommissioned officer and six privates, armored against light artillery, and armed with two machine guns placed for flanking as well as frontal fire. The backbone of the heavily defended portions of the frontier was the "independent" fortification, manned by an officer and thirty to thirty-five men, with deep underground entrances and compartments, ventilation and observation turrets, armored against medium artillery and armed with four or more machine guns, and mortars, antitank guns, and flame-throwers. Finally, at critical points along the Moravian-German border, between Troppau and Trautenau, were nine "fortification groups," in various stages of completion by the time of Munich. There were huge fortification complexes, largely underground, and expected to give protection against bombing.*

As for the field army, Colonel Stronge pronounced it "probably the best in the smaller states of Europe," but warned that "the process of replacing obsolescent arms with new models is far from complete though it is being pushed forward as rapidly as possible.† But in the air the Czechs were at a greater disadvantage, because of the comparatively small size of their air force and their country's narrow geographical confines. Furthermore, according to Beneš, civil air-raid defense was in a disorganized state because of interdepartmental jealousies. It was especially on the air side that Russian aid was counted on, and a program of extending and improving the Czech airfields was put under way but was still far from completion. Nor was it proposed to leave Germany unscathed; twenty Russian medium bombers were purchased and flown across Rumania to Czechoslovakia in April and May 1938.

But these arms were destined never to be used against Germany and, indeed, within the year they fell into German hands and were eventually turned against Britain and France. And, of course, they were not intended for use other than in a defensive holding operation awaiting relief, primarily from France with British backing.

General Eugène Faucher, Chief of the French Military Mission in Prague, is said to have remarked:

> The Sudeten-German Problem arose because Czechoslovakia had been abandoned. So long as nobody doubted that there were forces in Europe which could come to the aid of Czechoslovakia and maintain the order of the Peace Treaties, there were no question of Sudeten-German secession.

---

* The Czech fortifications are described and pictured in great detail in a memorandum by the engineering division of the German Army General Staff, compiled in 1941.

† Eisenlohr, in a report transmitted to Berlin in January 1938, described "the stupendous efforts being made to modernize the Army and strengthen the fortifications."

This observation tears off the veil and discloses the true motivations of the parties to the Sudeten "question" that so disastrously embroiled Europe. All of them were governed by purposes other than those which they openly avowed, and none was primarily concerned for the welfare of the Sudeten German people. Britain and France would surely have remained indifferent to and generally unaware of Prague's minority problems had they not thought it possible that concessions to the Sudeten Germans might forestall or at least delay intervention by the Reich. Beneš and his colleagues of course had an immediate interest in their country's domestic tranquillity; they were not unenlightened, and Prague's nationalities policies were much more permissive than those of her neighbors. But the Bohemians were pushy and insensitive and, as even the Czech apologist Hubert Ripka acknowledged, the Government's attitude was too often affected by "narrow-minded nationalism." It is certain that the principal explanation of the concessions to which Prague agreed during the summer of 1938 were only in small part the product of domestic concern. Primarily they were a response to the necessity of satisfying Britain and France, and secondarily to the hope of placating Hitler.

On the other side, the hypocrisy was much more crass, as Maxim Litvinov, for one, was well aware. At Geneva in May 1938 he admonished Halifax that Hitler had no more intrinsic interest in the Sudeten Germans than in the South Tyroleans, and was simply using the former as a pretext for territorial conquest. Two months earlier, as we have seen, Hitler and Henlein had agreed that the Sudeten issue would be exploited not to reach an agreement with Prague, but to destroy the regime.

With the benefit of this hindsight, the negotiations between the Prague government and the Henleinists, on which the attention of Europe's diplomats was focused from March to September 1938, appear as a pathetic, pointless charade. At the time only Hitler, Henlein, and their close associates knew the true inwardness of the situation; even Eisenlohr, judging from his dispatches, was unaware that Henlein had no intention of agreeing to anything, and was "negotiating" only as cover for the German diplomatic and military buildup. Litvinov had accurately diagnosed the situation, and from time to time Beneš, Hodža, or even Basil Newton wondered aloud whether the Henleinists were really seeking an agreement. But no one could be sure, and as long as a settlement acceptable to Henlein appeared to offer the possibility of staving off an aggressive move on Hitler's part, the British and French kept up strong pressure on Prague to go the limit by way of concessions.

This pressure took formal shape soon after *Anschluss,* in a message from Lord Halifax to Newton, directing the latter to "make an oral communication" to Krofta "in strict confidence, as early as possible tomorrow March 24, in the following sense":

> The obligations of Great Britain to Czechoslovakia are those of one member of the League to another . . .
> So far as France is concerned, His Majesty's Government are bound by . . . the Treaty of Locarno . . . to go to the assistance of France in the event of an unprovoked attack upon her by Germany.

His Majesty's Government intend to abide by the above-mentioned obligations . . . and . . . cannot see their way to add to them.

In view of the present situation, His Majesty's Government feel that in the interests of international peace every possible step should be taken to remove the causes of friction or even of conflict arising out of the present minority problem in Czechoslovakia, and they are confident that the Czechoslovak Government share this feeling. His Majesty's Government would be glad, at a later date, to exchange views with the Czechoslovak Government on this subject. . . .

The message was clear enough: Britain would make no promises of support in the event of a German attack against Czechoslovakia, strongly advised Prague to settle the minorities question, and indicated a desire to maintain a consultant status on the action taken in response to this counsel. To underline the lesson, with Halifax's approval Sir Samuel Hoare unofficially advised Jan Masaryk that Prague "should inform the British and French Governments of the utmost they could do to meet the wishes of the German minority and at the same time should invite British and French good offices."

Up to this time there had been little direct contact between the Henleinists and the Prague government. Although the Sudeten German Party was the largest in the Czech Parliament, Henlein himself was not a member, and Hodža had cited this circumstance as a reason for not receiving him officially. In September 1937 they finally met at the Prime Minister's private home, but the discussion was inconclusive and there was no follow-up. Henlein had little occasion to come to Prague, and his main contacts for advice and support outside the Sudetenland were across the border, in Germany. A man of limited ability in other respects, Konrad Henlein was a superb actor, and was able to present a courteous and even friendly face to Hodža while sending to Hitler horrendous reports of Czech mendacity and brutality.

During the winter of 1937–38, largely in response to diplomatic pressure from Berlin, Hodža prepared several draft statutes on minorities problems for presentation at the next session of the Parliament. These provided for a greater degree of local self-government and the delimitation of the counties on the basis of nationality, recruitment of public employees in proportion to the size and distribution of the national minorities, and guarantees of equal rights for all nationalities. Meanwhile Beneš and Hodža were also weighing the possibility of inviting the Sudeten German Party to quit the parliamentary opposition and take part in the Government.

On March 24, Hodža informed Eisenlohr that such an invitation would be extended following the local elections.* Four days later the Prime Minister, in a radio broadcast, announced the Government's intention to present the minorities bills. But that same day, March 28, found Henlein at the Reich Chancellery, receiving Hitler's instructions to press "unacceptable demands," and the following day Ribbentrop told the Sudeten delegation that their party should "avoid

* The first of the local elections was scheduled for May 22 and was, in part, the precipitant of the "May crisis."

entry into the Government." These directives were, of course, not known to
Beneš and Hodža and, when the Sudeten German Party appointed a parliamentary committee (headed by a Dr. Erich Kundt) to negotiate with the Government, Hodža willingly embarked on a series of meetings with them in the
hope that an agreed settlement could be reached. On April 22, Beneš told Newton that he planned to conduct "serious negotiations" with the Henleinists during May and June, and put an agreed program through Parliament in July.

These great expectations were given a rude jolt two days later by Henlein's
Karlsbad speech announcing the Sudeten German Party's eight demands, which
went much further than Hodža's minorities proposals and included points which
would be difficult if not impossible for Prague to accept. In addition, Henlein
called for a revision of the nation's foreign policy, "which had hitherto placed
the State among the enemies of the German people," and abandonment of the
view "that it was the particular task of the Czech people to form a Slav bulwark
against the so-called *Drang Nach Osten* [thrust to the east]." In an informational telegram to the Czech missions, Krofta flatly declared that Henlein's
demand that the Sudeten Germans be given separate "legal personality" was unacceptable, and the Czech press generally was outraged. Hodža, less upset than
Krofta, told Newton that, despite this new blow, he would try to continue the
negotiations, but he thought nothing "serious" would be possible until after the
local elections.

This indication of further delay was highly displeasing to London. Newton's
messages arrived there at the time of the Anglo-French conversations held late
in April, and triggered the decision to make a joint *démarche* in Prague. To underline the importance which his government attached to it, Newton, between
May 7 and 17, waited separately on Krofta, Hodža, and Beneš. The British
Minister made no bones about his dissatisfaction with the Government's minorities proposals, especially in view of the "great gulf to be bridged" between them
and the Karlsbad demands, and predicted "disaster" unless the negotiations
were resumed without delay.

Hodža promptly invited Henlein to Prague, but the May crisis intervened, and
on May 20 the Sudeten Germany Party announced the suspension of negotiations until "peace and order" had been restored. Henlein visited Hodža on May
23, but chiefly to state that negotiations could not be resumed until Prague had
rescinded the call-up and sent the troops home, a step which the Prime Minister
was quite unwilling to take so soon after the turbulence of the previous week.
Henlein also said that he "would communicate his demands in writing"—a
promise not altogether welcome to Hodža, who feared it might freeze the
Henleinists into a position which the Government could not accept. The two
men parted in agreement only "that they should remain in contact."

Early in June most of the Czech reservists were demobilized, and negotiations
were resumed. The Sudeten demands proved to be a complicated combination
of proposals some of which were susceptible to compromise, mingled with
others which were plainly unacceptable and probably so intended. At the root of
the conflict was the Henleinists' proposal to reconstitute the framework of gov-

ernment by shifting a large part of the legislative power from the national Parliament to "diets"—in the case of the Sudeten Germans a *Volkstag*—representing the several nationalities. Thus the national ministries for such matters as education and social welfare would be abolished, as these matters would be taken over in the area of such nationality by officials responsible to the "diet."* Viewed from Prague, such a system appeared fatally disruptive of national sovereignty and certain to lead rapidly to disintegration of the Czech state.

2

By mid-July the parties were still as far from agreement as ever, and Newton's dispatches to London were increasingly pessimistic. Up to this time Berlin had been lying low, but on July 19 the German voice was ominously raised. Weizsaecker sent for Henderson, and in London, Ambassador Dirksen called on Sir Alexander Cadogan, who had succeeded Vansittart as Permanent Under-Secretary at the Foreign Office. In both cities the burden of the German message was that the Czech Government's proposals were totally inadequate, and that British efforts to divert Prague from its "mistaken and dangerous course" had failed.

Shortly after the May crisis, the British Foreign Office had considered the possible benefit of appointing an individual or commission to investigate and report on the Sudeten problem, and in mid-June Halifax and Newton had agreed that the idea had merit but should not be openly broached unless the Prague-Sudeten negotiations were close to failure. That point now appeared to have been reached, and on July 18, Halifax instructed Newton to put to Beneš the proposition of a British-appointed investigator-mediator: "The person we propose for this task is Lord Runciman, who will need no introduction to President Beneš."† Newton was explicitly instructed to tell the President that, if the British proposal were rejected and the negotiations subsequently broke down, "His Majesty's Government may be constrained . . . to make public the nature of the suggestion and of the response."

When Newton put the proposition to Beneš on July 20, the President "seemed greatly taken aback and much upset, flushing slightly and hardly recovering his full equanimity by the end of a conversation which lasted nearly two hours." The proposal, Beneš declared, impinged on the nation's sovereignty, would "provoke a most serious crisis," and might even entail his own resignation. But Hodža took a less tragic view, and the French, whom the Czechs immediately

---

* A visiting British group who, in the course of an interview with Karl Hermann Frank, asked "how it could be possible for Sudeten Germans to practice a National Socialist philosophy within the Czechoslovak Republic" received the following reply: ". . . there should be absolute freedom in disseminating German and National Socialist culture. . . . A German view of History and in particular the official German view of the National Socialist world outlook should be taught in the schools. . . . The Sudeten Germans who, as a Germanic people, liked parading and marching should be allowed to do so. The personality of Herr Hitler should be permitted to be brought home to Sudeten Germans by pictures and other means and the Nazi flag should be allowed to be flown."

† Runciman had been President of the Board of Trade from 1931 to 1937.

consulted,* strongly advised prompt and unconditional acceptance. Prague informally agreed to the British proposal on July 23, and Lord Halifax then directed Newton to put it to the Sudeten leaders, and Henderson to inform the German Foreign Ministry and request their good offices in obtaining Henlein's agreement. Meanwhile the story had leaked to the press, and Ribbentrop stiffly declined to take a position on what appeared to be a *fait accompli*. But Dr. Kundt raised no objection from the Sudeten side, and on July 26, Prague gave formal approval and Chamberlain announced Runciman's designation in the House of Commons.

Accompanied by Frank Ashton-Gwatkin (a counselor in the British diplomatic service) and two junior assistants, Lord Runciman arrived in Prague on August 3, 1938. He at once began a round of conferences and dinners with Beneš, Hodža, Krofta, and representatives of the Sudeten German Party, which had designated for the purpose a "political staff" headed by Karl Hermann Frank and a "social staff" under the wealthy Prince Ulrich Kinsky. All parties appear to have spoken with considerable freedom, and the would-be mediator was soon discouragingly aware of the "great gulf" between the two sides. Government and Sudeten representatives alike were at great pains to make a favorable impression on the British group. Beneš and Hodža, of course, sought—at first with little success—to convince Runciman that they were going as far to meet the Sudeten demands as anyone could reasonably expect of them. The Sudeten representatives operated under guidelines dictated by Karl Hermann Frank:

> It is the duty of the Sudeten German Party to convince his Lordship that the nationality problem in Czechoslovakia cannot be solved within the State, and that the Czechs are in no way prepared to make concessions of a kind that would lead to a real pacification of the State. His Lordship must take away with him the impression that the situation in this State is so confused and difficult that it cannot be cleared up by negotiation or diplomatic action, that the blame for this lies exclusively with the Czechs, and thus that the Czechs are the real disturbers of peace in Europe.

During the first two weeks of their stay, the Runciman party's activities were largely self-educational and had no apparent impact on the Prague-Sudeten negotiations. The Hodža and Kundt delegations met twice, on August 11 and 17, and exchanged statements of position, but neither side came closer to the other. Then, during the third week of August, the march of events quickened.

The reason for this acceleration was fear that time was running out with Hitler's "patience" and that, failing substantial progress toward an agreement, the Fuehrer would use the Nuremberg Party Rally early in September as the occasion for pronouncements and decisions that would bring the crisis to a head. Beginning early in August, this anxiety was expressed repeatedly in reports from Sir Nevile Henderson to Lord Halifax, the content of which was transmitted to Runciman and Newton in mid-August. From then on, Lord Runciman was put

---

* The French had previously been informed of the Runciman project by Lord Halifax, who was in Paris from July 19 to 22 in connection with the royal visit.

under increasing pressure from London to "do something" before September 5 (the opening day of the Nuremberg rally) which might forestall Hitler's "taking the law into his own hands," as Halifax put it.

It is a fair assumption that similar reports were reaching the Prague government. Whether for this or other reasons, President Beneš also concluded that there was urgent need for drastic steps to break the impasse which the Hodža and Kundt negotiating groups had reached. Because of both constitutional limitations on his authority and personal tensions between Hodža and himself, the President had to move with care in taking the initiative. His first move, made about August 16, was to send word by circuitous channels* to Dr. Kundt that he was prepared to go far beyond the Hodža proposals and would welcome direct contact with Kundt's group. As President he could intervene only on Hodža's invitation, but thought that he could "induce the Prime Minister to make this request to him." For immediate steps, Beneš proposed to speed up the appointment of Germans as officials in the Sudetenland, raise a loan for the indemnification of damage suffered there, and make special budgetary provisions for the benefit of the German areas.

Dr. Kundt asked for time to consider the President's proposals and informed the counselor of the German Legation in Prague, Andor Hencke, who promptly took off for Berlin to obtain guidance from on high. He got it from Ribbentrop, arrogant as ever:

> Henlein had already received clear instructions, and it was not fitting that one gentleman or another kept appearing from Prague at short intervals to obtain decisions on individual questions. Henlein and his people must learn to stand on their own feet. The answer to the Benes proposal was contained in the general instructions given to Henlein, namely, always to negotiate and not to let the link be broken, on the other hand, always to demand more than could be granted by the other side.

Henlein himself, up to this time, had taken no direct part in the negotiations with Hodža and had not yet met Runciman, despite the latter's "urgent desire" for a discussion. The Sudeten Fuehrer, as was highly appropriate in view of his own professional past, had gone to Breslau at the end of July for the German Gymnastic Festival. Upon his return, he sequestered himself in the Bohemian forests, in accordance with the Sudeten German Party's tactics of holding their leader in reserve until "the final and decisive moment." Runciman, however, was increasingly importunate, and finally a meeting was scheduled for August 18 at the estate of Prince Max von Hohenlohe, a Sudeten German potentate and strong Henlein supporter.

When they met, Henlein was already apprised of Beneš' initiative and of Ribbentrop's instructions on how to handle it, but Beneš had not informed the British. Henlein did not bring up the subject, and the conference developed nothing new. Four days later, however, Ashton-Gwatkin (who was motoring in the Sudetenland) was invited to meet Henlein at Marienbad, to discuss a seven-

* Beneš used the President of the Supreme Court (Dr. Krejčí) and the Rector of the German University in Prague (Professor Fritz Sander) to convey his message to Kundt.

point program which Henlein coyly described as having "reached his Party through an indirect channel . . . allegedly from President Benes." The seven points embraced those already reported by Kundt to Hencke, with two important additions: the creation of three autonomous districts in the Sudetenland, to be administered by German officials, and the withdrawal of the Czech state police from the German districts "if all goes quietly."

Henlein told Ashton-Gwatkin that "he would be prepared to negotiate at once on this basis," but immediately added some further demands of his own. Despite this ominous echo of Oliver Twist, Ashton-Gwatkin was delighted with his host—"I like him. He is, I am sure an absolutely honest fellow"—and returned to Prague with, for the first time, some reason for hope that a settlement might after all be possible.

There was further cause for optimism the next day, August 23, when it became known that the difficulties between President and Prime Minister had been overcome, and that Hodža was in "entire agreement with the President in this last effort to reach a solution."* At least the constitutional obstacle had been surmounted, for on the mornings of August 24 and 25, Beneš held long conversations at the Hradschin with Dr. Kundt and another member of the Sudeten negotiating delegation, Dr. Wilhelm Sebekovsky. The first meeting accomplished little other than being an outlet for mutual recriminations, but at the second Beneš presented an "immediate program" based on his seven-point plan and asked his guests for an expression of attitude. Kundt and Sebekovsky replied that they had no authority to take a position, and it was then agreed that Beneš would put his program in writing for discussion at the next meeting.

The President was as good as his word and had his memorandum ready for the third conversation, on August 29. Ironically, it came closer to pleasing the Sudeten delegates than Lord Runciman, who was also given a copy and declared himself "disappointed" because it appeared to "dilute" the original proposals. Dr. Kundt, on the other hand, told Hencke that Beneš' plan "could in actual fact mean the fulfillment of the eight Karlsbad demands," and even Frank described it as "far reaching" though "unsatisfactory."

Following Berlin's instructions to the letter, on August 31 Henlein told Ashton-Gwatkin that the Beneš plan was "inadequate in its present form," and that Kundt would submit counterproposals on September 2. While these were being prepared, Henlein visited Berchtesgaden for fresh instructions from Hitler and Ribbentrop. Back at his home in Asch, on September 4 he received Ashton-Gwatkin, who was taking an increasingly active part in the pseudodrama. The Britisher was assured that the Fuehrer wanted a peaceful outcome, and preferred autonomy for the Sudetenland to a solution by plebiscite. Once again Ashton-Gwatkin was completely persuaded by his "honest, unpretentious" host, and returned to Prague encouraged to believe that the negotiations still had a fair prospect.

---

* Hodža was perhaps not as content as he represented to the British. On August 26, according to Hencke, Dr. Kundt had found the Prime Minister "displeased about the initiative taken by the President."

Meanwhile the British had made yet another scarifying *démarche* in Prague. Acting on instructions from Lord Halifax, Mr. Newton met with Beneš on September 3. Predicting dire consequences if no progress became visible before Hitler's speech at Nuremberg, Newton virtually accused the President and his colleagues of "merely maneuvering for position" while "counting on foreign support," and "spinning out the negotiations without any sincere intention of facing the immediate and vital issue." The Czech Government, Newton declared, "should go forthwith to the very limit of concession, which limit ought not to stop short of the eight Karlsbad points if a settlement could not be obtained otherwise." He scolded Beneš for not moving more quickly with the appointment of Sudeten Germans to official posts, and suggested that "a definite program of appointments should be put into execution at an early date according to an agreed timetable."

Much discomfited, the President complained of the vagueness of the Karlsbad points and expressed fear that the Henleinists would interpret them in such a way as to cause "the dissolution of the State." Newton rejoined by repeating Lord Runciman's earlier warning that "if it came to choice between acceptance of the Karlsbad program or war" there was no doubt that Britain would choose the former. Later in the day Runciman himself visited Beneš and underlined the gravity of the situation and the urgency of the steps Newton had recommended.

The immediate consequence of these pressures was that Beneš and Hodža produced a new program, based in considerable part on the counterproposals which Dr. Kundt had submitted on September 2, and specifically designed to meet Henlein's Karlsbad demands. Beneš agreed to them with great reluctance, and when delivering a copy of the plan to Runciman on September 6 told him that it "amounted to a capitulation and would in future years be regretted by Britain and France." The new proposals, which became known as the "Fourth Plan," were formally delivered to Dr. Kundt on the morning of September 7, and were the subject of anxious consideration by the Sudeten negotiating delegation that afternoon.

The reason for their concern was that the new plan did indeed embrace the Karlsbad demands, which the Sudeten delegates had repeatedly pointed to as the essential basis of a settlement. The delegation was unanimous in concluding that it could not be turned down, and dispatched them at once by courier to Hitler, who was now at Nuremberg, and to Henlein. Confronted with this virtually total acceptance of their demands,* how could the Henleinists continue

---

* There was complete agreement on all sides that the Beneš-Hodža Fourth Plan substantially met the Karlsbad demands. Newton so informed Halifax on September 7, and two weeks later, in identical letters to Beneš and Chamberlain, Lord Runciman declared that it "embodied almost all the requirements of the Karlsbad eight points." Karl Hermann Frank called it a "90 percent acceptance of Karlsbad demands," and other members of the Sudeten German Party's negotiating delegation spoke of 95 per cent. Ashton-Gwatkin told the Sudetens that the proposal "closely approximated" the Karlsbad demands. Newton advised London that on September 14 Beneš told him that "his last proposals conceded substance of Karlsbad program although he had refrained from saying so openly for fear of humiliating and antagonizing public opinion."

with the Hitler-dictated strategy "always to demand more than could be granted by the other side"?

Their solution of the dilemma was to fabricate a pretext for breaking off negotiations. A group of Sudeten German deputies was in Mährisch-Ostrau investigating the arrest of a number of Sudeten Germans on charges of gunrunning and espionage. Within a few hours after Hodža presented the Fourth Plan to Kundt, the entire Sudeten delegation waited upon Lord Runciman to charge that the deputies had been assaulted by the Czech police, and that evening Kundt informed Hodža that negotiations on the Plan would be suspended "until the Mährisch-Ostrau incidents had been liquidated."

Two British officials who investigated the "incidents" promptly concluded that it was "deliberately staged" by the Sudeten deputies, and Ashton-Gwatkin inferred that its purpose was to interrupt the negotiations until Hitler's Nuremberg speech. No doubt Beneš and Hodža knew or suspected as much, but they made no point of the provocation, and when Frank, through Runciman, presented his "terms for settlement of Mährisch-Ostrau and continuance of negotiations" Hodža promptly accepted them. The affair was "liquidated" during the evening of September 9, Hodža and Kundt met the next day to discuss implementation of the Plan, and it was agreed to resume formal negotiations on Tuesday, September 13.

But the charade was played out and the parties did not meet again. Sunday, September 11, was very turbulent, and on the twelfth Hitler closed the Nuremberg Party Rally with a speech which contained no explicit demands other than "self-determination" for the Sudeten Germans, but was laden with brutal denunciation of President Beneš and of the Czechs as an "irreconcilable enemy" of Germany. This triggered demonstrations and riots throughout the Sudetenland, accompanied by Henleinist efforts to seize official buildings and other violent episodes. Early in the morning of September 13, Newton informed London that the situation at Eger and Karlsbad was "ugly," with huge crowds in the streets and emergency details of police and army troops. Hencke passed on to Berlin a report that the Sudeten disturbances "have assumed the character of an insurrection." By noon the disorders in many Sudeten areas had reached such a pitch that the Czech Government declared martial law.

The Sudeten German Party reacted with a fine show of indignation at Prague's efforts to restore order. Following a meeting of Party leaders at Eger, Frank, speaking for Henlein, informed Hodža that negotiations would not be resumed unless martial law were rescinded, the troops withdrawn to their barracks, and the state police removed from all districts where the majority of the population was German. These demands were transmitted in the form of an ultimatum, to be accepted publicly within six hours, failing which the Party would "disclaim any responsibility for further developments."

The long-suffering Prime Minister replied, through Ashton-Gwatkin, that he would agree to these demands on condition that the Sudeten leaders would come at once to Prague "to discuss maintenance of public order." Shortly before midnight Frank telephoned Henlein's rejection of the condition. The time limit for the ultimatum expired, whereupon Henlein, who was directing his followers from his home at Asch, announced that negotiations were broken off and disbanded the negotiating delegation, the members of which had already left Prague and were at Eger.

Meanwhile, Ashton-Gwatkin had set out by car for Asch and Eger, where he arrived very early in the morning of September 14. At Eger he encountered Karl Hermann Frank, "so inflated with the eloquence of Nuremberg and his own importance that no common sense or sense of responsibility were to be gotten out of him." Shortly before noon he saw Henlein at Asch:

> Henlein repeated his refusal to treat with Hodza or send anyone to Prague unless Frank's four points were first unconditionally conceded. If so, negotiations could start again, but on a new basis—plebiscite. He did not wish to break off relations with the Runciman mission and thanked us for our efforts. We parted friends.

So, once Prague had been pushed (mostly by the British) to accept the Karlsbad program, Henlein raised the stakes, stimulated by Hitler's reference to "self-determination" in the Nuremberg speech. On this point the Czech Government would not yield, and it probably would have made little difference even had they been willing. A few hours before Henlein and Ashton-Gwatkin "parted friends," Neville Chamberlain had sent his famous message to Hitler declaring his readiness to come to Germany "with a view to trying to find a peaceful solution." Hitler replied affirmatively, and the focus of the crisis shifted away from Prague. The Runciman mission departed for London on September 16, while Henlein and many of his followers decamped to Selb in Germany (just across the border from Asch), where the Party established its headquarters and commenced the organization of a "Sudeten German Legion."

In a report on his mission written after returning to London, Lord Runciman put the "responsibility for the final break on Henlein and Frank." Ashton-Gwatkin, ever faithful to his friend from Asch, blamed "Hitler on the grand scale, and Frank on the small scale." Neither of the Britishers, it appears, ever realized that, from the Nazi-Sudeten standpoint, the negotiations had been a hoax ever since *Anschluss,* though there is a glimmer of perception in Ashton-Gwatkin's observation, ten days after the fact, that the Fourth Plan was "very favorable to the Sudetens—too favorable, in fact, for the extremists and the German Government, who must have counted on Czech obstruction."

Beneš and Hodža might, indeed, have been better advised to abandon their efforts to reach agreement with Henlein, and put through a unilateral program for betterment of the status of national minorities.* Such a course would at least have prevented the impression, prevalent in many quarters, that the Czechs were stalling. Still, it is at best very doubtful that Prague's internal policies, how-

* Such was the opinion, in retrospect, of Dr. Hubert Ripka, a leading Prague editor and Beneš supporter.

ever shaped, could have much affected the decisions of the great powers, governed as they were by fears and aims which Prague was powerless to modify.

What was finally left to the Czech Government was the hard choice to fight or not to fight, when it became apparent that the French would not willingly honor their treaty commitments.

CHAPTER 18

Among the Eastern Neighbors

1

In Central and Eastern Europe, Czechoslovakia had as neighbors the other countries of the Little Entente who were her allies against Hungary, Poland who was the ally of Czechoslovakia's ally France, and Soviet Russia, a conditional ally. The three smaller countries—Yugoslavia, Rumania, and Poland—were all the objects of intensive competitive diplomacy among the great powers of Europe, as the Munich crisis approached.

Could the Little Entente have been pulled out of the state of decay into which it had fallen by 1936? Could Yugoslavia or Rumania, formal allies of Czechoslovakia against Hungary, have been led to recognize the greater peril which all of the countries of Central and Eastern Europe now faced? As architect and moving spirit of the Little Entente, Beneš was keenly aware of its potentialities as a vehicle by which its members could make common cause against the German menace. Even after the stern lesson of the *Anschluss,* however, his efforts to gain new support from his eastern neighbors were no more successful than his attempt to reach a settlement with Henlein.

Painfully aware of the military and political significance of Germany's remilitarization of the Rhineland, six months later Beneš made a major effort to breathe new life into the Little Entente, at its meeting in the fall of 1936 at Bratislava. Stoyadinovitch was there for Yugoslavia, and Beneš strongly urged upon him that the Entente, consisting as it did of mutual assistance guarantees against Hungary only, be broadened into a mutual defense alliance operative against aggression from any quarter, and supplemented by a similar treaty between the Entente and France. But the Yugoslav strong man was already leaning away from France and collective security, and gave Beneš no encouragement.

The meeting reflected other disagreements among the members. The Czechs were by now aware that they had more to fear from Hitler than from Otto of Hapsburg; the Rumanians and Yugoslavs saw the comparison otherwise. Nor did Czechoslovakia's alliance with the Soviet Union sit well with her conservative, royalist partners in the Entente, which emerged from the meeting shaken rather than strengthened.

Disenchanted as he was with France and Little Entente alike, Stoyadinovitch went on a hunt for new friends, and soon found some. In January 1937, Yugoslavia and Bulgaria signed a pact of "inviolable peace and sincere and perpetual friendship," which undercut the former's obligation to aid Rumania, Greece, or Turkey in the event of an attack by Turkey, and was generally regarded as a move toward the side of the revisionist powers.* Far more important, however, was the agreement between Yugoslavia and Italy signed at Belgrade on March 25, 1937, which evidenced a sudden change for the better in the previously uneasy relations between the two countries.

There was reason on both sides to desire improvement. Despite the Rome-Berlin Axis and Stoyadinovitch's avowed wish for good relations with Germany, in Belgrade and Rome alike there was uncomfortable awareness of the growing power of the Third Reich, and concern that its future course of empire might turn toward the Adriatic. For Yugoslavia, a link with adjacent Italy began to look more attractive than the worn-out ties with distant and weakened France, while for both Italy and Germany the defection of Yugoslavia from the French alliance system was much to be desired.

And so, in December 1936, Ciano and Stoyadinovitch laid the groundwork for secret negotiations, which were pursued in Rome during the winter months and which reached the decisive stage early in March.† Finally agreement was achieved, and Ciano went to Belgrade for the signing ceremony and to review the whole European situation with Stoyadinovitch, who made a "profound impression" on the Italian:

> Stoyadinovitch is a Fascist. If he is not one by virtue of an open declaration of party loyalty, he is certainly one by virtue of his conception of authority, of the State and of life. His position in the country is pre-eminent. . . . Stoyadinovitch already has the marks of dictator in Yugoslavia, and is preparing to display them even more in the future.

The treaty itself contained mutual undertakings by the parties to respect their common frontiers, settle their differences peacefully, expand their trade, and (with obvious reference to Croatian separatists) "not to tolerate in their respective territories . . . activities directed against the territorial integrity or existing order of the other . . . or of a nature calculated to prejudice the friendly relations between the two countries." Privately, however, the discussions were much more specific, and Stoyadinovitch assured Ciano that Yugoslavia would give a negative answer to any suggestions that the Little Entente be used as a shield for Czechoslavakia against Germany.

Against this background, it is hardly surprising that Beneš made no progress with his plans, either when the Little Entente met in Belgrade a week after signature of the treaty, or when Beneš himself visited Yugoslavia a few days later. Talking with Stoyadinovitch, he received "a clear indication that in order to

---

* Greece, Rumania, Turkey, and Yugoslavia were parties to a mutual defense alliance called the Balkan Entente, which served the same protective purpose against Bulgaria's revisionist aims that the Little Entente served against Hungary's.

† Yugoslavia's principal negotiator was Dr. Ivan Subbotic, at that time his country's representative to the League of Nations. One of the stickiest problems confronting the parties was the presence in Italy, under police protection, of the Croat separatists who had been responsible for the assassination of King Alexander and Louis Barthou. Ciano and Subbotic had great difficulty finding a formula which would give Yugoslavia adequate security against future terrorist actions without appearing to implicate Italy in past crimes.

guard itself against a conflict between Germany and Italy on the one side and France on the other, Yugoslavia intended to make agreements with . . . the Axis." Then in September 1937, when Stoyadinovitch came to Prague for Thomas Masaryk's funeral, Beneš made a third and equally fruitless effort:

> I reproached him sharply for violating the obligations of the Little Entente when he concealed his negotiations with Mussolini, hypocritically coquetted with the Hungarians and negotiated with Hitler behind our backs. He excused himself very insincerely. I explained to him that the European crisis was rapidly approaching, that I was doing all I could to insure that France and the Soviet Union—which were and would be our powerful allies—should be prepared for it together with ourselves, that in the end there would come a catastrophic defeat for Germany and the rest. But I added that we all would have to hold out and stand faithfully together. . . . But he confessed that he had been invited to pay a political visit to Berlin. I . . . urged him not to go. He did not promise anything, however, and ultimately went to Berlin. . . .

Stoyadinovitch was in no mood to follow Beneš' lead.* There was, to be sure, no open break between Yugoslavia and the western powers and, after his trip to Prague, Stoyadinovitch visited both London and Paris, where he reaffirmed the Franco-Yugoslav Pact of 1927. But Italy was more congenial to him, and in December he was there for five days. In Rome he told Mussolini and Ciano that his journey to Paris and London had "produced no practical result"; Britain's weakness on land, he said, doomed her to a "position of inferiority," while France of the Popular Front had incurred his "deep dislike" by stirring up domestic opposition to him. But he had "overcome the crisis" and would move toward a more authoritarian regime. Relations between Yugoslavia and Hungary, he added, "have markedly improved recently."

All this was music to the Italians' ears, and Ciano unrolled more yards of red carpet. After a visit to the reclaimed Pontine Marshes, Stoyadinovitch was taken to Milan to be shown that "the regime has really permeated the masses and destroyed the Marxist strongholds." Political harmony was reinforced by Ciano's "personal liking" for the "strong, sanguine man" with a "resounding laugh and vigorous handshake," as well as a "weakness for pretty women" which Ciano indulged by arranging "a few dances with the prettiest women in Roman society."

In January 1938, Stoyadinovitch capped his tour of the European capitals with a visit to Berlin. His conference with the Fuehrer, Goering, and Neurath consisted mainly of a rambling Hitlerian monologue on the general state of Europe in which, as might be expected, the state of affairs in Austria and Czechoslovakia was deplored. The Yugoslav Premier responded with fulsome assurances of his country's friendship. "Yugoslavia," he declared, "would never under any circumstances enter into a pact against Germany or any kind of anti-German coalition" and "all of Yugoslavia relied on the word of the Führer."

---

* In August 1937, Ciano had sent Anfuso to deliver to Stoyadinovitch "photographic proof of the Franco-Czech conspiracy against him." The Italian cryptanalytic service was very successful at that time in decoding and deciphering diplomatic telegraphic messages of various nations, and it may well be that this was the source of the evidence with which Ciano sought to inflame Stoyadinovitch against his allies.

Furthermore, "his trip to Germany had been for the purpose of learning some-thing," and he would now "initiate some of the things he had seen here." Since the First World War, Yugoslavia had been separated from Germany by "the French spectacles," and now his country "had removed those spectacles."

While Stoyadinovitch was pulling Yugoslavia into close alignment with the Axis and parting company with Czechoslovakia, King Carol, for the third member of the Little Entente, was preoccupied with internal problems. The Lib-eral Party leader George Tatarescu, who had been Premier since 1933, was Carol's willing tool, but agrarian discontent was skillfully exploited by the Iron Guard with the slogan "one man, one acre." On the eve of the national elections in December of 1937, the National Peasant Party leader, Dr. Julius Maniu, sud-denly allied his party with the Iron Guard, with the result that the Liberal Party and the Peasant-Iron Guard opposition each polled about 38 per cent of the to-tal vote. Carol attempted a new parliamentary government headed by the poet Octavian Goga, leader of the reactionary and anti-Semitic National Christian Party (which had garnered only 9 per cent of the vote), but after a few weeks of anti-Jewish riots and retaliatory boycotts the Goga regime foundered in a welter of economic and political troubles, and on February 10, 1938, Carol dismissed him and appointed the Orthodox Patriarch, Miron Cristea, as Premier in a "provi-sional cabinet." Actually, Carol was moving rapidly toward royal dictatorship; the party system was abolished and replaced by a "Front of National Rebirth," and a new constitution was promulgated and affirmed by a yea-nay referendum in typi-cal totalitarian fashion. Viewing the Iron Guard as his most dangerous foe, Carol subjected Codreanu and his principal lieutenants to Moscow-type trials and subsequent imprisonment.*

Unlike Stoyadinovitch, Carol developed no personal animosity toward Czechoslovakia, and his relations with Beneš remained cordial. The King made a state visit to Prague in October 1936, and a year later he returned more in-formally to hunt in Moravia and confer with Beneš. But after the December 1937 elections Carol's seat on the throne was in virtually constant jeopardy, and he had neither strength nor inclination to leap to Czechoslovakia's defense against the growing German menace. The alliance between Prague and Moscow was displeasing to Rumania, faced as she was with Russian claims to Bessarabia. The new Rumanian Foreign Minister, Nicolas Petrescu-Comnene, had been the Ambassador to Germany since 1932, and on leaving Berlin told Weizsaecker that in his new office he would have "no other aim than to demonstrate even more forcefully than in the past his proven friendship for Germany."

Under these circumstances, Beneš could count on little effective support from Bucharest, either against Germany or in shoring up the Little Entente. Indeed, the last two meetings of the Little Entente—at Sinaia (in Rumania) in May and Bled (in Yugoslavia) in August 1938—witnessed its further erosion even as a bulwark against Hungarian revisionism.

This undermining of the Little Entente was the product of a scheme devel-oped in November 1937, when the Hungarian Premier and the Foreign Minister

---

* Codreanu and thirteen of his followers were "shot while trying to escape" in November of 1938.

(respectively Kálmán Darányi and Kálmán Kanya) were received by Hitler in Berlin. The object was to weaken Yugoslavia's ties with the Little Entente through an agreement by which Hungary would promise not to use military means to enforce her territorial claims against Yugoslavia, if the latter would accord cultural autonomy to the Hungarian minority. When Stoyadinovitch came to Berlin the following January, Hitler put this proposition to him, adding that Germany would be willing to guarantee fulfillment of the agreement by both parties.

Despite Stoyadinovitch's anxiety to court favor in Berlin, he drew back from this invitation to cut loose openly from his allies—a move which would have antagonized both Rumania and France—and deflected Hitler's proposal with the observation that "what he did with respect to Hungary he had to do within the framework of the Little Entente." Disappointed by this negative reaction, the Hungarians raised the stakes and informed Berlin that they were prepared to relinquish forever all claims to the territory which Yugoslavia had obtained from Hungary under the post-First World War treaties, in return for Yugoslavia's assurance of neutrality in the event of a Hungarian-Czechoslovakian conflict and a German guarantee of the settlement. The German Foreign Ministry transmitted the offer to Belgrade, but again with negative results; on May 19, Weizsaecker informed the Hungarian Minister in Berlin, Döme Stojay, that the proposal had been again "broached" in Belgrade but "so far had called forth no response."

Yugoslavia's continued silence drove the Hungarian leaders nearly frantic. As the prospects of a German invasion of Czechoslovakia increased, so did Budapest's appetite for a share in the fruits of conquest, by way of a free ride on Germany's back. Furthermore, Berlin was putting the Hungarians under increasing pressure to join in the hunt if they wished to share the game. In June and again in July 1938, Goering told Stojay that it "would be well if Hungary were at once to take an active part in any armed conflict between Germany and Czechoslovakia." When Admiral Horthy, accompanied by Kanya and the new Hungarian Premier, Bela Imredy, paid a state visit to Germany late in August (in the course of which the Regent broke the bottle in Kiel at the launching of the new heavy cruiser *Prinz Eugen*), Ribbentrop reminded Kanya that "anyone who had revisionist aims should take some part in what was being done," while Hitler, characteristically blunt, told Imredy, that "anyone who wanted to sit down at the meal must first help with the cooking."

But the Hungarians had the Little Entente to reckon with. Apparently they were not much worried about Rumania, but were deathly frightened by the prospect that, if they attacked Czechoslovakia, Yugoslavia would fulfill her treaty obligations and launch an assault across Hungary's southern border. Assurance of Yugoslavia's neutrality was a *sine qua non* of a Hungarian move; as Kanya told Mussolini in July, without "a military guarantee against a possible Yugoslav attack . . . no responsible [Hungarian] government could take the military initiative against Czechoslovakia."

Stoyadinovitch's unwillingness to shake hands with Hungary on this dubious bargain was in no way motivated by concern for Czechoslovakia, but rather by domestic considerations. Yugoslavia, like Czechoslovakia, was a mélange of nationalities; "self-determination" and "plebiscites" were concepts dangerous to both countries. Hungary was an uneasy and jealous neighbor. The Yugoslav intelligentsia was anti-Nazi, and many of the generals were pro-French and disapproved of Stoyadinovitch's affinity for the Axis powers; in May 1938 the Yugoslav General Staff advised the Government that Hitler was the country's most dangerous potential enemy. Under these circumstances, Hungary's renunciation of territorial claims against her southern neighbor did not appear, even to Stoyadinovitch, as valuable enough to warrant an open breach with France and the Little Entente, which would be widely regarded as a treacherous betrayal of Czechoslovakia.

Failing to make any headway through Berlin, the Hungarians sought assistance in Rome. Imredy and Kanya turned up there on July 18, seeking an Italian guarantee of aid in the event of a Yugoslav attack. It was an awkward problem for the Duce, since Italy's treaty ties with Hungary dated back to 1927, and as recently as January 1938 he had assured the former Hungarian Premier, Count Stephen Bethlen, that "it is clearly understood in Belgrade that we will not allow the Serbs to attack Hungary in defence of Czechoslovakia," while two months later Italy had signed the treaty of friendship with Yugoslavia.

Solution of the dilemma was not aided by the archaic and abrasive personality of Kanya, whom Mussolini regarded as "an old Hapsburg relic" and who openly used "Rumanian" as a synonym for "thievish" and referred to Stoyadinovitch as a "Balkan ruffian."* In any event, Mussolini was quite unwilling to jeopardize the new friendship with Yugoslavia by acceding to the Hungarians' plea. The problem had, in fact, been discussed between Stoyadinovitch and Ciano a few weeks previously in Venice:

> Stoyadinovitch . . . assured us that should a crisis arise and Italy make no move, Yugoslavia would do the same. He has not the least intention of dragging his country into a conflict with Germany to save Czechoslovakia, which is both unfriendly and an artificial creation, and even less of pleasing France, which is openly hostile to him. He asks of us only that we use our influence to prevent Hungary from taking the initiative in the attack. In such a case Yugoslavia would be obliged, much against her will, to abide by its pledges. . . . But if, as will happen in reality, Hungary does not take the initiative in the attack, and instead takes advantage of a crisis produced by Germany, Yugoslavia will remain completely indifferent to the fate of Czechoslovakia.

On this basis, Mussolini was able to advise Imredy and Kanya that "Hungary, by intervening in the conflict after the German attack, will run no risk of attacks on the part of the Little Entente." The Hungarians were far from satisfied, and Kanya railed at the Yugoslavs, "whom, with the old Ballplatz mentality, he in-

---

* Such language was hardly likely to please Ciano, who had found Stoyadinovitch politically impressive and personally attractive. Ciano's diary contains many references to Kanya's "manias," "Ballplatz mentality" (the Austrian Foreign Ministry) and "absurd prejudices against the Rumanians and Serbs." Kanya was no more popular in Berlin than in Rome; Weizsaecker wrote that "Kanya had a thorough knowledge of the Third Reich and hated it," while Ciano recorded that the Hungarian had "aroused personal enmities" among the Germans.

sists on calling Serbs." But in fact their situation was adequately clarified; Hungary would have to follow the German timing of any attack on Czechoslovakia, but if she took no unilateral initiative, Yugoslavia would stand aside despite the Little Entente commitments.

While covertly seeking to wean Yugoslavia from her treaty obligations, the Hungarians were simultaneously negotiating openly with the Little Entente as a group for an agreement whereby Hungary would give assurances of nonaggression in return for recognition of her equal military rights (that is, abolition of the Trianon arms restrictions*) and improved treatment of Hungarian minorities in the Little Entente countries. These discussions had begun in 1937, and were, continued in 1938 at the Sinaia and Bled meetings of the Little Entente Council.

The Sinaia Council was held in the wake of *Anschluss* and under the lengthening German shadow. Krofta, for Czechoslovakia, made an effort to have the members of Little Entente declare themselves a "factor with which Germany must reckon," but Stoyadinovitch blocked him, with Rumanian support, by insisting that the Sudeten question was an internal affair which Czechoslovakia would do well to settle. The Hungarian proposal was considered favorably but then put over for further discussion at Bled, where on August 21 and 22 the Council held what was to prove its last meeting.

The obstacle to acceptance of the Hungarian proposition was that while in Rumania and Yugoslavia the Hungarians' requests for their minorities could readily be met, in Czechoslovakia, they were virtually copying the demands of the Sudeten Germans, and even refusing reciprocal treatment for the 150,000 Slovaks in Hungary. Prague was prepared "to accept some discriminatory treatment as compared with her partners," but would not concede all that Budapest wanted. Accordingly, the Bled communiqué announced recognition of Hungary's "equality of rights in the matter of armaments" and the parties' "mutual renunciation of recourse to force," but signature of the agreement remained conditional on resolution of the Hungarian-Czech minorities issue. This, of course, was soon overtaken by the events at Munich, of which the Little Entente itself was one of the victims.

Rome reacted to the news of Bled with pleasure, Berlin with pain. Ciano rightly saw that it "marked a new phase in the crumbling of the Little Entente" and the isolation of Czechoslovakia. But Kanya, who hurried from Bled to join his regent at Kiel, found Ribbentrop very annoyed by Hungary's renunciation of the use of force, conditional though it was: "Hungary was blocking the road to intervention in Czechoslovakia and making it more difficult morally for the Yugoslavs to leave their Czech allies in the lurch." Kanya tried to wriggle out of his discomfiture by indicating that "the Hungarian demands on Czechoslovakia were so great that she would not comply with them," and therefore the agreement would never come into force, but the Germans were not mollified.

The story of these events is a pretty sorry chapter in the history of diplomacy,

* In March 1938, Darányi took advantage of the Austrian crisis to announce a new armament program which transcended the Trianon limitations. Negotiations for a general arms agreement, however, continued.

with Kanya and Stoyadinovitch, arrogant and mendacious as they both were,
the prime exhibits. Kanya was simultaneously offering Czechoslovakia a nonaggression agreement, assuring Berlin that it was really a hoax, and conniving
with Mussolini and Stoyadinovitch to enable Hungary to stab Czechoslovakia in
the back. Meanwhile Stoyadinovitch, sanctimoniously protesting his loyalty to
the Little Entente, gave Hungary the assurances she needed, provided only that
she waited for Germany to strike the first blow. But while Kanya's methods
were unscrupulous, his aims were consonant with the revisionist diplomacy to
which his country had been wedded since the First World War, while Stoyadinovitch, like Pilsudski and Beck, helped to tear up the protective mantle of Versailles and the French alliance system, and smooth the way for the German military machine that soon would level Belgrade and overrun his country.

Rumania's attitude was very different—an ambivalence born of a desperate
hope that the crisis would pass and spare her the necessity of agonizing decisions. On August 15, King Carol instructed Petrescu-Comnene to "express urgently" to Beneš "Rumania's wish that a solution of the Sudeten German problem satisfactory to Germany should be achieved." Two days later, in a long
report on the political situation, the German Minister, Wilhelm Fabricius,
predicted that Rumania would "make every effort not to be drawn into
conflict," but that if France and Britain were to take action Rumania "would associate herself with them." Despite his Hohenzollern blood Carol looked more
to Paris and London than to Berlin and thought that, if war came, "it will be
Great Britain whose power will in the end be victorious."

French military intervention would, however, at once present Rumania with
an immediate and highly uncomfortable question, as a by-product of the
Franco-Soviet and Czech-Soviet alliances. Rumania, like Poland, lay between
Russia and Czechoslovakia. If Russia were to come to Czechoslovakia's defense, Rumania would surely be confronted with demands to permit the passage
of Soviet troops and aircraft—a prospect which the Rumanian leaders, regardless of party, feared like the plague. It was in these terms that the issue was
drawn in Bucharest as the crisis deepened and war loomed.

2

While Germany was enveloping and swallowing Austria, and stepping up the
war of nerves against Czechoslovakia, the foreign policies of Poland—the ally of
Czechoslovakia's ally, France—remained hostile to the Czechs and essentially
unchanged by the ominous march of events. The conceptual touchstone of Poland's policies continued to be "equilibrium" between her two big neighbors, as initially established by the nonaggression pacts of 1932 with Russia and 1934 with
Germany. To maintain the precarious balance, Poland eschewed participation in
"blocs" such as the Little Entente or the Anti-Comintern powers—the first distasteful to Germany and the second to Russia—and restricted herself to the bilateral alliances with France and Rumania for mutual protection against Germany
and Russia respectively.

Even if the policy of "equilibrium" had been carried out with skill and integrity, it is hard to see how it would have protected Poland against Hitler's east-

ward drive. However that might have been, after the Rhineland remilitarization the Polish scales tipped decisively westward, as Beck and his collaborators concluded that Soviet Russia was both the weaker and the more hostile of the two powers, and that good relations with Germany were therefore both more valuable and more possible of achievement.* Early in 1936, Juliusz Lukasiewicz, then the Ambassador to Russia, reported that the Soviet leaders' attitude toward Poland remained hostile, and that "in view of the dangerous trend of Soviet policy it is absolutely necessary for us to continue our own policy of *détente* with Germany." A few months later Lukasiewicz, a close friend of Beck's, was transferred to Paris, but his successor in Moscow, Waclaw Grzybowski, was soon singing the same tune. In November 1936, reporting to Count Szembek, he described the "formidable dynamism" of the Soviet State and concluded that "despite their pretended desire for neighborly relations with us, the Russians hate us deeply and the Soviet drive is really directed against us."

Psychological factors played a large part in Poland's drift toward Germany. The authoritarian, anti-Semitic Polish Government found nothing offensive in a dictatorial, anti-Semitic Third Reich. The politicians and the press of the two countries strove to outdo each other in the violence of their denunciations of communism. Hitler, and Goering especially, courted and flattered the Polish leaders, and Goering came to Warsaw in February of 1937 and again a year later, full of compliments for Marshal Smigly-Rydz and assurances that Poland had nothing to fear from Germany. Superficial as these gestures were, compared to the frigidity in Moscow the German capital was warm indeed.

For all of this inclination toward Berlin, there were serious problems in the relations between the two countries. These concerned primarily the Versailles-born "Free City of Danzig" and treatment of the national minorities on each side of the German-Polish borders. Danzig was a German city, and soon after the advent of Hitler the city government was taken over by local Nazis, who clamored for reunion with the Reich and harassed the Polish officials and merchants in the exercise of their harbor and shipping rights. As for the minorities, there were three quarters of a million Germans in Polish Silesia and Pomerania, and almost twice as many Poles in Germany. There were repression and discrimination against these minorities on both sides of the frontier,† which had been not much alleviated by the 1934 nonaggression treaty, and a war of reciprocal denunciation raged in the newspapers of both countries.

With Austria and Czechoslovakia in the foreground of his aspirations, Hitler had good reason for wishing harmony with Poland. Accordingly, in June 1937, Neurath received the Polish Ambassador, Jozef Lipski, in order to propose a

* In a work utilizing Polish documentary sources unavailable to me, it is stated that up to 1938 it was the eastern rather than the western frontier which was the principal concern of the Polish General Staff. Budurowycz, *Polish-Soviet Relations 1932–1939*, p. 49, fn. 107.

† In Pomerania and generally in northern Poland the Germans, who were generally middle class and included many landowners and professional people, fared well enough. In Upper Silesia, however, the anti-German and energetic *voivode* (governor), Michal Grazinski, waged a campaign of "Polonization" which pinched the Germans badly and pushed many of them back to the Reich. The Poles in Germany, mostly peasants and day laborers, were easily victimized under the Nazis, who regarded all Slavs as inferiors or even "subhumans."

joint "declaration on minorities" which "would contribute to a relaxation of the atmosphere and set an example for the local authorities to follow," thereby "restraining the press and public opinion."

Beck and Lipski were not averse to the proposal, but saw in the German approach an opportunity to shore up the Polish position in Danzig by coupling the minorities declaration with another affirming compliance with the Danzig "statute" of 1920, on which Polish rights in the city were based. On Hitler's instructions, Neurath rejected this idea on the ground that, while the German Government had no intention of repudiating the Danzig statute, as a matter of principle it would not publicly acknowledge the validity of anything based on the Versailles Treaty. Lipski continued to press the point with both Neurath and Goering very sharply—more sharply, indeed, than Beck wished, and in the end Szembek was sent to Berlin to instruct Lipski that the minorities declaration should be signed on the scheduled date, regardless of any lack of success on the Danzig issue. Beck's reason for this decision was interesting: he wished to resolve the German-Polish minorities question before the Sudeten German issue became the focal point of German diplomacy, so that the German Government would not be able to link the two matters.

In the upshot, the impasse was broken by a compromise. Hitler, simultaneously with announcement of the minorities declaration, received Lipski and gave oral assurances that he did not intend to alter the Danzig statute, that Polish rights in Danzig would be respected, and that there would be no "surprise action" there on the part of the Germans.

Signature of the minorities declaration simultaneously in Berlin and Warsaw, on November 5, 1937, was an occasion of considerable ceremony. Hitler and President Mościcki received representatives of the Polish and German minorities and made amiable pronouncements; the Fuehrer gilded the event with the observation that "as an Austrian he well understood their situation," and a surprise amnesty for Poles under arrest for "political" infractions. His assurances to Lipski on Danzig were publicized in a communiqué stating that "it was confirmed during the conversation that German-Polish relations would not be disturbed by the Danzig question." Lipski departed well content and Hitler went off to the now historic "Hossbach" conference.

The minorities declaration was only hortatory; it contained no provisions for enforcement of the benevolent principles it proclaimed, and in fact did little to alleviate the condition of the minority populations in either country. Nevertheless, it marked the period when Polish-German relations, at least on the surface, were closest. In January 1938, Beck, en route to the League Council meeting in Geneva, stopped in Berlin for two days and had long conversations with Neurath, Goering, and Hitler, who gave the Polish Foreign Minister the usual *tour d'horizon*, reiterated his previous assurances about Danzig, and promised to scotch the local Nazis' move to put a swastika on the Danzig flag.

A month later Goering came to Poland to hunt boar in the forest of Bialowieza and to talk politics with Smigly-Rydz and Beck. To the Marshal of Poland, Goering extended (without result) Hitler's invitation to visit Germany, and stressed the congruence of German and Polish interests in raising a rampart against Soviet communism. The two meetings between Beck and Goering got much closer to the coming crises of 1938. Goering described the Hitler-Schuschnigg meeting at the Berghof, and his host disavowed any "political interests" in Austria. Beck did, however, express "serious interest" in the Czech problem and indicated Teschen—an interest which Goering promised "would not be infringed." The Polish Minister then suggested that the two countries' ten-year nonaggression pact of 1934 be extended, and Goering enthusiastically endorsed the idea, proposing a period of fifteen to twenty-five years.

But these friendly sentiments were about to be put to the stern test of events. On March 6, 1938, Beck arrived in Rome for what had been planned as an extended state visit-*cum*-vacation at Sorrento. Mussolini had a preconceived antipathy for Beck, Ciano found him "an unsympathetic character who produces a chill around him," and the Princess of Piedmont declared that "he had the sort of face you might see in a French newspaper as that of a ravisher of little girls." Given these reactions, it is hardly surprising that Beck's meeting with Mussolini was perfunctory, but on March 9 there came the news of Schuschnigg's plebiscite, and hosts and guest at once took more interest in each other.

By his own confession, Beck regarded Austria as "a problem which was remote to us and concerned us comparatively little," and Ciano, after his first conference with Beck, recorded that "as regards the *Anschluss* he displayed a lack of interest which seems to me out of proportion to the importance which the problem may assume for Poland." The plebiscite and the looming actuality of *Anschluss* considerably sobered both men, and they began to speak cautiously of a possible community of interest among Italy, Poland, Hungary, and Rumania as "reassurance against the hegemony of German influence."

Announcement of *Anschluss,* and the report of an incident on the Polish-Lithuanian border,* caused Beck to cut short his Sorrento holiday and hurry home. During his absence, the French Ambassador, Léon Noël, had made strong representations to Count Szembek about the necessity of supporting Schuschnigg's efforts to preserve Austrian independence, but had been brushed off by Szembek's rejoinder that this was an internal Austrian affair, and that there was no reason to think that her annexation by Germany was imminent. Five days later Szembek's prediction was proved wrong, but Warsaw put a good face on things; Szembek told the British Ambassador, Sir Howard Kennard, that *Anschluss* was "no surprise to us" and repeated that it was "an internal Austrian affair."

In Berlin, Jozef Lipski, one of the main architects of the German-Polish détente, was less serene. Like most of the Berlin diplomatic corps, he learned of the German march-in during Goering's mammoth reception at the Haus der Flieger, and was tactlessly twitted for looking gloomy by Prince von Bismarck, grandson of the Iron Chancellor. Lipski left the party "in a mood of utter disgust, convinced that the Reich was racing toward an inevitable catastrophe of war."

* A soldier of the Polish frontier guards who was about twenty yards on the Lithuanian side of the border was shot and killed by a Lithuanian guard during the night of March 10–11, 1938.

There were other worriers in the Warsaw government. General Kazimierz Sosnkowski, a former Minister of War, confided to Szembek his alarm that Germany was moving "too fast"; events suggested that "now it's Austria's turn, then it will be Czechoslovakia's, then ours, and finally that of France." Anatol Muhlstein, the Polish counselor in Paris, thought that *Anschluss* had cleared the way for Germany to annex the Sudetenland and make the rest of Czechoslovakia a "vassal state," and that the enfeeblement of France together with the dynamism of Germany had put Poland into "an extremely difficult and dangerous position."

But these fears, no doubt shared by others, did not work to change Polish policy toward Germany. Szembek and General Stachiewicz, the Chief of Staff, agreed that "the détente with Germany was the best guaranty that Poland would not be the country called upon to pay the price of appeasement." At the time of *Anschluss,* Smigly-Rydz acknowledged to Szembek that "after the absorption of Austria and Czechoslovakia, Germany might turn against Poland." Nevertheless, "in spite of this possibility, we ought to follow our policy of *détente"* and "sell Germany our neutrality for substantial advantages at Danzig."

This "what can we get out of it" attitude had, indeed, become the essence of Poland's attitude toward the prospective German conquests. Quite deliberately, Beck utilized the European focus on Austria as "cover" in order to turn the Lithuanian border incident to Poland's advantage. Upon his return to Warsaw, the Polish Government presented Lithuania with an ultimatum, to be answered within forty-eight hours, for the re-establishment of diplomatic relations.* The Lithuanians capitulated, and the Poles made much of this minor league victory, the fruits of which turned bitter a year later, when Germany annexed Memel.

What was to be gained from the Berlin-Prague confrontation? Beck had speculated on this as early as December 1936:

> Poland would have her choice among five solutions, of which two would be inacceptable; passivity, or alliance with Czechoslovakia against Germany. Of the other three, we might occupy Teschen, allow Hungary to take sub-Carpathian Ruthenia, and thus obtain a common frontier with the Magyars . . . or take Kaunas [the capital of Lithuania]; or occupy Danzig.

This was a diffuse and ill-considered menu, and by the spring of 1938 the Polish goals were a bit less dreamy. The Teschen question would not be settled through Berlin but, as befitted Poland's quasi-great power status, directly with Prague. There was no further talk of "occupying" Danzig, which surely would have precipitated war with Germany, but much reaching for new agreements with Germany that would reinforce Poland's security, not only in Danzig but generally. Warsaw's concern for some sort of reassurance was deepened by a swelling tide of minorities complaints in both countries, and the consequent and continuing battle of denunciation between the German and Polish newspapers.

---

* There had been no diplomatic relations between the two countries since 1920, when Poland occupied Vilna, which Lithuania claimed as her capital city. In forcing their resumption in March of 1938, Beck and his colleagues behaved with childish arrogance, rejecting French efforts to mediate the dispute and refusing even to grant the Lithuanians' appeal for a fifteen day delay in designating their minister and establishing a legation in Warsaw.

For the most part the discussion of ways to improve the situation was carried on outside normal diplomatic channels, at meetings between Lipski and Goering.* Late in August the latter again expressed approval of extending the 1934 treaty, and Lipski indicated a desire for better ordering of the Danzig situation. As formulated during Lipski's visit to Warsaw on September 13, 1938, the Polish "price" for neutrality in the Sudeten imbroglio comprised: (1) a joint Polish-German declaration certifying their common frontier as final, comparable to Hitler's statement in Rome with respect to the Brenner frontier; (2) extension of the 1934 agreement; and (3) a written German commitment on Danzig embodying Hitler's oral assurances to Lipski on November 5, 1937.

Interjection of the Danzig factor was a dangerous move, for during the negotiations preceding the November 5 declarations, Neurath had very bluntly told Lipski that "some day there would have to be a basic settlement of the Danzig question between Poland and us, since it would otherwise permanently disturb German-Polish relations," and that the "only possible aim of a discussion on this matter . . . would be the restoration of German Danzig to its natural connection with the Reich, in which case extensive consideration could be given to Poland's economic interests." It was a warning which Lipski and his superiors† would have done well to take more seriously, indicating as it did that a reopening of the Danzig situation would be likely to work out to Poland's disadvantage, as indeed happened two years later.

But all these fine plans to extract from Berlin a *quid pro quo* came to nothing. As Lipski boarded the night train from Warsaw to Berlin on September 14, 1938, he learned that Neville Chamberlain would fly to Berchtesgaden on the morrow, and sadly recorded: "The West had capitulated. It was too late to present our demands to Germany." Present them Lipski did, however, both to Goering and Hitler, but his premonition of failure was abundantly correct.

3

Given the assumptions and objectives of Warsaw's policy toward Germany and Czechoslovakia, it is not surprising that Poland's relations with France were far less harmonious than those between allies ought to be. The trouble was not solely due to disagreement over the need for preserving Czechoslovakia. The Blum government and the Franco-Soviet alliance were repugnant to the Polish governing group. With a population of 32 million, nearly four fifths that of France, and on the verge of recognition as a great power, Poland's view of France, as an acknowledged great power in retreat, was colored with both jealousy and scorn. The French failure to act against the Rhineland remilitarization aroused Warsaw's contempt and led to an entirely sound reassessment of the military value of the ties with Paris.

Instead of endeavoring to shore up the French security system, Warsaw

* On March 18, 1938, Lipski had raised with Ribbentrop the possibility of extending the 1934 nonaggression pact, which had first been mentioned during Goering's visit to Warsaw the previous month. Lipski found Ribbentrop both uninformed about and cool to the idea.

† The Lipski-Neurath conversation quoted in the text took place on October 18, 1937. Lipski's report of it to Warsaw does not mention the admonition quoted above, which is taken from Neurath's memorandum for the files.

turned in the opposite direction and embarked on a diplomacy which in many respects paralleled Berlin's, and inevitably hastened France's decline. Colonel Beck and his colleagues scoffed at the League of Nations and collective security, rejected the multilateral assistance pacts which Barthou and later Delbos attempted to establish, sneered at the Little Entente, and proclaimed their indifference or worse toward the two most immediately threatened countries, Austria and Czechoslovakia.

None of this made life any easier for Léon Noël, an energetic and aggressive diplomat who constantly strove to show the Poles the error of their ways. Neither Beck nor Szembek suffered tutelage gladly, and the result was that Noël's appearance at the Polish Foreign Ministry was far less welcome than that of Moltke, representing the very country against which the Franco-Polish alliance was directed. By the end of 1936, Noël's visits became a series of acrid altercations, no matter what the subject. In May of 1937, Szembek was countering Noël's complaints about Polish press attacks against Blum with expostulations over French newspaper criticism of Beck. Six months later Beck was peeved because Noël, of all the Warsaw diplomatic corps, was the only one who failed to send congratulations on the fifth anniversary of Beck's taking office as Foreign Minister.

In December 1937, when Delbos (who remained Foreign Minister until the spring of 1938) came to Warsaw on a visit of state, he was received with all due honors and decorated with the Grand Cordon of the White Eagle, but Beck's toast at the official banquet was so banal and tepid that Delbos had to water down his reply so as not to appear overeager. Noël urged Delbos to make strong remonstrances against the continuing feud with Czechoslovakia, but the latter had been rebuffed on the subject by Beck some months previously at Geneva, and in Warsaw the French Foreign Minister broached the question only tangentially and without the slightest success.

Beck and Szembek seemed almost to be getting a perverse pleasure from needling and frustrating Noël. Relations between France and Italy were very strained, and, on instructions from Paris, Noël beseeched Beck to call off his scheduled trip to Rome, only to be reminded that when Laval went to Moscow he did not take account of Beck's views. French efforts to smooth out the Polish-Lithuanian confrontation in March 1938 led only to a sharp altercation between Beck and Noël, in which the former declared that France had always taken a hostile attitude toward Poland's Lithuanian policies, and that her intervention in the current controversy was "clearly pro-Lithuanian." In Warsaw, it seemed, the French could do nothing right.

Indeed, despite Warsaw's ostentatious hostility toward Prague, the Czechoslovakian Ambassador to Poland got along much better than Noël. Dr. Juraj Slavik was a tactful and agreeable diplomat and, probably more important, a Slovak—a nationality much more acceptable to the Poles than were the Czechs. Even Beck treated him in friendly fashion, but the amity was strictly personal and accomplished nothing at the diplomatic level. Polish politicians and journalists continued to rage against Prague's treatment of the Polish minority in the Teschen area, although in fact they were faring better than their much more numerous compatriots in Germany. Late in 1937, Hodža made some conciliatory proposals, but this drew only rebuffs in the official publications of the Polish Foreign Ministry and General Staff, and Beck remarked acidly to Moltke that "fine words had often before been heard from Prague." Warsaw was also constantly accusing Prague of harboring Comintern "cells" that fomented subversive activities in Poland.

Early in 1937 the American Ambassador in Warsaw, John Cudahy, wrote to President Roosevelt that the feud between Poland and Czechoslovakia was so sharp that any joint military action was "out of the question." A year later Cudahy's successor, Anthony J. Drexel Biddle, reported his opinion that the Warsaw government had deliberately "kept alive her misunderstanding with Czechoslovakia in order to build up a "record" that would justify "letting her go down."

In May 1938 there was a slight easing of the tension after Slavik had assured Beck that the Polish minority would gain as much as the Sudeten Germans under the minorities statute then under consideration in Prague. On May 18, Beck went so far as to tell the British Ambassador that "he attached great importance to the assurance which . . . marked a great step in advance and he was highly satisfied at having received it." But two days later the "May crisis" erupted, and matters rapidly went from bad to worse. Press and officialdom took the German side of the issue, accused the Czechs of spreading false rumors in order to achieve an apparent diplomatic success, and redoubled their complaints about mistreatment of the Polish minority. "From that time on," Noël later wrote, "Colonel Beck worked openly in the campaign to bring about the destruction of Czechoslovakia."* Certainly Berlin was well pleased, for on May 31, Weizsaecker instructed Moltke to express appreciation for "the recent attitude of the Polish government."

Confronted with such obdurate hostility, Prague could do little to swing Warsaw toward its side. Furthermore, it is by no means clear how far Beneš would have been willing to tie his country to Poland even if the attitude in Warsaw had been more hospitable. Beneš might well have feared that alliance with Poland would automatically embroil Czechoslovakia if Germany went to war with Poland over the Corridor question.

According to Beneš, when General Gamelin passed through Czechoslovakia en route to Warsaw in August 1936, the President gave General Faucher (chief of the French military mission in Prague), for delivery to Gamelin, "a written invitation to the Polish Government to the effect that having in view the serious situation and the fact that a European crisis was well on the way, we should start preparations for Polish-Czechoslovak military cooperation." Beneš also declares that Gamelin presented the proposition both to President Mościcki and

---

* Part of the campaign of destruction was encouragement of Slovak separatism. When, at the end of May 1938, a delegation of American Slovaks visited Warsaw, they were treated to orations by Polish officials who attacked the Prague government for its discrimination against Slovaks, and one of whom declared that Czechoslovakia was "a fiction." These indiscretions provoked a retort from the leader of the American delegation, who emphasized that they had come to Europe not to destroy but to improve the unity of the Czech state.

General Smigly-Rydz, but received from the latter only the reply that such political matters lay outside a soldier's purview.

Neither Gamelin nor Faucher mentioned such a document in their subsequent writings or testimonies, but it is clear that if Gamelin made the approach requested by Beneš, it fell on deaf ears, for Beck and Szembek conferred in advance of Gamelin's arrival in Warsaw and agreed that, if the French general should endeavor to push Poland toward alliance with Czechoslovakia, he should be told that "this is unacceptable for us." Poland would assume obligations to no countries other than France and Rumania, and if Gamelin should inquire what Poland would do in the event of war between Germany and Czechoslovakia "we will refuse to answer"—just as Beck had refused when Laval put the same question a year earlier.

Whatever the truth may be about the events in Warsaw, there is no doubt that, on his way back to Paris, Gamelin was given a memorandum by Beneš inviting closer Polish-Czech relations, for discussion with Smigly-Rydz during the latter's impending visit to France.* The document was in eight paragraphs, the first four of which affirmed that Czechoslovakia had no understandings or arrangements with Soviet Russia or any other country that touched Polish interests. The fifth and sixth declared that since 1933 the Czech Government had three times proposed that the two countries join in a "treaty of friendship" but had never received any reply to these overtures. The seventh renewed the proposal and indicated that, once a friendly footing had been achieved, the military authorities of the two countries should establish collaborative relations, while the last paragraph invited negotiations on the minorities problem.

This, of course, was very far from being a proposal for a military alliance, and it would be wrong to saddle Beck with exclusive responsibility for the two countries' failure to effect one. It may well be, as Dr. Ripka wrote at the time, that Beneš would have avoided military commitments "towards a state which had so many unsettled disputes to resolve, both with Germany and with Russia." However that may be, even the limited *rapprochement* suggested by Beneš was unwelcome to the Poles. Smigly-Rydz read the Beneš memorandum and kept a copy, but told Gamelin that he could make no reply, as the document (which Lukasiewicz characterized as consisting of "muddled, vague suggestions that cooperation be broadened") was not in proper diplomatic channels. The Polish general did tell Gamelin that he "could not imagine Poland attacking Czechoslovakia" and that Czechoslovakia had no reason to fortify the Polish-Czech frontier.† But these limited assurances were coupled with reminders of the minorities and other issues dividing the countries, and the need for time to rebuild mutual confidence.

---

*The memorandum is dated August 28, 1936. Gamelin was given it in Vienna by an emissary of the Czechoslovak Legation in Austria.

†Gamelin contemporaneously described his Paris conversations both in a report to Daladier, the Minister of War, and in a letter to General Faucher, as well as later in his book *Servir*. The two generals conversed in French; Smigly-Rydz's language was ". . . qu'en aucun cas, il ne voyait la Pologne attaquant la Tschechoslovaquie," and that money spent on Polish-Czech border fortifications would be *vraiment de l'argent perdu.*

Rebuffs from Warsaw inevitably discouraged Beneš from making further efforts. After the Gamelin fiasco he told the French Minister, Victor de Lacroix, that no progress was possible so long as Beck remained in office. Smigly-Rydz was a brave soldier but no politician, and the Polish leaders were so obsessed by fear of Germany as to rule out any gesture of friendship toward Czechoslovakia. To Lacroix's entreaties that he rise above his personal resentment against Beck and persevere, Beneš reacted with glum silence.

In post mortem, Beck defended his refusal to join forces with Czechoslovakia on the grounds that:

(1) We were convinced that the Czechs would not fight and it was impossible to assist anyone who did not himself fight.
(2) The Western Powers were neither morally or materially ripe to engage themselves (proof: Munich).
(3) The attitude of Russia was then already most suspect.

The first two reasons, of course, ignore the question of the extent to which Poland's attitude was itself a factor in discouraging Czechoslovakia and the western powers from offering resistance to Germany. In any event, the justification was meretricious, for these reasons do not explain the way the Polish Government behaved. Polish diplomacy was not limited to avoiding a commitment to Czechoslovakia. Beck and his colleagues desired her destruction, were active agents in bringing it about, and in their franker moments made no bones about these hostile aims.

In August 1937, for example, Ambassador Lukasiewicz, one of Beck's closest lieutenants, bluntly told William C. Bullitt, the American Ambassador to France, that "Poland would look with approval on a German dismemberment of Czechoslovakia." In Rome, Beck "repeatedly" emphasized to Ciano that "the alliance with France will not operate in the event of a war produced by the Czech problem"—an assurance which he surely expected would be conveyed to eager ears in Berlin. Visiting Stockholm in the spring of 1938, Beck told the Swedish Foreign Minister, Rickard Sandler, that Czechoslovakia as a state was "artificial and in disagreement with the principle of national freedom." Throughout the six months preceding Munich, Beck, Szembek, and Lukasiewicz rebuffed every French effort to mitigate or qualify Poland's hostility toward Prague. Lukasiewicz, in his meetings with Georges Bonnet, decried the worth of the Czech Army, and threw cold water over all proposals in furtherance of the French commitment to Czechoslovakia.

In Warsaw, Sir Howard Kennard had concluded, by June 1938, that "the weakening of Czechoslovakia must now be regarded as one of the objects of Polish policy," and after an interview with Beck early in September he reported that Beck remained unsympathetic to Czechoslovakia's troubles. In July, Beck was at pains to assure Moltke that the "Polish Government had not modified its attitude toward Czechoslovakia nor did it intend to do so," and requested Moltke to pass this information to Ribbentrop. At about the same time Beck told Noël, who had presented a pleading note from Bonnet, that "the fate of the Czechoslovak state leaves us cold."

Beck's third post-stated reason for leaving Czechoslovakia to its fate—that "the attitude of Russia was . . . suspect"—is ambiguously put, but was in fact the reverse of the first two. Far from fearing that Russia would *not* come to Czechoslovakia's aid, Beck feared that she *would*. It was the same anxiety from which Rumania suffered: that they lay athwart the path of Russian assistance to Czechoslovakia, and that transit for Soviet troops would be demanded. But Poland's concern was much the deeper, for Rumania touched Germany not at all and Czechoslovakia only narrowly at the eastern end of Ruthenia, where transportation facilities were very poor, whereas Poland covered virtually all of Germany's eastern frontiers, and the Polish-Czech border stretched all the way to Moravia, with better road and rail access through Cracow and Katowice, permitting a much broader and more rapid flow of Russian troops and equipment.

Poland, like Rumania, had manifested a categorically negative attitude toward Russian transit whenever the idea was broached. Well aware of this attitude, General Gamelin, visiting Poland in 1936, had suggested to Smigly-Rydz the possibility of a Russian march through Lithuania toward Königsberg, which, with a simultaneous Polish attack from the south, would encircle East Prussia. But even this device for avoiding the passage of Russian troops through Poland was highly distasteful to Smigly-Rydz, who at once objected: "If the Bolshevists penetrate into Lithuania, just as if they penetrate Poland, they will never leave." Poland detested the Germans, but the Russians were "even more odious."

In a historical sense this was poetic justice, for part of Poland's old grudge against Czechoslovakia was the latter's refusal in 1920 to allow transit for Hungarian troops to come to Poland's aid against Russia. Nor were Polish fears that Russian guests might overstay their welcome anything but reasonable. And in 1938, when the transit question became a major and immediate one, the Poles abated their opposition not a whit, as Lukasiewicz made clear in May to both Bonnet and Bullitt, adding that if the Russians should attempt to pass through Poland, his government would declare war against them. Furthermore, he thought Rumania would do likewise, and if the Russians tried that path Poland would join Rumania in stopping them. In July, Beck was much annoyed that the Bucharest government had allowed the Czechs to overfly Rumania with military aircraft purchased in Russia, and later that month Szembek went to Bucharest to stiffen Comnene's spine against any concessions to Soviet demands.

In summary, there was hardly anything, short of an outright alliance with Germany, that Poland could have done to weaken the Franco-Czechoslovakian alliance that she did not do. Despite this, it is probably true that, if France had honored her commitment to Czechoslovakia and a European war had broken out over the Sudeten issue, Poland would have at least remained neutral and might even have joined with the western powers, particularly if Britain were fully involved. As Beck later wrote: ". . . in the event of a real European war with Germany we could not be on the side of Germany even indirectly."

If blame there be, the major blame for the Munich settlement is not Poland's. She had no treaty commitment; she was not a great power; she was in a desperate squeeze between Germany and Russia. But the diplomacy of Colonel Beck and his group, based as it was on the hope that Britain and France would do nothing and that Czechoslovakia would disintegrate under German pressure, was of great value to Hitler and a disaster for Czechoslovakia and those who tried to save her.

CHAPTER 19

The Road from Moscow to Prague
Runs through Paris

1

Shortly before the Sudeten crisis peaked, the German Ambassador in Moscow, Friedrich Graf von der Schulenburg, was queried from Berlin about the Russians' ability to intervene militarily. Schulenburg put the question to his military attaché, General Ernst Köstring (born in Moscow of German parents, and German military attaché there 1931–33 and 1935–41), who replied: "The Russian is very well able to intervene, especially with his air force. But whether he will or will not do so, is a question I must leave to the political officials!"

What an accurate answer to these questions would have been has remained to this day a matter of mystery and controversy. Soviet diplomatic and military archives have been opened only on a very restricted and selected basis. The few personal memoirs of Second World War Soviet generals deal with the prewar period aridly or not at all,* and the official Soviet history of those times is primarily a Communist indictment of the "imperialist" powers rather than an account of Russian policies. Public speeches and official statements are of course available and reflect the image which the Kremlin sought to project abroad. The memoirs and "now it can be told" accounts of émigrés and defectors are often distorted by hatred or the search for sensationalism, and are usually impossible to confirm. There are also the extensive but rambling and often obscure jottings by some apparently well-informed person, purportedly but not actually Maxim Litvinov, which were published in 1955 under the title *Notes for a Journal*.† In citing them I have put the purported author's name in quotation marks, and I have used them only to add detail to events that can be independently confirmed.

---

* The translated memoirs of Marshal Ivan Konev and General Vasili Chuikov do not touch the prewar period, and Marshal Georgi Zhukov's superficial account makes no mention of the 1937–38 executions of numerous Russian military leaders, nor of the military or diplomatic discussions and decisions of those years.

† The introduction, by the noted historian and Russian expert E. H. Carr, describes the provenance of these notes. He found it impossible to establish their authenticity as Litvinov's own work, but concluded that they "contain a substratum of genuine material emanating in some form or other from Litvinov himself," but also include "accretions added later by another hand or hands." General Walter Bedell Smith, former American Ambassador to Russia, contributed a "prefatory note" describing the work as "provocative and challenging" and approving Professor Carr's appraisal. In later years Professor Carr increasingly doubted the *Journal*'s authenticity and concluded that it was "faked" by some well-informed former Soviet diplomat.

Given this dearth of Soviet sources, the historian is perforce thrown back on the official dispatches and personal recollections of the ambassadors and other diplomatic representatives who were stationed in Moscow during the late thirties —Robert Coulondre for France; Schulenburg, General Köstring, and Second Counselor Gustav Hilger (who had also been born in Moscow) for Germany; Viscount Chilston for Britain; and, for the United States, William C. Bullitt until June 1936 and Joseph E. Davies for the next two years.* The short-comings of reliance on alien observers in a closed society are obvious, but since the reports of these men were their governments' main source of information, they at least assist us to see the Soviet Union as it was pictured at the time in the official circles of Paris, London, Berlin, and Washington.

As Max Beloff has aptly remarked, during the two years before Munich, So-viet policies appeared anomalous in that the Government's increasing involve-ment and activity, both in Europe and the Far East, was coincidental with do-mestic introversion and, except for Litvinov and his diplomatic colleagues, the virtual isolation of the Russian leaders from direct contact with the outside world. The principal causes of this withdrawal, no doubt, were the instabilities, suspicions, and conflicts that shook the Soviet hierarchy and precipitated the state trials and bloody purges which marked the years from 1936 through 1938.

To be sure, neither purges, state trials, nor executions were new in the Soviet Union. Communist Party "cleansings," with the expulsion or worse punishment of offenders, were a standard feature of the Soviet political system. The indus-trialization and agricultural collectivization programs of the Soviet "Five-Year Plans" were carried out with little regard for the human costs, and millions were killed or exiled to Siberia. Shortfalls from the announced goals of these pro-grams frequently triggered purges and trials in which sabotage and espionage by counterrevolutionaries and agents of foreign powers were charged as the expla-nation of failure to meet program goals. A prime example was the "Shakhty trial" in 1928, which was actually the first of the public "show trials," with fifty-three defendants (including three German engineers). It was held in the great Hall of the Trade Unions in Moscow, with press and diplomats in the audience and Andrei Vishinsky—the future "purge prosecutor" and Foreign Minister—as the judge.

Until 1936, however, with virtually no exceptions, there had been disciplining but no executions of prominent Party leaders or high officials. "Let not blood flow between you," Lenin had admonished his followers, and the injunction had been generally observed.

The causes of the Stalin bloodbath are complicated and murky. Underlying other circumstances, however, was the fact that the exiling of Trotsky and the political defeat of his sympathizers did not put an end to dissent within the

---

* Coulondre, Hilger, Köstring, and Davies published memoirs of their service in Russia, and Bullitt's brother Orville published the correspondence between the ambassador and President Roosevelt for that period. During the Bullitt and Davies years, excellent reports were sent by Loy Henderson and George Kennan, then of the embassy staff.

Party leadership. Numerous "old Bolsheviks" who had been close to Trotsky continued to object to the harshness of the economic policies, and a number of them—Zinoviev, Kamenev, Bukharin, and Rykov among others—were disciplined by demotion, dismissal, or temporary exile. A good harvest in 1933 alleviated the famine of the preceding year, and stimulated a strong current of opinion within the Party for reconciliation between the dominant Stalin group and the opposition, and an easing of the economic hardships incident to the Five-Year Plan. The leading spokesman of reconciliation was Sergei Kirov, Party leader of Leningrad and Stalin's close friend.

Stalin himself took no open position on the Kirov proposals, and the Party split widened. In the spring of 1933 the "hard-noses" succeeded in establishing a "Central Purging Commission," one member of which was Nicolai Yezhov, under whom three years later the political slaughter peaked. Nevertheless, at the Party Congress of 1934, Kirov scored a great personal success and was elected Secretary of the Central Committee, a position which called for his removal from Leningrad to Moscow. But he was assassinated by one Leonid Nikolaiev on December 1, 1934, and it is this episode which is often said to have triggered the great purges of 1936 to 1938.

There is no doubt that the Kirov murder greatly increased the intensity of the "cleansings" that were already under way in the lower Party circles throughout the Soviet Union. A few hours after the news of Kirov's death, a decree was issued authorizing special proceedings against "terrorists," without the presence of counsel and with immediate execution of those convicted. From Moscow a "closed letter" was soon issued denouncing the "evil murder" of Kirov and calling for intensified vigilance against "oppositionists."* But still there were few executions, and Stalin's lethal inroads on the Party and military leaderships did not assume large proportions until more than a year after Kirov was killed.

Furthermore, the truth about the murder has remained elusive. George Kennan, who was on Bullitt's staff at the time, declared in 1957 that Stalin had instigated the killing, but in his later *Memoirs* (1967) wrote more cautiously that allegations of his complicity "have never been specifically rebutted by the Soviet leadership." Bullitt himself, on the other hand, reported to Washington that the well-informed Estonian Minister, Baltrusaitis, was certain that there was a romantic relation between Kirov and Nikolaiev's wife, and that the shooting was a *crime de passion*. "Litvinov" and Stalin's daughter, Svetlana, both attest to Stalin's high regard for Kirov, and Svetlana thinks it impossible that her father was to blame.

The true inwardness of the affair remains uncertain. The light sentences initially given to the members of the secret police (NKVD) in Leningrad, who were responsible for Kirov's safety, did not prevent their later execution. Whatever the truth, it is clear that Stalin promptly moved to exploit the murder

---

* The impact of Kirov's assassination on the Party in the provinces is abundantly reflected in the "Smolensk Archive," consisting of the Party records in that city, which somehow had escaped removal or destruction and were seized by the Germans when they captured Smolensk in 1941. The records later passed into American hands and are the basis of Merle Fainsod's *Smolensk Under Soviet Rule* (1958).

by blaming it on opposition "enemies of the Soviet Union"* and intensifying his attack on Party dissidents. In February 1935, Yezhov was appointed head of the Party Control Commission with primary responsibility for the forthcoming purges, and he soon became Stalin's chosen tool in the NKVD, undermining the authority of Genrikh Yagoda, the titular chief.

These events occurred at a time when Stalin appears to have become embittered and more than previously suspicious in consequence of the suicide,† in the autumn of 1932, of his second wife, Nadezhda Alliluyeva, the mother of Svetlana, who later wrote that it destroyed Stalin's "faith in his friends and people in general." For a time he temporized, as Maxim Gorky and a few other close friends urged on him a policy of reconciliation. But Gorky's influence waned and he died in 1936, the year in which Yezhov replaced Yagoda as chief of the NKVD and the, first of the three public trials of the opposition leaders was held. Something, whether real or fancied, had pushed Stalin into a murderous fear of dissent, and the great purge, which was to take literally millions of lives, was launched.

The principal defendants in the first trial, during August 1936, were two old associates of Trotsky, Grigori Zinoviev and Lev Kamenev, who had been severely disciplined on previous occasions. They were tried jointly with fourteen obscure individuals, as members of a group described as the "Trotskyite-Zinovievite Terrorist Center," charged with responsibility for the murder of Kirov and plotting against Stalin's life, with Trotsky's complicity. All sixteen confessed their guilt; they were convicted, sentenced to death, and executed within twenty-four hours after imposition of the sentence. At about the same time another Central Committee "closed letter" was distributed describing the "Terrorist Activity of the Trotskyite, Zinovievite Counter-Revolutionary Bloc"; the scope and intensity of the nationwide Party purge escalated correspondingly, and a wave of utter terror swept through the Soviet governmental and Party bureaucracy.

Zinoviev and Kamenev had not only signed their own death warrants, but also implicated other old Bolshevik leaders with Trotskyite leanings. During the trial, in consequence, the prosecution announced the impending investigation of nine on whom new suspicion had been cast, including Nikolai Bukharin (a leading Communist theoretician, draftsman of the 1936 Soviet Constitution, and editor of *Izvestia*), Alexei Rykov (former Premier), Karl Radek (a leading Soviet journalist and head of the Comintern), and others of almost equal stature. Stalin, meanwhile, had left Moscow for a Black Sea vacation, and in

---

* The executions, reported in the Soviet press, which immediately followed the Kirov assassination aroused criticism in British trade union circles. The Soviet Ambassador in London, Ivan Maisky, publicly justified the stern measures on the basis that the murder showed the existence of a terrorist conspiracy in the Soviet Union.

† It has been said that Stalin killed Nadezhda, but Svetlana and "Litvinov" both describe her death as suicide with a pistol, though they differ on the circumstances. Svetlana states that her mother's death occurred after Stalin had addressed her roughly at a large banquet. "Litvinov" wrote that Nadezhda shot herself when grieved and distraught by the execution of a close friend, suspected of implication in a terrorist plot.

his absence, on what authority is not clear,* *Pravda* announced that the investigation of Bukharin and Rykov was being terminated for lack of incriminating evidence. This was little to Stalin's liking, and on September 25, 1936, from the Black Sea resort of Sochi, he sent a telegram to Molotov and other Politburo members demanding the replacement of Yagoda, who had old ties to Bukharin, by Yezhov. The change was announced the very next day, and the greatest butcher was now in the saddle—a man described by "Litvinov" as "a pigmy with the face of a murderer, a shifty look in his eyes and a perpetual twitching of the upper lip and left eye-lid . . . a sadist . . . pathological perversion with a sexual basis."

The clearing of Bukharin and Rykov won them a brief reprieve, and they were not among the seventeen defendants of the second show trial, held before the Military Collegium of the Supreme Court during the last week of January 1937, with Vishinsky as the prosecutor. This time the cast was headed by Radek, supported by Yuri Piatakov (Deputy Commissar of Heavy Industry), whom Bullitt had seen in 1933 playing "wild Russian dances" on the piano after a state dinner, with Stalin "standing behind him and from time to time putting his arm around Piatakov's neck and squeezing him affectionately") and Gregori Sokolnikov (head of the Soviet delegation at Brest-Litovsk in 1918 and former Ambassador to Britain), plus five less prominent ex-officials and nine obscure "spear carriers." The defendants were accused of being a "reserve cadre" behind the "Terrorist Circle" of the first trial, but now the emphasis shifted from terrorism to sabotage and espionage in behalf of Germany and Japan (the most probable foreign enemies), including causing railway accidents and industrial breakdowns. Once again, all confessed; thirteen were executed, while four, including Radek and Sokolnikov, were given prison sentences.

This crumb of leniency, however, was no sign of a general relaxation, for it was in 1937 and the early months of 1938 that the purge was at its worst. "Litvinov" called it "the complete physical annihilation of the more active opposition members and of all those connected with them, whether directly or indirectly" and described terrible scenes in Yezhov's office, where prominent "old Bolsheviks" were pistol-whipped and shot out of hand, and their wives and daughters stripped and raped. A number were tried and sentenced to death at secret sittings of the Collegium, and the official slaughter spread from Moscow over the entire country.

In January 1938 the third, last, and largest of the show trials was held, with Bukharin, Rykov, Yagoda, Nikolai Krestinsky (a member of the original five-man Politburo of 1918, former Ambassador to Germany, and until 1937 Deputy Commissar of Foreign Affairs), Christian Rakovsky (the leading Ukrainian among the "old Bolsheviks" and a former Soviet envoy to London and Paris), Arkady Rosengoltz (Commissar for Foreign Trade during the thirties), and fourteen others—all characterized by the prosecution as the "Anti-Soviet Bloc

---

* Kennan writes that the announcement was based on a decision of the Central Committee, while an anonymous "old Bolshevik" in a published *Letter* states that it was the result of pressure from members of the highest Soviet organ of decision, the Politburo.

of Rightists and Trotskyites." Treasonous acts on behalf of Britain and Poland as well as Germany and Japan were alleged, and this time the individual accusations were more disparate; Yagoda was charged with responsibility for the death of his predecessor chief of the NKVD, Rudolph Menzhinsky, and the "medical murder" of Gorky, while Krestinsky was taxed with treasonous contacts with the German Army while he was Ambassador to Germany in the early twenties, although what he did then in furtherance of the Reichswehr-Red Army collaboration had certainly been approved by the Politburo, and Radek, equally deeply involved in those events, had not been asked about them at his trial.

Krestinsky enlivened the proceedings by repudiating his pretrial confession, but after a recess recanted his recantation. Rakovsky and two others were given prison terms, and all the rest were shot. Thus, of fifty-four defendants in the three Moscow show trials, forty-seven were executed, including a dozen or more famous veterans of the Revolution. There were other trials in the provinces; General Köstring, who traveled widely in the Soviet Union, reported to his superiors on a trial at Alma-Ata which resulted in the execution of all nineteen defendants, and another in the Kuznetsk coal area, at which a poor production record was explained by the allegedly subversive activities of the seven defendants, of whom five were shot. How many Party and government officials and industrial or agricultural managers were liquidated in other proceedings is beyond the reach of useful speculation.*

At least equally catastrophic, on the military side, was the wholesale slaughter of leaders of the officer corps by the NKVD, which began in June 1937 and continued for more than a year. When the savage blow fell, the Red Army was on the upswing in size, morale, and technical proficiency. Soon after Hitler's coming to power and the end of collaboration with the Germans, the Soviet military budget was greatly increased, and the Red Army's standing strength jumped from little over half a million to nearly a million in 1934, 1,300,000 by the end of 1935, and 1,433,000 in 1937. The output of tanks and aircraft was approximately quadrupled between 1931 and 1937.†

Political responsibility for the armed forces had, since 1925, been committed to Klementi Voroshilov, Commissar for Defense, member of the Politburo, and one of Stalin's most trusted colleagues. The operational leader was Vice-Commissar Mikhail Tukachevsky, the "boy-general" and hero of the 1920 war

---

* The published estimates of executed anti-Stalinist Marxists run from 3 to 10 million, but such astronomical figures, if meaningful, must include ordinary workers and peasants who fell victim to ruthless enforcement of the economic policies.

In 1964, after the official downgrading of Stalin and his "cult of personality," *Pravda* reported that he had "destroyed" 1,108 of the 1,966 delegates to the 1934 Party Congress at which Kirov had scored his great success, and had "ruined" 98 of the 139 members of the Central Committee elected by that Congress.

† The annual figures given in the official Soviet *History of the Great Fatherland War of the Soviet Union* (Vol. I, p. 77, of the German edition) are:

	1930–31	1932–34	1935–37
Aircraft	860	2595	3578
Tanks	740	3371	3139
Artillery Pieces	1911	3798	5020

with Poland, now in his early forties. Little love was lost between Voroshilov and Tukachevsky, but under them the Red Army developed a professionalism and *esprit de corps* which, perhaps, were factors in their leaders' undoing. In 1935 the revolutionary designations of rank such as "Comrade Company-leader" gave way to the traditional military grades, and Voroshilov, Tukachevsky and three others—Blucher, Budenny, and Yegorov—were given the rank of Marshal of the Soviet Union. Within three years, three of the five had been executed as traitors.

In January 1936, Tukachevsky was in London with Litvinov as his country's official representative at King George V's funeral. On his way home he stopped in Paris for receptions and conferences in furtherance of the reborn Franco-Russian alliance. Through the rest of that year he was much in evidence in public places and at diplomatic gatherings,* but in February 1937 the alert and observant Coulondre reported to Paris that there were rumors of the marshal's "disgrace" or even arrest, and that he seemed to be out of circulation. On January 24, under examination at the second show trial, Karl Radek had stated that Tukachevsky, sometime previously, had sent General Vitovt Putna (another hero of the Polish war and military attaché in London at the time of King George's funeral) to Radek's office to pick up some documents, and that Putna had engaged him in conversation about the "Trotskyite center." Radek exculpated Tukachevsky of any knowledge of this discussion, but Coulondre thought the public coupling of the marshal's name with Radek's an ominous sign, and also inferred a decline in Tukachevsky's military prestige.†

But these signs of disfavor, if such they were, apparently were erased during the next few weeks. Once again the marshal was seen at official functions, and on March 23 he was at the American Embassy for a party given by the military attaché, Colonel Faymonville. Early in May he was again selected to go to London, this time for the coronation of King George VI.

At this point, however, things started to go very wrong. The designation for the coronation was revoked, and Admiral Orlov went instead. On May 11, 1937, as part of a publicly announced change in high military assignments, Tukachevsky was removed as vice-commissar and given a secondary command in the Volga District. At about the same time the authority of the political commissars attached to each Army unit, which had been greatly diminished, was ordered restored. On May 31, Vice-Commissar Gamarnik, Chief of Political Administration of the Red Army, committed suicide, and a week later he was described by *Pravda* as a "degenerate Trotskyite." Then on June 6, 8, and 9 came announcements of a half-dozen military appointments to posts already filled, without indicating the assignment of the officers thus replaced. One of

---

* Tukachevsky was a gregarious, vivacious, and versatile man, much given to the amenities of social intercourse, and an expert violin maker.

† Until January 1937, Tukachevsky shared the title "vice-commissar" only with Jan Gamarnik, Chief of Political Administration of the Red Army. On January 29, 1937, two new vice-commissars were named: Admiral W. M. Orlov (naval) and General J. I. Alksnis (air). Coulondre's inference was based on Tukachevsky's apparently diluted role in the commissariat.

these was Tukachevsky, who was replaced in the Volga District by General Efremov.

Against this background, the simultaneous announcement that Marshal Tukachevsky and seven generals (of whom Putna was one) had been arrested came as no surprise to the well informed. But there was no lack of shock on June 13, when the Soviet press revealed that all eight had been convicted by a special military tribunal under the "Kirov" statute of December 1, 1934, and shot the next day as agents of hostile foreign powers and members of a conspiracy "to partition the Soviet Union and restore a government of landlords and capitalists."*

It was only the beginning of a virtual massacre of the officer corps that continued for many months. Two more of the 1935 marshals—Yegorov, the Chief of Staff, and Blucher, commander in the Far East—"disappeared," as did the Navy and Air Force chiefs, Admiral Orlov and General Alksnis, and many others of high rank and good repute in military circles.† As "Litvinov" put it: "After every executed Marshal we must shoot several hundred officers of his staff. . . . Blood calls for more blood. . . . The flower of our army command has been shot and Yezhov has already arrested half of the judges who passed sentence on Tukachevsky and his unfortunate comrades." If the official Soviet history of the war is to be believed, from May 1937 to September 1938, "as a sacrifice to Stalin's despotism . . . about half of the regimental commanders, nearly all of the brigade and divisional commanders, all the corps commanders and chiefs of military districts, members of the war council, and leaders of political administration in the military districts, the great majority of the political officers of the corps, divisions, and brigades, about a third of the regimental commissars, and many instructors at the high and middle-grade military schools, were eliminated."

Such a torrent of arrests, imprisonments, and executions could not last indefinitely, and by the summer of 1938 the flow had diminished. According to "Litvinov," Yezhov boasted that he would soon arrest Voroshilov, who retaliated with threats to "shoot him personally, like a dog" and demanded that Stalin remove him. In July 1938, Lavrenti Beria was appointed Vice-Commissar of the NKVD and Yezhov was eased out of office and disappeared, according to rumor, into a mental home. Beria became and remained chief until his execution in 1953, in the political turmoil after Stalin's death. His yoke was not easy, but, in "Litvinov's" words, with the passing of Yezhov "one can breathe more freely."

It was announced that Tukachevsky and all the victims in his group had

* In addition to Tukachevsky and Putna, the victims were Generals Yakir (commander of the Leningrad District), Uborevitch (commander in White Russia), Kork (commandant of the Frunze Military Academy), Eideman (chief of civilian defense), Feldman (chief of personnel in the Commissariat of War), and Primakov (commander of the Kharkov-Kiev District).

† Not all of those who disappeared were executed. General A. V. Gorbatov, a corps commander who, by his own account (*Years off My Life*) was arrested in October of 1938, interrogated under torture, and sent to a prison camp in Siberia, was reinstated in his rank and command level in March 1941 and served with distinction throughout the war. Another such case was that of General Konstantin Rokossovsky, and no doubt there were others who survived the ordeal and served again.

confessed, but there was no public confessional—no parade of self-accusing military traitors. The thrust of the charge was treasonous contacts with the Germans, but public proofs were never offered. In the Soviet press, the military purge was treated comparatively laconically; some officers were denounced, others simply disappeared. The basis of selection is not at all clear and, in view of the magnitude of the holocaust, no doubt personal vendettas, mistakes, and even sheer chance played a part. As Coulondre and the American chargé d'affaires (Loy Henderson) noted, the civilian defendants in the show trials included a high proportion of Jews, but the available information points to no such factor at work in the military purge.*

What were the reasons for this murderous onslaught, which Stalin must have known would cripple the leadership of the Red Army at a time of considerable foreign peril? Granting the unlikely assumption that Tukachevsky was leading a ring of traitorous conspirators, this would not begin to explain the enormous sweep of the lethal operation. Nor was there much indication of connection between the Army leaders and the so-called "rightist" opposition in the Party. At the third show trial Bukharin, Rosengoltz, and (after initial denials) Krestinsky linked Tukachevsky and others of his group with their own "conspiracy," but their testimony was wholly unconvincing and was given months after the generals had been shot.

The basic reasons for the military purge appear to have been comparable to those which, at about the same time, moved Hitler in the Blomberg-Fritsch crisis —an awareness that the higher commanders had values and traditions independent of and partially in conflict with Party supremacy, and were an obstacle to dictatorial absolutism. The Red Army of the Revolution had been in large measure Trotsky's creation. Tukachevsky and his contemporaries had made their reputations in the days of Lenin and Trotsky, and owed nothing to Stalin. Voroshilov and Budenny were "Stalin men," but most of the other generals, Communist as they may have been, felt mutual professional loyalties more than personal allegiance to the Party leadership, somewhat in the manner of the German officer corps, with which they had had close and valued ties. In all probability they regretted the severance of those relations, which came at a time when Stalin's policies were generating disagreement: agricultural collectivization, with its concomitant civil turbulence and other costs, and (again in parallel with the Army-SS rivalry in Germany) the growth of the NKVD as a formidable paramilitary rival. Bitter conflict between the Army and NKVD leaders in Spain immediately preceded the military purge and may have contributed to Stalin's determination to carry it as far as he did.

Perhaps fearing resistance, Stalin skillfully prepared for his move by transfers that removed the marked officers from their friends and supporters, and minimized the possibility of organized opposition. As in Germany, the Red Army had just been greatly expanded, and the new troops and junior officers were of a younger generation, freshly indoctrinated by the Party, and unlikely to succumb to the wooing of dissident generals with their roots in another era. But

* There were, to be sure, a number of Jewish generals including, in the Tukachevsky group of eight, Yakir and Feldman. All but two of the fourteen defendants in the Zinoviev-Kamenev trial were Jews.

15. Joseph Paul-Boncour, French Foreign Minister in the Blum cabinet, March–April 1938. *National Archives*.

16. Stanley Baldwin in 1937, shortly after he resigned as Prime Minister and became Earl Baldwin of Bewdley. *Radio Times Hulton Picture Library*.

17. Admiral Sir Ernle Chatfield, Chief of the Naval Staff, with (left) Sir Samuel Hoare, First Lord of the Admiralty. *Radio Times Hulton Picture Library.*

18. Marshal Henri Philippe Pétain, Hero of Verdun, cabinet minister in various posts, and the dominant figure in post-World War I French military policy. *Radio Times Hulton Picture Library.*

19. At the Kaiserhof Hotel in Berlin: Ambassador Nevile Henderson with Heinrich Himmler and Alfred Rosenberg. *Bundesarchiv.*

20. Hitler, followed by his principal military adjutant, Colonel Friedrich Hossbach. *Bundesarchiv.*

21. General Hans von Seeckt, Chief of the Army Command 1920–26, and (right) General Werner von Fritsch, Commander-in-Chief of the German Army 1935–38.

22. General (later Field Marshal) Werner von Blomberg, Minister of Defense 1933–35, Minister of War and Commander-in-Chief of the Wehrmacht 1935–38.

23. General Ludwig Beck, Chief of the Army General Staff 1935–38.

24. General Franz Halder, Chief of the Army General Staff 1938–42.

25. General Wilhelm Adam, Commander-in-Chief on the western front at the time of Munich.

26. General Gerd von Rundstedt, the senior German field commander at the time of Munich.

27. General Fedor von Bock, Commander-in-Chief of the German forces that occupied Austria.

28. General Walter von Reichenau, commander of the German armored and mobile formations.

29. The "Tribune of Honor" in Vienna, for celebration of *Anschluss*. Heinrich Himmler is talking with the Fuehrer, behind whom is General von Bock (in helmet). General Halder is behind Hitler's left arm. Behind Himmler, General Milch of the Luftwaffe (looking at wristwatch) is giving the time to General von Brauchitsch. At the extreme right is Artur Seyss-Inquart, and at his right (bowler hat and glasses) the retired Austrian General von Kraus, a victorious commander in World War I. On Bock's right is Kurt Daluege, chief of the German regular police. *Library of Congress.*

30. Charles and Anne Lindbergh with Hermann Goering, 1937. *National Archives.*

resistance, as far as we know, there was none. There is a strange fatalism about the Red Army's meek acceptance of the disgrace of its heroes and the slaughter of its leaders which suggests that these soldiers, able as many of them were and proud of their profession, had become so accustomed to Party supremacy as virtually to paralyze the will to resist.

Hitler bent the German officer corps to his will by despicable trickery, but bloodlessly, and at small cost in professional talent. Stalin, pursuing analogous ends, decapitated the Red Army and decimated the officer corps. Politically, he won a crushing victory, but at a terrible price, which was paid by the Russian people in the summer and fall of 1941, when the Wehrmacht struck and the Red Army was put to the test of a major war.

2

Soviet Russia's role in the Munich crisis must be viewed through the lens of the purge. To the members of Russian officialdom, these bloody events were much the most important of the years 1936 through 1938. Friendship with Stalin gave no guarantee of safety; Bukharin, Gamarnik, and other victims had been close to the dictator, and their sons and daughters had romped with his children at the country *dachas* that were so much a part of Moscow official life. Only obscurity offered a measure of security; virtually everyone discharging official responsibilities lived in more or less constant fear. A British journalist summed up the temper of those times with a mordant pun: "Habeas corpus has become habeas cadaver."

The purges affected the Soviet Union's foreign presence and policies in two ways. Russia was militarily weakened and administratively disorganized, as her leaders well knew, and these circumstances diminished both their disposition and their ability to conduct a dynamic foreign policy. At least equally important was the effect of the purges on other governments, and the consequent decline in Soviet prestige and in the heed paid to Soviet pronouncements and commitments.

The show trials and the military executions made a lamentable impression on virtually all the foreign diplomats and journalists in Moscow. Ambassador Davies, who spoke no Russian and was newly on the scene, was an exception; a few weeks after his Moscow debut he attended the Radek trial and reported to Washington his opinion that the prosecution had proved the conspiracy charged and (quite wrongly) that most of the other diplomats agreed. A year later, after the Bukharin trial, Davies reported (pointing to his own legal experience in support of his opinion) that the defendants had been proved guilty beyond a reasonable doubt. But Davies' views provoked General Köstring's scorn, and, as George Kennan's and Charles Bohlen's memoirs reveal, Davies' own staff thought him a travesty of a diplomat. Davies was not in Moscow when the Tukachevsky group were shot; Chargé Henderson reported that not one diplomatic mission or foreign observer in Moscow thought the officers guilty of the crimes charged.

This is not to say that the critical foreign observers thought the defendants innocent of opposition to Stalin's policies or, perhaps, to Stalin himself. On the contrary, both Coulondre and Köstring, perhaps the most knowledgeable of the onlookers, stressed the likelihood that the principal defendants were, indeed, dissidents. "The worst lies are those that rest on a basis of truth," wrote Coulondre. "What seems certain is that the accused were not guilty of the crimes charged in the indictments. But that they were shown as hostile to the Stalin regime, and that they more or less conspired *à la Russe* is plausible and even probable." The charges of treason, sabotage, and espionage were intended, Coulondre inferred, as necessary in order to convince the mass of Russians that these draconic measures were necessary. If such was Stalin's purpose it apparently was successful, for the much-traveled Köstring reported no signs of public shock or disbelief.

The evidence of opposition to Stalin, formidable as the trials and executions made it appear, nevertheless failed to impress foreign observers as indications of instability of the regime; rather they concluded, and rightly, that Stalin was destroying his opponents and cementing his authority. Equally widespread, however, was the conclusion that, as a factor in European affairs, Russia was greatly weakened. Coulondre recorded the "general opinion" of the diplomatic corps that "weakened by the self-administered purge, the Soviet Union is presently of no account in Europe; she will no longer join in political combinations." The French military attaché, Lieutenant Colonel Simon, regarded Yakir and Uborevitch (both executed with Tukachevsky) as the ablest of all the Soviet generals. Colonel Firebrace, the British military attaché, thought that the "gigantic purge, which has smitten all ranks," as well as "the general disorganization in civil life caused by the civilian purge," had had "a serious weakening effect" on the Army. "It may well be doubted," he wrote, "whether there are now available men who are capable of commanding armies in the event of war," and he found general agreement with his diagnosis among his opposite numbers, including Köstring and the Czech attaché, Colonel Dastich.

These reports were soon reflected in downward reassessments of Russian strength in Berlin and London, as well as in Paris, where William Bullitt, who had left Moscow in 1936 disgusted and angered by his hosts, wrote to President Roosevelt, in the fall of 1937, that the Russians were now "out of the picture," and that "all hope that they might help Czechoslovakia has been abandoned."

While it may well be doubted that any Russian was bold enough to tell Stalin that, as a result of his purges, his country was "out of the picture," it is virtually certain that he and his close advisers—Voroshilov, Zhdanov, and Molotov among others—were acutely aware of their diminished international standing and military power. Even in the summer of 1941, three years after the worst of the purge, only 7 per cent of the Red Army's officers had trained in the advanced military schools. Of the senior revolutionary commanders only Voroshilov, Budenny, Shaposhnikov (successor to Yegorov as Chief of Staff), and Timoshenko were left, and of these the first two had little professional prestige. In 1938, the Army's command problems must have been truly desperate.

Whatever was going on inside the Kremlin, on the outside the Russians gave every indication of a pathological xenophobia. Gone were the days when commissars and generals would visit the foreign embassies and fraternize in the glow of vodka and champagne. The entire diplomatic corps was virtually isolated from unofficial contact with Russians; as Köstring put it, "no doctor, roofer, milkmaid, workman, language teacher, or washerwoman any longer dares to come inside the house." The numerous German engineers and technicians in the Soviet Union were subjected to arrest and deportation or harassed into leaving "voluntarily." In the fall of 1937, invoking the principle of parity, the Soviet Government required the closing of fourteen consulates maintained by Germany, Italy, Japan, and Poland. These might all have been considered "unfriendly" nations, but in January 1938 similar demands were made on Afghanistan, Iran, Turkey, Sweden, and Norway, and even Czechoslovakia was required to close its newly established consulate in Kiev.

Under these drastically restricted contacts with foreigners, the Commissariat of Foreign Affairs became virtually the only channel of communication between the Kremlin and the world beyond Soviet borders. Litvinov and, in his absence, Vice-Commissar Vladimir Potemkin (former Ambassador to France and successor to the purged Krestinsky) spoke to the foreign diplomats in Moscow. Abroad, Litvinov as the Soviet representative at Geneva and, much less prominently, Ambassador Ivan Maisky as the Russian member of the Non-Intervention Committee in London were the only Soviet officials whose voices were regularly heard in the arena of international diplomacy.

To the outside world, Maxim Litvinov was the symbol of Soviet foreign policy, and during the months leading to Munich he continued, indefatigably, to stress the need for international collective action to check German aggression. Was Litvinov the architect of this policy or a mere mouthpiece for his political superiors? Was the policy genuine, or was it a façade behind which Stalin pursued quite different aims?

The answers to such questions, speculative as they must be, depend in part on an assessment of Litvinov's political stature. He was an "old Bolshevik" revolutionary, three years senior to Stalin, and a dedicated Communist responsive to Party discipline. But he never attained high Party standing, perhaps because he lived abroad after the 1905 revolt, married an Englishwoman, and did not return to Russia during the 1917 revolution, but stayed in London as the agent of the new regime. Thereafter his entire career was in diplomacy, which many of his Party colleagues regarded as a secondary aspect of revolutionary politics. Lenin and, for some time, Stalin appear to have allowed Litvinov a considerable freedom of action, but he had no following within the Party and never was chosen for the Politburo. No doubt his political insubstantiality was also a good protective mantle, for Stalin had no reason to fear him. It is reasonable to conclude that on the main elements of foreign policy Litvinov had no independent authority and was wholly subject to Party directives, but that, as a highly articulate and experienced diplomatic technician, his opinions carried weight, and within the general directives, he had wide latitude to handle the details of their execution.*

* A frequent and knowledgeable observer of Litvinov in Geneva, the Deputy Secretary-General of the League of Nations, wrote: "Litvinov rarely asked for time to consult his government; he seemed always ready to decide on the spot when to press his argument, to propose a compromise, or to resign himself to accepting the majority view. It was clear that he had at least as free a hand as was generally given to the Foreign Ministers of the democratic powers." Walters, *A History of the League of Nations* (1952), pp. 358–59.

When Ambassador Bullitt first arrived in Moscow at the end of 1933, Stalin, Voroshilov, and Litvinov all told him that they expected to be attacked by Japan during the coming spring. Litvinov very confidentially disclosed that the French had approached them with proposals for a defensive alliance against Germany, to be coupled with Russia's entry into the League of Nations.* He explained that his government was favorably considering the proposal because, given the Japanese peril in the east, it was vitally necessary to secure the western frontier against the possibility that Germany and Poland might later join forces with Japan.

This fear was the genesis of "collective security" as viewed by the Kremlin, and, if the initial impetus was from the Japanese, they were soon replaced by the Germans as the main focus of anxiety, as the Japanese became mired in China and German power and truculence grew. "There is not the slightest doubt," wrote the German counselor in Moscow, Gustav Hilger, "that a deep fear of Hitler's Germany was the essential guide to Soviet foreign policy in the mid-1930's."

The Japanese, to be sure, remained a problem and a menace, and there was constant friction between the two governments over fishing rights, arrests of Soviet citizens, and border incidents which at times developed into small wars. But in March of 1935 the sale of the Russian-owned Chinese Eastern Railway to the Japanese puppet state of Manchukuo removed a major source of irritation. During the early thirties the Soviet Government had faced eastward and looked back over its shoulder at Europe, but, despite the continuing border battles, by 1937 the posture was reversed. Soviet aid to Chiang Kai-shek, and the Sino-Soviet nonaggression treaty of August 1937, helped to ensure continued Japanese preoccupation with China. But the military aid did not approach the quantity which Chiang had expected, and Litvinov explained frankly to Coulondre that the reason for this parsimony was to avoid antagonizing Tokyo. As Moscow saw it, the principal danger was in the west, and there was no desire to provoke a conflict with the Japanese which would require moving troops from west to east.

3

Recognition of Nazi Germany as the greater peril did not, however, solve all of Moscow's foreign policy problems in Europe, and the outbreak of the Spanish Civil War soon presented one which could not be met by recourse to collective security. In power terms, collective security in Europe meant Britain and France, and both of those countries soon espoused an international policy of nonintervention. The Kremlin, with no stomach for distant military adventures and eager to preserve its newly won place in the European concert of powers, promptly joined in the Non-Intervention Agreement.

But on August 5, 1936, the same day that Litvinov agreed in principle to the nonintervention proposals, a mass meeting in support of the Spanish Government was held in Red Square, launching a nationwide campaign to raise money

* Litvinov was referring to his discussions in Paris in July 1933 with Joseph Paul-Boncour, the French Foreign Minister.

for the Loyalist cause. Before the end of the month, the Soviet trade unions had raised 12 million rubles, and by the end of October four times that amount. There seems no reason to doubt that the popular sentiment was genuine, but such campaigns did not occur in Russia without official sanction. Meanwhile the Comintern was rallying volunteers all over Europe for the International Brigades.

All this transpired right at the beginning of the major purge. The Zinoviev-Kamenev trial took place late in August, and a few weeks later came the Party clearance of Bukharin and Rykov, which led Stalin to replace Yagoda with Yezhov. Bukharin remained editor of *Izvestia* during the remainder of 1936, constantly stressing the need to check the spread of Fascism and thus, by implication, endorsing aid to the anti-Franco forces.

It seems clear that, as Colonel Simon reported to Paris on August 8, the Spanish Civil War split the Soviet leadership. According to Simon's information, Stalin favored staying out of the trouble, so as not to offend Hitler and Mussolini, whose aid to Franco had become common knowledge. Other Party figures, however, urged support for the Loyalists and, as Simon rightly inferred, were being called Trotskyite—a very dangerous word—for their pains.

But the picture of a Socialist regime assailed by a reactionary junta of rebel generals, backed by black Fascists and brown Nazis, was simply too much for the left side of the Soviet throat to swallow. Stalin apparently feared that continued indifference to the fate of the Spanish Government would play into his opponents' hands, and decided (more or less copying the German tactics) to come out openly in favor of the Loyalists and give them a limited amount of military support, camouflaged as "volunteer" as far as possible, while simultaneously playing the noninterventionist game. The new Soviet Ambassador to the Madrid government, Marcel Rosenberg, arrived there late in August, with a salute to President Azaña as symbol of "the freely expressed will of the Spanish people to live . . . under the shelter of their democratic institutions," and six weeks later President Kalinin and Stalin sent greetings respectively to Premier Caballero and the Spanish Communist Party, wishing them "success in their fight for liberty" against "the oppression of the fascist reactionaries."

Material aid was already coming. The funds contributed by the Soviet trade unions were used to buy food, clothing, and medicines which arrived by ship at Alicante late in September.* In Rosenberg's wake, and in the guise of "volunteers," came a stream of Soviet military officers and technicians, as well as a few pilots, who flew in defense of Madrid against the September bombings. In line with nonintervention, however, on August 28 the Kremlin had issued an order prohibiting the export of arms to Spain and, until late October, whatever military aid had been sent was small and hidden.

But meanwhile, in the Non-Intervention Committee, Maisky had developed a tactic for justifying open Soviet assistance to Madrid. On October 7 the Soviet chargé in London, S. B. Kagan, had made a statement to the committee accusing Germany and Italy of furnishing military aircraft to the rebels, and declaring

---

* The goods were shipped in the Soviet vessels *Neva* and *Kuban;* the Germans and Italians charged, the Russians denied, that the ships also carried munitions of war.

that unless these violations of nonintervention were "immediately discontinued," the Soviet Government would "consider itself free of the obligations" of the agreement. On October 23 the threat was made good when Maisky told the committee that the nonintervention agreement had "turned out to be an empty, torn scrap of paper" that had "created a privileged situation for the rebels which was certainly not the purpose of the agreement." Since the Soviet Government was "unwilling any longer to bear responsibility for a situation which is clearly unjust to the legitimate Spanish Government and the Spanish people," it was "compelled now to declare that in accordance with its statement of 7 October it cannot consider itself bound by the agreement for non-intervention to any greater extent than any of the other participants of the agreement."

Fifty Soviet tanks and thirty instructors were already on their way to Spain, and in November twenty-five fighter aircraft were sent. The total amount of military equipment eventually provided from Russia was considerable, but, according to the official Soviet history, only 557 military personnel accompanied the arms.* Beyond question, the Russian assistance was crucial in enabling the Government forces to stabilize the front and prolong the war, but it was not enough to give them superiority. The Russians could certainly have done more, but it seems plain that Stalin's appetite for an outright Loyalist victory was as weak as Hitler's for a Franco triumph.

Both dictators were pleased to see Britain and France at odds with Italy, since Hitler smelled opportunity for conquest in Central Europe, while Stalin saw in these capitalist embroilments a safeguard against a "gang-up" of democratic and Fascist powers against the Soviet Union. Both were willing enough to have the civil war drag on without a clear-cut victory for either side, and use the opportunity to test new weapons. Hitler was enabled to pose as the protector of Catholic Spain against the Communist barbarians, while Stalin emerged as international champion of the workers against Fascism.

Stalin was, nevertheless, fearful of appearing as the instigator of Communist revolution in Spain, lest he antagonize the western democracies. On December 21 he, with Voroshilov and Molotov, wrote a joint letter to Caballero which was almost childish in its gratuitous assumptions and recommendations that Spain should follow "its own path, in many ways different from the road traversed by Russia" and join forces with the "urban petty and middle bourgeoisie" and "republicans," and in its approval of the possibility "that the parliamentary path will turn out to be a more effective means of revolutionary development in Spain than in Russia."

On the whole, the Soviet involvement in Spain was not a happy one for the Kremlin. As early as December 15, 1936, Coulondre reported that the Soviet Government "wanted to be out of Spain," fearful as it was of diplomatic isolation, what with Italy and Germany supporting Franco more or less shamelessly and Britain and France sanctimoniously preaching nonintervention but doing

---

* The figure is not out of line with Louis Fischer's estimate (*Russia's Road from Peace to War*, p. 279), based on personal observation. Of the 557 there were 141 pilots, 107 tank troops, and 106 communications, engineering, and medical specialists—all nominally "volunteers" for service in Spain.

little to enforce it. As with the other interventionist countries, there were troubles with and among the Soviet representatives in Spain, as well as with the individualistic and divided Spaniards. Like his German opposite number, General Faupel, Ambassador Rosenberg was too easily drawn into Spanish politics, and in February 1937 he was replaced and, upon his return to Russia, suffered the fate of many other Soviet diplomats recalled during the purges. There was constant friction between the head of the Soviet military mission, General Ian Berzin, and the NKVD emissary, Alexander Orlov.* Moscow continued to send military supplies to the Loyalists, and Soviet vessels en route to Spain were sunk by Italian submarines in the late summer of 1937, before the Nyon Conference. But during the spring of 1937 both Coulondre in Moscow and Corbin in Paris reported an unmistakable though unavowed Soviet trend toward disengagement, and as the war went on the Kremlin did nothing calculated to restore the Republic's fading prospects. Increasingly, the emphasis shifted from the battlefield in Spain to the green table in London, as Maisky played the role of gadfly, exposing the hypocrisy and ineffectiveness of the nonintervention system.

Internal and military insecurity resulting from the purges, and fear of diplomatic isolation as the only great power supporter of the Loyalist government, largely explain the Kremlin's waning interest in Spain. It may be, as Louis Fischer writes, that Stalin never intended to assume a continuing obligation in Spain, but only to sustain the Government until "given time France and England might recognize the folly of appeasement and join the Soviets in blocking Fascist-Nazi-Japanese aggression." If that was indeed his purpose, the experiment was a failure, and within the Kremlin the Anglo-French reaction to the Spanish Civil War must have been chalked up along with Manchuria, Ethiopia, and the Rhineland, on the debit side of the collective security ledger.

Indeed, for all of Litvinov's eloquence at Geneva, and Maisky's acridity in London, in retrospect it has become clear that the Kremlin's attitude toward collective security as the basis of Soviet diplomacy was at all times ambivalent and due to be scrapped without compunction whenever it might appear that some other policy offered better protection against foreign attack. Since Germany was the greatest danger, the obvious alternative to collective security against the Nazis was security bought by agreement with them—a policy which, when used in London, was labeled "appeasement" by many and was the object of various other pejoratives in Moscow.

The ambivalence surfaced within a few months after the German Army training centers in Russia had been closed down, when Stalin took pains to make it clear that there was nothing ideological about his disenchantment with the Third Reich. Addressing the Party Congress in January 1934, he explained: "Of course we are far from enthusiastic about the fascist regime in Germany. But fascism is not the issue here, if only for the reason that fascism in Italy, for example, has not prevented the USSR from establishing the best relations with that country. . . . The point is that Germany's policy has changed." This was a

* According to secondary sources, General Berzin, the former chief of Red Army intelligence, was recalled and later executed during the military purge, while Orlov (a pseudonym), fearing a like fate, defected.

clear enough signal that, if Hitler could be persuaded to abandon his anti-
Sovietism, the Kremlin was quite prepared to meet him at least halfway.

Covert and private approaches to the Germans continued to be made by generals soon to be purged as well as by Stalin and his henchmen. Reporting to the
Party's Central Executive Committee in January 1936, Molotov declared "quite
frankly that the Soviet Government would have desired the establishment of
better relations with Germany than exist at present," and went on to bemoan
the inconsistency between Berlin's "plans of conquest" and "criminal propaganda" against Russia, and the recently concluded trade and credit agreement
between the two countries. Two months later, just after the Rhineland remilitarization, Molotov gave an interview to the correspondent of *Le Temps,* in
which he denied any Soviet "irreconcilability to the present rulers of Germany"
and declared that "the chief tendency, and the one determining the Soviet Government's policy, thinks an improvement in Soviet-German relations possible."

If these publicly extended olive branches were not fully leafed, the private
approaches were more explicit. Despite Hitler's repeated and violent public diatribes against communism, in 1935 Krestinsky and Radek (both still in favor)
urged on the Germans a multilateral *Ostpakt* of mutual assistance, and at about
the same time the Soviet commercial attaché in Berlin, David Kandelaki (an old
friend of Stalin's), unsuccessfully endeavored to raise his commercial discussions with Schacht to the political level.

Tukachevsky was singing the same tune. At a German Embassy reception in
October 1935 he expressed deep regret at the break between Red Army and
Wehrmacht, and declared that if the two countries were to march together they
"could dictate peace to all the world." The following February, Gekker, Feldman, and some twenty other generals visited Köstring to see his travel films, and
all lamented the good old days of collaboration. But the most remarkable demonstration came on March 7, 1936, the day of the Rhineland remilitarization,
which happened to fall on the day of a memorial celebration at the Italian Embassy. There Köstring encountered Radek, Tukachevsky, and other high
officials and officers. One and all congratulated the German general ostentatiously, and the Soviet marshal put a goblet of champagne into Köstring's hand
and drank with him to the Reich's "great stride," adding his opinion that "in a
few weeks Germany could put enough troops into the Rhineland to attack
France."

That outburst no doubt was stimulated by the bottle and anyhow, as Köstring
silently reflected, probably nothing would have given Tukachevsky more satisfaction than to see France and Germany at each other's throats. The Red generals could drink with the French likewise, as Tukachevsky himself had done
three weeks before in Paris, where, hosted by Gamelin, he had raised his glass
to the *"renforcement de nos forces militaires."* And that fall, when Generals
Schweisguth and Vuillemin came to Russia to attend the maneuvers, Voroshilov
and several Foreign Ministry officials were at great pains to convince their
guests that Hitler's intention was to strike westward, and Tukachevsky strongly
urged general staff discussions for joint planning against the Germans.

Certainly the Kremlin wanted to reap maximum benefits from the Franco-

Soviet alliance, but in Moscow there was growing distrust of both France's actual strength and her willingness to turn a paper treaty into military reality. In March 1935, Tukachevsky, writing in *Pravda* on Germany's military expansion and aggressive aims, had declared that "the French army, with . . . its hastily assembled units, and slow rate of expansion by stages under mobilization, is already incapable of active opposition to Germany," and in the autumn of 1936, Voroshilov told General Schweisguth to his face that France "had lost ten to twelve years." Writing to Alexis Léger on November 11, 1936, Coulondre remarked that France was giving the Russians an impression of powerlessness (*"impuissance"*), and reported that, when presenting his credentials to Kalinin, the Soviet President had observed: "I know well that your government favors technical collaboration, but *voilà*—there is the opposition of the services."

But if France was weak and indecisive, and if in London and Paris appeasement was in the saddle, neither did the signals to Berlin stir any response, and the Anti-Comintern Pact, the Axis, and the German posture in Spain all appeared incompatible with a Nazi-Soviet *rapprochement*. Nevertheless, Coulondre, in March 1937, was still concerned about the possibility; the Russian attitude toward Germany, he reported, was a combination of admiration and fear. Given the diplomatic and military tradition of Russo-German collaboration, there were latent international forces which, though masked by ideological factors, could suddenly throw the two countries together.

For foreign consumption, collective security remained Soviet policy throughout the Munich period. But by the end of 1937 it was fraying badly, and Stalin was already preparing the home front for the possibility of a change. During 1937 and 1938 he was supervising the preparation of a new treatise for Party indoctrination, which was finally published in September of 1938 as a "Short Course" in Communist Party history. Its significance as a harbinger of Soviet foreign policy has been pointed out by Robert Slusser; the work "virtually ignores the policy of collective security in the late twenties and early thirties" and, as regards the period 1935 to 1937, it "discounts any possibility of effective action against the aggressors on the part of the Western powers." The League of Nations and mutual assistance pacts are "portrayed as props of no great value" as compared to the Soviet Union's own military defenses, and there is sharp criticism of Trotsky, Bukharin, and Radek for their initial refusal to sign the Treaty of Brest-Litovsk, thereby exposing the infant Soviet Union to "the blows of German imperialism."

The reader was left to draw for himself the inference that a treaty with Germany might once again be necessary. But the work as a whole is strong testimony to the accuracy, if not the authenticity, of "Litvinov's" attribution to Stalin of the view that, if Germany were about to strike, it was vital that Russia not "receive the first blow," and that therefore the lines of communication between Moscow and Berlin must be kept open.

4

Hitler proclaimed *Anschluss* on March 13, 1938, the same day the Bukharin-Rykov trial ended. Litvinov promptly pulled out the collective security stop and opened the swell box. His press statement of March 17 coupled "I-told-you-sos" with the proposal of an immediate international conference:

> The Soviet Government has voiced a warning that international inaction and the impunity of aggression in one case could inexorably lead to the repetition and multiplication of similar cases.
>
> Unfortunately international developments have justified these warnings. They received new confirmation in the armed invasion of Austria and in the forcible deprivation of the Austrian people of their political, economic, and cultural independence. . . .
>
> The Soviet Government . . . is prepared immediately to take up in the League of Nations or outside of it the discussion with other powers of the practical measures which the circumstances demand. It may be too late tomorrow, but today the time for it is not gone if all the States and the Great Powers in particular take a firm and unambiguous stand in regard to the problem of the collective salvation of the peace.

Before he launched this epistle, obviously intended particularly for London and Paris, Litvinov sought to raise the pressure in those capitals through meetings with several of his resident diplomats. To Davies he expressed the view that England was largely to blame, citing the Halifax visit to Germany the preceding November. Czechoslovakia was now gravely endangered, and France would have to come to her defense, "otherwise it would be the end of France." England would then be drawn in willy-nilly. To Viscount Chilston the next day (March 15) he repeated that Czechoslovakia was next on Hitler's list, and blandly informed the noble lord that "Herr Hitler was not afraid of any active opposition owing to the weakness shown by Great Britain and France in various stages of German menace in the past and the absence of collective security and failure of the League Powers to make a front against the aggressors." On the same day Potemkin received the Czech Ambassador, Zdenek Fierlinger, and explained that whether France would face up to or evade her treaty obligations depended on whether England would support her; as for the Soviet Union, nobody would be able to reproach her for nonperformance. Later, at a diplomatic reception, Litvinov told the press that Russia would fulfill her treaty commitment to intervene in defense of Czechoslovakia if France did, and when asked how this would be done, in the absence of a common frontier with either Germany or Czechoslovakia, replied that "some sort of corridor was certain to be found."

On March 23, however, when Davies again came in, the Soviet Foreign Commissar was far less sanguine. The crisis would erupt during the coming summer, and Czechoslovakia might give in because she had "no confidence in France." Unless Britain should change her present policies, Germany would dominate Europe, and the only other truly independent states in Europe would be Britain and the Soviet Union. With surpassing frankness, Litvinov then declared: "France has no confidence in the Soviet Union, and the Soviet Union has no confidence in France." Truer words were never spoken, as Litvinov put his finger squarely on the frailty of the Franco-Russian-Czech alliances.

Perhaps Litvinov had forewarning that his proposals of March 17 had fallen on stony soil in London. On March 24, addressing the Commons on the looming Czech crisis, Neville Chamberlain declared that Litvinov's proposed conference, appearing as it did "to involve less a consultation with a view to settlement than a concerting of action against an eventuality which has not yet arisen," would lead to British military commitments which his government was "unwilling to accept," and would "aggravate the tendency toward the establishment of exclusive groups of nations which must, in the view of His Majesty's Government, be inimical to the prospects of European peace."

It was a very sharp rebuff, and Litvinov did not again take the initiative on the international scene until early September. Diplomatic exchanges with the concerned countries individually continued, however, and a few preliminary military steps were taken. The Czech Colonel Frantisek Moravec came to Moscow to co-ordinate interchange of military information, and late in March the newly promoted Marshal G. I. Kulik* headed a Soviet military mission to Czechoslovakia. Late in April forty bombers were sold to Czechoslovakia and subsequently were delivered by flying them across Rumania.

Throughout the pre-Munich months, Soviet officials continued to assure the Czechs, and anyone else who asked, that Russia would give Czechoslovakia aid in the event of a German attack, but always subject to the condition, as stipulated in the Soviet-Czech treaty, that France was fulfilling her primary commitment. On April 23, Fierlinger reported that there had been a Kremlin conference attended by Stalin, Molotov, Voroshilov, Kaganovich, Litvinov, and the Soviet Ambassador to Czechoslovakia, Sergei Alexandrovsky, at which the ambassador was authorized to inform Beneš that, in agreement with France, the Soviet Union would take "all necessary measures relating to the security of Czechoslovakia." It was added that the Red Army and Air Force were in shape to fulfill this commitment, and that Russia would continue to aid Czechoslovakia as long as she "does not abandon her democratic policy."† Public statements reaffirming Russia's firm intention to observe her treaty commitment to Czechoslovakia were made early in May by President Kalinin when receiving a Czech labor delegation, and later that month by Ambassador Alexander Troyanovsky, addressing the American-Russian Chamber of Commerce in New York City.

On May 9, the Council of the League of Nations met in Geneva, and Litvinov found himself in the company of both Lord Halifax and the newly appointed French Foreign Minister, Georges Bonnet. According to the latter's account, he at once pressed Litvinov to say what Russia would do in view of the lack of any

---

* During the military purge three Red Army generals were promoted to Marshal of the Soviet Union: Shaposhnikov (the new Chief of Staff), Timoshenko (commander in the Caucasus), and Kulik, a "political" general who was appointed a Deputy Commissar of Defense. Kulik is sharply criticized in the official Soviet history for failure to make adequate preparations for war.

† It is perhaps significant, however, that the day after Fierlinger's report of this conference, *Izvestia* carried an article deploring the lack of "consistent and honest French policy based on the pact with the USSR," which "would have meant . . . unequivocal defeat for the fascist aggressors." Instead, the writer declared, France was being dragged in the wake of England.

common frontier with Czechoslovakia and whether she was prepared to force a passage across Poland or Rumania. Litvinov replied that she would do no such thing, since Moscow had no desire for war with either country. However, Litvinov observed, France had a treaty of alliance with Poland and of friendship with Rumania, and was therefore in a good position to obtain their permission for Russian transit. Litvinov's impression, as subsequently conveyed to Fierlinger, was that Bonnet had little interest in the possibility of Russian action, and was "groaning" over Polish and Rumanian obduracy rather than doing anything likely to prove effective in bringing those countries into the lineup. Simultaneously Schulenburg and the British chargé in Moscow were reporting their opinion that the Russians had no stomach for war and were making no effort to persuade the Rumanians to allow transit.

As for Halifax, Litvinov read him a lecture critical of Britain's entire policy vis-à-vis Germany. London, he declared, was wholly mistaken in viewing the Sudetenland as the root of the Czech-German problem; Hitler cared no more for the *Sudetendeutsch* than for the Germans of the Tyrol, and was simply using them as a cover for German aggrandizement. Litvinov's diplomacy was increasingly limited to put-downs and other jabs at London and Paris, and a few weeks later it was the French who suffered his tender mercies. On June 5, he instructed the Soviet Ambassador in Paris, Jacob Suritz, to point out to the Quai d'Orsay that, if Germany were to attack Czechoslovakia, Poland would probably take the opportunity to rip off Teschen, and to inquire whether, if Russia intervened militarily to check the Poles, France would come to Poland's aid, pursuant to the Franco-Polish treaty of 1921.*

Bonnet referred the question to his *jurisconsulte,* and eventually replied that, under the Czech-Soviet treaty, Moscow would be under no obligation to aid Czechoslovakia against Poland unless France were already doing so, in which case France and Russia would, of course, be on the same side. But when Coulondre relayed this answer to Litvinov, the response was: "That's true, but there is another hypothesis; which is that, for one reason or another, the Soviet Union might intervene even though France had done nothing." This was a plain enough intimation of Litvinov's doubt that France meant business, but Coulondre sensed a more sinister intimation in Litvinov's pursuit of this question. Was it possible that Russia would consider attacking Poland other than in concert with Germany? If Czechoslovakia were destroyed by Germany, and Poland by Germany and Russia, France would be left friendless in Eastern Europe, to face a triumphant and dominant Germany. Such was the degree of mistrust between the two nominal allies, on whose support Czechoslovakia's survival depended.

None of Litvinov's thrusts appeared to have accomplished anything by way of stiffening backbones in London or Paris. Meanwhile, Coulondre's efforts to persuade his superiors of the necessity of Franco-Russian general staff talks likewise came to nothing. Late in July, Moscow's attention was drawn again to the Far East, where heavy fighting broke out between Soviet and Japanese troops

---

* Litvinov had earlier put the same question to Coulondre, who immediately gave the same answer which the Quai d'Orsay gave later.

near Lake Khasan on the Russian-Manchokuoan border, only temporarily quieted by an inconclusive truce on August 11. A week later the needling policy was resumed when Maisky, returning to London after a home leave, called on Lord Halifax with information that "there was a good deal of disappointment among members of the Russian Government at , . . . the undue weakness of the Western democracies." In Moscow's view, neither Britain nor France was firm enough with Germany, "in whose policy there was at least 50% of bluff." Once more he drew a blank; Halifax replied that "there was no question" of Britain taking a stiffer position. Maisky pronounced it unfortunate that London "had not found it possible to be more precise," and declared that, if Germany should attack Czechoslovakia, his government would "certainly do their bit."

Litvinov sang a very different tune, however, when on August 22, Count von der Schulenburg came in to sound out the situation. When the German indicated that his country would not attack the Czechs unless "provoked," Litvinov practically laughed in his face, declaring that "even the wildest Czech hotheads" would take care not to provoke Germany, and that in a war between two countries so disparate in size there would be no doubt who was the "aggressor." He pooh-poohed Berlin's concern for the Sudeten Germans and accused the Reich government of aiming at Czechoslovakia's "annihilation." As for the consequences, Litvinov predicted categorically that France would mobilize, Britain would "follow France's lead," and the Soviet Union "would keep her word and do her best." Schulenburg's efforts to discover what her "best" would consist of, given the lack of common frontiers with either Germany or Czechoslovakia, were, not surprisingly, unsuccessful.

If, as is probable, Litvinov was whistling in the dark, there were no outward manifestations of uncertainty. By the end of August it was apparent in all the informed European capitals that Germany was marshaling her forces, and on September 1 the French chargé, Jean Payart (Coulondre was on leave), waited on Potemkin, telling him that Paris had had no luck in asking Warsaw and Bucharest to permit the passage of Russian troops: so what would Moscow do if the crunch came? The next day Litvinov dispatched a telegram to Alexandrovsky in Prague, with copies to Paris and London, stressing the urgent necessity of Franco-Soviet-Czech staff talks, and reaffirming that, *if the French became engaged,* Russia would do likewise. The message was coupled with a suggestion that the Czech question be brought before the League of Nations, in order to persuade Rumania to grant transit to the Russians.

When Maisky received his copy of Litvinov's message, despairing of rousing Halifax to action and in order to spread knowledge of his government's position, the ambassador took himself first to Winston Churchill, and subsequently to Lloyd George and Arthur Greenwood, deputy leader of the Labour Party. Churchill reacted by summarizing Litvinov's declarations in a letter to Halifax, who replied on September 5 in what Churchill calls "a guarded manner," dismissing Litvinov's proposal of recourse to the League as not "helpful."

For the second time, Soviet efforts to deal with the crisis through collective security had crashed on the British rocks, and in Moscow the effect was immediately noticeable. Coulondre, back in Moscow, saw Potemkin on September 11 and found him utterly unresponsive to questions and proposals about the by now full-blown crisis. The next day Fierlinger told Coulondre the reason: the Kremlin "did not believe that France and England were willing to make war for Czechoslovakia and, under these conditions, judged it advantageous to maintain reserve."

While Coulondre and Potemkin were meeting in Moscow, Litvinov and Bonnet were once more together in Geneva, and once more Bonnet put the question he had asked the previous May. The Soviet Foreign Commissar had nothing new to say; Russia would not cross Polish or Rumanian frontiers without those governments' consent. If Bonnet had been unable to obtain their permission, nothing remained but to bring the whole matter before the League, and develop international pressure which might at least persuade Rumania to accede. Bonnet's subsequent discussions with the Rumanian Foreign Minister (Petrescu-Comnene), who was also in Geneva, gave no basis for thinking that Rumania would yield, whatever the views of the League.

Such was the state of relations between the western powers and the Soviet Union when, on September 13, Neville Chamberlain invited himself to Germany.

5

Probably the Kremlin will never open, if they exist, the archives recording the discussions within and conclusions reached by the Politburo during the course of the Czech crisis. But I believe that the documents we have reviewed, read in the context of the circumstances which the Soviet leaders confronted, are sufficient to ground a substantially accurate analysis of their intentions and probable actions if Czechoslovakia had stood firm and had been attacked by Germany in the fall of 1938. The exercise is especially necessary because of the tendentious and often careless judgments which have been expressed, and the irrelevancy of some of the factors which have often been emphasized.

In part the confusion has arisen from failure adequately to distinguish between what Russia, assuming her sincere wish to do everything possible to aid Czechoslovakia, *could* in fact have done, and what she probably *would* have done, given the limitations on the possible. The first question can be answered with reasonable accuracy on the basis of objectively determinable circumstances, while the second can be dealt with only on the basis of inference verging on speculation.

A glance at a map of Europe for 1938 is almost enough by itself to demonstrate the small importance of the question, to which Bonnet appeared to attach such importance, of transit for Russian troops across Rumania to Czechoslovakia. William L. Shirer accuses Bonnet of not really trying to obtain the Rumanian Government's consent; Charles R. Foster is critical of the Soviet Government on precisely the same ground. Winston Churchill wrote that there were two railways from Russia into Czechoslovakia, which "might well have supported Russian armies of thirty divisions." But one of the lines of which he wrote ran through the southeastern corner of Poland, and the other through

Hungary, before entering Czechoslovakia. The chances of inducing either of these countries to permit the transit were virtually nil.

There was also a railway which ran directly from Satu Mare in western Rumania into Czechoslovakia's eastern province, Ruthenia.* But it was a single-track line which hugged the Hungarian border, within easy artillery range. There was no double track east of Sillein (near the Slovak-Moravian border), and from Sillein the main line westward divided, the northern one almost touching the Polish border at Teschen and the German at Oderberg, and the southern line running through Bratislava, adjacent to both Hungary and Austria.

The German military attaché in Prague, General Rudolf Toussaint, told George Kennan that it would have taken the Russians three months to get a division into Slovakia by way of Rumania. He was not far wrong, but the transportation difficulties were not the most important point. Sending Russian ground forces into Czechoslovakia by that route would have been military insanity, even if the Rumanians had gladly consented. Prague was as far from Rumania as it was from France; the Russians would have had to traverse over three hundred miles in Ruthenia and Slovakia, no doubt under constant aerial attack, to reach Moravia and the dubious pleasure of finding themselves virtually surrounded by the Germans.

The main obstacle to effective Russian aid to Czechoslovakia was not that those two countries lacked a common frontier—there was, after all, no common Franco-Czech frontier either—but that there was no Russo-German border. The great powers could have best aided Czechoslovakia not by sending reinforcements into that narrow and partially encircled land, but by attacking Germany directly and making it impossible for her to concentrate her major forces against Czechoslovakia without taking unacceptable risks of invasion and defeat elsewhere. And the country which blocked a Russian threat to eastern Germany was not Rumania but Poland. In the over-all strategic picture, the issue of Rumanian transit was insignificant.†

In March 1936, according to Bullitt, Tukachevsky told him that "at the present moment the Soviet Union would be unable to bring any military aid to Czechoslovakia in case of German attack." As long as Poland stood in the way, that judgment was perhaps overstated but not far from the truth in 1938 as well. The Soviet Air Force might have provided some help, but, given the distances involved, the range and capacity of military aircraft at that time, and the vulnerability of the Czech airfields to bombardment by the Luftwaffe, it could not have played a decisive role.

There was, to be sure, the possibility of avoiding the Polish obstacle by the route to East Prussia through Latvia and Lithuania—countries that could have

---

* In fact there were two lines from Rumania into Ruthenia, but one of them dead-ended in Rumania and was useless for through traffic. It joined the line from Satu Mare near Chust, and from Chust westward there was only a single-track line for the next two hundred miles. See map, p. 708.

† I do not, of course, mean to say that ground transit across Rumania would have been valueless. Russian advisers and technicians and limited quantities of munitions could have been sent through and, if the Russians had attempted to base air force units in Czechoslovakia, road and rail access would have been useful and perhaps crucial for the transportation of the ground staffs and equipment, and antiaircraft weaponry.

offered only token resistance and probably would have attempted none. The Red generals had at one time been worried that Germany might use that avenue for an attack, but early in 1936, Budenny told Bullitt that the Red Army had made "preparations" to block such a move and that anyhow the corridor was too narrow for the maneuvering of large forces. The space limitations would, of course, equally hamper the Russians, and there was also the risk that the Poles might not stand idly by; when Gamelin, visiting Poland in 1936, had suggested that the Russians might use this route, Smigly-Rydz had objected vehemently. In February 1937 the French Deputy Chief of Staff, General Paul Henri Gerodias, made the same proposal to Potemkin (at that time the Soviet Ambassador in Paris), whose response was utterly noncommittal. There is no evidence that the Soviet leaders ever seriously considered an offensive through the Baltic countries, which, from a military standpoint, was an attack through the neck of the bottle, justifiable only on the unlikely assumption that Poland could remain a neutral barrier between the two warring giants.

Some but probably not much air support, accordingly, was about all that Russia had to offer Czechoslovakia by way of immediate military aid.* It should be remarked, however, that these limitations on what the Soviet forces could do had no unique connection with Czechoslovakia; they would have been equally operative in case of war between Germany and France or, indeed, any war in which Russia and Germany were antagonists and Poland neutral. The hostility between Russia and Poland was, from the French standpoint, the major weakness of the Franco-Soviet treaty, as apparent in 1935, when the document was signed, as it was in 1938.

Given these circumstances, it is easy to understand why the Soviet Government limited its treaty commitment to Czechoslovakia so that it would come into force only if the French were fulfilling their own, and why in 1938 Moscow's repeated declarations of support for Prague invariably incorporated the condition of French participation. For if the French should default and the Czechs should nonetheless resist, it was plain that Poland would do nothing to aid them and might, indeed, attempt to annex the Teschen district by force. Russia might (as she eventually did) threaten the Poles in order to keep them out of Czechoslovakia's back door, but that would only indirectly have helped the Czechs against the Germans.

It is, therefore, absurd to attach much importance to the statements, by Maisky and the Soviet historian Trukhanovsky, that Stalin informed Beneš, through the Czech Communist leader Klement Gottwald, that Russia would assist Czechoslovakia even if France did not. Perhaps such a message was sent,† but if so it was surely for Party propaganda purposes, as the use of Party rather

---

* This was all that the Czechs expected, according to Colonel Moravec, the Czech Army's military emissary to the Soviet Union in 1938, who subsequently wrote of his experiences in his book *Nous avons été trahis* (Prague, 1940).

† The story's credibility suffers from the fact that Maisky (*Who Helped Hitler?*, p. 79) says that the message was sent early in September, while Professor Trukhanovsky (quoted in Fischer, *Russia's Road from Peace to War*, p. 311) placed it "in the second half of May, 1938." The official Soviet history of the Second World War makes no such claim, but does say that Beneš and Hodža were anti-Soviet and did not want Russian help, and that only Gottwald stood firmly for independence.

than diplomatic channels indicates. Regular diplomatic intercourse between Moscow and Prague through Fierlinger and Alexandrovsky was open and in constant use for discussion of the looming crisis, and a seriously intended assurance would have been extended by the usual means. Given the Polish barrier, the commitment would in any event have been an empty one. It is altogether beyond belief that the suspicious, cautious, and eminently realistic Stalin would have led his country into war with Germany while the western powers stood aside and gloated. That, indeed, was the very contingency which the Kremlin was most anxious to avoid.

What, then, would the Russians have done if France had honored her guaranty to Czechoslovakia by declaring war against Germany? Despite repeated Soviet urgings there had been no Franco-Soviet staff talks. Tukachevsky and Voroshilov had both vented their low opinion of the state of French arms, and "Litvinov" quotes the Soviet military attaché in Paris, one Krantz-Vientzov, to the effect that "the French were suffering from a state of complete passivity. . . . They had no air force . . . no tanks . . . no strategy. . . . Their defence was based on the ideas of the senile Pétain with his out-dated Verdun psychology. . . . They want to bury themselves behind the Maginot Line. . . . They are going back from Napoleon to Vercingetorix. . . ." Authentic or not, this was an only slightly unfair appraisal.

Given this distrust of French military capacity and the ambivalent attitude in London, the Russian leaders would have had ample reason for caution in committing themselves to war with Germany. However, it was Moscow that had been sounding the loudest trumpet calls for collective action and, with France at war to defend Czechoslovakia, the Soviet Government would have been utterly discredited had it failed to give her some kind of support.

Bearing in mind the Kremlin's reaction to the somewhat comparable Spanish problem in 1936, it can reasonably be inferred that the Russians would have done two things. They would have deployed substantial forces along their western frontier, in order to restrain Poland from invading Teschen, increase the pressure on Rumania to allow transit, and keep the Germans concerned about the security of East Prussia. They would also have sent observers, advisers, and technicians to Czechoslovakia and, if reasonably safe airfields remained available, a few squadrons of bombers, to be used in combat with Czech markings and, perhaps, Czech crews. These steps would have been of only slight immediate benefit to Czechoslovakia, but they would have been more than a token of good faith and would have been at least as effective as anything the French would have been likely to accomplish at the outset.

But Russia would not have immediately declared war or undertaken direct military action against Germany. Rather she would have used the League of Nations and other diplomatic procedures to temporize and keep her options open as the situation developed. The suspicious and crafty Stalin would certainly have envisaged the possibility that Czechoslovakia would be quickly overrun, and that France, confronted with a military *fait accompli,* would give way and make peace. Much would have depended on whether Britain came promptly to France's support or herself played a waiting game. Basically, the Russians would wait to see whether or not France and Britain were irrevocably committed to putting down the Germans and ending the menace of the Third Reich.

The full involvement of France was also crucial in its bearing on the Polish problem. The Polish leaders viewed with pleasurable anticipation the prospect of Czechoslovakia's dismemberment, and did everything possible to discourage France from doing anything to prevent it. But if, contrary to their expectations, France had committed herself to the Czech cause, the Poles would have found themselves in a very uncomfortable situation. Colonel Beck himself later wrote that "in the event of a real European war we could not be on the side of Germany." Talking to Gamelin in 1936, Smigly-Rydz allowed the possibility that Poland might make landing fields available to Russian aircraft. Under the pressures of a war in alliance with France and, however uneasily, with Russia, the Poles would surely have conceded much more and made Russia's effective participation against Germany possible.*

Accordingly, the way the "Munich issue" was drawn in Moscow might be fairly summarized as follows: First, war between Germany and the western democracies was not unwelcome to the Kremlin, since it both eliminated the possibility of an "imperialist" alliance against the Soviet Union and deflected Germany, the greatest danger, to the west. Consequently, unlike France and Britain, Russia did not strongly press the Czechs to avoid a German attack by concessions to the Sudeten Germans. Second, the Kremlin had a low opinion of French military power, and did not expect the western powers to go to war to save Czechoslovakia, or the Czechs to fight without support from France. Third, if Czechoslovakia had resisted without French aid, Russia would have concentrated forces on the western border to restrain Poland, and might have sent "volunteers" and what supplies it could, if the Czechs were able to hold part of their territory, in the hope that world sympathy for the Czechs' plight might shame the French into action. Fourth, if France had declared war in support of Czechoslovakia, Russia would have deployed more troops, sent more aid, and made serious preparations for war, but would have temporized until it became clear whether or not France and Britain meant business. Fifth, if France and Britain became irrevocably committed, Russia would have joined forces with them in order to put an end to the German peril.

In short, the road from Moscow to Prague ran through Paris. But, as we will now see, the road from Paris to Prague was equally circuitous.

---

* Indeed, the Germans might have resolved the problem by crushing Poland and confronting the Red Army. Whether in that event the Soviet Government would have fought, or whether Hitler and Stalin would have made a deal as they did in 1939, would probably have depended on how the war was going in Western Europe.

CHAPTER 20

The Road from Paris to Prague
Runs through London

1

After the German march into the Rhineland, the crucial question for France was whether the disaster she had suffered would act as a tonic or a narcotic. Thus confronted with the results of a purely defensive posture, would the French generals shake off the dead hand of Pétain? Could the Quai d'Orsay reestablish its independence of Whitehall? Could *la belle France* recapture the *esprit* of her heroic years, or would this latest German coup raise a wave of defeatism and strengthen the hands of those who professed to fear the Bolshevist more than the Nazi menace?

In the French press the theme last mentioned was prominent if not dominant, and politicians on the right were virtually unanimous in counseling their fellow-countrymen to view the new situation with equanimity. This was, to be sure, in keeping with the general trend among French conservatives; the more significant reaction was among some of those who had clearly perceived the menace of the German move.

During the Rhineland crisis, no one in the inner circles of the French Government had advocated military action more insistently than Alexis Léger. As he was the senior permanent official of the Quai d'Orsay, the effect of the event on his thinking was of considerable and continuing importance. Two weeks after the German entry, Léger was visited by Edwin Wilson, the new counselor of the American Embassy, who found the Secretary General in a mood of "intense gloom." The American Ambassador, Jesse Isidor Straus, reported to Washington Léger's view that, if Britain should continue to balk at effective action through the League Council, the consequences for Europe would be:

. . . an entirely new line-up in Europe since it would mean that all ideas of collective security had been abandoned; that Central and Eastern Europe must look after themselves while the Little Entente must necessarily turn to Germany as the great power in its region . . .

It seems to be this . . . state of affairs that Léger fears very much will be the outcome of the difficulties . . .

Léger said that if Hitler succeeds this time, it is "definitely the last, not the next to last, test" and means giving to the Hitler regime an almost unparalleled position in the European scene and that Hitlerian dreams of some mystic Carlovingian Europe would have a better chance of coming to pass.

Two months later William C. Bullitt, still accredited to Russia but soon to be transferred to France, visited Paris and found Léger's "gloom" thickened virtually to desperation:

> After a long statement which consisted largely of criticisms of the British for unwillingness to support France in resorting to force . . . Léger said that completion by Germany of the line of fortifications on the French and Belgian positions would place a Chinese Wall across Europe. France and England would be barred from Central and Eastern Europe and all the states of Central and Eastern Europe could be at the mercy of Germany . . . .
>
> There could be only one future for Central Europe if the fortifications should be completed—domination by Germany . . .
>
> I replied that from everything I knew about French public opinion it would be totally impossible to persuade the people of France to make war on Germany because of the construction of the fortifications . . . Léger . . . finally admitted that if the Germans during the period while they were constructing the fortifications should refrain from hostile acts and statements, it would be impossible for the French Foreign Office to arouse the French people to prevent the building of the fortifications.
>
> I then asked Mr. Léger what hope he had. He said that he could see no hope except that the Germans would conduct themselves so arrogantly and foolishly that they would arouse the people of France to a realization of the need for armed intervention and also perhaps the people of England.
>
> I derived the impression from this conversation with Léger that the French Foreign Office has in fact no constructive ideas whatsoever.

Bullitt's judgment was harsh—perhaps overly so—but basically correct. In retrospect, Léger himself acknowledged that in his mind the Rhineland was the turning point. For him the battle was already lost, and he had no program for retrieving the situation, save to cling to the British and hope for the best. Of course, Léger did not openly repudiate collective security or the French alliances in Eastern Europe, but he had been quite serious in telling Edwin Wilson that the Rhineland was "the last, not the next to last, test" of those policies, and now it seemed apparent to him that they had failed.

If Léger, the professional diplomat, was gloomy and resigned, Gamelin, the professional soldier, was defensive and unrepentant. Sometime in April, Flandin had occasion to confer with General Schweisguth, Deputy Chief of the Army General Staff and, whether on impulse or by plan, the Foreign Minister let loose a tirade against the attitude of the Army leaders "who, every time any immediate, energetic measures are proposed, raise objections." Schweisguth having reported the episode to Gamelin and the Minister of War, General Maurin, the latter promptly waited on Flandin to seek clarification of the complaint.

The matter was of immediate moment, for Hitler, once the Rhineland was safely in hand, had stepped up the pressure on Austria, posing the demands which ultimately led to the Austro-German Agreement of July 11, 1936. What should France do in the event of a German military move against Austria? On

April 23, Vice-Admiral Abrial, Deputy Chief of the Naval Staff, and General Joseph Georges, representing Gamelin, met at the Quai d'Orsay to discuss the problem with Paul Bargeton, chief of the political section, substituting for Léger, who was unexpectedly detained elsewhere.

Most of the meeting comprised a rather desultory discussion of a proposal to reinforce the French division at Nice with tanks and motorized artillery, while informing the Italians that the purpose was to assure them of French military support should they move to protect Austria's independence against the German threat. But General Georges, on Gamelin's instructions, took advantage of the occasion to read the Foreign Ministry a lecture, clearly intended as a reply to Flandin's criticisms:

> General Gamelin wishes the Quai d'Orsay to understand quite clearly that the present organization of our army is such that, without mobilization, we can occupy our defensive lines and repulse an attack, but any offensive action in an enemy country is impossible. Without mobilization we have a "static" army; to give it the dynamism necessary for an offensive, mobilization is essential. In 1914 our cavalry divisions were on a war footing and provided immediately the necessary security; we don't have them now. Divisional reconnaissance forces don't exist in peacetime. Requisitioning the transport and the arrival of reservists is necessary for their establishment.
>
> No offensive action in an enemy country can be undertaken before the twelfth day of mobilization.
>
> When the politicians speak of entering an enemy country without mobilization, they forget that we don't have the army for such a policy.

This was, of course, a bald reiteration of the same military limitations which had so exasperated Flandin, Paul-Boncour, and the other interventionists during the Rhineland crisis, and which largely accounted for the French Government's failure to take any military counteraction. Despite the catastrophic consequences, neither Gamelin nor Georges acknowledged the grievous sluggishness of their military machine, or suggested that corrective measures might be in order. The lessons of the Rhineland, so recently writ so large, were lost on them.

A week later the three service chiefs (Gamelin, Durand-Viel for the Navy, and Maurice Pujo for the Air Force) met for a general exchange of views. The preliminary elections of April 26 had already forecast the victory of the Popular Front in the second round scheduled for May 3, but under the French election laws the new government would not take office until June. What should be done if on May 3 the Germans, exploiting the interregnum, should stage a Nazi *Putsch* in Austria?

Gamelin woodenly prescribed the dispatch of a division to Italy, in accordance with his arrangements made with Badoglio prior to the Italo-Ethiopian War; Durand-Viel remarked that this could hardly be done as long as the League sanctions against Italy were in effect. Gamelin changed the subject, declaring that if Germany fortified the Rhineland, and if the Low Countries' neutrality were respected, France would be unable to invade Germany. Poland and Czechoslovakia would thus be laid open to a German attack.

What, then, was the answer? Harking back to the First World War, Gamelin proposed a large-scale landing in Salonika.* Admiral Durand-Viel, in a master-piece of understatement, observed that such a maneuver could hardly be impro-vised, and it was agreed that General Georges and Admiral Abrial would con-jointly pursue the project.

Apparently the plan died aborning, as indeed it should have. If the generals really believed that the Rhineland remilitarization would reduce them to such a desperate and costly scheme, assuredly they should have advised the Govern-ment that mobilization was a cheap price to pay to avert its necessity. The mere notion of sending a sufficiently large striking force by sea, past a possibly hostile Italy, in order to march clear across the Balkans to succor Poland or Czechoslovakia, was an eloquent demonstration of Gamelin's strategic bank-ruptcy.

It was a season of fantasy, recrimination, and dissension: Flandin accusing the generals of obstructionism, Gamelin deriding the politicians for naïveté while he daydreamed, and Abrial describing the Quai d'Orsay as a scene of "great uncertainty and even disarray." Reporting to Berlin early in April, the German chargé d'affaires, Dirk Forster, declared that:

> Never during all the time I have been living in Paris have I known a period when views on the international situation and on what France ought to do were as divergent and, in individuals, have changed so frequently. . . .
> It cannot yet be foreseen how the conflict of emotions will resolve itself . . . It is therefore more likely that France will for the time being continue to pursue her policy of semi-solutions and that the tense atmosphere will con-tinue.

In the spring of 1936, France's greatest need was for men capable of unifying and revitalizing the country, and after May 3 the immediate question was whether the new Popular Front government would be able to provide that lead-ership.

2

The Popular Front has been much blamed for the French débacle of 1940. No doubt it contributed to the downfall, but the question remains whether there is warrant for saddling it with the major responsibility, for it included men of in-contestable patriotism and competence, and its achievements were far from negligible.

Like most French governments, however, it was a coalition—though now of the "left"—and suffered from internal disputes. Furthermore, the elections reflected the increasing polarization of French politics, for the parties of the right held their strength, while the Communist and Socialist gains were at the expense of the center.

The Socialists emerged from the elections as the largest single party, and their

* French and British forces landed in Salonika (capital of Greek Macedonia) in October 1915, primarily in order to relieve their beleaguered Serbian allies. They remained through the war but made little progress until its final months, when, under General Franchet d'Esperey, they brought about the capitulation of Bulgaria.

leader, Léon Blum, formed the new government. The Communists (who had nearly doubled their popular vote and raised their representation in the Chamber of Deputies from ten to seventy-two) promised to support Blum but refused to participate in his government, which thus became a combination of Socialists and Radical Socialists, who (to paraphrase Metternich's famous critique of the Holy Roman Empire) were neither radical nor socialist. They were predominantly *petit bourgeois* and in many ways rather "conservative"; temperamentally they were closer to the center than the left. The Radicals had lost heavily in the elections but were still the second-largest single party, and their leaders included such famous figures as Edouard Herriot (who did not join the Blum cabinet), Camille Chautemps, and the Party leader, Edouard Daladier. Chautemps and Daladier were both former premiers, but Blum, though long a deputy and an expert parliamentarian, had never held cabinet office.

In forming his government, Blum assigned most of the important domestic positions to fellow-Socialists: Finance (Vincent Auriol) and Agriculture (Georges Monnet), as well as Interior and Economy. The Radicals were given the Quai d'Orsay (Yvon Delbos) as well as all three of the service ministries. Daladier was Vice Premier and Minister of National Defense as well as of the Army, while Alphonse Gasnier-Duparc took the Navy and Pierre Cot the Air Ministries. It is an open question whether an inversion of this division of labor between Socialists and Radicals would have been better; however that may be, the domination of foreign and military affairs by the Radicals did not have good results.

The incoming government was sore beset even before it took office. Contemporaneous with the elections there was a "flight from the franc" monetary crisis, and a wave of "sit-in" strikes at the Nieuport, Renault, Citroen, and many other factories, with which the holdover Sarraut government was powerless to cope. When Blum presented his cabinet to the deputies on June 6, there were about a million workers on strike, and France was approaching a state of chaos.

There can be no gainsaying the vigor and address with which Blum tackled these crises. On June 7 he and the organizational representatives of labor and management (the *Confédération Générale du Travail* and the *Confédération Générale de la Production Française*) signed the so-called "Matignon Agreement,"* under which the *C.G.P.F.* acknowledged the right of collective bargaining and agreed to a 7 to 15 per cent wage increase, while the *C.G.T.* agreed to urge the strikers to return to work as soon as their employers had accepted the agreement. The wave of strikes nevertheless continued for another ten days, but by late June the worst was over. Meanwhile the decline of the franc had been temporarily checked by Blum's promise not to devalue it, and to refrain from any "monetary *coup d'état*."

During the first few weeks of its existence, the Blum government proposed and put through Parliament a program of labor, financial, and other measures that the British and American press, with the early days of the Roosevelt administration freshly in mind, commonly referred to as France's "New Deal."

* The accord took its name from the Hôtel Matignon, where the Premier's office was located.

Laws safeguarding collective bargaining and requiring fifteen-day paid holidays were passed by both Houses almost unanimously, and the forty-hour-week law by two-to-one majorities. A Keynesian public works bill was approved (in the Senate only grudgingly) to diminish unemployment and increase purchasing power. The Bank of France, long ruled by the two hundred largest shareholders (unpopularly known as "the two hundred families") under statutes dating from Napoleonic times, was "democratized" by transferring effective control to the Government. In August, a law establishing procedures for the nationalization of arms manufacturing companies was approved, virtually without opposition.

But the Government's program was by no means limited to social measures. Léon Blum was a doctrinaire Marxist but no pacifist, and in later years was heard to voice regret that France had not waged "preventive war" when Germany started to rearm. To be sure, there was little rapport between the Popular Front and the French officer corps, but there is every evidence that Socialists and Radicals alike, hating and fearing Nazi Germany as they did, were earnestly desirous of bolstering the French military position.

Within the Blum cabinet, this determination was immediately reflected in Daladier's designation as Minister of National Defense—a new position*—as well as of the Army (*Guerre*). Daladier's return to cabinet office was accompanied by a presidential decree of June 6, 1936, charging him with the duty of "coordinating the actions of the three departments of War, Navy, and Air." His responsibilities were to include not only the combined employment of ground, naval, and air forces, but also "the planning and execution of armament programs, industrial mobilization, budgetary planning, and international arms conventions." The decree also created a "Permanent Committee of National Defense" (*Comité Permanent de la Défense Nationale,* or *C.P.D.N.*) under his presidency, to include the two other service ministers, the three chiefs of staff, and Pétain, who was designated by name.

On June 25, 1936, Gamelin submitted to Daladier a "Note" formulated by the War Council,† embodying an overview of France's military situation in the light of the Rhineland remilitarization. Taking account of German rearmament since 1933, and the answering French armament program of 1934, the note concluded that Germany had not yet achieved "marked superiority," and that a German attack in the west could be successfully opposed, *assuming* that France's British, Belgian, and eastern allies came to her support, that there was no threat from Italy such as to divide the French forces, and that France's current armament program was vigorously prosecuted. The Note warned, however, that the "equilibrium" could be shattered by accelerated German military growth, or by Italy's friendship turning into "uncertain neutrality, or hostility." It was vital, accordingly, to "maintain our military arrangements with Italy"—

---

* François Pietri had held this position in 1932 during the six-month government of André Tardieu, in which there was no Minister of War. Pétain held both the National Defense and the War titles during the six-day "government" of Fernand Bouisson in June 1935. These were the only precedents for the office.

† The *Conseil Supérieur de la Guerre,* comprising the marshals and the senior Army generals. The report was based on discussions at Council meetings on May 16 and June 4, 1936.

i.e., the Gamelin-Badoglio understandings—as well as to consolidate the Franco-Polish alliance, so as to immobilize on the eastern front a substantial part of the German forces.

On the day after transmission of this note, the new Permanent Committee of National Defense held its first meeting. Blum was present to inaugurate the body, and Daladier led off with a lengthy disquisition on the need for interservice co-ordination, pointing out that Germany, Italy, and Britain all had supraservice co-ordinating or command agencies, and touting the decree of June 6 as a means to that end. Blum then raised the second question on the agenda: whether or not to send war matériel to Czechoslovakia. Pétain at once took a negative stance, observing that all the landing fields in Czechoslovakia were targeted by the Germans and in case of war would be immediately destroyed. Daladier replied that France had already stocked 450,000 cartridges and more than 400 tons of bombs at Czech air bases, and that, in view of the Franco-Czech relationship, it would be difficult to hold back on military aid. Pierre Cot, the new Air Minister, strongly supported Daladier and proposed to send the Czechs sixteen heavy bombers, to be stationed at Brno in southern Moravia, where, he thought, there would be less danger of their destruction. The Czech "platform," he argued, offered the only means of attacking Berlin.

Cot, who had served briefly in 1933–34 as Air Minister in the Daladier, Chautemps, and Sarraut cabinets, then opened up a fundamental problem of French air power: Germany's superior industrial resources. The Luftwaffe was approaching a strength of 3,000 aircraft, he declared, and France would have difficulty in exceeding a third of that: "It is therefore necessary to pursue a policy of industrial collaboration with our friends, to wit Britain, the Soviet Union, and the Little Entente." Russia was of special importance since she alone had air bases and aircraft plants beyond the reach of German bombs, but she badly needed technical assistance, which France and Czechoslovakia ought to provide.

The discussion then turned to the question of interservice command and co-ordination, on which the attitudes and proposals differed little from those contemporaneously voiced in military circles of the other powers. Cot, declaring that the air arm was no longer supplementary but a major service, called for a unitary air command and opposed its "fractionalization" by allotting parts of it to the Army and Navy; the naval Chief of Staff, Admiral Durand-Viel, doubted that the independent Air Force could do much to help the Navy, and insisted that the Navy have its own aircraft for reconnaissance; Gamelin, too, wanted Army command of air reconnaissance. The interchange was contentious and inconclusive, and it ended only when Cot reminded the group that the immediate question was whether or not matériel should be sent to Czechoslovakia. This was finally approved.

During the ensuing summer of 1936, Gamelin and his Chief of Staff, General Colson, drafted an accelerated Army armament program for submission to Daladier. Gamelin's instructions to Colson—transmitted just *after* the German announcement of August 24 increasing the term of compulsory military service to two years—envisaged an increase in the career components of the Army, an increment of three infantry divisions, the formation of two tank divisions, and an increase in the number of motorized infantry divisions. Under these guidelines, Colson drew up a detailed schedule for the procurement of tanks, antitank guns, and new types of field artillery.

The recommendations were generally approved by the Cabinet on September 7, 1936. The premise of its action was that "demographic" factors made it impossible for France to match Germany in the size of the armed forces, and that it was therefore necessary "to put our efforts into the quality of personnel and equipment." To augment the career elements and provide the new weapons, 550 million francs were made immediately available, and an over-all budget of some 14 billion francs was approved for the four-year period 1937–1940.

Meanwhile Cot had been at work on an enlarged aircraft construction program. When he took office in June 1936, he found in effect the same "Plan I" which he himself had formulated in 1933 during his first term as Air Minister. "Plan I" contemplated a front-line strength of 1,000 aircraft and a ready reserve of 200 more, to be replaced by new planes every five years, and thus requiring an annual production of only 250 aircraft. In September, Cot secured Cabinet approval of his "Plan II," calling for a doubling of the Air Force within three years, by the construction of 2,400 new aircraft at an average pace of 800 per year.

These measures certainly laid the basis for a greatly improved French military position. The questions remained whether they would be vigorously and efficiently implemented, and whether, in view of the Wehrmacht's dizzy pace, even these steps might be too little and too late.

Problems of time likewise afflicted the diplomacy of the Popular Front. Blum and his Party colleagues took office imbued with traditional social-democrat antitotalitarianism and internationalism, and were strong supporters of general disarmament and collective security through the League of Nations. Laudable or not, these formulas were no longer particularly promising. Had the Popular Front been in power during the early thirties, it may be that disarmament would have made some headway, and if Blum instead of Laval had been Premier in 1935, perhaps the League sanctions against Italy would have turned the course of history. But by the summer of 1936, in the wake of Manchuria, Ethiopia, and the Rhineland, these ideas were badly frayed.

If at first Blum and the new Foreign Minister, Yvon Delbos, were insufficiently aware of the grievous state of French diplomacy, they soon were better informed. On June 30, Bargeton submitted a memorandum on "French security," assessing the value of France's Eastern European treaties. His analysis was devastating:

Among the five countries each having with France a treaty called an "alliance," there are few who consider themselves allied to one another. There is no need to mention the state of relations between the Soviet Union and Poland and between Poland and Czechoslovakia; the reciprocal suspicions of Poland and Rumania, born of the Polish-Russian hostility, which renders the Polish-Rumanian alliance fictive; the lack of any mutual assistance agreement among the states of the Little Entente, except as against Hungary; and the situation of Yugoslavia, hypnotized by fear of Italy and continuing to ignore the Soviet Union, to say nothing of other rivalries and disparities, less apparent but persistent.

These considerations lead one to think that—were there no other reasons to discard a "policy of alliances"—such a policy is not practicable, because it requires, above all, that in fact the participants are allied among themselves. The result of the present situation is not merely weakness. It also serves to focus on France every move made to disrupt the peace, since France constitutes—and how insufficiently—the only link among the countries which would be disposed to oppose such moves.

It was a succinct and frightening analysis of France's diplomatic weakness, omitting, however, one further and vitally important feature: the less France could count on her eastern allies, the greater was her dependence on the support of Britain. Whitehall's powerful influence on the Quai d'Orsay had already been exercised during the Rhineland crisis, with disastrous consequences for the French military and diplomatic posture. And before the Popular Front government was two weeks old, Britain's diplomatic dominance was again made manifest in connection with lifting the League sanctions against Italy.

Mussolini had proclaimed the annexation of Ethiopia and the birth of "Empire" on May 9, after the Popular Front electoral triumph but while the caretaker Sarraut cabinet was still in office. Sarraut, Flandin, and Paul-Boncour all agreed that it would be wise to waste no time in "liquidating" the Ethiopian affair by lifting the League sanctions and bringing Italy back into the European and, more particularly, the Locarno or even the Stresa circles. It was a move best accomplished in concert with Britain and, since the Popular Front government would be taking office early in June, Blum was preliminarily consulted. Despite his dedication to collective security, the Premier-to-be had no objection "in principle," but he was concerned lest the British, primarily responsible as they were for the sanctions, might resent any French initiative for their cancellation. Nevertheless, on May 23, Paul-Boncour (pinch-hitting for the ailing Flandin as Foreign Minister) directed the French Ambassador in London, Charles Corbin, to propose immediate consultations on the question.

The response was not encouraging. On June 3, Eden told Corbin that Britain could not possibly propose lifting the sanctions or join with France in such a move. A few days later, when Delbos took over the Quai d'Orsay, he assured Sir George Clerk (the British Ambassador in Paris) that "France would take no initiative on sanctions, and would join in whatever proposition the British government might advance." Delbos' reward for his deference was Neville Chamberlain's speech denouncing continued sanctions as "the very midsummer of madness," and the British Cabinet's decision on June 17, without prior notice to the French, authorizing Eden to propose at Geneva that the sanctions be abandoned. Eden, rather condescendingly, apologized to Corbin, but the fact remained that London had first repulsed Paris, and then done independently just what the French had proposed be done jointly. Once more France had lost the initiative to Britain, and all that Blum could now say was "Me too!"

Louis Barthou was the last French Foreign Minister who had pursued an independent foreign policy, but that was in 1934, before the worst of the bad things happened. By the summer of 1936, French diplomacy was, perhaps, mired beyond extrication. However that may be, the Popular Front government was not likely to work miracles in foreign affairs, as Blum was concentrating on domestic problems, while Daladier and Delbos brought more caution than imagination to their respective ministries.

Nor was the Blum government favored by fortune. Even as it took office, south of the Pyrenees events were shaping a course which was to rob the Popular Front of its *élan* and even of its self-respect, and in which, once again, France was soon swinging to a British rhythm.

3

When Premier José Giral's cry for help reached Blum on the morning of July 20, it was sympathetically received within the Popular Front government. The Spanish appeal was signed "fraternally yours" and plainly was addressed to Blum as a fellow-Socialist,* but the responsible Radical ministers—Delbos, Daladier, and Cot—joined willingly in formulating a program of military aid to the Madrid regime. In this there was nothing illegal, for any national government was entitled under international law to supply arms to another. Nor was it surprising, inasmuch as France and Spain were on friendly terms and their respective governments were politically compatible.

Well aware, however, of the ideological features of the Spanish revolt and their likely repercussions in France, Blum and his colleagues made no announcement of their decision to aid Madrid. But Giral's telegram had been sent *en clair* through the Spanish Embassy in Paris; the ambassador and most of the staff were strongly predisposed toward the rebels, and the military attaché, Major Antonio Barroso, soon divulged the tenor of the communications between Madrid and Paris to the French right-wing press.

Meanwhile, Blum, Delbos, and Léger had gone to London for the Anglo-Franco-Belgian conference of July 23, in which the three participants sought to salvage something from the wreckage of Locarno. Upon arrival at his hotel, Blum† was approached by the famous journalist André Géraud ("Pertinax"), who asked the Premier whether or not it was true that France would send arms to the Madrid government for use against the Franco rebels. When Blum replied affirmatively, Géraud commented that such a policy would be unfavorably

---

* The *Front Populaire* in France was matched by the *Frente Popular* in Spain.

† There are evidentiary discrepancies about the date of Blum's arrival in London. His own postwar testimony (July 1947) indicates that he had planned to go there with Delbos and Léger on July 22, and a memoir written in 1964 by Blum's erstwhile *chef de cabinet*, André Blumel, states that he did just that. Others, however, have written that Delbos, Léger, and Massigli of the Quai d'Orsay went to London on the twenty-second, and that Blum joined them there the following day. It is the fact that Blum was not present at the first session of the tripartite conference on July 23, but was there for the afternoon session. The American Ambassador, Jesse Isidor Straus, reported to Washington, on the basis of "a reliable press contact who obtained his information from a member of the Supreme War Council," that Blum went to London not to attend the tripartite meeting, but, as a result of a telephone call on July 22 from Corbin, to urge the premier to come in order to discuss the Spanish situation with Baldwin and Eden. This, of course, is in direct conflict with Blum's and Blumel's testimony, and is not borne out by the record of Blum's conversations in London.

viewed in London. The Spanish question was not raised during the tripartite conversations, but when Anthony Eden came to bid Blum good-bye, he put the same question that Géraud had asked and, getting the same answer, responded: "It's your affair, but I ask you one thing only: be prudent."

While Blum and his colleagues were in London, in France the ultraconservative *Echo de Paris* and other rightist newspapers had published full details of the Government's plan to aid the Spanish Republic, and right-wing journalists such as Henri de Kerillis were loud in their denunciations. Blum was warned by a telegram from the Quai d'Orsay that trouble was brewing in the Senate. Even so, he was stunned by the storm which these revelations had raised, the severity of which was immediately apparent upon his return to Paris.

Camille Chautemps, former Premier and presently Minister of State, was among those awaiting Blum on the morning of July 24, at Le Bourget. All wore grave faces and uttered ominous warnings, the burden of which was abundantly confirmed when Blum consulted other Radical leaders. Jules Jeanneney, President of the Senate, told Blum that no one could understand why France should risk war over Spain when she had just yielded over the Rhineland, and that it was generally believed that the British would give no support to any Spanish involvement. Edouard Herriot, grand old man of the Radical Party and presently President of the Chamber, beseeched Blum "not to get mixed up in there."* Meanwhile the Spanish Ambassador, Juan Francisco Cárdenas y Rodríguez de Rivas, and most of his staff had resigned their posts with ringing condemnations of the Republicans as Communists and murderers or worse, and Fernando de los Ríos arrived in Paris as a special emissary of the Madrid regime to obtain the armaments requested by Giral.

That same evening, July 24, Blum invited Ríos to his home for a meeting with Delbos, Auriol, Daladier, and Cot. The Spaniard soon sensed that the Foreign Minister had little stomach for the aid program, and after the meeting Cot sought him out to explain that Delbos was adamant in his opposition to using French pilots to fly military aircraft into Spain. Since there were very few qualified Spanish pilots, Cot suggested that the planes be turned over to them at Perpignan in southeastern France, from where it would be only a short flight to Spanish airfields.

But the following day the political clouds were even more threatening and that afternoon the Cabinet met to discuss the situation. Blum was still determined to assist the Madrid government, but by now it was apparent that the Radicals, with the exception of Cot, were all fearful of the consequences, both domestic and foreign, of French involvement. The immediate upshot was a rather untidy compromise. Publicly, it was announced that all export of war materials to Spain, whether by the French Government or French private industry, was banned, with the exception of unarmed aircraft furnished to the Spanish Government privately. The war materials in process of assemblage to fill the requests previously made by Madrid—comprising aircraft, bombs, artillery, and machine guns—would be delivered to the Mexican Government with the secret understanding that Mexico would deliver them to the Spanish Government.

* *"Ah, je t'en prie, mon petit, ne vas pas te fourrer là-dedans."*

So matters stood until July 30, when two Italian bomber aircraft crashed in French Morocco, en route to aid Franco. This evidence of Italian intervention on the rebel side encouraged Blum to tell the Senate Foreign Affairs Committee that, if Italy or Germany should openly aid Franco, the French Government would feel free to throw off the restraints it had been observing and take whatever steps the national interest might require.

The new situation disclosed by the appearance of Italian aircraft on the Franco side further complicated the already difficult problem confronting the Popular Front government. Militating against French aid to Madrid were London's disapproving attitude, fear that France might find herself fighting Italian (and, as soon became apparent, German) troops on Spanish soil, with great risk that the conflict would spread and escalate, and the deep antipathy of the French right and much of the center to the leftist Spanish regime. But German and Italian aid to the rebels also deepened the sense of obligation which the French Socialists and many Radicals felt to support Spanish Republicans against Spanish Fascists and monarchists. The Communists, like the extreme right, did their best to fan the flames which some feared might light a civil war.

Apart from the ideological factors, there were also important military considerations. The Rhineland episode had exposed the sorry state of French arms, and a heavy military involvement in Spain would drain resources which were already woefully inadequate. On the other hand, a dictatorial Spain overrun with Germans and Italians might seriously threaten both the lifeline between European and African France and Anglo-French naval control of the eastern Mediterranean.

Blum himself seems not to have been overborne by the British admonitions, but among the Radical ministers (except for Cot) and at the Quai d'Orsay they carried enormous weight. Léger, still distraught as a result of the Rhineland surrender and determined above all to maintain the entente with Britain, now came forward with a proposal which, he hoped, might keep the two powers on a common course and serve as a basis of compromise within the French Government. Delbos embraced the suggestion ardently, and so was born the policy which came to be known as "nonintervention."

The Delbos-Léger program was presented at a Cabinet meeting on August 1—the second called to consider the Spanish situation. It was a stormy affair* and was inconclusive in that the Cabinet decided to ride off in two directions at once. The Quai d'Orsay plan was embodied in a telegram from Delbos to the French diplomatic representatives in London and Rome, instructing them to approach the British and Italian governments with a proposal for "the adoption of common rules of non-intervention," to be extended as rapidly as possible to additional countries. The pro-Madrid view, for which Pierre Cot had emerged as the most militant spokesman, was recognized in the withdrawal (temporary, as it proved) of the June 25 Cabinet order banning the shipment of arms to Spain.

---

* According to Jean Zay, then a junior minister, the strongest proponents of aid to Madrid were Auriol and Maurice Violette, a Minister of State. Characteristically, Daladier sided with the noninterventionists, but with much grumbling and condemnation of the policy as *néfaste*.

Cot promptly effectuated the dispatch of some fifty-five aircraft, including fifteen fighter planes,* to the Spanish Republicans.

The difficulty with these two policies, as the British soon pointed out, was that the one tended to weaken the other: if France were to take the lead in sponsoring international nonintervention, it was necessary to set a good example. Blum, however, had not lost hope of swinging the British toward a more benevolent view of the Madrid regime. Surmising that London might be more receptive to military than ideological arguments, he took advantage of a visit from a Labour member of Parliament, Philip Noel-Baker, to hold forth on the dangers which a Franco victory, achieved with Italian and German support, might portend for both French and British interests in the eastern Mediterranean. Noel-Baker pointed out that in England Parliament and Cabinet alike were on holiday, and that the only person who might be able to convoke an emergency cabinet meeting was the permanent secretary, Sir Maurice Hankey, who might be approached through the Admiralty.

Thus prompted, Blum took the unusual step of sending the Naval Chief of Staff, Admiral Jean François Darlan, to London to meet with his opposite number, Admiral Lord Chatfield, and thereafter, it was hoped, with Hankey. Darlan was selected because Blum and Cot had found a measure of support for their anti-Franco views in the Ministry of Marine, and it was thought that Darlan could deal with Chatfield on a "sailor-to-sailor" basis. But when the two admirals met on August 5, Chatfield, though formally courteous, was frigidly unresponsive to Darlan's concern over the consequences of a Franco victory, and wholly unco-operative about arranging a meeting with Hankey. The Darlan "mission" was a total failure, and the rebuff increased Blum's feeling of uncomfortable isolation in the European community, where only Soviet Russia and Czechoslovakia were openly supportive of Madrid.

Meanwhile Delbos had launched his nonintervention plan in all the major European capitals. The British Government, whose attitude had greatly stimulated the French initiative,† of course approved and supported Delbos' efforts. But of the other powers who really mattered, the Germans and Russians indicated agreement only "in principle," the Italians made dilatory and argumentative responses, and the Portuguese demanded international guarantees against "communist" attack as the price of adhesion. Then, on August 7, Sir George Clerk admonished Delbos *sans ambages* (bluntly) that French deliveries of arms to Madrid might "compromise the whole thing."

Such was the situation on August 8, when the Cabinet met for the third and decisive review of the Spanish problem. By this time the participants were well aware that German as well as Italian aid was going to the rebels, and Cot, with some support from Gasnier-Duparc, argued strongly for continuing the flow of

---

* The other aircraft comprised thirty reconnaissance and ten transport planes. Cot subsequently wrote (in *Le Procès de la république*, II, p. 315) that Daladier sent other war matériel at the same time; I have been unable to find any record of what, other than the fifty-five planes, was furnished.

† According to Alexander Werth (in *France and Munich*, p. 98), "a witty Labour M.P." remarked of nonintervention that "the mother of this monster was French, but its father British."

French matériel to the Republicans. But he failed to carry the day because, according to his own assessment, the majority feared to antagonize London or face the internal political warfare which open and systematic military aid to Madrid and its *Frente Popular* would precipitate. So, on the announced basis that the response to France's nonintervention proposal had been "encouraging," the July 25 ban on military exports to Spain was reinstated, and the flow of matériel stopped over the bitter protests of the Republic's new Ambassador in Paris, Alvaro de Albornoz. "Nonintervention" was reaffirmed as France's basic policy toward Spain,* and Delbos continued his efforts to bring the Italians and other stragglers into line.

In a formal sense he was successful, and a month later the "International Committee for the Supervision of the Measures for Non-Intervention in Spain" held its first meeting. But it met not in Paris, where the idea originated, but in London, at the Foreign Office, and under British chairmanship—or, perhaps one should say, one-upmanship.

Meanwhile the Popular Front leaders, hands tied by their sponsorship of nonintervention, had to grind their teeth and watch helplessly as German and Italian aid poured into Franco Spain. Soon Blum was confronted with serious disaffection in the ranks of his followers. Cries of *"Des avions pour l'Espagne!"* and *"Blum à l'action"* drowned out the speakers at Popular Front rallies, and on September 3, the famed revolutionary heroine Dolores Ibarruri, better known as "La Pasionaria,"† galvanized a large audience of workers at the Vélodrome in Paris.

Thus it transpired that fellow-Marxists Léon Blum and Joseph Stalin found themselves in converse postures. The Georgian tyrant, inward-focused and fearful of foreign ventures, was pushed reluctantly into supporting the Spanish Republicans by pressures from the rank and file of the international party which he headed. The French humanitarian, idealistic and eager to aid his Spanish ideological comrades, withstood both his natural inclinations and the demands of his followers for fear of fomenting internal dissension and alienating his country's primary ally.

At least Blum confronted his dilemma more bravely than did Stalin. Three days after La Pasionaria's sensational appeal, Blum made an unscheduled appearance before a mass meeting at the Luna Park organized by the militant Socialist Federation of the Seine Department, in order to explain himself to his disgruntled followers. Did they not realize that he knew and shared their feelings? Did they really think that three months in office had so changed him? If he had done as he had done, it was because he thought it necessary. To be sure, international law permitted France to send arms to Madrid, but it also allowed other countries to recognize the Burgos government and furnish Franco with

---

* There was interesting and little-noted precedent for internationally agreed nonintervention in Spain (described in Watters, *An International Affair* (1937), pp. 13–26). In 1873, during the so-called "Carlist" war in Spain, a mutual policy of "noninterference" in Spain's domestic embroilments was informally agreed among the governments of Britain, France, and Germany.

† It was a fitting irony that La Pasionaria had picked up Pétain's famous *"Ils ne passeront pas!"* of Verdun, and turned it into the *"No pasarán!"* of Madrid.

weapons. France could not possibly do as much for the Republicans as the dictator governments could do for the rebels. The international nonintervention agreement was accordingly not only a peaceful solution, but also one which, in the long run, would work to the benefit of Madrid.

It was a courageous and skillful performance and, no doubt, a sincere one as well. Blum had come to believe in nonintervention. The flaw in his reasoning was, however, the same one which afflicted Chamberlain's appeasement analysis, for both were based on the erroneous belief that, if Britain and France set a good example, Germany and Italy would behave like gentlemen. If the Axis countries had respected the nonintervention convention, things might indeed have worked out as Blum predicted.

But before many weeks had passed, nonintervention was exposed for the cruel mockery that it was. Blum was increasingly oppressed and, from time to time, nearly overcome with chagrin and anguish. He never flagged in his overt dedication to the nonintervention principle, but, as the full measure of German and Italian aid to Franco became apparent, his government quietly adopted a policy which he called "relaxed nonintervention":

> . . . that is to say, we voluntarily and systematically closed our eyes to contraband and even, after a time, we practically organized it . . .
>
> One of the highest administrative officials at that time, who had previously been connected with the customs service, was the chief organizer of this contraband traffic which, for about a year and a half, was extremely active . . .

Two of the Popular Front ministers have given additional information on the nature of "relaxed intervention." Vincent Auriol, the Finance Minister, later wrote that he aided Madrid "by facilitating the transit of arms that were being sent from Mexico, Russia, and other countries." On the air side, Cot's account is more detailed in stating that, during 1937, France sent to Spain some 130 aircraft, of which two thirds were warplanes. This was accomplished chiefly by private sales to Finland, Brazil, and other countries who were actually routing the planes to Republican Spain. In addition, Cot allowed foreign aircraft en route to the Republicans to land and refuel in France, and made French air training schools available to Republican pupils and instructors.

Cot wrote this description during 1943 or 1944, just after he had been under attack at the Vichy Government's Riom trial for having weakened the French Air Force by sending French aircraft to Spain. His reply was that the planes sent to Spain in 1936 and 1937 "had long since been outmoded" before the outbreak of the Second World War; only three of the aircraft sent to Spain were built as late as 1936. But, of course, in defending himself against the Riom accusation, Cot was likewise acknowledging the inadequacy of what was sent to Spain. While France was sending obsolescent Potez and Dewoitine machines to the Republicans, on the other side Goering's men were trying out the latest German Messerschmitt 109's, Heinkel 111's, Dornier 17's, and Ju 87 Stukas, which were to be staple aircraft of the Luftwaffe in Poland and France and over Britain.

The contrast highlights the halfhearted, ambivalent quality of Blum's policy toward Spain. The aid sent was not enough to put the Republican forces on a parity with the Nationalists, but it was more than enough to arouse violent protests from the right and force the Popular Front leaders into implausible and embarrassing prevarications. Furthermore, clandestine help to Madrid did nothing to allay the exasperation and frustration of the left, and as time passed the utterly ignoble and farcical character of "nonintervention" sapped the morale and vigor of the Popular Front and eroded Blum's stature as a moral and intellectual leader.

4

France's troubles south of the border were coincidental with others across her northern frontier. Belgium, since 1920 bound to France by a military agreement, and one of the five Locarno guarantor powers, was moving toward a neutral status which might greatly complicate or even compromise France's strategic situation vis-à-vis Germany.

The causes of this change of heart were various. In large part, it was a consequence of France's uncertain handling of the Rhineland crisis, and of Catholic dislike for the Franco-Soviet alliance. These factors were, no doubt, aggravated by Belgium's increasing affliction with friction between the Flemish in the northern and the French-speaking Walloons in the southern provinces. The *Flamands* were congenitally opposed to the Government's ties with France and favored a closer relation with the Netherlands.

Little more than a month after the Rhineland remilitarization there were strong indications of a basic shift in Belgium's foreign policy. On April 14, Mr. Dave Morris, the American Ambassador in Brussels, reported to Washington that the Belgian Prime Minister's *chef de cabinet,* Viscount de Lantsheere, had stated:

> Public opinion in Belgium is coming more and more to demand that Belgium's position as a guarantor . . . shall be strictly limited to League obligations . . . the Belgian Government will probably endeavor in concluding any new pact to limit its obligations as a guarantor to agreements to defend its own territory. Belgium does not want to be a guarantor for France. Belgium has no alliances with Eastern European countries . . . and does not wish to be drawn into struggles originating in Eastern Europe, or in fact in Western Europe either if it can possibly keep out of them.

Two weeks later these sentiments were reflected in a speech by the Belgian Foreign Minister, Paul Henri Spaak, which called for "an immense military effort and a policy of independence" as the only way to regain the security lost by the Rhineland remilitarization. On May 1, Ambassador Morris informed the State Department that Belgium was leaning away from France and toward Britain, and that pressure to end the Franco-Belgian military alliance, previously emanating mostly from "Flemish extremists," was now supplemented by a more general belief that "it was not safe to put too much dependence on French aid."

The Quai d'Orsay does not appear to have been made aware of the strength of this trend until July 9, 1936, when Ambassador Jules Laroche reported to Delbos that a high official of the Belgian Foreign Ministry favored limiting any new treaty replacing Locarno in such a way that Belgium's independence and territorial integrity would be guaranteed by the signatory powers, but that Belgium would not undertake the responsibilities of a guarantor. Laroche added that this proposal was to be taken seriously, "as it corresponds to the mentality of the Flemish majority."

Laroche had correctly gauged the indicators, for two weeks later Mr. Spaak took occasion at a dinner for the foreign press correspondents to announce that his country would now follow a policy of "realism," and "cooperate for peace without undertaking commitments that exceeded Belgium's capacity." And then later in September, at Geneva, Spaak confronted Delbos with a definite proposal that Belgium should be relieved of its affirmative treaty obligation and become a neutral guaranteed country.

On October 14, 1936, in an address to his ministers in council, Leopold III stamped the royal seal on the new policy, which was to be "exclusively and integrally Belgian." No matter how swift the aid from an ally, it could not come until after Belgium had sustained the brutal shock of the aggressor's attack. Belgium must therefore arm herself, as Holland and Switzerland were doing, so as to discourage any invasion. She must also eschew any unilateral alliance, and that meant that no country should plan to use Belgian territory as the base for an attack against another. Remilitarization of the Rhineland, the King declared, "has put us in much the same position that we occupied before the War"— meaning that France could no longer protect Belgium against being overrun by Germany any better than she did in 1914.

There ensued some months of diplomatic exchange, oral and written, between Brussels and Paris. The Belgian move was most unwelcome to the French. A neutral Belgium meant that, in the event of war between France and Germany, Belgium need not participate unless invaded by one of the belligerents and, since in fact there was no likelihood of attack except by Germany, Belgian "neutrality" was a one-way street from Germany into France. The Maginot Line had not been extended beyond the Luxembourg border precisely because of the Pétain doctrine that northern France could best be defended in Belgium. Aerial attacks against the Ruhr from both Britain and France would be gravely hampered if Allied planes could not overfly Belgium. Furthermore, if and when the Allies thought their ground forces capable of mounting a large-scale offensive, it was Belgium that was thought to offer the most promising base for invading Germany.

These considerations, to be sure, applied only to a Franco-German war in which Belgium was not invaded. But Belgian "neutrality" might also and disastrously affect France's ability to come to Belgium's aid if the Germans should again choose that avenue of attack. For a joint Franco-Belgian defense of Belgium would require the closest and most trusting collaboration in defense planning, and constant contact between the French and Belgian general staffs—a course of conduct wholly appropriate between allies, but much less compatible with the role of a truly neutral Belgium. Such staff discussions had in fact been held both recently and for many years past. On May 15, 1936, the Belgian Army Chief of Staff, General E. M. van der Bergen, had come to Paris for detailed studies with Gamelin and the French air and naval chiefs. On July 18 Gamelin's deputy, General Schweisguth, had returned the visit and been given a tour of Belgium's newly planned fortification sites. As the French viewed it, military common sense demanded the continuation of these consultations if France was to remain in a position to give effective aid to the Belgians.

During the fall of 1936 and the ensuing winter, the French pressed these arguments through both diplomatic and military channels. Gamelin summoned the Belgian military attaché and pointed out:

> . . . the Germans could readily mount a surprise attack and that, in such a case, if the Belgian general staff had not called upon us preventively, we would be unable to support a defense of the Albert Canal, Liège, and the Luxembourg frontier.

The Belgians were not without answers to these arguments. Initially, they pointed out that the new policy comtemplated a large rearmament program, including modernization of the fortifications near the German border; these, they said, would relieve the French of necessity of themselves taking over part of the Belgian border defenses. However, this point could not conceal the obvious fact that Belgian rearmament plus alliance was better for the joint defense than rearmament with neutrality. In an effort to reconcile the French to the less desirable alternative, the Belgian Premier, Paul van Zeeland, came to Paris during the winter of 1936–37 for secret conversations with Blum, Chautemps, and Delbos. A few weeks later the talks were continued, with Spaak also present, at Zeeland's home in Brussels. It became apparent that the Belgians wished to explain their policy privately and personally rather than publicly or officially. Essentially, their point was that Belgian rearmament depended on the passage of a "military law" and the furnishing of credits by the Belgian Parliament and that, given the domestic political situation, neither law nor credits would be voted unless the military alliance with France were terminated.

It was a bitter pill for the French; Blum subsequently described his deep chagrin at "this new symptom of a progressive dismantling of all our European positions." But he and his colleagues had little leverage, especially since the British appeared to be undisturbed by the new Belgian attitude. The best he could do was to inform Zeeland and Spaak that France would now have to look to her own defenses along her Belgian frontier, and that the degree of aid which France would in future be able to give Belgium would depend on the extent of the Belgians' own rearmament effort and continued close relations between the two countries' general staffs.

The Belgian Government showed no sign of altering the position it had taken, and on March 19, 1937, Delbos submitted to the British a memorandum which, in substance, acknowledged that it would be best to adjust to the new circumstances and release Belgium from her guarantor obligations, while continuing to insist on general staff contacts. So it was agreed, and on April 24, Britain and France published a "declaration" addressed to the Belgian Government. Taking account of Belgium's assurance that she would defend her territory against any aggression, the two signatories acknowledged her release from all obligations to them under Locarno or subsequent agreements, and reaffirmed their own toward her. This was coupled with a "verbal communication" from the French Government pointing out that the "promptness and efficacy" of French assistance would depend upon the necessary prior "technical conversations"—a euphemism for general staff discussions.

In October 1936, immediately after King Leopold's address, General van der Bergen had assured the French military attaché, General Reidinger, that "the Belgian general staff would continue to concert with" its French colleagues and was counting on the support of French troops. But before the end of the month there was a disturbing report from Reidinger that the King had ordered that munitions stored in southern Belgium be removed to the north, apparently with the notion of preparing a "national redoubt" based on Antwerp—a plan which obviously contemplated, in the event of a German attack, a Belgian withdrawal *away from* instead of toward the French forces. A few weeks later Reidinger was complaining that Premier van Zeeland's aim was entirely focused on keeping Belgium out of any conflict between France and Germany, and that he showed no understanding of the need for preparing a joint Franco-Belgian strategy in case Belgium was invaded.*

Meanwhile, general staff contacts were in fact suspended. In January 1937, the Belgian military chiefs declined invitations to the annual banquet of French reserve officers resident in Belgium, an affair which it had been their custom to attend. Then, on February 15, came an outright rebuff. Cot had directed the French air attaché in Brussels, Colonel Hébrard, to ask the Belgian air staff for information on the results obtained from experiments with grenades dropped in low level flight. The Belgian air chief, General Duvivier, categorically refused the request, on the basis of a general staff order "forbidding the passing of confidential information to any foreign military person, regardless of nationality."

After the Anglo-French declaration of April 24, the staff situation was somewhat eased. Publicly, Mr. Spaak announced that the declaration "had brought to an end the period that we might call 'the hour of military accords,' and I am pleased with that result." Privately, however, he told Laroche that general staff contacts could be resumed, but "with the greatest prudence and in absolute secrecy."

And that was the footing on which the matter was left. From the French standpoint, secret contacts were certainly better than none at all, but the general strategic position was gravely impaired. Plainly, the loyalty of their former ally had been much diminished by the *flamand-wallon* schism, and King Leopold and his entourage were giving ear to the anti-French sentiments of the *Flamands*. Consequently, it was virtually certain that, if France should come to blows with Germany over Czechoslovakia, Belgium would remain neutral, as indeed she did when war came in 1939. Since the likelihood was that neither France nor Britain would disregard Belgian neutrality, this gave the Germans virtual assurance of a peaceful frontier from Luxembourg to the North Sea—a

---

* Reidinger's information was based on the report of a conversation between Zeeland and the American naval attaché in Brussels, Lieutenant Commander J. A. Gade.

glacis comprising Belgium and the Netherlands, protecting the Ruhr against attack on the ground or from the air.* It likewise meant that any French attack must come south of Luxembourg, on the frontiers which would in due time be protected by the West Wall. And finally, it meant that if Germany should decide to attack by way of Belgium, and made preparations with adequate secrecy, the Wehrmacht would initially confront only Belgian forces.

The ominous significance of the Belgian shift was not lost on France's eastern allies. Indeed, the Polish Ambassador in Paris, Juliusz Lukasiewicz, went so far as to tell Bullitt that it was the consensus within the Polish foreign service that Belgian neutrality had made the Franco-Polish alliance "virtually useless."

5

So France refused the aid so desperately needed by her friendly neighbor across the Pyrenees, and her former ally in the north declined the help that France was so eager to give. Nor was the outlook any more favorable on the Alpine frontier in the southeast, for Mussolini was unmoved by Blum's initial propitiatory gestures, and now Spain was widening the gulf between Paris and Rome, while strengthening the Rome-Berlin Axis. "So collapsed the plans for close collaboration with the Belgians and the Italians, which I had so carefully nurtured in 1935," wrote Gamelin in retrospect. "Henceforth both our flanks were threatened, and our prospects for an eventual offensive were gravely compromised." A more comprehensive analysis of France's diplomatic *débacle* was presented to his superiors in August of 1936 by the new German Ambassador in Paris, Count von Welczeck:

> During the past two months he [Blum] has suffered a series of disappointments and failures. . . . With regard to Italy, the French concessions . . . have obviously not achieved the desired result. Italy has not only not offered any *quid pro quo* but instead, in the French view, she is working in ever closer collaboration with Germany. The reestablishment of relations of alliance with Poland, which was so systematically stressed by the Government, has not been realized either. . . . The efforts to restore and increase French prestige among her allies in Central Europe and the Balkans have been grievously frustrated by the conclusion of the German-Austrian Agreement.† . . . The position of Czechoslovakia, in particular, is regarded with increasing uneasiness. . . . Above all, however, the precipitate developments in Spain have confronted the Blum Government with extremely difficult problems which are scarcely capable of a solution satisfactory to them . . .

While the Blum government was suffering these diplomatic shocks, their domestic program was also coming apart at the seams. The strikes aggravated conservative distrust of a Socialist government and, despite Blum's reassurances and his government's promise not to devalue the franc, the flow of capital abroad

---

* In order to make the Belgian neutrality cheese more binding, on October 14, 1937, the German Government issued a unilateral "declaration" engaging itself to respect Belgium's territorial integrity, and to give aid to Belgium in the event that she was attacked by some other power.

† The reference is to the agreement signed by Schuschnigg and Papen on July 11, 1936.

continued unchecked, and the index of industrial production declined steadily. By September 1936 the gold reserves in the Bank of France had fallen from 66 to 50 billion francs, and devaluation could no longer be staved off. At the end of the month, in agreement with the American and British governments, the franc was "realigned" at about 30 per cent of its former gold value.

The immediate results were helpful, and for the next six months industrial production rose substantially. But the primary purpose of the devaluation—to reverse the flow of capital—was not achieved. In order to curb speculative profits, "returning" capital in gold or foreign currency could be exchanged for francs only at the old rate, so that there was no profit incentive. Furthermore, the forty-hour-week law, now being put into effect on a broad basis, accelerated rising prices and diminished production. The new military program, adopted in September in response to the German announcement of the two years' military service requirement, was an additional strain, and in February of 1937, Blum was obliged to announce a governmental "pause," with postponement of salary increases and the public works program.

Meanwhile the Spanish Civil War was continuing to work its poison throughout the Socialist and Communist left wing of the Popular Front. The fraudulence of "nonintervention" became ever more blatant, and in December 1936, Blum was obliged to acknowledge, in a speech in the Chamber, that "some of our hopes and expectations have been, in effect, betrayed." He nevertheless continued to defend his policy on the ground that nonintervention, however imperfect, was the best safeguard of European peace, and he had no difficulty in winning Parliament's approval. But the policy was costing him dear, not only in outright disaffection on the left, but in sapping the morale of the entire Popular Front; as D. W. Brogan put it: "For the *Front Populaire,* the Spanish war was the Spanish ulcer."

Foreign and domestic trouble alike deepened the suspicions and exacerbated the hatred of Blum and his leftist supporters which was so pervasive among the parties and interests of the right—the grouping sometimes called the *Front National.* France was dangerously polarized. Blum's Jewishness fanned anti-Semitism, and even some Jews denounced him as a bad Jew, bad for France. Ugly episodes such as the Salengro suicide in November 1936 and the Clichy riot in March 1937 cast a pall over the regime.*

---

* Roger Salengro, the Socialist Minister of the Interior, was charged by the right-wing press with having been a deserter during the First World War. Despite proof, confirmed by Gamelin, that Salengro had been acquitted of the charge, the press campaign continued. On November 17, 1936, in a fit of depression, he committed suicide; the right promptly labeled this a confession of guilt.

Much of the rightist opposition to Salengro stemmed from his approval of the decree of June 18, 1936, abolishing the "Fascist leagues," including François de la Rocque's *Croix de Feu.* This organization was promptly reorganized as a political party—the *Parti Social Français.* In the evening of March 16, 1937, the *P.S.F.* held a meeting in the suburb of Clichy, which provoked a counterdemonstration by Popular Front workers. A riot resulted, in the course of which there was a clash between the workers and the police. Six workers were killed and many were injured, including Blum's *chef de cabinet,* André Blumel, who had gone there to assist in restoring order. Blum himself later appeared at Clichy in dress clothes and top hat (he had been at the Opéra), cutting a figure which many thought ridiculous.

What with Spain, Clichy, and the "pause," Blum was rapidly losing strength on the left. On the right he was faring even worse. The pause did nothing to mollify conservative financial circles, and his political opponents viewed it as a sign of weakening and retreat, which indeed it was. Faced with a downward turn in industrial production and continued weakness in the franc, Blum was turning toward the right. On March 5, 1937, the Cabinet approved a series of deflationary measures including a cutback on government spending and the appointment of a conservative and financially orthodox committee of financial advisers. There were new howls of protest from the left, and the right, smelling victory, did nothing to ease Blum's plight.

Nothing seemed to work. In June the flight of capital resumed; on the fourteenth two of the financial "wise men" resigned. Charging that the country's financial troubles were largely caused by "political intrigue and financial speculation," Blum went to Parliament demanding a law giving the Government emergency powers "to assure financial stabilization and economic development." The Chamber approved it by a comfortable majority, but the Senate balked, and Blum, unwilling to precipitate a constitutional crisis or dissolve Parliament, submitted his government's resignation on June 21, 1937.

Thus Blum's year of power, on which he had embarked with such high hopes, ended in failure at home and abroad. His was the last prewar effort to reunify and reinvigorate France by restructuring the body politic. The task was too much for him, and perhaps for anyone else, given the troubles inherited from his predecessors and the march of events beyond the borders. As Nicholas Paxton has remarked, there was "simply no basis for a national defense coalition" in the France of 1936. The *union sacrée* of 1914 could not be repeated, for the right feared Bolshevism more than Hitler, and the left was traditionally pacifist.

Yet perhaps a more adventurous, or even a more brutal, man might have done better. Blum was highly intelligent and personally courageous, but with his high, rather girlish voice and mincing manners (Bullitt described to Roosevelt the Premier's "little fluttery gestures of the hyper-intellectual queer ones") he did not give the impression of personal strength. He was too ideological and principled to resort to political expediency for his own ends, and his hatred of violence and anxiety to avoid crises led him to compromises on Spain and domestic social issues which took the heart out of the Popular Front and eventually destroyed his own capacity for leadership.

6

Léon Blum stepped down but not out, and the Popular Front, with Camille Chautemps as Premier, stayed on at least in name. Indeed, the alliance of Socialists and Radicals was still the only possible base for a government that the Parliament elected in 1936 would support. Blum himself remained in the Cabinet as Vice-Premier; in effect he simply changed places with Chautemps. Delbos stayed at the Quai d'Orsay and Daladier at the War Ministry, and, with one notable exception, the new Cabinet looked much like the old one.

The exception involved the return to Paris of a man who would become one of the two principal French figures of the Munich period. Georges Bonnet, at the right end of the Radical Party spectrum, had been sharply critical of Blum and Auriol when the franc was devalued, and for his pains had been sent to Washington as ambassador. But he had been Finance Minister in Chautemps' short-lived cabinets in the early thirties, and now the new Premier called him back to serve both as Minister of Finance and of National Economy, replacing Auriol and another Socialist, Charles Spinasse.*

Chautemps and Bonnet were much more acceptable to the Senate and the bankers than their predecessors, and were promptly given the emergency powers which had been denied to Blum and Auriol. Bonnet at once embarked on a policy of financial retrenchment; the franc was again devalued, taxes were raised, and government spending was reduced. These measures were more effective in restoring financial stability than in stimulating industrial production, and the benefits were correspondingly temporary, but the French economy puttered along without new crises until the end of 1937.

It was a government of drift. In sharp contrast to the ardent, idealistic Blum, Chautemps was the political "trimmer" par excellence. Suave and courteous, he was adept at compromise, nonideological, and virtually devoid of long-range goals.† Since he was not a Socialist and felt no affinity for the Spanish Republicans, he suffered none of the pangs of conscience that so preyed on Blum. As Delbos and Léger at the Quai d'Orsay were the principal architects of "nonintervention," the Chautemps government as a whole was much less concerned than its predecessors at the prospects of a Franco victory. Indeed, late in August of 1937, Delbos went so far as to tell Bullitt that he "did not care in the least whether Franco should win or not . . . provided he should ship out of Spain the Italian and German forces now there." Two months later Bullitt reported that Chautemps, in private conversation, had echoed these sentiments.

But if Chautemps and Delbos were at one in their indifference to the internal Spanish outcome, they were in sharp disagreement about how to get rid of the Axis intervenors, especially the Italians. Chautemps, following the British lead, sought a *rapprochement* with Italy, while Delbos thought this impossible and favored a strong line. The Premier once described himself to Bullitt as "the only pro-Italian member of his Government"; Delbos was equally frank with Bullitt in revealing that "he loathed Mussolini intensely and believed that Chautemps' attempts to reach reconciliation with Italy would be interpreted by Mussolini as a sign of weakness."

It seemed to make no difference which of these contradictory policies was foremost at any particular moment, for Mussolini was not to be cajoled, and the British would join in nothing that he might take as a threat. Certainly the Duce made it all but impossible for the French to make a friendly move; in Au-

---

* Auriol was transferred to the Ministry of Justice, while Spinasse was dropped from the Cabinet.

† Why did President Albert Lebrun call on Chautemps to form a government instead of Daladier, who was the leader of and strongest figure in the Radical Party? According to Georges Lefranc (*Histoire du Front Populaire*, p. 256), the choice was decisively influenced by Blum, who preferred the affable Chautemps to the mordant, saturnine Daladier, and who also thought that Daladier would be less acceptable to the left wing of the Popular Front.

gust 1937 he made an open mockery of nonintervention by publicly celebrating the victory of Italian forces at Santander, while simultaneously he aroused French anxiety for the security of their African empire by sending five divisions to Libya. When the Quai d'Orsay sought to replace the French Ambassador in Rome, Mussolini insisted that the new one be accredited to Victor Emmanuel as both King of Italy and Emperor of Ethiopia, and when the French refused he withdrew the Italian Ambassador from Paris, leaving the representation of both countries in each other's capitals to chargés d'affaires. Then on December 11 he pulled Italy out of the League of Nations

Mussolini thumbed his nose at the French, while the British put them in leading strings. The French Navy's worries about the Italo-German threat to French communications with North Africa were sincere and not dispelled by the repulse which Darlan had suffered at Chatfield's hands in August 1936. Two months later the French naval staff prepared a careful analysis of the situation in the Mediterranean, and the necessity of Anglo-French naval co-operation. They submitted it to the British naval attaché, Captain Hammill, but the response from the British Admiralty was that "they will do nothing without orders from their government." The French recommendations were simply ignored. Then, in September 1937, Delbos and Massigli came up with the idea of a joint Anglo-French occupation of Minorca to counterbalance the Italian military presence in Majorca. Eden replied that British public opinion would not tolerate such a step.

The French then proposed less drastic measures: an Anglo-French naval concentration off the principal port, Mahón, of Minorca; reopening the Franco-Spanish frontier to the passage of arms for the Republican government; denunciation of the Non-Intervention Agreement on the ground that it was being systematically violated by the Axis powers. Eden listened courteously, raised objections, and the British Cabinet disapproved all the French proposals. The English, concerned above all to avoid any step which might increase the danger of war, rejected any measure which embodied an element of threat or open accusation against Germany or Italy. The French were equally reluctant to do anything that might suggest a rift between themselves and the British, and the result was to perpetuate and underline the Quai d'Orsay's subjection to Whitehall. Even Chautemps, who certainly was no mover or shaker, complained to Bullitt that London was "counting on the readiness of France to support England at all points," and that consequently France "had no control over the course of events."

Given this unbroken succession of setbacks on their Belgian, Italian, and Spanish borders, it is not surprising that from time to time the French leaders indulged the hope of a *rapprochement* with the country that was the source of all their fears. Even Léon Blum, despite his deep hatred of Nazism, entertained the idea, and when Hjalmar Schacht came to Paris in August 1936, hoping to persuade the French Government to co-operate in giving Germany access to overseas raw material sources, Blum took the opportunity to discuss the possibility of a general détente. On this occasion Schacht was more amiable than ordinarily, and the conversation was not altogether unpromising. But the diplomatic follow-through came to nothing, and when Blum and Schacht met again in May 1937, the banker was his usual stiff-necked self. They parted on a sour note, and the Premier told Bullitt that Schacht "was definitely less conciliatory than he had been in a previous visit to Paris and he expected no constructive results whatsoever."

Other German dignitaries visiting Paris were less abrasive. In June 1937, General Ludwig Beck, a perfect gentleman, came to view the World's Fair and commune with Gamelin on the inevitable Bolshevization of Europe should France and Germany be stupid enough to go to war. Two months later came Goering's deputy General Milch, not renowned for affability, and General Ernst Udet, the great airman who could charm any bird off any tree. Cot had pleasant talks with both, and Udet was decorated at Rheims.

Appeasement in London strongly favored *apaisement* in Paris.* But in the latter capital, the leading diplomatic exponent of Franco-German *rapprochement* was the American Ambassador, William C. Bullitt, who was at that time greatly trusted by and in close personal touch with President Roosevelt—a circumstance well known in Paris, which gave Bullitt a very favored status with French politicians of many persuasions.† Bullitt loved France but not her principal allies; he had disliked the English since childhood, and his service in Moscow had left him deeply hostile to the Kremlin. A strange combination of romanticism and realism, he was rightly skeptical of France's military strength, well knew the strength of "isolationist" sentiment in the United States, and saw no avenue to Europe's salvation from communism other than by a reconciliation between France and Germany, which he ardently hoped his Great Friend in the White House might be able to effectuate. Throughout his very influential tenure in Paris, Bullitt urged this view on his French friends and his superiors in Washington alike, and tended to grade French politicians on the scale of their "realism" in recognizing the necessity of bringing their country and Germany together.

In fact, during 1937 the French got along much better with the Germans, whom they feared, than with the Italians, for whose military prowess they had less than no respect. Partly this was because Mussolini was throwing his weight around flamboyantly, while Hitler was still shrewd enough to be more discreet about his Spanish involvement; partly because François-Poncet in Berlin and Count Johannes von Welczeck in Paris were polished professional diplomats,

* A curious variant on the general "appeasement" school of diplomacy was reflected in the attitude of Sir Eric Phipps, who succeeded Sir George Clerk as Ambassador to France in February of 1937. Phipps had just previously been Ambassador in Berlin, and arrived at his new post filled with loathing of the Nazi regime, as was duly reported by Bullitt. The new emissary made no secret of his view that there was no possibility of agreement with Hitler except on his own impossible terms, but had little faith in the French Army, and thought that it was idle to resist Germany until Britain had rearmed.

† In July 1937, when Franklin D. Roosevelt, Jr. (then twenty-two years of age) came to Paris on summer holiday, he expressed to Bullitt a desire to meet "the heads of the French Government," whereupon Bullitt "had a little luncheon for him at Chantilly, which consisted of Chautemps, Blum and Delbos." Bullitt reported to the President that F.D.R., Jr., "not only spoke excellent French but also had things to say which interested everyone," and that Chautemps "turned somersaults on the lawn."

and as Foreign Minister the jovial Neurath was certainly easier to get along with than the flighty, feisty Ciano.

But at the bottom this was all irrelevant. To be sure, Hitler would have been happy enough to preserve at least the appearance of cordial relations with Britain and France, provided that they did not obstruct his aims in Central and Eastern Europe. But that proviso, of course, is what Munich was all about.

7

There remained only Eastern Europe as a theater for the exercise of French diplomacy, and in the fall of 1937, Foreign Minister Delbos went there on a tour of visits to France's allies. The agenda was to include Warsaw, Bucharest, Belgrade, and Prague—but not Moscow.

Late in November, before Delbos' departure for Warsaw, he accompanied Chautemps on a two-day visit to London for talks with Chamberlain, Eden, and Halifax. It was the first meeting between the political leaders of the two countries since the Blum-Delbos trip to London in June 1936, and the first since Neville Chamberlain's advent as Prime Minister.

At the onset of the conference, in the morning of November 29, 1937, Lord Halifax favored the guests with a long description of his recent visit to Germany. The French listened politely and offered no criticism, but after his return to Paris, Chautemps complained to Bullitt that Halifax "had made one blunder of the first water in his conversation with Hitler" by implicitly acknowledging Britain's lack of direct interest in Central Europe.

After Halifax had finished, Delbos expressed the opinion that the Germans' next step would be *Anschluss*, followed by annexation of the Sudetenland. Chamberlain asked how, short of force, these things could be prevented. Delbos replied that a firm Anglo-French show of opposition might make Germany more reasonable, eliciting from Chamberlain a short lecture on British public opinion, which, he said, "would not at any price run the risk of a war for Czechoslovakia, a distant country with which England had nothing in common," and which "thinks that the Sudeten Germans are not being fairly treated by the Czech government."

After the luncheon recess Chamberlain declared that "it was desirable to seek an accord with Germany on central Europe no matter what her objectives were, even if she wished to absorb some of her neighbors, in the hope of deferring the execution of these projects until, in the long run, they might become impossible of achievement." He recommended that Delbos, when in Prague, should urge Beneš to make concessions to the Sudeten Germans. Chautemps remarked that Delbos' task would be easier "if he could say that he spoke for both France and Britain, and that the Czechs, once they had done everything possible to satisfy the legitimate demands of the Sudeten Germans, could count on the *sympathie* of Britain and France if nevertheless they were the victims of aggression."

Chamberlain and Eden at once took alarm and stated that Britain "could give no assurance of her course of action in case of aggression." Most certainly, however, Delbos "would be fully justified in saying that, the more the Czechs gave proof of good will, the stronger would be their position *vis-à-vis* the German demands."

There followed some desultory talk of Austria, Italy, and the former German colonies, and the conferees then formulated a communiqué which reaffirmed the policy of nonintervention in Spain, and proclaimed the "community of attitudes and views which so happily characterize the relations between France and the United Kingdom." And then, just as the French were on the point of departure, Chamberlain took Chautemps aside and admonished him on the "lamentable state" of French aviation. England, in contrast, had "a large program which would not be completed for two or three years," whereas France "had no modern planes and no means for their mass production." All this was only too true; it was also a shrewd blow at the French case for a British guarantee to Czechoslovakia.

All in all, it was a remarkable foreshadowing of the Chamberlain strategy which would lead to Munich. Nevertheless, the French put a good face on things. On December 1, Bullitt found Delbos "for the first time in the past year extremely satisfied with himself and full of confidence" and "enormously pleased that Chamberlain had said to him that he could speak for Great Britain as well as France on his trip which begins tomorrow to Poland, Rumania, Yugoslavia, and Czechoslovakia."

Two days later, as Delbos' train stopped in Berlin en route to Warsaw, Neurath was on hand to greet the French Foreign Minister (who was accompanied on his trip by Charles Rochat, chief of the European Division of the Quai d'Orsay). There were mutual felicitations and expressions of desire for a peaceful future, and Neurath permitted himself to remark half jokingly that the Italians would not be pleased by his friendly gesture. Delbos was a nervous man and, for a diplomat, unusually susceptible to flattery; he was delighted by Neurath's attentions and made much of them in his statement to the press in Warsaw.

The sharper eyes of François-Poncet, however, did not fail to note a deeper significance. Barthou had ridden through Berlin in 1934 and Laval in 1935 without receiving any such courtesy. The former had been on his way to Moscow and the latter from Moscow, while Delbos was going no further east than Warsaw and Bucharest, and "this consideration was not unrelated to Neurath's decision." It was a thought-provoking analysis; were the *beaux yeux* of Neurath worth enough to France to offset the scowls in Moscow, where Litvinov was reminding the correspondent of the *Temps* that two could play at this game of *rapprochement* with Germany, and grumbling to Ambassador Coulondre that France was alienating herself from Russia?

As Delbos and Rochat took their course around the eastern capitals, it became apparent in Poland, Rumania, and Yugoslavia alike that the people of those countries were much more stirred by the French presence than were their official hosts. In Warsaw, as we have already seen, Colonel Beck was distinctly circumspect in his formal toast, and even stressed the freedom of each party to the French-Polish alliance to "pursue his own ends and defend his own interests." Much to Ambassador Noël's distress, Delbos did not strongly press the question of Poland's relations with Czechoslovakia; probably it would have accomplished little had he done so, for when the matter arose Beck attacked the Czechs not only for their treatment of the Polish minority, but for allowing Prague to be used as "the central source of Comintern propaganda in Poland," and showed no disposition to ameliorate the situation.

In Rumania, the official reception was much warmer, but the internal political situation was unstable and the results of the visit correspondingly uncertain. King Carol and the Prime Minister, George Tatarescu, both had long-standing personal and cultural ties with France and paid Delbos every possible courtesy, but times were changing fast and ominously. Early in 1936, while visiting Paris, Carol had told his friend and legal adviser, Joseph Paul-Boncour, that in the event of a war involving Germany on one side and France and the Soviet Union on the other, Rumania would permit Russian troops to pass through her territory. By the middle of 1937, however, when the King was again in Paris, his intentions were much less clear* because, as he told Paul-Boncour, "many things had happened," and a few days later, in London, he told his English hosts that he was not "in France's pocket" and wished closer contact with Britain.

By the time Delbos arrived in Bucharest, neither King nor ministers were willing to enlarge Rumania's commitments. At his final meeting with Tatarescu, the Prime Minister reminded him that, if Rumania's foreign policy from time to time disappointed him, it was because "France has not always acted in its own true image," especially in Laval's policy toward Italy and in connection with the Rhineland.

Feted but empty-handed, Delbos went on to Yugoslavia, setting off an explosion of pro-French demonstrations many of which turned into anti-Stoyadinovitch riots: In Belgrade the crowds, waving French flags, broke through the police cordons, and it took a burst of gunfire, and a bloody toll of demonstrators, to disperse them. The conversations with Stoyadinovitch were arid and at times recriminatory, particularly as regards the Yugoslav Government's new amity with Italy, and neither the Prime Minister nor the Regent, Prince Paul, made an effort to conceal their low opinion of the left-wing element in French politics, and of France's Soviet ally.

On his way from Belgrade to Prague, Delbos remarked to an accompanying journalist: "At last we are going to see some real friends." No doubt it was a relief, but Delbos still had to perform the task to which he had committed himself in London: persuading the Czechs to make suitable concessions to the Sudeten Germans.

He was not the sort of man capable of sharp pressure with friends. Beneš already knew about the London discussions and was well prepared with maps, historical explanations, a presentation of what was being done about schools and government jobs for the Sudetens, and reasons why other things could not

---

*Nevertheless, according to Gamelin, King Carol repeated in October 1937 his promise to give passage to Russian troops to Czechoslovakia, through the northern part of Rumania. This was on the occasion of Gamelin's visit to the Rumanian Army maneuvers and, whether or not the King went as far as Gamelin subsequently recalled, it is clear from the contemporaneous reports of the French Minister and military attaché that the King "firmly declared that France could count on the Roumanian Army."

be done. The Czech President also gave a good account of the state of Czech defenses, which, he declared, could hold the Germans in check "for several months." None of this suggested a willingness to go further in mollifying the Germans than had been previously intended.

Delbos arrived at the Gare de l'Est on the morning of December 19, 1937, and told the press that he had had an "excellent" trip. But he was whistling in the dark. By the end of 1937, French diplomacy was bankrupt on all fronts, and within a few weeks Delbos would want nothing more than to escape from the crushing responsibilities and insoluble problems of the Quai d'Orsay.

8

A few blocks away, at the Ministry of War on the Rue St. Dominique, things were equally gloomy. In retrospect, General Gamelin recalled 1937 as "a black period," in which "one felt the tightening grip of destiny, and inability to escape the powerless condition in which we were mired."

Why was France "mired" (*enlisée*)? Some have blamed the Popular Front—the strikes that accompanied its ascent to power and sporadically plagued its stewardship, the forty-hour week, the pacifism of social democracy. The evidence, even today, is incomplete and inconclusive, and of course the question is at bottom comparative. Would a regime of the center and right have done better? After all, it was on the right that the strongest defeatism—in the sense of nonresistance to German aggrandizement—was to be found.

However that might have been, the Popular Front—with either its Socialist or its Radical foot foremost—was in power throughout the last three prewar years and *politically* must bear responsibility for the military conditions that led to France's defeat. But whether this was primarily due to the debilitating effects of socialism, pacifism, and proletarian self-interest, or to the stagnation of France's military leadership, remains a question. No doubt both factors contributed to the eventual *débacle,* but the records now available strongly suggest that the last-mentioned was considerably the more significant.

One of the Army's difficulties was that responsibility for arms procurement was divided among the Chief of the General Staff, the directors of the various branches, such as artillery and infantry, and a War Ministry official with the title of Secretary-General—a "controller" with extensive powers over budgetary and administrative matters, bitingly described by General Weygand: "Because he was the controller, he was uncontrollable; because he was not a combatant, he was incompetent; because he was neither a Minister or Commander-in-Chief, he was irresponsible." From October of 1936 until May 1940 this crucial position was filled by Robert Jacomet, who for ten years had been a League of Nations staff specialist on disarmament, and whom Daladier brought to the War Ministry as a consultant during the summer of 1936.

In his postwar writings and testimony before a parliamentary commission of inquiry, Jacomet discussed at length the French armament program and its problems during the Popular Front years, including the strikes and the forty-hour week. As a responsible official and close associate of Daladier, he of course had a stake in laying the blame elsewhere, but his analysis finds considerable confirmation in other quarters. According to Jacomet the strikes of 1936 were indeed a negative factor but not a very important one; the Army General Staff estimated that it had set back the arms manufacturing program by about two months, but the rate of production was then so low that in absolute terms little was lost, and that little soon made up. Jacomet's assessment was generally confirmed by the then General of Engineers Martignon, who at the time was initially responsible for armament contracts, and who described the 1936 and 1938 strikes as "bothersome" but mitigated by the availability of other suppliers, and suggested that the strikes had actually been a useful stimulus to broadening the Army's procurement base.

The effect of the forty-hour law, according to both Jacomet and Martignon, was much more damaging, not so much in consequence of the limit itself, but because its provisions for overtime work were cumbersome and difficult to invoke if there were unemployed workers in the vicinity of the factory in question. Much of the labor in arms factories calls for special skills not usually possessed by the unemployed, and in such circumstances production could be raised (apart from costly and slow training programs) only by overtime work. The forty-hour law, intended primarily to spread employment, unfortunately resulted instead in a national five-day workweek, with results injurious to rearmament, but probably much more damaging to the over-all national economy.

A far greater impediment to rearmament than strikes or the forty-hour week was the debilitated technical condition of the French war industries. Lulled by the Versailles limitations on German arms and the assurance of support from Allies, the French government had not given the armorers enough orders to keep them healthy. By 1936, according to Jacomet, Schneider-Creusot was the only French firm capable of turning out cannon steel shaped to fine specifications, and most of their machine tools were obsolete. The state's orders did not furnish enough capital to justify expansion or modernization, or tooling up for mass production.

The negative impact of all these factors in conjunction was of course immense, but by no means equally so among the three services. Strategically, their effect on the Navy was insignificant, on the Air Force catastrophic, and on the Army injurious to be sure, but far less so than might have been expected.

Throughout the period since the First World War, the French Navy had received the lion's share of the funds made available to the military services for the new construction.* After 1936, it no longer enjoyed this favored status, because of the more pressing needs of the Army and Air Force. Likewise, naval construction was especially hampered by the administration of the forty-hour-week law, because of the need for special skills and the limited number of workers who can be efficiently employed on board ship. Nevertheless, despite the acceleration of naval construction in Germany and Italy, France remained, until the outbreak of war in 1939, the second naval power in Europe, with modern capital ships (*Richelieu* and *Jean Bart*), battle cruisers (*Dunkerque* and *Strasbourg*), and aircraft carriers (*Béarn*)

Like Britain, France was concerned about Germany's submarine strength

---

* According to Jacomet, during the period 1918–36 the Navy received 42 per cent, the Army 31 per cent, and the Air Force 27 per cent of these funds.

(though less so, since France was economically more self-sufficient than Britain), but otherwise she had nothing to fear from the German Navy. Conversely, the French Navy could do nothing directly in aid of France's eastern allies. In the Mediterranean, France had the Italian fleet to concern her, but, firmly allied as she was with Britain, the Italian threat was a very minor matter in comparison to France's other worries.

The reason for this heavy investment in new ships was the belief that, with the British fleet divided among the Atlantic, Mediterranean, and Far Eastern danger areas, and confronting the new Italian and German naval units, France could not rely primarily on England and must pull her own weight. It was a sound enough premise, but (as Cot lamented in retrospect), considering the immediate menace of the Luftwaffe and the woeful inadequacy of the French Air Force in 1936, it would have been wiser to skimp on the naval side in order to enlarge and expedite the aviation program.

Since there had been no military aircraft construction (other than prototypes) between 1918 and 1934, that program had to be started vitually from scratch. As Jacomet put in his postwar testimony:

> The lack of any coherent air policy put the aeronautical industries under the burden of an uncertain future, and drove away the specialists . . . In default of orders, the companies could not give research and experiments the attention they deserved, and no adequate effort was made to modernize their tooling; aeronautical production remained in a handicraft [*artisanal*] stage. Everyone neglected the fundamental rule of air power that, since equipment obsolesces very rapidly, everything depends on speedy modernization, that is to say on a well-equipped industry.

The modest Plan I of 1934 called for an annual production of only 250 to 300 new aircraft. Cot's Plan II, approved in September 1936, called for a construction rate of 800 per year, but the aircraft were of the same types as theretofore. In 1936 these Blochs and Potezes and Dewoitines compared not unfavorably with those of other countries, but the mid-1930's was a time of rapid advance in aircraft design, and by 1937 the French Air Force was getting planes which were indeed new but already obsolete.

Small as was Plan II compared to the air armament programs under way in Germany, Britain, and Italy, it was beyond the immediate capacity of the starved French aircraft industry. Reorganization and expansion were a necessary prerequisite, and the nationalization law was at hand as a possible basis. But the Air Ministry, and the Air Force as an independent arm, dated only from 1933, and Cot doubted that his administrative and technical resources were sufficient to justify expropriation and government operation. Instead, the airplane body and engine plants were grouped in six (five for bodies, one for engines) "National Societies of Aeronautic Construction," retaining a measure of competition subject to Ministry co-ordination, and with industry committees for the joint purchase of raw materials, labor negotiation, and research. Certainly there was a measure of improvement, but in 1936 and 1937 the Government failed to furnish the necessary credits for plant expansion, and the amounts borrowed from banks for this purpose during 1936 and 1937 were wholly inadequate. If the Air Ministry had been as well established politically as the Ministries of War and Marine, things might have been different, but the Air was still very much the junior arm; in 1936 it received only 22 per cent and in 1937 30 per cent of the over-all defense budget,

Of course, Cot was quite right in pointing out to the Permanent Committee of National Defense, as he did at its first meeting in June of 1936, that even with maximum effort and efficiency France could not keep pace with Germany and must rely on allies and friends. Both on this occasion and a CPDN meeting a month later, Cot urged that the deficit be made up in part by purchasing aircraft abroad, mentioning primarily the Soviet Union and secondarily Britain. Rather surprisingly, Cot was strongly supported by Pétain, and there was no objection from the others present, although Cot quite unnecessarily ruffled Gamelin by embellishing his plan with the prediction that, in view of the German fortifications sure to be built in the Rhineland, the Air Force would be the only French arm capable of offensive action.

The foreign purchase plan, involving as it did both diplomatic and financial factors, was beyond the competence of the CPDN to inaugurate, and in fact Cot had already laid it officially before the Quai d'Orsay in a letter to Delbos, wherein the United States, as well as Russia and England, was mentioned as a possible source, and requested that Delbos present the matter to the Cabinet. After two months and a prod from Cot, Delbos dispatched a cool reply, admonishing against any moves that might suggest an "encirclement" of Germany, and reminding Cot that the recently enacted neutrality legislation might inhibit purchases in America. On October 22, Cot responded in an edgy letter, accusing Delbos of intruding on technical questions within the exclusive competence of the Air Ministry, and indicating that further elaboration of a purchasing program would best be handled by an interministerial committee.

It was not a propitious start. The Air Ministry sent technical missions to both Russia and the United States, but political objections frustrated Cot's proposals for co-operation with the Soviet Union, and Bonnet, after he became Finance Minister, refused Cot the credits necessary for aircraft purchases in the United States. The British had none to spare, and the consequence of all these difficulties was that no foreign aircraft purchases were made in 1936 or 1937.

Cot was well aware of the shortcomings of his Plan II, and in December 1936 he and the new Air Force Chief of Staff, General Féquant, submitted to the CPDN a Plan III, calling for the allocation of 175,000 men to antiaircraft defense, and a Plan IV for enlargement of the Air Force, all to be accomplished by a trebling of Air Force credits. These plans were of such scope that their realization would have cut deep into the financial and manpower resources of the Army and Navy, and were far beyond the capacity of French industry to fulfill. Cot himself appears to have submitted them as a basis for study and modification rather than as immediately feasible proposals.* Whatever his hopes, they were thoroughly dashed on February 15, 1937, when the CPDN rejected them

---

* At the CPDN meeting at which Plans III and IV were rejected, Cot acknowledged that Plan III was unrealizable "from the three-fold viewpoints of finance, industry, and manpower," and that Plan IV was out of reach because even Plan II was being accomplished only with difficulty.

entirely, declaring that "there was no present reason to modify or extend the plan for increasing the Air Force."

By the end of 1937, the Air Ministry under Cot had doubled the size of the Air Force, but with planes that were already obsolete. A start had been made in reorganizing the aircraft industry, but it was still turning out only about fifty combat planes a month; Germany was producing seven to ten and England four times that amount, and even the scorned Italians' output was double or treble that of the French. Cot's efforts to obtain sufficient financial credits for major expansion had failed, as had his hopes for foreign purchases. All this he duly reported early in December 1937 to the CPDN, and to Premier Chautemps, when the latter returned from London with Chamberlain's admonitions ringing in his ears. What was to be done? Cot proposed a doubling of the Air Force budget, immediate construction of new factories, and authority to purchase 200 war planes and 500 aircraft engines abroad.

It was Cot's last *démarche* as Air Minister. He was energetic and intelligent, but lacked political clout and did not succeed in "getting things done." When Chautemps reorganized his government in January 1938, Cot was moved to the Ministry of Commerce and succeeded at the Air Ministry by Guy La Chambre.*

Financially, La Chambre fared considerably better than Cot. In 1938, for the first time, the Air Force, with 42 per cent, had the largest share of the defense budget, and in 1939 it had just over half. In March 1938 he readily won approval for his Plan V, envisaging an approximate doubling of the combat aircraft strength (4,740 in Plan V as against 2,400 in Plan II), with 2,600 in planes in the front-line units and the rest in reserve. At about the same time, La Chambre arranged for the purchase in the United States of 200 Curtiss P-36 fighters, deliverable in the summer of 1939.

No doubt the German annexation of Austria, which occurred while Plan V was under discussion, smoothed the path to its approval. But there were other reasons for La Chambre's success where Cot had failed. La Chambre in the past had served as Under-Secretary of the War Ministry, and subsequently as Chairman of the Army Commission of the Chamber of Deputies. In that capacity he had supported Daladier and Gamelin against the criticisms of De Gaulle, voiced through Paul Reynaud. Naturally, La Chambre got along much better with Daladier than had the disputatious and often tactless Cot, with his penchant for aerial striking forces and insistence on complete independence for the air arm.

This new harmony was highly advantageous to the Air Force financially, but much less so operationally, for the result was to commit the air arm to the same purely defensive strategy and tactics to which the Army generals were wedded. When La Chambre and the new Chief of the Air Staff, General Joseph Vuillemin, took office, Gamelin was delighted to be told that they, "breaking with the ideas of M. Pierre Cot," were abandoning the idea of a big striking force, and would give priority to fighters for defensive use.

This decision was reflected in the structure of Plan V, which, out of the 2,600

---

* La Chambre and Cot both testified before the Assembly's postwar inquiry into the causes of the French defeat. Not surprisingly, each sought to put substantial blame on the other, and both agreed that major responsibility lay with the Air Force generals.

first-line aircraft, envisaged 1,100 fighters and 600 reconnaissance and observation aircraft, compared to 875 bombers.* Furthermore, five sixths of the last would be level-flight bombers to operate behind the enemy front; only 72 dive bombers and an equal number of assault bombers, suitable for battlefield use, were contemplated. This, of course, eliminated the tank-dive-bomber team which the Germans were even then developing as the tactical basis of their offensive strategy—the very weapons which defeated France in 1940.

These shortsighted blunders bore their bitter fruit when war came, but at the time of Munich they were largely irrelevant because France then had but the shell of an air force. Quite rightly, during 1938 La Chambre put his main investment into plant expansion and modernization, the benefits of which were not realized until 1939 and 1940. According to General Vuillemin's report, there were barely 700 combat aircraft including fighter, bomber, and reconnaissance types, available in metropolitan France in September 1938. Antiaircraft defenses were virtually nonexistent. Vuillemin, a brave flyer in the First World War, was no hero in 1938, but his warning that the Air Force could neither attack nor defend effectively was well grounded.

And so it came about that France, having by victory and Versailles deprived Germany of the air arm for fifteen years, let the same weapon fall from her own hands. She was thus victimized by a combination of parsimony, lethargy, and senility, the consequences of which weighed heavily, and probably decisively, when the French Government confronted the Sudeten crisis.

9

Strikes and the forty-hour week hampered Army as well as Air Force production, and in June 1936 neither arm had any significant quantity of new weapons. So, too, France's inferiority of industrial resources as compared to Germany limited the Army as much as the Air Force. Nevertheless, both at the time of Munich and when the war came, the French Army, in size and equipment, suffered under no such inferiority to the German Army as did the Air Force to the Luftwaffe. Indeed, taken overall, the French ground forces were as well equipped as the German and, in September 1938, significantly larger. The Army's shortcomings were doctrinal and organizational rather than material.

There were several reasons for the Army's more favorable situation. As in Germany it was the major arm, to which the nation's military and patriotic tradition was dedicated. It had not been so badly starved for credits during the lean years as the air arm, and had been maintained at a numerical strength three to four times that of the Reichswehr. Many kinds of army weaponry do not become obsolete nearly as rapidly as aircraft; at the end of the First World War

---

* The actual course of procurement aggravated the plight of the bomber force. Despite its complicated construction and inferiority to the best German and British fighters, the Morane 405 was promptly selected for mass production. But the air generals, dissatisfied with the bomber prototypes, tinkered with them endlessly, with consequent grievous delays in quantity manufacture. The Air Force never purchased even the 72 dive bombers authorized by Plan V. Curiously enough the Navy, less demanding, bought somewhat more than that number, using both French and American types, and these actually flew in support of the Army during the Battle of France.

the French Army was richly endowed with rifles, sidearms, artillery,* and much other equipment which retained its military value between the wars. These stocks partially offset Germany's greater resources since, owing to the Versailles limitations, the Wehrmacht had to start its rearmament with much less equipment and from a much smaller base. As Jacomet put it: "We had our artillery, our infantry arms, and military stores and . . . because of the existence of these stocks, we were able to concentrate our efforts on modern weaponry. . . ." Accordingly, a large part of Daladier's 14-billion-franc budget of September 1936 was earmarked for tanks, antitank guns, and other new artillery.

Another and equally important circumstance was that, in contrast to the Air Force, the Army had already selected and approved the prototypes for most of the new weaponry—mortars, antitank guns, tanks of various weights, armored reconnaissance cars, and heavy artillery—in 1935 and 1936, before the Daladier budget was approved. This meant that, while the Air Force received little or no new equipment before 1939, the Army took into service between 1936 and 1938 close to 100 heavy tanks (heavier than anything the Germans had), 50 medium tanks (there were already thrice that number in French North Africa), and some 1,200 light tanks, as well as considerable quantities of artillery.

At that same time the Germans, to be sure, had a considerably larger nucleus of armored vehicles which they designated "tanks" (Panzerkampfwagen), but the great majority of them were very lightly armored and mounted only machine guns, while the French "light" tanks were twice as heavy and mounted both machine guns and a small (37-millimeter) cannon. In 1938, the Germans had no more than 300 comparable tanks, and as yet had no model equal to the heavy French Char Bs. It is true that the German tanks were faster and more maneuverable than the French, but taken overall in 1938 the French tanks were clearly superior and, even in 1940, were acknowledged on both sides to be approximately equal to the German, both in numbers and quality of equipment.†

This is not to say that France could have long maintained any such measure of military equality with Germany, nor is it to deny that France would have been much stronger, both in 1938 and 1940, had her military production not been limited by the antiquated state of her industry, the forty-hour week, and other factors for which the political and business leaders of the country were primarily responsible. Furthermore, there were at least two grievous errors in the Army's rearmament program, one being the failure to provide the ground forces with antiaircraft artillery, and the other a needless and very damaging lack of antitank mines.

Despite all these things, the ground forces were very substantially endowed with

* The famous French 75-millimeter field gun, which was the staple of French artillery in the First World War, was still very usable in the Second, and with modernizing alterations proved a very useful antitank weapon.

† Needless to say, the question has been endlessly discussed in the postmortems. But General Heinz Guderian's estimate of Germany's effective western tank strength at something less than 3,000 is approximately equal to the French totals as reported by Gamelin and Jacomet, and he confirms the French advantage in armor and armament and the German tanks' greater speed.

new military equipment between 1936 and 1940, and the political stimulus for this rejuvenation was the Popular Front. It was Pétain, as Minister of War in the conservative Doumergue government of 1934, who cut the military budget; it was Daladier, as Minister of War under a Socialist Premier, who in 1936 secured the financial credits and launched the new Army program.

No doubt Daladier should have procured even more than he did for the Army, but that failure, it should be repeated, was not the primary cause of the French military disaster. That lay rather in the collapse of the air arm and the lack of an adequate organizational and tactical framework for the use of the tanks and other new weaponry. Of these two factors the second was the more fundamental, for had there been sound military doctrine there probably would have been no such total failure in the air.

The fatal defect in French planning for the use of the ground and air forces was failure to provide for a strong striking force, capable of rapid movement, and utilizing modern tanks and ground attack aircraft as the spearhead, supported by mobile infantry and artillery. Such a force was the logical embodiment of ideas that had been given currency by British military writers such as Basil Liddell Hart and General J. F. C. Fuller in England, and were being given practical application in Germany by Generals Oswald Lutz, Heinz Guderian, and other architects of the Wehrmacht's panzer forces.

In France, Charles de Gaulle was preaching the same gospel, but he was only a lieutenant colonel. Within his own profession, De Gaulle was a voice crying in the wilderness, but in public life he found an eloquent spokesman in the person of Paul Reynaud, who gave strong support to De Gaulle's ideas in the Chamber of Deputies, as well as in books and articles. Most unfortunately, De Gaulle coupled his tactical proposals with the idea that the striking force should be entirely composed of professional soldiers—an elite group.* This unnecessary adjunct (the Germans did very well without it) was out of keeping with the republican tradition of the "people in arms." It was especially uncongenial to the Socialist and other parties of the left, and gave De Gaulle's military critics an avenue of attack quite irrelevant to the tactical and strategic content of his program.†

There has been considerable misunderstanding about the nature of the French generals' opposition to De Gaulle and Reynaud. The generals did not object to tanks, and William L. Shirer appears to have been mistaken in attributing to Gamelin an unwillingness to establish armored divisions. Indeed the first "mechanized division" had been established in 1933 when Weygand was Chief of Staff, and in April 1936, on the basis of Gamelin's report, the Army's *Conseil Supérieur* acted to create a second mechanized division to replace one of the four existing cavalry divisions. The establishment of each mechanized division included 100 light and 100 medium tanks, and Gamelin's report envisaged the sub-

* De Gaulle's famous book, published in 1934, was entitled *Vers l'Armée de Métier* (Toward the Professional Army).

† For example, on July 21, 1936, the chief of Daladier's military cabinet, General Bourret, submitted a memorandum attacking Reynaud's concept (adapted from De Gaulle's) of the *"armée de métier,"* especially on the ground that the existence of an elite force would weaken and demoralize the main body of the Army.

sequent establishment of a third mechanized division (as was in fact done in 1938-39) to match the three armored divisions which Germany had formed in 1935.* In December 1937 it was again Gamelin who proposed the creation of a heavy armored division (*division cuirassée*).

The issue at the Rue St. Dominique, then, was not whether tank divisions should be formed, but what use should be made of tanks generally. In Germany, the command basis for a major striking force was laid in 1937 and 1938, by the creation of new armored and motorized corps, and an over-all group command for mechanized forces† under General Walther von Brauchitsch, the future Army Commander-in-Chief. That was the sort of armored force, under a corps command, for which De Gaulle and Reynaud were pushing, but the Army command would have nothing to do with what seemed to many of the French generals so extravagant a notion, and Gamelin's postwar efforts to portray himself as approving of the corps command but not of the *armée de métier* aspect of the De Gaulle thesis bear the taint of afterthought.

Of course, an effective striking force could not be created simply by putting a lot of tanks in one unit; the problem was not simply one of command, and tanks alone were not enough. There would have to be fighter cover and antiaircraft guns to protect the force from enemy aircraft, dive bombers and other ground-attack planes to assail the enemy's defenses, antitank guns and other defensive artillery, radio communications from command to tanks and between the tank command and the supporting units, a speedy and flexible refueling system, and many other necessary appurtenances.

Most of these things the French lacked, because this was not the way they planned to use their tanks. The bulk of the light tanks were distributed among the infantry divisions in individual battalions. The medium and remaining light tanks formed the light mechanized divisions which were replacing the old cavalry divisions and were under cavalry command; there was no independent tank branch of the service. The heavy tanks were destined for the armored divisions, but there was no coherent plan for their use.

Apart from these material and organzational shortcomings, there was a failure of energy and will. Gamelin was intelligent and more progressive than most of his colleagues, but his acceptance of the tank divisions was cautious and ana-

---

* Shirer's strictures (*The Collapse of the Third Republic*, pp. 318–19) on Gamelin appear to be based on a misunderstanding of his report, insofar as it declared that tank attacks could not succeed unless strongly supported by artillery and infantry, and that the German divisions could not break through a well-organized front. In fact, the first conclusion was quite in line with German experience, as the German panzer division included a regiment each of artillery and motorized infantry and an antitank gun battalion as well as two tank regiments. At the time Gamelin prepared his report, the existing German tanks were armed only with machine guns, which no doubt explains the second conclusion.

† In March 1937 the French military attaché in Berlin, General Gaston Renondeau, reported to Paris that the purpose of the new Group Command was "to study the organization and employment of a mass comprising: large armored units, and motorized infantry and reconnaissance forces."

In the plan of attack against Czechoslovakia and in Poland, the Germans generally used the panzer divisions separately, each in a mechanized corps which included motorized infantry to follow up the tank spearhead. For the Battle of France, however, two or even three panzer divisions were put under a single corps headquarters, and two armored corps under a "panzer group" for the major assaults.

lytical rather than dynamic. The Army "Instructions" distributed in August 1936 (the year after Gamelin became Chief of Staff) informed the French soldier that, despite all the technical advances since the First World War, the Pétain "Instructions" of 1921 were still sound and "remain the charter for tactical employment of our major units." The light mechanized divisions were described under the heading "Cavalry," and the tank was described, essentially, as an improved horse.

It might have been expected that the Spanish Civil War would blow away some of the cobwebs in the Rue St. Dominique, but its consequences there seem rather to have been soporific. The German planes sent to Spain in 1936 were obsolescent, and the tanks then available were, as already noted, nothing more than armored machine-gun carriers. During the early months of 1937 it was the common opinion in informed circles that the German equipment in Spain was inferior to what had been sent in from France and Russia. The German military attaché in Paris, General Erich Kühlenthal, repeatedly admitted to his American opposite, Colonel Horace H. Fuller, that the German planes and tanks "were somewhat of a disappointment." There were other reports to the same effect, and in May 1937, Daladier told the CPDN that the war in Spain "had shown our superiority in aviation and tanks."

The lulling effect of such reports, accurate as they were presently but misleading in portent, was increased by the publication in 1938 of a book, *The Lessons of the War in Spain,* by a French military observer, General Maurice Duval. In a preface, Weygand hailed Franco as a great leader and approved Duval's declaration that there was little for France to learn in Spain about tanks because the combatants' other arms were too primitive. Duval's conclusion was that the Spanish experience furnished no support for the "futurists" of warfare, and there was no doubt that the futurists he had in mind were De Gaulle and Reynaud.*

What about the oft-repeated epigram on the unwisdom of leaving the conduct of war exclusively to soldiers? Should not the responsible Popular Front ministers have detected and corrected the generals' subservience to the past? Their failure to do so was not the consequence of unawareness of the issues that De Gaulle and Reynaud were raising. Blum himself had read De Gaulle's book and, while repelled by the "professional" aspect of his thesis, was attracted by his concept of large armored units. In October 1936, through the good offices of a mutual friend (Colonel Emile Mayer), Blum received the lieutenant colonel and offered him a post in Daladier's military cabinet. De Gaulle refused, preferring to fulfill his assignment to the new *Centre des Hautes Etudes Militaires,* and the meeting proved fruitless. De Gaulle's complaint that the large new appropriations for tanks and planes were not to be used for the establishment of large armored formations were brushed aside by the Premier with the observation that these questions were the responsibility of Daladier and

---

* A year later Pétain was helping to perpetuate the old ways in a laudatory preface to General Narcisse Chauvineau's *Is Invasion Still Possible,* which undertook to reaffirm Pétain's old concept of the virtually unbreakable "continuous front," and which scoffed at De Gaulle's ideas.

Gamelin. A few years later he blamed himself for not having followed through to ensure that the new funds would be used for "De Gaulle-type" armored divisions.

So Blum passed the buck to Daladier, who proved to be no more favorable to the De Gaulle proposals than was Gamelin. The political showdown came late in January 1937, when the Chamber of Deputies debated the question whether rearmament should be designed for a military establishment which could immediately attack and thus carry the war outside of France, or whether its primary purposes should be to protect France against invasion by winning "the battle of frontiers." Reynaud seized the occasion to criticize the Government's defensive strategy, and to propose the armored corps, utilized as an attacking force—"the iron tip of the lance of which the national army is the wood".—as the best counter to Germany's armor, and the only means by which France could effectively aid her eastern allies.

Daladier, as Minister of War and National Defense, made the main reply for the Government. The German armored corps, he declared, had not revolutionized the art of war. The Spanish Civil War had shattered "the immense hopes which some people had rested on certain devices." And why? "One always forgets the potency of fire-power. . . . Look at Madrid. On all sides the gun-fire . . . stops the advance of the tanks, which are pierced like froth." He was resolutely opposed to the creation of an armored corps;* it would be difficult to find the necessary personnel, it would disrupt the unity of the Army, and it would not be effective:

If by chance, after some local successes which I recognize as possible, these waves of armor were finally to be broken [décimées], and if once again the great law of war—that an offensive should never be launched without a large accumulation of men and weapons—then what, in the rout of your specialized corps, would be the fate of the nation?

Daladier was strongly supported by Guy la Chambre, then chairman of the Chamber's Army Commission, and the Government's military program was approved by an overwhelming majority. On neither right or left was there any significant support for Reynaud. Pétain and the other heroes of the First World War spoke with too loud a voice; their authority overbore the doubts which some of the civilian leaders entertained, and choked off the inquiries which they might otherwise have undertaken, confronted as they were by the ominous developments in Germany.

Daladier was by no means unaware of the strategic consequences of France's lack of a striking force. At a meeting of the CPDN in March 1938, just after *Anschluss,* Paul-Boncour put the question with which London was forever taxing Paris: "You say you will aid Czechoslovakia but, as a practical matter, what will you do?" To which Daladier replied:

* According to Gamelin (*Servir,* vol. 1, p. 263), Daladier also declared himself opposed to establishing armored divisions, a circumstance which the general found puzzling. Perhaps Gamelin's memory played him false, inasmuch as Reynaud's recollection was that Daladier, during the debate, favored the establishment of armored divisions but opposed their use en masse.

Initially, France can give Czechoslovakia no direct aid.

The only help she can give is indirect: by mobilizing, to hold German troops on our frontiers.

The problem thus presented is to know whether, in these conditions, Germany will have enough other forces to undertake an action against Czechoslovakia.

What Daladier did not say was that France's lack of an armored force virtually resolved the "problem." Had there been such, the Germans would have had to commit substantial forces, probably including both armor and aircraft, to the defense of their western frontier, seriously depleting their concentration against Czechoslovakia. With no such force to fear, and knowing the French plan to take a defensive posture, the Germans could feel reasonably secure in leaving only light screening forces in the west—as indeed they did in September when war threatened.

This was a disastrous strategy not only for Czechoslovakia (and Poland a year later) but for France as well. The Czechs could not be expected to hold out against Germany unaided, and the Wehrmacht's freedom to deploy virtually its entire strength against them would greatly abbreviate both their life expectancy and France's respite. Even more important, the French strategy played into Hitler's hands by enabling him to pick off his opponents one by one. The main point of France's eastern alliances was to confront Germany with a two-front war and the necessity of dividing her forces.

Charles De Gaulle had accurately prophesied the shape of things to come when he met with Blum in 1936. What would France do if Hitler should march on Vienna, Prague, or Warsaw? "According to circumstances," De Gaulle replied, "we shall have a limited call-up or a full mobilization. Then, peering between the battlements of our fortifications, we shall watch the enslavement of Europe." And that was exactly what happened in 1938 and 1939, after which it was France's turn.

10

The end of 1937 was also the end of Chautemps' brief period of political calm. Christmas and the New Year were marred by sit-in strikes, and the franc weakened again. In mid-January Chautemps, whether by clumsiness or design, repudiated Communist support for his policies, and the Socialist ministers, loyal to the Popular Front idea, resigned and brought down the Government. President Lebrun turned first to Bonnet, who failed because the Socialists would not promise him their support, and then to Blum, who was unable to form the broadly based left-to-center Government—"from Thorez* to Reynaud"—which he thought necessary. The upshot was that Lebrun recalled Chautemps, who formed a government of Radicals only. So the shift was "from Chautemps plus to Chautemps minus," as the wags put it.

Chautemps made an immediate show of activity by the promulgation of two decrees, the first of which expanded the functions of the Minister of National Defense, and the second gave Gamelin the title "Chief of Staff of National De-

* Maurice Thorez, the Communist Party leader.

fense." All this was more impressive on paper than in effect, for Gamelin was given no national defense staff, and his peacetime powers were limited to the "co-ordination" of strategic studies and plans. As in other countries, the air and naval arms fiercely resisted any subordination to the Army, and Daladier himself was hostile to the idea of an armed forces "generalissimo."

Meanwhile, what little was left of Delbos' diplomatic world was tumbling about his ears. On December 28 came the political upheaval in Rumania, with the dismissal of the ministers with whom Delbos had dealt during his visit to Bucharest two weeks before, and their replacement by the anti-Semitic Goga government. The New Year dawned with a harbinger of stormy diplomatic weather in London, when the Francophile Vansittart was kicked upstairs. Then in February came the news of Anthony Eden's resignation as Foreign Minister, and the rejoicing in Axis circles was echoed in the French right-wing press. Two days later Neville Chamberlain, addressing the House of Commons, in effect repudiated the idea of collective security and served notice on Austria and Czechoslovakia that they had nothing to hope for from the League of Nations—or, by implication, from Britain:

> If I am right, as I am confident I am, in saying that the League as constituted today is unable to provide collective security for anybody, then I say we must try not to delude small weak nations into thinking that they will be protected by the League against aggression—and acting accordingly when we know nothing of the kind can be expected.

It was a terrible blow to Delbos, for it strongly suggested that the policies to which he had clung—close entente with Britain and support for the League—were now, with Eden's passing, openly repudiated in London. To make matters much worse, these discouraging events in supposedly friendly quarters coincided with the mounting Austrian crisis.

In the Chamber of Deputies, which debated foreign policy during the last week of February, Chautemps and Delbos put a bold face on things. France's determination to fulfill her obligations to Czechoslovakia was reaffirmed, and Delbos described Austrian independence as "an essential element of European equilibrium . . . a question of European security, as well as international honour." The other speakers, except for ex-Premier Pierre Flandin (who, in the wake of a visit to Berlin, was increasingly appeasement-minded) and a few others, echoed these sentiments, and the Chamber resoundingly approved the Government's announced policy of "respect for treaties within the framework of collective security and the League of Nations."

But it was all wind, for none of the speakers offered any plausible strategy for saving Austria.* Nor, it appeared, did anyone else, and in the diplomatic corridors Austria was already regarded as surviving only at Hitler's pleasure. As early as April 1937, immediately after the announcement of Belgian neutrality, Delbos and Sir Eric Phipps, lunching with Bullitt, had agreed that "Hitler could now take Austria at anytime he might choose without creating serious interna-

---

* Most of them lamented the rupture of the Stresa Front and the alienation of Mussolini over the Ethiopian question; it would be well if Italy would "return to the Brenner" in support of Austria. By February of 1938, of course, these were wishful, wistful dreams.

tional complications." In November, the Quai d'Orsay had been inept enough to inform Papen, visiting Paris, that, while France would surely fulfill her treaty with Czechoslovakia, she "would view with disfavor any change in the status of Austria"—a distinction the import of which can hardly have been lost on Papen. Chautemps was no less unguarded; on December 4, 1937, Bullitt reported a conversation that morning, in the course of which:

> Chautemps said that he would . . . say something . . . to me which was highly indiscreet. So far as he was concerned he looked with considerable equanimity on the possibility that Germany might annex Austria because he believed that this would produce an immediate reaction of Italy against Germany. Czechoslovakia was a different matter. The French could not permit Germany to overrun an ally.

Considering that German annexation of Austria would greatly endanger the "ally" by well-nigh surrounding Bohemia, this would have been an extraordinary misjudgment* even if there had been some chance of cooling Mussolini's ardor for the Axis. But others, capable of a soberer assessment, were equally disinclined to take any initiative in behalf of Austria. The unhappy Delbos, after another rebuff in London, informed Bullitt on February 21 that "the British Government had made it clear that Britain would do nothing to prevent the absorption of Austria by Germany," and that "France could not alone attempt to protect Austria."

Meanwhile Gamelin, privately informed of the substance of the Hitler-Schuschnigg interview, had pointed out to Daladier the grave military consequences of a German occupation of Austria:

> The fortifications which our allies have since 1934 built on their northern frontier would lose all their value. An attack from the Vienna area, up the Moravia River valley, would not only render Bohémia indefensible when taken from the rear, but also put Moravia in a bad position. When the Germans complete their fortifications facing us . . . they would be the masters of central Europe, and we would be unable to intervene effectively.

Daladier saw the point but asked what allies France would have, since Italy was on the wrong side, Belgium was neutral, and England would undoubtedly "bow once again before the *fait accompli*." There were no helpful answers to these questions, and on February 21, dining with Bullitt, Daladier expressed his belief that "nothing effective could be done to save Austria."

On March 10, apparently piqued by the Socialists' refusal to support his quest for plenary power to deal with the worsening financial situation, Chautemps resigned.† The previous day Schuschnigg had announced the plebiscite, and two days later German troops were in Austria. Gamelin and various historians have

---

* It says little for Bullitt's perspicacity that, a few weeks after this conversation, he was able to describe Chautemps (in a private letter to President Roosevelt) as having "more common sense than any other French politician."

† There has been much speculation about Chautemps' motivation for his "resignations" in January and March 1938, as neither was necessary in a parliamentary sense. In March it was charged that he resigned when he saw that *Anschluss* was imminent, rather than confront the crisis—an accusation which he vigorously denied.

made much of the fact that France was without a government at the time of *Anschluss,* and have suggested that this circumstance determined Hitler's timing of the event.* But the Chautemps cabinet continued to function in a caretaker capacity, and there is no reason to believe that the course of events would have been any different if Chautemps had resigned earlier or later. Apart from his personal indifference to the fate of Austria, Chautemps, though a skillful parliamentary maneuverer, was no leader in matters of principle or policy, and his government was too narrowly based to take drastic action. Given the attitudes of Britain and Italy, his successor, whoever it might be, was not likely to be in any better position to take the initiative.

On March 11, when the news of the German entry into Austria reached Paris, Chautemps closeted himself with Daladier and Delbos. In later years Daladier claimed that he, in agreement with Gamelin, urged military action, but that Delbos insisted on obtaining Britain's agreement to participate. This, of course, was speedily refused, and it is wholly unlikely that Daladier or Gamelin was really willing for France to act alone. Gamelin was not present, but was told late that afternoon that no military action would be taken. He did not see Daladier until the following day; by that time there was no longer any question of fighting for Austria, and Gamelin contented himself with asking for funds to extend the Maginot Line.

11

While the outgoing ministers were wringing their hands over the *Anschluss,* Léon Blum was making a second effort to form a "government of national unity," now projected as "from Thorez to Marin" (a leading conservative politician). To the opposition parties he eloquently pleaded the gravity of the hour, and won the support of Mandel, Reynaud, and others of the moderate right. But it was not enough to carry the day when they voted,† and Blum was obliged to fall back on a cabinet comparable in its political spectrum to the first Popular Front government of 1936. He was well aware that it would not long endure, and in the event it lasted less than a month.

Delbos was not a member of the second Blum government; he was profoundly depressed, and for several weeks had been making no secret of his desire "to be out of office as soon as possible." In his place Blum selected

---

* See, e.g., Gamelin, *Servir,* vol. 2, pp. 315–16: "Hitler always knew remarkably well how to time his moves by exploiting our internal political crises." See also Werth, *France and Munich,* p. 62, and Shirer, *The Collapse of the Third Republic,* pp. 326–29. In fact, it was Schuschnigg's plebiscite which triggered Hitler's decision, and there is no evidence that the political situation in France contributed significantly to the timing.

† An important force in blocking Blum's Union Nationale was the tycoon François de Wendel, President of the Comité des Forges, regent of the Banque de France, and senator from Meurthe-et-Moselle. He shared Vansittart's views that Germany was the great danger and that Italy should be swung to the Allied side, but welcomed Hitler because he would show Germany's true colors, and Nazi anti-Semitism because it would swing the Jews to France's side. A close friend of Mandel, Wendel nevertheless refused to join him in favoring military action against Germany's remilitarization of the Rhineland, and welcomed Bonnet's selection as Foreign Minister in 1938. But after the "May crisis" he swung to Mandel's side in support of Prague, and regarded Munich as a disaster for France—"Waterloo, Sadowa, Sedan, Munich!"

Joseph Paul-Boncour, who had served briefly as Premier five years earlier, and subsequently as Foreign Minister and delegate to the League of Nations. He was a strong supporter of collective security, had urged a military reply to Hitler's move into the Rhineland, and might have been expected to revive the independent diplomacy of Barthou, had he been given time. But he lacked political strength, perhaps because much of his attention was devoted to literary pursuits and his career at the bar,* and as both an all-out supporter of the League and a convert to socialism, Paul-Boncour had few friends on the right.

Nevertheless, during his brief tenure the Quai d'Orsay spoke with a fresh voice, and a louder one than before or after. On March 14, the day after the new government was installed, Blum and Paul-Boncour formally received the Czech Ambassador, Stefan Osusky, and assured him that *Anschluss* had in no way altered French commitments to his country, and that, in the event of a German attack, they would be honored. Paul-Boncour then instructed Ambassador Corbin, in London, to report these renewed undertakings and ask the British Government to describe their intentions in the premises.

On March 15, at Paul-Boncour's urging, Blum convened the CPDN to consider not only the Czech situation but the Spanish question as well; following the Republicans' New Year's success at Teruel, the tide had turned decisively against them, and by mid-March, Franco was threatening to break through to the Mediterranean coast south of Barcelona, now under heavy aerial attack. Paul-Boncour had been studying the Quai d'Orsay dossiers on Spain and, impressed by the extent to which British influence had shaped French policy, thought it time for a reassessment of "nonintervention," particularly since rumors of new German troop arrivals in Spain were current.

Blum opened the CPDN meeting by calling on Paul-Boncour, who at once put the question which the British had previously posed:† if Germany were to attack Czechoslovakia, how would France aid her ally? Daladier gave the negative response already quoted, and Gamelin added that France could hold more German troops on the western front by attacking, although the German fortifications (which, at the time, were in fact virtually nonexistent) would turn this into "an operation of long duration." Blum raised the possibility of Russian aid, but Gamelin and General Vuillemin (newly appointed Air Force Chief of Staff) both scouted its value; Poland and Rumania were unlikely to facilitate the passage of Soviet ground forces, and the Germans would destroy the few usable Czech airfields.

Blum then turned to the Spanish problem: could France back up an ultimatum to Franco, bidding him within forty-eight hours to renounce foreign military support or face the consequence of French intervention to whatever extent was deemed necessary? Gamelin and Vuillemin replied that no such step should be taken without calling up the reserves and making preparations to face a general war. Paul-Boncour then asked what effect a French occupation of Spanish

---

* Paul-Boncour had been retained by the royal family of Yugoslavia at the French trial of King Alexander's assassins, and was often of counsel to King Carol of Rumania.

† Most recently on March 12, when Corbin called on Halifax, who had replaced Eden as Foreign Minister, to inform him that Blum would soon be in office and would propose Anglo-French consultations on how best to deal with the post-*Anschluss* situation.

Morocco would have in Spain, and Gamelin for the first time answered a bit more affirmatively saying that it would have "an important moral effect" and would also safeguard France's use of the Strait of Gibraltar; it could be accomplished by partial mobilization of the troops in Algeria. Paul-Boncour next projected seizing the Balearic Islands, and Admiral Darlan opined that it could be done with one division of ground troops.

The naval minister, César Campinchi, referring to France's weakness in the air, now asked "what would be the effect, on the conduct of the war, of Germany's total mastery of the air?" Vuillemin's reply was a crusher: "In fifteen days our aviation will be annihilated." La Chambre revealed that French aircraft production was running at about forty per month, and Pétain gloomily compared this to an estimated German production rate six times that amount.

All this was pretty dismal, but Paul-Boncour was not to be shaken from his pursuit of the Spanish situation, and he now asked "what would be the consequences of a total victory for Franco, in collusion with Germany and Italy?" Gamelin "pulled out of his brief-case" a long memorandum directly on the point, which he read to the gathering.* Its thrust was that the consequences would be extremely grave; the communications of both Britain and France with Africa and the Near East would be in jeopardy, the south of France and French North Africa would be subject to air attack, and part of the Army would have to be deployed on the Spanish frontier.

The reaction of Léger, architect of nonintervention, was that France could not permit such a state of affairs to come about. Daladier, however, declared that "one would have to be blind not to see that intervention in Spain would unleash a general war." France should not intervene "except by reason of some new circumstance, such as an important reinforcement from a foreign country." Léger agreed and pointed to the risk that Britain would repudiate French intervention. Blum asked whether, short of military intervention, France could not give "intensified aid" to Spain, to which Gamelin replied that this would deplete France's own resources and might well not succeed in its purpose, given the "ineptness" of the Republican forces. After further desultory discussion, the participants appeared to be in agreement that intervention in Spain was too risky a course, and the meeting adjourned with essentially negative conclusions on the possibilities of effective aid to either Prague or Madrid.

It was a distressing meeting, and Paul-Boncour was particularly shocked to hear Vuillemin blandly dismiss the Czech airfields as inadequate for Russian planes, without showing the slightest interest in rectifying the deficiency. In retrospect, the minutes are especially sad reading because the pessimistic assess-

* "Intervention in Spain" was on the agenda for the meeting, but it is not clear how Gamelin happened to have a memorandum (undated) on the precise point of Paul-Boncour's question. Neither Gamelin's nor Paul-Boncour's memoirs indicate any prior contact between them on the subject, and the latter's use of the phrase "pulled out of his brief-case" suggests that Gamelin's production of the document came to him as a surprise. Gamelin appears to have been, up to this time, remarkably indifferent to the military implications for France of the Spanish Civil War, and there is virtually no reference to it in his memoirs other than in connection with this memorandum, which, being on the letterhead of the "Chief of Staff of National Defense," must therefore have been finished after January 21, 1938.

ments of Gamelin and Vuillemin were, for the most part, factually accurate. Reflecting in his memoirs on the negative tone of his comments, Gamelin observed, rightly enough, that "the role of the technicians is to show the statesmen just what the difficulties are, for only the statesmen can provide the means of their resolution." But what he failed to say was that the technicians mislead the statesmen unless they also portray the dangers of doing nothing, for there are circumstances in which action may be hazardous but inaction fatal. That, indeed, was precisely what Gamelin had failed to do at the time of the Rhineland occupation.

The result of the meeting of March 15 was that "nonintervention" remained the official policy, but the clandestine arms traffic across the Pyrenees to Republican Spain was allowed to grow. "Relaxed nonintervention" of this sort had continued under the Chautemps government; now it was further relaxed and reached its peak under the second Blum government. Paul-Boncour did not again project the possibility of doing more, and, as the Madrid government's fortunes waned and turned hopeless, the Spanish question was overshadowed by the gathering storm in Central Europe.

In London, meanwhile, the King's ministers had been mulling over Corbin's inquiry, and on March 24, Sir Eric Phipps waited upon Paul-Boncour to present a note embodying the British reply. No, Britain would not join France in publicly declaring her intention to aid Czechoslovakia against German aggression, nor would she privately undertake any such commitment. The military situation was unfavorable: "His Majesty's Government do not press for any answer to the question Lord Halifax put to M. Corbin on the 12th of March as to what would, in the French view, be their method of rendering assistance to Czechoslovakia if the need arose; this is, however, a problem upon which His Majesty's Government have been reflecting, and they cannot say the result of their reflection is encouraging." In these circumstances, the best course would be for France to join with Britain in urging the Czech Government "to bring about a settlement of questions affecting" the Sudeten Germans. In accordance with his instructions, Sir Eric orally added the thought that eventually the German Government should be brought into the discussions of the Sudeten question.

Paul-Boncour was fond of repeating Talleyrand's comment that an alliance between England and France was as necessary as that between horse and rider, but that it was better not to be the horse. A joint and public warning to Germany, he insisted, would be the best means of preserving peace. France would assist Czechoslovakia by attacking Germany in the Rhineland. The insufficiency of French and British rearmament would only be aggravated by sacrificing the Czech forces, and anyhow time was working against the western powers, for German strength was augmented by each successful aggression. He agreed that the Czechs should be given counsels of moderation, but only privately, for any public admonitions would only serve to encourage Hitler to ask for more. On no account should Germany be approached directly on the Czech minority problem, as "this would be a terribly dangerous precedent for all countries with German minorities." All of which amounted to a judgment that the men of Whitehall were talking through their hats, and was hardly calculated to make Paul-Boncour popular with Chamberlain and Halifax.

Unfortunately, Paul-Boncour was more logical than politic. Few men like to be shown up, and his very directness soon worked against him. Someone privy to the discussions of the CPDN—according to Paul-Boncour an ex-officer in Pétain's entourage—leaked a distorted account of the meeting, and soon the air was filled with accusations that Blum and Paul-Boncour had decided to send the French Army into Spain.* Sir Eric Phipps, florid and suspicious, waited on the Foreign Minister to inquire whether it was really true that France was about to flout British policy by intervening in support of Madrid, and received for his pains not only a denial but a sharp reminder that, once Britain saw German and Italian troops around Gibraltar, she might better understand how France felt about their presence in the Pyrenees. However inaccurate, these accusations were damaging, and they reflected distrust of the Popular Front ministers' policies not only in Spain but in Central Europe as well; the commitment to Czechoslovakia grew increasingly unpopular as the possibility increased that France might be called upon to make good.

Late in March, Paul-Boncour summoned to Paris the French ambassadors in Central and Eastern Europe, and consulted them both individually and as a group on the problem of how to aid Czechoslovakia. Léon Noël, from Warsaw, declared that France was powerless to give effective help, citing the instability of the Blum government, the insufficiency of industrial resources, the weakness of the Air Force, and the adverse attitude of the Polish Government. According to Noël, all of his ambassadorial colleagues congratulated him for speaking their minds, while some of the Quai d'Orsay functionaries accused him of defeatism. Whatever the general sentiment, Paul-Boncour was not deflected from his course, and sent the ambassadors back to their posts with instructions to proceed on the basis that there would be no more concessions to Germany.

But it was Paul-Boncour's last sally. On April 4, Blum presented in the Chamber a request for power to carry through an ambitious program of fiscal reform and industrial expansion, based in large part on a greatly elevated rate of rearmament.† It passed the Chamber by a narrow margin, but on April 8 the Senate rejected it by a vote of 214 to 47. Blum and his cabinet at once resigned.

So ended the last serious effort by a French government to re-establish French power and cast off the British leading strings. Blum and Paul-Boncour had pointed a way to these goals, but theirs was an intellectual demonstration rather than a political achievement. There were simply not enough Frenchmen who thought they wanted to make the sacrifices essential to a national resurgence, or confront the hazards of blocking the Nazi march of conquest. France wanted a government that would take an easier course, and that is what they were about to get when President Lebrun, much vexed by the third cabinet crisis in three months, sent for Edouard Daladier.

---

* According to Paul-Boncour, the Pétain informant was a former ordnance officer and extreme rightist. Major Georges Loustanou-Lacau. He also named the British press attaché, Charles Mendel, as a source of hostile and mendacious accusations.

† Blum himself had taken the Finance portfolio in his second government, and the plan was largely the work of his under-secretary, Pierre Mendès-France, and his *chef de cabinet,* Georges Boris.

CHAPTER 21

Edouard Daladier: Man of Indecision

1

The government which Edouard Daladier formed in April of 1938 lasted through the Munich period, the destruction of Poland, and until March 1940, a few weeks before the Battle of France. Throughout his premiership Daladier retained the portfolios of National Defense and War, which he had held since June 1936. French premiers are ordinarily not as powerful as British prime ministers, and Daladier's grip on his government was by no means as tight as Neville Chamberlain's. But Daladier was also the leader of the dominant Radical Socialist Party and he, more than any other Frenchman, bears the political responsibility for the course his country took in the immediate prewar years.

His political soubriquet was "Bull of the Vaucluse," but though solidly built and often gruff in manner he was temperamentally no bull—his cop-out as Premier during the February 1934 riots was not soon forgotten, and perhaps that is why he had not been called earlier during the Blum-Chautemps game of musical chairs. His choice as War Minister in the Popular Front cabinet, however, was expectable, for he had served in that capacity from 1932 to 1934, and had led the Radical Party into the Popular Front coalition. Furthermore, in 1914 he had left the mayoralty of his native Carpentras to serve first as an infantry sergeant and later as lieutenant during the 1914–18 war, and throughout his career the Army was his favorite public concern.*

Daladier was highly intelligent and educated—he had taken a remarkable degree in history and classics and been a university professor before entering national politics—but he was not soigné like Chautemps and Blum. The Daladiers were a family of bakers, provincial petit bourgeois, and their prize offspring continued to speak an earthy patois. Daladier found his humble origin politically useful, and similarly exploited his own taciturnity, as the deputy from Orange, once the principality of William the Silent. Daladier's ability, industry, and incorruptibility, coupled with shrewd political sense, were the basis of his rapid political ascent and his only once-broken grip on ministerial office from 1924 to 1940. But the one break—from 1934 to 1936—was the consequence of his brief and disastrous second premiership, and was indicative of his crucial

---

* As Premier, Daladier continued to use the War Ministry office on the Rue St. Dominique, and he called his government the "Government of National Defense."

failing: in the clutch he recoiled from hard decisions, and let others take over. So it had been in 1934, and so it was to be again in 1938.

Daladier's lonely social and working habits were, perhaps, another drawback. His wife died in 1932; he did not remarry, and lived in a small apartment with his sister and his two sons, seldom entertaining. His social contacts were rather closely managed by his intimate friend, the Marquise de Crussol, who, according to Pertinax, brought him gossip which exacerbated his dislike of Blum and distrust of Reynaud. In public life he appears to have had numerous contacts but few confidants, and he was perhaps overprotected in his office by his devoted *chef de cabinet* and fellow *Vauclusien,* Marcel Clapier. High office did not broaden his international outlook; he was the French equivalent of a "little Englander," disliked the Treaty of Versailles because it entangled France with Eastern Europe, and, according to Beneš, he had little use for the Slav countries with which France was allied.

Despite their long association as War Minister and Chief of Staff respectively, Daladier and Gamelin were not close collaborators. Before Daladier took office as War Minister in 1936, Gamelin had been accustomed to deal with his predecessors Pétain, Maurin, and Fabry, all of whom were professional soldiers. Pétain's practice was to receive Gamelin at a regularly fixed time, while Maurin and Fabry were old comrades whom Gamelin could visit or telephone at his pleasure. But Daladier was a busy party leader; Gamelin could see him only by special appointment, often had to wait in the antechamber, and once inside found his conversations constantly interrupted by phone calls and visiting politicians. Daladier's military *chef de cabinet,* General Bourret, was not congenial to Gamelin, who found himself seeing Daladier less and less, with sometimes a full month between meetings. In the fall of 1936, Daladier and Gamelin were together on field trips to study extension of the Maginot Line and a better rapport was established.* But in Paris communication remained difficult, and suffered further in April 1938 when Daladier became Premier, retaining the National Defense and War portfolios.

The Socialists agreed to support the Daladier government (thus preserving the façade of a "popular front") but declined to join it, and Daladier sought a broader base by turning to the "right center" parties, bringing Reynaud, Georges Mandel, and a few other conservatives into lesser Cabinet posts. The major assignments all went to the Radicals, with La Chambre and Campinchi remaining at the Air and Naval ministries, and Georges Bonnet taking over the Quai d'Orsay.

The selection of Bonnet to replace Paul-Boncour was a sharp swing of the diplomatic weather vane, and a highly significant turn in the events leading to Munich. Both men were well known to the Premier; Bonnet had been Finance Minister and Paul-Boncour Foreign Minister in Daladier's 1933 government, and Daladier had been War Minister in Paul-Boncour's preceding government. In

---

* Together with his brusqueness and reticence, Daladier was possessed of a simplicity and directness which many found attractive; witness his effect on the young Captain Stehlin at Munich. This undeniable charm was still manifest in his old age, as will be apparent to anyone fortunate enough to view Marcel Ophuls' documentary film *Munich, ou la Paix de Cent Ans,* made in 1968, when Daladier was eighty-four years old.

view of the opprobrium which time has heaped on Bonnet's discharge of his office, the motivation of Daladier's choice has been much scrutinized, and he himself subsequently gave quite dissimilar explanations.

In 1951, responding to an inquiry on the point from the parliamentary investigating committee, Daladier wrote that Bonnet's selection was based on his having been president of the 1932 Stresa Conference on European economic reconstruction, and the good relations with President Roosevelt and other leading Americans which he had developed in 1937 as Ambassador to the United States. Seventeen years later at the age of eighty-four, talking with Marcel Ophuls, Daladier again mentioned the Washington contacts, but put the main emphasis on Bonnet's support from "bourgeois circles, heavy industry, and high finance," of which the new government had need.

Paul-Boncour, writing in 1945, described his long meeting with Daladier on the morning of April 10 (the day the new government was formed) as exclusively concerned with foreign policy. Daladier referred to the political opposition which Paul-Boncour's intransigence had aroused, and the latter replied that a yielding policy would lead to the destruction of both Czechoslovakia and Poland and leave France isolated and at Germany's mercy. They parted, and a few hours later Daladier telephoned:

DALADIER: I have reflected. The policy you have formulated is admirable and worthy of France, but I do not think we have the means to carry it out. I will take Georges Bonnet.
PAUL-BONCOUR: If you wish to pursue the other policy, you could not make a better choice. Good luck, my friend!

Most men are prone to color the past to their own credit, and Paul-Boncour wrote with the benefit of hindsight. Perhaps the interchange was not so sharply focused, but it probably followed those lines, and certainly the change from Paul-Boncour to Bonnet foreshadowed precisely the policy shift which the former defined.

But of course foreign policy was only one, and perhaps not the principal, reason for Daladier's choice. He was franker in 1968 than he had been in 1951; Bonnet was a political asset, Paul-Boncour a liability,* and after the "cascade of cabinets" from January to April, Daladier needed all the political strength he could muster if his government were to survive much more than a few weeks.

2

As it was, the French Parliament and public reacted with relief to the prospect of a more stable regime. The Parliament with virtual unanimity confirmed the Daladier government, and on April 13 voted the extraordinary financial powers previously denied to Blum. Strikes were settled and the franc steadied. The right-wing press, too, greeted the new government cordially, but there were

---

* According to Alexander Werth (*France and Munich*, p. 131), then the *Manchester Guardian* correspondent in Paris, there was "very good reason for saying that . . . the British Government made it very plain to M. Daladier . . . that it would consider the reappointment of M. Paul-Boncour to the Quai d'Orsay as eminently undesirable." As will appear in the next chapter, Werth's suspicion was well founded.

ominous notes struck: the Franco-Czech alliance was widely denounced and on April 12, Professor Joseph Barthélemy, a noted authority on constitutional law,* argued in *Le Temps* that the demise of Locarno had rendered the Franco-Czech treaty legally obsolete. Although the Quai d'Orsay, via an inspired editorial in *Le Temps,* immediately repudiated Barthélemy's analysis, the professor's article provided a plausible legal basis for spokesmen of appeasement such as Flandin.

Bonnet had hardly time to warm his new chair at the Quai d'Orsay when he was confronted by Sir Eric Phipps with new admonitions from London, stressing the dangers of the Czech-German situation, and urging Paris to join in strong representations to the Czech Government for settlement of the Sudeten minorities problem. Sir Eric found the new Foreign Minister compliant and even subservient. The very next day, April 14, Bonnet replied that, if the British did not find the Czech proposals "sufficiently far-reaching," the French minister in Prague would be instructed to join with the British "in urging modifications thereof upon the Czechoslovak government." Bonnet did not even reserve the Quai d'Orsay's right to make its own appraisal of the Czech offer to the Sudetens; that was a matter for London to determine. Ten days later the inadequacy of the Czech minorities program, as viewed by the Germans, became abundantly apparent when Konrad Henlein made his Karlsbad speech embodying the "eight demands."

The consequence of these developments was that on April 27, Daladier and Bonnet, accompanied by Léger and Rochat, were on their way to London by air. The French, it seemed, were forever going to London; the British rarely appeared in Paris. Shortly before his departure, Daladier had handed Gamelin a note asking the general to "specify the military action France could take against Germany and in support of Czechoslovakia, on the basis that mobilization is only the first step." Gamelin's reply, dispatched the next day, was a masterpiece of emptiness. After pointing out that "the military had not been party to the adoption of the mutual assistance pact" and that there was no "corresponding military convention," the Chief of Staff wrote:

> If the government so decides, the army and air force can act offensively under the conditions anticipated in our operational plans.
>
> It is clear that the power of our offensive will depend on whether or not the attitude of Italy requires us to leave forces in the Alps and North Africa.
>
> The effectiveness of the aid to Czechoslovakia also depends on the aid which could eventually be furnished by . . . Rumania and Yugoslavia, the Soviet Union, Poland, and the British Empire. But these questions are initially presented on the diplomatic level.

Presumably this document reached Daladier during the London discussions, but it can hardly have been of much help to him. And help he surely needed. Bonnet had dealt with the English leaders at the Lausanne Conference in 1932; Neville Chamberlain thought him "clever, dull, ambitious, and an intriguer." It was Daladier's first major encounter with "perfidious Albion," and the men opposite him were hard-boiled in manner to the point of truculence.

---

* Professor Berthélemy later served as Minister of Justice in Pétain's Vichy Government.

The conferees met four times on April 28 and 29. The agenda was, of course, dominated by the Czech situation, but Spain and Italy were the subjects of the opening exchanges. The British complained about the military aid which the French were allowing to slip through the Pyrenees to Madrid; the French gave their usual reply stressing the dangers presented by Axis troops in the peninsula, but agreed to resort once more to "nonintervention" as a means of getting them out. British and Italian representatives had recently signed the protocol for a treaty which would include recognition of the Ethiopian conquest, and it was understood that France would seek a comparable agreement with Italy.

When, toward the end of the first session, the conversation turned to the central question, it took a course which the French had not anticipated. Chamberlain, presiding, did not open the next item on the agenda—"Czechoslovakia" —but declared that it would be "more convenient" to discuss first the military staff contacts for which the French had been pressing. Furthermore the British, authors of the agenda, had inscribed this matter as "contacts between the British and French *air* staffs." Taking the lead, Halifax declared that, in the event of war with Germany (Italy, in deference to the nascent Anglo-Italian treaty, was ruled out as a potential enemy), British participation would chiefly be "by sea and in the air." Since war with Italy was not in question, there was no need of naval staff talks "at present." Air staff conversations would be conducted for "coordination of the two air defence systems" and to plan for basing "a British advanced striking force in France." As for the ground forces, "with the best will in the world" Britain could at the outset send only two incomplete divisions to France. Halifax left to implication the conclusion that for such small potatoes no Army Staff consultations were called for, and when he had finished the French were swept off to lunch.

When the conferees returned to the green table, Daladier objected forcefully to the limits of the British proposals. Warfare involved all branches of the armed forces; it could not be compartmentalized. The British should motorize the two divisions to be sent, and Army Staff contacts were essential. Especially in view of the Spanish situation, the French Navy would be operating in the Atlantic as well as the Mediterranean, and the naval staffs ought now to make the contacts which "would immediately become necessary in time of war."

Daladier's military logic was unassailable, but the British remained adamant. Since there was simply no answer to Daladier's argument for Army Staff talks even if only two British divisions were sent, Chamberlain fell back on the possibility that there would be none at all: "He could only say that the Government of the day might decide to do so [*i.e.,* send them], or they might not." Army Staff talks, therefore, could only be "hypothetical" and of dubious utility. As for the Navy, there was "no particular objection in principle," but "His Majesty's Government could not help feeling that there was really nothing special requiring discussion." Furthermore, such talks might excite "Italian or German suspicions that we were now devising fresh military, naval, or air combinations designed to injure those two powers."

For two hours that afternoon Daladier, with an occasional assist from Bonnet or Corbin, struggled to shake their ally's negative attitude. Finally Chamberlain grudgingly agreed that his government "would not be unwilling" for Army contacts to be established through the military attachés, as long as it was clearly understood that this involved no commitment to send any ground forces whatever to France in the event of war. But regarding naval talks the English would not budge, and the day's work ended without a mention of Czechoslovakia.*

On the second day, however, the conferees talked of little else. Again Halifax lead off, this time reiterating the position already taken in the note presented to Paul-Boncour on March 24. His Majesty's Government would assume "no fresh military commitments." Czechoslovakia could not be protected against German aggression, and it was therefore essential that Britain and France join in urging Beneš to make a settlement with Henlein, "on a much broader basis than they had hitherto envisaged."

Apparently irked by the many hours of English admonition, Daladier now began to talk like Paul-Boncour, and threw at the British all the arguments which that gentleman had unsuccessfully advanced to him less than three weeks earlier. Henlein, said Daladier, was really seeking "the destruction of the present Czechoslovak State"—a government which "had done more for the minorities than any other European State." Germany was prepared to "tear up treaties and destroy the equilibrium of Europe"; yesterday it was the Rhineland and then Austria, today it was Czechoslovakia, and tomorrow it would be, perhaps, Rumania. If the present military situation was poor, it certainly would not be improved by sacrificing the Czechoslovak Army. If Russia was weakened by the purge, still it had the "strongest air force in Europe." Concessions to the Sudeten minority should be made, but the only way to save the peace of Europe was for Britain and France to make it clear that "they could not permit the destruction of the Czechoslovak State."

Chamberlain replied harshly and adroitly, pretending that Daladier was giving way to anger, which the Prime Minister professed to share—it "made his blood boil to see Germany getting away with it time after time and increasing her domination over free peoples." But "such sentimental considerations were dangerous." Britain and France were not "sufficiently powerful" to risk a war, and anyhow the picture was not "really so black as M. Daladier had painted it." Chamberlain "doubted" that Hitler "really desired to destroy the Czechoslovak State" or "bring about the *Anschluss* of the Sudeten districts with Germany."

Bonnet (whether sincerely or fearful of displeasing Daladier) and Halifax now took up the cudgels in support of their chiefs, and Daladier closed the morning session with further argument that a firm and public position against further German aggression must be taken, lacking which "he could only regard the future with the greatest pessimism." After lunch, however, everyone was a bit more tractable. Chamberlain agreed "in principle" to naval staff talks at some future date, after Hitler's forthcoming visit to Italy. Halifax, while reiterating his government's unwillingness to enlarge its commitments, suggested that it might make a *démarche* in Berlin to inform the Germans that they were seek-

---

* That night the French were guests of the King and Queen at Windsor Castle, and, according to uncharitable journalists, Bonnet was so delighted with the attention that the next day "he could talk of nothing else."

ing a peaceful solution, but that "it took two to reach an agreement." This would be done simultaneously with a joint Anglo-French *démarche* in Prague to spur Beneš to greater concessions.

On that basis the conference ended. The official communiqué was innocuous; the participants tipped their hats to the Anglo-Italian agreement, "appeasement" in the Mediterranean, and the prospect of withdrawing "foreign participants" from Spain. General staff contacts would continue "as might be necessary." Czechoslovakia was not named, but the participants proclaimed their "general agreement in the action that might most usefully be taken" to ensure peace in Europe.

Actually, the French were probably more upset by the British attitude on staff talks than on Czechoslovakia. If Daladier had really hoped to force the British into a joint undertaking to defend Czechoslovakia, he would have taken Paul-Boncour with him rather than Bonnet. The Bull of the Vaucluse had snorted and kicked up the dust, but he did not want to charge. Ten days after his return from London, Daladier, asked by Bullitt whether France would go to war for Czechoslovakia, replied: "With what?" The French Air Force, he declared, was so weak that it would be "impossible for France to go to war," adding that "he had considered the position of Czechoslovakia entirely hopeless since the annexation of Austria by Germany." And on May 10, Chautemps, now Vice-Premier, told Bullitt that, in the event of a German attack on Czechoslovakia, "aside from protesting, France would do absolutely nothing."

The essence of the French leaders' attitude was immediately conveyed to Berlin by a British journalist acting as a confidential agent of the German Embassy in London,* who saw Daladier shortly after his arrival in London on April 28. According to the agent, Daladier expressed the greatest eagerness that Britain put pressure on Prague without delay, as he expected a showdown within a matter of months. France "had her hands tied" by her treaty with the Czechs, which made it all the more essential that Britain act: "The peace of Europe probably depends at this moment on the Czechoslovak issue and on what your Government, and especially Mr. Chamberlain, will do in that direction."

3

Dark as were Czechoslovakia's prospects for British or French military support after the London meeting, the decisions reached there did not mean that the unhappy country was to be pitched headlong into the German jaws, or that the French Government's reluctance to fulfill its treaty commitments would be openly avowed. Both London and Paris wished to save by negotiation as much of Czechoslovakia as possible, and in neither capital was there any illusion that concessions on Czechoslovakia would eliminate the Axis peril. Furthermore, there was no certainty that the British program would succeed in getting the

---

* The German archives do not reveal the identity of this individual, and it is, of course, possible that he was a double agent. See DGFP-D-II-Nos. 143 and 1470 of April 30 and May 6, 1938, recording the agent's conversations on this occasion with Daladier and subsequently with Count Fernand de Brinon, a French journalist used by Daladier as an unofficial contact with Berlin, convicted of high treason and executed in 1947.

western democracies off the hook; Czechoslovakia might not yield enough to satisfy Hitler, and Germany might then attack Czechoslovakia so brutally as to make it politically impossible for France to leave her in the lurch.

Daladier, indeed, was more than half persuaded that Paul-Boncour was right in his forecasts, and that giving in on Czechoslovakia would be merely exchanging a bad situation soon for a worse one later. But if he foresaw that the loss of Czechoslovakia would greatly increase France's military peril, this failed to spur him sufficiently to speed and modernize the rearmament program. He was not unaware of the generals' conservatism,* but gave De Gaulle and Reynaud no support. When he became Premier his time and energies were sorely taxed, and fiscal problems greatly affected his approach to rearmament.

On May 10, Gamelin laid before the Premier a new program calling for three additional infantry divisions, an enlarged call-up of recruits, and immediate expenditures for defense against air attack. Ten days later he supplemented this with a request for funds for the immediate establishment of three armored divisions, and three more as soon as possible thereafter. This program reached the Cabinet on the eve of the "May crisis" in Czechoslovakia, which certainly underlined the urgency of the military situation. Nevertheless, Daladier rejected, on grounds of cost, all of Gamelin's major requests. The general thought seriously of resigning in protest, but was dissuaded by Pétain. As Pertinax put it, Gamelin "was not impelled by a burning passion for getting results." Unfortunately, he and Daladier resembled each other in this respect, and the result was that the pre-Munich months saw no major expansion of the French arms program.

On the diplomatic front French activity, after the London discussions at the end of April, was more than ever circumscribed by the Chamberlain government, sometimes with humiliating consequences. The protocol for the Anglo-Italian treaty was signed in Rome on April 16, 1938, and that same day the French chargé in Rome, Jules Blondel, waited upon Ciano with Bonnet's note inviting negotiations for a Franco-Italian counterpart. Ciano agreed readily enough, but indicated that nothing could be finalized until after Hitler's visit, scheduled for early May. The Fuehrer came and went, but instead of continuing the negotiations, Mussolini, speaking at Genoa, delivered himself of a vigorous attack on France, in which he stressed the opposing Spanish policies of the two countries and cast doubt on the prospects of reaching an agreement. Bonnet's attempts to revive the negotiations were ignored, and that gentleman unhappily but accurately concluded: "After Mussolini had the agreement with England in his pocket, he lost interest in concluding one with France."

Worse was to come. Despite the British complaints during the London talks, Daladier had kept the Spanish border open, and on May 9 he boasted to Bullitt that he had told Chamberlain that the road to Madrid would be open until the Germans and Italians withdrew from Franco Spain. Early in June, however, the British renewed the pressure to close the frontier in the hope of persuading the

---

* On July 1, 1936, just after he returned to the War Ministry in the first Blum government, Daladier told the Deputies' Army Commission: "I know very well that the French Army is very traditionalist."

Axis powers to reciprocate. On June 13, Chamberlain told the House of Commons that, despite the bombings of British ships in Spanish loyalist harbors, his government would take no retaliatory action, and on the same day the American Ambassador in Rome, William Phillips, reported that "Monsieur Baudoin, a well-known French banker, has arrived unofficially in Rome . . . to convince the Italians that the French Government has for all practical purposes closed all Pyrenees frontiers and also to ascertain whether it would not be possible to reopen the Franco-Italian negotiations." In fact, and in consequence of the British request, Daladier had closed the Spanish border that very day, but the negotiations were not resumed, nor were the Axis troops withdrawn from Spain. Once again, the French Government had followed the British lead into a blind alley.

In the scales of strategy, Italy and Spain together were far outweighed by Russia; apart from Britain, the Soviet Union was the only major power from which France might hope for aid against Germany. Barthou had laid the basis for the pact that Laval unenthusiastically signed, and when Blum came to power he was eager to give military meaning to the diplomatic document by embarking on the staff talks which the Russians had been inviting. In November 1936, Blum directed the Army Staff to approach the Soviet military attaché, General Ventzov, and ascertain the prospects for useful general staff negotiations.

The task was entrusted to General Victor Schweisguth, then the Deputy Chief of the Army General Staff, who had headed the Army mission to the Soviet maneuvers in September.* Its fulfillment was delayed because of Ventzov's replacement by General Semenov, with whom Schweisguth conferred twice early in 1937. After returning to Moscow for instructions, on February 17 Semenov brought a verbal reply: if transit through Poland and Rumania were available, Russia would attack Germany's eastern frontier; if not, she would "send troops by sea"; in either case, she would contribute oil and other war materials and engage in naval and aerial warfare. Semenov then threw back to the French the same questions they had put to him, and received an equally vacuous reply: If Germany were to attack the Soviet Union, France "would intervene with all her forces."

In the afternoon of the same day, Blum himself entered the discussions through an interview with Ambassador Vladimir Potemkin, but this resulted in no significant clarification† of either Soviet or French intentions. Blum, no

---

* General Schweisguth was not predisposed in favor of military collaboration with the Soviet staff. His report on his mission concluded that the Soviet Army was "insufficiently prepared for war against a major European power," and that its employment against Germany was "very problematic." He also inferred a Soviet policy to push Germany and France into war, so that the Wehrmacht's initial blow would be directed westward and leave the Soviet Union, like the United States in 1918, "arbiter of the fate of an exhausted Europe." Blum remarked the difference between Schweisguth's unfavorable appraisal and a much more positive assessment by General Loiseau, who had witnessed the Red Army maneuvers in 1935.

† Potemkin specified that Soviet troops would be sent by sea to France, and that his government could furnish manganese, foodstuffs, and armaments as well as oil. In reply to General Gerodias' question about the possibility of a Soviet offensive through Lithuania, Potemkin replied that the Soviet staff had considered only "passage through states friendly to France," and that if there were other possible hypotheses, it would be up to France to develop them.

doubt, was sincere in his approach, but plainly the military men were sparring. When Schweisguth asked Semenov for further details on the scope and speed of Soviet action, the Russian answered that these were technical questions "which could not be answered until the two governments decided to hold staff conversations." However, he was returning to Moscow on March 20, and would report the questions to Marshal Yegorov, the Chief of Staff. Semenov said he would return to Paris early in April, but the French never saw him again. In the Soviet Union the purge was reaching its peak; Yegorov soon "disappeared," and Semenov's assistant told the French that his superior had undergone a "serious operation."

It is apparent that the Russians, who were very desirous of the staff talks, suspected that the French were trying to extract information without committing themselves to the staff contacts. The suspicion was well founded. Neither Daladier nor Delbos shared Blum's enthusiasm for the project, and the generals were even less enthusiastic. Daladier, when transmitting to Delbos a copy of Schweisguth's report on the Red Army maneuvers, told the Foreign Minister that any Franco-Soviet talks should be preceded by a Franco-Czech agreement on their scope and added:

> . . . under present circumstances these staff conversations, likely as they are to alarm certain friendly powers and to furnish Germany with a plausible pretext to charge an attempt at her encirclement, in my opinion present serious disadvantages, of which you better than I can understand the significance.

Delbos needed no reminder that the British would take a dim view of strengthening Franco-Soviet ties. Like Schweisguth, he also suspected that the Russians might, for their own benefit, foment hostilities between France and Germany, and he warned Coulondre of this possibility when the latter departed to his new post in October 1936. A year later, Moscow was significantly omitted from the eastern capitals which Delbos visited on his grand tour, and while in Warsaw he went so far as to tell the Soviet chargé, Vinogradov, that the French government was *"stupifié"* by events in Russia, which were destroying civil and military administration and putting "grave difficulties" in the way of Franco-Soviet co-operation.

At the Rue St. Dominique, Gamelin, originally favorable to the Soviet alliance, was cooling markedly. In May 1937, the Army General Staff prepared a memorandum of "reflections on the possible consequences of a Franco-Soviet military contact," the thrust of which was that, under existing circumstances, the hazards greatly outweighed the benefits. French security, it was declared, "rests above all on a close entente with England," and this would be gravely jeopardized by a Franco-Soviet military agreement. Furthermore, in view of the unfriendly attitudes toward the Soviet Union prevalent in Poland, Rumania, and Yugoslavia, such an agreement might well split the Little Entente and pitch Poland into the arms of Germany. Accordingly, no military connections with Russia should be established except in the unlikely events that Poland and Rumania sought Soviet support against Germany and that London gave its approval. On June 9, as a result of Tukachevsky's public disgrace, the French

General Staff composed a supplementary "note" pointing out the dangers of holding military talks with individuals who might disappear at any moment.

The French generals were quite correct in their assessment of the British attitude; London lost no opportunity to remind them that Moscow was not a respectable neighborhood. In April 1937, Ambassador Corbin reported that Sir Robert Vansittart, "among the Foreign Office chiefs least prejudiced against the Soviet Union," had read him a lecture on the perils of a Franco-Soviet military pact, which would surely reinforce British fears of Communist influence in France. A month later Eden was singing the same tune to Delbos, by remarking emphatically "the inopportunity, at this time, of any apparent move toward Franco-Soviet solidarity." And in February 1938, Neville Chamberlain, alarmed by a rumor (attributed to Reynaud) that London "favored the inclusion of a Communist in the French Government and military conversations between the French and Russian general staffs," telephoned Premier Chautemps to say that any such report "was the exact contrary of the truth."

To be sure, there was much substance in the points made in the French General Staff memoranda. It was indeed true that the Soviet army leadership had been weakened by the Stalin purge, that Russia had no common frontier with Germany, and that neither Poland nor Rumania was likely to grant passage to Soviet troops. For all these reasons there was little prospect of immediate, decisive aid from Russia to France in the event of war with Germany. But the same was true of Britain. If Russia had no direct access to Germany's eastern frontier, Britain had virtually no troops to deploy on her western borders. Against Germany the British Navy was primarily a defensive weapon, and in 1937 it was by no means clear that the Royal Air Force was as much of a threat to Germany as the Russian. It had been apparent all along that, if France and Germany should come to blows over Czechoslovakia, the French would have to rely initially on their own strength and await the time when Britain or Russia or both could mobilize and deploy their greater resources. No doubt, for reasons of trust and proximity, France was right to rely primarily on Britain, but it was no part of wisdom to allow Whitehall to dictate a policy that greatly diminished the possibility of Russian aid, which both of the western democracies would badly need once Germany struck.

The French General Staff's assessment of the eastern situation was even less shrewd, placing as it did the major emphasis on Poland and the Little Entente. A Czech-Polish combination against Germany would have been worth something, but that possibility had foundered on the rocks of Polish obstinacy. The Little Entente was already split and useless against Germany. Excessive concern for feelings in Warsaw, Bucharest, and Belgrade was bound to antagonize Moscow, with the prospect that it would be not Poland, but Russia, that would turn from France and make an arrangement with Hitler.

That, of course, is exactly what happened in 1939, but the danger signals were already visible even before *Anschluss*. On Christmas Day of 1937, Litvinov gave an interview to the Moscow correspondent of the Paris *Le Temps,* in which he declared that a Russo-German *rapprochement* was "perfectly possible," especially since the Soviet Government had no stake in Versailles or in maintaining the European *status quo*. A few weeks later he was telling Coulondre that, quite obviously, Paris was moving away from the Franco-Soviet alliance, and was responsible for a chilling of the relations between the two countries. "In determining our ultimate attitude toward the Soviets," Coulondre advised Delbos, "we must realize that if the Soviet Union is not with us, it will be against us."

With this background of mistrust and rejection, by the time that Georges Bonnet met for the first time with Maxim Litvinov—at Geneva on May 12, 1938—there was little basis for meaningful discussion between the two. Bonnet asked Litvinov the same questions that Blum and Schweisguth had put to Potemkin and Semenov a year earlier, and got much the same answers: Poland and Rumania were France's allies, and it was up to France to arrange passage for Soviet troops going to the aid of Czechoslovakia. Bonnet took up the matter with the Rumanian Foreign Minister, Petrescu-Comnene (who was also at Geneva), but without success.

Blum and Paul-Boncour might perhaps have re-established a measure of French credibility in Moscow, but Daladier and Bonnet had no stomach for such a course. On May 20, 1938, Ambassador Coulondre, recalled to Paris for consultation, made a determined effort to persuade his superiors of the vital need for three-way talks among the French, Czech, and Soviet general staffs. According to his account, over the course of the next three days* he succeeded in obtaining verbal approval of such talks from Daladier, Bonnet, Léger, and Gamelin. On May 23, Bonnet showed signs of uncertainty but finally reaffirmed his approval, and Coulondre returned to Moscow "thinking that I had finally taken a forward step."

But he was soon disillusioned. Whether because Coulondre's superiors had been stringing him along, or were shaken by the May crisis, or dissuaded by the British,† or on account of some combination of these factors, the French Government did absolutely nothing. On July 1 the Czech Ambassador in Moscow, Zdenek Fierlinger, showed Coulondre a report from his colleague in Paris, Stefan Osusky, that the French Government was eschewing staff contacts with the Russians "in order not to arouse the susceptibilities of the English conservatives." And when Coulondre returned to France for his vacation early in August, Daladier told him that the Government's policy was "above all to maintain a close entente with Britain, and take account of English prejudice against Bolshevik Russia."

Such was the negative state of French policy toward the Soviet Union when, a few weeks later, the Munich crisis arose.

4

It would, of course, be quite wrong to saddle London with the entire blame for the timidities and deficiencies of French diplomacy during the prewar years.

---

* This was precisely the period of the "May crisis" in Czechoslovakia, which, strangely enough, Coulondre does not mention in connection with his stay in Paris. Since his account is based on personal notes, the likelihood of an error in dating his Paris visit seems remote.

† Coulondre himself attributed his failure to a report, by the French journalist Geneviève Tabouis, that he had come to Paris to urge a Franco-Russian military agreement, which he thought had stimulated a strong negative reaction in London.

Certainly there were more than enough Frenchmen who shared the Chamberlain government's antipathy toward socialists and communists, whether in Paris, Prague, Madrid, or Moscow, and who extrapolated this distaste into the view that there was more to fear from Red Russia than Brown Germany—that Hitler might even serve as a barrier against the spread of Bolshevism. Such opinion led naturally to the conclusion that the Franco-Czech treaty was no longer legally or morally binding, and that a war fought to keep the Sudetenland part of Czechoslovakia would be the height of folly. These contentions were lent respectability by the pronouncements of Professor Barthélemy, ex-Premier Flandin, and others, and were featured in the conservative press most frequently and vociferously during the weeks immediately following *Anschluss*.*

To be sure, the Daladier government was not openly based on any such viewpoints; on the contrary, Daladier and Bonnet publicly reaffirmed France's commitment to the defense of Czechoslovakia. Nevertheless, the Premier was well aware that his government owed its popularity primarily to its "moderate" stance on international as well as domestic problems.

The selection of Bonnet was a signal that the Government would not follow the bold program of Reynaud and Paul-Boncour, and would seek accommodation with the Axis powers rather than attempting to construct a broad front to preserve the European *status quo* against Axis incursions. Bonnet needed no British instructions on appeasement, for he had his own reasons for subscribing to its wisdom. Furthermore, and apart from the substance of his policies, Bonnet's personality was such as to weaken both the Quai d'Orsay and the Government as a whole by sowing dissension and distrust. He had no rapport with Léger and inspired such repugnance at the Rue St. Dominique as to move the usually mild-spoken Gamelin to denounce his appointment as "profoundly unfortunate, because he never ceased to play an equivocal role," and to describe him in retrospect as:

> . . . a very intelligent man but without profound convictions, one could even say without morality.† He never regarded anything but his momentary personal interest, and had a natural taste for intrigue. Over and over again I found that I could not take his word for anything. He had, nevertheless, a strong influence, if not authority, in political circles. . . . He was, within the Daladier ministry which in fact included a number of valuable members, an evil ferment [*mauvais ferment*]. I should add that, if I distrusted him from the start, given what I knew about him in various connections, I only by degrees realized the baneful influence which he embodied and exercised. The British did not hide from me how they felt about him.

Such a spokesman was hardly likely to strengthen the voice of France in other countries, or deal effectively with their representatives in France. Perhaps even more than in most capitals, in Paris this was a lamentable deficiency. Ever since

---

* The concatenation of *Anschluss*, which showed the danger of war over the Sudetenland to be imminent, with the re-establishment of a Blum—i.e., Socialist—government, which of course was anathema to the conservatives, no doubt explains the virulence of the French press on these issues during the early spring of 1938.

† Bullitt, in a letter to Roosevelt dated January 10, 1937, described Bonnet as highly intelligent and well versed in financial and economic matters "but not a man of character."

the Franco-Prussian War, French security vis-à-vis Germany had been depend-ent on the support of allies, and the personalities and methods of allied diplo-mats were unusually important—unduly so, unless there was a firm hand on the tiller at the Quai d'Orsay.

The five countries (other than Czechoslovakia) most closely tied to France by treaty or tradition were Belgium, Britain, Poland, Russia, and the United States. As the Sudeten crisis mounted, the only one of these five whose repre-sentatives were urging France to fulfill her obligations to Czechoslovakia was Red Russia—the one country whose urgings to that end were bound, for do-mestic political reasons, to fall on deaf ears in French governmental circles. Officially or unofficially, the influence of the four others was exerted to persuade France *not* to honor her commitment, and in two cases—Poland and the United States—these views were presented by ambassadors of unusual forcefulness.

The impact on the Quai d'Orsay of this mass of diplomatic opinion was espe-cially great during and just after the May crisis in Czechoslovakia. To the gen-eral public, this affair appeared as a setback for Germany, and in its wake there was a noticeable softening of the French press's attitude toward Czechoslovakia. Behind the scenes, however, the Czech partial mobilization was the target of vast disapproval, and the French leaders were made painfully aware that their country might find itself virtually isolated should the crisis lead to war. The Bel-gian Government, for example, informed Ambassador Bargeton that in such event their army would conduct maneuvers on the French frontier "to demon-strate that, if you enter our territory in order to aid the Czechs, you will confront the Belgian army."

The behavior of the Poles was even more distressing. On May 22, Bonnet called in the Polish Ambassador to ask whether his government would be willing to "make a *démarche* in Berlin" similar to the warning which the British Government delivered there, and to inquire what Poland would do in the event that France and Britain should go to war with Germany in defense of Czechoslovakia. Ambassador Juliusz Lukasiewicz—a handsome, articulate, ar-rogant diplomat, fully wedded to Beck's policies—treated the questions with polite scorn. Of course he would put them to Warsaw, but Britain had made no similar request for Polish action in Berlin, and "we do not discuss with the Ger-man government the problems of other countries." As for what Poland would do "in case of a French-British-German conflict over Czechoslovakia," Lukasie-wicz "reminded" Bonnet that this eventuality lay outside the reach of any Polish treaty obligations, and it was doubtful "that my government could now take on any commitments."

Bonnet wheedled his auditor with protestations that he considered Poland to be France's "most important ally in the continent," and that "the role of Soviet Russia . . . would be geared to our needs, or would not be taken into account at all," all of which merely led Lukasiewicz to conclude that "Bonnet is aware of the likelihood that we would cripple possible Soviet Russian actions." Cer-tainly nothing Bonnet said had any helpful effect in Warsaw, for two days later, when Lukasiewicz brought Beck's reply, its content was negative and frosty. Poland would make no *démarche* in Berlin; if the "Czech problem" led to war,

Poland "must reserve the right of examination and decision"; furthermore, any concessions made by Prague to the Sudeten Germans must be matched by comparable benefits to the Polish minority in Teschen. This response, far from giving any support to the French position, notably failed even to convey any assurance that Poland would not join the fray on the German side.

The United States was bound to France not by treaty, but by the traditions symbolized by the names of Lafayette and Pershing. "Isolationism," given legal form by the Neutrality Acts of 1935 and 1937, was the order of the day in America; nevertheless, it was apparent that, in the event of war, American sentiment would be strongly favorable to the European democracies. If Britain and France were hard pressed, there would be every reason to hope for material aid from across the Atlantic and perhaps a repetition of 1917.

The prospect of ultimate American assistance was thus enormously important to the French. But could it be expected if France were at war not because the Germans had attacked her, but because she had attacked Germany to save Czechoslovakia? Ambassador Bullitt, who spoke with the strongest voice in the Paris diplomatic corps, was an avowed foe of the Franco-Soviet pact and an advocate of Franco-German conciliation. He was friendly with Lukasiewicz (both had been ambassadors to the Soviet Union and came from there to Paris in 1936) and made no secret of his admiration for Poland's policy toward Germany. In 1937, Bullitt twice visited Warsaw,* and made free to tell Beck and Szembek and others that French aid to Czechoslovakia would be "illusory," and that Soviet Russia was far more dangerous to Poland than was Germany.

Francophile as he was, Bullitt nonetheless shared the prevalent American determination to avoid military involvement in Europe's wars. Just a week before the May crisis, he had been at pains to caution Guy La Chambre that "in case of war between France and Germany, public opinion in America would be overwhelmingly in favor of application of the Neutrality Act" and that President Roosevelt "would have no choice but to apply it and prevent the delivery of planes and munitions." The May crisis itself utterly horrified Bullitt, and prompted his letter to Roosevelt of May 20, quoted in the first chapter of this book, in which the ambassador suggested that the President take the lead in bringing about a four-power conference to settle the Sudeten dispute. Bullitt prefaced his proposal by writing:

> I hope this letter reaches you before Europe blows up. At the moment, it looks to me as if the Czechs had decided that in the long run it would be better for them to have general war rather than give the Sudeten a sufficient autonomy to satisfy either Henlein or Hitler. They will shoot some Sudeten,† and Hitler will march across the Czech border.

---

* With sublime inconsistency, Bullitt told Szembek that the four "great European powers (England, France, Germany, and Italy) could maintain peace," and then told Beck that he "categorically" opposed the idea of a Four Power Pact (which involved the same four powers and was anathema to the Poles) and that Poland could count on American support in opposition to the project.

† In this and subsequent Bullitt dispatches there is an anti-Czech tone that had not previously been evident. Two days later Bullitt was warning the State Department that "Benes can throw the Continent into war by shooting some more Sudeten," and expressing his belief that "Benes prefers war to real concessions."

The question of whether or not all Europe shall go to war is . . . becoming a question of whether or not France will march when the Germans cross the Czech frontier . . .

I feel it would be an unspeakable tragedy if France, to support Czechoslovakia, should attack the "Siegfried Line". . . . There could be only one possible result; the complete destruction of western Europe and Bolshevism from one end of the Continent to the other. . . . If you believe, as I believe, that it is not in the interest of the United States or civilization as a whole to have the continent of Europe devastated, I think we should attempt to find some way which will let the French out of their moral commitment.

That "way" was, of course, exactly what Chamberlain and Halifax (for whom Bullitt had little use) were also seeking, and they were as alarmed as he was by the May crisis. Plainly worried that the French might not react with proper restraint, Halifax coupled an admonitory message to Berlin with another directed to Paris, embodying a very sharp reminder that if France should intervene it would be at her own risk:

1. It is of utmost importance that French Government should not be under any illusion as to the attitude of His Majesty's Government, so far as it can be forecast at the moment, in the event of failure to bring about peaceful settlement in Czechoslovak question. . . .

. . . . . .

4. If . . . the French Government were to assume that His Majesty's Government would at once take joint military action with them to preserve Czechoslovakia against German aggression, it is only fair to warn them that our statements do not warrant any such assumption. . . .

. . . . . .

6. His Majesty's Government . . . would therefore hope that they might be given an opportunity of expressing their views before any action is taken by the French Government which might render the position more acute or have the result of exposing them to German attack. . . .

Even before reading this warning to Bonnet, Sir Eric Phipps had told him that the Czechs "had put themselves in the wrong" and that Bonnet ought to "speak most severely to M. Osusky." Like Bullitt, Sir Eric was increasingly impatient with the Czechs, and as the final crisis approached, his dispatches increasingly reflected the attitudes of the French conservatives. On this occasion he found Bonnet "only too anxious to follow any lead we may give at Prague with a view to averting war," and soon Bonnet was telling Phipps that "if Czechoslovakia were really unreasonable the French Government might well declare that France considered herself released from her bond."

Bonnet was a loose talker and Phipps a close listener. Ten days later Halifax, much disturbed by the slow progress of the Sudeten-Prague negotiations, instructed Phipps to remind Bonnet of his remark about "release from the bond," and to indicate that "the moment has now come for a warning to be given to the

Czechoslovak Government on those lines." The next day (June 1) Bonnet promised Phipps that he would tell the French Minister in Prague (Lacroix) to convey the threat directly to Beneš, but the instructions actually sent to Lacroix from the Quai d'Orsay did not fulfill Bonnet's promise, and merely urged Beneš to approach the Sudeten problem "in a spirit largely of conciliation."

Quite incautiously, Lacroix revealed to the British Minister (Basil Newton) the limited and bland nature of his instructions and of his interview with Beneš, all of whch Newton dutifully reported to Halifax. Vastly displeased by Bonnet's failure to perform as promised, the noble lord at once directed Phipps to put the Foreign Minister on the spot by asking him what had been the result of the promised instructions. Bonnet wriggled out of the corner by claiming that he had communicated with Beneš through Osusky rather than Lacroix,* and once again assured Phipps that he would "continue to support us at Prague whenever we feel that it is necessary."

These were items in a constant stream of hortatory and admonitory messages from Whitehall to the Quai d'Orsay, which reached flood level after the May crisis. To all of them Bonnet responded affirmatively and even obsequiously, but for all his cleverness and long political experience he was not a firm or reliable person, and usually found it easier to join Phipps in lamenting Beneš obstinacy than to take a strong line with Beneš himself. Lord Halifax had a low opinion of the French in general and of Bonnet in particular, and was rapidly coming to the conclusion that diplomatic pressure on Beneš to make concessions to the Sudeten minority would not resolve the Czech-German problem. On May 30 he instructed Phipps to raise with Bonnet the project of an international commission to mediate the Sudeten question, and on June 17 he told Phipps to broach, a much more radical proposal under which Czechoslovakia, like Belgium, would be freed of her treaty obligations to assist France and Russia in the event of a German attack on either of these countries, while Czechoslovakia herself would remain the beneficiary of French and Russian guarantees, to which would be added a German commitment to respect her national and territorial integrity.

Bonnet's response to the mediation project was vaguely affirmative, but his reaction to the treaty proposals was noncommittal and dilatory, and eventually negative. Indeed, by mid-June there were signs that Halifax's unremitting hammering and lecturing were beginning not only to irritate the French officials, but also to raise question in their minds about the wisdom of pushing the Prague government so fiercely. In London, Corbin warned both Halifax and Sir Alexander Cadogan (Vansittart's successor) that Beneš was generally following the counsels of Britain and France, and that if despite such good behavior the pressure were increased, he might be driven "to desperation" and "let events take any course they might." A month later Daladier told the British chargé, Roland Campbell, that urging Prague to make further concessions, with no sign of reci-

---

* Bonnet was still the gay deceiver. His message via Osusky was not transmitted until June 9, the day after Lacroix saw Beneš, and it did not contain any threat of "release from the bond," although it did strongly urge speed in resolving the Sudeten minority question.

procity from the other side, "might be misinterpreted in Germany as a sign of weakness," in which case "the consequences would be highly dangerous."*

As spring turned to summer, the French leaders' attitudes toward the Czech problem were diverse and often ambivalent. On the surface, there had been a noticeable stiffening in support of their ally. Daladier, who shortly after the April meetings with the British had told Bullitt that "it was impossible for France to go to war to protect Czechoslovakia," on June 22 told him that, if the Czechs made a reasonable offer to the Sudetens and it was rejected, "France should not hesitate to go to war if Germany should invade Czechoslovakia . . . whether England liked it or not." A few days earlier, after talks with Gamelin and Inspector General Edouard Réquin, Bullitt had advised President Roosevelt that "public opinion in France had solidified to such an extent that if the German Army should cross the Czech frontier, France would mobilize at once and march against Germany. Gamelin is certain of this and so is Réquin, and there are few politicians who disagree." And a month later, after conversations with President Lebrun "and nearly all members of the Government and a number of generals," Bullitt reiterated his prediction that "France will go to war if the German Army enters Czechoslovakia."

But in fact there were at least a few politicians who disagreed with these assessments—for example Jean Mostler, Chairman of the Foreign Affairs Committee of the Chamber, and the still-influential Joseph Caillaux, Chairman of the Finance Committee of the Senate, both of whom, on June 14, told one of Phipps's subordinates that "France would never fight for Czechoslovakia." If Daladier and Gamelin were serious in their contrary statements to Bullitt, their behavior otherwise was passing strange. It was at that very same time that an invitation to Beneš to visit France was withdrawn, and that the Czech Chief of Staff, General Ludvik Krejcí, was discouraged from coming to Paris to discuss co-ordination of the Czech and French mobilization plans.† Likewise, it was during these same weeks that the French, under British pressure, closed the Spanish frontier. The political ban on military staff contacts with the Russians remained in effect and, while Bonnet repeatedly begged the Poles to give a formal commitment that they would not attack the Czechs, he never, according to Lukasiewicz, "attempted to pressure us to change our minds about allowing Soviet troops to march through our territory." In no significant way did the French government's actions lend credibility to Daladier's bold words to Bullitt.

Nevertheless, disregarding the counsels of Ambassador Noël that Prague

---

* Probably the French disposition to ease the pressure on Prague was in part the work of the able and articulate Osusky, who, less abrasive than Lukasiewicz, was equally secure in his dealings with Bonnet. Osusky strongly urged that France, allied with Czechoslovakia and in large part dependent on her for military aid against Germany, was in a very different situation from that of Britain, and should not be drawn in Britain's diplomatic wake.

† These two rebuffs are described in Beneš' *Memoirs* (pp. 34 and 42). According to Beneš, he was told that his invitation was withdrawn because "one of the items on my progamme was the unveiling of a memorial to the Czechoslovak Army of 1918," which Berlin would regard as "a provocation." There is no mention of these episodes in the French diplomatic documents so far made public, but there is no apparent reason to doubt Beneš' account.

should be warned of the fragility of French support, on July 12 Daladier took occasion in a public speech to reaffirm that France's "solemn agreements with Czechoslovakia are, for us, ineluctable and sacred."* Corbin explained to Halifax that the reason was Daladier's conviction that "the only sure method of preventing Herr Hitler from aggression against Czechoslovakia was to leave him in no doubt that France would honor her obligations towards that country "

Quite possibly Daladier was right, but he who is uncertain of his own intentions rarely sounds convincing. Halifax took the reaffirmation with good grace, but perhaps this was partly because the Chamberlain government was about to use quite different tactics.

5

On July 19, 1938, King George VI and Queen Elizabeth arrived in Boulogne to pay the first British royal visit to French shores since 1918. It was also their own first royal trip outside of Britain, and it was thought significant of the close relations between the two countries that Their Majesties had not followed the tradition of going first to one of the Dominions. They stayed in Paris for three days, and on the return trip the King unveiled the Australian war memorial on the Somme.

The weather was glorious and festooned Paris looked her loveliest. Their Majesties stayed at the Quai d'Orsay Palace, and Georges Bonnet was in seventh heaven, greeting them at Boulogne, shepherding them around Paris and Versailles, and throwing a magnificent dinner party for them on the last night of their visit, after which the royal couple appeared on the balcony of their apartment to acknowledge the passionate acclaim of huge crowds gathered on the banks of the Seine and on the Alexander III Bridge. For once, ceremonial and sincerity seemed happily joined, and the King, whose French was equal to the needs of the hour, declared it impossible to recall a period in which their relations were more intimate.

But if the brilliance of the occasion blinded the public and many of the participants to the perils besetting them, there was at least one who was not so dazzled. Lord Halifax had accompanied his sovereigns, and on July 20 he was closeted briefly with Daladier and Bonnet, and disclosed his intention to propose to Beneš that the British send an "investigator and mediator" to Czechoslovakia. The individual in question was to be Lord Runciman, and his terms of reference were purposely vague: ". . . our responsibility would begin and end with finding him and turning him loose at Prague to make the best that he could of the business." This information was conveyed to the French in the context of a reiterated warning that Britain stood committed to nothing by way

---

* The speech was delivered at a Paris banquet of the Provence and Languedoc Association. Late in April 1938, Bonnet had sent Noël, who had served in Prague before his transfer to Warsaw, to visit the Czech capital and make a confidential report on the situation. Noël's assessment was very pessimistic (in line with his expressions at the Paul-Boncour conclave a few weeks earlier), and in reporting his conclusions to Bonnet, with whom he enjoyed confidential relations, Noël recommended that the Czechs be warned that "France was not in condition to make war" and could not fulfill her engagements.

of aid to Czechoslovakia, reinforced by mention of South African and Indian opposition to anything "that might involve the British Empire in war."

The communiqué issued after the meeting was even blander than most such documents, and announced only the "complete harmony" of the participants' views. But in fact the meeting signalized the virtually total elimination of the Quai d'Orsay in the management of what might be called the "Sudeten Problem Resolution Company." Having functioned up to now as Chairman and Vice-Chairman of the Board, Chamberlain and Halifax were now taking over, in addition, the positions of President and Executive Vice-President. So complete was their disregard of French views and feelings that they had not even bothered to consult the French in the selection of the person who was to fulfill the "mediator's" role.

Bonnet's feelings do not appear to have suffered, but it is more than doubtful that Daladier was much pleased. In his postwar testimony, Daladier confined himself to the rather acrid comment about Runciman that "no one knew whether he was arbitrator or mediator, expert or advisor." But Léon Blum, who (as well as Herriot, Chautemps, Léger, and Corbin) was invited to a postconference luncheon at the Quai d'Orsay, was certain that the Premier was exceedingly disgruntled:

> I can testify, in consequence of the tête-à-tête that Daladier and I had during the luncheon—the conversation between Lord Halifax and Georges Bonnet being prolonged—how suspicious he was of this proposition, which he knew was being discussed over our heads or on the other side of the door, how hostile he was to the idea of this mission, the fatal consequences of which he rightly foresaw, and moreover a few minutes later, in my presence, he categorically rejected Lord Halifax's proposal that the inquest be a joint Anglo-French one, and that Lord Runciman be joined by a French collaborator.*

But if Daladier took so jaundiced a view of the Runciman plan, he did nothing to stop it. When the Czech leaders were confronted with the British proposal and at once sought advice from Paris, Bonnet and Léger advised Osusky in no uncertain terms that Prague should agree immediately and unconditionally. The Czechs promptly complied, and ten days later Runciman arrived in their capital city.

With the dispatch of the Runciman mission, the French Government lost what little room for initiative it had left. As Pertinax pointed out, France had really no alternative but to await and accept Runciman's recommendations, while Germany would remain quite free to reject them. Meanwhile, the Quai d'Orsay could do little but mark time. Lukasiewicz soon noticed that his visits to Bonnet had taken on a "stereotyped character," as the Foreign Minister had little to communicate other than the course of the Sudeten-Prague negotiations which Runciman was encouraging and evaluating.

---

* It is virtually certain that Halifax made this suggestion out of belated politeness and with every expectation that it would be declined, in as much as the British internal documents prior to July 20 show quite clearly that Halifax was planning on the dispatch of a British "mediator" only. Furthermore, in Prague, Mr. Newton proposed the sending of Lord Runciman to President Beneš that same day, July 20.

If August was Runciman month in Czechoslovakia, it was, as always, holiday month in France. "Runciman and Czechoslovakia seemed a million miles away . . . during that beautiful summer of 1938," Alexander Werth recalled. The Riviera, swarming with people from Menton to Marseilles, "had never had such a wonderful season before." The combination of paid vacations and legal holidays resulted in extensive factory shutdowns throughout the month. Meanwhile, both the Quai d'Orsay and Rue St. Dominique were receiving ominous reports of German troop movements and reserve call-ups.

The sight of his countrymen laying down their tools and heading for the sunny beaches, while Germans were jumping into uniform and working frantically on the Siegfried Line, finally moved Daladier to do more than grumble. On August 21, in a nationwide radio address, he announced suspension of the forty-hour week in defense plants, and begged the nation to get back to work. An immediate result was the resignation of his Ministers of Labor and Public Works. Ironically, his choices to replace them were two of the most appeasement-minded men in the Parliament, and Anatole de Monzie, the new Minister of Public Works, was known as a savage critic of the Franco-Czech alliance. Once again, it appeared, the Bull of the Vaucluse had taken one step forward and two backward.

On August 24, General Vuillemin returned from an official visit to Germany, full of frightening news about the pace of German aircraft production, and repeating to all and sundry his gloomy prediction, first given voice at the CPDN meeting the previous March, that in the event of war with Germany the French Air Force would be destroyed in fifteen days. Worse still, when he had told Goering that a German invasion of Czechoslovakia would mean war with France, the Fat One had flown into a rage! Then, on August 29, the Fuehrer himself appeared at Kehl, across the Rhine from Strasbourg, in the course of an inspection trip along the Franco-German frontier.

That same day Georges Mandel, Minister of Colonies and, like Reynaud, a strong opponent of appeasement,* told Osusky that the Rue St. Dominique had reliable information that Czechoslovakia would be attacked during the last ten days of September. And the next day, August 30, Lieutenant Colonel Fernand-Georges Gauché, chief of the famed Deuxième Bureau (intelligence section of the Army General Staff) informed the British military attaché that the German Army was "in process of mobilization," and that "from the military point of view, Germany is ready for immediate war against Czechoslovakia . . . and it rests entirely with the political side if it is to be averted."

Alarmed and with good reason, on August 25 Bonnet had sent René Massigli to ask Gamelin what measures he was taking to meet the threatening situation. The general replied that "our system is ready, it's only necessary to press a button to start it"—which was a figurative reply at best, since French mobilization was far from a rapid process. On the twenty-ninth Gamelin thought it time to touch the first button, and recommended to Daladier that the class of

---

* As events were soon to prove, the three conservatives that Daladier had brought into his cabinet—Reynaud, Mandel, and Paul Champetier de Ribes—were the staunchest governmental advocates of resistance to German aggression and fulfillment of France's eastern treaty obligations.

reserves due to be released in September be kept on duty, and that the class just previously released be recalled in the fortified zones, along with the special fortification troops. It was the beginning of the traditional defensive *couverture,* and on September 2 the Cabinet gave its approval. In accordance with Daladier's instructions, General Colson informed General Kühlenthal of the steps being taken, explaining that they were necessitated by the German troop deployments. On September 5 the French Government issued a communiqué revealing the recall of troops on leave and the call-up of fortress troops, together with cautions against panic and assurance that "the general situation appears to lead toward a discernible *détente.*"

At the Quai d'Orsay, meanwhile, Bonnet was still hopeful that Runciman's activities could lead to a compromise that would avert the threat of war. Time and again he assured Phipps that the French Government would support "any solution proposed by Lord Runciman . . . whether pleasing to the Czech Government or not." He told Bullitt the same thing on August 26 and Welczeck on September 1, adding on the latter occasion that "if M. Beneš would not accept Lord Runciman's verdict France would consider herself released from her engagements to Czechoslovakia."

To increase the pressure on Hitler, Bonnet now seized upon the dedication of a monument at the Pointe de Grave (near Bordeaux, where the first American units had landed during the First World War) as a lever to extract some helpful official statement from the United States. Bullitt and Bonnet were to be the two principal speakers. A few days before the ceremony, scheduled for September 4, Bonnet pressed Bullitt to repeat a phrase from a speech made in February of 1937, to the effect that while America hoped to stay out of war, "it was always possible that some country might be crazy enough to draw her in." The State Department objected, but Bullitt took the matter to Roosevelt, and with his approval declared at Pointe de Grave that "if war should break out in Europe, no one could predict whether or not the United States would be drawn in."

So far so good, but Bonnet's effort proved counterproductive because, in his own speech, he badly overplayed his hand by coupling a reaffirmance of France's "faithfulness to the commitments she has made" with a portrayal of the United States as her comrade-in-arms:

> One is inclined to say that it is the fate of France's arms and America's arms to be assembled under the same banner whenever they are called upon to defend those principles which our two countries consider to be the most precious heritage of mankind. The one friend is irresistibly compelled to rush to the help of the other friend who is in danger.

Given the conjunction of the occasion and the speakers, in the context of the rising tension in Europe and neutralist sentiment in America, such talk was bound to arouse apprehension in Washington. Five days later, in a press conference at Hyde Park, President Roosevelt rather brutally dashed the expectations that Bonnet had sought to excite:

> Ambassador Bullitt's speech does not constitute a moral engagement on the part of the United States toward the democracies. . . . To include the United

States in an alliance France-Great Britain against Hitler is one hundred percent false.

Bonnet, of course, was much upset by the dénouement, but he had only himself to blame; particularly as a recent ambassador in Washington he should have known better. The Nazi press, of course, had a field day with Roosevelt's disavowal, and the French position was further weakened.

Bonnet fared little better at Geneva, where he betook himself on September 11 for the opening of the League of Nations' annual session, and where he again encountered Litvinov and Petrescue-Comnene. Their conversations were a virtual replay of what the three had said to each other in May; Litvinov held fast to his position that it was up to France to persuade her Polish and Rumanian allies to grant passage to Russian troops. Petrescu-Comnene once more turned a deaf ear to Bonnet's plea.*

Despite these diplomatic failures, the French Government was still maintaining a firm posture. On September 8, Daladier received (separately) both Phipps and Bullitt and told them, very positively, that, if Germany attacked Czechoslovakia, France would "march." To Phipps he explained that "this will not be for the *beaux yeux* of the Czechs" but because "after a given time, Germany would, with increased strength, turn against France." Nor would the conflict be "a case of stalemate in the Maginot and Siegfried lines," for the German fortifications were not yet formidable, and Gamelin was "convinced that he would be able to undertake a series of limited offensives."

The Premier's representations to Bullitt were equally categorical but much less buoyant. France, he said, would mobilize and attack Germany "if the foot of a German soldier should cross the Czechoslovak frontier," and "however England might wobble or vacillate there would be no vacillation on the part of France." Personally, Daladier "had fought the Versailles Treaty to the utmost" and thought "that the Czechs had been most brutal in their treatment of the Sudeten." The day before, he had called in the German chargé d'affaires, Dr. Curt Braeuer,† and told him all these things, hoping to convince Hitler that France was not bluffing. Bullitt found Daladier "completely calm and posed as all Frenchmen are" and prepared to joke about the prospects of "our being blown simultaneously into the air from both sides of the Seine." But "he was fully aware that a French attack on the German line would be very costly and would not get very far." With Gallic logic, he declared that "the world was indeed insane," but insisted that "France was bound in the interests of honor and public decency to make such an attack."

Gamelin, for his part, was stepping up the military preparations, though not very rapidly. On September 7, a presidential decree was issued covering "the general organization of the nation in time of war," which committed the war's

---

* Paul-Boncour, who was at Geneva as chief of the French delegation, sent personal word to Beneš that he should swing the Poles to his side by ceding the Teschen area, and then lay the Sudeten problem before the League of Nations. The later proposal was in line with Litvinov's view of the action to be taken if Poland and Rumania refused passage to Soviet troops—an attitude which Paul-Boncour thought "wholly correct."

† Ambassador Welczeck had gone to Germany early in September and did not return to Paris until after the Munich crisis.

"general direction" to the Government, the co-ordination of air and ground operations to the Chief of Staff for National Defense (Gamelin), and the direct conduct of operations to the three service commanders-in-chief. The *couverture* call-ups continued, and on September 8 preparations were begun for the "reinforced *couverture,*" involving the mobilization of divisions stationed in the French interior and their movement to the frontiers. On September 11, Gamelin called in Kühlenthal to explain once more that "we are by reason of the steps you are taking, obliged to act ourselves."* And the next day, a few hours before Hitler's closing speech at the Nuremberg Party Rally, Gamelin, accompanied by Generals Georges and Billotte (who were to be the field commanders on the northeastern and Alpine fronts, respectively), met with Daladier to discuss the military plans and prospects.

The Premier put two questions to the generals. What could they do on the ground to aid Czechoslovakia? How great a danger to Paris was the Luftwaffe?

As to the first, Gamelin replied that nothing could be done before Czechoslovakia had lost a large part of her territory, but that the Army was confident of the ultimate outcome, and all could be restored by the peace treaty as had been the case with Belgium, Serbia, and Rumania after the First World War. Since Belgium was no longer open to French troops and the Rhine-Black Forest front was hopeless, the attack would have to be launched between the Rhine and the Moselle. This would lead to a frontal engagement between French and German forces of approximately equal size—fifty to sixty divisions each. The attack could be launched seven or eight days after the first day of mobilization; Georges thought it would take ten days, and warned against hopes of quick victory.

As for Paris, even with good antiaircraft the city's security could not be guaranteed, but this consideration should not govern the military decision. This was a question of civilian morale, and with British help there could be retaliation against the great cities of the Ruhr; Germany was more vulnerable to air attack than France.

The generals, it is clear, neither denied the possibility of offensive military action nor even advised against it. Still, the prospect they described was not very inviting. It would be a long, hard war.†

What impression the generals' presentation made on Daladier we do not know. What we do know is that twenty-four hours later Sir Eric Phipps found him a very much more uncertain man than he had seemed on September 8. Of course, after the meeting with the generals, the Premier, presumably, listened to Hitler's speech, which was certainly violent in tone. But the Fuehrer had announced no action and made no specific demands, and his verbal assaults appear insufficient as a major cause of Daladier's faltering.

Perhaps at the earlier meeting the Premier had been bluffing, and that is just

* It was a friendly conversation, at the conclusion of which the two reminisced about the personal qualities of Generals Mangin and Touchon, of First World War fame.

† As will appear, Gamelin and Georges grossly overestimated the strength of the German forces which Hitler planned to deploy on the western front while Czechoslovakia was under attack.

what Phipps inferred in his report to Halifax. There are indeed indications, in both Phipps's and Bullitt's reports of their meetings on September 8, that Daladier was talking as he did in the hope that the words would reach Hitler's ears and dissuade him from resorting to war. But other factors, including the attitude of Phipps's own government, may well explain Daladier's shift as not a seeming but a genuine change of heart.

On August 31, when Corbin informed Lord Halifax of France's precautionary military measures, his tidings evoked no expressions of approval, but only the usual reminder that Britain would not commit herself to any supporting action in behalf of Czechoslovakia. Three days later, Phipps quizzed Bonnet, on the basis of reports circulated by Flandin, about the alleged warmongering activities of Herriot, Reynaud, and Mandel.* On September 5 the ambassador warned Bonnet against any concerted Franco-Soviet diplomatic action, because it would be "likely to infuriate Hitler." On the seventh Lord Halifax asked Corbin for assurance that if a situation arose calling for French fulfillment of their treaty obligations "the French Government would still be prepared to consult us before taking any action involving them in hostilities against Germany." He coupled this with an expression of opinion that if Hitler should foment a Sudeten secessionist movement, and send German troops in to support it, "the French people . . . and the British people would not wish to embark upon protracted hostilities against what would have appeared to be a secessionist movement on the part of the Sudetendeutsch." That same day the London *Times,* regarded by many as closely allied with the Chamberlain government, published an editorial proposing cession of the Sudetenland. After Daladier's statements to Phipps and Bullitt on September 8, Halifax told Corbin that he "did not think that British opinion would be prepared, any more than I thought His Majesty's Government would be prepared, to enter upon hostilities with Germany on account of aggression by Germany on Czechoslovakia," and reiterated "the urgency of our desire that the French Government should . . . consult us before embarking upon measures that might involve them in war." And on September 10, when Bonnet called in Phipps and squarely faced him with the question whether, if France should "march," Britain would join her, Phipps promised to refer the question to Halifax but replied at once that "the question could not be answered in advance and without reference to the nature of the German aggression."

It would be more than surprising if this unremitting barrage of admonition and remonstrance from France's major ally, whose government appeared to be taking absolutely no precautionary military measures, had failed to have a chilling effect on Daladier's morale. Everything emanating from Whitehall seemed to confirm the dire predictions of defeatist politicians like Flandin and Cailaux. Daladier had to worry about the home front as well as the international scene, and by the time of Hitler's Nuremberg speech there was a swelling chorus of political and journalistic voices calling for a peaceful solution, even at the cost of Prague's capitulation.

---

* Bonnet denied that either Herriot or Reynaud was "bellicose" but "admitted" that Mandel was "doubtless prompted by his Jewish origin."

During the first ten days of September, French public opinion was generally firm in support of Czechoslovakia. There were exceptions among the extreme right partisans of peace-at-any-price—the "Resigned Nationalists," as Charles Micaud described them. For example, the *Times* editorial of September 7 was anticipated on the sixth by Emile Roche in *La République,* who wrote that if Germans and Czechs could not live together, they "must be separated." But when Daladier told Phipps, on September 8, that "the internal situation was excellent" even though the public fully realized the gravity of the situation, he reflected the views of most observers, including Léon Blum, with whom Phipps lunched the following day. There were few strikes, and the reservists were joining their units without a trace of complaint. Indeed, through most of the crisis, it was Alexander Werth's impression that the French people were far more stable than their press or politicians.

However that may be, *articulate* French opinion soon became sharply divided among *bellicistes* (war hawks), *bonnetistes* (supporters of Bonnet), and those who could not make up their minds. The annual Nazi Party Rally at Nuremberg began September 5, and on the tenth Goering delivered a violent diatribe against the Czechs which badly shook the fainthearted, and *bonnetiste* voices began to drown out the others. Daladier himself later testified to the impact of all this on his own state of mind:

> I shall long remember those September days, when one saw two-thirds of the French press, if they did not take the German side, at least take sides against Czechoslovakia, and declare that the treaty was no longer valid because the Locarno pact had been torn up, and the lamentable spectacle presented by numerous deputies, in groups which were almost always deeply divided on the matter, and who sent me contradictory delegations, some opposing mobilization and others urging me to go to war, and charging from the Ministry of War to the Elysée Palace, bringing disarray and demoralization everywhere.

The Cabinet met on the afternoon of September 12 but decided nothing, since everyone was waiting for the Fuehrer to drop the second shoe that night. The bang was not as loud as had been feared, since neither a plebiscite nor cession nor any specific concession was demanded. But the tone was vicious, and the speech triggered riots in the Sudetenland that could readily furnish Hitler with an excuse for armed intervention. Germany's military posture was increasingly minatory, and it was high time to answer the hard question: should France mobilize? To Hitler even more than to most men actions spoke louder than words, and it was of no use for Daladier to talk tough to Minister Braeuer if the French Army did not prepare to back his words by deeds.

Accordingly, the French Cabinet meeting on September 13 was crucial. It is well known that the members were sharply divided; that Reynaud and Mandel, with variable support from Champetier de Ribes, Campinchi, Zay, and Queuille, advocated full or partial mobilization, both as a matter of security and to convince Hitler that France meant business, and that Bonnet, Chautemps, Monzie, and Pomaret were the apostles of appeasement and the most determined opponents of mobilization. In the upshot, the *bonnetistes* carried the day with a vacillating, melancholy Daladier and a majority of the Cabinet,* and shortly after the meeting ended Bonnet told Phipps that "no further military measures were contemplated, and peace must be maintained at any price."

Despite his success in the Cabinet, the French Foreign Minister was in a state of nerves bordering on panic. Greatly alarmed by the reports from Czechoslovakia, he telephoned Phipps during the course of the meeting to "beg" that Runciman forthwith announce that he was about to propose a compromise plan; the "whole question of peace or war," he declared "may now be only a matter of minutes instead of days." A few hours later he renewed the plea that Runciman do something to calm the situation, and pressed the point so frantically that Phipps reported that "His Excellency seems completely to have lost his nerve and to be ready for any solution to avoid war." After telling Phipps the result of the Cabinet meeting, Bonnet criticized the "bellicose attitude of certain press" on the ground that such writing "was calculated to raise French hopes unduly." Phipps advised Halifax that "M. Bonnet's collapse seems to me so sudden and so extraordinary that I am asking for an interview with M. Daladier." Lukasiewicz, who saw the Foreign Minister later that evening, described his mood as one of "depression and helplessness."

The Premier, when Phipps saw him early that evening, was in better control of himself than Bonnet, but "gravely perturbed by the bloodshed in Czechoslovakia," and echoing Bonnet's view that minutes counted, and his plea that Runciman act quickly. Phipps reported:

> I finally asked M. Daladier point blank whether he adhered to policy expounded to me by him on September 8. He replied, but with evident lack of enthusiasm, that if Germans used force French would be obliged also. He added, however, that of course he would have to be sure regarding rights and wrongs of recent bloodshed in Czechoslovakia . . . he spoke bitterly of M. Benes, as did M. Bonnet previously. . . .
>
> To resume, M. Daladier of today was quite a different one to the M. Daladier of September 8, and tone and language were very different indeed.
>
> I fear French have been bluffing, although I have continually pointed out to them that one cannot bluff Hitler. . . .

As Phipps left, Daladier said that "he would perhaps telephone to the Prime Minister." What the Premier had in mind stemmed from a proposal which Léger, on his own responsibility, had put to Phipps two days earlier: that a four-power conference (Britain, France, Germany, and Italy) should be convoked "for a general settlement of all outstanding questions." Léger confided to Phipps that Bonnet would probably favor the idea, but that Daladier would fear left-wing opposition; if the British were to sponsor the project, however, the French Government would certainly accept it. Léger brought the matter up again in a telephone conversation with Phipps early on September 13, and Emile Roche had already taken the same line in La République: "Perhaps this is

---

* No record of the meeting has become available. There are descriptions of its course in Werth's *France and Munich* (pp. 251–55) and Wheeler-Bennett's *Munich* (pp. 102–3), both based on undisclosed sources. Bonnet, Reynaud, and Zay do not describe the meeting in their memoirs, nor does Monzie in his published diary entries.

the time for the four great nations who hold in their hands the heritage of Occidental civilization to act in full agreement." Later on the thirteenth Bonnet repeated the proposal to Phipps.

When Phipps saw Daladier at the end of the day, the Premier approved the conference idea but expressed preference for a three-party meeting, eliminating Italy. As related in the opening chapter, this was the same lineup that François-Poncet had unsuccessfully proposed in June, and the Britisher was no better impressed with the idea in Daladier's mouth.

Nevertheless, at about nine o'clock that evening, Daladier attempted to convey the three-nation plan to Chamberlain by telephone. Years later Daladier wrote that he spoke to Chamberlain, but communication was badly hindered by a poor connection. The Frenchman had no English and the Englishman little French, and if they did talk,* it must have been, as Cadogan recorded, a hopeless effort. Cadogan insisted that the message be sent through Phipps.

The ambassador, with true British nonchalance, had gone to the Opéra Comique. Summoned to the Rue St. Dominique, he was closeted with the Premier for some time. Emerging, he vouchsafed to the waiting newsmen only the cryptic observation "This bickering [*chamaillerie*] has got to stop!" In fact, Daladier had dictated to him a "very urgent" message for transmission to Chamberlain:

> Things are moving very rapidly and in such a grave manner that they risk getting out of control almost at once, and neutralizing all the reasonable measures undertaken by France and Great Britain, such as the Runciman Mission, pressure on M. Benes, etc., which I am keeping up more than ever.
>
> Entry of German troops into Czechoslovakia must at all costs be prevented. If not France will be faced with her obligations, viz.: automatic necessity to fullfill her engagements.
>
> To avoid this I propose two things:—
>
> 1. Lord Runciman to make known his plan publicly and immediately.
> 2. Can he also bring the two parties together in his presence?
>
> Should the above procedure not be sufficient I propose:
>
> 3. An immediate proposal to Hitler for a meeting of the Three Powers, viz.: Germany for Sudetens, France for the Czechs, and Great Britain for Lord Runciman, with a view to obtaining that pacific settlement advocated by Hitler in his speech last night. After that settlement a more general settlement with other additional Powers participating might be contemplated.
>
> Do you agree to my above proposals, or would you suggest any others?

This message was the first direct contact between the two leaders since their April meeting in London, and it was Daladier's first and last attempt to take the initiative in resolving the Sudeten crisis. It was not a good effort, for it was both tardy and maladroit. The idea of the British Government as a representative of

---

* Sir Thomas Inskip's diary states that Chamberlain refused to talk to Daladier. Cadogan's diary is ambiguous on the point. Bullitt reported to Washington that Daladier had spoken to Chamberlain, but that the latter's poor French then required transmission of the message through Phipps.

Runciman was ludicrous, and the prospect that Hitler would join a conference outnumbered two to one was nil. Furthermore, Daladier had delayed his move too long, for Neville Chamberlain already had a different plan, foreshadowed in his answer to Daladier, which was dispatched to Phipps early in the morning of September 14:

> Prime Minister fully recognizes immediate urgency of action in view of pace at which events are moving. He has considered the two courses of action proposed by you, and thinks with you that either or both may be found useful. But before deciding on your proposals, Prime Minister is exploring tonight another possibility of direct action in Berlin on which he should be in a position to inform you fully tomorrow. We have some hope that it might be helpful on wider lines you suggest.

September 14 dawned over a very tense Paris. Talking to Bullitt, Phipps labeled the Daladier plan "not a happy one," but believed that Hitler might agree to attend a conference if Italy were included. The French, he thought, "since yesterday had weakened greatly in their support of the Czechs" and by now "were ready for peace at almost any price."

Bullitt then paid a visit to Bonnet, who was still overwrought and labeling "absolute folly" Runciman's failure to issue his report, which was "the single thing which would calm the Sudeten" and prevent incidents which would cause Hitler to "march in." While Bullitt was there, Daladier telephoned Bonnet with a report that "the Czechs without informing the French government in any way had issued orders for the mobilization on the German frontier of a number of motorized divisions." For weeks Bonnet had been rightly alarmed because the Germans had been deploying battle-ready formations on the Czech frontier, and it is a measure of his blindness to moral and military considerations alike that he now characterized it as "outrageous" that the Czechs should take countermeasures without consulting the French Government.* The Czechs, he complained, "had failed to play straight so often with France that the French would be fully justified in washing their hands of their obligation to the Czechs."

At midday Phipps waited upon Bonnet, to convey Halifax's answer to the question Bonnet had put on September 10: if France should be obliged to march against Germany, would Britain march with her? The answer was a repetition of the oft-expressed unwillingness of the British to commit themselves in advance. But much had changed since the question was asked, and Phipps reported that Bonnet "seemed genuinely pleased by the negative nature of your reply to his question"—no doubt because, as he had told Phipps the day before, he found Britain's refusal to take a pat position "useful with certain bellicose French ministers." Bonnet went on to tell Phipps that "France would accept any solution of the Czechoslovak question to avoid war," and to that end "we must therefore make most far-reaching concessions to the Sudetens and to Germany . . . in spite of Czechs and Soviets . . . in order to forestall any aggression by Germany."

Not until that evening was the mystery of Chamberlain's other "possibility of

---

* In fact the Czechs had not mobilized but had declared martial law in the riot-torn Sudeten regions.

direct action in Berlin" made clear in Paris. Halifax's message was that his Prime Minister had decided to "offer to go at once to Germany to meet Herr Hitler in a last effort to find a peaceful solution." Indeed, the offer had already been made to and accepted by the Fuehrer, and Chamberlain would be on his way to Germany the very next morning. The Prime Minister hoped "that French Government will trust him never to lose sight of the common aims and policies of the two Governments, French and British, who have worked so closely together during the crisis."

In France, as virtually everywhere, there was wide acclaim for Chamberlain's dramatic move. Bullitt reported that the news of his visit to Hitler "has been received by all circles in France except the Communists, other agents of the Soviet Government and certain Jews, with intense satisfaction and a relief that approaches gayety." Léon Blum was not one of the "certain Jews"; he saluted Chamberlain's decision as one which "stirs our minds and our imagination" and "marks a noble and bold step in the will for peace."

Monsieur Bonnet made an immediate recovery from his nervous disorder and sent his government's "warm thanks . . . for the magnificent gesture of the Prime Minister in going to Berchtesgaden." The Foreign Minister assured Phipps "that he would strongly advise his Government to accept any proposal regarding Czechoslovakia that Mr. Chamberlain might make, whether it were accepted by the Czechs or not." Carte blanche to Runciman in August, carte blanche to Chamberlain in September. Bullitt found Bonnet:

> . . . of course delighted. The chief aim of Bonnet's foreign policy has been to engage England's intervention in the affair of Czechoslovakia. . . . Chamberlain's personal visit to Hitler is therefore a personal triumph for Bonnet and he is gleeful.

But Bullitt was wrong in telling Washington that only Communists and Jews were opposed to or less than enthusiastic about the Chamberlain journey. Hard-nosed nationalists of the Clemenceau-Poincaré type—writers such as Henri de Kerillis of *Epoque* and Emile Buré of *Ordre*—were exceedingly disenchanted. Others, including Reynaud and Herriot, admired Chamberlain's boldness but feared that his trip to the Nazi summit would only make Hitler more self-confident and demanding.

And Daladier? Publicly, his reaction was a rather forced effort to claim for himself some of the credit for the step which was now so widely praised. His statement on September 14 declared:

> At the end of yesterday afternoon . . . I took the initiative to establish a personal and direct contact with Mr. Chamberlain with the object of examining with him the possibility of adopting an exceptional procedure which would allow for the examination with Germany of the most effective measures to assure a friendly solution. . . . I am therefore particularly happy that the two Governments see eye to eye.

But the Premier was putting a good face on things; his response when Phipps first brought him the message announcing Chamberlain's trip was quite different, as the ambassador reported:

M. Daladier did not look very pleased after I had delivered my message. He said he hoped the Prime Minister's interview would produce good results; but that his own proposal had been for a conversation *à trois*. It had several times been suggested to himself to have a meeting with Herr Hitler but he had always refused as he had felt a representative of Great Britain should be present.

That Daladier had abundant cause for discomfiture is obvious. Consider what Bullitt was simultaneously reporting to Washington:

> It is certain that the French Government will support any arrangement that Chamberlain may be able to make with Hitler. As I have pointed out repeatedly . . . the only reason why the French have been ready to go to war on behalf of Czechoslovakia is because of the point of honor involved. The feeling here today is that Chamberlain will take care of that point of honor completely and that the French Government will be justified in the eyes of its own people and the world in following his lead, whatever that lead may be and however unpalatable to Czechoslovak authorities.

But of course Chamberlain could not "take care of" the "point of honor completely" or, indeed, at all. The picture thus painted—though Bullitt seemed blind to it—was that France had made a promise to Little Brother and now was calling in Big Brother to bully Little Brother into forgoing fulfillment of the promise. This was no honorable discharge of France's obligation, and Daladier was an honorable man.

In any event, honor was not the only thing at stake. Another was security. Four of France's bastions—German disarmament, the Rhineland, the Belgian alliance, and Austrian independence—had fallen in less than four years, and now a fifth was threatened. If the Czech fortified border regions were lost to Germany, the Franco-Czech alliance would be militarily valueless. What sort of deal with Hitler would Chamberlain accept? From the standpoint of French military security it was a crucial question, and it was a terribly dangerous answer to say, as Bonnet was telling anyone who would listen, that France would accept any plan that Chamberlain might bring back from Hitler's Bavarian fastness, where Schuschnigg had so recently come to grief.

It is not unlikely that Daladier's dissatisfaction was mixed with the relief that most Frenchmen were feeling. But he, and others well informed and equally introspective, must have realized that it was relief generated by a cop-out. France, not Britain, was the ally of Czechoslovakia. France, not Britain, would bear the brunt of the fighting for many months if war should come. It was the French Government that should be calling the shots for France, instead of letting Chamberlain call them for her.

Edouard Daladier was an intelligent and incorruptible French patriot with very considerable political ability, but his will could not sustain the reach that his intellect perceived. In 1938 he confronted a threat to the country he loved far graver than the one that had bested him in 1934. Once again he said *merde* to what he saw, and shifted the burden of decision to other shoulders. It would all depend on London.

CHAPTER 22

Neville Chamberlain As Diplomat

1

By the spring of 1936, sixty-eight-year-old Stanley Baldwin was a very tired man. Since February he had been suffering periods of acute fatigue, and on April 30 his friend Tom Jones found him taking pills "for nervous exhaustion." The Prime Minister was still able to pull himself together for political and public occasions, but his general condition did not improve, and on July 7 he confessed to Jones that he was "far too tired" to seek relaxation at the theater or even at private musicals: "If he were equal to it he would ask Myra Hess, but he was not."

Baldwin's doctor, Lord Dawson of Penn, found nothing organically wrong with him, and it appeared that his malaise had resulted from the accumulated strain of years of high office and responsibility, aggravated by acute political problems of the moment. His cabinet had suffered a sharp decline in prestige following the Hoare-Laval affair, and in May, Baldwin made matters worse by bringing Hoare back to office as First Lord of the Admiralty a few weeks after the latter had delivered a fulsome encomium of the Prime Minister in the Commons. The collapse of the Ethiopian cause and the lifting of sanctions gave Lloyd George the opportunity for his devastating denunciation of the Government of "cowards "

Ethiopia was only one of Baldwin's troubles. Winston Churchill's constant criticism of the rearmament program had small appeal to the Labour benches, but was beginning to take effect among the Conservatives. Hitler's remilitarization of the Rhineland aroused little public unrest, but in governmental circles there was general awareness that Britain's weakness had been exposed and exploited. Dissatisfaction with the pace of rearmament was intensified rather than allayed by the surprising choice of Inskip as Minister for the Coordination of Defense.

Humiliation in Ethiopia and uneasiness about rearmament resulted in the emergence of a group of prestigious ex-ministers, including Austen Chamberlain, Leo Amery, Lord Lloyd, and, of course, Churchill, who were increasingly critical of Baldwin's leadership—or, more accurately, the lack of it. Abroad, Britain was in the undignified posture of vainly seeking face-saving concessions from both Hitler and Mussolini, as compensation for legitimatizing the former's larceny and the latter's robbery. It was, indeed, a springtime of discontent in the sceptered isle, and the Prime Minister was visibly weakening under the strain.*

For many years Baldwin had relied on his annual summer holiday at Aix-les-Bains to restore his physical and nervous reserves. Now he was counting on Aix again; on July 15 he told Tom Jones that he would "drag himself across the Channel as soon as he can and fall asleep in the first village in France he comes to and then crawl to Aix," arriving there in mid-August. But ten days later he cracked. The staff at Downing Street found it "impossible to get a decision on anything out of him." Lord Dawson ordered a period of complete rest, and the trip to Aix was canceled. Instead, the Prime Minister would leave London at the end of the month and go into seclusion first at Gregynog Hall in Wales, and later at Lord Lothian's Blickling Hall.

With great fortitude, on July 28 and 29 Baldwin carried through long meetings with a deputation of his Conservative critics, headed by Austen Chamberlain and Winston Churchill. Then he departed the London scene and did not return to Downing Street until October 12. Parliament rose early in August, and the Cabinet did not meet again until September. Baldwin designated no deputy; Neville Chamberlain took the main burden on domestic matters, and Eden (or, in his absence, Halifax) handled foreign problems. And it was while official London was about to settle into its usual summer snooze that the Civil War spread across Spain.

2

In Britain, as in France, the Spanish tragedy divided public opinion, with the right generally pro-Franco and the left pro-Loyalist. In both countries, too, the left was sharply split on what could and should be done to help Madrid. But there ended the similarity between the reactions to the Spanish war in the two countries. The crucial differences, of course, were that Britain was governed by a right-wing and France by a left-wing government, and that the Conservative government was based upon a recent three-to-one parliamentary victory over their Labour opponents, while Blum's power, resting on an unstable coalition of Communists, Socialists of various hues, and bourgeois Radicals, confronted a fiery and powerful conservative opposition.

In the British political arena, accordingly, disagreement with national policy toward Spain was largely confined to the minority party. Early in September a Labour delegation headed by Hugh Dalton went to Paris to confer with Blum, whose arguments for nonintervention proved persuasive, partly on the basis that he thought it would work to the benefit of the Loyalists. Nonintervention was endorsed by a more than three-to-one vote at the opening of the Labour Party's Annual Conference early in October, but after hearing Spanish Republican guests give evidence of German and Italian aid to Franco, the Conference resolved that, if deliberate violation of the Non-Intervention Agreement became clear, the Spanish Government should regain the right to buy arms. As time

---

* It was during this period of increasing fatigue that Tom Jones was endeavoring to bring about the meeting between Baldwin and Hitler which the latter so much desired. As related earlier, Eden scotched the project, but Baldwin's poor health and spirits may well have contributed to his acquiescence in Eden's advice.

passed some clamored for aid to the Spanish Government without saying what kind of intervention they favored,* while others continued to support nonintervention. Thus were the Popular Front's problems in France mirrored in British Labour circles.

But all of this Labour toing and froing was of little consequence to the Baldwin government. It would be fair to say that some members were pro-Franco, some were "plague on both their houses," and that no one supported the Spanish Government. But with the possible exception of the Navy, all were agreed that Britain should stay out of the Spanish mess. And so when, at the last Cabinet meeting (July 29) before the summer holidays, Anthony Eden reported that the Spanish Ambassador had suggested that Britain or the League might intervene "to stop the bloodshed," everyone agreed that no such interference could be considered.

A few days earlier Stanley Baldwin had made his only contribution to the formulation of British policy by instructing Eden "that on no account, French or other, must he bring us in to fight on the side of the Russians." In fact Moscow's sympathy for the Loyalist cause did not manifest itself until a week later, while German Junkers aircraft were already winging their way to aid Franco. As usual with foreign affairs Baldwin's approach to the problem was ill-informed and superficial; as usual, too, what he said reflected feelings and preconceptions common to many of his countrymen, by whom the Spanish Government was seen as "Red" or "Russian."

Furthermore, the first days of the Civil War took such a course as to fix on the Loyalists the major blame for the appalling massacres that accompanied the fighting. The Royal Navy, while evacuating Britons resident or caught in Spain, had the first close look at the ugly realities. Nearly all of Spain's major seaports, including Barcelona, were in Loyalist hands. In Barcelona the strongest hands were Anarchist and, in the wake of victory over General Goded's rebel forces, thousands were executed and virtually all the city's churches were burned. These were the sights the British sailors saw and the tales the evacuees told when they were home. It was not until later that comparable evidence of Nationalist atrocities was common currency outside of Spain.

For many years, British officialdom had been accustomed to dealing with a Spain of bishops, grandees, and bemedaled officers. Franco Spain fitted the pattern. Republican Spain, with its proletarian, leftist physiognomy, was an unpredictable and unsavory newcomer to the European scene. The British Ambassador in Paris, Sir George Clerk, was so sure of the Whitehall attitude that, without consulting his superiors, he told Delbos that the Madrid government was a mere screen for "extreme anarchist elements," and urged that France embargo the frontier and stick firmly to nonintervention.† Visiting the Foreign Office two weeks later (August 20) the American Ambassador, Robert

---

* About 2,000 Britishers "intervened" as volunteers in the Republican armies. Over 500 of them were killed. The Franco supporters were not so self-sacrificial; about 600 Irishmen fought with the Nationalists, but not more than a dozen Englishmen.

† Sir George's confidence was not misplaced, for after reporting the conversation to London he received a reply approving his language and congratulating him on the "good results" obtained.

Bingham, was informed that there was "no effective government in Spain, and that the so-called government was completely at the mercy of its violent left-wing supporters."

It is hardly surprising, therefore, that when Admiral Darlan came to London early in August to alert his British counterparts to the dangers of a Spain beholden to Germany and Italy, his arguments fell on deaf ears. The First Sea Lord, Admiral Chatfield, made no secret of the Navy's partiality to Franco,* and was insensitive to the perils Darlan portrayed. When the Frenchman referred to intelligence reports about Italian activities in the Balearics, Chatfield blandly denied that he had any comparable information, although in fact he did.

Favored though Franco might be in some quarters, there was no official sentiment for intervention in his behalf. Many found the two sides equally repulsive, and welcomed a war in which, as Hoare put it, "Fascists and Bolshevists would kill each other off." For Harold Nicolson, Madrid was "a mere Kerensky Government at the mercy of an armed proletariat," but "Franco and his Moors are no better." Winston Churchill thought the government of Communists and Anarchists the more evil of the two, but drew from the "Spanish convulsion" the conclusion that for Britain and France there was only one answer: "Send charitable aid under the Red Cross to both sides, and for the rest, keep out of it and arm."

Given this atmosphere of revulsion, the French proposal for an international nonintervention pact was warmly welcomed in London.† The Foreign Office joined eagerly in Delbos' efforts to bring the dictator nations into the fold, and when reports of German and Italian aid to Franco caused some wavering in Paris, Whitehall was quick to counsel emphatically against any change of front. On August 19, without waiting for adherence to the pact by the dictator countries, Eden announced a British embargo on arms to Spain in order, as he wrote to Baldwin, that "we might, by setting an example, do our best to induce . . . Germany and Italy to follow suit." And when the French proposed London as the seat of the Non-Intervention Committee, Eden willingly acquiesced.

The Cabinet held its first postholiday meeting on September 2 and accepted without question Eden's report on the progress of nonintervention; a week later the committee met for the first time. Later that month Eden went off to the League meeting in Geneva, where he refused to be impressed by photographic evidence proffered by the new Spanish Foreign Minister, Alvarez del Vayo, of German and Italian aid to Franco. On October 9, Eden was in Paris, conferring with Blum and agreeing that nonintervention "was the correct policy" regardless of new charges of Nazi and Fascist transgressions. Back in England, he told a Sheffield audience that "impatience" about the Non-Intervention Committee "has not been balanced by the production of any practical alternative proposals

---

* On April 29, 1937, Liddell Hart encountered "at a dinner party" the Director of Naval Intelligence, Rear-Admiral Sir James Troup, and "was staggered at the vehement way he proclaimed his pro-Franco bias to members of the foreign diplomatic service in London."

† When it arrived on August 2, Eden was vacationing in Yorkshire but was in close touch with the Foreign Office, where Halifax was temporarily in charge. Baldwin seems to have been completely out of the picture until August 19, when Eden (who had returned to London on the sixteenth) sent him an informatory letter.

for dealing with the situation." If this was damning with faint praise, it nevertheless indicated that Eden would not easily be shaken from the noninterventionist position.

Indeed from the British standpoint, *if nonintervention were to be fact and
not fiction,* there was much to be said for it. A century earlier Wellington,
enlightened by Peninsular War experiences, had declared: "There is no country
in Europe in the affairs of which foreigners can intervene with so little advantage as those of Spain"—a verdict to which Hitler would have nodded gloomy
assent in 1940 when he tried to cash Franco's check. Yet this gave no warrant
for indifference, for if Italy lay athwart Britain's Mediterranean passages, Spain
could threaten those and also Britain's sea-lanes to the Cape of Good Hope. As
Liddell Hart put it: "A friendly Spain is desirable; a neutral Spain is vital."

If Britain should back the losing Spanish horse, friendship and neutrality
would both be lost, and even if she backed the winner, those attitudes might be
undermined by the loser's hate. Neutrality is generally the surest begetter of reciprocal neutrality. But suppose other nations—Germany, Italy, Russia—were
of a different mind? In August the British Chiefs of Staff drew up for the Cabinet a report on "the extent to which British interests would be affected and what
action His Majesty's Government might take in the event of Italy taking some
action which might upset the existing balance in the Western Mediterranean."
The "Summary of Conclusions" included the following:

(i)   Our interests in the present Spanish crisis are the maintenance—
        (a) of the territorial integrity of Spain and her possessions, and
        (b) of such relations with any Spanish Government which may
            emerge from this conflict as will ensure benevolent neutral-
            ity in the event of our being engaged in a European war;

(ii)   Open intervention by Italy in support of the insurgents in Spain
        would precipitate a major international crisis;

(iii)   The occupation by Italy of any territory in Spain itself would be
        detrimental to British interests;

(iv)   The Italian occupation of any part of Spanish Morocco, and par-
        ticularly of Ceuta, would be a threat to vital British interests;

(v)   The Italian occupation of any of the Balearic Islands, Canary
        Islands, and/or Rio de Oro, is highly undesirable from the point
        of view of British interests, but cannot be regarded as a vital
        menace;

(vi)   Any of the contingencies specified in (ii) to (v) above would be
        injurious in greater or lesser degree to French interests;

(vii)   The conclusion of any Italo-Spanish alliance would constitute a
        threat to vital British interests;

(viii) The threat of effective action, other than action in a diplomatic
        sphere, to thwart Italian designs would involve a grave risk of
        war;

(ix)   Italy is the only Power whose forces are mobilised and ready for
        immediate action. Her preparedness for the initial phase of hos-
        tilities, *vis-à-vis* Great Britain, is greater than it was nine months
        ago.

RECOMMENDATIONS

Our recommendations may be summarised as follows:—

(i)   The principle that should govern any action on the part of His Majesty's Government should be that it is most important to avoid any measures which, while failing to achieve our object, merely tend further to alienate Italy;

(ii) We should press for the earliest possible conclusion of a non-interference pact in Spain, embracing France, Russia, Portugal, Germany, Italy and the United Kingdom;

(iii) If no general agreement can be reached, we should impress on the French the desirability of giving no cause for intervention by Italy;

. . . . . .

(vii) We should make it known to Signor Mussolini that . . . any alteration of the *status quo* in the Western Mediterranean must be a matter of the closest concern to His Majesty's Government in order that he may be under no misapprehension as to the consequences of any action that he may take to disturb the existing balance.

What is most remarkable about this document is that it is exclusively concerned with the Italian threat and makes no mention of Germany, whose forces were at that time the more extensively engaged in Spain. The preoccupation with Italian seizure of the Spanish African or island possessions strongly suggests that the paper was primarily the work of the Admiralty. Echoes of the failure of sanctions and eagerness to avoid another clash are audible in the first two "recommendations," while the program as a whole appears to be based on little more than a hope that, if Britain and France refrained from any action which might "alienate" Italy, she would behave herself in Spain. Certainly the final assessment that Mussolini would not intervene if he were warned and given no "cause" by France was as poor a prediction as Munich later proved to be.

But probably the Chiefs of Staff were not quite so naïve as that suggests. There is a revealing phrase in the second "conclusion," with its qualified forecast that "open" Italian intervention "would precipitate a major international crisis." Of course, in fact it did not; after Guadalajara and Santander, Italian participation in the war was as open as the skies. At the time the report was written, however, Rome was still maintaining the pretense, and the language of the second conclusion suggests that the Chiefs of Staff were not so much worried about the *fact* of Italian intervention as about the appearance of things—an attitude which, once again, is strikingly premonitory of Britain's policy in the Sudeten crisis. It also closely parallels the view later voiced by Halifax:

The immediate practical value of the [Non-Intervention] Committee . . .

was not great. I doubt whether a single man or gun less reached either side in the war as a result of its activities.* What, however, it did was to keep such intervention as there was entirely unofficial, to be denied or at least deprecated by the responsible spokesman of the nation concerned, so that there was neither need nor occasion for any official action by Governments to support their nationals. After making every allowance for the unreality, make-believe, and discredit that came to attach to the Non-Intervention Committee, I think this device for lowering the temperature caused by the Spanish fever justified itself.

If a devout High-churchman like Halifax could find this rationalization of international "unreality" and "make-believe" satisfying, small wonder that his colleagues had few qualms. But in fact it was a long jump from supporting nonintervention as a desirable international policy to defending the sham which resulted. The hollowness of Britain's espousal of sanctions in the Ethiopian affair had just been exposed. How would her credit rating be affected when Mussolini scornfully ripped off the veil of "nonintervention" and the ugly realities became common knowledge? How would Britain's strategic situation be altered if Franco should ride to victory on German and Italian shoulders?

3

On October 12, 1936, Baldwin returned to No. 10 Downing Street after his ten weeks' vacation, rested but nervously fragile. His domestic antennae, however, had lost none of their old sensitivity, as Anthony Eden, recounting their first meeting in three months, has memorably described:

. . . Naturally I was impatient to deploy the course of events and to take counsel with him, particularly about the Spanish civil war, which had become so international a menace since our last talk together. Baldwin listened for a while, but his mind was evidently not on the subject. I thought his unconcern exasperating. At a pause in my dissertation Baldwin astonished me by saying: "Have you had any letters about the King?" "No, not as far as I know," I said, "why should I have?" "Well," Baldwin went on, "I wish you would inquire. I expect that you have had some. I fear we may have difficulties there." He added: "I hope that you will try not to trouble me too much with foreign affairs just now." After three months without a comment from the Prime Minister, I found this an astonishing doctrine and suspected at the time that it was another example of Baldwin's reluctance to face the unpleasant realities which were our daily fare at the Foreign Office. But I was wrong. When I got back to my room I found that there had been letters from overseas, where there was no press restraint, such as our own newspapers had voluntarily assumed, and where both foreign and British subjects were at liberty to express

---

* The noble lord's assessment of the consequence was far wide of the mark. But for "nonintervention," French aid to Madrid would surely have been much more extensive— with what effect on the flow of German or Italian aid to Franco is uncertain. In the event, "nonintervention" greatly favored the rebels, both because of Russia's geographical remoteness, and because the negative attitudes of Britain and France discouraged the Soviet leaders from sustaining what rapidly became a solitary position.

their opinions and anxieties. These wrote of the King and Mrs. Simpson and her impending divorce suit and they were critical.

Baldwin had at once sensed the dangers for the country and Empire of any action by the Crown which might divide its peoples. . . .

For the next two months, Baldwin had little time or mind for anything other than the affair of the King and the object of his heart's desire. The Prime Minister did not wholly disappear from the parliamentary scene; in October he spoke in support of nonintervention in Spain, and the following month he defended his government's rearmament record both in the House and at a second meeting with the Austen Chamberlain-Churchill deputation. But he was a tired man working under great strain, and it was in the House on November 12 that he made the unguarded reference to the East Fulham by-election which later cost his reputation so dear at the hands of Churchill and others. Harold Nicolson, a sympathetic listener, recorded that "by the end of his speech his voice and thought limp as if he were a tired walker on a long road."

But the old pro was husbanding his energies for nearer matters. Dedicated as he was to the Crown, it was an extraordinary irony that Edward VIII's abdication was Baldwin's salvation, and the occasion of his last great triumph. When Mrs. Simpson sued her husband for divorce, and Edward revealed to Baldwin his firm intention to marry the lady, the Prime Minister (having taken extensive soundings both at home and in the Dominions) had already concluded that neither English nor Empire opinion would accept Mrs. Simpson as the King's wife either morganatically or as Queen. A constitutional crisis was inevitable unless Edward would either break off the affair or abdicate.

Give up Mrs. Simpson the King would not, and the efforts of Beaverbrook, Churchill (whose "line," according to Harold Nicolson, was "let the King choose his girl"), and a few others to round up a "King's party" came to nothing.* On December 10, 1936, the King abdicated, and Baldwin's explanatory speech in the House glowed with his old magic with simple English. It was a great performance by the worn and weary man, and when he encountered Harold Nicolson in the House later that evening he responded to congratulations by saying: "I had a success, my dear Nicolson, at the moment I most needed it. Now is the time to go."

In fact, he did not "go" for another five months. However great his tactical and forensic triumph, abdication was a sour note on which to finish, and Baldwin decided to stay on for the coronation of George VI. That event was calendared for May 12, and Baldwin's resignation for May 28, 1937.

Thus, for these many months the British public's attention was diverted from foreign problems and centered first on King Edward VIII's abdication and then on the pleasant prospect of George VI's coronation. A grave crisis had been averted and the image of royalty restored, but all this was basically irrelevant to the Axis menace and the Spanish Civil War. These dangers were in no way re-

---

* According to Baldwin's longtime confidant Viscount J. C. Davidson, Ribbentrop, who was in London at the time of the abdication, made a telephone call to Hitler (which the Foreign Office "unscrambled") predicting that the abdication would precipitate riots and even the fall of the Government.

ceding, but Baldwin was unable or unwilling to take much part in their handling. The consequence was that his government remained for ten months in the essentially leaderless condition in which it had been left by his nervous collapse in the summer of 1936. Neville Chamberlain was now the heir-apparent, but he was in the uncomfortable situation of carrying responsibility without authority, and he did not as yet venture to interfere with Eden's control of the Foreign Office.

It was during this period when the reins of authority were hanging loose that rifts appeared within the Cabinet which were to lead a year later to Eden's resignation and contribute greatly to an intensification of appeasement policies. Initially, the argument lay between the Foreign Office and the Admiralty.

In November 1936, Germany and Italy had recognized the insurgent regime as the legitimate government of Spain, and shortly thereafter Franco announced what amounted to a blockade of Barcelona and other Loyalist-held ports. The British admirals, true to their preference for Franco and their horror of offending Mussolini, wished to acknowledge the blockade by granting Franco belligerent rights and cease protecting Spain-bound British shipping—steps which would have been of great value, both diplomatic and military, to the insurgents. The Foreign Office, partly because neither France nor the United States contemplated such measures, and partly to preserve a more neutral posture, proposed instead that British ships be forbidden to carry arms to Spain, but that the Royal Navy continue to protect them when carrying legitimate cargo. At a lively meeting of ministers on November 22, Eden's views prevailed over those of Hoare, the First Lord of the Admiralty.

This was the first of a series of episodes that brought Hoare to the view that Eden viewed the Spanish conflict "as one between absolute right and absolute wrong in which the dictator should at all costs be totally defeated and democracy totally defended." Nothing that Eden said or wrote warranted such a characterization; indeed, in the fall of 1936 Eden was doing his best to suppress information about Axis transgressions in Spain. On October 14 he told the Cabinet that "the Italians were breaking the rules in the Balearic Islands," but that "the moment was particularly inopportune for raising the matter in the Non-Intervention Committee." Five weeks later, answering questions on nonintervention breaches in the House,* Eden declared: "I wish to state categorically that I think there are other governments more to blame than those of Germany or Italy." It was apparent that he was referring to the Soviet Union, and it is hard to believe that Eden did not know full well that Russian aid to Madrid was little and late compared to what Italy and especially Germany had sent to Franco.

Uneasiness between Eden and other members of the Cabinet was also noticeable at their meeting on November 4, during a general discussion of defense policy. Hoare led off by remarking the continuing poor state of British arms, and by a recommendation "to get Italy out of the list of countries with which we had to reckon." His view won immediate approval from Chamberlain, Mac-

* During October, accumulating evidence of German and Italian aid to Spain caused the Labour Party executives to endorse a policy favoring "complete commercial liberty to Republican Spain" under the slogan "Arms for Spain."

Donald, Inskip, Halifax, and others; the Colonial Secretary (Ormsby-Gore) opined that there was "a feeling in the country that we were tied up too much with France and that that had prevented us getting on terms with the dictator Powers." In conclusion the Cabinet agreed that the Foreign Office "should in the light of the discussion adopt a policy of improving relations with Italy."

To all this Eden responded that "the attitude suggested by the First Lord [Hoare] might be mistaken for flabbiness," and cautioned his colleagues against kowtowing to the Italians. But he did not oppose the basic policy of reconciliation with Italy,* and shortly thereafter commenced the negotiations which culminated, early the following year, in the so-called "Gentleman's Agreement" between the two countries.

The title was supplied by Mussolini, who made the first advances; it denoted an "understanding" rather than a pact, giving expression to mutual respect for the interests of each country in the Mediterranean. The Quai d'Orsay was eager that France should be a party to it, but Ciano was unenthusiastic, and Eden moved ahead alone despite the French anxieties. As signed on January 2, 1937, by Ciano and the British Ambassador in Rome, Sir Eric Drummond, the Agreement recited that the two powers "disclaim any desire to modify . . . the status quo as regards national sovereignty of territories in the Mediterranean area" and "undertake to respect each other's rights and interests in the said area," as well as to "discourage any activities liable to impair the good relations" between the signatories. In a separate note Ciano undertook that: "So far as Italy is concerned, the integrity of the present territories of Spain shall in all circumstances remain intact and unmodified."

The ink was hardly dry on these documents when events reconfirmed that at least one party to the Gentlemen's Agreement was no gentleman. On January 4, Anthony Eden returned from a short vacation to find on his desk reports that a large number of Italian "volunteers" had just arrived in Franco Spain. This did not, to be sure, violate the stipulations on the territorial status quo, but it was certainly calculated "to impair the good relations" between the two countries.

Eden and Mussolini had gotten along badly when they met during the Ethiopian crisis, and now the Foreign Secretary felt, with reason, that he had been had for a sucker. He now prepared a Cabinet paper describing the dangers consequent on the Italian moves, and a program of action to counter them:

> . . . I proposed that we should offer the services of the Royal Navy to supervise at sea all approaches to ports and harbours, both round the Spanish coast and in Spanish overseas possessions, to prevent either volunteers or war material entering these territories. The other nations would be asked to agree that our ships should be entitled to visit and search merchant vessels or send them into a convenient port, if inspection could not be completed at sea. To bear witness to our impartiality, I proposed that each British ship employed

---

* However, at the next Cabinet meeting (November 11) Eden took exception to the statement that the reconciliation policy had been adopted "in the light of the discussion" at the previous meeting, on the ground that improved relations with Italy was already Foreign Office policy. He also warned that British forces in the Mediterranean would have to be maintained and that Italian anti-British propaganda would probably continue.

in this task would carry a naval officer of one of the countries which had signed the Non-Intervention Agreement.

In making this offer, Great Britain would call upon the Soviet, German, Italian, Portuguese and French Governments to carry out their pledges to stop the flow of volunteers, and upon the last two Governments to close their frontiers with Spain. We would discuss with the French the advisability of inviting neutral officers to cooperate in the frontier control. His Majesty's Government, for their part, would state publicly that the Foreign Enlistment Act would be strictly enforced, to prevent the enrolment of any British volunteers.

Eden supported his plan not solely in terms of Britain's Mediterranean interests, but of her general strategy vis-à-vis the dictator nations:

> The Spanish civil war has ceased to be an internal Spanish issue and has become an international battle-ground. The character of the future government of Spain has now become less important to the peace of Europe than that the dictators should not be victorious in that country. The extent and character of the intervention now practised by Germany and Italy have made it clear to the world that the object of these powers is to secure General Franco's victory whether or not it represents the will of the Spanish people. . . .
>
> It is therefore my conviction that unless we cry a halt in Spain, we shall have trouble this year in one or other of the danger points I have referred to. It follows that to be firm in Spain is to gain time, and to gain time is what we want. We cannot in this instance gain time by marking it. It is to be remembered that in the language of the Nazi Party any adventure is a minor adventure. They spoke thus of the Rhineland last year, they are speaking thus of Spain today, they will speak thus of Memel, Danzig or Czechoslovakia tomorrow. It is only by showing them that these dangerous distinctions are false that we can hope to avert a greater calamity.

Baldwin and Halifax reacted favorably, and on January 8 the former convened an informal meeting of ministers (these plus Hoare, Simon, Inskip, Duff Cooper, and a few others) to consider Eden's program. His apology for the short notice given his colleagues failed to mollify Sir Samuel Hoare, who launched a frontal attack on the entire conception:

> Sir Samuel Hoare said that he would not complain of the short notice when events were moving so quickly, but it would certainly have been easier if a proposal involving every kind of Naval issue had been discussed first either between the Ministerial Heads of the Departments or their Staffs. Some preliminary discussion, at any rate, would have been desirable. As a first preliminary observation, we appeared to be getting near a situation where, as a nation, we were trying to stop General Franco from winning. That was the desire of the Parliamentary Parties of the Left; but there were others, including perhaps some members of the Cabinet, who were very anxious that the Soviet should not win in Spain. It was very important to hold the scales fairly. He recalled that at the last Meeting of the Cabinet before Christmas the feeling had been opposed to an international blockade. He thought it possible that the feeling had been even stronger against a blockade by British forces. As a second preliminary observation he said that the Navy was always prepared to

undertake any duty imposed upon it by the Cabinet, as had been shown during the past year, when they had been working under great strain. He wanted to make clear that the Navy was always prepared to do its duty. But at the same time it was his duty to inform the Cabinet as to what was involved in the decision they were asked to take: as to what were the prospects of success or otherwise; and as to whether it was not liable to embroil us with one or other of the European Powers.

There were special dangers inherent in a blockade of the Spanish coast, which was even harder than the blockade of Germany in the War. The Spanish coast was 1,600 miles long. . . .

It speedily became apparent that Hoare was much closer than Eden to the temper of the Cabinet. Despite their earlier encouragement, neither Baldwin nor Halifax gave the Foreign Secretary any help, and the others were unanimously hostile to the plan, largely from fear that such an undertaking might "embroil" Britain with one or more of the transgressing powers. Instead, Hoare proposed that Eden endeavor to "induce" the other parties to the Non-Intervention Agreement to forbid their nationals to volunteer. Inskip, with what in retrospect was astonishing naïveté, recommended that, rather than trying to stop Germany and Italy from sending more aid to Franco, Britain should stop her own nationals from volunteering, in the hope that Hitler and Mussolini would then follow suit.

Eden warned that Germany and Italy might "in effect, conquer Spain," and that the Hoare-Inskip proposals would be ineffective. But he made no headway with his colleagues, and when the discussion was renewed the following day, it was decided to leave the problem to the Non-Intervention Committee and work to strengthen its hand in stemming the flow of "volunteers."

It was a bad setback for Eden,* which clouded his relations with his Cabinet colleagues at the very time when his performances in Parliament and as a public speaker were greatly enhancing his public standing. Furthermore, his failure to carry the day doomed what was probably the last chance to make nonintervention something more than a sham. The consequence was, of course, the Non-Intervention Committee's control plan, which was soon punched full of holes. Even before it was launched, Guadelajara at once disclosed the presence of large Italian formations and fired Mussolini's angry determination to send enough "volunteers" to avenge the defeat, while in London his ambassador, Dino Grandi, flatly refused to participate in any Non-Intervention Committee discussion of withdrawing "volunteers."

April brought the news of deplorable Italian massacres of Ethiopians in Addis Ababa, and later of the German bombing of Guernica. Waves of anti-German and anti-Italian feeling swept over the country and heated the parliamentary debates. The insurgents' Basque offensive was under way, and Franco endeavored to blockade the port of Bilbao, precipitating new disputes between the Admiralty, which wished to keep British ships out of harm's way, and the

* Corbin, well informed on the matter, reported to Paris that the Foreign Office staff was much upset, and that the British ministers were so anxious to avoid incidents that they tended to draw a veil of silence over unpleasant questions.

Foreign Office, which insisted upon their being given protection. Eden won this argument, but not without trouble from Simon as well as Hoare.

Privately, Eden expressed horror at the atrocities, and declared that he now hoped the Spanish Government would prevail. But in Cabinet he bemoaned the questions in the House that were "calculated to irritate Signor Musso," and wanted to persuade the BBC to stop broadcasting daily bulletins on Spain—for once winning "much sympathy" from his colleagues for the difficulties caused him by "ill-timed publicity methods." And, for all his bitter disillusionment with the fruits of the nonintervention policy, he continued to support it in the House, in diplomatic discussions, and in private.

The other major military-diplomatic problem which rose during this last year of the Baldwin regime was the attitude of Belgium, changing under the pressure of the Rhineland remilitarization and the influence of King Leopold III. On October 2, 1936, London had been fully advised of the serious military consequences, as viewed in Paris, of a neutral Belgium, guaranteed by the other Locarno powers but not herself a guarantor, and two weeks later the French anxieties were confirmed by King Leopold's address to the Council of Ministers.

Eden was miffed that the King had spoken out on the question without consulting the protecting powers, but neither he nor any of the other ministers were much alarmed. At the Cabinet meeting of October 21, the consensus was that the speech contained nothing "especially new" and that "France would sort it out with Belgium and we need do nothing."

On November 6, Ambassador Corbin tried to convince Eden that "from a military point of view, this development was of capital importance for our defense and for the security of Belgium which, in the event of a conflict between France and Germany, would sooner or later be invaded by the German Army." But Eden was not impressed; the British "military experts" did not share the French view: "The Foreign Office had just received a new report from which it appears that the maintenance of Belgian neutrality would be much more advantageous for France and England than Belgium as a field of military operations." The force of this assessment, of course, depended on German respect for Belgian neutrality, and it is remarkable that the Chiefs of Staff were willing to base their judgment on so dubious a forecast.

A week later Eden told Corbin that he was reluctant to push Belgium to the limit, and on December 9 the Foreign Secretary put before the Cabinet a proposal that Britain and France should accept the Belgian position, while asking the Belgian Government to undertake to "resist not only a violation by the German army of Belgian territory, but also of Belgian air by German aircraft," and to "remove the present uncertainty on their attitude toward [military] cooperation with the French." The Cabinet approved the basic position but struck out the second request, thus depriving the French of official British support for their desire to maintain close staff relations with the Belgian armed forces.

Brussels gave London formal assurance that she would treat aerial incursions as no less an invasion than ground attack—a point of obvious moment to the British—but the French continued to insist that staff contacts were essential to effective discharge of their obligation to come to Belgium's aid. Eden feared that

Belgium might sign a bilateral nonaggression pact with Germany if the situation were allowed to drift. On March 22, by arrangements which Eden initiated, King Leopold came privately to London for an informal discussion of the treaty situation, and two days later the Government sent a note through Corbin, advising France to postpone the question of staff contacts until after Belgium had been relieved of her guarantor obligations. A month later this was accomplished by the joint Anglo-French declaration of April 24, 1937.

The next day Eden went to Brussels, where he was warmly received, but found his hosts unwilling to agree to "staff conversations which they regard as compromising, for they believe—rightly or wrongly—that if they do not so compromise their independence Belgian soil may escape the next war."* The rebuff to the French was softened, however, by Foreign Minister Spaak's private assurances that "necessary technical exchanges" through "discreet and fruitful contacts" would take place.

In responding to the Belgian maneuver, it was Britain and not France— discredited and weakened as the latter was in Belgian eyes—that had the leverage in Brussels. Very possibly it was wise to free Belgium from her guarantor commitments rather than try to hold her willy-nilly, but Cabinet and Chiefs of Staff alike assessed the military consequences very superficially, and Eden seems to have made little effort to convince the Belgians that whether or not they were neutral would, in the event of war, make little difference to Hitler, for whom their country was both the route for an end run around the Maginot Line, and an airfield within a few minutes' flight of the English coast.

In strategic terms, these events in Spain and Belgium during the last year of Baldwin's primacy were as dangerous to Britain as to France. But the French at least realized that they were getting hurt and complained loudly, while the British leaders were so determined to stay out of trouble until rearmament was well advanced that they tended to turn away from immediate difficulties and accept too readily the conclusion that, for the moment, nothing should be done.

Eden made one effort to break out of this cunctative strategy, but found no support and estranged powerful colleagues. Stanley Baldwin virtually withdrew from the foreign arena, though he was by no means blind to the looming dangers. Five days before his retirement, during the Imperial Conference, which followed the coronation of George VI, he gave the Dominion prime ministers a gloomy summary of German and Italian moves and motives, concluding: "We have two madmen loose in Europe. Anything may befall."

Determined men, however, can play some part in determining what "may befall" even when madmen are at large. On May 28, 1937, Stanley Baldwin became Earl Baldwin of Bewdley, and was succeeded as Prime Minister by Neville Chamberlain, a determined man and the master architect of Munich.

---

* The quoted words are from *The Diplomatic Diaries of Oliver Harvey* (entry for April 27, 1937), Eden's private secretary, who was with his chief in Brussels. Harvey also recorded the opinion of Sir Noel Charles, counsellor at the Brussels embassy, that despite her assurances Belgium would not forcibly resist German overflights if there were no ground invasion.

4

"Before Chamberlain became Prime Minister," wrote Anthony Eden in quarter-century retrospect, "I would think it true that he and I were closer to each other than to any other members of the Government, exchanging opinions on many Cabinet matters without any disagreement. . . . I was not at all surprised when he mentioned that he was soon to take over from Baldwin and added the hope that I would continue with my work at the Foreign Office. Nor was I dismayed when he said with a smile 'I know you won't mind if I take more interest in foreign policy than S.B.' We both knew that no one could have taken less."

The handsome young Foreign Secretary was to be both surprised and dismayed within a few months, as his relations with the new Prime Minister rapidly worsened, ending in Eden's resignation in February 1938. But he would have been less surprised at this dénouement had he been privy to the thoughts Neville Chamberlain had been confiding to his diary and to his cherished sisters Hilda and Ida, especially since his return to the Exchequer in 1931, for these intimate entries and letters reveal a pent-up tide of self-confidence and arrogance that boded no good for those, friend or foe, who stood out against him.

However, the confidence and arrogance were nourished by great ability, remarkable energy and drive to get things done, and truly formidable conscientiousness. On these qualities of intellect and will, the testimony of his contemporaries is convincing. William (later Lord) Strang of the Foreign Office, no friend of the Munich settlement, saw him as "a man of cool, calm mind, strong will, decisive purpose, wholly devoted to the public cause and with a firm confidence in his own judgment." Chamberlain's close friend Hoare remarked his "clear-cut mind and concrete outlook," which "had an astringent effect upon opinions and preferences that had hitherto been only sentiments and impressions." Leo Amery, who turned against him when war came, recalled him as a "first rate debater" and "essentially a man of action; even more, perhaps, of administration." Sir Horace Wilson has described his unflagging industry and contempt for political bonhomie: "He read papers assiduously, generally from beginning to end, and seemed never to tire, whatever the hour. After the usual harassing day he would start on tightly packed boxes of papers at 11 P.M. or later, and not go to bed until he had finished them. These seemed to him more important than becoming 'friends' with possible opponents or critics. Vain the efforts to get him to attend the Derby, Wimbledon, Lords. 'It would be humbug and I won't be party to it.'" Chamberlain's Minister of Labour, Ernest Brown, congratulated his chief on "what a comfort it has been to hard-pressed departmental ministers to know that, when their subjects have to be discussed, whoever else has not read their papers and digested them, one man had—the Prime Minister." Sir John Simon, not the least critical of men, praised his ever-readiness to aid and guide his colleagues: "Neville Chamberlain . . . would go in to the matter as though it was his personal problem, test it at every point, listen in a businesslike fashion to what one had to say, and then state his conclusions with the finality of a General Manager conducting his company's affairs."

These comments give the impression of a highly competent but grim and graceless man, and many saw him that way. Oliver Harvey wrote that he had "none of Austen's charm and that even in a small party . . . he was quite incapable of making any pleasant personal impression; he is a sort of robot." But his formidable manner was at least partly due to shyness, and with those few who were able to approach him closely—Baldwin, Halifax, Hoare, Eden before the split—he was capable of deep friendship. He was sensitive to and knowledgeable about the beauties of nature and classical music, and almost absurdly fond of fishing. His political opponents in the Conservative and Liberal parties were quick to pay tribute to Chamberlain's ability, integrity, and humanity: barely six weeks after Duff Cooper resigned from the Government in protest against the Munich settlement, he was happy to declare publicly that "The outstanding qualities of Mr. Chamberlain are courage, consistency and logic." Winston Churchill regarded him as "the ablest and most forceful Minister, with high abilities," and extolled him in Shakespeare's words as the "pack-horse in our great affairs." Perhaps the most moving words of praise were uttered by a frequent target of Chamberlain's tongue, Sir Archibald Sinclair, the Liberal Party leader:

> Even in the heat of the most controversial debates we have been forced to pay tribute to his humanity as a social reformer, to his courage and high sense of public duty, and to his unsparing devotion to the cause of peace.

The affinity for social reform was inherited from his father Joseph, one of the most powerful figures of turn-of-the-century Britain. Neville was devoted to his father's memory, as he was to his elder half-brother, Austen. It was a proud, close Birmingham family, in which the members were all expected to do well as a matter of course, and help each other to do even better—in this respect, if perhaps no other, resembling the Boston Kennedys. Unlike his father and half-brother, who had entered Parliament when forty and twenty-nine respectively, Neville stuck closer to Birmingham and did not stand for Parliament until his fiftieth year. Furthermore, he had been forty-five in 1914 and was never in uniform. He had hated Rugby School, attended a small engineering college in Birmingham instead of one of the great universities, and so had none of the "old school tie" associations then so characteristic of English upper-class society. Consequently he entered Parliament much older than most of the newcomers, and without the bond of experiences shared at school, at the front, or in politics. These factors go far to explain his reticence and difficulty in finding common ground with most of his colleagues, as well as his anxiety to make up for lost time by superior ability and application.

Under all these circumstances, it is not surprising that, when his efforts and talents were speedily recognized and rewarded with high office, he developed an aggressive, uncompromisingly partisan personality in the House, and a dominant, often domineering, one in ministerial consultations. He could not temper the force of his blows in debate, or conceal his determination to prove himself right and his colleagues, if they differed, wrong. R. A. "Rab" (later Lord) Butler, who became Under-Secretary for Foreign Affairs after Eden's resignation, has graphically described the contrast between Chamberlain's and Baldwin's methods:

> I found the Prime Minister temperamentally incapable of forming a nationally based administration. By nature and by intention his approach to political problems was the exact opposite of Baldwin's. Whenever I thought of this approach I always found myself comparing it to a "ton of bricks." Talking to him day after day about statements and answers in the House, I got to realize that, if one phrase or one word were out of place, an order would be given, the builder's lorry would be tipped, and if one didn't watch out the ton of bricks would descend on one's own head. Shortly after I took office I described his attitude in less metaphorical prose to my parents, who were in India: "He frequently redrafts in pencil with very little hesitation and very little crossing out. He does not like vague and polite phrases but wishes to go straight at the Opposition and express exactly what he means. The traditional soothing of Members by such phrases as 'the honourable and gallant gentleman will be aware' is usually erased. There is no doubt, however, about his loyalty to his friends and his courage." In the Commons itself, where I used to sit next to him, he could not conceal his impatience with the Labour and Liberal leaders. He would fidget and fume expletives in a manner which brought to my mind the famous physical eccentricities of Dr. Johnson. . . .

Leo Amery described Chamberlain as "an autocrat with the courage of his convictions," adding that Chamberlain's manner and "corvine" features gave an appearance of "contempt" for the Labour members, who hated him for it. Halifax, writing with the charity of close friendship, echoed the same themes:

> He and Baldwin, of course, were very different characters. Chamberlain was resentful of criticism from those who sat in Parliament as his supporters. . . . This was partly due to his sensitiveness, which was greater than a casual friend would have guessed, and made him judge criticism more harshly than it might always deserve. It seemed to him akin to insubordination, and no team could get on without discipline. . . . Stanley Baldwin's method was dissimilar from Chamberlain's and was quite his own. When a supporter had made a violent speech and voted against him, S.B. would meet him presently in the Lobby and would greet him genially with, "Well, old chap, I expect you feel better after that." And the least result was that all the sharp edge and eastwind were taken out of the attack.

And Baldwin himself saw things much the same way after Chamberlain had been Prime Minister nearly a year:

> In the House, the PM is supreme. He is a far better debater than I: he hits his opponents hard and our backbenchers are enthusiastic. All good as far as it goes. But the Labour fellows say "We are back in the Party dogfight. The PM's are A-1 partisan speeches but if he talks as if he were on the hustings, so can we. And there never can be a national foreign policy so long as he is there.

Chamberlain's heavy-handedness with those of whom he disapproved was strikingly revealed during the abdication crisis when, critical of Baldwin's cautious tactics, he persuaded his senior colleagues to join him in proposing a letter to the King instructing him that his "association with Mrs. Simpson should be terminated forthwith," on pain of the entire Government's resignation should that advice be refused.* Baldwin, far wiser and more sensitive to personal and popular reactions, suppressed the letter, which he was sure would provoke the King to do precisely the opposite of what was demanded, and put the Government in the position of blackmailing the sovereign.

Anthony Eden was not unaware of these less gracious qualities in his new chief; indeed, a few weeks before the changeover he had privately deprecated one of Chamberlain's attacks on Sinclair, fearing that "when Neville Chamberlain became Prime Minister affairs would go less smoothly in the country than with Baldwin—there would be better administration and more discipline in the Cabinet, but he would not be able to resist scoring off the opposition." But he was on the best of terms with Chamberlain, and on balance thought the change would be very much for the better: "He had a grip of affairs which Stanley Baldwin never had," he told Oliver Harvey, and in his own memoirs Eden recorded that "he looked forward to working with a Prime Minister who would give his Foreign Secretary energetic backing." In March 1937, Eden was reassuring the American Ambassador, Robert Bingham, that Chamberlain had supported Eden and the League in not lifting the sanctions after the capture of Addis Ababa, and was "not so far to the right as many people thought." True, in June 1936 Chamberlain, with his "midsummer of madness" speech, had forced Eden's hand on lifting the sanctions, but he had apologized handsomely, and Eden concluded that "Chamberlain having been such a steadfast colleague" the "lapse" must have been "accidental."

But in fact it was no accident; in his diary Chamberlain recorded:

I did it deliberately because I felt that the party and the country needed a lead, and an indication that the government was not wavering and drifting without a policy. . . . I did not consult Anthony Eden, because he would have been bound to beg me not to say what I proposed. . . . He himself has been as nice as possible about it, though it is of course true that to some extent he has to suffer in the public interest.

This entry is one of a large number of passages in Chamberlain's diary and letters to his sisters which reveal, beginning in the early thirties, his emerging self-image as the indispensable man, superior to any of his fellow-ministers. His abundantly justified self-confidence was increasingly edged with condescension, sometimes verging on contempt, for his colleagues, and a growing disposition to take over their responsibilities and himself make decisions that were properly theirs. Consider a sampling of Neville Chamberlain as he saw himself in the years immediately preceding his primacy. Writing to Hilda in October of 1932:

* J. C. Davidson, Baldwin's close friend and Chancellor of the Duchy of Lancaster in his cabinet, recorded that Chamberlain "wanted the Cabinet to send for the King and reprimand him as if he were a naughty schoolboy." Davidson left the cabinet when Baldwin retired, because of lack of confidence in Chamberlain, whom he described as "a good Lord Mayor of Birmingham in a lean year"—a poor assessment, no doubt colored by personal dislike.

It amuses me to find a new policy for each of my colleagues in turn.

From his diary, May 12, 1934:

Unhappily it is part of my nature that I cannot contemplate any problem without trying to find a solution for it. And so I have practically taken charge of the defense requirements of the country.

From his diary, March 8, 1935:

I am more and more carrying this government on my back.

To Hilda, March 23, 1935:

As you will see I have become a sort of Acting P.M.—only without the actual power of the P.M. I have to say "Have you thought" or "What would you say" when it would be quicker to say "This is what you must do."

From his diary, December 8, 1935, ruminating on why he should not retire:

I suppose the answer is that I know no one that I would trust to hold the balance between rigid orthodoxy and a fatal disregard of sound principles and the rights of posterity.

To Hilda, November 14, 1936:

This is another case of my doing the P.M.'s work but as he won't or can't do it himself, someone must do it for him.

Shortly before he became Prime Minister, Chamberlain told Lady Nancy Astor "that he meant to be his own Foreign Minister." It was a comment that would have amused and perhaps alarmed brother Austen, who, as the author of Locarno, was the elder statesman of British foreign policy, and who once, in the dinner company of Anthony Eden, had responded to the soon-to-be Prime Minister's observations on the future of Austria with the admonition: "Neville, you must remember you don't know anything about foreign affairs."

It was, of course, true that Neville Chamberlain's ministerial accomplishments had lain primarily in the domestic area, and no doubt many of his contemporaries would have shared Tom Jones's impression that the new chief was "rather a dark horse, especially in foreign affairs." In fact, however, his "track record" was longer than was generally realized, and foreshadowed much of what he did as Prime Minister.

In the early 1930s, when Chamberlain began to express himself officially on foreign policy, his views were in close harmony with those of Eden. Unlike the younger man, Chamberlain had no personal experience of the horrors of trench warfare, but he had been deeply involved in hospital and refugee work in Birmingham, had lost dear friends and relatives to the war (including a younger cousin with whom he had particularly close ties*), and fully shared Eden's

* Norman Chamberlain, the son of Neville's father's brother Herbert, who had served with him on the Birmingham City Council and was killed in action in December 1917. Neville Chamberlain's only book was a privately printed memoir of Norman, whom he described as "the most intimate friend I ever had."

hatred of war and determination to do everything possible to prevent its recurrence.

War was not only horrible; it was wasteful, and as Chancellor of the Exchequer, Chamberlain bore primary responsibility for the budget and the general economy. Massive rearmament meant high taxes, government controls, and the production of things useless except to kill. Moved by such practical but genuine idealism, Chamberlain clutched eagerly at collective security as a means of avoiding war and the strains of preparing for war. In the spring of 1934 he went so far as to propose an "international police force" to keep the peace, and was bitterly disappointed when his colleagues failed to rally to his standard. When Mussolini launched the Ethiopian invasion, Chamberlain encouraged Hoare to take a firm position at Geneva, and strongly supported the sanctions policy. Even as late as May 1936, with the Italians in Addis Ababa, Chamberlain thought that sanctions should be maintained because "the time has not yet come for the League to own itself beaten."

But it was, in fact, the League's failure in Ethiopia that caused Chamberlain, like many others, to give up on collective security as the solution of Britain's defense problems. His "midsummer of madness" speech in June 1936 was of small importance in the Ethiopian affair, for Eden himself was already convinced that sanctions had failed. But it symbolized a basic shift in Chamberlain's thinking, which now led him toward a policy of what he at first called "localizing the danger spots in the world by means of regional agreements." What he really had in mind was some kind of arrangement with the Germans, who he had declared as early as 1934 to be "the *fons et origo* of all our European troubles and anxieties." Now, in April 1936,* he noted in his diary that if the League should abandon sanctions or other forceful means of peace-keeping, that "would make it easier for Germany to come into the League, and I was anxious that Halifax should visit Berlin and get into touch with Hitler as soon as possible." At the time, of course, Eden was Foreign Secretary and Halifax held the sinecure post of Lord Privy Seal; Chamberlain's private tapping of Halifax for the future Berlin mission suggests his belief, long before it blossomed into actuality, that the Yorkshire nobleman would be the more congenial guest in Nazi society and better able to make friends with the Fuehrer.

This desire to reach an accommodation with Germany by no means reflected any susceptibility on Chamberlain's part to the lure of Nazism. He was especially shocked by the murder of the Austrian Chancellor Dollfuss (whom he had met and liked at Lausanne in 1932), and vented his feelings in a letter to his sister Hilda: "That those beasts should have gotten him at last, and that they should have treated him with such callous brutality, makes me hate Nazi-ism, and all its works, with a greater loathing than ever before."

Yet there was something narrow and superficial in his condemnation of the dictators, reflected a year later, when the Ethiopian crisis loomed, in his writing that "it does seem barbarous that in these days it should still be in the power of

---

* That same month he wrote: "I don't believe myself that we could purchase peace in a lasting settlement by handing over Tanganyika to the Germans, but if I did I would not hesitate for a moment to do so."

one man, for a whim or to preserve his personal influence, to throw away the lives of thousands of Italians." The probable fate of the Ethiopian victims of Fascist aggression was not in the forefront of Chamberlain's mind.

More important, he continued to regard the Axis leaders as men with whom one could bargain and trade, and he seems never to have grasped the irrational, tide-like quality of Hitlerian Nazism. The Soviet Ambassador in London, Ivan Maisky, recounts that in July 1937 Chamberlain longingly remarked that "if only we could sit down at a table with the Germans and run through all their complaints and claims with a pencil, this would greatly relieve all tensions." And Strang wrote in retrospect that Chamberlain was "dominated" by two ideas: hatred of war and "the belief that the German and Italian dictators were men whose word could be relied on; that it was possible to come to agreements with them which could transform the international situation for the better and give peace to Europe; and that by his personal influence with them he could hope to bring such agreements about."

Chamberlain's intention to be his "own Foreign Minister" and his eagerness to stabilize relations with Germany and Italy through direct negotiations with the dictators, coupled with his generally masterful disposition, spelled inevitable trouble for his relations with Anthony Eden. Whatever his merits or defects, Eden's faith in Hitler's or Mussolini's promises had been pretty much dispelled, and he was no longer disposed to hand over the *quid* unless he had the *quo* in hand.

At the time Chamberlain became Prime Minister, neither of the two appears to have realized that their ways were bound to part. As a matter of course, Chamberlain asked Eden to stay on, and the latter was blissfully blind to the changes in store for him.

5

Chamberlain marked his advent as Prime Minister by a considerable reshuffling of the Cabinet, but it was mostly musical chairs, for there were no new faces in the major offices. Ramsay MacDonald departed with Baldwin, and Halifax was named Lord President. Simon replaced Chamberlain at the Exchequer, Hoare left the Admiralty to succeed Simon at the Home Office,* and Duff Cooper left the War Office (where he had not distinguished himself) for the Admiralty. Two junior ministers were promoted; Leslie Hore-Belisha from the Ministry of Transport to the War Office, and Oliver Stanley from Education to the Board of Trade, replacing Lord Runciman, who left the Cabinet. Lord Swinton at the Air Ministry and Inskip as Coordinator of Defence, like Eden, stayed on.

Soon after becoming Prime Minister, Chamberlain met informally with the Conservative backbenchers† to outline his prospective foreign policy. He told them that he thought it uncertain whether the German challenge could be

---

* Hoare requested the Home Office, which was senior to the Admiralty in the Cabinet hierarchy, prompting Winston Churchill to remark that Hoare was "the first man I've ever known to prefer Jack Ketch to Jack Tar."

† During his last few months at the Exchequer, Chamberlain, on recommendation of the Chief Whip (Captain David Margesson), took on a new parliamentary private secretary,

deflected and war averted, but that, if not, he believed that he could detach Mussolini from Hitler and thus break up the Axis. "If only we could get on terms with the Germans, I would not care a rap for Musso," he wrote at about the same time. Italy was to be feared only in conjunction with Germany, and if British advances in Berlin should prove unrewarding, the thing to do was to settle the issues with Mussolini by diplomacy, and thus avert the prospect, which the Navy especially feared, of war with both Germany and Italy.

True to these intentions and shortly after he took office as Prime Minister, Chamberlain had an official invitation for a visit to England sent to Neurath. The personable Baron had been Ambassador in London before his appointment as Foreign Minister; he would be easier to talk with than the tactless, humorless Ribbentrop, and no doubt Chamberlain hoped that he and the German could sit down together and check off the points at issue "with a pencil." Rather gracelessly Neurath agreed to come to London on June 23, but a few days before the scheduled date he postponed the trip, following German charges that the cruiser *Leipzig* had been attacked by "Spanish-Bolshevist" submarines.*

Frustrated at the northern end of the Axis, Chamberlain turned his attention southward, finding Mussolini in one of his less bellicose phases. On June 19, Ciano assured Sir Eric Drummond that Mussolini was "willing to come to an understanding with Great Britain on the basis of an agreement which is complete and clears up all points—beginning naturally with recognition of the empire [Ethiopia] in order to remove any possibility of misunderstanding and friction in the future." Despite his dislike for the Duce, Eden had been tempering his public references to Italy, and on July 21 had his reward in the form of a visit from Dino Grandi, who declared that Mussolini was ready to embark on conversations as a basis for "permanent friendship" between the two countries. Furthermore, he was the bearer of a personal message from the Duce to the Prime Minister, with whom Grandi was now given an appointment for July 27, 1937.

Eden was not present, Grandi did not leave a copy of the Duce's message (apparently embodied in a four-page letter), and Chamberlain had difficulty "in distinguishing what was Grandi and what was Mussolini." The ambassador was at pains to explain Italy's recent reinforcement of her Libyan garrison from fear of a British attack,† but the only specific request he put forward was the one already mentioned to Ambassador Drummond by Ciano: *de jure* recognition of

---

Lord Dunglass (later the Earl of Home, who thereafter surrendered his peerage and, as Sir Alec Douglas-Home, served during the sixties, as Prime Minister and Foreign Minister). In an interview with me in 1974, Sir Alec described his chief responsibility to Chamberlain as "keeping the back-benchers happy"—an important task since Chamberlain was very reticent and "no good in the smoking-room."

* There may well have been other reasons for the postponement (which amounted to cancellation) of the visit, as Ribbentrop can hardly have relished the prospect of being upstaged by Neurath.

† On July 22, Grandi had delivered a like justification for the Libyan reinforcement by way of message from Mussolini to Hore-Belisha, for which the protocol base was that the Duce held the War portfolio in the Italian Government. Grandi recommended close staff contacts between the two powers, in order to lighten their respective military expenditures in the Mediterranean and give Italy "a line of escape from the German menace" which might lead to a "re-establishment of the Stresa front." The British Army General Staff was

the Ethiopian conquest. Chamberlain assured Grandi of Britain's peaceful intentions, affirmed his readiness for conversations, and then "asked whether a personal note to the Duce would be appreciated." Grandi welcomed the idea, and Chamberlain at once wrote and handed to the ambassador a letter expressing regret that "Anglo-Italian relations were still far from the old feeling of mutual trust and affection" and a willingness "to begin conversations at any time."

Mussolini replied promptly and cordially, with an appropriate reference to Austen Chamberlain (with whom he had been on very friendly terms) and assurances that he was ready for conversations. "The interests of Italy and Great Britain," he wrote, "are not opposed to each other in the Mediterranean or elsewhere. On the contrary, through their peaceful co-existence they can be responsible for a most active spur to the development of our relations." On August 8, Chamberlain, delighted with his apparent success and intoxicated by his new feeling of power, confided to his family:

> . . . I can look back with great satisfaction at the extraordinary relaxation of tension since I first saw Grandi. Grandi himself says it is 90 per cent due to me and it gives one a sense of wonderful power that the Premiership gives you. As Chancellor of the Exchequer I could hardly have moved a pebble: now I have only to raise a finger and the whole face of Europe is changed.

But the face of Europe soon darkened again. Two days after the Prime Minister penned this extraordinary effusion, a British tanker was attacked off the Spanish coast by aircraft which the Foreign Office knew were based on Majorca, where the Italians were in full control. Throughout the rest of August there were frequent submarine attacks on ships of various nationalities, and it soon became common knowledge that the Italians were responsible. On August 25, Mussolini publicly mocked nonintervention by his telegram to Franco celebrating the contribution of "Italian legionary troops" to the capture of Santander.

While all this was going on, Anthony Eden was on holiday in Hampshire, with Halifax pinch-hitting for him at the Foreign Office. Upon his return to London at the end of August he pointed out to Chamberlain and Halifax that Italian actions hardly signified a sincere desire for *rapprochement,* and that there was little point in starting conversations, or conceding recognition of the Ethiopian conquest *de jure,* as long as Mussolini was keeping the Mediterranean in such an uproar. Eden's hand was strengthened by the submarine attack on the destroyer *Havock* and the sinking of the tanker *Woodford,* and on September 2, the Government announced that more destroyers would be sent to the western Mediterranean to protect British shipping. Meanwhile Eden was concerting, with the French, plans for what became the Nyon Conference, from which Germany and Italy absented themselves, and in consequence of which the Italians suspended their submarine "blockade."

Nyon was generally regarded as an Anglo-French diplomatic triumph, and

inclined to regard the Italians' fears as genuine, while Eden, Vansittart, and Hankey thought it more probably a device to deter the British from strengthening their own Mediterranean forces.

Chamberlain joined in the congratulations which Eden received when he returned to London. But in fact the Prime Minister was displeased. On September 12, the day after the Nyon conferees reached agreement, he wrote: "I am not too happy about the Foreign Office who seem to have no imagination and no courage. . . . I am terribly afraid lest we should let the Italian situation slip back to where it was before I intervened. The F.O. persist in seeing Mussolini only as a sort of Machiavelli putting on a false mask of friendship in order to further nefarious ambition. If we treat him like that we shall get nowhere with him and we shall have to pay for our mistrust by appallingly costly defence in the Mediterranean." And after the conference was over, Chamberlain recorded his opinion that "We have had a great success at Nyon, but at the expense of Anglo-Italian relations."

These were by no means the new Prime Minister's first adverse reactions to Eden's conduct of affairs. Less than two weeks after he took office, according to Hankey, Chamberlain was "very annoyed" because Eden had "chucked a spanner into a most critical situation" at the Imperial Conference.* The Prime Minister's distrust of Eden's attitude toward Italy must have developed rapidly, for he wrote his letter to Mussolini without consulting Eden, and later recorded that: "I did not show my letter to the Foreign Secretary for I had the feeling he would object to it." A few days later (August 1, 1937), referring to his "double policy" of rearmament and appeasement, Chamberlain qualified his optimism for its success with the condition "if only the Foreign Office will play up," and went on to remark what he thought were signs of jealousy in that quarter regarding newspaper references to the "Chamberlain touch" in British foreign policy.

During the summer of 1937, Chamberlain kept his displeasure under wraps, and Eden appears to have been unaware of any such problem until his return to London on September 22 from Nyon and Geneva. The Prime Minister's felicitations were at once coupled with a pointed suggestion that Eden take "a really good holiday" and cancel his plans for a major political speech scheduled for October 15 at Llandudno in Wales.† Eden confided to Harvey that there was "a difference as to methods" between himself and Chamberlain, who, he now believed, "had a certain sympathy for dictators whose efficiency appealed to him."

Whatever disagreement existed was still kept within the family. Ambassador Corbin, a shrewd and experienced observer of the British official scene, reported to Paris on September 22 that Chamberlain and Eden were working well together, and on October 8 Chamberlain, addressing the Conservative Party Conference, paid high tribute to Eden's conduct of his office. A month later, however, the "differences," for the first time, turned acrimonious.

The initial cause was Halifax's invitation to visit Germany for the International Hunting Exposition. Eden's approval was lukewarm, while Chamberlain's

---

* The Imperial Conference was held in London following George VI's coronation. What the "spanner" was Hankey did not specify; Captain Roskill thinks (*Hankey: Man of Secrets*, pp. 280–81) that it had to do with a proposed Pacific Pact.

† On the insistence of the chairman of the Conservative Party, Sir Douglas Hacking, Chamberlain acceded to Eden's keeping his engagement to make the speech, which was duly delivered.

was enthusiastic to the point that he grew very impatient with the cautions emanating from the Foreign Office: "But really, that F.O.!" he exploded in a letter of October 24 to his sister. "I am only waiting for my opportunity to stir it up with a long pole."

A few days later the Prime Minister took to his bed with gout and was unable to attend the opening of Parliament. In his absence, Eden was to make the principal government speech on foreign policy, and Chamberlain sent word via Eden's parliamentary private secretary, James P. L. Thomas, that "he hoped he [Eden] would say nothing to upset the dictators." Thomas did not deliver the message,* and Eden used the occasion to criticize Italy for supporting Germany's colonial claims without herself offering to contribute to meeting them. Chamberlain was vastly annoyed, and recorded on November 6:

> It contained unfortunate passages, from my point of view, and shows again a characteristic of the Foreign Office mind which I have frequently noticed before. They never can keep the major objects of foreign policy in mind, with the result that they make obstructions for themselves by endeavouring to give smart answers to some provocative foreign statement. . . .
> Mussolini had been more than usually offensive with his remarks about bleating democracies, and his outrageous allusion to the Colonies. But Anthony should never have been provoked into a retort which throws Germany and Italy together in self-defence, when our policy is so obviously to try and divide them.

Eden, too, was increasingly irritated, both by what he regarded as Chamberlain's overeagerness for the Halifax trip (which was to be carried out even though Hitler would not be in Berlin to receive him, and a trip to the Berghof would therefore be required), and by the slow pace of British rearmament in comparison to the Germans' achievements. A consequence of these disagreements was two very unpleasant meetings. On November 8, according to Harvey's account:

> A.E.'s conversation with the P.M. went very badly. P.M. stiff . . . complained that F.O. never made genuine effort to get together with dictators. A.E. said it was useless and impossible to do so unless and until we were strongly armed, complained of the spirit in which rearmament was being undertaken and urged the necessity for buying abroad.

On November 16 there were more mutual recriminations, and after Eden again attacked the handling of rearmament, the Prime Minister advised his colleague, who had influenza, "to go back to bed and take an aspirin." This interchange was followed by a letter in which Chamberlain attributed Eden's concern about rearmament to his illness and hoped that he would shortly be able to take a holiday.

Lord Halifax departed to Berlin the next day, and his discussions with the Nazi leaders raised no important new questions. Following his return, Cham-

---

* It was on this occasion that Eden's two principal secretaries, Thomas and Oliver Harvey, first began to discuss privately the idea that Eden might be obliged by Chamberlain's interference to resign from the Cabinet, and on November 7, Harvey raised the possibility in a confidential memorandum to Eden.

berlain and Eden had what the latter regarded as a "satisfactory" talk, and they collaborated well and in full mutual agreement for the meetings with Chautemps and Delbos at the end of November. At the Cabinet meeting on December 1 they again were in complete harmony in assessing the French ministers' visit, and in formulating the Cabinet's conclusion that "steps would be taken with a view to a start being made with the proposed conversations with Italy." A week later Eden had another "very satisfactory talk" with Chamberlain, finding that the Prime Minister was "in absolute agreement about Germany—viz. no settlement except a general European settlement."

The period of good feeling lasted through December. Both Chamberlain and Eden had come to the conclusion that it was time for a change in the office of Permanent Under-Secretary to the Foreign Office. Vansittart had held the post for seven years, his prestige had been shaken by his involvement with Hoare and Laval, and some of the ministers and senior civil servants thought he was deteriorating in self-control and insight. So it was now arranged, with Eden's full agreement, that Vansittart would be replaced by Sir Alexander Cadogan and given the new title of Chief Diplomatic Adviser to His Majesty's Government—a post devoid of executive responsibilities which would keep Sir Robert honorifically employed and available for consultation when needed.*

Eden had planned to go on December 28 to Madeira for the "long vacation" that Chamberlain had been urging him to take. However, important negotiations were in prospect for joint action with the United States in the Far East. The Prime Minister's anti-American feelings were rarely hidden, while Eden regarded the development of Anglo-American co-operation as a matter of the first importance. Fearing that Chamberlain, who was to take over the Foreign Office in his absence, might be too "heavy-handed" and "upset the Americans for good"—a hunch which was to prove not entirely groundless—Eden decided to go no further than the South of France, to which delightful part of the world he repaired on January 3, 1938.

On the Riviera, Sir Anthony found not only sun and tennis, but Winston Churchill and David Lloyd George as well. During a pleasant luncheon, these vivacious and powerful-spoken gentlemen congratulated Eden on his firm stand at Nyon, reinforced his distrust of Mussolini, and strongly opposed recognizing the Ethiopian conquest de jure. These counsels were given at a more crucial moment than the lunchers realized; that same day (January 14) Eden had a call from Cadogan asking him to return to London at once to deal with a new matter too secret for discussion by telephone.

Back in London the following evening, Eden learned that the problem arose from a proposal by Roosevelt that he would summon the entire Washington diplomatic corps to the White House on January 22 and urge that the governments represented should all agree on a program for reduction of armaments, equal access to raw materials, and respect for the laws of war. The President planned to do this only if assured of "wholehearted" British support, and he wanted an answer by January 17.

* Hierarchically, the post was parallel to those of Sir Horace Wilson as Chief Industrial Adviser and Sir Frederick Leith-Ross as Chief Economic Adviser.

Chamberlain set little value on the prospects of collaboration with the United States, and had nothing but scorn for American diplomacy. He had not much liked Roosevelt's famous "Quarantine" speech,* and he was immediately and strongly hostile to this new proposal, which he saw as cutting athwart his own efforts to reach a settlement with the dictators. In his diary he recorded:

> The plan appeared to me fantastic and likely to excite the derision of Germany and Italy. They might even use it to postpone conversations with us, and if we were associated with it they would see in it another attempt on the part of the democratic bloc to put the dictators in the wrong. There was no time to consult Anthony, for in view of secrecy on which Roosevelt insisted in emphatic terms I did not dare to telephone. Therefore, after consultation with Wilson and Cadogan, I sent a reply deprecating immediate publication. . . .

The "deprecating" reply described Chamberlain's hope to reach a settlement with Italy involving *de jure* recognition of the Ethiopian "empire," and suggested that Roosevelt postpone his conclave pending the outcome of these efforts. Chamberlain struck out the final portion of Cadogan's draft promising British support if the President was determined to go ahead, and with this deletion the message sent was, as the Under-Secretary of State, Sumner Welles, described it, "a douche of cold water."†

Eden's assessment of the situation was directly contrary to Chamberlain's. He thought nothing more important for Britain's long-term diplomacy than to involve the United States in European matters, and had returned from the Riviera with his doubts about the value of conversations with Rome underlined by his talks with Churchill and Lloyd George. Apart from his anger at not having been consulted, he thought the Prime Minister's reply much too chilling and likely to set back his efforts to tighten the London-Washington bonds.

On Sunday, January 16, Eden went to Chequers for a meeting with Chamberlain which turned into an altercation far more serious than those of the preceding November, when the Halifax visit had been the irritant. Now there was a basic issue of foreign policy between them, and it was sharpened two days later by Roosevelt's reply to Chamberlain's "douche of cold water," for the President expressed strong disapproval of granting *de jure* recognition of Ethiopia's subjugation and pointed out the bad psychological effect this would have on Anglo-American efforts to mobilize sentiment against Japanese imperialism in China.

Chamberlain's reaction to Eden's views had not been sweetened by the information that his Foreign Secretary had been consorting and consulting with Churchill and Lloyd George, and now two other personal factors were estranging them. The more important was the growing role in foreign policy of Sir Horace Wilson, whom Baldwin had brought into the inner circle of advisers,

---

* In October 1937, in a speech at Chicago, Roosevelt denounced international lawlessness and spoke of a "quarantine" for offending states. Chamberlain read the speech with "mixed feelings" and commented that there was "something lacking in his analogy" since "patients suffering from epidemic diseases do not usually go about fully armed."

† The American Embassy in London appears not to have been involved in this episode, probably because Ambassador Bingham had recently died and his successor, Joseph P. Kennedy, was not yet on hand.

and who stayed on under Chamberlain with an office at No. 10 Downing Street and closer access to the Prime Minister than any other senior official. Although his title of Chief Industrial Adviser remained unchanged, Wilson's activities were not correspondingly limited, and Chamberlain used him extensively as a consultant and, at times, an executant in the field of foreign policy.*

Wilson's handling of these responsibilities has been defended by Sir Samuel Hoare as wholly in line with the standards of an "orthodox, conscientious and efficient civil servant." But the records and recollections of others seem rather to establish that he was more of an echo and agent of Chamberlain's views than a truly "nonpolitical" adviser, and that sometimes his tactics were abrasive or devious. When J. P. L. Thomas became Eden's parliamentary secretary, Wilson and Warren Fisher privately told him that Vansittart was an "alarmist" influencing Eden against appeasement, and asked Thomas to serve as a "bridge" to create better "understanding" between the Foreign Office and the Prime Minister's staff—a suggestion which Thomas indignantly rejected because "they expected me to work behind the back of my own chief."

Whether or not Wilson instigated Chamberlain's distrust of the Foreign Office, he certainly encouraged it and openly voiced his own criticism of the "negative approach of the F.O. and failure to make approaches to dictators." Now that the Roosevelt proposal had precipitated a Chamberlain-Eden split over the *de jure* concession to Italy, Wilson paid a call on Cadogan, to say that the Prime Minister was "rather horrified" at Eden's attitude: he had thought that, before going to France, Eden "accepted idea of negotiations with Italy on the basis of de jure recognition," but "now finds he is opposed and thinks he has 'run out.'" Rather incautiously Cadogan suggested that Wilson speak directly to Eden, perhaps not realizing that for the Chief Industrial Adviser to lecture the Foreign Minister on the conduct of foreign affairs was all too likely to cause an explosion. Eden has described the outcome of Wilson's visit:

> . . . eventually I told Sir Horace that if ever it fell to my lot to cross the road to Downing Street, and I had there to deal with an industrial problem, I would send for him and almost certainly take his advice, for I knew that he understood industrial affairs, but I asked him to believe me that he did not understand foreign affairs. The meeting did not end well and I doubt whether mine was a wise comment.

The other exacerbating personality in the immediate situation was Lady Ivy Chamberlain, the widow of Sir Austen.† Benito Mussolini seems to have had a way with British Foreign Ministers (other than Eden) and their wives. In his early years as Duce, he had been befriended by Lord and Lady Curzon, to whose encouragement he owed his knowledge of English. A few years later, Sir Austen and his lady also found the Italian dictator very personable, and the three enjoyed warm relations. Lady Ivy also found Fascism most impressive,

---

* Indeed, after Vansittart's "elevation" as Chief Diplomatic Adviser, Chamberlain frequently brought Wilson to ministerial foreign policy meetings to which Vansittart was not invited.

† Sir Austen Chamberlain had died on March 16, 1937.

and shortly before Christmas of 1937, bedecked with the Fascist Party badge, she was in Rome, lunching with Ciano.* This odd couple effusively agreed with each other that their respective countries should seek "complete agreement, without a shadow, and meant to last," but Ciano reflected in his diary that Eden's recent statements were not "encouraging" and that "we had better sharpen our swords."

Lady Chamberlain met with Ciano again on New Year's Day, armed with a letter from her brother-in-law reaffirming his desire for conversations. Whatever Ciano may have actually said (his diary is noncommittal), his guest was moved to write to her brother-in-law that Ciano had declared the present moment "psychological" for a settlement.

If Chamberlain saw anything irregular about this diplomatic correspondence through in-laws, it did not prevent him from waving Ivy's letter under Eden's nose, to reinforce his arguments for pushing ahead on talks with Rome despite Roosevelt's messages. When the Prime Minister revealed that he had penned his own letter to Lady Ivy on Downing Street notepaper and sent it by ordinary mail, Eden suggested, not without reason, that very probably the Italian intelligence service had read it before delivery. This provoked a storm of Chamberlainian indignation, and the two fell into a wrangle that led Chamberlain to observe that "there was a deep difference" between them. Eden began to doubt whether he could remain in office, but, as Chamberlain and Cadogan both pointed out to him, the secrecy in which Roosevelt had wrapped his proposals would have made it impossible for Eden to explain publicly the circumstances leading to a resignation.

The forum of controversy now shifted to the Foreign Policy Committee of the Cabinet, which met four times on January 19, 20, and 21.† The first meeting went very badly for Eden. Chamberlain described Roosevelt's proposal as "detestable" and read from Lady Chamberlain's letter, and his views were strongly endorsed by Halifax, Simon, and Inskip. Eden had some support from the younger ministers, but it was plain that the Prime Minister had the upper hand with his colleagues, whose hostile attitude toward Eden was now even more apparent than it had been the previous winter during his arguments with Hoare over Spain.

The following morning Wilson's sharp tongue was wagging briskly, telling J. P. L. Thomas that the Roosevelt plan was "woolly rubbish," and that he was encouraging Chamberlain to pour cold water on it and move ahead with Italy. Thomas, perhaps injudiciously, pointed out the risk that news of the Roosevelt proposal might leak at the American end, in which event Chamberlain would be in the public posture of turning down Washington in order to appease the dictators. This threw Sir Horace into what Thomas described as a "towering rage," in the course of which he threatened that "if America produced the facts he

---

* That sententious young man recorded in his diary: "I am too much of a patriot to appreciate such a gesture from an Englishwoman at the present time."

† Hankey's original records of these meetings appear to have been destroyed but prior to their disappearance were examined by the research assistant working on the memoirs of Lord Avon (Eden). Her notes have survived and are the basis of the account in Roskill, *Hankey: Man of Secrets* (1974), pp. 299–301.

would use the full power of the Government machine in an attack upon A.E.'s past record with regard to the dictators and the shameful obstruction by the F.O. of the P.M.'s attempts to save the peace of the world." Later that day Wilson dropped in on Cadogan, who was beginning to wonder "what he's at or whether he's quite straight."

Such episodes among the subordinates did nothing to ease the tension between the principals. Nevertheless, the immediate crisis was resolved without an open split. There was much more and bitter argument, but at the fourth Foreign Policy Committee meeting, in the afternoon of January 21, it was agreed to send Roosevelt two messages, one welcoming his plan and promising full support, and the second setting forth the case for *de jure* recognition as part of an over-all Mediterranean settlement. Thus the "choice between the U.S.A. and Italy" was avoided by choosing both. Eden was not altogether happy about the compromise, but Roosevelt's reaction was cordial, and on January 25, Eden went to Geneva, for a League Council meeting, in a fairly cheerful mood. Early in February, Roosevelt postponed his program because of uncertainties arising from the Blomberg-Fritsch-Neurath shake-up in Berlin, and eventually he abandoned it.*

But it was only a brief calm spell, and the culprits who whipped up the final storm were Benito Mussolini and Neville Chamberlain. No sooner was Eden on his way to Geneva than the Prime Minister was again writing to Lady Ivy, and on February 1, Ciano's diary recorded:

> I took Lady Chamberlain to see the Duce, and she showed him an important letter from Neville Chamberlain. Two points: Great Britain is coming around to the idea of a formal recognition of the Empire; conversations can begin at the end of the month. Mussolini approved and agreed. Lady Chamberlain will write to her brother-in-law to inform him of the Duce's reactions, which were definitely favorable. He showed himself in full sympathy with the project of an agreement and said that he intends to make one which will be complete and durable and able to serve as a basis for co-operation between the two Empires. He dictated to Lady Chamberlain the terms of her letter.

The sincerity of Mussolini's protestations of goodwill may be gauged by the concomitant Italian actions in the Spanish conflict.† A few days before Lady Ivy's visit, the Italian Navy had exploited a relaxation of the Nyon patrols by resuming the submarine blockade, and had sunk the British ship *Endymion;* on February 4 another Britisher, the *Alcira,* was sunk by air attack. On February 2, Mussolini wrote to Franco a letter which, according to Ciano, "reinforces our obligations if Franco means to fight, but opens the way for us to disengage ourselves if the Generalissimo is going to insist on a long-drawn war of nerves." On

---

* Winston Churchill subsequently wrote that Chamberlain's handling of the Roosevelt program destroyed "the last frail chance to save the world from tyranny other than by war" (*The Gathering Storm*, pp. 254–55), and Eden wrote in a similar vein (*Facing the Dictators, 1923–1938*, p. 645). If in retrospect these estimates of the President's plan appear extravagant, it is nonetheless apparent that, for the long pull, American support against the dictators was vital for the survival of the European democracies, and that Eden was quite right to insist on encouraging Roosevelt's initiative.

† Ciano's diary indicates that during this period, whether by stealth or cryptanalysis, the Italians were reading some British diplomatic messages.

the same day the Duce "intensified the air raids" on the Spanish coast "which are breaking the nerve of the civil population," and which caused such carnage in Barcelona that a written description led even Ciano to record that "I have never read a document so realistically horrifying."

The renewed sinkings produced a resumption of full-strength Nyon patrols, and British and French announcements that any submerged submarines encountered in their respective areas would be sunk. Sinkings and Barcelona bombings alike aroused indignation in the British press and the House of Commons, and underlined Eden's concern about the wisdom of embarking on conversations with Rome under such circumstances—doubts which were reinforced by exasperation when he learned that the Neville-Ivy correspondence was again in bloom.

However, on February 4, Grandi had come to Eden with the news that Italy would resume its part in the Nyon patrols, and had spoken understandingly about the need to resolve the Spanish problem as part of a general settlement. Eden was sufficiently encouraged to tell Grandi that if the two of them could make preliminary progress on Spain and other prickly issues such as the Italian radio's anti-British broadcasts, the basis might be laid for more formal conversations to follow.

Chamberlain appeared to agree with this program, and for the next two weeks things were amicable enough. The Prime Minister had turned his attention to the betterment of relations with Germany, and on February 12 the Hitler-Schuschnigg meeting brought the Austrian question to the front of the stage. On these matters the two men were in general accord, and on February 13 *The Times* carried a denial "on the highest authority" of any differences, while Chamberlain was writing to his sister that rumors of a split were "mendacious and vicious," and that "I saw Anthony on Friday morning and we were in complete agreement, more complete perhaps than we have sometimes been in the past."

The final crisis began on Wednesday, February 16, when Grandi refused, on the pretext of a golf engagement, Eden's request that he come to the Foreign Office, while transmitting to Downing Street, through unofficial channels,* a request for a meeting with the Prime Minister. Grandi's move was apparently stimulated by a telegram from Ciano with instructions which were elaborated in a letter directing the ambassador to speed up the negotiations. In the letter (which did not reach Grandi until the morning of February 18), Ciano pointed to the imminent possibility that Hitler might march into Austria and announce an *Anschluss,* after which "it would be impossible to prevent the entire world interpreting our policy of *rapprochement* with London as a journey to Canossa under German pressure."

Eden did not like the idea of a Chamberlain-Grandi meeting, and was even more strongly opposed to opening formal conversations in Rome. But Chamberlain was adamant, and an appointment for Grandi was arranged for the late

---

* The channel was Sir Joseph Ball, research director of the Conservative Party, who enjoyed confidential relations with both Chamberlain and Wilson. Ball was well acquainted with Grandi and had another source of information at the Italian Embassy in the person of one Dingli, a Britisher who acted as legal adviser to the embassy.

morning of February 18. The previous evening, a message came from the indefatigable Lady Ivy, reporting that Ciano, at lunch with her, had asked whether she had any further word from London, and on being answered in the negative had declared: "Today an agreement will be easy, but things are happening in Europe which will make it impossible tomorrow."

Meanwhile Eden had sent Chamberlain a memorandum categorically opposing any British commitment to open formal conversations. Chamberlain was much impressed by Lady Ivy's intimation of urgency and its possible bearing on the Austrian situation, while Eden strongly suspected that Mussolini had already sold out Austria for "some kind of *quid pro quo* from Berlin." Eden's attitudes triggered a strong negative reaction from the Prime Minister, who foresaw apocalyptic consequences if conversations were not promptly begun:

> This note [from Eden] convinced me that the issue between us must be faced, and faced at once. In my view, to intimate now to Grandi that this was not the moment for conversations would be to convince Mussolini that he must consider talks with us "off" and act accordingly. I had no doubt at all that in his disappointment and exasperation at having been fooled with, as he would think, so long, Italian public opinion would be raised to a white heat against us. There might indeed be some overt act of hostility and in any case the dictatorships would be driven closer together, the last threads of Austrian independence would be lost, the Balkan countries would feel compelled to turn towards their powerful neighbours, Czechoslovakia would be swallowed, France would either have to submit to German domination or fight, in which case we should almost certainly be drawn in. I could not face the responsibility of allowing such a series of catastrophes to happen and I told Horace Wilson on Friday morning that I was determined to stand firm, even though it meant losing my Foreign Secretary.

The meeting with Grandi on February 18 must be well-nigh unique in diplomatic annals, for it appeared to pit the Foreign Secretary against a *de facto* alliance between the Prime Minister and the ambassador of a potential enemy power. Chamberlain seemed bent on extracting statements and representations from Grandi that would support him on the issues between him and Eden. Chamberlain asked the ambassador point blank whether or not there was any understanding between the Fuehrer and the Duce envisaging German absorption of Austria; Grandi answered in the negative. Chamberlain asked whether, if an Anglo-Italian settlement were not reached, Italy would be obliged to adopt policies hostile to the western powers; Grandi answered in the affirmative. Chamberlain inquired finally whether a prompt and public announcement of the commencement of conversations in Rome might favorably affect the results, and Grandi declared that it was so. After each of these replies Chamberlain looked toward Eden, as much as to say: "I told you so!" When Eden controverted any of Grandi's statements, Chamberlain played the part of peacemaker, putting his Foreign Secretary and the Italian Ambassador on the same level, and Grandi played up to the opportunity thus presented with great skill, for, despite all his general assurances to Chamberlain, he offered no commitment whatsoever with respect to either Austria or Spain.

Eventually, Chamberlain suggested an adjournment so that he might confer with Eden, and a resumption of the talks in the afternoon. Grandi departed, and Chamberlain and Eden then fell into a bitter confrontation: "Anthony, you have missed chance after chance. You simply cannot go on like this." To which Eden replied that Chamberlain was right "if you have faith in the men you are negotiating with." When Grandi returned that afternoon, he was told that the Cabinet would consider the situation over the weekend, and that the Prime Minister would see him again on the following Monday. Grandi, for his part, agreed to ask Rome whether a British formula for the withdrawal of volunteers from both sides in Spain would be acceptable.

When the Cabinet met on Saturday afternoon, Chamberlain opened the discussion, stating that he had long believed better relations with Germany and Italy were vital to British security; that Italy had recently shown herself more amenable; that the Austrian situation had increased Mussolini's need for friends and introduced an element of urgency; that Grandi had denied any Austrian deal between the dictators, and that he but not Eden believed the denial; that "the present occasion provided one of the opportunities that came at rare intervals and did not recur," and that he wished to tell Grandi on Monday that conversations could be commenced, and he hoped to get this information immediately to Hitler, who was to address the Reichstag on Sunday.

Eden responded that, while it was possible that the German threat to Austria was driving Mussolini to "our side," he thought it more likely that a deal had already been made, and that Mussolini's interest in conversations was to get the prestige of *de jure* recognition to compensate for what would be regarded as an Italian setback in Austria. Since the Duce had offered nothing on Austria, Spain, or anti-British radio propaganda, there was no evidence of his good faith. Eden was willing to continue informal talks with Grandi in the hope of improving the Spanish situation, but was definitely opposed to formal conversations in Rome, which was what Mussolini was demanding, until a resolution of the Spanish question was in sight.

One by one Simon, Halifax, Hoare, Inskip, Swinton, and Hore-Belisha supported Chamberlain. Of the senior ministers, only Lord Zetland (India) was on Eden's side, while the juniors were divided. Eden then declared that he could not support the Prime Minister's policy in the Commons, and when Chamberlain stated that he could not accept any other conclusion, the meeting was adjourned to Sunday afternoon.

Sunday morning Wilson telephoned Thomas "to say that all was up and that Anthony should resign for reasons of health." Thomas "asked why, when Anthony was so thoroughly fit," and received the reply: "Because it would be better for him and what is more, it would be better for you if you persuaded him to do so." This psychological warfare proved ineffective, though others also suggested, without success, that Eden follow that course.

Shortly after noon, Chamberlain and Eden conferred privately and agreed that "it was in the national interest for us to part." Chamberlain then said that "it was only fair" for Eden to know that the Italians had accepted the British formula for the withdrawal of volunteers from Spain. Eden, having heard nothing of this, expressed astonishment, whereat the Prime Minister said that he could not reveal the source of his information. In fact, the source was, once again, Sir Joseph Ball. Perhaps because of embarrassment at the irregularity of the channel, Chamberlain made no use of the news at the ensuing Cabinet meeting.

When the ministers realized that Eden's resignation was indeed confronting them, there were expressions of dismay, and efforts to patch up the dispute. A few of the junior ministers contemplated resigning with Eden, and Ormsby-Gore (Colonies) offered to give up his post so that Eden might remain in the Cabinet in another capacity. Halifax proposed a compromise under which conversations would be commenced, but no *de jure* recognition would be granted until the Spanish problem had been settled. Eden was pressed very hard to accept this, but eventually held to his decision. After the meeting he sent his letter of resignation to Chamberlain, who accepted it with expressions of "profound regret." Viscount Cranborne (the parliamentary Under-Secretary of the Foreign Office) and J. P. L. Thomas also gave up their offices, and Lord Halifax took Eden's place, at first on a temporary basis. On Monday, Eden and Cranborne made their resignation speeches in the Commons, and the next day, February 22, 1938, Eden delivered up his seals of office to the King.

There were many public expressions of support for Eden, and undoubtedly his resignation embarrassed the Government politically; on the Opposition's motion of censure that followed the debate, about fifty Government supporters abstained. Chamberlain did not handle the debate well, and distressed even his allies by describing the League of Nations as something to be laid aside for better times—a comment well designed to encourage the dictators and discourage the smaller nations. But the Prime Minister was more than strong enough to shake off the critics, and he mounted by far the heavier guns. Except for Lord Zetland, whose influence was limited to Indian affairs, Eden had been supported in the Cabinet only by a few junior ministers, to whom Chamberlain referred slightingly as "the Boys' Brigade." Popular as Eden had become, he was in no position to challenge Chamberlain for the Conservative Party leadership, and the higher levels of both the military and civil services were on Chamberlain's side.

The Royal Navy, confident though it was of its superiority to the Italians, was sympathetic to Franco, distrustful of the French, and anxious to eliminate any Italian menace to the Mediterranean routes. General Pownall, Director of Military Operations and intelligence, recorded that Chamberlain would "rally all commonsense people to his side." The Chiefs of Staff, dismayed at the prospect of simultaneous war with Germany, Italy, and Japan, strongly favored immediate steps to strike Italy from the list of potential enemies. Hankey thought Eden had been "swayed by a lot of sloppy people in the F.O.," and Vansittart, fearful though he was of the German menace, thought Chamberlain right in seeking reconciliation with Italy. Independent-minded Conservatives like Amery and Duff Cooper, who later fell away from Chamberlain, sided with him against Eden on this occasion.

Halifax and several other ministers strongly opposed Eden's resignation because they thought there was no difference "in principle" between him and Chamberlain, and this was not surprising, for the two men shared many attitudes. Both were supporters of Baldwin's decision to stand pat at the time of the Rhineland remilitarization. Neither showed any inclination to bring Russia into the European conclave; in May 1937, Eden counseled Delbos against strengthening Franco-Soviet relations on the ground that the public reaction in England would be adverse, while Chamberlain's hostility to the Soviet Union was outspoken, and not until 1939 did he even grudgingly recognize any legitimate role for the Russians in the resolution of European problems. Eden came eventually to the conclusion that, in view of Franco's dependence on Italian support, a Government victory would be less dangerous to British interests, but he remained a firm supporter of nonintervention and repeatedly poured cold water on French proposals to lift the arms embargo or take other steps to aid the Loyalists. While he did not share Halifax's near-contempt for the French, Eden at times treated their representations cavalierly and took unilateral action which disturbed the Quai d'Orsay. No more than his colleagues did Eden sense the negative impact of Belgian neutrality on defense against a German attack in the west. He was not opposed in principle to seeking a détente with Germany and Italy, and fully agreed with the Baldwin-Chamberlain policy of avoiding a military confrontation until British rearmament was further advanced. After the Hitler-Schuschnigg meeting on February 12, when his differences with Chamberlain were nearing the breaking point, Eden was as cautious as his colleagues in his reaction to the Austrian situation, telling them that "he did not want to put himself in the position of suggesting a resistance which we could not in fact furnish."

In short, the disagreements that arose over the Halifax visit to Germany and the opening of talks in Rome were tactical rather than strategic. But tactical disputes can, of course, be exceedingly important, and Eden was surely justified in concluding that he was being asked to use methods which he thought were bound to fail, and was losing the elbowroom for the exercise of his own judgment which a foreign secretary is entitled to claim.

The dispute over the Roosevelt proposal, on the other hand, acquired strategic dimension as soon as it was cast in terms of Italy *or* the United States. But the issue was not resolved on an "either-or" footing, and it is doubtful that the argument would have reached so sharp a pitch if Chamberlain had not gotten the matter off on the wrong foot with an ill-considered response sent without consulting his Foreign Secretary. Retrospectively, indeed, it appears that perhaps all of the policy issues in conjunction might well have been insufficient to precipitate a split if Chamberlain had refrained from exploiting Eden's absences and using private channels, through individuals such as Lady Chamberlain and Sir Joseph Ball, for diplomatic communication. One is led to wonder whether Chamberlain was resorting to these abrasive and humiliating tactics for the very purpose of getting rid of Eden.

But it is unlikely that this was so, at least until the last few weeks of Eden's tenure. Whatever his other faults, Chamberlain valued friendship, and his diary and letters reflect genuine fondness for Eden and respect for his ability. But the Prime Minister's supreme confidence in his own rightfulness, and his impatience with subordinates who moved too slowly or disputatiously, led him to "take charge" in ways that Eden soon found offensive. Other ministers accommodated themselves to Chamberlain's dominance. But Chamberlain was either insensitive or indifferent to the circumstances that Eden was high-spirited, had his own political base, and was far more experienced than his chief in diplomatic matters. Then, bent as Chamberlain was on reconciliation with Mussolini, came reports through Lady Ivy and others* that in Rome Eden was regarded with "strong dislike and distrust," and the Prime Minister concluded that his Foreign Secretary was more of a liability than an asset.

To be sure, Chamberlain paid a political price for Eden's departure. The leading Conservative independents, Churchill and Amery, were relics of the First World War who had been out of office since the twenties; now their slender ranks would be reinforced by a handsome, forty-year-old ex-Foreign Secretary. Still there were only thirty to forty Conservative dissidents, and they were quite unable to make a dent in Chamberlain's decision-making.

But if in Britain the political effect of Eden's resignation was limited, on the European Continent the impact was immense. Ciano was "at a party at the Colonnas'" when he "learned of Eden's fall," and he recorded: "There was a general cheer at the news. The Prince and Princess of Piedmont [the King's son and daughter-in-law] were there, and the Prince insisted on drinking several toasts with me. From the Colonnas' I gave instructions for the press not to be too triumphant—we don't want to turn Eden into a victim of Fascism." In London, the German chargé d'affaires, Dr. Ernst Woermann, described Eden as having a "pro-French attitude" and a "lack of understanding for Germany and Italy." From Berlin, Nevile Henderson sent Eden a personal letter predicting that his own task would now be easier, since the Germans regarded Eden as a *Deutschenfresser* —a "devourer of Germans"—while François-Poncet, much more discerning, informed Paris that "M. Eden is detested by the Nazis," who would regard his departure as a "confirmation of their calculations and an indication that they have no need to fear that an Anglo-French intervention would compromise their operation in Austria."

The French Ambassador also wrote that the Germans saw Eden's resignation as a setback for France, and in this respect the French themselves were in full agreement. On February 21, Premier Chautemps told Bullitt that Chamberlain had now eliminated Eden, Vansittart,† and Cranborne—"the three Englishmen closest to the Quai d'Orsay"—and that the British Government "would be inclined to make ever-increasing concessions to Germany."

It is certainly too much to say that if Eden had remained Foreign Secretary there would have been no Munich. To be sure, he was critical of the agreement

---

* Sir Henry ("Chips") Channon, an M.P. who had recently visited Italy, when summoned by Chamberlain on February 7, 1938, for a private report, declared that "Italy wanted to be friends with us and the only drawback to better relations was Anthony Eden." According to Channon, the Prime Minister then "smiled enigmatically." At about the same time, in Washington, the Italian Ambassador (Fulvio Suvich) was portraying Eden to Sumner Welles as the obstacle to an Anglo-Italian settlement.

† Chautemps was presumably unaware that Eden and Chamberlain acted in full agreement in removing Vansittart from his seat of power.

when Chamberlain brought it home, but in March 1937 he had told Ambassador Bingham that Britain could not give Czechoslovakia a guaranty because it "would split British public opinion." However, there can be no doubt that Hitler was well pleased with Chamberlain's replacement of Eden by Halifax, or that the Fuehrer gave weight to this episode as he assessed the danger of Allied intervention should he fall upon Czechoslovakia.

6

Fatigued and loath to linger through the aftermath of his resignation, Eden went to his sister's villa on the French Riviera, where he remained until early April. At the Foreign Office, now headed by Halifax, Cranborne was replaced as Under-Secretary by R. A. ("Rab") Butler, who had held that position at the India Office and (currently) the Ministry of Labour. Inasmuch as Halifax was in the House of Lords, Butler now became, except for the Prime Minister himself, the principal government spokesman on foreign affairs in the Commons.*

Once rid of Eden's opposition, Chamberlain lost no time in telling Grandi that Britain was ready for discussions, to be held (as the Italians had insisted) in Rome. Drummond (who had become Lord Perth) would be brought back to London for instructions, and the negotiations could commence upon his return to Rome, early in March.

Meanwhile, the Prime Minister turned his attention toward the northern end of the Axis, which he rightly continued to regard as much the more important. During his visit to Germany, Halifax had repeatedly been told that the colonial question was the only issue between Berlin and London, and when he recounted his conversations to the Cabinet on November 24, 1937, Chamberlain and Eden both opined that colonies loomed larger than before in the German mind, and the matter would have to be dealt with. Halifax favored an effort to strike a "bargain of a colonial settlement at the price of being a good European."

These tactics were based on a rather naïve extrapolation of what the Germans had said to Halifax, for it should have been realized that they had singled out colonies as the only issue on the assumption that Britain would not interfere with German expansion in Central and Eastern Europe. Chamberlain and Halifax were prepared to give Hitler his head there if he would stick to "peaceful" means of attaining his ends, but the Fuehrer, no more than the Duce in Ethiopia, was likely to respect such a limitation. Hitler and Goering had both indicated to Halifax that the colonial question was not urgent, and it was quite plain that the short-fused powder keg was in Central Europe, not Central Africa.

Nevertheless, the Foreign Office and the Colonial Office staffs were set to work up a plan for a colonies proposal to Germany. It was not an easy task. In March 1937 the Colonial Secretary, William Ormsby-Gore, had circulated a

---

* Halifax was replaced as Lord President of the Council by Viscount Hailsham, previously Lord Chancellor, who in that capacity gave way to Viscount Maugham. Eden's private secretary, Oliver Harvey, stayed on with Halifax, a circumstance to which historians are indebted for the continuation of Harvey's *Diplomatic Diaries*. Butler chose as his parliamentary secretary another diarist, Sir Henry ("Chips") Channon, an unabashed Chamberlain idolizer.

memorandum pointing out some of the obstacles. The former German colonies were all held as mandated territories under League of Nations supervision, and subject to guarantees for the benefit of the native populations. Britain, France, and the other mandatory powers had undertaken responsibilities toward these peoples which could hardly be discharged by turning them over, like so much freight, to another sovereignty—especially to the Third Reich, which was not a member of the League of Nations and espoused views about superior and inferior races that boded ill for fulfillment of the mandate guarantees.*

These difficulties no doubt explain the complicated nature of the plan which the Prime Minister unveiled before the Foreign Policy Committee on January 24, 1938. No territory was to be returned to German sovereignty. Instead, Germany was to share with Britain, France, Belgium, and Portugal in the administration of a wide belt of territory across south central Africa. The northern border would lie "roughly to the south of the Sahara, the Anglo-Egyptian Sudan, Abyssinia, and Italian Somaliland," and the southern "roughly to the south of Portuguese West Africa, the Belgian Congo, Tanganyika, and Portuguese East Africa." This ambitious project "would be based on complete equality of the powers concerned and of their all being subjected to certain limitations" in administering the lands within the belt. Germany "would be brought into the arrangement by becoming one of the African colonial powers . . . and by being given certain territories to administer." Which these would be the plan did not specify.

Chamberlain introduced his program by stressing the need for following up the Halifax visit in order to demonstrate sincerity and the desirability of opening up the German colonial question simultaneously with the Anglo-Italian conversations so as to show that "we were directing our efforts to secure a general appeasement." He was "convinced that no satisfactory general settlement with Germany was possible which excluded some colonial concessions." His plan would put German colonial administration under international control and ensure that it would not be used to raise "native armies." If the Cabinet approved, Henderson would sound out Berlin, and the Prime Minister "could see no reason" for the Germans to reject a plan which "gave them what they so strongly insisted on, namely equality of opportunity and treatment."

It was an ingenious scheme, but with its obvious defects it evoked mixed reactions among the committee members. Eden, whose relations with Chamberlain were at the breaking point over the Roosevelt episode, forbore any general criticism but insisted that no colonial concessions be considered except as part of a general settlement with Germany. The principal opposition came, surprisingly, from Simon and Hoare, generally to be found among the Prime Minister's steady supporters. The former pointed to the large territorial losses which Belgium and Portugal might face, and tried—unsuccessfully—to tie Chamberlain down on how the German share would be carved out. Hoare tartly observed that the Government seemed about to do precisely what it had always refused to do: treat the colonial question in isolation from other issues. Chamberlain de-

---

* Ormsby-Gore also inveighed against the "colonial guilt lie" and paying "danegeld," and predicted that colonial concessions would not put an end to German demands.

nied this, but further discussion brought out that both he and Ambassador Henderson had been contemplating a "point-by-point" handling of German questions, with the colonial issue "in the fore-front." Ormsby-Gore and Malcolm MacDonald, the Dominions Secretary, queried other facets of the project, and there was little support for Chamberlain's optimism about Germany's acceptance.

These doubts were reinforced on February 3, when Henderson, summoned home for consultation, met with the committee. The ambassador thought that the Germans would not be "greatly thrilled" by the proposals unless some territory were given them outright. Simon then remarked that, while the return of colonies to Germany was a "concrete proposition," the *quid pro quo* from Germany was "abstract and indefinite." Well it might be; Henderson had seen Neurath before returning home, and had been told in no uncertain terms that the German "claim to the return of colonies could not be the subject of bargaining," and other issues must be discussed quite "independently." When their conversation turned to "contributions to appeasement" which Germany might make, Neurath had slammed the door on any thought of rejoining the League of Nations unless the Covenant were greatly modified, and had declared that Britain had no right to "interfere in the settlement of our relations with Austria"; that country "was behaving badly and he could make no promise of any kind with regard to her."

Despite these discouraging factors the committee proceeded to consider how the proposal should be presented to the Germans, and immediately confronted the problem of what Henderson should say if (as was virtually certain) they should ask what part of the territory would be assigned to them. Chamberlain, who had been ducking this central issue, was much opposed to any discussion of specific territory, and endorsed Halifax's suggestion that, when the Germans put the question, Henderson "would have to reply that they must proceed on the assumption that they would be satisfied in this respect." In reply to Henderson's further question, Chamberlain indicated that "the idea of returning some African territory to Germany in full sovereignty was not absolutely excluded."

While the committee was meeting, Berlin was in the throes of the Blomberg-Fritsch affair. On February 12 the Hitler-Schuschnigg meeting at the Berghof brought the Austrian situation to center stage, and a week later came the Cabinet crisis that led to Eden's resignation. It was not until March 1 that Henderson was able to tell Ribbentrop—now the Foreign Minister—that new instructions had come from London, and that he would "appreciate an early audience with the Chancellor." And it was not until the next day—*after* Henderson had seen Ribbentrop and it was too late to draw back—that Chamberlain put before the full Cabinet the proposals about to be made to Hitler. Their advantages, he claimed, were that they "could be presented to the world not as handing back to Germany her former colonies as a right, but as a new plan based on higher ideals," and that "it avoided one of the most formidable criticisms, namely, the handing over of natives from one Power to another as though they were chattels without regard to their interests." The Prime Minister added that "it had not been thought necessary to give particulars to the French at the present stage," and they were being told only that Henderson would "take soundings as to the German attitude toward the colonial question."*

For all this careful preparation, it was a badly packaged and ill-shapen proposition that Henderson presented to Hitler and Ribbentrop on March 3, 1938. Sir Nevile began by stressing the need for secrecy—"no information would be given the French, much less the Belgians, Portuguese, or Italians, concerning the subject of the discussion"—and that no agreement could be reached except on the basis of "reciprocity"; Germany must give "positive cooperation" in order to "reestablish peace and security in Europe." As an indication that Austria and Czechoslovakia were countries where Germany could manifest "cooperation," Henderson read from his instructions a paragraph querying the significance of the recent Hitler-Schuschnigg meeting, and remarking that such events "have aroused apprehension in many quarters which must inevitably render more difficult the negotiation of a general settlement." He then referred vaguely to disarmament and "a limitation on bombing planes" and then, at long last, baited the hook with the colonial proposals. Here again he read from his instructions† and concluded by asking Hitler:

> . . . first, whether Germany was prepared in principle to participate in a new colonial regime as provided for by the British proposal, and
> second, what contribution she would be prepared to make to the general peace and security of Europe.

The Fuehrer's answers were immediate, direct, and defiant. "The most important contribution to the peace and security of Europe," he declared, "would be the suppression of the inflammatory international press . . . represented in large numbers in England. Perhaps nobody had been oftener and more grievously offended by England than he." As for Austria and Czechoslovakia, "Germany would not tolerate any interference by third powers in the settlement of her relations with kindred countries or with countries having large German elements in their population, just as Germany would never think of interfering in the settlement of relations between England and Ireland." The Austrian situation was "intolerable," and "if England continued to resist German attempts to achieve a just and reasonable settlement, then the time would come when one would have to fight."

In vain Henderson tried to check the angry, minatory torrent of words. Limitations of armaments, including a ban on aerial bombing, were all out of the question because "one could place about as much reliance upon the faithful observance of treaties by a barbarous creation like the Soviet Union as upon the comprehension of mathematical formulas by a savage." As for the proposed new colonial regime, it seemed very complicated: "Why not solve the colonial

---

* The Cabinet "took note" of the Prime Minister's statement, without formal action approving the plan.

† Henderson elaborated the written instructions by describing the proposed territorial belt as "bounded on the north by the fifth degree of latitude and on the south by the Zambesi River." This area would have included the entire Belgian Congo, most of Portugal's African empire, French Equatorial Africa, Northern Rhodesia, Kenya, and Uganda, and the former German colonies under League mandate in Tanganyika (British), and the Cameroons (French and British), as well as the southern part of Italy's new Ethiopian "empire."

problem in the simplest and most natural way, namely, by returning the former German colonies?" Anyhow, there was no hurry about this matter; he did not want to press the issue and was willing to "wait quietly for 4, 6, 8, or 10 years."

When Henderson reiterated that Germany must also make a "contribution," Hitler replied that "his contribution to these problems consisted of the Berchtesgaden Agreement with Austria." Ribbentrop broke in to complain of the attitude of the British Minister in Vienna, Sir Michael Palairet, to which Henderson weakly replied that Sir Michael's statements "did not necessarily represent the opinion of the British Government."*

When Henderson's report of his encounter was received in London, Cadogan described it in his diary as "*completely* negative," and Harvey in his as a "complete rebuff." The German reaction should not have come as a surprise, for essentially Hitler had been told that, if he behaved himself in Central Europe, he would be allowed to play with the other children in Central Africa—an attitude which the proud and prickly Fuehrer was bound to regard as an insufferable condescension, and anyhow the colonies, in his eyes, were not worth a pfennig compared to Austria and Czechoslovakia. His response was no momentary spasm of irritation, and its calculated character is borne out by Ribbentrop's informational message to Ciano: "The Fuehrer was very hard and the results absolutely negative."

In London the question now was, as Cadogan put it, "whether to try and administer oxygen to the conversations to keep them alive, or whether to announce what we have done in all good faith to show . . . that we have done our best and that it is not *our* fault." The problem was considered in the Cabinet on March 9, after Halifax had treated his listeners to the gist of Henderson's report: "Hitler had been at his worst and Herr Ribbentrop had been thoroughly unhelpful. . . . The German Government appeared to be set head-on to achieve its aims in Central Europe, and did not want to tie their hands by talks. That left Britain in a rather dangerous position."

Despite all this, Chamberlain and Halifax did not want to abandon pursuit of the Fuehrer's favor. Ribbentrop was due in London the next day to say his good-byes as ambassador,† and Halifax intended to greet him with "a mixture of disappointment, reproach and warning." He would "speak very frankly" to his guest, but "would intimate" that the rebuff had "made no difference to the British desire to improve relations."

The next morning Ribbentrop arrived at the Foreign Office, where he was met by a crowd shouting: "Release Niemöller!"—the dissident German pastor imprisoned in May 1937. Ribbentrop's remarks largely echoed Hitler's state-

---

* The text is based on the account by Paul Otto Schmidt, the official interpreter. At this point, Schmidt's memorandum attributes to Henderson the statement that he "had himself often advocated *Anschluss*." On seeing Schmidt's rendition, Henderson denied the statement; he had only (like Sir Michael) "expressed personal views which may not have been entirely in accordance with those of my Government." At his request, the entire paragraph was stricken from the Schmidt memorandum.

† Ribbentrop's successor as ambassador, Herbert von Dirksen, did not arrive in London until early May 1938; in the interval, first Ernst Woermann (the counselor) and then Theodor Kordt (who succeeded to Woermann's position in April) served as chargé d'affaires.

ments to Henderson, but there was an important new element. The previous day Schuschnigg had announced the plebiscite scheduled for March 13, and Ribbentrop took occasion of the meeting to denounce it as "a fraud and a swindle" and "a violation of the letter and spirit of the Berchtesgaden Agreement."

Halifax then delivered his planned "between sorrow and anger" lecture, apparently without much effect on his visitor.* As for the plebiscite, Halifax "assumed the German Government would . . . take all measures in their power to restrain Nazi followers from any action which might interfere with the smooth and free holding of the plebiscite." Ribbentrop replied that he did not know what action his government might be taking, and declared that the best thing Britain could do "would be to use your influence with the Austrian Chancellor to cancel the plebiscite"—a virtual taunt which drew Halifax's retort that "it seemed impossible to say that the head of an independent state could not have a plebiscite if he wanted to." As the German left the building, the crowd was shouting: "Ribbentrop get out!"

The next day—Friday, March 11, while German troops were secretly assembling on the Austrian borders—Chamberlain gave Ribbentrop a farewell luncheon at No. 10 Downing Street. After the meal the two spoke privately, and Chamberlain asked his guest to tell Hitler that "it had always been his desire to clear up German-British relations" and he "had now made up his mind to realize this aim." Shortly thereafter messages were brought to the Prime Minister disclosing the German ultimatums to Schuschnigg, which demanded cancellation of the plebiscite and his own resignation in favor of Seyss-Inquart.† Chamberlain then took Ribbentrop, together with Halifax, Cadogan, and Woermann, into his study and declared the situation disclosed by the messages "extremely serious" because of the "threat" behind the ultimatums. Halifax, "somewhat excited," according to Ribbentrop, condemned the threat of force as "an intolerable method." Ribbentrop professed ignorance of the actual state of affairs, but replied that cancellation of the plebiscite and the replacement of Schuschnigg were both desirable developments. Later that afternoon Halifax went to tea at the German Embassy and read Ribbentrop another lecture, describing the German tactics as "an exhibition of naked force." But he got nothing for his pains; by this time it was known that Schuschnigg had resigned, and Ribbentrop hailed this development as "much the best thing that could have happened." Such was the onetime champagne salesman's characteristically arrogant farewell to official Britain.

Meanwhile from Vienna came, via Ambassador Palairet, a plea from Schuschnigg for "immediate advice as to what he should do," and Halifax answered that, while strong representations had been made to Ribbentrop, the

---

* Cadogan, who was present during the latter part of the meeting, recorded that Halifax read "a lecture—or a sermon—not too frightfully well," and that Ribbentrop was "quite hopeless and wooden and useless." The next day, the acrid diarist remarked that "Ribbentrop was so stupid it mattered very little what anyone said to him."

† Winston Churchill was a guest at the luncheon and observed Chamberlain's preoccupation when Cadogan handed the messages to him. But Churchill's statement (*The Gathering Storm*, p. 271) that the messages reported the German invasion of Austria is inaccurate, as that did not take place until the following day.

British Government "cannot take the responsibility of advising the Chancellor to take any course of action which might expose his country to dangers against which His Majesty's Government is unable to guarantee protection." And that same day a dispatch came from Henderson stating his disbelief "that at this stage Hitler is thinking in terms of *Anschluss* or annexation." Less than twenty-four hours later, German troops were halfway from the border to Vienna.

Henderson was, of course, instructed to protest the German actions "in the strongest terms," and warn that they were "bound to produce the gravest reactions of which it is impossible to foretell the issue." The only result was another rebuff, this time from the deposed Neurath, substituting for the absent Ribbentrop:

> In the name of the German Government I must state in reply that the British Government is not within its right in claiming the role of a protector of the independence of Austria . . . the form of the relations between the Reich and Austria can only be regarded as an internal affair of the German people which is no concern of third Powers. . . . For this reason the German Government must from the outset reject as inadmissible the protest lodged by the British Government. . . .

Within that government there was no lack of verbal condemnation of the forced *Anschluss*. Halifax was genuinely shocked and, according to Harvey, prevailed upon the reluctant Geoffrey Dawson, editor of *The Times* ("who will do whatever H. tells him"), to denounce Germany's behavior. Cadogan labeled it "infamy," and Chamberlain, in the Cabinet, described the "manner" in which Hitler had brought off his coup as "distressing and shocking" and "a typical illustration of power politics."

But there was an immediate scramble to lay the blame on others. Henderson attributed Austria's fate largely to "Dr. Schuschnigg's ill-conceived and ill-prepared folly," and was reckless and weak enough to say as much to Hermann Goering.* Chamberlain, too, explained the timing of the event as resulting from Schuschnigg's "blunder," which had given Hitler his opportunity. Cadogan emptied most of his wrath on Vansittart ("an idiot with an idée fixe—all facade and nothing else") for having constantly harped on the danger to Austria "when we can't do anything about it." In the Cabinet on March 12, Chamberlain by implication laid blame on the absent Anthony Eden: ". . . it might be said with justice that we had been too late in taking up the conversation with Italy." Grandi had said that "Signor Mussolini would have moved troops to the Brenner Pass at the time of the Berchtesgaden talks, but he had not felt sure of his position in the Mediterranean." In a letter to his sister the next day, Chamberlain made the inference explicit: "It is tragic to think that very possibly this might have been prevented if I had had Halifax at the Foreign Office instead of Anthony at the time I wrote my letter to Mussolini." And he added: ". . . what a fool Roosevelt would have looked if he had launched his precious proposal.

---

* For this inexcusable gaffe, the ambassador drew a well-deserved rebuke from Halifax, who reminded the errant emissary that such an "admission" must inevitably "diminish the force of the protest" which Henderson had been instructed to make.

What would he have thought of us if we had encouraged him to publish it, as Anthony was so eager to do? And how we too would have made ourselves the laughing-stock of the world."

Only a man reaching desperately for self-justification could have written these words.* The Prime Minister was not alone in this search; Halifax and Cadogan ended the day's work of March 11 with a talk in which they "agreed our consciences were clear." Chamberlain and Halifax had cut a poor figure, wining and dining Ribbentrop while Hitler killed off Austria. But of course it was quite true, as Chamberlain told the Commons on March 14, that "nothing would have arrested this action by Germany unless we and others with us had been prepared to use force to prevent it."

This no one, least of all Chamberlain, was prepared to do. He was on the road to peace by appeasement, and the fork to Berlin had been blocked, first by the scornful rejection of his colonial offer, and then by *Anschluss*. "For the moment we must abandon conversations with Germany," he told his sister, and now "we must show our determination not to be bullied by announcing some increase in rearmament, and we must quietly and steadily pursue our conversations with Italy."

7

Viewed from London, the prospects for appeasement certainly appeared better in Rome than in Berlin. Grandi, Ciano, and the Duce himself had all exhibited eagerness to begin discussions. Chamberlain and Halifax wished to sustain the momentum generated by Eden's departure; the Prime Minister wanted to reach an agreement "as rapidly as possible"—perhaps within ten days—and not allow the talks to be "prolonged by the discussion of details."

But there were some awkward problems. The French, already annoyed by the British Government's refusal to make a joint *démarche* to Berlin on the Austrian situation, were now seriously miffed by what appeared to be a unilateral British policy toward Italy. On February 26, Ambassador Corbin read the newly ensconced Halifax a lecture which must have given that aristocratic Francophobe considerable discomfort, though he was suave enough not to show it. General expressions of goodwill were not enough, Corbin told Halifax; France's confidence would be gravely undermined if she were confronted by *faits accomplis* or given last-minute notice of vital decisions. As for Italy, France too would like to improve relations, and had the right to full information about British plans for the forthcoming talks, and participation in matters of mutual concern. All this spelled trouble, for it was quite plain that Mussolini wished to negotiate with Britain only and would object to any involvement of the French.

An even more difficult problem was, of course, Spain. Defending his policies in the Commons when Eden resigned, Chamberlain had promised that "a settlement of the Spanish question" would be "an essential feature of any agreement at which we might arrive." But Lord Perth (in London for consultation and in-

---

* They were, however, matched in converse by Harvey's reflection that, if Roosevelt's plan had been launched when first proposed, "these events in Austria would not have occurred."

structions during late February and early March) declared that, if the possibility of agreement should hinge on the Spanish question, it "would have to be postponed for a very long time." This seemed more than probable,* so in view of Chamberlain's commitment to Parliament the Government, as Harvey put it, was "indeed in a fix," since the Prime Minister wanted a speedy resolution which would warrant him in promoting *de jure* recognition of the Italian empire to appease the Duce.

These conundrums were reflected in the vagueness of Perth's instructions, which were, in general, to bargain empire recognition against Italian withdrawal from Spain, reduction of troop strengths in Libya, and cessation of anti-British radio propaganda. These were the important items in the package which Lord Perth presented to Ciano on March 8, but their lack of precision was exposed by the ambassador's inability to answer a crucial question. What was to be regarded as "concrete progress" in the evacuation of Italian troops from Spain, which was to be a condition precedent to giving effect to the agreement? Lord Perth could only say that he would raise the question with London.

Ciano recorded his "first impressions" as "not too bad," but added that "Chamberlain is more interested than we are in achieving agreement." Certainly this attitude emerged during the bargaining, for Ciano yielded nothing. Would Italy concede a "change in tone" toward France? For ideological reasons that would be "difficult." Would Italy evacuate her forces from the Balearics, a gesture which would "arouse a widespread and most favorable response among the British public"? This was a "strange" suggestion, for Italy had no land forces there, and the Non-Intervention Committee "dealt only with land forces." Anyhow, the proposal "could not be considered." Other British requests were treated with "the utmost reserve."

Before the two met again, the Chautemps government fell and Austria became part of Germany. Both of these events threatened Chamberlain's prospects of achieving the agreement he so greatly desired.

. The impact of *Anschluss* was discussed at a Foreign Policy Committee meeting on March 15, after Chamberlain had observed that Hitler's "violent actions" had "strengthened the hands of those persons . . . who urged that we should cease to have any dealings of any kind with the dictators." He himself, to the contrary, thought "recent events had confirmed . . . that his policy was a right one." But "it would be necessary to warn Count Ciano that the whole position had been very much altered by Hitler's action in Austria and that more in the way of guaranties of good faith would be required from Italy than had previously been contemplated." Simon agreed and Malcolm MacDonald added: "Public opinion was already asking why Italy had failed to intervene in the Austrian crisis, and it was generally thought that there must be some secret and discreditable bargain under which, in return for a free hand in central Europe,

* In Cabinet on March 2, Chamberlain sought to gloss over the Spanish problem by declaring "that the Italian Government was very eager to withdraw their troops and would do their utmost to facilitate an agreement." Events soon disproved this prediction; if the Prime Minister really believed what he had said, Eden was certainly right in diagnosing their disagreement as turning on whether there was room for "faith in the men you are negotiating with."

Hitler had given Mussolini a free hand in the Mediterranean and in particular in Spain."

It does not appear, however, that any of these sentiments were conveyed to Ciano, who maintained his negative attitude toward all British requests for some Italian concession to sweeten the deal. Nor did London find it easy to answer Ciano's question concerning the meaning of "progress" on the Spanish question. In the upshot the prerequisite was left undefined; the negotiators busied themselves with other issues and by the end of March were close to the final wording of an agreement which would not, however, come into force until "a settlement of the Spanish question" had been achieved.

Meanwhile, the Anglo-Italian *rapprochement* appeared to be threatened from Paris, where the second Blum government, with Paul-Boncour at the Quai d'Orsay, had taken office simultaneously with *Anschluss*. London officialdom was disappointed by the narrow base and poor longevity prospects of the new Cabinet, and the elevation of Paul-Boncour sent a shiver of apprehension through Whitehall. Because of the Austrian crisis and the increased danger to Czechoslovakia, Paul-Boncour proposed that he visit London to discuss both the Czech and Spanish situations. Sir Eric Phipps sent in a negative recommendation, approved by Halifax on the basis of a memorandum by Sir Orme Sargent:*

> I would like to support most strongly Sir E. Phipps' view that we should definitely not allow French ministers to come to London during the weekend to discuss Spain and Czechoslovakia. M. Paul-Boncour at the Quai d'Orsay is a disaster and an invitation to him would only strengthen his position, whereas it must be our sincere wish to see him out of office at the earliest possible moment. In fact, I should go so far as to say that any thing we can do to weaken the present French Government and precipitate its fall would be in the British interest.
>
> As regards Spain I am not competent to speak, but I cannot believe for a moment that the advantages of a personal interview between the Secretary of State and M. Boncour would outweigh the kudos which would accrue to M. Boncour by being received by Lord Halifax under present circumstances.

By March 30, Phipps was rightly predicting the imminent fall of the Blum government and licking his chops over the anticipated departure of that "alarmingly light weight, Paul-Boncour." As a devotee of collective security and an outspoken foe of the dictators,† the latter was certainly uncongenial to the Chamberlain-Halifax appeasement policies. And so, when it appeared that Daladier might keep Paul-Boncour at the Foreign Ministry, Phipps at once went into action, as described in his "most confidential" letter of April 11, 1938, to Halifax:

> We were nearly cursed by having Paul-Boncour again at the Quai d'Orsay. Not only the Socialists, but also Herriot wanted him to remain there.
> I therefore had Daladier and Paul Reynaud informed indirectly that it

---

* Assistant Under-Secretary at the Foreign Office, and in 1946 Cadogan's successor as Permanent Under-Secretary.

† Phipps noted that he had been in the gallery at the Chamber of Deputies "years ago" when Paul-Boncour referred to Mussolini as *"ce César de Carnaval"*—a description which, on Raymond Poincaré's urging, he changed in the official transcript to *"César de fortune."*

would be most unfortunate if Paul-Boncour were to remain, not only because of his mad hankering after intervention in Spain, but because it seemed highly desirable for France to get on to better terms with Italy, and this the author of "ce César de Carnaval" would be unable, even if he were not unwilling, to do.

Paul Reynaud was convinced by my message and used his influence with Daladier in the desired sense. Daladier himself was in full agreement, but hesitated a great deal owing to inevitable considerations of electoral and political expediency. Finally, after an interview of over an hour with Paul-Boncour, he did the right thing, or rather the semi-right thing, for I should have much preferred Chautemps, who wanted the Quai d'Orsay, to Georges Bonnet, who got it. However we must be grateful for being spared Paul-Boncour, who was a positive danger to the peace of Europe.

I am always most particularly careful to avoid intervening in any way in French politics, but this time I felt it was my duty to take a certain risk, though it was a very small one as my messages were quite indirect and I can always disavow them.

Phipps's fears about Paul-Boncour's interventionism in Spain were, in fact, largely unfounded, but thinking as he did, there loomed the danger of vastly increased French aid to the Spanish Loyalists, and counteraction by Mussolini which might end all prospects of an Anglo-Italian (to say nothing of a Franco-Italian) agreement. Diplomatically, however, Phipps's conduct was, to say the least, most unusual; one can readily imagine the reaction in London if Ambassador Corbin had sought to influence the selection of a Foreign Secretary. Halifax, however, was well pleased with what Phipps had done:

> I am most grateful to you for having taken the action which you did, for I quite agree that if Paul-Boncour had remained at the Quai d'Orsay it might have been disastrous. Certainly Bonnet is not an ideal choice, but I should imagine that his weaknesses are more the result of personal ambition than of misguided principles. In other words, he is far less dangerous!
> I agree also that you are right in being most careful to avoid intervening in French politics; but I have not the slightest hesitation in warmly approving the hint you conveyed to Daladier on the subject of the late Foreign Secretary!

A far more difficult obstacle than Paul-Boncour or even *Anschluss,* however, was the Duce himself, who chose mid-March as a time to order heavy bombing attacks on Barcelona. On March 20 the British and French governments addressed a protest on this score to Franco,* and the same day Lord Perth waited upon Ciano to point out that the raids "might produce a state of opinion hostile to the continuation of the Anglo-Italian negotiations." Ciano replied that "operations are initiated by Franco, not by us"; Italy might "exercise a moderating influence, but we could make no promises." As both Harvey's and Cadogan's diaries reveal, by March 19 the British had "secret information" that

---

* The following day in Washington, Secretary of State Cordell Hull issued a statement in the name of "the whole American people" voicing "horror at what has taken place at Barcelona."

the orders for these attacks came from Rome, and Ciano's diary confirms the accuracy of their intelligence:

> The truth about the air raids on Barcelona is that the orders for them were given to Valle by Mussolini in the Chamber a few minutes before he made his speech on Austria.* Franco knew nothing about them, and asked yesterday that they should be suspended for fear of implications abroad. Mussolini believes that these air raids are an admirable way of weakening the morale of the Reds. . . . He is right. He wasn't very worried when I informed him of Perth's *demarche.* In fact he said he was delighted that the Italians should be horrifying the world by their aggressiveness for a change, instead of charming it by their skill at playing the guitar. In his opinion this will send up our stock in Germany too, where they love total and ruthless war.

Bombing Barcelona augured ill for a "settlement of the Spanish question"—from the British standpoint, the keystone of the agreement. Awareness that Ciano was lying in his teeth about responsibility was ill calculated to maintain that "faith" in the Italian leadership for lack of which Eden had disappointed Chamberlain. Nevertheless, Lord Perth plugged away at the negotiations, while Mussolini, jealous of Hitler and humiliated by *Anschluss,* vented his feelings by slaughtering the Catalonians, in order to prove his manhood to the Germans. Perth's remonstrances accomplished little if anything; on April 6, Mussolini ordered the bombers in the Balearics to attack the areas behind the Loyalist lines, while Ciano recorded that "Franco doesn't want air raids on cities, but in this case the game is worth the candle."

On March 30, Halifax told the Cabinet that the Rome conversations were going well, and that the Italians wanted to sign the agreement before Hitler's forthcoming visit. Two weeks later the final draft was submitted to the Cabinet, and on April 16, Ciano and Perth signed the documents, consisting of a protocol, eight annexes, and an exchange of notes, including several to which Egypt was also a party.

Most of this elaborate documentary structure related to matters of less than first importance, such as reaffirmation of the "Gentlemen's Agreement," renunciation of aggressive actions on the Arabian peninsula, and Italian adherence to the London naval treaty of 1936. More significant, at least to London, was Italy's agreement to reduce her troop strength in Libya at the rate of 1,000 men per week "until the . . . effectives reach peace strength"—and "ultimate diminution" of "not less than half the numbers present in Libya when our conversations commenced." Most important for the British was Italy's confirmation of "full adherence to the United Kingdom formula for the proportional evacuation of the foreign volunteers from Spain," and of her pledge "that if this evacuation has not been completed at the moment of the termination of the Spanish Civil War, all remaining Italian volunteers will forthwith leave Spanish territory and all Italian war material will simultaneously be withdrawn." As *quid pro quo,* the British Government, in order to remove "such obstacles as may at present be held to impede the freedom of member States as regards recognition of

---

* The speech in the Chamber was delivered March 16. General Giuseppe Valle was Chief of the Air Staff and Under-Secretary for Air. Mussolini was himself the Minister for Air.

Italian sovereignty over Ethiopia," would "take steps at the forthcoming meeting of the Council of the League of Nations for the purpose of clarifying the situation of member States in this regard."

But although the documents were all duly signed, the agreement they embodied did not then come into force. The entire transaction was subject to the stipulation "that His Majesty's Government regard a settlement of the Spanish question as a prerequisite of the entry into force of the Agreement between our two countries." And what would such a "settlement" be? That was the question which Clement Attlee, the Labour Party leader, put to Chamberlain on May 2 when the Prime Minister laid the agreement before the House of Commons. "I prefer not to give a definition of it" was the reply, and when Attlee described the situation as "ridiculous" and declared that "the House is entitled to know," Chamberlain calmly admitted that he could not "tell the House even when this Protocol and Annexes will come into effect," and expressed confidence that "the situation will clear itself up as time goes on." He hailed the agreement as marking "the beginning of a new era" and, over the disapproving shouts ("Matteotti" and "new horrors") of the Opposition, saluted Mussolini for his "new vision and new efficiency in administration and in the measures which they are taking to improve the conditions of their people."

Chamberlain was right that the Spanish situation would be clarified "as time goes on," but in private he was soon singing a very different tune about the personal merits of the Duce, whose behavior worsened after the agreements were signed. For a few weeks, to be sure, things went smoothly enough. On April 19, Ciano agreed to open discussions in furtherance of the Franco-Italian agreement which both Paris and London so ardently desired.* Withdrawals of troops from Libya were commenced. On the British side, Halifax went to Geneva, where on May 12 the League Council accepted his proposal that recognition of Italian sovereignty in Ethiopia be regarded as a matter "for the individual Members of the League to determine . . . in the light of their own situation and their own obligations."

Two days later, Mussolini gave Britain and France their reward in a speech at Genoa. The Duce extolled Nazi-Fascist collaboration, referred repeatedly to the sanctions "which we have not yet forgotten," and expressed doubt that the pending talks with the French would "reach a conclusion" because "we are on opposite sides of the barricade" in Spain, where "they desire the victory of Barcelona; we, on the other hand, desire the victory of Franco." Ciano noted that, "carried away by the crowd," his chief had departed from the text and given "a very strong, anti-French speech" in the course of which "the crowd hisses France" and "laughs, ironically, at the agreement with London."

It was the same sort of behavior which had made a mockery of the "Gentlemen's Agreement," and the consequence was to cut off the French talks

---

* The French, suspicious of bilateral talks between London and Rome, had all along wanted tripartite talks, though they were skeptical of the possibility of any genuine *rapprochement* with Mussolini. The British did their best to bring in the French; Ciano told the new German Ambassador, Hans Georg von Mackensen (son of the old field marshal), that during his sixteen negotiating sessions with Perth, the Englishman had made fourteen requests for French participation, all unsuccessful.

and endanger the prospects of the agreement with Britain, for whatever "settle-ment of the Spanish question" meant, this was certainly not it. On May 18, Lord Perth came to protest ("very politely and with a certain bitterness," ac-cording to Ciano) the blow to British hopes, but Ciano was adamant that Italy would make no agreement with France that so much as mentioned Spain. A few days later Ciano told Mackensen that the French talks would not be resumed so long as France was "sabotaging non-intervention."

For all this, at the end of May, Chamberlain was still wearing his rose specta-cles and writing his sister that "Anschluss and the Anglo-Italian Agreement to-gether, have given the Rome-Berlin Axis a nasty jar and in our future conti-nental and European policy we may hope for a good deal of quiet help from Italy." What followed immediately was neither quiet nor helpful. In Spain, the bombing of towns and villages behind the Loyalist front was intensified, and raids on Barcelona were resumed. On June 3, Perth was again protesting, and Ciano again deflecting the blame to Franco. Quite unabashed, the Count seized the occasion to claim that Italy had now "fulfilled her pledges in a loyal manner" and it was high time "to put into force the Agreements of 16th April."

Chamberlain, perhaps, would have liked nothing better, but the Genoa speech and the bombings had seriously undermined his political base at home; public opinion in the western democracies was not yet ready to accept the rightfulness of urban bombardments. To make matters worse, British ships in Spanish waters were again under attack by Nationalist bombers, and by mid-June sev-eral had been sunk and a number of British seamen and Non-Intervention Com-mittee observers killed. On June 9, Cadogan briefed Joseph Kennedy on the sit-uation, and the ambassador reported to Washington:

> Last night I saw Cadogan and asked him what his Government was plan-ning to do in connection with the bombing of British ships in Spanish waters. He said that the situation had the Cabinet almost distracted. It has been de-cided to discuss with the French the question of an armistice in Spain. . . .
> Beyond this question of arranging an armistice, he said, the British feel they are frankly up against it. British shippers are crying for protection and the country is beginning to feel without realizing what the result might finally be that this Government is not courageous and . . . that England's great pres-tige is rapidly diminishing. Cadogan said that the Prime Minister's answer so far has been that it is much more courageous to proceed along his line of pol-icy and take the charges of cowardice than it is to take up a position which would mean war in three or four places at once simply because Great Britain does not approve of the bombing. The British, Cadogan said, are not very proud of any solution that they are thinking about . . . but there is a feeling that they will try any idea that anybody suggests which still adheres to the principle of not going to war.

Despite the rising tide of public and parliamentary anger over the attacks on British shipping, Chamberlain, with Admiralty support, opposed any counter-measures. "I have been through every possible form of retaliation," he wrote privately on June 20, "and it is absolutely clear that none of them can be effec-tive unless we are prepared to go to war with Franco, which might quite possibly lead to war with Italy and Germany, and in any case would cut right across my policy of general appeasement." Unwilling to face the dangers thus envisaged, and unable to put the Agreement into effect because of adverse public opinion, the Chamberlain government was, as Harvey put it, "in a jam over Spain, exactly as A.E. said we would be."

Desperate for a solution, the Foreign Policy Committee instructed Lord Perth to propose to Ciano either that Italy unilaterally withdraw her forces from Spain or that the two countries work jointly to bring about an armistice. It is hard to believe that anyone in London expected these proposals to be acceptable in Rome, and Ciano's reaction was predictably negative, though he agreed to refer the question to Mussolini. On July 2 he handed Perth the Duce's written answer. A unilateral withdrawal was unacceptable, and an armistice no less so "unless the Reds surrender at discretion." There would be no resumption of Franco-Italian talks until the Anglo-Italian Agreement had become effective. Delay in that accomplishment was unfortunate, but it was not Italy's fault. By Mussolini's direction, Ciano added orally that Italy would now resume "complete liberty of action with regard to the conditions already observed by us"— i.e., evacuation of troops from Libya and cessation of "displeasing" propaganda —and that the Duce expected "a precise answer" to his memorandum.

If it was Mussolini's intention to shock and insult the denizens of Whitehall and Downing Street, he succeeded admirably. "A frightful telegram," Cadogan called it, and Harvey described it as "blackmailing," adding that "I have rarely seen such an offensive communication." In Cabinet, Chamberlain tried to pass it off as something to be treated lightly, because "dictators were liable to gusts of ill-temper," but privately he wrote that "Mussolini is behaving just like a spoilt child, and it is difficult to know how to deal with him." Talking with Ambassador Kennedy on July 5, the Prime Minister declared that "Mussolini is in a very bad mood; he is constantly baiting the French and when the English ask him to do business with the French he resents the British attitude." Kennedy's report of the talk continued:

> Chamberlain of course is inwardly very sore that he has to take all this nonsense from Mussolini but he reiterates again and again, "my job is to try to keep England out of war if I possibly can; therefore I am doing a lot of things that are difficult for me to do." He is hopeful Mussolini's attitude may change and . . . said that Mussolini assures him that since the English agreement he has not shipped any men or ammunition to Spain. Chamberlain has no reason to disbelieve this although he would not bet his life on it.*

Despite all this exasperation, the British replied *suaviter in modo*. On July 11, 1938, Perth came to the Palazzo Chigi with a note from London expressing "surprise" at the contents of Mussolini's *aide-mémoire* but disclaiming any intention "to begin a controversy on the subject" or to "make the situation more difficult." Rome was reminded that "settlement of the Spanish question" was a *"sine qua non"* of the agreement, and since other alternatives had been rejected

---

* Chamberlain's caution was well advised, for in June, Mussolini had doubled the flow of reinforcements to Spain.

by Italy, "nothing can be done except to wait until the evacuation plan is put into action."

Thus matters reached an impasse. On July 18, Mussolini told Mackensen that the agreement was "well on its way toward petering out," because "Chamberlain was lacking in the courage that was indispensable to bold action." "Anglo-Italian discussions are obviously a thing of the past for the Duce," the German Ambassador concluded, and in fact nothing was done on either side to revive the agreement until mid-November, six weeks after Munich.

Appeasement had failed in Rome, not as quickly as in Berlin, but more publicly and humiliatingly. To Berlin, Chamberlain had offered an interest in the colonies Hitler said he wanted; to Rome, he had offered recognition of the "empire" Mussolini had already taken. In neither case was the bid nearly high enough; both dictators had bigger aims in view and wanted things which were not Britain's to give.

No doubt Chamberlain sincerely wanted good relations with Fascist Italy, but his reasons were not such as to bring them about. "If only we could get on terms with the Germans, I would not care a rap for Musso," he had written in 1937. The British leaders did not want the Duce's help; they merely wanted him tucked away in a neutral corner, so that if they found themselves at war with Germany (or Germany and Japan), the Royal Navy would not need to worry about the Mediterranean. Though never publicly acknowledged, it was plain enough that Britain's Italian policy was primarily intended to split the Axis* and thus remove Italy from the list of likely enemies.

For Mussolini, the agreement with England was attractive chiefly to better his bargaining position with Germany. *Anschluss* had been a blow to Italian prestige, Hitler was coming to visit him in May, and the Duce thought he would be strengthened by a demonstration that his friendship was desired in London as well as Berlin. Additionally, he was happy to give Chamberlain a lift over Eden† and, if possible, trouble the relations between England and France. But he nourished ambitions in the Mediterranean area which Britain, with her protectorate in Egypt and friendships or alliances with France, Portugal, and Greece, was bound to oppose. Germany, much as Mussolini disliked her presence on the Brenner, was unlikely to obstruct his Mediterranean objectives, and in May the Duce made it clear to his son-in-law, who did not entirely agree, that an alliance with Germany was to be the basis of Italian security against France and England.

Crudely put, Mussolini's policy was to string the British along. On June 22, at the very time when he was pressuring London to give effect to the agreement, he told Ciano:

---

* Joseph P. Kennedy, a man not devoid of shrewdness, thought that internal politics were also moving Chamberlain after the *Anschluss*: ". . . the British know they must bring in a successful negotiation with Italy to save their political faces and they are going to make every effort," he wrote to Hull on March 23, 1938.

† On March 9, 1938, the French chargé in Rome, Jules Blondel, reported that Mussolini would agree to a text that Chamberlain "could present to his public opinion as a diplomatic success," and thus avoid a setback which might bring Eden back to office, or even an election which would produce a Labour government.

. . . we shall not modify our policy toward Franco in the smallest degree and the agreement with London will come into force when God pleases. If indeed it ever will.

And so the flow of volunteers to Spain was augmented and the bombing of Barcelona was resumed, not withstanding the unfavorable effect of this behavior on the agreement's prospects.

If it was Mussolini's object to make Britain look weak and ridiculous, he certainly succeeded. The humiliation perhaps peaked on June 28, when His Majesty's Ambassador came to the Palazzo Chigi to ask the Duce's son-in-law to use his influence to persuade a Spanish rebel general to stop bombing British ships. The dictators, it appeared, could twist the Lion's tail to the breaking point, and the Lion would only mew.

CHAPTER 23

Neville Chamberlain As Armorer

1

Neville Chamberlain was a patriotic, proud Englishman, and if he pursued these policies of appeasement, it was because he firmly believed that Britain was not ready for war with the Axis powers. What was, in fact, the state of British arms in 1938, as the Munich crisis loomed?

Chamberlain's own large responsibility for that state dated back to the spring of 1934, when, as Chancellor of the Exchequer, he had taken the lead in cutting back the arms program recommended by the Defence Requirements Committee, and making air defense the focal point of rearmament. In foreign affairs, Chamberlain had to await his ascendance to the prime ministership before establishing his dominance. In arms matters his control of the purse-strings and force of character, the lesser caliber of the service ministers, and Baldwin's declining activity combined to give Chamberlain as Chancellor the principal Cabinet role in defense matters—a leadership which the Minister for the Coordination of Defence, Sir Thomas Inskip, was neither able nor inclined to challenge.

Early in 1936, when the DRC's third report came up for review, Chamberlain had joined forces with Lord Weir to reduce the proposed expenditures and once again subordinate the Army's demands to those of the RAF. Since he shared Weir's view that a strong bomber force would be a more effective deterrent to German air attack than air defenses, Chamberlain was cool even to Army pleas for antiaircraft artillery. When General Hastings "Pug" Ismay, then Hankey's deputy, came before the CID in 1936 asking for an additional hundred antiaircraft guns, Chamberlain complained that less than a year previously an increase had been approved: "Was there no end to this importunity?" Chamberlain appeared to believe that Britain's security could be ensured with air and sea power—an attitude which professional army officers could hardly be expected to endorse. On January 27, 1936, during consideration of the DRC proposals, Lieutenant Colonel Henry Pownall, an Assistant Secretary to the CID, entered in his diary a powerful condemnation of Chamberlain as an arbiter of the arms budget:

> There was a further and most dangerous heresy—the Chancellor's. That of limited liability in war. They cannot or will not realize that if war with Germany comes again . . . we shall again be *fighting for our lives*. Our efforts

must be the maximum, by land, sea, and air. We cannot say our contribution is "so and so"—and no more, because we cannot lose the war without extinction of the Empire. The idea of the "half-hearted" war is the most pernicious and dangerous in the world. It will be 100 percent. . . . In God's name let us recognize that from the outset—and by that I mean *now*. The Chancellor's cold hard calculating semi-detached attitude was terrible to listen to. . . .

But it was music to the ears of many of his fellow-countrymen, both within and without the Government. The defense program unveiled in February 1936 could, in the words of the White Paper, go forward "without impeding the course of normal trade." It was a rearmament pace which satisfied even a man like Lord Weir, who, for all his energy, ability, and dedication to the task in hand, was still unwilling to "take the whole life and industry of this nation and organise it for war preparation."*

But the German march into the Rhineland came less than a week after the White Paper. While the Chiefs of Staff assessment was overpessimistic and strategically incompetent, its unrelieved gloominess at least rang a loud warning bell. The Air Staff, envisaging the possibility of a sudden air attack on London which "might quickly paralyze the control of national life and the national war effort," weighed the comparative merits of evacuating the entire government from London against dispersing it in "protected accommodations" in the London area.† The service ministries made hasty studies of the forces available in the event of war, and were appalled by the scanty contents of the cupboard. A CID subcommittee opined that if Germany should attempt a "knock-out blow," "the results, judging from the 1914–1918 war, would be catastrophic," with London "untenable" and the nation's food supply cut off by "attacks on the ports."

These Rhineland reverberations, ominous as they were, had no immediate effect at Cabinet level. On March 25, Sir Thomas Inskip, newly emerged from comparative obscurity by his appointment as Minister for the Coordination of Defence, reminded the Chiefs of Staff that rearmament was still subject to the noninterference with "normal trade" limitation, though he recognized that, if Germany rearmed with "dangerous speed, that policy might have to be reconsidered." A month later, however, Inskip told the Cabinet that he "had been considering how far the assumption of 'peace conditions' . . . was compatible with the growing anxieties of the international situation." Moved by Eden's pleas for increased speed in rearmament, Inskip now warned his colleagues that "he might have to ask for authority to adopt more drastic measures," such as enforced industrial priority for government orders.

Neville Chamberlain saw no need for hasty change. In February, writing privately, he had claimed the lion's share of credit for the new rearmament pro-

---

* See his letter of May 13, 1936, in reply to Winston Churchill's letter chiding him for lending his reputation "to keeping this country in a state of comfortable peace routine."

† It was concluded that evacuation was too "risky," since the attack might be so sudden and heavy that transportation would be so dislocated that removal of "44,000 officials plus essential documents" would be impossible.

gram, which, he thought, would in a few years produce "an air force of such striking power that no one will care to run risks with it." Inskip's suggestion that business-as-usual might have to be abandoned "should wait until major policy decisions had been reached."

Inskip's concern was shared by others not so amenable to Chamberlain's influence. His elder half-brother Austen was urging a secret session of the Commons on the defense situation, and Churchill was stoking up for a fiery speech which Baldwin feared might cause a "panic." These pressures led to the extraordinary Conservative deputation, led by Austen Chamberlain and Winston Churchill for the Commons and the Marquess of Salisbury for the Lords, which Baldwin received on July 28 and 29, 1936. Chamberlain was on vacation; Baldwin was flanked by Halifax, Inskip, and several CID staff members, including Hankey and Pownall.

Churchill led off on his favorite theme: the alarming rate of the Luftwaffe's growth, and the need for greater speed in augmenting both the RAF's frontline strength and Britain's aircraft production capacity. His statement of the Germans' numerical strength did not differ significantly from the Air Ministry's, but he quite outdid them in overestimating the weight of bombs that the Luftwaffe could drop on London.* Lord Trenchard and Leo Amery also spoke to the air question (ineffectively, Pownall thought), and then Sir Edward Grigg gladdened Pownall's heart with a vigorous attack on the Government's neglect of the Army.

The second session opened with several members of the deputation inquiring whether, in the event of war, Britain was committed to France to send an expeditionary force. Baldwin, to their great relief, answered that there was no such engagement. Lord George Lloyd (an eminent peer closely aligned with Churchill) then called attention to the decline in Britain's merchant marine, and recommended government assistance to the industry in order to relieve a shortage which might, under war conditions, prove fatal. Churchill then spoke at length on the need to organize British industry "to turn over from peace to war," closing with a warning that "we are separated by at least two years from any appreciable improvement in the material process of national defence," and condemnation of the Government's policy of avoiding interference with "ordinary trade."

To this barrage of questions and criticism, the ministers had few defenses. Baldwin was at the end of his tether (he left London for his ten-week convalescence almost immediately after these meetings), Chamberlain was absent, Halifax knew little of such matters, and Inskip had been only a few months in office. The Prime Minister's response was diffuse and defensive; rearmament had been delayed by the Ten-Year Rule, economic depression, and the public's pacifism and faith in collective security. If greater efforts had been made in 1934, "you might have lost the General Election," whereas "the one thing in my

---

* Churchill declared that the Germans could "drop at least 500 tons a time on London," causing an average of 5,000 deaths, 15,000 wounded, and 5 million pounds' damage.

mind was that necessity of winning an election as soon as you could and getting a perfectly free hand with arms."* As for the present:

> The worst of it is none of us knows what goes on in that strange man's mind. I am referring to Hitler. We all know the German desire as he has come out with in his book to move East, and if he should move East I should not break my heart. . . . I do not believe he wants to move West. . . . But what if the man went mad? . . . if he does it before we are ready I quite agree the picture is perfectly awful . . . every effort of our work and diplomacy must keep us out of it if it can be done. . . . If there is any fighting in Europe to be done, I should like to see the Bolshies and the Nazis doing it.†

Inskip then declared, fatuously enough, that it was unimportant whether Germany had 2,000 or 3,000 or 5,000 aircraft since "the fact is she has made herself supremely strong." Rearmament was necessarily slow, but if war could be held off until the middle or end of 1938, Britain would be in a "very much happier position." The former Attorney General did not stand up well under Lord Lloyd's cross-examination on arrangements for the safe storage of oil; he hedged and then was obliged to concede that nothing had been done. His claims that plans had been made to import the nation's food supply through the western ports, so as to avoid the hazardous North Sea and Channel approaches, appear in retrospect to have been spurious.‡

In conclusion, Baldwin assured his visitors that their points would all be considered, and he would meet them again in the autumn. Before leaving London, the Prime Minister directed that the several ministries concerned should submit memoranda dealing with the issues raised, and these were in hand on November 23, when he and Inskip* received the deputation for the third and last time.

Essentially these reports differed in detail but confirmed in principle the deputation's arguments. Aircraft production was indeed behind schedule but not so far as Churchill had stated. There was less merchant shipping than in 1914, but not so much less as Lord Lloyd had alleged. The slowing effect of the "noninterference" policy was painfully evident; Churchill's suggestion of a ban on aircraft deliveries to foreign countries could not be adopted because of Govern-

---

* This passage is strikingly anticipatory of his speech in the Commons the following November, which Churchill then condemned so harshly but seems not to have noticed in July. It appears to have its origin in "some rough notes" which Pownall had prepared for Baldwin, and which included: "State of country a year or two ago did not permit the Government to embark on a large programme of armaments. Had they done so they would in all probability have lost the election with results which would have been catastrophic to defence."

† A sentiment echoed in a different context some twenty years later by another father figure, Dwight Eisenhower, when he expressed his preference for wars of "Asians against Asians."

‡ See Roskill, *The War at Sea*, vol. I, pp. 38–39 (1954): "Not until early in 1939 . . . was this important matter [i.e., protection of merchant shipping in the coastal waters] forced into the foreground. To divert all the shipping to the west coast ports was not practicable, because the handling facilities at the latter were inadequate and the strain on the inland transport system would have been intolerable."

* According to Roskill (*Hankey*, vol. 3, p. 240), Neville Chamberlain was also present, but if that is so the Chancellor must have been uncharacteristically quiet.

ment policy that "deficiencies of the Defence Forces should be made up with the least possible interference with the export trade," while re-equipment of the Regular Army and reserves was under a "handicap" because industry was operating on a "business-as-usual" basis and was "very busy with their normal orders."

Baldwin and Inskip argued that things were not as gloomy as the deputation had thought, and were unyielding on the need to avoid emergency measures which would upset the country. The members of the deputation, in varying degrees, remained unsatisfied, and Churchill insisted on retaining his freedom to criticize.

Whatever impression this Conservative deputation made on the other ministers, it appears to have made virtually none on Neville Chamberlain. "If we were now to follow Winston's advice and sacrifice our commerce to the manufacture of arms," he wrote in mid-November of 1936, "we should inflict a certain injury on our trade from which it would take generations to recover, we should destroy the confidence which now happily exists, and we should cripple the revenue." Baldwin had been more concerned about the political and psychological consequences of rearmament; Chamberlain, now moving into the leading position as decision-maker, looked to the economic aspects. Neither man was blind to the military perils to which Churchill pointed, but both found reasons to keep rearmament within limits which Churchill and others thought dangerously low, and this remained the major focus of strategic disagreement in high political circles, where Chamberlain's voice was dominant.

The latter part of 1936 was a period in which other fundamental defense issues emerged or were sharpened. Churchill was pressing for the establishment of a Ministry of Supply to expedite war production, but Chamberlain, Weir, and the leading Cabinet members opposed this as "an instrument of total war, not a peace-time proposition," and it was not done until 1939, after Hitler had entered Prague. The Air Ministry was confronting a crucial double dilemma: should its resources be invested in expansion of the RAF as rapidly as possible, or should more emphasis be given to the increase of production capacity, to ensure greater output at a later time? Would the Germans more likely be deterred from bombing Britain by the fear of an RAF counterattack or by a strong defense that could inflict heavy losses on the Luftwaffe in the air? The Admiralty and the Air Ministry were still wrangling over control of marine air operations, and were in sharp disagreement over the defensive value of the convoy system, which the Navy favored but the Air Staff feared because "to mass ships in convoy would result in heavier losses from air attack" by bringing "large numbers of vulnerable targets close together"; these two problems were resolved, as will be seen, in 1937.

Neville Chamberlain's main defense preoccupation at this time was determining the proper role of the Army. "I cannot believe that the next war, if it ever comes, will be like the last one," he had written in February 1936, "and I believe our resources will be more profitably employed in the air, and on the sea, than in building up great armies." On October 25, 1936, he elaborated his views:

> I must really have some decision as to the future function of the regular and territorial armies. . . . In my view, apart from any other considerations, we had not the manpower to produce the necessary munitions . . . to man the enlarged Navy, the new Air Force, and a million-man Army. . . . We should aim at an Army of 4 divisions plus 1 mobile division. . . . Territorials should be kept fo A.A. defence.*

Chamberlain's concern lest Army expansion should absorb funds better invested elsewhere may well have been sharpened by new and alarming reports about the Luftwaffe. Early in October, Swinton had informed the CID that German pilot training and aircraft production were increasing rapidly, and that first-line strength would probably rise to 4,000 planes. Later that month the Joint Planning Subcommittee sent an extremely gloomy report to the Chiefs of Staff on "the situation in the event of war with Germany in 1939," in which the Luftwaffe again loomed as the principal threat.

On November 4, 1936, these problems were the subject of long discussion in Cabinet. Inskip described the proposed Ministry of Supply as the largest problem, but opposed it as "a declaration of martial law in time of peace," unnecessary unless war was coming in six months. Chamberlain, Swinton, Hoare, and Duff Cooper joined in a chorus of opposition. Eden alone confessed concern that war might come before rearmament, at the present pace, had paid dividends. Chamberlain closed the meeting with a lecture on "the mounting cost" of rearmament, and a warning to his colleagues that their departments should not try to slip into their budgets any "developments of convenience which had been refused in the past."

A month later the Cabinet was the scene of a sharp confrontation when Duff Cooper came in with a request that re-equipment of the Territorial Army be authorized. Chamberlain at once objected that, when the defense program had been approved the preceding February, it had been agreed that re-equipment of the Territorials would be postponed for reconsideration in three years' time. No decision had been made to re-equip the Territorials at all and: "The fact that successive Chiefs of Staff and Secretaries of State for War had taken the view that in the event of an attack by Germany on France, we should be prepared to send a land force to Belgium or France did not weigh very much with him as the War Office was the interested department." It would be "madness to add to our commitments," and it would probably be wiser to increase the Air Force for use abroad, and keep the Territorials at home.

Inskip came to Duff Cooper's defense, pointing out that, if the Territorials were to be re-equipped in three years, plans must be made in advance; Duff Cooper's request was not to send the Territorials to Europe, but to make them capable of going. Chamberlain warned that the proposal could add 90 million

---

* The Territorial Army was composed of civilians who volunteered for military training on an annual basis, and was roughly equivalent to the organized reserve components of the Army of the United States. "A.A.," of course, meant "antiaircraft."

pounds to the defense budget, provoking Duff Cooper to petulance: "if the Territorial Force was not to be re-equipped, it might as well be abolished." After more barbed exchanges, Baldwin asked that a decision be postponed for further study, and the Cabinet agreed to ask the Chiefs of Staff "to consider further the role of the British Army in time of war."

The Chiefs of Staff (at that time Admiral Chatfield, Field Marshal Deverell, and Marshal of the Royal Air Force Ellington) saw no reason to modify the views they had long held. On January 28, 1937, they advised the Cabinet:

> We are agreed that it is doubtful whether the German Army could be stopped by the sole agency of any air forces which the French and ourselves could ever oppose to it and that the Allies must therefore be capable of putting considerable land forces into the field for that purpose.*

Accordingly, plans were in preparation to send the five-division Regular Field Force to the continent within fifteen days of the outbreak of war. The Territorial Army should be re-equipped so as to be ready within four months, and the Cabinet was urged to approve "the principle of its modernisation" so that "the present basis of production of supply can be broadened."

Duff Cooper underscored the last point by circulating to the Cabinet a memorandum from Sir Harold Brown, Director General of Munitions Production at the War Office:†

> I can, of course, appreciate the magnitude of the issues involved and the difficulties of arriving at definite conclusions, but I must point out the danger of delay from the point of view of material.
>
> If we are to get within the next two years any substantial quantity of major equipment other than that already approved . . . it is essential to provide at once for their production. . . . I have made provisional arrangements for meeting such forward requirements as I have been able to ascertain, but, so far, none of these forward requirements has received the necessary approval, and I cannot proceed with schemes which are now becoming very urgent without such approval as will satisfy the Treasury.

All this came before the Cabinet on February 2, 1937, with a compromise proposal by Inskip under which the Territorial Army would be given only enough modern equipment for training purposes. If the Chancellor of the Exchequer should approve, said Inskip, Sir Harold Brown could proceed on that basis and avoid delay in placing important orders.

But Chamberlain was not to be hurried, and insisted on a statement of costs before final action:

> Admittedly, national safety came before finance, but the bill for armaments was running up very heavily. . . . There was, perhaps, some alleviation in

* Three weeks earlier the Deputy Chiefs of Staff (W. M. James, Major General R. H. Haining, and Air Marshal Christopher Courtney, with Hankey as Chairman) had submitted to their chiefs a report coming to essentially the same conclusion.

† Engineer Vice-Admiral Sir Harold Brown, who had recently retired as Engineer-in-Chief of the Fleet, was appointed to this post in the War Office in September of 1936, on the strong recommendation of Lord Weir.

the international situation, and the dangers of overloading the programme beyond the material capacity of the nation had to be considered. Was it really
necessary to stick rigidly to a date in 1939 for completion of our programme?

The result was that Inskip's compromise was approved only in principle, and
the whole matter was thrown back to the War Office for an estimate of the
costs. Chamberlain was well pleased with the result:

> I have at last got a decision about the Army and it practically gives me all
> I want. The Regular Army is to be armed *cap à pié* with the most modern
> equipment, to be ready to go anywhere at any time. But we are not committed
> to sending it anywhere, anywhen. The Territorials are to be given similar
> equipment, but only in sufficient quantity as to enable them to
> train. . . . The War Office have renounced all ideas of a continental Army
> on the scale of 1914–18.

The last sentence was true only as limited by the final phrase. With the
slaughter of Passchendaele still in living memory, no one wanted and few envisaged a British Expeditionary Force comparable to that of the First World
War. But the Army leadership had *not* renounced the idea of a substantial continental force—say twelve to twenty divisions—while Chamberlain was thinking
of very much less or even none, and this basic strategic disagreement was to last
well into 1939.

Duff Cooper returned to the Cabinet with his cost estimates on April 28,
1937: 205 million pounds for the five Regular Army and the two Territorial antiaircraft divisions; 9.25 million for training equipment for the twelve Territorial
infantry divisions; and 43 million for full war equipment for four of these
twelve, to ready them for active service on four months' notice. Sir Harold
Brown had advised him that, as a practical matter, only the first two programs
could be carried out in three years. Therefore the four-division Territorial project would involve no additional immediate expense, but it was essential to plan
for it. Otherwise, if war came, the Territorials would immediately lose their training weapons, which might serve to equip two divisions for combat, leaving the ten
others trained but unarmed. Inskip added that Duff Cooper's program, while
larger than his own compromise plan, fell far short of the Chiefs of Staff request
that all twelve of the Territorial infantry divisions be fully equipped.

Chamberlain embarked on a long, destructive analysis of the War Office proposal. The Army was pyramiding its demands, starting with "very small but perfectly equipped Regular Army," then arguing for four similarly equipped Territorial divisions, and "eventually this was doubled again." Manpower and money
were both in short supply, and "he thought it only right to warn his colleagues that
an approach by the Admiralty for a much larger Naval Programme was foreshadowed." In view of all this "further time was necessary to examine these
questions . . . in the light of both the financial situation and the man-power
position." Inskip pressed for an immediate decision of this issue, which "had
been dragging on ever since" the previous December, but the matter was put
over to the Cabinet's next meeting, a week later.

On May 5, in what was to prove his last major effort as Secretary for War,

Duff Cooper put the issue to his colleagues very squarely: ". . . his proposals had been based on military advice the rejection of which placed a good deal of responsibility on the Cabinet." He understood that the Chancellor's objections were not military but arose from the financial and manpower aspects. But the Territorial Army would need only 277,000 men to bring it up to strength, and the entire Army requirement of 500,000 was "not excessive." As for the financial side, 43 million pounds spread over three years "did not seem an impossible amount." The Inskip two-division compromise his military advisers thought "most unsafe." Inskip ruefully admitted that "he had no alternative but to accept what the Chancellor of the Exchequer would agree to," but declared that he felt the force of the Army's verdict that training is no good unless you can use those who are trained, and that without weapons the trainees would be valueless.

The Chancellor would not be budged:

He could not accept the question at issue as being a purely military matter. Other considerations entered into it. He himself definitely did challenge the policy of their military advisers. . . . Our contribution by land should be on a limited scale. . . . His suggestion, therefore, was to approve so much of the . . . proposals as had already been agreed, and to proceed to the consideration, in comparative leisure, of the proper *role* of the Army in the light of other considerations.

Duff Cooper expostulated that the role of the Army "had been under investigation ever since he had been a member of the Cabinet, and for six months before." What would be learned from a further inquiry? But his protests were unavailing; the Cabinet approved the funds for the Regulars and the antiaircraft divisions, but for the infantry Territorials authorized only the 9.25 million for training equipment. These programs were to be completed by April 1940, but even at this Chamberlain balked, noting that he "reserved" as to the date of completion, which had not been discussed. The further investigation of the Army's role was referred to a recently formed Defence Plans (Policy) Committee.* And so ended Duff Cooper's earnest but unsuccessful struggle for a viable field army.

The Admiralty bid for a "much larger Naval Programme," about which Chamberlain had forewarned his Cabinet colleagues on April 28, was the natural product of the Navy's concern over the possibility of simultaneous war with Germany and Japan. As the service responsible for maintaining communications among the Dominions and colonies, the Navy was especially sensitive to the ties of empire. Perhaps stimulated by the approaching Conference of Dominion Prime Ministers scheduled for May 1937, in April the Admiralty revived a naval construction program originally formulated in 1935 and based on

---

* This was a Cabinet committee, the membership of which largely overlapped that of the DPRC and the CID. It was formed in February 1937 and met four times between April 19 and July 23, but then sank into desuetude. The role of the Army was considered at its third meeting, on July 13, but no action was taken.

a "new" standard of required naval strength—essentially a two-ocean Navy—which would have increased the prospective size of the fleet by about one third:

	Present "One-Power" Standard	"New" Standard
Capital Ships	15	20
Aircraft Carriers	10	15
Cruisers	70	100
Destroyers	16 flotillas	22 flotillas
Submarines	55	82

When the First Lord (Sir Samuel Hoare) brought this ambitious but strategically sound proposal before the short-lived Defence Plans (Policy) Committee on May 11, Chamberlain declared that "in the main" he agreed with the Admiralty's case—a reaction the less surprising in view of his family's traditional solicitude for Empire solidarity, and his own frequent statements that British rearmament should be concentrated on sea and air power. But the two-ocean program would have doubled the cost of the fleet and entailed a permanent annual expenditure of 100 million pounds.

And so, "in view of the immense implications of the proposals," they met the same fate as those for equipping the Territorial Army. The committee agreed that the program should not go to the Cabinet until it had been studied "in greater detail together with those of the other services," a process which lasted until the following December.*

In applying the brakes both to the Territorials' re-equipment, which he thought superfluous, and the two-ocean Navy, which he favored, Chamberlain was governed by his growing conviction that financial considerations required fixing an upper limit to the total of defense expeditures. He was willing to approve a figure far above the costs in past years, for he deeply believed in the urgent necessity of speedy rearmament. But, from his standpoint, the system by which each service submitted estimates which are reviewed by the Cabinet and approved to the extent that military necessity warranted was resulting in uncontrolled totals which were mounting to a point which threatened Britain's economic security. The remedy, he concluded, was to fix the maximum sum which the economy could tolerate, and then ration it among the services. Administration of this rationing process was the primary task he had in mind for the Minister for Coordination of Defence, Sir Thomas Inskip.

Chamberlain was already laying the basis for the rationing concept in the Cabinet meeting of February 3, 1937, when, commenting on Inskip's progress report, he observed that tool shortages and other bottlenecks "showed that even the present programmes were placing a heavy strain on our resources" and that any additional strain "might put our present programmes in jeopardy." A week later he told his colleagues that some of the rearmament program would have to be

---

* Postponement of this decision did not stop the Chiefs of Staff, with Inskip and Hankey present, from assuring the Australian and New Zealand delegates to the Imperial Conference, on June 4, that in the event of war simultaneously with Japan and Italy "no anxieties or risks [in the Mediterranean] . . . can be allowed to interfere with the dispatch of a Fleet to the Far East."

paid with borrowed funds, and that the total "would come as a surprise to the public, and perhaps as a shock to financial circles." This "would do no harm," as it was high time the people realized that they could not get arms without paying.

All this was by way of prelude to the Defence White Paper of February 1937, which envisaged an expenditure of 1,500 million pounds over the next five years. Even that, Chamberlain told the Commons on February 17, might not be enough, but it is plain that he intended the figure not only as notice of the problem's magnitude, but as a means of guarding against its enlargement, for on April 28 he used it to oppose the Territorial Army equipment request, and simultaneously "warned the Cabinet that we were approaching the time when he would have to propose a fixed limit to which the Services would have to conform." None, it appears, dared mention King Canute.

A month later Chamberlain became Prime Minister, and it was left to his successor as Chancellor of the Exchequer, Sir John Simon, to fill in the details of the new procedures. Formally submitted to the Cabinet on June 30, 1937, these called for (1) new estimates from each of the services of the time and money required for "completion of their programmes"; (2) review of these estimates by the Treasury; (3) review of the estimates and Treasury comments by the DPRC, which would "determine priorities between conflicting claims" and "recommend to the Cabinet maxima for the expenditure by each Department year by year"; and (4) postponement of "decisions on new projects of major importance" pending completion of these procedures. In explaining the plan, Simon added that the permissible total would include Home Office expenditures for air-raid protection, and that after all the required procedures had been completed, "a Committee of the Cabinet would have to . . . work out how the rationing of the Defence Services was to be accomplished."

It is astonishing, at least in retrospect, that this proposal failed to arouse a storm of opposition, envisaging as it did reassessment of matters already discussed at length, a three-level review system, and indefinite postponement of such urgent "new projects" as the two-ocean Navy. But Swinton, Inskip, and Hore-Belisha (newly ensconced at the War Office) were the only listeners who voiced doubts or questions, and Hore-Belisha's sole concern was assurance that the previously approved Army program would not be subject to reconsideration. Simon's answer was equivocal. . . . "programmes that had been approved in principle by the Cabinet and in detail by the Treasury" would not be affected, but those approved only by the Cabinet might still be "reserved for approval in detail by the Treasury Inter-Service Committee."

Neville Chamberlain, whose brainchild this all was, made clear the kind of rationing process he envisaged:

> . . . when the matter had come before him as Chancellor of the Exchequer, what he had in mind was that it would be necessary to arrive first at a global total of the expenditure contemplated. . . . The next stage would be to obtain from the Treasury some idea as to the amount that could be spent . . . and then a second process might arise as to how the available money was to be subdivided between the various departments. . . . Then each Gov-

ernment Department would have to say for itself which items within its own estimates should be reduced.

The Cabinet then approved the new dispensation. To be sure, the changes thus wrought were in part psychological; as a Treasury official* rightly observed, "all Treasury control is in substance a form of rationing." Funds are never unlimited, and to give to one must mean that there is less for others. But up to this time, in theory at least, if a service established the urgent necessity of an expenditure to the satisfaction of the Cabinet, the Treasury was expected to find a way to fund it, whereas the consequence of a Treasury-fixed maximum, from which distributive shares would be cut, was that even if a service was able to show an urgent necessity which required exceeding its allotment, the answer was that to grant this demand would require diminishing the share of another service whose claims might be equally urgent and necessary.†

Apart from all this, the new procedures were laden with the probability of delay. Sir Thomas Inskip plaintively observed that "the existing system at any rate resulted in getting things done," and expressed fear that now "all decisions would be held up until the global sum had been arrived at." His apprehensions were all too well founded, for nearly six months passed before he was able to return to the Cabinet with the fruits of the new review procedures.

2

Thus Chamberlain, upon his advent as Prime Minister, reinsured his own dominance, and the primacy of economic factors, in rearmament decision-making. Simultaneously he cemented his control by the Cabinet shifts which substituted Leslie Hore-Belisha for Duff Cooper at the War Office. The former had served under Chamberlain at the Treasury, and it was on his recommendation that Baldwin brought Hore-Belisha into the Cabinet as Minister of Transport. Hore-Belisha was personally beholden to the Prime Minister and very dependent on his continued favor, for at the age of forty-three he had no independent political base, and as a Jew, a bachelor of somewhat flamboyant manner, and an inveterate headline grabber, he was unlikely to find warm welcome in stuffy Army circles. But whatever his shortcomings, Hore-Belisha was undeniably energetic, and Chamberlain sent him to the War Office in the expectation that he would bring about "drastic changes" which were long overdue, since "the obstinacy of some of the Army heads in sticking to obsolete methods is incredible."‡

* Sir Richard Hopkins, Second Secretary of the Treasury, on April 28, 1938.

† Chamberlain's indication that each service would "say for itself" what reductions it should make was illogical and dangerous. If the Cabinet should review defense investments to be made, surely it should also review proposals *not* to make investments previously described as urgently necessary for national security.

‡ The War Office and Foreign Office were the two departments which Chamberlain held in low esteem. Although the Admiralty appeared in no need of a shake-up, still it is strange that Chamberlain gave it to Duff Cooper, with whom he had no rapport and who had been opposing him so vigorously over the Territorials' re-equipment. Duff Cooper in his memoirs acknowledged that his War Office tenure had brought him "little credit," and that he was "astonished" when Chamberlain offered him the Admiralty. Eden thought his record "disappointing," and Harvey described him as "bone-idle"—an impression perhaps fostered by

For Chamberlain, reform of the War Office had the double attraction that it was badly needed and much cheaper than expansion of the Army. Hore-Belisha did not disappoint his chief; by early August, Chamberlain was congratulating himself that his new War Secretary was "doing what I put him there for and has already stirred the old dry bones up till they fairly rattle. Things are even worse at the War Office than I feared. . . ."

They were indeed. Recruiting for the Army was so slow that it was under its authorized strength by some 60,000 men. Unlike the Navy, in which sailors could serve for twenty years and earn a pension, the Army offered no career. Early in August, Hore-Belisha announced the first of a series of personnel reforms, including provision for long-term enlistments and pensions, to make service more attractive. Beneficial results were immediate. In October he announced plans to raise the status of Territorial officers, whose upper rank limit was brigadier, and who were never given divisional commands. Over the vehement objections of Deverell and other high-ranking regulars, two Territorial officers, Sir John Brown and C. F. Liardet, were designated respectively as Deputy Director of the Territorial Army and Commander of the London Territorial Division, each with the rank of major general.

In these and other matters, Hore-Belisha drew heavily on the counsel of the noted military historian and journalist Captain Basil Liddell Hart.* Duff Cooper had effected the introduction early in June, and on August 18, Hore-Belisha invited Hart to his summer home for the first of many long consultations that blossomed into what the former liked to call their "partnership." The close relationship lasted for nearly a year and, however fruitful, was more than a little anomalous in that the Captain retained throughout the "partnership" his position as military correspondent for the London *Times*. In fact, there is little evidence that either function interfered with the other, but the irregularity of his status, together with the pungency of his criticism, no doubt contributed to the resentment of his influence which soon developed in high Army circles.

This hostility was, no doubt, aggravated by the circumstance that during the early months of the "partnership" its chief subject matter was personnel—appointments, promotions, and changes in the top leadership. It was bad enough that the Secretary was concerning himself with decisions of this sort, which traditionally had been left to the Chief of the Imperial General Staff (CIGS), but far worse that Hore-Belisha was taking guidance from a rank outsider!

The necessity of a new approach was plain enough, for the selection process at the higher levels was hidebound and ridden with prejudices—against Jews, social nonconformists, and officers prematurely interested in modern gadgets

---

Duff Cooper's leisurely, social life-style; he and his wife (the beautiful and famous actress Diana Manners) were often seen with the Prince of Wales and at glamorous gatherings, and he (like Churchill and Harold Nicolson) mixed politics with literary and historical pursuits. As Liddell Hart put it, "Duff Cooper had delightful qualities, but was not a dynamic man."

* Hore-Belisha was also in close touch with Lord Weir, whose advice was largely concerned with supply problems but who agreed with Liddell Hart in urging a shake-up at the higher command levels to bring younger men to the fore.

such as tanks, which threatened the old cavalry tradition.* High appointments were handed around among a close circle of seniors on an "old Buggins' turn" footing.

It was just the sort of system which Chamberlain wanted Hore-Belisha to break up, and after a few months of obstruction to his changes from Deverell and the Adjutant General, Sir Harry Knox, the Secretary was nothing loath. By the end of November, Hore-Belisha had concluded that he could make no headway with the incumbent leadership. On December 2, 1937, having cleared his proposals with the Prime Minister and the King, Hore-Belisha announced the retirement of Deverell, Knox, and the Master-General of Ordnance, Sir Hugh Elles. General Lord Gort, who had been Hore-Belisha's military secretary and, at fifty-one, was twelve years younger than Deverell, succeeded him as CIGS, and with the other new appointments the accent was also on youth.†

The press generally applauded this evidence of a "new broom" at the War Office, and Hore-Belisha received much praise from Chamberlain and his Cabinet colleagues. But many of those who congratulated him were increasingly put off by his overexuberance and extravagance, and the records of his talks with Liddell Hart show him as lamentably subject to autointoxication. He had done the right and courageous thing but was reaping a harvest of dislike which, in the end, was to destroy him politically and, more immediately, diminish his influence on the course of Britain's rearmament.

Meanwhile, early in November, the two partners had begun work on the basic question—the role of the Army in the event of war with Germany—which the Cabinet in May had remanded for further study. It was a subject on which Liddell Hart had a long track record. A year earlier, at a meeting with Deverell in the course of which the CIGS had put forward the firmly held War Office view that in the event of a major war Britain would need a large army (for which 5 million men were said to be available) in order to "go all out with the resources of the nation," Hart's reaction had been critical: Of what use was "mass"? To what use would such an army be put? Then, in his book *Europe in Arms,* published in 1937, he had answered his own questions. The Army's only "essential" functions were defense of the homeland and "policing" the overseas territories:

> Anything beyond this is not a strategic obligation, although it may be prompted by political considerations. The use of a field force to prevent hostile air and submarine bases being established close to our coast may be desirable strategically, but it is not strictly essential. Its value should be weighed against its cost. . . . Its practicability should also receive due attention. . . . Can it be sufficiently effective under the modern conditions of warfare and limitations of geography?

* I well remember, when billeted with a retread British cavalry officer during the Second World War, being told of a dispute in the Cavalry Club over the eligibility for membership of officers of armored units. According to my informant, it was resolved on the basis that they would be eligible only if their units had in the past been horsed.

† Liddell Hart had earlier given his partner tables showing that the average age of the Army leaders was considerably greater in 1937 than it had been in 1914. Knox, who was in his sixties, was succeeded by Major General C. G. Liddell, fifty-four. Elles' duties were taken over by Sir Harold Brown, and the two departments (Munitions Production and Ordnance) were merged.

Weighing these factors, together with the probability of late arrival on the continent and insufficient attacking power:

> . . . the balance seems to be heavily against the hope that a British field force might have a military effect commensurate with the expense and the risk.

Such doctrine, anathema to the Army leaders,* was music to the ears of Neville Chamberlain, who congratulated the author both in person and in writing, reiterating his conviction that Britain should "never again send to the Continent an Army on the scale of that which was put in the field in the Great War." On October 29, Chamberlain wrote Hore-Belisha, calling attention to Liddell Hart's book and especially the chapter on "Role of the British Army." Surely the Prime Minister must have concluded that, with such a counselor, his War Secretary was in safe hands.

Hore-Belisha, who had previously read the book and needed no convincing,† replied that he was "impressed" by the author's "general theories." And so it was with little regard for the Army leaders' views on the "Continental Commitment" and re-equipping the Territorials, for which Duff Cooper had fought,‡ that the partners set about composing the memorandum on "The Role of the British Army." Its conceptual basis, in line with Liddell Hart's writing and the Prime Minister's views, was that the Army's responsibilities, in order of priority, were (1) "defending . . . [Britain] against attack from without and preserving order within," (2) performing "the same dual function for the territories of the Empire," and (3) protecting "our foreign interests."

As eventually completed by Liddell Hart, the memorandum was almost exclusively concerned with the first two missions. Since the "risk of sea-borne invasion by a foreign enemy" was "negligible," home defense could be adequately secured by the antiaircraft and Territorial infantry divisions. The bulk of the field army would be distributed among the Empire territories most susceptible to land invasion by potental enemies, and the possibility of undertaking offensive operations against Libya, Italian Somaliland, the Balearics, and the Dodecanese was discussed. A short concluding section on "foreign commitments" stated that two infantry divisions and one mobile division would be available to aid France, but *only* if the actions against the Balearics and Dodecanese were not undertaken. *If* an expeditionary force were to be sent to France, then, instead of infantry divisions, tank and machine-gun battalions should be organized as two

* Discussing Chamberlain's opposition to the "Continental Commitment," in his diary entry for January 3, 1938, Pownall wrote: ". . . the writings of the ineffable Liddell Hart have done great harm."

† In September, after observing French Army maneuvers and visiting the Maginot Line, Hore-Belisha noted: "When the French realise that we cannot commit ourselves to send an Expeditionary Force, they should be all the more induced to accelerate the extension of the Maginot Line to the sea." Had his French hosts seen the note, their reaction would surely have been choleric.

‡ In July 1937 before Hore-Belisha started consulting Liddell Hart, he had revived the request for funds to equip four Territorial divisions. As might be expected, Simon turned him down, and he did not carry the matter any further.

mobile divisions, which would aid the French more than "the whole Field Force of the present pattern."

The "Continental Commitment" was dwindling, and it now came close to disappearing altogether. On November 15, Hore-Belisha informed his partner that "the Cabinet was moving toward the discontinuance of our Expeditionary Force for the Continent," and asked Liddell Hart for a memorandum on what "economies could be effected if this were done." The following night the Secretary called from Buckingham Palace, saying that "he had told Chamberlain of the line he was taking about the role of the Army, and the P.M. was delighted— said: 'Now we can get on.'"

Liddell Hart subsequently provided a memorandum proposing the creation of armored forces in Egypt and India, and augmenting the armored components of the Field Force held in Britain. These ideas, as he was well aware, "proved extremely unpalatable in the higher military quarters." Pownall described the proposal as a "terrible solution, most unsatisfactory and the answer to no problem, whether of the Middle East or of the Continent." But that was the "role of the Army" when Inskip presented his "rationing" program to the Cabinet in December. The French, of course, were not told, and apparently they did not learn of it.

3

So, under the plans evolved in 1937, the small British Army would be modernized but not much enlarged, and would not be intended for continental employment. The Navy was already large, new construction was authorized, and the question of a further increase to two-ocean strength, put forward in April, had been postponed. The RAF was growing, but the Luftwaffe was growing faster and was the only weapon with which Germany could launch a "knockout blow" against the heart of Britain. How the RAF could best be designed and used to deter the launching or deflect the force of that blow was, from 1936 on, the overriding military issue.

Throughout 1937, RAF expansion continued to be governed by "Scheme F," adopted in 1936 with aim of assuring, by March 1939, a home-based air force with a front-line strength of 1,736 aircraft. It had been put forward as adequate to fullfill Baldwin's "parity" pledge to the Commons in March 1934 that the Government would "see to it that in air strength and air power this country shall no longer be in a position inferior to any country within striking distance of our shores." But even as Scheme F was announced, the parity claim was rickety,* and by October 1936, when Swinton foresaw a 4,000-plane Luftwaffe, it was plain that Scheme F, which was aleady behind schedule, would not suffice.

The political importance of Baldwin's parity pledge was manifest in the nature of the proposal, embodied in "Scheme H," which Swinton submitted to the Cabinet on January 14, 1937. Essentially, the plan was to increase the front-line strength of the home ("Metropolitan") air force by holding in Britain ten

---

* The Air Staff had anticipated that the Luftwaffe's front-line strength in the spring of 1937 would be over 1,500 aircraft, and on that basis the DPRC, in February 1936, thought it likely that Germany would thereafter move toward "a figure of [not] less than 2,000 first line aircraft."

squadrons allocated under Scheme F to overseas use, and transferring about half of the aircraft reserve contemplated by Scheme F to form additional front-line squadrons. By this means, it was hoped to show a Metropolitan front-line strength of 2,422 aircraft by April 1939, thus redeeming Baldwin's pledge at the expense of overseas needs, and with wholly insufficient reserves to make good operational losses.

So tough-minded an administrator as Swinton would hardly have advanced so desperate a step except under strong pressure. Its force was reflected in the Cabinet discussion on January 27, a large part of which was concerned with devising a formula which would enable Inskip to answer questions in the Commons about parity without seeming to whittle away Baldwin's pledge. Swinton, however, had more substantial ends in view, for he coupled his plan with warnings that Scheme F was running slow, Germany had the capacity to achieve a 2,500-plane combat force by 1939, and acceleration of British production would be difficult if not impossible without departing from the "noninterference" policy by transferring skilled labor from civil to military production and working the aircraft factories on double shift.

The force of the warning was considerably weakened, however, when Swinton disclosed to the Cabinet (as he was obliged to do) some figures on German production plans which had been given confidentially by Milch to the Deputy Chief of the Air Staff, Air Marshal Christopher Courtney, during the latter's recent visit in Germany. These indicated that by the fall of 1938 the front-line strengths of Luftwaffe and RAF would be virtually identical, at 1,755 and 1,736 aircraft respectively.

Since these figures, if accepted, indicated that parity would be preserved for another eighteen months even under Scheme F, it was more comforting to believe than disbelieve this information, which Goering's air force deputy had so thoughtfully furnished. Probably lulled also by Sir Samuel Hoare's observations that naval figures from Berlin had proved truthful, and Chamberlain's declaration that there was "perhaps some alleviation in the international situation," the Cabinet, on February 24, held to the "noninterference" pace, turned down Scheme H,* and Scheme F remained the order of the day.

During the next few months, the Air Staff turned its attention to other things. Chatfield had reopened the old running sore—naval control of the Fleet Air Arm, which had been confirmed as part of the RAF in 1923 on Lord Weir's recommendation. In March 1937, sharply pressed by the Admiralty, Baldwin directed Inskip to survey the problem anew. In July, Inskip recommended that the dispute be resolved by transferring all shipborne aircraft to naval control, and leaving shore-based planes with the RAF even if engaged in maritime operations. On July 29, over Swinton's objections, the Cabinet approved this solution. Nonbelievers in the aircraft carrier, such as Group Captain John Slessor, of the Air Staff, and of course Weir and Swinton, thought the decision very wrong, but the Air Staff took it with good grace, Chamberlain sternly warned the Navy

---

* In token recognition of Swinton's warnings, the Cabinet approved the preparation of land for the additional airdromes which Scheme H would have required, as well as increased recruiting of pilots and mechanics.

not to gloat, and at least the dispute was laid to rest at a time when continued friction could ill be afforded.

A few months later the less bitter but more significant controversy over the protection of seaborne trade was resolved, when the Air Force finally abandoned the old Trenchard view that convoys were especially vulnerable to air attack and could best be protected by attacking the enemy's air bases. On December 2, 1937, the CID approved an arrangement between Chatfield and Sir Cyril Newall (who had succeeded Ellington as Chief of the Air Staff in September) under which the RAF's Coastal Command would allocate some 340 aircraft to convoy and maritime reconnaissance duties, and Newall agreed that this force would not be diverted to other duties without prior approval by the Chiefs of Staff.

There were other significant technical and tactical advances during 1937. Radar (or, as it was then called, RDF, for radio direction finder), for the detection of approaching aircraft, passed from the theoretical to the practical stage, with a training program and, in August, authorization for the construction of twenty stations along England's southeastern shores. Experiments with the use of radar for navigation and antiaircraft gun aiming were commenced. Basic designs for the four-engined heavy bombers were settled, so that production could begin in 1938. The Air Staff's reliance on strategic bombing as a major offensive weapon was subjected to target selection and aiming tests. Lord Swinton's "shadow factories" sprouted across the land, greatly increasing future production capacity. Hurricanes and Spitfires emerged from the prototype stage, and in October 1937 the first production-line Hurricanes took to the air.

Still, aircraft production lagged well behind the Schedule F timetable, and there were especially discouraging delays with the Spitfire. Meanwhile the Air Ministry, like the other service departments, had commenced the general survey of future requirements which the Cabinet, on June 30, had called for in connection with Simon's review procedures. As a basis for this report, Group Captain Slessor, head of the Plans Branch of the Air Staff, made a "careful scrutiny of R.A.F. expansion *in actual performance* against the planned programme to which we were working," and embodied the results in a memorandum submitted to Newall on September 3, 1937. Slessor, newly arrived at the Air Staff,* was appalled. Not only was the Schedule F program increasingly in arrears, but Bomber Command's present strength in long-range bombers was under a hundred, compared to the Luftwaffe's 800 bombers, including some 200 new Heinkel 111s and Dornier 17s. He wrote:

> . . . the Air Staff would be failing in their duty were they not to express their considered opinion that the Metropolitan Air Force in general, and the Bomber Command in particular, are at present almost totally unfitted for war; that, unless the production of new and up-to-date aircraft can be expedited, they will not be fully fit for war for at least two and a half years; and that even at the end of that time, there is not the slightest chance of their reaching

---

* After the Second World War, Marshal of the Royal Air Force and Chief of the Air Staff. In May 1937, Slessor returned from foreign duty and succeeded Group Captain Arthur Harris as Director of Plans.

equality with Germany in first line strength if the present German programmes are fulfilled. . . .

Alarming analysis of this sort, coupled with news that the Army and Navy
were utilizing the report on their needs as a vehicle for increased cost estimates
which might squeeze the RAF out of its fair share of the 1500-million-pound
pie which would soon be cut, stimulated Swinton and Newall to prepare forthwith a new expansion program. Designated "Scheme J" and submitted on October 12, 1937, it called for completion by 1941 of first-line units with a strength
of over 3,000 aircraft, including 1,442 bombers and 532 fighters in the Metropolitan Air Force.

Apart from the substantial increase in the number of aircraft the principal
difference between Schemes J and F was the former's greater comparative investment in bombers. Numerically, the Metropolitan fighter strength was to rise
by 26 per cent and the bomber strength by 46 per cent, but in power terms the
change was even greater, for the Blenheims, Battles, and other medium bombers
were to be replaced as rapidly as possible by the four-engined heavies that
would come into production in 1938. Overall, Scheme J would cost £650
million as compared to 467 million for Scheme F.* The Air Ministry acknowledged that so large a program could not be undertaken without diversion of
labor and plant facilities from peacetime uses and (in a supporting memorandum
submitted in November) flatly urged abandonment of the noninterference policy, as well as purchasing Douglas bombers from the United States.

The proposed expansion was immense in comparison to Scheme F, now
nearly two years old, but not in light of the Luftwaffe's concurrent growth. Contemporaneous Air Staff estimates indicated that within one year the Germans
would have some 1,100 front-line bombers and 700 fighters, and that by the end
of 1939, more than a year before Scheme J would be fulfilled, the Luftwaffe's
front-line strength would rise to 3,240 aircraft with 1,450 bombers and nearly
1,000 fighters.†

Lord Swinton and the Air Staff were not alone in their concern. On October
14, the indefatigable Sir Maurice Hankey transmitted to Inskip a memorandum
warning that "it is not safe to allow the position of our defensive preparations,
especially in the air, to remain as at present," and arguing that the imposition of
compulsory industrial priorities was not politically so impossible as had been assumed, and in any event would be preferable to "late in the day panic measures." Three weeks later Eden wrote to Chamberlain that he was "profoundly
worried about the state of our rearmament" and urged that the British people
"are ready to make sacrifices and appreciate, perhaps more than some of our
colleagues, that we have got to meet the challenges of the dictators, and that to
do so we do have to be strong in armaments."

These were strong voices, but by this time the relations between Eden and

* Scheme J, like Scheme F, envisaged a 225 per cent aircraft reserve, thus abandoning the
device used in Scheme H to inflate the front line by depleting the reserve.

† These estimates were supported by Milch's own statements when he visited England in
October 1937, and admitted that the Luftwaffe had already achieved the strength which, according to his earlier representations to Courtney in Berlin, would not have been reached
until the fall of 1938.

Chamberlain were showing strain, and the former's reference to "our colleagues" was hardly likely to please the Prime Minister who had chosen them for his cabinet. The intrinsic strength of the Air Staff's case gave no assurance that Scheme J would survive the cold scrutiny of Simon and Chamberlain when it reached the Cabinet.

4

On July 29, 1937, at the last Cabinet meeting before the summer recess, Sir Thomas Inskip informed his colleagues that the service estimates and Treasury comments were not yet complete but should be available for consideration in October. However, some tentative sums were mentioned, and they were large enough to produce another lecture on economy from Chamberlain, who remarked that the annual maintenance of the contemplated forces (figured at 240 million pounds) "seemed likely to constitute a permanent financial burden which was altogether beyond what this country could find from revenue."*

On October 27 the promised documents were in hand. Simon confessed that he had been unable to fix "a figure the nation could afford," but stressed factors which foreshadowed difficulty in borrowing large sums. The Cabinet then threw the whole problem into Inskip's lap, specifying that he should be advised by Hankey, Sir Horace Wilson, three other high-ranking civil servants, and the Chiefs of Staff.

Wilson reflected Chamberlain's views and two of the civil servants were Treasury officers, so it could be expected that a majority of the civilian component would be predisposed against any substantial increase above the 1500-million-pound limit previously marked by Chamberlain. Hankey saw the priority order as (1) defense against air attack, with primary reliance on fighters rather than bombers; (2) naval protection of trade and blockade of the enemy; (3) defense of overseas bases; and (4) a continental expeditionary force. On the last point, Hankey came out on Liddell Hart's side of the controversy and favored discarding the Territorials as a reserve for the field forces, and restricting their role to home defense.

The crucial issue, of course, was Scheme J, and Inskip's memorandum to Swinton of December 9, 1937, showed which way the wind was blowing in the higher councils:

> As regards the Air Force I am satisfied that the present programme as represented in Scheme F. does not meet the case, but I am not satisfied that Scheme J. is one which I can recommend as it stands.

The first objection was, of course, the cost: "The Treasury give most cogent reasons for not increasing our expenditure above the lower limits" indicated by Simon. But Inskip supported the financial factor by a frontal attack on the Air Ministry's basic theory, which was that, while the RAF did not need "parity" with the Luftwaffe in numbers of fighters but only a number "adequate" to de-

---

* Two weeks earlier the Cabinet had turned down a CID proposal for national registration of occupational qualifications. Arguments that it was desirable as preparation for manpower allocation were rejected on the ground that it would create "political difficulties."

fend against a German "knockout blow" attempt,* it must have "parity" in strength of long-range bombers, so that Bomber Command could deal Germany as heavy blows as the Luftwaffe could strike against Britain.

Inskip virtually reversed the bomber-fighter strategic factor. Noting with agreement the Chiefs of Staff view that Germany, better prepared but shorter of staying power than Britain, must try for a quick victory by knockout, Inskip saw quite different strategic significance in terms of air power:

> I cannot . . . persuade myself that the dictum of the Chief of the Air Staff that we must give the enemy as much as he gives us is a sound principle. I do not think that is the proper measure of our strength. The German Air Force, as I have pointed out, must be designed to deliver a knock-out blow within a few weeks of the outbreak of war. The *role* of our Air Force is not an early knock-out blow—no-one has suggested that we can accomplish that but to prevent the German from knocking us out.
>
> It has occurred to me, therefore, that we ought to consider whether our Air Force programme could not be re-cast on somewhat different lines. Please do not think that I am driving my ideas to the extreme logical conclusion that we ought to have nothing but fighters at the outset of a war. That would be an absurdity. My idea is rather that we need not possess anything like the same number of long-range heavy bombers as the Germans. . . . They must come to this country to damage us. They are likely to concentrate on great centres, such as London, which provide an irresistible target. In fact, it would seem in accordance with strategical principle that the decisive place and the decisive time for the concentration of our own air force would be somewhere over our own territory at the outset of a war.

The Inskip memorandum was an odd mixture of perception and misperception, sense and nonsense. The Luftwaffe was *not* being designed to "deliver a knockout blow," but primarily as a tactical weapon for use against troops. There was no certainty that the Germans would attempt such a blow, especially if their purpose were conquest of a secondary power such as Czechoslovakia or Poland.

Probable or not, however, an all-out German air assault was possible and, in view of the RAF's weakness, the most immediate threat to Britain's survival. The Air Staff was still following the Trenchard-Weir doctrine that the fear of retaliation was the best deterrent, but this view, whatever its merits if Britain had an equal or superior striking force, simply could not be sustained when Bomber Command had less than a quarter the strength of the Luftwaffe's bombers. There was no possibility of achieving equality before 1941, and surely Inskip was right to challenge the structure of Scheme J and focus attention on defense against air attack.†

---

* The lack of need for "parity" in fighters arose from the circumstance that Germany, as a continental power with a large army, would need fighters for a much greater variety of purposes than would Britain.

† In his memoirs, entitled *The Central Blue* (1956), Slessor wrote (pp. 166–67): "It had always been an article of faith with the Air Staff that the counter-offensive was the most important element in our own defence. I think it must be admitted that we overstressed that doctrine to the extent of seriously underrating the efficacy of fighter defense and providing

The shortcoming of Inskip's memorandum was that, while dressed in the language of strategy, its real objective was financial economy. Inskip did not propose to increase the fighter and decrease the bomber components of Scheme J, but only to leave the fighter strength unchanged and cut back on the bombers. This meant that the fighter defense would be no stronger than the Air Staff had proposed, and that the development of an effective striking force would be delayed. Inskip endeavored to camouflage these factors by proposing not to reduce the *number* of bomber aircraft but to substitute "a larger proportion of light and medium bombers for our very expensive heavy bombers." The fighter force could perhaps be augmented without additional expense by "using our own bombers to supplement our own fighters," and Inskip added the remarkable notion that British bombers might drop "special light bombs" on German bombers. In conclusion, Swinton was invited to submit "a revised program" based on Inskip's conception.*

On the morning of December 22, 1937, Inskip's report (submitted a week earlier) came before the Cabinet. It opened by stating two basic and competing values: a stable economy which Inskip, following Chamberlain's oft-repeated doctrine, described as essential to Britain's ability to survive a long war, and which would be threatened by too much taxing or borrowing; and the danger of modern mechanized forces "capable of dealing a knock-out blow in a few weeks or months," which required such investment in arms as was necessary to' enable Britain to "avoid instant defeat."

Inskip attached a memorandum from Simon showing that continuation of the existing defense programs over the five years 1937–41 ("Hypothesis A") would cost £1605 million, while with the addition of the two-ocean Navy and Schedule J ("Hypothesis B") the cost would mount to £1884 million. The annual cost of maintaining these forces when completed would be £255 million under Hypothesis A and £301 million under Hypothesis B. Both hypotheses, though in varying degree, involved the danger of "building up the Defence Forces out of borrowed money to a level which it is beyond our power to maintain." Therefore the estimate must be cut back to £1500 million,† or else taxes would have to be raised.

After stating the defense priorities precisely as Hankey had ordered them in November (home defense, trade route protection, British overseas territories, and aid to allies), Inskip proceeded to the application of these policies and priorities to the several services. The two-ocean naval standard was to be

---

inadequate numbers of fighters . . . perhaps we may be excused for laying what we now know was too much reliance on the importance of a bomber counter-offensive as the major element in defence. Nevertheless, we did place more reliance on it than we were justified in doing with the bombers of the day."

* Two days later the Air Staff submitted a note sharply challenging Inskip's recommendations. The war could be won only by attack, it was declared, and to degrade the bomber force would be to accept permanent air inferiority to Germany. If, despite all, the funds for Scheme J were not made available, nevertheless the heavy bomber force must be built, albeit more slowly.

† The £1500-million figure for five years was based on anticipated tax revenues at existing rates of £210 million per annum, plus £400 million obtained from government loans, as authorized by Parliament in February 1937.

indefinitely postponed, despite the Admiralty's admonition that the present program "in no way represents the realities of the position" in the event of simultaneous war with Germany and Japan. The Army was to concentrate on home and empire defense, with additional funds for antiaircraft defense but none for continental employment; Inskip wrote, with wistful hope, that it would be "in Germany's interest" to honor Belgian neutrality. As for the RAF, Scheme J was dealt with much as indicated in Inskip's earlier memorandum to Swinton. Proposed increases for the overseas components were disallowed, since priority should go to home defense. For the Metropolitan forces, the requested enlargement of Fighter Command was approved, but Inskip declared himself "not wholly convinced" by the Air Staff's case for the Scheme J bomber force. He made no precise recommendation other than to suggest allowing "some increase in the present first-line strength, with reduced provision for reserves and greatly improved arrangements for war potential"—meaning by this last clause an expansion of "shadow" factory capacity.

It was not suggested in Sir Thomas' report that this program was militarily adequate, but only that it was the best that could be done within the economic guidelines. Lack of provision for an expeditionary force was especially disturbing:

> If France were again to be in danger of being overrun by land armies, a situation might arise where, as in the last war, we had to improvise an army to assist her. Should this happen, the Government of the day would most certainly be criticized for having neglected to provide against so obvious a contingency.

"What about the unfortunate troops?" Pownall mused sourly, when he read the foregoing passage. If the "contingency" was indeed "obvious," what was the justification for disregarding it? *Diplomacy* was Inskip's answer, as he cast the burden on the Foreign Office to mitigate the military perils: ". . . in the long run the provision of adequate defences within the means at our disposal will only be achieved when our long-term foreign policy has succeeded in changing the present assumptions as to our potential enemies." Alas, the assumptions could not be changed without reducing the hostile quantum, and it was asking too much of diplomacy to accomplish this, other than by extensive concessions, if Britain indeed lacked adequate means even for her own defense.

In the Cabinet meeting, Inskip added a few more thoughts. The two-ocean naval standard was presently impossible because of the "staggering cost," but perhaps the Admiralty might be helped by "the retention of ships which were due for scrapping." In dropping aid to the French to the foot of the priority list, he had drawn comfort from Hore-Belisha's statement that "France no longer looked to us in the event of war to supply an Expeditionary Force on the scale hitherto proposed." Inskip acknowledged that his proposals for the RAF "fell short of the Air Staff's demands," but "in view of the financial and economic outlook, he thought that they were the right course."

Chamberlain then adjourned the morning session, and the Cabinet met again late that afternoon for discussion and decision. Duff Cooper immediately, but without apparent effect, challenged the naval proposals, which, he said, did not even meet the previously agreed standard of strength, and he asked for more submarines and destroyers. Hore-Belisha, however, was all milk and honey, with congratulations to Inskip for his understanding attitude toward the Army's problems. In an apparent effort to mitigate the gravity of Inskip's warning about the "obvious contingency" that France might be in danger of being overrun, Hore-Belisha told his colleagues that the Maginot Line could be held with small forces, thus enabling the French to assemble large reserves, and reiterated his fatuous prediction that "if French realized that we could not commit ourselves to send an expedition they would be the more inclined to accelerate the extension of the Maginot Line to the sea."

Lord Swinton then served the group a large helping of food for serious thought. An air force could not be improvised at short notice, so decisions could not be postponed, and the Air Staff's Scheme J was "the minimum for security." The Government had told the Commons that "parity" meant an air force which would be "an effective deterrent" and "able to meet a potential enemy on equal terms." This did not mean a "mere mathematical comparison," and in formulating Scheme J the Air Staff had eliminated all German aircraft except "bombers that could be used against this country" and had "asked for an equal number of first-line machines to these." Inskip was proposing to cut back not only the first line but the reserve as well, while increasing shadow factory capacity. But "even if a firm . . . was fully equipped and jigged, it would take six months from the word being given before it could be in production, and that was apart from the risk of war damage." A 225 per cent reserve of ready aircraft would be necessary to make good operational wastage until the shadow plants started to produce, and therefore: "The only alternative to having both reserves and war potential was for the Air Force to go slow during the first six months of a war." That, of course, would lessen Britain's capacity to resist a knockout blow; nevertheless if, for financial reasons, a choice had to be made, Swinton agreed with Inskip that "the right course was to reduce the reserves and to go in for increased war potential."

Sir John Simon then repeated the arguments for the £1500-million ceiling, with a supporting interjection from Chamberlain that, if observing the limit required a departure from the parity pledged by Baldwin, he was prepared to defend such a step "if the Cabinet thought it necessary." Hoare, however, criticized Inskip's proposals as inadequate. He was reluctant to reject the opinion of the Air Staff and supported the Admiralty's pleas (he had been Duff Cooper's predecessor as First Lord) for additional naval construction. Eden spoke even more strongly for a bigger effort. He favored Scheme J and thought "we were concentrating too much on the defensive." He alone challenged Inskip and Hore-Belisha on the Army proposals; the idea of sending no ground forces to the continent until Britain was "safe at home" was muddled, for "if the Channel ports fall into the hands of Germany, the country would not be safe." He reminded Hore-Belisha that Daladier and Delbos had asked for two mechanized divisions, and asked whether these would be available, eliciting the response that this could be done only "by dividing the existing Division into two." Halifax then said a few words in line with those of Hoare and Swinton, but chiefly stressed the necessity of "every possible effort to get on good terms with Germany"—a task which "threw an immensely heavy burden on diplomacy."

Summing up the discussion, Chamberlain predictably "attached great importance to . . . the maintenance of our economic stability as an essential element in our defensive strength." True, the enemy might attempt a knockout blow, but "the evidence before him did not show that that was likely to succeed." The Cabinet then approved "the proposed defence priorities" and the "primary Army role" as set forth in Inskip's report, and "deferred a final decision on an increased standard of naval strength until next year." Despite Swinton's pleas for speed "no final decision was reached on policy for expansion of the Air Force," and Inskip was directed "to consult further" with Swinton. All the services were requested to submit their final estimates, so that Simon could prepare his forecast of defense expenditures by the end of February 1938.

It was an enormously important meeting,* both for what it rejected and what it left undecided: no continental expeditionary force, no two-ocean Navy for the present, no action on Scheme J, so that Scheme F remained in effect. The Cabinet had flatly rejected the views of the three Chiefs of Staff, supported by two of the three responsible ministers.† Right or wrong, the responsibility for these decisions was Chamberlain's, for nothing can be more certain than that if he had supported the military chiefs the Cabinet would have followed his lead.

The December 22 Cabinet and its aftermath dismayed the Chiefs of Staff. At their meeting on January 19, 1938, Admiral Chatfield, according to the minutes:

> said that he had the gravest misgivings. . . . It was only comparatively recently they had almost, as it were, been invited to spend up to the limit. Now a change had come over the position and money was less free for the defence services. For instance there was a proposal to impose a cut of £6 million on naval estimates. . . . It was difficult to say what had happened in the last few months to justify this swing of the pendulum. It was, in fact, even more surprising if regarded in the light of the grave world political situation, which appeared daily to grow more menacing.

Newall "expressed his entire agreement," adding: "A large cut amounting to £80 million, spread over 5 years was contemplated in the further expansion programmes of the RAF now under consideration. . . . we were trying to take wartime measures with peacetime machinery." Rather than ask for additional funds, however, the Chiefs decided to press the Government for greater speed in

---

* However, none of the participants' memoirs or other records thus far published (Chamberlain, Halifax, Simon, Hoare, Eden, Swinton, Duff Cooper, and Hore-Belisha) mention the meeting, so that the Cabinet minutes and memoranda are the sole available source.

† The third minister was, of course, Hore-Belisha. I have seen no indication that Gort's views were independently presented to the Cabinet, but Pownall's diary (entries for March 14 and April 11, 1938) makes it clear that Gort strongly favored the "Continental Commitment." Pownall's own reaction to the Inskip-Hore-Belisha "role of the Army" was sulphurous: *"My* view is that support of France is home Defence—if France crumbles we fall. Therein lies the fallacy of his [Inskip's] argument. And see how the argument is altered to fit the purse. The tail is wagging the dog."

the use of moneys already available, supported by memoranda from each service showing delays in rearmament caused "by the slow rate of production." Essentially, this was a protest against the noninterference policy.

But the Chancellor of the Exchequer felt no such urgency. The elimination of two-ocean navies, expeditionary forces, and bomber squadrons made him no less watchful of expenses for approved purposes or less insistent on bringing down the total to the stipulated level. "John Simon before leaving for the south of France wrote to me, turning down our proposals," Hore-Belisha noted in his diary on January 7: "This knocked me out." Two weeks later Duff Cooper recorded receipt of "a discouraging letter from the Chancellor of the Exchequer" who "wants us to reduce our estimates by £6,000,000 and I don't see how it can be done." Meanwhile the Air Staff, confronted with a Cabinet majority unwilling to approve Scheme J, submitted a program designated Scheme K, which (1) left Scheme F in effect for the overseas units, (2) cut back by about 20 per cent the proposed increase in front-line bombers, (3) provided full reserves for Fighter Command but little more than half the requested bomber reserves, and (4) cut in half the funds for production expansion.* Newall gloomily forecast that, in the event of war, "there would be a period when the Air Force would come to a standstill owing to lack of reserves and the [production] potential would consequently be useless (since the war would have been lost) if it were not destroyed."

When the Cabinet met on February 16, 1938, to consider Inskip's further report, two weeks had elapsed since Hitler's sacking of Blomberg, Fritsch, and Neurath, and four days since Schuschnigg's visit to the Berghof. The international atmosphere was increasingly laden with menace. Still, the Defense Minister was not much closer to a solution of the defense allocations than he had been in December. The service five-year estimates totaled nearly £1800 million, despite the Cabinet's December request that they be held to £1500 million. Such expenditures, Inskip wrote, "would definitely impair that economic stability which is a vital part of our defensive armour."

But Sir Thomas had had a perfectly splendid idea which would render it "happily unnecessary" to face the awful alternatives of exceeding the £1500-million limitation or failing to rearm adequately. The three services, he proposed, should be allowed to expand their expenditures through 1938 and 1939, but not to fix their programs beyond those years. He indulged the hope that before 1941 the international situation would improve and rearmament expense could be cut back. Surely it was a remarkable triumph of math over mind! On this basis, Inskip proposed a conditional elevation of the permissible five-year total to £1650 million, of which £80 million would go to the Home Office for civilian air raid protection, leaving £1570 million to be divided among the military services.

The Cabinet also had before them another memorandum on the role of the Army which Hore-Belisha had submitted on February 10, after more than a

---

* The comparative five-year costs were: Scheme F, £467.5 million; Scheme J, 650 million; Scheme K, £567.5 million.

month of work on it. Pownall's draft had not pleased the Secretary,* and late in January he started using Liddell Hart as unofficial editorial adviser.

The decision to drop the continental commitment had moved Hore-Belisha to promise—most imprudently, in Liddell Hart's view—that it would "save millions" in expenditures for tanks, and he had sent Chamberlain a construction prospectus calling for hundreds of light reconnaissance tanks but very few mediums and heavies. But the types of tanks needed would depend upon where and how the Field Force would be used, and if not in France, then where would it go, and for what purpose? To Egypt, said the General Staff, without saying why, but perhaps moved by the earlier decision that Empire defense took priority over aid to France. Furthermore, like the force previously destined for France, it would comprise one mobile and four infantry divisions, whereas (as Liddell Hart observed with some asperity) Egypt was especially suitable for a mobile force;† the staff was perpetuating Deverell's Field Force "with merely the difference that instead of being plunked into France it was to be plunked into Egypt." Liddell Hart's counsel prevailed to the extent that more mobile troops were to be posted to Egypt, but the finished document, he thought, still reflected the General Staff's traditional reliance on infantry at the expense of armor.

Little attention was paid to Army matters when the Cabinet met to consider these reports. Inskip was "disappointed" that the service figures were so high, and declared himself afflicted with a "heavy heart" at the necessity of raising the ceiling to £1650 million. Duff Cooper again attacked the rationing system and predicted that if the Navy were held to the prescribed limit there would be no forces available for the Far East. Swinton, as before, was the most articulate of the service ministers. Scheme J was the Air Staff's minimum proposal of "adequate insurance." Scheme K had been formulated only because his colleagues had failed to approve Scheme J; it "was not what the Air Force thought ought to be done, but what they thought would be the best value that could be got" for its cost. Inskip's proposal that the defense program be approved only for the first two years "would be of no value to the Air Ministry," since contracts had to be made "looking four or five years ahead."

Simon, Hoare, Halifax, Eden, and others also spoke, but no one except Duff Cooper directly challenged the rationing procedure. Inskip said that probably Swinton's concern about long-term contracts could be met with the aid of cancellation clauses. Chamberlain, summing up, acknowledged that Inskip's two-year procedure was "to some extent an evasion and a postponement of decision," but thought it justified "by his hope for some improvement in the international situation." The Cabinet then approved with expressed misgivings the five-year £1650-million ceiling subject to review after 1939. No action was taken on Scheme K.

---

* Hore-Belisha's preparation of this memorandum drove the General Staff nigh to distraction. Everything they produced was criticized as "woolly," and the paper went through five drafts before taking its final form.

† Apart from Egypt, Liddell Hart also proposed extensive armored additions to the Army forces overseas in other territories where mechanized forces could be advantageously used.

Despite the Cabinet's preoccupation with knockout blows from the air, the RAF got the smallest ration from Inskip's 1938 allocation—£103.5 million as compared to £106.5 for the Army and £123.7 for the Navy. Neither the estimates nor the Defence White Paper revealed much about the arguments and issues which had so beset the service departments and the Treasury during the preceding six months.

On March 7,1938, Neville Chamberlain arose in the Commons to present the Defence White Paper, based on defense estimates totalling £343.5 million. It concluded with a prediction that the five-year total would exceed £1500 million, but otherwise it contained not a word to indicate that anything might be amiss with rearmament, or to stimulate Parliament or public to greater effort: "The essential features of the policy underlying the defence programme remain unchanged, and what is needed is rather a survey of the progress achieved. . . ." True, there had been some setbacks by way of shortages of materials and skilled labor owing to "the policy to avoid as far as possible interference with the requirements of private industry," but there was no suggestion that the policy be changed; instead the Prime Minister recurred to his favorite theme—"economic and industrial stability." Likewise, he spoke with satisfaction of the Government's advice from the Chiefs of Staff—"never has planning for strategical purposes been brought to so complete a state as it is at present"—but of course the members were not told that those same Chiefs of Staff all thought the Government's program grossly inadequate.

The Prime Minister took occasion to respond to a question previously put to him by a Conservative M.P., Captain Harold Balfour, a First World War fighter pilot: Would the present RAF expansion program (Scheme F) "provide parity in front-line strength with any European air power within striking distance of our shores?" That, said Chamberlain was a "narrower view of parity" than Baldwin took in his 1934 pledge. First-line strength was "only one of a number of factors which go to make up the air power and air strength of which Lord Baldwin spoke." Aircraft reserves, production potential, access to raw materials, training, aircraft quality, and yet other elements had also to be considered. This, of course, was all very true, but as of March 1938 the inclusion of these other factors would not have served to better the RAF's situation vis-à-vis the Luftwaffe, and some of those in the know doubted that Britain could *ever* regain air parity with Germany.

Another member then reiterated the question on first-line strength, but Chamberlain brushed it off: he did not "propose to enter into details." And after another few hours of desultory debate, the Defence White Paper was approved by 347 to 133 votes.

Three days later Hore-Belisha presented the Army estimates in a speech which he and Liddell Hart had labored over for weeks. In describing the Army's role, "co-operation in the defence of . . . allies" was put last, and the Secretary pointed out in a general way that the "assumptions" which had governed during the Great War might no longer be valid. But of course there was no disclosure that the "continental commitment" had been virtually abandoned, if for no other reason than that the French had not been so informed.

Even as Hore-Belisha spoke, in Berlin the generals were improvising their plans for the march into Austria. Two days later, on Sunday March 13, Hitler announced *Anschluss*. For Britain the great question now was how the seizure of Austria would affect the Chamberlain government's pace of rearmament and national strategy.

CHAPTER 24

Neville Chamberlain: Man of Decision

1

The annexation of Austria was a nasty shock to the British Government—especially, perhaps, to Lord Halifax, who had so recently supped with the devil using a spoon now proved far too short. Yet there was also an undercurrent of relief that what had been feared had now happened, and therefore was no longer to be feared. Hitler had furnished "a typical illustration of power politics," Chamberlain told his cabinet on March 12, but "this thing had to come" and "at any rate the question was now out of the way." A month earlier, after Schuschnigg's trip to the Berghof, Cadogan had "almost" wished that "Germany would swallow Austria and get it over," and on April 22 he wrote to Nevile Henderson:

> Thank goodness, Austria's out of the way. I can't help thinking we were very badly informed about feeling in that country. . . . we should evidently have been very wrong to try to prevent *Anschluss* against the wishes of . . . a very considerable proportion of the population. After all, it wasn't our business: We had no particular feelings for the Austrians: We only forbade the *Anschluss* to spite Germany.

With such sentiments voiced in the highest Government circles, it is less surprising that *Anschluss,* despite the oratorical gusts of righteous indignation at Hitler's "methods," did not immediately affect the tempo of rearmament. This was not for any failure to perceive the *portent* of *Anschluss;* at the March 12 Cabinet meeting Chamberlain stated that the two questions posed were:

(1) What steps should be taken to guide public opinion?
(2) How were we to prevent similar action being taken in Czecho-Slovakia?

These questions naturally provoked discussion of "the possibility of some expansion and acceleration of our defence forces," in the course of which "the general view was that any such expansion and acceleration should be applied to our Air Force and Anti-aircraft defences." Chamberlain warned "against giving the impression that the country was faced with the prospect of war within a few weeks," and set the matter for discussion two days hence.

When the Cabinet met on the morning of Monday, March 14 (while Hitler was on the road from Linz to Vienna), they had before them memoranda from

Lord Swinton, urging an accelerated version of Scheme K designated Scheme L, and from Hore-Belisha, reporting the situation and prospects with respect to antiaircraft artillery.* To speed production, Swinton proposed that the larger aircraft factories be given priority for sufficient skilled laborers to work double shifts; this would raise production by 33 per cent and produce the front-line numerical strength envisaged under Scheme K within one year instead of three, and the necessary reserves in two years. Hore-Belisha also demonstrated the feasibility of greatly accelerated production if emergency labor measures were invoked.

Anschluss or no, the reaction from Simon and Inskip was agonized negation; the adoption of Scheme K would wreck the armament program recently adopted by the Cabinet and would "reduce the quota available to the Navy and Army very seriously." These expostulations were joined in by Ernest Brown, the Minister of Labour, and the Prime Minister then declared that Scheme K could not be adopted without further study.

Hore-Belisha then delivered himself of a long lecture (prepared with Liddell Hart's aid) on the imminence of war, the strength and efficiency of the German military machine, and Britain's present weakness and desperate need for accelerated rearmament, all supported by a reading from *Mein Kampf*. Lord Halifax (by this time Foreign Minister) administered a dash of cold water: ". . . the events of the last few days had not changed his own opinion as to the German attitude towards this country" and he "did not think it could be claimed that a new situation had arisen."

Chamberlain then declared himself convinced by the discussion that no decision could be reached that day. The meeting adjourned with the understanding that Inskip "should further investigate" the Swinton and Hore-Belisha proposals in consultation with them and Ernest Brown. And so the ministers separated with Scheme F and business-as-usual still in effect. In the House of Commons that afternoon, Chamberlain expressed "severe condemnation" of the "methods" Hitler had used in bringing about *Anschluss,* but as far as concerned rearmament, said only that the Government "would make a fresh review," and that "in due course we shall announce what further steps we may think it necessary to take."†

2

The Chamberlain government's policy to meet the looming crisis over Czechoslovakia was developed and put into effect during the ten days from March 15 to March 24, 1938. The laboratories in which its elements were analyzed were the staff of the Foreign Office and the Chiefs of Staff Subcommittee of the CID. The locus of decision-making was the Cabinet's Foreign Policy Committee.

---

* Duff Cooper, who was ill, submitted a letter proposing an immediate increase in the naval construction program. Chamberlain told the Cabinet that air expansion was more urgent, and no one appears to have supported Duff Cooper's request.

† The following day, in reply to a question, Chamberlain told the Commons that as yet he had nothing new to say on the subject of RAF expansion.

Several policies, alternative or conjunctive, had been proposed by leading members on March 14, during the Commons debate on Chamberlain's statement. Leo Amery, former minister and independent Conservative, urged the Government to seek allies among "those who will stand with us for the peace of Europe," and then to fish or cut bait on Czechoslovakia: "Let us either make up our minds that we must stand out . . . or let us say to France and Czechoslovakia and Germany . . . that the first German soldier or aeroplane to cross the Czech border will bring the whole might of this country against Germany." He did not say which,* but Arthur Henderson (former Foreign Secretary in MacDonald's Labour government) had no doubt that the Prime Minister should "make it plain" that the British Government stood behind France and Czechoslovakia.

It was Churchill, however, whose speech made the deepest impression. He supported Amery's call for a "clear and precise" policy and for a diplomacy that would attract allies. There should be no delay: "Why should we assume that time is on our side?" The dictators would gather strength by conquest. Rearmament was essential but not enough. And then, in a ringing passage:

> If a number of States were assembled around Great Britain and France in a solemn treaty for mutual defence against aggression; if they had their forces marshalled in what you may call a grand alliance . . . if that were sustained, as it would be, by the moral sense of the word; and if it were done in the year 1938—and, believe me, it may be the last chance there will be for doing it—then I say you might even now arrest this approaching war.

In Britain, as in France, *Anschluss* was linked with Spain, where Franco's victory was increasingly imminent, as symbols of the dictators' duplicity and ruthlessness. Sir Archibald Sinclair (the Liberal Party leader) went so far as to predict that "it is not Czechoslovakia which is the next victim on the list, but Spain," and urged his listeners to "unite in opposition to this Italian and German conspiracy to dominate Spain." The Duchess of Atholl wondered why Mussolini had not raised a finger to prevent *Anschluss,* and suggested that the dictators had made a deal over Austria and Spain "with results extremely dangerous to us," especially at Gibraltar. Pressure for review of nonintervention was mounting, and the Spanish question was the subject of discussion in the Cabinet and debate in the Commons.

Meanwhile, Liddell Hart had waded in with memoranda to Hore-Belisha declaring that "we are blind if we cannot see that we are committed to the defence of Czechoslovakia" since France's "military situation largely turns on the existence of a Czechoslovakian distraction to Germany's power of concentration in the West. . . ." But Liddell Hart coupled this verdict with the corollary that "the key to the military situation does not lie there but in Spain." German-Italian domination of Spain "would place heavy odds against the success of

---

* In his postwar memoirs (vol. 3, p. 238), Amery confesses that he was then uncertain whether Czechoslovakia could be effectively aided, or whether it would be wiser to let Germany move eastward.

Britain and France in a war with these powers. . . . A friendly Spain is desirable, a neutral Spain is vital."*

At the Cabinet meeting on March 16, Hore-Belisha (stimulated by a talk with the Duchess of Atholl) treated his colleagues to Liddell Hart's views, put forward as his own, and added a proposal that France should not be discouraged from intervening in support of the Spanish Government. This, of course, was directly contrary to the policy Eden and Halifax had been pursuing since the beginning of the Civil War, and Halifax stiffly retorted that "in an era of power politics" Britain should look to her own arms and not encourage the French to take the offensive. Hankey telephoned Pownall to ask whether Hore-Belisha "was reflecting the General Staff opinion," and was assured that "he was *not.*" Pownall, whose opinion of his minister was nearing rock bottom, recorded with evident pleasure that "H-B made a chump of himself" and "knows that he dropped a brick and that his colleagues don't think much of him over the incident"—accurate, no doubt, but it is ironic that Halifax, Sargent, and Phipps were heaping scorn on Paul-Boncour as "a disaster" with "a mad hankering after intervention in Spain" at the same time that Britain's War Secretary, and her most eminent military critic-journalist, were expressing comparable anxieties.

In the Commons that evening, the Opposition moved to condemn the "lack of any ministerial policy to counter a grave menace to British interests arising out of the armed intervention in Spain by certain foreign powers." The Labour and Liberal spokesmen were joined by a few from the Government benches,† but Chamberlain calmly declared: "We intend to continue in the future as we have in the past," and on the division the Government was upheld by the usual Party majority.

And so the effort to excise the Czech cancer by pricking the Spanish boil failed in London, as it had failed the previous day in Paris. By mid-March 1938, Franco was so close to victory that a reversal of nonintervention would probably have been ineffectual. Yet there was much force in Liddell Hart's argument that, by virtue of France's geographical adjacency and Anglo-French naval superiority, the two democracies were in a much better strategic position than the dictatorships to determine the outcome in Spain and to protect Allied control of the Strait of Gibraltar and use of the Mediterranean sea-lanes.

While the military staffs and Foreign Office officials were busy preparing their memoranda, there was a considerable inflow of information and exhortation from abroad. In Paris, Paul-Boncour was pressing Phipps for a British commitment to "stand by France" in the event of war over Czechoslovakia. From

---

* Since 1936, Liddell Hart had been preaching this doctrine, but *The Times,* strongly supporting nonintervention, had been unwilling to publish his views for fear of antagonizing Germany and Italy. Liddell Hart found that "Whitehall circles were very largely pro-Franco . . . and that was particularly marked at the Admiralty."

† Notably Harold Nicolson, who urged the House to focus on the military effect of a Franco victory "upon British interests and the security of this country." His diary records: "When I sit down, the Prime Minister passes along a message through Kingsley Wood asking, 'What do you want us to do?' I say, 'Occupy Minorca.' . . . 'Occupy Minorca,' whispers David Margesson (the Conservative Chief Whip) to Chamberlain. The latter flings back his head with a gesture of angered despair."

Prague came a dispatch from Minister Basil Newton gloomily predicting that Czechoslovakia would be "the next item" on the Nazis' program, and that "no scruples will deter them from pursuing their aims by fair means or foul." The Czech Government was counting on France and "early, if not immediate, British support," and if the British Government indeed proposed to support Czech independence, "the sooner Germany can be convinced that if she tried to intimidate Czechoslovakia, she will be barking up the wrong tree, the better." But Newton had "misgivings" about such a policy, since it was doubtful that such warnings would deter the Germans, and if war came "nothing that we or France could do would save Czechoslovakia from being overrun, and all we could hope to achieve would be to restore after a lengthy struggle a *status quo* which . . . would probably again prove unworkable." Czechoslovakia's political position was "not permanently tenable," and it would be best for her "to adjust her position to the circumstances of post-war Europe while she can still do so in more favorable conditions than will obtain later." Newton's words were soon to find echo in the highest circles of the Chamberlain government.

On March 17, Ambassador Maisky transmitted to Halifax Litvinov's statement condemning *Anschluss* as an act of aggression and "a menace to Czechoslovakia," and proposing "collective actions" by "all the States and especially the Great Powers" to protect world peace. This offer was generally in line with Churchill's concept of a "grand alliance" (though Churchill had not mentioned the Soviet Union as a participant), and at least called for a considered reply from those who were formulating British policy.

The Foreign Office studies, however, had already been completed, and in the event Litvinov's *démarche* got little attention in London. Neither did Paul-Boncour's adjurations; Halifax told Corbin that a consultation between the two governments "might be useful," but in fact he had no interest in such a meeting with the "disastrous" Foreign Minister of the rickety Blum government, and the British proceeded to their decision without any consultation with their French ally, whose interests were so nearly affected.

By March 16, Sir Alexander Cadogan had in hand memoranda from three* of his subordinates. These were the work of Sir Orme Sargent, Assistant Under-Secretary (and Cadogan's successor in 1946 as Permanent Under-Secretary); William Strang, head of the Central Department (and Sargent's successor in 1949); and Gladwyn Jebb, Cadogan's private secretary (and his successor in 1950 as Representative to the United Nations). These papers are noteworthy both for their diversity of outlook—the Sargent and Jebb efforts were almost antithetical—and for their high professional quality.†

Sir Orme Sargent, known as "Moley" to his colleagues, saw Hitler's Germany through Vansittart lenses. *Anschluss* was the first step in Germany's "policy of

---

* A fourth paper from Sir William Malkin, Legal Adviser to the Foreign Office, dealt with the juridical aspects of the Czech situation.

† The memoranda are in the Foreign Office records and are extensively quoted and ably analyzed in an unpublished student thesis by David R. Markham, *The Foreign Office and the Search for Peace* (Cornell University, 1973). They are discussed in Cadogan's diary entries for March 15 and 16, 1938, and in *The Memoirs of Lord Gladwyn* (1972), pp. 73–76. Sargent left no memoirs, and Strang's do not mention them.

expansion beyond her present borders" that would lead to the dismemberment of Czechoslovakia, dissolution of the Little Entente, severance of French and Russian ties with those countries, and the reduction of "all the weak and disorganized countries of the Danubian basin . . . to a position, both politically and economically, of vassal states." In consequence: ". . . if we and the French do nothing . . . the whole of Central Europe will be lost to us and France. In any future war not only will they not be allies but they won't even be neutral." Italy had been much weakened by the end of Austrian independence, and if an Anglo-Italian treaty were to be achieved, "when it comes to choosing between Germany or Great Britain, she is bound to consider Germany as the stronger power so far as she is concerned. . . ." Sargent did not explicitly propose a British commitment to France, but in conclusion recommended staff talks with France and Belgium; development of a "common policy" with France vis-à-vis Czechoslovakia, the other Danubian states, and Spain; and a broad diplomatic campaign to restore good relations with Japan and "cultivate" Poland, Russia, and "above all" the United States.

Where Sargent was afraid of the consequences of "doing nothing" about Czechoslovakia, Jebb described "the suggestion that we and the French alone should fly to the rescue of the Czechs" as "resembling suicide." Jebb's assessment of the Italian situation was directly contrary to Sargent's; *Anschluss* had "shaken the Axis," and Mussolini would be casting about for support against the German giant peering over the Brenner Pass. The solution for Britain and France was to countenance a Franco victory in Spain, recognize the Italian conquest of Ethiopia, enter into "a tacit understanding that we would *not* support Czechoslovakia," and guarantee the Brenner border between Italy and Germany.

Strang's study, which leaned heavily on Newton's dispatch, was the most comprehensive and measured of the three, and made much the deepest impression on Cadogan and Halifax. At the outset he raised a key question: the prospective attitude of the British public toward a German-Czech conflict over the Sudetenland. After all, the inhabitants of the Sudetenland were *German,* just as the Austrians and Rhinelanders were German, and self-determination was an appealing principle. It would be hard enough to persuade the average Briton to go to war to prevent Hitler from bringing all Germans within the Reich—i.e., if he were only a pan-German, and not a latter-day Napoleon. It would be quite impossible if there were credible evidence that the Czechs were abusing the German minority. Therefore, "if we are to work for the prevention of further untoward events in Central Europe, we must convince the Czechoslovak Government that they must satisfy His Majesty's Government and British public opinion not only that the Sudeten Germans enjoy the treatment to which they are entitled, but also such treatment as will leave the German Government with no reasonable cause for complaint." This could best be accomplished by "a neutral Commission, with powers to observe and report upon the situation of the German minority in Czechoslovakia."

Assuming that a sound psychological and moral basis was thus laid, would a British commitment "whether undertaken directly to Czechoslovakia, or indirectly to Czechoslovakia in the form of an undertaking to France" furnish "an effective deterrent to German action"? Perhaps so, but on the other hand it might increase the chances of war by provoking Hitler with what would appear as a direct challenge, or by encouraging the French and Czechs to actions which they might otherwise not dare to take.

Would it "be prudent in the present state of our military preparations to undertake any new commitment"? The Prime Minister had put that question to the Chiefs of Staff, but their answering report had not yet been rendered, and in formulating policy "full regard" must be paid to what they would say.

Leaving these vital questions spotlighted but unanswered, Strang proceeded to consider the three possible courses of action which he envisaged. The first was Winston Churchill's "Grand Alliance," which Strang rejected:

> This is an attractive proposal . . . but there is one decisive objection against it for our present purposes. In order to achieve it, it would be necessary to draw up a formal instrument in treaty form, and this would be a long and complicated matter. . . . The long and difficult negotiations which would be necessary to conclude the Grand Alliance would afford both a provocation and an opportunity to Germany to dispose of Czechoslovakia before the Grand Alliance had been organized.

The second policy was, essentially, the new commitment for which the French were asking: ". . . to assist France against Germany if her territory were attacked by Germany as a result of France fulfilling her treaty obligations to Czechoslovakia." Unlike the first, this could be done at once but, if extended unconditionally, would subject Britain to France's decision on the crucial issue of peace or war. Strang proposed, accordingly, that:

> if any undertaking of this kind is considered, our assistance to France should be subject to two conditions:
>   (i) that the Czechoslovak Government had satisfied us of their treatment of the Sudetendeutschen; and
>   (ii) that the French Government had sought our approval before going to the aid of Czechoslovakia.

The policy would be initiated by establishing a "Commission of Enquiry" either British or international in its composition (possible to be headed by Mr. Herbert Hoover) to investigate and publish a report on Sudetenland conditions, following which Britain would guarantee that:

>   (i) if we are in agreement with the Commission's report and recommendations, and satisfied that Czechoslovakia is complying with them;
>   (ii) if Germany uses force against Czechoslovakia to secure settlement of the Sudetendeutsch question; and
>   (iii) if, after consulting with and securing the approval of His Majesty's Government, France goes to the assistance of Czechoslovakia . . . and if in the ensuing war France's territory is threatened or attacked by Germany . . . then His Majesty's Government will give immediate assistance and support to France in defence of her territory.

It will be observed that, *as so worded,* this was no "guarantee" at all, for Britain was not bound to accept a Commission report favorable to Czechoslovakia unless she was "in agreement" and, even if so agreed, was under no obligation to support France unless she had given "approval" of French intervention. It is hard to believe that so experienced a diplomat as Strang would unintentionally have left such holes. Nevertheless, he appears to have thought that this second policy involved a real commitment, as his third proposal reveals:

> The third alternative course before us is a negative one, and is not advanced on its own positive merits, but rather on the strength of the objections to other alternative courses. It is briefly that we should decline to undertake any fresh commitment in regard to Czechoslovakia; that we should, on the contrary, try to persuade France and Czechoslovakia that the best course would be for the latter to make the best terms she can with Germany while she can perhaps still do so in more favorable conditions than would obtain later; that we should do our best to reach an agreement with Italy sufficiently attractive to her to induce her in the long run to abandon the "axis"; that we should perhaps confine ourselves to reaffirming the guarantees we have already given France in the Locarno Treaty to go to her assistance in the event of an unprovoked act of aggression by Germany.

This was, essentially, a combination of Newton on Czechoslovakia and Jebb on Italy—minus the latter's notion of giving Italy a guarantee of her border with Germany. Strang did not explicitly choose between the second and third alternatives, except by his indication that the only basis for the third was an assumption that Britain was too weak to do anything else. As we will see, the third alternative corresponded closely to the policy that the Government was soon to adopt.

In concluding, Strang discussed without deciding the very pertinent question whether, granting Britain's military unreadiness, "Germany's superiority in arms may be greater a year or two hence than it is now." Strang agreed that this "may well be true," but replied that "this is not a good argument for risking disaster now." The force of the point rested on the assumption that "unless we make a stand now, Germany will march uninterruptedly to hegemony in Europe," but such a conclusion "may well be based upon a more confident prediction of future events than the experience of history will support." To be sure, the future looked "black," but "at least there is an element of uncertainty in our diagnosis, and on the strength of that uncertainty we might at least refrain from the more hazardous course." On the other hand, it could well be argued that Germany's looming domination of Central Europe would isolate Britain and France and further discredit free institutions, wherefore "the two great democracies must rally their forces and make a stand at an early date before the situation deteriorates still further, and the obvious point to make a stand is over the continued independence of Czechoslovakia."

On the evening of March 16, Sir Alexander Cadogan sat down with these essays and started work on his own memorandum. He had made up his mind even before reading what his subordinates had written, and had probably known what to expect from each of them. This fastidious, reserved gentleman, prudent in his views and public expressions, revealed in his diary a much more passionate and hasty temperament, not always free from self-dramatization. On March 12 he had written:

> We are helpless as regards Austria—that is finished. We *may* be helpless as regards Czechoslovakia, etc. *That* is what I want to get considered. Must we have a death-struggle with Germany again? Or can we stand aside? Former does no one any good. Will latter be fatal? I'm inclined to think not. But I shall have to fight Van, Sargent and all the forces of evil. God give me courage. So far we've not done wrong.

On the fourteenth, Cadogan had a short discussion with Chamberlain and Halifax, finding them "rather on the line of Winston's 'Grand Alliance,'" which was not to Cadogan's liking. Reviewing the staff papers on the sixteenth, Cadogan described Sargent's as "his usual black picture" and Strang's as "more business-like," rightly concluded that Jebb's proposal to guarantee Italy's Brenner frontier "doesn't make sense," and finally "came down against a guarantee to Cz[echoslovakia]."

Cadogan's paper embodied three basic reasons for coming to this decision. The first was that, as a moral-political matter, Britain *should* not go to war to preserve Czech sovereignty over the Sudetenland. The Versailles ban on *Anschluss* had not been "inspired by any lofty altruistic motive" but "was aimed simply against the aggrandizement of Germany." Austrians were "at least Germanic," and many of them wanted *Anschluss*. And "the same *may* be said of the Sudetendeutsch." In any event, if Hitler wanted to incorporate them into the Reich, that "would not be an issue on which we should be on very strong grounds for plunging Europe into war."

If that was so, the case for supporting Czech territorial integrity must depend, not on the Sudetenland, but on what Hitler might do *after* annexing it, and Cadogan's second reason was the uncertainty that Hitler would do anything particularly harmful. Mere *economic* domination of Central Europe by Germany did not much trouble him: "Why should we wish to monopolize the Danubian market? And if Germany proves herself capable of developing this market, why should we (who have others) try to prevent her?" *Political* domination Germany might find difficult to achieve: "Do we really see Czechs, Hungarians, Rumanians, Greeks, Yugoslavs, and Turks united in crusade against the French?"

The third reason was that war was intrinsically useless:*

> On the whole, I certainly feel that it would be very difficult to choose any course of action that might plunge Europe into war now to avert what might be a war later on. To judge by our experience of the last twenty years, war solves nothing, and it, or rather the peace, having brought us to this pass. War now would wreck civilization almost as effectively as war two, three, or four years hence.

Recognizing, however, that Sargent's prediction of Germany's future course might prove correct, Cadogan stated the issue thus: "Shall we risk war now,

---

* Cadogan had remained at the Foreign Office during the First World War. Like Chamberlain, therefore, he lacked the bond of war experience which was felt by many of their contemporaries.

when the prospects are not too bad, or shall we put it off until our prospects, maybe, will be worse, but with the hope that in the meanwhile, 'something will turn up'?" His answer was that, "unless the C.O.S. can give us a much more reassuring report than I expect," Strang's third alternative should be adopted: no new commitment in regard to Czechoslovakia, an effort to reach an agreement with Italy,* and rearmament with priority to the air arm. "Things do change," he wrote in conclusion. "If we stand aside from Central Europe, we and the French may lose face, but the reverse may steel us to efforts that may make good some of our present deficiencies."

In his diary entry for March 16, Cadogan gave what amounted to a fourth reason for the no-new-commitment policy:

> I shall be called "cowardly" but after days and nights of thinking, I have come to the conclusion that it is the least bad. We *must* not precipitate a conflict now—we shall be smashed. It *may* not be better later, but anything may happen (I recognise the Micawber strain). . . . That is the policy of the line of least resistance, which the Cabinet will probably take. But I am convinced it is the lesser evil. Strang in his heart approves. . . .

Of course, if it was not a question of balancing risks now and later, but of certain defeat now, postponement was the only reasonable answer. But did war now mean certain defeat, or (what some might regard as just as bad) a terrible rain of death and destruction from German bombers over Britain? Or were these groundless fears?

The Foreign Policy Committee met on March 18 for what was to prove the crucial discussion. Halifax had circulated over his name a memorandum which embodied verbatim most of Strang's paper, and which the Foreign Secretary said was intended as a basis for discussion and formulation of the statement which the Prime Minister would present in the Commons the following week.

The discussion opened with Inskip's inquiry whether Germany would be satisfied with "taking over" the Sudetenland, or wished to "absorb" all of Czechoslovakia. Chamberlain replied that Hitler's policy was "to include all Germans in the Reich but not to include other nationalities," and cited Newton's dispatch for the prediction that "Germany would absorb the Sudeten German territory and reduce the rest of Czechoslovakia to a condition of dependent neutrality." Apparently alarmed by this turn of the conversation, Hankey broke in to remind the ministers that Czechoslovakia was an economic unit which would be destroyed by severance of the Sudetenland. But Inskip then cited Newton's description of Czechoslovakia as an "unstable unit," and declared that "he could see no reason why we should take any steps to maintain such a unit in being." Hankey produced another "reminder," that the German-Czech frontier was two hundred years old, and that the Sudeten Germans were immigrants. With Hankey getting much the better of this exchange, Chamberlain changed

---

* Cadogan criticized Jebb's proposed methods for drawing in Italy as "too crude," and was especially scathing of the Brenner guarantee notion: ". . . I cannot see Signor Mussolini accepting a guarantee of the Brenner Frontier. He would (and must) say he doesn't want it. We really can't suggest it: if two wayfarers are fallen upon by two highwaymen, it really is not much good for the two former offering to the two latter to guarantee the one against the other."

the subject by criticizing Strang's second alternative (conditional commitment to France) on the ground that it proposed action without any prior consultation with Germany, and declaring his agreement with Halifax "that on any such basis Germany would be certain to oppose the whole scheme." Malcolm Mac-Donald chimed in with a warning that the conditional commitment might involve Britain in a war which would cause the Commonwealth to "break in pieces," since "South Africa and Canada would see no reason whatever why they should join in a war to prevent certain Germans from rejoining their fatherland."

The tide of opinion continued to run strongly against any new commitment. Halifax, acknowledging that "we could not in our own interests afford to see France overrun," preferred to continue "the existing scheme of things," which "had the great advantage that we were able to keep both France and Germany guessing as to what our attitude in any particular crisis would be, and no doubt this in itself had a restraining effect both upon France and upon Germany." Inskip referred to the forthcoming Chiefs of Staff report and declared it to be "certain that Germany could overrun the whole of Czechoslovakia in less than a week." Hailsham thought a new commitment might cause Germany to "hasten on an attack" against Czechoslovakia or against Hungary and Rumania. Ormsby-Gore pronounced the commitment "a bad and dangerous one." Simon endorsed Newton's view that, even if Britain were victorious over Germany, there would be no reason to re-establish Czechoslovakia, which was a "very artificial creation with no roots in the past."

Only Oliver Stanley spoke in favor of the commitment, and even he was critical of the "very elaborate machinery" (referring to the proposed Commission of Enquiry) which Strang had conceived to protect Britain against being pulled into war against her will. He was immediately countered by Chamberlain and Halifax, and he drew no outright support from other ministers, though Hoare and MacDonald were ambivalent.

Toward the end of the meeting, Halifax and then Chamberlain came out categorically against the commitment. The Foreign Secretary relied primarily on arguments drawn from Newton and Strang, while the Prime Minister stressed the military factors. No "effective help could be swiftly brought to Czechoslovakia," and therefore "all we could do would be to make war on Germany, but we were in no position from the armament point of view to enter such a war and in his opinion it would be most dangerous for us to do so." Halifax then summed up, saying:

> . . . that the discussion pointed on the whole to the conclusion that we must decline to undertake any fresh commitment in regard to Czechoslovakia and that we must try and persuade Dr. Benes and also the French Government that the best course would be for Czechoslovakia to make the best terms she could with Germany while at the same time impressing on the French Government the imperative necessity in the general interest of arriving at some amicable and permanent settlement.

From this there was no dissent, though Stanley and MacDonald continued to talk vaguely about some "reassurance" to France. The Foreign Policy Committee took no formal action and adjourned to meet again on March 21, by which time it was expected that the Chiefs of Staff report would be available.

Returning from the meeting, Halifax told Cadogan that the committee had been "unanimous that Czechoslovakia is not worth the bones of a single British Grenadier,"* which was both inaccurate (since the committee had *not* been unanimous to any such effect even figuratively) and cynical. Cadogan's diary comment—"And they're quite right too"—was superficial as well, since it overlooked the possibility that Czechoslovakia might save a number of British Grenadiers from premature deposit in the ossuary.

The day before the scheduled meeting, Neville Chamberlain wrote a long letter to his sister Ida, which shows more clearly than the official records the considerations which had led him to his conclusion:

> . . . with Franco winning in Spain by the aid of German guns and Italian planes, with a French government in which one cannot have the slightest confidence and which I suspect to be in closish touch with our Opposition, with the Russians stealthily and cunningly pulling all the strings behind the scenes to get us involved in war with Germany (our Secret Service doesn't spend all its time looking out of the window), and finally with a Germany flushed with triumph, and all too conscious of her power, the prospect looked black indeed. In face of such problems, to be badgered and pressed to come out and give a clear, decided, bold, and unmistakable lead, show "ordinary courage," and all the rest of the twaddle, is calculated to vex the man who has to take the responsibility for the consequences. As a matter of fact, the plan of the "Grand Alliance," as Winston calls it, had occurred to me long before he mentioned it. . . . I talked about it to Halifax, and we submitted it to the chiefs of the Staff and the F.O. experts. It is a very attractive idea; indeed, there is almost everything to be said for it until you come to examine its practicability. From that moment its attraction vanishes. You have only to look at the map to see that nothing that France or we could do could possibly save Czechoslovakia from being overrun by the Germans, if they wanted to do it. The Austrian frontier is practically open; the great Skoda munition works are within easy bombing distance of the German aerodromes, the railways all pass through German territory, Russia is 100 miles away. Therefore we could not help Czechoslovakia—she would simply be a pretext for going to war with Germany. That we could not think of unless we had a reasonable prospect of being able to beat her to her knees in a reasonable time, and of that I see no sign. I have therefore abandoned any idea of giving guarantees to Czechoslovakia, or the French in connection with her obligations to that country.

It is noteworthy that Chamberlain's reason for rejecting the Grand Alliance was essentially military, and quite different from Strang's objection, which was the slow pace of treaty-making. Even more interesting is an ensuing portion of the letter, with its harbinger of a direct approach to Hitler in which Chamberlain imagined himself saying to the Fuehrer:

---

* Halifax's phrase was an amalgamated adaptation of Bismarck speaking of the Balkans —"They are not worth the healthy bones of a single Pomeranian musketeer"—and Frederick the Great—"No work of art is worth the bones of a Pomeranian grenadier."

"We can't go on talking about colonies . . . everyone is thinking that you are going to repeat the Austrian coup in Czechoslovakia. I know you say you aren't, but nobody believes you. The best thing you can do is tell us exactly what you want for your Sudeten Germans. If it is reasonable we will urge the Czechs to accept and if they do, you must give assurances that you will let them alone in the future." I am not sure that in such circumstances I might not be willing to join in some joint guarantee with Germany of Czech independence.

No joint guarantee with France, but perhaps one with Germany! It was not only an extraordinary reversal, but given the assumptions that the Sudetenland was separable and that Hitler would be satisfied, it was not illogical, and certainly riskless and face-saving. Britain's Man of Decision had decided what British policy with regard to Czechoslovakia would be. The road to that decision can be traced, right through the documents, from Newton to Strang to Cadogan to Halifax to Chamberlain, and virtually every British move in the oncoming Czech crisis is explicable and, indeed, inevitable in the context of the committee meeting of March 18 and Chamberlain's letter to his sister Ida.

The next day, Monday March 21, the Chiefs of Staff submitted their report on "Military Implications of German Aggression Against Czechoslovakia." "It is in this report by the Chiefs of Staff," writes Commander Kemp, "that we find the true background to Munich."* However, the Prime Minister and the Foreign Policy Committee had arrived at their decision before the report was received. Too much should not be made of this, for no doubt the ministers had a pretty good idea of what the report would be like. Nevertheless, it would be fair to say that the report itself played no part in the process of developing the policy, and served primarily as an instrument for persuading or cowing the doubters.

Despite its anticlimactic appearance, the report is well worth a reading. Not its least interesting feature was its scope, as fixed by the questions which Chamberlain had put to the chiefs in the following "hypothetical alternatives":

(a) That this country should concert with France, Czechoslovakia, Yugoslavia, Roumania, Hungary, Turkey, Greece, or any of them, an undertaking to resist by force any attempt by Germany to impose a forcible solution of the Czechoslovak problem.

(b) That this country should give an assurance to the French Government that, in the event of the French Government being compelled to fulfill their obligations to Czechoslovakia, consequent upon an act of aggression by Germany, the United Kingdom would at once lend its support to the French Government.

The assumption in both cases to be that Italy is at the best neutral, and possibly hostile; that there is considerable risk of Japan being hostile; that the following are neutral: Russia, Poland, Belgium, Holland, Denmark; that the U.S.A. Neutrality Act is in operation at the outset; and that the arrangement in either case would begin to operate at once.

* P. K. Kemp, *Key to Victory—The Triumph of British Sea Power in World War II* (1957), p. 26. The report was signed by Gort, Newall, and the Deputy Chief of Naval Staff, Admiral W. M. James.

The assumption in the second case to be that at the outset the following are neutral: Roumania, Yugoslavia, Hungary, Turkey, Greece.

The division of countries between those in the "concert" of the first alternative and those assumed neutral is curious, to say the least. Soviet Russia was the only country, other than France, bound by treaty to assist Czechoslovakia against Germany; she was one of the great powers, militarily more significant than all the small countries in the concert combined. Poland was tied to France in defensive alliance, and was militarily far stronger than any of the lesser countries in the concert except, perhaps, Czechoslovakia herself. Yet both Russia and Poland were assumed neutral. To be sure, there were geographical obstacles to Soviet aid to Czechoslovakia, but that was likewise true of Britain and France. So, too, Poland and Czechoslovakia were on bad terms, but would Poland stand aside if France were threatened with destruction? In this respect her situation was not unlike Britain's, for in each case the long-range hazards of a French defeat by Germany might be fatal. And, if the uncertainties regarding effective Russian or Polish participation in the "concert" were deemed such as to require their exclusion, what is to be said of the inclusion of Hungary—a defeated and *revanchiste* amputee of the First World War, *against* whom the Little Entente was directed?

The result of these terms of reference was that the Chiefs' report was written as if Russia, Poland, and the other "neutral" powers did not exist. So, too, it took no account of the possibility of a German attack through the Low Countries, which of course would have ended Belgian and perhaps Dutch neutrality. And the further result was that the "concert" contributed nothing of significance to the forces hypothetically arrayed, for Hungary was disaffected and ready to strike at Rumania, Yugoslavia (recently in *rapprochement* with Italy) had made it clear that to her the Little Entente was nothing but a protective league against Hungary, while Greece and Turkey were remote and irrelevant except in the event of Italian intervention. It is hard to believe that Chamberlain's questions to the Chiefs were not framed to garner ammunition to discredit rather than to examine objectively Churchill's Grand Alliance,* and indeed without Russia or Poland there was nothing "grand" about it.

As a military matter, accordingly, there was not much difference between the two "alternatives," and most of the comparisons and conclusions in the report applied equally to both. About one third of the sixteen pages comprised a quantitative comparison of the naval, air, and ground strengths of the "concert" as compared to those of Germany, Italy, and Japan. These, of course, showed naval superiority with the former and air superiority with the latter; the ground forces tabulations showed an enormous numerical superiority for the "concert," but the effectiveness of most of the Central European divisions was rightly discounted. Major emphasis was on the air components, and the key comment

* Churchill had laid himself open to this sort of destructive analysis by suggesting the Little Entente as the equivalent of a "Great Power," and mentioning the same countries (plus Bulgaria and minus Greece) that were included with the "concert" of Chamberlain's first alternative.

31. Sir Horace Wilson (center) with Italian Ambassador Dino Grandi (left). *National Archives.*

32. Colonel Józef Beck, Polish Foreign Minister 1932–39 (center). *National Archives.*

33. Kurt von Schuschnigg, Chancellor of Austria 1934–38. *National Archives*.

34. General Maurice Gustave Gamelin, Chief of the Army General Staff 1931–40. *National Archives*.

35. Georges Bonnet, French Foreign Minister 1938–39 (left), with Maxim Litvinov at Geneva. *National Archives*.

36. Anthony Eden, Foreign Secretary 1935–38. *National Archives.*

37. Jan Masaryk, Czech Minister to Great Britain 1925–38. *National Archives.*

38. Joseph P. Kennedy,
Ambassador to the Court of
St. James, 1937–40.
National Archives.

39. Lord Runciman, left,
and President Eduard Beneš,
at a meeting in Prague,
August 1938. *Keystone.*

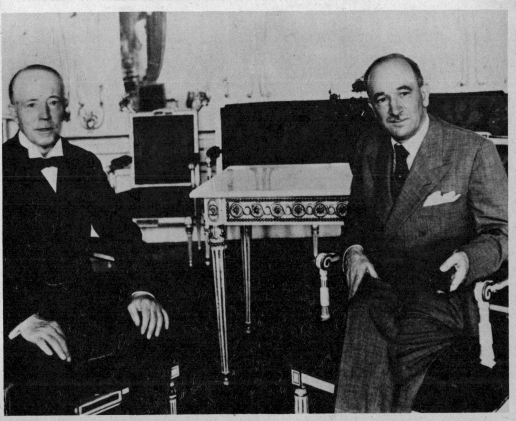

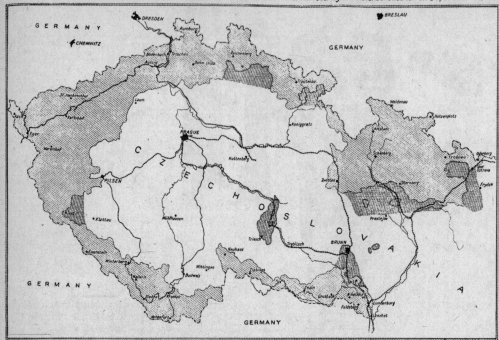

Sketch Map based on the Map annexed to the Agreement signed at Munich on September 29, 1938.

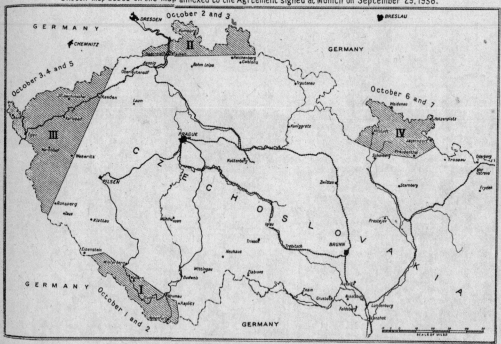

40. The maps included in the British White Paper presented in Parliament October 3, 1938.

41. October 1, 1938—troops of the 61st Infantry Regiment, 7th Division, crossing the Czech border at Klein–Philippsreuth, north of Passau. *Bundesarchiv.*

42. October 3, 1938—Hitler crosses the Czech border at Wildenau, just south of Asch at the western tip of Bohemia. The officer at far left, facing the camera, is General Wilhelm Keitel, Chief of the OKW. *Bundesarchiv.*

was that the RAF "cannot at the present time be said to be in any way fit to undertake operations on a major war scale."

Projecting these comparisons into possible Allied operations, the report found that Germany could be subjected to economic pressure by naval blockade, but that "this would not become effective for a long time," and therefore would not be an effective deterrent if the Germans thought they could achieve a quick victory. Neither by land nor by air could Germany be seriously hurt, and therefore:

> . . . no military pressure we can exact by sea, or land or in the air can prevent Germany either from invading and overrunning Bohemia or inflicting a decisive defeat on the Czechoslovakian Army. If politically it is deemed necessary to restore Czechoslovakia's lost integrity, this aim will entail war with Germany, and her defeat may mean a prolonged struggle. In short, we can do nothing to prevent the dog getting the bone, and we have no means of making him give it up, except by killing him by a slow process of attrition and starvation."*

The Chiefs then speculated on the course of German operations following the conquest of Czechoslovakia, which was treated as certain and speedy. Although "the Maginot Line is an enigma," they doubted that Germany "would be able to break through the French frontier defenses." Accordingly, since "she cannot face the prospect of a long war with confidence," Germany might try to bring matters to a speedy conclusion by attempting a knockout blow from the air before Britain was given "a breathing space to muster our resources."

Would such an attack succeed? The Chiefs anticipated that "the scale of attack which Germany could direct upon us in April this year (1938) is unlikely to be less than 400 tons per day," and Britain's air defense preparations were "very far from complete." A gloomy prospect at best, with outcome uncertain:

> The outcome of unrestricted air attack on this country by Germany is impossible to forecast with any accuracy. All we can say is that we are not in a position to prevent them dropping bombs in this country on the scale suggested above, which we think they might be able to sustain for not less than two months.

The Chiefs then assessed the effects of Italian and Japanese participation on the side of Germany. Italy would bring "a powerful addition in armed forces" but was dependent on seaborne supplies of oil and other essentials, and with these cut off she might prove "an embarrassment to her ally." But Britain would be obliged to reinforce Egypt, and France to leave substantial forces in North Africa, thus causing a "considerable diversion of allied forces from the main theatre." The Chiefs' conclusion was that Italian support to Germany would "appreciably enhance" Axis prospects for "a rapid success."†

---

* A draft of the Chiefs' report in the Air Ministry files (Air 9/87, piece 2) displays, following this paragraph, a hand sketch of a defiant dog wearing a swastika waistband and clenching in his jaws a large bone.

† It is hard to see how this conclusion followed from the Chiefs' premise, which was that the knockout blow by air attack against Britain (to which Italy could not substantially contribute) was the most promising German route to a speedy victory.

As for Japan, her advent on the side of the enemy "would produce a situation which neither the present nor projected strength of our defence forces is designed to meet." The Empire would be simultaneously threatened in Europe, the Mediterranean, and the Far East, the fleet would have to be divided, and the British position in the Near East "would become critical." The military implications of such a situation would give rise to "the deepest misgivings."

In conclusion, the Chiefs repeated that nothing could be done to protect Czechoslovakia from defeat and dismemberment, and added a prediction—diplomatic rather than military—that in the event of war "both Italy and Japan would seize the opportunity to further their own ends, and that in consequence the problem we have to envisage is not that of a limited European war only, but of a world war." The report ended with a thinly veiled plea for postponement of a confrontation, since presently Britain was "at a stage of rearmament when we are not yet ready for war."

Given the history of interchange between the Chiefs of Staff and the Cabinet ministers over the past several years, and the limits of the questions submitted by the Prime Minister, the conclusions in the report were virtually inevitable, and it is easy to see why Chamberlain and his colleagues felt no need to await the report before reaching their own conclusions. Year after year the Chiefs had pointed with alarm to the sorry state of British and the alarming growth of German arms, and year after year the Cabinet had replied by reducing their rearmament estimates. A few weeks earlier, on Chatfield's initiative, the Chiefs had renewed their warnings against "business as usual," only to be rebuffed again by the Chamberlain-Simon-Inskip combination. Against this background, it was not to be expected that the Chiefs, suddenly confronted with the possibility of war against Germany, and perhaps Italy and Japan as well, would react with anything other than dismay and revulsion. They may, indeed, have feared that any note of optimism in their report would undercut their pending requests for increased military appropriations.

If the conclusions of the report were expectable, however, they were likewise incomplete, for they did not deal with the military consequences of inaction. Especially since the stipulated Grand Alliance was too puny to count significantly in the scales of war, the two basic alternatives confronting Britain were to aid France and Czechoslovakia—and Russia if she honored her guarantee—against Germany, or to stand aside. Of course, Chamberlain had not asked the Chiefs for their views on the negative course, but surely any strategist worthy of the name would see that neither solution could be meaningfully assessed except in comparison with the other. How would Britain and France stand vis-à-vis Germany once Czechoslovakia, in a military sense, had been eliminated?

To be sure, it is possible, and even probable, that after focusing on this question the Chiefs would still have come down in favor of delay. Despite the bad state of ready armament in the spring of 1938, Britain's war potential was on the verge of big developments. The Navy was expanding and modernizing; the Army was beginning to get its antiaircraft weaponry; the RAF would sooner or later have fighters as good as and bombers better than anything the Germans could put into the skies, as well as a chain of radar defenses that would revolutionize aerial warfare. It was altogether natural that the military leaders would prefer to wait until the new tools were in hand.

But if natural it was quite wrong, with their country in the clutch of decision, to pass over these crucial issues in silence, and the Chiefs' report can hardly be regarded as a model of strategic analysis The military men were not, however, primarily to blame, but rather the ministers responsible for dictating the report's metes and bounds, and for bringing about the conditions under which it was written.

3

It remained only to frame the documents to put the no-commitment policy into effect, and the Foreign Policy Committee meeting of March 21 was largely devoted to Halifax's drafts of an aide-mémoire for the French Government, and the Prime Minister's forthcoming speech in the Commons. Stanley and Mac-Donald both thought the document for the French "cold and unsympathetic," a criticism with which Chamberlain expressed agreement. Various changes to "warm up" the memorandum and soften the blow were discussed; Halifax accepted many of them, though his anti-French bias was evident in his remark that "the French were never ready to face up to realities, they delighted in vain words and protestations." Stanley's efforts to develop the "warming" additions into a quasi-commitment were rebuffed by Halifax, who cited the Chiefs' report as showing "conclusively" that it "behooved us to take every step that we could and to use every argument that we could think of to dissuade France from going to the aid of Czechoslovakia." There was no dissent from the decision to reject the Soviet Union's proposal of an international conference.

On the next day, the program was submitted to the full Cabinet. It was presented by Halifax, who began by saying that he and the Prime Minister "had begun their examination with some sympathy towards the idea of a guarantee."* But the Chiefs' report, from which Halifax read the conclusory portions, was so "gloomy" that "whatever his sympathies and anxieties he felt he was not in a position to recommend a policy involving a risk of war." Rather France and Czechoslovakia should be persuaded that a settlement with Germany was essential. This would no doubt be "unpalatable" to the French, and "it was a disagreeable business which had to be done as pleasantly as possible." Chamberlain strongly supported these recommendations.

The leaders' proposals did not escape sharp criticism.† It was said that they were "tantamount to an invitation to Germany to take the next step in her programme"; that "we could not afford to stand aside and see France go under," and therefore it would be better "to recognize the inevitable and plunge

---

* Surprising as it is that Chamberlain had initially taken such a view, Halifax's statement is confirmed by Cadogan's diary for March 14 (quoted heretofore), as well as by Geoffrey Dawson's diary for March 21, recording that Chamberlain "said he had come clear around from Winston's idea of a Grand Alliance to a policy of diplomatic action and no fresh commitments."

† The Cabinet minutes covering the discussion of Halifax's presentation are in summary narrative form, and do not disclose the identity of the individual speakers. It may be assumed that the dissenting voices were those of Stanley and MacDonald, with some support from Duff Cooper and perhaps Swinton.

in at once to France's aid"; that the Chiefs of Staff had been "instructed to leave Russia out of the calculation" and "had not dealt with the prospective situation a year or two hence when the smaller nations of Central and Eastern Europe might all have collapsed before German aggression"; that "disadvantageous as might be the circumstances today for intervention, they would be still more so tomorrow."

Despite all these considerations, according to the minutes "the view that was accepted more generally and increasingly as the discussion continued was that the policy proposed by the Foreign Secretary and supported by the Prime Minister was the best available in the circumstances." The majority thought that "the people" were opposed to any new commitment, and expressions by "important representatives of the City of London" were "mentioned in this connection." The Dominions, except New Zealand, were likewise hostile to hazarding war. As for "the position two years hence," at least the RAF and the antiaircraft ground defenses would be in better shape. All in all, Chamberlain concluded: "It would be a mistake to plunge into certain catastrophe in order to avoid a future danger that might never materialize."

And so it was decided.* The Cabinet then turned to rearmament and put an end to the rule of noninterference with normal trade—the sole positive step taken in immediate consequence of *Anschluss*.

Later that day Halifax forewarned Ambassador Corbin that there would probably not be any commitment to aid France, but sugared the pill by observing that, in the event of war, it was likely that Britain would be drawn in "both on account of our own vital interests and of our attachment to France." And this was the essential content of the British aide-mémoire which reached Phipps on March 23, and was presented by him to Paul-Boncour the following morning. By then it was, of course, too late for the French to exert any influence on the decision, since Chamberlain was to make it public in his speech to the Commons that afternoon. The Russians were treated even more summarily in a letter, dated March 24, from Halifax to Maisky, which rejected Litvinov's proposed international conference on the ground that it was "designed less to secure the settlement of outstanding problems than to organize concerted action against aggression," a purpose which "would not necessarily, in the view of His Majesty's Government, have such a favorable effect upon the prospects of European peace."

In his speech in the Commons, Chamberlain was even sharper: "His Majesty's Government are of opinion that the indirect but none the less inevitable result of such action as is proposed by the Soviet Government would be to aggravate the tendency toward the establishment of exclusive groups of nations, which must . . . be inimical to the prospects of European peace." It is a measure of British antipathy toward the Soviet Union that, except for the Liberal leader Sir Archibald Sinclair, there was no criticism of the Government's decision to spurn Litvinov's bid for collaboration. Even Churchill, sponsor of the

---

* Harvey recorded Sir Orme Sargent's reaction to the decision: "He really feels all is lost. A mixture of utter contempt for the Government and profound anxiety as to the consequences."

Grand Alliance, ignored it, pointing again to the Little Entente and other small powers as the components.

Chamberlain's defense of the no-commitment policy was, in parliamentary and public terms, one of his most effective public utterances. A commitment to aid France if that country went to the defense of Czechoslovakia, he explained, would create a situation in which "the decision as to whether or not this country should find itself involved in war would be automatically removed from the discretion of His Majesty's Government. . . ."* British "vital interests were not concerned in the same degree as they are in the case of France and Belgium," and accordingly the loss of discretion was unacceptable. However, this did not mean that Britain would not intervene if the necessity arose:

> Where peace and war are concerned, legal obligations are not alone involved, and, if war broke out, it would be unlikely to be confined to those who have assumed such obligations. . . . The inexorable pressure of facts might well prove more powerful than formal pronouncements, and in that event it would be well within the bounds of probability that other countries, besides those which were parties to the original dispute, would almost immediately become involved. This is especially true in the case of two countries like Great Britain and France, with long associations of friendship, with interests closely interwoven, devoted to the same ideals of democratic liberty, and determined to uphold them.

In conclusion, Chamberlain declared that acceleration of rearmament was essential, as well as expansion of the program for the RAF and antiaircraft ground defenses. To this end, steps would be taken to ensure that rearmament work would "have first priority in the nation's effort."

Winston Churchill pronounced it a "very fine speech," and if it did not silence all the critics, it softened most of them. Churchill himself accepted the Prime Minister's arguments against an "automatic" commitment, but advocated a pledge of aid against a violent, unprovoked attack on Czechoslovakia, somewhat comparable to the conditional guarantee Strang had outlined in his memorandum. He was not satisfied with Chamberlain's statements on rearmament, and was thus moved to a magnificent peroration:

> . . . I have watched this famous island descending incontinently, fecklessly, the stairway which leads to a dark gulf. It is a fine broad stairway at the beginning, but after a bit the carpet ends. A little farther on there are only flagstones, and a little farther on still these break beneath your feet. . . . Look back upon the last five years—since, that is to say, Germany began to rearm in earnest and openly to seek revenge. If we study the history of Rome and Carthage, we can understand what happened and why. It is not difficult to form an intelligent view about the three Punic Wars; but if mortal catastrophe should overtake the British Nation and the British Empire, historians a thousand years hence will still be baffled by the mystery of our affairs. They will never understand how it was that a victorious nation, with everything in

---

* It is, of course, true of any defensive alliance that it may remove the parties' right to exercise discretion whether or not to become involved. The real reason for the no-commitment policy—that the Government *did not want* France to honor her treaty with Czechoslovakia, which a British commitment might encourage her to do—was not stated.

hand, suffered themselves to be brought low, and to cast away all that they had gained by measureless sacrifice and absolute victory—gone with the wind!

Now the victors are the vanquished, and those who threw down their arms in the field and sued for an armistice are striding on to world mastery. That is the position—that is the terrible transformation that has taken place bit by bit. I rejoice to hear from the Prime Minister that a further supreme effort is to be made to place us in a position of security. Now is the time at last to rouse the nation. Perhaps it is the last time it can be roused with a chance of preventing war, or with a chance of coming through to victory should our efforts to prevent war fail. We should lay aside every hindrance and endeavor by uniting the whole force and spirit of our people to raise again a great British nation standing up before all the world; for such a nation, rising in its ancient vigor, can even at this hour save civilization.

It was superb oratory, but the effect was fleeting. Chamberlain had no intention of "rousing the nation," and had succeeded in drawing most of the critics' sting. Harvey, no admirer of the Prime Minister, conceded that his "statement was not too bad and perhaps as much as could have been expected in view of the defence position." Another doubter, Duff Cooper, described Chamberlain's speech as "a great success," because "Without saying so definitely, he quite clearly implied that if France went to war we should go too. That was all that I wanted."

Press reaction was excellent; *The Times* of course was laudatory, the *Manchester Guardian* declared that "Mr. Chamberlain has overcome the enemies in his own camp," and in the *New Statesman,* J. M. Keynes urged the Czechs to negotiate a settlement with Germany. Chamberlain had achieved the effect he must have hoped for: most of his audience was either relieved that no commitment had been given, or pleased that the likelihood of British support of France, if war came, had been acknowledged. Neither Germany nor France had been told when or how the decision would be reached, so the "keep 'em guessing" tactic had been preserved. The Prime Minister had every reason to be gratified as he and Mrs. Chamberlain went off to join the Cadogans for a weekend party at Cliveden, where, according to the acidulous Permanent Under-Secretary, there was an "ordinary sort of crowd," and "the P.M." won the afterdinner game of musical chairs.

But the face which Chamberlain had thus put on British policy was a mask. The impression he had given was that the Government thought Germany and Czechoslovakia ought to reach a reasonable settlement; that in such a complex and remote situation, Britain would not bind herself by French decisions, but that if war came, she would, as a practical matter, have to join with France. This was not inaccurate so far as it went, but was misleadingly incomplete in that it did not reveal the Chamberlain-Halifax determination that the war situation *should not arise* over Czechoslovakia.* As Halifax had put it to his col-

---

* Duff Cooper recorded late in March that Hillaire Belloc, lunching wth him and friends, reported that Chamberlain had written a "poem" which went:

> Dear Czecho-Slovakia,
> I don't think they'll attack yer
> But I'm not going to back yer.

leagues on March 21, the vital thing was "to dissuade France from going to the aid of Czechoslovakia," and given that purpose any British commitment, no matter how conditional, would have been counterproductive.

Obviously the Blum-Paul-Boncour government was unlikely to be amenable to such dissuasion, and anyhow it was plainly doomed to a short life. It was devoutly to be hoped that their successors might be more receptive.

4

The lifting of the ban against interference with normal business, like the repeal of the Ten-Year Rule, removed a limitation on rearmament but did not constitute a new policy. How great a degree of "interference" would now be permissible? Would the rationing system be continued, and if so would the ration be enlarged?

It soon became apparent that, in the minds of the Prime Minister and the Chancellor of the Exchequer, the financial limits previously fixed should continue to be respected, and that acceleration rather than expansion was the end in view. The acceleration, furthermore, was to be accomplished by establishing production priorities for rearmament by voluntary rather than mandatory measures, and without creating a central procurement authority, such as a Ministry of Supply, which Churchill had been urging.

The armed services did, however, register some significant gains in the wake of *Anschluss*. But the second helpings were not evenly distributed among the three claimants, and as usual it was the Army that fared worst. Chiefly this was due to the Government's continuing opposition to a continental expeditionary force—an attitude which *Anschluss* seemed, if anything, to harden. On April 11 the CID concluded that military staff talks with the French were unnecessary because the possibility of sending an expeditionary force was so slight. Two days later the Cabinet decided that the French should be told "that they must not count on receiving a force of two divisions," and should base their plans on a negative assumption; the Prime Minister repeated Hore-Belisha's notion that this would spur them to complete the Maginot Line.

Within the accepted "role of the Army" there were, however, other tasks of greater moment, notably defense of British overseas territories and, as a first priority, ground defense (artillery, searchlights, barrage balloons, etc.) of Britain against air attack. This last was, of course, crucially important in surviving the feared knockout blow, and a generous governmental attitude toward such expenses might have been expected. Instead, when the War Office submitted an estimate of £347 million for the five-year period 1938–42, Simon and Inskip demanded a cut of £82 million, and only with difficulty were persuaded to accept a reduction by £70 million. This was accomplished by deep cuts in the amounts budgeted for Territorial Army equipment and for antiaircraft personnel and weaponry. The reduced estimate was approved by the Cabinet on April 27, but not without misgivings voiced by Hoare and other ministers, as well as less temperate objections confided by Pownall to his diary.

Whether or not the result would have been otherwise had Hore-Belisha been a different kind of man, the fact is that he did not fight for his estimates. Energetic and innovative as an administrator, he was unwilling or unable to stand up to his senior Cabinet colleagues, especially the Prime Minister; he would not "fight City Hall." Thus on April 9, informed of the Treasury's reduction of the Army's allocation, he wrote to Chamberlain that he had acquiesced "with a heavy heart," and invited attention to "the *extent* of our desire to cooperate."

After the "May crisis," there were signs that the question of a continental expeditionary force was being reconsidered. On June 17, *The Times* published an article by Liddell Hart, who had strongly influenced both Chamberlain and Hore-Belisha against such a force, noting "the increased tension in Europe" and predicting that it was likely to lead to a revision of the Government's policy. A British field force, Liddell Hart urged, should not be composed of the infantry divisions which Deverell and his predecessors had planned, but "a mechanized force" which would provide "a greater measure of insurance to France against the piercing of her defence."

By this time Liddell Hart's "partnership" with Hore-Belisha had been dissolved, and they rarely met. If the article made any impression on Hore-Belisha, it was not apparent from anything he did during the period before Munich. On August 30, when Chamberlain informed his colleagues of the gravity of the situation, Hore-Belisha reflected sadly that "all we could do at the outset would be to provide a force of two divisions which would be inadequately equipped for offensive operations. . . . We cannot at present put an army into the Field large enough to have any decisive effect."

Alfred Duff Cooper was quite a different sort of man, and had behind him the weight of the Senior Service. After *Anschluss* he restated his case for the New Naval Standard (a two-ocean navy, capable of offensive operations in both European and Far Eastern waters), and submitted a naval budget to 1942 of £435 million. Confronted in April with Treasury demand for an £80-million cut, Cooper replied in May with a memorandum attacking "the absurd new system of rationing the defence departments," and suggesting "that the sensible plan must be to ascertain your needs for defence first, and then enquire as to your means for meeting them." Simon prevented circulation of Cooper's paper to the Cabinet, and asked him to "put forward some proposal, as Hore-Belisha had done, whereby the money could be saved." The First Lord flatly refused, saying that if the Navy's mission was "to fight Germany and Japan," it simply could not be fulfilled within the Treasury allowance. A few days later, according to Cooper:

> My meeting with the P.M., Simon and Inskip . . . resulted in a long and profitless argument which at moments became, on the Prime Minister's side, rather acrimonious. I cannot help irritating him. The upshot was that the Chancellor [Simon] wrote me a letter asking for certain definite figures, which we are preparing for him. . . .

The May crisis then erupted, and it was not until July that the dispute came before the Cabinet. Inskip submitted a paper informing the members that the Admiralty had been offered a "ration" of £355 million, but that the First Lord had requested an additional £30 million to cover the approved naval program, and £50 million more if the New Standard was accepted. Inskip further explained that "the First Lord is now disposed to regard a system of rationing the Defence Departments as impossible to defend," adding that acceptance of that view would involve a reversal of policy, which was "not a good idea." The New Naval Standard had never been adopted by the Government, and he agreed with Duff Cooper that a decision on the size of the fleet was long overdue. He did not contest the Admiralty's estimate of its needs, but thought their program much too expensive. He recommended that the fleet should be "substantially less" than as envisaged in the New Naval Standard, and suggested a reduction in the number of capital ships to be laid down.

Duff Cooper lacked Hore-Belisha's administrative dynamism but was much more assured in dealing with his seniors, and when the Inskip report came before the Cabinet on July 20, he was in a truculent mood. Sea power was the backbone of Britain, he reminded his auditors, and if they rejected a standard which the Navy declared to be the minimum for security, "there would be such a storm in the House of Commons that the Government could not hope to survive." The rationing system did things the wrong way round, and anyhow it had already broken down.* He went on:

> It was really no use asking the Admiralty to work out a fresh Programme. They would have to be given completely new Terms of Reference. They had been asked to work out plans on the assumption of having to meet an enemy in the Far East and to hold the situation in Europe. If the Cabinet wanted a new programme they must give the Admiralty different assumptions. For his part, he was not prepared to suggest an alternative. . . . The position with the Dominions in this matter must be borne in mind . . . during the Imperial Conference a year ago the Dominions had been given a memorandum by the Chiefs of Staff Subcommittee which had been based on the assumption that we could send a Fleet to the Far East. There had been no suggestion of lack of money. The Dominions had been told nothing of the policy of rationing.

Simon responded rather feebly that the maintenance cost of the two-ocean Navy would be beyond the nation's means. But Duff Cooper had spoken effectively, and Hoare (his predecessor as First Lord and original proponent of the two-ocean fleet) came to his support with a declaration that the New Standard was both attainable and pledged to the Dominions. Its abandonment would be a "terrible shock" to them, and it ought to be adopted without fixing a time for its completion. MacDonald, Minister for the Dominions, agreed. In the event, the Cabinet approved neither the New Naval Standard nor the Inskip recommendation, and sent the matter back to Simon, Inskip, and Duff Cooper for further consideration.

They met on July 25 and, in effect, split their difference. The Admiralty was awarded a ration of £410 million and the Naval Staff was well pleased. Two days later, when the Cabinet approved the settlement, Duff Cooper was able to remark with some satisfaction that with this amount the New Naval Standard

---

* Later in the meeting Chamberlain, using a comparison which must have made some of his auditors wince, declared that the rationing system, like the Non-Intervention Committee, "was not a perfect weapon, but it was an effective one."

could eventually be reached. In the process, however, he had won more money than friends in high places.

No one questioned that the Navy knew what it needed if the money was available, but the Air Staff's judgments did not go unquestioned, and it was the air estimates which caused the sharpest and most significant controversy. After the rejection of Scheme J, Swinton had come back with Scheme K, which was still too much for the Chamberlain-Simon-Inskip phalanx to swallow. Then came *Anchluss,* the Air Ministry was encouraged to accelerate production, and Scheme L was presented as a speedier version of Scheme K, but on March 14 the Cabinet once again put the matter over for further consideration.

On March 29, Inskip addressed to all three service ministers an admonition that "acceleration" had to be held within their previously fixed "rations" from the £1570-million five-year total. Swinton immediately challenged him with a memorandum insisting that Scheme K was "the minimum response which the Air Staff advises it would be safe to make to Germany," but that since its fulfillment in 1941 would only match the Luftwaffe's anticipated strength in 1938, the acceleration proposed in Scheme L was "vital" so that the RAF could "maintain, throughout this dangerous period, the most effective fighting force possible." Shadow factory space had been "extended and equipped on a scale which will take a very large reinforcement of labour," and "general authority for the full programme" should now be extended.

But for Inskip, £1570 million was still the lodestar. "I should regret very much any decision which threw into the melting pot the whole question of defence expenditure," he wrote in his memorandum to the Cabinet, adding that if the Air Ministry's demands were to be met, the allocations to the other services would have to be adjusted accordingly. Simon came to his support with a lawyer's observation that *Anschluss,* "however serious," had not altered the Cabinet's February approval of the £1570-million ceiling. "Something more than Scheme F" but short of K and L should be authorized.

And so, in Cabinet on April 6, there was still another in the long series of confrontations between Swinton and the "higher powers." Inskip, as usual, bewailed the impasse between the military advisers and the Treasury, but came down firmly on the side of the latter. Without waiting for Swinton's reply, Chamberlain intervened with the suggestion that the gulf between the £505 million the Treasury was offering and the £567.5 million the Air Ministry was demanding had nothing to do with the Austrian crisis, but arose from Germany's ability to outstrip British aircraft production. The Prime Minister, who would have made a good trial lawyer, then put three questions to Swinton: Did he have a program within £505-million allocation? Could Britain "achieve parity without compulsory service and throwing over financial considerations?" If not, could a "formidable offensive force" be created simultaneously with such defensive strength "that we should not be at the mercy of a foreign power?"

Swinton, like Duff Cooper, refused to propose a program within the Treasury limit, saying that "we could not adopt anything less than 'Scheme L'," and that the "recent change of policy away from 'business as usual' meant an effective effort." As to the second and third questions, Scheme L would not give numerical parity, but "in two years' time we should be relatively stronger," and we "should not be at the mercy of Germany—as it might be said we were today—and we should possess a strong deterrent."

After the usual monetary grumbling from Simon, the Cabinet again put the matter over in hopes of a compromise. Meanwhile, however, Newall had written another note to Swinton, stating the issue in such categorical terms as to preclude, so far as the Air Staff was concerned, any part-way resolution:

> We are at the present moment temporarily in a position of immense strategical inferiority to Germany. In my belief we are today in no position to resist any demand by Germany, and if we attempted to do so I believe we should be defeated by the knock-out blow. . . . I feel strongly that the time for mincing words is past and that the Air Staff should state their view of the situation plainly. Their view is that unless the Cabinet are prepared to incur at the very least the full expenditure for Scheme L and possibly more, we must accept a position of permanent inferiority to Germany in the air. In that event we must be prepared to accede to any German demand without a struggle, since in the event of war our financial and economic strength, which the present financial limitations are designed to secure, will be of no use because we shall not survive the knockout blow.
>
> No one can say with absolute certainty that a nation can be knocked out from the air, because no one has yet attempted it. There can be no doubt, however, that Germany and Italy believe it possible, as there can be no other explanation for their piling up armaments to a level which they could not hope to maintain in a long war. When, as I firmly believe, the issue is that of the survival of British civilization, we cannot afford to take so great a chance for the sake of £60 or £100 millions.

This memorandum of April 5, 1938, must rank with Chamberlain's letter to his sister Ida of March 20 as a signpost to Munich. Newall gave no indication that the situation would be any better short of at least a year, and if the Czech crisis led to a showdown in 1938, his answer would be that Britain must "accede to any German demand" or suffer probable defeat via the knockout blow. Goering's Luftwaffe had become a thunderbolt which Hitler could hurl at his pleasure, and drive Britain to her knees.

Whether or not the memorandum was an accurate assessment of the Luftwaffe's potential, or even a competent judgment in the light of what the Air Staff knew or should have known, is quite another question. However these questions might be answered,* it is now clear that, if the Luftwaffe generals had been privileged to read Newall's memorandum, they would have been astonished.

Whatever else its import, Newall's note was uncompromising on Scheme L, and after the Cabinet of April 6 the tussle went on with ministerial meetings and memoranda galore. It finally came back to the Cabinet on April 27, with a report that the Prime Minister had asked Swinton how many aircraft could be produced during the next two years, and had been given figures of 4,000 the first year and 8,000 the second, which would largely fulfill Scheme L by 1940. Swin-

---

* They are discussed below, pp. 648–50, in the next chapter, pp. 709–13, and in Chapter 30, pp. 865–66.

ton had then been authorized to go ahead on that basis. The Cabinet confirmed this arrangement, which in substance meant that Scheme L was approved for the expenditures up to March 31, 1940, but not beyond. It was a meaningless limitation—for who could tell what would be going on by then?—but it served as a bookkeeping device to keep the authorized expenditures for the whole five-year period within the fixed limitations.

For Swinton it was a considerable victory financially, and for the RAF, Scheme L was certainly an advance on Scheme F. Considering the international situation and the Luftwaffe's growth, however, Scheme L was unimpressive, as it fell far short of numerical parity, and Bomber Command's striking force would be considerably smaller than the one envisaged under Scheme J, with reserves for only nine weeks of operations. Fighter Command, however, would have 38 squadrons of 16 aircraft with reserves for 16 weeks of fighting, and in the event the emphasis on fighters proved Scheme L's most valuable feature.

But getting the money was only half the battle. Swinton had based his production estimates on the assumption that the supply of labor would be "guaranteed," so that double shifts could be promptly started and maintained. *Anschluss* had not much diminished Chamberlain's distaste for mandatory measures. The Minister of Labour, Ernest Brown, was of like persuasion; immediately after *Anschluss* he had told the Cabinet that compulsion "would raise a most dangerous issue in its most dangerous form." Inskip had then reported a talk with Sir Alexander Ramsay (Director of the Engineering and Allied Employers' National Federation), who had warned that if large numbers of skilled workers were needed the trade unions would have to be consulted, and they might "make conditions, e.g. they might demand that the Government should undertake to use the arms in support of Czechoslovakia, or insist on the question being dealt with by the League." These were regarded (not surprisingly) as "impossible conditions," and the Cabinet agreed to take no action of a compulsory nature.*

Cabinet acceptance of Scheme L did nothing to change these attitudes. On May 18, Chamberlain told the Cabinet that British production could not catch up with German "unless we were prepared to undertake the tremendous measures of control over skilled labor as in Germany. . . . He doubted whether the nation would be prepared to go as far as that at the present time." This led to a bitter rejoinder from the Air Staff:

> If present arrangements continue, the programme must fail. . . . 4000 aircraft this year was based on the assumption of double shifting. At the present time there is no double shifting. . . . The Prime Minister says the country is not ripe for a Ministry of Supply, but a Government has a duty not only to follow its public opinion, but at times to lead it. . . . The Government are pledged [under Scheme L] to produce a first line of 2373 aircraft by 31/3/40. . . . this pledge cannot be fulfilled—unless the Government are prepared to

* The existence of a labor supply problem was not universally acknowledged. On May 25, 1938, Hugh Dalton, a member of the Labour Party executive and the Party's specialist on RAF matters, told the Commons that there was no shortage of skilled labor, and that there was unemployment among sheet metal workers and engineers.

continue to fob off their critics with a facade—an expedient which appears to be wearing thin with use. . . .*

But if the Air Staff was increasingly critical of the Government, in the Commons the Air Ministry itself was in virtual disgrace, and changes in high places were imminent. Lord Swinton had been under increasingly heavy fire since the fall of 1937, when parliamentary dissatisfaction with the state of British civil aviation forced him to appoint a departmental committee of inquiry headed by Lord Cadman.† In February 1938 the Cadman Committee reported that the ministry had seriously neglected the design and development of civil aircraft, and the Government's opponents seized on the report as the occasion for a general attack on the ministry's RAF production program as well. Sir Warren Fisher waded in with a personal letter to Chamberlain, declaring: "For some years we have had from the Air Ministry soothing syrup and incompetence in equal measure. For the first time in centuries our country is (and must continue to be) at the mercy of a foreign power."

Parliamentary dissatisfaction was deepened by the circumstance that Swinton, who had gone to the Lords as a viscount in 1935,‡ could not answer for his ministry in the Commons, and the Under-Secretary, Lieutenant Colonel A. J. Muirhead, was not of Cabinet rank. This threw an extra burden on the Prime Minister, and in March, Chamberlain tried to buttress the parliamentary position by giving Lord Winterton, Chancellor of the Duchy of Lancaster (a sinecure post), the additional title of Deputy Secretary for Air, with the responsibility of representing the Air Ministry in the Commons. Winterton was not a success in his new role; on May 12, presenting the new air estimates in the Commons, his stone-wall refusal to admit past mistakes and his implausibly optimistic assessment of the air situation alienated members on both sides of the aisle and greatly embarrassed the Government.

On May 16, Winston Churchill was attending a meeting of the Air Defence Research Committee "when a note was brought in to the Air Minister asking him to go to Downing Street. He desired us to continue our discussions, and left at once. He never returned. He had been dismissed by Mr. Chamberlain."

The Prime Minister was suffering from gout, which may explain the abrupt nature of the dismissal. His impatience with the situation in the Commons was natural, and no doubt intensified by a leader in *The Times* for May 12 critical of the aircraft construction program. Furthermore, Swinton was forceful and

---

* Meaning that without the compulsory measures necessary to procure the labor supply for double-shifting, the aircraft envisaged by Scheme L would not be produced, but the Government could create the "facade" of fulfillment by establishing the 2,373-strong front line without the reserves to back it up for operations.

† John Cadman, created Baron in 1937, was chairman of the Anglo-Iranian Oil Company, a director of the Suez Canal Company, and a frequent appointee to governmental boards and committees. The two other members were Sir Warren Fisher and Sir William Brown, Permanent Secretary to the Board of Trade, who had been Swinton's private secretary when the latter was President of the Board of Trade some years earlier.

‡ A man of many names was the beleaguered Minister for Air. He had started life as Philip Lloyd-Greame, but when his Yorkshire wife succeeded to the Swinton estates at Masham, by royal warrant he took the name of the first Baron Masham, Cunliffe-Lister. In 1935, Sir Philip Cunliffe-Lister was created Viscount Swinton of Masham, and in 1955 he became the Earl of Swinton and Baron Masham.

often abrasive, and had been pressing Chamberlain mercilessly for the measures necessary to speed production. And so, as Swinton later wrote: "He gave me no warning, he just sent for me and said I must go. . . . He offered me several alternative posts, including that of Lord President of the Council, but I naturally refused." With Swinton went Lord Weir, who resigned as soon as he heard of his friend's dismissal.* Winterton was shorn of his Air Ministry status, and Muirhead was transferred to the India Office—a clean sweep of the political leadership of the Air Ministry.

Lord Swinton was a man of great wealth and of enormous prestige in British ruling circles. His ministerial career dated back to 1922, when he had succeeded Baldwin as President of the Board of Trade in the Bonar Law government. His abilities were highly regarded by the professional airmen, as well as by Churchill and others who had been critical of the Government's air policies. The financial limitations were not his doing, and he had fought them hard and, in the end, with some effect. Air technology had made great strides under his ministry, and with the shadow factory scheme he and Weir had laid the basis for the remarkable production expansion which would bear fruit in 1939. Much of what he had done could not be made public, but those on the inside knew that an exceedingly able administrator had been sacrificed for political reasons at a time when his talents were sorely needed, and it is small wonder that Chamberlain begged him to remain in the Government. But Swinton had neither taste nor need for an honorary sinecure or a lesser position, and by this time he gravely doubted the wisdom of Chamberlain's continuing appeasement policies. So he took his leave.†

The physically diminutive Sir Kingsley Wood, who was transferred from the Ministry of Health to succeed Swinton, was Chamberlain's oldest and most loyal political supporter. They had both been elected to the Commons in 1918, and from 1924 to 1929 Wood was Chamberlain's parliamentary secretary at the Ministry of Health. It was at Chamberlain's suggestion that he had been brought into the Cabinet in 1935. As Under-Secretary, Muirhead was replaced by Captain Harold Balfour, a decorated First World War fighter pilot, barely forty, and with no prior ministerial experience. Kingsley Wood, in Balfour's words, was "a splendid little man but he admitted not knowing one end of an aeroplane from another." He was, moreover, the most ardent of all appeasers, distrustful of the French alliance, and even more anxious than the Prime Minister for friendship with Germany. His selection gave Chamberlain a faithful and able spokesman in the Commons, but since Wood had had no military service and had devoted his entire career to education, health, and other social welfare matters, it was curious if not bizarre, and lends credence to Swinton's statement that Cham-

---

* Weir's influence had been reduced in November of 1937, when the Defence Policy and Requirements Committee, of which he was a member, was abolished as a separate entity, and its functions taken over by the Committee of Imperial Defence.

† Swinton served in important nonministerial posts during the war, and in 1944 became (rather ironically in view of the Cadman report) the first Minister of Civil Aviation. His memoirs are disappointingly thin. Weir, too, returned to serve in consultative capacities at the Ministry of Supply, but never sought or accepted a position comparable in influence to those he held from 1935 to 1938.

berlain had said he had made the change because he "wanted a quiet political life and he didn't believe the war was coming."*

Despite these changes, the air front remained active for some little time. On May 25, Hugh Dalton, for the Labour Opposition, renewed the demand for an independent inquiry, buttressed by a powerful attack on the Air Ministry's record. A few weeks later Attlee, Dalton, and Greenwood met with Chamberlain and presented a written statement of their charges. "I assume that you have come to see me from patriotic, and not from political party motives" was the Prime Minister's salutation. But Kingsley Wood was more conciliatory than his chief, and soon greater matters absorbed public and parliamentary attention.

5

More important than these changes at the top was the evolution of operational thinking among the professional airmen during the year before Munich. Essentially this involved a growing realization that for at least three years Bomber Command would be unable to mount an attack on Germany sufficient to have much effect as a deterrent to the feared knockout blow, coupled with an emerging belief that Fighter Command might much sooner be able to mitigate substantially the impact of an assault by the Luftwaffe.

The RAF's sacred doctrine, nurtured by Trenchard and Weir since the end of the First World War, was that the bomber could not be stopped, and Britain's best protection therefore lay in the ability to retaliate so ruinously as to deter any other power from striking the first blow. All the alphabetically designated schemes from "A" through "L" called for bomber forces two or three times larger in numbers (and proportionately much more in cost and personnel, since bombers are more expensive and require bigger ground and flight crews) than the fighter forces.

Primary reliance on the bomber striking force as the major deterrent was still official gospel in the spring of 1938. During the Cabinet meeting of April 27, at which Scheme L was partially approved, when Halifax suggested a higher proportion of fighters, he was firmly put down by Swinton because, as he informed Newall:

> The Air Staff have always pressed not to be made to have fighters to the exclusion or reduction of bombers. In Cabinet Lord Halifax asked if we could not have *fewer* bombers and *more* fighters—you have always insisted on not sacrificing the counter-offensive. . . . When Sir T. Inskip asked us to limit the counter-offensive and confine ourselves to defence, the Air Staff opposed this strongly, and I insisted on their view. . . .

Considering the age and tenacity of this doctrine, it is nothing short of astonishing that so little attention had been devoted to basic bombing questions.

* Coincidentally with Swinton's removal, Ormsby-Gore's father died, and he found himself the fourth Baron Harlech and translated to the House of Lords. Chamberlain seized the occasion to remove him from the Cabinet—according to Harvey, because "P.M. . . . hates him and the whole Cecil connection" (Ormsby-Gore was married to Lady Beatrice Cecil of that famous family). The vacancies thus created at the Colonial Office and Ministry of Health brought about some other Cabinet shifts and new appointments, unimportant for present purposes.

What targets should be hit if they could be? What targets could be reached? What were the chances of hitting them when reached, and how hard must they be hit to knock them out?

It was not until 1937 that such questions began to be given systematic consideration by the Air Staff. Since the initial shape of the coming war could not be foretold—whether Germany would begin with an attempted knockout blow against Britain from the air or France on the ground, or stay on the defensive in the west and attack eastward—a number of alternative plans were prepared. They were in a numbered sequence designated "W.A." for "Western Air," and by the time war came there were no less than sixteen of them, but at an Air Ministry meeting on October 1, 1937, three were given priority:

W.A. 1. Attack on the German air striking force and its maintenance organization, including the aircraft industry. This plan would be especially important if the Luftwaffe attacked Britain.

W.A. 4. Attack on German military rail, canal, and road communications, to hinder and delay army concentrations and movements. This plan would be used if the German Army attacked the Low Countries or France.

W.A. 5. Attack on German war industry, including the Ruhr and oil resources. This would be "strategic bombing" in its purest form, and would work in conjunction with the naval blockade to wear Germany down in a long war.

Conceptually, these plans were all sensible enough. The difficulty was that the more the Air Staff and Bomber Command studied them, the clearer it became that the RAF lacked the capacity to carry them out, at least until the projected four-engined heavy bombers became available, which would not be until 1941 at the earliest. The RAF bombers of 1938 had neither the range nor load to operate effectively against Germany from British bases, the likelihood of finding and hitting their targets was beyond the capacities of the crews with the instruments then at hand, and losses would be prohibitive. German airdromes were too numerous and scattered, and damage to the factories would not affect the Luftwaffe's operations quickly enough. Predictions of the possible effect of W.A. 5 were more optimistic, but Air Chief Marshal Sir Edgar Ludlow-Hewitt, Chief of Bomber Command, estimated in March 1938 that a determined attack on Germany would wipe out his medium bombers in less than four weeks, and his heavies in less than seven. As Slessor later wrote:

We . . . were too optimistic on many counts—on the ability of the offensive to reduce the enemy attack at its source; on our ability to bomb unescorted by day or to find and hit targets at night; on the bombing accuracy to be expected; on the effects of a hit by the small bombs of the day and on the numbers required to ensure a hit; and on the results both moral and material to be expected from bombing of industrial objectives. . . . Other difficulties beset us . . . it became more and more obvious as war came nearer that the force likely to be at our disposal, before the new heavies could get into bulk production, was sadly inadequate to our needs, whether in technical performance, hitting power, training or ability to sustain operations in the face of war wastage of aircraft and crews.

The "other difficulties" to which Slessor referred involved questions of the legality of bombing operations which might cause civilian casualties. Of course, if the Germans were doing their best to flatten London, such issues would be academic, but suppose (as appeared increasingly probable) they stood on the defensive in the west while overrunning Czechoslovakia? Heavy German civilian casualties from British bombs would almost certainly lead to retaliation, and perhaps to a knockout attempt—the very thing the British were most anxious to avoid. Given the RAF's inferiority, their leaders and the civilian officials thought that restrictions on bombing would be advantageous to Britain, and on June 21, 1938, the Prime Minister told the Commons that the RAF would not "bomb civilians as such," would attack only "legitimate military objectives," and when doing so would use "reasonable care" to minimize civilian casualties. Although they approved, the Air Staff generally "regarded it all as a matter not of legality but of expediency," and deprecated the confusion with which the legalities afflicted operational planning.

For all these reasons, by the summer of 1938 the Air Staff had all but discarded the striking force as a present deterrent to the knockout blow. Naturally, this underlined the question of what might be expected of Fighter Command, and on March 11, Slessor sent the Assistant Chief of the Air Staff (Air Vice-Marshal Sholto Douglas) a questionnaire designed to clarify the state of fighter effectiveness against bombers.* It was answered, after discussions in which Douglas, Slessor, and several other Air Staffers participated, by Air Chief Marshal Sir Hugh Dowding, who headed Fighter Command from its establishment in 1936 and throughout the Battle of Britain.

In his answers to the detailed questions, Dowding replied that radar (still called RDF) and the high speed and rate of climb of modern fighters had greatly improved their ability to intercept bombers, at least in clear weather, when 60 per cent of the raids could be engaged. Radar would dispense with the necessity of continuous fighter patrols, and the fighter strength under Scheme K would be adequate to inflict prohibitive (10 per cent) losses on the German bombers.†

On Slessor's memorandum opposite his comment that the value of the fighter was declining, Dowding scribbled: "*No*. The 8-gun fighter is very much on top of the *unarmoured* bomber." Armoring the bomber or adding tail-gun turrets would present a problem, and more and bigger fighter guns or cannon would be required. On March 23, Sholto Douglas circulated Dowding's answers with a supporting memorandum:

> I do not agree that the value of the fighter in home defence is . . . declining. I think that within the last few months, what with the advent of the 8-

---

* Slessor accompanied the questionnaire with a memorandum in which he expressed his own view that the value of the fighter was declining, "although I am still convinced that it has great value, and probably rather more than the Air Staff are inclined to think." He added that as yet "we do not know much about the tactical performance of . . . the Hurricanes, or . . . the Blenheims."

† Though not stated, it is apparent that Dowding's answers were based on the assumption that the bombers would come without fighter escort. This was perfectly valid on the further assumption that the bombers would come from Germany, since the German fighters would lack the range to reach Britain.

gun fighter, R.D.F., and the Biggin Hill interception scheme,* the pendulum has swung the other way and that at the moment—or at any rate as soon as all our Fighter Squadrons are equipped with Hurricanes and Spitfires—the fighter is on top of the contemporary enemy bombers. How long this will be the case it is of course difficult to say, but that is my view at the moment.

But the squadrons were not yet equipped with Hurricanes or Spitfires, and the radar chain was in its early stages. Sholto Douglas was not talking about the fighter potential as of the time he wrote, but as of at least a year later.

These long looks into the mirror gave the RAF leaders, on the whole, an accurate assessment of their own present and potential capacities. It is, of course, remarkable—and some might say inexcusable—that after twenty years of Douhet-Trenchard-Weir bombing doctrine the RAF found itself with a "striking force" that could not effectively strike the one country whose identity as *the enemy* had been obvious for over three years. It is ironic that in pressing, over RAF objections, for more fighters the civilian ministers and civil servants like Halifax, Inskip, Hankey, and Fisher were right but for the wrong reasons, which were that fighters were cheaper and less disturbing to the financial "ration," and quicker to build so that front-line strength could be more quickly increased toward the politically magical "parity."

But what is most extraordinary is that the RAF leaders' enlightening reassessments of their own forces were accompanied by a continuing and egregiously exaggerated appraisal of the Luftwaffe's power to hit Britain. As Douglas and Slessor and Ludlow-Hewitt discovered one reason after another why their Wellingtons and Whitleys and Hampdens could scarcely dent the German war machine, it rarely if ever occurred to them that most of the negative factors would equally plague the Germans. True, the Heinkels and Dorniers were superior aircraft, but they also had to contend with the problems of distance, weather, target-finding, and aiming. Furthermore, the Air Staff knew that the Luftwaffe was primarily designed for tactical support of the Army rather than long-range strategic bombing, and that Goering had no intention of developing four-engined heavies comparable in range and load to those the RAF had in prospect.

There were, to be sure, occasional glimmerings of awareness that bombing problems worked both ways. Early in January 1937 the Joint Planning Staff expressed the opinion that, if Germany had not occupied northern France or the Low Countries, the danger to Britain from air raids launched from Germany would be small, and a few weeks later this conclusion was approved by the CID. But no such assessment was reflected in the Air Staff appreciations during the next year and a half, and in July 1938 they were estimating that the Germans could sustain a daily average of 600 tons of bombs on Britain during the first several weeks of the assault—a level which the Luftwaffe, operating from bases in France and the Low Countries, achieved on only a few days in 1941, and which Britain and the United States, with their far more numerous and heavier bombers, did not attain until 1943.

Not until the end of August, when the Czech crisis was approaching its cli-

* Biggin Hill was the principal fighter headquarters for the defense of the London area.

max, were more realistic assessments made. On August 30, Ludlow-Hewitt, observing that if Germany respected the Low Countries' neutrality their bombers would have to approach Britain via the North Sea, raised the question of how far this would "prove a deterrent to systematic attack in England." He cautiously remarked that the question was "impossible to assess in peace-time," but followed this with a warning that, if Bomber Command had to attack Germany by the North Sea route, the necessity of returning "in aircraft which may have been severely damaged" was "by no means an attractive prospect," and that it was "improbable that any really potent or vigorous air offensive can be effectively *sustained* against Germany by this route."

On September 12 the Air Staff dealt with Ludlow-Hewitt's question a little more definitely. Assuming that the entire German bomber force was directed against Britain, a daily average of 500 to 600 tons of bombs was theoretically possible, but "practical factors" made it very doubtful that any such figure could be achieved. By the North Sea route and respecting Belgian and Dutch air space, the range of the Heinkel made it unlikely that it could reach London or the Midlands except with a much decreased bomb load and extra fuel tanks. Furthermore, sustained operations across the North Sea "presupposes a very high standard of leadership, training, endurance and navigational skill on the part of the whole of the German Bomber Force, including their reserve flying personnel." The same obstacles that were troubling Bomber Command also confronted the Luftwaffe. If they were to cross the Low Countries, "we would get earlier warning," and if not, their bombers would have to take off from the same bit of northwest Germany and approach Britain from a single direction, which would make interception much easier. But these few rays of light did little to qualify the prophecies of doom, such as Newall's memorandum of April 5, 1938, that emanated from the Air Ministry during the months before Munich. To a degree, these forebodings were reasonable enough; even if the 600-ton estimate was wildly high, it was clear that the Luftwaffe would be able to drop a nasty mess of bombs on London, and nobody knew what the effect would be. Some of the professionals, like Slessor, were troubled by recollections of London under the Zeppelin strikes during the First World War.* But to focus exclusively on one's own weaknesses to the exclusion of the enemy's problems is hardly conducive to a sound strategy and may well induce a state of panic.

What the air marshals said and wrote did, indeed, help to beget an outlook in high civilian and military circles for which "panicky" is hardly an exaggerated description. On March 29, 1938, Harold Nicolson, no appeaser, consulted Malcolm MacDonald, one of his two (with Eden) "leaders." To Nicolson's remonstrances that Germany and Italy "are trying to chloroform us while they occupy strategic points to our disadvantage," and that Britain "should occupy Minorca," MacDonald replied that:

---

* In October 1915, Slessor, then a young pilot-officer, crash-landed near London after an unsuccessful attempt to attack a Zeppelin. The following evening he drove through London's East End with replacement parts for his damaged aircraft, and was harassed by a mob of Londoners angry at the Royal Flying Corps for its failure to protect the city against the Zeppelin raiders. As he later wrote, the episode made a lasting impression, and was "one of the fears that haunted me as Director of Plans" during the Munich period.

. . . we are really not strong enough to risk a war. It would mean the massacre of women and children in the streets of London. No Government could possibly risk a war when our defences are in so farcical a condition. . . . All we can do is by wise retreat and good diplomacy to diminish the dangers being arrayed against us.

Some weeks later, on May 16, Sir Warren Fisher took lunch with the new American Ambassador, Joseph P. Kennedy, and told him that "German war plans are on the supposition that if war were declared on Great Britain the issue would be decided within 30 days and that Germany is building an air force designed to demolish London in one fell swoop."* Others, equally highly placed, expressed themselves less colorfully but just as decisively. Sir Alexander Cadogan repeatedly declared that war must be avoided at all costs; if not, "we shall be smashed." General W. E. "Tiny" Ironside, a senior Army commander and later CIGS, wrote that going to war would be "to expose ourselves to annihilation for the sake of the Czechs," since "at no time could we stand up against German air bombing."

Thus, as the Czech issue assumed crisis proportions, the RAF leaders had completely lost faith in the value of their striking force. They were gripped by grossly exaggerated fears of what the Luftwaffe's bombers, operating from German bases, could accomplish against Britain, and thought it quite possible that their country could be crushingly defeated within a few months or even weeks. There was rising confidence that Fighter Command, when fully fledged, could beat off the assault, and a desperate insistence on the year of the peace necessary for its growth. All these fears and anxieties had been forcefully communicated to the political leadership, where they had had enormous impact.

6

The Chamberlain government's formulation, in March 1938, of policy regarding the Sudeten situation was accomplished without prior consultation with either France or Czechoslovakia. The Prime Minister's speech on March 23 and the contemporaneous Foreign Office aide-mémoire for Paris did, of course, acquaint the French with the Government's decision to give no new commitment. But these pronouncements fell far short of giving them a full description of the British position. They made no mention of the military staff talks for which the French had been pressing; they did not disclose the decision to limit Britain's continental commitment to two divisions or perhaps to send no ground forces whatever; they did not reflect the Government's determination to avoid war no matter what course events in Czechoslovakia might take.

Such a situation could not be continued, for the success of British policy depended on French co-operation. Rather than risk a war Czechoslovakia could be allowed to go down the drain, but not France. If the French and Germans went to war, willy-nilly Britain would be in it; even the most extreme appeasers knew that. *Ergo,* France must not go to war for Czechoslovakia. To that end,

---

* Of course the Germans were doing no such thing, and if Sir Warren believed such nonsense, he was a sadly misinformed senior civil servant. Kennedy passed this "information" on to Washington without comment.

the prospect of British aid must appear as dim as possible, short of shattering the Anglo-French entente.

A meeting of the heads of the two governments, which the French wanted, could be used to swing them into line, but not until the rickety Blum cabinet had been replaced by something more stable. Soon after Daladier took over and, with an assist from Phipps, ousted Paul-Boncour from the Quai d'Orsay, the invitation was issued for the meeting on April 28 and 29 in London.

The one issue on which the British had not yet firmly settled their own policy was that of staff talks. The Chiefs of Staff, especially Lord Chatfield, had strongly opposed any military conversations with the French. In February, Eden had been so aroused by a negative Staff memorandum that he insisted on a meeting at which he, with Chamberlain's support, imposed on the Chiefs a policy which recognized the necessity of military co-operation with France, if for no other reason than to secure air bases there for operations against Germany.*

But a week later Eden resigned, and the Chiefs now endeavored to restrict the scope of the talks to air matters. They had some success; when the matter came before the Cabinet on April 6, Halifax and Duff Cooper opposed naval contacts, on the ground that they might upset Mussolini. But Chamberlain, with a breadth of vision which he did not always exhibit, pointed out that "in a war with Germany, Anglo-French trade would be liable to attack in all parts of the world" and "therefore, that the conversations ought to extend to the Admiralty. . . ." As for the Army, the very poverty of the British contribution made it the more important that the French be consulted on its use. On his recommendation, the Cabinet approved "in principle" staff talks covering all three services, and referred to the CID all other questions with respect to their scope.

But the Chiefs were not yet licked, and the records of the CID meeting on April 11 and the Cabinet two days later are appalling reflections of strategic narrow-mindedness. The CID concluded that the talks should be limited to the Locarno stipulations—i.e., a German attack on France—and not be concerned with the situation if Germany attacked Czechoslovakia and France intervened. Italy and Japan were to be assumed neutral, and therefore the Mediterranean theater would not be considered, nor the Far East. It was likewise to be assumed that, in view of the strength of the Maginot Line, Germany would first attempt a knockout blow directed against Britain rather than France.

By treating these possibilities as limiting postulates, the CID was able to conclude that there should be neither Naval nor Army Staff conversations. The former were unnecessary since Italy was assumed neutral, and dangerous because they might cause Hitler to denounce the Anglo-German Naval Agreement. The latter were equally unnecessary since, if the knockout blow were directed

---

* The Air Staff had been much more favorable to staff talks than the other services, since most of its bombers could not reach Germany from Britain. As early as May of 1937, Slessor had complained that lack of knowledge of French intentions made it correspondingly difficult for the RAF to plan its moves in the event of war with Germany. The Army, on the other hand, thought that the French would use staff talks as a means of extracting a British continental commitment, and the Navy, worried chiefly about a German-Italian-Japanese coalition, feared that staff talks with the French would throw these potential enemies into each other's arms.

against Britain, the likelihood of any British expeditionary force was slight; this argument was to be "tactfully put" to the French!

On April 13 the Cabinet actually approved the CID's recommendations, but they were too preposterous to survive further reflection. Two weeks later, when the Cabinet met on the day before the French ministers were to arrive, Halifax asked for latitude to agree to Army Staff talks if the French insisted on them. There was some grumbling from Simon, and Lord Maugham, at least as confirmed an appeaser as Kingsley Wood, was worried that the talks might needle Hitler into attacking Czechoslovakia forthwith But Chamberlain strongly supported Halifax, observing that to refuse the French request "would seem rather churlish" and cause "an uncomfortable jar," and the Cabinet eventually agreed.

The British constructed the agenda for the conference to fit the purposes they had in view, with the results already described.* Essentially, Chamberlain and Halifax used the "latitude" on staff talks to grease the way to an accord on the far more fundamental problem of Czechoslovakia. Daladier insisted, at times angrily, that military conversations should embrace all three services. The British gave way on the army talks without much fuss, but on the naval side with obvious reluctance, and only "in principle"; Chamberlain subsequently told the Cabinet that the conference might have broken down if they had not finally conceded the point. It was not of much importance compared to the general Sudeten issue on which, after Daladier's blustering, the British quite carried the day.†

From the British standpoint, plainly, the purpose of the talks was not to make plans for the protection of Czechoslovakia against German aggression, but to concert an Anglo-French policy that would prevent that obligation from arising, by ensuring that Czechoslovakia would yield far enough so that Germany would not attack her. This attitude was freely enough expressed in British ministerial discussions, but of course not publicly avowed. Daladier (but not Bonnet) had too much pride to admit that this was indeed the policy, but in fact he was desperately eager to get his country off the hook of the Czech guarantee: after the conference the British were confident that his government would follow the British lead, and Chamberlain and Halifax were able to assure the Cabinet that the French had given way, and that "public opinion in France generally would be opposed to any form of military adventure."

With the French securely in tow, the focus of British concern shifted to Berlin and Prague. In the latter city, the question was simply whether the Czechs would move fast and far in their concessions to the Sudetens, and to this end London and Paris were to apply maximum pressure. Early in May instructions

---

* See Chapter 21, pp. 507–10. The disclosure that the British Field Force, if sent at all, would not exceed two partially equipped divisions, can hardly have surprised the French, for Hore-Belisha had told Gamelin substantially the same a few days earlier, when he stopped in Paris on the way home from visits to Italy and Malta.

† Writing to his sister shortly after the conference, Chamberlain remarked that "fortunately the papers have had no hint of how near we came to a break over Czechoslovakia." Other accounts fail to reflect so high a degree of tension. Lord Halifax took occasion to urge Bonnet privately to open Madagascar for settlement by German Jews, whose position was becoming "increasingly acute."

were issued from both capitals to their respective ministers in Prague, and by the middle of the month Newton and Lacroix had made strong representations to Beneš, Hodža, and Krofta.

With regard to Berlin, the question was much more difficult. Was Hitler really aiming at a resolution of the Sudeten question, or was he using it as a device to eliminate Czechoslovakia as an independent power, or even to destroy her completely? Hitler had told Henderson on March 3 that Germany could live at peace with Czechoslovakia if the Sudeten Germans were accorded "full equality" with Czechs, and British policy now proceeded on the assumption that it was at least reasonably possible that Hitler had meant what he said. Accordingly, on May 4 Sir Nevile Henderson was told to seek audience with Ribbentrop, and tell him that the British and French governments were "using their influence to promote a peaceful and equitable settlement of the Sudeten German question" by urging the Czech Government "to seek without delay a solution of the problem on comprehensive lines by direct negotiation with the Sudeten Germans." Henderson was then to ask the Germans to "use their influence with Henlein in the direction of moderation," and invite them to give London "some idea of the terms that would be likely from the German point of view to form the basis of an agreed settlement."

When Henderson received these instructions, Ribbentrop was with Hitler in Italy, and the ambassador delivered his message to Dr. Ernst Woermann, Chief of the Political Section, and the ranking Foreign Ministry official then in Berlin. Henderson was an impulsive and ill-disciplined man, deeply appeasement-minded and overeager to please his hosts, and his handling of this assignment well illustrates the disastrous representation which his government was getting from him at this crucial period.

Henderson had been explicitly told *not* to specify the content of a "solution . . . on comprehensive lines," and that only at a later date, and in the event that the prospects of a peaceful settlement appeared remote and Germany threatened to use force, should any warning of possible British intervention be given. The ambassador disregarded both instructions, telling Woermann (according to Henderson's own report) that the settlement in mind would turn Czechoslovakia into "a state of nationalities rather than a national state," and indicating that "if a *casus belli* was invoked there was no knowing how far the complication might spread." These statements he reported to London and was duly reprimanded by Halifax,* but according to Woermann's record of the conversation, Henderson also declared (and did not report to London) that in "his personal view of the situation . . . France was acting for the Czechs and Germany for the Sudeten Germans," while "Britain was supporting Germany in

* Henderson attempted to brush off the admonition by asserting his need for "a certain latitude in expression of personal opinion," but Halifax reiterated that he must follow instructions. The only result was that Henderson did not thereafter report his statements which transcended his authority. According to Harvey, Halifax and Eden had already concluded that Henderson had proved a bad appointment, and Cadogan, who at first had found him "very good," now wrote that he needed "a gentle jab in the mouth occasionally," and eventually thought that he ought to be recalled. But despite these egregious indiscretions, Henderson was allowed to remain as Britain's spokesman in Berlin throughout this crucial period.

this case and he urgently hoped that Germany would not refuse some kind of cooperation with Britain in this matter, which might then, perhaps, lead to cooperation in other questions also."

Such statements were hardly likely to impress Berlin with the dangers of a confrontation, and Henderson made matters much worse a few days later (May 11) when he saw Ribbentrop. The ambassador again violated his instructions by implying that Britain might become involved if war erupted over Czechoslovakia, and was at once rebuffed by the German's retort that his country would not be moved by "threats from third parties and would not even shrink from a European war," and would regard any military intervention by France as "a war of aggression." To this tirade the ever-anxious-to-please Henderson replied (according to Ribbentrop's record) "that he had not imagined that the German attitude would be any different, and he added the question whether I could imagine that British soldiers would again march into Germany."

Ribbentrop did, however, welcome the British action in Prague "in principle," and by suppressing the negative aspects of his reaction Henderson contrived a favorable report. The Minister for Foreign Affairs had been "unusually temperate," and the German reaction "quite as satisfactory as I anticipated."

Simultaneously, there were more soothing words from Konrad Henlein, who visited London on May 12 and 13, laying a thick coating of reassurance wherever he went. Only six weeks earlier he had received instructions from Hitler to press "unacceptable demands" on the Czech Government, and en route to England he stopped in Berlin to prearrange with Ribbentrop what he would say, and agree that he would "deny . . . that he is acting on instructions from Berlin." Vansittart (who at Henlein's request had invited him and arranged his agenda)* was completely taken in; he found himself talking to "a wise and reasonable man," and was greatly pleased by the visit "for if the situation created by it is handled promptly and if the Germans will desist from blocking tactics, we may really have turned a crucial corner in European history." Even Jan Masaryk professed himself contented with a settlement on the terms described by Henlein, and Halifax, on the basis of Vansittart's report, told the Cabinet that Beneš could get a settlement if he acted quickly, and that Henlein "had no instructions from Berlin." Shortly after quitting England, Henlein went to Berchtesgaden to report to his German masters.

The wave of false optimism thus generated was rudely broken a week later by the May crisis, which precipitated the British warning messages to Berlin and the unpleasant Henderson-Ribbentrop confrontations already described.† In London, the crisis reached climax on Sunday, May 22, and an emergency Cabinet meeting was held. The minutes reveal little of the members' reaction to Halifax's report; Duff Cooper sensed that the "general feeling seemed to be that great, brutal Czechoslovakia was bullying poor, peaceful little Germany," and his impression is partially confirmed by Cadogan's diary record that the Cabinet was "quite sensible—and anti-Czech!"

---

* Henlein also saw Churchill and Sir Archibald Sinclair, Harold Nicolson and a group of Conservative M.P.s assembled by him, and the Czech Minister, Jan Masaryk, who subsequently told Ambassador Kennedy that he believed Hitler had nothing to do with the visit.
† See Chapter 16, pp. 390–94.

In fact, London was badly scared. Chamberlain wrote to his sisters that "the Germans, who are bullies by nature, are too conscious of their strength and our weakness, and until we are as strong as they are, we shall always be kept in a state of chronic anxiety," and he even suggested that he would resign if there were anyone to take his place without "undermining confidence." Halifax and Cadogan anxiously "decided we must *not* go to war," and a telegram was sent to Paris, warning the French not to be "under any illusion" about the likelihood of British assistance "to preserve Czechoslovakia against German aggression."

But the next day the tension broke as quickly as it had gathered. The Czech elections were over, the Sudetenland was quiet, there were no more reports of German troop movements, and the British military attaché in Berlin reported that prolonged automobile reconnaissance of the region bordering Czechoslovakia had revealed nothing unusual.

Despite this comforting news, the key officials in London remained convinced that the Germans had been on the verge of some sort of military action—whether "to go for Czechoslovakia," as Harvey put it, or "some kind of monkey tricks," as Pownall recorded.* Wherever the truth lay, Chamberlain's conclusions, as disclosed in a letter to his sister Ida, were sufficiently alarming:

> The more I hear about last weekend, the more I feel what a damned close run thing it was. . . . I cannot doubt in my own mind, 1. That the German Government made all preparations for a coup. 2. That in the end they decided, after getting our warning, that the risks were too great. 3. That the general view that this was just what had happened made them conscious that they had lost prestige, and 4. That they are ventilating their spite on us because they feel that we have got the credit for giving them a check . . . but the incident shows how utterly untrustworthy and dishonest the German Government is, and it illuminates the difficulties in the way of the peace-maker . . .

If the notion that British firmness had stopped a German coup was, in all probability, mistaken, in any event Chamberlain and Halifax had no stomach for a second such experience. In their view, as they told the Cabinet on May 25, press reports of an Allied check to Hitler were most unfortunate, as they made it all the more difficult to settle the Sudeten affair peacefully. As we have already seen from Hitler's reaction to the May crisis, this diagnosis was quite accurate.

In London, the most significant consequence of the May crisis was a growing concern that diplomatic pressure on Prague might not be a sufficient stimulus to fruitful negotiations with Henlein, and that a settlement of the Sudeten question by granting extensive local autonomy, even if acceptable to Henlein, might not resolve the more important problem of German-Czech relations. Halifax laid some of the worrisome possibilities before the Cabinet on May 25, mentioning the possibilities of a plebiscite in the Sudetenland, and of neutralizing Czechoslovakia in the manner of Switzerland, so as to eliminate the alliances with France and Russia which were so distasteful to Germany.

* Pownall's (and no doubt the others') opinions were in part based on information from Admiral Sinclair, known as "C" (actually the head of M.I.6, the "Secret Service" for foreign intelligence), that some German military adventure had been commenced but was called off on Monday, May 23.

The Foreign Secretary lost no time in giving these reflections wider exposure. Strang was sent to Prague and Berlin for discussions with Newton, Henderson, and their staffs. On May 27 a telegram went out to those two emissaries asking them to feel out the German and Czech governments on a proposal "that an international commission be set up . . . for investigation of any incidents which might lead to trouble" in the Sudeten region. On May 30, Halifax directed Phipps to discuss with Bonnet the establishment, in the event of a Prague-Henlein deadlock, of an "international commission" to "investigate the cause of the deadlock and devise means for overcoming it." The next day Halifax was again telegraphing Phipps, suggesting that Bonnet should warn Beneš "that if through any fault of his, the present opportunity to reach a settlement is missed, the French government would be driven to reconsider their own position *vis-à-vis* Czechoslovakia."

At the time, none of these projects bore fruit. German reaction to the incident-investigating commission was negative. As we have seen,* Bonnet waffled and prevaricated on the warning to Prague, Newton did not think a plebiscite timely or that an alteration of the Bohemian borders was economically or culturally sound, Strang found no support for it in Berlin, and Halifax soon discarded it. But the idea of a commission to study and recommend a settlement met a much more congenial response from both the Berlin and Prague staffs and from Bonnet as well, and was the seed from which the Runciman mission sprouted six weeks later.

Throughout June and early July, while the discussions between the Prague government and the Henleinists spun out their futile course,† Halifax concentrated on questions which he regarded as more basic than the Sudeten question to a stable Central Europe. On June 1 he laid before the Foreign Policy Committee a memorandum on the danger that German economic domination of southeastern Europe would ultimately drag those countries into war on Germany's side, urging a British economic and financial counteroffensive in those lands. For once he and Chamberlain did not see eye to eye, and the Prime Minister sharply challenged both the assumption that "these vast areas would, in fact, pass under German domination," and that "it was possible for us to do something to prevent this happening." In the end an interdepartmental committee was set up to look into the possibilities, but it was much too late in the day for such a project to have any impact on the Czech situation.

The other focus of the Foreign Secretary's concern was Czechoslovakia's treaty situation. Newton had told Strang that "even if there were not a single German in Czechoslovakia, the root problem of German-Czech relations would still remain, viz., a Slav state thrust into the heart of Germany, and having treaties of mutual assistance with powerful states East and West." In Halifax's view,

---

* Chapter 19, pp. 519–20.

† The real attitude of Vansittart's "wise and reasonable" Henlein was manifested during his visit to Berlin early in June, when he put to Werner Lorenz the question: "What attitude should I adopt if the Czechs, under foreign pressure, suddenly accede to all my demands and present, as a counter-demand, entry into the Government?" Henlein's own proposed answer was: "I shall answer 'Yes' with the demand that the foreign policy of Czechoslovakia be modified. The Czechs would never accede to that."

as reported to the Foreign Policy Committee for its meeting on June 16, German antipathy to the Franco-Soviet guarantee was matched by French anxiety to be relieved of the uncomfortable dilemma of "dishonor or war." He concluded, accordingly, that Britain and France should be prepared with a plan for the "neutralization" of Czechoslovakia, to be put forward if the Sudeten negotiations broke down, or later if occasion arose.

Halifax's diagnosis was better than his therapy. He was, of course, quite right in supposing that the Sudetenland was not Hitler's real objective, and the French and Czech treaties with the Soviet Union had been one of the main targets of the Nazi press. But, as was soon to appear, "neutralization" would not have met Hitler's purposes, and anyhow it was a foggy concept which Halifax had not thought through.* Nevertheless, Phipps was instructed to raise the matter with Bonnet, and on June 30 was told to press for "an early expression of his views." But no answer was volunteered, and when, on August 10, the British chargé again pushed for an answer, Bonnet declared the issue premature and refused to be drawn into further discussion.

If these explorations by Halifax manifest reflective foresight, they lagged too far behind the march of events to be effective. By mid-July, Chamberlain and Halifax had concluded that the Prague-Henlein negotiations were making insufficient progress, and that Britain would have to take a hand. In June, Halifax had told the Cabinet that "in case the conversations broke down he proposed to have a wise British subject available to slip off quietly to Central Europe to try to get the parties together again," and had notified Newton and Phipps (who was instructed to inform Bonnet) of what he had in mind. Meanwhile Halifax had been casting about for the "wise British subject" and had finally† settled on Viscount Runciman, the sixty-eight-year-old shipping magnate who had been President of the Board of Trade in the Baldwin cabinet. Sir Horace Wilson, who recommended Runciman, described him as having "a puzzling demeanor which might, in certain circumstances, be of advantage," and added: "Someone would have to accompany him and do most of the work, but he could be relied on to put the results across."

The decision to launch the Runciman mission was precipitated by messages from Prague in mid-July, wherein Newton, after a meeting with Beneš, expressed the opinion that "the prospects of agreement with the Henlein party are poor," and that "the time has now come when we should consider offering advice of a more concrete nature" by sending "a mediator or investigator." On

---

* At the Foreign Policy Committee meeting Halifax declared that he was proposing a "joint guarantee" which "only holds good so long as all the guarantors were ready to give effect to it." Accordingly "in the case of Czechoslovakia there would have to be a number of guarantors, including Germany, and if Germany infringed her guarantee her fellow guarantors would then be free from their obligations." To this Simon caustically retorted that if neutralization "was that which Lord Halifax had just indicated, it would be obvious to all that our action was nothing more than window dressing."

† On June 22, Sir Horace Wilson had submitted to Halifax a list of names headed by Runciman's, which also included Lord MacMillan (a distinguished appellate judge), the historian H. A. L. Fisher, Lord Riverdale (a prominent industrialist), and Sir Norman Raeburn, K.C. Sir Horace's own first preference ran to MacMillan, with Runciman in second place. Runciman was not held in uniformly high regard.

July 18, Halifax instructed Newton to put the Runciman project to Beneš, and then went with the King and Queen to Paris, where he told the French about it. The Czech Government and the Henleinists both gave their assent, and the Runciman mission arrived in Prague on August 3, under the circumstances and with the consequences already described.*

Chamberlain announced the Runciman mission in the House of Commons on July 26, just before it broke for the summer recess. Runciman, he declared, would not be an arbitrator but "an investigator and mediator"; furthermore, he "would, of course, be independent of His Majesty's Government—in fact, he would be independent of all Governments" and "would act only in his personal capacity." But what the Prime Minister thus touted as an asset looked rather different to Runciman himself, who complained that "the Government were pushing me out in a dinghy in mid-Atlantic." Especially in retrospect the proclaimed design of the mission appears utterly preposterous. Since Runciman's personal opinion on the Sudeten issue carried no international weight, everyone must have realized that he would act only in Britain's interest, and his "independence" was only a fiction contrived to enable London to adopt or reject his recommendations as the Government saw fit.

With the dispatch of Runciman and the relegation of the French Government to a bystander's role, the focus of British diplomatic concern shifted to Berlin. Throughout June and July there was little sign of concern that Hitler might attempt a military solution; Chamberlain, indeed, seems to have been riding a wave of optimism. On June 18 he wrote to his sister that the Prague negotiations were going well, and added gloatingly that the Germans "have missed the bus† and may never again have such a favorable chance of asserting their domination over Central and Eastern Europe." Early in July he told Ambassador Kennedy that the Sudeten negotiations presented "no real prospect of difficulty for some time at least," and that there would be no military developments unless precipitated by an explosive border incident.

Ten days later the Prime Minister's hopes were raised even higher by unexpected news from Germany. Hermann Goering, who had hosted Halifax's visit the previous autumn, fancied that he could do a better job than Ribbentrop (whom he despised) at befriending the English, and through unofficial channels was angling for an invitation. The go-between was the Princess Hohenlohe,‡ and according to Harvey she was brought to Halifax by Sir Samuel Hoare's brother Oliver. She had been sent on this mission by Captain Fritz Wiedemann, who had been the adjutant of Hitler's regiment during the First World War and since 1934 the Fuehrer's personal adjutant. At her interview with Halifax it was agreed that Wiedemann would come to London on July 18 and discuss with the

* Chapter 16, pp. 403–10.

† The Prime Minister made a second and more unfortunate (because public) use of this phrase in the early spring of 1940, just before the German occupation of Norway and Denmark.

‡ Stephanie Princess Hohenlohe-Schillingsfürst, of a famous Franconian noble family, who acted as a sort of ambassadress-at-large for Lord Rothermere of the London *Daily Mirror*. Harvey described her as "a well-known adventuress, not to say a blackmailer."

Foreign Secretary and Cadogan the possibility of a Goering visit for a general discussion of Anglo-German relations.

Neville Chamberlain was delighted by this development. "What this means I don't know," he wrote to his sister, "but this is the most encouraging news from Berlin that I have heard of yet and I hope signifies that at any rate they mean to behave respectably for the present." He speculated happily on the possibility that Hitler wanted to steal a march on "his dear ally" Italy.

But the Fuehrer had no such thing in view. In all probability he regarded Wiedemann's trip as an interesting opportunity to probe the British official mind, for he briefed his adjutant with great care. There was to be no commitment for a visit by Goering, which Hitler regarded as untimely. Wiedemann was to complain about the hostility of the British press and other matters, and then tell Halifax that if the Sudeten question were not settled peacefully, Germany would resort to force: "And if he [Halifax] asks you how long I will remain peaceful, you can tell him until about March of 1939."*

Halifax received Wiedemann at home, with Cadogan interpreting. The conversation closely followed the course Hitler had prescribed. Although the Goering project was the supposed reason for the meeting, it was not discussed at length since Wiedemann could make no commitment, and Halifax at once made it clear that such a meeting would not be welcome until the Sudeten question was much closer to resolution. Wiedemann then indicated that Hitler might give assurance of no resort to force "limited to a definite period" (he appears not to have specified March 1939), but qualified it by indicating that "incidents" might occur which would require German intervention. The discussion went on for two hours in a friendly tone, and at parting Halifax told his guest to give Hitler his greetings and say that "the English Foreign Minister had only one goal, which was that one day the Fuehrer, as guest of the King at Buckingham Palace, would be greeted by the cheerio of the English masses."

Despite the unofficial and inconclusive nature of this meeting, and the virtual certainty that the appearance of Hermann Goering on English soil would arouse wide and vehement protest, Chamberlain entertained the possibility seriously enough to tell the Cabinet on July 20 (Halifax being in Paris with the King and Queen) that "the proposed visit by Field Marshal Goering was not likely to take place before autumn" and that "the proposed subject of the conversations was to be all questions outstanding between the two countries, which, of course, would include colonies." The Prime Minister also emphasized Wiedemann's assurance that Germany would take "no kind of forcible action" for a "definite period," which he thought "might be one of a year." Two days later, when Ambassador Dirksen saw him before going on leave, Chamberlain "several times expressed his satisfaction with the information received from Captain Wiedemann"—no doubt the very result for which Hitler had hoped.

Thus reassured that the peace of Europe was in no immediate danger, Chamberlain saw no reason to alter the course on which he had embarked, or to give

---

* This was said about six weeks after Hitler's order of May 30, under which military preparations for the attack on Czechoslovakia were to be completed by October 1, 1938.

any special warnings to the recessing Parliament. Nor does he appear to have felt any compelling need to improve Britain's international position diplomatically. Despite the British Government's mistrust of the French, and Chamberlain's own uninformed but accurate belief that the French Army was not all it was cracked up to be, he made no effort to develop or strengthen ties with the two nations—the Soviet Union and the United States—from which aid might come. For neither country did the Prime Minister have much use. "His dislike of the Soviet Union was unmistakable," reported Ambassador Dirksen after a meeting with Chamberlain on June 22, and on other occasions he and other officials were incautious enough to reveal to the Germans their desire to weaken the Franco-Soviet relations and "exclude Soviet Russia from any discussion of a European settlement." As for America, when he was consulted on a successor to the retiring ambassador Sir Ronald Lindsay, Chamberlain replied that "the Americans are so rotten" that "it does not therefore matter who we send there."

As Parliament was recessing, the Cabinet met on July 27* to be told about the Runciman mission and hear Halifax's encouraging report that "some of his advisers, who had been inclined to take rather a grave view of the outlook over Czechoslovakia, now thought that the war party in Germany had received a check at the end of May, and perhaps were receiving a further check by what was happening now, and for that reason there might be a better prospect of a peaceful issue to the affair."

The "advisers," whoever they were, had it backwards; on the issue of peace or war Hitler was the ultimate "party," and it was at the end of May that he set his mind on a speedy military solution. But of this there was as yet no inkling in London, as the M.P.s scattered for their vacations. Halifax dutifully remained in London, but Chamberlain went fishing in Scotland, Cadogan departed to spend August at Le Touquet, and British officialdom relaxed for the summer, hoping that Lord Runciman would keep the lid on things at least until the end of the holidays.

7

The Cabinet ministers were not alone in their belief that there was no imminent threat to peace; for the most part, the military were of the same opinion. In mid-June, Colonel "Mason-Mac" told his colleagues in the War Office that "the absorption of Austria is going to put the German army back two or three years," and that he reckoned 1943 "as the date by which Germany will be ready." The COS Committee minutes during the summer of 1938 reflect no feeling of emergency or apprehension about the Czech situation. At the meeting of July 25, indeed, Lord Gort expressed doubt that "if Germany considered war in the West as inevitable she would be so foolish as to get herself engaged on another front in the east." Even during August, the main concern of the Chiefs' meetings was not Czechoslovakia but Palestine, where the Jews and Arabs were in bloody conflict.

* The Cabinet met again the following day to say good-bye to its retiring Secretary, Sir Maurice Hankey. He was succeeded as Cabinet Secretary by a Treasury official, Sir Edward Bridges, as Secretary of the CID and COS (Chiefs of Staff) by General Sir Hastings "Pug" Ismay, and as Clerk of the Privy Council by R. B. Howorth.

The staff talks with the French which the Cabinet in April had forced on the reluctant Chiefs of Staff were in process through the service attachés. But the Chiefs were unwilling to raise them to a higher level, and the Army talks were confined to administrative questions relating to the initial assembly areas in France, and excluded the question of where British troops might be operationally concentrated and how they might be used.

Late in July the Foreign Office received a number of reports from secret sources indicating "that trouble may be in store for us in the autumn," and Strang forwarded them to Berlin for comment.* On July 27, Henderson replied, enclosing Mason-Mac's comments on the reports and his opinion that they did not establish a probability that Germany would attack Czechoslovakia in the fall: indeed, the military attaché could not "believe that the Führer or Göring have already made up their minds to march this autumn."

But a week later the future looked much blacker. It was almost as if Hitler had maliciously chosen Chamberlain's first cast in the trout stream as the moment to put his military machine in motion.

At the end of July the German Government announced that the entire Rhineland and large areas on the French, Czech, and Polish borders were "prohibited areas" forbidden to "the sojourn of active members of foreign armed forces," and that in September a number of divisions would be brought to war strength by calling up reservists, who would be held in service until November. On August 3, Henderson transmitted to London Mason-Mac's analysis of these steps, in which the colonel declared that they amounted to "little short of a partial test mobilization" which, given the international situation, was "desperately provocative" and made it "hard to see how at least Czechoslovakia can fail to mobilize in reply." The following day Henderson forwarded another Mason-Mac dispatch:

I have during the past month consistently endeavoured to discount rumours which ran contrary to my evidence and personal opinions, regarding intention on Germany's part to take military action against Czechoslovakia. The cry of wolf has often been raised. . . . I wish therefore to make it quite clear that although I am still of opinion that it does not necessarily follow that Herr Hitler has made up his mind irrevocably to employ force against Czechoslovakia this autumn the possibility that he may do so has now in my opinion become more real. The extent to which the Government have apparently forced the army command to undertake in September what is in effect very like "partial mobilization" can hardly fail in due course to produce a dangerous situation. . . .

Nevile Henderson was greatly alarmed by these developments, but as usual he opposed any *démarche*. His reaction was to urge on Halifax the need for immediate and greater concessions by the Czechs, and to tell a Wehrmacht intelligence officer (and no doubt other German officials) that "Great Britain would

* Strang asked Henderson to destroy his letter "in view of the nature of the sources from which the above information has been obtained." In all probability at least some of it came through "C" from secret intelligence sources. On July 28, Cadogan talked to Halifax "about secret stuff concerning German preparations," noting inconclusively in his diary: "I don't *think* I'm very much impressed by it on the whole."

not think of risking even one sailor or airman for Czechoslovakia, and . . . any reasonable solution would be agreed to, so long as it were not attempted by force."

But the German military measures had deeply alarmed Halifax and Chamberlain, who had fallen ill in Scotland and was convalescing in London. On previous occasions they had opposed French suggestions of a "strong line" in Berlin, but now they feared the German moves would provoke Czech countermeasures and destroy all hope for Runciman. On August 11, Halifax signed a memorandum, for the Prime Minister and himself, appealing to Hitler "not to do anything which might sterilize Lord Runciman's mission and prematurely [!] and unnecessarily create a fresh crisis in Europe," and specifically "so to modify his military measures as to avoid the dangers that we foresee. . . ." It was transmitted to Henderson with instructions that it be conveyed to Hitler "direct through his Chancery," with a copy to Ribbentrop.

Inasmuch as a few weeks earlier Hitler had sent Wiedemann to Halifax without informing Ribbentrop, there was ample excuse for the routing thus prescribed. Nonetheless, it might have been anticipated that the touchy Foreign Minister would find this procedure little to his liking. When Henderson, after delivering the memorandum to the Chief of the Reich Chancellery (Dr. Hans Lammers), presented a copy to Woermann for Ribbentrop, Woermann expressed "extreme astonishment at this procedure." Two days later Woermann summoned Henderson to tell him that Ribbentrop had been "unpleasantly surprised" and admonished the ambassador "to refrain in the future from the incorrect method which had been adopted for delivering the memorandum"; the "way to the Führer lay solely through the Reich Foreign Minister." Henderson, ever eager to side personally with his hosts, declared "in confidence" that "he, too, did not consider the matter correct," and failed to report his admission to London.

No doubt Halifax's memorandum would have had no better effect had it been sent through Ribbentrop. In any event, the *démarche* was a total failure; Hitler never even acknowledged its receipt, and Ribbentrop stiffly answered that "we cannot allow ourselves to enter upon any discussion about military matters."

Meanwhile the military picture grew darker. "The German situation worsened," wrote Pownall on August 22, "and I put it at even money that Hitler will barge into C-S before the end of September." Mason-Mac's official contacts on the Army staff,* with many of whom he was on good personal terms, pulled long faces and told him that the situation was very serious, while refusing him any further information about the extent of the reserve call-up or the nature and duration of the maneuvers.

Explicit and even more alarming predictions, however, were now coming in from very unofficial sources. On August 7, Mason-Mac reported a luncheon meeting with Viktor von Koerber, a retired cavalry captain and early Nazi, who now professed himself "rabidly anti-Hitler." Claiming "any number of friends

---

* The military attachés in Berlin conducted their day-to-day inquiries through the "Attaché Group," which was subordinated to the Chief of Army Intelligence, General Kurt von Tippelskirch. The Chief of the Attaché Group was Major von Mellenthin, and Mason-Mac was especially close to one of his juniors, Captain Silvius von Albedyll.

and acquaintances in the Army," Koerber declared that "war in September has already been decided upon by Herr Hitler and his intimate advisers." Mason-Mac was guarded in his response, but informed Henderson that Koerber's statements "may be worthy of credence." Two weeks later Mason-Mac was reporting a like prediction by an informant identified only as "Herr X," who declared that Hitler, addressing a gathering of Army commanders, "had announced his intention of attacking Czechoslovakia towards the end of September."

Between these two whisperers with less than full credibility came one with more impressive credentials—Ewald von Kleist-Schmenzin of the famous Prussian military and landed line, who arrived in London in mid-August with grave warnings which he conveyed to Vansittart, Churchill, and Lord Lloyd. War, he declared, was now "a complete certainty" unless Hitler were stopped. He exhibited amazement that the British did not know the crucial date, which he eventually specified as September 27. The Army leaders—"and I include even General von Reichenau"—were all opposed to war, "but they will not have the power to stop it unless they get encouragement and help from outside."

When Vansittart's memorandum of the talk with Kleist was shown to Chamberlain, he reacted very coolly: "I take it that von Kleist is violently anti-Hitler and is extremely anxious to stir up his friends in Germany to make an attempt at its overthrow. He reminds me of the Jacobites at the Court of France in King William's time and I think we must discount a good deal of what he says." But the Prime Minister was troubled and told Halifax that Britain ought "to make some warning gesture." What he proposed was "to send for Henderson and take care that everyone knew it." A few days later Halifax dispatched a telegram to Henderson informing him: "The Prime Minister and I wish to discuss the German-Czechoslovak question with you" and asking him "to reach London in time for a meeting on the morning of Monday, August 29."

Late in August the danger signals multiplied. In Berlin on the nineteenth the Italian Ambassador, Bernardo Attolico, warned Henderson that the situation "was far too dangerous for a policy of 'wait and see.'" Four days later the German chargé in London, Theodor Kordt, told Sir Horace Wilson that if Britain wanted "a reasonable solution of the Czechoslovak question . . . she must act quickly," and made it clear that Germany "would not agree to a solution which left the [Czechoslovak] State intact in its present extent." The next day a like message was delivered in distant Prague, where the German military attaché, Colonel Rudolf Toussaint, told his British opposite number, Lieutenant Colonel Stronge, that autonomy for the Sudetenland would no longer satisfy the Nazis, and that: "Nothing short of an 'Anschluss' was possible today."

The same day (August 23) came news that the German ministers in Belgrade and Bucharest had warned Czechoslovakia's two partners in the Little Entente that Germany would take "all necessary measures" unless the Czechs yielded, and that if France should come to their aid, the "German Government would regard such action as aggression." In Berlin, Mason-Mac was getting repeated warnings from the Attaché Group, and on August 24 he dispatched an extremely pessimistic analysis to his superiors, concluding: "Whatever we may decide to do or be forced to do there is the gravest possibility that we shall see the progressive test mobilisation now in progress developing into a general mobilisation as a consequence of Herr Hitler's possible declaration at Nürnberg. We have to decide whether the moment is ripe to say 'No' or whether we are prepared to let Herr Hitler attempt what he hopes to be a rapid and possibly bloodless victory over the Czechs."

The British Government's immediate reaction to these ominous reports was to reiterate, in a speech on August 27 by Sir John Simon at Lanark in Scotland, Chamberlain's March declaration that it was impossible to foresee the limits of a war provoked by the Sudeten issue. To say, in the face of the Wehrmacht's "progressive test mobilisation," no more than had been said in the wake of Goering's assurance at the time of *Anschluss* can hardly have seemed very minatory in Berlin. Furthermore, on the same day that Sir John spoke, the editor of the *New Statesman,* Kingsley Martin, published a piece recommending that if Lord Runciman failed to achieve an agreement:

> . . . the question of frontier revision, difficult though it is, should at once be tackled. The strategical value of the Bohemian frontier should not be made the occasion of a world war. We should not guarantee the status quo."*

Thus, during August the British Government had made four moves to avert the looming confrontation: the dispatch of the Runciman mission, the Halifax memorandum for Hitler, the open recall of Ambassador Henderson for consultation, and the Lanark speech. At the end of the month there was as yet no sign that any of these measures, singly or in conjunction, had had the slightest impact on Hitler's plans. Whatever those plans might be, there was much evidence that they included the use of force at the end of September if the Czechs had not yielded by that time. Chamberlain and Halifax were sufficiently aroused to send out a call to all available Cabinet members for a "Meeting of Ministers" on Tuesday, August 30.

It was not an official Cabinet meeting and there was no agenda, but despite the short notice all but four members† were on hand, as well as Henderson, recalled from Berlin. The Prime Minister opened the meeting by explaining that only the gravity of the situation had moved him to interrupt his colleagues' holidays, and then gave way to Halifax, who spoke at length.

The Foreign Minister began with a recapitulation of events since the last Cabinet meeting, and then invited his colleagues to consider two conflicting assessments of Hitler's intentions. The first, that "Herr Hitler, against the advice of the Army and of the moderate party, was determined to intervene by force"—in order "to wipe out the flavour felt by the events of 21st May," to achieve "a spectacular success for internal reasons," and because "he believed that a solution could only be achieved by force"—and reckoned that France could do little

---

* Kingsley Martin, whose voice had been one of the loudest demanding resistance to Hitler, later wrote that this article "was a mistake which I was never allowed to forget" and that his "self-reproach was bitter." He explained his action on the ground that he favored British military measures only in alliance with Soviet Russia, which did not appear likely to eventuate.

† The absentees were Lords Hailsham (Lord President), Zetland (India), and Stanley (Dominions), and Mr. Burgin (Transport).

and Britain would try to stop her from doing anything. The second, that Hitler was determined to settle the Sudeten issue in 1938, but had not yet decided to use force: "He was, however, determined to have everything ready . . . perhaps a mixture of bluff and reliance on force." Halifax did not say which alternative he espoused (he described the second as Henderson's view) but proceeded to discuss what Britain's response might be to each.

If the Fuehrer were bent on war, he said, "The only deterrent which would be likely to be effective would be an announcement that if Germany invaded Czechoslovakia we should declare war upon her." However, such a declaration "would probably have the effect of dividing public opinion, both in this country and the Empire." Furthermore, the deterrent purpose might fail, and, if so, were we ready to carry out such a threat? And he then repeated the negative arguments which he and Chamberlain had used after *Anschluss* to oppose such a guarantee, adding that even if Germany absorbed part of Czechoslovakia it might not be entirely to her advantage: "He had in mind the gathering force of world opinion particularly in the USA." He speculated inconclusively on whether France would declare war if Germany invaded Czechoslovakia. In the event of war, would Germany bomb France? Halifax "did not think that Germany would attack France unless forced to do so." Henderson ringingly chimed agreement, fatuously citing the vast numbers working on the Siegfried Line as proof that Germany would not attack France.

If Hitler was not determined on war, but only on a prompt solution by some means, there was no reason for a change of policy: "In effect we should try to keep Herr Hitler guessing; the fact that the present meeting was being held and the recall of our ambassador from Berlin would all be helpful." Halifax had considered "some rather dramatic action" involving the fleet, but had refrained because the First Lord had been away (a remarkably insufficient reason considering the gravity of the situation) and "action along these lines was not quite on all fours with the other action we were taking" (meaning, of course, the policy of conciliatory appeasement). The Prime Minister had considered summoning Parliament into special session, but this too was rejected, since it "might create the impression that we were on the verge of war" (which of course they were, unless determined to yield rather than go to war).

Halifax then revealed that "moderate Germans" were urging that Britain should publicly commit herself to resist any aggression, predicting that Hitler would then not dare to move and, indeed, his "regime would crack." This, in fact, had been the urging of "Herr X," Kleist, and other Germans, as well as Mason-Mac. But Halifax had "received these messages with some reserve" and "did not believe that the internal regime of one country was destroyed as the result of action taken by some other countries."

The Foreign Secretary concluded that the Government should continue "to keep Germany guessing as to our intentions" and "do all we could to forward the success of Lord Runciman's mission." This, of course, was no change of policy, and embraced the unspoken but implicit decision that, if Hitler were indeed bent on a solution by war, Britain would endeavor to restrain France from intervening, and let Czechoslovakia go under. Halifax ended with an admonition to his colleagues:

> There was no guarantee that this policy would be successful, but the only alternative was to make a direct threat* to Germany. He wished it to be clearly understood that if this policy failed, the Government would be told that if only they had had the courage of their convictions they could have stopped the trouble. They would be accused of deserting the principle of collective security and so forth. But these criticisms left him unmoved.

Describing Halifax's presentation as "full and masterly," the Prime Minister supported his view that no stronger statement of Britain's position should be made, despite the contrary views of others.† No state should "make a threat of war" unless willing and able to carry it out, which Britain was not. Furthermore, the threat might be ineffective with Hitler, who "was withdrawn from his Ministers, and lived in a state of exaltation." Presently the British press was backing the Government, but "if we were right up against war public opinion might well change suddenly," causing "disunity in this country, and in the Empire."

There followed a chorus of agreement from the senior ministers. Simon, Maugham, Hoare, Inskip, and MacDonald all endorsed the Halifax recommendations. Lord Maugham even questioned whether Britain should necessarily intervene if Germany invaded France, while Inskip wistfully opined that "if Germany overran Czechoslovakia, this would increase Herr Hitler's internal difficulties," and MacDonald "had little doubt that the Dominions would be in favour of holding this country back." Henderson (whom Hoare thought "overwrought") declared it "right and necessary" to reckon that Hitler had not yet decided on force, and condemned any "threat" as likely to strengthen the Nazi "extremists," who would accuse Britain of "moving towards a preventive war."

The first and only strong dissent came from Duff Cooper, who forcefully countered the Halifax and Inskip intimations that a Czech coup would weaken Germany: "On the contrary . . . it would enormously strengthen her, at any rate for the time being." In the event of a "European war" Britain would inevitably be involved, and it was a mistake to state the question as whether to go to war "for Czechoslovakia." Given the present situation:

> He thought that we ought to show that we were thinking of the possibilities of using force. He had discussed the matter that morning with the First Sea Lord from the point of view of what action we should take if we were con-

---

* Thus Halifax substituted the unpleasant word "threat" for such previously used expressions as "warning" or "making our intentions clear." British policy in 1914 had been much criticized by historians on the theory that a plain warning to Germany of the prospect of British involvement might have deterred the Kaiser's government from steps which helped to precipitate the First World War.

† Chamberlain read to his colleagues a personal letter from Robert Boothby, a Conservative M.P. and Churchill supporter, recounting a dinner conversation with four "German industrialists . . . all men of standing" who unanimously urged that the British Government issue "warnings . . . strong enough to enable the moderate elements and particularly the General Staff to make effective use of them" in combatting the war plans of the "gangsters."

templating immediate war. The Fleet was going to the North Sea in fourteen days' time. This time could be advanced by four or five days.

Duff Cooper also suggested bringing the ships' crews up to full complement, moving the battle cruiser *Repulse* from the Mediterranean to home waters, and other preparatory measures. But he got no support from the two other service ministers; Hore-Belisha thought "there was no way of preventing the Sudeten Germans from joining their compatriots," and Kingsley Wood opposed Duff Cooper's proposals and "thought that any statement that we should declare war on Germany if she invaded Czechoslovakia would divide the people of this country and that in a few weeks there would be a majority . . . against such a policy."

Of the junior ministers, Stanhope, Morrison, Brown, and Colville joined in the Halifax view without significant comment. Earl "Buck" De La Warr, the Lord Privy Seal, agreed that there should be no "threat" but "was not quite happy about the assumption that, if Germany marched, we could keep out of war," and gave Duff Cooper tepid support, as did Elliot, Oliver Stanley, and Winterton. Halifax then vetoed the First Lord's recommendation of a display of force by declaring it "not particularly desirable to play Germany's game," and the Prime Minister wound up the meeting by noting unanimity "that we should not utter a threat to Herr Hitler, that if he went into Czechoslovakia we should declare war upon him," and announcing that there was no decision on what Britain would do if Hitler attacked, and that meanwhile "nothing should be done in the nature of pinpricks."

The public announcement of the meeting said only that there had been a full statement of the international situation. This was in line with Chamberlain's expressed desire to avoid alarming the public. Indeed, there was little show of anxiety among the ministers themselves, even though the Nuremberg Party festivities were to begin within a week. Major General Pownall, Director of Military Operations and Intelligence, was on leave from September 3 to 23. Cadogan, golfing at Le Touquet, found enough in the newspapers to reflect, as the ministers met on August 30, that "a crisis is going on, and I ought to have been back," but he was not recalled. The Prime Minister and the Minister of Defence shortly departed to Scotland, where they were followed on September 4 by the First Lord of the Admiralty, who went to Drumlanrig, where he "stayed for three days, grouse-driving every day." Scotland was also the destination of the Home Secretary, serving as Minister in Attendance on King George VI at Balmoral Castle:* "As the King wished me to shoot on September 9, I stayed on for an extra day."

8

In the sense that the ministers on August 30 reached no new decisions, their meeting was a nonevent. Contrariwise, one might say that the fact they decided to do nothing, in the face of the news from Germany, was an extraordinary event.

---

* Hoare was preceded in this capacity by the Prime Minister, and succeeded on September 10 by Malcolm MacDonald.

Chamberlain had called the meeting to obtain ministerial approval of his leadership, and he got it. But he was a man of decision, and it would not have been in character for him to fail to react to the German threat. In fact he had been less than candid with his ministers, for he had up his sleeve a new card, which on August 30 had been seen by only four other men.

Two or three days before the end of August, Chamberlain discussed with Sir Horace Wilson the idea that the Prime Minister go to Germany and meet with Hitler, in an effort to resolve the Czech crisis peacefully.* On August 30, after the meeting of ministers, Sir Horace made the initial written record of the project:

> There is in existence a plan, to be called 'Plan Z,' which is known only to the Prime Minister, the Chancellor of the Exchequer, the Foreign Secretary, Sir Nevile Henderson and myself.
>
> It is to come into operation only in certain circumstances which have been discussed within the last few days, and were explained by the Prime Minister this morning after the cabinet to Sir Nevile Henderson, as it was essential he should know about it. The success of the plan, if it is to be put into operation, depends upon its being a complete surprise, and it is vital nothing should be said about it.
>
> If the circumstances do arise, an effort is to be made if possible to give Sir Nevile Henderson preliminary warning, and I have undertaken to telephone to him saying that 'Plan Z is emerging.' The object of this message would be to give him time to give us a lesson in geography.
>
> But no action is to be taken except on the authority of the Prime Minister, or, if he is not available, of the Chancellor of the Exchequer, the Foreign Secretary or myself.

The next day Sir Horace Wilson filed another memorandum elaborating the planned procedure:

> On being told that Plan Z is emerging, Henderson will ascertain where Hitler is, but will not say why he wants to know. If time permits Henderson would have a second message indicating time of arrival and authorising him to inform Ribbentrop. Again if time permits, we would like to do this before we make public announcement here that Plan Z has been put into operation. Place of arrival must be Berlin connecting with Henderson and Ribbentrop. (Schmidt† is reliable.)

It is plain from the discussion of the time factor that Plan Z was intended for a situation where only a few hours might be available before German troops would attack Czechoslovakia. More remarkable, it was contemplated that the Prime Minister would take off for Germany without invitation, and with no

---

* Keith Middlemas writes, on the basis of a later memorandum by Sir Horace Wilson (which I have not seen), that the meeting was "late at night at 10 Downing Street on 28 August" (*The Strategy of Appeasement*, p. 300). Ian Colvin writes (*The Chamberlain Cabinet*, p. 143, n. 1) that "Sir Horace does not recall the date, but has told me that it was either August 29th or 30th." The later date seems unlikely, as Wilson's memorandum, quoted above, is dated August 30 and indicates earlier discussion. Sir Alec Douglas-Home confirmed to me that the idea was the brainchild of Chamberlain and Wilson.

† Presumably a reference to Paul Otto Schmidt, the Foreign Ministry interpreter customarily assigned to Hitler's meetings with foreign dignitaries.

prior arrangements for meeting Hitler. This extraordinary feature may well account for Chamberlain's own excited hint in a letter of September 3 to his sister:

> . . . is it not positively horrible to think that the fate of hundreds of millions depends on one man, and he is half mad? I keep racking my brains to try and devise some means of averting catastrophe, if it should seem to be upon us. I thought of one so unconventional and daring that it rather took Halifax's breath away. But since Henderson thought it might save the situation at the 11th hour, I haven't abandoned it, thought I hope all the time that it won't be necessary to try it.

Chamberlain went to Balmoral, and for the next few days nothing more was heard about Plan Z.* Meanwhile on August 31 the service ministers met to consider preparatory military measures. In line with the decision to avoid "pinpricks" which might irritate the Fuehrer, only those steps which could be taken without publicity were approved. The services were to prepare papers on other measures which "it would be prudent to take, but which would involve some degree of publicity"; on these no action would be taken without the Prime Minister's approval.

On the same day Winston Churchill called on Halifax, proposing that Britain, France, and Russia jointly tell Hitler that "an invasion by Germany of Czechoslovakia would raise capital issues for all three Powers," and that Britain back up the warning with well-publicized naval measures (as Duff Cooper had unsuccessfully urged at the ministers' meeting). Wilson passed on Churchill's suggestions to Chamberlain, with a note describing them as "a mixture of diplomacy and threat," criticizing the inclusion of Russia as likely to infuriate Hitler, and warning that such a course would take Britain nearer to a commitment where "we might find ourselves . . . tackling Germany single-handed."

Churchill's ideas were not taken up, but Halifax himself, despite his firm opposition at the ministers' meeting to any "threat," was increasingly uneasy about the Government's remaining silent. Cadogan was still at Le Touquet, and his absence enabled the more activist Vansittart to move back into the higher councils, to the obvious displeasure of Chamberlain and Wilson. On September 1, in consultation with Vansittart and other Foreign Office officials, Halifax produced a draft of a speech which he proposed to deliver on either the third or fifth, with the dual purpose of lecturing the Czechs (to remedy what he thought a defect in Simon's Lanark speech, which was one-sided in that he had admonished the Germans but not the Czechs) and reinforcing the Lanark warning to Germany on the eve of the Nuremberg Party Rally, which was to open on Monday, September 5. In retrospect the draft seems innocuous enough, but it did stress the progress of British rearmament and described the British people as capable

---

* The idea of personal contact with Hitler occurred independently to Lord Weir, who wrote on September 2, in a letter forwarded by Wilson to Chamberlain: "World opinion and opinion in this country will expect that the big people, personally and directly, as soon as it is clear that the little people (Benes and Heinlein) . . . are likely to be the cause of starting the avalanche, will do something." The three "big people" were Chamberlain, Hitler, and Roosevelt, who should announce that there must be no war, and handle the situation on "direct personal grounds."

of "stern action on a wave of high resolve, if they had reason to think that it was in their power to protect a great cause from mortal injury."

Sir Horace Wilson was vastly displeased with the whole idea, and transmitted the draft to Chamberlain with the comment that "any intelligent journalist . . . could draw but one deduction, namely that we were threatening Germany." Halifax agreed to several deletions to meet Wilson's criticism, but the Prime Minister was not satisfied; one passage was "clearly a threat," another would "draw protests from Dominions," and the whole speech "out of place till after Nuremberg." Henderson and Newton also reacted to the draft unenthusiastically, and on September 6, Halifax wrote to the former that he had "more or less given up the idea of making a public speech."

However, the Foreign Secretary remained uneasy about the *status quo,** and on Sunday, September 4, at a meeting with Cadogan (back from Le Touquet), Vansittart, Wilson, and Sargent there was discussion of "the idea of a *private* warning to Hitler that we should have to come in to protect France." Cadogan "gave some support" to this proposal, on the ground that "Hitler has probably been persuaded that our March and May statements are bluff, and that's dangerous." On the next day, according to Harvey, Halifax turned against the idea. But on the evening of September 6, Sir Horace Wilson had an unexpected visitor whose message put matters in a new and much more ominous light.

His caller, who entered No. 10 Downing Street through the garden gate, was no less a person than Theodor Kordt, counsellor and at the time (in Ambassador Dirksen's absence) chargé d'affaires at the German Embassy, and the information he conveyed, putting "conscience before loyalty," was that "Hitler had taken his decision to 'march in' on 19th or 20th." When Wilson reported this to Halifax and Cadogan, they told him to bring Chamberlain back from Scotland "as soon as might be." The following morning Kordt again came secretly to Downing Street and told his story to Halifax, recommending that the British Government issue· a warning "that could not be clear and unmistakable enough," perhaps by a "broadcast to German nation."†

The same morning (September 7) *The Times* in its leading article declared that if the Sudeten Germans and Prague came to an impasse:

---

* Chamberlain told Inskip that "H. has become unsettled, no doubt under R.V.'s [Vansittart's] influence," but more likely the impetus was furnished by messages from Henderson on September 1 and 2 indicating that Ribbentrop believed that England would not "move under any circumstances," and reporting Weizsaecker's comment that "war in 1914 might possibly have been avoided if Great Britain had spoken in time."

† Kordt's information was confirmatory (except for the supposed date of the "march-in") of other intelligence recently received. Cadogan, on his return, had found "enough in the Secret Reports to make one's hair stand on end." On August 30, Lieutenant Colonel Gauché had told the British military attaché that the German Army was mobilizing so as to be "ready for immediate war against Czechoslovakia." On September 5 the British Minister at Bern reported information from Carl Burckhardt (the League of Nations Commissioner in Danzig) that Hitler had "decided to attack Czechoslovakia in about six weeks" and that the only hope for peace would be a letter from Chamberlain to Hitler "saying that if Czechoslovakia were attacked England would support her with all the forces at her command." On September 7, Robert Boothby transmitted to Vansittart a report that a "high" German general had said that a "plain declaration" from London might "prevent a war."

. . . it might be worth while for the Czechoslovak Government to consider whether they should exclude altogether the project, which had found favour in some quarters, of making Czechoslovakia a more homogeneous state by the cession of that fringe of alien populations who are contiguous to the nation to which they are united by race.

The Times had hinted at cession several times during the past few months, and what was published on September 7 was rather less than Kingsley Martin had written in the *New Statesman* eleven days earlier, but coming from *The Times* it was as a cannon to a squib. The Government promptly issued a statement that the piece "in no way represents the views of His Majesty's Government," but it caused great anxiety in both Paris and Prague, which was in no way eased when *The Times* reiterated the suggestion of territorial cession the next day. Kordt reported to Berlin the possibility that the proposal "derives from a suggestion which reached the Times editorial staff from the Prime Minister's entourage," a suspicion shared in some British circles.*

Chamberlain himself was in Scotland when the offending piece was written, but returned to London late on the seventh and the following morning held conclave with Halifax, Simon, Wilson, Cadogan, and (at Halifax's request) Vansittart. This meeting began the decision-making process which the Prime Minister employed throughout the Czech crisis. The Foreign Policy Committee of the Cabinet had not met since June 16, and would not be called together again until mid-November. Apparently Chamberlain found it too unwieldy and disputatious; at all events from this point on the "Big Four"—Chamberlain, Halifax, Simon, and (after his return to London on the tenth) Hoare—made the crucial decisions, usually meeting with Wilson, Cadogan, and Vansittart in attendance. The full Cabinet was reduced to a ratifying role, and the Parliament did not reassemble until September 28, on the eve of Munich.

The information from Kordt—which out of regard for his personal safety was very closely held and probably limited to Chamberlain, Halifax, Wilson, and Cadogan—indicated that on August 30 the ministers had accepted the wrong one of the two alternative assessments of Hitler's intentions which Halifax had put before them. Naturally, it now revived consideration of sending Hitler a private warning.

At the meeting on the morning of the eighth, however, Chamberlain opposed sending a warning, and said that "he should go himself." This, of course, was Plan Z, with which Cadogan now expressed agreement. Halifax then called in Vansittart, who was dead against the idea, likening it to the Emperor Henry IV's fabled trip to Canossa. No decision was reached, and the conference adjourned so that Chamberlain might draft a message to Hitler "saying he is coming," and Cadogan a private warning.

* Despite the Foreign Office *démenti* and Halifax's criticism of the piece in his talks with Corbin, Maisky, and Jan Masaryk, it appears that he was not ill-pleased. Geoffrey Dawson, who had written the piece on September 6 immediately upon his return from a month's holiday, recorded in his diary on the seventh: ". . . the Foreign Office went through the roof—Not so, however, the Foreign Secretary, who came and lunched with me at the Traveller's, and had a long talk. He is as much in the dark as everyone else, as to what is likely to happen next. . . ."

That afternoon Chamberlain summoned Inskip, who recorded in his diary:*

The P.M. then broached a proposal to me which he had discussed with Hx. and J.S. He thought something dramatic was needed to get out of the rut of exchanges of notes. What did I think of the idea of an offer by him to go to Germany and see Hitler. R.V. had fought the idea tooth and nail, "it was Henry IV going to Canossa over again." I was a little tepid about the proposal, and merely said it could do no harm. I was pledged to secrecy, as surprise and timing were vital to its success. Later the same day P.M. asked Kingsley Wood the same question, and I think also Malcolm MacDonald.

When the meeting resumed late in the afternoon, Chamberlain still disliked the warning message as redrafted by Cadogan and Vansittart. Furthermore, he himself had produced no draft, having decided not to give Hitler notice of his coming: "He seems to want simply to wait till after Nüremberg and then spring himself on Germany." It was a bizarre notion indeed that the Prime Minister should arrive in Germany uninvited and then, like a Martian emissary, ask to be "taken to your leader." No decision was reached that day.

While these agonizing conferences were under way on the eighth, the National Labour Executive was meeting at Blackpool, and Anthony Eden was on his way back from a vacation in Ireland, summoned by Vansittart for consultation with Halifax. The Labour Party leaders adopted a public declaration that: "The British Government must leave no doubt in the mind of the German Government that they will unite with the French and Soviet Governments to resist any attack on Czechoslovakia." Eden saw Halifax the following day and strongly urged that Hitler "in person" be informed that if there were a European conflict and France were involved, Britain would be in it "up to the neck." According to Eden, Halifax agreed, saying: ". . . my mind is moving on just such a project and indeed I was going to speak to Neville about a draft today."

These developments, reinforced by secret intelligence reports of German troop concentrations near the Czech borders, resulted in a decision late on September 9 to send a warning and at the same time start preparations for Plan Z. The message was wired to the Berlin embassy for forwarding to Henderson (in Nuremberg), and instructed him "at once" to read it to Ribbentrop and request that "it be transmitted without delay to Herr Hitler." The core of the message was generally in line with Eden's suggestions:

. . . The Czechoslovak Government has made proposals which, in the view of His Majesty's Government, go far to meet the claims put forward on behalf of the Sudeten Germans and therefore afford a reasonable and hopeful basis for negotiations. . . . If in place of this there were recourse to force, a situation would arise leading directly to a request from the Czechoslovak Government for assistance. In such circumstances His Majesty's Government are

* The only available records of these earliest "inner group" meetings are from the Inskip, Cadogan, and Harvey diaries. Unfortunately, all of these gentlemen sometimes neglected their note-making for several days and filled in the gaps later. Occasionally this led to dating errors. Inskip's diary puts his meeting with the Prime Minister on September 7, which seems unlikely, since Chamberlain was not recalled from Scotland until the evening of the sixth, and Cadogan's diary puts the disclosure of Plan Z to Vansittart on the eighth.

convinced that the French Government would consider themselves bound to discharge their Treaty obligations to Czechoslovakia.

France having thus become involved it seems to His Majesty's Government inevitable that the sequence of events must result in a general conflict from which Great Britain could not stand aside. In this connection the recent declaration made on behalf of the British Labour movement, in which they call upon the British Government to state "that they will unite with the French and Soviet Governments to resist any attack upon Czechoslovakia," shows how opinion in responsible Labour circles is moving. Whatever might be the issue of such a struggle, no one can doubt that the end must be disastrous to all concerned—victors and vanquished alike.

The use of the word "inevitable" brought the Government's position much closer to the "commitment" to which Chamberlain had been so deeply opposed, and the reference to Labour and the Soviet Government make it the more surprising that he consented to sending such a message. But it was destined never to be delivered.* Early on the morning of September 10, Henderson telephoned Cadogan, telling him that he was sending a report by courier and begging that his instructions to deliver the warning message be suspended pending consideration of his report.† A few hours later came a telegram from the Berlin embassy saying that Henderson thought the warning "would be ill-timed and disastrous in its effect."

By midafternoon the full report was in hand and was considered by the usual "inner group," now augmented by Sir Samuel Hoare, back from Balmoral. Henderson was "violently" opposed to the warning message, on the dual ground that it was superfluous, since he had already "made British position as clear as daylight to people who count," and that it would appear to the Germans as a repetition of the May 21 warning, and "drive Herr Hitler straight off the deep end." All the conferees except Vansittart agreed to accept Henderson's advice, and that evening Halifax wired Henderson: "In view of strong expression of opinion in your communications . . . and on understanding that you have in fact already conveyed to Herr von Ribbentrop and others substance of what you were instructed to say,‡ and that you are clear they can be under no misapprehension, I agree you need make no further communication."

Thus once again Halifax's attempt to speak more firmly to Hitler was aborted. In fact the Foreign Minister was playing a double game, for at the same time he was drafting warnings to Berlin he was denying Paris the commitment that the

* The fact that a warning message had been sent, together with much supporting detail, was leaked by someone "in the know" and reported in the *Daily Mail* on September 10.

† Henderson's communication facilities in Nuremberg were limited by the circumstance that he and the other foreign diplomats were required to live in their railway train compartments. A new wing of the Grand Hotel housed several distinguished British guests of the Fuehrer, including Unity Freeman-Mitford and her parents, Lord and Lady Redesdale, Sir Josiah Stamp and his wife, and Lord Brocket, chairman of the Anglo-German Fellowship.

‡ There appear to be no German records of what Henderson actually said to Ribbentrop, Goering, Goebbels, and other high officials to whom he spoke at Nuremberg. In general, he tended to placate the Germans, often expressing personal agreement with their points of view. SS Lieutenant Baumann, Henderson's escort during his stay there (September 7–11), reported that he "expressed his aversion to the Czechs in very strong terms" and "remarked with a sigh that Great Britain was now having to pay for her guilty part in the Treaty of Versailles."

French repeatedly requested. As a lame substitute for the warning message, Chamberlain held an off-the-record press conference on September 11, in which he insisted that the Germans had been sufficiently apprised of the possibility of British involvement. But the Prime Minister's heart was not in the warning strategy, for the same day he wrote to his sister explaining his continuing hostility to any categorical declaration that, if Germany should attack Czechoslovakia, Britain would at once declare war:

> . . . I am satisfied that we should be wrong to allow the most vital decision that any country could take, the decision as to peace or war, to pass out of our hands into those of the ruler of another country, and a lunatic at that. . . . There is another consideration . . . and that is the plan, the nature of which I think you have guessed correctly. The time for this has not yet arrived . . . but in the meantime I do not want to do anything which would destroy its chance of success because, if it came off, it would go far beyond the present crisis, and might prove the opportunity for bringing about a complete change in the international situation.

This was a foretaste of the "Peace for our Time" which Chamberlain proclaimed on his return from Munich, and reveals the expanse of the hopes which he was already lodging in Plan Z. Preparing for its execution began on September 9 with a letter from Wilson to Henderson warning him that the moment of decision was approaching, and continuing:

> We have in the meantime, with one eye upon Nuremberg, considered sending word to H. [Hitler] through you at once saying that X [Chamberlain] had it in mind to come and have a talk with him, and asking him in the circumstances not to say anything unpleasant in the course of his speech on Monday.*
>
> We thought, however, that there were a number of objections to this, perhaps the most important of which is that it would provide H with an opportunity to get Ribbentrop to write a lengthy reply raising all sorts of awkward questions and generally creating a fog through which it would be difficult to penetrate. We should then have shot our bolt and there would be nothing in reserve. We are therefore at the moment back on Z simpliciter.† . . . One point that we have been discussing today is whether X, on arrival in Berlin, is likely to be met by you with a statement to the effect either that H. would not see him or, (perhaps) is "ill" and cannot see him.
>
> This would be very awkward and would not look very well over here. What are your views about this, and what line do you think H would be likely to take? Would the kudos of a visit so appeal to him as to deter him from administering such a rebuff? In any case, would he think it worth while so to flaunt us, and so to exasperate world opinion, which undoubtedly would be all the more consolidated against him.
>
> If you think the risks of a rebuff are real, one alternative would be for you (on hearing from us) to let H know that X proposes to come arriving at B [Berlin] at such a time and for you to ask H to fix the hour at which he

---

* Monday, September 12, when Hitler would give the concluding Nuremberg speech, which the British, French, and Czechs were awaiting with apprehension.

† Meaning the plan that Chamberlain should arrive in Berlin without prior notice of his coming.

would be ready to see X. This would give H time to say "No" if he wanted to, and for you to convey that answer before X left here. It would therefore eliminate the risk of a rebuff.

On the other hand if the answer *was* no, X would never have an opportunity of putting his case and the last chance of peace might be lost. There would also be some lessening of the dramatic effect of a surprise on which X sets a certain store. We should very much like you to think this over carefully and give us your views as soon as possible.

Henderson replied the same day, giving his opinion that: "The moment for X is not come. . . . Here at Nuremberg it would be out of the question." On the remarkable notion of Chamberlain's coming uninvited, the ambassador for once showed himself more stable than his chiefs:

> While I greatly doubt H. being ill and refusing to see X, he might think things had gone so far that German honour would not allow him to stop. I do not think that the risk should be run, as such a rebuff to X could not be tolerated. I feel I should have to advise you on this when you telephoned about Z, and that Z should not function until *after* you have telephoned. H will presumably go to Berchtesgaden as soon as Nuremberg is over.
>
> I feel much more certain that the answer would not be no if there was previous arrangement: and *I don't really like the idea of proceeding without previous arrangement.* I would not advise it unless it was practically impossible to hope to save the situation except by a departure at the very moment itself.
>
> I don't believe that the "kudos" aspect would appeal much if H felt that German honour (his idea of it) had been so injured that action alone could satisfy it.

These counsels reached London on the afternoon of September 10. From then until late on the thirteenth, Plan Z was the focus of discussion by the inner group, and the subject matter of various drafts of messages from Chamberlain to Hitler, as reflected in Cadogan's diary entry for Sunday, November 11:

> After breakfast rewrote H.J.W.'s [Wilson's] draft for "Plan Z". . . . Discussed my redraft with H. [Halifax] before the huddle at 12. Huddle jiggered draft about. . . . Back at F.O. 2.30 to rewrite draft again. All sorts of bothers and questions. Huddle again at 5.30. Re-draft approved —with further alterations. . . ."

Chamberlain's original idea of an unannounced landing in Berlin (it must have been this feature which "rather took Halifax's breath away") was discarded at the latest by September 12, when he sent a long letter to Runciman outlining the plan. After observing "that we must be prepared for the possibility of a sudden change for the worse," he wrote:

> I have been considering a sudden and dramatic step which might change the whole situation. The plan, which is known here as Z, has been imparted to Henderson, and I have discussed it with Halifax and a few of my colleagues. I do not propose to reveal it to the Cabinet until the last minute as its virtue lies in the element of surprise and the smaller the number of persons in the secret the less likelihood there is of a leakage. . . .
>
> The plan is that I should inform Hitler that I propose at once to go over to

Germany to see him. If he consents, and it would be difficult for him to refuse, I should hope to persuade him that he had an unequalled opportunity of raising his own prestige and fulfilling what he has so often declared to be his aim, namely the establishment of an Anglo-German understanding preceded by a settlement of the Czechoslovakian question.

True to his intention thus revealed to Runciman, the Prime Minister said nothing about Plan Z* when the Cabinet met that same day. He told his colleagues that their meeting, "announced in advance, will assist in keeping public opinion steady," and then called on Halifax to tell them what had transpired since the ministers' meeting of August 30. The Foreign Secretary traced the events which had led to the dispatch of the warning message on September 9 despite the negative decision on August 30, stressing the distinction between public and private warning, and the ominous nature of the information after the thirtieth. He recounted Henderson's objections to delivering the message, and the decision on the tenth to accept his advice, despite Churchill's recommendation that the Government should say that if Germany "set foot in Czechoslovakia we should at once be at war with her." Anthony Eden, however, "had expressed complete agreement with the line taken."†

Halifax concluded by remarking, with characteristic vagueness, that "Herr Hitler was possibly or even probably mad." If he had decided to attack Czechoslovakia, it was doubtful that any ultimatum would stop him. The wise course "was to await Herr Hitler's speech and then review the situation."

There was, indeed, very little the Cabinet could decide at that moment; as Duff Cooper acidly recorded: "The Cabinet was called at the worst possible moment—too late to take any action before Hitler's speech, too soon to consider the new situation which that speech might create." He tangled sharply with Chamberlain over the withdrawal of the warning message on the sole advice of Henderson, and suggested that the Cabinet should now authorize its utterance, but the matter was not pressed to a vote.

It was a diffuse and feckless meeting (which probably was what Chamberlain wanted) until the very end, after Kingsley Wood had suggested, and the others approved, that the Chiefs of Staff submit an updated assessment of the military situation in the event of war with Germany. Oliver Stanley then asked that their report should also include an analysis of the situation a year hence, if Germany were now allowed to overrun Czechoslovakia and expand her influence in southeastern Europe. From a military standpoint this was, indeed, a crucial

---

* Inskip and Kingsley Wood were cautioned before the meeting by Wilson "to be careful not to mention it, either in or out of the Cabinet."

† Whether or not deliberate, this was a misrepresentation of Eden's views. Harvey recorded that on September 10 Eden was "very worried at the decision not to send a further warning," and that when he saw Halifax the next day "he saw the point of not sending warning in view of Henderson's advice but he mistrusted the man's judgment: he urged that the Government should announce further naval movements." Eden himself wrote in his diary on the tenth that he believed Henderson's advice "to be wrong"; on the eleventh he wrote Halifax lamenting the Government's failure to announce the naval measures he had advocated; and on the twelfth *The Times* published Eden's letter declaring: "In any international emergency that threatened the security of France this country would be found at the side of the French Republic, whatever the consequences."

question, which the Chiefs should have been asked to confront at the time of *Anschluss*.

After approving Halifax's noncommittal answer to Bonnet's inquiry whether, if France "marched," Britain would march with her,* the Cabinet adjourned to await the Fuehrer's words from Nuremberg. Meanwhile Wilson had roughed out the contents of alternative messages to Hitler to launch Z, one on the assumption that the "speech is deplorable," the other that "the speech appears moderate." In either case, Henderson should "resort to every measure to ensure that the message reaches Herr Hitler himself with the least possible delay," if necessary by asking for "an immediate audience," whether Hitler was in Berlin or Berchtesgaden. The Prime Minister "might decide to be ready to start at once on receipt of a not unfavourable reply," while if unfavorable "the plan could not be executed, but it might be thought advisable to publish the correspondence." Wilson concluded "that the spectacular effect on public opinion everywhere of making the journey *by air* is likely to be considerable."

The Big Four met after Hitler's speech, and agreed that it "pulls no triggers," as Cadogan put it. There was some discussion of defense measures, after which the decision-makers adjourned "to sleep on" the situation.

They awoke to a very dark day. Hitler's speech "pulled triggers" in the Sudetenland, where riots forced the Czech Government to declare martial law, whereupon the Henleinists suspended negotiations with Prague and issued a virtual ultimatum to the Government. Henderson telephoned a message interpreting Hitler's speech as a declaration that "failing immediate grant of autonomy to the Czechs he will march." Phipps reported that Bonnet had "completely lost his nerve" and was in a sudden and extraordinary state of "collapse." British secret intelligence sources reported that German embassies and legations had been told that Czechoslovakia would be invaded on September 25, and there were new reports of troop concentrations.

In this charged atmosphere the Big Four met morning and afternoon, but there apparently was little discussion of Plan Z. Instead, there was extensive talk about plebiscites in the disputed areas, the possibilities of which Halifax had been studying for some time. They presented many difficulties: in which areas should they be held? Would the Czechs agree to them without "some form of guaranty from this country?" Would not the plebiscites "be hailed as a maximum triumph for Hitler?" Despite all these shortcomings they were seen as preferable to a war.

The conferees also discussed two proposals emanating from the French. Bonnet was pushing for immediate promulgation of a "Runciman plan" to resolve the crisis. This idea was viewed with reserve, as whatever he produced would "be labelled as the British plan." Léger had proposed a four-power (Britain, France, Germany, Italy) conference, but it was doubted that Hitler would see any attraction in this other than the "exclusion of Russia."

At six o'clock the Big Four met with the service ministers and Chiefs of Staff to discuss further military measures. Duff Cooper immediately proposed mobilizing the fleet. He acknowledged that the meeting had no authority to take such a step, but urged that "only facts would impress Germany" and "we might be able to preserve peace, and such action could not be construed as a provocative measure, as we should only be defending our own shores." Chamberlain was opposed ("quite rightly," Cadogan thought) but allowed that it could be discussed in Cabinet the following day. Duff Cooper doubted the wisdom of waiting, and urged a Cabinet meeting that night, but could not move his colleagues. The conferees then discussed a number of specific proposals, but few were approved (three of the Navy's eleven) as Chamberlain shrank from any steps involving publicity.

Later that evening came Daladier's futile effort to speak to Chamberlain on the telephone, after which, at about ten o'clock, the Prime Minister met with Halifax, Wilson, and Cadogan. Whether or not Chamberlain had already decided to put Plan Z into operation that evening is a matter of speculation. The Big Four had agreed on September 10 that a move of such moment would require Cabinet approval, and Chamberlain had only a few hours earlier rejected Duff Cooper's suggestion of a Cabinet meeting that evening. At all events, he now announced his decision to proceed, and took the lead in drafting a telegram to Hitler. Before dispatching it, however, Wilson sent a note to Sir John Simon: "Do you think it would be well to summon Cabinet before doing this? If so, call tonight." The Chancellor of the Exchequer wrote back: "I do *not* think it is necessary. Cab. will trust P.M. S.H. agrees."

The famous message was:

In view of increasingly critical situation I propose to come over at once to see you with a view to trying to find a peaceful solution. I propose to come across by air and am ready to start tomorrow.

Please indicate earliest time at which you can see me and suggest place of meeting. Should be grateful for your early reply.

Henderson was alerted by telephone and informed that: "Our intention is to make no public reference . . . until the Chancellor has had the opportunity of sending reply which we hope we may have at earliest possible moment."

It would indeed have been awkward for Chamberlain had there been any public reference at that time, for the British constitutional rule is that the Prime Minister must secure the sovereign's consent to his leaving the country, and as yet the King had no knowledge of Plan Z.* Chamberlain was not unmindful of the requirement, and some time on September 13 prepared a letter to the King (who was still at Balmoral) which described Plan Z in much the same language that he had used in his letter of the twelfth to Runciman. At the end of the letter to the King, Chamberlain expressed the hope that if the plan were adopted, he would have the King's permission "to absent myself from the country . . . in a last attempt to save the peace of Europe."

---

* On September 6, Chamberlain had written to the King: ". . . I have a 'hunch,' as J. P. Morgan says, that we shall get through this time without the use of force. . . . I don't think we have fired the last shot in our locker." No doubt Plan Z was in the Prime Minister's mind as he wrote the second sentence.

After dispatching the telegram to Hitler, Chamberlain added to the King's letter a postscript:

> Events on the Continent of Europe have moved so rapidly and the situation appears to have become so critical that I have sent a personal message to Herr Hitler that I propose to travel to Germany by air and I am ready to start tomorrow. . . . I trust that my action will have your approval.

Since the message had already gone to Hitler, the King was, of course, confronted with a *fait accompli*. Highly unlikely as it is that the monarch would have withheld permission, this was unnecessarily cavalier treatment of the Constitution and the sovereign. The letter did not reach King George until the afternoon of the fourteenth, when he gave his approval by telephone.

The Cabinet was called together the following morning, before any reply had been received. The Prime Minister began by claiming that Hitler's speech had vindicated the decision not to send another warning, since the Fuehrer had said nothing "irrevocable." The speech, he observed, had "pointed" toward a plebiscite, and "it would be difficult for the democratic countries to go to war in order to prevent the Sudeten Germans from saying what form of government they wanted to have."

Chamberlain then unveiled Plan Z, explaining that "the vital element in this plan was surprise" and therefore "he had thought it better to postpone mentioning it until the last moment." He continued: "Up to yesterday afternoon . . . he had had it in mind that this plan . . . should be put into effect probably towards the end of the present week. On the preceding afternoon, however, events had started to move rapidly. . . ." He then recapitulated the events in Czechoslovakia and Paris, as a basis for explaining why he had launched Plan Z without consulting the Cabinet:

> In these circumstances the Prime Minister said that he and the Foreign Secretary, with the advice of the Chancellor of the Exchequer and the Home Secretary—themselves two former Foreign Secretaries—had decided that plan 'Z' should be put into operation at once. A telegram had accordingly been despatched to Sir Nevile Henderson.*
>
> The Prime Minister said that his hand had been forced, since a position had been reached in which, unless plan 'Z' was put into effect quickly, it could not be adopted at all. He hoped that the Cabinet would feel that he had not gone beyond his proper duty in taking this action on the advice of those of his colleagues whom he had mentioned, but without consulting the full Cabinet.

This was shrewdly put, but in fact Chamberlain had said nothing to explain why a delay of twelve hours would have been dangerous, or why the Cabinet could not have been called the previous evening, as Duff Cooper had recommended. Nevertheless, Simon's judgment that the Cabinet would "trust" the Prime Minister was sound; only Walter Elliot grumbled about being rushed to a decision without prior consultation and declared that "we were being led by pressure to do something which we would not have done of our own free will." Duff Cooper declared that "he had intended to propose the mobilization of the

---

* Copies of this telegram were distributed to the Cabinet members.

Fleet" but that this "was now out of the question, and he much preferred plan 'Z'." Why he thought the two moves incompatible he did not say, and he joined in "unanimous and enthusiastic" approval of the plan. Simon then bestowed what Inskip called "his usual shower of compliments" on Chamberlain, predicting that "if he comes back with the seeds of peace with honour, he will be immediately acclaimed as having carried out the greatest achievement of the last twenty years." The Prime Minister gave suitable thanks, and stowed away the Disraeli phrase for future repetition when opportunity offered.

When the Cabinet adjourned there was still no word from Hitler. He and Ribbentrop were in Munich, and Henderson had given the Prime Minister's message to Weizsaecker in Berlin for forwarding to Ribbentrop, who would present it to the Fuehrer. The reply came in midafternoon: The Fuehrer would be happy to receive the Prime Minister at the Berghof on the following day, September 15, and he was invited to bring Mrs. Chamberlain "if he so wishes." The agreed public communiqué was issued that evening, and next morning the Cabinet members and other British and foreign dignitaries gathered at Heston Airport to give the Prime Minister (who took Wilson and Strang with him) a good send-off.

Thus the Prime Minister set in train the events leading directly to Munich. Plan Z was his own conception (with an assist from Wilson), and he had put it into execution without the prior approval of either King or Cabinet.

Undeniably, Neville Chamberlain was a man of decision. He was also a man of courage, moved by his own vision of what he could do to make a safer and happier world for all mankind. His spirit, at least, was worthy of the tribute paid him by the Poet Laureate, John Masefield:

> *As Priam to Achilles for his son,*
> *So you, into the night, divinely led,*
> *To ask that young men's bodies, not yet dead,*
> *Be given from the battle not begun.*

Part V

THE CONFRONTATION: 1938

CHAPTER 25

The Wehrmacht:
On the March but Out of Step

1

"The Führer signs Directive Green," wrote General Jodl in his diary on May 30, 1938, "wherein he decides to destroy Czechoslovakia in the near future, and thus starts military preparations all along the line." Jodl continued:

> The previous intentions of the Army must be considerably changed so as to envisage an immediate breakthrough into Czechoslovakia on X-day [the first day of the attack] together with an attack by the Luftwaffe. . . .
> Once again the opposition becomes acute between the Führer's perception that we must do it this year, and the Army's opinion that we cannot do it yet, as the Western powers would surely interfere and we are not yet a match for them.

Within the Army, the weightiest voice expressing this negative view was that of the Chief of the General Staff, General Ludwig Beck. Since Hitler had ordered that preparations for the attack be completed by October 1 "at the latest," there remained only four months to resolve the conflict and, if the Fuehrer's decision remained unaltered, put the plan into execution.

Beck's disapproval of Hitler's program was no secret in high Government circles. Three years earlier he had denounced the *Schulung* plan for a surprise assault on Czechoslovakia, and the previous November he had forcefully criticized Hitler's presentation at the "Hossbach" meeting. Within a few weeks after *Anschluss* it became apparent that Hitler intended to lose no time in disposing of Czechoslovakia, and on May 7, Beck presented to Brauchitsch the first of what became a series of memoranda condemning Green. The gist of Beck's case was that, in the event of an attack on Czechoslovakia, Germany could count on no reliable or strong allies, and would face the united forces of Britain and France backed by the arsenal of America, as well as of Russia. For such a struggle the Wehrmacht was unready, and the war economy insufficient. Accordingly, for the time being the Czech problem could be approached only within the framework of a solution acceptable to Britain.

Three weeks later Beck attended the meeting of May 28, at which Hitler announced his "smash Czechoslovakia at the first opportunity" policy. No doubt wisely, Beck said nothing at the time,* but the next day he composed a written response, which he read to Brauchitsch on May 30. He conceded Germany's need for more territory, and that Czechoslovakia must eventually be reduced in size. But he repeated his earlier arguments about the danger of Anglo-French intervention and Germany's unreadiness to face a major war. Furthermore, declared Beck, the military leaders were not being sufficiently consulted, and Hitler was moving rapidly toward "untenable propositions" which might seal Germany's fate.

The same day that Beck laid these views before Brauchitsch, Hitler signed the revised Green directive, with the October 1 deadline. This precipitated still another memorandum from Beck, dated June 3, which criticized the new directive as "militarily unsound" and based on an over-estimate of the Wehrmacht's strength. Confronted as he now was by a direct order from on high, however, Beck was moved to add an admonition "that the military bases of the order will not withstand conscientious examination . . . and that the General Staff of the Army must explicitly decline responsibility for its narrow, insufficient military bases, so far as concerns the Army."

In assessing the prudence of these memoranda, one must first inquire: whom were they intended to influence? It must be remembered that the Chief of the General Staff no longer carried the authority pertaining to that office in the days of Hindenburg, when he was the chief military adviser to the Kaiser and issued orders in the name of the All Highest. Beck was Chief of Staff to Brauchitsch, the Army Commander-in-Chief, and had no access to the Fuehrer except through Brauchitsch; indeed, Beck had had only occasional personal contact with Hitler.

But even assuming that Brauchitsch would pass Beck's papers on to Hitler, they were poorly calculated to influence a man who saw himself as touched with strategic genius and had little respect for the political wisdom of generals. If Hitler was the intended reader, it was naïve to hope to achieve anything by lecturing him on what England or France or Russia or Italy would or would not do about Czechoslovakia.

This aspect of the situation was not lost on Keitel, whom Brauchitsch consulted about the handling of the Beck memoranda. Keitel was no strategist and

---

* To controvert the Fuehrer in the presence of so many other officials would have been counterproductive, and to take such an initiative in the presence of his own Commander-in-Chief (Brauchitsch) a grave breach of protocol. According to Hitler's Army adjutant, Captain Gerhard Engel, Beck attended the meeting only reluctantly and after a direct order from Hitler. Engel and Schmundt had both urged Beck to attend, but Beck had told Engel that Halder would come in his stead, and later asked Schmundt to say that Beck was working on a memorandum that Hitler would soon read. It is doubtful that Schmundt would have delivered such a message.

was putty in Hitler's hands, but he had some administrative sense, and on his advice Brauchitsch suppressed the political portions and sent on to Hitler only the parts discussing the comparative military strengths of the powers involved. Even these precautions failed of their purpose; as Keitel later wrote: ". . . the only result was a very sharp protest from Hitler that the data were not objective and that the balance of strength had been depicted far too favourably for the enemy. . . . It was another disaster for the Army and resulted in a further loss of confidence in Brauchitsch. . . ."

Beck, however, had a considerable following in the General Staff, particularly among the older officers. He could not, of course, instruct his subordinates to oppose official directives, but there were other ways to make his views known. As Chief of the General Staff, Beck had authority to select and define the subject of the annual General Staff exercise—the *Generalstabsreise*—and for the spring of 1938 he had chosen a hypothetical attack on Czechoslovakia and posed as problems how best it could be executed, and how long it would take to achieve victory, taking into account the probability that France would honor her treaty and attack Germany from the west. The upshot of the exercise was that the French broke through the German screening forces and arrived in strength near Frankfurt, where the Wehrmacht sustained a catastrophic defeat.

At the end of the exercise came a concluding conference, addressed by both Beck and Brauchitsch.* The former delivered, with great emphasis and earnestness, an analysis of the exercise which many if not all those present sensed as a warning against the dire consequences of plans germinating in the High Command. Brauchitsch made only a few formal remarks, neither endorsing nor disavowing the implications of Beck's speech.

A vivid account of this episode is given in a book, published a quarter of a century later, by the then Lieutenant Colonel Edgar Röhricht,† operations staff officer of IV Corps in Dresden: "There stood the Chief of the German General Staff, in the eyes of the world the prototype of militarism, in the circle of his colleagues, with his alarm-call against a looming war. . . . Stronger than all of his arguments, for me, was the adjuring quality of the words, spoken from an imperious command of conscience."

But at the festive dinner which followed, it became apparent to Röhricht that the listeners were not all of one mind. Old and close friends of his included both Major Rudolf Schmundt (Hossbach's successor as adjutant to Hitler) and Lieutenant Colonel Hans Jeschonnek, chief of operations on the Luftwaffe General Staff, and soon to become, at the age of forty, Goering's Chief of Staff. Schmundt was "the son of a Potsdam general" and an "idealistic old-Prussian type" who had greatly revered Beck. His few weeks with the Fuehrer had turned his head completely; to Röhricht's astonishment Schmundt loudly criticized both the exercise, which "failed to take account of the dynamics of the new times," and Beck himself as "a ridiculous petitioner at the Geneva table." For his part,

* None of the accounts of this meeting gives its date or location. The scheduled duration of the *Generalstabsreise* was from April 27 to May 10.
† Röhricht, *Pflicht und Gewissen* [Duty and Conscience] (1965), pp. 119–23. During the war, Röhricht served as Chief of Staff of the First Army and later as a corps commander. and rose to the rank of lieutenant general.

Jeschonnek denounced "the hierarchy of everlasting yesterdays," declaring scornfully: "The blind will see as soon as Beck will! Thirty days for those ridiculous Hussites! As if there wasn't any Luftwaffe! Schlieffen set back military technique by 20 years, and on the Marne we paid the price. For Beck, our squadrons are only a troublesome appendix. But all of you will soon see the most stupendous things!" And so the wrangling continued, with the anti-Beck sentiments generally coming from the younger officers. Time, the expansion of the Army, and Hitler's successes had destroyed the legendary unity of the German General Staff.

2

Far from exercising any restraining influence on the Fuehrer, Beck's address (which must have been reported by Schmundt) and his memoranda only aroused Hitler's anger and contempt. "What kind of generals are these, that I as head of the State have to push into war!" the Fuehrer was reported as saying, and: "I do not demand that my generals understand my orders, only that they obey them." But for the time being he took no action to replace Beck, probably for fear that such a step might cause public alarm.*

Beck's predictions of French and British intervention, if Hitler heard them, surely troubled him not a whit. On such a matter Hitler had little use for any judgment but his own, and the diplomatic intelligence reaching him through Ribbentrop gave little cause for concern. Both London and Paris seemed bent on staying in his good graces. Immediately after the Anglo-French talks at the end of April, rather than using them to make a show of fresh determination, Halifax had been at pains to assure Kordt that Britain had made no new commitments. In virtually every conversation with German diplomats, the British and French representatives stressed their determination to bring such pressure to bear on the Czechs that Germans wishes vis-à-vis the Sudeten question would be amply fulfilled.

Unofficial and perhaps unpremeditated comments by British officials also reinforced, in German minds, the conclusion that Allied talk of armed intervention was largely bluff. On April 22, "Rab" Butler, newly designated Under-Secretary for Foreign Affairs, described himself to Kordt and Woermann as one of the "intelligent" but not "intellectual" younger generation who did not share the antiauthoritarian views of the "intellectuals," and who "fully understand that Germany had to pursue her national aims in her own way." Germans and Englishmen were of the same blood, constituting a "bond of unity," and it was "inconceivable" that there should be another Anglo-German war. As to Czechoslovakia, England was "aware that Germany would attain 'her next goal.'"

Chamberlain's selection of Butler and his heavy reliance on Sir Horace Wilson (whom the Wilhelmstrasse had categorized as "decidedly pro-German")

---

* Hitler had been personally well disposed toward Beck ever since 1930, when the latter testified in support of three lieutenants in his regiment at Ulm who were charged with spreading Nazi propaganda (see pp. 84–85). By 1938, however, Hitler regarded Beck as "imprisoned in the ideas of the 100,000-man Army," and he told Engel that he could work better with Halder, who had a "modern" outlook, and that Beck's "days were numbered."

were regarded in Berlin as reflectors of the Prime Minister's own predilections. Such inferences were no doubt strengthened by Sir Nevile Henderson's ingratiatory ad libs such as his rhetorical question to Ribbentrop, on May 11, whether it could be imagined "that British soldiers would again march into Germany." Ten days later Daladier, meeting at his home with Count von Welczeck, added to the accumulation of ineptitude by revealing his own anti-Semitism and declaring that he had not made the alliance with Czechoslovakia and was "certainly not happy about it." Then on June 3 *The Times* tentatively proposed a plebiscite for the Sudetenland, and again Berlin's informants suggested that it represented official thinking (as, indeed, it did). If the British were willing to see mayhem committed on Czechoslovakia by plebiscite, was it credible that they would go to war to prevent its being accomplished by military force?

3

Thus persuaded that there was little danger of Allied intervention in support of the Czechs, Hitler pushed ahead vigorously with the military preparations. The three matters which appeared most important were (1) to assemble the German forces in a manner which would not tip his hand too early, (2) to devise a deployment which would enable the Wehrmacht to inflict a decisive defeat on the Czechs at the earliest possible moment, so as to confront their allies with a *fait accompli,* and (3) to rush construction of fortifications on the western borders, so as to discourage the French and enable that front to be held with weak forces if, contrary to expectations, France should attack.

While the first two were primarily planning tasks, the third required the immediate mobilization of manpower and materials. It was to this project—known variously as the "West Wall," "Limes" (after the Romans), and the "Siegfried Line"—that Hitler first turned his personal attention.

He was by no means unfamiliar with fortification problems. Ever since the First World War there had been a sharp division of opinion among the Army leaders between those who favored a linear defense system along the German borders, and those who favored areas fortified in depth at places where attacks were likely to occur and where the terrain was favorable for defense. In the mid-1930s Generals Blomberg, Keitel, Manstein, and Fromm favored the first course, while Fritsch, Beck, and the Army fortifications specialist General Otto-Wilhelm Förster* were of the other opinion. When rearmament got under way the issue had to be resolved; the contending generals were unable to do so, and in October of 1935 they put the matter up to Hitler, who accompanied them on a tour of the fortifications then under construction near the Polish frontier.

The Fuehrer decided on the fortified-area concept, and fixed a period of fifteen years for the completion of a general system of fortifications. But a few months later the Rhineland was remilitarized, and the focus of fortification activity was shifted from the Polish to the French frontier, while the time allowance for completion of the plans was reduced first to ten and then to four years.

Only a beginning was made on the western fortifications during the two years

* Förster, from 1933 to November 1938, was Chief of the Army Inspectorate of Fortifications and Engineers.

following the Rhineland remilitarization. Blomberg ruled that there would be "no Maginot Line" in the west, and he and Fritsch moved conservatively and authorized only the construction of obstacles (rather than fortifications) on the border between the Mosel at Luxembourg and the Rhine at Karlsruhe, and behind the Rhine south of that city; construction on the Rhine itself was forbidden, and the importance of camouflage was stressed. Allocations of materials and funds for these purposes during 1936 and 1937 were small, partly because of expenditures to construct the famous *Autobahnen*. By the time of *Anschluss* only a few hundred small concrete emplacements had been built. On March 9, 1938, Hitler personally approved extension of the obstacle construction on the Belgian and Dutch frontiers, under a two-year program.

In fact, prior to the May crisis there is no evidence that Hitler had been greatly concerned about the pace of fortification work in the west. On May 27, however, he summarily ordered an acceleration of the program so as to complete, by October 1, 1,800 large gun emplacements and 10,000 pillboxes (*Bunker*), to be distributed so as to provide protection for eleven divisions. Revising his 1935 decision, Hitler called for a linear defense system along the French and Belgian frontiers. To expedite these ambitious designs, the Army was to assign more fortification engineer troops to the task; the State Labor Service (*Reich Arbeitsdienst,* or RAD) was to commit 50,000 men, and the General Inspector of Roads, Dr. Fritz Todt, was to be put in charge of "a large part of the concrete construction." Brauchitsch passed on these orders to General Wilhelm Adam, heading Group Command 2 in western Germany, who was directly responsible for their execution.

General Adam was a Bavarian, sixty-two years old, fourth in seniority of all Army generals on active duty, and in the event of war was to be in command of the German ground forces on the western front. Since he had passed most of his peacetime service in Munich and Berlin, and had been Chief of Staff* when the Nazis came to power, he was well known to Hitler and many Party leaders, who regarded Adam as a supporter of Schleicher and Hammerstein and did not trust him. But he was basically unpolitical, amiable, and of such outstanding military competence that he was highly regarded not only by Beck and the OKH staff, but also by Keitel and, especially, Jodl, a fellow-Bavarian who had been Adam's pupil at the War Academy.

Exceptionally and often amusingly blunt, Adam made no bones about telling Brauchitsch that Hitler's order was absurd and betrayed a weakness for figures at the expense of realities. Effective fortification could not be obtained by sowing concrete along the French border the way a gardener seeds the lawn. Adam was an adherent of the "fortified-area" school and, as he put it in his memoirs, Hitler was imagining a Roman boundary wall (*limes*), while a twentieth-century soldier should rather think in terms of a battlefield in which fortifications aid the defender. They should not follow the political boundary, but be placed (perhaps miles back of the frontier) so as best to exploit the terrain and open up fields of

---

* Because of the Versailles Treaty restrictions, Adam's title was "Chief of the Troops Department," but he performed the functions of Chief of Staff to the commander of the Reichswehr, at that time General Kurt von Hammerstein-Equord.

fire. Camouflage was vital, and the construction should provide for ventilation, protection against gas, and other necessities.

Given all these problems and more, Adam told Brauchitsch, Hitler ought to be satisfied if by October he had good plans for the fortifications, and a few of the important emplacements had been built. Brauchitsch answered only by declaring that he had Hitler's orders.

The leader of the RAD was Konstantin Hierl, a Bavarian and a former general staff officer who had resigned from the Army to join the Nazis in 1924; Adam had known him for many years and had less than no use for him. Dr. Todt had a much more attractive personality and had achieved a deserved reputation for his design of the *Autobahnen,* but what did he know of Vauban's art of fortification? And as for Brauchitsch, that gentleman had exposed himself for what he was: Hitler's yes-man and no true commander-in-chief.

Hitler now aggravated these tensions by sending Hermann Goering to inspect and report on the state of the western defenses. The Fat One had already, in his capacity as Luftwaffe Commander-in-Chief, established (on June 1) a "Western Air Defense Zone," intended to comprise secondary fortifications and anti-aircraft installations. Eager to reap personal credit for the western defenses, Goering arrived* at the northern end of the front (Trier) in his luxurious private train, with Milch, Hierl, and a large staff.

It soon became apparent that his main purposes were to find fault with everything and turn the trip into a personal political triumph. At every stop the SA and SS were out with banners and the populace with flowers. Goering, totally ignorant of the subject at hand, criticized everything, pulled rank, and shouted down the juniors. After two days Adam had had enough; he took his leave, and Goering went on with the staff.†

Upon his return, Goering delivered himself of a report to Hitler which, according to Keitel, "was one long accusation against the Army from beginning to end; virtually nothing had been done, what had been done was inadequate, and there was hardly the most primitive defence system." Hitler reacted like a spoiled child who had forgotten to do his homework. He had throughout been personally involved in the fortifications work, had repeatedly altered the fundamentals of the program, and had done nothing to expedite it until the May 27 order. Adam had no responsibility for the embryonic state of the fortifications, as he had taken command in the west only in April.

The fact was, of course, that Hitler had been caught short by his own sudden

---

* Adam was notified on June 8 of Goering's coming, and Goering reported back to Hitler on June 14.

† The principal junior staff officer was Captain Reinhard Gehlen, later chief of intelligence for the West German Government. In 1938 he was serving in the operations and fortifications sections of the Army General Staff, and was assigned as a specialist to the Goering party. He later wrote (Gehlen, *The Service* [1972], pp. 22–23): "Goering made no secret of his criticism. . . . No sooner had I opened my mouth to answer Goering's criticism than he interrupted me, referred to me as a 'young man,' and silenced me."

Adam's recollections of Goering are varied. In 1933, Ernst Roehm had warned him that Goering was "intelligent but unreliable," and in 1938, Adam found him intolerable—boasting of his Cranach at Karinhall, and clutching Adam's arm in fright when their automobile skidded. But when Adam's younger son was killed early in the war, Goering sent a letter of condolence and after Adam's retirement was solicitous for his comfort in Garmisch.

decision to resolve the Czech situation in 1938. Goering's bad report now gave Hitler an excuse to blame everything on the Army and shift his principal reliance to Todt and Hierl.

Meanwhile Adam had sent reconnaissance teams to lay out a plan for the location of the various types and sizes of fortifications. For construction manpower, he had available the nine infantry divisions and other units comprising Group Command 2, and by mid-June over 50,000 troops, supplemented by RAD units, were at work. Later that month Brauchitsch called Adam to Berlin for a report, and immediately thereafter came a summons to the Berghof for a meeting with Hitler.*

Adam arrived with his fortifications specialist, General Richard Speich, and was received preliminarily by Schmundt (referred to in Adam's memoirs as *Bürschchen*—a young rogue), who declared that Hitler was displeased about the lack of progress on the West Wall and suggested that Adam make an optimistic report. It was exactly the wrong thing to say to Adam, who retorted that he would tell the Fuehrer no fairy tales. Schmundt then disclosed that Hitler was considering taking Group Command 2 out of the OKH chain of command and subordinating Adam directly to himself (a device which Hitler repeatedly used during the war); Adam opposed this idea and stressed the value of unity in the High Command.

When Hitler appeared, Adam told him that the western fortifications did not yet—and could not in the short time since the May 27 order—amount to much in operational terms. He remarked the insufficiency of supplies and spoke disparagingly of Hierl and Todt as military engineers. Vastly displeased, Hitler interjected: "Todt is the right man—for him the word impossible does not exist!" He bombarded Adam with production statistics, and insisted that the bunkers be ready in three months. At the ensuing luncheon Hitler denounced foreign meddling in "German matters," and repeatedly declared that "England will come over to me."

Militarily, the confrontation was an impasse; neither dictator nor general worked any change in the other's opinion. Two weeks later, when Adam noted a statement circulated in the OKH that 10,000 bunkers and 1,800 fortified emplacements in the west would ensure "quiet" (*Ruhe*), he brusquely warned OKH that such construction would not provide that sort of guarantee.

Hitler, for his part, was chiefly concerned to prevent Adam's views from infecting others, and to justify his own orders. On the night of June 30 he dictated a lengthy memorandum on "the question of our fortifications," which he circulated the next day to OKW, the three service commands, and the fortifications inspectorate.

"It is essential that these conclusions be given effect forthwith," began this lit-

---

* In his memoirs Adam dates his meeting with Brauchitsch as June 28, and with Hitler as June 30. However, the calendar kept by Oberstuermbannfuehrer (equivalent to Lieutenant Colonel) Max Wuensche, Hitler's SS adjutant, records Adam as meeting with Hitler at the Berghof on June 21, 1938. Brauchitsch's travel schedule shows him to have been away from Berlin from the seventeenth to the thirtieth of June. Adam's diary is not wholly reliable for specific dates; when I interrogated him in Nuremberg in 1948, he specified June 26 as the date of the meeting with Hitler, who was at the Berghof on all three of the mentioned dates.

tle-noted but remarkable document. There followed many pages of "principles," the gist of which was that large fortifications could be a waste of men, time, and materials, since their existence induced concentrations of enemy heavy artillery that usually neutralized them, that the basic purpose of fortifications was not to save the lives of the occupants but to ensure the strongest possible defense against enemy attack, and that for this purpose a decentralized system of small fortifications was the most efficient. He then dealt seriatim with the five "enemies" of fortifications—infantry, artillery, tanks, gas, and mines—among which infantry was primary and tanks the most dangerous. Against the former, concrete machine-gun emplacements were the best defense. These should have a free field of fire in all directions and be so constructed that the defenders could emerge when the attackers came to close quarters, and supplement the firepower with rifles and grenades. Tanks should be dealt with by obstacles, mines, and heavy artillery.

On the strength of these generalities, Hitler based his order for 10,000 concretized bunkers, each to accommodate twelve to twenty men. He ended his opus with the admonition that the focus should not be on perfection, but on the most that could be done in the time remaining.

Only superficially was the conflict between Hitler and Adam one of military technology. Adam thought that risking a war with France and England in 1938 was sheer lunacy, and that if a West Wall were to be built it should be designed for maximum usefulness in the future, when Germany was a match for the western allies. Hitler, on the other hand, was determined to put down the Czechs that year and wanted the most protection in the west that could be gotten in four months. Apart from the short-term operational value of the wall in the unlikely event of a French attack, he wanted a show of activity that would impress the French and discourage them from going to war at all.*

The two men's goals were so disparate that one would have expected Hitler to replace Adam with a more tractable commander, but he did not. Nor was Förster relieved of his post, though Hitler continued to rail at his incompetence. But Hitler left the issue of subordination, as between Adam and the Todt-Hierl combination, wholly unresolved; Adam continued to report to OKH, and the two civilian officials to Hitler.

The Fuehrer's memorandum of July 1 was never given the form of an order fixing the pattern for the construction of the West Wall, so it was every man for himself. Adam's engineers continued to work in accordance with the Army's policies. Todt built giant emplacements. The inevitable result was a mishmash in which optimum location and effective camouflage were impossible, and long-term plans had to be discarded. As Förster later put it, the West Wall was "an improvised border defense line." But whatever its shortcomings, in 1938 the

---

* It was, no doubt, with this end in view that General Bodenschatz (Goering's personal liaison with Hitler) informed Captain Stehlin early in June that Germany was building a defense line from the North Sea to the Swiss border, thirty miles deep and comprising "a multitude of shelters for men armed with anti-tank guns and concretized so heavily as to give security against the heaviest artillery." Working on the project, he declared, were 100,000 men of the RAD and 60 battalions of engineer troops. The French Embassy duly passed this information on to Paris.

West Wall served Hitler's purpose, for the Anglo-French allies were mightily impressed.

4

Apart from its immediate significance, Hitler's memorandum of July 1, 1938, was an unmistakable sign of the change that had overtaken the German High Command since the departure of Blomberg and Fritsch, and a remarkable harbinger of Hitler the Warlord (*Feldherr*) as he would behave throughout the war. The German Chief of State, be he Emperor or President, had always been the Supreme Commander, but it could not be imagined that the Kaiser, or Ebert, or even Hindenburg would compose overnight a thirty-five-page essay on fortifications. Hitler, plainly, meant to be Supreme Commander in detail as well as in the large.

The West Wall was a central but by no means the only field of his interest. Searching questions about Czech arms and fortifications poured out of the Berghof and were answered by the OKW staff. On June 24, Hitler was at the maneuver area at Grafenwoehr (in Bavaria near the Czech border) for artillery tests. A few days later Todt and Hierl were at the Berghof, and on July 4, Förster and General Karl Becker, Chief of Army Ordnance, together with Hierl, Speich, and Luftwaffe General Kitzinger, commander of the Western Air Defense Zone. In mid-July, strolling in the hills near the Berghof with Engel, Hitler let loose a blast against Becker: "A good technician and even better professor, who understands nothing of the needs of the troops!"*

Hermann Goering, meanwhile, was whipping up the pace of arms production. On July 8 he gathered the leading aircraft manufacturers at Karinhall and delivered a long pep talk, in the course of which he revealed the possibility of war over the Sudeten question and spoke darkly of "the fate which would befall us if we lost the war" and glowingly of the prospect that victory would make Germany "the greatest power in the world." A few days later Goering and Carl Krauch of the huge I. G. Farben chemicals combine promulgated the "Karinhall" or "Krauch" plan for vastly expanded production of gasoline and industrial oils, rubber, light metals, and explosives.

And what of General Ludwig Beck, as the war-like pace quickened? His subordinates were faithful and supportive, but his role in decision-making steadily dwindled as Hitler and then Brauchitsch, sensing the direction of the wind, bypassed the Chief of the General Staff in favor of his deputy, General Franz Halder.

So Beck once more took pen in hand, and on July 16 produced the fourth and last of his warning memoranda. Execution of the Green plan, he predicted, would lead to world war, to a war unwanted by the German people, and to catastrophe for Germany. Victory over Czechoslovakia in a few days, as postulated by Hitler, would be impossible, and Anglo-French intervention a certainty. The

---

* General Becker, apparently from distress that Hitler found him inadequate, committed suicide in 1940.

western front could not possibly be held with the available troops. It was the responsibility of the military leaders to prevent such a disaster.

In a handwritten draft of this document, Beck had stated that he, as Chief of the General Staff, was unwilling to carry out Green. This declaration was replaced in the final version by a sharp demand that preparations for war be stopped. Beck further stated that all the section chiefs of the General Staff shared his views. In conclusion, Beck proposed that Brauchitsch call a meeting of all the commanding generals and discuss the situation with the Navy* and Luftwaffe commanders, after which a united front against war should be presented to Hitler.

After transmitting his memorandum to Brauchitsch, Beck supplemented the document with the oral observation that, if Hitler proved adamant, the generals should resign in a body: "History will burden these leaders with blood-guilt if they do not act in accord with their specialized political knowledge and conscience." Their action would be supported by all "upright civil officials," he predicted. Three days later, Beck was again closeted with Brauchitsch, making detailed recommendations of methods by which the *démarche* to Hitler should be made. At long last—unhappily, much too late—it had begun to dawn on Beck that he was confronting a problem far broader and deeper than how to put an end to Green. At last he realized that the menace of war was not simply a momentary, mad idea of Hitler's but was an intrinsic part of an evil and dangerous political and social system. Beck was face to face with the Third Reich itself.

Accordingly, his proposals to Brauchitsch on July 19 went far beyond anything that he had yet written. The Army generals must seek allies among the surviving better elements, including the "good generals" of the Luftwaffe, civilian ministers, and even the more respectable and reasonable Nazi Party officials. All these should be warned of the perils of the situation. So reinforced, and avoiding any appearance of conspiracy, the coalition should meet the SS and the radical Party leaders head-on and "re-establish orderly conditions." There was to be no *Putsch,* and Hitler would remain; the keynote was reform: "For the Führer, against war, against 'boss rule,' peace with the Church, free expression of opinion, an end to the 'Cheka,' restore justice in the Reich, cut in half contributions to the Party, no more building of palaces, housing for the people, Prussian cleanliness and simplicity."

During the balance of July, Beck continued to press his views upon Brauchitsch and give vent to them among his colleagues. Ribbentrop and Himmler, Beck thought, were egging Hitler on to war. Goering, however, "was not a warmonger" and might be approached. As for timing, Hitler might perhaps be more willing to listen to reason toward the end of September, after the hysteria of the Nuremberg *Reichsparteitag* had tapered off. The *démarche* would undoubtedly

---

* Views comparable to Beck's were being circulated within the Naval Staff by Vice-Admiral Gunther Guse. So far as appears from the available documents, neither Guse nor other like-minded naval officers were in contact with Beck. However, Beck and Guse were well known to each other and may have had informal contacts.

cause acute political tension and possibly domestic violence. Therefore, General von Witzleben, the commander of the Berlin Military District, and Count von Helldorf, the Berlin police chief, should make joint preparations to preserve order.*

Brauchitsch, who agreed with his chief of staff at least as far as the latter's views on Green were concerned, transmitted the July 16 memorandum to Hitler. The Fuehrer's reaction was prompt and intemperate. Discussing the document two days later with Todt, Schmundt, and Engel, he called it "mendacious" and "childish in its reckoning of French strength." He would not let Beck take him for a fool; he would show how wrong Beck was and lay it under his nose! A few days later he drowned the defenseless Brauchitsch in a flood of optimistic armament statistics.

The hapless, weak-kneed Commander-in-Chief now found himself ground between two millstones. He was incapable of standing up to Hitler, but the pressure from Beck, backed as he was by the Army General Staff, could not be ignored. Then, on July 26, Hitler ordered a meeting of the corps and higher commanders at the Jüterbog artillery proving grounds (about forty miles southwest of Berlin) for August 15. Beck, anticipating that Hitler would exploit the occasion to advance his war policy, insisted that Brauchitsch call a conference of the leading generals at an earlier date. He prevailed, and the gathering was called for August 4, 1938.

Historians and other commentators on the Third Reich have often wondered out loud why the German generals never formed a common front of resistance against Hitler. The meeting of August 4 in Berlin was the one and only occasion when the senior generals of the Army came together other than on Hitler's call and discussed the formation of a united front in opposition to the Fuehrer's policies. It was an unprecedented event, altogether out of keeping with the traditions of the officer corps, and the very fact of such a meeting is eloquent testimony that Beck's warnings were deeply troubling to many of the military leaders.

Distrusting Brauchitsch's firmness and powers of expression, Beck prepared a speech for him to deliver at the meeting, and to use in subsequent discussions with Hitler. It consisted chiefly of an analysis of the military situation and probable attitude of each country that might be involved in a European crisis, in order to demonstrate Germany's isolated position. England was confronted with an Italian threat in the Mediterranean, wanted quiet in Europe, and was not in good military repair. However, she would follow the French on the Czech problem, her "imperial resources" gave her the depth for a long war, and she could count on American logistic support. France, bound by treaty to support Czechoslovakia, was "the strongest military power in Europe," with manifold superiority over Germany. By the fifth day of mobilization she could put on the western front three times as many divisions as the Reich could muster. Germany was quite unable to hold the French in the west while fighting the Czechs in the southeast. America was a country of tremendous military potential, and

---

* Beck, Witzleben, and Helldorf were all later involved and lost their lives in the attempted *Putsch* of July 20, 1944.

her attitude was irretrievably favorable to England. Poland was interested in detaching the Teschen area from Czechoslovakia, but the Poles hated Germany and could not be counted on to side with her against France and England. In Russia the purges had weakened the Army, but in a long war she would be a powerful enemy. Japan was preoccupied in China and in no position to aid Germany against Russia, England, or the United States. Italy was ill prepared for war and could give Germany no decisive relief; General Pariani (the Italian Chief of Staff) was especially opposed to war with England and France. Belgium, normally neutral, was subject to Anglo-French pressure and would surely allow the French to march through and threaten the Ruhr.

For all these reasons, Germany could not possibly prevail in a world war in her present state of preparation. The question was not one of peace or principle, but of timing; *the German Army would not be ready until 1941*. The generals' judgment of the military situation must govern, and Brauchitsch must demand that Hitler act in accordance with their views.

It was a strong speech, but Brauchitsch was not the man to deliver it. Instead, Beck's memorandum of July 16 was read to the assemblage—whether by Brauchitsch or by Beck himself is not clear.* Brauchitsch then asked Adam for a statement of his opinion and a description of the defensive situation on the western front. Adam characterized Hitler's plan as a "war of desperation"† and pictured the West Wall as such a "jumble" that it was useless for defense. In view of the Army's planned concentration against Czechoslovakia, Adam would have only five regular and four reserve divisions, with no air or armor and little artillery, and if the western powers should attack he would soon be overrun. He finished by saying: "I paint a black picture, but it is the truth."

Beck congratulated Adam, and Brauchitsch urged him to tell Hitler the same story when next they met. Others spoke and, according to Weichs, the consensus was "that the mood of the people and the Army was generally against a war, and that the organization, training, and equipment of the troops would be sufficient for a war against Czechoslovakia, but not against the European great powers." Apparently there was absolutely no dissent from the military analyses of Adam and others, but two generals—Reichenau, and Busch of VIII Corps—questioned Beck's recommendation of outspoken opposition to the Fuehrer. Reichenau observed that all wars are dangerous, that Hitler would take the right course, and that generals who individually crossed him would "incur disad-

---

* Two participants—Adam and General Maximilian von Weichs, commander of XIII Corps—have left written accounts of the meeting. Adam, both in his memoirs and in an affidavit submitted to the Nuremberg war crimes tribunal, stated that Beck did the reading. Weichs, in his unpublished memoirs, states that Brauchitsch read Beck's memorandum, and adds that Brauchitsch opened the meeting by declaring that he was first apprized of Hitler's decision to attack Czechoslovakia by a memorandum from Colonel Jodl. According to Weichs, Brauchitsch professed to be deeply shocked that such a vital decision had been made without consulting himself or Beck, and even proposed that Jodl should be stripped of his General Staff insignia for bypassing his superiors.

† Adam also spoke of Germany's vulnerability to air attack and the probable air superiority of the enemy. Considering the state of the French and British air forces at that time, this is surprising; it is possible that Adam had in mind that the Luftwaffe's concentration against Czechoslovakia would leave Germany open to bombardment from the west.

vantageous consequences." Busch spoke in generalities about obedience and loyalty. Beck sharply controverted Busch, arguing that a General Staff officer ought to take a stand on military-political questions of such moment.

Brauchitsch closed the meeting by saying that all were united in their opposition to war. But there was no decision to take any particular action,* and Weichs heard Rundstedt urge Brauchitsch to conduct the "negotiations" with Hitler in such a way as not to endanger his own standing with the Fuehrer—an admonition of which Brauchitsch had no need. There is no evidence that the Commander-in-Chief did anything at all to follow up the meeting, which he apparently regarded simply as a means of getting other generals to attempt to influence Hitler toward caution.

Why did nothing come of this extraordinary military convocation, at which there was such general agreement that Germany could not successfully confront the western powers? Adam, reflecting in later years, thought it was because the senior German officers were cursed with mediocrity—none had the "holy fire," and there were no outstanding personalities. Furthermore, many of them were overfond of the pomp, prestige, comfort, and decorations that came with promotion, and saw war as an avenue to these perquisites.

If Beck was comparatively immune to the blandishments of preferment, he was no exception to Adam's verdict on the lack of charismatic leadership among the generals. His professional home was the General Staff; he had had only short periods of troop command and, with his reticent personality and melancholy mien, was not the man to dominate the old field generals like Rundstedt, Bock, Leeb, and List, who were his seniors on the rank list. Furthermore, in matters of military technique he was an arch-conservative. The rising group of "tank" generals who, in Germany as in Britain and France, had fought hard for their place in the sun, had little use for Beck. Heinz Guderian, the Army's leading armored force commander in the early years of the war, later wrote of Beck:

> His was an upright character, a calm, almost too calm, and thoughtful man of the old school. . . . He had no understanding for modern technical matters. Since he invariably chose men with much of his own attitude to fill the more important General Staff posts, and even more so to form his own close circle, as time went on he erected—without wishing to do so—a barrier of reaction at the very center of the army which was to prove very difficult to overcome. He disapproved of the plans of the armoured force: he wanted the tanks to be employed primarily as infantry support weapons. . . . Leaving the whole argument of armoured troops aside, however, Beck was above all a procrastinator in military as in political matters. He was a paralyzing element wherever he appeared. He always foresaw all the difficulties and required time to think everything over. . . . He had a number of adherents at the centre, but no influence over the Army as a whole and even less in the other services.

---

* As the meeting broke up, Adam overheard one of the officers (Kluge or Liebmann, he could not remember which) suggest that all "generals with two stars" (the insignia of a *General,* the equivalent of a lieutenant general in the American military hierarchy) should resign.

There were deeper reasons for Beck's failure than his own limitations as a leader. They emerge in a long personal letter to Beck from General Erich von Manstein, perhaps the ablest German general of the Second World War, equally successful in staff work and field command. Manstein had been Beck's deputy from 1936 to March 1938, when he was transferred to a divisional command, and had the highest regard for his former chief. Visiting Beck in mid-July, Manstein was distressed to find him so frustrated that he was seriously contemplating resignation, and on July 21 wrote to dissuade him.

The major theme of Manstein's letter was that Beck's difficulties stemmed chiefly from a faulty military command structure—faulty in that Hitler was leaning on Keitel and his staff at OKW for military advice and assistance, instead of on Brauchitsch and Beck. The OKW, he declared, "must be eliminated from the exercise of military leadership, and the necessary preponderance of the Army in that leadership be established as the basis for mutual trust between the Führer and the Army." In achieving this vital readjustment, no successor to his position would have as much respect and authority as Beck.

In support of this thesis, Manstein dealt first with the major issue upon which Hitler and Beck were sharply divided: "The *basic question* of whether and *when* we can solve the Czech question, taking into account the possible intervention of the Western powers." Essentially, said Manstein, this was a problem not for Beck, but for Hitler:

> In this matter, as I see it, the *military responsibility* is limited to clearly presenting to the Führer whether and when we can accept French military intervention (I don't think we can contemplate the possibility of English intervention) and what military consequences it entails. Only if no agreement between the political and military leadership can be reached on this question is military responsibility involved.
>
> I believe that the decision *whether* a Western military intervention is to be expected is for the political leadership alone. If the Führer in judging the political situation concludes that we should intervene in Czechoslovakia sooner rather than later (*i.e.* before we are fully prepared militarily), because he thinks the Western powers are less likely to intervene now than later, that is his decision and responsibility alone. The military precondition is only that a successful operation against the Czechs is possible, and that there will be enough military power to spare to make French intervention unlikely. The military leadership is responsible only for a quick success against Czechoslovakia, and for actions that will discourage the French. . . .
>
> I thus believe that this *basic* question which, I have the impression, particularly burdens the general's [i.e., Beck's] sense of responsibility, must be viewed as follows: there must be clear understanding between the political and military leaders about the consequences of so risky a step, but the final responsibility is the Führer's alone. After all, so far he has always judged the political situation correctly.

Manstein next dealt with the "overhasty" construction of the western fortifications, pointing out that here, too, political issues were involved, and Hitler might be counting on their deterrent effect on the French. Most of the remainder of his letter concerned the manner in which the German forces should be deployed to ensure maximum surprise and a speedy breach of the Czech fortified line, which was another area of disagreement between OKW and OKH. Noting parenthetically that Beck was as dedicated as anyone else to a successful resolution of the Czech question, Manstein reiterated the necessity of reforming the military command structure and urged Beck to use the deployment controversy as a vehicle for convincing Hitler that the major political-military link must be between him and the Army, to the exclusion of OKW. Only if this realignment proved impossible should Beck consider resignation.

If few of the generals could have articulated the governing considerations so lucidly and forcefully as Manstein, there can be no doubt that it reflected conscious and subconscious motives and apprehensions that were pervasive among them. It would have been hard to find a German officer who did not favor a "solution" of the "Czech question" and the "Polish Corridor" and a powerfully armed Reich. By 1938 the main obstacle to achieving these goals were the danger of intervention by the western allies. It was the same hazard that had threatened open rearmament in 1935, remilitarization of the Rhineland in 1936, and *Anschluss* only a few months earlier. In each case Hitler had confronted the danger, and in none had it developed into a threat, much less into force. "After all, so far he has always judged the political situation correctly," wrote Manstein.

Beck was violating Manstein's injunction that the issue was one for the political leadership alone; he thought Hitler was wrong, and that the Allies would be at Germany's throat if the Czechs were attacked. But the Fuehrer's so far unbroken record of successes gave him a leverage in the officer corps that quite overbore Beck's warnings.

The Chief of Staff was unmoved by Manstein's letter and replied that the time was long past for the course of action that his former deputy recommended: "I can only say today, as I have for a long time, 'too late.'"* And for Beck indeed it was, for his military career had but a few more weeks to run its course.

5

How and when Hitler learned of the senior generals' meeting is not clear, but it is altogether improbable that he long remained ignorant of it. He was due to meet them himself on August 15, but he did not await that day before taking countermeasures. Apparently thinking that a younger group might be more responsive to his views, on August 10 he summoned to the Berghof the officers who, if war came, would be serving as chiefs of staff to the principal field commanders. It was an unprecedented and insulting procedure to go directly to the subordinates and address them out of the presence of the commanders to whom they were responsible, but there is no indication that Brauchitsch or anyone else raised objection.

The twenty-or-so invited officers arrived in the morning, and were received in the Berghof's famous reception room with the gigantic picture window overlooking Salzburg. General Gustav von Wietersheim, who was to be Adam's wartime chief of staff, was there, together with Manstein, Salmuth, and Ruoff (who

---

* The quotation is from a reply drafted by Beck on July 31 and conveyed orally to Manstein on August 8.

were to be chiefs of staff to Leeb, Rundstedt, and List respectively) and the chiefs of the four air fleets. In addition to the chiefs of staff, the guests included Jodl from the OKW, Jeschonnek from the Luftwaffe General Staff, and Hitler's military adjutants.*

After Hitler had expatiated on the view, the party went to the dining room. Manstein, who sat beside Hitler, found him withdrawn and taciturn, but finally drew him into a conversation about the paintings in the Munich Haus der Deutschen Kunst.† After the meal Hitler held forth for two or three hours on the reasons why he had decided to deal with Czechoslovakia presently, mentioning oppression of the German minority and that country's hostility, which made it a potential enemy of the Reich in any war. England was not yet rearmed, and France was suffering domestic difficulties; neither country wanted to go to war for the Czechs. Poland and Hungary were waiting to pluck the carcass, and the Red Army, since the purges, was in no shape to fight.

When Hitler had finished tea was served, and he then threw the meeting open for discussion. Much to his annoyance, it soon became apparent that he was far from having persuaded the Army chiefs, who generally shared the views of their commanders. In the course of the colloquy General von Wietersheim, the ranking officer present,‡ attributed to Adam the opinion that with the available forces the West Wall could not be held against a French attack for more than three weeks. Hitler exploded with rage and roared at Wietersheim that, if the generals were as courageous as the musketeers, then "I assure you, Herr General, that the line will hold not for three weeks but three years." After this outburst, there was no stomach for further discussion.*

In his diary, Jodl ruminated disconsolately on the meeting's unhappy course:

> The cause of this despondent opinion, which unfortunately enough is held very widely within the Army General Staff, is based on various reasons.
>
> First of all, it is restrained by old memories; political considerations play a part as well, instead of obeying and executing the military mission. That is certainly done with traditional devotion, but the vigour of the soul is lacking because at bottom they do not believe in the genius of the Fuehrer. And one does perhaps compare him with Charles the XIIth.
>
> And since water flows downhill, this defeatism may not only cause immense

---

* The exact composition of the group is not clear. Jodl's diary states that it comprised the *Armeechefs,* the four air fleet chiefs, Jeschonnek, and himself. Since the Green plan called for ten armies and an army group, the guests would thus have totaled seventeen plus the adjutants. But at least two of the Army chiefs (Apell and Sodenstern) were not invited (perhaps because the roles of their particular armies were subsidiary), while at least one corps chief of staff (Olbricht) was present, and perhaps others.

† Manstein in his book *Aus einem Soldatenleben, 1887–1939* (pp. 336–39), Jodl in his diary, Salmuth in his testimony at Nuremberg, and Wietersheim in response to my interrogation of him at Nuremberg (February 13, 1948) have left accounts of the meeting. It is also described in Adam's memoirs, on the basis of information Adam got from General Olbricht.

‡ In the spring of 1938, Wietersheim had been promoted to two-star rank and given command of the newly formed XIV Corps (motorized). In the event of war, he was to transfer to Adam's army group as Chief of Staff.

* Wietersheim's remark put the ceiling on his military career. He led XIV Corps with ability until his retirement in 1942, but was never promoted in rank or given a higher command.

political damage, for the opposition between the generals' opinions and those of the Fuehrer is common talk, but may also constitute a danger for the morale of the troops. But I have no doubt that somehow the Fuehrer will be able to boost the morale of the people in an unexpected way when the right moment comes.

As Manstein later wrote, ". . . this was the first and last time that Hitler after a presentation of his views and decisions to a large group, permitted a discussion." Five days later, at Jüterbog, no such liberties were allowed. The operational purpose of the gathering was to witness demonstrational infantry attacks on concrete bunkers at Jüterbog, and the effect of heavy artillery fire on the bunkers at the nearby Kummersdorf proving ground, but this all led up to Hitler's address to the senior commanders in the officers' mess.

On this occasion, Hitler began with an autopanegyric of the kind that was soon to become more frequent and fulsome in his speeches. Since the start of his political life, it had been his unshakable purpose that Germany should attain predominant power. He had his great self-trust to help him, and great things awaited his auditors in the coming years. It was his main fear that he might be done away with (*zustossen*) before he could carry out the decisive moves. The vital thing was greater *Lebensraum,* and now the country had the necessary bases for action; national unity, rearmament, the Rhineland, and Austria.

Next Czechoslovakia—the "Soviet Russian aircraft carrier"—must be eliminated. Armies were never strong enough to suit their leaders, and success depended on rightly gauging the politico-military balance. So far he had always been right in his assessments. The other powers would not intervene: "Gentlemen, with that possibility you need not concern yourselves." English threats were bluff, as her efforts at compromise showed, and she would keep out as long as Germany showed no sign of weakening. And then, in conclusion: "Fortune must be seized when she strikes, for she will not come again! . . . I predict that by the end of the year we will be looking back at a great success!"

All this was delivered with the greatest assurance, and even General Curt Liebmann (commander of the War Academy, and no Hitler-lover) confessed that while listening it was difficult to sustain contrary convictions, and that many of the auditors were "more or less" persuaded. Certainly no objections were audibly raised, and Beck concluded that his own effort was done for. Three days later he asked Brauchitsch to be relieved of his duties as Chief of Staff, and on August 21, Hitler gave his approval but insisted that the resignation not be formally announced and that it be given no publicity. Beck, like Fritsch limited by personal reticence and perhaps mistaken patriotism, complied.

And so, when the British ministers held their first "crisis" meeting on August 30, they had no idea that on August 27 the Chief of the General Staff of the German Army had resigned in protest against Hitler's plan to attack Czechoslovakia. Beck had summoned the section chiefs of the General Staff to his office, read them a short lecture on the historic "independence" of the General Staff, and quietly departed. He remained, for the time being, on the active list, hoping for a field command, and even allowed himself to be publicly and falsely paraded as Chief of Staff at the maneuvers in East Prussia, and at a luncheon on September 15 for the foreign military attachés.* Beck had been true to the dictates of his own mind, but lacked the fire and force to transmute dangerous thought into bold action.

6

Despite the strong current of dissent among the Army generals, verging in some cases on disobedience or revolt, preparations for the attack went forward rapidly and, in most respects, smoothly and efficiently. There was, of course, no question of the Wehrmacht's capacity, in due course, to destroy the Czech forces, but that was only the beginning of the problem, since the real danger was Anglo-French intervention. Hitler repeatedly assured the generals that this would not happen, but his almost hysterical insistence on rushing construction of the West Wall showed his anxious hope that the military measures would increase the probability that his prediction would prove accurate.

Indeed, it is far from clear whether or not Hitler, in the spring of 1938, really expected that the Sudeten question would be resolved by armed combat. Manstein, in his letter to Beck, ruminated on the possibility that Hitler was using military threats as a means of pressuring the Czechs into concessions to the German minority that would eventually undermine the Prague government and cause it to crumble, as had Austria, or of frightening the French and British into abandoning Czechoslovakia, as in fact happened.

Equally unclear is whether Hitler intended, at least after the May crisis, to go through with the attack against Czechoslovakia even if it finally appeared that the western powers would surely come to her aid. A draft for a new directive to the armed forces, dated June 18, states that "I shall, however, only decide to take action against Czechoslovakia if, as in the case of the occupation of the demilitarized zone and the entry into Austria, I am firmly convinced that France will not march and therefore Britain will not intervene either." The draft was initialed by Keitel, Jodl, and Zeitzler but, so far as appears, was never signed or issued by Hitler.

Assuming that the German tactics were to bully Czechoslovakia or her allies into conceding the German demands without a fight, those ends would be served by ostentatious fortification of the western front, the announced formation of additional divisions and air squadrons, the appearance of full-strength, combat-ready units near the Czech borders, and the threat or commencement of mobilization. But if these minatory gestures did not break the Czechs' will to resist, they would alert Prague to the imminence of an attack and destroy any prospect of surprise. In view of the political tension between the two countries, strategic surprise was of course impossible, but if the Czechs could be kept uncertain whether an attack was really intended, and if so *when* it would come, a considerable measure of tactical surprise might be gained, which would enhance the hope of a speedy breakthrough of the Czech defenses, and a swift victory which would confront the Allies with the politically desirable *fait accompli*.

* On the basis of a dispatch from Ian Colvin, the *News Chronicle* on September 15 reported Beck had resigned.

This incompatability between the tactics of threat and surprise was remarked by Manstein in his letter to Beck:

> As I see it, in our situation we can be successful only through *either* political pressure *or* military surprise. If one mixes both, the military surprise will be sacrificed to the political pressure. Yet on this surprise is built and must be built the entire Army operation, as long as a quick success appears necessary because of the political risk, and as long as the way of brute force, i.e. the powerful attack without regard for the time factor, is out of the question because of our lack of offensive strength in the East and of effective defense forces in the West, as well as our lack of reserves of any kind for a long war.

Of course, the incompatability between threat and surprise was not total; considerable military pressure could be exerted without triggering a Czech mobilization or a full-strength manning of the fortifications. But the tension between them presented a continuing politico-military problem, and as preparations continued, the balance fluctuated. At the outset, the OKH attitude was to keep options open. In May the higher field commands were told "that there were two alternative operational possibilities: "Normal Case," after a systematic mobilization in the troops' home stations, and "Special Case," whereby assault troops would be assembled during field exercises near the Czech border and hurled across the frontier in a surprise attack, to be followed by larger units brought up from areas well back of the border.

In Hitler's mind, the surprise factor was dominant. His Green directive of May 30 stated:

> For the military operation it is essential to make full use of surprise as the factor most important for victory, by means of appropriate measures taken before the war, and a speed of action unexpected by the enemy. . . . If notable successes are not achieved in the first few days of ground operations, a European crisis will certainly develop. Realization of this ought to give commanders of all ranks the incentive for resolute and bold action. . . .
>
> The basic principle of surprise must not be endangered by the time unavoidably necessary for moving the bulk of the field army by rail. . . .
>
> The first task for the Army is therefore to employ as many assault columns as possible simultaneously with attacks by the Luftwaffe.
>
> These assault columns, constituted in conformity with their missions, must comprise troops which can be rapidly committed because of their proximity to the frontier, motorization, and special measures for their readiness.

This was all very well, but left two major tactical problems to be solved. How could the bulk of the German Army* be assembled in the general vicinity of Czechoslovakia without a regular mobilization, which if ordered would at once precipitate a Czech mobilization and greatly diminish if not destroy the surprise factor? How could the troops for the initial breakthrough assault be deployed in

---

* In Germany, as in most other countries, the divisions and other large units of the regular Army were not maintained at full combat strength during peacetime. They were brought to strength by calling up trained reserves. Other reserves might be used to form additional divisions or other units. These steps were the essence of "mobilization," usually accomplished by an order requiring designated reserves (classified by age group, branch of service, etc.) to report to placement depots for assignment to particular units.

proximity to the Czech frontiers without likewise triggering Czech defense measures, including immediate manning of the fortifications?

The first difficulty was met by a most ingenious system of substantial mobilization without any formal order or other indication that the troops were to be made ready for actual combat. Large-scale maneuvers were scheduled at training grounds near Czechoslovakia—Grafenwoehr in Bavaria, Königsbrück in Saxony, Neuhammer in Silesia—and several age groups of reservists were called up during the summer, under orders to remain in service beyond the usual six-week training period and until the maneuvers had been completed. They were brought to the training grounds, where they were used to complete regular divisions already there or form new ones. Except at the highest level, neither officers nor men knew anything of Green, and assumed that these were simply longer and larger summer maneuvers than had been customary.

The second problem had not been satisfactorily resolved at the time of Manstein's letter to Beck, in which he pointed out that "the appearance of strong mobilized units at the border will lead to immediate military counter-measures" which would deprive the Germans of the advantage of surprise and endanger the prospect of quick victory. Manstein's proposed solution, to which the subsequently planned deployment closely corresponded, was:

> The tactical assault over the border should be carried out with extensive use of the Luftwaffe and, as far as possible, with small units near the border who would be taken there in one night direct from their stations or from nearby training-grounds. These would be followed in the same night by reinforced regiments from the motorized infantry divisions (if necessary also by armored units) which would be standing ready in the interior under camouflage. They have the task of holding the gaps made in the fortifications by the initial assault, as well as to widen them and take the fortifications set back from the border. . . . At the same time deployment of the combat-ready divisions would begin.

Numerous other devices were adopted to conceal the preparations for the attack; as Keitel later wrote: "Every imaginable but inconspicuous makeshift had to be exploited; hastily improvised ammunition and supply columns were camouflaged as being connected with the manoeuvres, and the railway movements as being linked with the Reich Party Rally." Early in August came the decree (already mentioned) barring all foreign military personnel from entering "prohibited zones" which included the Rhineland, a sixty-mile-wide belt on the east bank of the Rhine between its confluence with the Main (at Mainz) and the Swiss border, a twenty-five-mile-wide strip along the Bavarian-Czech border, and most of Germany between the Oder and Poland. Maneuvers to which the military attachés and foreign military missions were invited were held in East Prussia, hundreds of miles from the crucial Czech and French border areas, during mid-September, shortly after the Nuremberg Party Rally.

As camouflage, these measures worked beautifully. The reactions and reports of Britain's experienced and perceptive military attaché, "Mason-Mac," do indeed reflect increasing concern over the reserve call-ups and "prohibited-area" order, but they also disclose his complete uncertainty whether they foreshadowed an actual attack, and if so, when it would come. On August 16 the British attaché in Prague, Colonel Stronge, reported that the Czech General Staff, "while admitting that the general situation must naturally cause anxiety are not unduly apprehensive," and Ambassador Newton was told at the Foreign Ministry that "military maneuvres in Germany were not causing exceptional anxiety in Czechoslovakia as they were not considered to have added greatly to normal and constant German menace."

Not until September 10 did Colonel Stronge observe that the Czech General Staff "were becoming increasingly anxious regarding their own lack of any precautionary measures in view of present great strength and state of preparedness of German Army." By that time Germany's concealed mobilization was well under way, and the scheduled date for the attack less than three weeks off.

7

Throughout the summer of 1938, the German Army regulars were engaged in exercises focused on the tactical problems precipitated by the Green plan. In this special training, the center piece was *fortifications*. It was not only the construction and use of the fortifications on the western front, but also the development of weapons and tactics for overcoming the Czech defenses modeled in part on the Maginot Line, which provided the subject matter.

The Czech fortifications had been carefully reconnoitered both from the air and, by telephoto lens cameras, from the German side of the border.* Reproductions were constructed at the troop training areas and artillery proving grounds, where the technique of infantry attack could be tested and the effects of artillery and aerial bombardment studied.

The center of this research was at Jüterbog and Kummersdorf under the charge of General Walter Model, chief of the technical section of the Army General Staff, and it was he who led the demonstrations which Hitler witnessed there on August 15 before his address to the commanding generals. Adam and Beck both thought that Model had staged the exercise so as to favor the attacker and give Hitler a false idea of the infantry's strength, and Adam called Model a "will-o'-the-wisp" (*Irrlicht*) and a Nazi-follower. Anyhow, the Fuehrer applauded,† and Model climbed into his good graces, slated for rapid promotion and a field marshal's baton.

But the Army's handling of the West Wall continued to arouse his criticism and, especially after his June encounter with Adam, outspoken derision. At Bayreuth for the Festival early in August, a visit to Winifred Wagner was interrupted by the arrival of Captain Claus of Förster's staff with a new model of a *Bunker*. Hitler at once rejected it: "Not strong enough, too complicated. A masterpiece of German architecture, but of no practical use." He rained taunts on

---

* A special high altitude reconnaissance unit under Captain Theodor Rowehl (anticipatory of the American U-2s thirty years later) did the aerial photography. Captain Reinhard Gehlen, with an OKW intelligence officer, took long-range pictures "using a giant telephoto lens of about 1,000-millimeter focal length" by which they "secured information on the thickness of the concrete even at ranges of twenty miles and more."

† General von Weichs thought that Hitler showed "undeniable technical understanding" and made valuable suggestions.

the Army technicians, calling them "stonecutters," and declared that big construction firms would do a better job, rejecting all contrary arguments from Schmundt and Engel. Two weeks later in Berlin, a layout of the plan for the West Wall elicited another outburst against Förster and the Army's delays.

In mid-August another dispute erupted, involving the RAD units and Todt's civilian laborers.* Many of the RAD workers were in the reserves and liable to call-up. In the event of a French attack, the presence of a large civilian labor mass in the combat zone would seriously interfere with operations. On July 28, OKH advised OKW that the workers, with the trucks and horses they were using, must be out of the fortified zone by September 24, since the operation against Czechoslovakia might take place at the end of that month.

On August 12, however, Todt telephoned Adam's chief of staff, General Georg von Apell, and told him that Hitler had declared an early break-off of the fortification work "out of the question," and that the work was to continue "at least until October 1st, probably until October 15th, in short, up to the first shot." Indignantly Adam wired Brauchitsch: "I suspect that OKW has not yet or not with the necessary clarity informed the Führer on the true state of affairs and the obvious conclusions therefrom. I propose, therefore, that a speedy decision by the Führer be secured through OKH."

If Brauchitsch acted on Adam's suggestion, Hitler gave him short shrift. On August 18, OKW informed OKH that: "The Führer has ordered that the construction of the Western fortifications, on the present scale of effort, be continued right through mobilization, as long as it is not necessary to stop the French in the West by military measures." The RAD units were to be maintained intact as long as French inaction would permit, and the mobilization difficulties pointed out by OKH dealt with by suitable planning. The order flew in the face of the military necessities as Adam saw them, and was to lead to another sharp conflict at the end of September, when war seemed imminent.

Late in August, the Fuehrer decided to make a personal tour of the western defenses. He traveled in his special train with Keitel, Brauchitsch, Jodl, Himmler, Bormann, Hierl, Todt, and a host of junior officers, minor dignitaries, adjutants, and other aides. The inspection began at the northern end of the fortifications near Aachen, where Adam met the party on the morning of August 27, and ended three days later at the Swiss border.

This was Adam's first opportunity to speak with Hitler since August 4, when Adam had promised Brauchitsch to tell Hitler the true facts about the western defense situation. Once he found himself inside Hitler's car, the blunt old Bavarian lost no time in bringing matters to issue, in a direct and peremptory manner. The conference compartment was crowded, with insufficient room to spread the maps, and Adam began by declaring that his briefing was for the Fuehrer and his military advisers, and that the civilians—including Himmler,

---

* As General Inspector of Roads, Todt fell within the framework of Goering's Four Year Plan, and his subordination to Goering was accentuated by the fact that Todt allowed himself to be put into the uniform of a Luftwaffe brigadier general. But he was in constant conflict with Goering and rapidly established an independent relationship with Hitler. For his work on the West Wall, Todt established the "Organization Todt" as his own labor force, and it endured under that name.

Hierl, and Todt—should leave. Despite a few sneers, Adam carried his point (though the three just named, unbeknownst to Adam, crept back into the compartment later), but Hitler was put in a bad humor from the start.

"As Commander-in-Chief in the West I have responsibilities, and I want to speak openly about the difficulties," Adam began. "Let's get to the point," Hitler interjected. Adam proceeded to describe the current state of the fortifications, observing that in May, when the speed-up was ordered, he had hoped to get the work half done by the fall, but in view of delays in the delivery of materials, one third was the most that could be expected in 1938. Adam then recalled that at Jüterbog Hitler had analyzed the political situation, but that as he was the responsible commander in the west, his own obligation was to treat the most dangerous possibility as probability—i.e., the western powers would intervene. Furthermore, his own belief was that if Germany attacked in the east they would indeed do so.

This last remark was too much for the Fuehrer. "We have no time to listen to this stuff," he shouted. "You understand nothing. The English have no Army reserves, the French are internally embroiled." There came the usual flood of statistics about Germany's superiority in steel production. As soon as Adam could get a word in he remarked, with evident sarcasm: "If things are as you say, I have no need to worry about the Western front. I suggest we go into the field." Hitler glared ominously but finally said: "Agreed," and the tour began. Brauchitsch, at whose personal request Adam had made this *démarche,* had said not a word.

The party set off in automobiles, Adam in the lead car with the officer who knew the route, Hitler in the second car with the commander of the unit to be visited, and the others bringing up the rear—an order which Adam stuck to throughout the tour. They drove through the Eifel, the hilly, wooded lands between the Rhine and the Low Countries, stopping at various points for briefings by Adam and the unit commanders. At noon they rejoined the train for a luncheon of stuffed eggs. Adam observed that only Hitler's eggs were stuffed with caviar, and after the meal he commented to Bormann that the Fuehrer was fond of this delicacy. That worthy agreed this was so, but declared that because of the expense the Fuehrer did not eat it. "What can you say to such a big lie?" Adam wondered in his memoirs.

As in the case of the Goering tour, there were large popular demonstrations along the way, and Adam thought much of it spontaneous; the people were very loyal and had willingly given up their homes to make way for the fortifications. Toward the end of the first day the group reached Saarbrücken, which was situated very close to the French frontier and in such terrain that Adam had located the fortifications east of the city. Hitler now declared that he would give Saarbrücken another* gift, and ordered that the Wall be laid to the west of the city. Adam regarded this decision as "tactical nonsense—a Greek gift."

On the second day, the tour passed through the Rheinpfalz to Bühl in southern Baden. Several more times Hitler did what he had done in Saarbrücken. He

---

* After the German victory in the Saar plebiscite of 1935, Hitler had provided for the construction, at Reich expense, of a large theater in Saarbrücken, capital of the Saarland.

had no patience with terrain factors, and insisted on moving the line of the Wall westward, to cover in more towns.* The tension between him and Adam was intensified.

That evening Hitler held a long military conference in his private car. During the first two hours, only Brauchitsch, Keitel, Adam, Jodl, Colonel Kurt von der Chevallerie of the OKH General Staff (who made a record of the discussion), and Brauchitsch's adjutant, Major Siewert, were present. Hitler began with his usual catalogue of Anglo-French weakness and German strength, including the observation—very curious in the light of subsequent events—that "the tank arm has passed its peak," and therefore the antitank artillery and mines on the western front would provide defense against an armored attack.

Adam then pointed out that, with the infantry presently earmarked for his use, each division would have at least a twenty-kilometer front, and that he would have no reserves. Brauchitsch rejoined that "if everything in the Southeast went according to plan, the three divisions of the OKH reserve and the first eight replacement divisions would be made available for the West." Adam raised the possibility that the French would attack through and with the support of Belgium and Holland, in which case, unless reinforced, "I must abandon the Palatinate [the Rhineland south of the Saar] and turn to counter-attack against Belgium and Holland." Hitler would have none of that: "The Palatinate must not be given up. The attack against Czechia will not be broken off. I intend in this case to attack and defeat Holland, the weakest opponent, first."†

Nothing daunted, Adam declared that "in the operational area there can be only one master," and therefore after mobilization the Western Air Defense Zone (established by Goering on June 1 and commanded by Luftwaffe General Karl Kitzinger) must be put under his command. Furthermore, he insisted, "no conditions" should be placed on his authority to concentrate his troops in the combat zone, so that they would be familiar with the terrain in the event of a French attack. Goering was not there to explode at the first request, and Hitler evaded the second by assuring Adam that he would authorize deployment of the western forces "in good time, if an attack by France appears possible."

The conversation then turned to the vexing issue of when civilian labor should be cleared from the fortified zone. Hitler declared, reasonably enough, that a "premature breaking off of the work is politically risky," because it would disclose the imminence of a military crisis. He agreed, however, that the civilians should be out of the advanced positions by the end of September, and this controversy was temporarily resolved.

After a break the conference was resumed shortly before midnight, with the additional presence of Förster, Speich, Kitzinger, and Dr. Todt. The discussion chiefly involved the supply of gravel and other construction material, and when Todt stated that acceleration of the work required an increased flow, Hitler gave his needs priority over all others. The Fuehrer closed the meeting by declaring

* In his memoirs, Adam states that he did not carry out these orders. German maps of the West Wall show it as divided at Saarbrücken, with one line east and the other west of the city.

† At this point in his record, Chevallerie noted: "The Führer did not speak about the forces to be committed and the timing calculations involved."

himself "greatly impressed by the work accomplished," and "convinced that German troops could not be bombarded out of these positions."

On the third day the group continued up the east bank of the Rhine to the Swiss border. "The impression of the attitude of both the population and the workers is very strong," Jodl recorded. "The work done in the short period is tremendous. It is a pity that we could not have started work four weeks earlier." Bidding Adam good-bye, Hitler professed as his only regret "that I am the Führer and Reichschancellor and not the Commander-in-Chief of the Western front." To others, he declared that "the man who could not hold the fortifications is a scoundrel [*Hundsfott*]!" The next day, August 30,* he flew from Freiburg to Munich for dinner with Martin Bormann at his favorite Osteria restaurant, and then went on to the Berghof, to prepare himself for the Nuremberg Party Rally and what was soon to follow.

8

During June, July, and most of August the principal Green activities were planning, training of the regular units for special assault operations, and construction of the western defenses. During late August and September the calling-up of reserves, filling out the divisions to combat strength and forming new ones, creation of new commands, and deployment of troops were carried out at an increasing tempo.

In the summer of 1938, the German standing Army comprised forty-seven regular divisions, of which three were armored.† The reserve components were very small. Not only did Germany (like France) experience the "white years" from 1915 to 1918 when the birthrate was very low, but also, owing to the Versailles restrictions, there was no conscription from 1919 to 1935. Accordingly, the greater part of the male population under the age of thirty-five had had no military training, and the veterans of the First World War had had none since 1918 and were past the usual age for front-line service. In 1938 most of the trained reserves were needed to bring the regular divisions to combat strength, and only eight additional divisions for the front line were formed from reserve components, while twenty-one *Landwehr* (overage) divisions, useful primarily for rear-area or static defense assignments, were formed from the thirty-five- to forty-five-year age group.

For higher command purposes in peacetime, the forty-seven regular divisions were distributed among eighteen corps commands, and the corps in turn were subordinated to five group commands; these last were the highest field headquarters, and their commanders-in-chief reported directly to OKH. In wartime,

---

* On September 1, Engel sent to OKW and OKH a list of seven instructions concerning the fortifications which Hitler was giving in consequence of his inspection trip. None was of much importance.

† Of the forty-four infantry divisions, four were motorized, three were mountain divisions, and three were "light" divisions, an experimental mobile type (later converted to armored divisions) which included one armored battalion. There was also a cavalry brigade in East Prussia. A fourth light division and a fourth panzer division were in process of formation, and there were three militarized SS regiments.

the group commands would become "army group" or "army" headquarters, and the corps might remain such or be upgraded to "army" level.* For Green, command of the field Army was to be distributed among one army group and ten armies.

The single army group, under Adam, was to command all forces on the western front; it was formed from Group Command 2, the headquarters of which were moved from Kassel to Frankfurt am Main in July. Under Adam would be three armies: the Seventh, in the south on the east bank of the Rhine; the First, based in Wiesbaden, to defend the Rhineland between Karlsruhe and Trier; and the Fifth, in the north, opposite the Low Countries. Liebmann was given command of the Fifth Army, and General Hans Seutter von Loetzen, who had retired in 1933, the Seventh Army. He was an old friend of Adam's, and as a former commander of Group Command 2 and a longtime resident of Stuttgart was doubtless familiar with the defense problems of his area. Originally it was planned that Adam himself would command the First Army as well as the army group. But he did not like the idea, and the result, surprisingly enough, was that Beck was given the assignment.

The seven other armies were immediately subordinate to OKH. Two were given purely defensive roles in the east. In East Prussia, General Georg von Küchler's I Corps was to be reconstituted as the Third Army, and on the other side of the Polish Corridor in West Prussia and Pomerania, the Fourth Army would guard against the unlikely possibility of a Polish attack. In another surprising selection, Hammerstein was called from retirement to assume this command.

The five remaining armies were to be deployed in an arc around Bohemia and Moravia, from the German-Polish border on the north to the Austro-Hungarian border on the south. The Second Army was based in Upper Silesia, in position to strike southward across the narrow waist of Czechoslovakia, just west of the border between Moravia and Slovakia. The Eighth Army was concentrated in the Dresden area, north of Prague. The Tenth Army was drawn up along the western frontier of Bohemia, northeast of Nuremberg. The Twelfth Army, based at Passau, covered the southeastern frontier of Bavaria and the Austrian border north of Linz. The Fourteenth Army was at Vienna, ready to attack northward into Moravia, opposite the Second Army, and thus make a pincer.†

All but the Twelfth Army were constructed from the peacetime group commands: the Second from Rundstedt's Group Command 1 at Berlin; the Eighth from Bock's Group Command 3 at Dresden, the Tenth from Reichenau's Group Command 4 at Leipzig, and the Fourteenth from List's new Group Command 5

---

* An "army group" (the highest field combat command) generally comprised two or more "armies," an "army" two or more corps. The "army" was not a peacetime component. But although lower than an army group, it was a much larger headquarters. The army group's major function was to exercise command over its armies, while the army was responsible for supply, security, and numerous administrative functions as well as for command of its component units.

This chain of command was not invariable; a corps, division, or even a regiment might operate under direct command of an army group or of OKH, without responsibility to any intermediate headquarters.

† There were no armies numbered 6, 9, 11, or 13.

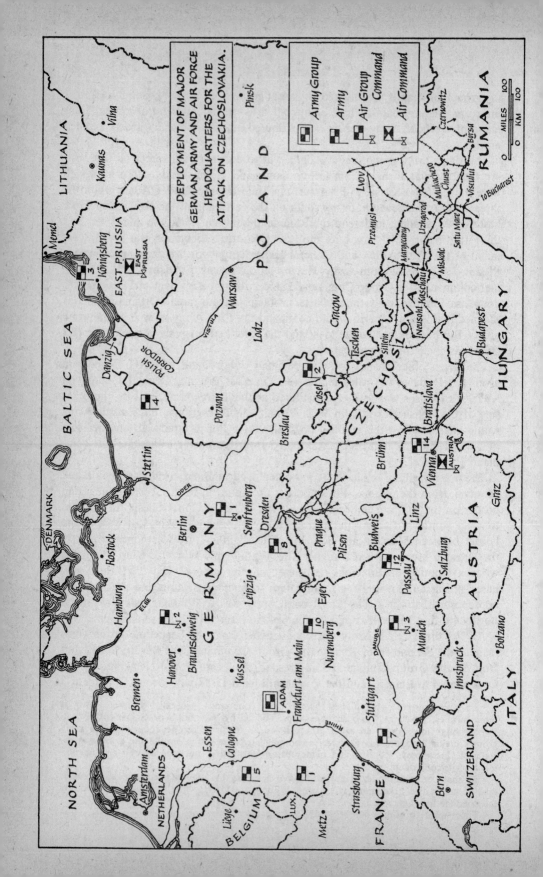

DEPLOYMENT OF MAJOR
GERMAN ARMY AND AIR FORCE
HEADQUARTERS FOR THE
ATTACK ON CZECHOSLOVAKIA.

Army Group
Army
Air Group
Command
Air Command

at Vienna. To lead the Twelfth Army, Leeb was recalled to duty. As he had had no headquarters or staff since his retirement at the time of the Blomberg-Fritsch shake-up, a special "Working Staff Leeb" was established at Munich in April.*

On paper, ten armies made a brave show, but three of them were little more than paper, and one (the Third, in East Prussia) was remote from the field of operations. An "army" is a headquarters, staffed to direct and administer to the units assigned to it, but it is not a combat formation and is no stronger than its components. The Fifth and Seventh armies in the west and the Fourth along the Polish Corridor were skeleton headquarters, established only so as to be available to receive and lead such troops as might be assigned in the improbable event of an enemy attack in their respective areas. In the west the area of greatest risk was the Rhineland border between Karlsruhe and Luxembourg, where the First Army was to be deployed. For the entire western front, Adam and his three army commanders had only five regular and four reserve infantry divisions, plus the overage *Landwehr*.

Subtracting the three regular divisions in East Prussia, the five in the west, and the reserve and *Landwehr* units left about thirty-seven divisions for the operation against Czechoslovakia—four fifths of the regular Army. As planned in August by Brauchitsch and Halder, the main punch would be delivered by Rundstedt's Second Army from Silesia and the Fourteenth and Twelfth Armies (List and Leeb) from Austria and southern Bavaria. These would attack toward each other, with the objective of meeting between Olmütz and Brünn, thus pinching off Bohemia and Moravia from Slovakia, and encircling the main body of the Czech Army. Airborne troops were to be dropped at Freudenthal in front of Rundstedt's army to speed its advance.†

Much smaller and of course more mobile than the Army, the Luftwaffe's deployment for Green was simpler. The highest field headquarters, directly subordinate to Goering as Commander-in-Chief of the Luftwaffe, was the Air Force Group Command (corresponding to an army group), of which there were three, located in Berlin (1), Brunswick (2), and Munich (3).‡ Each was supposed to be an air force in miniature, with all major operational types of aircraft, communications and supply units, and subordinate commands for airfields, transport, repair and other ground services, and antiaircraft artillery (*Flak*). The combat aircraft were organized in five "flight divisions," of which two each were in Group Commands 1 and 2, and the fifth in Group Command 3, which also comprised the Western Air Defense Zone.

As in the case of the army groups and armies, these top Luftwaffe commands were only as strong as the components assigned to them. Group Command 2, under General Helmuth Felmy, comprising Flight Divisions 3 and 4, was not to

---

* *Arbeitsstab Leeb* consisted at first only of Leeb himself and Colonel Günther Blumentritt as operations officer (both on a part-time basis), with the expectation of Manstein as chief of staff later on. As the headquarters developed, it was redesignated Army Group Command z.b.V. ("for special purposes") and was to become the Twelfth Army for operational purposes.

† See the chart of the Army's order of battle and the map of its dispositions, pp. 1006–7 and 708.

‡ There were also three smaller headquarters directly under Goering called Air Force Commands—one in East Prussia, one in Austria, and one for marine aviation. These had no important role in Green.

DEPLOYMENT OF GERMAN ARMY AND AIR FORCE
HEADQUARTERS FOR "GREEN," LOCATION OF
CZECH FORTIFICATIONS, AND GENERAL
LOCATION OF CZECH FORCES.

Leipzig

GERMANY

Chemnitz

Senftenberg

7
Sorau   Sagan

Görlitz

IV   X

Dresden

8

Freiberg

XI

Herrnhut

VI

Eibenstock   I

Hof

Saaz

Prague   I

I

Kolin

Bayreuth   Wildenau   Eger

XVI

Grafenwöhr   Mies   Pilsen

CZECHO

Iglau

10

Schwandorf   XIII

Rötz

V

Regensburg

Kl. Philippsreuth   Budweis

Straubing

DANUBE   Freyung   Böhmisch-
Krummau

VII

Vilshofen   Glöckelberg

12

Landshut   Passau

IX

Linz

3

Munich

AUSTRIA

Salzburg

palacios

0   MILES   50

0   KM   50

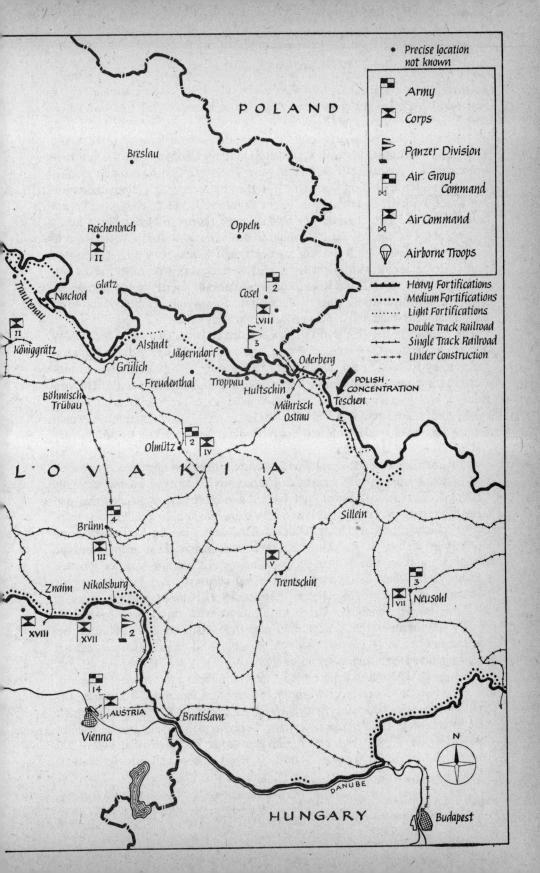

be involved in the attack against Czechoslovakia. Like Adam's army group, it was for defense against a possible attack from the west and had only small forces immediately available.

The main body of the Luftwaffe was allocated primarily to General Albert Kesselring's Group Command 1, covering eastern Germany and the northern Czech frontier opposite Silesia, Saxony, and Thuringia; and secondarily to General Hugo Sperrle's Group Command 3 in Bavaria and Austria, along the southern Czech borders. In addition to Flight Divisions 1 and 2, Kesselring's command included Flight Division 7,* in which the airborne troops had been newly assembled under the command of General Kurt Student. These forces were to provide air support for Rundstedt's, Bock's, and Reichenau's armies. Sperrle's Group Command 3, with Flight Division 5, would work with Leeb's and List's armies in the south.† If the western powers attacked, Sperrle would also be responsible for the southern part of the western front, while Felmy would cover Belgium and Holland and handle operations against Britain.

The primary goal of the Luftwaffe, as detailed in Hitler's Green order of May 30, was to destroy the Czech Air Force, and its bases as well, so as to prevent their use by Russian or French aircraft. Additionally, the Luftwaffe was to provide close support for the Army's breakthrough and paralyze the Czech Government by attacks against "its communications systems" and "centers of mobilization and administration." This third mission, if broadly interpreted, would entail widespread destruction and heavy civilian casualties and could even include leveling the Hradschin.

While the pertinent documentation is scanty, it does not appear that any such rain of terror was actually envisaged. Ruthless as Hitler was, he was certainly anxious to avert Anglo-French intervention, and must have concluded that pictures and reports of Prague and Pilsen crumbling into rubble would not be helpful in localizing the war. General Bodenschatz, describing the Luftwaffe's plans to Captain Stehlin at the Munich Conference, made them seem fearsome enough without any mention of terror-bombing. Hitler's aim was the quickest possible victory and the appearance of a *fait accompli,* and for this purpose elimination of the Czech Air Force, destruction of its bases, and assistance to the Army in overcoming the Czech fortifications must surely have been given priority. Furthermore, Hitler's May 30 directive stipulated that "industrial establishments are to be spared" as far as possible, and "reprisal attacks against the population are subject to my approval."

On July 11, 1938, Kesselring issued a general directive for the deployment of Air Force Group Command 1.‡ About 150 reconnaissance and 50 courier aircraft were transferred to the Army's direct command, and 200 fighter aircraft were allocated to the defense of eastern Germany against air attack. Against Czechoslovakia, Flight Divisions 1 and 2 together could marshal about 200 fighters, 600 level-flight bombers, and 200 dive bombers and other ground-at-

---

* Flight Division 6 was not established until 1939.

† Flight Divisions 1 to 5 were commanded respectively by Generals Ulrich Grauert, Wilhelm Wimmer, Richard Putzier, Hellmuth Bieneck, and Ludwig Wolff.

‡ Presumably there was a parallel order from Sperrle to Group 3, but it has not come to light.

tack aircraft. *In toto,* Kesselring had nearly half of the Luftwaffe's combat units at his disposal. Sperrle's forces for Green included the same types of aircraft but were much smaller.*

In August, Kesselring set up his combat headquarters at Senftenberg in eastern Saxony. Forward airfields had been built and equipped as jumping-off bases (*Absprungshafen*) for the attack. On receipt of the code word "Albert" the combat units were to move to these advanced bases, and "Starflight" was the signal for the assault, to be carried out in close timing with the ground forces. The new German dive bomber—the Junkers 87, better known as the Stuka— was still in short supply, and to augment the ground-attack strength, five groups (about 150 aircraft) of obsolescent biplanes, which had been used effectively for this purpose in Spain (Heinkel 45s and 51s, Henschel 123s), were hastily thrown together. Three of these were deployed in Silesia behind Rundstedt's sector, and the other two went to Sperrle, for use in support of Leeb's army.

For those times, the most novel item in the Green plan was the airborne landing to be undertaken by Flight Division 7 under General Student, a First World War aviator who had stayed in the Army, specializing in air planning, until his transfer to the Luftwaffe in the early thirties. In the summer of 1938, when the project was conceived, Flight Division 7 was a newly established and hastily improvised command. Its infantry components comprised one battalion each from the Luftwaffe and the Army trained for parachute operations, Army Regiment No. 16, specially trained for combat after being landed by airplane or glider in enemy territory, and a few volunteers from the SA Regiment *Feldherrnhalle,* mostly untrained. Air transport was to be furnished by some 150 Junkers 52 transports. The landing was to be made at Freudenthal, about 15 miles inside Moravia, to clear the way for the Third Armored Division, of VIII Corps in Rundstedt's army, advancing on Olmütz.

All in all, the Luftwaffe was ready and able to strike heavy blows and rapidly win command of the air over Czechoslovakia. But it had serious weaknesses; many of the units were newly formed, and there was a great shortage of trained crews. There were practically no reserves; all the ready aircraft had been put into the front line. Heavy losses could not be made good, and consequently the Luftwaffe was unable to sustain a protracted campaign.

As for the German Navy, except for a few armed vessels on the Danube which were to be put under Army command, it had no part in Green. In the Baltic and North seas, it was to be on the alert against Russian or British intervention, but defensive measures were to be as "inconspicuous" as possible, so as to avoid all provocation.

Late in August, Admiral Raeder advised Hitler that only one pocket battleship and eight submarines were ready for war. The Fuehrer replied that this didn't matter at all, since he knew that England would remain neutral.

9

Hitler's assurances to Raeder were, of course, exactly those which Beck had refused to accept. By the end of August, Beck was gone, but he was by no

* No documentary summary of Sperrle's strength has come to light. Inferentially, it would appear to have comprised about 150 level-flight bombers, 100 fighters, and 60 or more ground-attack aircraft.

means the only skeptic, nor were these doubts confined to the Army. At the Foreign Ministry the second man, State Secretary Ernst von Weizsaecker, was very much of Beck's opinion.

Early in June 1938, and probably in reaction to Hitler's Green directive of May 30, Weizsaecker submitted a memorandum to Ribbentrop predicting that a military attack on Czechoslovakia would lead to war with France and England, and to Germany's ultimate defeat. Czechoslovakia, he urged, must rather be eliminated by diplomatic means, invoking slogans such as "self-determination for the Sudeten Germans," which would win sympathy and support in Britain. A month later, moved by further information on the military plans, Weizsaecker repeated these views orally to his chief, urging that "the situation must be made plain to the Führer." According to his memorandum record of the meeting, Ribbentrop "agreed with what I had said."

Ribbentrop's agreement was short-lived. Later in July he enjoined Weizsaecker that the Foreign Ministry should tell "all and sundry" that Germany was ready to "run the risk of a full-scale war with the Western Powers and win it too." France would be "decisively beaten," and raw materials were on hand "for a war of no matter what duration." The State Secretary replied rather acidly that German diplomats should talk in a way that would "obtain credence," and that "even if it was our business to fool foreign countries, it was nevertheless our duty not to dupe one another." But despite these cogent warnings, on August 3 a circular went out to the German foreign missions generally in line with Ribbentrop's instructions.

Later that month, the differences between the two men came to a head. As recorded by Weizsaecker:

During a conversation with Reich Minister von Ribbentrop on August 19 he explained to me that the Führer was firmly resolved to settle the Czech affair by force of arms. He described the middle of October as the latest possible date because of technical reasons governing air operations. The other powers would certainly not make any move and, even if they did, we should accept their challenge and defeat them also. I refuted this whole theory, as previously, and remarked that we must reach the political stage of a falling off in British interest in the Czech affair and also of British tolerance before we could take up the matter without running an unjustifiable risk. Herr von Ribbentrop sought to represent the question of responsibility in such a way that I was responsible to him alone, he to the Führer alone, and the Führer solely to the German people, while I maintained that it was necessary to be deeply rooted in the theory of such a policy in order to carry it out to the best advantage. Herr von Ribbentrop declared that the Führer had never yet made a mistake; his most difficult decisions and acts (occupation of the Rhineland) already lay behind him. It was necessary to believe in his genius, just as he, R., did from long years of experience. If I had not yet reached the stage of blind belief in the question under discussion—as I expressly told Ribbentrop —then he desired of me, in a friendly manner and urgently, too, that I should do so. I should certainly regret it later, if I did not succeed in doing so and the facts then contradicted me. . . .

Ribbentrop then informed his deputy that if war came "the Führer intends to move into Czechoslovakia himself at the head of the leading armored division," and that "the Foreign Minister is to accompany him into action," leaving the diplomatic responsibilities to Weizsaecker. With this absurd fantasy, Weizsaecker's efforts to convert his chief came to an end. Many of the career Foreign Ministry officials shared Weizsaecker's views, and he encouraged them to take steps, through Theodor Kordt in London, to apprize the British Government of Hitler's plans. Weizsaecker also maintained contact with Beck's successor as Chief of Staff, General Franz Halder, who was equally convinced of the unwisdom of risking a military confrontation with the western powers, and was discreetly discussing with a few like-minded officers the possibility of steps to prevent Hitler from doing so.

Franz Halder, who had succeeded Manstein during the Blomberg-Fritsch crisis when Manstein was sent off to field duty, and who now stepped into Beck's shoes as Chief of the General Staff, was a prissy, schoolmasterish officer, constantly torn between professional ambition and dismay at Hitler's military presumption. A Bavarian, a commoner, and physically unimpressive, Halder was less upsetting to the Fuehrer's ego than the taciturn, tight-lipped Prussian "vons" like von Fritsch, and held his position for four years until Hitler let him go in the fall of 1942. Halder had risen steadily if not spectacularly in the Army and, if he lacked Manstein's capacity for bold and original operational plans, was a staff officer of acknowledged competence. He was not a dominating personality, and under stress was likely to shed a few tears. Less philosophical than Beck, he was perhaps more inclined to make decisions and take action. A prideful man, he fumed and fussed when Hitler overrode his counsels, and in the fall of 1938 he was seriously disaffected. But his rebellious streak was constantly at war with his hope to be bracketed in military history with Moltke and Schlieffen as a great Chief of Staff.

Such was the man at the center of what is now referred to in the histories of those years as the "Halder plot" of 1938. The scope of this "plot," if it merited that description, remains somewhat obscure, and it appears that the plans for carrying it out were never developed with the precision which so dangerous and important an enterprise should have entailed. But it is certain that soon after he became Chief of Staff, Halder did indeed engage in secret conversations both within and without the Army, the object of which was to head off Hitler from his risky military designs and remove him from power if necessary.

There were already a number of military and civilian officials who were consulting discreetly to this same purpose. Probably the most cohesive group was composed of officers in Admiral Wilhelm Canaris' OKW intelligence division. Canaris himself played a protective rather than active role; the leader of the group was his deputy, Lieutenant Colonel Hans Oster. Outside the Army, the most active dissident was Dr. Carl Goerdeler, the former Mayor of Leipzig, and others included the disgruntled and demoted Hjalmar Schacht, Ulrich von Hassell, who had been sacked as ambassador in Rome at the time of the Blomberg-Fritsch crisis, and a police official, Hans Gisevius.

Among these and others who were in touch with them, the degrees of courage and resolution varied widely. Many of them were to lose their lives after the July 1944 attempt on Hitler's life, and some of those who survived, notably Schacht, later presented conflicting claims to leadership, bespeaking jealousy and friction among the participants. These circumstances add greatly to the difficulty of describing or assessing the 1938 "plot" with any assurance of accuracy.

In retrospect, however, it is clear that there was a basic difference in motivation as between Halder and the Goerdeler-Oster confederates. These latter, whether from principle or resentment at their treatment, had turned against Hitler before *Anschluss*. Halder, like Beck, on the other hand, was chiefly moved by his conviction that Green would be militarily disastrous because of Allied intervention. The Goerdeler-Oster people wished to *exploit* the Army's internal crisis over Green to get rid of Hitler and change Germany's political face and structure; Halder and Beck wished to abort Green and stave off the military defeat which they feared would otherwise ensue, and, if Hitler were to come around to their point of view, they would abandon all thought of a *Putsch*.

Given this divergence of purpose, it is not surprising that Halder appeared ambivalent and irresolute to the others, and that there was sharp disagreement on the timing of the proposed coup. Since his object was to avoid war in the west, Halder was unwilling to move until he felt that such a war was momentarily imminent. The others felt that to wait so long might be to miss the crucial opportunity and see all possibility of resistance swept away by the tides of war. Since everything depended on the Army, however, the keys to action were in Halder's hands.

Despite his exalted title, Halder alone was powerless. The Chief of Staff commands no troops and can give orders only in the name of the Commander-in-Chief. But Halder knew his chief well enough not to try to involve him. Brauchitsch was personally beholden to Hitler, and his shaky support of Beck's efforts had shown him up as a man of little intestinal fortitude; furthermore, he was about to marry as his second wife a lady of strong Nazi sympathies, and he was in no mood for mutiny.

In fact, even if Brauchitsch had joined in the plot, the difficulties of organizing and executing a successful military revolt would still have been enormous. An army is a chain of command, and the higher an officer's post, the further he is removed from the men who do the shooting. In peacetime the fighting units are scattered in garrisons and camps throughout the nation, and to concentrate an effective force requires the communication of orders and *obedience,* and this in turn depends on unity of purpose. Even in the days of Seeckt and the tiny Reichswehr, the generals had been divided when confronted with the Kapp-Lüttwitz and Hitler-Ludendorff *Putsche*. Brauchitsch carried little clout with the senior generals, Halder less. Some, like Reichenau, Schobert, and Busch were avowedly pro-Hitler. The junior officers and most of the troops reflected popular sentiment, generally idolatrous of the Fuehrer. Goering's Luftwaffe was beyond hope of enlistment in any rebellious enterprise.

Halder was well aware of these factors. The troops, in his view, were as unreliable for revolutionary purposes as the general population. It was clear that, if confronted by conflicting orders from Hitler and a rebellious military junta, the Fuehrer's commands would soon carry the day.

Still, with a number of highly placed officers deeply convinced that Hitler's policies threatened ruin to the Fatherland, perhaps some way could be found to cut him off from the levers of power and stop his apparent rush toward war. If he and his subservient satraps and functionaries like Goering, Goebbels, and Himmler and the security police could be suddenly rounded up and held incommunicado, so that no conflicting orders could go out to the various commands, maybe the organizers of the coup could achieve the necessary momentum and take control of the State machinery. Obviously, the focus of such a venture must be Berlin, and its success would depend on Hitler's presence in the capital.

The highest field commander in Berlin was the senior field commander in the entire Army, General Gerd von Rundstedt, whose Army Group Command 1 comprised four corps areas (I, II, III, and VIII) covering East and West Prussia, Pomerania, Mecklenburg, Brandenburg, and Silesia. Prestigious and competent, had he chosen to lead no doubt many would have followed, but he had always been passive on crisis issues and, at sixty-three, was professionally and temperamentally desiccated. Socially the Nazis were little to his liking and he often made cutting comments about them, but it was all superficial.

Late in July, Adam, visiting Berlin, encountered Halder, and after they had found themselves at one on the need for a change of regime, Adam agreed to probe Rundstedt's views on the situation. The result was a flat rebuff, coupled with praise for the Fuehrer.

Berlin itself was in the III Corps area, commanded by General Erwin von Witzleben, and with him the plotters had more success. The postwar accounts of Halder, Schacht, and Gisevius all agree that Witzleben was strongly anti-Nazi and joined eagerly in the plan to forestall a war by deposing Hitler. Three years older than and senior in rank to Halder, Witzleben was to be the military commander of the *Putsch*—the man in whose name the orders would be issued, and the leader of the forces that would carry it out. As corps commander Witzleben had few troops under his immediate command, but he brought with him into the enterprise General Walter Graf von Brockdorff-Ahlefeldt, commander of the 23rd Infantry Division, garrisoned in and near Berlin.* This division was to play the key role in the plan by occupying the Reichschancellery, the buildings of the other major ministries, and the wire and radio communications centers,

---

* What it was about Witzleben and Brockdorff that moved them to accept these crucial assignments, in what amounted to a military revolt, is not clear. Brockdorff served ably as a divisional and later a corps commander during the early part of the war, and died of illness in 1943. Witzleben and most of the other officers involved in 1938 (not including Halder) participated in the attempt against Hitler in July 1944, and paid for its failures with their lives. The lucky ones were shot, while Witzleben and some others were strangled with piano wire. Witzleben was a field soldier rather than staff officer, and is said to have been of a forthright and venturesome disposition, but not particularly intellectual. He was not motivated by professional dissatisfaction, for he had been promoted rapidly, and was made a field marshal in 1940. However, he was retired from active duty in 1942, apparently because of disagreement with OKW over military policies in occupied France.

and taking as prisoners Hitler, Goering, Himmler, Goebbels, and all other high officials in a position to obstruct the success of the venture.

Outside of Berlin, other generals were ready to join: in the west, Adam and Beck; in the east, Colonel Paul von Hase of the 30th Infantry Regiment at Landsberg-an-der-Warthe, and General Friedrich Olbricht, Chief of Staff of IV Corps in Dresden; in the south, General Erich Hoepner, commander of the 1st Light Division. Apart from the Army officers, Gisevius apparently obtained the adherence of Wolf Graf von Helldorf, chief of the Berlin police, and Arthur Nebe, head of the Reich criminal police and a general in the SS.

From this conspirational welter, according to Gisevius and Halder, the rough outline of a plan had emerged by early September. Halder, with his deputy, General Karl-Heinrich von Stülpnagel, would give the signal for the revolt when it appeared that Hitler was about to attack Czechoslovakia, and use the leverage of the General Staff to swing Brauchitsch and the rest of OKH into the revolutionary camp. Under Witzleben's over-all command, Brockdorff-Ahlefeldt's 23rd Division, and such police forces as Helldorf, Nebe, and Gisevius could control would take over the machinery of government in Berlin and cut off Hitler and other Nazi leaders from communication with the rest of Germany. Simultaneously, Witzleben, Halder, and their like-minded colleagues in the provinces would try to spread the fires of military revolt throughout Germany, and if necessary find troops to aid Witzleben in Berlin.* Meanwhile Schacht, Gisevius, and disaffected ex-officials such as Hassell would make plans for a civilian government to replace the temporary military regime.

10

If Hitler or any of the principal Nazi officials knew of these conspiratorial doings, no evidence of their awareness has come to light. Of course Hitler well knew that Beck, Adam, and some of the other generals distrusted his judgment on the likelihood and consequences of Anglo-French military intervention. But throughout the months from *Anschluss* to Munich not a single general or civilian official was removed because of opposition to Green or any like cause, and Hitler never showed any anxiety that he might be the object of forceful opposition.

This rather surprising failure of Hitler's secret intelligence may be partly explained by the forced inactivity of the plotters. Their plan was operable only if Hitler was in Berlin, from where he had departed on August 26 after his reception of the Hungarian Regent, Admiral Horthy. From August 27 to 30, Hitler was touring the western fortifications, from then until September 4 he was in Munich or at the Berghof, from the fifth to the thirteenth at the Nuremberg Party Rally, and then again at Munich or the Berghof until September 21. He

---

* There was special concern about the motorized SS Regiment *Leibstandarte Adolf Hitler* near Munich, which, it was feared, might move toward Berlin and threaten Witzleben's hold on the capital. If this happened, Hoepner's division, which included an armored battalion, was to block the way to Berlin. The second General Staff officer of Hoepner's division was Captain Klaus Graf von Stauffenberg, who in 1944 was the bomb planter in the July 20 attempt on Hitler's life. Whether or not in 1938 he was privy to Hoepner's involvement in the "plot" is not clear.

met Chamberlain at Godesberg on the twenty-second, and finally returned to Berlin two days later.

Apart from the matter of Hitler's whereabouts, for Halder and the other dissident generals the prospect of Allied military action was a *sine qua non* of the project, and Halder would not give the signal until that was momentarily imminent. Furthermore it was by no means certain that Hitler would launch Green in the face of Allied military opposition.

On that issue, Hitler had continued, throughout August, to play his cards close to his chest. He had ordered the Wehrmacht to be *prepared* to execute Green by October, but had not said that this would be the date of the attack. On the very day that the Green directive was issued (May 30), in response to an inquiry from Mussolini about the Germans' "final aim regarding Czechoslovakia," the Duce was told only that Hitler regarded Henlein's Karlsbad demands as "reasonable" but was not convinced that the Czechs were negotiating in good faith, and that it was "difficult today to form any clear notion or make dispositions going beyond this program." Berlin placed little trust in Rome.

With the German military leaders, Hitler simply took the position that France and Britain would not intervene, and that they should not trouble their heads about political matters. If, like Adam, they questioned these assurances, he tried to blow them out of the water with a broadside of statistics. Of course, plans were written up (under the code name Red) for defense in the west, and the frenzied rush to pour concrete for the Siegfried Line (or West Wall) showed clearly enough that Hitler was concerned about the western powers, as did his insistence on a speedy breakthrough into Czechoslovakia, to resolve the issue before the Allies could react militarily. Still, the whole enterprise was initially based on the premise that *Germany would not find herself at war with France and Britain.* Some of the officers exposed to Beck's and Adam's views may have had nagging doubts about this forecast, but they do not appear to have been numerous. And, of course, throughout August and the first half of September, most of the field officers and troops thought they were on extended maneuvers, and had no idea of their eventual mission.

Meanwhile, Hitler and Goering were carrying on a shrewd psychological campaign against the Allies, especially the French, intended to convince them of the Luftwaffe's overwhelming might, and the Fuehrer's firm intention to solve the Sudeten problem in the near future and react immediately and brutally against any further Czech "provocation." These were the themes dinned into young Captain Stehlin's ears by General Bodenschatz, as well as by Goering's sister Olga Riegele, with whom Stehlin had a remarkably close relationship.

To make sure that Paris got the message, the French air chief, General Joseph Vuillemin, was invited to pay the Luftwaffe an official visit. François-Poncet and Colonel Geffrier (the air attaché) both advised against acceptance at a time when Czechoslovakia was being so openly threatened, but Bonnet insisted that Vuillemin go.

The French general was impressively feted, but, as Stehlin had expected, he was subjected to "a pageant of German military power calculated to kill any French intention to use its admittedly weak air force, even though it was the only way that Czechoslovakia could be given immediate aid." Vuillemin was taken to airdromes and experimental stations and through the Messerschmitt and Heinkel factories, and plied with beer, served by young Bavarian girls "to whose charm the French chief of staff was very susceptible," while Udet, a great raconteur, kept him mirthful. At the Heinkel plant in Oranienburg, Udet took Vuillemin aloft in a slow plane, while a prototype Heinkel 100, which had just broken the world speed record, raced by. At Karinhall, Goering asked his guest what France would do "if we are obliged to attack Czechoslovakia." Vuillemin replied, with dignity, that France "would be faithful to her word," but on the way back to the French Embassy he repeated to François-Poncet his earlier prediction that, against the Luftwaffe, the French Air Force would not last fifteen days. And that was the word he carried back to Paris, reinforced by personal observation.

As August lengthened and the Wehrmacht's preparations approached the critical phase, the questions of how best to justify and to time the attack called for decision. On August 26, Jodl sent Hitler, via Schmundt, a memorandum on the military problems raised by Hitler's insistence that the attack be launched without warning following an "incident" which Germany could treat as "provocation":

> The *Luftwaffe's* effort to take the enemy air force by surprise on their peace-time air fields . . . justifies its objection to all preparatory actions prior to the X-order,* and its demand that the X-order itself be issued late enough on X-day minus 1 so that the fact of Germany's mobilization will not be known in Czechoslovakia on X-day minus 1.
>
> The *Army's* effort leads in the opposite direction. Its view is that OKW may take, between X-day minus 3 and X-day minus 1 such advance measures as will ensure a rapid and smooth mobilization. OKH also demands that the X-order be given to the Army not later than 2 p.m. on X-day minus 1.
>
> To the foregoing it may be said:
>
> Operation *Green* will be set in motion by means of an "incident" in Czechoslovakia which could give Germany cause for military intervention.
>
> Fixing the time for this incident by *day* and *hour* is of the utmost importance.
>
> It must take place in general weather conditions favorable for our superior Luftwaffe to go into action, and at such an hour that reliable news of it can be known to us by mid-day of X-minus 1.
>
> It can then be spontaneously met by issuing the X-order at 2 p.m. on X-day minus 1.
>
> On X-day minus 2 the Wehrmacht will receive only a warning.
>
> If the Führer intends to act in this manner, any further discussion is unnecessary.
>
> For in that case no advance steps may be taken before X-day minus 1 which cannot be innocently explained, as otherwise the incident would appear to have been staged by us. Absolutely necessary advance measures must thus

---

* I.e., the order for the attack. "X-day" is the day on which the attack is to be launched; "X-day minus 1" is the previous day.

be ordered well beforehand, and camouflaged with numerous exercises and maneuvres. . . .*

The purpose of these notes is to show how deeply the Wehrmacht is interested in the incident, and that it must be informed in good time of the Führer's intentions—so far as the Abwehr is not responsible for arranging the incident.†

I request that the *Führer's decision* on these points be obtained.

On the day (the twenty-sixth) this inquiry was transmitted, Hitler was in Berlin saying good-bye to Admiral Horthy, and that evening left for his visit to the west front. Schmundt did not give Hitler the memorandum until after he had completed the tour and arrived in Munich on the thirtieth, where he promptly approved Jodl's schedule.

Despite Adam's orneriness, Hitler returned from the trip full of zeal for the fray, and apparently confident that Britain and France, even if they intervened, could do the Reich no harm. In Munich, Friedrich Bürger (Henlein's representative in Berlin) reported his conversation with the Fuehrer:

England bluffs and plays for time. He [Hitler] will not receive an English envoy."‡ A British attack is not to be expected, and if—then Germany is well prepared. England has no fighters that can overtake the fast German bombers. England has no ships that can attack the German coasts. English flak shoots lower than German by 3000 meters. . . . If France should attack, a slight correction in the West would be made. The Western fortifications are enormously strong.* Now is the best time to attack Czechoslovakia—in December it would be too late, as he had made clear to Henlein.

There was more of the same on September 1, when Hitler received Konrad Henlein at the Berghof: "Long live war—and even if it lasts two to eight years." The next day the Fuehrer spent most of the morning conferring with Henlein and Ribbentrop, and after lunch with Goebbels, Speer, Bormann, and Bodenschatz. In the course of all this, he ordered Henlein to have the Sudeten Germans provoke some "incidents" in Czechoslovakia on the following Sunday.

The pot was beginning to boil, and on September 3, Brauchitsch and Keitel were at the Berghof to review the military plans. The former reported that the troops would be moved up to their jumping-off areas on September 28: "From then they are ready for action. When X-day becomes known, the troops will

* The omitted paragraphs pointed out that it would be impossible to warn diplomatic representatives in Prague before the first air attack, even though the consequences of their being victims might be very serious, especially if representatives of friendly or truly neutral powers were killed.

† The "Abwehr" was the OKW intelligence branch, and if it staged the "incident" the other sections of the OKW could, of course, be readily informed.

‡ Probably the reference is to Theodor Kordt's report of his conversation with Sir Horace Wilson on August 23, when Wilson had "mentioned the possibility that a special envoy of the British Government might transmit to the Führer a proposal for a peaceful and generous settlement."

* The quoted text is from Helmuth Groscurth's diary, based on Bürger's report. At this point Groscurth interpolated *"völliger Unsinn"*—completely nonsensical or, more idiomatically but less politely, "full of s—t."

conduct their exercises in the opposite direction."* Brauchitsch added that he must know the time of X-day by noon on September 27. Hitler expressed some misgivings about the two-day march between the troops' assembly points and the assault areas, and ordered extensive camouflage maneuvers to conceal the pending attack, but expressed no reservations about the stipulated date.

The Army's plan of attack, however, did not meet with his full approval. In August Halder had provided Hitler with a map and memorandum of the proposed deployment and objectives of the attacking forces, which he had been mulling over. Now he took strong objection to the basis of the Army plan, which was to use the Second Army in the north and the Twelfth and Fourteenth armies in the south to make a pincer, cutting Czechoslovakia in two and trapping the main body of its forces in the western part.

The basis of the Fuehrer's objection was that this was just what the Czechs would be expecting, and would be guarding against by fortifying the border opposite the Second Army most strongly and keeping an assault force east of Prague ready to counterattack. Therefore the prospects for the Second Army were the least favorable; furthermore, the Fourteenth Army's thrust would fail because of poor transportation in Austria. He feared a "repetition of Verdun" for the Second Army, which would "bleed to death for a task which cannot be accomplished."

For these reasons, Hitler proposed to shift the *Schwerpunkt* of the German assault to Reichenau's Tenth Army, opposite the western end of Czechoslovakia. Here, he said, the Czech fortifications were weaker and further back of the border, and there was more prospect of support from the "Henlein people." Therefore all the armored and motorized divisions should be assembled under the Tenth Army for an easterly thrust toward Prague: "Once we are through there, the south front . . . opposite the 12th Army will collapse. One army in the heart of Bohemia will be decisive."

Brauchitsch expressed some reservations because of the condition of the newly motorized divisions and the lack of trained leaders, but he voiced no fundamental objections. Upon return to Berlin, however, Brauchitsch and Keitel found Halder adamantly opposed to Hitler's plan. The Army was so weak in medium artillery, Halder said, that the armored divisions had to operate separately so as to ensure that the infantry could break through at the critical points.

Without having brought the matter to a conclusion, Keitel went off to the Nuremberg Party Rally, where, according to his later account:

. . . Hitler inquired of me whether the General Staff had amended its operational plan in accordance with his wishes. I telephoned Halder and he said they had not: they had not been able to amend it in time as the orders had had to go out. I asked Hitler for permission to fly to Berlin to speak with Brauchitsch personally; I made the excuse that for security reasons it would be imprudent to use the telephone. I determined on no account to return to Nuremberg without having achieved my purpose. I spoke alone with Brauchitsch and he saw the position in which we both now found ourselves; he promised to speak at once to Halder along these lines. But when I called on

* I.e., toward instead of away from the Czech border.

him two hours later to pick up his final decision . . . he rejected any prospect of making any alterations; that was quite impossible, and I would have to tell Hitler that.

There was trouble brewing, and it concerned not only the Army's deployment for Green. Goering, saying to Hitler: "So the OKW is working against you,"* had brought him a collection of antiwar statements by officers of both OKH and OKW. While in Berlin (on September 8) Keitel gave an order to the OKW staff that no political reports or alarming intelligence should be given to either the Army or the Luftwaffe without his personal approval.

Jodl, meanwhile, was having an uncomfortable conversation with Halder's deputy, General Karl-Heinrich von Stülpnagel, who came in to request that the Army be given five days' advance notice if Green were to be undertaken. Jodl agreed to this, with the qualification that meteorological predictions were reliable for only two days and therefore the plans were subject to change until X-day minus 2. Stülpnagel then remarked that ". . . now for the first time he wonders whether the original basis of the plan is being abandoned. It presupposed that the Western powers would not finally intervene. It gradually seems as if the Führer would stick to his decision even though he may no longer be of that opinion. It must be added that Hungary is at least uncertain and Italy, according to Canaris' report, is holding back."

Stülpnagel was in Halder's dissident group and may perhaps have been probing for ulterior reasons, but Jodl in his diary recorded parallel concern: "I must admit that I too am worried, when comparing the changing assessments of our political and military potential as between the directives of 24 June, 5 November, and 7 December 1937 and 30 May 1938 with the latest pronouncements."

For the Fuehrer-faithful Jodl, however, the answer was a stiff upper lip and good security: "Nevertheless, one must realize that other nations will do all they can to put us under pressure. And as only a few people have the strength to withstand such pressure, only a very small circle of officers should have news that arouses anxiety, rather than have it circulated in ante-rooms, as has been the case."†

The following day, September 9, Brauchitsch and Halder were summoned to Nuremberg for a showdown meeting with Hitler on the Army's deployment for Green. The conference began at ten in the evening, following a session of the Party Congress, and lasted until half-past three the next morning. Disinclined to

---

* Goering's charges against OKW apparently concerned reports of General Georg Thomas' economic branch on Germany's material shortages, and by Admiral Canaris on his recent trip to Italy during which he met with the Army Chief of Staff, General Alberto Pariani. According to Canaris' report, Pariani counseled forcefully against war, and indicated that Italy would take no part. After hearing of Keitel's order, Groscurth noted in his diary: "The Admiral's report on his Italian trip must be *immediately* withdrawn."

† Anxiety was not confined to the Army. After Stülpnagel's departure, Keitel and Jodl received Jeschonnek and two other Luftwaffe General Staff officers, also concerned about advance notice of X-day. The subsequent discussion revealed that: "The Luftwaffe begins to have doubts about Student's success [referring to the proposed airborne operation at Freudenthal] and is looking for another place; this would weaken the *Schwerpunkt* [i.e., the Second Army's drive] and undermine confidence in the leadership." Keitel and Jodl opposed changing the airborne plan, and Freudenthal remained the chosen area.

treat Halder, of whom he had a good opinion, too abruptly, Hitler allowed the new Chief of Staff to present the Army plan without interruption, as recorded in Schmundt's* notes:

> General Halder explains the basic plan of Operation *Green*. Mission: To prevent the withdrawal of the Czech Army from Bohemia-Moravia. To destroy it. To bring about a rapid decision.
> Mission can be accomplished by pincer attack toward Olmütz and Brünn by 2d and 14th Armies. Transportation difficulties in Austria, so *Schwerpunkt* with 2d Army.
> The Czech borders can be only lightly held. Withdrawal of the Czech forces is certain. Multiple defensive lines on terrain favoring defense will delay follow-up attacks and give the Czechs time to withdraw, so as to hold a "rump" area.
> That must be prevented. The Bohemian-Moravian heights, which would confront the attacker [from the west] would favor these Czech tactics.
> The pincer attack makes it possible to attack these heights from the rear.
> This operation will definitely succeed.

Halder went on to controvert Hitler's proposal to shift the *Schwerpunkt* from the Second Army to the Tenth Army. Opposite the Second Army, he declared, the Czech fortifications were weak, and no armored forces would be encountered. If, contrary to expectations, the attack in this section failed, there would be no "bleeding to death," for the deployment would be flexible and rear formations would be brought to points where initial success had been achieved. On the southern front, the Twelfth and Fourteenth armies would work together and cause the weakly held Czech front to collapse. Once through the line, the Twelfth Army would swing eastward and strike toward Brünn. In contrast, the Tenth Army confronted a strongly fortified line near Pilsen, and the roads were bad. Tanks would have to break through and secure bridgeheads for the following forces.

Hitler then repeated much of what he had said a week earlier, including references to "Verdun" and "bleeding to death." But it became plain that he now viewed the Tenth Army attack not as a substitute for but as an addition to the Army plan:

> There is no doubt that the planned pincer operation is the most desirable solution and should be carried out. But its success is nonetheless too uncertain to be depended on. Especially as a rapid success is necessary from a political point of view. The first eight days are politically decisive; within that time large territorial gains must be achieved.
> Our artillery (21 dm. howitzers) is not strong enough against the fortifications. Where an attack is expected, there can be no surprise.

Furthermore, the Fuehrer had abandoned his proposal to concentrate all the armored and motorized divisions under the Tenth Army. The three available armored divisions would remain where the Army had assigned them: one each (the 1st, 2nd, and 3rd panzer divisions) respectively with the 10th, 14th, and 2d ar-

---

* In addition to Hitler, Brauchitsch, Halder, and Keitel, the adjutants Schmundt, Engel, and Below were present. Todt joined the group toward the end of the meeting.

mies. Of the four motorized divisions, one (the 29th) would remain, as planned, with the Fourteenth Army in Austria, where rail transportation was inadequate.

However—and this was the only major shift on which Hitler insisted—the Tenth Army, which already had the 20th Motorized Division, would now get the 2nd and 13th as well, transferred respectively from the Second and Twelfth armies. Hitler's point was that in the narrow waist of Czechoslovakia opposite the Second Army the objectives were not far enough away to warrant the use of motorized troops, and that since the Twelfth Army had no tanks, it had no use for motorized infantry, the prospective use of which was to follow up an armored breakthrough.* This reinforcement of Reichenau's army would create "two chances for victory."

With this major issue settled, Todt was called in for a discussion of the West Wall supply and worker-evacuation problems. In fact, Brauchitsch and Halder had come off fairly well, as the armored forces were left as they had planned, and the exchange of divisions would not seriously weaken the pincers attack. But Schmundt's notes conveyed nothing of the bitterness of the affair. Keitel, who was quite convinced that Hitler would get what he wanted in Czechoslovakia without a war, regarded the whole dispute as a waste of time, and saw the outcome as a "defeat" for Brauchitsch and Halder. Engel called it a "disaster" for the generals, and it is plain that Brauchitsch, and Halder even more, were vexed and humiliated at being lectured and overruled by a man they regarded as a military tyro. In retrospect Halder cuts an absurd figure—dancing with indignation at the alteration of his military plans while secretly plotting the overthrow of the man who was doing the amending.

After Brauchitsch and Halder had left in a huff, Keitel "yessed" Hitler in a ludicrous fashion, which produced only new charges of the Army's fear and cowardice from the Fuehrer. Admiral Canaris brought back to Berlin disturbing reports of chaotic conditions in Nuremberg, and of Hitler's apparent determination to settle the Sudeten issue by war.

The prime source of the ill-feeling was Hermann Goering, since February a field marshal and thus the ranking officer of the Wehrmacht. He and his acolytes were busy with talebearing against the Army. Milch revealed that General Liebmann, the head of the War Academy and slated to command the Fifth Army on the western front, had lamented the weakness of the western fortifications.† General Kitzinger, commander of the Western Air Defense Zone, had sent Hitler a report that General Erik Hansen, chief of the operations section of the General Staff, had made "less than optimistic" remarks about the western front.

Goering was seeking and relishing every opportunity to deride or talk down to the Army. According to General von Weichs, who (as commander of the XIII Military District, of which Nuremberg was the center) was in charge of the Army parade and demonstration troops assembled for the occasion, it had be-

---

* Hitler suggested that in the Second and Twelfth armies the motorized divisions be replaced by ordinary infantry divisions brought to the front in trucks and buses. This was in fact done, the two divisions being the 9th Infantry from Giessen and the 30th from Lübeck.

† When Milch disagreed with these strictures, Liebmann retorted: "You may be a brilliant airman but about army tactics you know nothing."

come the custom for the ranking officer present at Nuremberg to visit the troops' encampment. Now this assignment fell to Goering, who took occasion to address the officers at a breakfast reception in a most insulting fashion: "I know you are afraid of the Czech bunkers," Goering told them, "but just throw your hearts over them and you will make it." The officers, most of whom as yet knew nothing about Green, took this for what it was: an accusation of cowardice. Weichs lacked the fortitude to denounce the slur openly, and his later complaint to Brauchitsch was ineffectual.

Monday, September 12, was the last day of the Rally. It was also the day scheduled for the Wehrmacht demonstrations, and so most of the senior generals were in the audience when Hitler closed the Congress with his long-awaited speech. Adam and some of his friends were seated behind Wilhelm Ohnesorge, an elderly postal official and an early and fanatical Nazi who had been rewarded by appointment as Reich Postal Minister. When Hitler announced the award of 100,000 marks to Todt for his work on the West Wall, Adam and his neighbors responded with derisive laughter, bringing glares from Ohnesorge. During the Fuehrer's speech, Ohnesorge turned and exhorted the generals to applaud. "Are we in the theater?" Adam sardonically inquired.

Such goings-on reflected deep malaise in the upper reaches of the officer corps, and the next day Keitel returned to Berlin in what Jodl described as a very excited state "because of his bad experiences in Nuremberg." He called together all the department and section chiefs, recounted some of the bad reports about the OKW which had reached Hitler, and declared that he would not tolerate any criticism, reservations, or pessimism within the organization. Sadly, Jodl reflected in his diary.

Thus a cold and frosty atmosphere prevailed in Nuremberg, and it is distressing that the Führer has the whole people behind him except for the leading Army generals.

Only by acts can they repair the damage they have done by lack of spirit and disobedience. It is the same problem as in 1914. There is only one disobedience in the Army and it is that of the generals, and in the last analysis it springs from their arrogance. They can no longer believe or obey because they do not recognize the genius of the Führer, in whom some of them still see the corporal of the World War and not the greatest statesman since Bismarck.

At noon on September 14, there was a false report of a general mobilization in Czechoslovakia. It was soon corrected by more accurate news that a few reservists had been called up for temporary duty. Meanwhile negotiations between Henlein and Prague had broken down, and many Sudeten Germans were pouring over the border into Germany. Late that afternoon Hitler (who had gone to Munich after Nuremberg) authorized calling up the border guard reserves* along the Czech borders.

---

* These were the so-called VGAD (*Verstärktes Grenzaufsichtsdienst*), meaning reinforced border watch, composed largely of former regular soldiers serving as customs or other civil officials in border areas. They were organized so as to be available to man border defenses within a few hours after call-up, and were roughly comparable to the French *frontaliers* in the vicinity of the Maginot Line.

Thus the winds of war were rising rapidly when, at nine o'clock that evening, the German radio announced that the British Prime Minister, Sir Neville Chamberlain, would meet next day with the Fuehrer at the Berghof.

11

Despite the Fuehrer's apparent eagerness for war when talking privately with Henlein and Bürger at the beginning of September, he had continued to guard his words in public and diplomatic discourse right up to the time of Chamberlain's arrival in Berchtesgaden. Early in September, in response to repeated and increasingly irritated inquiries from Mussolini about his plans in regard to Czechoslovakia, Hitler sent a wordy memorandum which Prince Philip of Hesse (the usual intermediary) read to the Duce and Ciano on September 7. Despite all the public talk of Axis solidarity, it told the Italians virtually nothing. The Fuehrer declared that he himself did not want "to take the initiative" but would "intervene immediately, in spite of all threats from Great Britain and France, even at the risk of war with both these powers, should it come to fresh intolerable provocation." Therefore the Fuehrer could not give the Duce the date of a prospective attack on Czechoslovakia "because he does not know this himself," but would "explain his attitude in detail when he makes his big speech at the Party Rally."

But the speech on September 12, for all its brutal invective, explained nothing more. Hitler denounced the Czech actions in the May crisis as an "infamous encroachment" on the "rights" of a "Great Power," demanded "justice" for the Sudeten Germans, but made no precise demands and uttered no specific threat.

In fact, what Hitler said either publicly or privately was not a trustworthy reflection of his intentions, which, in all probability, fluctuated considerably in the course of the crisis he was fomenting. It was in his interest to tell Henlein and Bürger that he would soon attack the Czechs whatever the consequences with the western powers; how else could he expect them to engage in the provocations and produce the "incidents" he required as a justification for intervention? It was likewise natural that Hitler would refrain from explicit ultimatums that would precipitate Czech mobilization and eliminate the surprise factor. It was equally expectable that he should assure the generals that Britain and France would not go to the Czechs' aid, while telling London and Paris that he would resolve the Sudeten issue regardless of whatever they might do. Finally, it was in keeping with his aims that he not formulate any specific demands for, as we will soon see, *he did not want demands to be met*. Hitler was bent not on accepting but on *taking*.

The planned course of German military action, however, had become clear. Exploiting an instigated "provocation" on the part of the Czechs, the Army and Luftwaffe would achieve a quick breakthrough into the heart of Bohemia-Moravia before the main body of the Czech forces could withdraw to Slovakia and—even more importantly—before there was time for any meaningful Anglo-French intervention. And in early September of 1938 the crucial question was how great a likelihood of such intervention did Hitler perceive, and how great a likelihood was he prepared to confront in carrying out the military plan.

Internal counsels continued to play little part in his assessment. Beck had been banished, and there is no evidence that Halder, despite his conspiring, ever advised Hitler against the venture. Weizsaecker was walled off from Hitler by Ribbentrop. On September 1 the Minister of Finance, Count Schwerin von Krosigk,* addressed a memorandum to Hitler warning that the Reich was "heading towards a serious financial crisis" partly because of the prevalent "war psychosis," and predicting that Britain, "judging from my knowledge of England" (he had been at Oxford as a Rhodes scholar), was not bluffing and would go to war in aid of Czechoslovakia. There is no evidence that Hitler was at all affected by Krosigk's advice.

From London and Paris, the signals during the first half of September were mixed, but overall not very alarming. On August 27, Sir John Simon had reiterated Chamberlain's earlier statement that if war broke out over Czechoslovakia it was impossible to foresee how far it might spread. But, thanks to Sir Nevile Henderson, no new diplomatic warning came from London in early September. On September 10, Rear Admiral J. A. G. Troup, the Director of Naval Intelligence, told the German naval attaché (Captain Leopold Siemens) that the fleet had mobilized its minesweepers and layers because of the European "situation," and this information appears to have greatly alarmed the attaché. But this was so small a step that it can hardly have caused much concern in Berlin, especially since *The Times* had just published its famous editorial suggesting cession of the Sudetenland to Germany, upon which Theodor Kordt commented, in his report to Berlin, that it might have been inspired from within Chamberlain's entourage. On September 12, Kordt sent in a report of a conversation between a German embassy official and Joseph P. Kennedy, in which the American Ambassador declared, on the basis of recent talks with Chamberlain and Halifax, that it was now his "firm conviction that if France intervened Britain would intervene too." But this was only a contingent prediction, and it is unlikely in any event that Kennedy's views made much impression in Berlin.

As for the French, General Vuillemin had declared that France would honor her commitments but, under the circumstances, what else could he have said? Early in September, Daladier and Bonnet held private talks with Welczeck and Braeuer in which they stressed France's commitment of "honor" to support Czechoslovakia if she were attacked, but these declarations were buried under a pile of protestations of "understanding" for German demands in the Sudetenland, and abhorrence of war. On September 2, General Colson, the French Army Chief of Staff, said much the same things to the German military attaché, General Kühlenthal. Berlin reacted coolly and told Kühlenthal to discontinue the conversation with Colson. Then on September 11, Gamelin called in Kühlenthal and told him that French military precautions would be "intensified," and would include "a general ban on leave, the recall of men on leave . . . and other preparatory measures" including the calling up of reserves "in large numbers." But Gamelin virtually apologized for these steps by observing that "these measures

---

* Schwerin-Krosigk and Franz Guertner, the Minister of Justice, were by 1938 the only Cabinet members who had held office under Papen and Schleicher, before Hitler's coming into power.

would in no way amount to what Germany had set in motion, according to reports reaching him."*

Such a remark was hardly calculated to fill the Germans with apprehension. The realists in Berlin would look beyond the words spoken to the steps taken by the western powers. They knew that by this time the French and British had a pretty good idea of the scope of the Wehrmacht's moves toward mobilization. If, faced with such reports as Allied military attachés were transmitting, Britain was only mobilizing a few minesweepers, and France was avowedly doing much less than Germany, it was plain that neither France nor Britain was preparing for a swift and vigorous military response to Green.

Furthermore, by mid-September the preparations for Green were rapidly approaching a point at which it would be very difficult for Hitler to call it off. To be sure, the deployment time schedule was so constructed that the attack could be ordered postponed at any time until the day before the planned date. Even if the intention to attack was firm, this flexibility was militarily necessary, since the Luftwaffe was to play a vital role in the initial assault, and a "provocation" was to provide the excuse. Unfavorable weather for aerial bombardment, or a miscarriage of the "provocation," might require a brief postponement.

In theory, the entire plan could also be called off for a long period, or indefinitely, at any time up to the last day. But there were two factors—one political and the other military—that limited Hitler's freedom of decision to abort Green once the machinery for its execution started to resolve.

The political factor was essentially psychological. During the final stages of Green, the circle of knowledge that an attack on Czechoslovakia was imminent would be enormously widened. The assault troops would be moving to the jump-off areas. Maps of the Czech frontier areas, showing the location of the fixed defenses and the objectives for each day's advance, would be distributed to the attacking units. Luftwaffe formations would be flown to the fields from which the attacking aircraft would take off, with maps of the targets. Railway and other transportation schedules for the mobilization and deployment along the Czech borders would go into effect. The Henleinists would be urged to more and bolder instigations, on the basis of assurances that the Wehrmacht would soon be there. In May, the false appearance of a German setback had driven Hitler to fury. It is easily imaginable how humiliated he would have been if, once this grand program was begun, the curtain were to be rung down because of the threat of outside intervention. And indeed, apart from the shattering effect of such an anticlimax on the Fuehrer, it would have been a sharp blow to Germany's military and diplomatic prestige.

The military limitation was that the all-important surprise factor in Green could not survive a long period of maximum tension and "provocation." The longer this phase lasted, the greater the likelihood that Prague would mobilize and man the defenses in full strength, jeopardizing the speedy breakthrough on which Hitler was counting to chill any Allied inclination to intervene. The at-

---

* This last comment is not reflected in Gamelin's later account of the meeting (*Servir*, vol. 2, pp. 342–43). But whether or not he actually said it, that is what was reported by Kühlenthal to Berlin.

tack would have to follow hard on the heels of the "provocation" which would furnish the excuse.

In simile, once the ski jumper was fairly started down the run, it would be too late to abort the takeoff. By mid-September, Green was not quite yet so irreversibly in process, but the point of no return was not far distant. The reinforced regimental groups which were to make the initial assault were being assembled in their final training areas. The armored and motorized troops were being readied for their dash to the front from assembly points well back of the frontier. The four reserve divisions destined for the western front were being mobilized. Antiaircraft and reconnaissance units were transferred from the Luftwaffe to the Army units they would support. On the fourteenth the border guard was called up, and on the fifteenth the RAD was put under the Army's command.

Of course, it cannot be surely stated what Hitler would have done if, on September 14, he had received news of general mobilization in France and Britain, instead of Chamberlain's wish to come to Germany. But there is little doubt that, failing some equally unexpected and sensational development, Green would have gone ahead according to plan. Indeed, on September 14 Ribbentrop ordered that families of the legation and consulate staffs in Prague "should be evacuated gradually and unobtrusively." In all probability on or about September 28, after some prearranged "provocation," the Wehrmacht would have attacked Czechoslovakia.

12

The Nuremberg Party Congress ended on September 12, and the following day Hitler went to Munich, where he remained for the next two days. The first news of Chamberlain's message asking for a meeting came early on September 14, when Sir Nevile Henderson handed the text to Weizsaecker in Berlin, with the request that it be immediately forwarded to Hitler through Ribbentrop, who was also in Munich at the Vier Jahreszeiten Hotel. At about half-past nine Weizsaecker dictated the message to Ribbentrop, and later Schmidt provided a translation.

An hour or so later Ribbentrop went with the text to Hitler, who apparently was visiting at the Martin Bormann home in Pullach, a nearby village. Chamberlain's move took him completely by surprise. *"Ich bin vom Himmel gefallen"* is the phrase he is said to have used to describe his own reaction.*

Hitler and Ribbentrop apparently considered recognizing Chamberlain's seniority by proposing that the meeting take place in England, but that notion was discarded for obvious reasons. They likewise rejected the idea of a meeting on Hitler's yacht *Grille,* and finally settled on the Berghof, where Schuschnigg had

---

* Literally "I have fallen from heaven" but signifying utter astonishment. The remark is quoted in most of the Hitler biographies and works on Munich, sometimes as being what Hitler said when Ribbentrop brought him the news. Perhaps he did, but the only authority for the attribution is Sir Lewis Namier's statement (*Diplomatic Prelude, 1938–1939,* p. 35) that Hitler used this expression at a later date when telling to an unnamed "foreign diplomat" the story of Chamberlain's visit.

come to grief, as the right setting in which to receive the British Prime Minister, who was invited to fly to Munich on the morrow.

The Fuehrer did not wait in Munich to greet his distinguished visitor. After authorizing the border guard call-up he left Munich and went to the Berghof, summoning Keitel and Henlein to join him there, and leaving Ribbentrop in Munich to meet Chamberlain and escort him to Berchtesgaden. And so the scene was laid for the first of the three confrontations that culminated two weeks later at Munich.

CHAPTER 26

Chamberlain At the Berghof

1

On the evening of September 14, when it was announced from London and Berlin that the British Prime Minister would fly on the morrow to Germany and meet with the Chancellor of the Reich, much of the world heaved a great sigh of relief. It still lacked a few weeks of twenty years since the 1918 Armistice, and few had stomach for another Great War, which, it was generally believed, would start with cities crumbling to rubble under skies darkened by bomber clouds.

In England especially, relief was mixed with acclaim for the initiative and pluck of the elderly Neville Chamberlain, who had only once before been aloft in an aircraft, and then only for a few minutes. In fact the venture was bolder diplomatically than aeronautically, though in the planes of those times a six-hundred-mile flight was no joyride. But for Chamberlain to commit his own prestige and perhaps his country's course to an unprepared summit confrontation, on an unpredictable and bellicose dictator's home ground, was unconventional and venturesome indeed.

The unimpressed might have said, with reason, that it is too soon to cheer the high jumper until he has cleared the bar, but that was not how most Britons saw it at the time. As darkness fell on September 14, a large crowd was gathering on Downing Street, and when the announcement came there was prolonged and heartfelt cheering for the Prime Minister. The following morning the press was virtually unanimous in praising his initiative; the *Daily Herald,* for example, called it "an effort to stave off war which has seemed to be growing dreadfully near and, as such, it must win the sympathy of opinion everywhere, irrespective of Party." Even Harold Nicolson, no admirer of Chamberlain's policies, recorded his own reaction as "one of enormous relief." Theodor Kordt summed it all up in his dispatch to Berlin:

> Never have I witnessed such a sudden change of atmosphere as took place yesterday in the whole of Great Britain when Chamberlain's visit to the Führer was announced. Until evening the entire British population was sunk in deep depression called forth by the decision, no less serious, to take up arms under certain circumstances. Now things had taken a completely unexpected turn which offered the hope of a peaceful settlement. . . . It is no exaggeration when the newspapers report that men and women wept for joy in the streets.

At Heston Airport early in the morning of the fifteenth, Halifax and his Lady and Cadogan were there to bid their chief Godspeed, as well as Corbin, Kordt, and assorted dignitaries including Lord Brocket, chairman of the Anglo-German Fellowship.* To the press, the Prime Minister explained:

> I am going to meet the German Chancellor because the situation seems to me one in which discussion between him and me may have useful consequences. My policy has always been to try to assure peace, and Herr Hitler's ready acceptance encourages me to hope that my visit will not be without result.

The party took off in two planes, one carrying two typists and two "detectives,"† the other with Chamberlain, Sir Horace Wilson, and Sir William Strang of the Foreign Office. Halifax was left in charge at home, and Sir Robert Vansittart, the Chief Diplomatic Adviser to the Government, was left in charge of nothing in particular, while the Chief Industrial Adviser accompanied the Prime Minister in a conspicuously diplomatic role.

The bumpy flight took over three hours, in the course of which (according to the late Sir John Wheeler-Bennett) Wilson regaled his chief with a selection from the laudatory messages that had arrived at Downing Street. But what did those who praised expect him to do? Some undoubtedly hoped that the Prime Minister would at last tell Hitler off, and make it clear that if he disturbed the peace he must reckon with British might; others, better attuned to Chamberlain's views, thought otherwise. But surely most of the onlookers did not know what they wanted Chamberlain to do other than lift the threat of war. And that, of course, raises the question of what Chamberlain himself planned to do and say once he found himself head to head with Hitler. Did he in fact have a considered strategy, and if so what was it?

It is clear from what he later said that he saw his trip in part as a mission of inquiry to "find out in personal conversation whether there was any hope of saving the peace"—in other words, to hear from Hitler's own lips what were his terms for calling off the impending attack on Czechoslovakia. Wheeler-Bennett, who of all the authors of books on "Munich" had the best access to those who participated, declared that Chamberlain had no thought of military resistance, and thus implies that he was prepared to accept whatever terms Hitler might specify.

But it is hard to believe that the Prime Minister, accustomed as he had grown to dominating his fellow-men, saw his role as so passive and negative as Wheeler-Bennett suggests. Surely he intended to negotiate an "arrangement" with Hitler, and the question is, what sort of deal had he in mind? There are three presently‡ available sources that throw some light on the question: notes

---

* Lord Brocket, who had been an official guest at the Nuremberg Party Rally and was "deeply impressed" by a talk with Hitler, assured Kordt that "the task of conciliation would succeed."

† Sir Horace Wilson's word. It would be interesting indeed to discover what the detectives did while in Germany, and what if anything passed between them and the Nazi security police, but these matters have not come to light.

‡ The Chamberlain papers have not yet been fully available for historical purposes, but are in use by Mr. David Dilks for a biography of Chamberlain.

composed by Sir Horace Wilson during the gestation of Plan Z; the letters that Chamberlain wrote to Lord Runciman on September 12 and King George VI on the thirteenth; and what he told the Cabinet on September 14, before Hitler's reply had been received.

The Wilson notes, written September 10, are perhaps the most interesting, as prepared only for Chamberlain's consideration rather than for the record, and as showing what was in mind before Hitler's Nuremberg speech. The first set of notes, entitled "points which might be useful," listed five propositions to be advanced:

1. The Czech proposals* go far to meet the Sudeten claims, and are a "reasonable and hopeful basis for negotiations."
2. "In view of the doubt that exists in some quarters as to the *bona fides* of those who have put forward the proposals," Britain would assist in "translating the proposals into a settlement which meets the justice of the Sudeten claims."
3. Britain would assist in implementing the settlement.
4. "In view of the character of the proposals and of the offers under 2. and 3., no case exists for resort to force."
5. If there were resort to force, "this would involve . . ." consequences to be specified on a play-it-by-ear basis.

The second set of notes dealt with questions likely to be raised by Hitler. The Czech-Soviet treaty? A matter for Czechs and Sudetens to sort out together. The Franco-Soviet treaty? Suggest that it stems from French "uneasiness about future manifestations of German policy." British policy was "to bring about such a change in the European situation as would put an end to this state of uneasiness," and in that connection Britain and Germany should be "the two pillars that support orderly civilization against the onslaught of disruptive Bolshevism." Nothing should "weaken the resistance that we can jointly offer to those who threaten our civilization." Was British financial aid to Turkey designed to block German commercial expansion in southeastern Europe? Certainly not, so long as Germany operated on an open-door basis.

Then there was an added section, consequent upon the Prime Minister's asking what should be said about the remaining unsettled issues in Czechoslovakia. Wilson cautioned his chief not to get into the position of appearing to negotiate with Germany in behalf of Czechoslovakia. Therefore he should not go into details, but suggest that, since Lord Runciman had now come so near to closing the gap, the "interested parties" should "agree to ask Runciman now to become the arbitrator." Since there were possibilities of friction prior to the "changeover," perhaps "some form of international police" should cover the interim.

These notes furnished the basis for Chamberlain's letter of September 12 to Lord Runciman. The theme of Britain and Germany as the two pillars of a peaceful, non-Communist Europe was incorporated, leading up to the proposal that Runciman be the arbitrator.† If this proved acceptable to Hitler, Cham-

---

* The reference must be to Prague's "Fourth Plan," of September 7, which, as all sides agreed, substantially met Henlein's Karlsbad demands.

† Lord Runciman promptly replied that he would undertake the assignment "with great reluctance and as the last resort."

berlain would then raise for discussion "the existing treaties between Czechoslovakia, France, and Russia," and he would not "despair of finding a solution acceptable to all, save perhaps Russia." The letter on September 13 to the King incorporated most of this and added nothing; it shows only that Chamberlain felt able to send the same letter after Hitler's Nuremberg speech as the one written before it.

But at the cabinet meeting the following morning, the idea of a Runciman arbitration appeared less promising, and the prospect of a plebiscite was coming center stage. Indeed, even before revealing Plan Z to the Cabinet, Chamberlain observed that Hitler's speech "pointed" toward a plebiscite and that it would be difficult to resort to war to prevent one. Then, after describing Plan Z, he went on, according to the Cabinet minutes:

. . . he thought that the right course was to open by an appeal to Herr Hitler on the grounds that he had a great chance of obtaining fame for himself by making peace in Europe and thereafter by establishing good relations with this country, which was always his aim.

After some such opening it might be pointed out that if Germany was to have the goodwill of the British people, it was essential that the present dispute should not be settled by force. We were neither pro-Czech nor pro-Sudeten German. Our business was to keep the peace and find a just and equitable settlement. Negotiations had continued for a long time. Thanks, however, to pressure from ourselves and France, M. Benes had gone much further than had been expected. At this point there would probably be a tirade against M. Benes and a statement that it was impossible to have any confidence that M. Benes would carry out his promises.

The Prime Minister said that he thought that at this point reference might be made to the suggestion that some international body should be set up to supervise the fulfilment of any agreement reached. To this Herr Hitler might retort that no agreement had yet been reached and that matters could not go on indefinitely. The Prime Minister had had in mind to propose as a solution that the two parties should agree to put their views before Lord Runciman and to accept Lord Runciman as the final arbitrator.

The Prime Minister said he would, of course, have to make it clear that he could not answer for M. Benes. At the same time he would undertake to put all the pressure he could on M. Benes, and that the French would do likewise.

This, said the Prime Minister, was the idea with which he had started. But he now felt that Herr Hitler might say that, while this might have been acceptable a week ago, nothing could now settle the matter except a Plebiscite. The Prime Minister thought that the Cabinet would have to consider very carefully what should be said to any such demand.

Some people might take the view that the demand for a Plebiscite should be rejected out of hand. That was not his view, nor the view of the Foreign Secretary. He thought it was impossible for a democracy like ourselves to say that we would go to war to prevent the holding of a Plebiscite. . . .

Unlike Gertrude Stein's rose, a "plebiscite" is not self-defining. The previous May, Halifax had given some attention to the problems which a Sudeten plebiscite would present, and the subject had arisen again during the last few days in the Big Four meetings. The Prime Minister now acknowledged these difficulties

—how were the plebiscite areas to be delineated, what regard should be paid to "strategic and economic considerations," and how to deal with areas of "mixed populations"? But he indicated that in his opinion such obstacles would have to be overcome, since "he doubted whether Czechoslovakia would ever have peace so long as the Sudeten Germans were part of the country." From the Czech standpoint this was, obviously, a most ominous remark.

The Prime Minister then mentioned favorably a suggestion originated by Simon that "the Sudeten Germans should at the outset be given a wide measure of autonomy in specified areas, with the option of a Plebiscite after a given period," which would "ensure that the Plebiscite took place in a better atmosphere." He next undertook to deal with the awkward fact that Czechoslovakia, bereft of the mountainous and fortified Sudetenland, would be well nigh incapable of self-defense, so that the Czechs "might prefer to die fighting rather than accept a solution which would rob them of their natural frontiers":

> The Prime Minister said that the only answer he could find was one which he was most unwilling to contemplate, namely, that this country should join in guaranteeing the integrity of the rest of Czechoslovakia. This would be a new liability, and he realized that we could not save Czechoslovakia if Germany decided to overrun it. The value of the guarantee would lie in its deterrent effect. The sort of arrangement he contemplated was that Czechoslovakia should be guaranteed by France, Russia, Germany and ourselves, and should be relieved from liability to go to the assistance of the guarantor countries and would become a neutral State. This would help to clear up the situation in Central Europe. . . .

At least in retrospect, it is a preposterous notion that Britain should prefer to guarantee an indefensible rather than a defensible Czechoslovakia, or entertain hope that Russia would join in so extravagant a commitment. And this passage was followed by one even stranger, in its assumption that Germany could be induced to accept a gift of the Sudetenland by the prospect of friendship with Britain:

> The Prime Minister pointed out that the inducement to be held out to Herr Hitler in the proposed negotiations was the chance of securing better relations between Germany and England. This chance would be lost if Herr Hitler had recourse to force now. He could say that if a solution was found to the present difficulty, we might presently be able to deal with the problems which affected both countries.
>
> In this connection the Prime Minister referred to the statement which Field-Marshal Goering had made to Sir Nevile Henderson to the effect that if once the present difficulty was settled, we in this country would be surprised at the moderation of German demands.

A few of the ministers were troubled by the prospect of a plebiscite, and warmed to Simon's suggestion for its postponement. None held out hope for a Runciman arbitration,* but none offered serious objection to the general line

---

* The Minister of Transport, Leslie Burgin (who had been educated on the Continent and had served as a delegate to the League in 1935), warned Chamberlain privately that Berlin would be most unlikely to accept a non-German arbitrator, and that it would be very unwise to make any such suggestion to Hitler.

the Prime Minister proposed to pursue. He left London in a glow of approbation and, in all probability, confident that he could bring the Fuehrer to terms, on the assumption that Czechoslovakia could be persuaded to cede to Germany Sudeten areas to be determined by plebiscite, and that this settlement would also serve as the starting point for a general Anglo-German understanding. In short his task was to convince Hitler that he could get what he wanted without fighting, or, more accurately, that what he could get without fighting was what he wanted.

2

What Adolf Hitler wanted or expected to get out of the meeting is by no means clear. He was taken by surprise, and it may be that he had little purpose other than to take Chamberlain's measure as a leader, and impress his guest with his own determination to bring the Sudeten Germans into the Reich.

What does appear certain is that the Chamberlain message, together with the escalatory turmoil in the Sudetenland and Henlein's flight to Germany, gave Hitler cause for worry that events were outstripping his military timetable, which still had two weeks to run before the tentatively scheduled X-Day. This concern was reflected in Berlin, where Keitel and Jodl met with the Army and Luftwaffe Chiefs of Staff early on the morning of the fifteenth to consider "what could be done if the Führer wants to advance the date due to the rapid development of the situation." As Jodl's diary tells us:

> Result: it cannot be done. The former plan for *Green* can only be put into operation if all the troops return to their garrisons. Also railway preparations last 10 days unless one orders mobilization of the Reichsbann [State Railway]. The new railway schedule comes into force on September 28th. Thus we are bound to the date the Führer has chosen, taking into account that the work in the West should be continued as long as possible. On the request of General von Stülpnagel this conclusion is telegraphed to the Berghof. . . .

At half-past nine Keitel departed to fly to Berchtesgaden, and the remaining conferees turned to discussing the latest time of day for which the attack could be ordered. It was agreed that this was seven in the morning, and that the order must have been given by 8 P.M. the previous day: "In case of bad weather the Luftwaffe will try, by a coded radio message, to stop all or at least part of the attack."

Meanwhile at the Berghof, Hitler was getting bulletins on the famous Pilgrim's progress. Keitel arrived shortly after noon, and briefed the Fuehrer on the staff deliberations in Berlin. At four in the afternoon Chamberlain reached Berchtesgaden, and an hour later he was at the Berghof.

3

Whatever thoughts preoccupied Neville Chamberlain as his aircraft approached Munich, he appeared to his junior assistant Strang "as always, aloof, reserved, imperturbable, unshakably self-reliant." At the Munich airport his party was joined by Sir Nevile Henderson, and Ribbentrop was there to escort him, accompanied by General von Epp, the *Reichsstatthalter* of Bavaria, Dörnberg, the Chief of Protocol,* and Paul Otto Schmidt, the official interpreter. Chamberlain inspected an honor guard—"Death's head corps" troops, according to Wilson, whose note to this effect shows no awareness that these were SS *Totenkopf* concentration camp guards formed into armed battalions. Driving from the airport to the Munich railroad station, Chamberlain "felt quite fresh and was delighted with the enthusiastic welcome of the crowds who were waiting in the rain, and who gave me the Nazi salute and shouted 'heil' at the tops of their voices all the way to the station." A special train was waiting to take the party to Berchtesgaden; Schmidt recalled that:

> We lunched in Hitler's dining car on the way. . . . The scene is still very clear in my memory. During almost the whole of the three hour journey troop transports rolled past, making a dramatic background, with soldiers in new uniforms and gun barrels pointing skywards. . . . †

At Berchtesgaden the Prime Minister reviewed another SS honor guard (this time the *Leibstandarte Adolf Hitler*). The party was taken briefly to the Grand Hotel and then by automobile to the Berghof. A few days later Chamberlain described what followed in a letter to his sister Ida:

> . . . The entrance of the house is on one side opening on to a sort of terrace, from which a flight of steps descends to the road. Half way down these steps stood the Führer, bareheaded and dressed in a khaki-coloured coat of broadcloth with a red armlet and a swastika on it, and the military cross on his breast. He wore black trousers, such as we wear in the evening, and black patent-leather lace-up shoes. His hair is brown, not black, his eyes blue, his expression rather disagreeable, especially in repose, and altogether he looks entirely undistinguished. You would never notice him in a crowd, and would take him for the house painter he once was. After saying some words of welcome, he took me up the steps and introduced me to a number of people, among whom I only distinguished General Keitel, a youngish pleasant-faced, smart-looking soldier. We then entered the house, and passed along a very bare passage through a smaller room to the celebrated chamber, or rather hall, one end of which is entirely occupied by a vast window. The view, towards Salzburg, must be magnificent, but this day there were only the valley and the bottoms of the mountains to be seen.
>
> At the opposite end is a raised dais, on which a large round table was laid for tea. . . . On the walls were a number of pictures by old German and Italian masters. Just behind me was a large Italian nude.
>
> We sat down, I next to Hitler, with the interpreter on his other side. He seemed very shy, and his features did not relax while I endeavoured to find small talk.

---

* Frh. von Dörnberg is the towering uniformed official who appears in many official photographs of those times, and who (in Schmidt's description) "like a Furtwängler, was the expert conductor of the diplomatic audience at such a meeting."

† According to Ward Price (who was in the dining car in which Chamberlain spent most of the trip lunching on Starnberger See trout, roast beef with Yorkshire pudding, and several wines) troop trains were visible only during a short stop at Rosenheim, and Chamberlain did not see them because his back was to the window.

I.   I have often heard of this room, but it's much larger than I expected.

H.   It is you who have the big rooms in England.

I.   You must come and see them sometime.

H.   I should be received with demonstrations of disapproval.

I.   Well, perhaps it would be wise to choose the moment.

At this H. permitted himself the shadow of a smile.

After we had finished tea, H. asked abruptly what procedure I proposed. Would I like to have two or three present at our talk? I replied that, if convenient to him, I would prefer a *tête à tête*. Thereupon he rose, and he and I and the interpreter . . . walked upstairs, and through a long room with more pictures (and more nudes), till we arrived at his own room. This was completely bare of ornament. There wasn't even a clock, only a stove, a small table with 2 bottles of mineral water (which he didn't offer me), 3 chairs, and a sofa. Here we sat and talked for 3 hours.

Except for Henderson, none of the British spoke German, and Hitler spoke no foreign language. Schmidt's inclusion on the *"tête à tête"* was essential, but it is noteworthy that Ribbentrop did not participate, and remarkable that Chamberlain took not one of his colleagues with him, if for no other reason than to check and supplement his own recollection. Schmidt's memoirs partly explain the situation:

> After conventional remarks about the weather, the size of the room, the possibility of Hitler visiting England, and Chamberlain's journey, Chamberlain asked rather abruptly whether Hitler would speak to him alone or whether he wanted the support of his advisers. "Of course Herr Schmidt must be there as interpreter," said Hitler, "but as an interpreter he is neutral and forms part of neither group." I already knew that Chamberlain would express the wish to speak to Hitler alone. With Hitler's knowledge this had been settled between the English and the Germans beforehand, behind Ribbentrop's back. Both sides felt that our Foreign Minister would prove a disturbing element in any endeavour to achieve a friendly settlement between England and Germany. Hitler too had noticed the wounded vanity aroused by the English in his former London Ambassador. He had therefore agreed to the plan to exclude him which had the approval of Henderson and Weizsäcker and the warm support of Göring.
>
> Ribbentrop therefore remained angrily in the background, while I went with Hitler and Chamberlain to the office on the first floor. It was the same simple, almost bare, room in which Hitler and Halifax had got on so badly a year before. This conversation also, on which hung the issue of peace or war, was not conducted in an exactly serene atmosphere, and sometimes became quite stormy. It lasted nearly three hours. . . .

The consequence was that Schmidt's notes were the only ones made on the spot, and the only official record of the talk.* Chamberlain opened by stressing his long-standing aim to improve Anglo-German relations, and Hitler replied

---

* Chamberlain dictated a "minute" (described by him as a "bare record") of the conversation after dinner that evening. He also described it in his September 19 letter to Ida, and Schmidt did likewise in his memoirs (*Hitler's Interpreter*, pp. 92–94). There are few important discrepancies among the several accounts.

that he shared this aim, but "in recent years his faith in the possibility of a rapprochement had suffered a severe blow." Chamberlain then suggested that they explore the general "situation" before approaching the Sudeten question (according to his own recollection, he proposed "leaving, perhaps, the Czechoslovak problem till tomorrow"), adding that "many Englishmen regarded the Führer's speeches solely as words, behind which were concealed carefully laid plans"—a view which the Prime Minister personally disavowed.

This gave Hitler the opening for a long monologue, in which at the outset he rejected the idea of postponing discussion of "the Sudeten German question, which at the moment had left the sphere of theoretical expressions of opinion, since the situation was moving from hour to hour to an open crisis," in which "300 Sudeten Germans had been killed." The situation "demanded instant solution," so that "it would be better if we started at once on it." Chamberlain responded: "All right, go ahead."

Without interruption Hitler then spoke at length of his commitment to the German people to end "the suffering caused them by the Treaty of Versailles." At the same time he had conciliated Germany's neighbors with the Polish treaty, the guarantees to Holland and Belgium, the renunciation of Alsace-Lorraine, and the Anglo-German Naval Agreement. But this last item was based on "the mutual determination never again to make war on the other contracting party," and if "England were to continue to make it clear that in certain circumstances she would intervene against Germany, the precondition for the Naval Agreement would cease to hold, and it would be more honest for Germany to denounce the agreement." This roused Chamberlain to inquire "whether this denunciation would be contemplated by Germany before a conflict broke out," to which Hitler replied affirmatively.

Hitler now came to his main point:

> Germany had . . . put forward a general demand in all clarity: in any circumstances return to the Reich must be made possible for the 10 million Germans who lived in Austria and Czechoslovakia, and whose earnest desire it was to return to Germany. In the case of the 7 million Germans in the Ostmark this demand had been met. The return to the Reich of the 3½ million Germans in Czechoslovakia he would make possible at all costs. He would face any danger and even the risk of war for this end. Here the limit had been reached where the rest of the world could do what it liked; he would not yield a single step.

Chamberlain appears to have absorbed this demand without a blink of doubt or word of protest, and immediately asked whether "the difficulties with Czechoslovakia would be at an end with the return to the Reich of the 3½ million Sudeten Germans"; in England "the question was being asked whether this was all that Germany demanded or whether he did not aim beyond this at the disintegration of the Czechoslovak State." Hitler's reply was far from categorical. He first declared that "he did not want a lot of Czechs, all he wanted was Sudeten Germans." But this protestation was followed by the observation "that apart from the demands of the Sudeten Germans similar demands would, of course, be made by the Poles, Hungarians and Ukrainians living in Czechoslovakia, and that in the long run it would be impossible to ignore these demands." He added that Czechoslovakia was "a spearhead in his side," thus prompting Chamberlain to inquire whether, after annexation of the Sudetenland, "would the remainder of Czechoslovakia be still regarded as a dangerous spearpoint in Germany's flank?" Hitler replied "that this would be the case so long as the Czechoslovak State had alliances with other countries which made it a menace to Germany," adding that "Czechoslovakia had already become a great expense to Germany, for she had made it necessary for Germany to make her Air Force twice as strong as she had originally intended." It is hard to believe that this last sally (which is not recorded in Chamberlain's own notes) was other than tongue-in-cheek, but Chamberlain gave no sign of grasping its absurdity.*

Again yielding rather than trying to stem the torrent of demand, Chamberlain now asked whether, if Soviet-Czech relations "were modified, so that Czechoslovakia were no longer bound to go to the assistance of Russia if Russia were attacked, and on the other hand Czechoslovakia were debarred from giving asylum to Russian forces in her aerodromes or elsewhere; would that remove your difficulty?" The reply, as recorded by Schmidt, was evasive: "Czechoslovakia would, in any case, cease to exist after a time for, apart from the nationalities already referred to, the Slovaks were also trying with all their energy to detach themselves from that country.†

Chamberlain then endeavored to raise some "practical" problems about fixing the bounds of the areas to be ceded:

> The Sudeten Germans did not live in a compact area, but were fairly scattered, and even if one were to hand over to Germany those areas in which 80 percent of the total population was German, there would always remain quite a number of the inhabitants of the remainder . . . who were of German origin. It was therefore not only a question of a new delimitation of frontiers, but, ultimately, also of a transfer of certain parts of the population.

Hitler promptly scotched this attempt to limit the cession to the 80 per cent German areas: ". . . in every place where there was a majority for Germany, the territory in question would have to go to Germany."‡ The minorities left on each side of the new boundaries thus established could then be interchanged. But he added that these discussions "were of a purely theoretical nature, since the march of events was continuing at a rapid pace." Czech atrocities against the Sudeten Germans were forcing him to act without delay.

Chamberlain met this rebuff by proposing "a joint appeal to both parties in Czechoslovakia, so as to provide the opportunity for mutual discussions . . . in a quieter atmosphere." Hitler rejected this idea out of hand: ". . . he could not be expected to give the victims of Czechoslovak persecution reprimands." He

---

* Hitler also made mention of "colonies" and Memel, but not in a demanding way.

† Chamberlain's minute was to the effect that the Hungarian, Polish, and Slovak minorities would secede, "and what was left would be so small that he would not bother his head about it."

‡ Although Chamberlain probably did not realize it at the time, the change from an 80 to a 51 per cent basis would mean that nearly twice as much territory and a third more population would be ceded to Germany.

grew excited, describing the Czechs as "cruel and cowards at heart," and insisting that if Britons were "being enslaved by an inferior people," Chamberlain's "blood would boil just like that of the German in the case of Czechoslovakia." In the face of "three hundred Sudetens killed" things had to be set right at once: "I do not care whether there is a world war or not, I am determined to settle it soon."

This tirade was too much for the long-suffering Prime Minister, who now asked "why the Führer had let him come to Germany when the Führer was apparently determined to proceed in one definite direction and would not consider an armistice." Hitler calmed down, but only to use Chamberlain's question as the springboard for his demands:

> Would Britain agree to the secession of these areas and an alteration in the constitution of Czechoslovakia, or would she not? If Britain would agree to a separation of this kind, and this could be announced to the world as a fundamental decision of principle, then, no doubt, it would be possible to achieve a large degree of pacification in the areas in question. . . . The conversations could continue on these lines, but the Prime Minister must first state whether he could or could not accept this basis. . . .

In other words, yielding to Hitler's demands was the price, not of peace, but of continuing the conversations! Chamberlain, of course, had no authority to make any such commitment. He "expressed his satisfaction that the root of the question had now been reached," and then (according to his own minute of the conversation) continued:

> I said that I was not in a position to give such an assurance in behalf of the British Government who had not authorized me to say anything of the kind, and moreover I could not possibly make such a declaration without consulting the French Government and Lord Runciman. But I could give him my personal opinion, which was that on principle I had nothing to say against the separation of the Sudeten Germans from the rest of Czechoslovakia, provided that the practical difficulties could be overcome.

On this basis, Chamberlain now proposed that the discussion be adjourned while he returned to England for consultation, and then return to Germany to resume the conversation. Hitler at once agreed, insisting that he would be glad to spare Chamberlain a second trip by meeting in England, but "anti-German demonstrations would complicate rather than simplify the situation." However, he would shorten the Prime Minister's next journey by holding the next meeting in "the lower Rhine district, Cologne or Godesberg."

Chamberlain then asked "what would happen in the meanwhile, and whether it was not possible to take measures to prevent a further deterioration of the situation." Hitler, of course, already knew from Keitel and Jodl that Green could in no event be launched before September 28 at the earliest, but he now made great play about the "great military machine which Germany had built up" and which could not be stopped "once this machine was in motion." However, failing serious incidents, "he would not give the order to set the machines in motion during the next few days." Shameless before Chamberlain's apparent ignorance of the true state of military affairs, Hitler urged his guest to "bring Czechoslovakia to stop her mobilization measures," which might precipitate "a second May 21st."

The two leaders then agreed upon a short press communiqué:

The Führer and Chancellor of the Reich held a conversation today with the British Prime Minister, in the course of which a comprehensive and frank exchange of views took place about the present situation. The British Prime Minister returns to England tomorrow in order to consult the British Cabinet. In the course of a few days a further conversation will take place.

It was indicative of the attitude of both principals that the communiqué made no mention of Czechoslovakia, of France, or even of Lord Runciman.

4

While the two leads were in confrontation upstairs, below in the reception room the numerous seconds, tense and no doubt bored, were in desultory conversation. As usual at these encounters, the British were heavily outnumbered. In addition to Keitel and Ribbentrop, a large Foreign Ministry delegation* had come from Berlin, including Weizsaecker, Walter Hewel (Ribbentrop's liaison officer to Hitler), Friedrich Gaus (the legal adviser), and Ambassador von Dirksen, who had been on leave from his London post since late July.

Wilson engaged Ribbentrop in a discussion of the British Civil Service, making rather heavy weather of it, as the Foreign Minister was very sullen. No doubt all were relieved when, at about eight o'clock, Chamberlain and Hitler reappeared. Both were in a good mood; Chamberlain later wrote to Sister Ida that:

On the way downstairs he [Hitler] was much more cordial than on going up. He asked what time I had to leave, with a view to my seeing his scenic beauties in the morning, and when I said I must go early, since lives were being lost, he said "Oh well, when all this is over you must come back, and I will take you to my tea house at the top of the mountain."† . . . I had established a certain confidence, which was my aim, and on my side, in spite of the hardness and ruthlessness I thought I saw in his face, I got the impression that here was a man who could be relied upon when he had given his word.

The British party and Schmidt then were driven down the mountain to Berchtesgaden, where the interpreter went to work dictating his notes of the conference. At the Grand Hotel Chamberlain told the press that the talk had been "very friendly and that he would return to consult his colleagues." Ribbentrop and Weizsaecker remained at the Berghof for another hour or so, to be regaled by the Fuehrer with an account of his success. As Weizsaecker later described the occasion:

* According to Ward Price, there were thirty Foreign Ministry officials attendant on Ribbentrop.
† The reference is to the famed "Eagle's Nest," which was on the summit of the Kehlstein and was on the point of completion.

Hitler gave a lively and joyful account of the conversation. . . . He clapped his hands as after a highly successful entertainment. He felt that he had managed to maneuver the dry civilian into a corner. . . . Hitler then enlarged to us on his more remote and highfalutin plans, such as his intention to see through to the end in his own lifetime the inevitable conflict with our enemies.

Hitler had good reason for satisfaction. Since the Army could not move before the twenty-eighth, he had given away nothing by agreeing to stay his hand for a few days. While Chamberlain had been unable to make a formal commitment, he had expressed his own agreement to a cession of the Sudetenland. "If the Czechs refused, then the way would be free for the Germans to march in." If they yielded, they would be left virtually defenseless, and the Czech State would probably disintegrate. And so, after dinner, Hitler relaxed by watching a movie, *Vier Gesellen* (Four Companions), which he did not like, and to bed at midnight.

But at the hotel things were not going so smoothly. Schmidt was busy dictating his record, frequently interrupted by Sir Nevile Henderson, impatient to get the memorandum in order that Chamberlain could report in detail to his cabinet on the morrow. Suddenly a very angry Ribbentrop appeared and ordered him to deliver his record to Hitler and no one else, and left Schmidt the unpleasant task of so informing the British. Chamberlain, disgruntled and probably fatigued, declared that he would certainly have his own interpreter at the next meeting,* and had to spend the evening dictating his own account of the meeting.

The next morning Chamberlain sent Hitler a note informing him that Lord Runciman had been asked to appeal for restraint on both sides, and urging the Fuehrer to use his influence in the same direction. He then proceeded to Munich by automobile with Ribbentrop (still out of sorts) and Schmidt. Wilson followed in the next car with Dirksen, who was full of praise for the good impression Chamberlain had made on Hitler. At stops along the way Schmidt, Hewel, and Weizsaecker were all singing the same song; the last-named, of course, gave no indication of Hitler's reaction as he had witnessed it the night before. Chamberlain was cheerful, and, during a short stop at the Chiemsee, asked what fish (almost his only recourse for small talk) were caught there. *Renken,* he was told—cold-water fish local to Bavaria.

In Munich, Chamberlain stopped briefly at the Königsplatz to view the new Fuehrerbau, to which he was destined to return two weeks later. He lunched at the airport seated next to General von Epp, who spoke English learned, he explained, in China during the Boxer uprising. Chamberlain's other luncheon neighbor, the President of Bavaria (one Seibert) then apologized for his English, which was poor "because he had never had the opportunity to visit China."

During the meal Wilson took occasion to tell the still sulking Ribbentrop that he had checked with the Runciman mission about the three hundred dead Sude-

---

* The text gives Schmidt's version of this contretemps. According to the British documents, Chamberlain was told only that he could not have the record until Hitler had first seen it. There were subsequent sharp exchanges between Henderson and Weizsaecker, and the British apparently got the Schmidt record on September 21, on the eve of the Godesberg conference.

ten Germans with which Hitler had belabored the Prime Minister, and had been assured that the story was "nonsense" and that there had been *no* casualties whatever. Ribbentrop made no comment, and Wilson told Henderson that, in view of the Foreign Minister's attitude, it would be well to get in touch with Goering "as soon as he could possibly manage to do so."

After lunch the British party enplaned and returned to London.

5

If Hitler felt anxiety or uncertainty about the situation caused by Chamberlain's visit, this was not reflected in his schedule during the next few days. At noon on the sixteenth he conferred with Keitel (who then returned to Berlin) and later with Todt, and at half-past four paid his first visit to the Eagle's Nest, then going by the name *Kehlsteinhaus.* On his return to the Berghof he met with Henlein and Lorenz on Sudeten matters; at eight o'clock he saw Ribbentrop (probably to get report of the latter's drive to Munich with Chamberlain), and then watched a motion picture.

There is little record of the discussions, but much of their substance can be inferred from other developments. During the day the Foreign Ministry instructed the German missions in the "friendly" capitals (Rome, Warsaw, and Budapest) to inform Ciano, Beck, and Kanya confidentially about the Hitler-Chamberlain meeting, and informed all the missions that:

> Autonomy for Sudeten Germans is no longer being considered, but only cession of the region to Germany. Methods of doing this are still to be arranged. Chamberlain has indicated personal approval. He is now consulting British Cabinet and is in communication with Paris. Further meeting between Führer and Chamberlain planned for very near future. Führer does not wish expected leakages about the conference to originate on German side.

Konrad Henlein, before leaving Czechoslovakia, had informed Ashton-Gwatkin that the Karlsbad demands were now obsolete, and that there could now be no settlement except "on the basis of a plebiscite." On September 15, Henlein (now on German soil) issued a "proclamation to the Sudeten Germans, the German people, and the whole world" that "the Czech people's system of oppression had reached a climax" and that "We wish to live as free Germans! We want peace and work again in our homeland! We want to return to the Reich!"

The Henlein-Lorenz conference with Hitler in the evening of the sixteenth probably concerned the military disposition of the many Sudeten Germans who had crossed into the Reich. According to Jodl's diary entries, the original plan had been that the Sudeten refugees who were militarily trained would be taken into the German Army reserves. But on the seventeenth Hitler directed that instead they be formed into a Sudeten *Freikorps,* and an OKW staff officer, Lieutenant Colonel Friedrich Köchling, was assigned as military adviser to Henlein. The *Korps* was to be armed with Austrian weapons, and its mission was to "protect" the Sudeten Germans in Czechoslovakia and restore peaceful conditions.

Giving every appearance of calm and relaxation at the Berghof, on the seven-teenth Hitler conferred with Himmler and Ribbentrop at midday, later with the British Daily Mail correspondent Ward Price (his favorite channel for feeding the British press),* and then took these guests, together with Goebbels, Himmler, Bormann, and some lesser functionaries, up to the Eagle's Nest. On the eighteenth he saw General von Reichenau (probably to tell the general about the meeting with Brauchitsch and Halder at Nuremberg). On the nine-teenth he was again at the Eagle's Nest, and the next day he conferred with Kanya and Imredy of Hungary and Lipski of Poland, and that evening went to Munich en route to the second meeting with Chamberlain, at Godesberg.

Meanwhile the preparations for Green were developing smoothly. In Berlin, orders were given to strengthen the border guards on the Czech frontier, and to begin a secret accumulation of empty railroad cars to be available for military transport by September 28.

There is not the slightest evidence that Chamberlain's visit to the Berghof resulted in any slackening in the pace of preparations for Green. Colonel Walter Warlimont, who returned from a field command to OKW at about this time, was told by Jodl "that the object of the military preparations then in train was not merely the incorporation of the Sudetenland in the Reich but the complete extinction of Czechoslovakia as an independent state." Hewel reported similarly to Erich Kordt.

It appears certain that Hitler would have preferred to proceed with Green and crush the Czechs rather than settle for the Sudetenland. But was he, after meeting with Chamberlain, disposed to risk war with Britain and France in order to gain the greater prize?

Nothing Hitler did or is reported to have said at the time provides a sure an-swer. Even if bent on war, he also wanted surprise, and if this were to be achieved he could neither refuse to receive Chamberlain nor close the door to negotiations, for either course would have both alerted the Czechs to the proba-bility of imminent attack, and increased the likelihood of French and British ac-tion in their support. Perhaps, as Erich Kordt suggests, Hitler was still per-suaded by Ribbentrop's insistence that England was "bluffing," and discounted the danger of a general war. But the true state of his intentions, which probably fluctuated, cannot now be certainly determined.

6

At Heston Airport, Chamberlain's party was met by Halifax and several other ministers, Theodor Kordt, and a general crowd of several hundred. According to Kordt, Chamberlain declared that he had "had a great time," and Wilson and Strang both professed themselves "highly satisfied with their visit." Kordt's dis-

---

* In a short conversation at the Berghof with Price, Hitler declared: "I am convinced of Mr. Chamberlain's sincerity and good will. I can't tell yet whether he can put it through. But a solution has got to be found—so oder so." At the *Kehlsteinhaus* they had a longer talk, in the course of which Hitler stated: "If we have to march in, they [the Czechs] are finished. If they make the necessary concessions to the Sudeten in time, they can carry on their own affairs as they like." Later Hitler denied any desire for German expansion in southeastern Europe. In retrospect, it is plain that the purpose of these statements was to quiet British fears and stimulate them to put pressure on the Czechs.

patch must have made pleasant reading in Berlin. At the airport microphone, Chamberlain described his talk with Hitler as "frank" and "friendly," and declared himself "satisfied now that each of us fully understands what is in the mind of the other." He continued:

> You won't, of course, expect me to discuss now what may be the results of that talk. What I have got to do now is to discuss these with my colleagues. . . .
> But I shall be discussing them tonight with my colleagues and with others, especially Lord Runciman. And later on, perhaps in a few days, I am going to have another talk with Herr Hitler.
> Only this time he has told me that it is his intention to come half way to meet me—he wishes to spare an old man another long journey.

At this revelation of the Fuehrer's magnanimity the crowd, according to Kordt, "broke out into spontaneous applause."

The Prime Minister was driven directly to Downing Street, where he arrived shortly after six o'clock and went straightaway into conference with the "inner Cabinet" (Halifax, Simon, and Hoare) plus Vansittart, Cadogan, Wilson, and (a later arrival) Runciman. The day before, while their chief was closeted with Hitler, the three ministers, with Cadogan and Sir Edward Bridges (Hankey's successor as Cabinet Secretary) had considered ways and means of fixing the new Czech-German boundaries. Simon still clung to his idea of Sudeten "autonomy for a period of years, to be followed by a plebiscite." If Hitler insisted on an immediate plebiscite, British and other neutral troops "under the supreme control of British officers" would be needed to keep order. Or instead of a plebiscite, the new borders might be fixed by ethnographic statistics; or districts "indubitably German" might be ceded at once, with plebiscites confined to doubtful areas. Perhaps certain areas strategically valuable to the Czechs could be returned in exchange for concessions elsewhere.*

Chamberlain's report of his talk with Hitler speedily rendered most of these proposals academic: Simon's plan, however desirable, "no longer stood a chance." The Prime Minister "was satisfied that it was impossible to go to war to prevent self-determination, more especially now that Herr Henlein said that the Sudeten Germans wanted to go back to the Reich." Now, he thought, it was simply a matter of whether "that return be carried out in an orderly or a disorderly manner." France would not oppose a plebiscite, so could not Lord Runciman simply announce it as the only possible course?

At this point the noble lord himself arrived, fresh from an interview with Beneš that morning. It had been a pretty sharp exchange; Beneš had expressed fear that his country had been "sacrificed" at Berchtesgaden, and Runciman had

---

* The conferees also discussed, and discarded as politically "extremely difficult," a plan of Dr. Jaroslav Preiss, an influential Czech banker, to resolve the crisis by granting the Karlsbad demands, suppressing local communism, and denouncing the Czech-Soviet treaty. Preiss had pointed out to the German minister, Eisenlohr, that cession of the Sudetenland would leave "a united Czechoslovak State attached by race with Russia and by sentiment with Social Democracy," which would be a "continuing anxiety for Germany." Eisenlohr and Hodža had apparently found the Preiss proposal inviting, and after Preiss had discussed it with Ashton-Gwatkin, it was transmitted to London for urgent consideration.

retorted that his host "had done more than anybody else to sacrifice his country." The Czech President, Runciman told his colleagues, was a prevaricator: "People did not regard him as honest. He was an intensely clever man." As for the present situation in Czechoslovakia, however, it was quiet and under control. There had been some trouble in Eger and Asch, where Runciman "thought these people rather liked to row," and arms were being smuggled in from Germany. As a solution, Runciman favored the Karlsbad demands, denunciation of the Czech-Soviet treaty, and a commercial agreement with Germany.*

Halifax asked him whether Czechs and Germans could ever live together happily. "No," Runciman answered, and launched into a diatribe: "Czechoslovakia provided horrid stories of irregularity, graft and corruption. The behavior of the Government to minorities had been outrageous. . . . not merely with the Germans, but also with the Hungarians. Altogether it was an ugly story." Chamberlain then inquired whether the Hungarians and Poles would follow the lead of the Sudetens and, when Runciman replied affirmatively, Halifax asked whether, in that case, Czechoslovakia could still exist. Runciman answered that "once you started to examine the makeup of particular provinces you found that they were all terribly mixed . . . the country would be reduced to a very small area." Could the Czech Army withstand a German attack? The Czech generals, said Runciman, thought they could hold out for six to eight weeks.

All in all, it was a confused report. In one breath Runciman had declared that Czechs and Germans could never live together, and that the Czech State would disintegrate once the Sudetens seceded, and in another he had advocated a plan based on the Karlsbad demands which would have left the State intact. Beneš was described as a mendacious menace, but the country was under firm control and could give a good military account of itself.

None of this was of much help to Chamberlain, who had returned from the Berghof convinced that the Sudetenland could be ceded without mortally wounding Czechoslovakia. The conferees broke up at about nine o'clock, having decided only to say nothing to either Paris or the press. The Prime Minister, manifesting remarkable tirelessness, went to Buckingham Palace to report to the King† whom he assured that only the intervention of his visit had prevented an immediate attack on Czechoslovakia. There is no reason to doubt Chamberlain's sincerity in making this claim, but of course, as we now know from the German records, it was quite unfounded.

The Cabinet met the following morning with Lord Runciman, whose report opened the proceedings. It generally corresponded to what he had said the previous evening, and was equally confusing in its conclusions: Czechoslovakia could not continue to exist as at present, and the Czechs were "responsible for most of the trouble," but the two sides had been close to agreement, which had

---

* This was essentially the Preiss plan, described in the preceding footnote.

† While Chamberlain was in Germany, the King (who had served in the Navy during the First World War) had drafted a personal letter to Hitler, as "one ex-Serviceman to another," urging him to spare the youth of Britain and Germany from the horrors of a second world war. The King put the idea to Halifax, who courteously doubted its efficacy, and the draft was laid aside.

failed because of the "close connection between the Sudeten Germans and Berlin," of which Runciman confessed he had been unaware.

The Prime Minister then told his own story, much as he had told it the night before to the inner circle. Duff Cooper, on the whole a hostile auditor, recorded his impression:

> Looking back upon what he said, the curious thing seems to me now to have been that he recounted his experiences with some satisfaction. Although he said that at first sight Hitler struck him as "the commonest little dog" he had ever seen, without one sign of distinction, nevertheless he was obviously pleased at the reports he had subsequently received of the good impression that he himself had made. He told us with obvious satisfaction how Hitler had said to someone that he had felt that he, Chamberlain, was "a man."
> But the bare facts of the interview were frightful. None of the elaborate schemes which had been carefully worked out, and which the Prime Minister had intended to put forward, had ever been mentioned. He had felt that the atmosphere did not allow of them. . . . From beginning to end Hitler had not shown the slightest sign of yielding on a single point. The Prime Minister seemed to expect us all to accept that principle [self-determination] without further discussion because the time was getting on.

Inskip, a respectful source, left a memoir almost as negative:

> The P.M. was astonishingly fresh and alert . . . He described the welcome of the crowds, the Guards at the Brown House, the reception by Hitler,—"the commonest little dog he had ever seen"—in a khaki-coloured tunic of good cloth, a red band with a black swastika; black evening trousers and high laced boots beneath the trousers. His house barely furnished, a number of modern German and Italian pictures. . . . There were very many pictures of women with nothing on. . . . Hitler became excitable as he talked, but no signs of insanity were shown. While he talked his common appearance was forgotten, and the P.M. was impressed with his power. The P.M. had come to the conclusion that though Hitler was determined, his objectives were strictly limited. . . .
> The P.M. thought the atmosphere was too heated and electric to allow him to bring forward any of the plans, such as J.S.'s [Simon's] proposals, discussed with the Cabinet. P.M. said he must go home and consult his colleagues. . . .
> The impression made by the P.M.'s story was a little painful. H. had made him listen to a boast that the German military machine was a terrible instrument, ready to move now, and once put into motion could not be stopped. The P.M. said more than once to us he was just in time. It was plain that H. had made all the running: he had in fact blackmailed the P.M.

Chamberlain concluded his account by stressing the "desperate urgency" of the situation: "If he had not gone he thought that hostilities would have started by now." There was still great need for a speedy resolution, for "a man as excitable as Hitler might easily be carried away by some unfounded report." But Hitler had been "most favourably impressed," and this "was of the utmost importance, since the future conduct of these negotiations depended mainly upon personal contacts." As for the details of the settlement, he thought that "Herr Hitler would not prove too difficult." He asked the Cabinet for agreement in principle, and suggested that Parliament not be summoned until "that course would be helpful."

But the Cabinet's agreement was not so readily forthcoming. At Halifax's instance it had already been decided to call the French to London for consultation, and Lord Hailsham thought that should be done before any course of action was settled. Duff Cooper, Stanley, Elliott, and Winterton expressed varying degrees of dissatisfaction and, since the sitting had already lasted nearly three hours, the meeting was adjourned to midafternoon.

When it reconvened, Simon at once called for an endorsement of Chamberlain's statements to Hitler. Lord Maugham undertook to support him by declaring that no vital British interest was involved. This fired up Duff Cooper, who "argued that the main interest of this country had always been to prevent any one power from obtaining undue predominance in Europe; but we were now faced with probably the most formidable power that had ever dominated Europe, and resistance to that power was quite obviously a British interest." He did not believe that the Sudetenland was Hitler's last goal, and saw "no chance of peace in Europe so long as there is a Nazi regime in Germany." Despite all this, and the vehemence of his rhetoric, Duff Cooper did not oppose a plebiscite, if the Prime Minister would make clear to Hitler that it was only an agreement in principle, and subject to the stipulation of "fair conditions with international control."

Duff Cooper's presentation was so ambivalent that Inskip could discount his position as not really different from Chamberlain's. As for the First Lord's talk of one-power dominance of Europe, that meant that Britain would not be fighting for Czechoslovakia but "to check Herr Hitler," and the result, said Inskip, could be changes in the state of Europe "which might be satisfactory to no one except Moscow and the Bolshevists." Lord Zetland pointed out that the lesson of self-determination in the Sudetenland would not be lost on India, but then echoed the fear that war would profit "those who controlled the destinies of Russia." General agreement with the Prime Minister's policy was also voiced by MacDonald, who wanted "reasonable" conditions, and Hoare, who thought Britain should get a *quid pro quo* from Hitler.

The strongest negative expressions then came from the Lord Privy Seal, Earl "Buck" De La Warr, who had returned from Geneva to attend the meeting.* He raised no objection to the principle of self-determination, but denounced an immediate plebiscite forced by German threats both as "unfair to the Czechs and dishonourable to ourselves," and declared that a less than honourable peace would soon beget war. He urged that no concession be made until Germany had demobilized, and otherwise he was "prepared to face war now in order to free the world from the emotional threat of ultimata."

Lord Hailsham, old and ailing, lumbered to the Prime Minister's defense, declaring that "like it or not" Germany dominated the continent, and "we have no alternative but to submit to humiliation." Winterton replied that such an argu-

---

* Because Halifax thought it unwise to leave London at that time, De La Warr headed the British delegation to the League, with "Rab" Butler as the senior representative of the Foreign Office.

ment would logically lead to surrendering the Isle of Wight, but declined to reverse the logic and support war as the solution.

Halifax, in an obvious and conspicuously unsuccessful effort to raise the level of the discussion, now said:

> If the alternative to acceptance of the Prime Minister's proposal was war, then, he asked himself, what was the ultimate justification for war? In his view, he would fight for the great moralities which knew no geographical boundaries. But there was no greater urge to fight for Czechoslovakia than to fight Japan because of the bombing of civilians in Canton. If the matter was looked at from the point of self interest, he would distinguish between the attack on Czechoslovakia and an attack, say, on the Isle of Wight.

Of course, it was equally possible to distinguish "from the point of self interest" between Czechoslovakia and Canton. But the Foreign Secretary opined that war over Czechoslovakia would be "preventive," and "the theory of a preventive war meant that we should have a bad war every 20 years, in order to prevent a war from occurring five years later." Somehow, he drew from all this the conclusion that "we should accept the principle of the transfer of these peoples." Having thus cast his vote for the dismemberment of Czechoslovakia, he warned his colleagues that "it was very important that we should avoid allowing the French to say that they had come to London and found that we had decided to give the show away."

One by one the other ministers—Hore-Belisha, Kingsley Wood, "Shakes" Morrison, Colville, Brown, and Stanhope—fell into line. The only remaining quasi-dissident was Oliver Stanley, who echoed Duff Cooper's prediction that the Government was staving off an evil day for a worse one in the future, but was no more willing than the First Lord to reject "self-determination" in favor of war.

The Prime Minister, "most grateful" for his colleagues' support, summed up. Mockingly he expressed surprise that the First Lord had not ended his speech by saying that Britain should fight; that had been left to the Lord Privy Seal to voice.* As for De La Warr's proposal that Germany be required to demobilize before discussing terms "the only result would be that Herr Hitler would order his troops to march straight into Czechoslovakia." He assured his colleagues that suitable conditions for applying the principle of self-determination would have to be obtained through negotiation, but "rather deprecated any attempt to tie his hands too closely by fixing precise limits beyond which he should not go, when he resumed the negotiations." It was quite possible, he warned, that Britain would be obliged to guarantee the remainder of Czechoslovakia, much as he and Halifax disliked any such "commitment in a distant country.".

In deference to Halifax's reminder that the French should not be confronted with a *fait accompli,* the Cabinet took no formal action. But it was plain enough that the Prime Minister had carried the Cabinet a long way down the road on which he had set his feet.

To his sister, Chamberlain wrote: "We had two Cabinets lasting five hours

---

* A sharp thrust, pregnant with the implication that Duff Cooper, the only senior minister among the dissidents, had left it to a junior (De La Warr) to stick his neck out.

and finally overcame all critics, some of whom had been concerting opposition beforehand." The Cabinet did not adjourn until close to six o'clock, but his day was not yet over, for he now (with Halifax and Wilson) met with the Labour opposition, represented by Walter Citrine, Herbert Morrison, and Hugh Dalton. The National Labour Council had just voted full support for Czechoslovakia, and Citrine opened the meeting by declaring that many Labourites "thought that British prestige had been gravely lowered by Chamberlain going to see Hitler." Chamberlain of course contradicted this, and then gave an account of the Berchtesgaden meeting, rather exaggerating his own vigor of utterance, and describing Hitler variously as a "most extraordinary creature," a "man who would be rather better than his word," and—because of Hitler's concern about Chamberlain's age—as "having another side, besides the gangster, which it is worth trying to cultivate." As justification for conceding the principle of self-determination, Chamberlain cited "the weakness of France" and especially the "appalling" state of the French Air Force.

The Labour delegates were not impressed, and in the ensuing colloquy there was sharp disagreement on the likelihood of Soviet support and on other elements of the situation. Dalton directly challenged the Government's strategy in much the same vein that Duff Cooper and De La Warr had followed. All in all the ministers had a rough passage, but surely Chamberlain had not expected Labour support for his initiative, and his confidence remained unshaken.

After these unwelcome visitors had departed, the indefatigable Prime Minister received Ambassador Kennedy and told his story all over again. Kennedy's reports to Washington often appear to reflect more of his own outlook than those of his sources, and it is hard to tell whether or not his rendition of Chamberlain's now four-times-told tale is true to its general tenor. Whatever the reason, Kennedy's record, much more than the other accounts, stresses Chamberlain's distaste for Hitler's personality: "Chamberlain came away with an intense dislike . . . he is cruel, overbearing, has a hard look and . . . would be completely ruthless in any of his aims and methods." As for the immediate future, Chamberlain had little confidence in the French, who "do not want to fight and will probably blame the whole thing on the British." The Czechs would "talk big but probably accede," while asking for a "guarantee of protection for the maintenance of the balance of the state." If an agreement with Hitler based on "the principle of self determination" could be reached, Chamberlain wanted it to comprise "orderly elections and protection of peace and order while the plans are being worked out." If other countries would join in the peace-keeping force, he might later ask whether the United States would participate.*

So ended the three days of the "Berchtesgaden phase" of the Munich cycle. Hitler had hoodwinked his visitor into believing that Germany was on the brink of an attack, when in fact the Wehrmacht could not move for another two weeks. With this and other pressures, he had caused Chamberlain to abandon, without ever proposing, the plans which he had had in mind, and Chamberlain

---

* Kennedy also reported Chamberlain's opinion that he had just put the Labour leaders "in a box." The ambassador had himself seen Citrine, Morrison, and Dalton, who had "made it very clear that they were going along with Chamberlain."

had immediately given his personal acquiescence to a solution by "self-deter-mination" which, whether by plebiscite or outright cession, would tear away Czechoslovakia's fixed defenses, both natural and artificial. Twenty-four hours back in London had sufficed to convince the Prime Minister that his program would be approved by the Cabinet and that, given the general state of public feeling, he had little to fear from political opposition.

But Neville Chamberlain was still a long way from the end of his chosen road to peace. All he had gotten from Hitler was a conditional agreement to postpone a military solution for a few days, so that a plan based on self-determination could be formulated. Already the difficulties in the way of this were mounting, for his trip to the Berghof had triggered demands from Poland and Hungary that their territorial claims be settled at the same time.

Daladier and Bonnet were due in London on the morrow. A program would now have to be developed which the French would actively support, and then join in forcing Prague to swallow the bitter pill. Thereafter the plan would have to be presented to Hitler at Godesberg, and the details of its execution settled. And all this had to be accomplished in a few days lest Hitler, sitting like Jove on his mountaintop, should lose patience and hurl his thunderbolt.

CHAPTER 27

The Lone Eagle, the Voice of America, and the Voice of Empire

1

Before following the further course of events between Berchtesgaden and Munich, it will be well to take account of the major non-European influences which affected London and Paris during these crucial weeks. It is impossible to attribute precise weight to these factors, and it may be that the British and French governments would not have behaved very differently even in their absence. But the pressures from abroad were substantial, were remarked by the protagonists, and have their place in any balanced account of those times.

For both Britain and France, of course, the American presence loomed large. No one feared that the United States would join the Axis powers, but what, if anything, might Washington do to aid the western Allies? Again, both Britain and France were imperial powers. Both countries, and Britain in particular, relied heavily on their overseas dominions and colonies as major reservoirs of military and economic power. What could be expected from them in 1938, in the event of war?

Such questions would occur to any well-informed person spinning a global map. What is more remarkable is that there was a third force, important enough to be mentioned in the same breath with America and the British and French empires, which now came into play in the person of a private individual—Charles Augustus Lindbergh, world-renowned hero of the first nonstop airplane flight from New York to Paris.

Prior to the epochal solo flight in May 1927 which brought him the sobriquet "Lone Eagle," Lindbergh had been a barnstorming stunt aviator and parachutist, a cadet at the Army Flying School and thereafter a junior officer in the Army Service Reserve, and a contract air mail pilot. His cultural heritage, however, was richer than his career might suggest. His father took a law degree at the University of Michigan and became a significant figure in Minnesota politics; he served five terms in Congress and in 1918 was the Nonpartisan League's gubernatorial candidate. His mother held bachelor's and master's degrees from Michigan and Columbia respectively and was a high school science teacher. Both were exceptionally strong-minded and independent, intensely private, and in the father's case principled to a degree that many found stiff-necked.

Their son showed no interest in his parents' academic, legal or political pursuits, but from an early age was absorbed in high speed transportation and the cultivation of his own physical endurance and induration. His early exploits with motorcycles and airplanes were frequent and extremely hazardous, but a close observer would have noted that they were not truly reckless, but motivated by a desire to improve his skills or opportunities, and that his approach to new problems was systematic and highly intelligent.* And no doubt it was these qualities and capacities that enabled him to survive the elements, alone in his tiny single-engined *Spirit of St. Louis,* and arrive safely at Le Bourget. Here, aided by his boyish good looks (he was twenty-five), engaging grin, and directness of manner, he was at once transmuted from an obscure aerial adventurer into an object of worldwide adulation—"this boy of divine genius and simple courage," as Ambassador Myron T. Herrick described him in a cable to President Coolidge.

But as events soon proved, courageous and a genius Charles Lindbergh might be, but he was certainly not "simple." He accepted praise with poise but hated crowds and grew increasingly impatient with the press. When asked to speak, he gave his opinions on what was needed for the development of American aviation. His life style changed abruptly as he consorted with the rich, published a best-selling account of his flight (*We*), and took lucrative consultancies to the big airplane companies. He wooed and won Anne Morrow, daughter of Dwight Morrow, Ambassador to Mexico and a former partner in J. P. Morgan & Company. Promoted to colonel in the Air Corps Reserve, he spent little time on military matters; he continued to fly far and wide, but usually to survey new routes and test new aircraft models for the commercial companies.

In the course of all this Lindbergh eschewed his father's political progressivism and absorbed the views of the bankers and corporate officials who had taken him into their offices and estates.† The barnstorming, practical-joking kid of the early twenties faded away, but he did not go soft; his skills and physical prowess were unimpaired, and he and his wife, who had learned to pilot, navigate, and handle the radio, undertook arduous and hazardous missions—"the Lone Eagle and his mate," as they were dubbed by the journalists he scorned.

As Lindbergh's ease and confidence grew, he ceased to think of himself as a mere aeronautical expert. In 1930 he met the famous French medical scientist Alexis Carrel, an eccentric and flamboyant genius, whose philosophy was dedicated to the proposition that all men are not created equal, and that much might be gained by the selective breeding of an elite, and the "humane disposition" of criminal and insane types. They formed a close friendship, and Lindbergh went to work in Carrel's laboratories on the development of a "mechanical heart."

---

* Lindbergh's longtime personal lawyer, the late Walter Fletcher, of Davis, Polk & Wardwell, described his client to me as "the most intelligent man he had ever met." From one who had surely met many top-notch lawyers, academics, and businessmen this was extraordinary and perhaps inordinate praise.

† As was subsequently revealed in the hearings of the Senate Banking and Currency Committee conducted by Ferdinand Pecora, J. P. Morgan & Company maintained a "preferred list" of individuals to whom they sold stock well below the market price. Lindbergh was among those so favored, together with such notables as Bernard Baruch, General John J. Pershing, Supreme Court Justice Owen J. Roberts, and former President Calvin Coolidge.

Even earlier Lindbergh had begun to raise his voice on political issues. In October 1928 he publicly endorsed the presidential candidacy of Herbert Hoover. Five years later, after Senator Hugo Black had exposed fraud and collusion in the award of air mail contracts to the big airlines (including TWA, with which Lindbergh was closely associated), President Franklin Roosevelt ordered the cancellation of all the contracts and directed the Army Air Corps to carry the mail. Promptly Lindbergh dispatched and publicized a telegram to the President declaring that his action deeply affected "the industry to which I have devoted the last twelve years of my life," condemned "the largest portion of our commercial aviation without just trial," and would "unnecessarily and greatly damage all American aviation." This was not the counsel of a technical expert, but the judgment of a moral and legal philosopher.*

Such was the man whose firstborn infant son was kidnaped on March 1, 1932, from the Lindbergh home near Hopewell, New Jersey. Ransom was paid, but six weeks later the baby was found dead in woods barely a mile from the home. Three years passed before Bruno Richard Hauptmann was convicted of the kidnap-murder in a trial at Flemington, New Jersey, which press and public turned into a macabre circus.

Meanwhile Anne Lindbergh had given birth to another son, Jon, who now had to be kept at home under armed guard because of threats, press intrusions, and hate mail. Lindbergh wrote to a friend that Americans were a "primitive people" that lacked "discipline" and had low "moral standards. . . . It shows in the newspapers, the morbid curiosity over crimes and murder trials." Secretly he booked passage for himself and family to England. They docked at Liverpool on the last day of 1935. A few weeks later they rented the Harold Nicolsons' "cottage" in Kent, and while they were getting settled the Wehrmacht marched into the Rhineland.

In England the Lindberghs found the privacy they sought. But they continued to move in exalted circles, and in May they dined with the King and Mrs. Simpson, the Baldwins, the Duff Coopers, the Mountbattens, and other denizens of the top drawer. And then, early in June, Lindbergh received a letter from the American military attaché in Berlin which brought him into the mainstream of this account of Munich.

2

During the years between the great wars, the United States Army in general, and its intelligence service (never a favorite with career officers) in particular, were lamentably underfunded and undermanned. The Air Corps was part of the Army, and the military attachés were responsible for intelligence on air matters. But in Berlin, despite the unveiling of the Luftwaffe and its obviously rapid growth, the attaché, Major Truman Smith (an infantryman with no air experience) had as his sole assistant for air matters Captain Theodore Koenig, an able pilot, but lacking both technical training and intelligence experience. Early in

* Subsequently Lindbergh testified before a Senate committee in favor of a bill to return the air mail to private operators. The Army Air Corps had suffered numerous crashes and fatalities in its ill-prepared effort to carry the mail, and Roosevelt soon returned the task to the airlines with, however, greatly reduced subsidies.

1936, Smith asked that Koenig be replaced by a technically qualified officer, but it took over a year to accomplish this.

In May of 1936, Mrs. Truman Smith called her husband's attention to a news report of Lindbergh's visit to a French aircraft factory.* It soon occurred to the major that a Lindbergh visit to Germany might be welcome to the Luftwaffe hierarchy and open up contacts and areas of information presently beyond Koenig's reach. He cleared the project with his embassy and with Colonel Friedrich-Karl Hanesse, chief of the military attaché section of the Air Ministry. On May 25 he wrote to Lindbergh extending "in the name of General Göring and the German Air Ministry an invitation to visit Germany and inspect the new German civil and military air establishments," and adding: "From a purely American point of view . . . your visit here would be of high patriotic benefit." Lindbergh accepted with alacrity, observing that he wished to avoid "the sensational and stupid publicity which we have so frequently encountered in the past," and that "I thoroughly dislike formal functions and have not attended one for several years"—thus relegating the recent banquet with the King and Mrs. Simpson to "informal" status. On July 22, 1936, he and his wife flew to Berlin, where they were received by German and American dignitaries and hosted by the Truman Smiths.

The Lindberghs remained in Germany for ten days, and if their distaste for "formal functions" was unfeigned, they must have had a very thin time, as there were one or more such nearly every day, accompanied by much publicity. There were lunches and dinners at the Air Club, teas at the American Embassy and at the Caecilienhof with the former Crown Prince, a reception given by the Lord Mayor of Berlin, an enormous luncheon given by Goering at the Air Ministry, and on August 1 the opening of the Games in the Olympic Stadium.† The social occasions were not without professional value, however, as they gave Lindbergh opportunity to talk with Goering, Milch (who at once told the American that Germany would build an air force "second to none"), Udet, Bodenschatz, and other high-ranking Luftwaffe officials, but none of these discussions produced any important intelligence.

The visits to Luftwaffe stations and aircraft factories were somewhat more useful. Lindbergh visited, in succession, the Richthofen Squadron fighter base at Döberitz (near Berlin), the Luftwaffe research institute at Adlershof (also near Berlin), the Heinkel plants at Warnemünde and Rostock, and the Junkers factory at Dessau. At Döberitz, Lindbergh saw only obsolete biplanes, and his hopes of seeing the new Messerschmitt fighters (of which only a few prototypes were then in existence) were disappointed, though the squadron commander,

---

* While living in England, the Lindberghs frequently went to France, primarily to visit the Alexis Carrels. Lindbergh's contemporaneous correspondence reflects liking for the French, but dismay verging on contempt for their inefficiency and lack of leadership.

† The Lindberghs saw Hitler in the stadium but did not meet him then or on any of their later visits to Germany. The Fuehrer was at the Berghof or in Bayreuth throughout the latter part of July. The emissaries from Franco arrived in Berlin just two days after the Lindberghs, and it was during their visit that Hitler and Goering decided to aid the Spanish insurgents, and that the first group of Junkers 52s went to Morocco to ferry troops to the Spanish mainland. German security was good enough so that neither the Lindberghs nor the American Embassy got any hint of these events.

Colonel von Massow, gave him the operational specifications. At the Heinkel factories Lindbergh and Smith saw the new He 111 bomber (Heinkel's most successful type), as well as fighter and dive-bomber prototypes that never saw service.* In Dessau they were given a preview of the Ju 87 dive bomber—the dreaded Stuka of the early war years.

The lean, spartan, highly principled, and terribly earnest American Hero indeed cut a curious figure in company with the Nazified Luftwaffe hierarchy, especially with such *bons vivants* as Goering and Udet. Yet he got along with most of them very well, and plainly he admired their achievements. How seriously his German hosts took him as a person, rather than an exhibit, is open to some question; certainly he did not escape the keen ear and acid pen of the ubiquitous Bella Fromm,† who recorded in her diary:

> On Friday Mrs. Dodd gave a cocktail party in honor of the American aviator, Colonel Charles. A. Lindbergh. The Lindberghs are here as guests of the government. . . .
>
> Lindbergh seems impressed. He appeared pleased when . . . Milch, the unspeakable rat who disgraced his mother's name by inventing the story that he is the son of his Aryan mother by an Aryan lover instead of his Jewish father, patted him on the shoulder. And when a genuine prince, Louis Ferdinand, linked arms with him, his face beamed with happiness. I heard him say to Captain [*sic*] Udet: "German aviation ranks higher than that in any other country. It is invincible." . . .
>
> Axel von Blomberg, son of the Minister . . . and Colonel von Hanesse . . . told me that they considered Lindbergh a very important personage and that the government here was taking great pains to impress him.
>
> "He's going to be the best promotion campaign we could possibly invest in," said Blomberg.
>
> It was an early hour of the day but Loerzer, as usual was already slightly drunk.
>
> "Wonder what the hell is the matter with that American?" he remarked. "He'll scare the wits out of the Yankees with his talk about the invincible *Luftwaffe*. That's exactly what the boys here want him to do. He's been saying that the Russian air force is not worth worrying about, and that the English have very few machines, and those few mediocre. Yet they were pretty nice to him in England, I hear." . . .
>
> Frau von Widkum had been at the gala dinner Duke Adolf Friedrich von Mecklenburg gave in honor of the Lindberghs.
>
> "He seems rather naive, this North American Colonel," she said with a trace of asperity in her tone . . .
>
> Wolfgang von Gronau, president of the Aeroclub, told me: "That was a

---

* These included the He 112 fighter and the He 118 dive bomber, unsuccessful competitors of the Me 109 and Ju 87 respectively. While Lindbergh was at Rostock, Udet was slightly injured in parachuting from a plane which disintegrated while he was testing it. Truman Smith's report describes the plane as an He 112, but, according to Ernst Heinkel's memoirs, it was an He 118 which Udet was power-diving.

† Diplomatic columnist for the *Vossische Zeitung*. Strongly anti-Nazi and Jewish, Mrs. Fromm had highly placed friends who protected her and helped her to leave Germany in 1938. Extracts from her diary were published in 1942 under the title *Blood and Banquets*. Her slurs on Milch's parentage are disputed by Milch's biographer, David Irving, in his *Rise and Fall of the Luftwaffe*, pp. 327–29.

surprise speech of Lindbergh's at the club's dinner in his honor. First he mentioned the grave and fearful danger of modern air warfare and then he praised the powerful German *Luftwaffe*. . . ."*

In fact, Lindbergh had not been greatly impressed by the quality of most of the German aircraft types he saw. The He 111 he thought comparable to American and British bombers of the same category, and the He 112 inferior to the Spitfire (which the British must have shown him soon after its birth, as the prototype first flew on May 5, 1936). But the airfields, the factories, and the energy which suffused the whole air establishment mightily impressed him, as speedily became manifest on his return to England. Undoubtedly his wife reflected his views when she wrote, a few days after they left Berlin: ". . . There is no question of the power, unity, and purposefulness of Germany. It is terrific. I have never in my life been conscious of such a *directed* force. It is thrilling when seen manifested in the energy, pride, and morale of the people—especially the young people."

Lindbergh himself wrote to American friends in the same vein; he found Germany "in many ways the most interesting nation in the world today" and (remarkably) a "stabilizing factor" in Europe. Early in September the Lindberghs visited the Harold Nicolsons, and Charles projected his impressions into opinions which his host recorded:

Lindbergh has just returned from Berlin where he had seen much of German aviation. He has obviously been much impressed by Nazi Germany. He admires their energy, virility, spirit, organization, architecture, planning and physique. He considers that they possess the most powerful air-force in the world,† with which they could do terrible damage to any other country, and could destroy our food supplies by sinking even convoyed ships. He admits that they are a great menace but he denies that they are a menace to us. He contends that the future will see a complete separation between fascism and communism, and he believes that if Great Britain supports the decadent French and the red Russians against Germany, there will be an end to European civilization. He does not see any real possibility of our remaining in the centre between right and left.

In December, Nicolson took Lindbergh to the House of Commons for lunch with Ramsay MacDonald and, more importantly, Sir Thomas Inskip. The latter took notes on Lindbergh's description of the Luftwaffe, but, according to Nicolson's record, his guest soon launched into higher strategy: "Lindbergh tells us that there is no known defence against air attack. For the first time in warfare 'all fortification is useless' "—so much for the Maginot Line and West Wall-to-

---

* Mrs. Dodd was the wife of the American Ambassador. Axel von Blomberg, a Luftwaffe junior officer, was the son of Field Marshal Werner von Blomberg, Minister of War and Commander-in-Chief of the Wehrmacht. Bruno Loerzer was Goering's closest friend from his First World War days and, like Udet, had been taken from civilian aviation into the Luftwaffe with high rank. Lindbergh gave a prepared speech at the Air Club lunch on July 23 in which he warned against the destructive power of modern aircraft.

† This estimate does not quite square with contemporaneous letters in which Lindbergh wrote that the United States had "nothing like the margin of leadership today which we have held in the past," and that it would not "take very much more political bungling to remove the margin of leadership which we still hold in America."

be alike. "There only remain deterrents," Lindbergh continued: "We must exploit our deterrents in terms of night-bombers at 30,000 feet guided only by the stars. [!] He and Inskip get off into technicalities, and I observe that Inskip . . . regards him (as he is) as a person whom he wants to talk to again. . . ."

Lindbergh had thus been enabled to air his views in high political circles, but he saw no sign that his warnings had been taken to heart, and his correspondence early in 1937 reflects growing disenchantment with the English, who, in comparison to the Germans, seemed complacent and inefficient. Invitations to the Astor estate at Cliveden brought him into contact with people who shared many of his views.

Meanwhile in Berlin, Truman Smith had a succession of visits from prominent American aviation figures, including manufacturer-designers like Glenn Martin, Lawrence Bell, and Igor Sikorsky. In August 1937, Major Arthur Vanaman replaced Koenig. But Smith was awaiting a second opportunity for a Lindbergh visit, and in September of 1937 it came in the form of an invitation from Colonel Hanesse to attend the Lilienthal Congress to be held in Munich in mid-October. Once again Lindbergh accepted willingly, and he and his wife landed at Munich-Prien airfield on October 11, 1937,* for a two-week stay in Germany.

From a military standpoint, this second visit to Germany was the most important of the five which Lindbergh made before the Second World War. After the Congress finished, the Lindberghs went to Berlin, where they again were houseguests of the Truman Smiths. On October 16, Udet took Lindbergh to the Luftwaffe testing base at Rechlin in Pomerania,† where seven aircraft were drawn up on the field for his inspection: the HE 111 and Do 17 bombers, Ju 87 and Hs-123 dive bombers, Me-109 fighter, Fiesler-Storch liaison plane, and a Focke-Wulf training plane. With the exception of the later-developed Ju 88 bomber and the Me 110 and Fw 190 fighters, Lindbergh thus saw all the major types of propeller-driven aircraft which the Luftwaffe used in the Second World War. He was allowed to sit in the cockpits, and to fly the Storch, which he found superior to comparable American planes. The Do-17 and especially the Me-109 made a deep impression on him.

On the eighteenth and nineteenth Lindbergh and Vanaman were taken to the Focke-Wulf plant to inspect helicopters, and then to the Henschel and Daimler-Benz aircraft factories. Lindbergh then spent several days with Colonel Smith preparing a "General Estimate as of November 1, 1937" which Major Smith transmitted to Washington over his own signature, but which was mostly Lindbergh's work. Smith later wrote that it was deliberately written in a dramatic

---

* While in the Munich area, the Lindberghs stayed at an old *Schloss* in the foothills of the Bavarian Alps, inconveniently far from Munich, as guests of the Baron and Baroness Cramer-Klett. They were strongly anti-Nazi, and apparently were selected for this honor by friends in the Luftwaffe who thought (rightly) that it would give them some protective coloration.

† This secret base was closed to foreign military attachés, so Lindbergh was unaccompanied by Vanaman or any other American. Lindbergh was allowed to make notes, which he later made available to Vanaman, who used them as a basis for his reports to Washington.

style in order to attract high-level attention.* Neither was it lacking in bromides and homiletics:

> Germany is once more a world power in the air. Her air force and her air industry have emerged from the kindergarten stage. Full manhood will still not be reached for three years.

> The astounding growth of German air power from a zero level to its present status in a brief four years must be accounted one of the most important world events of our time. What it portends for Europe is something no-one today can foretell and must be left as a problem for future historians.

> The reasons which have permitted this miraculous outburst of national energy in the air field, are many. Among them are:

> . . . . . .

> 3. The vision of General Goering who from the start planned a *fantastically* large Air Force and Air Industry and who at the same time possessed the energy to convert his plans into reality.

> . . . . . .

> 5. The wise realization of the German air authorities at the start of their rearmament that other nations, especially the United States, were far in advance of them, both in scientific knowledge and technical skill. This humbleness of spirit has been one of the chief strengths of Germany. The old adage that self-dissatisfaction is true strength has never been better exemplified than in the German air development from 1933 to 1937.

> It is difficult to express in a few words the literally amazing size of the German air industry. The twenty-three known airplane concerns with their forty-six identified plants have a potential annual plane production of probably 6,000 planes. There is every reason to believe that the plants identified only give a part of the picture and that the truth, could it be known, would show a still higher potential production. The scale of the German airplane motor industry is no less impressive. It is ever and again the size of this industry, which forces the foreigner,—and even the American who is accustomed to think in big terms,—to pause, ponder and wonder as to the future. . . .

> Behind this industry stands a formidable group of air scientists, with large and well equipped laboratories and test fields, constantly pushing forward the German scientific advance. This advance is remarkable. The fact that the United States still leads in its air science and manufacturing skill must not be allowed to overshadow the German achievements between 1933 and 1937 and above all, not to lead to an underestimate of what Germany will achieve in the future.

> In four brief years, Germany could not accomplish everything. The extraordinary technical excellence of American aviation had been built up as a result of 19 years' uninterrupted progress since the Armistice. To equal this accomplishment in 48 months would be miraculous. In truth, it has not been achieved. Yet, because on November 1, 1937 the American technical level,

---

* The effort was at least partly successful; when Smith returned to Washington that fall, General Malin Craig, the Chief of Staff, questioned him at length about the report.

which is but one phase of air power, has not been reached, is no ground for the United States to adopt the British policy of smugness. If so, we shall be doomed to the same position of air inferiority with respect to Germany, as France now finds herself in and which Great Britain just as certainly will find herself in tomorrow—unless she realizes her own shortcomings. . . .

The actual November 1st strength of the German Air Force is probably from 175 to 225 squadrons. If we take a mean between these figures of 200 squadrons, we find Germany to at present possess

1800 first line planes in units,
600 first line planes in reserve units

or a total of 2400 planes. . . .

The level of flying ability reached by the German air power still leaves much to be desired, both by our standards and theirs also. While good potential pilots, the Germans must still be rated as unrefined. However, they have made great progress since 1933. The present flying of units would be still better, were it not for the air force expansion. Units have given up about half of their trained men every six months to form new units. There is also a marked shortage of efficient squadron and group commanders, which has adversely affected training standards. . . .

In general, the German air power has now reached a stage where it must be given serious consideration as a powerful opponent by any single nation. Qualified officers who have had the opportunity to inspect recently the British, German and French air forces, believe that:

1. Technically Germany has outdistanced France in practically all fields.
2. Germany is on the whole superior to Great Britain in the quality of her planes, but is still slightly inferior to Great Britain in motors, but rapidly closing the gap.
3. Both Great Britain and France are still superior to Germany in the training levels of their respective Air Forces, but Germany has cut down greatly the gap separating her from these rivals, during the past 12 months.

Despite the overblown style and the preposterous attribution of humility to a Luftwaffe led by the likes of Goering, Milch, and Udet, much of this report stands up pretty well in retrospect. The Lindbergh-Smith estimates of the Luftwaffe's present strength and the potential output of the aircraft factories were not far wrong, and the personnel shortcoming had not escaped attention.

But the report had a crucial flaw of omission. The authors had wholly failed to grasp that the Luftwaffe, in its organization, training, and aircraft selection, was not a strategic but a tactical force, designed to support the Army but not to carry out Douhet-type long-range bombing. There were few four-motored aircraft and no true heavy bombers, even by the standards of those times. This failure to grasp the essential character of the Luftwaffe goes far to explain the exaggerated predictions of destruction which Lindbergh was soon spreading far and wide.

The Lindberghs spent the winter in the United States and returned to England only briefly, before moving in June to a rather Spartan house on a small island off the Breton coast, near the Carrels. But it was a very social spring season, and Lindbergh had frequent opportunity to preach his gospel of German aeronautical prowess—to Inskip and others at the Astors' Cliveden; to Ambassadors Bullitt and Kennedy, Thomas Jones, and George Bernard Shaw at the Astors' London town house; to Lord Halifax, Hore-Belisha, and Henry and Clare Luce at the American Embassy; to various guests at the Astors' ball for the Royal Family; to others at a Buckingham Palace ball. Most emphatically of all, perhaps, to Harold Nicolson on May 22,* whose diary entry relates:

> Lindbergh is most pessimistic. He says that we cannot possibly fight since we should certainly be beaten. The German Air Force is ten times superior to that of Russia, France, and Great Britain put together. Our defences are simply futile and the barrage-balloons a mere waste of money. He thinks we should just give way and then make an alliance with Germany. To a certain extent his views can be discounted, (a) because he naturally believes that aeroplanes will be the determinant factor in war; and (b) because he believes in the Nazi theology, all tied up with his hatred of degeneracy and his hatred of democracy as represented by the free Press and the American public.† But even when one makes these discounts, the fact remains that he is probably right that we are outmastered in the air.

Despite the social and intellectual recognition he was receiving, Charles Lindbergh's opinion of the English was sinking ever lower. On April 2 he wrote in his diary:

> The contrast between an English aircraft factory and an American or German factory is understandable. The English simply do not seem to have equivalent ability along those lines. God! How they will have to pay for it in the next year. The country has neither the spirit nor the ability needed for a modern war. . . . It is not only in aviation that they are behind. . . . And the people show little sign of changing. They need an entirely new spirit, if British greatness is to endure.

Lindbergh's favorable impression of Hurricanes and Spitfires did nothing to reverse this current of disapproval. Later in April he and the American air attachés in London were communing sadly about "the condition of English military aviation and the rearmament program in general," and lamenting that England "seems hopelessly behind in military strength in comparison to Germany." Why? "I believe the assets in English character lie in confidence rather than

---

* This was at the time of the German-Czech May crisis. Anne Lindbergh recorded that her husband "gets Harold Nicolson and evidently pummels him with gloomy aviation data." Lindbergh's own diary (the published extracts from which begin in March 1938) states that Nicolson was "very anti-German," and that "I took Germany's side, possibly too ardently as is usually the case in arguments of this kind."

† In 1966, when Nicolson's *Diaries and Letters* were published, this passage led to sharp controversy between Lindbergh and Sir Harold's son Nigel, as recounted in Moseley, *Lindbergh* (1976), pp. xxiii–xxx. Lindbergh took exception to the phrases "believes in the Nazi theology" and "hatred of democracy," as well as the attribution to him of the view that the Luftwaffe was "ten times superior" to the combined forces of the other powers, when in fact he stated only that it was "stronger" than that of the other nations combined. Nicolson's rendition may be loose or hyperbolic, but as a historical matter, the impression which Lindbergh made on his listeners is more important than his precise words.

ability; tenacity rather than strength; and determination rather than intelligence. . . . It is necessary to realize that England is a country composed of a great mass of slow, somewhat stupid and indifferent people, and a small group of geniuses." After his move from England to Brittany, he had a like conversation at the American Embassy in Paris with Bullitt and the military attachés (June 23):

> In a conflict between France, England, and Russia on one side, against Germany on the other, Germany would immediately have supremacy of the air. . . . Germany has developed a huge Air Force while England has slept and France has deluded herself with a Russian alliance.

During the last two weeks of August, apparently by arrangements made through Colonel Raymond L. Lee (the American military attaché for air in London), the Lindberghs visited the Soviet Union. They were royally received, and Lindbergh examined most of the Soviet military aircraft types and visited numerous air bases and airplane factories. He thought the aircraft "not as good as the similar designs of the United States, Germany, and England," but "good enough to be used effectively in a modern war." Returning from Russia, the couple spent the first week of September in Czechoslovakia. Lindbergh was "greatly impressed" by the Czech generals but concluded "that Czechoslovakia is not well equipped in the air" because their planes, pursuit and bomber alike, were "too slow for modern warfare."

The travelers arrived in Paris on September 8, and had planned to return to their Breton home the next day, but changed their plans in order to accept a dinner invitation from Ambassador Bullitt.

3

Up to this time Lindbergh's pronouncements had been those of an influential but unofficial American. Now, however, chiefly as a result of actions taken by Ambassadors Bullitt and Kennedy, Lindbergh's opinions appeared to become a part, by no means unimportant, of the official voice of America.

Lindbergh's views on the European crisis paralleled closely those of Bullitt, whose genuine love for the French was transmuted, politically, into fear for their fate if they tangled militarily with Germany. Now that sad prospect was imminent, and on the day the Lindberghs landed at Le Bourget, Daladier had told Bullitt that "if German troops should cross the Czechoslovak frontier," France would attack Germany, even though "he was fully aware that a French attack on the German line would be very costly and would not get very far."

It was in this dismal atmosphere that Bullitt invited the Lindberghs and the American military attaché, Colonel Horace Fuller, to dinner on the ninth, together with the French Minister for Air, Guy la Chambre. Lindbergh summarized the ensuing conversation:

> The French situation is desperate. Impossible to catch up with Germany for years, if at all. France is producing about forty-five to fifty warplanes per month. Germany is building from 500 to 800 per month, according to the best estimates. England is building in the vicinity of seventy per month.

France is hoping to have 2,600 first-line planes by April, 1940. Germany is probably building that many every three or four months. One is forced to the conclusion that the German air fleet is stronger than that of all other European countries combined. . . . M. La Chambre apparently realizes this fact. The French are also deficient in antiaircraft guns, and the people of Paris are not equipped with gas masks. Yet the French Army is apparently ready to attack on the old Western front if Germany invades Czechoslovakia. It is suicide. . . .

La Chambre reported these ominous judgments to his Cabinet colleagues, and they seem to have been partly responsible for the "sudden" and "extraordinary" collapse of Bonnet that Phipps reported to London on September 13:

Mr. Bonnet was very upset and said that peace must be preserved at any price as neither France nor Great Britain were ready for war. Colonel Lindbergh had returned from his tour horrified at overwhelming strength of Germany in the air and terrible weakness of all other Powers. He declares that Germany has 8,000 military aeroplanes and can turn out 1,500 a month. M. Bonnet said that French and British towns would be wiped out and little or no retaliation would be possible.

To be sure, three weeks earlier General Vuillemin had brought back from Germany comparable reports on the Luftwaffe. But Lindbergh gave confirmation from a neutral and presumably expert source. At all events, the Lindbergh pronouncements continued to reverberate in Paris; as the British military attaché, Colonel Fraser, put it in a report on September 21:

. . . . pointed at Paris (and at London) is the threat of the German Air Force, and the Führer found a most convenient ambassador in Colonel Lindbergh, who appears to have given the French an impression of its might and preparedness which they did not have before, and who at the same time confirmed the view that the Russian Air Force was worth almost exactly nothing.*

The day after the Bullitt-La Chambre dinner the Lindberghs flew back to Brittany. Their quiet was interrupted on September 19 by a telegram from Ambassador Kennedy requesting their presence in London as soon as possible. They left the next day and were at lunch with the Kennedys on September 21 the day before Chamberlain's scheduled flight to Godesberg to resume his negotiations with Hitler.

Kennedy and Lindbergh had met at the Astors' in May, and hit it off well; Lindbergh had found the ambassador "not the usual type of politician or diplomat," and his views on the European situation "intelligent and interesting." In fact the ambassador's views were somewhat mercurial, and his reports and diplomatic dealings quite unsophisticated, but in general he and Lindbergh were like-minded on the major issues, and no doubt that is why he had summoned the famous flyer at this critical juncture.

---

* This considerably overstated the opinions Lindbergh recorded while in the Soviet Union. Daladier, meeting with Phipps on September 13, described Lindbergh's estimate of the Russian air strength as "unduly pessimistic," since the Premier "had reason to believe the Russians had 5,000 aeroplanes."

4

Prior to Kennedy's appearance on the diplomatic scene, there was little other than his wealth and Irish Catholic lineage on which to draw conclusions about Joseph P. Kennedy's views on international issues. These two attributes suggested both that he was politically conservative, and that it was surprising that he had been selected as Ambassador to the Court of St. James especially by a President whose New Deal was veering leftward. But Franklin Roosevelt had a love, sometimes childish, for the unexpected move, and no doubt chuckled at the prospect of a son of the old sod riding so high in the domain of His Britannic Majesty.*

Publicly, Kennedy was an immediate success in his new role. He was able and gregarious, colorful of speech, had a large and handsome family, and within a week of his arrival in England (March 1, 1938) shot a hole-in-one at Stoke Poges. A month later he sensibly ended the snobbish practice of presenting American debutantes to the Queen. In Britain and at home alike, the new ambassador got a very good press.

But for all his attractive qualities and remarkable financial and administrative abilities, Joseph P. Kennedy was no diplomat. Masterful and accustomed to lead, he could not accommodate himself to the role of spokesman for policies determined by others. He gossiped and dealt in personalities indiscreetly. Openly contemptuous of the State Department,† he sometimes did not report his discussions with foreign officials, and when he did there might be considerable discrepancies between his versions and those of the other conferees. He carried on a large volume of private but revealing correspondence, and expressed opinions to the press which he had not vouchsafed through official channels. In short he regarded himself not as an agent of the State Department, but as an autonomous American diplomatic operative, loosely responsible to the President.

It soon appeared that Kennedy was considerably more isolationist than either the President or the Secretary of State. Scheduled to give his first public ambassadorial speech on March 17, Kennedy submitted to Washington a draft containing such phrases as: "Our people do not see how we could usefully participate in the adjustments of international relations" and "the great bulk of the [American] people is not now convinced that any common interest exists between them and any other country." Secretary Hull, with Roosevelt's approval, considerably modified Kennedy's language on the ground that it was "entirely too isolationist,"‡ but Kennedy was able to preserve his main theme,

---

* According to Postmaster General Jim Farley, Roosevelt thought it unlikely that a hardboiled Irish multimillionaire would be taken in by the slick English.

† Secretary of the Interior Harold Ickes, a guest of the Kennedys during his honeymoon early in July 1938, recorded in his diary that the ambassador "inveighed eloquently against the 'career boys' in the State Department. He insisted that the State Department did not know what was going on in Europe and that there was no use trying to keep the State Department informed. He complained that everything leaked through the State Department and that nothing got through to the President straight unless he sent it to the President direct."

‡ Hull was preparing a speech for delivery at the National Press club on March 17, the day before Kennedy's scheduled appearance at the Pilgrims' Club in London, in which Hull would stress the danger of not fulfilling international responsibilities. Kennedy had the gall to suggest that the Secretary's speech be postponed, giving as a reason that, in the wake of *Anschluss,* Hull's speech might be misunderstood in England.

that United States policy would be governed by national self-interest, and that the country would act militarily only if directly threatened. A few weeks later he wrote to the isolationist Senator William E. Borah:

> The more I see of things here, the more convinced I am that we must exert all our intelligence and effort toward keeping out of any kind of involvement. As long as I hold my present job I shall never lose sight of this guiding principle.

Like Neville Chamberlain, Kennedy was business-oriented, and viewed war in general as wasteful of life and property, destructive of prosperity, and leading to the spread of Bolshevism. He viewed with horror the likelihood of American involvement in a European war and, so inclined, fell enthusiastically into line with the British Government's appeasement policy. He admired Chamberlain and especially Halifax, and frequently boasted of his close relations with them. The British leaders did, indeed, go out of their ways to keep Kennedy well informed, but despite the politically harmonious relationship, neither Chamberlain nor Halifax appears to have valued his counsel or had much use for him personally.*

Perhaps the most naïve of Kennedy's actions were his efforts to assume the role of conciliator between his own country and Nazi Germany. On May 31, Ambassador von Dirksen reported to Berlin:

> Mr. Kennedy, the United States Ambassador here, is not a career diplomat, but a private business man, very rich, and a close friend of President Roosevelt. On various social occasions he has repeatedly turned the conversation to the point that he would like to do his very best to improve German-United States relations; he had the intention of undertaking a tour of study of Germany; he also wished, during his next stay in Washington, to discuss the European complex of questions with President Roosevelt . . . he would not merely restrict his activities to Britain, but . . . would report on the entire European situation.

Kennedy disclosed that he would soon go to Washington, and wished first to confer with Dirksen so as to be better informed on German-American relations. Accordingly (Dirksen having meanwhile received instructions from Berlin), on June 13 the two ambassadors conferred at length. As reported by Dirksen, much of what Kennedy said was indiscreet and even bizarre:

> We . . . touched upon Kennedy's trip and its purpose . . . to give President Roosevelt detailed information about European conditions; Kennedy added that if he did not believe an improvement could be achieved in Europe, he would resign from his position here. However, he was convinced that this was possible, and he believed above all that the United States would have to establish friendly relations with Germany.

---

* The Foreign Secretary may well have been put off by Kennedy's indiscretion, which permitted him to vent to Halifax his dislike for Harold Ickes and his distrust of Roosevelt's domestic economic policies. See Koskoff, *Joseph P. Kennedy* (1974), p. 129. In response to my inquiry, by letter of August 16, 1974, Sir Alec Douglas-Home (Chamberlain's parliamentary secretary at the time) stated: "The relations between Mr. Kennedy and Mr. Chamberlain were not as I recollect very close." According to Cadogan, Chamberlain "had an almost instinctive contempt for the Americans."

Kennedy seemed to be strongly convinced of the strength of his position; he said that neither Secretary of State Hull nor any of the other Cabinet members or influential persons could jeopardize his position. He also felt absolutely secure as to his constituency and number of votes [*sic*]. The only one whom he had to recognize as superior was President Roosevelt. Roosevelt himself, like all Presidents, was on bad terms with the State Department and did not have much use for it. . . .

The President was not anti-German, but desired friendly relations with Germany. However, there was no one who had come from Europe and had spoken a friendly word to him regarding present-day Germany and her government. When I remarked that I feared he was right in this, Kennedy added that he *knew* he was right. Most of them were afraid of the Jews and did not dare to say anything good about Germany; others did not know any better, because they were not informed about Germany.

Although he did not know Germany, he had learned from the most varied sources that the present Government had done great things for Germany and that the Germans were satisfied and enjoyed good living conditions. The report by the well-known flier, Colonel Lindbergh, who had spoken very favorably of Germany, made a strong impression upon Ambassador Kennedy, as I know from an earlier conversation with him. Lindbergh and his wife spoke to me in the same manner regarding their impressions of Germany and of German aviation when I became acquainted with them recently at a court ball in Buckingham Palace.

As an illustration of how wrong impressions regarding Germany were being spread, Ambassador Kennedy related that recently "Johnnie" Rockefeller, a very influential and sensible man, had told him that according to a report by one of the leading professors of the Rockefeller Institute the limited amount of food available in Germany was being reserved mainly for the army, with the result that the rest of the population had to suffer want. As far as he knew, the professor who made the report was a Jew. He—Kennedy —had set Rockefeller right.

When he spoke favorably of Germany, people would have absolute confidence in his statements, because he was a Catholic.

. . . . . .

The Ambassador then touched upon the Jewish question and stated that it was naturally of great importance to German-American relations. In this connection it was not so much the fact that we wanted to get rid of the Jews that was so harmful to us, but rather the loud clamor with which we accompanied this purpose. He himself understood our Jewish policy completely; he was from Boston and there, in one golf club, and in other clubs, no Jews had been admitted for the past 50 years. His father had not been elected mayor because he was a Catholic; in the United States, therefore, such pronounced attitudes were quite common, but people avoided making so much outward fuss about it. . . .

The overwhelming majority of the American people wanted peace and friendly relations with Germany. The average American took a very simple view of problems of foreign policy; there were only 3-½ million Jews in the United States all told, and the overwhelming majority of them lived on the east coast. Elsewhere, however, the anti-German sentiment was—as mentioned above—by no means widespread; neither did the average citizen of the

United States have any particular liking for England; regarding England he only knew that she had not paid her war debts, and that she had deposed her King because he wanted to marry an American; he had no prejudice against Germany.

The two agreed that "the decisive point" was that democratic and totalitarian states "could maintain wholly satisfactory friendly relations." Kennedy then remarked that "Chamberlain in particular was extremely anxious for a settlement with Germany," and subsequently added that "in economic matters Germany had to have a free hand in the East as well as the Southeast." Dirksen concluded his report by opining that Kennedy was "sincere," and stressing the high regard in which he was held in London.

Kennedy appears not to have reported either of these conversations to the State Department, but no doubt he used them to his own purpose when he met with Roosevelt a week later at Hyde Park. Back in London the following month, Kennedy lost no time in renewing contact with Dirksen, with whom he met on July 20. On this occasion the German found Kennedy "much more worried and pessimistic" than before; American public opinion about Germany "had deteriorated appreciably," the economic situation was so unstable that J. P. Morgan "had even mentioned giving up his business," and the likelihood of war over Czechoslovakia, which would eventually involve the United States, had "a pretty firm hold on him." President Roosevelt, however, "thought calmly and moderately," and Kennedy added the remarkable pronouncement that the President "would be prepared to support Germany's demands vis-à-vis England or to do anything that might lead to pacification."*

The discussion then turned to Kennedy's desire to visit Germany, which met with a generally favorable reaction in Berlin. Kennedy, however, went off with his family to Cannes, and when he returned on August 20, the looming Czech crisis swept these plans aside. Extraordinary as they were, Kennedy's statements probably did little damage, as the German Foreign Ministry apparently did not take them seriously and was getting much more reliable reports on the American scene from Ambassador Dieckhoff in Washington. But Kennedy's blarney (as he probably regarded much of what he said) cannot have done the Allied cause any good and leaves no mystery about the Kennedy-Lindbergh affinity.

After returning to his post, Kennedy saw the Prime Minister on August 30, and "appeared surprised" when told that a German attack on Czechoslovakia might be imminent. His dispatch to Secretary Hull was confined to what Chamberlain had said, but the British account reported him as declaring that if Hitler attacked Czechoslovakia "it will be hell," predicting that if France and Britain went to war "the United States would follow before long," and finally stating that President Roosevelt had decided "to go in with Chamberlain; whatever course Chamberlain desires to adopt he would think right." The next day Kennedy saw

* This appears to be the only Dirksen discussion which Kennedy reported to the State Department, writing: "His [Dirksen's] manner was a revelation to me. He definitely gave me the impression that Hitler was decidedly in the mood to start negotiations with England." Since nothing was further from the truth, either Dirksen was misinformed or stringing Kennedy along, or Kennedy misunderstood what was being said to him.

Halifax, who asked what would be the American reaction "if the Germans went into Czechoslovakia, with the Czechs fighting them, and England did not go along." Kennedy replied that "a great deal would depend on the attitude the President would take as to whether he thought England should be encouraged to fight or whether he would contend that they should stay out of war until the last possible minute." The ambassador concluded his dispatch:

> I would appreciate some opinion from you as to policy of handling the British attitude if Hitler marches and England decides not to. I think that Chamberlain and Halifax would appreciate your reaction and judgment as to what should be done on this as far as the United States goes.

Perhaps intoxicated by his access to the seats of decision, Kennedy next gave an exclusive telephonic interview to the Hearst Boston *Evening American,* saying that he had just met with Halifax, and that Americans should "keep cool" and "not lose our heads," because "things aren't as bad as they seem." The British public was "very strongly behind the Cabinet" and there would be no war "during the rest of 1938."

On the same day (August 31) Kennedy submitted to Washington the draft of a speech he was shortly to deliver in Scotland,* in which he proposed to say:

> I should like to ask you all if you know of any dispute or controversy existing in the world which is worth the life of your son, or of anyone else's son? Perhaps I am not well informed of the terrifically vital forces underlying all this unrest in the world, but for the life of me I cannot see anything involved which could be remotely considered worth shedding blood for.

Admirably humane as were these sentiments, they did not sit well in Washington and neither did the press story. Hull and the President himself both rapped the ambassador's knuckles for the interview with the *Evening American,* and Hull reminded Kennedy that "the recent public speeches and public statements of the President and myself, which were prepared with great care, accurately reflect the attitude of this Government toward the European and world situation, and that it would not be practicable to be more specific as to our reaction in hypothetical circumstances." The paragraph quoted from the speech draft was ordered stricken as too isolationist for a President who was trying to give moral support to the western Allies without jeopardizing his own domestic political base.†

Kennedy was now in the presidential doghouse. Talking to Henry Morgenthau, Secretary of the Treasury, and Hull on September 1, the President paraphrased the offending paragraph in the Aberdeen speech draft as "I can't for the life of me understand why anybody would want to go to war to save the

---

* The occasion was the laying of a memorial stone in Aberdeen Cathedral to the memory of Samuel Seabury, the first Episcopal bishop in the United States.

† Speaking at Queen's University in Kingston, Ontario, on August 18, 1938, Roosevelt had declared that the United States would not tolerate foreign domination of Canada, and that the time was past when controversies beyond the seas did not interest or threaten Americans. Of course, the relations between Britain and Czechoslovakia were hardly comparable to those between the United States and Canada, but Roosevelt told the Canadian Governor-General (Lord Tweedsmuir) that he had made the statement because it seemed "to fit in with the Hitler situation" and might have "some small effect in Berlin."

Czechs," and remarked: "Who would have thought that the English would take into camp a red-headed Irishman? The young man needs to have his wrists slapped rather hard." Roosevelt then described Chamberlain as "slippery" and "interested in peace at any price if he could get away with it and save face."

As manifested by his statement to the Boston *Evening American,* at the beginning of September, Kennedy discounted the likelihood of war.* Ten days later, when the ambassador next saw Chamberlain and Halifax, the Nuremberg Party Rally was bringing the crisis to full boil. After seeing the Foreign Secretary on September 10, Kennedy reported to Hull his opinion "that the British are, much against their will, veering away from the stand of keeping out." The ambassador's impression was, of course, a mistaken one, but plainly the danger of war was increasing and Kennedy appears to have concluded that the best chance of preserving peace lay in convincing the Germans that Britain would fight and that America would, in all probability, be drawn in.

Without further instructions from Washington, and without reporting most of his own doings, Kennedy told Halifax that "it was essential to take every possible step to avoid misunderstanding in Herr Hitler's mind," expressed approval of the fleet moves which had been announced, raised the possibility of inducing the Russians to demonstrate by concentrating air forces near their western border, and arranged to call on the Prime Minister "in order to encourage German speculation regarding the fact that the two countries were apparently keeping in such close touch." On September 12, Kennedy told the German counselor of embassy, Selzam, that, as a result of his talks with Chamberlain and Halifax, he had "completely altered his previous opinion" and now was convinced "that if France intervened Britain would intervene too"; there was now "a new glint in Chamberlain's eyes and in those of Sir Samuel Hoare and the others," and this time "they mean business." If war came, Kennedy would work to keep his country out of it, but "America would nevertheless intervene in the end." In this situation, it "depended on Hitler whether there was to be chaos . . . or whether he became a benefactor of mankind" through his "extraordinary achievements" in the "social and economic field."

It is most unlikely that these maneuvers had any impact in Germany, and they were soon robbed of any force by the Prime Minister's trip to Berchtesgaden. Publicly, Hull described his government's attitude as that of a deeply interested observer. Privately, Roosevelt took a negative attitude, predicting that the Hitler-Chamberlain talks would only postpone "the inevitable conflict." Writing to Ambassador William Phillips in Rome, he opined that "ninety percent of our people are definitely anti-German and anti-Italian in—sentiment— and incidentally I would not ask them to be neutral in thought." In Cabinet on September 16 and talking to Ickes the next day, the President complained that Chamberlain was "for peace at any price," and predicted that Czechoslovakia would be left in the lurch by Britain and France, who would "wash the blood from their Judas Iscariot hands."

* On September 2, Kennedy told the beautiful young American painter Ione Robinson (whom he had met on the *Normandie* two months earlier) that "nothing was going to happen in Prague because Mr. Chamberlain was such a capable man," and that "it was utterly ridiculous to have a crisis in Europe over a minority question."

These strong presidential sentiments were unknown alike to the general public and Kennedy himself when, on September 19, he sent an urgent message to Lindbergh to come to London as soon as possible. By that time it appeared that the issue of peace or war would depend on whether or not the Czechs would accept the terms which London and Paris were putting to them, and what Britain and France would do if Prague refused.

5

By 1938, the greater English-speaking portions of the British sovereign conglomerate had become virtually independent "Dominions," and the Empire was fading into the Commonwealth. India was increasingly restless under the Raj, and newborn Eire, struggling to be Gaelic, was ostentatiously neutral in European power politics. In the councils of Whitehall it was the distant Dominions— Australia, Canada, New Zealand, and South Africa—whose voices counted for most in the formation of British foreign policy. And in 1938 these voices, if with varying strength, were all counseling peace.

The resident spokesmen for the Dominions were the High Commissioners in London—Stanley Bruce (a former Prime Minister) for Australia, Vincent Massey (elder brother of the famous actor Raymond Massey) for Canada, W. J. Jordan for New Zealand, and Charles Te Water for South Africa.* The commissioners were not ambassadors, and their main contact with the British Government was not the Foreign but the Dominions Office.

The very cautious attitude of the three large Dominions toward their involvement in European conflict was made manifest at the time of the Rhineland remilitarization. Australia said nothing officially, but on March 30, 1936, Richard Casey, the Federal Treasurer, wrote to Hankey that "the sooner all the shackles are removed from Germany the better," and that Britain should "get France to cool down and accept the Rhineland position." Canada, having declined to become party to Locarno, likewise kept official silence, but Vincent Massey betrayed his own feelings in his diary, recording on March 14 his view that there should be no effort to dislodge the Germans, adding: "We have suffered enough in the past from French vindictiveness against Germany and French pedantry in the interpretation of contracts." From South Africa the Prime Minister, General J. B. M. Hertzog, telegraphed that if Britain took any military action against Germany the Union would "feel compelled to withhold its support," and Hertzog's diary notes read: "Today and the following days Great Britain must choose between hegemony with France and the leadership of the British Commonwealth of Nations."†

In May of 1937, at the Imperial Conference following the coronation of

---

* There was also a High Commissioner for the Irish Free State, W. J. Dulanty, whose government was not only neutralist but anti-Commonwealth, and who once remarked that attending meetings with his fellow-commissioners made him feel "like a whore at a christening."

† Charles Ritchie, a secretary in the Canadian Legation in Washington, had opportunity in 1937 to read "secret telegrams sent by the Dominion governments to London during the Rhineland crisis." In *The Siren Years: Undiplomatic Diaries 1937–1945* (1974), p. 16, he described these messages as "an eye-opener to me," because there was not much "rallying around the Mother Country in time of danger."

George VI, there was opportunity for direct interchange between the British and Dominion leaders in the context of the developing European crisis, and in the lengthening shadow of the League's failure in Ethiopia. General Hertzog, who "never changed his opinion that the unholy work of Versailles must be undone," was the most outspoken appeaser, telling the Conference:

> I am glad that no further obligations have been undertaken . . . and that Great Britain is free in respect of Eastern Europe, Austria, Czechoslovakia, Danzig, Memel, etc. . . . I maintain that peace in Europe can be assured today and should be assured if Great Britain approaches Germany in the same spirit of friendly cooperation which she has shown to France since 1919. . . . Great Britain's attitude towards Germany is far too much one of cold, repelling indifference compared with the warm welcome given to France.

And Hertzog added that if war came because of unwillingness to rectify Versailles "South Africa cannot be expected to take part in the war."

For Canada, Prime Minister Mackenzie King was almost equally explicit: "There was in Canada a great dread lest the country should be committed at the Imperial Conference to some obligation arising out of the European situation." King and Vincent Massey were both strong spokesmen for appeasement and subsequently supported the Munich settlement. According to Massey's private secretary, Charles Ritchie, King was basically opposed to the Commonwealth concept, and deeply suspicious of any systematic concert of purpose with Britain.*

Australia, facing an expanding Japan and fearful that Germany might demand return of the mandated territories in New Guinea, was much more Empire-minded than Canada or South Africa, but her spokesman, R. G. Casey, was openly sympathetic to allowing Germany to incorporate Austria and the Sudetenland in the Reich. New Zealand, a member of the League Council and strongly supportive of collective security, secretly informed the British: "If Great Britain was at war, New Zealand would be at war. The New Zealand Government did not believe in collective security [only] for the League of Nations, they believed in collective security for the British Commonwealth of Nations as well."

Welcome as were the warmer attitudes of the Pacific Dominions, they spotlighted the lack of unity within the Commonwealth. Came the *Anschluss* and Hertzog's reaction was to remind Britain that, if she became involved in war by policies "which South Africa could not wholly approve," the Union would not feel bound to join in. Through Massey, Canada likewise counseled restraint.

On March 20, Malcolm MacDonald† told his colleagues of the Foreign Policy Committee: "If we found ourselves engaged in a European war to prevent

---

* After the conference, Mackenzie King went to Germany and a meeting with Hitler on June 21. He was deeply and favorably impressed not only by the Fuehrer but by Goering and Neurath as well, and returned to Canada persuaded that the peace of Europe lay in the hands of Hitler and Chamberlain.

† MacDonald began 1938 as Secretary for the Dominions. On May 16 he was replaced by Lord E. M. C. Stanley and shifted to the Ministry for the Colonies in place of Ormsby-Gore, who was dropped from the Cabinet on succeeding to his father's baronetcy. In October, when Lord Stanley died, MacDonald became Secretary for both Dominions and Colonies.

Germans living in the Sudeten districts of Czechoslovakia from being reunited with Germany, on this issue the British Commonwealth might well break in pieces."

As the Czech crisis intensified, cautionary signals from the Dominions multiplied. Late in March, Hertzog wrote to Chamberlain advocating a revision of the Versailles Treaty, and early in May he was objecting to Anglo-French staff talks. Two weeks later, during the May crisis, the Australian Foreign Minister (William Hughes), speaking in the House of Representatives, expressed the hope that British representations to Prague would lead to a peaceful solution, and in London neither Bruce nor Te Water showed any sympathy for the Czechs. In July the Australian Attorney General (Robert Menzies) visited Germany, and after his return the Government instructed Bruce to suggest in London that Czechoslovakia be urged to make "the most liberal concessions it could offer."

On September 1, sensing the approaching climax, Hertzog completed a draft of a resolution declarative of Union policy "in the event of war in Europe with England as one of the belligerents":

The existing relations between the Union of South Africa and the belligerent parties shall, so far as the Union is concerned, remain unchanged and continue as if no war were being waged. . . .*

Hertzog made no immediate official use of the draft, but showed it privately to the Defense Minister, Oswald Pirow, and to General Jan Smuts, at that time the Minister of Justice and leader of the South African Party, which, with Hertzog's Nationalist Party, comprised the "United Party"—the electoral vehicle of the coalition government. Smuts, one of the fathers of the Commonwealth idea, had spoken in the House of Assembly on August 25, denying the existence of any automatic obligation on the Union's part to support Britain in a European war, but expressing his personal opinion that in such event the Parliament would vote to go to Britain's assistance.† Smuts and Hertzog were political opponents of long standing, and the Prime Minister had reason to fear that Smuts might reject the draft. Perhaps moved more by tactical considerations than inner conviction, Smuts joined with Pirow in approving it and, thus reassured, Hertzog held it for use if war seemed imminent.

Whatever the effect of these overseas developments on the decision-making process in London, they now began to be cited by the Chamberlain government in support of its appeasement policies. In July and August, Halifax had used the Dominions' attitude to oppose French demands for a strong *démarche* in Berlin, and on September 7 the British chargé in Washington (Mallet) justified, to the State Department, British pressure on Prague by saying: ". . . it was becoming

* The ensuing qualifying clause preserved pre-existing "contractual relations" with Britain concerning the naval base at Simonstown (on the Cape of Good Hope) and obligations arising from South Africa's membership in the League of Nations or "the free association of the Union with the other members of the Comonwealth."

† Smuts's prediction was accurate. When war came a year later, by a narrow voting margin in Parliament, South Africa joined Britain, and Smuts replaced Hertzog as Prime Minister.

clearer that the Dominions were isolationist, and there would be no sense in fighting a war which would break the British Empire while trying to assure the safety of the United Kingdom." Five days later, in Cabinet, Halifax quoted Vincent Massey to the effect that "a minority in Canada might be in favour of our taking some forward action," but "the majority would be against . . . in the hope that we should not become involved in a war."

When Neville Chamberlain went to the Berghof, applause was heard from every corner of the Commonwealth. From then on, Malcolm MacDonald met almost daily with the High Commissioners, to keep them informed and solicit their views, which remained unanimously in favor of all possible concessions in order to avoid war. Their attitude, and the issue gripping politically conscious Britishers, was epitomized in an unpremeditated colloquy between Vincent Massey and Harold Nicolson, encountering each other at a London club on September 16, while Chamberlain was returning from the Berghof:

NICOLSON: Well, are the Government going to give way?
MASSEY: It is better to have smallpox three years from now than at once.
NICOLSON: Yes, but if we have it now, we shall recover; if in three years, we shall die.

CHAPTER 28

The Hard Sell

1

When the French delegation arrived in England on the morning of Sunday, September 18, 1938, the principal members were not equally pleased with the situation. Georges Bonnet, so recently in a state of near-collapse, had revived rapidly after the news of Chamberlain's pilgrimage, and on September 16 the Polish Ambassador, Juliusz Lukasiewicz, found the Foreign Minister "wholly relaxed and full of hope that war could probably be avoided." Daladier's feelings, as we have seen, were ambivalent, compounded of shame at France's loss of control of her own destiny, and relief that responsibility had been shifted to British shoulders.

More immediately, Daladier was disgruntled by the silent treatment Paris had been getting from London, as September 15 and 16 and the morning of the seventeenth passed with no information about the Berghof conference and no move toward consultation between the two capitals. Finally, in the afternoon of the seventeenth, Halifax, as if acknowledging a boring reminder—"Oh yes, the French of course; tell them to come at once"—sent a terse message through Phipps: "His Majesty's Government would be very glad if President of Council and Minister of Foreign Affairs would come immediately to London for discussion." Simultaneously, Cadogan was authorized by Chamberlain and Halifax to see Ambassdor Corbin and "tell him something—not too much."

The explicit invitation to Bonnet had been suggested by Ambassador Phipps (by now thoroughly appeasement-minded) on the ground that Bonnet "more than certain other French Ministers, realizes the weakness of France owing to the lamentable condition of her air force." Phipps's distrust of the government to which he was accredited was strikingly manifest in his private letter to Halifax, advising that at some point during the coming conversations Daladier and Bonnet should be questioned separately:

> The famous Lindbergh report on the various European air forces might be a peg on which to hang a question as to the real state of the French, and possibly Russian, air forces. Bonnet almost collapsed when he mentioned this report to me, whereas Daladier affected hardly to have heard of it. Which spoke the truth? or were both lying, the one from funk and the other from over-assurance?
>
> Veracity is not, I regret to say, the strongest point of the average French

politician, but there is a rather better chance of extracting the truth from him when he is not in the presence of another Frenchman. . . .

Lindbergh's gloomy predictions to La Chambre were still echoing through French official corridors, and, just before Daladier took off for London, that other apostle of air despair, General Vuillemin, had a letter with "new pessimistic information" put into the Premier's hands at Le Bourget. But on the Army side of the military issue, Daladier's advices, if not exhilarating, were not so dismal. On September 12 he had met with Gamelin and two top field commanders (Georges and Billotte), who had indicated that the French Army could launch an offensive between the Rhine and Moselle within ten to twenty days after the outbreak of war. This, to be sure, would not lead to a conquest of the German Army before the Germans would have overrun "an important part" of Czechoslovakia's territory.*

Meanwhile the Czechs, fully aware of the advancing state of German preparations, were increasingly fearful of a surprise attack which would prevent their own mobilization. On the seventeenth, Foreign Minister Krofta warned his European ambassadors of the danger, emphasizing that his government wished to do nothing that would hinder Anglo-French efforts to preserve peace. The next day Gamelin received a personal message from General Faucher pointing out "the very grave consequences that could result" from a failure to mobilize, and posing Beneš' urgent request for advice. The French delegation had already gone to London; Gamelin gave Krofta no answer but informed the Quai d'Orsay, which relayed Beneš' inquiry to Daladier.

There was other and quite different news from Prague. On September seventeenth, Léon Blum was visited by Jaromir Nečas, an old friend who was the Minister for Social Security in the Czech Government. Nečas was the bearer of a handwritten note from Beneš, together with a map showing the placement of the Czech fortifications and the general location of portions of the Sudetenland which could be ceded to Germany without seriously diminishing the country's defensive capabilities. In the note, Beneš stressed the necessity of absolute secrecy, in view of the likely catastrophic effect of its contents becoming known, and described the plan (which would have envisaged the cession of four to six thousand square kilometers with a population of perhaps a million Germans) as the last possible concession to Hitler, to be allowed only as a matter of dire necessity.

Blum sent the document to Daladier, who received it just before his departure for London. Meanwhile, Bonnet had received substantially similar information from Minister Lacroix, who had seen Beneš on the fifteenth.

In his postwar testimony, Daladier professed to have been "singularly embarrassed" by the Beneš "proposition," which he felt obliged to disclose to Chamberlain, and which "was another argument in favor of the London thesis." As we will see, however, the Beneš proposition played no significant part in the en-

---

* After the war Daladier testified that the generals had told him that "the Germans could crush Czechoslovakia in a matter of days." This is not borne out by Gamelin's records, which show rather that this consequence was predicted only if the Czechs tried to defend Prague, while estimating a much more prolonged defense if they fell back into Moravia.

suing Anglo-French conversations. Beneš had rightly anticipated that Britain and France would want his government to make additional concessions, and it made sense for him to convey secretly to them how far they could go territorially without fatally undermining Czechoslovakia's defensive position. Daladier is more to be blamed for abandoning than Beneš for advancing the proposal, and the Premier's later lamentations can only be regarded as another example of his unhappy tendency to shirk decisive responsibility and blame others for the consequences.*

On the French home front, during the three days between the announcement of Chamberlain's trip and the London meeting, enough had leaked out so that it was generally known that Hitler had delivered an ultimatum backed by the threat of war, and that he had demanded cession to the Reich of at least a large part of the Sudetenland. Press comment soon made it appear that French public opinion as a whole, including most of the right and, except for the Communists, the left, was ready to accept this solution. The dissenters included the intransigent nationalist Kerillis, who, in *Epoque,* described the crisis as a "diplomatic Verdun" and predicted nothing but disaster from Daladier's summons to London. At the other end of the political spectrum, the Communist *L'Humanité* was equally pessimistic. But the big journals—*Paris-Soir, Petit Parisien, Le Temps, Le Figaro, Paris-Midi, Information, Le Matin, L'Action Française,* and even the Socialist *Le Populaire*—were all for peace, even at the expense of democratic Czechoslovakia.

2

Prime Minister Chamberlain, in person, greeted the French delegation when it arrived at Croydon, and escorted them to 10 Downing Street, where the conference was held. Daladier and Bonnet were accompanied by Léger, Rochat, and Jules Henry† from the Quai d'Orsay staff, and were joined in London by Ambassador Corbin and the secretary of embassy, Roland de Margerie. Even with these reinforcements, at the green table the French party of seven was outnum-

---

* After Munich, Beneš (in a letter to Lacroix dated January 20, 1939) denied that he had even made any offer of cession, and Wheeler-Bennett (*Munich: Prologue to Tragedy,* p. 115, n. 1) accepted the explanation that Beneš had merely "recounted the occasion of the offer which President Masaryk made at the Peace Conference in 1919." Wheeler-Bennett gave no source for this version, and he wrote in 1948, nearly twenty years before the text of the Nečas memorandum was published in German translation. Nittner, *Dokumente zur Sudetendeutschen Frage 1916–1967* (1967), p. 224. Nittner gives no source, but Daladier's papers include a French translation, which closely corresponds to the Nittner text. I do not know the fate of the original document, which contained an injunction that it be destroyed. Lacroix testified postwar in line with the explanation credited by Wheeler-Bennett, but his own message to Bonnet on September 17 clearly shows that Beneš was not merely recalling past history. The Nečas map confutes Wheeler-Bennett, as does the French Foreign Ministry journal for September 20, which reveals that on September 20, Beneš asked Lacroix for an answer to his proposal for limited cession. Furthermore, the same information was transmitted to London by Ambassador Newton, whose source was Hodža rather than Beneš, and on the nineteenth Beneš told Jan Masaryk that Nečas was on his way to London to see Attlee. All in all, therefore, it is beyond doubt that Beneš did indeed put forward the proposal for use as a last resort.

† Jules Henry served in the French Embassy in Washington from 1920 to 1937, when he returned to France as Bonnet's *chef de cabinet.*

bered by their hosts. Chamberlain and Halifax were flanked by the two other members of the inner Cabinet, Simon and Hoare, and six civil servants: Vansittart, Wilson, Cadogan, Strang, Edward Bridges (Secretary to the Cabinet), and Frank Roberts (Central Department).

Chamberlain lost no time in getting down to business, and for the benefit of the French gave what must have been at least his sixth account of his talk with Hitler. It differed little from the earlier versions, except that Chamberlain read passages from Henderson's report of his meeting with Goering the previous day, as added assurance that Hitler would make no military move pending resumption of negotiations. The Prime Minister summarized the situation by saying that once Hitler decided to go into Czechoslovakia "nothing could be done to stop him," and that the only way to avoid violence was to accept his demand for "self-determination" for the Sudeten Germans. He concluded by asking the French to state "their views on the decision which had now to be taken."

Daladier was not so easily drawn. He pointed out that the upshot of the Chamberlain-Hitler meeting confronted the French Government "with facts and proposals which had never hitherto come under consideration," whereas the British had already been deliberating them and also had received the advice of Lord Runciman. Therefore, he "felt that it was for His Majesty's Government rather than for the French Government to express their views on the proposal under consideration."

The colloquy then turned into a sort of diplomatic tennis, the game being to keep the ball in play without answering the basic question and thus put the responsibility for giving in on the other side of the net. Chamberlain cited Runciman's view that it was all Beneš' fault for conceding too slowly, and, thus having impugned France's ally, he declared that, since it was not Britain but France that was bound by treaty, it was up to the guests to say whether the treaty made acceptance of self-determination impossible. Daladier replied with a warning against resort to plebiscite, since the reach of the self-determination principle would extend to Poland, Hungary, and Rumania, and enable Germany to destroy Czechoslovakia and other Central European states as well. Chamberlain was obliged to admit this likelihood; London "had already been told by the Hungarian and Polish Governments that they desired similar treatment for their minorities." Daladier declared that, especially without consultation with his Cabinet colleagues, "it seemed to him difficult to accept the principle and method proposed," and asked point-blank whether the British were prepared to go along. Chamberlain produced "a secret paper which had just been put into his hands, showing that German military preparations, far from slackening off after his visit to Herr Hitler, had intensified," and asked Daladier "whether he had any possible alternative to propose." Daladier did not offer any; he stressed both France's treaty obligations and his opposition to a plebiscite, "which was so dangerous for Czechoslovakia and for the peace of Europe," and again asked "what conclusions had been reached by the British Government who had had more opportunity to examine the position."

Lord Halifax now intervened with an admonition that the French, by "the very fact of . . . obligations towards Czechoslovakia," were entitled and "even bound" to say whether or not their treaty precluded acceptance of Hitler's conditions for continuing the negotiations. Without explicitly stating his government's conclusion, he pointed out that Czechoslovakia could not be protected and, even after an Allied victory over Germany, would probably not be reinstituted with the same borders, thus clearly implying that Hitler's conditions should be met.

After two and a half hours of sparring, Chamberlain proposed an adjournment for lunch, and Daladier agreed with alacrity. Privately, the British were scornful of their guests. Chamberlain later told the Cabinet that the French had kept passing the ball into the British court and that "the darkest hour was before lunch," while the morose Cadogan referred to "Daladier and Bonnet and their circus" and complained: "We had to listen to Daladier, with voice trembling with carefully modulated emotion, talking of French honor and obligations." But there was plenty of reason for cynicism on both sides, and it is hard to believe that none of the British squirmed when Halifax unctuously declared: "Nothing was further from their thoughts than that the French Government should fail to honour their obligations to the Czechoslovak Government."

The leaders of the two delegations lunched together and finally came closer to the issue.* Daladier maintained his opposition to a plebiscite but volunteered (presumably on the basis of the Nečas-Lacroix messages from Beneš) that the Czech Government could be persuaded to agree to an outright cession of some of the Sudetenland. Bonnet suggested that Britain should join in a guarantee of Czechoslovakia thus weakened, and after lunch the deliberations were largely devoted to these two themes.

Since Newton had transmitted to London much the same information that Lacroix had sent to Paris, Daladier's suggestion of Czechoslovakia's willingness to cede territory probably came as no surprise to Chamberlain. The difficulty, with which the first part of the afternoon meeting was chiefly concerned, was that the size of the cession contemplated in Prague was totally inadequate to meet Hitler's demand for all areas "where over 50 percent of the inhabitants were Sudeten Germans."

Daladier counterproposed final resolution of the new border by an "International Commission" which would "lay down a frontier which would correspond as far as possible with the ethnical frontier, but should at the same time take into account Czechoslovak requirements in respect of defence and security." Chamberlain warned that the guiding principle would have to be "the presence of a majority of Germans in any given area," but agreed to the idea of "adjustments by the international commission, who would take into account the difficulties which M. Daladier had in mind." For domestic political reasons, the Prime Minister was very eager to find a solution which Prague would accept voluntarily, and he hoped to create the impression that by supporting the Czechs' objections to a plebiscite they had been induced to accept Hitler's territorial demands:

---

* No record was made of the luncheon conversation; the text above is based on Chamberlain's report to the Cabinet the following morning.

Mr. Chamberlain . . . pointed out that the idea of a territorial cession would be likely to have a much more favourable reception from the British public if it could be represented as the choice of the Czechoslovak Government themselves and it could be made clear that they had been offered the choice of a plebiscite or of territorial cession and had preferred the latter. This would dispose of any idea that we were ourselves carving up Czechoslovak territory.

Daladier then turned to the question of a guarantee, declaring it "a vital question for the French Government":

They could hardly bring pressure to bear on the Czechoslovak Government to agree to the cession of part of their present territory unless they could assure them of some sort of international guarantee of what remained of the Czechoslovak territory after the amputation of the Sudeten areas. He also thought it was quite essential that Germany should be a party to this international guarantee of the neutrality of Czechoslovakia.

Chamberlain "did not know what he could say about the German guarantee," and described a British guarantee as "a very grave departure" from the Government's previous position. Without an army, and considering the distance between the two countries, how could it be enforced? And if Britain were to consider such a step, then perhaps the Czech treaties with Soviet Russia and France should give way so that the country might occupy "a position of neutrality somewhat similar to that taken up by Belgium."

Halifax chimed in with a reference to Chamberlain's speech after *Anschluss,* in which he had declared it "quite impossible to allow the direction of British policy to be placed in the hands of any other country," especially since the Dominions would be necessarily involved. Accordingly:

If, therefore, we were to consider the guarantees . . . he would like to see associated with them some undertaking on the part of the Czech Government that in issues of peace and war they should accept the advice of His Majesty's Government, and that if they did not accept it His Majesty's Government would then be automatically absolved of their guarantee.

If the record is accurate, the French were either too polite or too stunned to comment on this preposterous proposal, which would have vitiated the guarantee and left the Czechs, vis-à-vis Britain, exactly where they already were. Perhaps realizing that his Foreign Secretary needed straightening out, Chamberlain announced that the guarantee "was a very serious question for the British Government and he and his colleagues would therefore like to retire to discuss it."

After a considerable adjournment, the meeting was resumed at seven-thirty, but only briefly. Chamberlain announced that the British delegation had agreed that their government "must give the assurances for which the French Government had asked." Furthermore, they had prepared a draft "in the form of a message to the Czechoslovak Government" which embodied the guarantee. He proposed an adjournment so that the French could consider the draft during dinner, and the delegations parted until ten-thirty in the evening.

At this final session, the French accepted the substance of the British draft. There was much discussion, but apparently no significant changes were made. Chamberlain wanted to send the message to Prague immediately; he stressed the danger of delay and pointed out that his delegation had taken decisions without consulting their Cabinet colleagues. But Daladier insisted on submission of the proposition to the French Cabinet, while promising Chamberlain that he would have an answer by noon of the following day. It was finally agreed that the text could be immediately telegraphed to the British and French ministers in Prague, and held by them until they were authorized by telephone to "make their *démarche.*"

Not content with all this, Chamberlain asked Daladier: "What would be the position if Dr. Beneš said 'No' in reply to our representations?" Daladier "did not think such a reply would be possible" but, with a last flicker of pride, declared that if the settlement were to "fall through" the Franco-Czech treaty "would come into force." Still pressing, Chamberlain asked whether it would thus be left to Beneš "to take a decision which would certainly involve France and might perhaps also involve . . . [Britain] in war"—thus raising explicitly the possibility that Britain might not join with France. Daladier replied that "the strongest pressure would have to be brought to bear on Dr. Beneš" to ensure acceptance. And then, shortly after midnight, the conference was ended.

In the small hours of September 19, the agreed message was telephoned to Basil Newton for delivery to Beneš as soon as the French Cabinet had approved it:

1. The representatives of the French and British Governments have been in consultation today on the general situation, and have considered the British Prime Minister's report of his conversation with Herr Hitler. British Ministers also placed before their French colleagues their conclusions derived from the account furnished to them of the work of his Mission by Lord Runciman. We are both convinced that, after recent events, the point has now been reached where the further maintenance within the boundaries of the Czechoslovak State of the districts mainly inhabited by Sudeten-Deutsch cannot in fact continue any longer without imperilling the interests of Czechoslovakia herself and of European peace. In the light of these considerations both Governments have been compelled to the conclusion that the maintenance of peace and the safety of Czechoslovakia's vital interests cannot effectively be assured unless these areas are now transferred to the Reich.

2. This could be done either by direct transfer or as the result of a plebiscite. We realise the difficulties involved in a plebiscite, and we are aware of your objections already expressed to this course, particularly the possibility of far-reaching repercussions if the matter were treated on the basis of so wide a principle. For this reason we anticipate in the absence of indication to the contrary that you may prefer to deal with the Sudeten-Deutsch problem by the method of direct transfer, and as a case by itself.

3. The areas for transfer would probably have to include areas with over 50 per cent. of German inhabitants, but we should hope to arrange by negotiations provisions for adjustment of frontiers, where circumstances

render it necessary, by some international body including a Czech representative. We are satisfied that the transfer of smaller areas based on a higher percentage would not meet the case.

4. The international body referred to might also be charged with questions of possible exchange of population on the basis of right to opt within some specified time limit.

5. We recognise that if the Czechoslovak Government is prepared to concur in the measures proposed, involving material changes in the conditions of the State, they are entitled to ask for some assurance of their future security.

6. Accordingly His Majesty's Government in the United Kingdom would be prepared, as a contribution to the pacification of Europe, to join in an international guarantee of the new boundaries of the Czechoslovak State against unprovoked aggression. One of the principal conditions of such a guarantee would be the safeguarding of the independence of Czechoslovakia by the substitution of a general guarantee against unprovoked aggression in place of existing treaties which involve reciprocal obligations of a military character.

7. Both the French and British Government recognise how great is the sacrifice thus required of the Czechoslovak Government in the cause of peace. But because that cause is common both to Europe in general and in particular to Czechoslovakia herself, they have felt it their duty jointly to set forth frankly the conditions essential to secure it.

8. The Prime Minister must resume conversation with Herr Hitler not later than Wednesday, and earlier if possible. We therefore feel we must ask for your reply at earliest possible moment.

Thus once more Chamberlain and his inner group committed Britain to a course of action and confronted their colleagues with a *fait accompli,* of which the guarantee proved the most touchy part when the Cabinet met the next morning and were told what had been done. Hore-Belisha was especially disturbed; he thought the amputated Czechoslovakia would be economically and strategically unstable, and "it was difficult to see how it could survive." Britain was incapable of implementing the guarantee, which was no "solution" but only "a postponement of the evil day" and "there was a risk that we were putting our signature to something which might involve us in dishonour."

The discussion turned acrimonious, and Inskip thought that Chamberlain was "tired and dispirited." With the aid of Simon and Maugham he sought to limit the scope of the guarantee, pointing out that it covered only "unprovoked aggression," while freely admitting that it would be difficult to implement: "Its main value would lie in its deterrent effect."

How a guarantee which could not be implemented could serve as a deterrent the Prime Minister did not say. It was all pretty lame, but there was little the Cabinet could do about it. Unity with France and an answer satisfactory to Hitler were the two essentials, and the French had been assured that the guarantee would be given. Chamberlain had taken the reins, and no one wished to move him out of the driver's seat. Even Duff Cooper and Winterton were in accord, the former declaring that the "prospect of war was so appalling that 'postponement of the evil day' was the best course."

Leslie Burgin raised the question of compensation for Czechs living in the areas to be ceded, and Chamberlain had to admit that the matter had not been discussed with the French. Oliver Stanley then made four practical suggestions to guide the coming negotiations with Hitler: (1) that the bare majority determinant demanded by him was reasonable for a plebiscite but too low for an outright cession; (2) Germany should compensate both Czechs and Germans who wished to leave the ceded areas; (3) the German Army should demobilize as soon as the International Commission was set up; and (4) Henlein's Sudeten "corps" should be disbanded. As Inskip noted, these proposals were "all of them good, but of doubtful value unless Hitler was agreeable." Chamberlain ignored the merits of Stanley's proposals, declaring that "it was no use returning to Hitler with the intention of imposing conditions," but indicated that "if all went well" he might achieve (3) and (4).

Simon, in his usual role of flatterer-in-chief, assured his colleagues that the Anglo-French meeting had removed the basis for any claim that the Government was preventing the French from fulfilling their commitment, and declared that "they had gone away with heart and courage restored to them by the Prime Minister." On this slightly sour note of unity the Cabinet endorsed the Berchtesgaden understanding and the agreements with the French, and adjourned. Without waiting for word from Paris, Chamberlain telephoned via Henderson a message to Hitler: "I have now got so far with my consultations that I anticipate that it will be possible to resume my conversations with Your Excellency on Wednesday September 21."

Oliver Harvey was among those at Croydon early that morning to bid the French delegation Godspeed, and, far from finding them "with heart and courage restored," he thought "they looked wretched." Immediately following their return to Paris, the Cabinet assembled at the Elysée Palace. Bonnet and Chautemps spoke in favor of the "Anglo-French" plan. According to Daladier's postwar testimony, there was general regret at the "sad necessity" which confronted the ministers, but, in view of the British attitude and lack of desire to go to war without British aid, the Cabinet was unanimous in approving the course of action as settled in London.*

Shortly after noon the British were informed of the French Cabinet's action. In accordance with instructions from London and Paris, at two o'clock on September 19, Messrs. Newton and Lacroix waited upon Beneš and delivered the joint message.

3

Eduard Beneš had first learned of Chamberlain's Berchtesgaden trip on September 14, by telephone from Jan Masaryk. "It's impossible" was the President's immediate comment.

---

* Alexander Werth wrote (in *France and Munich,* p. 263) that there were "reservations" by Reynaud, Mandel, and Champetier de Ribes, and that Reynaud extracted from Bonnet a promise not to press the Czechs to accept the plan. A cryptic note in the Daladier papers lends substance to Werth's account, but if Bonnet in fact made such a promise, he broke it within the hour when he met with the Czech Minister, Stepan Osusky. At London, the French had agreed that the strongest possible pressure should be brought to bear on Prague.

By the morning of the nineteenth, however, Beneš knew, in general, what he had to expect from his diplomatic visitors. Enough of the content of the Anglo-French agreement had leaked into the London and Paris newspapers, or otherwise come to his knowledge, to prompt him to telephone Ambassador Jan Masaryk in London and warn that the Czech Government would never accept such a proposition. Furthermore, Bonnet had already told Osusky the essentials of the Anglo-French plan, and the Czech Ambassador's report was probably on Beneš' desk. It concluded with Bonnet's warning that "the British Government was so cautious" that, if Prague rejected the plan and war between Germany and Czechoslovakia ensued, France "would refuse support." No wonder Osusky, so often the recipient of French assurances, told the newsmen outside the Quai d'Orsay that Czechoslovakia "has been sentenced without even being heard."

Despite these forewarnings, Newton found Beneš "greatly moved and agitated" by the message. The British Ambassador's report continued:

> His first comment was that as his Government had not been consulted when questions of such deep concern to it had been discussed he did not propose to reply. He was moreover a constitutional President and must refer the matter to his Government, and also, to Parliament. My French colleague drew his attention to critical and urgent nature of the question and I was able to reinforce his remarks. . . . President seemed to be impressed though later on he indicated that he would not be able to reply today.
>
> Speaking with self-control but with great bitterness he showed that he felt that, after all the efforts which he and his Government had made, they were being abandoned. I pointed out to him that at least he was being offered a new and important guarantee by His Majesty's Government. . . .
>
> Dr. Beneš listened with attention but showed that he felt guarantees which he already possessed had proved valueless. He said he did not believe proposed solution would prove final or be anything more than a stage toward eventual domination by Germany and develop further German ambitions. . . .

Nevertheless, Newton told London that he thought Beneš was "more likely to accept than to refuse and . . . very receptive to any reason which will help him to justify acceptance to his people." The ambassador's impression was fortified by his military attaché, Colonel Stronge, who had previously visited the Czech General Staff and had been apprized of their opinion that since "Czechoslovakia was being betrayed by France and abandoned by Britain, it would be suicidal to fight Germany single-handed," and therefore "it was not proposed to resist." This information came as a great relief to Lacroix, who "had been afraid there might be an immediate mobilization."

There is no available documentation on the Czech Cabinet's initial reaction, but the account by Beneš' close associate, the journalist Hubert Ripka, is credible:

> When the Czechoslovak Ministers, assembled at the President's Palace, were informed of these incredible proposals, they were all—and, I would emphasize, all without exception—unanimously in favor of rejecting them. To answer France and England with a rejection of their proposals was not easy,

for it was necessary to take into consideration all the possible consequences which might arise from such a rejection. . . . The Government immediately consulted the military authorities, and invited General Syrový, the Inspector-General of the Czechoslovak armed forces, and General Krejčí, Chief of the General Staff, to attend its discussions. The generals thought that it would be extremely dangerous to risk measuring our forces with those of Germany, unless the help of France were assured.

It was a cruel dilemma, sharpened by the overwhelming evidence of public opposition to accepting the terms. Beneš played for time, slightly encouraged by signs of dissension in both Britain and France. Jan Masaryk, very popular in London, was telling Eden and De La Warr and even Runciman that the plan was unacceptable. Eden conveyed his "distress" to Halifax and, according to Masaryk, he and others advised the Czechs to refuse a prompt answer on the ground that the Czech Parliament must pass on so vital a matter.*

Churchill visited Halifax, who gave him a pessimistic account of the French military situation, whereupon Churchill took off for Paris to consult Reynaud and Mandel. Churchill found them on the brink of resignation but persuaded them to stay in office so that the French Government would not be "weakened by the loss of its two most capable and resolute men." Léger, as always both critical and cautious, told Osusky on the twentieth that he accepted the Anglo-French proposition "in principle" but "with the greatest reserve," so that Chamberlain could break off the negotiations with Hitler, presumably if proper conditions and guarantees were not embodied.

Not unmindful of his big eastern ally, Beneš contacted the Soviet Ambassador, Sergei Alexandrovsky, and asked him to get Moscow's answer to the question whether the Soviet Union would support Czechoslovakia if the French did so. Of course the answer, from Potemkin, was affirmative; the Russians had repeatedly declared that they would honor their conditional commitments if the French fulfilled theirs, and on the twenty-first, at Geneva, Litvinov reiterated his government's intention in a speech to the League Assembly. Beneš also met with Klement Gottwald, leader of the Czechoslovak Communist Party, who told the President that if there was a question of the Soviet Union doing more than was called for by its conditional guarantee, the request should be precisely formulated and submitted. At this time, however, Beneš took no such action.

But neither the Soviet attitude nor the stirrings of the doubters and dissenters in London† and Paris had any effect on the march of events. As soon as the French Government's agreement was in hand, Cadogan sent word to Henderson —on what basis other than overconfidence does not appear—that "the Czech reply will be available this afternoon," and that the Germans should be alerted to make arrangements for the second Chamberlain-Hitler conference, which had been scheduled for Wednesday, September 21.

* Eden in *The Reckoning* (p. 29) describes a telephone conversation with Masaryk on September 19, but says nothing about giving such advice.
† According to Harvey, disagreement extended to the Royal Household, where King George VI's private secretary, Sir Alexander Hardinge, was "horrified" at the government's attitude. The King himself was unhappy; on September 17 he wrote to the assistant private secretary, Sir Alan Lascelles: "The French arrive tomorrow and if they won't stand up to Hitler how can we and the world must be told it is their fault and not ours."

Within the hour Henderson telephoned Hitler's suggestion that they meet in Godesberg. Halifax had already directed Newton to "emphasize the urgent need for a reply from President Beneš tonight or tomorrow," since Chamberlain's trip "cannot be postponed beyond Wednesday, and he would be in a most difficult situation, and indeed it might be disastrous, if he should have to go without any answer from Prague." But the afternoon passed without any response, and toward its end Chamberlain was obliged to inform Hitler that the time for their meeting could not yet be fixed. Henderson, of course, was beating the drums for an immediate response, and just before midnight Halifax had to warn him that Prague might not "give in a few hours final answer on . . . such vital decision."

The morning of Tuesday the twentieth passed with no word from the Czechs, who were still casting about for help. As Beneš put it to Masaryk, what was needed was a "formula" meaning neither "yes" nor "no," so that Prague could throw the issue into further negotiation. In Washington the chargé was vainly pleading with the State Department for a statement of support for the Czech position.

Early in the afternoon word leaked out that, instead of accepting the Anglo-French proposals, the Prague government planned to invoke the German-Czech arbitration treaty. Immediately Newton and Lacroix were sent into action to impress upon the Czechs "the dangers of bargaining and giving any excuse for precipitating war." Lord Runciman, shorn of his spurious "independence," was busy drafting a report for the purpose, as he himself put it, of doing "everything to make the P.M.'s position easier."

In Paris, Phipps suggested to Bonnet that "the moment seemed to have come when we should inform M. Beneš that, unless his reply was an acceptance pure and simple, France and Great Britain would wash their hands of Czechoslovakia in the event of a German attack." This caused consternation at the Foreign Office where, as Harvey recorded, "it was feared that it would be used as evidence that we had pressed the French Government to evade their treaty obligations"—which, of course, was precisely what had happened. Meanwhile, in view of the delay, Ribbentrop himself had suggested that the Godesberg meeting be postponed to Thursday the twenty-second. The British readily agreed,* and a communiqué to that effect was issued, although no reply from Prague had as yet been received.

It finally came at eight o'clock in the evening of September 20. On its face, it was a rejection of the Anglo-French proposals, on the ground that they had been "drawn up without previous consultation with representatives of Czechoslovakia," that the proposed cessions would mutilate Czechoslovakia economically and militarily, and that if carried out, the "question of peace would in no way be settled." Instead, the Czechs invoked the arbitration treaty with Germany, and declared themselves "ready to accept whatever arbitral decision

---

* Henderson advised London that the Germans would "hold the situation," and that the one-day delay was "a good risk to take." Of course it was; the German attack could not have been launched for another week, which no doubt was why Ribbentrop was moved to suggest the postponement.

might be made." The note concluded with a "new and last appeal" to the French and British governments "to reconsider their point of view."

But the Czechs did not say that they would fight rather than accept the Anglo-French plan, and the closing appeal for reconsideration left the door open for acquiescence if London and Paris remained adamant. When Krofta handed the document to Newton, he remarked that "a door was left open," and Newton, refusing to treat it as final, admonished the Foreign Minister that the appeal to arbitration was "folly," and that "refusal or evasion at this last moment meant the destruction of their beautiful country, while acceptance meant retention of most of what mattered to Czechs and Slovaks." Newton then advised London:

> I have very good reason . . . to believe that . . . reply handed to me by Minister for Foreign Affairs should not be regarded as final. A solution must be imposed upon Government as without such pressure many of its members are too committed to be able to accept what they realize to be necessary.
> If I can deliver a kind of ultimatum to President Benes . . . he and his Government will feel able to bow to *force majeure*. It might be to the effect that in view of His Majesty's Government the Czechoslovak Government must accept the proposals without reserve and without further delay failing which His Majesty's Government will take no further interest in the fate of the country.

This, of course, was precisely the attitude which Phipps was urging on Bonnet and which greatly troubled Whitehall, not for its actuality but its appearance. But the "ultimatum" idea was now approved in London. A midnight conference at Downing Street, of Chamberlain, Halifax, Wilson, and Cadogan, produced a reply, described by the last-named as "driving the screw home on poor Czechs," which was but little softer than what Phipps and Newton had proposed:

> You [Newton] should at once join with your French colleague in pointing out to Czech Government that their reply in no way meets the critical situation which Anglo-French proposals were designed to avert. . . . You should urge the Czech Government to withdraw this reply and urgently consider an alternative that takes account of realities. . . . On basis of reply now under consideration I would have no hope of any useful results ensuing from a second visit to Herr Hitler, and Prime Minister would be obliged to cancel arrangements for it. . . . If on reconsideration Czech Government feel bound to reject our advice, they must of course be free to take any action that they think appropriate to meet the situation that may thereafter develop.*

Meanwhile, through Lacroix, messages were passing between Prague and Paris, the true import of which still remains in controversy. As Lacroix was preparing his report on the Czech arbitration counterproposal, Hodža summoned him and asked if it was certain that, in the event of war, France would stand aside (*"se déroberait"*). Lacroix, according to his own account, proposed that he put the question to Paris; Hodža replied that this might take too long, and then

---

* According to Harvey, this last sentence "was designed to meet the danger of Phipps's suggestion—we do not say in so many words that we will wash our hands of them."

stated: "I assume *a priori* that France will not march, and if you can get tonight a confirming telegram from your government, the President of the Republic will yield. It is the only way to save the peace." Hodža added that he was speaking with the approval of Beneš and the General Staff.

Lacroix telegraphed this information to Paris, adding, that "the Czech leaders need this protection in order to accept the Anglo-French proposition." Of course, such a message would involve an explicit repudiation of France's obligations under the treaty with Czechoslovakia, and the French were at first in doubt whether to do this without Cabinet approval. But Daladier and Bonnet, after President Lebrun's approval had been obtained by telephone, authorized Lacroix to tell Beneš that, if his government refused the Anglo-French terms, Britain would stand aside; that without Britain, French aid would be ineffective; and that therefore France would also refuse support (*"la France ne s'y associera pas"*).*

On the basis of this interchange, and particularly of Lacroix's telegram following his talk with Hodža, Bonnet and others gave currency to the story that the French Government did not, on its own initiative, repudiate the commitment to Czechoslovakia. Rather, it was said to have been done at the insistence of the Czech Government, which had decided voluntarily to accept the Anglo-French plan but wished the French repudiation for domestic political reasons—i.e., to quiet its critics by claiming that the Anglo-French terms had been accepted only under the pressure of the French betrayal.

There is no basis for such an interpretation of this episode. The Czech military chiefs had indeed stressed the danger in taking on Germany single-handed, but there is no evidence that the Czechs were reluctant to defend themselves if France made good on her treaty commitments.† Bonnet, on the other hand, was of all the French and British leaders the most anxious to avoid war at all costs, and had already told Osusky that France would stand aside from any conflict which might result from a rejection of the Anglo-French plan. For the Prague government it was obviously essential, both for informed decision-making and for the record, to know *with certainty* whether or not France would come to their aid if they refused that plan and were then attacked by Germany.

Accordingly, the motivation for Hodža's inquiry is abundantly apparent. Whether, by the evening of September 20, the Czechs were already sure that the French would let them down and were primarily seeking official verification, or whether they were still uncertain and sought a categorical statement of French intentions as a basis for their own decision, is a matter of conjecture. Probably

* For Bonnet's account of the episode, see his *De Washington au Quai d'Orsay*, pp. 246–53, which should be compared with Werth, *France and Munich*, pp. 267–69; Ripka, *Munich: Before and After*, pp. 86–93; Wheeler-Bennett, *Munich: Prologue to Tragedy*, pp. 120–26; and Pierre Comert's testimony in *Temoinages*, vol. 8, p. 2178. Bonnet wrote that Léger and Jules Henry were with Daladier and himself when the decision was made; Comert, chief of the Quai d'Orsay's press office, testified that Léger was not present and that Bonnet consulted his own "brain trust."

† It seems clear that, until receipt of the Anglo-French terms, the Czech leaders fully expected to be soon at war, which no doubt accounts for Jan Masaryk's urgent telephone requests to have his personal funds transferred out of Czechoslovakia.

both reasons were operative, and neither supports the Bonnet interpretation, which can surely be labeled a deliberate distortion.*

In any event, the midnight deliberations at Downing Street and the Quai d'Orsay led to the same conclusion, and the two ministers were instructed, in substance, to make it clear to Beneš that unless the Anglo-French terms were promptly accepted, Czechoslovakia would be on her own, confronting, in the words of Halifax's message to Newton, "a situation for which we could take no responsibility." Pursuant to Newton's instructions to "act immediately at whatever hour," he and Lacroix waited on President Beneš at about two o'clock in the morning of Wednesday, September 21. The British *démarche* was available in writing; Lacroix delivered his tidings orally, and Beneš insisted on written confirmation that France would not honor her obligations. After more than an hour of this confrontation, Beneš promised an answer by midday.

At six o'clock that morning, Beneš met with the Cabinet ministers, the heads of the political parties represented in the Government, and Generals Syrový and Krejcí. No contemporaneous record of the deliberations is available.† However, both Beneš and the Minister of the Interior, Josef Cerny, subsequently wrote about the proceedings, and their accounts are mutually confirmatory.

Beneš' account of the nocturnal visits of Newton and Lacroix aroused great indignation, and the initial reaction was to reject the Anglo-French proposals, move the civil government offices from Prague to Moravia and Slovakia, and fight it out. But further discussion (in which Beneš did not take an active part) raised doubts. Some, incredulous of the positions taken in London and Paris, wished to send special delegations to the two capitals. Then the two generals were asked to answer the question: "Shall we or shall we not go to war without allies?" The answer was:

> . . . considering Germany's preparations, the annexation of Austria, the hostility of Hungary and Poland, and the attitude now revealed on the part of Britain and France, our only capacity, from a military point of view, was a brief and difficult defense. How things would actually develop could not be predicted, but they could not recommend a single-handed war against Germany. What the Soviets would do by way of practical military action was not clear. As far as they knew, Moscow had given no precise information of this kind.

According to the Czech chief of military intelligence, General Frantisek Moravec, Krejcí was asked how long his forces, without French and British support, could hold out, and he replied: "About three weeks." According to Cerny:

---

* On September 22, Osusky informed Beneš that Bonnet had told the French Cabinet that Prague had requested the ultimatum for domestic political "coverage." The next day Beneš sent an indignant denial to Osusky and authorized its delivery to Daladier and the three "pro-Czech" ministers—Reynaud, Mandel, and Champetier de Ribes.

† But such a record is probably in the Prague archives, for the annotators of Beneš' memoirs published in Prague in 1968 corrected Beneš' erroneous statement that the meeting began at eight o'clock by referring to the "Government protocol" stating that the meeting lasted from six to eight-fifteen in the morning.

President Beneš, at the request of the Government and the political representatives, again called the Russian Minister [Alexandrovsky] to ascertain the final standpoint of the Soviet Government; after a prolonged, very emotional discussion with the Minister he informed the meeting that "the Soviets are willing to help Czechoslovakia in case of an attack by Nazi Germany, but only if France, Czechoslovakia's ally, also comes to her rescue." In the face of this news and the adamant attitude of both the French and British Ministers, the Government and all chairmen of political parties, on the recommendation of President Beneš, unanimously accepted the Franco-British proposals.

In his memoirs, Beneš also wrote that if the French would not fulfill their commitments Moscow would take the matter to the League of Nations and "abide by the decision." When Beneš complained that this would take too long, Alexandrovsky brought further word that, if Czechoslovakia submitted a plea to Geneva, that would be enough to warrant Soviet aid.

But all this was of little import, for Beneš had already decided against going to war with the Soviet Union as the only ally. As he viewed it, his country would then be regarded as a "Soviet satellite," there would be domestic difficulties with the Agrarians and other conservatives, and Poland and Hungary, together with "reactionary circles in the West" might join forces in a "war to the death against Bolshevism," and side with Nazi Germany against Russia.

Accordingly, later that morning Newton and Lacroix were informed that the Czech Government's "reply is affirmative" and that an official note accepting the Anglo-French terms "will be sent as soon as possible."

But it took all day to play out the miserable scene. At eight-thirty in the morning Beneš called in Lacroix and read him a draft statement, which was expected to be delivered to both ministers "shortly afterward." Then at ten Beneš told Lacroix by telephone that "difficulties had been experienced with leaders of political parties." Osusky telephoned to Beneš, urging the President not to allow himself to be rushed into capitulation, and describing the French declaration as "not decisive." By noon the statement was still undelivered; Lacroix had already warned Beneš of the "extremely serious consequences which would follow from any delay now," and Newton told Hodža that he "could not wait much longer before warning my compatriots to leave the country."

The immediate difficulty in Prague was that, while the Cabinet had ratified the decision to yield, the issue had still to be presented to the so-called "Coalition Twenty"—the parliamentary representatives of the political parties included in the Government. According to Ripka's account:

After a detailed report by the Prime Minister, this body also, after a session lasting till 1 p.m., took note of [i.e., accepted] the decision made by the President of the Republic and the Government. The depression which prevailed . . . defies description, and it was only with the greatest self-sacrifice and internal revulsion that the fatal decision was accepted. It was generally felt that it would be an inadmissible adventure to embark on a struggle with Germany in the state of absolute isolation, to which we had been reduced by the defection of our Western friends and allies. This opinion was shared also in competent military circles.

It is true that a certain group of politicians and soldiers did not agree with the capitulation and insisted that the honour and interest of the nation . . . demanded that we should fight Germany if she attacked us, even if we had to fight alone. . . . In any case, whether they were right or wrong, the Czechoslovak politicians who were ready to risk war, even in isolation, were in an absolute minority. It was evident that the policy of resistance which they advised would entail mortal danger for the nation, because . . . we were not only isolated, but almost completely surrounded. For, side by side with Germany . . . Poland and Hungary were preparing to act against us.

Meanwhile, both the Quai d'Orsay and Whitehall were fuming, though the heat was greater in London, where Neville Chamberlain was readying himself for his flight to Godesberg the following morning. On Halifax's instructions, at about midafternoon Cadogan telephoned to Jan Masaryk, asking the ambassador immediately to telephone to Beneš, "pointing out that Prime Minister has arranged to leave for Germany tomorrow morning, and that it is essential that acceptance by Czechoslovak Government be received without delay." Masaryk replied that he had just been in touch with Beneš, who had told him that the acceptance was being drafted and would be delivered to Newton and Lacroix by four o'clock.

In Paris, Bonnet's main concern was the written answer, to the question originally put by Hodža, which the President had demanded of Lacroix during the early morning conference. This presented the Quai d'Orsay with exactly the same problem that had been resolved in London by the midnight message to Newton: how to tell the Czechs that the treaty would be dishonored without saying so "in so many words." Bonnet was equal to the problem; the resulting document stated:

> France, in agreement with England, has put forward the only plan which she judges sufficient, under present circumstances, to prevent a German entry into Czechoslovakia.
>
> In rejecting the Franco-British proposition, the Government of Czechoslovakia takes responsibility for bringing about Germany's recourse to force. It likewise shatters the Franco-British solidarity which has just been established, and thus renders French aid ineffective. These are the advices which have already been given, notably by I myself [i.e., Lacroix] since July, and on the 20th of September by M. Georges Bonnet to M. Osusky.
>
> Czechoslovakia thus assumes a risk which we have consciously guarded against. Czechoslovakia ought herself to understand the conclusions which France could justifiably draw if the Franco-British proposal is not immediately accepted.

So it was left to the Czechs to "understand" what the French Government was ashamed to say. In this they found no difficulty of comprehension, but Beneš still had a card—not very strong—to play. He asked for a "further written declaration by French and British Governments that if Czechoslovakia accepts Anglo-French proposals and if nonetheless Germany attacks Czechoslovakia the two Governments will come to her assistance." It was surely not an unreasonable request, but English if not French patience was exhausted. Newton "pointed out to Dr. Benes that it was extremely dangerous to make new conditions for acceptance at the last moment." At his urgent request, Beneš transformed the "condition" into a "wish."

And so, at about five o'clock in the afternoon of September 21, Newton and Lacroix were summoned to the Foreign Ministry, where Krofta handed them the Czech Government's note of acceptance, constituting the basis of consent on which Neville Chamberlain would go to Godesberg:

> The Czechoslovak Government, forced by circumstances, yielding to un-heard-of-pressure and drawing the consequences from the communication of the French and British Governments of September 21, 1938, in which both Governments expressed their point of view as to help for Czechoslovakia in case she should refuse to accept the Franco-British proposals and should be attacked by Germany, accepts the Anglo-French proposals with feelings of pain, assuming that both Governments will do everything in order to safeguard the vital interests of the Czechoslovak State in their application. It notes with regret that these proposals were elaborated without previous consultation with the Czechoslovak Government.
>
> Deeply regretting that their proposal of arbitration has not been accepted, the Czechoslovak Government accept these proposals as a whole, from which the principle of a guarantee, as formulated in the note, cannot be detached, and accept them with the further assumption that both Governments will not permit a German invasion of Czechoslovak territory, which will remain Czechoslovak up to the moment when it will be possible to carry out its transfer after the determination of the new frontier by the International Commission referred to in the proposals.
>
> In the opinion of the Czechoslovak Government, the Franco-British proposals imply that all details of the practical realization of the Franco-British proposals will be determined in agreement with the Czechoslovak Government.

4

"I have always believed that Benes was wrong to yield," Winston Churchill wrote in his classic account of the Second World War's approach:* "He should have defended his fortress line. Once fighting had begun, in my opinion at that time, France would have moved to his aid in a surge of national passion, and Britain would have rallied to France almost immediately." Perhaps so, and there were some in Prague who nursed such hopes and urged resistance. But even Hubert Ripka, who was one of them, soon questioned his own earlier optimism:

> After what we have seen take place during the weeks which followed, it is perhaps doubtful whether the hopes which were entertained by some of us were justified. It is more probable that we would have shared a fate similar to that of Republican Spain, to whose help neither France nor England came, even though their vital interests were evidently at stake.

* *The Gathering Storm* (1948), p. 302.

There is no doubt that the sights and sounds of the Wehrmacht clobbering a courageously resisting small nation, and perhaps laying its cities in ruins, would have shocked a world not yet hardened to such carnage. But how strong would the political impact have been? Guernica and Barcelona were widely deplored but did not measurably influence British or French policies toward Spain. Unlike physical waves, which diminish in strength as they spread from the point of origin, waves of horrified indignation mount higher as they leave the area of responsibility. No doubt such a spectacle would have been denounced from every pulpit and platform in America, where there was no likelihood of involvement. But what would have been the impact on the decision-making process in France and Britain?

Of course the brutal assault *à outrance* which Hitler had planned would have raised waves of high feeling in Britain and, to a lesser degree, in France. In England, the divulgence of the Anglo-French terms had already raised what Cadogan described, on the twenty-first, as a "Press campaign . . . against 'Betrayal of Czechoslovakia.' " But the English leaders, whatever their lack of judgment and prescience, were men of strong moral fiber, and they were profoundly convinced that they were doing the right thing. Cadogan's own diary reaction to the press criticism is indicative; it was "inevitable, and must be faced." And he added: *"How* much courage is needed to be a coward!"

Furthermore, for the Czechs to have rejected the plan and taken to their guns, thus exposing France and Britain as fair weather friends and precipitating wrenching controversy in both countries, would surely have aroused resentment as well as sympathy, especially in France, where virtually all the press except on the extreme left and right had lined up solidly behind the Anglo-French plan.

But however one reads the might-have-beens, it was asking too much of the Czechs that they should unilaterally call the turn of such dire and far-reaching issues. It was unrealistic to expect the soldiers and statesmen in Prague, however sturdy, to engage a determined and encircling foe ten times their strength, with Poland and Hungary snapping at their heels, on the speculative possibility that Britain and France would be shamed into action.

Perhaps that is the way Beneš saw the issue. He knew his Europe very well, and was wise enough not to overvalue the cries of anguish and sympathy generated by the sacrifices Britain and France were demanding. For even the anguished and sympathetic were, for the most part, quite unready to confront the threat that Hitler was posing to the European order. Léon Blum spoke for most of them when he wrote in *Le Populaire* on September 20:

> War has probably been avoided. But under such conditions that I who have never ceased to struggle for peace, I who have for many years dedicated my life to it, cannot feel joy. I feel myself torn between a sense of cowardly relief and shame.

CHAPTER 29

The Godesberg Ultimatum

1

Sir Alexander Cadogan, pouring out his feelings to his diary on the night of September 21 and ruminating on the courage of necessary cowardice, concluded his entry: "We must go on being cowards up to our limit, but *not beyond*. I have tried to impress this. But what of the future?" The answer depended, of course, on where the "limit" was to be drawn, and whether the line was visible to Sir Neville Chamberlain, as he packed his bags for the flight to Godesberg and his second rendezvous with the Fuehrer.

The Prime Minister, to be sure, was well aware that Prague's acceptance of the Anglo-French proposal was only the beginning of a resolution of the crisis. Hitler might well put forward additional demands, and there were numerous questions which the Anglo-French plan did not cover, of which two—the Polish and Hungarian claims, and the timing and method of transferring to Germany the territories to be ceded by Czechoslovakia—were the most important.

On September 19, shortly after the Anglo-French memorandum was presented to Beneš, Halifax called in Cadogan and other staff members to discuss the transfer problem. He apparently hoped that Hitler would accept "a joint German-Czech Commission with a British Chairman to supervise the transfer of territory," and Harvey recorded acidly: "He is very anxious to have British troops sent to show the flag. He believes naïvely that a few British regimental bands marching up and down the Sudeten areas would suffice to keep order."

A much more realistic note was struck by Sir Orme Sargent, who accurately foresaw the likelihood that Hitler, faced with acceptance of his Berchtesgaden demands, would ask for more, such as the cession of Sudeten minority areas "contiguous to the majority districts," control of Czechoslovakia's foreign relations, and satisfaction of the Polish and Hungarian demands. Sargent's memorandum, circulated September 20, stimulated Cadogan to draw the "limit" to which he later referred in his diary:

> I should have thought it was quite clear that we have gone to the limit to satisfy what Hitler said were his claims, on the ground that . . . they were not entirely unjustifiable. If he goes beyond them, he will have gone beyond our limit, and there will be nothing more to be done but to oppose them . . . and events will take command. . . .

That same day the Prime Minister turned his attention to these problems, at a meeting with the inner circle of ministers and staff. The proposed gambit for Godesberg was not very positive; Chamberlain would report Beneš' agreement to a transfer of territory and solicit Hitler's "views" on "the steps . . . to be taken to give effect to the whole settlement." Such an approach would, of course, give Hitler the initiative at the outset of the negotiations. This would diminish whatever prospect there was of extracting the concessions from Hitler which the conferees thought would be desirable "from the point of view of public opinion in this country," such as an increase in the necessary percentage of Sudeten Germans in the areas to be ceded, withdrawal of German troops from the frontier, and disbanding the Henlein "Legion."

The focus of discussion was order-keeping in the territories to be ceded or subjected to plebiscite. Halifax's desire to use British troops had run into difficulties; the Chiefs of Staff had advised that three divisions would be necessary. Britain had nothing like that many troops to spare, and it appeared "most unlikely that other neutral countries would consent to send troops." Sudeten German forces "were likely to come to blows with certain sections of the people." Occupation by the German Army "had the political disadvantage that it looked as though Germany was being allowed to enter into possession at once before she had made any concessions herself"—which of course was not only the appearance but the actuality.

The conferees finally agreed to seek Beneš' consent to occupation of the "German districts" by the Wehrmacht, and of the "mixed districts" by local police and Czech troops, with numerous British "observers" also present. To redraw the German-Czech frontier, a three-member commission—Germany, Czechoslovakia, and Britain—would be set up: "Italy had no interest in the matter and had better be kept out of it. France would probably be glad not to be represented on the Commission." The British member would be chairman and would decide all issues on which Germany and Czechoslovakia could not agree. Considering all that had gone before, it does seem that Chamberlain and his colleagues were in a dream world if they seriously hoped that Hitler would consider such arrangements.

The conferees also discussed the promised guarantee of Czechoslovakia, and decided that Russia should be asked to participate, but that Germany should make a separate nonaggression pact with Czechoslovakia. Cadogan thought the meeting a "waste of time," since Hitler would probably refuse to discuss details, "and unless he accepts broad settlement, we needn't bother about them." He even had trouble staying awake, but Sir John Simon, ever the lawyer, was "in his element."

When the Big Four met again the following morning, the initial focus was on Polish and Hungarian claims. The decibel level of these had been rising steadily since the Berchtesgaden meeting, the theme being that whatever the Sudeten Germans were to get must likewise be given to the Poles in Teschen and the Hungarians in Slovakia and Ruthenia. The Polish ambassadors in London and Paris were camping in Halifax's and Bonnet's anterooms, and were far from satisfied with the answers they were getting from the two foreign ministers, both of whom tried vainly to persuade their guests to put off the settlement of these issues until after the Sudeten crisis had been resolved.

What was to be done if Hitler should raise these issues at Godesberg? Chamberlain agreed that he would try to exclude them from the discussion, and that if Hitler insisted, he would break off the meeting and return to London to consult the Cabinet. Cadogan, momentarily reassured, recorded that the Prime Minister "seems agreed he can't go further than he has gone, and he can't champion Poles and Hungarians. This is *essential*. I hope he'll stick it."

The conferees then returned to the vexed question of policing the Sudeten areas pending the cession, and sent for Hore-Belisha and Lord Gort. Their report on the possible use of British troops was gloomy. Considering the size and geographical dispersion of the Sudeten areas, three divisions would be needed; Britain could at most supply one, and even for that would have to call up some of the Army Reserve. Furthermore, it would take three weeks to assemble and dispatch such a force and, as Gort pointed out, "it would mean locking up in Central Europe half of the force which we had immediately available for despatch overseas." Hore-Belisha remarked other disadvantages. Weak and scattered forces would be helpless against serious disturbances; the purpose would not be to use the troops, but only to "show the flag." If there were real trouble, the troops would have to withdraw to barracks, and this would not be "calculated to raise the prestige of British arms." While it would be possible to send a force, Hore-Belisha thought it definitely undesirable. The conferees weakly agreed to ask Beneš for his "views."

While the senior ministers were planning for Godesberg, Lord Runciman, whom Harvey found "quite broken down . . . rather pathetic," had been working on his report. It took the form of nearly identical letters, dated September 21, 1938, to Chamberlain and Beneš, and was the third subject discussed by the Big Four meeting that morning. Although Runciman supported Chamberlain's preference for outright cession rather than a plebiscite, and there were other portions of the text sufficiently parallel to the Anglo-French plan so that the conferees could record that "in effect, his Report supported the action by His Majesty's Government," there was an obvious and crucial difference. Instead of proposing, as Hitler had demanded, that all areas in which the Sudeten Germans constituted a bare majority be ceded to the Reich, Runciman advocated that only those "frontier districts" where the Sudeten Germans were "an important majority"* be ceded, and that in areas "where the German majority is not so important . . . an effort be made to find a basis for local autonomy within the frontiers of the Czechoslovak Republic. . . ."

Since Chamberlain was convinced that a settlement could only be secured on Hitler's bare majority basis, publication of the Runciman recommendation, far from making the Prime Minister's task any easier, would rather have served to heighten the wave of public opposition to the Anglo-French settlement which was beginning to rise in Britain as more of the Berchtesgaden news leaked out.

---

* The report did not quantify "important." Ashton-Gwatkin and perhaps Runciman had in mind a figure of 80 per cent, which was the same measure that Chamberlain had unsuccessfully proposed at Berchtesgaden.

It is not surprising, therefore, that the conferees decided to suppress the letters for the time being.

Of course, in theory Runciman was an "independent" mediator, and if he had really been such he presumably would have sent his letter to Beneš at the same time that he delivered it to Chamberlain. But not until the following day did he send it to Jan Masaryk for dispatch to Beneš, and then only with the admonition that "for the time being" it should be regarded as confidential and that Beneš should be informed accordingly.

In the afternoon of the twenty-first the Cabinet held its final meeting prior to Godesberg. Halifax brought the members up to date; the Czechs had not yet officially accepted the Anglo-French terms but were expected to momentarily. He then reported the growing pressure from the Hungarians and Poles, and Chamberlain declared his intention to resist vigorously any efforts Hitler might make to bring these questions into the discussion. Hoare described the matter as a test of Hitler's sincerity, and the Cabinet readily agreed that if the Fuehrer continued to press the Polish and Hungarian claims, the Prime Minister should break off the talks and return to London for further consultation.

The problem of transitional order-keeping within the Sudetenland proved much more difficult. The Prime Minister's suggestion that German troops be allowed to move at once into the heavily German areas met with sharp criticism from several members, including Duff Cooper, who took the lead in opposition:

> . . . there must be a decent interval, in order to enable those who wanted to leave to do so. We couldn't abandon the Czechs and still more the German Social Democrats etc. to the tender mercies of the Nazis. . . . I felt that we had reached the limit. Not a shadow of concession, not a word of goodwill, had we received in return. Since the Prime Minister's visit the German press had grown steadily more violent. Hitler could have restrained it had he wished. . . . I hoped that when the Prime Minister saw Hitler he would say . . . that he was bringing him Czechoslovakia's head on a charger. . . . Further he could not go. He would prefer, if it were necessary to go to war. . . .

But what was the alternative? Hore-Belisha and Gort had made an unanswerable case against the dispatch of a British force, and no one made the obvious suggestion that the Czechs be left in control of their own sovereign territory until the transfer. There was talk of an international force, but where was such to be found? In the end it was agreed that no German troops should be allowed to cross the border without Prague's consent,* but the problem should be put to Beneš, and he should in any event be asked to withdraw the Czech Army and state police from the Sudeten border areas, and leave peace-keeping responsibility to the local *gendarmerie*.

After the Cabinet had adjourned, and just after Prague's formal acceptance of the Anglo-French terms had been received, Halifax instructed Newton to urge

---

* In his diary Hore-Belisha recorded: "We were all dead against any proposal to allow German troops to cross the frontier during the transitional period and it was agreed that there should be some form of international force." The records do not reflect a unanimous view, but the Cabinet did agree that "if the Prime Minister could not conclude a satisfactory settlement on this matter, he would consult the Cabinet again."

Beneš to withdraw the state police, and asked for his views on the future use of British, "international," or German troops. On its face this was only an inquiry, but the trend of Halifax's thinking was reflected in his accompanying suggestions:

> I think regular German troops would at least be preferable to Henlein's Freikorps, who would be likely to work off private grudges and to commit outrages on political opponents.
>
> We may, therefore, have to try to facilitate the entry of German troops at an early date into a defined area and to eliminate all danger of clash with the Czechs. It would, of course, be best if Dr. Benes himself would suggest that, in districts which will obviously pass to Germany, he no longer desires to retain responsibility for maintenance of order, and that German troops should be employed.

"Best" perhaps for the convenience of the powers, but "best" for those inhabitants of the Sudetenland, German or Czech, who did not relish passing under Nazi rule? Their fate seems not to have been in the forefront of the mind of Lord Halifax, churchman, horseman, rich man, and Foreign Secretary.

While Halifax was composing this message, Beneš was sending, via Lacroix, an agonized appeal that whatever agreement was reached at Godesberg* should ensure that no German troops be allowed across the old frontier until the new one was officially established. In Prague huge crowds were marching toward the Hradschin, protesting the capitulation and some calling for a military dictatorship. General Jan Syrový, one-eyed hero of the First World War, told them that a dictatorship would do no good: "You do not know the causes which forced the Government to make its decisions. We cannot lead the nation to suicide." But the next morning the Hodža government resigned and was replaced later that day by a new one headed by Syrový.

Shortly before eight o'clock in the morning of September 22, the Foreign Office received a telephoned report from Prague that Asch (a town at the extreme eastern tip of Bohemia, with a largely German population) had been invaded and occupied by Henlein's *Freikorps*.

In France that morning *Paris-Midi* told its readers: "Mr. Chamberlain is leaving for Germany with a plan in his pocket. Let Germany make no mistake about it: this plan provides for certain limits beyond which England will not go."

Where this journal got such information was not disclosed. In fact, Chamberlain's preparation for the encounter hardly deserved to be called a "plan," beyond his intention to report Prague's acceptance of the Anglo-French terms and then observe Hitler's reaction. His staff failed to come up with a firm program for interim control of the Sudeten areas, or a procedure for considering the Polish and Hungarian claims. Above all he wanted peace; it was altogether probable that the Fuehrer would set a high price. The Prime Minister was batting on a very sticky wicket, and Hitler might well make it difficult for him to insist on "limits beyond which England will not go."

---

* Beneš asked that Chamberlain be informed of the plea before his departure for Godesberg. The text found its way into Chamberlain's files, but whether he saw it before leaving, or ever, does not appear.

2

At half-past eleven in the morning of September 21, Hitler's Army adjutant, Captain Engel, telephoned to OKW that "the Fuehrer five minutes ago received news that Prague has accepted unconditionally." An hour and a quarter later OKW passed this information to the staff section chiefs, with instructions that preparations for Green were to be continued, but also plans should now be made for a peaceful entry.

If up to this time it is difficult to tell where Hitler's intentions lay as between war and a peaceful annexation of the Sudetenland, it appears clear that, at least after learning of Prague's acceptance of the Anglo-French terms, he paid serious heed to the possibility that a bloodless resolution of the crisis *might* be preferable to the losses and uncertainties of war. But it is most unlikely that he had as yet made a firm decision, and there was no slackening in execution of the Green program for an attack. Indeed, on the twenty-first the 7th Infantry Division in Bavaria, and no doubt other units there and elsewhere, were assembling in their preliminary stations the forces that were to make the initial assault. The French military and air attachés, well informed by aerial and road reconnaissance and consular reports, continued to observe the concentration of German forces all along the Czech frontier.

There was, however, one respect in which things were not developing in accordance with the original Green plan. Hitler's decision to form the Henlein *Freikorps* instead of putting the Sudeten German "refugees" into the Army reserves resulted in the creation of an undisciplined, nondescript force eager to display its prowess and settle old scores. There were tempting opportunities for raids across the Czech border, especially in those areas, such as the Asch-Eger district, which were nearly 100 per cent German and which lay outside the Czech fortifications and would have been indefensible in the event of war. Sudeten control of Asch during the night of September 20–21 may initially have been accomplished locally, but was soon buttressed by the *Freikorps* and perhaps also by German SS and SA units and extended to Eger and Franzsenbad. To avoid provocation, the Czechs made no effort to expel the invaders, but warned Britain and France that these incursions greatly increased the danger of clashes with Czech soldiers in the area.

The German Army command was also vastly displeased by these activities. Not only were they of no military value; far worse, they were wholly inconsistent with the purpose of achieving at least an element of surprise in the initial attack on the Czech fortifications. Provocational pinpricks along the frontier were altogether likely to cause the Czechs to mobilize and man the fortifications in full strength, which was just what the Wehrmacht leaders wished to avoid. Jodl's disquiet was reflected in his diary entry for September 20:

> The Freikorps begins operations, of such extent that they may have, and may already have had, harmful consequences to the Army's future plans (bringing stronger units of the Czech Army near the border). By conferring with Lt. Col. Köchling I try to bring these activities into controlled channels. Toward evening the Führer also intervenes and limits the operations to

groups of not more than 12 men, subject to approval of the Army corps head-quarters.*

These problems would vanish, of course, if the crisis were to be resolved nonmilitarily. Considering the breadth of opposition within the High Command to involvement in a European war, it is safe to infer that the OKW and OKH staffs turned willingly to drawing up lists of conditions which the Czechs would have to meet in order to earn a peaceful settlement.

After the Berchtesgaden meeting, Ribbentrop's staff had submitted a memorandum on procedures for conducting a plebiscite, and on the twenty-first the OKW, proceeding on the assumption that the Czechs would agree to cession of the Sudeten German districts and plebiscites in the mixed German-Czech districts, compiled a list of twenty-five demands which should be considered for imposition on Prague. These included the immediate withdrawal of all Czech troops and police and the surrender of all fortifications in both types of districts, occupation of the ceded area by German troops, and of the plebiscite areas by German police pending the arrival of an international police force, demobilization of the entire Czech Army, prohibition of any future fortification construction, pardon and release of all Germans and Sudeten Germans imprisoned for espionage, and numerous other equally drastic requirements and restrictions.

Meanwhile, Hitler was giving his own primary attention to the Hungarian and Polish minority claims. At Berchtesgaden he had told Chamberlain that "in the long run it would be impossible to ignore these demands," but had given no indication that he would insist on their settlement in connection with the Sudeten problem. Now, however, both he and Goering took steps to persuade the Hungarian and Polish governments of the necessity of pressing their demands immediately and forcefully, if they expected to profit by the Sudeten crisis.

The two countries were not equally bold, for Hungary was much weaker than Poland and was further inhibited by the agreements linking the Little Entente, which would have required Yugoslavia and Rumania to go to the aid of Czechoslovakia if she were attacked by Hungary. On September 16, Goering invited the Hungarian Minister, Döme Sztójay, to Karinhall, and sought to allay these fears by giving his personal assurance "that Yugoslavia would take no action if Hungary were to march, not on the first day [of the German attack], but say three or four days later."† Goering criticized Hungary for "not doing enough in the present crisis," and urged on Sztójay that his country should

* The effect was immediate, as evidenced by a *Freikorps* document of September 21, reporting that during the previous night their units had attacked and damaged the "Masaryk building" on the Silesian frontier and burned the Czech customshouse at Neuendorf, while: "The other actions were terminated by the Supreme Headquarters of the Wehrmacht."

† Three days earlier the Yugoslav Minister in Rome, Bosko Cristich, had told Ciano that if Hungary were "the first to take up arms" against the Czechs, Yugoslavia would be obliged "to keep faith with its pledge to the Little Entente," but: "Should Hungary, however, support and follow up a German intervention, Yugoslavia would consider herself freed from all obligation." This conversation was known to the Germans, and later on the sixteenth Woermann passed the information on to Sztójay.

demand "in clear terms the detachment of the Hungarian region from Czecho-slovakia."

The Poles, on the other hand, needed no persuasion. On the same day, when Goering met with Ambassador Lipski, he found that the Pole had already informed Weizsaecker that "the Polish Government would categorically request" a solution of the Teschen situation. Lipski informed Warsaw that Goering was obviously "anxious to separate Slovakia from the rest of Czechoslovakia, in order thus to create a Czech state economically dependent on the Reich."

On September 19, Hitler summoned to Berchtesgaden for the following day the Hungarian Prime and Foreign Ministers, Bela Imredy and Kalman Kanya, and separately requested Lipski to come later the same day. The Hungarians were given the rough edge of the Fuehrer's tongue and told in no uncertain terms what to do:

> First, the Führer reproached the Hungarian gentlemen for the undecided attitude of Hungary in the present time of crisis. He was determined to settle the Czech question even at the risk of a world war. Germany demanded the entire German area. He was convinced that neither England nor France would intervene. It was Hungary's last opportunity to join for, if she did not, he would not be in a position to put in a word for Hungarian interest. . . . He presented two demands to the Hungarians: (1) that Hungary should make an immediate demand for a plebiscite in the territories she claimed, and (2) that she should not guarantee any proposed new frontiers for Czechoslovakia.

Imredy apologetically explained his government's delay by pleading surprise at the speed of Hitler's program, and promised that he would now demand a plebiscite, make military preparations, and decline any border guarantee until "all Hungarian demands had been satisfied."* Hitler went on to give his guests further indication of his views, and of how he would handle Chamberlain at Godesberg:

> In his opinion, the best thing would be to destroy Czechoslovakia. In the long run, it was quite impossible to tolerate the existence of this aircraft carrier in the heart of Europe. . . . The Führer declared further that he would present the German demands to Chamberlain with brutal frankness. In his opinion, action by the Army would provide the only satisfactory solution. There was, however, a danger of the Czechs submitting to every demand. . . . The Führer states that Germany would give no guarantees unless every country concerned took its share in them. . . . The Führer then stressed once more that he would put forward the German demands at Godesberg with the starkest realism. If, as a result, disturbances started in Czechoslovakia, he would then start military operations. It would, however, always be preferable if the pretext for this were provided by the Czechs.

* The Hungarian Minister in London presented his government's demands to Halifax on the evening of the same day, and on the twenty-first the Hungarian Government called up two classes of Army reserves.

The Hungarians departed with this earful, and at four o'clock that afternoon Lipski was received. At least according to Lipski's account,* Hitler treated him with complete courtesy and there was no lecturing.

Hitler opened the interchange by declaring that, while he had no definite information about the proposals which Chamberlain would bring to Godesberg, he had reason to think that the principle of Germany's claims would be honored.† However, there was a report that "the settlement . . . will be executed not by self-determination [i.e., plebiscite] but by a new delineation of frontiers" [i.e., cession]. Hitler "declared that he preferred a plebiscite and is standing firm on it. He would of course insist on a plebiscite in order to secure votes for people who left the territory after 1918. The status of 1918 must be restored. Otherwise, it would mean acceptance of Czechization, which has been underway since 1918." Hitler's real point was, of course, that a plebiscite in which Sudeten Germans who had left the area since 1918 would be included while Czechs who had since entered would be excluded, would establish a frontier much more favorable to Germany than a line drawn on the basis of present majorities.

Hitler then told Lipski, as he had the Hungarians, that a forceful occupation of the Sudetenland would be the best solution. "However," Lipski reported, "in case his claims are recognized, it would not be possible for him not to accept them before his people, even if the rest of the Czechoslovak problem remained unsolved." What, then, should be done about the Polish and Hungarian claims? Lipski replied by stating the geographical bounds of the claimed Teschen area, and declaring that Poland was prepared to use military force if necessary. He and Hitler then agreed that neither country would join in guaranteeing the new Czech borders until all the minority claims were satisfied, and the Fuehrer added that Italy should be brought into the guarantor group in order "to counterbalance the French and British guarantees."

The rest of the talk was desultory and inconclusive. Lipski, under instructions previously received from Warsaw, also endeavored to raise some nagging problems of German-Polish relations, including Danzig and the Corridor, but he made little progress because "the Chancellor was very much absorbed by his approaching talk with Chamberlain." After the interview a communiqué was issued which confirmed only the fact of the meeting without revealing anything of the discussion.

From these conversations and the settlement memoranda composed by the Foreign Ministry and the High Command, it is possible to gauge Hitler's plans for the Godesberg meeting. He could not, in any event, move militarily for an-

---

* It appears that, for some reason, there is no official German record of Hitler's conversations on this day. Lipski's official report and accompanying personal notes are available, but the only available record of the meeting with the Hungarians is a memorandum by Erich Kordt based on information received by telephone from Brücklmeier, a Foreign Ministry official at the Berghof, where he was apparently acting as liaison officer for the ministry in Berlin.

† On the day of the meeting (September 20) *The Times* of London and other journals carried fairly accurate summaries of the Anglo-French proposals, apparently based on information leaked in Paris.

other week, so he would have to avoid a total rupture of the negotiations. He was by no means insensitive to domestic feeling, and realized that, if he were offered most of what he had been claiming, it would be dangerous to resort to war for the purpose of getting even more. But his previously held belief that Britain and France would go very far to avoid war had been abundantly confimed, and he was reasonably certain that he could get more than he had stipulated at Berchtesgaden.

Since the destruction of Czechoslovakia was his goal, what Hitler wanted at Godesberg was a temporary settlement which would so weaken that country as to assure its speedy collapse and absorption by the Reich. Hence the preference for a plebiscite, which (if the 1918 voting basis were adopted) might tear off more land and peoples than a cession on a current 50 per cent basis. Hence his incitement of the Poles and Hungarians, whose claims would narrow the bounds of Slovakia and Ruthenia and further demoralize Prague.

Hitler had yet another purpose, not fully articulated in the records, but reflected in his repeated statements that a solution by military force would be best. The Wehrmacht was mobilizing and was deploying its forces near the Czech border. It would be difficult if not impossible to hold these legions indefinitely poised on the brink of attack, and once they were withdrawn the capacity for instant action would be lost and the crisis would be resolved, not by German might, but by treaties and international commissions. Such an outcome would have been intolerable to Hitler; the Wehrmacht must be the major agent of the take-over.

These were the aims—far more specific than Chamberlain's—which must have been in Hitler's mind as he left the Berghof in the evening of September 20 and proceeded, via Munich, to Godesberg. How much did he know about the contents of the package with which Chamberlain would present him? He knew, of course, what had appeared in the press about the Anglo-French proposals, and that Prague had accepted at least enough of them to make Chamberlain think his trip worthwhile. But there is good reason to believe that Hitler knew much more than that.

At least since mid-September and probably long before that, a German intelligence unit of the Air Ministry* had been intercepting the telephone calls between the Prague government and its diplomatic outposts in London, Paris, Berlin, and, no doubt, other capitals. Transcribed and if necessary translated, these intercepts were circulated to Hitler and high military and diplomatic officials.

On September 26, during a meeting with Sir Horace Wilson, Hitler declared that intercepted Czech calls from London to Prague revealed that Jan Masaryk was urging Beneš not to yield. The following day Goering had about twenty intercepts delivered to the British Embassy, whence they were sent to London. Of course, these particular messages were selected in order to support Hitler's charge and foment British anger at the Czechs, but even this handful is enough to establish that Hitler could confidently expect Chamberlain to propose cession

---

* Known as the *Forschungsamt* (research office) and primarily occupied with tapping telephone lines, opening mail, etc.

of the Sudetenland by treaty rather than plebiscite, at a line to be fixed, on a bare German majority basis, by some sort of international body. Very likely he knew much more.

Hitler arrived at Godesberg at about ten o'clock in the morning of September 22. As he settled into his favorite Rheinhotel Dreesen (the proprietor was an old Nazi supporter, and it was from here that Hitler had launched the Roehm purge four years earlier), he had little reason to fear surprise in the coming confrontation. Nevertheless William Shirer, who saw the Fuehrer that morning on the hotel terrace, thought him "highly nervous." He was sure he could push Chamberlain back, but he did not know how far, and the ready date for Green was barely a week ahead.

3

"A peaceful solution of the Czechoslovakia problem is an essential preliminary to a better understanding between the British and German peoples; and that in turn is the indispensable foundation of European peace," Neville Chamberlain told the journalists gathered at Heston Airport to see him off, and added: "European peace is what I am aiming at, and I hope this journey may be the way to get it." Like a week earlier, a crowd of diplomats and supporters had gathered to wish him success, but there was more tension on this second occasion. Geoffrey Dawson of *The Times* told Theodor Kordt that "if Chamberlain were to return without an understanding based on the Anglo-French plan, public opinion would turn against him," and the editor and the diplomat were agreed, as Kordt reported to Berlin, that "opposition to Chamberlain's policy is increasing."

Wilson and Strang again accompanied the Prime Minister, and the team was augmented by Sir William Malkin, Legal Adviser to the Foreign Office, whose presence indicated that Chamberlain anticipated the possibility that treaties or other diplomatic documents might be drafted. The party arrived at the Cologne airport shortly after noon, and were joined by Nevile Henderson and the first secretary of the embassy, Ivone Kirkpatrick, whose excellent German would enable him to serve as the British party's interpreter and recorder.*

Ribbentrop and the local gauleiter, Joseph Grohe, were at the airport to greet the Prime Minister, who emerged from the aircraft grasping the umbrella that was to become the Munich talisman of peace. The SS *Leibstandarte Adolf Hitler* regiment provided a guard of honor for him to inspect and a band to play *God Save the King*. The British were then driven to the super-de luxe Kurhotel Petersberg, on the east bank of the Rhine opposite Godesberg. The hotel, on an eminence near the famous *Drachenfels,* commands a lovely view of the river and surrounding countryside, and from the terrace Chamberlain could see across to the Dreesen, where his host awaited him. The proprietor also owned the famous Eau de Cologne, and the sumptuous accommodations included, according to Kirkpatrick, "no fewer than fifteen samples of his products."

After lunch the British, escorted by police launches, were ferried across the

---

* According to Kirkpatrick, he was included in the party only because of the rumpus over Schmidt's record of the Berchtesgaden meeting.

Rhine to Godesberg. The riverbanks were thronged as far as the eye could see; in Godesberg the street crowds were quiet, and Kirkpatrick thought it "easy to see that there was no desire for war." At the Dreesen a sizable group of German dignitaries—Ribbentrop, Goebbels, Himmler, Weizsaecker, Keitel, Gaus, Dörnberg, Dirksen,* and others—filled the lobby. Kirkpatrick's account continues:

> Suddenly there was a murmur: "Der Führer kommt." Conversation stopped, everyone shrank towards the walls, a door opened and Hitler strode in, looking neither to the right nor the left. He walked up to Mr. Chamberlain, shook hands and led him up a staircase preceded by an S.S. guard. Schmidt and I, clasping pencils and paper, followed. . . . We walked along a passage, the guard threw open a door and we entered a room containing a long table covered with green baize. It was a very long table, which could conveniently have sat twenty people or more. Hitler stalked to the top of the table, Mr. Chamberlain sat on his right, Schmidt and I on his left. Beyond, a long vista of green baize and empty chairs. There was a moment of silence and Hitler then gestured to the Prime Minister as if to say: "Your move."

Thus, as at the Berghof, the Godesberg meeting began tête-à-tête, but this time with two reporters instead of one. Both Schmidt and Kirkpatrick made records of the discussion, which, fortunately, tend to confirm rather than confute each other.

In response to Hitler's gesture, Chamberlain described, at considerable length and without interruption, the Anglo-French plan which Prague had accepted. It was shrewdly presented, in that Chamberlain made frequent reference to what Hitler had said and demanded at the Berghof, so as to create an atmosphere of contractual obligation on Hitler's side. But the Prime Minister also made an attempt to better the deal from the Czech standpoint by proposing a Sudeten percentage of 80 per cent for cession without question, and 65 per cent as a guide to the international commission in drawing a frontier which would take political, economic, and military factors into account. He also raised several ancillary points such as population exchange, compensation to Prague for state property in the ceded areas, and German assumption of a proportionate share of the Czech public debt.

Hitler than asked, although he must have known that the answer would be affirmative, whether or not the terms so described were those which Prague had accepted. After Chamberlain's "Yes," Hitler replied: "I am very sorry, but all that is no longer any use."†

After what Kirkpatrick recalled as "a long pause of pained silence," Hitler went on with what sounded like a prepared statement. It consisted largely of a long diatribe against Czechoslovakia as an "artificial structure" from which the

---

* Dirksen, still on leave from his London post, had ridden in the car with Sir Horace Wilson en route from Cologne to the Petersberg. Wilson told the ambassador that Chamberlain "was in a position to make proposals to Hitler which would surely satisfy him," adding that the Prime Minister should be given "time to bring the entire business to a successful conclusion." At lunch on the Dreesen terrace Dirksen passed this information on to Ribbentrop, who, when the ambassador repeated Wilson's warning that Chamberlain should not be hurried, "banged the table with his fist and called out 'Three days.'"

† The quoted language is Kirkpatrick's recollection of Schmidt's oral translation; the German, according to Kirkpatrick, was: "*Es tut mir leid, aber das geht nicht mehr.*"

component nationalities other than the Czechs wanted to escape. At the Berghof, Hitler explained, his own first concern had been the Sudeten Germans. Now, however, Poland and Hungary had put their claims, with which he fully sympathized. So far as he was concerned peace in Europe could not be established until these other claims had been settled.

Chamberlain interjected that it was precisely because the Fuehrer at Berchtesgaden had stressed the urgency of the Sudeten problem that this question had been given priority. To this Hitler had no good answer, and he shifted his main thrust to the urgency of a prompt solution: "He must emphasize that the problem must be settled definitely and completely by October 1st at the latest." The "unstable" situation in Czechoslovakia rendered the immediate prospects there unpredictable, with violence and civil distress all too probable.

The Prime Minister replied that he was "both disappointed and puzzled" by the Fuehrer's attitude. At Berchtesgaden the principle of self-determination had been put forward, and now he had obtained the agreement of his cabinet, and of the French and Czechs, so "he could rightly say that the Führer had got from him what he had demanded." In order to achieve this "he had risked his whole political career," and now was being "accused by certain circles of having sold and betrayed Czechoslovakia." As to the incidents stressed by Hitler, Kirkpatrick had just brought him information "to the effect that German troop formations had crossed the frontier at Eger." After Hitler denied this, Chamberlain put the ball in Hitler's court by asking what proposals he might have to make in the interests of peace.

Hitler answered that there was but one possibility, which he then described, generally in line with what he had told Lipski and the Hungarians two days earlier. A line must be drawn "along the language frontier"; all Czech military, police, and civil agencies must be immediately pulled behind the line, and the area thus evacuated would be occupied by German troops. Subsequently there would be a plebiscite covering the entire area, in which all Germans who had left it could vote, but not the Czechs who had entered it. The plebiscite could be conducted by an international commission, and he would hand back any districts where the majority vote went against cession to Germany. There would be no compensation to Prague for Czech state property, since it "had duly been paid for by the taxes of the local inhabitants." All Sudeten prisoners of the Czech police must at once be released. There would be no guarantees or nonaggression pacts on the part of Germany until the Polish and Hungarian claims were settled.

The colloquy waxed argumentative and repetitious. Chamberlain stressed the political difficulties which Hitler's proposals would raise in England, to which Hitler replied that he had problems of his own. The Fuehrer was on the offensive at every turn of the talk, and while Chamberlain did not yield, he was forced to abandon his initial effort to get anything above the bare majority line, and readily agreed to requiring the Czechs to release Sudeten prisoners. The Prime Minister tried repeatedly to limit the plebiscite to areas where the vote might be close, but Hitler would have none of that.

Finally Chamberlain asked to be shown the "language boundary" which

Hitler had in mind, and to this end the meeting was moved to a downstairs room where maps were laid out on a table. Here the principals and their interpreters were joined by Wilson, Henderson, Ribbentrop, Weizsaecker, and Werner Lorenz, a high-ranking SS officer who had charge of the registration and repatriation of ethnic Germans. Hitler, well briefed, showed where he would draw the line bounding the area for immediate occupation. The conversation grew desultory. Near the end, Hitler declared that the Wehrmacht was prepared to move "at a moment's notice" (which, of course, was not the case), but that he would instruct Keitel to take no action while the talks were going on. It appeared clear that Chamberlain and Hitler were nowhere near an agreement, and finally the Prime Minister decided that he had had enough, and the British party got into their cars and returned to the Petersberg, with the understanding that the talks would be resumed at half-past eleven the following morning.

How Hitler spent the evening we do not know; presumably he reviewed the situation with Ribbentrop and others. He had outlined his terms to Chamberlain, and the next move was up to the guest. Uncertainty of the outcome is reflected in Keitel's instructions, telephoned to OKW and OKH in Berlin, that the date for launching Green could not yet be fixed, but would not be sooner than September 30 unless "improvised," which meant an unopposed entry into Czechoslovakia. Military preparations were to continue according to plan, and four reserve divisions were to be sent to the western front.

Upon returning to the Petersberg, Chamberlain telephoned to Newton in Prague, instructing him to urge upon Beneš the necessity of calm local conditions during the negotiations. After dinner he telephoned Halifax and reported on a "most unsatisfactory" interview. To be sure, the new boundary proposed by Hitler "corresponded very closely to the line we have been considering," but Hitler was insisting on speedy occupation to that line by German troops, and the Prime Minister "had been unable yet to make Herr Hitler appreciate that British and French opinion could not accept this solution." Chamberlain "was considering writing him a letter tonight with a view to putting this beyond all doubt"; he "might then have to return tomorrow"; but he was "still reflecting on the wisdom of this course of action."

The Prime Minister's indecision was understandable, for he had had a long, tiring, and unexpectedly disappointing journey. Furthermore, he had not followed the course envisaged in Cabinet the previous day. Hitler had insisted on resolving the Polish and Hungarian claims as a prerequisite to a final settlement with Czechoslovakia, and on sending German troops at once into Czech territory; the Cabinet had agreed that under either of these circumstances the Prime Minister should adjourn the meeting and return to London to consult his colleagues. Having disregarded these understandings and remained at the Petersberg, Chamberlain now faced the problem of how to cope with Hitler's intransigence.

At breakfast the following morning, it was decided to send Hitler a letter before meeting with him again. According to Wilson, the purpose was to draw a reply, which would get the Fuehrer on paper with specific demands. Chamberlain's letter, however, consisted only of objections to Hitler's insistence that the areas in question should "in the immediate future" be occupied by German troops:*

> . . . I do not think you have realized the impossibility of my agreeing to put forward my plan unless I have reason to suppose that it will be considered by public opinion in my country, in France and, indeed, in the world generally, as carrying out the principles already agreed upon in an orderly fashion and free from the threat of force. . . . Even if I felt it right to put this proposal to the Czech Government, I am convinced that they would not regard it as being in the spirit of the arrangement which we and the French Government urged them to accept and which they have accepted.

Instead, Chamberlain suggested that Prague might be asked "whether they think there could be an arrangement under which the maintenance of law and order in certain agreed Sudeten German areas would be entrusted to the Sudeten Germans themselves—by the creation of a suitable force, or by the use of forces already in existence, possibly acting under the supervision of neutral observers." This proposal was still another departure from the Cabinet's conclusions,† which envisaged the use of an international force. In light of the War Office's gloomy assessment of this course of action, however, Chamberlain can hardly be blamed for disregarding it. In fact, there was little room for choice other than to let in the Germans, or leave the Czechs in control until the new boundary was settled. Since it was out of the question that Prague and Berlin would agree on either course, the impasse was unlikely to be resolved other than forcefully.

On receiving the letter, Hitler sent word that he would reply in writing. The scheduled morning meeting was canceled. Hitler sat down with Ribbentrop to prepare his answer, while across the Rhine the British fidgeted, with nothing but the lovely view to distract them. In the river below they could see the yacht aboard which Hitler had planned a Rhine cruise with his guests. They sat down to what Kirkpatrick recalled as "a rather grim lunch," in the course of which the Prime Minister "discussed the theatre and spoke of his early days in Birmingham."

Finally Hitler dictated a reply—too long for a timely written translation—and sent Schmidt to deliver it by hand and translate verbally. The interpreter left the Dreesen at about three o'clock and half an hour later was pushing his way through a horde of journalists at the Petersberg, ignoring shouted questions, such as "Do you bring peace or war?" He was taken to Chamberlain's room, where he translated the letter in the presence of Wilson, Henderson, and Kirkpatrick.

The Fuehrer's response yielded nothing. It opened with a diatribe against the

---

* Mr. Kirkpatrick (the junior member of the party) was unhappy about the British position on this issue, thinking that: "If we were prepared to agree to the cession of the territory, it seemed illogical to object to its military occupation . . ." He showed drafts of a "compromise" to Wilson on the morning of the twenty-third, but was told "that the Prime Minister was resolved not to give an inch on this particular issue and that it was hopeless to think of any compromise."

† Ashton-Gwatkin, well informed as a result of his experience as a member of the Runciman mission, had advised strongly that "the Sudeten Germans were not to be trusted, and . . . might commit outrages on the people they were supposed to protect."

iniquities of the Czechs, reaffirmed the need of immediate steps to rescue the Sudeten Germans from "Czech tyranny," and rejected Chamberlain's suggestion of Sudeten German order-keeping as "practically impossible in consequence of the obstacles put in the way of their political organization in the course of the last decade, and particularly in recent times." The same considerations, he wrote, applied to "the other nationalities in this State." Responding directly to Chamberlain's professed inability to lay the German demands before his cabinet, the Fuehrer concluded by reaffirming his determination to use force if it proved "impossible to have the clear rights of the Germans in Czechoslovakia accepted by way of negotiation."

There appeared to be little reason for further discussion, but Chamberlain wanted a more precise statement of Hitler's demands than the letter afforded. Late in the afternoon, Wilson and Henderson went across to the Petersberg and handed Ribbentrop a second letter from Chamberlain:

> In my capacity as intermediary, it is evidently now my duty—since Your Excellency maintains entirely the same position you took last night—to put your proposals before the Czechoslovak Government.
>
> Accordingly, I request Your Excellency to be good enough to let me have a memorandum which sets out these proposals, together with a map showing the areas proposed to be transferred, subject to the result of the proposed plebiscite.
>
> On receiving this memorandum I will at once forward it to Prague and request the reply of the Czechoslovak Government at the earliest possible moment. . . .
>
> Since the acceptance or refusal of Your Excellency's proposal is now a matter for the Czechoslovak Government to decide, I do not see that I can perform any further service here, while on the other hand it has become necessary that I should at once report the present situation to my colleagues and to the French Government. I propose, therefore, to return to England.

Ribbentrop told the British emissaries that Hitler would receive the Prime Minister and explain the requested memorandum. Once more Chamberlain and his colleagues dined and waited. At last they were told that the documents would be ready by half-past ten in the evening, when they would be expected at the Dreesen.

4

Chamberlain at the Petersberg had much more restless waiting than his Cabinet colleagues in London, who had few idle moments. "All these days have been awful—from 9:30 till about midnight—practically no break and one's mind gripped the whole time with this one awful obsession," Cadogan recorded on the twenty-third, adding: "We have been, at intervals, discussing war preparations (which is not cheering)."

Halifax, now in charge on the home front, met with Simon and Hoare during the afternoon of the twenty-second, and the inner Cabinet group was now augmented by Inskip and Malcolm MacDonald; Vansittart and Cadogan were also present. The matter of most immediate concern was the news that Henlein's

Freikorps had taken control of Eger and Asch, and what this portrayed by way of other incursions on Czech territory. Since the eighteenth, Prague had been refraining from ordering mobilization, in deference to London's request and assurance that the Wehrmacht would not attack during the negotiations.* Alarmed by the seizure of Egar and Asch, the British ministers now gave consideration to withdrawing their previous advice to Prague.

Sentiment at the meeting favored lifting the advisory ban, but it was decided to consult Paris first. Daladier and Bonnet, on Léger's recommendation, agreed that the previous advice should be withdrawn, and Newton was then instructed to inform the Prague government, after nine o'clock that evening, that "French and British Governments cannot continue to take responsibility of advising them not to mobilise." At the same time, however, Chamberlain was urging the Czechs to do nothing that would interfere with the progress of the Godesberg talks. Consequently, and on the basis of telephone messages from Horace Wilson, the instructions to Newton were countermanded.

Meanwhile, considerable tension was developing within the Cabinet. Chamberlain left most of the liaison functions to Wilson, who seemed to take delight in keeping London on short rations of information about the doings in Godesberg. What little news trickled in from Wilson was distributed only to the inner group, which now included Inskip but none of the service ministers. Duff Cooper, already disaffected, grew more and more irritated at being kept in ignorance of developments, especially when it began to appear that the Godesberg talks were not going well and the likelihood of war was increasing:

> We went to a cinema after dinner [in the evening of the twenty-second], but before going I rang up the Resident Clerk to know if there was any news. He told me that they had sent a telegram to Prague to the effect that we could no longer be responsible for advising the Czechs not to mobilise. I couldn't stay at the cinema for more than a quarter of an hour as the inanity of it got on my nerves. I walked home and sent for the latest telegrams. . . . I rang up the Private Secretaries at Downing Street; nobody was there. I rang up the Foreign Office and learnt that Halifax, Simon, Hoare, MacDonald and Inskip were in conference and that there had been a message from Horace Wilson from Godesberg which was "not too good." I sent a message to the effect that we Service Ministers were being put in a very difficult position. The country might be within twenty-four hours of war and we were not being given the latest information which was available to some of our colleagues.
>
> After half an hour, having received no reply, I rang up again and learnt that the Ministers had dispersed. With some difficulty I got onto the Cabinet Officers and spoke to Ismay [Secretary of the CID]. He told me that he himself had given the message to Tom Inskip, who had immediately got up and gone home to bed.

* On the morning of the eighteenth, having learned of the German concentrations near the frontier, the Czech Government informed Newton that mobilization was thought necessary but would not be ordered pending consultation with London and Paris. Later that day Halifax replied, urging that the Czechs "abstain from mobilisation measures pending further negotiations." He also instructed Henderson to inform the German Government accordingly, and indicated that London's advice to Prague was based on "assurances given to Prime Minister by the Chancellor."

In fact, the inner group meeting that evening had accomplished little. The members listened to a report of Halifax's telephone conversation with the Prime Minister, and of Inskip's informal inquiries to the Chiefs of Staff concerning what military measures would be taken if war broke out. The Chiefs had said nothing of fresh importance; only the Navy, which would sweep the seas clear of German shipping and establish a blockade in the North Sea, was ready for offensive action.

Early in the morning of the twenty-third the ministers were confronted with a telegram from Godesberg expressing the view that the "suspension" of Czech mobilization should be continued until after the scheduled meeting with Hitler. During the morning there were two murky telephone calls from Wilson, in the first of which he enlightened his listeners with the observation that there was "fog all around" which would "clear one way or another during the day," and in the second reported that the meeting with Hitler had been postponed. Wilson also told them that two telegrams were on the way which would "be enough to go on with in the light of previous messages" and "enable the boys to go on playing marbles."

The cavalier attitude in Godesberg was too much even for the usually tractable Halifax, who had been greatly alarmed by the Eger-Asch episode. The French were equally anxious; early in the afternoon Daladier sent via Léger a message pointing out that "if things have gone badly at Godesberg we shall incur a terrible responsibility in not withdrawing the advice" not to mobilize. At about the same time, Halifax telephoned to Godesberg a message that: "In light of your information and ours, we are profoundly disturbed at . . . your telegram [requesting that the "suspension" be maintained during further discussion with Hitler] and we feel that this decision must now be reversed. We propose to make necessary communication [to Prague] in this sense at 3 p.m. today."

At two o'clock Nevile Henderson telephoned to Halifax a message that: "We expect reply to this morning's letter [from Chamberlain to Hitler] at any moment and think you should wait a little longer before making the communication." But this was not intended as a firm prohibition, for the message continued: "In any event communication should point out that such action by them [i.e., the Czechs] may very well precipitate action by others."

The inner ministerial group met at three o'clock; the text of Chamberlain's morning letter to Hitler had been received and was read,* and at four o'clock Newton was authorized to inform Prague that the advice against mobilization was withdrawn, but that the Government should be cautioned in line with the Prime Minister's instructions.

The conferees also took note of complaints from other ministers who were being left in the dark, and Simon undertook to "give them the latest facts" that afternoon. Halifax announced that he had instructed R. A. Butler, who was in Geneva at the League meeting, to sound out Litvinov on the Soviet Govern-

---

* During the meeting, Horace Wilson telephoned that Hitler's reply was still awaited, and added: "We received a telegram from the Foreign Office [Halifax's "profoundly disturbed" message] which spoilt our luncheon"—astonishing language for a civil servant to use to the Secretary of State for Foreign Affairs.

ment's intentions, and Malcolm MacDonald reported on his conversation at noon with the Dominion commissioners, who had shown no stomach for war. Deeply concerned by the increasing prospect thereof, Halifax telephoned to Godesberg: "We are sure that you have in mind the necessity of a period of at least some days for precautionary stage which includes measures such as mobilisation, before entry into hostilities. If you are anticipating a breakdown in your negotiations will you consider whether some Cabinet action authorizing further precautionary steps should not be taken forthwith. . . . until mobilisation is ordered the defences against air attack cannot be ready."

Later that afternoon Simon met with half a dozen of the "outer" ministers (including Duff Cooper and Kingsley Wood) and brought them up to date. Duff Cooper found Simon "in a robust mood, prepared for the fray" but wondering how Chamberlain would react to the impasse: "If the worst comes to the worst, will he be ready to go to war?" Upon leaving the meeting Cooper returned to the Admiralty and "took it upon myself to authorise the recalling of men from leave, the bringing of all crews up to full complement, the despatch of 1,900 men to the Mediterranean to bring that Fleet up to establishment and to man the Suez Canal defences, and also one or two minor measures."

Meanwhile in Prague, Newton had delivered the releasing message at five o'clock, and Lacroix followed suit an hour later. Beneš promptly called the nation's political and military leaders to meet at the Hradschin, and it was unanimously agreed that immediate mobilization was necessary. At half-past ten that evening the Prague radio announced the call-up of all classes of men up to the age of forty.

When the weary members of the inner group reassembled at half-past nine, they received messages from Newton reporting that the Czechs had been duly informed, and from Chamberlain stating that he would depart the following morning,* and that decisions on British mobilization should await his return. The exasperating Wilson had purported to cut off further communication by a message that: "We shall not speak again tonight: we have got a lot to do."

Halifax, who had been consulting with Vansittart, now told his colleagues that the "Godesberg conversations should end on some simpler and stronger note than . . . the P.M. seemed to contemplate." He produced a draft of a message, strongly favored by Hoare, which the conferees agreed should be sent at once and *en clair* so that Chamberlain would get it before his meeting with Hitler:

> It may help you if we give you some indication of what seems predominant public opinion as expressed in press and elsewhere. While mistrustful of our plan [i.e., the Anglo-French proposal] but prepared perhaps to accept it with reluctance as alternative to war, great mass of public opinion seems to be hardening in sense of feeling that we have gone to limit of concession and that it is up to the Chancellor to make some contribution. We, of course, can imagine immense difficulties with which you are confronted but from point of view

* A note in the British records reveals that on the morning of the twenty-third the Prime Minister's aircraft crew had been alerted to the possibility that they might be required to fly "anywhere." Possibly Chamberlain had some thought of going from Godesberg to Prague.

of your own position, that of Government, and of the country, it seems to your colleagues of vital importance that you should not leave without making plain to Chancellor if possible by special interview that, after concessions made by Czechoslovak Government, for him to reject opportunity of peaceful solution in favour of one that must involve war would be an unpardonable crime against humanity.

This text, with the concluding phrase later made memorable at the Nuremberg trials, was the last counsel received by Neville Chamberlain from his own government as he started across the Rhine to Godesberg for his next confrontation with the Fuehrer.

5

When the British party arrived at the Dreesen at about half-past ten o'clock, the hotel was much quieter than on the first occasion. Hitler, flanked by Ribbentrop, Weizsaecker, and Schmidt, met with Chamberlain, Wilson, Henderson, and Kirkpatrick in a small dining lounge, while Strang, Malkin, and what Strang described as like "the domestic establishment of some great barbarian chieftain of German heroic legend" hung about the halls.

Hitler opened the meeting with politenesses about his guest's efforts in behalf of peace. Chamberlain thanked him courteously but immediately asked for the promised document stating the German position. Ribbentrop handed it over, and Hitler remarked that "it contained essentially ideas and suggestions which he had already stated in the course of previous conversations." He characterized the present occasion as the first on which Britain had acted "in a spirit friendly to Germany" on "the one remaining question at issue," and predicted that an agreement "might well be regarded as a turning point in Anglo-German relations."

The immediately ensuing dialogue between the principals was confused, largely because the Germans had not done their visitors the courtesy of furnishing them an English translation of the document. Chamberlain knew no German and had to rely on scribbled notes handed to him by Henderson, as he and Kirkpatrick hastily perused the paper. The Prime Minister complained that Hitler had failed to abide by the Berchtesgaden understanding, and was contributing nothing toward a solution; Hitler replied that this was not a problem which he, as a German, could be expected to view "objectively." However, as soon as Chamberlain was made aware that the Germans were demanding that the Sudetenland be evacuated by the Czech forces and handed over to German occupation by September 26, he declared this time schedule "quite impracticable" and expressed amazement that "Herr Hitler would deliberately gamble away all chances of working together, the prospect of peace and a happy future for Europe for the sake of avoiding a delay of a few days." Hitler retorted that "he sincerely believed that the shorter the time limit the greater the chances of definite acceptance."

At this point a message was brought in to Ribbentrop, who announced in what Kirkpatrick described as "portentous tones" that the Czech radio had just carried Beneš' order for general mobilization.* Hitler then declared that of course this development had "settled" the whole affair, plainly implying that the only solution now was for the Wehrmacht to take over and seize the Sudetenland. Chamberlain challenged this conclusion, and the two fell into a wrangle over which country had mobilized first, at the conclusion of which Hitler quoted a German proverb: "Better an end even with terror than terror without end." Chamberlain then asked whether the German document was Hitler's "last word," and was told that indeed it was, and furthermore that the Czech mobilization compelled him now to take "the appropriate military measures." The Prime Minister leaned back and, in a resigned tone, declared that "in that event there was no purpose in negotiating any further. He would go home with a heavy heart, since he saw the final wreck of all his hopes for the peace of Europe. But his conscience was clear; he had done everything possible for peace. Unfortunately, he had not found an echo in Herr Hitler."

Ribbentrop met this attack by accusing Chamberlain of rejecting the German document without having read it. The Prime Minister replied that Hitler himself had stated at the outset that it embodied his earlier proposals, so that there was apparently nothing new.

Despite these unpleasantnesses, it now became apparent that neither of the principals wanted to break off negotiations. Chamberlain declared that if the Fuehrer "would hold his hand until a reply was received, he would undertake to transmit the memorandum to the Czechoslovak Government." After explanation of "hold his hand" as meaning refraining from "invasion" of Czechoslovakia, Hitler promised not to take such action "as long as the negotiations were in progress."

Horace Wilson, who had been perusing the memorandum, now called attention to its "timetable," which envisaged Czech evacuation of the Sudetenland beginning September 26 and finishing by the twenty-eighth. Chamberlain again lamented the "deplorable" public effect of so "peremptory" a schedule, and characterized Hitler's document as "an ultimatum and not a negotiation." Henderson interjected: *"Ein Diktat!"* Whether weakly or insolently, Hitler pointed out that it was entitled "Memorandum." Chamberlain acidly observed that he was "much more impressed by the contents than by the title," and added that Hitler "was behaving like a conqueror." Hitler retorted: "No, like an owner of his property," and then asked if Chamberlain had read the memorandum. The Prime Minister answered that "he had already seen a pencilled translation of the most important passages . . . he did not want to read any more of the memorandum, and if he did it would not make him change his opinion."

Tempers were getting very short, but the tension was somewhat relieved when the British briefly withdrew for consultation and for a pause in the colloquy to allow Schmidt to give an oral translation of the document into English.† It

---

* Schmidt's record describes the British as "extremely taken aback" by this news, but in view of their earlier communications with Halifax they can hardly have been greatly surprised.

† At about this point, the Schmidt and Kirkpatrick records differ in the order and content of the discourse. The Kirkpatrick version is fuller and probably more accurate chronologically, as Schmidt was doing the oral translation, which must have limited his time and attention for record-keeping.

consisted of two introductory paragraphs, six paragraphs of specifications, a brief "appendix" of additional specifications, and a map showing the areas to be occupied by Germany on the twenty-sixth, and those to be subsequently subjected to plebiscite. When Schmidt reached the six specifying paragraphs, described in the memorandum as German "demands," Chamberlain interjected that this was "precisely the sort of language he had in mind when he criticized the tone of the memorandum." Hitler said that he was willing to substitute "proposals" for "demands." The fifth paragraph of "demands," rechristened "proposals," provided for final settlement of the new frontier by a "German-Czech commission" and, at Chamberlain's request, Hitler agreed to provide in the alternative for "a German-Czech or an international commission."

Chamberlain then raised once more the issue of the time schedule. After some back-and-forth, Hitler, with an air of great magnanimity, agreed to eliminate the September dates and fix October 1 as the date for completing Czech evacuation of the Sudetenland and its occupation by the Germans, adding that his guest was "one of the few" or "the only man" to whom he had ever made a concession."*

Chamberlain next made an effort to restrict the initial German occupation to areas where the Sudeten German population had an 80 per cent preponderance. Hitler refused. The Prime Minister then put "one last question," arising out of the circumstance that the area to be occupied would contain "Czechs and even some Germans who had worked against *Anschluss* with the Reich." What protection would they have? "He did not suggest that they would be necessarily beaten and mishandled, but the question would certainly be addressed to him in England, and he would be grateful if Herr Hitler would provide him with an answer." It was a miserably flaccid probe, and Hitler replied only that the Saar plebiscite should serve as a reassuring example, but that any "Communist atrocities" or "murders of Germans" in the occupied areas would naturally be punished. This was far from reassuring, but Chamberlain did not pursue the inquiry, and a few moments later, at almost half past one in the morning of September 24, the meeting ended.

On the way out of the Dreesen, Hitler and Chamberlain had a brief tête-à-tête. Schmidt, who interpreted, recalls that they discussed the prospect of a general Anglo-German settlement after the Sudeten problem was resolved, and that they "parted in a thoroughly amiable atmosphere"—an impression not shared by Weizsaecker or Kirkpatrick. Ribbentrop testified at Nuremberg that his recollection was that Chamberlain said he would recommend that Prague comply with the German memorandum. The Reich Foreign Minister was far from being a reliable witness, but subsequent events lend credibility to his account.

Despite the vehemence of his initial objections to Hitler's demands, the Prime Minister's negotiation had accomplished only two minor revisions in the language of the memorandum, and a seventy-two-hour extension of the time allowed the Czechs to complete their evacuation of the Sudetenland. He had failed to win any revision of the boundaries shown on the map which accompa-

---

* Neither Schmidt's nor Kirkpatrick's records report this statement, but Schmidt's, Kirkpatrick's, and Henderson's memoirs all agree that some such thing was said by Hitler.

nied the memorandum, or any protection or economic relief for the Czechs and anti-Nazi Germans in the Sudetenland. As revised at the conference, the German document read as follows:

MEMORANDUM

Reports which are increasing in number from hour to hour regarding incidents in the Sudetenland show that the situation has become completely intolerable for the Sudeten German people and, in consequence, a danger to the peace of Europe. It is therefore essential that the separation of the Sudetenland agreed to by Czechoslovakia should be effected without any further delay. On the attached map (the map will be brought along by the delegation) the Sudeten German area which is to be ceded is shaded red. The areas in which, over and above the areas which are to be occupied, a plebiscite is also to be held are drawn in and shaded green.

The final delimitation of the frontier must correspond to the wishes of those concerned. In order to determine these wishes, a certain period is necessary for the preparation of the voting, during which disturbances must in all circumstances be prevented. A situation of parity must be created. The area designated on the attached map as a German area will be occupied by German troops without taking account as to whether in the plebiscite there may prove to be in this or that part of the area a Czech majority. On the other hand, the Czech territory is occupied by Czech troops without regard to the question whether, within this area, there lie large German language islands, the majority of which will without doubt avow their German nationality in the plebiscite.

With a view to bringing about an immediate and final solution of the Sudeten German problem the following proposals are now made by the German Government:—

1. Withdrawal of the whole Czech armed forces, the police, the *gendarmerie,* the customs officials, and the frontier guards from the area to be evacuated as designated on the attached map, this area to be handed over to Germany on October 1.
2. The evacuated territory is to be handed over in its present condition (see further details in appendix). The German Government agree that a plenipotentiary representative of the Czech Government or of the Czech Army should be attached to the headquarters of the German military forces to settle the details of the modalities of the evacuation.
3. The Czech Government discharges at once to their homes all Sudeten Germans serving in the military forces or the police anywhere in Czech State territory.
4. The Czech Government liberates all political prisoners of German race.
5. The German Government agrees to permit a plebiscite to take place in those areas, which will be more definitely defined, before at latest November 25. Alterations to the new frontier arising out of the plebiscite will be settled by a German-Czech or an international commission. The plebiscite itself will be carried out under the control of an international commission. All persons who were residing in the areas in question on October 28, 1918, or were born there prior to this date will be eligible

to vote. A simple majority of all eligible male and female voters will
determine the desire of the population to belong to either the German
Reich or to the Czech State. During the plebiscite both parties will withdraw their military forces out of areas which will be defined more precisely. The date and duration will be settled by the German and Czech
Governments together.

6. The German Government proposes that an authoritative German-Czech
commission should be set up to settle all further details.
Godesberg, September 23, 1938.

APPENDIX

The evacuated Sudeten German territory is to be handed over without
destroying or rendering unusable in any way military, commercial, or traffic
establishments (plants). These include the ground organization of the air
service and all wireless stations.

All commercial and transport materials, especially the rolling stock of the
railway system, in the designated areas, are to be handed over undamaged.
The same applies to all public utility services (gas works, power stations,
etc.).

Finally, no foodstuffs, goods, cattle, raw material, etc. are to be removed.

From the Petersberg, Chamberlain telephoned to Newton an English translation of the memorandum, directing him to communicate it to the Czech Government, "intimating that I undertook to place it before them," and adding "that at
the beginning and end of a very long conversation the Chancellor in reply to a
question from me intimated that proposal in this memorandum constituted his
last word." Colonel "Mason-Mac," who had arrived independently at the
Petersberg, volunteered to hand-carry the German text and the map to Prague.
The colonel requested one of the aircraft that had brought the British party
from London, but for some reason this was denied, so he had to make his own
way by air, automobile, and on foot—an adventurous journey which was later
to assume considerable importance.

After an early breakfast, Chamberlain was driven to Cologne and flown back
to London. Hitler lingered at the Dreesen until the afternoon, when he flew to
Berlin (where he had not been since August 26) and immediately busied himself with military matters.

For the second time, Hitler could feel that he had had the better of Chamberlain. The seventy-two-hour time extension was, of course, no concession at
all, for September 30 had already been fixed as the earliest day for launching
Green, and the assembly, transportation, and deployment schedules precluded
any attack in force before October 1. Chamberlain had agreed to transmit the
German demands, without substantial change, to Prague. Whether or not he
said that he would urge the Czechs to accept, his willingness to serve as a transmission link showed that he was desperately anxious to avoid war and would
continue to press for a settlement which would come close to meeting Hitler's
terms.

Nevertheless, the Fuehrer suffered a sharp blow while at Godesberg, delivered not by Chamberlain but by Beneš with the support of Halifax. This was the Czech mobilization, which spelled the failure of the Wehrmacht's elaborate effort to conceal the preparations for attack and gain the benefits of surprise.

For this fiasco, Hitler was personally responsible. It was he who canceled the original plan to absorb the Sudeten German refugees into the Army reserve, and who authorized Henlein to set up a separate organization outside the regular chain of command. In military terms, the "actions" of the *Freikorps* were of no more value than the depredations of rowdy boys at Halloween. But the Eger-Asch incursions finally brought home to Halifax the dangerous folly of pressuring the Czechs to stay on a peacetime basis, and triggered the very defensive measures which it had been a prime part of the Green plan to avert. Hitler had repeated the kind of mistake that he had made three weeks earlier at Saarbrücken, in ordering Adam to defend the indefensible—the same sort of mistake that he was to make again and again throughout the war: indulging political and sentimental factors to the grave detriment of military considerations.

It was no minor blunder, and if there had been war instead of Munich, it would have cost the Wehrmacht dear. Total mobilization of the Czech forces could not, to be sure, be completed in a few days. But by the time the Wehrmacht would be ready to strike, the Czech fortifications would be manned, supporting troops deployed, and air-raid preparations made in Prague and elsewhere. German losses would be far heavier, and German penetration into Czechoslovakia slower, than would have been the case if the ill-trained Sudeten Germans had been held in check, for in that event Halifax would not have taken the initiative to lift the "ban," and the Czech mobilization would have been further delayed.

6

Returning to the Petersberg in the small hours of the morning on the twenty-fourth, Chamberlain was asked by an anxious onlooker: "Is the position hopeless, sir?" The weary Prime Minister replied: "I would not like to say that. It is up to the Czechs now." The plain implication was that it was "up to the Czechs" to accept the German terms if war were to be averted.

When Chamberlain arrived at Heston Airport some ten hours later, his statement to the press was more circumspect: "I trust all concerned will continue their efforts to solve the Czechoslovakia problem peacefully, because on that turns the peace of Europe in our time." This expression spread the responsibility generally, but the statement reveals that Chamberlain was already regarding the issue as not primarily one of fairness to the Czechs but of surmounting an obstacle to a prolonged time of peace.

After leaving Heston, Chamberlain lunched with Halifax, and at half-past three o'clock met with his usual chosen few—Halifax, Simon, and Hoare. Inskip and MacDonald were again relegated to the outer circle, but Vansittart, Cadogan, Wilson, and Strang were present. Most if not all the participants had by this time read Hitler's "Memorandum" and Cadogan, for one, reacted (in his diary) explosively:

Hitler's memo. now in. It's awful. A week ago when we moved from "autonomy" to cession, many of us found great difficulty in the idea of ceding people to Nazi Germany. We salved our consciences (at least I did) by stipulating it must be an "orderly" cession—i.e. under international supervision, with safeguards for exchange of populations, compensation, etc. Now Hitler says he must march into the whole area *at once* (to keep order!) and the safeguards—and plebiscites! can be held *after!* This is throwing away every last safeguard that we had. P.M. is transmitting this "proposal" to Prague. Thank God he hasn't yet recommended it for acceptance.

After recounting his Godesberg experiences, Chamberlain presented his "analysis" of the situation. There was not much difference, he said, between the new boundaries as envisaged by Hitler and those of the Anglo-French plan. "The most difficult part was the immediate occupation by German troops, which was very difficult to deal with politically. . . ." However, "having once agreed to cession, the sooner the transfer took place the better." The Sudeten Germans could not keep order; the Germans could.

Thus the Prime Minister now held out to his colleagues as an advantage the very feature of Hitler's program which he had denounced so vehemently at Godesberg. The inconsistency is not so surprising as it first appears. The creation of an international policing force would take time and was uncertain at best. The same was true of a British force. It was true that the Sudeten Germans neither would nor could keep order, and Hitler would never accept the only reasonable solution—to leave the Czechs in control until the internationally supervised plebiscites were held—which Newton had recommended the previous day. Of course an immediate entry would be tragic for the Czechs and anti-Nazi Germans in the Sudetenland, but this is not what troubled Chamberlain most. Rather it was the *political* difficulty of selling such a process either to the Prague government or the British public.

By the time he reached London, Chamberlain appears to have concluded that the selling job must be done, and he used the inner group meeting as the starting point. Hitler, he told his colleagues, had said that the Sudeten Germans "were asking for protection, they have been beaten up, and he was resolved that they should have protection." Chamberlain was sure that Hitler would fight if these terms were rejected, in which case "Czechoslovakia would be overrun," and the Poles and Hungarians "would snatch what they could and there would be an end of the country."

Besides, the seriousness of the situation "lay less in what was immediately involved, but in what might lie beyond. Did Herr Hitler mean to go further?" The Prime Minister answered his own question:

The Prime Minister was satisfied Hitler was speaking the truth when he said that he regarded this as a racial question. He thought he had established some degree of personal influence over Herr Hitler. The latter had said to him: "You are the first man in many years who has got any concessions out of me." Herr Hitler had said that if we got this question out of the way without conflict, it would be a turning-point in Anglo-German relations. That, to the Prime Minister, was the big thing of the present issue. He was also satisfied that Herr Hitler would not go back on his word once he had given it.

On this occasion, the Prime Minister prevailed easily. Hoare rather lamely suggested that the Government "might find difficulty" in getting the German proposals accepted without "something to put on the other side" of the bargain,* but Halifax replied that, in his view, the disadvantages of acceptance were not enough "to justify us in going to war," and Simon offered no objections. The effect of all this on Cadogan, however, was cataclysmic:

> Meeting of "Inner Cabinet" at 3:30 and P.M. made his report to us. I was completely horrified—he was quite calmly for total surrender. More horrified still to find that Hitler has evidently hypnotized him to a point. Still more horrified to find P.M. has hypnotized H. [Halifax] who capitulates totally. P.M. took nearly an hour to make his report, and there was practically no discussion. J.S. [Simon]—seeing which way the cat was jumping—said after all it was a question of "modalities," whether the Germans went in now or later! Ye Gods! And during Thursday and Friday J.S. was as bellicose as the Duke of Plaza Toro. . . . I gave H. a note of what I thought, but it had no effect. . . . I told J.S. and Sam Hoare what I thought: I think the latter shares my view, but he's a puny creature. . . .

But the Cabinet meeting which followed, at half-past five that afternoon, was a different story. Chamberlain repeated his account of Godesberg, explaining Hitler's rejection of the Anglo-French terms on the basis of his "intense dislike of the Czechoslovaks," and the abrupt tone of Hitler's letter as due to the habit of Germans "to express themselves curtly."

The Prime Minister then gave "his views on the position." They consisted of arguments for accepting Hitler's demands. His initial indignation at Godesberg had been "modified" by further conversation with Hitler:

> In order to understand people's actions it was necessary to appreciate their motives and to see how their minds worked. . . . Herr Hitler had a narrow mind and was violently prejudiced on certain subjects, but he would not deliberately deceive a man whom he respected and with whom he had been in negotiation, and he was sure that Herr Hitler now felt some respect for him. When Herr Hitler announced that he meant to do something it was certain that he would do it. In the present instance Herr Hitler had said that if the principle of self-determination was accepted he would carry it out. The Prime Minister thought that he was doing so, although he had odd views as to the proper way to give effect to the principle. He did not believe that Herr Hitler thought that he was departing in any way from the spirit of what he had agreed to at Berchtesgaden.

Had Hitler indeed deceived Chamberlain so completely, or was Chamberlain deceiving his colleagues in order to win acceptance of Hitler's demands? How-

---

* Privately Hoare wrote that Chamberlain made the Germans "make some alterations; why did he not make them make more?" The statement in Hoare's memoirs (*Nine Troubled Years*, p. 312) that "the meeting of the four Ministers at once decided that Hitler's new demands were unacceptable" finds absolutely no support either in the record of the meeting or in Cadogan's contemporaneous diary entry.

ever that may have been, this certificate of good character was now used to lend credibility to Hitler's assertion that his objective was "racial unity and not the domination of Europe," where he had "no more territorial ambitions" once the Sudeten issue was settled. Furthermore, "Herr Hitler was extremely anxious to secure the friendship of Great Britain," and he had also said that settlement of the Sudeten question "might be a turning-point in Anglo-German relations." It would be a "great tragedy," the Prime Minister thought, "if we lost this opportunity of reaching an understanding with Germany on all points of difference between the two countries." He had now "established an influence over Herr Hitler," who "trusted him and was willing to work with him," and that was "the big thing in the present issue."

From this vision of a *Pax Germanica-Britannica,* Chamberlain shifted to the horrors of a confrontation. There was "no chance of getting a peaceful solution on any other lines," and the Cabinet should "examine very carefully the differences between the [Anglo-French] . . . and the present proposals, and should consider whether those differences justified us in going to war":

> That morning he had flown up the river over London. He had imagined a German bomber flying the same course. He had asked himself what degree of protection we could afford to the thousands of homes he had seen stretched out below him, and he had felt that we were in no position to justify waging a war today in order to prevent a war hereafter.

Chamberlain then minimized the impact of immediate German occupation, and ended by repeating his well-worn argument that Czechoslovakia could in no event be saved from present destruction. Just before concluding, however, he remarked that his colleagues should not "think that he was making any attempt to disguise the fact that, if we now possessed a superior force to Germany, we should probably be considering these proposals in a very different spirit." But this undermined what he had said earlier, for if yielding the Sudetenland was to lead to an Anglo-German settlement and an era of European peace, what did it matter whether Britain was weaker or stronger than Germany? Why should not Britain have yielded happily if thrice Germany's strength? It was a signal flaw in the logic of the presentation, but at the time it passed unremarked.

When the Prime Minister had finished, Hore-Belisha asked whether, if Prague rejected the German demands, "should we still hold out the hand of friendship to Germany?" Shrewdly, Chamberlain did not answer the question as asked, but said that *"if war broke out"* the hand of friendship would be withheld,* and that if the French decided to back the Czechs, "the next point would be to ascertain what action they proposed to take." Oliver Stanley remarked that Prague was likely to ask for advice before deciding what to do, and Chamberlain replied that this made it desirable to consult with the French Government. That brought Halifax into the discussion, and it was soon agreed that the French should be informed of Hitler's terms, and invited to come to London for consultation.

---

* Hore-Belisha's memoirs (p. 143) reveal that he did not realize that Chamberlain had answered a different question.

43. October 3, 1938—A military picnic near Eger in western Bohemia. At center, General von Reichenau is offering a bowl of meat stew to the vegetarian Fuehrer, who refused it and ate only the apples. On Hitler's left sits Konrad Henlein, and next to him General Keitel. On Reichenau's right are Himmler and (leaning over the table) General Heinz Guderian, commander of XVI Corps, who hosted the meal. *Library of Congress.*

44. October 7, 1938—the reviewing stand for a parade of Sudeten Germans in northern Moravia, near Jägerndorf. From left to right: Robert Ley; Karl Hermann Frank; Konrad Henlein; the Reich Sports Leader, Von Tschammer und Osten; Wilhelm Frick; Hitler; Bernard Rust, Minister of Education. *Bundesarchiv.*

45. October 9, 1938—German motorized troops entering Saaz. *Bundesarchiv.*

46. October 19, 1938—Hitler is greeted at Krummau, in the southwestern Sudetenland. Saluting is General Eugen Ritter von Schobert, commander of VII Corps. *Bundesarchiv*.

47. At Mies, west of Pilsen: A "medium" fortification, armed with two machine guns and manned by a noncommissioned officer and four to six men. *Bundesarchiv*.

48. An "independent" fortification in the Sudetenland, manned by an officer and thirty to thirty-five men, and armed with one double-barreled and three single-barreled machine guns, a 47-millimeter antitank gun, and a flame-thrower. *Bundesarchiv*.

49. The effect on a machine-gun embrasure of experimental fire from a German antitank gun. *Bundesarchiv*.

50. A Czech fortification at Saaz exploded, as the graffito says, by the 1st Company of Engineer Battalion 24, from Riesa in Saxony. *Bundesarchiv*.

51. Paris, November 1938—left to right: Lord Halifax, Neville Chamberlain, Georges Bonnet.
Fox Photos Ltd.

52. Rome, January 1939—left to right: Ciano, Halifax, Chamberlain, Mussolini. *Imperial War Museum.*

53. German motorcycle troops in Prague crossing the famous Charles Bridge over the Moldau. *Bundesarchiv.*

54. On the Wenzelsplatz (Václavské náměstí) in Prague: from left to right Constantin von Neurath, the newly appointed "Protector" of Bohemia and Moravia; Dr. Emil Hácha, successor to Beneš as President of the Czechoslovak Republic; General Walter von Brauchitsch, Commander-in-Chief of the German Army; General Milch, Goering's deputy in the Luftwaffe command; General Johannes Blaskowitz, commander of the German troops that occupied Bohemia. *Bundesarchiv.*

Duff Cooper then made a strong statement, the gist of which was that Hitler could not be trusted, that the public would not accept his demands and in, that event the Prime Minister's "influence" over Hitler would evaporate; that the Czechs would fight, and that Britain should at once order general mobilization to support them, which would "make our position clear to the German Government and might yet result in diverting them from war." Hore-Belisha and Elliot (Minister of Health) supported Duff Cooper's general view but recommended only partial mobilization.

Chamberlain strongly argued that the situation was not "so urgent that a decision was required that night," and thought that a "decision should be taken in respect of Herr Hitler's proposals" before undertaking additional defense measures. Winterton stressed the need for speed but agreed that the issue could go over to the morrow, and Halifax, Inskip, Simon, and MacDonald added their voices in support of Chamberlain's views. Halifax added that he had seen Jan Masaryk, who had declared that his country "would sooner go down fighting than accept" the German demands; the Foreign Secretary had pointed out that war might produce even worse consequences for Czechoslovakia, and urged that its leaders "take their time before reaching a decision."

Duff Cooper returned to the charge, but after a bit more colloquy it was apparent that the members were divided, and the Cabinet adjourned until the following morning, having decided only that the French should be invited to London, and that "discussion of further defence measures, including general mobilisation, should be postponed until a decision has been reached on the policy to be adopted in regard to Herr Hitler's proposals." Once again Chamberlain had prevailed on the most immediate issue, but it was clear that his basic policy was, for the first time, running into strong opposition.

Halifax, however, was not among the doubters; when he came out of the meeting Cadogan found him "completely and quite happily defaitiste-pacifist." Later that evening Cadogan drove Halifax home "and gave him a piece of my mind but didn't shake him." As for Cadogan, his "playing fields of Eton-white man's burden" standards were utterly outraged:

> I know we and they [the French] are in no condition to fight: but I'd rather be beat then dishonoured. How can we look any foreigner in the face after this? How can we hold Egypt, India and the rest?
>
> Above all, *if* we have to capitulate, let's be honest. Let's say we've been caught napping: that we can't fight now, but that we remain true to all our principles, put ourselves straight into war conditions and *rearm. Don't*—above all—let us pretend we think Hitler's plan is a *good* one. I've never had such a shattering day, or been so depressed and dispirited. I can only hope for a revolt in the Cabinet and Parliament.

When the Cabinet reassembled at half-past ten the following morning (a Sunday), Halifax announced that the French ministers would "be available for discussion at about 5 P.M. that same day." Eden, he reported, had urged rejection of the German terms as reported in the press. Answering a question, Halifax said that "no news had yet been received from Prague"; he had informed the

Czech Government that any reply to the German memorandum should be transmitted through Chamberlain, and that if it was "desired to send a special representative to London to discuss matters we should be very happy to receive him preferably on Monday." Chamberlain then answered a few questions* about the German memorandum.

Prompted by Oliver Stanley's suggestion that "the first question is to settle whether we should advise the Czechoslovak Government to accept the present offer," Halifax took the floor, and it soon became apparent that Cadogan's views had had an impact on him:

> Yesterday he had felt that the difference between acceptance of last Sunday's proposal and the scheme now put forward a week later for its application did not involve a new acceptance of principle. He was not quite sure, however, that he still held that view. What made him hesitate was that it might be held that there was a distinction in principle between orderly and disorderly transfer with all that the latter implied for the minorities in the transferred areas. . . .

> While he did not altogether share the First Lord's views as to the "March to the East," he nevertheless felt some uncertainty about the ultimate end which he (Lord Halifax) wished to see accomplished, namely, the destruction of Nazism. So long as Nazi-ism lasted, peace would be uncertain. For this reason he did not feel that it would be right to put pressure on Czechoslovakia to accept. We should lay the case before them. If they rejected it he imagined that France would join in, and if France went in we should join with them. . . .

> The Foreign Secretary concluded by saying that he had worked most closely with the Prime Minister throughout the long crisis. He was not quite sure that their minds were still altogether at one. Nevertheless, he thought it right to expose his own hesitations with complete frankness.

Chamberlain gave no oral reply—indeed, he did not speak again that morning—but, while the colloquy continued, scribbled a note to Halifax:

> Your complete change of view since I saw you last night is a horrible blow to me, but of course you must form your opinions for yourself. However, it remains to see what the French say.
> If they say they will go in, thereby dragging us in I do not think I could accept responsibility for the decision.
> But I don't want to anticipate what has not yet arisen.

Halifax replied on another slip:

> I feel a brute—but I lay awake most of the night, tormenting myself and did not feel I could reach any other conclusion at this moment, on the point of co-ercing CZ.

---

* One of these related to the appendix, which would have prohibited the removal of "foodstuffs, goods, cattle," etc., from the areas to be occupied by Germany. This, said Chamberlain, "related only to the period up to the occupation by German troops." Thereafter these matters would be regulated by the proposed German-Czech commission. Making all allowances for the advantages of hindsight, it is hard to believe that such an answer could have been given or taken seriously.

The Prime Minister wrote "Night conclusions are seldom taken in the right perspective" on Halifax's slip and passed it back. Halifax took up a third slip and answered: "I hope you don't think I agree with Buck [De La Warr]! I should like the Czechs to agree on the facts—but I do not feel entitled to coerce them into it." This slip also came back to him with Chamberlain's rejoinder:

> I can't help feeling that there is some confusion. What pressure *can* we put on the Czechs except the negative one of saying that we are not coming in unless the French are in it? What we should do is to discuss frankly with the French the position. If in the end they do go in we must still be in Mar. 24 position.*
>
> What D.C. [Duff Cooper] and O.S. [Oliver Stanley] want us to do is to *encourage* French and Czechs to resist and *promise* them our help. That I will not myself consent to.

As this interchange reveals, Chamberlain saw Paris rather than Prague as the key to the problem. What troubled him about Halifax's note, apart from the bare fact of his closest and most influential colleague's defection, was that the Foreign Secretary might not join wholeheartedly in exerting the necessary pressure on Daladier.

While Chamberlain and Halifax had been passing their slips back and forth, Lord Hailsham had been delivering a long recitation of Germany's broken promises—in 1935 to respect the Locarno obligations; in 1936, after the Rhineland reoccupation, to assert no further territorial demands in Europe; after the Austrian *Anschluss,* to respect Czechoslovakia's territorial integrity. Hitler simply could not be trusted. He joined Halifax in opposing any "pressure" on the Czechs.

One after another, the members expressed their views or temporized. Simon, Maugham, Kingsley Wood, Stanhope (Education) and Burgin (Transport) came out squarely in support of the Prime Minister. Duff Cooper, Winterton, De La Warr, Oliver Stanley,† Hore-Belisha, and Elliot joined Halifax and Hailsham in opposing any effort to push the Czechs to accept the German terms, and most of them were far more bellicose than the two senior ministers, almost to the point of recommending war now rather than later. Inskip, MacDonald, Zetland (India), Colville (Scotland), and Morrison (Agriculture) all purported to disapprove putting "pressure" on the Czechs, but at the same time advocated "laying the facts" before the Prague government. All five believed that it was better to accept Hitler's terms rather than go to war, and it was plain that, if it came to a vote, they would be in Chamberlain's corner. Hoare declared that "the proper course was not to put any pressure on the Czechs either to accept or to reject those proposals." He suggested further consultation with the Chiefs of Staff, discussions with France and Russia, and counterproposals (of an unspecified nature) to Hitler.

---

* The reference is to Chamberlain's speech in the Commons on that date, stating his policy of no fixed commitment to join France in a war against Germany precipitated by the Sudeten issue.

†The President of the Board of Trade. Lord Stanley, Secretary for the Dominions, was ill and did not attend these meetings; he died a few weeks later.

During these exchanges, Halifax had received and reported a message from Jan Masaryk asking an opportunity to present "an urgent message from his Government" at the meeting with the French ministers; this was agreed to. Later there was a luncheon adjournment, and when the meeting was resumed at three o'clock Halifax announced that the French Cabinet was in session and that Daladier could not be expected in London until the evening.

When every member had expressed himself, Chamberlain spoke at some length. He began by minimizing the differences of opinion, and urging that "faced with a critical situation . . . it was important that the Cabinet should present a united front." He then took essentially the line reflected in his earlier exchange of notes with Halifax: it was up to Prague, not London, to accept or reject Hitler's terms; no decision was possible until the French intentions were known; therefore the immediate question was "the attitude we should take up at the forthcoming interview with the representatives of the French Government and with the Czechoslovak Minister." In the last analysis, "it seemed likely that Czechoslovakia's attitude would be determined by the attitude of France." He disagreed with Duff Cooper's view that the Czechs should be encouraged, by the promise of military support, to reject Hitler's terms, because "we could not take that course this afternoon unless the whole Cabinet was united in support of it, and it was evident that this was not the case." He doubted that Hoare's suggestion of counterproposals was promising.

From all this, the Prime Minister drew the conclusion that the Government should remain in essentially the position he had outlined on March 24 in Parliament. In the discussions with the French and Masaryk, he would decline to say that Britain either would or would not declare war on Germany if Prague rejected the terms. But he would put forward "the full facts of the situation, as we saw them, in their true light."

Tactically, it was a masterly presentation—Chamberlain at his most persuasive. But of course the members did not all see the situation in the same light; there was no consensus on the "true light." Chamberlain was temporizing, and that was what the majority of his colleagues wanted.

The dissenters, however, were not silenced. Oliver Stanley urged that "immediate steps . . . be taken to set on foot further precautionary measures" and declared that "the time had come when we should define our policy in clear and unmistakable language." France should be assured that if she was "prepared to support Czechoslovakia energetically, we should join" her. Duff Cooper thought "that there was a risk of a marked difference of opinion" and spoke of resigning, but was dissuaded by Chamberlain from "any precipitate action." He and Stanley then "expressed some anxiety that the attitude to be adopted" in the conversations with the French (now scheduled for nine o'clock that evening) "had not been more fully defined," and Stanley suggested that the conversations "be divided into two parts." First the views of the French would be ascertained, and then the talks should be temporarily adjourned so that the Cabinet could be reassembled for further consultation "before any formal decisions were reached."

The Prime Minister accepted this suggestion,* and the Cabinet so agreed. It was left to Chamberlain and Halifax to decide whether to see Masaryk before or after meeting the French. The Cabinet adjourned at about six o'clock to await the expected recall.

7

Jan Masaryk was an ebullient, charming man, and a favorite guest of many leading Britons. As befitted the son of Thomas Masaryk, the minister was intensely proud of his country and its heritage, and even after his government accepted the Anglo-French proposals, he continued to hope for some development that would preserve Czechoslovakia's territorial integrity and capacity for self-defense. Curiously enough, the first thing to give him satisfaction was Lord Runciman's report—which had certainly been intended by its signatory to help Chamberlain rather than the Czechs, but which (probably due to Ashton-Gwatkin's influence) laid the blame for breaking off the Sudeten-Czech negotiations on the Henleinists, and proposed cession of only those parts of the Sudetenland where the Germans were an "important" majority. On the morning of the twenty-third Masaryk telephoned Beneš, describing the report as "very interesting" and "absolutely orderly and honorable," but not to be published until further notice from the British.

The news that the Godesberg conference was going badly was music to Masaryk's ears and far from unwelcome to Beneš, for it raised the possibility that France and Britain might reach an impasse with the Germans and perforce lend greater support to the Czech cause. These hopes, strongly entertained by Masaryk, were reflected in several of his telephone conversations with Beneš, and so immediately became known to the German government through Goering's intercepts.

Although the Foreign Office had received by telephone an English translation of Hitler's ultimatum early in the morning of September 24, there appear to have been difficulties with the transmission or encipherment when London relayed the message to Prague and Paris. Newton was unable to deliver the text in Prague until six o'clock that evening, and Phipps in Paris not until ten o'clock. Consequently, when Masaryk telephoned Beneš shortly before noon to inquire about the "plan," Beneš had not yet seen the document. Masaryk reported a rumor that under Hitler's plan the Czechs would have to withdraw from the fortifications and allow the Germans to "march in." President and minister agreed emphatically that such a procedure was out of the question. Masaryk spoke enthusiastically about the pro-Czech attitude of the British press.†

Very shortly after this conversation, Cadogan gave Masaryk a copy of the Hitler memorandum. Masaryk took it immediately to Eden, who advised him to go at once to Halifax to get a statement of the British attitude. Halifax saw him

---

* At about this time Hore-Belisha passed a note to Chamberlain asking "why should not the French Ministers meet the whole Cabinet." Chamberlain passed it back with a penciled reply: "Perhaps at the 2nd meeting, but not at the first."

† At the end of the conversation Beneš spoke of the strain he was under, and Masaryk counseled his President that "the main thing was to sleep well and avoid constipation."

promptly, but there was no meeting of the minds; Masaryk was intransigent, and the Foreign Secretary, not yet swayed by Cadogan, told the minister that rejection of Hitler's terms might lead to even worse consequences for Czechoslovakia.

Meanwhile, Mason-Mac was en route to Prague, carrying the German text of Hitler's memorandum, with the map showing the areas to be immediately occupied by German troops and the additional plebiscite regions. The colonel himself found it "difficult to understand why the Prime Minister undertook to ensure the delivery of this shocking document," but volunteered for the task because the German-Czech frontier was closed and "it seemed to me that a soldier who knew the country would have the best prospects of getting through."

On the morning of the twenty-fourth Mason-Mac (in company with Ian Colvin in a Lufthansa plane) flew to Berlin, where he took an automobile with a German driver and, in company with the Czech assistant military attaché, drove to the frontier at Zinnwald, which they reached at dusk, and found the road across the border solidly blocked. There was rifle fire coming from nearby woods, where men of Henlein's *Freikorps* were sniping at the Czech border patrols. But the telephone line from the Czech guardhouse to Teplitz-Schönau (a small city a few miles beyond in Bohemia) was working, and the Czech officer arranged with the regimental commander there to give them a car for the last lap to Prague. Guided by a Czech customs official, Mason-Mac and his companion struggled through the woods for two hours. From Teplitz-Schönau to Prague they made slow progress because of military traffic and roadblocks, and did not reach Prague until quarter past eleven. The German memorandum and map were delivered to the Czech Foreign Ministry shortly before midnight, and Mason-Mac then retraced his steps to Berlin.*

At eight o'clock the following morning, September 25, Beneš called in Lacroix and told him that the Czech Government would abide by the Anglo-French proposals but would go no further. He requested that the French refuse to approve the German demands, and so inform London. Later that day he instructed Osusky to conduct discussions with the French on the basis that Prague would adhere absolutely to the Anglo-French proposals, which offered hope of eventual amelioration through the international commission, but would firmly refuse to evacuate the fortifications.

Shortly after half-past eight the same morning Masaryk conducted a telephone conversation with Beneš which must have been of great interest to the eavesdropping Germans:

M. Mr. President, after lunch I will be meeting the top leaders here, and it would be desirable that I say something in your name to the English and French . . . the situation is grotesque . . . another effort will be made here, do you understand? By the Conservative Party, and we must kill it right away! . . . So I want your authority. If Daladier comes here, I will say that I have a communication from you for him and the English. In it, I

---

* Much to Mason-Mac's chagrin, he found a guard of honor drawn up for him on the German side of the frontier, and was thanked by a general for acting as Hitler's messenger under hazardous circumstances.

will say that . . . we have shown good will and accepted their plan
. . . but regret that we cannot accept this document.

B. I agree, and will telegraph you the details.

M. Have you seen the map?

B. Yes . . . it means we put our whole state into Hitler's hands. . . .

M. No one has given me the map; it's a big rascality. . . .

B. A plebiscite is expressly called for, and under their occupation
. . . Mährisch-Ostrau and Witkowitz are connected to the rest [of the
country] by a slim neck. . . . The connection between Bohemia, Moravia, and Slovakia is a neck sixty kilometers wide.

M. Then I can say we can't accept it. . . .

B. That you can say. You have full approval for this.

M. I will be with the Foreign Minister and I will certainly say that. I must ask
you in this historic moment for your approval. You and Syrový, etc.*

B. Yes . . . The main thing is that we not be asked to evacuate our own territory. . . . We can't weaken on this. . . .

So armed with authority, Jan Masaryk composed a letter to Halifax embodying his government's refusal of the Godesberg terms, and presented it to Chamberlain, in the presence of Halifax,† after the Cabinet recessed and before the
meeting with the French, to whom Masaryk delivered a copy. More a reflection
of emotional patriotism than an instrument of diplomacy, it opened with a reference to "the unbelievably coarse and vulgar campaign of the controlled German
press and radio against Czechoslovakia and its leaders, especially Mr. Beneš." It
continued with a reminder to the addressee that "the so-called Anglo-French
plan" had been accepted in Prague only "under extreme duress" and despite "its
many unworkable features," and on the understanding that "it was the end of
the demands to be made upon us." Even after these sacrifices "the vulgar German campaign continued," and now the Godesberg meeting had produced "a
new proposition." After study, the Czech Government had found that:

> It is a *de facto* ultimatum of the sort usually presented to a vanquished na-
> tion and not a proposition to a sovereign state which has shown the greatest
> possible readiness to make sacrifices for the appeasement of Europe. . . .
> The proposals go far beyond what we agreed to in the so-called Anglo-French
> plan. They deprive us of every safeguard for our national existence. We are to
> yield up large proportions of our carefully prepared defences and admit the
> German armies deep into our country before we have been able to organize it
> on the new basis or make any preparations for its defence. Our whole na-
> tional and economic independence would automatically disappear with the

---

* There is no published mention of a Syrový government meeting to consider the Godesberg terms, and one writer (Thompson, *The Greatest Treason: The Untold Story of
Munich*, p. 213) suggests that Masaryk acted without authority from Prague. The quoted
telephone conversation indicates otherwise. Mobilization was under way, the Czech
ministers were busy, and it may well be that Beneš consulted them by telephone, thinking a
meeting unnecessary in view of the obvious unacceptability of the Godesberg terms. In his
memoirs, Beneš wrote that he and Jan Masaryk discussed rejection of the Godesberg terms,
and that the Masaryk letter of September 25 was composed by Masaryk on the basis of
that discussion.

† There appears to be no British record of this meeting, but it is confirmed by its mention
in Strang's memorandum written the following day.

acceptance of Herr Hitler's plan. The whole process of moving the population is to be reduced to panic flight on the part of those who will not accept the German Nazi regime. They have to leave their homes without even the right to take their personal belongings or even, in the case of peasants, their cows.

And Masaryk the son concluded, with pardonable grandiloquence:

My Government wishes to declare in all solemnity that Herr Hitler's demands in their present form are absolutely and unconditionally unacceptable to my Government. Against these new and cruel demands my Government feel bound to make their utmost resistance and we shall do so, God helping. The nation of St. Wenceslas, John Hus and Thomas Masaryk will not be a nation of slaves.

We rely upon the two great Western democracies, whose wishes we have followed much against our judgment, to stand by us in our hour of trial.

CHAPTER 30

If at First You Don't Succeed . . .

1

By the early evening of September 25, Neville Chamberlain's peace-keeping efforts had suffered what appeared to be decisive setbacks. Confronted at Berchtesgaden with demands far more extensive than he had expected, he had hammered the Czechs into accepting them, only to suffer humiliation at Godesberg, where Hitler had spurned his accomplishments and presented new and even more onerous terms. Convinced that it was nevertheless better to accede than go to war, he had returned to London hoping to persuade his colleagues of the wisdom of this course, but had encountered a sharply divided cabinet, with two of the three service ministers and Halifax, the most senior and hitherto a supportive member, among the doubters. Probably Chamberlain could still swing a majority behind his policies, but on such grave issues, especially after Eden's resignation, that was not enough. And now, just as he was about to meet with the tortured French leaders, Jan Masaryk had handed him Prague's categorical rejection of the Godesberg terms, in a declaration ringing with the invocation of Bohemian kings and martyrs.

Furthermore, the tide of public sentiment was turning, unmistakably, against the Prime Minister. Halifax's admonitory telegram of the twenty-third had referred to "public opinion as expressed in press and elsewhere" and was not based on any systematic inquiry; the techniques of opinion-testing were then in their infancy. But two young pioneers of the art were conducting a survey which, crude and limited as it was by today's standards, shows plainly enough that Halifax was essentially right.*

Even after *Anschluss* the British public remained predominantly apathetic or confused about foreign policy, with no strong current for or against the Government's policies.† But the indifference was dissipated by Hitler's Nuremberg speech and the announcement of Chamberlain's flight to Berchtesgaden; newspaper space devoted to foreign affairs was doubled, and there was a pronounced swing of opinion in favor of Chamberlain. A poll in an urban, working-class,

* Charles Madge and Tom Harrison, *Britain by Mass-Observation* (Penguin, January 1939). The conclusions are based on the work of some 1,500 amateur "observers," constituting an organization called Mass-Observation.
† In March 1938, Mass-Observation put the question "What do you think about the country's foreign policy." Of those asked, 35 per cent did not answer at all, and 26 per cent gave uncertain, confused replies. Slightly under 20 per cent declared themselves satisfied, and slightly over 20 per cent dissatisfied with the policy.

pro-Labour district showed 70 per cent in support of and only 10 per cent opposed to the Prime Minister's action.

But the publication on September 20 of the gist of the Anglo-French proposals produced a strong anti-Chamberlain reaction. On the twenty-first and
twenty-second a poll of 350 persons on the question "What do you think about
Czechoslovakia" produced an indignantly anti-Chamberlain response from 40
per cent as compared to 22 per cent in his support (nearly a third "didn't
know"), and among the males two thirds of the responses were negative and
plainly anti-Government. There were angry demonstrations; walking home in
the evening of September 22, Duff Cooper encountered a "vast procession . . .
marching down Whitehall crying, 'Stand by the Czechs' and 'Chamberlain must
go.'"

There is no indication that any of this opposition—whether from the press, the
public, the Labour Opposition, or his own Cabinet colleagues—had any persuasive effect on Neville Chamberlain or substantially altered his conception of the
course his country should pursue. He was not the man to yield lightly, and these
developments he regarded simply as political obstacles to be faced and overcome. And if it were to be asked where, beyond his own strong conscience and
confidence, he found the most solid support and encouragement, it would be
from the British military leaders and the spokesmen for the Dominion governments, who were proving as impervious as Chamberlain himself to the changing
currents of public opinion.

At the Cabinet meeting on September 12, Kingsley Wood had suggested an
updated military assessment, and the Chiefs of Staff responded on the fourteenth, with an "Appreciation of the Situation in the Event of War Against Germany."* Since on this occasion the Chiefs were not asked to analyze Churchill's
"grand alliance" concept, their report was organized quite differently from the
one submitted in March after *Anschluss*. However, the new "Appreciation" was
generally parallel to the March document in its temper and thrust. In both, the
conclusion rested on assumptions that Italy and Japan were potential enemies;
in the earlier report Soviet Russia was stipulated as neutral, while the later one
posited that: "The attitude of the U.S.S.R. is incalculable, and it is unsafe to assume that Soviet Russia would go to the assistance of Czechoslovakia." As we
have seen, it is altogether probable that the Kremlin's assessment of French and
British intentions was substantially similar.

The body of the report was in two parts, the first entitled "Factors Affecting
the Situation." On a long-term basis, the German war economy was vulnerable
to a naval blockade, and "purely from an economic point of view, Italian intervention should prove more of a liability than an asset to Germany." But France
too would find herself in an "extremely serious" economic situation which could
be relieved only by British and American aid. Militarily, "at sea, Great Britain
and France have a marked advantage over Germany," but "on land and in the

---

* In large part the document was based on a paper submitted the day before to the
Chiefs by the Joint Planning Committee. A slightly revised version of the Chiefs' report
was printed and circulated on October 4, 1938.

air they are at a disadvantage." Indeed, "Germany will probably be able to dispose as great, if not greater, strength than the combined strength of the three Allies."*

The Chiefs "assumed that Germany's most probable course of action would be to occupy the whole or part of Czechoslovakia, whilst standing on the defensive in the West." It was estimated that "20 regular divisions (including 8 armoured, motorized, and light divisions) are already concentrated opposite the Czechoslovakian frontiers, ready to move at instant notice, and these are likely to be reinforced by some reserve divisions." Furthermore "practically the whole of her air force would be available for this operation." These forces would conduct "an encircling advance" which would soon overrun Pilsen and Prague. On these bases, the Chiefs concluded that the Wehrmacht could occupy "the whole of Western Czechoslovakia, including Bohemia, Moravia, and Silesia . . . without any appreciable delay," and then proceed "at will" to eliminate Czechoslovakia from the war.

The second part of the report, entitled "The Intervention of France and Great Britain," began with a survey of essential British defensive measures—protection of merchant shipping against U-boats, activation of antiaircraft resources in Britain, and the commitment of land forces primarily to the defense of Britain, Egypt, and Palestine. In the air: "All our available Metropolitan air strength must be devoted to operations against Germany with the primary aim of the defence of the United Kingdom." Nothing could be spared for overseas defense, "and this would leave our defence against Italian air attack on Egypt very weak."

Turning to the offensive possibilities, the positive side was exclusively naval. German shipping would be driven off the seas and contraband controls instituted, "but we cannot expect any immediate effect from this action." On land, the report was a confession of bankruptcy: "The conduct of the war on land would be the responsibility of the French." And then, astonishingly: "We do not know whether they intend to stand on the defensive on the Maginot Line, or to attempt an offensive across the frontier. . . ." Such was the consequence in crisis of the Chiefs' long and stubborn opposition to staff talks with the French.

But the authors of the report were not without an opinion, which was that "Germany will be able to spare adequate forces to hold her fortified line in the West against attack"—a view not entertained by General Adam, whose meager forces would have to do the holding. To these enterprises Britain could at the outset at most "provide a force of two divisions which would be inadequately equipped for any offensive operations."

In the air the factors were more complex, but the immediate prospects little better. While it could be assumed that Germany would initially commit most of

* The report does not clarify the basis of this conclusion, but states: "Precise figures of the armed forces of the several belligerents are available, but we have not thought it appropriate to include details in a paper of this scope." Elsewhere it was stated that Czechoslovakia "possesses 21 divisions . . . and this number might possibly be doubled within a few days by reserve divisions." In their March report the Chiefs had allowed the French only fifty-three divisions, and on that basis Germany could probably have matched the Allied total. But in fact the French had nearly double that divisional capacity.

the Luftwaffe to the conquest of Czechoslovakia, this should not be regarded as opening the way for an Allied air offensive. German air power was "considerably greater than our own." If concentrated against Britain, it "might be able to maintain a scale of attack amounting possibly to as much as 500–600 tons per day* for the first two months of the war," though this estimate was qualified by reference to distance, North Sea weather, and the necessity of diverting some of the Luftwaffe to operations in France and Czechoslovakia.

On balance, the Chiefs thought it would be "unwise to initiate air attack upon industrial targets in Germany," since they would not be heavy enough "to produce decisive results" and "must inevitably provoke immediate reprisal action on the part of Germany at a time when our defence measures at home . . . are very far from complete." Once again, the authors had to confess: "We have no knowledge of whether the French have given consideration to the question of a strategic bomber offensive" but left no doubt of their opinion that any such action would be highly imprudent.

All of the foregoing was used to support essentially the same conclusion that had been reached in March: nothing could be done to protect Czechoslovakia against destruction, and her reconstitution could only be achieved at cost of "a prolonged struggle" to defeat Germany. There was real danger that such a conflict would bring in Italy and Japan as additional enemies, and that would create a situation "which neither the present nor the projected strength of our defence forces is designed to meet, even if we were in alliance with France and Russia, and which would, therefore, place a dangerous strain on the resources of the Empire."

It is noteworthy that the Chiefs did not touch on the problem which, in Cabinet on September 12, Oliver Stanley had posed for their consideration: what would be the military situation a year hence, if Germany had destroyed Czechoslovakia in the meantime? Despite a reminder on the sixteenth from Inskip, it appears that the Chiefs never did speak to this very pertinent question. However, on the twentieth General Sir Hastings "Pug" Ismay, then Secretary to both the CID and the Chiefs of Staff subcommittee, submitted a short memorandum on the matter to Inskip and Horace Wilson.

Ismay acknowledged that six to twelve months later Germany's margin of superiority on land and perhaps in the air would be substantially increased. He argued that the German Army's strength would still be insufficient for a quick victory over France, and that Germany's only hope for a speedy triumph was "a knock-out blow from the air." Even though the Luftwaffe's over-all strength would continue to increase more rapidly than that of the RAF, Britain's defenses against air attack would within a year "have made a big advance on our present position." On these bases he concluded that by delaying the war "we shall have heavily insured ourselves against the greatest danger to which we are at present exposed; indeed by substantially reducing Germany's only chance of a rapid decision, we shall have provided a strong deterrent against her making the attempt." From this it followed "that, from the military point of view, time

---

* The comparable estimate in the March appreciation was 400 tons per day.

is in our favour" and "If war with Germany has to come, it would be better to fight them in say six to twelve months' time, than to accept the present challenge."* Ismay's reasoning rested, of course, on the premise that there was a real risk of a speedy defeat inflicted by the Luftwaffe; if that were not so, his analysis would be worthless.

According to Inskip, Chamberlain saw the Chiefs' "Appreciation" just before he went to Berchtesgaden. In view of their past attitude he can hardly have been surprised by their conclusions, and they provided him with expert military judgment in support of his policies. If there were dissenters among the uniformed leaders, they did not raise their voices, and there were many who joined the chorus. General Sir Edmund "Tiny" Ironside,† for example, declared it "madness to expose ourselves to annihilation for the sake of the Czechs," and on September 22 pronounced Chamberlain "right" and Churchill "wrong," since Britain could not possibly "stand up against German air bombing." Three days later he acknowledged that Germany would be greatly strengthened by the elimination of Czechoslovakia, but "I am still of the opinion that we should go to any length to put off the struggle."

The Air Staff, especially, was suffused with such views. As one of its able members, Sir John Slessor, wrote in retrospect, "the possibility of what was referred to as the 'knock-out blow' bore heavily on the minds of the Air Staff." Therefore they urged that war be postponed at almost any cost and, if that proved impossible, England's slender military resources be conserved until greater strength had been attained. For the French the RAF leaders had almost as little use as the Germans had for the Italians; their Chief of Staff, Sir Cyril Newall, upon hearing that General Gamelin was considering "carefully executed offensives" against the Germans, was greatly alarmed and suggested immediate staff conversations with the French for the purpose of dissuading them from such rash measures.

The early bad news from Godesberg prompted Inskip to ask the Chiefs for a memorandum on "what action, both offensive and defensive, could and should be taken immediately in the event of Great Britain breaking with Germany in the course of the next few days." Their reply, on September 23, was a two-page document declaring that they were "most strongly of the opinion that immediate general mobilisation is a first, and vitally essential, measure." No doubt mindful that, while the Prime Minister was in Godesberg, such authorization was unlikely to be granted, the Chiefs attached a list of defensive measures which could be taken without ordering mobilization.

Meanwhile Inskip had sent them a further request, for their answer to the question: "Assuming that all the proper measures, including mobilisation, have

---

* An unofficial but notable opinion to the contrary was voiced by Liddell Hart, who urged that "although the strategic ground for a stand was much less favourable than over Abyssinia in 1935, over the Rhineland in 1936, or over Spain in the last two years, it was better to make a stand now than to postpone it—as the situation was likely to be worse the following year if Czechoslovakia was abandoned." During this period Liddell Hart was in close touch with Eden, Churchill, and the Labour Opposition.

† At that time commander of the Eastern Command in England; Chief of the Imperial General Staff during the first nine months of the war.

been taken to put us into a state of preparedness for war, what is the military action we are in a position to take in order to bring pressure on Germany?" The answer was to be based on the assumption that Italy "may at any moment join Germany," and that "Japan will be on the lookout for an opportunity to exploit the situation." The reply—the last formal report the Chiefs were to make before Munich*—was submitted on the twenty-fourth, the day that the Prime Minister returned from Godesberg.

For the most part, this last report was only an updating and recasting of those portions of the September 14 "Appreciation" dealing with Anglo-French offensive operations. Britain's naval blockade would "bring pressure, immediate but slow in effect, on Germany by interrupting her seaborne trade, except in the Baltic." As for the German Navy, the "British Fleet will endeavour by sweeps in force to destroy any enemy forces operating in the North Sea and, aided by air and submarine forces, would hope to cut off naval forces attempting to reach the Atlantic." The RAF would seek to base "a high proportion" of its bombers in France so as to bring the Ruhr and Hamburg within easier reach, but the earlier recommendation against initiating any provocative action such as bombing Germany, until Britain's air defenses were greatly strengthened, was reiterated.

The one noteworthy change related to land warfare and involved French rather than British action. On September 23 a letter from Colonel Fraser (the military attaché in Paris) reached the War Office, specifying the distribution of the German Army divisions "as given to me by" General Henri Dentz, Deputy Chief of the Army General Staff. The report showed, reasonably accurately, the concentration of most of the German Army on the Czech border, with only nine divisions in the front line on the western front. "This might be described as a thin *couverture*," Fraser wrote, "and by no means able to hold the French if they really meant business." And the reason for this "thin *couverture*," according to Fraser, was that "Hitler is convinced, in spite of all statements to the contrary, that the threat of his Air Force is sufficient to keep the French, and consequently ourselves, quiet under all circumstances."

Apparently in consequence of this information, the previous judgment that "Germany will be able to spare adequate forces to hold her fortified line in the West" was dropped, and instead it was stated: "We have always assumed that the Germans would occupy the Siegfried Line in sufficient strength to balance the French Army. Our latest information, however, is that the Germans at present have only eight or nine Divisions on their Western Frontier. Consequently, opportunities will arise for offensive operations by the French Army unless the Germans take steps to redress the balance by transferring troops from the Eastern to the Western front, immediately it is evident that France is coming in. . . . Whether the German General Staff have gathered sufficient experience to carry out these movements with the expedition of the last war is open to doubt."

* This report, like its predecessors, was based largely on a draft submitted by the Joint Planning Subcommittee, composed of the Chiefs' planning subordinates.

This was an astonishingly tepid reaction to a major change of scene,* for it showed that Britain and France *could,* if sufficiently energetic, bring immediate help to the Czechs. A speedy concentration of force on the German frontier between Karlsruhe and Luxembourg would have confronted Hitler with the choice of moving troops from the Czech border to the west, or leaving Adam, with no armor and little air strength, to defend the western front in unfinished fortifications and outnumbered four or five to one.

Of course, exploitation of the opportunity was primarily a French responsibility. But none of the military men appears to have even suggested the advisability of immediate staff contacts with the French to assess the situation.† And the reason must have been that in London, as in Paris, the last thing the generals were looking for was an opportunity for prompt offensive action.

Considering the depth of the uniformed leaders' opposition to risking a war, it is curious that two of the three service ministers were among the dissidents in the Cabinet. But it is more curious than significant, for neither Duff Cooper nor Hore-Belisha carried much weight in the Cabinet, and the latter was not respected in his own ministry. In Cabinet Hore-Belisha spoke of Britain's moral obligation to the Czechs, but there is no evidence that the information from Dentz made any impression on him, or that he took any practical steps (as Duff Cooper did) to strip for battle.

And if the Army or Navy ministers were prone to kick against the pricks of Chamberlain's leadership, at the Air Ministry everyone was in his corner. Swinton's force and independence were sorely missed; Kingsley Wood was Chamberlain's most devoted follower and was heard purveying predictions of half a million casualties in three weeks if the Luftwaffe were loosed against Britain. Harold Balfour,‡ who had succeeded Winterton as Under-Secretary for Air in May, was at one with his chief, and happy to proclaim himself in later years "a man of Munich."

Small wonder, then, that the Prime Minister used the Luftwaffe as his front line of persuasion with his Cabinet colleagues, and invited them to "consider whether the protection which we could afford today to the people of this country against German bombs was as effective as the protection which we might be able to offer in the future."

2

If the generals, admirals, and air marshals were fully mobilized behind Chamberlain's policy, the spokesmen of the Dominions, except New Zealand, were

---

* General Pownall, who returned from leave on the twenty-third, was equally cautious in his reaction to this news: "All this may give France a bit of a loophole to do *something* against Germany—the latter may have overdone their Eastern concentration at the expense of the West—it is certainly a bit risky even if their Siegfried Line is in fairly good shape by now. Fortifications are no good if the men are too thin on the ground."

† Inskip referred to this development at the Cabinet meeting on the morning of the twenty-fifth, remarking that it was "clearly of the first importance to ascertain the real facts as to France's intentions." The only such effort, prior to Munich, was made at the meetings with Gamelin the following morning.

‡ An ex-RAF officer, commercial aviation executive, and Conservative member of Parliament.

out in front pulling him along. When the High Commissioners met with Malcolm MacDonald on September 23, after bad news had come from Godesberg, all expressed the hope that Chamberlain would go a long way to reach a compromise with Hitler. The following day, with the text of Hitler's ultimatum before them, MacDonald described the Government's objections to its terms, but the discussion made it clear that all of the High Commissioners favored accepting the German demands. In his diary, Vincent Massey recorded: "All four of the H.C.s (Jordan of N.Z. is at Geneva) take a view on the basic issue rather different from MacDonald's emphasis. We are all prepared to pay a higher price for peace than he. Bruce . . . feels very strongly that the German proposals can't be allowed to be a *casus belli* & says so on behalf of his Govt.* Te Water & Dulanty speak with great vehemence as well. I take the same line. . . ."

On the twenty-fifth Bruce, by telephone and in person, sought to bring MacDonald around to the commissioners' point of view. Massey was especially upset by the increasingly anti-German tone of the British press, and noted in his diary:

> Greatly perturbed at the mood of the morning papers on the crisis. Extreme condemnation of German proposals given to Chamberlain at Godesberg. Little or no appeal to calm judgment. "Now is the time to remove the menace of Hitler," "It has to come sooner or later." These mark the growing feeling in the streets. . . . Can we let war break out—universal war with all its appalling consequences—over the method by which the Sudeten territory—already enclosed—is to be actually transferred? It's unthinkable.

Eager to check the dangerous trend, Massey sought out Geoffrey Dawson of *The Times,* who readily agreed that "something must be done." At Massey's suggestion Dawson talked with the other High Commissioners, and Bruce took steps to have the Australian Government send a "helpful" message to Chamberlain.

Malcom MacDonald saw to it that the High Commissioners' views were fully reported to the Cabinet that same day, describing them as convinced that since they had "accepted the principle of transfer a week ago . . . we ought now to accept proposals which merely concerned the method of giving effect to that principle." This distinction between "principle" and "method," which certainly held small comfort for the Czech and anti-Nazi residents of the Sudetenland, was becoming the formula most frequently invoked in support of giving Hitler his way. MacDonald himself embraced it as the basis for his personal conclusion that "the present terms should be accepted."

3

When the Prime Minister looked toward Europe, he saw virtually nothing to sway him from the counsels of the British Chiefs of Staff and the Dominion

---

* The Australian attitude was a bit eclectic. On the twenty-fourth Bruce told MacDonald that in Australia there would be "little enthusiasm" for sending troops to fight in Czechoslovakia or "anywhere in Central or Eastern Europe," but that there would be "a really enthusiastic response to an appeal for men to fight 'the dirty Italians,' in defence of Egypt, the Suez Canal, and Palestine."

commissioners. If war came, the main initial burden of its conduct would fall on France, and for the French as allies Chamberlain had little use. He was no military man but had a shrewd if uneducated hunch that the French lacked the will to fight, and that their army was far from being that "greatest army in the world" in which so many democrats put so much hope.

The information coming from France confirmed Chamberlain in these views. Colonel Fraser's report received September 23 described an interview on September 20 with Colonel Gauché, who had informed Fraser: "Of course there will be no European War, since we are not going to fight." Gauché "went on to say that they could not face the risk of the German air threat—since their material was so superior that they (the French) were powerless to deal with it."

Another report from Fraser concerned his meeting on the twenty-third with General Dentz, who had predicted that Hitler at Godesberg would make new demands, including satisfaction of the Polish and Hungarian claims and the division of the remainder of Czechoslovakia into two demilitarized states comprising respectively Bohemia and Slovakia. Fraser had inquired: "What then, since you don't intend to fight?" and had "suggested that the situation had deteriorated since Colonel Lindbergh's visit and his stories of the German Air Force." In response: "General Dentz did not react; he merely pointed out that French cities would be laid in ruins and that they had no means of defence. They were now paying the price of years of neglect of their Air Force."*

Colonel Fraser was only reporting what leading French General Staff officers were telling him, but his chief, Ambassador Phipps, was editorializing freely and selecting his sources from defeatist circles. On the twenty-fourth he reported Flandin's view that "all peasant class were against war," and added his "own impression" that if a vote in the *Parlement* on going to war were to be taken that day, "the issue would be doubtful." The next day he passed to London the views of Joseph Caillaux, Premier in 1911, a proponent of Franco-German *rapprochement* throughout his long political career, bitter opponent of long-dead Clemenceau and Poincaré, and in 1938 President of the Finance Commission of the Senate and as pro-German as ever. He now told Phipps that "a large majority of French are against the war," that "a large majority of the Senate would vote against it," that "a small majority of the Chamber might be for it" since "A number of legislators are paid by Soviets," and that in the event of war "From the air our towns will be wiped out, our women and children will be slaughtered . . . Heavy bombardments of factories around Paris may cause another Commune."

A third message, dispatched on the twenty-fourth, conveyed Phipps's "purely personal impressions":

> Unless German aggression were so brutal, bloody and prolonged . . . as to infuriate French public opinion to the extent of making it lose its reason, war now would be most unpopular in France.

* In Cadogan's diary under date September 22, and apparently on the basis of these messages, he wrote: "News from France shows more and more the badness of their military (air) position and their growing disinclination to fight. So the Dictators will have it *all* their own way."

I think therefore that His Majesty's Government should realize extreme danger of even appearing to encourage small, but noisy and corrupt, war group here.

All that is best in France is against war, *almost* at any price (hence the really deep and pathetic gratitude shown to our Prime Minister). Unless we are sure of considerable initial successes we shall find all that is best in France, as well as all that is worst, turn against us and accuse us of egging French on to fight what must have seemed from the outset a losing battle.

To embark upon what will presumably be the biggest conflict in history with one ally, who will fight, if fight she must, without eyes (Air Force) and without real heart must surely give us furiously to think.

The Foreign Office staff took a very dim view of this sort of diplomatic reporting. According to Strang, the message "struck us with a sense of outrage." Harvey wrote: "I have never seen anything like the defeatist stuff which Phipps is now sending us. He is either not reporting honestly feeling in France or else is taking no trouble to find out opinions which may be unpalatable to H.M.G. It is tragic that at such a time we have three such wretched ambassadors (Rome, Berlin and Paris)." Cadogan promptly requested Phipps to report on the views of other "public men," including Gamelin, Pétain, Herriot, Blum, Reynaud, and Laval, and asked whom Phipps meant to include in his "noisy and corrupt war group." Surely he did not refer to "all those who feel that France must carry out her treaty obligations to Czechoslovakia." Who, then, comprised it, and "what are your reasons for describing it as corrupt?"

The rebuke had immediate impact on the tone of Phipps's dispatches.* But the "corrupt war group" message found favor in the highest circles, and Chamberlain read it aloud at the Cabinet meeting on the twenty-fourth, just after his return from Godesberg.

Viewed from Downing Street, the Russian prospect was even bleaker than the French. The Soviet Government, it was thought, could do little; if it could, it would not; even if it could and would, it was an unwelcome ally, since any success it might achieve would spread Bolshevism in Europe. If the Kremlin refused to make commitments, it showed that its leaders would do nothing to help; if they made promises, it would be only for the purpose of fomenting strife among the other great powers.

Despite this gloomy assessment, on September 23 the bad news from Godesberg moved Halifax to send a message to "Rab" Butler, who, with Lord De La Warr, was heading the British delegation at Geneva, asking that Litvinov be approached in order to obtain "any precise indication of what action Soviet Government would take in event of Czechoslovakia being . . . involved in war with Germany, and at what point they would be prepared to take it."

Thinking back on Chamberlain's curt rejection of the Soviet bid for joint action in March after *Anschluss,* and the British Government's cool attitude to-

---

* On the twenty-sixth Phipps replied that the "corrupt war group" meant "the Communists who are paid by Moscow and have been working for war for months," and excused the offending telegram on the ground that it had been sent before the terms of Hitler's ultimatum became known in France.

ward comparable Soviet proposals early in September, Litvinov must have derived wry satisfaction from this belated exhibition of British interest in Soviet views. Furthermore, only three days earlier Litvinov, in an address to the League Assembly, had committed his country "to fulfill our obligations under this [the Czech-Soviet] pact and, together with France, to afford assistance to Czechoslovakia with ways open to us." Such assurances, he added, had been extended directly to the Czech Government, and the Soviet military authorities stood "ready immediately to participate in a conference with representatives of the French and Czech War Departments, in order to discuss the measures appropriate to the moment."

On the twenty-third Litvinov recurred to the subject in a public statement before a committee of the League Assembly, in order to explain the conditional nature of his country's obligation to give military support to the Czechs, pointing out (as was the fact) that the Czech Government "had at the time insisted that Soviet-Czech mutual assistance should be conditional upon assistance by France." If France took no action, the Soviet Government "might come to the aid of Czechoslovakia only in virtue of a voluntary decision on its part, or in virtue of a decision by the League of Nations," but it had no *duty* to act independently of France's fulfillment of her obligations, and the Czech Government had raised no such question.

Because the Czech crisis kept the senior British ministers in London, the British delegation to the League was a curious mix. The only Cabinet member was "Buck" De La Warr, the Lord Privy Seal, who was one of Chamberlain's scorned "boys' brigade" and a dissenter from the appeasement policies. He shared the leadership with the Under-Secretary of the Foreign Office, "Rab" Butler, an able man with a crooked smile and a strong fancy for himself as a realist. With him at Geneva was his parliamentary private secretary, Henry "Chips" Channon, a wealthy social butterfly and ultra-Conservative M.P., anti-Semitic, violently anti-Soviet, pro-Franco, idolatrous of Chamberlain, and scornful of the League of Nations as "almost a joke," with "bars and lobbies . . . full of Russians and Jews who intrigue with and dominate the press."*

Shortly after the League committee meeting on the twenty-third, De La Warr and Butler met with Litvinov and Ambassador Maisky, whom Litvinov had summoned from London to join the Soviet delegation. The Britishers asked whether Litvinov could "develop further" what he had said publicly, and "in particular at what point Soviet Government would be prepared to intervene."

Litvinov's reply, according to Butler's report to London (which coincides in all important respects with the account in Maisky's memoirs), included the following:

* Channon, from a wealthy Chicago family, married into the Guinness fortune and was naturalized a British subject. Few took him seriously, but Butler enjoyed the association with a *bon vivant* with "a useful nose for gossip, and a great sense of friendship." Published extracts from his diaries tell the reader that he and Butler shared faith in Chamberlain and Halifax because: "Either would do an even dishonest deed to reach a high goal," and that after Anthony Eden's resignation as Foreign Secretary no one in the Government wore Homburg hats, only bowlers. On September 21, Channon left Geneva to visit his "old friend" Prince Paul, Regent of Yugoslavia.

He said that he could say no more than that if French came to the assistance of the Czechs Russians would take action. . . . He said that they might
desire to raise the matter in the League; this would not alter the proposition
that he had stated, namely, that Czechoslovakia Pact would come into force.
He said that he welcomed the fact that we had asked him to talk to us. He
had long been hoping for conversations between Great Britain, France and
Russia, and he would like to suggest to us in this informal conversation that a
meeting of the three powers mentioned, together with Roumania and any
other small Power who could be considered reliable, should take place away
from the atmosphere of Geneva, and preferably in Paris, to show Germans
that we meant business. . . . He would be ready then to discuss military and
air questions, upon which he was not posted, since he had been away from
Russia for such a time. He could not therefore tell us to what extent Russian
army was mobilized or air force ready to assist Czechoslovakia. . . .

If Halifax had a serious desire to explore Russian military preparations, he
had certainly bungled things. It was absurd to ask such questions without preparatory forewarnings, reasons for asking the questions, and prior decisions on
what might be told reciprocally. It was absurd to put such questions to the Foreign Minister at Geneva. It was absurd to have them propounded by second-
flight officials having no authority or responsibility for military affairs. It is easy
to imagine the reaction at Whitehall if some inconspicuous Soviet bureaucrat
had showed up at Geneva, or London, and put comparable questions to Butler
or Halifax.

Halifax must have been aware of these *bizarreries,* and it is hard to believe
otherwise than that the affair was more of a ploy than a probe. The meeting
with Litvinov would enable the British Government to say, if asked, that it had
been in direct communication with the Soviet Foreign Minister, and that he had
been unable or unwilling to say what military steps his government had in mind,
in case Germany attacked Czechoslovakia. Far from trying to explore seriously
the possibilities of helpful military action by the Russians, the British were gathering ammunition to support their contention that no effective help could be expected from Moscow. This analysis is confirmed both by London's failure to
pick up Litvinov's bid for a meeting at which the military situation could be
seriously explored, and by Butler's memoirs, in which he recorded his belief that
"the Russians themselves did not mean business," largely on the basis of Litvinov's rejection of questions which Butler himself would have been unable and
unwilling to answer had they been put to him.*

The British knew perfectly well, without talking to Litvinov, that the political
geography of Eastern Europe made direct action by Russia against Germany
very difficult. Of course it was true, in a sense, that the Russians "did not mean

---

* Butler's account (in *The Art of the Possible,* pp. 69–72), absurdly tendentious, blames
Moscow for the conditional nature of its commitment, although his own government would
not even go that far. He accuses Litvinov of being "deliberately evasive and vague," while
Chamberlain was still sticking to his March 24 formulation intended to keep the Germans
and French "guessing" what Britain might do. At the very time of his meeting with Litvinov, the British Chiefs of Staff were confessing their ignorance of whether the French
Army would attack or stand on the defensive, and the British Government had not yet decided whether or not to send an expeditionary force to France.

business," but this was in large part due to their accurate perception that the last thing either France or Britain wanted was "business" if that meant war. It was, after all, France and not Russia that had encouraged the Czechs and other Central European countries to rely on France and the Anglo-French entente to protect them against Germany. The most charitable description that can be applied to the Chamberlain-Halifax-Butler attitude on the Soviet aspect of the Sudeten crisis is that it was a case of a black pot calling a gray kettle black.

But Litvinov had one real piece of news for his British interlocutors. Earlier that day Moscow had informed Warsaw that in the event of a Polish attack against Czechoslovakia the Soviet-Polish nonaggression pact would be denounced.

The Soviet *démarche* had in fact been made that morning, when Litvinov's deputy, Potemkin, summoned the Polish chargé d'affaires and handed him a note. The Poles had replied defiantly a few hours later, but also denied that they had concentrated troops on the Czech border. Nothing came of this crossing of swords, since Prague was already preparing to accept the Polish demand for cession of the Teschen area.

For the event of war, however, Moscow's move was the only effective step taken by any of Czechoslovakia's "friends." The Czech Chief of Staff, General Krejčí, was deeply concerned by the possibility of a Polish military incursion which would outflank and disrupt his army's deployment against Germany. Potemkin's warning confronted Warsaw with the danger that any hostile move they might make toward Czechoslovakia might bring Soviet troops (which appear to have been already concentrated on the Polish frontier) pouring into eastern Poland, to much of which the Soviet Government would lay claim as pre-Soviet Russian territory.*

All of this is not to say that these things would surely have happened had the Czechs stood firm. However, some of them might have, and with peace and war in such uneasy balance, Soviet intentions and capabilities deserved scrutiny by the western allies. But Moscow's twice-repeated offer to join in a military assessment of the situation fell on deaf ears in London. There is virtually no mention of the Russian factor in the Cabinet minutes during the critical period, and, with one exception shortly to be mentioned, Chamberlain and his colleagues simply ignored the Soviet Union in their policy determinations.

From Italy, the best that Britain could hope for was an unfriendly neutrality, and in September, on the face of things, there was more unfriendliness than neutrality. The Anglo-Italian Agreement, by which Chamberlain set such store, still languished in the limbo where Mussolini's arrogance and indifference had dumped it in July. And since September 18, Mussolini had been giving a series

* If the Poles were unable to stop the Russians, the Germans would have soon confronted Soviet troops on the borders of East Prussia or even Silesia. According to information transmitted on September 25 from Moscow to France via the Soviet air attaché in Paris, there were thirty Russian infantry and an unspecified number of cavalry divisions deployed along the western frontier. On that same day the Riga correspondent of the New York *Times* reported large Soviet troop concentrations in White Russia and the Ukraine "ready to break through at the start of hostilities."

of speeches in the cities of northeastern Italy, in a crescendo of support for the German claims against the Czechs.

In fact the Duce, while putting up a brave and bellicose front, was being pulled inexorably into the wake of the Fuehrer, by virtue of whose conquests he hoped to profit. But he was fiercely jealous of Hitler, and as August passed with no official word from Berlin about his Axis partner's plans, Mussolini grew increasingly resentful and restive. Between August 20 and September 3 he and Ciano made three unsuccessful efforts through their ambassador in Berlin, Bernardo Attolico, to extract information from the Wilhelmstrasse. Ciano concluded, rightly enough, that "the Germans do not want to let us into the game."

A few days later, however, Prince Philip of Hesse brought to Rome a vague, turgid memorandum from Hitler, obviously designed to placate his overly inquisitive fellow-dictator without telling him anything specific. If there were "fresh intolerable provocations" from the Czechs, the Fuehrer would "intervene immediately, in spite of all threats from Great Britain and France," but he was "unable to state any definite time because he does not know this himself."

On September 12 (the last day of the Nuremberg Party Rally) came a message from Berlin proposing a Duce-Fuehrer meeting at the Brenner Pass "on any day, but not later than September 25th."* When Ciano telephoned this news to Mussolini, the Duce replied: "It is an idea which I do not reject. We will talk about it." But the next day Mussolini sent word that he wanted the meeting postponed "until the beginning of October" because until then he would be "occupied with visits to the provinces"—an unlikely reason, since these visits were all scheduled for cities conveniently near the Brenner. Berlin did not respond, and after Munich there remained no reason for such a meeting.

Gradually the Germans were becoming less secretive, and Ribbentrop now sent word that Berlin would welcome Italian press support for the view that the Karlsbad demands "have now been superseded and only a radical solution, on the principle of self-determination, can put an end to the Czech crisis." Dictator though he was, Mussolini was still a journalist at heart and often wrote unsigned articles for *Popolo d'Italia* which everyone knew came from his pen. The prompt result of Ribbentrop's request was an official *Informazione Diplomatica* published on September 13 and a "Letter to Runciman" in the *Popolo,* both urging that Karlsbad be forgotten, and the "letter" recommending "a plebiscite . . . not only for Sudeten Germans but for all nationalities who ask for it." And on September 15, while Hitler was taking precisely that position with Chamberlain at the Berghof, Ciano was saying the same to Sir Noel Charles, the British chargé in Rome.

Mussolini's tour of northeastern Italy was to commence with a speech in Trieste on September 18. In the wake of Berchtesgaden he felt the need of further information, and accordingly, on the sixteenth, Attolico was again importunate at the Wilhelmstrasse, asking guidance so that the Duce's remarks

---

* To the best of my knowledge, Ciano's diary is the only source of this puzzling episode, and there is no documentation indicating Hitler's purpose. The proposal, according to Ciano, was initially made by Goering, and subsequently confirmed "in Hitler's name." Goering was opposed to a war-like solution of the crisis, and perhaps he hoped that Mussolini would exercise a moderating influence.

would be "in full agreement" with German policy. In Ribbentrop's mind Godesberg was looming, and on the seventeenth he informed the ambassador that the Czech situation was now "intolerable" and required "an immediate radical solution," that immediate withdrawal of all military and police forces from the Sudetenland was "the primary requisite," that the only possible solution "would be the liberation of all foreign nationalities" from Czech rule, and that "Germany will settle this problem one way or another, by peaceful means or by military intervention."

Of these secret interchanges between Berlin and Rome, the British, presumably, knew nothing. But of course they heard very clearly Mussolini's pronouncement in Trieste that the Czech problem could only be resolved by "Plebiscites for all the nationalities which demand them." Furthermore, events were now assuming "the headlong movement of an avalanche, so that it is necessary to act speedily if it is desired to avoid disorders and complications." A peaceful solution was desirable, but if there was to be "a general division of forces for and against Prague, let it be known that Italy's place is already chosen."

There were, to be sure, a few less ominous signs. On September 3, Sir Noel Charles, after reading an alarming dispatch from Paris about the extent of German mobilization and the likelihood that Italy would side with Germany, informed London that "there are no indications here to suggest that Italy might be preparing for large scale military operations in the near future." Both the Army and the Air Force were in the course of reorganization and creation of new units that would "involve dislocation of the military machine for some months." Indeed, Mussolini himself stated, in his speech at Vicenza on September 26: "Up to now, Italy has taken no military measures."

But as the Duce went from city to city, the tone of his speeches hardened, with more and more references to Italy's might, and her unity with the Reich. At Padua on September 24, after the bad news from Godesberg, he laid all the blame on Prague, for mobilizing and for replacing Hodža with "a general who, everyone says . . . is too friendly with Moscow." If things came to a showdown between the democracies and the totalitarian powers, the former "will not find themselves faced by two separate countries, but by two countries which form a solid *bloc*."

Of course, memories lingered of Italian fence-sitting in 1914, and most of Mussolini's bombast about the Italian martial spirit was discounted in London as bogus. But with Ethiopia and Spain in the immediate background, what the Duce was now saying and repeating was far from incredible, and raised a strong possibility that in the event of war, eventually if not immediately, Italy would become an enemy nation.

None of the lesser European countries offered much by way of encouragement. Switzerland, the Low Countries, Scandinavia, and the Baltic countries were ostentatiously neutral. The Little Entente was cowed, Greece and Turkey remote, Poland and Hungary were doing their best to make bad matters worse. Spain was deeply indebted to the Axis and, exhausted though she was, could provide her benefactors with useful air and naval bases, and perhaps even threaten Gibraltar. On September 25, Cadogan learned that Franco would declare his neutrality, and this news he accurately described as a "crumb of comfort."

4

And what of the United States, when the news of an apparent impasse at Godesberg was flashed across the Atlantic? Free from any feeling of responsibility for the crisis, or of obligation to commit life or property to its resolution, the pundits of the press were in the catbird seat, loudly denouncing the villainy of the Axis, the cowardice of the Allies, or both. Public sentiment was overwhelmingly anti-German and pro-Czech, but no one suggested that America should *do* anything about it.

Officially, Washington's position remained one of rigorous neutrality, and this attitude was not merely formal, but reflected the general belief of officialdom that the people, for all their dislike of the Nazis, would strongly oppose any American involvement. Furthermore, the dynamics of American foreign policy were focused on the Pacific and Far East; the fleet was in the Pacific, and the United States had a military presence in the Philippines and in China, where the naval gunboat *Panay* had been sunk by Japanese gunfire some months earlier. In the corridors of the State Department, machinations in Tokyo* caused much more concern than events in Central Europe. In short, there was nothing tending to shake Chamberlain's long-held opinion that the Americans would talk big but do nothing.

But if Washington was officially silent, there were two famous Americans who were talking, one very secretly, and the other to anyone who cared to listen. The latter was Charles Lindbergh, who reappeared on the London scene at the invitation of Ambassador Kennedy, and the former was Franklin D. Roosevelt.

On September 19 the President telephoned to the British Ambassador, Sir Ronald Lindsay, and asked him to come to the White House that evening under mandate of "absolute secrecy" extending even to the State Department. But it was plain that Roosevelt expected his observations to be reported to the Foreign Office, as Lindsay promptly did:

> He [the President] said the Anglo-French note to Czechoslovak Government was the most terrible remorseless sacrifice that had ever been demanded of a State. It would provoke a highly unfavourable reaction in America. He himself was not disposed to blame the French or British Governments whose difficulties he completely understood. He spoke in a most friendly and appre-

* On September 14, the Japanese Ministry of Foreign Affairs issued a press statement praising Hitler's Nuremberg speech, supporting self-determination for the Sudeten Germans, and denouncing the Comintern, which was said to be "pulling the strings behind the Czechoslovak Government." A few days later the ministry assured the British Ambassador, Sir Robert Craigie, that the statement did not signify alignment with Germany and Italy against Czechoslovakia, but only against the Comintern. Both Craigie and the American Ambassador, Joseph Grew, thought it likely that Japan would avoid involvement, but the press statement was not reassuring, and the British Government (especially the Admiralty) remained concerned over the possibility that Tokyo would exploit the European crisis with new moves in China or further south.

ciative manner of the Prime Minister's policy and efforts for peace. If the policy . . . proved successful he would be the first to cheer. He would like to do something to help it but was at a loss to know what. . . . Today he would not dare to express approval of the recommendations put to the Czechoslovak Government. He would be afraid to express disapproval of German aggression lest it might encourage the Czechs to vain resistance. He thus felt unable to do anything. . . .

Roosevelt then predicted that the Czechs would fight; "his general staff told him they would be overrun in three weeks." If the Czechs gave in to the demands, Germany would go on to Denmark, the Polish Corridor, or Rumania. More probably Chamberlain's policy would fail and there would be war: "In this case, in his opinion, even if Great Britain and France and Russia were fighting loyally together they would be beaten if they tried to wage war on classic lines of attack."

But there was a third possibility, which the President described as "the very secret part of his communication and it must not be known to anyone that he has even breathed a suggestion." Otherwise "he would almost be impeached and the suggestion would be hopelessly prejudiced." His idea was:

Assuming present expedients would only delay crisis for a short time if at all, Western Powers might choose to call a world conference for the purpose of reorganising all unsatisfactory frontiers on rational lines. They should invite active heads of States to attend including Herr Hitler. He himself would be willing to go to it *but not if it was held in Europe.** That he would never do. But he would go half way and attend a conference in the Azores or some other Atlantic Island. . . .

The President then turned military strategist. Assuming that the western democracies were forced into a war,†

. . . he believed that they should carry it on purely by blockade and in a defensive manner. . . . The Powers should close their own frontiers to Germany, stand on an armed defensive and call on all other States adjoining Germany to adopt the same line of non-intercourse. The blockade line should be drawn down the middle of the North Sea through the Channel to Gibraltar and the Mediterranean should be closed at the Suez Canal also. Should any of the adjoining Powers refuse to join in this policy of non-intercourse . . . its supplies from overseas would be rationed. He believed that they would indeed protest against this, but that they would acquiesce fairly easily, and would make the rationing system work as it did in the last war.

When Lindsay noted a resemblance between such a strategy and sanctions, the President replied that:

. . . any suggestion of sanctions must be most carefully avoided. Blockade must be based on loftiest humanitarian grounds and on the desire to wage

* This stipulation appears to reflect Roosevelt's memory of the unhappy domestic political consequences of Woodrow Wilson's diplomatic sojourns in Europe.

† Much of this part of Roosevelt's statement was a repetition of views he had expressed in the presence of Harold Ickes two days earlier, and of Henry Morgenthau that same day.

hostilities with minimum of suffering and the least possible loss of life and property, and yet to bring enemy to his knees. In this connection he mentioned bombing from the air. He said only defense to this was to retaliate in the same way; but bombing from the air was not the method of hostilities which caused really great losses of life.

Roosevelt then declared that as President he had authority to declare the proposed blockade "effective" and exclude American shipping from the forbidden zones. This led to a discussion of the Neutrality Act, and Roosevelt suggested that its prohibitions might be evaded if the Allies should refrain from declaring war, and call their operations against Germany "defensive measures or anything plausible." Finally he turned to the possibility of direct American participation. The President:

. . . showed himself quite alive to the possibility that . . . the United States might again find themselves involved in a European war. In that case he regarded it as almost inconceivable that it would be possible for him to send any American troops across the Atlantic even if his prestige were as high as it had been just after the 1936 elections. But it was just possible that if Germany were able to invade Great Britain with a considerable force, such a wave of emotion might arise, that an American army might be sent overseas.

From the British standpoint, this was a pretty depressing conclusion to what may most charitably be described as a rambling and naïve presidential discourse. Much of it must have struck the British recipients as bizarre if not worse, such as picturing Hitler sitting in the Azores with Roosevelt and other chiefs of state and rectifying "unsatisfactory frontiers," or basing a strategy of starvation and fiery death for the German people on "loftiest humanitarian grounds." But in fact the idea of a war waged principally by blockade and bombing was approximately what London had in mind. Politely acknowledging the President's "confidence," Halifax agreed that, in the event of war, his government's "major role would probably be enforcement of blockade as President foresees," but pointed out that Italy's position presented complications, and it might be "necessary to choose between a neutral Italy with an ineffective blockade and a hostile Italy with an effective blockade."

But however one might assess the merits of Roosevelt's views, his remarkable meeting with Lindsay appears to have made no impression whatever in London. In part this may have been due to the secrecy on which Roosevelt insisted,* but Chamberlain's anti-Americanism was deep-seated, and Roosevelt's discursive observations can hardly have carried any weight with the Prime Minister. Indeed, there is virtually no mention of the United States in the records of those days until September 26, when the President issued his first peace appeal.

While Roosevelt was whispering secretly, Lindbergh was calling loud and clear. He and his wife arrived in London late in the evening of September 21, and the next day lunched at the American Embassy with the Kennedys. It was a

---

* In his reply (sent while Chamberlain was at Godesberg), Halifax assured the President: "I will observe complete secrecy in the matter." Who else saw the Lindsay dispatch is not clear; there is no mention of it in the published portions of the Cadogan and Harvey diaries. Presumably Kennedy knew nothing of it.

tense moment; that morning Prague had indicated its consent to the Anglo-French terms, but formal acceptance had not yet been received, and the next day Chamberlain was to fly to Godesberg.

In the presence of their wives, ambassador and aviator "discussed the crisis and the aviation and general situation in Europe," with Lindbergh opining that the English "can't realize the change aviation has made," and that "this is the beginning of the end of England as a great power." Anne Lindbergh recalled the men talking "about air warfare and how long it would take to 'level' a city like London or Paris (Germany is perfectly able to do it)." Walking down traffic-swollen Piccadilly after lunch, she felt "as though I were watching the dead, seeing the doomed."

Later that afternoon Charles Lindbergh returned to the embassy for talks with Kennedy and the counselor, Herschel Johnson.* In the course of these discussions, Lindbergh was asked to put his views in writing, and this he accomplished that evening and the following morning in the form of a letter to the ambassador, the substance of which Kennedy cabled to Washington:

> I feel certain that German air strength is greater than that of all other European countries combined, and that she is constantly increasing her margin of leadership. I believe that the German factories are now capable of producing in the vicinity of 20,000 aircraft each year. Her actual production is difficult to estimate. The most reliable reports that I have obtained vary from 500 to 800 planes per month. . . .
>
> I do not believe civilisation ever faced a greater crisis. Germany now has the means of destroying London, Paris, and Praha if she wishes to do so. England and France together have not enough modern planes for effective defense or counter attack. . . .

The Lone Eagle did not confine his counsels to questions of air power:

> It seems to me essential to avoid a general European war in the near future at almost any cost. I believe that a war now might easily result in the loss of European civilization. . . . A general European war would, I believe, result in something akin to Communism running over Europe and, judging by Russia, anything seems preferable.
>
> I am convinced that it is wiser to permit Germany's eastward expansion than to throw England and France, unprepared, into a war at this time. . . . For the first time in history a nation has the power either to save or to ruin the great cities of Europe. Germany has such a preponderance of war planes that she can bomb any city in Europe with comparatively little resistance. England and France are far too weak in the air to protect themselves.

What circulation Kennedy gave to Lindbergh's letter in England is not clear;†

---

* Johnson had been on the staff of Anne's father, Dwight Morrow, when the latter was Ambassador to Mexico.

† One of Lindbergh's biographers has written (Moseley, *Lindbergh,* pp. 228–29) that Chamberlain had "a summary of Lindbergh's views with him" when he went to Godesberg. This appears unlikely; Chamberlain departed London early in the morning of September 22, while Lindbergh (according to his own diary) completed his letter to Kennedy that morning, had it typed, and left it with Herschel Johnson for delivery to Kennedy.

Kennedy subsequently told Walter Winchell that he had made it available to Chamberlain and that it was an important factor in the Prime Minister's decision to avoid war. That is probably a gross exaggeration, but it is certain that Lindbergh's views immediately gained wide currency among influential Britishers. No sooner had he completed his letter than the ambassador was arranging interviews with Air Ministry officers. That evening (September 22) he dined with Group Captain Slessor, chief of the Plans Branch, who made a detailed memorandum of the conversation.

Much of what Lindbergh said was a repetition of what he had written to Kennedy, but was even more far-ranging. Freely admitting that "he was not a military expert," the great aviator tossed off opinions on complicated strategic questions with seeming abandon:

> He is convinced that our only sound policy is to avoid war at almost any cost. He spoke with admiration of Mr. Chamberlain, and said he felt that he had taken the only possible course; he felt that the present situation was largely the fault of the unwise attitude of France, Great Britain, and the United States at Versailles. . . . His whole attitude was that Germany was immensely formidable in almost every way both in her spirit, her national organization and particularly her Air Force which, he says, is incomparably the strongest in the world and stronger than that of France, the United Kingdom and the United States of America put together. . . . He said he felt gravely doubtful if Britain and France could win a war now (not only on account of the air factor), especially if Italy came in, who he said was "darned formidable in conjunction with Germany and could tie us up in the Mediterranean". . . . He said he thought the German Air Force could "flatten out cities like London, Paris, and Prague," and asked us how we proposed to defend London if it was under a curtain of low cloud and fog.*

On the following day Lindbergh lunched with Air Marshal Sir Wilfred Freeman (the Air Staff member for Development and Production), and then went with him for further discussions with staff officers at the Air Ministry. In a sense he was carrying coals to Newcastle, for the Air Ministry already entertained hopelessly exaggerated estimates of the Luftwaffe's long-range bombing capacity. But what he reported tended to confirm rather than correct these errors of intelligence and assessment,† and Lindbergh's outpourings to the Air Ministry soon reached Cabinet level. At the morning meeting on September 25, Kingsley Wood informed his ministerial colleagues about Lindbergh's visit, cau-

---

* Slessor apparently did not answer the question. If intent on probing the basis of Lindbergh's opinion, he might have asked his guest what targets he thought the German bombers might be able to find and hit in the course of a six hundred-mile round-trip mission (eight hundred if the Low Countries' neutrality was to be respected) to a target area obscured by "low cloud and fog." These distances were at or beyond the extreme loaded range of the German bombers of 1938.

† Slessor, for one, thought that Lindbergh "was probably overestimating their [the Germans'] capacity and underestimating their difficulties to some extent, possibly owing to successful propaganda," and advised Newall to take what Lindbergh said "with a pinch of salt." Nevertheless, Slessor found "much truth in his story," and was reinforced in his own opinion that, even though "by delaying the war Germany might get relatively stronger," still "in addition to the relative there was the absolute factor, and he [Lindbergh] did not feel that either ourselves or France yet had the absolute minimum for defence."

tioning them that "he had perhaps become an unwitting tool of the Germans," but describing his account of the German, Russian, and French air forces as "fair, if somewhat superficial."

If some professional airmen, while agreeing with Lindbergh's conclusions, were shrewd enough to see that he was not a dispassionate or expert military analyst, most of his other auditors were not. The news of his views traveled far and fast, even before his return to England. On September 10, Ione Robinson, vacationing in Scotland with a party that included such luminaries as Bernard Baruch and Admiral Sir Roger Keyes (hero of the Zeebrugge naval raid in 1918, retired admiral of the fleet, and Conservative M.P.), recorded that her fellow-vacationers, although neither pro-Chamberlain nor pro-Cliveden, "have been affected by the rumors circulated in England by Lindbergh. He claims, after looking over Russia's air fleet, that he found it in a chaotic condition, without leadership. . . . these observations of Lindbergh are sufficient for them to put the Russians in the ash-can."

Back in England, the Lindberghs cut a wide swath. Alfred Lesley Rowse of Oxford recalled: "Great play in those days, I remember, was made of Lindbergh, treated as omniscient in air matters, who was able to assure us that the Russians couldn't fight anyway. Dawson* quoted Lindbergh to me: he was made much of by the Cliveden set." At lunch in a London club with editor Kingsley Martin and others, Lindbergh "terrified us all by his account of the coming destruction of London." Lord Robert Brand (a prominent banker) was showing his friends a letter from Lindbergh saying that the air power of Germany was greater than that of all the European nations combined and could not be prevented "from laying the great capitals level with the ground."

On Monday the twenty-sixth the Lindberghs went to Cliveden and spent the evening with the Astors, the ubiquitous and well-connected Welsh diarist Thomas Jones, and other Astor friends and relatives. Lord Astor and Jones declared that "it was necessary for England to fight if Germany moves into Czechoslovakia"; they were countered wildly by Lady Nancy Astor, and more calmly by her son William and the Lindberghs. For a while Jones stuck to his guns, saying: "There are some things that are worth more than life." But he was soon won over, and later recorded: "Since my talk with Lindbergh on Monday I've sided with those working for peace at any cost in humiliation, because of the picture of our relative unpreparedness in the air and on the ground which Lindbergh painted, and because of his belief that the democracies would be crushed absolutely and finally."

The morning after the Cliveden dinner Jones, perennial purveyor of information and arranger of meetings that he was, went to work spreading the Lindbergh gospel. He immediately put "all that I have learned from authoritative people" before Stanley Baldwin (whom he found "for peace at any price"), and urged him to speak in the Lords to "save the country from war." He took Lindbergh to lunch with a group of his friends to give them the flyer's views on

---

* Geoffrey Dawson of *The Times,* who learned of Lindbergh's views from Kennedy on September 23: "Looked in on Joe Kennedy . . . and found him very vocal and excited and full of strange oaths. He had had Lindbergh with him, didn't see how we could go to war effectively."

Great Britain's military position. That afternoon he "borrowed one of the Astor cars and sent Lindbergh . . . to see L.G. (Lloyd George)" so that his famous fellow-Welshman "might learn at first-hand what an air expert thought of our chances."*

Thus Charles Lindbergh's views on the Sudeten crisis attained wide currency and influence in British ruling circles, while those of his President were known only to Lindsay, Halifax, and perhaps Chamberlain. It would be hard to say whether pilot or President showed himself the more naïve, and certainly nothing was lost by the secrecy surrounding Roosevelt's meandering mishmash.

Despite Kennedy's subsequent claims, there is little reason to think that Lindbergh's activities were a factor in Chamberlain's determination to avoid war, but he certainly swung influential people to that policy and provided ammunition for the arguments of those already so minded. Unfortunately, and despite his unquestionable sincerity, what he brought to England at that critical juncture was a mass of misinformation and misjudgment, the product of his lack of military expertise, gullibility, susceptibility to certain aspects of German life-style, and distaste for British casualness and Russian sloppiness. What England most needed at that moment was the capacity for calm and informed appraisal of the many factors in the crisis. Instead, Lindbergh came crying doom and destruction, and counseling only the hopelessness of anything other than surrender to the German juggernaut.

5

And so, at home and abroad, all these voices were whispering or shouting in Neville Chamberlain's ear: "You are right. Stick at it. There must be no war."

As he viewed the situation on the evening of September 25, the first problem to be dealt with was presented by the letter rejecting the Godesberg ultimatum which Jan Masaryk had handed to him and Halifax. The news that Prague had refused his demands, Chamberlain feared, might so provoke Hitler that he would reject out of hand any proposals for compromise, or even order his troops to attack Czechoslovakia without further delay. The tone of Masaryk's letter, with its reference to the "unbelievably coarse and vulgar campaign of the controlled German press and radio," increased the danger of an explosion.†

* Jones's efforts did not bear all the fruit he had expected. Baldwin did not address the Lords until October 4, after the meeting at Munich. Lindbergh and Lloyd George had no meeting of the minds; the former Prime Minister thought war "unavoidable," and Lindbergh thought his reasoning "not very clear."

Another supporter of Lindbergh's views, according to Hugh Dalton (whose memoirs do not disclose the identity of the "intermediary") endeavored to arrange an appearance by Lindbergh before Labour Party executives, but Dalton rejected the proposal on the ground that "we knew exactly what he would say, and did not wish to hear this pro-Hitler and anti-Russian story once again."

† For some hours there was doubt whether Masaryk's letter constituted the official Czech reply, which Prague had indicated would not be ready until September 26. Late in the evening of the twenty-fifth, the Czech Foreign Ministry told the British Legation that Masaryk's letter was the reply, but that a further explanatory memorandum was in preparation. On learning of this, Masaryk telephoned Prague and objected vehemently, with the consequence that early in the morning of the twenty-sixth Beneš directed Krofta to inform the British and French ministers in Prague that Masaryk's note was his government's official answer, and there would be no further explanatory message.

The Prime Minister started to lay the basis for further pressure on Prague when he and Halifax received Masaryk, by expressing surprise that the Czech troops were not being withdrawn from the border fortifications. Masaryk replied that the border had been manned only the day before on the advice of the English and French, and would not now be evacuated—an interchange which he reported to Beneš in a coded telegram, adding: "It is unfortunate that this stupid, badly informed little man is the English Prime Minister, and I am convinced by this that he won't be much longer."

Chamberlain also requested Masaryk to ask Beneš whether his government would be willing to participate in an international conference to resolve the Sudeten question. By telephone (in a communication with Beneš intercepted by the Germans) Masaryk put the proposal to his chief. Beneš thought it a hard question and expressed concern that the purpose would be to start with what his government had already accepted, and ask for new concessions. He and Masaryk finally agreed that if all previous deals were off, and the conference was directed toward finding a "new basis," he would be willing to participate.

Having thus made it plain to the Czechs that London was not resigned to war, steps were next taken to prevent publication of the Masaryk letter. At Halifax's direction, Strang phoned Masaryk and the legation in Prague, to remind the Czechs that they had agreed to transmit their reply to Hitler's ultimatum through Chamberlain, and emphasizing that release of the letter "might destroy all hope of further negotiation, of which even now we did not despair."

Masaryk assured Strang that "there was no intention of publishing the letter at this stage,"* but this did not stop him from holding a press conference in the evening of the twenty-fifth at which he displayed the map attached to the Godesberg ultimatum and explained the reasons for its rejection by his government. Thus the London *Times* and the New York *Times* on the twenty-sixth published the full text of the Hitler document. The London *Times* also printed the map, and an editorial describing the terms as "quite incapable of fulfillment," with an accompanying letter from Leo Amery vehemently denouncing the entire course of German conduct.

Chamberlain was made aware of Masaryk's press disclosures during the evening of September 25. Again fearful of their effect on Berlin, the Prime Minister called in Kordt and asked him "to transmit the following strictly confidential information": "Reports to be expected in immediate future in British and foreign press on final Czech rejection of German memorandum are not last word. Chamberlain asks that statement on result of his action be awaited. The immediate publication of the [Hitler] memorandum is . . . the work of the Czechoslovak Legation here. Downing Street is indignant at this arbitrary action." Simultaneously in Berlin, Henderson was sent to Weizsaecker to convey Chamberlain's request "that the Führer should take no notice of any reports on the course of

* Masaryk had, however, already read at least part of the letter during a telephone talk with Leo Amery, so its existence must have been known of in political circles. In Prague the British request was respected, but on September 26 the Czech Government published a long communiqué detailing its economic, military, and political objections to the Godesberg demands. This communiqué, apparently, embodied the memorandum which Prague had planned to send to London to supplement the Masaryk letter.

his present negotiations with the French and Czechs unless they came directly from himself. Any press or other messages which might appear should be disregarded as pure guesswork."

So seeking to keep the issue in suspense in Berlin and Prague, the Prime Minister turned his attention to his guests arriving from Paris.

6

As the news from Godesberg changed from puzzling to disquieting to ominous, the mood of the French stiffened. Even Bonnet approved the decision to withdraw the Allies' request that the Czechs not mobilize; even Phipps reported that "since Hitler's last demands have become known here, there is a distinct change in the attitude of public opinion. The press to-day is practically unanimous in declaring that the Anglo-French proposals must be considered as the limit of concessions to Hitler."

On September 23, Daladier conferred at length with Gamelin, who once again pointed out that Belgian neutrality and the Rhine would confine the probable area of French attack to the border between the Rhine and the Moselle, where the Germans had been building the Siegfried Line. Daladier, according to his postwar notes, referred to reports submitted by the French air attaché in Berlin, Colonel Hubert-Marie-Joseph Geffrier, and his assistant, Captain Stehlin, indicating that the defenses were not very strong.* That evening it was agreed to call up two "categories" of reserves, comprising some 600,000 men, sufficient to bring the Maginot Line up to full war strength and (together with earlier call-ups) deploy fourteen divisions along the frontier. The following morning Gamelin told Colonel Fraser that Daladier had concluded that "the only way to save peace now was to demonstrate that France was prepared to fight."

And so on September 24, while Chamberlain was flying home from Godesberg, in Paris the main hall of the Gare de l'Est, under Albert Herter's grand painting *August 1914,* was crowded with the families and sweethearts of reservists boarding trains for Strasbourg, Metz, and other points east. Alexander Werth, an eyewitness, was "impressed by the deep unity of the French people in a moment of danger," and thought that they "were certainly showing an infinitely better spirit than either the newspapers or the politicians."

When the French Cabinet met in the afternoon of September 25, Daladier was equipped with a report from the Deuxième Bureau on Hitler's ultimatum, advising him that it would entail the abandonment *"quasi-total"* of the Czech fortifications, and the near-severance of Moravia from Slovakia. According to the Premier, the Cabinet unanimously decided that the German demands must

---

* Geffrier had transmitted to La Chambre on August 2, 1938, a report on the western fortifications, based on his and Stehlin's aerial observations and French consular reports, stressing the intensity of effort on the fortifications but expressing the opinion that only the light fortifications could be completed in the near future. According to Stehlin, Gamelin was irritated by and critical of this report on the ground that the air attachés were analyzing matters beyond their competence. After Hitler's Nuremberg speech, in which he claimed that the Line would be completed before the winter, Geffrier and Stehlin reported that the Line could not be completed before the fall of 1939, and that Hitler had greatly exaggerated its present defensive power.

be rejected, and it was on that basis that he and his diplomatic colleagues went to London that evening.*

They arrived at Croyden at about seven o'clock, and met with their hosts at 10 Downing Street some two hours later. No less than seventeen sat at the table. The Prime Minister was flanked by Halifax, Simon, Hoare, Vansittart, Wilson, Cadogan, Bridges, Strang, and Roberts, while Daladier had with him Bonnet, Léger, Rochat, and Henry from Paris and Corbin and Margerie from the embassy. As at the meeting a week earlier, Chamberlain opened with an account of his meeting with Hitler, but on this occasion he had put it in writing, which he read aloud "to save time." It added nothing to his previous narratives, and concluded with the statement: "The Prime Minister left Hitler in no doubt as to the judgment which would be pronounced by public opinion on the terms of the memorandum."

Daladier then reported that the French Cabinet had unanimously rejected several features of the Hitler memorandum, stressing the immediate occupation of much of the Sudetenland by German troops, the provision for plebiscites in areas less than 50 per cent German, the lack of protection for Czechs and "democrats" living in the areas to be ceded to Germany, and Hitler's apparent intention "to destroy Czechoslovakia by force, enslaving her, and afterwards realizing the domination of Europe, which was his object." He and the Prime Minister then had a lengthy and inconclusive exchange about the interpretation of the Hitler document, in which Chamberlain sought to show that it was not as bad as Daladier had painted it. Chamberlain then put the big question: "Accepting the objections raised by M. Daladier, what did he propose to do next?" A sharp colloquy ensued:

> M. Daladier proposed that our next step should be to say to Herr Hitler that he should return to the Anglo-French proposals.
> Mr. Chamberlain asked what should be done if Herr Hitler refused.
> M. Daladier said that in that case each of us would have to do his duty.
> Mr. Chamberlain thought we should have to go a little further than that. . . .
> M. Daladier said he had no further proposal to make.
> Mr. Chamberlain thought we could not fence about this question. We had to get down to the stern realities of the situation. Assuming that the Czech Government . . . said they would not accept Herr Hitler's proposal, then . . . their reply would have to be transmitted to the German Government by the British Government. We could accompany this reply with counter-proposals, for example, referring the matter to a conference as M. Daladier had suggested.
> M. Daladier interjected that he had not made any proposal for a conference. . . .
> Mr. Chamberlain continued by stating that . . . we must . . . consider the probability that, on receipt of a reply on the lines now under consid-

---

* The unanimity may not have been so solid as Daladier indicates. Gamelin (*Servir*, II, p. 350) later wrote that Daladier told him that day that Bonnet was threatening to resign. Phipps reported to London that afternoon: "I understand on excellent authority that MM. Daladier and Bonnet have gone to London with their position marked out and that they have a limited mandate beyond which they must consult their colleagues."

eration, Herr Hitler, instead of temporizing any further, would interpret it as a rejection of his proposals and say he would march into Czechoslovakia. Mr. Chamberlain wished to know what the French attitude would be in such an event.

M. Daladier replied that Herr Hitler would then have brought about a situation in which aggression would have been provoked by him.

Mr. Chamberlain asked what then.

M. Daladier thought each of us would do what was incumbent on him.

Mr. Chamberlain asked whether we were to understand from that that France would declare war on Germany.

M. Daladier said that the matter was very clear. The French Government had always said . . . that, in the event of unprovoked aggression, France would fulfill her obligations. It was because the news from Germany had been bad that he had asked 1,000,000 Frenchmen to go to the frontier. They had gone calmly and with dignity, conscious of the justice of their cause.

Mr. Chamberlain said that no doubt M. Daladier had considered what the next step should be after that. It would be of great assistance . . . to hear from M. Daladier whether the French General Staff had got some plan, and, if so, what that plan was.

M. Daladier said . . . it was not possible for France to send help directly to Czechoslovakia by land, but France could naturally assist Czechoslovakia by drawing the greater part of the German Army against France.

Whether because bound by his cabinet's instructions or for some other reason, Daladier had told Chamberlain nothing that was not already known to all present. Chamberlain insisted on the need for further information, and turned the cross-examination over to Sir John Simon.* Was the French Army contemplating an invasion of Germany? Daladier replied that he would bring General Gamelin "to give to another conference a full technical explanation of the plans which he had already drawn up." Simon pressed; he "did not wish to appear to be playing the strategist for he was only an ordinary public man," but it was important to know whether the French would simply "man the Maginot Line and remain there without any declaration of war," or would they take "active measures." Daladier answered that "that would depend on many things." Simon asked whether the French Air Force would be used over Germany, and Daladier, by now somewhat nettled, replied that "he would consider it ridiculous to mobilize French land forces only to leave them under arms doing nothing in their fortifications" and it would be "equally ridiculous to do nothing in the air." Simon pressed on, with occasional unctuous apologies, making a mixed impression on the auditors. Wilson recalled: "Meeting with French painful. Daladier in a panic," while Cadogan recorded: "J.S. was turned on in his best manner to cross-examine French as to what they would *do*. Awful. But French kept their tempers. . . ."

Eventually Daladier suggested that Hitler be informed that an international commission was being immediately set up to draw the new boundary within "a

---

* In contrast to the first Anglo-French meeting, Halifax took no part in the discussion, perhaps because of the rift between him and the Prime Minister revealed at the morning Cabinet. Simon had been foursquare for Chamberlain and was a leading barrister and, subsequently, Lord Chancellor.

week or ten days," after which the areas to be ceded could be occupied by German troops. "No honest man could object to such a procedure and retain his sincerity." Hoare gave him some support, but the Prime Minister at once knocked out the proposal on the double ground that Hitler would not accept it and that such a commission could not be so rapidly constituted. Chamberlain followed this up with blunt references to "disturbing accounts of the condition of the French Air Force," and to "the tone of the French press" as "not very bellicose." To all of this Daladier made emphatic but diffuse reply,* and then turned questioner on his own part. Did the British accept the Hitler plan? Did they plan to pressure the Czechs to accept? Did they think "that France should do nothing?"

Chamberlain answered that it was up to Prague, and not London, to accept or reject Hitler's terms; that the Czechs had already rejected those terms, and Britain "could not exert pressure . . . since we had no means to compel them to reverse their decision"; and that it was for Paris, not London, to decide what France should do. Daladier was either too slow, shrewd, or polite to comment that Chamberlain's second response was, in the light of the pressure previously focused on Prague, utterly preposterous, or that the Prime Minister's answer seemed to him as uninformative as his own had seemed to the Prime Minister.

Midnight was fast approaching. It was agreed that Gamelin would come to London on the morrow to join in the deliberations. Chamberlain then asked the French to withdraw "for half an hour whilst the British Cabinet met" and the conference was temporarily adjourned. The Knights of the Green Table had not acquitted themselves with distinction, but once again the Prime Minister had kept the issue open.

However, exposing Daladier's lack of a feasible plan accomplished nothing toward resolving the crisis, and it was high time for Chamberlain to come forward with a program of his own. He had one, and he unveiled it at the midnight Cabinet meeting which now ensued.

Chamberlain, aided by supplementary comments by Simon, Hoare, and Halifax, reported on the meeting with the French. This evoked from Duff Cooper the sour comment that "the British Ministers had appeared to have contested the French point of view on every point . . . without making any positive contributions themselves." Inskip expressed doubt that Gamelin could answer "what was strictly a political question, namely what decision the French Government would take if and when hostilities broke out." A few other members made noncommittal observations. The Prime Minister then put forward his plan:

> He suggested that . . . he should write a personal letter to the Führer saying that he had received intimation that the Prague Government were likely to reject Herr Hitler's proposals and making one last appeal to him. He proposed to ask him to agree to the appointment of a Joint Commission, with German and Czech members and a British representative. This Commission would not start *de novo,* but would consider how the proposals accepted by

---

* In the course of these remarks, Daladier mentioned and contested the report on the Soviet Air Force of "Colonel Lindbergh, who had been much quoted recently."

the present Czech Government could be put into effect in an orderly manner and as quickly as possible, without shocking public opinion. This further move would once more demonstrate to the world how hard we had tried to preserve peace. If it was unsuccessful, we should lose nothing by it, and it . . . might also help to rally the Dominions to our side. There was a chance that it would be accepted, although he could not pretend that he thought it was likely to be accepted.

Chamberlain proposed that Sir Horace Wilson, as his confidential adviser, should go to Berlin* and, with Henderson, present the letter to Hitler. And then came the final and salient feature of his plan:

> If the letter failed to secure any response from Herr Hitler, Sir Horace Wilson should be authorized to give a personal message from the Prime Minister to the effect that if this appeal was refused, France would go to war, and that if that happened it seemed certain that we should be drawn in.

This implicitly recognized a British commitment to support France militarily if she went to war in fulfillment of her treaty with Czechoslovakia—just what the French had been seeking without success since *Anschluss*. Duff Cooper listened with pleased amazement. Simon, MacDonald (who described the plan as "essential if we were to secure the cooperation of the Dominions"), and others voiced full approval of the program. No one raised any objection to the commitment to join with France. Chamberlain said that he would communicate it "confidentially" to the French ministers, and "felt sure that they would agree to it willingly."

And so the meeting adjourned on an upbeat note, despite the Prime Minister's prediction that Hitler would reject his proposal. The British rejoined the French briefly and arranged to meet again at ten o'clock the following morning.

Displaying remarkable resilience, the Prime Minister was up and doing business by nine o'clock, with the letter to Hitler already drafted. Shrewdly judging that communication with Daladier might be more fruitful without an audience, he described his plan to the Premier at Downing Street in a conversation *à deux*, with Corbin as interpreter. If the letter drew no response, Sir Horace was to say to Hitler:

> The French Government have informed us that, if the Czechs reject the memorandum and Germany attacks Czechoslovakia, they will fulfill their obligations to Czechoslovakia. Should the forces of France in consequence be-

---

* While the Cabinet was meeting, another British emissary was already in Berlin. Sir Frederick Maurice, a retired major general and President of the British Legion, had proposed to Halifax that "a mixed force of German and British ex-Service men" should occupy the Sudetenland prior to the entry of German troops to supervise the plebiscites and keep order. In the evening of the twenty-fifth he was flown to Berlin and, through Kordt, the Prime Minister requested that Hitler receive him personally. Hitler treated the general courteously, but on the twenty-sixth Ribbentrop sent word via Kordt that the Fuehrer considered the proposal impracticable "in its present form" because it "would take far too long." Hitler proposed instead that detachments of the Legion be sent into the plebiscite areas "as soon as the German and Czech troops have been withdrawn from them to allow the plebiscite to take place." According to Ribbentrop, Maurice approved this suggestion; however that may be, the discussion was not followed up after Munich.

come engaged in active hostilities against Germany, we shall feel obliged to support them.

Chamberlain then asked Daladier "whether he had any comments to make on the proposed oral statement or whether it would embarrass him in any way." One may well wonder what the Premier's real feelings were; this was the very reassurance he had sought for the event of war, but the reassurance likewise deprived the French Government of an excuse for not going to war. However that may be, Daladier responded that "he was absolutely in accord with the proposed statement and had no comment to make on it."

Meanwhile General Gamelin, Halifax, Bonnet, and Léger were waiting in the anteroom. Gamelin was now asked to join the two principals, and shortly thereafter Inskip came in. According to Chamberlain's subsequent report to the Cabinet,* Gamelin declared that the Army would "launch an attack in about five days," at points which had already been determined, and the Air Force would attack "industrial targets near the frontier," even though "France was aware she would suffer heavily from [German] air attacks." Germany and Czechoslovakia each had some thirty-four divisions facing each other, and Gamelin "thought that the Czechoslovak Army would give a good account of themselves," and if forced to retire could "maintain a fighting force" in Slovakia and Ruthenia.

In the west France had twenty-three divisions on the frontier, the Germans only eight, and the Siegfried Line was "far from complete" and "in many respects improvised." But the conclusions Gamelin drew from this were far from bold; his armies would be "in a position to make an attack which would at least draw off troops from Czechoslovakia." Gamelin also spoke of Italy and its poor morale and capacity for endurance, whereat Chamberlain interjected: "If we go to war, Italy will not."

The conference at Downing Street ended shortly before eleven o'clock, and Gamelin was then escorted to Inskip's room in the Cabinet Offices, where the CID was situated. Inskip, Kingsley Wood, Hore-Belisha, Gort, and Newall were the ranking participants, supported by Ismay, Slessor, and Brigadier F. G. Beaumont-Nesbitt, the Deputy Director of Operations and Intelligence; Gamelin was accompanied only by Lelong.†

The French military chief told his hosts that France could mobilize 5 million

---

* There is no official record of this meeting, and considerable confusion about who participated and what was said. Bonnet later wrote that Lord Gort was also present, and General Albert Lelong (the French military attaché) recorded Bonnet as present—certainly erroneously, as Bonnet himself wrote that he was elsewhere with Halifax and Léger, and Gamelin wrote that Bonnet was deliberately excluded because "c'est lui qui décourage tout le monde."

The British Cabinet minutes record the Prime Minister as reporting that he received the military information from Daladier, but the annexed memorandum by the Prime Minister referred to in the minutes attributes (surely correctly) the information to Gamelin. There is little similarity between Chamberlain's and Gamelin's descriptions of what Gamelin said. It appears to me that part of Gamelin's account covers what he later told the British army and air ministers and Chiefs of Staff, and in the text I have followed the Chamberlain memorandum, except for the Chamberlain "interjection" which Gamelin describes.

† Despite the Navy's obvious interest in the air and ground prospects, especially if a British expeditionary force might be sent across the Channel, no representative of the Admiralty was present. Possibly Inskip wished to exclude the prickly Duff Cooper.

men and put 100 divisions into the field. Already 1.5 million men were mobilized, but "nothing more could be done until full mobilisation was ordered." There were presently fifteen divisions on the German frontier, and ten in reserve. Then came the key disclosure:

General Gamelin said he had no intention of sitting behind the Maginot Line and waiting for a German offensive. It was his intention to advance immediately into Germany and to continue to advance until he met really serious opposition. He would then, if necessary, withdraw to the protection of the Maginot Line, leaving it to the Germans to break their strength against the permanent fortifications. In reply to a question whether his attack would take place immediately on the outbreak of war or after a certain delay, he explained that on the one hand immediate action would be to the advantage of France in view of the fact that the Germans had only 8 divisions on their western frontier. On the other hand, in view of the menace from the air, a delay of four or five days would be required to enable Paris and the principal French towns to be evacuated. On balance, however, he would attack as soon as possible.

According to General Lelong, Gamelin added that:

. . . the French and Czechoslovak armies were the only ones ready for action: they constituted the *couverture* for the whole world which, it must be hoped, would align with the democratic powers. It was vital not to be smashed separately by taking ill-considered action. France could play her part. But, to win the war, she would have need of help.

Gamelin apparently delivered himself of these pronouncements with calm assurance, but it was a most disquieting presentation. It was, of course, plain that he had learned nothing from the 1936 experience, for France still had no quick-striking force and could take no offensive action until the whole machinery of mobilization had run its cycle. Even so, with such overwhelming superiority on the Rhineland front, what was to stop the French Army once through the embryonic West Wall, which Gamelin described as "improvised," from turning north into the Ruhr industrial area, so vital to German strength? Would not such a move put the Germans to the choice of transferring large forces from the Czech front or leaving the Ruhr to the French? What would make it "necessary" for the French to withdraw behind the Maginot Line at the first "serious opposition?" Why should Gamelin expect the Germans to be so foolish as to "break their strength" against the Line? Why did he think it necessary to delay his attack pending the evacuation of Paris and other cities since, as he told the British, the German long-range bombers were "disposed in a ring around the Czechoslovak frontier"? In view of the weakness of the French Air Force, was not the best defense against German attack on French cities a strong ground offensive, which would force the Luftwaffe to focus its strength in support of the Army rather than against cities far behind the French lines?

Scrutinized as a whole, Gamelin's statement gave the impression that he had no intention of a sustained offensive to exploit Germany's weakness in the west, but rather a face-saving *essai* which might draw at least some troops from the Czech front and bring Britain and Russia into the war as allies, after which the

French would withdraw at the first sign of trouble and sit behind the Maginot Line until foreign reinforcements were at hand. The more the British listened, the less they liked what they heard. Slessor found Gamelin "a most likeable person, a courtly and confident old soldier, but . . . as far removed from reality as he later proved to be." And when the full import of his presentation was grasped at Cabinet level, there was, as will soon appear, great distress.

At noon the three ministers departed to a Cabinet meeting, and the discussion turned to other aspects of the situation. Gamelin contemplated almost with equanimity, the probability of Italian hostility, acknowledging only that this would divert French troops from the German front and increase the need for British reinforcements. He did not think Russia was in a position to help very much, but attached great importance to the attitude of Poland, describing it as "the key of the whole situation." Of course it was true that a Polish attack, other than for the limited purpose of seizing Teschen, could play havoc with the Czech Government's plan to retreat and hold out in the eastern part of their country; likewise, if Poland should join forces with France, Germany would have faced new and possibly insuperable military problems. But by the twenty-sixth the combination of Prague's offers to cede the Teschen area and Moscow's threats to Poland's eastern frontier made the first of these eventualities unlikely, and the second was out of the question, short of a complete change in Poland's attitude.

The last part of the meeting was not without embarrassment for the British, as Gamelin stressed that his planning was, of necessity, closely linked with the prospects of British aid in the air and on the ground. This knowledge, he said quite rightly, would be especially important in the event of Italian intervention or of the Low Countries being drawn into the war by a violation of their neutrality. Gort and Newall were obliged to reply "that they were not in a position to answer these questions until they had received instructions from the Cabinet." On that rather futile note the conference ended, and after a pleasant luncheon with his hosts (who expressed themselves very unfavorably with respect to Bonnet) General Gamelin returned to Paris.*

Meanwhile the two diplomatic delegations had reassembled at Downing Street, and the Prime Minister had repeated to all what he had earlier told Daladier about the Wilson project. Daladier had been given a copy of the letter which Wilson was to present, but it would not now be made public, "to avoid anything which he [Hitler] might regard as a public humiliation." Daladier gave full approval to the plan.

Halifax, Bonnet, and subsequently Daladier then discussed the Teschen question and, after Bonnet had assured the British that Beneš had, in principle, agreed to the cession of that area to Poland, it was agreed that the two countries would join in a *démarche* to Warsaw making plain their condemnation of any aggressive military action on the part of Poland.

Chamberlain then announced that Sir Horace Wilson would be "leaving the

---

* Liddell Hart encountered General Lelong just after Gamelin's departure and was told that the French Army might be ready for a major offensive by the spring or summer of 1939, and that Gamelin thought Poland a "key to the situation."

aerodome in a few minutes," and obtained agreement to a communiqué which disclosed only that he was bearing "a personal communication to the German Chancellor." A second communiqué noted Gamelin's visit and declared "full accord" between the French and British ministers. The French departed after lunch and were back in Paris in the late afternoon.

At the noon Cabinet meeting, Chamberlain reported on his morning talks with Daladier and Gamelin, and informed his colleagues that Wilson was already en route to Berlin with the "personal message" and the text of the oral statement to be made if the Fuehrer were adamant. All of this the Cabinet unanimously approved, and Duff Cooper took pains to state that he was "in entire agreement with the policy now adopted."

Hore-Belisha then endeavored to get a Cabinet commitment for the dispatch of a British force to France in the event of war. He was blocked by Simon, who described this matter as "an issue which was still entirely open," and Inskip, quoted Gamelin to the effect that "the French dispositions had been made independently of any British assistance by air or land."*

MacDonald reported on a meeting he had had that morning with the Dominion High Commissioners, who "had all said in the strongest possible terms that . . . if there was any chance of peace by negotiation the opportunity should not be lost." All of them thought "acceptance of Herr Hitler's proposals was better than war," while recognizing that if Britain became involved in war, "the Dominions would join in too." Chamberlain had had a telephone call from the Prime Minister of Australia, Mr. J. A. Lyons, approving the efforts to reach a peaceful settlement and describing the present issue as evolving a "method of procedure rather than principle."

The Cabinet discussed emergency defense measures, approved Chamberlain's plan to address the nation by radio on the evening of the twenty-seventh, and (prodded by a pointed letter from Winston Churchill) directed that Parliament be called to meet on the twenty-eighth. The Prime Minister was authorized, if necessary, to order full mobilization without summoning the Cabinet. Meanwhile they would await the results of the Wilson mission, in which the Prime Minister placed only modest hopes; he thought there was "just a chance that it might have some result," and reminded his colleagues that they might get some indication that evening, from the radio broadcast of the speech Hitler was to make in Berlin.

After adjournment the CID met with many Cabinet members sitting in, and the Government finally got down to the business of preparation for war. The discussion covered such matters as the distribution of food which would be required by city evacuation plans, oil stocks, issuance of gas masks, and the construction of bomb shelters and trenches. The Army called up the Home Army units for air and coastal defense. Despite what was regarded as "a very grave risk," merchant shipping was not recalled from the Mediterranean,

---

* This was literally true since, lacking any British commitment, the French had no other basis on which to plan. But at the morning meeting with the service Chiefs, Gamelin had emphasized his need for information about the time and scale of British assistance, and Hore-Belisha was quite right to stress the need for a decision as the basis for joint planning for the event of war.

so as not to antagonize Italy. Mobilization of the fleet was considered but post-poned for later decision. The RAF alerted Fighter Command, called up some auxiliary squadrons, and made preparations for sending an Advanced Air Strik-ing Force to bases in France. As Duff Cooper put it, the CID at this meeting "took dozens of decisions which would have taken months or years to get through in peacetime." Considering the apparent imminence of war, it was little enough, and dangerously late.

The Foreign Office reacted to the day's events with surprising force and puz-zling diction. While the CID was meeting, Lord Halifax authorized issuance of a statement to the press:

> During the last week Mr. Chamberlain has tried with the German Chan-cellor to find the way of settling peacefully the Czechoslovak question. It is still possible to do so by negotiations.
>
> The German claim to the Sudeten areas has clearly been conceded by the French, British and Czechoslovak Governments, but if in spite of all efforts made by the British Prime Minister a German attack is made upon Czecho-slovakia the immediate result must be that France will be bound to come to her assistance, and Great Britain and Russia will certainly stand by France.
>
> It is still not too late to stop this great tragedy, and for the peoples of all nations to insist on settlement by free negotiations.

The purport was abundantly clear, but for an official Foreign Office release it was strangely worded. It referred to the preceding negotiations as between Chan-cellor and Prime Minister, with no reference to the discussions with Prague. It read as if the boundaries of the "Sudeten areas" to be ceded had been deter-mined, which of course was not the fact. It referred to the third intervening country not as the "Soviet Union" but as "Russia," which was both inaccurate and diplomatically gauche. Furthermore, there appears to have been no notice to or consultation with the Soviet authorities about the release, which did, nevertheless, comport with what Litvinov had told De La Warr and Butler in Geneva three days earlier.

These odd features were, as we will shortly see, promptly exploited by French anti-intervention spokesmen, who endeavored to discount the statement as unau-thorized or even spurious.*

7

Adolf Hitler returned from Godesberg, in the afternoon of September 24, to a Berlin that was teeming with army ants. The Fuehrer immediately closeted him-self with Keitel, who emerged with the hardly earth-shaking decision to set up

---

* In a private letter to Churchill dated July 24, 1947, Halifax wrote ". . . greatly to my surprise, Neville was much put out when the Communiqué appeared, and reproached me with not having submitted it to him before publication. I never understood then, and I don't understand now, why he should have been vexed—unless it was that he thought it 'provoca-tive' and not fully consistent with his desire to make a further conciliatory appeal to Hitler." Hoare's later statement (in *Nine Troubled Years*, p. 318) that the Government is-sued a repudiation is quite without foundation; on March 1, 1939, in response to a ques-tion, R. A. Butler inserted the text in Hansard (col. 1230) as the "official communiqué of the Foreign Office." Churchill later wrote (in *The Gathering Storm*, pp. 308-9) that he participated in its preparation.

the Border Watch (VGAD) on the Czech and French frontiers. The following day Hitler ordered that two SS companies be sent to reinforce the Henlein *Freikorps* units occupying Asch. This was a detail even further from the core of the grand plan, and Hitler's preoccupation with these apparent trivia suggests that, militarily, he was temporizing.

In fact, Hitler's grip on the throttle had slackened, and his reluctance to fix a firm date for the attack (X-day) had injected considerable confusion into the High Command. Keitel's note of May 30 transmitting the basic Green directive had specified October 1 as the date by which preparation for the attack must be completed, but did not say that the operation would begin on that day. During July transportation schedules had been worked out envisaging September 28 as the ready day, and, as we have seen, at the time of the Berchtesgaden meeting with Chamberlain, the OKW advised Hitler that the date could not be advanced.

Already, however, there was much uncertainty. In August, IX Corps (and presumably all the other field commands involved in the initial attack)* ordered its assault units to reach their final deployment positions by September 26 and be ready to attack on the twenty-eighth. But on September 9 and 10, OKH orders went out postponing until September 30 the assault units' arrival in their final positions. However, on September 21, OKH sent an order to Leeb's headquarters calling for their arrival early on September 27, which was to be a day of rest, after which the troops would be ready to attack.

On the evening of September 22, Jodl received word from Keitel, who was with Hitler at Godesberg, that the attack would not come before September 30. Either OKH was not informed of this or saw no reason to delay the troop movement schedule, for on September 24, while Hitler was returning to Berlin, the assault units, presumably pursuant to the OKH order of September 21, began their two-day march to the final deployment areas, close to the Czech border. There were other signs of imminent hostilities; military police units were called up on the twenty-third, the next day Leeb ordered XIII Corps to set up a "propaganda company" to be ready for action in two days, General von Manstein sent word that he would arrive in Munich on the twenty-fifth to take over as Leeb's chief of staff, and at midday on the twenty-sixth VII and XIII Corps established advanced headquarters near the frontier.†

These moves were bringing the German assault troops into battle deployment along the Czech frontier four days before the end of the month, and Hitler had promised Chamberlain that he would not act militarily before October 1. It is difficult to believe that he did not learn of the deployment soon after his return to Berlin. However, it was not until the morning of the twenty-sixth that steps

---

* Virtually all of the field command documentation now available for the period in question comes from the war diaries and other files of VII, IX, and XIII Corps.

† There is no doubt that staffs and troops came up to the border meaning business. The VII Corps began its war diary at midday on the twenty-sixth, with an introductory note stating that the Czechs had knowledge of the corps' plan of attack and had strengthened their defense line in the correct way to block it. Therefore the corps commander, General von Schobert, shifted the main body of his forces and the focal point of the planned attack further to the southeast.

were taken to avert the risk of a premature engagement, by means of an order from OKW through OKH to stop the advance because, as Jodl recorded, "it is not yet necessary and the Führer does not in any case intend to march in before the 30th."

And so, VII and XIII Corps staffs had barely reached their combat headquarters at noon on the twenty-sixth when they received orders to stop the advance and withdraw the troops to a distance of one to two days' march from the combat deployment areas. The assault units of the 7th Infantry and 1st Mountain divisions, having just completed a two-day march in full combat gear, had to spend the twenty-seventh, the day of rest, withdrawing some ten miles to the rear. There was much grumbling, and the 7th Division's operational report commented sourly on the apparent "uncertainty" and "lack of foresight" of the higher command, which had caused this marching to and fro and made a bad impression both on the troops and on the civilian population in the border areas.

It was a real foul-up, but its cause is by no means clear. Was it simply that Hitler was inattentive to the relation between the pace of deployment and his diplomacy? Or did something occur on the morning of the twenty-sixth that moved him to pull back the assault units? He knew (from telephone intercepts) by the evening of the twenty-fifth that Prague had rejected his ultimatum. That evening or the following morning he received Chamberlain's message that the Czech response was not the last word, and was informed that Sir Horace Wilson was coming with a personal letter from the Prime Minister. Perhaps these developments caused him to order the withdrawal, to avoid the risk of an unplanned frontier clash that would leave him no options.* Whatever the reasons, it is apparent that Hitler by this time realized that Green might involve him in a war with the western powers, and that he did not want such an outcome.

During these few days there were other doings in the higher military circles of which Hitler was not fully aware, or perhaps wholly ignorant. Late in August the Luftwaffe Chief of Staff, General Stumpff, had directed the commander of the 2nd Air Group Command in Brunswick, General Helmuth Felmy (whose sphere of operations included the Low Countries and Britain), to prepare operational plans for the eventuality of military intervention by Britain. On September 22, Felmy submitted a memorandum to the Luftwaffe High Command (OKL) which presented a very pessimistic assessment of the possibility of effective air action against Britain from German airfields. A successful air war against England would be possible, Felmy wrote, only after occupation of the Low Countries' coastal areas. The range of German bombers with a 1,000-pound bomb load was only 430 miles, and the crews were not trained for overseas operations. Therefore: "With the means available we cannot expect to achieve more than a disruptive effect. Whether this will lead to an erosion of the British will to fight depends on imponderable and certainly unpredictable factors. With the means now at hand a war of annihilation [*Vernichtungskrieg*] against England is out of the question."

---

* During the afternoon of the twenty-sixth Jodl noted in his diary: "It is important that we do not permit ourselves to be drawn into military action because of false information, before Prague replies."

Goering, highly displeased, penned an angry note on Felmy's document:* "I have not asked for a memorandum weighing the existing possibilities of success and pointing out our weaknesses; these things I myself know best of all. What I requested is information on the manner in which you expect to obtain maximum effect with the projected resources, and what conditions you require for that purpose." But the contents can hardly have surprised him, and in 1939 the OKL staff submitted very similar estimates.

Assuming that Goering mentioned Felmy's report to Hitler, it can hardly have much affected his decisions at the time of Munich, as the Fuehrer had little faith in the ability of air power alone to bring down a major foe, and there is no evidence that at the time of Munich he was contemplating a bombing assault against Britain. But Felmy's assessment indeed stands in extraordinary contrast with the lugubrious predictions of death and destruction which were emanating from the Air Staff in London at that same time.

The Fuehrer's return to Berlin on September 24 put him within reach of the Halder-Witzleben plans to seize him and overthrow his regime if such action appeared to be the only way to prevent war with the western powers. Reports that the Godesberg talks had not gone well were spreading, and this combination of circumstances led to a flurry of meetings among the Berlin members of the dissident group, comprising primarily Witzleben, Halder, Brockdorff-Ahlefeldt, and Oster on the military side, and Schacht, Helldorf, and Gisevius among the civilians.†

The initial success of the planned enterprise depended on the ability of Witzleben, Brockdorff, and Helldorf, with the troops and police under their command in the Berlin area, to seize and remove from the scene of action Hitler and his principal supporters such as Goering, Hess, Himmler, Bormann, and Goebbels, and take control of all communication facilities and other instruments of central administrative control. Then it would be necessary to rally enough support from military commanders and civilian officials in the rest of Germany to shore up the new regime and beat off whatever counterattacks were mounted by elements loyal to the Fuehrer. Ultimate success depended above all on a carefully planned and timed program, and the determination to move swiftly and ruthlessly.

All the surviving participants agree that Witzleben, Brockdorff, and Helldorf stood ready to launch the coup upon word from Halder that the time had come. But evidence of the preparation essential to so weighty and hazardous a step is lacking. Brockdorff died of illness in 1943, and Witzleben, Karl-Heinrich von Stülpnagel, Hoepner, Helldorf, Hase, Olbricht, and others apparently involved in the 1938 affair were executed during or in the wake of the July 1944 attempt on Hitler's life. The main survivors were Halder, Schacht, and Gisevius, and

* General Felmy remained in Goering's black book, and in January 1940 was discharged from the Luftwaffe on the pretext of the loss in his operational area of a courier plane carrying secret documents. In 1941 he was recalled to active duty in the Army, and after the war he was tried and convicted at Nuremberg for war crimes committed in Greece by troops under his command.

† Carl Goerdeler, then and later a leading member of the civilian opposition, was traveling outside Germany during August and September 1938.

the last two named, in postwar testimony and writings, have given voluble support to the seriousness of the plan. But Schacht knew little of its military aspect, and Gisevius, although he claims to have been close to Witzleben and Brockdorff, was *persona non grata* to Halder, and his postwar writings show little comprehension of the military factors.*

Halder testified and talked extensively about the matter, but by his account he left the operational details to Witzleben, and concerned himself chiefly with governing the "pace" of the enterprise. For Halder this was the crucial matter, for the object of the coup was to prevent Germany from involvement in a war for which, as Halder believed, her resources were insufficient. If the Czech crisis could be resolved peacefully, so much the better, and there would be no basis for a coup. To ensure timing which would be neither premature nor tardy, Halder planned to give the signal immediately after Hitler had fixed the date of attack, during the two-day interval between the order and the assault itself.

If Hitler had fixed X-Day and Halder had then pushed the button, what arrangements had Witzleben and Brockdorff made to seize Hitler and control of Berlin? Witzleben had, as corps troops directly under his command in the Berlin area, a cavalry regiment and smaller units of antitank and engineer troops. Brockdorff, whose headquarters were in Potsdam, had an artillery regiment and several smaller units directly under him and, through a subordinate general, three regiments of infantry. What steps had the two confederates taken to ensure that these subordinate officers and troops would obey orders to seize government buildings, if necessary by storm, and arrest Hitler and the other Nazi leaders? What preparatory conversations had been conducted with the junior officers who would be in immediate command of the men? No evidence of these seeming essentials has emerged in the forty years since Munich, and this vacuum must generate suspicion that the "Halder plot" had very little engine under the hood.

Furthermore, while the *Putsch* was to begin in Berlin, it would have to spread or die. Yet the efforts to involve the field commanders appear to have been at best desultory. Adam, as commander-in-chief in the west and a key figure, had made his sympathies known to Halder at the end of July, but never heard another word about the matter, despite his vehement and open disapproval of Hitler's policies. Beck, who was to command an army on the western front in the crucial Rhine-Moselle sector, seems not to have been involved, and he even appeared, ostensibly as Chief of Staff (although he had already resigned), at the mid-September army maneuvers in East Prussia to which the foreign military attachés were invited, thereby aiding Hitler's purpose to preserve the appearance of harmony within the High Command.

* A good example of Gisevius' misapprehensions is his statement (in *To the Bitter End*, p. 295) that "Halder had at his disposal both prerequisites for a *coup d'état*" in that "In the first place, he commanded the army—and certainly a part of the soldiery would obey his orders," and "In the second place, he always had access to the person of the Führer." As Chief of Staff, Halder commanded only the members of his staff; he had no troop command authority whatsoever. He was subordinate to Brauchitsch and had access to Hitler only on the invitation of Brauchitsch or Hitler himself. During the period in question, he saw Hitler only a few times.

However, there must have been some contact between the Berlin plotters and their sympathizers in the field. On September 26 or 27, Lieutenant Colonel Edgar Röhricht in Dresden, about to go forward to the combat headquarters of IV Corps, was asked by the chief of staff, General Olbricht, to delay his departure. If "the plans work out," said Olbricht, OKH would not send the code word for the attack; furthermore several motorized units would be sent "in another direction." Not surprisingly, a pointed colloquy ensued:

RÖHRICHT: A *coup d'etat* [*Staatsstreich*], then!

OLBRICHT: Call it what you will! More an act of self defense! We're only involved in that the code word will not reach us.

RÖHRICHT: The Luftwaffe begins the attack, and what then?

OLBRICHT: (shrugs)

RÖHRICHT: And so Goering will enthusiastically begin his war and behind us
   a couple of divisions will be diverted in the direction of Berlin, which
   makes me wonder what the practical result will be. And the rest of us, here
   on our local front, will stand transfixed, with the gun on the ground. And
   what goes on at the main attack points? It will be unimaginable confusion!

OLBRICHT: That is why I want you here with me! We will probably soon face
   decisions, that must be resolved coolly and quickly.

RÖHRICHT: I fear that these decisions relate to our troops more than to us
   personally. Do you think, General, that we have units in our area that are
   immediately willing.to be thrown into war against Hitler, particularly as no
   one has been prepared for such a turn-about?

OLBRICHT: (shrugs) Who can say?*

Whether Hitler had no inkling of the conspiracy or, suspecting something, took no countermeasures is unknown; considering the number of officers who were privy to it, either conclusion is surprising. But if he knew nothing of the plot, Hitler was well aware of widespread opposition among the military leaders to pre-cipitating a major war, and it is altogether probable that this contributed to the nervousness and indecision which he displayed during these few days between Godesberg and Munich.

On the diplomatic as well as the military front, the Fuehrer was coming under increasing pressure. Ever since the Berchtesgaden meeting had revealed the seriousness of the Sudeten crisis, General Franco had been complaining and criticizing in a most ungrateful manner,† and on September 26 his ambassador, the Marqués de Magaz (who had been informed that both Ribbentrop and Weizsaecker were too busy to see him), told Woermann that a European war would have a "catastrophic effect on Nationalist Spain," since Spain had "relia-ble information" that in such event France intended to invade and occupy much of the country: "The Spanish Government was therefore under the necessity of

---

* Shortly after this colloquy, public announcement of the Munich conference resolved the two officers' dilemma. Olbricht was a leading participant in the abortive July 20, 1944, *Putsch,* and was shot that evening. Röhricht survived the war and in 1965 published the memoirs (*Pflicht und Gewissen*) from which the above and other extracts are taken.

† Ambassador Stohrer reported on September 16 that there was great dissatisfaction at Franco's headquarters "because when choosing moment for settlement of Sudeten question we did not appear to take into consideration the cause of Nationalist Spain. . . ."

making an attempt to open negotiations with England and France concerning the neutrality of Nationalist Spain if a war broke out."

For Franco in 1938, as in later years, gratitude was all very well in the private sector, but was not a viable principle of international intercourse. On consideration, Weizsaecker concluded that "Spanish neutrality seemed to us preferable to any participation by Spain in the war"—a policy which Hitler abandoned two years later, after the fall of France. But apart from the material consequences, Franco's eagerness to avoid involvement certainly conveyed that if things came to scratch he was in no hurry to throw in his lot with his Axis benefactors. Mussolini and Ciano were "disgusted," and Ambassador Mackensen described the latter as in a state of "intense indignation" over Franco's "direct betrayal of the common cause," while in Berlin, Woermann told Magaz that Franco's handling of the situation had "left somewhat of a nasty taste."*

Desertion by an ingrate protégé might be more annoying than alarming, but for the long pull the United States was quite another matter. From Paris, Ambassador Bullitt had been pleading with his great friend in the White House to do something to save the peace and avert the fate he feared for the France he deeply loved. In Prague, after receiving Hitler's ultimatum, Beneš called in the American Minister, Wilbur J. Carr, and begged him "to transmit to President Roosevelt his personal appeal to urge the British and French Governments not to desert this country and permit it to be destroyed and thus bring nearer a greater conflict vital to them as well as to the peace of the world."

Neither Beneš' plea nor Bullitt's latest suggestion of a five-power conference at The Hague met with favor in Washington. Henry Morgenthau recorded that Roosevelt had liked Bullitt's idea but that Hull opposed it, and the President dropped it for fear of "untoward domestic effects." However, Hull's objections to the issuance of an appeal for peace were overridden because, as Roosevelt put it: "It can't do any harm. It's safe to urge peace until the last moment." And so, after an evening of drafting, the President's statement was released in the small hours of September 26. The signed text was sent to Berlin, Prague, Paris, and London, but the text left no doubt that Adolf Hitler was the prime addressee.

After rehearsing the shattering world consequences of war, emphasizing the impartial position of the United States, and reminding the recipients of "the solemn obligations of the Kellogg-Briand Pact of 1928," the statement concluded:

> On behalf of the 130 millions of people of the United States of America and for the sake of humanity everywhere I most earnestly appeal to you not to break off negotiations looking to a peaceful, fair, and constructive settlement of the questions at issue.
>
> I earnestly repeat that so long as negotiations continue differences may be reconciled. Once they are broken off reason is banished and force asserts itself.
>
> And force produces no solution for the future good of humanity.

* On September 27, in a press release from Burgos, Franco announced his regime's neutrality.

The statement reached London while the French were still there; Daladier and Chamberlain at once replied with fulsome expressions of agreement, and Beneš joined in the chorus of approbation. Since everyone knew that Hitler was the only recipient threatening imminent force, and the President's letter showed that an attack on Czechoslovakia would arouse massive international disapproval, the difficulty in drafting an adequate German reply was much greater. Furthermore, the Fuehrer had a very full schedule, with Sir Horace Wilson due that afternoon and the speech in the Sportspalast scheduled for the evening, and his reply did not go out until the following day.

8

The letter from Chamberlain to Hitler which Sir Horace Wilson was carrying to Berlin was largely the product of the proposal for "an international conference attended by Germany, Czechoslovakia and other Powers" which Chamberlain had put to Masaryk on September 25, when the latter presented his letter rejecting Hitler's ultimatum. Masaryk and Beneš discussed the proposal by telephone that evening and again at midday on the twenty-sixth, agreeing that it would be a mistake to shift from negotiations in which Britain and France were involved to bilateral talks between Berlin and Prague, and that it would be equally unwise to utilize the Anglo-French plan as the basis of such talks, since Prague would then be "bargained down" from what was already a very unsatisfactory resolution. Instead, other friendly powers must participate in the conference, which would seek a "new basis" of settlement.*

Utilizing Chamberlain's hand-written suggestions, during the evening of the twenty-fifth Wilson produced a draft which, with minor emendations, comprised the signed letter which he took to Berlin. The text was not shown to Masaryk, but Newton was instructed to "explain to the Czechoslovak Government that the communication which is being made to the German Chancellor through Sir Horace Wilson in no way prejudices the position of the Czechoslovak Government. The proposal is simply to substitute a process of negotiation between the Czechoslovak and German Governments for violent military action."

In fact, Wilson was already meeting with Hitler by the time the Czech Government's reply to Chamberlain's inquiry was received in London. In line with the Beneš-Masaryk telephone discussions, Prague agreed to a conference in which Germany and Czechoslovakia "among other nations" would participate, and in which the "many unworkable features" of the Anglo-French plan could be reviewed.

Chamberlain's letter said nothing about reopening the Anglo-French terms, and was infirm on the participation of countries other than Germany and Czechoslovakia. The opening paragraphs informed Hitler (who no doubt knew already from the intercepts) that Czechoslovakia had rejected the Godesberg

---

* The Beneš-Masaryk telephone conversation, begun at 12:53 P.M. on the twenty-sixth, is the last one for which a German transcript is presently available, since the existence of the intercepts was divulged to Sir Horace Wilson that afternoon, and the transcripts now in the Public Records Office in London were delivered to the British Embassy on the twenty-seventh.

terms, reminded him that Chamberlain had warned him of this outcome, and summarized Prague's reasons for refusal. After a reference to Hitler's previously expressed view that it appeared "impossible" to settle the Sudeten question by negotiation came the operative paragraph:

> On the contrary, a settlement by negotiation remains possible and, with a clear recollection of the conversations which you and I have had and with an equally clear appreciation of the consequences which must follow the abandonment of negotiation and the substitution of force, I ask Your Excellency to agree that representatives of Germany shall meet representatives of the Czechoslovakian Government to discuss immediately the situation by which we are confronted with a view to settling by agreement the way in which the territory is to be handed over. I am convinced that these discussions can be completed in a very short time and if you and the Czechoslovakian Government desire it, I am willing to arrange for the representation of the British Government at the discussion.

Armed with this document and a personal note to Hitler in which Chamberlain declared that "Sir Horace Wilson has my full confidence and you can take anything he says as coming from me," as well as a memorandum of the oral statement which, as agreed in Cabinet and with the French, Wilson was to make if the letter drew no helpful response from Hitler, the trusted emissary arrived in Berlin and, after a brief consultation at the embassy, proceeded to the Chancellery, accompanied by Henderson and Kirkpatrick. The Fuehrer, flanked by Ribbentrop and Schmidt, received them at five o'clock.

Hitler was under great tension, and the meeting was stormy and, at times disorderly. Schmidt later wrote that it was the only time he had seen Hitler "lose his nerve." Wilson made matters worse by attempting, even before Chamberlain's letter was read, to "explain the background" in a lecturing manner, and by describing British opinion as "profoundly shocked" by Hitler's Godesberg terms. The result was that Wilson's remarks, and Schmidt's reading in German the text of the letter, were continually interrupted by angry Hitlerian interjections and by numerous gestures and expressions of extreme impatience and disgust.

The letter, when Schmidt was allowed to translate it, did nothing to mollify the dictator, as it began on an "I told you so" note, and continued with a description of the Czech objections. When Schmidt read the words "wholly unacceptable," Hitler abruptly rose and made for the door, muttering that there was no use in further talk, and that the time for action had come. "It was an exceptionally painful scene," Schmidt wrote, "especially as Hitler seemed to realize when he reached the door how impossible his behavior was, and returned to his seat like a defiant boy." Poor Schmidt, usually in good control of the interchange on such occasions, gave up in desperation, and "everybody talked at once except Kirkpatrick and me."*

When the reading of the letter was finally concluded, Hitler said at once that a Czech representative should be sent to Germany, "but it must be clearly un-

* There appears to be no German transcript of the meeting. Kirkpatrick's notes reflect the difficulties under which he was laboring as record keeper.

derstood that he came on the basis of the acceptance of the German memorandum and that there was no alteration in the German decision that the territory should be handed over and should be free of Czechs before the 1st of October." Furthermore, he continued, there would have to be an affirmative reply "within two days," that being by Wednesday the twenty-eighth. "Midnight, Wednesday?" asked Henderson. "No, by 2 p.m.," was the reply. To the British, it appeared that Hitler was moving up the date for the attack, but in fact he had to give the order for troop movements and other measures by the twenty-eighth in order to make possible an attack on the thirtieth.

Wilson was making no headway, but (as he explained in a message to Chamberlain that evening): "In view of intense emotion and frequent references to tonight's speech it seemed better not to deliver special message. . . ." Instead, Wilson obtained Hitler's assent to renewing the discussion on the morrow. Hitler suggested that Wilson attend the assemblage in the Sportspalast that evening, and when Wilson answered that pressures of time would prevent this but that he would listen to the speech on the radio, Hitler admonished his guest "that he must go in person or he would not get an impression of the intense feeling animating the German people." As the British were departing, Hitler disclosed the German interception of the Beneš-Masaryk telephone conversations, attributing to the latter scurrilous characterizations of Chamberlain and Wilson, and exhortations to Beneš to play for time and await the overthrow of the Chamberlain government.

Back at the embassy, Wilson and Henderson ate in the dining room, while Kirkpatrick supped from a tray in front of the radio, making notes on "as truculent a speech as Hitler ever made." Listening too were General von Schobert and his VII Corps staff in their combat headquarters at Vilshofen near the Bavarian and Bohemian frontier; the Lindberghs, Astors, and other guests at Cliveden, where two German boys summering in England did the translating; and millions of high and low degree and all political persuasions all over Europe and across the Atlantic.

Joseph Goebbels introduced his Fuehrer to a packed audience of Nazi Party leaders and hacks in the Sportspalast. Hitler spoke for over an hour, starting in a low key and indulging in his customary historical introduction, but soon modulating into a hymn of hate against Beneš, whose name he mentioned, always with a snarl, over thirty times. It was as if Hitler felt that Czechoslovakia was too small to serve as a hate symbol and was using Beneš instead—"In this name is concentrated all that which today moves millions, which causes them to despair or fills them with fanatical resolution"—exactly what Hitler's own name was doing. Flattering words for Poland, sorrowful but not hopeless words for Britain, reassuring words for France, encomiums for Mussolini, and then a crescent diatribe against "this Czech State," which "began with a single lie and the father of this lie was named Benes." This state was now the "Bolshevist canal" into Europe, and Beneš had begun a "reign of terror" against the Sudeten Germans: "Whole stretches of country were depopulated, villages burned down, attempts were made to smoke out Germans with hand-grenades and gas." As for the present, "now two men stand arrayed against one another: there is Mr. Benes and here stand I," and in conclusion: "Now let Mr. Benes make his choice." A cynical Beneš might have even been amused at finding himself thus portrayed as the major foe of the dictator of the most powerful country in Europe.

It was a wild and woolly oration, and in the audience William L. Shirer, like Schmidt that afternoon, thought that it reflected a man who had "completely lost control of himself."* After his speech, according to Shirer:

> . . . Goebbels sprang up and shouted into the microphone: "One thing is sure: 1918 will never be repeated!" Hitler looked up to him, a wild, eager expression in his eyes. . . . He leaped to his feet and with a fanatical fire in his eyes that I shall never forget brought his right hand, after a grand sweep, pounding down on the table, and yelled with all the power in his mighty lungs: *"Ja!"* Then he slumped into his chair exhausted.

But for all the sound and fury, Hitler did not slam the door on Chamberlain. His references to the Prime Minister were friendly, and he expressed willingness to guarantee Czechoslovakia after the Polish and Hungarian claims were resolved, and to allow the British Legion to police the plebiscite areas. He repeated his assurance that "when this problem is solved there is for Germany no further territorial problem in Europe," and that after the Czech minorities problems were settled "I have no further interest in the Czech State. . . . We want no Czechs!"

Noting all this, Wilson at once telephoned to London his opinion that the speech was "not so violent as was expected" and, despite Hitler's insistence, at their meeting, that there be no departure from the Godesberg terms, recommended that the Czechs send an emissary to Berlin. He also, perhaps under Henderson's influence, expressed doubt that "it is either necessary or wise to deliver that special message tomorrow."

Neither suggestion met with favor in London; Chamberlain replied: "After violent attack on Benes we feel it is useless to ask Czech Government to approach Germans with fresh offer," and: "We do not consider it possible for you to leave without delivering special message, in view of what we said to French, if you can make no progress. But message should be given more in sorrow than in anger."

The Prime Minister, after hearing Hitler's speech, had issued a statement to the press, the text of which he transmitted to Wilson with the suggestion that it be discussed with Hitler at the next meeting:

> I have read the speech of the German Chancellor and I appreciate his reference to the efforts I have made to save the peace.
> I cannot abandon those efforts. . . .
> It is evident that the Chancellor has no faith that the promise made will be carried out. . . .

---

* Shirer, broadcasting "from a seat in the balcony just above Hitler," also thought the crowd responsive but lacking any "war fever." "The crowd was *good-natured,* as if it didn't realize what his words meant."

Speaking for the British Government we regard ourselves as morally responsible for seeing that the promises are carried out fairly and fully and we are prepared to undertake that they shall be so carried out . . . provided that the German Government will agree to the settlement of terms and conditions of transfer by discussion and not by force.

I trust that the Chancellor will not reject this proposal . . . which . . . will satisfy the German desire for the union of Sudeten Germans with the Reich without the shedding of blood in any part of Europe.

The odd consequence of this statement was that France remained bound to defend Czechoslovakia against a German attack, while Britain undertook to ensure Germany against a Czech refusal to turn over the Sudetenland! Odd or not, the statement increased the pressure on Hitler by making a resort to arms appear utterly wanton. But it had no perceptible effect on the Fuehrer's intransigence when he again received the British group, shortly after noon on the twenty-seventh.

Obedient to his instructions, Sir Horace referred to the Prime Minister's announced assumption of "moral responsibility" for the execution of the Czech obligation, and asked whether, in the light of that commitment, "had the Führer any message for Mr. Chamberlain?" Hitler answered that he had no further message, other than to thank the Prime Minister "for all his efforts."* Wilson then told his host that there was "one more thing to say and he would try to say it in the tone which the Prime Minister would have used had he been himself present." He and many other Englishmen greatly desired a general Anglo-German settlement, and the issue of events immediately confronting them might "have a far-reaching effect" on the two countries' future relations. And then came the "special message":

If Germany attacked Czechoslovakia, France, as Daladier had informed us and as he had stated publicly, would fulfill her treaty obligations. If that meant that the forces of France became actively engaged in hostilities against Germany,† the British Government would feel obliged to support France.

Hitler declared that this amounted simply to a declaration that if France attacked Germany, Britain would join in the assault: "He could only take note of this communication." Wilson read the message again, and Hitler repeated his observation. Instead of pointing out that the *démarche* was contingent on a prior German attack on Czechoslovakia in full awareness of the Franco-Czech alliance, Wilson resorted to a mere quibble: "The French had not said they would attack Germany, but only that they would fulfill their treaty obligations to Czechoslovakia. In what form they would do this, he did not know."

One can almost excuse Hitler for being angered by such mumbo jumbo. Excitedly he denounced France and Britain for encouraging the Czechs to refuse his terms: "In the event of a rejection of the memorandum, I will smash [*zerschlagen*] Czechoslovakia! In six days we will all be at war with one an-

---

* Both Schmidt and Kirkpatrick made records of this meeting. They do not differ importantly; Kirkpatrick's is a little fuller.

† Here Hitler interjected: "That means if France attacks, since I have no intention of attacking France."

other, and only because the Czechs refuse a proposal for the execution of obligations they have already undertaken. I have made preparations for all emergencies! It is not for nothing that I have spent 4½ billion marks on the Western fortifications!"

According to Schmidt's record, Wilson wanted to continue the interchange but was dissuaded by Henderson. The British took their departure, in the course of which Wilson, alone with Hitler and Schmidt for a moment, declared that he would "still try to make those Czechos sensible." After what must have been a very tense lunch at the embassy, Wilson left for Tempelhof and the homeward flight.

9

"Frightful afternoon—the worst I have ever spent" was Sir Alexander Cadogan's recollection of September 27, 1938, post meridiem. *"Schwerster Tag"* ["Hardest day"], Jodl wrote in his diary the following morning. Not only for those in the know, but for the hundreds of millions of the Western world, September 27 and the daytime hours of the twenty-eighth were the crest of the crisis. After Hitler's speech in the Sportspalast, everyone knew that Godesberg had been a failure, that Hitler's terms had been rejected in Prague, and that the Fuehrer had staked his prestige on taking the Sudetenland by October 1. In the confronting countries, the people saw gas masks distributed, slit trenches dug in the parks, and young men marching as to war. The inner circles also knew that the Wilson mission had failed, and that Britain had given Germany the warning that Sir Edward Grey had been much blamed for not giving in 1914. It suddenly became apparent that, if a European war were to be averted, someone had to give, and that the antagonists were locked into positions that made new concessions difficult if not impossible.

Adolf Hitler was probably under the heaviest pressure, for in the Sportspalast he had publicly declared that the Sudetenland would be in German hands, by "peace or war," on October 1. If it had to be by war, the military measures for the attack had now to be put in motion. At one-twenty in the afternoon of the twenty-seventh, accordingly, Hitler gave the order that the assault units should again move forward to the combat deployment areas from which they had been withdrawn on the twenty-sixth. These troops were to arrive at their destinations late on the twenty-eighth or early on the twenty-ninth, which was to be a rest day, and make ready to carry out the attack on the thirtieth.*

Later on the afternoon of the twenty-seventh Hitler also authorized mobilization of the five regular divisions which were to be the core of Adam's defensive force on the western front. In order to make the troops already at his disposal combat-ready (involving such matters as camouflage, fields of fire,

---

* In order to make these marches and countermarches "understandable" to the troops, General von Schobert circularized within his VII Corps an explanation that they were necessitated by the "political situation." Most of his assault troops completed the rearward march ordered on the twenty-sixth only by late afternoon of twenty-seventh. Accordingly, he allowed them the daylight hours of the twenty-eighth to rest, and directed that the second forward march begin on the evening of the twenty-eighth.

equipment, stores, and the location of headquarters), Adam had previously ordered that the probable combat area be cleared of Todt's construction workers.

Todt protested violently and appealed successfully to Hitler, whose order on the twenty-seventh "strictly reserved" to himself the decision to pull out the workers and make room for the troops, who were presently to be deployed *behind* the fortifications.* In this, Hitler was probably moved by a desire to get the last possible minute's work done on the fortifications, a shrewd hunch that the French would not attack very soon if at all, and a reluctance to alarm them by the appearance of German combat units at the frontier.

At the southern end of the Axis, Hitler's fellow-dictator was getting very restive. Hitler had kept him poorly informed, and now the possibility of war, which Mussolini had been discounting, was real and imminent. On the twenty-fifth he discussed with Ciano the possibility of a meeting with Ribbentrop "to clarify the conditions of Italian intervention." The following day came news from Berlin that Wilson's mission had failed and that Hitler had demanded Czech acceptance of the Godesberg terms by the afternoon of the twenty-eighth. "It is war!" Ciano recorded. "May God protect Italy and the Duce."

On the morning of the twenty-seventh Mussolini conferred with his service ministers, and then brooded in the presence of Ciano. What would the Anglo-French military tactics be? As for the Germans, the Duce probably knew even less about their plans than the British knew about those of the French. "In any case," wrote Ciano, "the Duce wants to settle forthwith the basis of the political understanding with Berlin and to create organs of military co-operation. With this end in view he proposes a meeting between me and Ribbentrop."

Confronted with this probably unexpected request, Berlin suggested "bringing the soldiers too." It was decided that Ribbentrop and Keitel would meet with Ciano and the Italian air and ground chiefs (Generals Giuseppe Valle and Alberto Pariani) in Innsbruck at noon on the twenty-ninth—a gathering which, of course, was aborted by Munich itself.

Apart from the military problems, Hitler, during these last days, was chiefly concerned with his public image, both domestic and international. Although the German press had carried no mention of Roosevelt's appeal, Hitler had not forgotten it, and after the Sportspalast speech he sent an answer.† Long and rambling, it was addressed to the history of the Sudeten issue rather than the immediate situation, concluding with a declaration that Czechoslovakia, not Germany, was "to blame" for the crisis, and therefore: "It now rests, not with the German Government, but with the Czechoslovak Government alone, to decide if they want peace or war."

Hitler was also showing increasing concern about the home front; no doubt

---

* Adam was scornful of the order, and declares in his memoirs, which are replete with references to the OKH staff as "letter carriers [*Briefträger*] for Hitler," that he disregarded it, deeming it militarily impossible. Despite Adam's distrust of Hitler and close relations with Beck, there is no evidence that in September 1938 he had any plans other than to defend the western front to the best of his ability.

† Hitler's reply is dated September 27, but the cable office stamp shows its receipt in Washington as 9:14 P.M. on September 26. The discrepancy is no doubt accounted for by the time zone differential, and suggests that Hitler composed or edited the text of the letter late in the evening of September 26, after the speech.

the concocted accounts of Czech atrocities in the Nazi press had chiefly the purpose of inciting a war-like domestic attitude. With X-Day barely forty-eight
hours away and, despite Goebbels' prodding, few signs of popular enthusiasm
for war, on the twenty-seventh Hitler ordered what Jodl described as a "propaganda march" of motorized troops through the central governmental blocks of
Berlin. It was staged early that evening, with what were, for Hitler, very disappointing results. An eyewitness of the scene outside the Reich Chancellery
wrote:*

> About two hundred people are standing in the square outside the Reich
> Chancellery . . . clustered tightly together, they are staring tensely at an
> uninterrupted procession from Unter den Linden past the historic balcony:
> cannon, baggage trucks, horses, tanks, soldiers. Soldiers without end. Steel
> helmets low on their foreheads, eyes rigidly to the front, they sit their saddles,
> crouch on wagon seats and limbers, march heavy-footed along the asphalt.
> The balcony door upstairs opens. Hitler comes out bareheaded, his hands
> in the pockets of his tunic. He moves quickly to the railing. A couple of
> officers follow at a respectful distance. I recognize Raeder, and see the gold
> embroidery on several generals' uniforms in the twilight.
> I steal a glance at the faces of those around me: tight lips, wrinkled brows.
> They stand there with their tails between their legs, with the embarrassed,
> guilty look of people who know perfectly well that they don't want to do as
> they must.
> Not a hand is raised anywhere.
> The tanks roll, the people keep silent, and the Führer, uncheered, vanishes
> from the balcony. White-gloved SS men shut the doors, and draw the curtain
> inside the window.

Quite possibly this episode deepened Hitler's concern over the way the over-
all situation was developing. Whether or not that was so, it is clear that Hitler
was having second thoughts about the manner in which he had received Sir
Horace Wilson, and the abruptness of his denial that he had any reply to Chamberlain's letter other than a general expression of thanks for the Prime
Minister's efforts.

Soon after Wilson's departure Hitler decided to send Chamberlain a written
reply. Most of his letter† was repetitive of his previous arguments that the
Godesberg terms were not significantly different from the Anglo-French proposals. The demand for immediate occupation of the Sudetenland he justified as
"no more than a security measure intended to guarantee a quick and smooth
achievement of the final settlement."

* The eyewitness was the German writer and anti-Hitler activist Ruth Andreas-Friedrich,
author of *Berlin Underground 1938–1945* (1947). See the like account in Shirer, *Berlin
Diary* (1941), pp. 142–43. Their impressions are confirmed by Schmidt (*Hitler's Interpreter* [1951], p. 105), who recorded that several of Hitler's adjutants told him that the
Fuehrer "found the scene most disillusioning," and by Erich Kordt (*Wahn und
Wirklichkeit* [1948], p. 124), who reports Hitler's remark after observing the silent specta-
tors: "With these people I cannot make war."

† The letter was transmitted through Henderson and was received by telephone in London at 8:40 P.M. A draft found in the Wilhelmstrasse files bears editorial corrections in
Weizsaecker's handwriting, and Schmidt recalls preparing the translation into English. All
this indicates the probability that the letter was drafted before the silent public reaction to
the military display, which occurred at twilight.

None of this was helpful, but in conclusion, after accusing Prague of "using" the occupation proposal only to obtain English and French support and thus foment a "general warlike conflagration," Hitler wrote:

> I must leave it to your judgment whether, in view of these facts, you consider that you should continue your efforts, for which I should like to take this opportunity of once more sincerely thanking you, to spoil such maneuvres and to bring the Government in Prague to reason at the very last hour.

It was Hitler's last communication to his potential enemies prior to Munich, and it plainly shows that he did not want war with the western powers. The last sentence, though not phrased as a request, was a legible signal that Hitler was still holding back his attack, waiting to see what more the Prime Minister could extract from Prague.

10

The Czechs were not in a mood for further concessions. Fatigued they were, and the grinding uncertainty, consequent upon awareness that they were not the masters of their own destiny, added greatly to the strain. But mobilization had gone smoothly, and the country was solidly aligned behind the decision to fight with the support of their allies. There was no disposition to make independent proposals to Berlin, and after rejecting the Godesberg terms there was little for the Czech Government to do but complete its preparations* and react to the hints and warnings emanating from their western friends.

France, in contrast, was a nation riven ever deeper by the mounting crisis. True, the reservists went dutifully to their units, but with a shrugging *c'est la guerre* rather than a cheering *pour la patrie*. And as news of the impasse at Godesberg spread, the flight from Paris began. Alexander Werth has described the exodus:

> It started on Sunday [the twenty-fifth]. Thousands of cars were speeding West and South. . . . On the great main roads to Dijon and Nevers and Rennes the hotels were beginning to profiteer on a big scale. . . . On and on they would drive away from the danger zone. . . . Soldiers on the road would jeer at them as they drove past. . . . On Tuesday the opening of schools was postponed from October 1 to October 10. . . . There was no longer any excuse for leaving the children in Paris. Train services were doubled and trebled; immense crowds were assembled at the railway stations. . . . There were long queues outside the savings banks. . . . Trenches were being dug in the Parc Montsouris. . . . and at the Louvre pictures were being packed up. . . .

* For a description of the scene in Prague during the days immediately preceding Munich, see the account in G. E. R. Gedye, *Betrayal in Central Europe* (1939), pp. 439–66, and Ripka, *Munich: Before and After* (1969), pp. 194–216. In his memoirs Beneš disclosed that on September 26 General Syrový (Krejčí was then in Moravia) persuaded the President to move from the Hradschin to a locality a short distance from Prague, on the grounds that the city was likely to be bombed. Shortly thereafter news of fresh approaches by Chamberlain to Hitler made the bombing appear less imminent, and Beneš returned to the Hradschin.

Public confusion and fear were matched by dissension and rancor among the nation's leaders and press spokesmen. A good example of the lengths to which the *anti-bellicistes* went to discredit their opponents is the treatment which the Foreign Ministry and much of the press gave to the British Foreign Office communiqué of September 26, which for the first time officially declared that, if France came to Czechoslovakia's assistance against Germany, Britain and the Soviet Union would "certainly stand by France." The Agence Havas dispatch from London quoting the text reached Paris late in the evening of the twenty-sixth. Instead of emphasizing the undeniable importance of this declaration, Bonnet, in response to inquiries, merely stated that he had no "confirmation" of its authenticity. Thereupon a number of the large, appeasement-favoring Paris dailies denounced the communiqué as *"fausses nouvelles"* (fake news) or a *"mensonge"* (lie) supporting this accusation by its odd wording and lack of a personal signature. The result was that the release, which the Foreign Office had intended as reassurance to the French, lost much of its impact.*

The virulence of language used by the defeatists was increasing dangerously. In the afternoon of the twenty-seventh, the streets of Paris were adorned with a poster signed by former Premier Flandin, which informed the readers: "You are being deceived! During recent weeks and months, occult forces have been operating a clever device to render war inevitable." The text continued with a denunciation of military mobilization, which would lead to the massacre of millions of Frenchmen. This came so close to counseling disobedience to the call-up orders that the police tore down the posters and confiscated the issue of the Fascist *Liberté* which had carried the text on its front page.

Such was the atmosphere which Daladier and his party found upon their return to Paris in the afternoon of the twenty-sixth. Early in the evening Bonnet sent for Phipps and put to him three questions, all based on the assumption that France, as a result of a German attack on Czechoslovakia, would mobilize and engage in "an act of war" against Germany. In such event, would Britain:

1. Mobilize immediately and at the same time as France?
2. Introduce conscription
3. Pool the economic and financial resources of the two countries?

Bonnet explained to Phipps that "he and M. Daladier had thought it best to put these questions after their return rather than verbally, so as to give time for His Majesty's Government to consider them carefully. They would be glad, however, for very early replies."

The excuse was plainly spurious, as the sooner such questions were put the more time there would have been for their consideration, and putting them orally would have made possible immediate clarifying discussion. It is quite pos-

---

* In his postwar testimony, Bonnet defended his "reserve" about the communiqué primarily on the ground that Phipps had told him that it was the work of Vansittart, intended to impress Berlin, and that the British Government's policy remained unchanged. The comments he attributed to Phipps are in character, but Bonnet's excuse entirely overlooks that, so far as it concerned Britain, the communiqué only bore out the declarations Chamberlain had made to Daladier that morning, and that Wilson was to make to Hitler. It seems clear that Bonnet rightly feared that the British guarantee of support would reinforce the arguments of the *bellicistes,* and took steps to diminish its public and political effect.

sible that Daladier knew nothing of Bonnet's move, which may well, as Phipps implied in transmitting the inquiry to London, have been instigated by the *défaitiste* Caillaux, who had raised similar questions when talking with Phipps the previous day. The Bonnet inquiries, like his treatment of the Foreign Office communiqué, appear in retrospect as an effort to disparage the value of the newly given British guarantee of assistance.

Of course, the ministers did not all share Bonnet's views, and for the French Government the question now was what action to take in the wake of the decisions reached in London and of Hitler's Sportspalast tirade. Early in the morning of the twenty-seventh Daladier and Gamelin conferred, and the general, after bringing the Premier up to date on the military discussions in London, told him that the result of allowing Hitler to crush Czechoslovakia would be to add thirty divisions to the German forces available against France or Poland, and greatly to enlarge Germany's economic resources through domination of Central and Eastern Europe. *"Nous aurons reculé pour plus mal sauter"* (in essence, "We will have retreated to a worse position"), Gamelin declared, and added that "even if peace is preserved by our holding aloof, in ten years France would be only a second class power."

That was all very well, but what was to be done here and now? Gamelin's memoirs mention no discussion of full mobilization. Instead, he spoke of the necessity that the Czech Army avoid encirclement by giving up Prague and most of Bohemia at the outset and withdrawing into Moravia, and of the risk that Poland might disrupt this strategy by attacking in the rear, at Teschen. On these matters Gamelin offered to intervene on a personal basis with Syrový and Smigly-Rydz.

Daladier approved the idea, and Gamelin at once sent, via the Czech military attaché, a message to Syrový counseling him in line with these views. The advice was given on a purely personal basis "as a friend," and the message began with the statement: "In the present situation I cannot enter into relations with the Czechoslovak general staff"—given the time and circumstances a wretched confession of French hesitation and lassitude. Through the French military attaché in Warsaw, Gamelin sent a letter to Smigly-Rydz, reminding him of their conversation in 1936, when the Polish marshal had promised that his country would never be ranged against France, and pleading for a solution of the Teschen issue by agreement with Prague.*

Later that morning the Cabinet met. According to Bonnet, he and Daladier had a preliminary consultation *à deux,* in which they decided, despite "alarming reports," not to initiate general mobilization. In his memoirs, Bonnet described mobilization as "one of those grave steps which, according to our agreements with London, would not be taken without previous consultation with the British Government." Certainly there was no such formal commitment; possibly there was some such informal understanding, but this appears unlikely, since that very

---

* The answers to these letters were overtaken by events. On the twenty-ninth, while the Munich conference was under way, Syrový replied that "the Czechoslovaks knew how to make the sacrifices necessary to save the bulk of the army." After the settlement and the Polish occupation of Teschen, Smigly-Rydz answered in what Gamelin called a "bittersweet" tone, which ended the friendly relations between the two.

evening the British Cabinet authorized mobilization of the Royal Navy without any thought of prior consultation with Paris.

In any event, the Cabinet approved only the call-up of additional classes without general mobilization, and the continuation of efforts to solve the crisis peaceably. Bonnet described the discussion as "confused," and immediately after the meeting Chautemps told Bullitt that "since the French Cabinet this morning had no knowledge of the nature of Hitler's reply to the message from Chamberlain transmitted yesterday by Sir Horace Wilson it had been impossible to come to any definite conclusions as to what policy should be followed." Obviously, the initiative still lay with London, and Paris was reluctant to make other than following moves.

11

After listening to Hitler's Sportspalast speech, Chamberlain and his inner group foregathered to review the situation. Despite the violent tone, Simon and Vansittart both thought it a "mark time" speech, and the group agreed that it did not require immediate mobilization. Then, however, Wilson's message describing his first interview with Hitler was read, and it was the consensus that if at the second meeting the Fuehrer were "equally uncompromising," mobilization would be necessary. The Prime Minister then suggested, and himself drafted, the public statement assuring Hitler that Britain and France would hold themselves responsible for Prague's compliance with its promises. In conclusion, the conferees discussed bringing Mussolini into the situation, but decided the risk of a refusal was too great.

Tuesday, September 27, had been planned as a day of Britannic rejoicing, for the great liner *Queen Elizabeth*—the largest of her kind ever built—was launched that day at Clydesbank in the presence of the Queen. His Majesty King George VI was not there, as it was thought that his presence in London might be necessary. In fact, the forenoon and early afternoon passed rather quietly in higher Government circles, as everyone was waiting for the news of Wilson's second meeting with Hitler.

For the English people, however, it was a day of great tension. Hore-Belisha toured the London antiaircraft defenses, trench-digging and the distribution of gas masks continued, and that evening there were radio announcements of the formation of the Auxiliary Territorial Service (the women's Army auxiliary) and the temporary closing of the Underground for "special structural work."

The bad news of Wilson's second encounter with the Fuehrer arrived in midafternoon. Wilson himself, accompanied by Mason-Mac, arrived soon thereafter, and so began Cadogan's "frightful afternoon," as he described it in his diary:

> Small meeting of Ministers, frightened out of their wits by Gamelin's conversation, by a telegram from Phipps about French feeling, and Malcolm M. and Bruce on subject of Dominions. P.M. came in and out. Unfortunately Mason Macfarlane M.A. in Berlin also here, and he painted gloomy picture of Czech morale. What does he know about it? Also meeting with Chiefs of Staff who were called in. Not very reassuring. But P.M. authorized Backhouse

to mobilise Fleet. But all this produced a glacial period in Ministerial feet. . . .

The "small meeting," which began at half past four in the afternoon, was in fact not so small, as MacDonald and Inskip had been restored to membership in the inner circle, and the Chiefs were also present, as well as Wilson and Cadogan. Mason-Mac and Bruce came in later, but the former's views on Czech morale had been telephoned to the War Office the previous evening. Based on his observations during his courier trip carrying the Godesberg ultimatum, Mason-Mac reported: "Gain general impression Czechs' morale not very good. Certainly not if forced to fight alone."

Mason-Mac's opportunities for observation had been very limited, and the second quoted sentence was a very significant limitation on his verdict. Nevertheless, the Chiefs of Staff reported it to the ministers at the beginning of the meeting, and then expressed anxiety that the French might undertake an offensive against Germany "which would not be likely to achieve any effective result." It was agreed that the French should be told not to take any major offensive action without first consulting London.

Admiral Sir Roger Backhouse (Chatfield's successor as Chief of the Naval Staff) then repeated his previous warnings that, for effective defense at sea, the fleet would have to be mobilized well before the outbreak of hostilities. Chamberlain dared no longer to temporize on this, and it was agreed that naval mobilization would be ordered the next morning.

Prior to the meeting Halifax and Cadogan had prepared a new proposition—a "time-table," as Cadogan called it—for submission to Berlin and Prague, as a further effort to stave off hostilities. This was approved; in brief, it provided for German occupation of Eger and Asch "outside the Czech fortified line" on October 1; meetings of German and Czech plenipotentiaries and an International Boundary Commission on October 3; entry of German troops on October 10 into the zones in which the plenipotentiaries had completed arrangements for the hand-over; entry of German troops by October 31 into the remaining areas within the frontiers finally determined by the Boundary Commission; "as soon as possible" thereafter negotiations for "revising Czechoslovakia's present treaty relationships and instituting a system jointly guaranteeing the new Czechoslovakia."

Colonel Mason-Mac then entered and added to his prior report his opinion that the Czech Army's matériel preparations were incomplete, the defenses in the south opposite Vienna and Linz (many miles from the ground he had covered on his trip) ill-prepared, and the Czech frontier guards "scared stiff." The French military attaché in Berlin, Mason-Mac reported, was doubtful of the resistance that the Czechs would put up, and he himself thought "it would be very rash to base any policy on the assumption that the Czechs would fight like tigers." The Germans, he opined, were planning a pincers attack to cut Czechoslovakia in two and, while there was much dislike of the prospect of war, he "thought that there would be more enthusiasm for war than seemed possible a month ago."

MacDonald then brought the Australian High Commissioner, Stanley Bruce, into the meeting. MacDonald, it appeared, had suggested that the High Commissioners put their views in writing. Te Water of South Africa had done this,* but Bruce thought it "a very dangerous course," since "any views now committed to writing would be likely to take the line that the terms of the German memorandum were not a sufficient cause for a world war," and if war came this "would subsequently prove very embarrassing." Bruce's main point was that the British Government must decide whether "the matters in dispute were now relatively small," in which case they should "at all costs be settled by negotiation," or whether "the point in dispute was really a challenge between the idea of force and peaceful negotiation," in which case "the challenge was to be taken up" and in due course the Dominions "would come to share" that view. Irrespective of its moral validity, it is hard to see how this statement can have been of much assistance to the British ministers.

Sir Horace Wilson then described his second meeting with Hitler, and recommended that the Czechs should be urged to withdraw voluntarily to permit German troops to occupy the areas up to the line stipulated in the Godesberg memorandum—"complete capitulation," as Cadogan pointed out. Chamberlain asked that this proposal be passed over and considered that evening by the full Cabinet.

Finally the ministers considered the proposed White Paper which Chamberlain had promised Attlee to make available for the morrow's meeting of Parliament. The intention had been to lay all the relevant official documents before the members, but there was a very embarrassing problem which, the ministers decided, required the omission of a key paper:

> It was decided to print the White Paper . . . subject to the excision of the message sent by the Czechoslovak Government accepting the Franco-British proposals. This document . . . referred to the strong and continuous pressure put upon the Czechoslovak Government by the French and British representatives. If this was printed it would lead to a demand for the telegrams to the French and British Ministers at Prague urging them to apply pressure. These could not be printed at this stage.

In the course of or immediately after the meeting, messages were sent to Henderson, Phipps, and Newton embodying the Halifax-Cadogan "time-table" proposal. Henderson was instructed to submit it "immediately" to Hitler, adding that the French Government approved "a scheme on these lines," and that it had been "intimated" to the Czech Government that "this affords the only means of securing an orderly transfer of the territories which they have agreed to concede." Phipps was told to urge the French Government "to support us in this endeavor to secure a reasonable procedure for settlement."

* In the morning of the twenty-seventh Te Water had delivered to the Prime Minister a message from Hertzog "that he and his colleagues feel that the Berlin proposals should be accepted," and reiterating "that South Africa cannot be expected to take any part in a war over Czechoslovakia." Later that morning after studying Hitler's speech, Hertzog sent a further message that "if after this an European war is still to take place, the responsibility for that will not be placed upon the shoulders of Germany."

As for the Czechs, if Chamberlain and Halifax were fearful of informing Parliament about past pressures, there was no hesitation about renewing and reinforcing them now. At quarter to six o'clock Chamberlain wired Beneš:

> I feel bound to tell you . . . that the information . . . from Berlin makes it clear that German forces will have orders to cross Czechoslovak frontier almost immediately, unless by 2.0 p.m. tomorrow Czechoslovak Government have accepted German terms.
>
> That must result in Bohemia being overrun and nothing that any other Power can do will prevent this fate for your country and people, and this remains true whatever the ultimate issue of a possible world war. His Majesty's Government cannot take responsibility of advising you what you should do but they consider that this information should be in your hands at once.

In fact, this conveyed no new information. The Czechs well knew that a German attack was imminent and that they could not long hold Bohemia. It is hard to believe, as the rest of that sentence seems to say, that Chamberlain really meant that Bohemia would remain overrun by Germans "whatever the ultimate issue" of the war; the phrasing betokens fatigue and near-panic.

A quarter of an hour later Halifax instructed Newton to present the "time-table" immediately, and "most earnestly urge" the Czechs to accept it. The "only alternative" would be "the invasion and dismemberment of their country by forcible means, and though that might result in general conflict entailing incalculable loss of life, there is no possibility that at the end of the conflict, whatever the result, Czechoslovakia could be restored to her frontiers of today."

These were terrible warnings; even Bonnet recorded that their tone "froze him." But they were also more than a little spurious; surely the territorial settlements at the end of a "general conflict" were beyond the range of vision of Halifax or anyone else. The noble lord seemed to be saying that, even after victory over Germany, the Allies would not reconstitute the very Czech borders that France and the Soviet Union were treaty-bound to protect, and his plain purpose was to portray military success as valueless and saddle Prague with responsibility for "incalculable loss of life."

Chamberlain was to broadcast at eight o'clock, and half an hour earlier the electricians came into the Cabinet room to rig the microphone. The Prime Minister, Halifax, Wilson, and Cadogan adjourned to Wilson's room to consider his draft of a telegram to Beneš advocating what Cadogan called "complete capitulation," tantamount to acceptance of the Godesberg terms. Halifax and Cadogan opposed it, and at eight o'clock "Poor P.M. (quite exhausted) said 'I'm wobbling all over the place' and went in to broadcast."

He began by acknowledging the many letters he had received—"Most of these letters have come from women"—expressing "their gratitude for my efforts" and "their prayers for my success." Then came the much-quoted and oft-criticized passage:

> If I felt my responsibility heavy before, to read such letters has made it seem almost overwhelming. How horrible, fantastic, incredible it is that we should be digging trenches and trying on gas masks here because of a quarrel in a faraway country between people of whom we know nothing. It seems still

more impossible that a quarrel which has already been settled in principle should be the subject of war.

Chamberlain next described his success in getting Prague's agreement to "the substance of what Hitler wanted," his surprise when confronted at Godesberg with the demand for immediate occupation, and declared plaintively: "I must say that I find this attitude unreasonable." He would not abandon his efforts for peace, but "at this moment I see nothing further I can usefully do in the way of mediation."

Shifting to the home front, the Prime Minister called for volunteers for air-raid defense and other duties, but told his listeners not to be "alarmed" by the announcement of military call-ups, for these were "only precautionary measures" which "do not necessarily mean that we have determined on war or that war is imminent." Then in conclusion:

> However much we may sympathize with a small nation confronted by a big and powerful neighbour, we cannot in all circumstances undertake to involve the whole British Empire in war simply on her account. If we have to fight it must be on larger issues than that. . . . Armed conflict between nations is a nightmare to me, but if I were convinced that any nation had made up its mind to dominate the world by fear of its force, I should believe it must be resisted. Under such domination life for people who believe in liberty would not be worth living. . . .

The Prime Minister phrased the test in libertarian terms, but essentially this was a recasting of Eyre Crowe's 1907 "balance of power" formulation. Was Britain now, as in 1914, confronting a nation so bent on domination? Chamberlain left the question unanswered, saying only "War is a fearful thing, and we must be very clear, before we embark on it, that it is really the great issues that are at stake . . ." and that his listeners should "await as calmly as you can the events of the next few days."

To whom was Chamberlain talking? If Hitler was the principle target, the text was in line with Chamberlain's tactics—a reiteration that the Fuehrer could have what he wanted without war, so why did he insist on provoking a war? But for the home front this was a lugubrious, desperate, and confusing message. The first part seemed to say that a war for faraway people "of whom we know nothing" would be senseless, while the conclusion sounded a faint note of the necessity of resisting a latter-day Napoleon. But if Hitler was indeed that, Britain above all needed a trumpet call, and that was an instrument Chamberlain could not play.

While the Prime Minister was speaking, Halifax dispatched the message to Paris, agreed at the ministers' meeting, warning the French against precipitate military action. Phipps was asked to deliver it at once to Bonnet or, preferably, Daladier:

> General Gamelin made it plain to us . . . that, in his view, if German forces now invaded Czechoslovakia, Czech resistance is likely to be of extremely brief duration. This disturbing estimate is confirmed by our Military Attaché in Berlin, who has just returned from Czechoslovakia and reports

that he is convinced that morale is poor and that resistance will prove to be feeble. The Attaché has just reached London and has reported his visit to me personally. If therefore our efforts for peace fail . . . we may expect to be faced in a very short time with a *fait accompli,* so far as Czechoslovakia is concerned. No declarations or actions of France or ourselves in the meantime can prevent this sudden and overwhelming result. . . .

. . . In this situation, having regard to the identity of intents of our two countries, it is necessary that any action by France in discharge of her obligations and by ourselves in support of France should be closely concerted. . . .

We would be glad to know that French Government agree that any action of an offensive nature taken by either of us henceforward . . . shall only be taken after previous consultation and agreement.

Of course, it was not only sensible but essential that major military moves be made in consultation and, if desirable, with co-operation between the Allies. But considering the British Chiefs' long and obstinate opposition to staff talks, and their inability to deploy more than two underequipped divisions at the outset, the admonition to the French was presumptuous, to say the least. Furthermore, Gamelin had *not* said in London that Czech resistance would be "of extremely brief duration," but rather that if the Czechs withdrew from Bohemia in good time, they could give a good account of themselves and maintain a front further east.* But the thrust of the message was altogether welcome to Bonnet, to whom Phipps delivered it, and who happily gave the required assurance, adding that in his view "it behooves us both to be extremely prudent and to count our probable and even possible enemies before embarking on any offensive act whatever."

After the ministers' meeting, Gort and Mason-Mac returned to the War Office to confer with Pownall and General Sir Ronald Adam, the Deputy Chief of Staff. In view of their conclusions, which "were much influenced by the views of Mason-Mac," Pownall that evening produced an "appreciation" which was the military leaders' last word of advice prior to Munich. In fact, its content was more political and psychological than military. German morale could be "sustained" for a considerable period; feeling in the House of Commons was likely to be "bellicose," which was "the more unfortunate in that members have no knowledge of the military situation"; Czech resistance "even in the best circumstances, cannot be prolonged"; the attitude of the Dominions was "far from helpful," except for New Zealand; Italy was "uncertain," and from the Soviet Union "little is to be expected in our aid."

On the military level, Pownall remarked the country's unpreparedness, but thought "a period of even six months, *provided full pressure of work were maintained and financial obstructions removed,* would go a long way to provide at least our essential needs" and make Britain "reasonably secure against defeat." On that basis, the season was propitious, since the coming winter months would both dull the edge of enemy air raids and provide time to strengthen de-

---

* Gamelin, when apprized of this portion of Halifax's telegram, subsequently took pains to correct Lord Halifax's misapprehension in personal conversation, and made the correction a matter of record in a letter to Daladier. Gamelin blamed the affair on Bonnet.

fenses. Nevertheless, the timing also "has advantages from the German point of view," for reasons Pownall did not intelligibly explain. In conclusion:

> . . . from the military point of view the balance of advantage is definitely in favor of postponement. This is probably an exception to the rule that "no war is inevitable," for it will almost certainly come later. Our real object is not to save Czechoslovakia—that is impossible in any event—but to end the days of the Nazi régime. This is not our selected moment, it is theirs; we are in bad condition to wage even a defensive war at the present time; the grouping of the powers at the moment makes well nigh hopeless the waging of a successful offensive war.

It was a hastily drawn paper, but even allowing for time pressures the analysis was superficial. Nothing in the body of the document supported the conclusion in favor of postponement, except a highly speculative suggestion that Italy would be a less likely belligerent in "a later war . . . fought on some other pretext." The present was plainly *not* Hitler's "selected moment" for a general European war; much as the Fuehrer wanted to smash the Czechs, his dealings with Chamberlain over the past two weeks had made it obvious that he did not want to confront the Anglo-French alliance. But it may be doubted that, at this late stage, the document had much effect on the course of events or on the decisions reached when the Cabinet met at half-past nine that evening—their last gathering before Munich.

Chamberlain began by reading a dispatch from Henderson recounting a meeting with Goering which the ambassador thought made it obvious that "the die is cast" and "British mediation at an end," and predicted for Czechoslovakia "the same fate as Abyssinia." This was followed by a report of Mason-Mac's pessimistic opinion of Czech will to fight, and then by a reference to Te Water's memorandum and the reading of a telegram from the Australian Prime Minister, J. A. Lyons, urging that the Godesberg terms be accepted. Furthermore, the High Commissioners had all visited Downing Street that afternoon and recommended "further pressure" on the Czechs. MacDonald, when called upon to amplify this report, was obliged to add that the British High Commissioner in Australia thought that Lyons "underestimated the strength of feeling in Australia against acceptance of Herr Hitler's proposals."

Wilson reported on his Berlin mission, and then told the Cabinet that, as matters now stood, the only hope of preventing a German military conquest of Czechoslovakia was for the Czechs to withdraw their forces immediately from the areas specified in the Godesberg memorandum. If they did so, the Germans might be expected to stop at the line they themselves had fixed, and the Czechs "would have the benefit of Herr Hitler's public declaration that Sudeten German territory represented the last of his territorial aims in Europe," as well as of the Anglo-French guarantee. Wilson laid before the Cabinet the draft of a telegram to Beneš laying out this proposal as one which "it would be wise" for him to consider.

The plan was vehemently attacked by Duff Cooper, who also accused the Prime Minister of presenting facts which "all tended to one conclusion," and excluding "other facts which tended the other way." Oliver Stanley put questions

which elicited from Simon the admission that Wilson's proposal "amounted to
acceptance of Herr Hitler's memorandum." Halifax then described to his colleagues the "accelerated time-table" which he had already circulated to Berlin,
Prague, and Paris, and went on to say that "he would feel great difficulty" in approving Wilson's telegram. In view of the decisions reached with the French they
would surely have to be consulted* before accepting this "complete capitulation
to Germany." Nor should Britain press the Czechs "to do what we believed to
be wrong." Finally (and this was probably the clincher) "we could not adopt
this suggestion unless we assured Czechoslovakia that Germany would stop at
the red line [on the German map accompanying the Godesberg ultimatum], and
he would feel some difficulty in giving such assurance."

Chamberlain at once conceded that "the Foreign Secretary had given powerful and perhaps convincing reasons against the adoption of his suggestion."
Simon, as usual, then swung into line, and the Cabinet agreed that the Wilson
proposal should not be transmitted to Prague.

At this point Hitler's reply to the letter Wilson had carried to Berlin was
brought in and read aloud. The reaction was that the Fuehrer's message might
"afford some ground on which a further proposal for a peaceful settlement
could be based," but that this would require careful consideration before determining what if anything ought to be done.

There followed some discussion of what the Prime Minister should say on the
morrow in addressing the Commons. It was agreed that the members should be
told of the new commitment to support France and the terms of the "special
message" delivered by Wilson to Hitler. Chamberlain "did not, however, propose to commit himself to . . . the effect that, if Germany invaded Czechoslovakia, we should at once go to war with Germany."

Finally, the Prime Minister announced the decision taken that afternoon to
mobilize the fleet. The Cabinet adjourned, and Duff Cooper rushed out to telephone the Press Section of the Admiralty so that the information could be
released to the morning newspapers.

Meanwhile, in Prague, Newton had presented the "time-table" to Beneš, who
said that "he would immediately convoke Government to make a decision." A
few hours later, in Berlin, Henderson presented it to Weizsaecker for transmittal
to Hitler. The German official commented that the plan was "out of date" and
unlikely to be accepted, and in reporting to London, Henderson characterized
the proposal as "quite useless here since there is not the slightest chance Herr
Hitler will accept it or even consider it."

After the Cabinet had adjourned, a message came in from Prague in which
the military attaché, Colonel Stronge, differed sharply from Mason-Mac's

_____

* Apparently someone in London—possibly Wilson—had been in touch with Bonnet
about the plan, for when Bullitt met Bonnet late that afternoon, the Frenchman told him
"under the seal of absolute secrecy" that the "French Foreign Office and the British Foreign Office were engaged in working out a plan to give to Germany before October 1st full
possession of the regions which Czechoslovakia had promised to turn over to Germany."
Bullitt expressed his astonishment and told Washington that in his opinion "Daladier positively will not assent to any such proposal." Daladier made no mention of it when Bullitt
saw him later that evening.

disparaging report on the morale of the Czech forces. Mason-Mac's impression, said Stronge, was based on his encounters with the Czech border guard, a paramilitary organization wholly inferior to the Czech regulars who, Stronge reported, "have confidence in their cause, their leadership and their equipment" and, given the support of "powerful allies even if these cannot immediately act on their behalf," would probably "render a good account of themselves."

Thirty years later, in a letter to *The Times,* Stronge attributed Mason-Mac's hasty and ill-informed judgment to "his natural tendency to act on impulse." In effect, Mason-Mac had followed in Lindbergh's footsteps; he had given ammunition to those on the Allied side bent on averting a military showdown. This is the more curious because Mason-Mac's personal view of Nazi Germany bore no resemblance to Lindbergh's. The British colonel hated the regime, talked semiseriously of assassinating the Fuehrer, and thought Henderson a naïve fool and Munich a disaster.

The Mason-Mac episode reveals more about those in London to whom he talked than it does about the talker. Stronge was the responsible military observer in Prague, yet little or no attention was paid to his riposte to Mason-Mac. The latter's gloomy assessment, the superficiality of which should have been apparent to any discerning listener,* was seized upon with avidity because it was what his listeners wished to hear. They did not want encouraging news; they wanted news which would justify capitulation. And so Mason-Mac was brought in person before the Prime Minister and his inner circle, called the tune for Pownall's War Office "appreciation," and was quoted as an authority in Cabinet and in Halifax's message intended to slow down the already muscle-bound French generals. There is no doubt that the real fear in London was that, if the French should move aggressively, the Germans would be the more likely to rain bombs on London.

12

While the British Government was staggering through what was certainly not its finest day, in Washington the President had called a special Cabinet meeting to consider what if anything further might be done, in the light of the reply from Hitler to the President's peace appeal. According to Ickes, Harry Hopkins "thought it would be a mistake to make any further effort," but Roosevelt was getting contrary advice from the State Department, as well as from Ickes himself. Bullitt, in a long telephone conversation with Welles in the morning of the twenty-seventh, had raised again his earlier idea of an international conference at The Hague, and had reported that Daladier was still hoping that the deadlock might be broken in some such manner.

The Bullitt-Daladier ideas for a five or six European power conference at The Hague, with an American representative participating, had some attraction for Roosevelt, but Hull opposed it and, according to Morgenthau, the President rejected it for fear of "untoward domestic effects." Instead, he tentatively fa-

---

* Writing thirty years later, General Kenneth Strong, who was Mason-Mac's deputy at the time, described the latter's report as "superficial, because of the speed with which his task had been undertaken."

vored a less detailed proposal of a conference comprising the countries "directly interested" to be held in a "neutral European capital," and on the afternoon of the twenty-seventh Welles telephoned the gist of the plan to Bullitt and Kennedy, with instructions to get Daladier's and Chamberlain's reactions and suggestions. Simultaneously, Ambassador William Phillips was requested to convey a "personal and confidential" message from Roosevelt to Mussolini, soliciting the Duce's aid in securing "continuation of the efforts to arrive at an agreement of the questions at issue by negotiation or other pacific means rather than by resort to force."

Kennedy telephoned later in the Washington afternoon that Chamberlain held out little hope of swaying Hitler but had no objection to another appeal. The President then settled down with Hull, Welles, and Adolf Berle (Assistant Secretary of State) to edit Welles's draft, and at about half-past nine that evening it was signed and given to the State Department for dispatch to Hitler.* Exploiting the Fuehrer's lengthy rehearsal of grievances dating back to Versailles, Roosevelt began with a sharp reminder that: "The question before the world today, Mr. Chancellor, is not the question of errors of judgment or errors committed in the past. It is the question of the fate of the world today and tomorrow." And then, after a reference to reports from "responsible statesmen" that "an agreement in principle has already been reached," came the passages quoted at the beginning of this work suggesting an immediate conference "of all the nations directly interested" to be held "in some neutral spot in Europe."

On the morning of Wednesday, the twenty-eighth, Roosevelt's letter shared the headlines with Chamberlain's radio address and mobilization of the fleet. By law, mobilization had to be authorized by an Order in Council from the Privy Council, and this was done at half-past ten o'clock. Duff Cooper found the King "very cheerful, envisaging the war with great equanimity," but the monarch must have been keeping a stiff upper lip, for the night before he had written to the Queen Mother: "It is all so worrying, this awful waiting for the worst to happen."

The Prime Minister was up betimes that morning, and by ten o'clock messages which he himself had drafted were on their way to Hitler and Mussolini. The first, quoted in part in the first chapter, proposed a five-power conference in Berlin, and concluded with stiffer language than Chamberlain had previously used to the Fuehrer: "I cannot believe that you will take the responsibility of starting a world war which may end civilisation for the sake of a few days' delay in settling this long-standing problem."

The message to Mussolini was *not* the initial or decisive stimulus to the Duce's intervention. The previous day, as related in the first chapter, Lord Perth had suggested that Mussolini be asked to act as peacemaker, and the Foreign Office, in reply, had authorized Perth to inform Ciano of the "time-table" proposal, and suggest that Mussolini "use his influence" to induce Hitler to accept.

---

* Copies were transmitted to London, Paris, Prague, Rome, Warsaw, and Budapest. As the message was being transmitted, a telegram was received from Bullitt reporting that Daladier was "delighted" by the President's move.

Perth acted on this at ten o'clock in the morning of the twenty-eighth, with consequences described in Ciano's diary:

> He says, with much emotion, that Chamberlain appeals to the Duce for his friendly intervention in these hours, which he considers the last in which something might be done to save peace and civilization. He repeats the guarantee already offered by England and France for the return of the Sudetenland. I ask Perth whether I am to regard his *démarche* as an official invitation to the Duce to assume the role of mediator. Yes. In that case there is no time to lose—the offer deserves to be given consideration. I tell Perth to wait for me at the Palazzo Chigi. I go to the Duce. He agrees at once on the impossibility of meeting Chamberlain's request with a flat refusal. He telephones Attolico: "Go to the Führer and tell him, having said that in any eventuality I shall be at his side, that I recommend that the commencement of hostilities be delayed for 24 hours. Meanwhile I undertake to study what can be done to solve this problem." I go back to the Palazzo Chigi. I inform Perth that hostilities are to begin today* and confirm that our place is beside Germany. His face quivers and his eyes are red. When I add that nevertheless the Duce has accepted Chamberlain's request and has proposed a delay of 24 hours, he bursts into a sobbing laugh and rushes off to his Embassy.

At noon the Foreign Office received Perth's report that Mussolini had asked Hitler to hold off for twenty-four hours. At his embassy Perth received Chamberlain's "personal message" to the Duce, describing his "last appeal" to Hitler, embodying the offer to go to Berlin for a five-power conference to settle the Sudeten issue, and concluding:

> I trust Your Excellency will inform German Chancellor that you are willing to be represented and urge him to agree to my proposal which will keep all our peoples out of war. I have already guaranteed that Czech promises shall be carried out and feel confident agreement could be reached in a week.

So armed, Perth hastened back to the Palazzo Chigi, where, according to Ciano's diary:

> He brings with him . . . a concrete proposal for a Conference of Four† with the task of reaching a radical solution of the Sudeten problem within seven days. It cannot be rejected—by rejecting it Hitler would draw the hatred of the world upon himself and have the sole responsibility for the conflict. Palazzo Venezia—the Duce decides to support the English request, particularly as the Führer has now, at Mussolini's desire, had a phonogram of instructions made. I telephone to Perth, to inform him, and to Attolico, to give him directions. Naturally I cancel the meeting with Ribbentrop and Keitel arranged yesterday.

---

* This, of course, was not the case, as the German assault troops were still moving up and would not have been ready for attack until the night of September 30.

† Chamberlain had in fact proposed a conference of five (Britain, Czechoslovakia, France, Germany, and Italy), not four. No doubt Ciano wrote the entry some hours, at least, after the events related, and in this instance reflecting subsequent developments. Other evidence suggests that the "phonogram" was not received in Rome as early as the entry suggests.

And so, at one o'clock that afternoon, Perth was able to inform London by telephone that Hitler had agreed "to postpone mobilisation for 24 hours" and that Mussolini would "support with Herr Hitler, and advise acceptance of proposals for a conference in Berlin and ask to be represented." That much Chamberlain knew when he rose to address the House of Commons,* although of course he did not know that Mussolini had already been promised a "phonogram of instructions" comprising, presumably, the memorandum hastily prepared by Goering, Neurath, and Weizsaecker, as described in the second chapter.

The French Government also tried to make its voice heard in Rome, but Ciano rebuffed Chargé Blondel's approaches. In Berlin, François-Poncet, the urbane dean of the diplomatic corps, was treated more respectfully. Bonnet, on receiving Phipps's report of the British "time-table" proposal, had commented that it was not "sufficiently far-reaching to satisfy the German Government," and had instructed François-Poncet to seek a personal interview with Hitler and present proposals under which Germany would occupy a larger area on October 1.

Shortly after eight o'clock in the morning of the twenty-eighth, François-Poncet telephoned Weizsaecker and requested the audience with Hitler. The new French proposal, as he described it to Weizsaecker, contemplated the immediate German occupation of several zones on the northern, western, and southwestern frontiers of Bohemia, including the fortifications therein. The plan had not yet been made known to Prague, but if acceptable to Berlin, the Czechs would have to yield or be told to shift for themselves.

François-Poncet then telephoned Henderson, and it is illustrative of the confusions and misunderstandings of that hectic morning that he gave the British Ambassador a very different impression of the new French proposal than he had given Weizsaecker. Henderson reported to London that the French proposed to allow immediate German occupation of "Egerland as a whole" instead of (as in the "time-table") only that portion lying outside the Czech fortifications.

The French proposals were welcomed by Henderson, who, as he reported to London, "ventured to tell" François-Poncet that "His Majesty's Government would accept this modification and that he might say so." In other words, both ambassadors, *without informing Prague,* were ready to concede immediate territorial concessions that would breach the Czech fortified line in advance of any general settlement. But whether the French Government had in fact authorized any such under-the-table deal remains uncertain,† and both the "time-table" and the French "improvement" were shortly superseded by the Munich settlement.

---

* The idea of an appeal to Mussolini was also suggested by the Australian Prime Minister in a telephone call to Chamberlain in the morning of the twenty-eighth, and in a telegram received at quarter past one. Mr. Lyons also offered to have Mr. Bruce fly to Rome to make a personal presentation. A note in the British file states that Chamberlain had already decided to invoke Mussolini's aid.

† Later on the twenty-eighth Phipps reported to London that, according to Léger, there had been a "misunderstanding" about the French offer, which had been "carefully drafted so as not to include Czech defenses" in the area to be surrendered on October 1. Halifax, too, queried Henderson on the area described as "Egerland as a whole."

After telephoning Weizsaecker and Henderson, François-Poncet "had a map drawn with the districts admittedly German heavily colored in red," which he proposed to use to show Hitler "how very much he could gain without a general conflagration." But by ten o'clock no word had come, and he sent his military attaché, General Renondeau, to OKH to inform the military leaders "of the message I was charged with but as yet unable to deliver." He also telephoned Henderson "to say that he feared the worst since he had no answer to his request for an audience." The Britisher at once telephoned Goering, who, after hearing a description of the situation, said that he would go immediately to Hitler, to ensure that the new proposals were considered. Shortly thereafter Henderson received Chamberlain's morning message to Hitler, and François-Poncet got word that Hitler would receive him at eleven o'clock.

Around the entrance to Hitler's office at the Chancellery was a disorganized, excited gathering of officials. Ribbentrop and Weizsaecker were both there, as well as Neurath, who, without any request from Hitler, had left his estate and come to Berlin to make known his views on the crisis. As described by Schmidt:

> . . . in the neighboring rooms and passages there was the high-pressure activity of a time of crisis. Ministers and generals, with their train of Party members, who had hurried round to consult Hitler, were sitting or standing everywhere. None of these discussions were held as part of formal meetings. Hitler strolled the rooms, speaking now to one, now another. Whoever happened to be near could get at him, but nobody could actually get a word in. To anyone who wanted, or did not want, to listen, Hitler made long harangues about his view of the situation. It was just a series of shorter Sports Palace speeches. Only now and then Hitler withdrew to his office for a longer discussion with Ribbentrop, Goering, or one of the generals—Keitel in particular.

When François-Poncet entered this hurly-burly, he found Hitler with Ribbentrop and Schmidt. Armed with his map, the ambassador (who spoke fluent German) displayed the large amount of territory that the Reich could acquire without a war. "Why then should you take this risk when your essential demands can be met without war?" Ribbentrop interjected unhelpful, bellicose comments, but François-Poncet persisted, and both he and Schmidt got the impression that Hitler was shaken.

Meanwhile Mussolini had telephoned to Attolico instructions to see Hitler and propose a twenty-four-hour postponement of hostilities. Attolico went at once to the Wilhelmstrasse, where, in the absence of Ribbentrop and Weizsaecker, he was received by Erich Kordt, the *chef de cabinet* and brother of Theodor Kordt. "I have a personal message from the Duce for the Fuehrer, and must see him quick, quick, quick,"* Attolico explained, and was told to go directly to the Chancellery. There the ambassador was informed that François-Poncet was with Hitler, but he persuaded an SS adjutant to carry in a note saying that he was there with a message from Mussolini. Hitler and Schmidt came out to meet him, and the latter translated the message suggesting the post-

* Attolico spoke very little German and customarily used English in conversation with English-speaking German officials.

ponement. After a brief pause for reflection, Hitler replied that "since Mussolini requested it he would delay affairs 24 hours." Attolico, who was expecting another call from Mussolini "at noon sharp," excused himself and hurried back to his embassy.

Hitler resumed his meeting with François-Poncet, but he was visibly preoccupied and inattentive. Soon he ended the interview by telling the ambassador that he would have an answer to the French proposals early that afternoon.

Goering and Neurath then came into the room and presented arguments for a peaceful resolution of the crisis.* Attolico reappeared, fresh from his second conversation with Mussolini, during which the Duce had told him about Chamberlain's morning message with the prediction that the whole thing could be settled in one week, and had instructed the ambassador to return to Hitler and say that Mussolini thought this would be such a "grandiose victory" that "there was no point in precipitating hostilities."

Hitler had not yet received Chamberlain's message, and "appeared puzzled and said that nobody had yet spoken to him about the problem being solved in one week and he thought there was some confusion." Attolico therefore said he would return to his embassy and bring back to Hitler a copy of the Chamberlain message.

Shortly after Attolico had departed on this errand—it being by now just past noon—Henderson came in, bringing the message in question. After Schmidt had translated it, Hitler replied that he would have to consult Mussolini before giving "a definite answer." He told Henderson that at the Duce's request mobilization had been postponed for twenty-four hours, and added that it was doubtful that there would be any necessity for Chamberlain to visit Germany again. All this Henderson telephoned to Cadogan at half-past two o'clock that afternoon.

Henderson's interview had been interrupted by Attolico's third appearance with a copy (now superfluous) of Chamberlain's message and further word from Mussolini that, if Hitler so desired, Italy would be represented if Chamberlain's conference proposal materialized. To this Hitler answered that at Godesberg he had gotten the impression that his demands were acceptable to Chamberlain, but that the Prime Minister had "slipped back" under the pressure of hostile British public opinion. Therefore, Hitler would agree to a conference only if Mussolini attended in person.

Attolico rushed back to his embassy to call Mussolini, and Hitler sat down to lunch with a large group of military and civilian officials. Weizsaecker thought that "the general feeling of relief was obvious," and also recalled that "Dr. Goebbels said at the table—after the conference plan put forward by London and Paris had been approved—that the German people were after all averse to war, as one had seen the day before when a motorized division had passed through Berlin." During the meal Attolico came to the Chancellery for the fourth time, and when Hitler went out to meet him essayed a few words of German—*"morgenelfuhr Mussolini"*—so imperfectly that Hitler laughed. Mussolini

---

* At some time that morning Goering and Ribbentrop had a tempestuous altercation, as the Foreign Minister continued to urge Hitler to stand fast and yield nothing.

would come in person, Attolico reported,* and then returned to his embassy for a well-earned lunch.

Shortly after Attolico's departure, at about three o'clock, the invitations to Munich were sent via Henderson and François-Poncet to London and Paris. The memorandum requested by Mussolini was translated and handed to Attolico for transmission to Rome. Thus were set in motion the events described in Part I of this work.

It had been a Day of the Diplomats; as far as the records and memoirs disclosed, the German military leaders played no substantial part in the final counseling and decision-making. But they were very busy, for the day began with every indication that the attack would be launched within little more than forty-eight hours, and until late in the afternoon the preparations continued unabated. During the day OKW issued orders giving the Army full control of the frontier guard and police in the frontier areas, subjecting the Henlein *Freikorps* to OKH command as soon as the Army crossed the frontier, transferring four SS *Totenkopf* battalions to Army command for defensive use on the Upper Rhine, and preparing for the reception of refugees from the prospective combat areas on the Franco-German border. The assault units were marching toward their final deployment areas, under orders to be ready to attack on September 30. The final order for the attack was to be given not later than noon on September 29.

Meanwhile, what of the Halder plotters? At Nuremberg, Erich Kordt, who was privy to whatever plot there was, testified that shortly before noon on the twenty-eighth he was visited by Helldorf's deputy, Count Fritz von der Schulenburg, who discussed with him the question whether the *Putsch* should be attempted at once or the following day. Kordt had twice that morning been to the Chancellery, knew that the security was poor and that Hitler and most of the higher Nazi leaders were there, and consequently favored immediate action, but Schulenburg said that the other plotters wanted to wait another day.

Gisevius wrote that Colonel Oster had procured a copy of Hitler's letter of the twenty-seventh to Chamberlain, which all the conspirators regarded as conclusive evidence that Hitler was bent on war, that Halder and Witzleben thereupon decided to act at once, and that each of them separately urged Brauchitsch to join the *Putsch*. According to Gisevius, the Commander-in-Chief said that he would make no decision until he had verified that Hitler intended to attack, and went to the Chancellery to confront the Fuehrer. A few hours later came the news of Munich, and the plot was abandoned.

This story is implausible. As we have seen, Hitler's letter was not the intransigent, defiant document that Gisevius depicts. More important, Halder—the pacemaker of the enterprise—had no need to rely on diplomatic correspondence, as he was the immediate recipient and, in large measure, the executant of Hitler's military directives. He knew full well that the assault units were

---

* Several of the accounts by participants in the Berlin events of September 28 refer to telephone conversations between Hitler and Mussolini. Attolico's statement is explicit that there was no direct contact between the two dictators; throughout, the ambassador was the intermediary. Hitler's departures to speak with Attolico apparently gave François-Poncet and others the erroneous impression that he was talking with the Duce.

on their way to the combat zone, but he also knew that the attack would not be launched without a further order, to be given by noon of the preceding day which, as matters stood, was September 29.

It is, to be sure, quite true that the news of Munich and the probability of a peaceful settlement put an end to the plans for an immediate *Putsch*. But it appears altogether probable, assuming the existence of a serious plan, that on the twenty-eighth Halder realized—rightly, as events proved—that until noon on the twenty-ninth there was still a possibility that diplomatic developments might abort the attack. Since he, in contrast to some of his fellow conspirators, was concerned not with overthrowing Hitler but with forestalling a war which he thought would be disastrous for Germany, he insisted on waiting another day, to see whether or not the die would finally be cast for war.*

13

Why did Hitler draw back from war and invite a diplomatic settlement at Munich? Obviously there was no singly decisive cause, but the primary reason is apparent. Things had not worked out as he had planned, and the premises of Green had not been established.

As we have seen, the basic theory of Green was an attack in which "the surprise element is the most important factor," and whereby the Wehrmacht would overrun Czechoslovakia so rapidly that her allies would confront a *fait accompli*. It had never been Hitler's plan to precipitate a European war in which the Reich would confront other major powers.

By the end of September the surprise factor had been lost. The concentration of German forces without a formal mobilization had been smoothly managed but could not pass undetected, and coupled with the German press campaign against Prague and Hitler's Nuremberg speech—actions which presumably Hitler felt necessary to awaken a war spirit at home—it aroused the state of alarm abroad which prompted Chamberlain's trip to Berchtesgaden two weeks before the Wehrmacht would be able to strike.

Still the Czechs might have been caught unprepared, because their chief supporters urged them not to upset the green table by mobilizing. But Hitler made the stupid blunder of allowing Henlein to set up the *Freikorps* outside military command channels—a move which was politically unnecessary and was unwelcome to the Army—and the ensuing occupation of Asch and Eger triggered Halifax's conscience and resulted in mobilization of the Czech forces. By the end of September the Bohemian fortifications were fully manned and the bulk of the Czechoslovak Army was in the field, fully alert to the prospect of imminent attack.

Despite all this, it was plain to Hitler that Britain and France would go to great lengths to avoid war, and, once embarked on negotiations, he ruthlessly

---

* It is altogether probable, however, that Halder, and perhaps Witzleben, had some contact with Brauchitsch on the twenty-eighth. Jodl's diary entry for that date notes that "Brauchitsch entreats Keitel, stressing his responsibility, to do all he can to persuade the Führer not to invade the Sudeten German region." Very likely Brauchitsch acted on Halder's urging, and it is characteristic of the former that he went to Keitel instead of directly to Hitler.

pressed his bargaining advantage. No doubt after Berchtesgaden he found it difficult to believe that Chamberlain would grant him the bulk of his demands but would go to war rather than yield to the new demands at Godesberg. In this he underestimated the strength of the British sense of order and fair play, as reflected by Halifax much more than Chamberlain. When the Fuehrer finally realized that there was indeed a point at which Britain would stand and fight, he felt trapped, and exploded in panic in the Sportspalast and with Sir Horace Wilson.

Then came the apathetic public reaction to the propaganda parade in the early evening of the twenty-seventh, the following morning's news that the British had mobilized the fleet, and the atmosphere of crisis that enveloped the Chancellery. François-Poncet and Henderson came with new offers which would enable Hitler to save face. Goering counseled peace, and Hitler knew that many of the generals on whose leadership he would have to depend thought the Wehrmacht quite unready for a major war. Finally Mussolini joined the chorus.

Chamberlain's pertinacity had reaped its reward. He never gave up, and by following every failure with another effort, he finally pushed Hitler into a position in which no one—not even Goering and Mussolini—would regard a refusal to compromise as rational.

And so, at almost half-past six o'clock in the afternoon of the twenty-eighth, orders went out from the OKH that the assault units were to stop short of their combat deployment areas, so positioning themselves that on receipt of the code-word *Erntedank* (Harvest Festival) they could reach those positions on the thirtieth by a six-hour march. Simultaneously the German radio network carried the announcement of the next day's meeting in Munich.

At that moment, in Dresden, Colonal Röhricht was sitting gloomily in a *Bierstube* with General Olbricht, Baron von Waldenfels,* and their wives. In a vain effort to cut the tension Olbricht was telling old jokes, and the empty laughter grated on Röhricht's nerves.

The loudspeaker blared the news of Munich. The Baron slapped his hand on the table and turned to his wife: "Let's go to the Bellevue Hotel! Gertrud, now we should dance!" And the next day the four men of Munich danced their quadrille.

---

*Röhricht's memoirs do not further identify the Baron, who was probably General Wilhelm Freiherr von Waldenfels, commander of the Dresden army training center.

Part VI

POSTLUDE AND RETROSPECT

===========

CHAPTER 31

Peace With Honor

1

At noon on September 30, about eight hours after the Munich Agreement had been signed, Ivone Kirkpatrick telephoned to London and spoke to Gladwyn Jebb at the Foreign Office. He first gave Jebb the metes and bounds, as shown on the map attached to the agreement, of the four zones which the Wehrmacht was to occupy from October 1 to 7. These zones, Kirkpatrick then declared, "amount to less than half of the Godesberg areas," and all the remaining areas to be ceded "have to be determined by the International Commission." Among "other good points" in the agreement Kirkpatrick stressed that: "The International Commission is to consist of an Englishman, Frenchman, German, Czech and Italian, an arrangement which will ensure fair play for the Czechs. On paper the Czechs' side have a majority of one."

Kirkpatrick went on to instruct Jebb in the "line which should be emphasized to the press":

> . . . there will be fair play and the Commission will be purely objective. The Czechs cannot claim that their case will be prejudiced.
>
> The Delegation are happy in this respect—that they have at least gotten the very best terms for the carrying out of the proposals which Czechs had already accepted. . . . it would have been difficult to believe earlier on that we should get such good terms for the Czechs.*

This telephone message foretold the description of the Munich Agreement, which Neville Chamberlain was about to put before his Cabinet colleagues and Parliament. Immediately after his triumphant return to 10 Downing Street and

---

* Mr. Kirkpatrick's satisfaction, if genuine, was short-lived. In his memoirs he described the Munich conference as "in every way a sad affair. I can remember no redeeming feature."

his pronouncements of "peace with honour" and "peace for our time," he met with the Cabinet in his now familiar role of adventure-teller. Before he spoke, Sir John Simon paid tribute "on behalf of the whole Cabinet," whose members felt "profound admiration and pride in their Prime Minister." Chamberlain thanked them, with the assurance that "as things had turned out, he felt that they could safely regard the crisis as ended." The conference had been "badly run" and the inkpot for the signatures had been empty, but the terms obtained were "a real improvement."

The Prime Minister said that he had suggested the addition of a Czech representative, but had been told that delay was impossible. Mussolini had arranged for his reception in Rome on the next day, and: "This had fixed the latest hour at which Signor Mussolini could leave Munich."

Chamberlain then outlined the difference between the Munich agreement and Hitler's Godesberg ultimatum. The Czech evacuation of the ceded territories would not have to be completed by October 1, but would stretch over the first ten days of that month. This, to be sure, was something of an improvement on Godesberg. But, as Chamberlain next indicated, most of the other important matters were left unresolved in the agreement and were to be settled by the International Commission, which was given authority to fix the bounds of the remaining territory to be occupied by the Germans on October 10, the area in which plebiscites would be held, the final determination of the new frontiers, and the settlement of "all questions which may arise out of the transfer of territories."

Although in fact there was no way to determine how much had been gained or lost at Munich until the International Commission had acted, the Cabinet was suitably impressed. Even Duff Cooper pronounced the differences between Godesberg and Munich considerably greater than he had previously realized, but he nonetheless thought them "not good enough" and indicated that he would probably resign his post. The Prime Minister, fresh from both royal and public accolades, showed no anxiety at this prospect, and the First Lord did indeed resign the next day.*

During the weekend of October 1–2 the inner group of ministers held what proved to be its last two meetings. Before them on Saturday was a letter from Jan Masaryk depicting the "economic aspect of the situation created by the Four Power decisions," predicting the arrival of "about 1,000,000 people, escaping from the ceded territory," and asking that the British Government guarantee a £30-million loan to Czechoslovakia: "The above-mentioned amount . . . would have been spent by Great Britain in a very short while if she had to take part in a war, in the avoiding of which my country is making the utmost sacrifices." The ministers discussed the matter as if this were a worthy charity for which they wished due credit at the Great Bar, wherefore they decided to say nothing to the French, who if informed might "take the credit for themselves." No conclusion was reached and the request was referred to the Cabinet.

The conferees also considered the Government's defense of the agreement in

---

* Harvey, in his diary, described Duff Cooper's resignation as "certainly courageous," while Cadogan noted acridly: "Good riddance of bad rubbish."

the forthcoming Commons debate. Sensing the importance which the International Commission was assuming in making a case for the agreement, and that it was composed of three supposedly "pro-Czech" and two "anti-Czech" members, the ministers decided that "it would be necessary to take the line" that disagreements would be decided by majority vote, "although this point had not been specifically provided for in the Agreement." Aware that the Government was on shaky ground, the ministers also agreed that "it would be a mistake to enter into a detailed discussion . . . of the terms of the Munich Agreement, or to invite detailed comments on its provisions."

There was inconclusive discussion of the guarantee of the new Czech borders referred to in the annex to the agreement. But the most immediately troublesome problem was the provision in the agreement that "international bodies" would occupy the plebiscite territories until the plebiscite was completed. Should these be regular troops, or ex-servicemen like the British Legion, who could be easily supplied but would be useless in the event of any real trouble? How should such forces be sent in? If through Germany, would it not look as if British contingents were "supplementing the German advance"?

When the Cabinet met in the morning of October 3, the principal item of business was Masaryk's letter. Chamberlain thought the prediction of a million refugees was "guesswork" and that, since the Germans would prevent "incidents," most of the refugees would return to their homes. Nevertheless, the request should be entertained with sympathy and generosity. Simon, ever unctuous, agreed with his chief but declared that Britain had no legal obligation, and indeed the moral obligation ran in the other direction, as by Britain's efforts "a world war had been averted and thereby Czechoslovakia had been saved."

In the Commons on October 3, Chamberlain made his public defense of Munich, following and expanding on what he had said to his colleagues. The members had before them a White Paper reprinting the text of the agreement and its several annexes and supplemental declarations, together with two maps, the first showing the four zones to be occupied during the first week of October, and the second the areas demanded by Hitler in the Godesberg memorandum. The juxtaposition was shrewd, for the Munich zones composed only a minor fraction of the Godesberg demands. But it was also deceptive, as Anthony Eden pointed out during the debate, because the Munich map did not show the additional areas, to be determined by the International Commission, which would be occupied on October 10, and which might or might not approximate the Godesberg line depending upon the commission's decision.

Indeed, with one major exception, the International Commission was the basis of all the differences in outcome, as between Godesberg and Munich, which Chamberlain paraded before the Commons. The "Godesberg Memorandum," the Prime Minister declared, was "in fact an ultimatum," whereas the Munich decisions were taken on the responsibility of the four Powers and would be carried out "under international supervision." Under Munich "the line up to which German troops will enter into occupation is no longer the line as laid down in . . . the Godesberg Memorandum. It is a line which is to be fixed by an International Commission." Plebiscite areas and conditions of evacuation would likewise be determined by the Commission.

The major point unrelated to the commission was: "The joint guarantee, which is given under the Munich Agreement to the Czechoslovak State by the Governments of the United Kingdom and France against unprovoked aggression upon their boundaries" and which "gives to the Czechs an essential counterpart which was not to be found in the Godesberg Memorandum. . . . It is my hope and belief that under the new system of guarantees, the new Czechoslovakia will find a greater security than she has ever enjoyed in the past."*

In the Lords, Halifax laid even greater emphasis on the guarantee provisions. Well aware that the failure of the existing French commitment to protect Czechoslovakia raised doubts about the value of new assurances, the Foreign Minister gave three reasons why things would be better this time:

> The first is this. Nothing has been more persistently pressed upon me during the last two or three anxious months than this. If only Great Britain would say clearly and unmistakeably for all to hear that she would resist any unprovoked aggression on Czechoslovakia, no such unprovoked aggression would be made. We never felt able to use that language; but . . . the deterrent value of such a statement will be in full force under such a guarantee as we have expressed our willingness to give. The second thing . . . is this. To guarantee a Czechoslovakia including within her borders restless and dissatisfied minorities was one thing; to guarantee Czechoslovakia when those explosive minority questions have been adjusted is quite another. And lastly, the guarantee itself is reinforced and buttressed by two other vital elements. First, Germany and Italy have expressed their readiness to guarantee Czechoslovakia when the other minority questions have been settled; and secondly, Great Britain and Germany have mutually expressed their desire to resolve any differences between them through consultation.

It would be fair to say that the guarantees and the International Commission were the two prime features of the Munich Agreement on which the Government relied to differentiate it from Godesberg and to persuade the Commons to endorse their policy. During the ensuing discussion, the guarantees came in for considerable comment and inquiry; this was hardly surprising, since the Government spokesmen acknowledged that the guarantees were not yet formally in effect, and Halifax warned that it had not yet been decided whether they "should be joint or several," or "what states should be invited to assume" these obligations, or "in what circumstances" they would arise.

What is indeed surprising is that, despite the authority to fix the new boundaries and determine the conditions of evacuation which the Government was attributing to the International Commission, there was virtually no discussion of the composition of that body during the ensuing debate, nor any inquiry about what it had been doing during the several days it had been in existence. Duff

---

* The Prime Minister went on to recommend that the Czech request for financial aid "should meet with a sympathetic and even a generous response," and to report that Prague was being informed that "we are prepared immediately to arrange for an advance of 10 million."

Cooper, whose resignation speech preceded Chamberlain's, made no mention of the commission, although (as his diary reveals) he was well aware that the British member was Nevile Henderson, "who in my opinion has played a sorry part in the whole business and who is violently anti-Czech and pro-German." Indeed, the late First Lord was strangely blind to the frailty of the Government's case, for he declared that between Godesberg and Munich: "There are great and important differences, and it is a triumph for the Prime Minister that he was able to acquire them." Nevertheless he had resigned because of "deep differences between the Prime Minister and myself throughout these days" in that Chamberlain had talked to Hitler with "sweet reasonableness," when the only effective language would have been "the mailed fist."

Except for Hugh Dalton's forceful attack from the Opposition benches, the strongest indictments of the Government's policy came from the dissident Conservatives, especially Amery, Churchill, and Eden. The last named was the only speaker to point out that all the comforting talk about the International Commission was premature "until we see how they work out." Amery scoffed at reliance on "guarantees given on the run," and declared his disbelief "that the student of history will note any substantial difference between Godesberg and Munich." Churchill, undeterred by angry interruptions from Government supporters, labeled Munich "a total and unmitigated defeat," and warned that it was not the end: "This is only the beginning of the reckoning. This is only the first sip, the first foretaste of a bitter cup which will be proffered to us year by year unless, by a supreme recovery of moral health and martial vigour, we arise again and take our stand for freedom as in the olden times."

The parliamentary basis of the debate was a resolution "That this House approves the policy of His Majesty's Government by which war was averted in the recent crisis and supports their efforts to secure a lasting peace." On the party division it carried by 366 ayes to 144 noes, but thirty Conservatives abstained, including Churchill, Amery, Eden, Duff Cooper, Harold Nicolson, Sidney Herbert, Harold Macmillan, and Admiral Sir Roger Keyes.

In the French Parliament, convoked for a brief "exceptional" session on October 4, Munich had an even easier passage. Unlike the British Parliament, which had met the day before Munich and heard Chamberlain's report on the course of the crisis, the French legislators had not been recalled, and thus Daladier had a lot of ground to cover in his presentation. He did it summarily, and the whole debate on Munich in the Chamber of Deputies lasted only six hours.

Like Chamberlain, Daladier proclaimed Munich a definite improvement on Godesberg, citing primarily the projected guarantees and the International Commission, which "has been created in order to avoid arbitrary unilateral decisions. We hope thus to substitute legal procedures for forceful solutions." Again like Chamberlain, Daladier made no reference to the composition, procedures, or actions of the commission, by now five days old.*

* Interviewed thirty years later, Léger observed that the zonal map agreed upon at Munich was "not bad" (which was quite true) and took credit to Daladier and himself for obtaining the provisions for an International Commission with a three-to-two composition

The only opposition came from the Communists and the intransigent right-wing nationalist Henri de Kerillis. Daladier had anticipated some Cabinet resignations, but the doubters—Reynaud, Mandel, and Champetier de Ribes—stayed in office and sat silent in Parliament. Flandin did not think it necessary to speak in support of an agreement which meshed so well with his own opinions; he sent a congratulatory telegram to Hitler, which the Fuehrer graciously acknowledged on October 2, with thanks for Flandin's "efforts in support of an *entente* and full collaboration between France and Germany." The Chamber approved the agreement by 535 to 75 votes, and of the 75 votes 73 were cast by the Communists and two by Kerillis and Bouhey, a Socialist.

2

The first meeting of the International Commission began in Berlin at five o'clock on the afternoon of September 30, even before Chamberlain disembarked at Heston Airport. Such expedition was possible because a supplemental declaration adopted at Munich had prescribed its membership as "the Secretary of State in the German Foreign Office, the British, French and Italian ambassadors accredited in Berlin, and a representative to be nominated by the Government of Czechoslovakia." Prague at once designated their minister in Berlin, Dr. Mastny.

The Munich records disclose nothing of the background of this decision to repose the commission's authority in Weizsaecker and the diplomatic representatives of the four other nations. Yet it was a stipulation of the greatest importance, for it robbed the commission, from the outset, of any intrinsic authority. Weizsaecker would get his orders from Hitler via Ribbentrop, and the others would follow instructions from their respective capitals. Not one of the members could vote or take any significant action on his own responsibility. The commission, in other words, was a body for negotiating and recording, but not for decision-making.

On the face of the Munich Agreement it appeared as if the four signatories had transferred the decisions on certain vital issues to another source of authority. But in fact they had done nothing of the kind; they had simply postponed the final decisions on issues too difficult to resolve at Munich and, by giving their Berlin diplomats a high-sounding group name, papered over the fact that future decisions would be made by the same people who had met at Munich. This enabled Chamberlain and Daladier, with superficial plausibility, to tell their respective parliaments that the commission rather than Hitler would make these decisions.

But whether or not that was so still depended, as it had all along, on how far the British and French were willing to go in supporting the Czechs against the Germans. The answer to that was obvious: not very far. London and Paris had already agreed to territorial cessions which would leave Czechoslovakia militarily indefensible and economically rickety. Britain and France having yielded

---

favoring the Czechs. The real disaster, he declared, was that the Allied representatives on the Commission yielded to German pressures. In fact, as will be seen, they yielded to instructions from their own governments.

so far, it did not stand to reason that they would take a stand that might blow up the agreement and raise again the threat of war. Hitler had only to indicate that he was prepared to take what the commission would not give him, and he was altogether likely to get his way.

Furthermore, the new *mise en scène* was highly unfavorable to the Czech "side." Although the agreement did not so state, the designation of three Berlin ambassadors clearly implied that the signatories intended the German capital to be the seat of the commission. At Munich (and Berchtesgaden and Godesberg) Hitler had been confronted, on a plane of at least nominal equality, by national leaders. In Berlin, diplomatic civil servants would negotiate with the Fuehrer's subordinates, in the shadow of his authority. All facilities and means of communication would be under German control.

All these circumstances, boding so ill for the Czech cause, were from the outset well known to the leaders of the British and French governments, to whom the International Commission was little more than a face-saving device.

3

For the diplomatic dénouement, accordingly, the scene shifted from Munich to Berlin. In order to get the British, French, and Italians back to the capital in time for the commission's opening session, the Germans provided an official aircraft, and early in the morning after the night before, Weizsaecker and the three ambassadors enplaned and returned to Berlin.

The commission began its proceedings, at about half-past five o'clock, even though the Czech delegation had not yet arrived. On François-Poncet's nomination, Weizsaecker was made chairman, and at the latter's suggestion a military subcommittee was established to regulate the transfer of the zones shown on the Munich map. The subcommittee met at once; Britain, France, and Italy were represented by their military attachés, and Germany by General Karl-Heinrich von Stülpnagel (chief of operations of the Army General Staff) and—nominally subordinate but, as soon became apparent, the real voice of authority—Colonel Walter Warlimont of the Wehrmacht High Command. Soon the Czech delegates arrived, and Captain Stehlin (attached to the military subcommittee) noticed "with emotion" that the Czech officers' uniforms were covered with French medals—the *Légion d'Honneur,* the *Croix de Guerre,* and the *Médaille Militaire.* At the second session, however, the French decorations had disappeared, in silent but conspicuous rebuke to "us who had abandoned them."

The most immediate task facing the commission was to determine the conditions for Czech evacuation and German occupation of Zones I and II, scheduled for transfer on October 1–2 and 2–3 respectively. These questions, which concerned chiefly the disposition of Czech state military property in the zones, were referred to the military subcommittee. François-Poncet cited reports that the Henleinists were causing "incidents" near the border, but there was no immediate confirmation. The meeting went on until nearly midnight, and in its course the commission decided to send the Italian and British assistant military attachés (Majors Badini and Strong) to observe the evacuation and occupation movements and ensure that the governing conditions were complied with. The meeting ended with no important disagreement, but Henderson's report to London revealed an attitude which well warranted Duff Cooper's misgivings about him:

> The best help which the British press could give would be to write nothing awkward calculated to encourage the Czechs to resist. It is perfectly obvious from now on that such incidents as do occur will be indicative of Czechs' resistance. Germans have nothing to gain by creating trouble but Czechs have and they will certainly try to make what capital they can out of incidents. This should be clearly realized by the British press.

The following morning (October 1), those returning from Munich by train arrived in Berlin. For some, including William L. Shirer, it had been an unpleasant trip:

> Most of the leading German editors on the train were tossing down the champagne and not trying to disguise any more their elation over Hitler's terrific victory over Britain and France. On the diner Halfeld of the *Hamburger Fremdenblatt*, Otto Kriegk of the *Nachtausgabe*, Dr. Boehmer, the foreign press chief of the Propaganda Ministry, gloating over it, buying out all the champagne in the diner, gloating, boasting, bragging. . . . When a German feels big he feels *big*. Shall have two hours in Berlin this evening to get my army passes and a bath and then off by night train to Passau to go in to Sudetenland with the Germany army—a sad assignment for me.

Hitler and Goering also returned to Berlin in their trains, with Goering in the lead so that he could be on hand with Goebbels at the Anhalter station when, in midmorning, the dictator's train pulled in. Accolades to the Fuehrer "on behalf of the entire German people" were the order of the day, joined in by Heinrich Himmler of the SS, Viktor Lutze of the storm troopers, Keitel of the Wehrmacht, cabinet ministers galore, and Konrad Henlein from the "liberated" Sudetenland. Congratulations poured in from all the cardinals of German Catholicism, from Admiral Horthy and Bela Imredy of Hungary, Prince Konoye of Japan, Pierre Flandin of France, Lord Rothermere of England, and Archduke Joseph of Liechtenstein. Despite all this praise, the Fuehrer was far from pleased with the compromises he had felt obliged to accept at Munich, and now was determined to push his advantages to the utmost.

The commission, faced with the necessity of fixing the evacuation conditions for all four zones before October 6 (when the occupation of Zone IV would begin), met twice on October 1 and again on the third. The problem of removing heavy weaponry from the Czech fortifications rapidly enough to meet the zonal occupation schedule gave the military subcommittee much difficulty but was ultimately resolved without a major dispute.

However, other and even more important issues remained, and it soon became apparent that the Germans knew what they wanted and were determined to get it. Their delegates were on home ground and could get their instructions promptly. Furthermore, they had no disposition to be conciliatory, and many of them—especially the military, greatly enjoying their first opportunity since 1918 to lord it over the French and British—were insufferably arrogant. Even Weizsaecker was embarrassed by the behavior of "certain experts from the General Staff" who "behaved like victors after a battle." The temper of the meetings emerges vividly in Captain Stehlin's account:

Despite the efforts which we the English, French and Italians made to limit the German demands, the German [military] delegation, directed by General* Warlimont, wasted no time in letting us know, in the bluntest fashion, that the occupation of the Sudeten areas would be carried out in accordance with the orders of the Wehrmacht High Command.

The directives that the other three delegations received from their governments were alike. They were vague, imprecise, they advised conciliation, and that meant surrender. Furthermore, the answers to our questions were tardy, and the Germans turned this to their advantage and did what suited them. Three times, in the course of our meetings, we saw Warlimont rise and leave with his colleagues, and come back a few minutes later and begin his statement by saying: "The High Command of the Wehrmacht has decided that. . . ." Hitler's arrogant designs stood out in bold relief. The *détente* following Munich was of short duration. The atmosphere again became terribly heavy. . . .

The temper of the International Commission meetings which I attended left no doubt of the harshness of which the Germans would give proof in future discussions. Referring to the orders to which we were subjected, the ambassador [François-Poncet] reported to our government that, under cover of the agreement of the Four Great Powers, the Germans had conducted themselves in the Commission with the insolence of victors toward the vanquished.

The commission's most important task was to determine the "predominantly German" areas, over and above the four zones specified at Munich, to be occupied by October 10. For the working-out of this matter, the commission established a subcommittee on "plebiscites and frontiers" of which the German member and chairman was a second-level diplomat, Herbert Count von Richthofen.†

Here was the real crunch, and on Sunday, October 2, while elsewhere the men of Munich were resting on their laurels, Adolf Hitler summoned the German delegates and gave them their marching orders, the gist of which was that the boundary he had demanded at Godesberg, the rejection of which by the Czechs had precipitated the final crisis and the Munich conference, should be adopted as the line for October 10 purposes.

This directive was bound to produce a clash, for Beneš had given Mastny strict instructions to stick to the Anglo-French proposals and refuse to accept the line shown on the Godesberg map. The Germans' tactics for achieving their aim were manifested on the morning of October 3, when Subcommittee C held its first meeting. The room was packed with Germans, including a number of

---

* Warlimont was in fact a colonel at the time.

† Richthofen had been serving as Minister to Belgium. The International Commission established three subcommittees, designated (A) military, (B) finance and economics, and (C) plebiscites and frontiers. The other members of Subcommittee C were Sir George Ogilvie-Forbes (counselor of the British Embassy), Count Magistrati and M. Menthan of the Italian and French foreign services, and for Czechoslovakia General Husárek and M. Heiderich, the Czech delegate to the League of Nations.

Army officers led by Major Bernhard von Lossberg of the Army General Staff, and Sudeten Germans, for whom the principal spokesman was a vintage Nazi, Hans Krebs, who had been made an honorary *Gauleiter*. As subsequently described in Sir Nevile Henderson's report to the Foreign Office:

> The proceedings of the subcommittee were confused and frequently noisy, and the chairman was quite incapable of maintaining order. At one point no fewer than seventeen German representatives were present. . . . Gauleiter Krebs was permitted to take a prominent part in the discussions, and it was not uncommon for four or five of the Sudeten Germans and Czech representatives all to be shouting at once. At two critical points in the discussions Major von Lötschberg* intervened, and, standing stiffly to attention, rapped out orders which effectively silenced the other German representatives.

The Germans' initial demand for the Godesberg line was rejected by all the other delegates, including the Italians, whose attitude was often surprisingly sympathetic to the Czechs. Interpretation of the Munich language was the threshold problem, and the Czechs argued—persuasively to all the subcommittee members except the Germans—that "predominantly German" meant more than a bare majority, perhaps 75 per cent. They produced a map with a line drawn on this basis, using the most recent (1930) census figures. The Germans countered with a map line based on a 51 per cent German-Czech ratio, using the last (1910) pre-First World War census, arguing that the original sin of subjecting the Sudeten Germans to the Czechs had been committed in 1918, and that population changes since that time should be disregarded.

Despite these differences of principle the Czechs and Sudetens, by reciprocal concessions, managed to agree on a portion of the line. But Major von Lossberg overruled the Sudetens on one of their key concessions, and things began to go very badly. On the next day (October 4) Mastny brought the issues before the commission, where they proved no less obstinate. Weizsaecker was adamant for 51 per cent and the 1910 census, Mastny equally so for 75 per cent and the 1930 census. Attolico and Henderson were inclined to support the Germans, while François-Poncet proposed a compromise at 66.66 per cent based on an averaging of the 1910 and 1921 censuses. Neither the Czechs nor the Germans liked this solution, and the meeting adjourned with the issues unresolved.

Late that evening François-Poncet was summoned by an angry and excited Ribbentrop, who told him that Hitler "was accusing the British and French delegates of going back on the Munich decisions" and threatening to order the Army to occupy up to the Godesberg line unless the Czechs, by noon the next day, had agreed to 51 per cent on the 1910 census. A new crisis was in the making, and anxious requests for instructions were telephoned to Paris and London the following morning. Daladier promptly informed François-Poncet that the Germans were right. "Predominantly German" meant a simple majority as of 1918, and the ambassador was admonished to do nothing that would "spoil the effects of Munich." Halifax agreed on the majority question but in-

---

* There is no officer by this name in the German Army lists, and it is certain that this is an erroneous rendering of Lossberg.

formed Henderson that to use the 1910 census "seems grossly unfair" and that the 1921 census was greatly to be preferred.*

This message, however, did not reach Henderson until the afternoon of October 5, and the ambassador had already committed himself. On the particular issue, he thought "the German contention was actually the better grounded of the two theses." More generally, however, he favored extending the new frontier far enough so that few Sudeten Germans would be left within the new Czech borders, and Hitler would have the less excuse for future complaint. The International Commission he regarded as useless for the protection of Czech interests, since Hitler felt no obligation to comply with its decisions, and confrontation would cause a collapse of the entire Munich structure. The Czechs, he thought, would be well advised to make their own peace with Hitler by direct negotiations.

Under all these circumstances, the result was a foregone conclusion. The method, however, was hardly edifying. Once again, as at Munich, the Czechs were excluded from the decisive conference. At noon on October 5 the three ambassadors went to Ribbentrop's office, and the four signed a protocol with an attached map, fixing the line for occupation by October 10 on the basis of a simple majority according to the 1910 census. The line so drawn closely corresponds to the Godesberg lines.

Later in the day the Czech delegates were summoned and shown the map, to which they, of course, raised vigorous objection. If they had expected further support from their erstwhile protectors, their hopes were soon dashed. As Weizsaecker put it:

> The Czech representatives were then, at a suitable moment, confronted with the protocol of the midday session . . . which the four Powers had already agreed on and were committed to.

And so, at the very time that Chamberlain and Daladier were defending the Munich settlement to the deputies and the Commons, and claiming that it was a great improvement on the Godesberg terms, their ambassadors in Berlin were carrying out instructions to concede to Hitler substantially what he had demanded at Godesberg. The Czech delegates referred the issues to their government, but Prague had nowhere to turn, and at the International Commission meeting next day Mastny announced that his government "noted the decision of the four great Powers with profound sorrow" but accepted the lines so fixed and would carry out the necessary measures.

The capitulation in Berlin passed virtually unnoticed by the world press.† Attention was centered on other events—on the parliamentary debates in London

* The census instruction was due to Vansittart, and was strongly disapproved by Cadogan, who noted on October 5: "A hourouche before lunch, when it appeared International Commission had gotten into deadlock over percentage and census. We have to give way (because it was given away at Munich). Van in a splutter, and got H. [Halifax] to agree to tell N.H. [Henderson] to stick up for something we can't get. And of course we didn't."

† On October 13, 1938, the London *Daily Telegraph* reported that Hitler had "obtained, through the machinery of Munich, a still larger slice of Czechoslovakia than he had sought by the method of the ultimatum at Godesberg."

and Paris, the Hungarian demands for a slice of Slovakia, and the changes in the Prague government. President Beneš resigned on the evening of October 5, following a cabinet reshuffle in which Foreign Minister Krofta, long associated with Beneš' policies, was replaced by Frantisek Chalkovsky, a Beneš opponent then serving as Minister to Italy, who set out at once to court the Germans' favor by every possible means. The days of reliance on France and Britain were over; as General Syrový (who became acting Chief of State after Beneš' departure) put it to a Franco-British delegation: "In this affair, messieurs, we have been willing to fight on the side of the angels. Now we shall hunt with the wolves."

It remained to be seen whether the pro-German reorientation of Prague's policies, coupled with Beneš' resignation, would serve the Czechs any better than what had gone before. The Munich misery was not over; the questions of plebiscites and guarantees were still open, and until they were resolved the new frontier could not be finally determined, nor its future security assessed.

4

Meanwhile the Wehrmacht was making its way into the Sudetenland. General von Leeb was in command of the troops opposite Zone I, and the leading units went over the border at two o'clock in the afternoon of October 1; Leeb himself led the 100th Mountain Regiment across the frontier at Glöckelberg, north of Passau.

The evacuation rules envisaged a three kilometer-wide "neutral" zone between the retiring Czechs and advancing Germans. Czech liaison officers were to be present when the Germans crossed the border so that the two armies' movements could be co-ordinated. However, most of these officers never made it to the frontier, as en route they were disarmed and imprisoned by the Henleinists. On learning this, the Germans freed the Czechs, agreed on a schedule of movements, and escorted them back to the neutral zone.

Despite the cloudy, wet weather, the populace (over 90 per cent German) hung out the flags and gave the German troops a joyous reception—six months after Austria, a second *Blumenkrieg*. Actually there were few Czech troops in Zone I, which lay outside the principal fortifications, and most of the trouble arose from Henleinist attacks on withdrawing Czech gendarmes and customs guards. According to a British military observer sent from Prague, all the casualties were suffered by the Czechs.

Adolf Hitler, busy in Berlin during the entries into Zones I and II, arrived in Hof on the morning of October 3 and crossed the border at Wildenau, a few miles south of Asch in Zone III, where he was met by General Guderian, commander of XVI Corps. The Fuehrer and his entourage drove through Asch toward Eger, stopping for a field-kitchen meal alfresco with Reichenau, Guderian, Keitel, Himmler, Henlein, and other dignitaries. Unhappily, there was meat in the stew; the vegetarian dictator munched apples and requested a change in the menu for the remainder of his visit.

Hitler traveled through the Sudetenland under the protection of an escort battalion commanded by the then little-known Colonel Erwin Rommel, whose military writings the Fuehrer admired. After an enthusiastic reception in Eger, he returned to Hof for the night, and the next day visited Karlsbad, where he made a short speech (intended, according to one listener,* for "the lachrymal glands of the German people") in the theater. As Guderian described the scene:

> He walked through the ranks of the guard of honor into the theater, where he was greeted by the populace. Outside the rain poured down in sheets, but inside the theater the most touching scenes now took place. The women and young girls in their national costume burst into tears, many knelt down, and the cheers were deafening.

Bloodless conquest and pretty *Mädchen* throwing flowers and bestowing kisses induced a general euphoria and expansiveness among the troops at all levels of rank. Major Strong, acting out an intelligence officer's dream as he circulated, happily noting unit insignia and details of armament, walked through Hof seeking General von Reichenau's headquarters. Strong encountered the general himself: "I saluted and said I was looking for the High Command. He drew up and said 'Why look further? *I am the High Command* and I know everything.'" The next day Groscurth spent two hours listening to a Reichenau monologue while the general "drank one glass of champagne after another."† Hitler, he declared, had already decided to take care of the Czech state in its entirety "in the foreseeable future." The Fuehrer was a genius and if he played poker "would win a hundred thousand marks every evening." The general staffs of the Army, Navy, and Luftwaffe ought to be abolished and replaced by a single Armed Forces General Staff. The military outlook for Germany was bright; soon Hitler would be making new moves, and he, Reichenau, was slated for even higher rank and responsibility.

It was in Zone IV, which General von Rundstedt's troops entered on October 6, that the attack by General Student's airborne troops was to have been attempted. As a demonstration exercise, the operation was carried out on the seventh, with the Fuehrer himself as a spectator. The landing area was near Freudenthal, behind the main Czech fortifications, which were to have been taken from the rear by troops landed in gliders towed to the scene by the Luftwaffe's workhorse aircraft, the Junkers 52.

The maneuver was carried out on schedule and without serious accident, and the three hundred aircraft made an impressive show. But it was not war; there was a military band to greet the "invaders," and Groscurth reported that the residents of Freudenthal had spent the last two days leveling the ground and cutting down maple trees to make a clear landing strip.

During the next three days, the German forward units moved further in to the line fixed by the International Commission. More troops marched in, from Aus-

---

* Major Helmuth Groscurth of the Wehrmacht Intelligence and Security Service, whose published diary contains the most detailed account of the German occupation of the Sudetenland.

† A year earlier Reichenau, who spoke excellent English, had impressed Anne Lindbergh as "one of those completely rounded, charming, cultured men of wide experience, great strength, and concentrative ability, combined with fineness of perception and breadth of vision." Groscurth found him much less attractive, because he did not offer his three auditors anything at all to drink and talked critically of the Army command to junior officers.

tria as well as through the four zones, and by October 10 there were some twenty-four divisions in the ceded areas. But the Army's dominant role in the occupation dwindled as many of the divisions returned to their home bases in Germany, and on October 21, Hitler ordered the re-establishment of civil administration, nominally headed by Konrad Henlein as Reich Commissioner for the Sudetenland.

As the occupation progressed and thousands of members of civilian and paramilitary agencies poured into the Sudetenland, the German image changed rapidly and radically. The regular troops, finding themselves in friendly territory, behaved correctly,* but many of those who followed were of a different ilk, and soon the heavy heel of Nazism was leaving its imprint everywhere.

Three regiments of armed SS troops† had gone in behind the assault units, and they lost no time in making themselves objectionable to the Army and a brutal menace to those Czechs and Jews who remained in the occupied districts. Groscurth encountered some of the SS *Leibstandarte* on the road, driving like maniacs "with no regard for on-coming traffic, the only undisciplined troops." A week later (October 12) in Reichenberg, Groscurth found the divisional staff greatly exercised because the SS *Germania* insisted on trying to extend the occupation beyond the October 10 line. In this (General von Bock's) area, relations between the populace and the Army were good, but the Luftwaffe and Nazi Party agencies were already ill-regarded. There was trouble because German soldiers were spending their money in Czech and Jewish shops, and promptly there were orders, executed by the Henleinists, that all such businesses be placarded to assist the boycott. The tables were turned with a vengeance; whatever discrimination the Sudeten Germans had suffered now recoiled a hundredfold on the remaining Czechs.

Soon malicious mischief gave way to murder of Czechs and Jews beyond the demarcation line. The German divisional commander, General Erich Raschick, pulled the *Germania* back from the border and started to set up a court-martial to try the perpetrators on criminal charges, whereupon Himmler withdrew the regiment from the Sudetenland to the SS's own bases in Germany. The Army security service reported these atrocities to the High Command, but there is no record of punitive or other corrective action. Well-intentioned Army officers began to realize that it did not pay to try to enforce ordinary rules of lawful behavior against Himmler's men.‡

Perhaps the saddest feature of the whole scene was that thousands of Czech and Jewish refugees, expelled by or fleeing from the German-occupied areas, were turned back and refused asylum in the remaining Czech territories. Many

---

* Even so anti-Nazi an observer as the late G. E. R. Gedye (*Betrayal in Central Europe* [1939], p. 477) wrote that "to its credit, the German Army declined to share in the orgy of beastliness indulged in by Reich-German and Sudeten Nazis alike."

† These were the SS regiments *Leibstandarte Adolf Hitler* in Zone III, *Deutschland* in Zone I, and *Germania* in Zone II.

‡ General von Weichs, commanding XIII Corps at Marienbad, had a like experience after he learned of the brutal abuse of a female Czech secretary under interrogation by Gestapo agents. He instituted an investigation which confirmed the event, but his report to higher headquarters resulted only in a rebuke because "I had attempted to pit one government arm against another, which was harmful to the prestige of the Reich."

of them had to find whatever shelter they could—a barn or even a ditch—in the neutral zone along the demarcation line. A few hundred even tried to return to the Sudetenland, where five hundred "suspects" had already been arrested by the Henleinists or the Gestapo in Bock's area alone.

For this harshness, the Czechs had reasons. As summarized by Gedye:

> It is the business of those who made these people refugees, Britain and France, to save them, not ours. We appeal to their representatives on the Berlin Commission, we appeal direct to London and Paris for something to be done in the way of providing an asylum for these people, and we get no reply. . . . It is not our job to play philanthropist to the victims of Franco-British dictation.

Newton reported this sorry situation to London on October 12. A week later the Foreign Office responded by instructing Newton to urge Prague to admit the refugees "on humanitarian grounds." The Czech authorities replied that "a favourable decision would be greatly facilitated if His Majesty's Government could arrange for emigration of these persons." In his report to London on the twenty-second, Newton commented:

> I am sure you will agree that these arguments are reasonable. . . . Even though these refugees may be Czech citizens their living room has been taken over by the Reich and living room left for the real Czechs is likely to be seriously overcrowded. While the accommodation of extra Jews may be an inconvenience for other countries it may for the Czechs be not only an economic but a political danger. There is already evidence of this in continuance of anti-Jewish campaign in Czech [language] broadcasts from Germany.

On October 26, Halifax forwarded Newton's dispatch to Berlin, with instructions for the chargé in Henderson's absence, Sir George Ogilvie-Forbes:

> You will see that reports that German authorities in Sudeten area are expelling Jews appear to be authenticated. . . . Jews are squatting in deplorable conditions in no man's land between Czech and German lines. . . . the practice of expelling Jews in this manner is not only inhumane, but also contrary to the intentions of the Munich Agreement, Article 7. . . . Please approach German Government in your capacity as a member of the International Commission . . . and urge them to refrain from such expulsions.

Ogilvie-Forbes promptly addressed an "urgent personal appeal" to Weizsaecker, but nothing came of it, and two weeks later the officially inspired anti-Jewish demonstrations and depredations in Germany which became known as "Crystal Night" sent a new wave of refugees into Czech territory. On November 15, Halifax told Ogilvie-Forbes to "renew your representations," adding despondently that "While realizing the uselessness of general protest . . . against treatment of Jews I am anxious to do everything we can when good grounds for intervention exist." There certainly were good grounds, but the intervention proved, as Halifax anticipated, utterly futile.

Eventually Prague allowed most of the refugees to enter, and early in 1939 it was estimated that they numbered about 170,000 of whom 12,000 were Social Democrats and other anti-Nazi Germans, and 7,000 were Jews. London had advanced £10 million to Prague, but what was needed more than money were visas from other countries willing to receive some of the refugees, and of these there were few indeed—a token few hundred to Britain, a couple of thousand to Australia.*

Negotiations for an Anglo-French loan to Czechoslovakia, against which the British had advanced the £10 million, continued through the winter of 1938-39. The French public was indifferent and their government, ever practical, was reluctant to subsidize a country being drawn into the German orbit. The British were more concerned about anti-Semitic measures which the Prague government, under great pressure from Hitler himself, was considering. In view of all that had happened, Halifax showed little sensitivity in urging the Czech leaders to risk the Fuehrer's displeasure by defying his wishes with respect to the Jews. Toward the end of January 1939, a £16-million program of financial assistance to Prague was agreed upon by London and Paris, but six weeks later the German occupation of all of Bohemia and Moravia rendered these plans academic.

5

After settling the October 10 boundary in the manner already described, the International Commission turned its attention to determining what areas should be subjected to plebiscites. In fact, no one wanted them very much because, under the Munich terms, they would require the presence of international peace-keeping forces. Hitler did not want foreign troops messing around in or near the newly occupied areas. The British, who had originally proposed their legion of ex-servicemen, had second thoughts as they reflected on the cost and inconvenience, and the probable inability of untrained, overage veterans to handle any real trouble. The Czechs rightly feared that any change in the October 10 line would be to their disadvantage, and Hitler himself had declared in a speech in Berlin on October: "By 10 October we shall have occupied all the areas which belong to us." There appeared to be a good chance that the plebiscites might be dispensed with, and the final boundary settled approximately on the basis of the October 10 line.

Nevertheless, on that very day Henderson, in discussion with Weizsaecker, got the impression that Ribbentrop and others might be pressing for plebiscites in the German-speaking areas around Brünn and Olmütz, where the Moravian "waist" connecting Bohemia with Slovakia had already been greatly narrowed by the October 10 occupation. This news was altogether too much even for that archengineer of appeasement. Henderson had justified his signature on the October 5 protocol in order to "pin the Germans down to a line of their own choosing," and now they were coming unpinned. The ambassador found this intolerable and read Weizsaecker a very stiff lecture:

> I . . . spoke with the utmost gravity. I said that I personally would never agree to plebiscites being held for such a purpose and would if it were suggested withdraw from the International Commission pending instructions from my government. . . .

* Because of strict statutory limits on immigration, the American Legation in Prague could do little or nothing to alleviate the refugee problem.

The Czechs were down and out, Germany had got all she wanted and if she could not behave with decency it would be useless to go on negotiating. Having accepted the big transaction I did not imagine we would go to war over Brünn and Olmütz but at least I would not be a party to further ungenerous spoliation.

As far as plebiscites were concerned Henderson's fears were unfounded. The next day, conferring at Godesberg, Hitler instructed Ribbentrop to ask for no plebiscites, to wind up the International Commission as soon as possible, and settle all future questions by direct negotiations with Czechs. On October 13 the International Commission formally recorded a unanimous agreement that there would be no plebiscites.

That same day Chalkovsky arrived in Germany; he was received by Ribbentrop in Berlin and, on the fourteenth, in Munich by Hitler. To both the Czech sang the same song: Masaryk and Beneš had been fools and worse to guide their country into anti-German paths, and now "Czechoslovakia would make a complete *volte-face* in her foreign policy." The Fuehrer received this information with bare toleration. Czechoslovakia must find her "proper place" and recognize that British and French guarantees were "worthless." She must "not play any tricks with Germany," and if she were to deviate from the straight and narrow path, "in 24 hours—no, in 8 hours—*mache ich Schluss!*"*

A few days later Henderson went home on a long sick leave, and François-Poncet was transferred to Rome, both, no doubt, believing that at least the frontier question had been settled. But the final line remained to be fixed, not by plebiscite but by the International Commission, on the recommendation of a German-Czech Frontier Committee. The Czechs were desperately hoping that the Munich Agreement's authorization of "minor" departures from an ethnographic line might be allowed them for the benefit of their east-west railway traffic. On the other hand, German occupation troops had already gone across the October 10 line at a great many points.

Throughout October the German delegates refused to meet to resolve these issues, waiting on Hitler's review of their proposed demands. He finally got around to the matter on November 8, and a meeting of the Frontier Committee was called two days later. The Germans put on a brutal performance; Baron von Richthofen castigated the Czechs for presuming to request any revisions in their favor, and declared that "the Reich Government does not intend in any circumstances to give up any of the occupied area," whereas "the Reich Government for its part still has claims to put forward." He then produced a map on which the German claims were shown by a new red line. There were no negotiations; the Czechs were simply told to assent "within a day or two," and their chief delegate hurried off to Prague for instructions.

Such was the result of the direct negotiations which Henderson had thought would best serve the Czechs' interests, and which Chalkovsky had resorted to in his meetings with Ribbentrop and Hitler. From an ethnographic standpoint the new German demands were indefensible, as the areas in question were over-

* "I'll finish her off!"

whelmingly Czech. Chalkovsky declared himself struck "like a bolt from the blue," but his remonstrances to the Wilhelmstrasse elicited only the response "that the German demands admitted of no bargaining and that the Czechoslovak Government would be well advised to accept the demands in the form in which they were presented." And so, just before midnight on November 11, the Prague government secretly informed Berlin that the German demands would be "accepted in principle."

The Czechs, in fact, had been pushed to a point where they were afraid to make an open appeal for British or French support. On November 17, Sir George Ogilvie-Forbes was visited by Mastny, who told him "in great confidence" about the German demands, under which "territory populated by about 6000 Germans and 50,000 Czechs" would be ceded to Germany.* In his dispatch to London, after reporting this conversation, Sir George observed:

> In this eventuality the question arises as to what should be my attitude. There are three alternatives: 1. to accept; 2. refuse; 3. refer for instructions.
> 1. If I were to accept, it would appear to be truckling to an unreasonable demand and out of accord with the terms and spirit of the Munich Agreement which did not contemplate annexation of predominately Czech territory.
> 2. To refuse would be regarded by the Germans as contrary to His Majesty's Government's policy of Anglo-German *rapproachement* as regarded at Munich.
> 3. . . . Reference for instructions might be regarded by the Germans in their present mood as an attempt to hold up the proceedings of the Commission; but rather than be rushed into agreeing to such a settlement I would insist upon referring to you. . . .
> As I have no indication that the Commission will meet in the near future it would not surprise me were the Germans suddenly to summon it and present it in their usual dictatorial manner with a *fait accompli* to be approved merely as a matter of form. . . .

Sir George's apprehensions were well justified. On November 21 he was called by Ritter (acting as chairman of the commission in Weizsaecker's absence) and informed that there would be a meeting that very evening to sanction the new frontier "agreed upon between Czechs and Germans." The meeting would be "brief and of course purely a matter of form." Before going to the meeting, Sir George consulted with his French and Italian colleagues; all were of the opinion that:

> . . . as the Czechs have already signed an agreement with Germans . . . Commission has no alternative but to endorse it. Had the Czechs protested and appealed to the Commission before signing the case would have been different. But it is no good being more royal than the King.

Accordingly when the International Commission, a few hours later, held its last meeting, Sir George Ogilvie-Forbes joined with the four other members in

---

* The Germans' own figures showed 39,443 Czechs in the newly ceded territories, and that after the final settlement about 475,000 *Volksdeutsche* would remain in rump Czechoslovakia, while 675,000 Czechs would "fall to Germany."

signing a resolution that the line on Ritter's map should constitute the final frontier under Article 6 of the Munich Agreement. It is doubtful that the end would have been any different had the Czechs appealed to the commission; a procedure which had brought them nothing in early October was unlikely to show any better results in late November. Once the British had swallowed what Henderson called "the big transaction," it was out of the question to launch a major war over border shifts, no matter how indefensible, involving less than fifty thousand Czechs.

Munich had landed Britain and France in a diplomatic cul-de-sac. It was painfully humiliating to Sir George and a few others in the Foreign Office, but these events passed virtually unnoticed by the world at large. Even the Czechs were losing the fine edge of resentment; just before the final meeting, Mastny told Sir George that there was "no alternative but to sign" and that he was "quite resigned" to Sir George's concurrence in the settlement.

And so the International Commission adjourned, *sine die* and, altogether too literally, not with a bang but a whimper. In Cabinet the next day (November 22), Neville Chamberlain reported to his colleagues; "The result might be described as a compromise in which Czechoslovakia conceded everything and gained nothing. A further 30,000 Czechs and 6000 Germans had passed under German rule. The result was to be deplored but there was nothing we could do in the matter. The International Commission had confirmed the result."

6

The Prime Minister's profession of helplessness in the face of German demands was characteristic of his and Halifax's attitude toward enforcement of the Munich terms. On October 19, Halifax had told the Cabinet that "the Czech Government would have to come to terms with Germany on both economic and political matters." A week later, confronted in Cabinet with reports that German troops had crossed the October 10 line at three hundred places, Halifax responded that "he hoped, without much conviction, that the Germans would behave reasonably," but anyhow Britain "had no particular *locus standi* in the matter" and couldn't help. With regard to Polish and Hungarian claims against the Czechs, the Foreign Secretary thought Britain's best course would be to maintain that these matters were "not our concern."

In fact, of course, they were. An annex to the Munich Agreement provided that if "the problems of the Polish-Hungarian minorities in Czechoslovakia" were not settled by agreement between those governments, they would "form the subject" of another four-power meeting.

The Poles, however, were not disposed to be patient in pressing their long-standing claim to the Teschen district in the northeastern corner of Moravia. Warsaw's prideful aspirations to "great power" status made the prospect of subjecting the Polish claims to the judgment of the four Munich participants vastly irritating, especially to the arrogant Colonel Beck. On October 1 an ultimatum was dispatched to Prague demanding cession of part of the claimed area within twenty-four hours, and the remainder in ten days. Geographically the total area

was not great, and the beleaguered Czechs, with no stomach for resistance, capitulated within a few hours and accepted the Polish demands in their entirety.

The Hungarian claims were very much more extensive, comprising a large
part of southern Slovakia and, at its eastern end, Carpatho-Ruthenia in its entirety. Efforts to settle these issues by direct negotiation between Prague and
Budapesth proved unsuccessful, and at the end of October the two countries
submitted their differences to arbitration, not by the four powers as envisaged in
the annex to the Munich Agreement, but by Germany and Italy.

For both military and diplomatic reasons, Hitler was not disposed to give full
support to the Hungarian claims. When the Munich crisis was boiling up, Hungary had been reluctant to range herself on the German side, and the Fuehrer
did not readily overlook such insubordination. More important, he did not welcome the idea of a Polish-Hungarian frontier, which the cession of Ruthenia to
Hungary would have provided. The German aim was to establish dominance
over Slovakia and Ruthenia, thus keeping open a road through Central Europe
to Rumania and the oil-fields of the Ploesti region.

On November 2, Ribbentrop and Ciano met the Hungarian and Czechoslovak
delegations at the Belvedere palace in Vienna, and handed down their decision.
An unbroken strip of southern Slovakia and Ruthenia, with over a million inhabitants of mixed nationality, was peeled off and ceded to Hungary, but
Czechoslovakia retained the Slovak capital (Bratislava) and northern Ruthenia.

Thus the Hungarian claims were adjusted without the advice or participation
of Britain or France. They did not object, nor, in view of Hitler's attitude on
this particular matter, did the Czechs. Mussolini and Ciano were delighted with
the opportunity to appear as arbiters of Central European issues, and the
Vienna award was widely portrayed as yet another proof of declining French
power and prestige.

7

The final settlement of Czechoslovakia's new borders brought into effect the
last remaining unexecuted part of the Munich Agreement, in the annex relating
to "an international guarantee of the new boundaries of the Czechoslovak State
against unprovoked aggression." Addressing the Commons on October 4, Sir
Thomas Inskip had announced: "His Majesty's Government . . . feel under a
moral obligation to Czechoslovakia to treat the guarantee as being now in
force." But no treaty or other formal document had been drawn up, as Britain
wished her obligations to be part of a multination agreement. The second paragraph of the Munich annex provided that: "When the question of the Polish
and Hungarian minorities in Czechoslovakia has been settled, Germany and
Italy for their part will give a guarantee of Czechoslovakia." That time had now
arrived, and on November 5, Chalkovsky told Newton that he was "very anxious to obtain as soon as possible guarantee of all four Munich powers."

The promised guarantee had, as we have seen, been one of the strongest talking points in defense of Munich during the debate in the Commons. A few
weeks later, however, the British Government's attitude underwent a marked

change, as the initial euphoria gave way to a less rosy perception of the new situation.

Chalkovsky's request moved Halifax to submit to the Cabinet, on November 12, an analysis of the questions which would have to be considered in putting the new guarantee into treaty form. Should the participants include only the four Munich signatories or other neighboring powers such as Poland, Hungary, and Rumania? In particular, should Soviet Russia be asked to join, as had been envisaged in the Anglo-French proposals? How should it be determined that an "unprovoked aggression" had occurred? Should the guarantee remain effective if Slovakia or Ruthenia broke away from Prague? Most important of all, should the guarantee be "several," so that each guarantor would be bound to assist Czechoslovakia regardless of what the other guarantors might do, or "joint," so that no guarantor was obligated to act unless the others acted likewise?

Only the last question was handled decisively in Halifax's memorandum. In his view, the Cabinet had decided on September 21, when the Anglo-French proposals were approved, that so far as Britain was concerned the guarantee must not be several, "on the ground that we cannot accept a position in which we might be called upon to implement our undertaking single-handed."* On the other hand, he recognized that if there were multiple signatories, including one or more possible aggressors, "a strictly joint guarantee, which would only become operative if all the guarantors agreed to act, would, from the point of view of Czechoslovakia, not be worth the paper it was written on." To meet the problem, Halifax proposed that the obligation of each guarantor should be contingent on the willingness of a specified number of additional guarantors (say three others out of six in all) to take action.

At its next meeting, the Cabinet referred Halifax's memorandum to the Foreign Policy Committee, and the subject was also put on the agenda for discussion with the French, during talks scheduled to be held in Paris on November 24. It was at this meeting (for which the London delegation comprised Chamberlain, Halifax, Cadogan, and Strang) that the crucial Allied decisions were taken.

The conferees discussed at some length whether countries other than the Munich signatories should participate, and eventually agreed to put the question to the Czechs before reaching a decision. Lord Halifax then said, almost as an afterthought, that:

> there was one further point: if and when the guarantee were to be given by the four Munich Powers, His Majesty's Government considered that their obligation should be drawn so as to make it a joint guarantee. The obligations should . . . only come into force as a result of a decision by three of the four Powers.

It at once became apparent that this was, to the French, a new and shocking idea. The existing French treaty commitment to Czechoslovakia was in no way

* In fact, Inskip's statement in Commons had already put Britain in this position as a matter of "moral obligation," for he had said that, in the event of unprovoked aggression, "His Majesty's Government would certainly feel bound to take all steps in their power to see that the integrity of Czechoslovakia is preserved."

dependent on the action of other states. Neither the Anglo-French proposals nor the Munich Agreement described the projected new guarantees as either "joint" or "several" but simply as "international," and the French (and, presumably, the Czechs) had assumed that these would be as binding as the existing French guarantee. It was now obvious that the British had never informed either Paris or Prague about the "joint" limitation which, according to Halifax, the Cabinet had approved on September 21.* Furthermore, if the joint factor were to be applied as Halifax had stated it, the obvious consequence was that if Germany attacked Czechoslovakia, Britain and France would have no obligation to go to her assistance unless Italy—Germany's Axis partner—joined in the protective action.

Small wonder, then, that Daladier and even Bonnet objected vigorously that Halifax's proposal diminished the value of the guarantee far below its pre-Munich level. Chamberlain replied that "it was too dangerous so to arrange the guarantee that it might happen that France and Great Britain would have to go to war because of action on the part of the other two guarantors," and that the stipulation for a guarantee effective only with the participation of three out of the four "would protect France and Great Britain from such a risk." That was certainly true, but the guarantee was for the benefit not of Britain and France but of Czechoslovakia, and it was obvious that the Halifax formulation would make it virtually valueless to the Czechs.

Daladier remarked acidly that if that was what Britain had had in mind "it would have been better not to undertake a guarantee like that undertaken at Munich." He went on to remark that the territorial loss to Czechoslovakia as determined by the International Commission was "a much more serious thing" than even Godesberg had envisaged, and that: "If France were now to refuse to guarantee what remained of Czechoslovakia, her position would be still worse." Halifax then paid lip service to "the moral question" but declared that his position was not "out of conformity with the letter of the Anglo-French declaration." Bonnet, often receptive to such arguments, nevertheless retorted that "it was hardly in conformity with the spirit."

Of course, the declared purpose of the new guarantee was to give better security to the Czechs to compensate them for the sacrifice of their own defenses, and the British position that this could be accomplished by a guarantee far feebler than its predecessor was preposterous. As a practical matter, however, it made little sense for the British and French to assume the same obligations from which they had just escaped so narrowly, and the French, for all their show of indignation, had no more stomach than the British for an undertaking to defend a now undefendable Czechoslovakia. Pharisaical French, Jesuitical British.

In the end, accordingly, the French were brought around to Chamberlain's shrewdly phrased proposal that the Halifax formulation should be put before the Czechs. If they accepted such an arrangement, "that would satisfy all par-

---

* Nor had Parliament been informed of any such decision. In the Lords on October 4, Halifax had mentioned the question whether the guarantee should be "joint or several," describing it as one that "will require more careful consideration than it has yet been possible to give. . . ."

ties," and Prague would be better off with "a guarantee which would bring in Germany and Italy willingly rather than a sham guarantee which could not work if it were really wanted." This transformed the arrangement from one in which the deterrent effect would be achieved not by protective military force, but by co-opting the likely criminal as one of the police, and thereby shaming him into mending his ways.

Thus once again the Prime Minister carried the day over initial French objections. After considerable discussion in Cabinet and the Foreign Policy Committee over the wording of the inquiries to be made in Prague, on December 3 Newton was sent instructions embodying the Halifax line. The Czechs were invited to express their views on participation by countries other than the Munich signatories, but on the nature of the guarantee it was to be made clear that the British Government "was not prepared to consider a guarantee which might oblige them, alone or with France, to come to the aid of Czechoslovakia in circumstances in which effective help could not be rendered," such as a case in which "either Germany or Italy were the aggressor and the other declined to fulfill the guarantee."

As things worked out, London and Paris could have spared themselves most of the argument and acrimony over the joint-or-several issue. When Newton explained the situation to Chalkovsky on December 10, the latter "seemed hardly to have appreciated the importance of distinguishing between an individual guarantee and various forms of collective guarantee." The Czech Foreign Minister was "very guarded and reluctant to express opinions," but he plainly recognized the "major importance" of German participation and was chiefly interested in speed:

> Finally Dr. Chalkovsky begged me to emphasize to you [i.e., Halifax] the importance of giving the guarantees as soon as possible. Their form and extent were less important than promptitude. Until they were in force the Czechoslovak people . . . would find it difficult to settle down to the future with any sense of security.

Chalkovsky's reticence and impatience are alike understandable. When he had been received by Hitler in Munich on October 14, the Fuehrer had given no direct answer to the question whether he would guarantee the new frontiers. But he had told Chalkovsky that "British and French guarantees were as worthless as the treaty of alliance with France or the pact with Russia had been during the crisis and that the only really effective guarantee was one by Germany." Hitler had threatened his guest with utter and speedy calamity for his country if it made a single hostile move. With the German sword hanging over his head, Chalkovsky cared little about the terms of the guarantee, for all he wanted was something, almost anything, that would speedily put Germany in the role of guarantor.

But Prague's hopes were in vain, for already there were signs that Hitler had no intention of entering into any guarantee whatever. On December 6, while visiting Paris, Ribbentrop told Bonnet and Léger that German participation in a guarantee "was dependent on whether German-Czech relations were placed on an entirely new basis," and expressed fear that "a four-power guarantee would mean a certain temptation for Czechoslovakia to follow once more in the old paths of the Benes policy." Two weeks later Weizsaecker greeted the new French Ambassador in Berlin, Robert Coulondre, with the information that "the destiny of Czechoslovakia lay in the hands of Germany" and that "nothing other than a German guarantee had any significance for Prague." He smilingly suggested that the matter be "forgotten," and Coulondre's protesting references to the Munich promises drew only the reaction that "the political situation was a new one and Czechoslovakia was quite dependent on Germany." On December 28, Weizsaecker sang the same tune to the Italian chargé d'affaires, Count Massimo Magistrati, and on January 21, 1939, when Chalkovsky came again to Berlin, his references to the possibility of a frontier guarantee drew very cold rejoinders from Ribbentrop.

Despite these rebuffs the Czechs continued to press for a guarantee, and at long last, on February 8, the British and French governments each submitted a *note verbale* in Berlin, referring to the Munich annex and suggesting that "the time has now come to regularize the guarantee in question." Two weeks later no answer had been received, and the Czechs circulated a memorandum to all four Munich powers formally requesting action on the guarantee.

The Czechs never had the courtesy of a written reply.* To the British and French, the German Government replied by *note verbale* dated February 28, the bulk of which was written by Hitler himself. "The assumption of . . . guarantee obligations by Great Britain and France in favor of Czechoslovakia," the two powers were told, "does not appear, in the opinion of the German Government, to provide a sure safeguard against the emergence or deepening of antagonisms [between Czechoslovakia and her neighbors] and the conflicts which might possibly result therefrom. . . . The German Government is fully aware that, in the last analysis, the general development in this European zone falls first and foremost within the sphere of the most important interests of the German Reich . . ."

Ambassador Coulondre received the note on March 2 and forwarded it to Paris with the observations that "Decoded, this message means that the Western powers no longer have any right to look in the direction of central Europe" and that "the document is far from reassuring as to the immediate views of Nazi policy with regard to Czechoslovakia."

Exactly two weeks later German troops entered Prague, and the question of an international guarantee, joint or several, became moot.

8

Such were the ignominious demises of the International Commission and the international guarantee—the two features of the Munich Agreement chiefly relied on by the British and French governments to justify their acceptance of Munich as a great improvement on the rejected Godesberg ultimatum.

---

* On March 3 Weizsaecker summoned Mastny and described the contents of the German reply to the Anglo-French *note verbale,* with an indication that this adequately embodied the German view of the Czech request for a guarantee.

In retrospect, the puzzling aspect of this sorry record is that so little public attention was paid it, especially in Britain, where the debate in Parliament had obliged the Government to state its case for Munich with some particularity. The Government, to be sure, did all it could to keep the details of the International Commission's doings out of the press, and their penchant for secrecy was greatly favored by the fact that Parliament adjourned on October 6 and did not reconvene until November 1, by which time most of the commission's work was finished. But even within Government circles astonishingly little was said, and the Cabinet only rarely adverted to the commission's doings, although one might have thought that the doubters, such as De La Warr and Oliver Stanley, would have sought to follow closely the administration of the agreement and ride herd on their leader for the disasters that ensued. Only Vansittart, again losing influence, seems to have spoken out. On October 11 he wrote:

> In my opinion the proceedings of the International Commission have been scandalous. It never even made an attempt to get a compromise between population figures of 1910 and 1918, *as instructed*. It has simply reproduced Godesberg, after we had flattered ourselves publicly on having got away from it. Over three-quarters of a million Czechs are now apparently to be under German rule. It is a shame.

To be sure, events in the commission and the Sudetenland did not pass wholly unnoticed. When Parliament reconvened there was a quite brisk debate on the Czech situation, with strong criticism from Attlee, Sinclair, and others chiefly directed to the use of the 1910 census in fixing the October 10 line, and the fact that the result was worse than Godesberg. "This, then, is peace with honour," said Vyvyan Adams, a Conservative backbencher, "when Munich exceeds Godesberg; when young women Jewish refugees are, I am told, lying exposed to pneumonia on the damp ground between Sudetenland and the new unfortified Czechoslovakia. . . ."

There were other sharp words, but the debate did not really catch fire. Attlee and Sinclair were spokesmen for the opposition, and the heavy guns among the Conservative dissenters—Churchill, Amery, and Eden—did not go into action.

The Prime Minister, barely ruffled, stood off the attacks on the dual ground that the Czechs had accepted the new frontier, so that the commission's hands were tied, and that the alternative to acceptance would have been war. No one rose to point out that the second reason implied that Hitler would have disregarded commission decisions that were not to his liking, and revealed that since the other signatories were not prepared to back up their votes militarily, the commission was powerless. No one suggested that the juxtaposition of the two reasons indicated that Prague had consented only because of lack of support from her "allies."

Chamberlain did not disclose that Czech assent had been procured by presenting her with an ultimatum from the same four powers that were Munich signatories, issued after a meeting from which her representatives were excluded. That and other ugly details were (to borrow from the Watergate vocabulary of a later era) "deep-sixed."

After this discussion (on the issue of which no vote was taken*), parliamentary interest in the execution of the Munich terms waned. Within the Foreign Office the fiction that Munich was a compromise wore so thin that, by December 3, Ogilvie-Forbes could write to Strang:

> I entirely agree with Troutbeck [First Secretary to the legation in Prague] that all questions arising out of the Munich Agreement have been and will be decided at German Nazi dictation. It is pathetic to see the trouble taken by members of the Foreign Office . . . on questions of frontiers, economics and options, all in vain. The Ambassadors' Commission might as well be dead for all the use it is. . . .

To virtually all complaints about the commission the Government replied blandly that the Czechs had consented, and therefore the Munich terms were not being violated. It was a performance smoother but no more palatable than that of Georges Bonnet, speaking to his electoral constituents at Périgueux: "There is one criticism which I refuse to accept: that is that France was not loyal to her signature. France's signature is sacred. Czechoslovakia wasn't invaded, was she?"

During the winter of 1938–39, such parliamentary interest as persisted was focused on the projected international guarantee. On all searching questions, the Chamberlain government simply "stonewalled," refusing to answer, or denying the factual basis of the inquiry. Neither the Cabinet decision that Britain would give only a joint guarantee, nor the outcome of the French discussions, nor the Newton-Chalkovsky exchanges, nor the approach to the German Government, were disclosed in answer to questions in Parliament. On February 21, in response to a member's question "whether the British guarantee for the integrity of Czechoslovakia continues several or has become joint," R. A. Butler declared himself "unable to make any further statement on this subject," although the joint limitation had been the core of the British position since the previous November.

The basic reason for all this secrecy was, of course, that the Munich Agreement, in the eyes of the British and French governments, was a cloak of respectability, and that disclosure of the emptiness and futility of the commission and the guarantee would have torn gaping holes in the cloak. In retrospect, what is most offensive about the British Government's policy at and after Munich is that its leaders had no intention of effectively opposing whatever the Germans might insist on in execution of the agreement, while publicly proclaiming that the three-two "pro-Czech" majority in the commission and the international guarantee would give the Czechs justice and security. In this betrayal, Britain well deserved the Napoleonic epithet "perfidious Albion."

The German occupation of Bohemia and Moravia on March 15, 1939, tore the cloak to shreds. Even then Chamberlain failed to disclose that Berlin, two weeks earlier, had refused the Munich-promised guarantee, thus dealing a

---

* The debate on Munich was rather overshadowed by the ensuing debates on the Anglo-Italian treaty (on which the Government prevailed in the division on a party basis), Spain, and rearmament.

deathblow to the entire guarantee concept, and raising a warning signal of great danger to the remnants of Czechoslovakia's sovereignty. But since the German move immediately followed a declaration (German-fomented) of Slovakia's independence of Prague, Chamberlain was able to construct verbal defenses for Britain's failure to intervene. He explained to the Commons that Inskip's "moral" guarantee had been in effect "until yesterday." However, Slovakia's secession was an internal disruption of the state which was the object of the guarantee.* Indeed, that state had ceased to exist, and therefore "His Majesty's Government cannot accordingly hold themselves bound by this obligation."

* Halifax's memorandum of November 12, 1938, had presciently remarked: "Were Slovakia or Ruthenia to break away from Czechoslovakia and . . . establish independent States . . . it is clear that a new position would arise and it might be argued that the guarantee we have given to the new Czechoslovak state would no longer apply."

CHAPTER 32

Peace For Our Time

1

The first person who had an opportunity to talk with Neville Chamberlain upon his return from Munich was Lord Halifax, who rode with him during the triumphal journey from Heston Airport to London. Shouts of acclaim and a rain of flowers made conversation difficult, but during a lull Halifax managed to slip in a bit of advice, "which was that by the time he met the House of Commons on Monday [in three days' time] he ought to have reconstituted his Government, bringing in Labour if they could join, and Churchill and Eden." According to Halifax, the Prime Minister "seemed surprised, but said he would think it over." However, no such thing was done, and subsequent events make it doubtful that Chamberlain gave Halifax's proposal much thought.

Other urgent recommendations soon came in from two of the ministerial "doubters," Stanley and De La Warr. In separate letters on October 3, they declared themselves ready to accept and defend the Munich settlement, but registered strong dissent from its portrayal as "peace for our time" and urged immediate intensification of rearmament. The Prime Minister replied that he was unwilling "to pledge myself to any particular programme of armaments" until the situation had been reviewed in the "light of recent events." When Lord Swinton told Chamberlain that he would support Munich only on the basis that it had purchased time for rearmament, the Prime Minister replied: "But don't you see, I have brought back peace!"

This issue—what effect the Munich crisis should have on the pace of rearmament—surfaced in Cabinet at the end of the meeting on the morning of October 3, when Walter Elliot observed that "one view which was strongly held in certain quarters was that we must never again allow ourselves to get into the position in which we had been in the last few weeks, and that every effort should be made to intensify the rearmament program." Halifax at once supported this opinion, as did Winterton later on. Once again, Chamberlain's response as reported in the minutes was at best equivocal:

> Ever since he had been Chancellor of the Exchequer, he had been oppressed with the sense that the burden of armaments might break our backs. This had been one of the factors which had led him to the view that it was necessary to resolve the causes which were responsible for the armament race.

He thought that we were now in a more hopeful position, and that the contacts which had been established with the Dictator powers opened up the possibility that we might be able to reach some agreements with them which would stop the armament race. . . . For the time being . . . we should relax no particle of effort until our deficiencies had been made good. That, however, was not the same thing as to say that as a thank offering for the present *détente,* we should at once embark on a great increase in our armaments program.

The Prime Minister was equally noncommittal during the Commons debate which began later that day. Neither he nor Inskip, in their speeches supporting the agreement, said a word about acceleration or expansion of the existing rearmament program. Others, especially Churchill, Eden, and Amery, did so, but in his summing up at the end of the debate Chamberlain gave them scant comfort, saying only that he would not now commit himself to any such plans "until I have had time for a little reflection, as to what further it may seem good to ask the nation to do. . . ."

It had already become apparent, as Eden observed in the Commons, that "There is a difference of view as to whether the events of the last few days do constitute the beginning of better things, as my right honorable Friend [Chamberlain] hopes, or whether they only give us a breathing space, perhaps of six months or less, before the next crisis is upon us." To be sure, the Prime Minister confessed to the House that his declaration of "peace for our time" had been the product of fatigue and overexcitement. But he did seriously believe that Munich had not only resolved the immediate crisis but also had opened a way to enduring peace. With this outlook, he was unmoved by pleas for intensified rearmament, and complained privately on October 22 that "A lot of people seem to me to be losing their heads and talking and thinking as though Munich had made war more instead of less imminent."

For the same reason he turned a deaf ear to the arguments of Halifax and others for a "Government of National Unity" which would include Labour, Liberal, and dissenting Conservative ministers. Some changes there would have to be, for Duff Cooper had resigned, Lord Stanley (Dominions) died a few weeks after Munich, and Hailsham was old and failing. Lord Runciman was rewarded with Hailsham's sinecure as Lord President, Lord Stanhope (a close friend of Chamberlain's) was promoted from Education to the Admiralty, and Malcolm MacDonald took the Dominions as well as the Colonial Office. The only significant shift was that the troublesome De La Warr was moved to Education, and replaced as Lord Privy Seal by the very able Sir John Anderson, who was given responsibility for co-ordinating the various agencies (Air, War Office, Home Office) concerned with civilian defense.

Given the gulf between Chamberlain and the Conservative dissidents, and his lack of interest in broader political support at a time of public adulation, it is easy to see why he made no move to bring in Churchill or even Eden. As he wrote privately in mid-October, if Eden were in the Cabinet "he would do what he did before, always agree in theory, but always disagree in practice. . . . I have had enough trouble in my present Cabinet."

This disagreement over the significance of Munich for the shaping of British policy was not primarily between the proponents and the opponents of Munich itself, although of course the critics generally saw it as a warning. But many of those who most emphatically approved Chamberlain's determination to resolve the crisis peacefully, even at high cost, thoroughly disagreed with the Prime Minister's insistence that Munich had improved the long-term prospect. At the Foreign Office, in addition to Halifax himself and, of course, Vansittart, Cadogan regarded rearmament as the "vitally necessary first step" on which future policy must be based. Strang, too, described rearmament as "the first essential," and this view was generally shared among the senior staff.*

This attitude was, not surprisingly, also prevalent among the service leaders. With virtual unanimity, they welcomed Munich as an instrument to delay the outbreak of a war which was inevitable and probably imminent, and for which preparations must speedily be made. General Pownall, for example, recorded on October 3:

> There is a remarkable degree of agreement throughout the country that we cannot take Hitler's assurances as guaranteeing "peace in our time". . . . The ruin of Czechoslovakia does not improve the military position, far from it. . . . we cannot rely on any breathing space longer than six months. We may get two years, if only because Germany will not *deliberately* enter a war against England until she feels she can support a long war. . . .
>
> We are now examining the "lessons" of the past two weeks, of which there are plenty. The first and foremost lesson is that we must *expect* to have to send troops to help the French. The General Staff have consistently held this view and now is the time to raise the question again. . . .

An expeditionary force to France meant more troops, more equipment, and of course much more money. What would Chamberlain's attitude be in the aftermath—or afterglow—of Munich?

A systematic review of Britain's military situation was launched by the CID on October 6, when the three services were asked to report on deficiencies exposed by the Munich crisis, and on how far the existing rearmament programs would be completed by August 1, 1939. Recommendations for acceleration of the present program were also requested, and Inskip undertook to discuss with the service ministers "any changes in defense policy which are now considered necessary." On October 19, Inskip told the Cabinet that these reports would soon be submitted, and added a warning that any substantial acceleration of the rearmament program might require "a somewhat drastic use of compulsory powers" in order to commandeer the necessary workers and production facilities.

On October 21, Inskip transmitted to the Cabinet the three services' predic-

---

* Cadogan's views were initially set forth in a memorandum submitted to Halifax on October 14, 1938. Strang, Sargent, Ashton-Gwatkin, and others produced individual analyses of the post-Munich scene, and these were all utilized by Cadogan and Strang in preparing the document submitted to the Foreign Policy Committee of the Cabinet, which met (for the first time since June) on November 14.

tions of their situation as of August 1, 1939,* explaining that he had chosen that date both because by then the rearmament program would be about three years old, and that it would be "about the time of year at which the possibility of an outbreak of war is at its highest." In his covering letter, Inskip stated that the reports raised two major questions: should the scope of the existing defense programs be enlarged, and should a Ministry of Supply be established? With regard to the first, Inskip remarked ominously "that the financial implications even of the present program are so grave that it has been a question whether they do not threaten that stability which is . . . probably our strongest weapon in war." Concerning the Ministry of Supply, Inskip set forth arguments pro and con, with negative implications.

Meanwhile the three service staffs were preparing their showings for expansion of the existing rearmament programs, and both the Air Ministry and War Office memoranda presented the Cabinet with major problems. The Air proposals were set forth in a memorandum signed by Kingsley Wood on October 25, entitled "Relative Air Strengths and Proposals for the Improvement of this Country's Position" and embodying what became known as "Scheme M"—the last of the prewar RAF expansion programs. Under Scheme M, first priority was given to fighter production. Scheme L had envisaged a front-line home strength of 608 fighters, in 38 squadrons, by March 31, 1940; Scheme M called for 640 fighters, in 40 squadrons, by March 31, 1939, and an eventual strength, in 1941, of 800 in 50 squadrons. No increase in the *number* of Britain-based bombers was envisaged, but the medium bombers called for under Scheme L were to be replaced by heavies, so that by 1942 the "striking force" would comprise 1360 heavy bombers in 85 squadrons, capable of very much greater range and lift than the mixed force provided for in Scheme L.

At the War Office, the staff prepared a memorandum entitled "Role of the Army in the Light of the Czechoslovak Crisis," which Pownall described as "going back nearly to the proposals of two years ago which were not accepted and for which we never got the money." The pre-Munich Army would have been barely able to send two partially equipped divisions to France. The new staff plan provided for a ready (fourteen-day) expeditionary force of six divisions (two mobile and four regular infantry); two lightly armed "colonial" divisions for overseas garrisons to be ready in a month; four Territorial Army divisions ready for the continent in four months; four more (two of which mobile) ready in six months, and three more in eight months. The estimated total cost of the program was over £200 million, of which £70 million was requested as a "first instalment" to cover the first ten divisions for the continent and the two colonial divisions.

In his memorandum of October 21, Inskip gave the Cabinet his opinion of the service demands. For the Navy "no material change is requisite." Any substantial RAF expansion would encounter grave problems in the procurement of

---

* These showed, in essence, that the Navy would be in a good state of readiness except for antiaircraft protection, but that both the Army and the Air Force would still suffer from serious deficiencies of various sorts.

trained personnel. Accordingly, "only in regard to the Army may there be some ground for looking again at the programme."

With all of the foregoing before the Cabinet on October 26, the ministers decided to refer the whole problem to an *ad hoc* subcommittee on Defence Programmes and Acceleration, chaired by Inskip and comprising also Simon, Hoare, Brown (Labour), and the three service ministers. Pownall recorded a description of their reaction to the Army's proposals:

> We got our paper on the Role of the Army before the Cabinet sub-committee this week—*and* how they hated the idea and shirked the plain issue. Only Inskip showed the least sympathy and he quite a lot. Simon was studiously polite . . . but he didn't like the cost; one could hardly expect him to. . . . E. Brown was violent but confused. Sam Hoare thoroughly beastly. . . . H-B [Hore-Belisha], I must say, took them on pretty well, considering he hasn't really much knowledge of the subject and no background from which to argue.

Despite the last-named's efforts, the Army program got nowhere, as Kingsley-Wood "produced the theory that the question was outside their terms of reference," and the subcommittee passed the buck by referring the Army program to the CID, where it languished for some weeks. On November 1 Chamberlain told the Commons: "We are not now contemplating the equipment of an army on a continental basis."

During its meeting on October 26, the Cabinet also discussed the proposals to establish a Ministry of Supply, favored by some both within (Hore-Belisha) and without (Churchill) the Cabinet. Chamberlain dismissed the project as "unnecessary at the present time, though it might be discussed later." On the thirty-first, after the Prime Minister declared that the Minister for Coordination of Defence was able to take care of supply problems, the Cabinet rejected the idea. Chamberlain went on to give his colleagues the rationale for what he planned to say in the Commons when it assembled on the morrow:

> Our Foreign Policy was one of appeasement. We must aim at establishing relations with the Dictator Powers which will lead to a settlement in Europe and to a sense of stability.
> There had been a good deal of talk in the country and in the press about the need for rearmament by this country. In Germany and Italy it was suspected that this rearmament was directed against them, and it was important that we should not encourage these suspicions.
> The Prime Minister said that he proposed to make it clear that our rearmament was directed to securing our own safety and not for purposes of aggression against other countries.
> A good deal of false emphasis had been placed on rearmament, as though one result of the Munich Agreement had been that it would be necessary for us to add to our rearmament programmes. Acceleration of existing programs was one thing, but increases in the scope of our programmes which would lead to a new arms race was a different proposition.

Taking his lead from the Prime Minister, Simon sent the Cabinet a memorandum on the Air Ministry's proposed program, which, he said, would involve additional expenditures of nearly £350 million—"so costly as to raise serious doubt whether it can be financed beyond 1939/40 without the gravest danger to the country's stability." Acknowledging that "purely financial claims" should not be given priority over "urgent and definite needs for material defense," Simon shrewdly proposed:

> . . . that a sharp distinction should be drawn between the total figures of the . . . *fighter* programme and the total figures of the . . . *bomber* programme. The Cabinet should be invited as a decision of policy to author-ize an intensive concentration on the production of fighters up to the full figures proposed with particular regard to getting the maximum production possible within 1939. . . . So far as the bombers are concerned I suggest that the Cabinet should give general approval to the placing of numbers sufficient to avoid substantial dismissals in the factories concerned. . . .

On November 11, 1938 the Subcommittee on Defence Programmes and Ac-celeration reported to the full Cabinet on the proposals of the three services. The Navy made no major demand, and its requests for additional small naval craft (chiefly escort vessels and minesweepers), air defense, and carrier aircraft were approved without difficulty. The Army's major proposal for an expedi-tionary force was still bottled up in the CID, and at this time Hore-Belisha was requesting only additional antiaircraft weaponry; this too, being purely de-fensive, was readily approved.

The focus of debate was, then, the Air Ministry's Scheme M, since it was the only proposal which seriously challenged the Prime Minister's policy of "accel-eration but no expansion." Essentially, the Cabinet decided to draw the line as laid down by Simon: fighters—yes to the full amount asked; bombers—no, ex-cept enough to hold the plants and workers available for the future. Kingsley Wood, striving valiantly to fill Swinton's big shoes, made a strong pitch for Scheme M, but Chamberlain supported Simon in opposition to the bomber por-tion:

> As regards our bomber strength, he [Chamberlain] thought it was rather difficult to represent this part of our force as in any way defensive.* Everyone would agree that we must have bombers, but he thought it was undesirable to stress this side of the programme.
> The Prime Minister said that he . . . felt very uneasy about the proposal that we should concentrate on the type of very heavy bomber now proposed. He . . . recalled . . . the satisfaction which had greeted the first building of "Dreadnoughts" by this country. . . . Before long other countries had started to build Dreadnoughts, and we had been forced to rebuild the whole of our Battle Fleet. . . . He could not help wondering whether the proposal to con-centrate on building Manchester and Halifax bombers would not result in Germany producing a super-Halifax. These heavy bombers cost as much as four fighters.

* This, of course, was directly contrary to the long-standing Air Ministry position that the deterrent effect of British bomber strength was the best protection against bomber attacks directed at Britain.

The Cabinet's decision to give priority to fighter production was, as the events of 1940 would prove, a fortunate one, albeit displeasing to the Air Staff at the time.* But the reasons which moved Chamberlain to delay the bomber program —cost and reluctance to antagonize Hitler—were the same reasons that underlay his unswerving opposition to expansion of the Army in order to support the French. Unlike the heavy bombers, provision for a British continental field force was an essential element of any plan for the defense of France and the Low Countries against a German attack, and Chamberlain's negative attitude was symptomatic of his continuing overoptimism and mistaken faith in Munich's peace-generating potential.

Three days later came the "Crystal Night" harassments of Jews which, if nothing else, demonstrated the Nazi government's utter indifference to foreign opinion. It was poor thanks for Chamberlain's concern for German feelings about "offensive" rearmament, but the Prime Minister was unshaken. On November 22, outlining to the Cabinet his plans for the forthcoming Paris conversations, Chamberlain declared that he would make it very clear to the French that, in the event of war, they could expect no more assistance on the ground than the two divisions that had been mentioned before Munich. Hearing of this, Pownall complained to his diary that: "Chamberlain went off to Paris with his ideas fixed in his head but without consulting the CID or the Chiefs of Staff as to whether his views were correct in the new circumstances of the time."

It is hard to describe Chamberlain's conduct at the Paris talks (November 24) as other than stubborn and graceless. He lectured Daladier on France's low aircraft production, blandly ignoring the fact that the British Army was in at least as poor a state as the French Air Force. When Daladier declared that two divisions of ground troops were not enough, and that the British units ought, as far as possible, to be motorized, the Prime Minister responded that since London was "now the most vulnerable capital in the world" first priority was being given to the antiaircraft defenses. Since the gun factories were fully occupied with antiaircraft artillery, they could not provide the field army with modern artillery. England was also deficient in tanks because it has taken "a long time to decide on the right type of tank." The Prime Minister made no new commitment, and warned his hosts that "the strength of any force which would come to the assistance of France must be limited by the fact that its equipment, both of medium and heavy artillery, was not complete," and that the available equipment "was obsolete." Under these circumstances there was no point in talking about additional troops.

Daladier did not press the demand beyond asking that the two divisions be dispatched within eight days after the outbreak of war. Chamberlain made no reply. Earlier in the meeting he had raised the possibility that Germany might first attack Britain rather than France, and demanded confirmation (which was readily given) that in such event France would come to Britain's aid. Later in

* In a contemporaneous (undated) memorandum to Kingsley Wood, Newall insisted that the new heavy bombers would be "the sole means by which we can endeavor to minimize our inferiority in striking power as compared to the Germans," and that without them, when the next crisis arose "we will once more find that our negotiations are at a grave disadvantage owing to the menace of the powerful German Air Force hanging over London."

the meeting (as we have already seen) Halifax discomfited the French greatly by insisting that the guarantee to the Czechs be joint rather than several.

Toward the end of November, Hore-Belisha saw Chamberlain privately and endeavored to persuade him to a more realistic view of the Army's needs. He got nowhere, and apparently the Prime Minister asked him "as our Army was so small was it worth worrying whether it was ready or not?" Pownall was highly indignant: "A maddening attitude in 'The Coroner' (as the backbenchers call him) for we know we shall be sent if there is a war in Western Europe—the only point therefore is whether our men shall be properly equipped for it—or ill equipped and slaughtered."

In December, Hore-Belisha tried his hand at revising the "Role of the Army" memorandum so as to make it more palatable to his colleagues. In the CID his presentation gained support from Halifax, but it was not enough to prevent that body from bouncing the document back to the Chiefs of Staff, where it remained until the following February.

Thus the only significant impact of the Munich crisis on British rearmament was the acceleration and expansion of the production of fighter aircraft and antiaircraft weaponry. Of course, there is no gainsaying the importance of those measures, but their strategic effect was limited to diminishing the danger of the much-feared "knockout blow" from the Luftwaffe. Guns circling London and short-range fighters based in England would play no part in continental warfare. Britain's capacity to assist France or the Low Countries was not measureably increased.

Considering the continuing probability that, if Britain were forced into war, the cause would be a Franco-German war, and recalling also Chamberlain's hunch that the French Army was overrated, it is nothing short of astonishing that he remained so adamant in his opposition to making provision for effective aid to their ally. There is no doubt that the reason was what Chamberlain himself said: that in his view Munich had lessened the danger of war and thus the need for rearmament.

Whatever the reason, the record is clear enough that the Munich crisis failed to cause the British Government to take any significant steps to enable their country to participate in warfare on the continent. With the aid of Simon, Hoare, and Inskip, the Prime Minister succeeded in blocking every proposal directed to that end.*

2

The British, German, and French military leaders were all pleased that Munich had at least temporarily averted hostilities, for none of them thought his country as yet sufficiently prepared for a major war. The French and British were in full agreement, likewise, that the cession of the Sudetenland had consid-

* In the face of the record in general, and in particular Chamberlain's opposition to the bomber portion of Scheme M, Harold Balfour (who, as Under-Secretary for Air, must have known of many if not most of the events set forth above) nevertheless wrote (in *Wings over Westminster* [1973], p. 111): "Never from No. 10 did any order come to slow up anything. On the contrary we were encouraged and supported to redouble our efforts." The service staffs would have found such a verdict preposterous.

erably worsened their military situation vis-à-vis Germany. The Germans agreed with that too, but of course they (with the exception of the most determined members of the resistance group) found the alteration greatly to their liking. On hearing the news from Munich, Jodl recorded in his diary:

> The Munich accord is signed. Czechoslovakia as a power factor is eliminated. . . .
> The genius of the Führer and his determination not to back away even from world war have again won victory without the use of force.
> It is to be hoped that the unbelievers, the weak, and the doubters have been converted and will stay so.

Hitler himself, as we have seen, was less well pleased. On October 9 he first gave public expression to his post-Munich truculence in a speech at Saarbrücken, where he dedicated the new Saarland-Theater.* First paying tribute to Mussolini as "the one true friend whom we possess today," he observed that in a democracy such as England there could be a dangerous change of leadership at any time: "It only needs that in England instead of Chamberlain, Mr. Duff Cooper or Mr. Eden or Mr. Churchill should come to power, and then we know quite well that it would be the aim of these men immediately to begin a new World War." Furthermore, the English had better mind their manners: "It would be a good thing if in Great Britain people would gradually drop certain airs which they have inherited from the Versailles epoch. We cannot tolerate any longer the tutelage of governesses! Inquiries of British politicians concerning the fate of Germans within the frontiers of the Reich . . . are out of place. We for our part do not trouble ourselves about similar things in England."

Because of these dangers from the democracies, Hitler told his audience, he would now "continue the construction of our fortifications in the West with increased energy." The next day he toured the nearby fortifications, and then went to Mainz, where he embarked on a Rhine steamer to Godesberg.

En route Hitler appears to have toyed with the idea of disregarding the newly fixed Czech frontier and marching right on to Prague, for he telegraphed a series of questions to OKW in Berlin, of which the first was: "What reinforcements are necessary in the present situation to break all Czech resistance in Bohemia and Moravia?" Keitel consulted the five army group commanders and replied that Rundstedt and Bock each wanted an additional motorized division and Leeb wanted two plus an armored brigade, while List and Reichenau wanted nothing, and the Luftwaffe also could handle the task with the forces presently available. Keitel added OKW's own view that the operation could be begun without these increments "in view of the present signs of weakness in Czechoslovakia's powers of resistance."†

The operation would have presented few military difficulties. Some twenty-four German divisions were in the Sudetenland, while the Czech Army had

---

* General Adam, still in command in the west, received Hitler in Saarbrücken; it was their last personal encounter, and a very cool one. A week later Adam sent his letter of resignation to Brauchitsch.

† The other questions concerned the time which would be required to procure and deploy the requisite forces.

pulled back out of its fortifications and was in a virtually helpless situation. But it is doubtful that Hitler, for all his ruthlessness and scorn for treaty commitments, seriously considered so treacherous and shocking a move. He had no desire for so sharp a confrontation with Britain and France at that time, and contented himself with the issuance, on October 21, of an interim secret directive to the Wehrmacht requiring that preparations be made "to smash the remainder of Czechoslovakia at any time should her policy become hostile towards Germany." In that event the objective was to be "the swift occupation of Bohemia and Moravia and the cutting off of Slovakia."

On October 13, Hitler visited the Krupp works in Essen, and then returned to Berchtesgaden. Here, in his retreat atop the Kehlstein, on October 18 the Fuehrer received a farewell visit from François-Poncet, who was being transferred to Rome.* The Fuehrer did not generally care much for diplomats, but he had a soft spot for the suave, articulate Frenchman. The meeting lasted over two hours; Ribbentrop was also present but said little.

Most of the time was spent discussing the stabilization of Franco-German relations by formal recognition of their mutual frontiers, agreement to consult on future problems between the two countries, and a joint guarantee of Belgium. Britain and Italy might be asked to join in four-power discussions of economic problems, and proposals for "the humanization of warfare." This was all very loose, but in conclusion it was agreed that the "experts" at the Wilhelmstrasse and Quai d'Orsay would "explore the suggestions furnished" by the discussion in order to "establish concrete formulas."†

The friendly tone of the conversation did not inhibit Hitler from a sharp attack, punctuated by "violent outbursts," on "Britain's selfishness and the ingenuous ideas she possessed concerning the superiority of her rights over those of others." As for Munich, the Fuehrer was deeply disappointed by its aftermath: "The crisis was not over; unless conditions changed it would soon break out anew. Britain echoed 'with threats and calls to arms' . . . that . . . clearly revealed to him what was Britain's attitude."

Accounts of the interview which the French passed on to London played down its anti-British character, but Hitler soon reiterated his sentiments publicly. On November 6, addressing a mass audience at Weimar, Hitler twisted the lion's tail again, with especially sharp references to Churchill and Eden. His hostile remarks greatly puzzled General Heinz Guderian, who, as the senior military officer in the area, was seated at Hitler's table for the tea party which followed the speech, and who asked Hitler "why he had spoken so sharply against England":

> His attitude, I discovered, was based on what he took to be the improper behavior toward himself of Chamberlain at Godesberg and the deliberate rudeness of certain prominent visitors who had come to see him. . . . He went on angrily to describe what he regarded as the rebuffs that he had re-

---

* He was replaced in Berlin by Robert Coulondre, transferred from Moscow.

† François-Poncet spoke excellent German, so no interpreter was present, and no official record of the talk was made. The only firsthand account is the ambassador's own in *The Fateful Years*, pp. 280–88.

ceived, and said that the English were not really interested in honestly establishing friendly relations with Germany.

To be sure, Hitler had taken a strong personal dislike to Chamberlain, but that was only a small part of the reasons for his post-Munich attitude. The root cause was his resentment against British meddling in Central and Eastern Europe, since he regarded British rearmament, other than naval, as undertaken solely to hold him in check there. German rearmament might threaten everyone, but by the same token it was not pointed in a single direction. However, Hitler well understood that if British bombers flew over and British soldiers landed in Europe, Germany would be their target. Probably he did not know that Chamberlain was doing his best to limit rearmament to "defensive" weaponry, but he was sure that Churchill and Eden would not relinquish Britain's historic role as a continental power-balancer, and that essentially accounts for his ire.

Furthermore, Hitler's concern was practical and immediate, for he planned shortly to take further steps which would test whether or not Britain was still determined to play the "governess." The same secret directive of October 21, which laid the basis for the taking of Prague, also called for readiness to occupy the Baltic port of Memel, which had been part of East Prussia prior to Versailles but was now Lithuanian. And on October 24, Ribbentrop, lunching in Berchtesgaden with Ambassador Lipski, had for the first time put forward the suggestion that Danzig (a "free city" under League of Nations control, with a predominantly German population but of vital importance for Polish maritime commerce) should be reunited to the Reich, and that Germany should be granted an extraterritorial road-railroad strip across the Polish Corridor from Pomerania to East Prussia.

Quite possibly Hitler would have been more likely to achieve his ends by soothing England with fair words instead of railing like a fishwife. Cadogan had advised on October 14: "We must cut our losses in central, and eastern Europe —let Germany, if she can, find there her 'lebensraum', and establish herself, if she can, as a powerful economic unit." A month later he wrote that Munich had shown "that we cannot any longer aspire to police Europe as we did in the post-Versailles-Covenant era, or join in crusades where our direct interests are not threatened."

Ambassador Kennedy (prone to exaggerate) reported on October 12 that Halifax had told him that Britain should "let Hitler go ahead and do what he likes in Central Europe," and that "reasonably soon Hitler will make a start for Danzig, with Polish concurrence, and then for Memel, with Lithuanian acquiescence, and even if he decided to go into Rumania it is Halifax's idea that England should mind her own business." Throughout the Foreign Office, there was a tendency to write off Central and Eastern Europe and concentrate on safeguarding British influence in Western Europe and the Mediterranean.

Accordingly, despite the Saarbrücken and Weimar harangues and the International Commission débacle, Chamberlain and Halifax continued to think of following up Munich with some kind of general settlement with Germany, based on the appeasement policy. And so they might have continued to think had it not been for Crystal Night, whereby the hardening of Hitler's outlook and strategy started to pervade the whole body politic of the Third Reich.

On November 7, 1938, a young German Jew named Herschel Grynszpan had shot and mortally wounded the Third Secretary of the German Embassy in Paris, Ernst vom Rath.* The German press immediately laid responsibility on "the infamous underground activities of Jewish propaganda," and accused British "war-mongering politicians" as instigators of the killing. Early in the morning of November 10, Goebbels and Heydrich organized a "spontaneous" orgy of looting, arson, and harassment of Jews, their synagogues, homes, and businesses throughout the Reich. Some Jews were killed, many injured, and thousands arrested. When it was found that most of the broken windows had been insured by "Aryan" insurance companies, Goering convened a meeting of high officials (Goebbels, Heydrich, and others) to cope with the unexpected problem. The Government confiscated all insurance money payable to Jews, a billion-mark fine was levied on the Jewish communities, and new measures were decreed to "eliminate Jews from the economic life of Germany and Austria" and "Aryanize" their properties.

The worldwide press reaction was shock and horror, especially in Britain and the United States. From London, Ambassador von Dirksen, who on October 31 had advised Berlin that "it can be expected that Chamberlain will shortly make proposals to the Führer for a continuation of the policy initiated at Munich" as applied to armaments and colonies, on November 7 reported that his prediction "no longer applies now." The "intensification of the anti-Jewish movement in Germany," Dirksen wrote, had caused "pessimism" in the sections of the British public who actively supported Anglo-German friendship, and a deterioration in the Prime Minister's position which would make it "impossible for Chamberlain to consider carrying out his plan of settlement with Germany on a broad basis."

Dirksen was right in concluding that Crystal Night was a monkeywrench thrown into Chamberlain's plans, but what was the British Government to do about it? On November 14 the Foreign Policy Committee was convened to consider the whole range of Anglo-German relations. Halifax (who had already sent instructions to Ogilvie-Forbes to register a sharp protest against German press accusations that Churchill, Attlee, and Duff Cooper were among those who had instigated the killing of Rath†) was armed not only with reports on

---

* There had been recent disagreement between the German and Polish governments with respect to the latter's new limitations on the issuance of passports to Polish Jews resident in Germany, in consequence of which the Germans in October expelled some 17,000 Jews of Polish nationality to Poland, under harsh physical circumstances. Grynszpan's parents were among them, and it was apparently (though a personal connection with Rath has been suggested) in demonstrative revenge that the son went to the German Embassy intending to kill the ambassador and instead shot Rath. The episode stimulated the composition of Michael Tippett's oratorio, *A Child of Our Time*.

† Dated November 11, Halifax's message directed Ogilvie-Forbes to deliver the protest personally to Ribbentrop or Weizsaecker. Both of them proved to be unavailable so that it had to be presented to Woermann, the Under-Secretary. The protest declared that the "scurrilous attacks" were out of harmony with "the Declaration which the Prime Minister and Chancellor signed in Munich," and requested steps "to prevent the publication of further articles of this kind." In an interview with a Reuter's representative, Goebbels repudiated the accusation, but the German press did not print the disavowal.

the anti-Jewish depredations, but also with secret intelligence reports from Germany. These portrayed the Nazi leaders as convinced that they "had Europe in their pocket" and that British rearmament was "not to be taken seriously"; Hitler as saying that it was "astonishing how easy the democracies make it for us to achieve our goal"; and a friendly German diplomat as concluding that Britain was "so completely unprepared that only the most superhuman effort on her part can make any impression and save the Empire."

Like the portrait of Dorian Gray, Chamberlain's vision of Munich was turning into a hideous face of riot and war. Halifax sadly confessed "that in present circumstances no useful purpose would be served by a resumption at the present time of the contemplated Anglo-German conversations, though it was possible that some progress might be made in discussion with Signor Mussolini." MacDonald, whose staff had been working on possible solutions of Germany's claim for the return of her former colonies, declared that "events in Germany had made it impracticable to do anything in this direction for the time being and the Government might be forced to make a statement to that effect." Hoare gloomily suggested that "unless something were done there were signs that the House of Commons and the country might get out of hand." The conferees wondered whether there was any form of retaliation which would hit Germany hard enough, and discussed British Guiana and Australia as possible refuges for German Jews.

The Prime Minister first tried to put a good face on things, expressing surprise at the "mild press reaction" and the lack of public demand for immediate action. That was fortunate because "it must be recognized that we could do nothing except pinprick and what useful purpose would that serve? The Germans are now much stronger and more arrogant than they had been and anything in the nature of threats could only result in our hand being called. In present circumstances we were not in a position to frighten Germany."

As for future relations with Germany, the Prime Minister, for the first time since Munich, was gloomy*—"very much concerned at the disappointing way in which things had developed in Germany since the Munich settlement." He did not quarrel with his Foreign Secretary's conclusion that the road to Berlin had been closed, at least for the moment, and followed Halifax's lead in suggesting, as a dual course of action, accelerated rearmament and an approach to Italy by personal visit in order to have "a heart to heart talk with Signor Mussolini . . . and help him, if he so desired, to escape from the German toils."

Chamberlain's recommendation of rearmament acceleration was an empty one, for he made no specific proposals, and spoke strongly against the establishment of a National Register of occupational skills, which was the next item on the committee's agenda.† *Rapprochement* with Italy was already under way,

---

* On November 10, while Goebbels and Heydrich were organizing Crystr \ Night, Chamberlain happily passed on to his sister a report from the Astors' son William, who had returned from a trip to Berlin with the impression that "Hitler definitely liked me [Chamberlain] and thought he could do business with me."

† Sir John Anderson, the new Lord Privy Seal, was charged with developing this proposal, strongly favored by Hoare. At the next Committee meeting (November 21) it was decided to proceed with a voluntary occupational register and lay the basis for a compulsory register in the event of war.

and two days later (November 10) in Rome Ciano and Perth signed a declaration bringing into effect the long-delayed Anglo-Italian Agreement. At the same time Mussolini sent word that he would welcome a visit by the Prime Minister during the second week of January 1939.

Diplomatically, Britain was again where she had been the previous March, when Hitler's angry rejection of the colonies proposal, followed by *Anschluss,* had caused Chamberlain to look away from Berlin and toward Rome *faute de mieux.* But now the odd situation was arising that, while Britain had the better relations with Italy, France was doing better than Britain in Berlin.

At François-Poncet's farewell meeting with Hitler, it had been left to Ribbentrop to come forward with specific proposals for the betterment of Franco-German relations. By coincidence, the German proposal for a Franco-German agreement, comparable to the Hitler-Chamberlain declaration signed at Munich, was first presented to Bonnet on November 7, the day that vom Rath was shot. The ensuing anti-Jewish outbreak in Germany was sharply criticized in the French press, but the German Government's wrath was focused on Britain, and both Paris and Berlin went ahead on the agreement project as if nothing untoward had occurred.* On November 21, Ambassador Coulondre presented his credentials to Hitler, and four days later (the day after the Anglo-French talks) the German press announced that Ribbentrop would shortly go to Paris for the signing ceremony.

Meanwhile François-Poncet arrived in Rome and on November 29 was received by Mussolini. The interview was not without its tension; despite the ambassador's effort to flatter his host on his contribution to the Munich settlement, Spain was still a stumbling block, and the Duce strongly implied that not much progress could be made until France's internal situation was more stable. The next day François-Poncet was in the audience when Ciano addressed the Italian Chamber of Deputies on foreign policy, at the conclusion of which there was an outburst of shouted demands for "Tunis! Djibouti! Corsica! Nice!" The demonstration was in line with instructions which Mussolini had given to Ciano on November 14, and was plainly welcomed and undoubtedly organized by the Fascist Party.

The French, of course, were greatly incensed, but Chamberlain and Halifax were at least equally upset. In the Anglo-Italian Agreement, the Italian Government had disclaimed all desire to modify the territorial *status quo* in the Mediterranean region, and now, only two weeks later, they were staging a demonstration for the "return" of French territories. It was almost too much, and on December 12 Chamberlain sent word to Lord Perth that he was "beginning to feel considerable difficulty about his projected visit to Rome."

It was in such an atmosphere, with Berlin castigating London, Rome screaming at Paris, and much of the world still shaken with fear and disgust at the spectacle of Crystal Night, that Ribbentrop arrived in Paris on December 6 to take the lead in what must have been one of the emptiest diplomatic ceremonies of all time. That afternoon at the Quai d'Orsay he and Bonnet signed a "Decla-

---

* Bonnet's memoirs attribute some delay, on the part of Berlin, to the killing of vom Rath, but they do not even mention Crystal Night as a factor in the negotiations.

ration" that "peaceful and good neighborly relations between France and Germany constitute one of the essential elements for . . . the maintenance of general peace"; that "between their two countries there is no territorial question outstanding"; and that their two governments "are resolved, with reserve as to their particular relations with third Powers, to remain in contact with regard to all questions interesting their two countries and mutually to consult should the later evolution of those questions threaten to lead to international difficulties."

Ribbentrop and his party were taken around Paris, under heavy security guard, to a succession of lunches, dinners, and ceremonial calls, and to the Arc de Triomphe for a wreath-laying on the tomb of the *Soldat Inconnu*. Needless to say, the German's presence in Paris evoked no popular acclaim, but it passed without untoward incidents.

The business conference, in which Bonnet and Léger confronted Ribbentrop and Welczeck, accomplished nothing. At the outset Ribbentrop declared "that he would not hold any *official* conversation about Jews as Herr Hitler felt so strongly in the matter." He mentioned the issue of colonies, but Bonnet declared that "the question could not now be raised." Léger broached the promised guarantee to Czechoslovakia, and Ribbentrop was evasive. Ribbentrop later claimed that Bonnet had said that France was no longer interested in Eastern Europe, and Schmidt (who was present to interpret*) confirmed this in his memoirs; Bonnet's contemporaneous account of the meeting, however, specified that he had "reserved all French rights" in Central and Eastern Europe, and Léger told Coulondre that Bonnet had said no such thing as Ribbentrop claimed.†

This frigid, fruitless encounter did nothing to better the prospects of "appeasement." Every approach and concession by the Western democracies seemed to be rewarded with a rebuff or slap in the face from the dictatorships, and now it was the turn of Berlin to strike the next blow. Three days after Ribbentrop left Paris, Dirksen transmitted to Halifax a letter announcing that his government, in accordance with the Anglo-German Naval Agreement, was notifying the British Government of their intention to increase their submarine tonnage to parity with that of the British Commonwealth. No reason was given other than "the necessity of paying increased attention to the protection of their maritime communications in the event of war-like complications."‡ On December 14, Lord Stanhope (the new First Lord) told the Cabinet that this would require Britain to build two destroyers for every additional large German submarine. Of even more moment was the possible political effect; he "feared that public opinion might take the view that Germany was definitely against us and that there was no hope of any real appeasement."

The Naval Agreement required discussion prior to exercise of the Germans' right to increase their submarine strength to parity with Britain's, and on De-

---

* In his memoirs Bonnet denied that Schmidt was present, but Schmidt's memorandum of the conversation adequately establishes his participation.

† Ribbentrop's French was only fair, and it is possible that Bonnet said something which the German misunderstood.

‡ As described in Chapter 10, under the agreement the Germans agreed to limit their submarine tonnage to 45 per cent of the total tonnage of the British Commonwealth, unless a situation arose which, in the German Government's opinion, made it necessary for Germany to build up to parity.

cember 30 a British delegation headed by Vice-Admiral A. B. Cunningham, the Deputy Chief of Staff, met in Berlin with a group led by Rear Admiral Otto Schniewind, Chief of Staff of the Naval War Staff. It was a courteous and even friendly conference of naval professionals, but on the issues the Germans were adamant. Cunningham predicted that disclosure of the German plan "would have a profoundly disturbing effect on public opinion," and asked that a lesser increase be specified. Schniewind replied "that the estimation of absolute requirements in the submarine category was not a matter of arithmetical calculation, but one mainly dependent on political issues. The Führer, after full consideration, and bearing in mind that the German Navy was the only Navy now subject to quantitative limitation, had decided to make full use of all the opportunities allowed by the Anglo-German Agreement."

This "political" reason was plainly not within the intendment of the agreement, but there was nothing the British could do about it. They fell back on a request that, since the Germans could not build up to 100 per cent of the British strength except over the course of several years, the public announcement should specify yearly percentage increases. But agreement even on this point proved impossible, and the delegations parted with the understanding that no details of the German proposals would be published "at present."*

Thus the year 1938 ended with still another British effort at compromise encountering nonnegotiable German demands. Appeasement was coming apart at the seams,† and the best one could say about "peace for our time" was that it had survived into 1939.

3

Ominous as were the Fuehrer's speeches, the anti-Semitic riots, and the enlarged U-boat program, behind the scenes there were even more dangerous developments during the last quarter of 1938. Hitler's October 21 directive to the Wehrmacht to prepare to smash "the remainder of the Czech State" was accompanied by a political strategy directed to the same end, in which Slovakia would take over the destructive role previously fulfilled by the Sudetenland. On October 7, Ernst Woermann submitted a memorandum to Hitler discussing the

---

* An agreed communiqué was published in the German and British press on February 3, 1939.

† There were other disquieting emanations from Germany during the last six weeks of 1938. On November 24, Oswald Pirow, the South African Minister of Defense, visited Hitler at the Berghof. When Pirow described the Jewish situation as the main obstacle to good Anglo-German relations and rather naïvely begged his host to make some kind of gesture of co-operation in resolving it which would strengthen Chamberlain's hand against the "war party" in England, Hitler reacted with a long tirade against Britain and the Jews, ending with a threat that "if Britain rearmed, he would rearm twice as fast." Pirow went on to Rome, where he urged Mussolini to "mediate between Hitler and the Jews," causing the Duce to describe his guest to Ciano as "an outstanding example of the rapidity with which a race living in another latitude could deteriorate."

On December 8, Baldwin spoke at a meeting to launch the "Lord Baldwin Fund for Jewish Refugees." Immediately there were violent attacks on Baldwin in the German press and, when Chamberlain included a defense of Baldwin in the advance text of his speech to the Foreign Press Association on December 13, Dirksen and the other invited German guests declined to attend, on the ground that Chamberlain would discuss "subjects which entailed criticism of German affairs."

merits, from the German standpoint, of an independent Slovakia, as compared to an autonomous Slovakia within the Czech, Hungarian, or Polish nations. Woermann concluded that: "An independent Czechoslovakia would be constitutionally weak and would therefore best further the German need for penetration and settlement in the east."

Overt German support for Slovakian independence, on the heels of Munich, would have been too brazen a repudiation of its terms. Since Hitler had no desire to strengthen Poland or Hungary, Slovakia's autonomy within the sovereign ambit of Prague appeared as the best immediate solution, and that remained Germany's official policy for the next four months.

However, clandestine aid was soon given to the Slovakian independence movement, which developed in the wake of Munich. In mid-October, Goering received the Slovakian Minister of the Interior, Ferdinand Durcansky, who declared that in Slovakia the "Jewish problem will be solved as in Germany," and that the Slovaks "want full independence, with very close political, economic, and military ties with Germany." Goering's reaction was that "efforts of the Slovaks for independence should be suitably supported," since "a Czech State minus Slovakia is even more completely at our mercy" and German air bases in Slovakia would be "very important for operations in the East."

Thereafter Himmler's Security Service gave secret financial support to the Slovakian independence partisans. On December 17, Hitler issued a second directive to the Wehrmacht on "liquidation" of Czechoslovakia, which made it clear that this was to be brought about by political means and threats rather than force:

> This operation is to be prepared on the assumption that no appreciable resistance is to be expected.
> Outwardly it must be quite clear that it is a peaceful action and not a warlike undertaking.
> Therefore the action must be carried out *only* with peacetime forces, without strengthening from mobilization. . . .
> Likewise, the army units for the march-in must generally not leave their regular stations until the night before the crossing of the frontier and must not, as was previously planned, deploy on the frontier. . . .

Late in November, another target appeared on the Wehrmacht's list, by way of a Fuehrer order that "preparations are also to be made for the occupation of the Free State of Danzig by German troops." The operation was to be carried out from East Prussia with naval support, and using Army units other than those earmarked for the taking of Memel, "so that both operations can, if necessary, take place simultaneously." It was stipulated that the operation must be conducted as a surprise raid, taking advantage of a favorable political situation, and not as a war against Poland.

Thus before the end of 1938 the Wehrmacht had three operations for territorial acquisition in preparation. It is clear that Hitler expected to carry out all three without precipitating a major war. But there was danger that, even if Poland were to be confronted with a sudden *fait accompli* in Danzig, she might declare war, and therefore Hitler ordered intensified work on the eastern fortifications.

These designs were held very secret, but of course they were known to Halder and others in the OKH. The "Halder plot" was dead, and no objections were raised. Adam and Beck were both retired in October, the former of his own volition, the latter because Hitler required it. Neither Witzleben (who succeeded to Adam's command in the west) nor Halder saw the slightest hope for resistance after Hitler's Munich triumph.

While the Nazi press was shrilly denouncing the British for daring to rearm, in Germany the pace was redoubled. There was no worrying about financial stability or the effect of rearmament on British opinion. On October 14, Goering called in his chief economic subordinates and announced that Hitler had ordered him "to carry out a gigantic program compared to which previous achievements are insignificant." Within the shortest possible time "the Air Force is to be increased fivefold," the Navy should expedite its construction schedule, and "the Army should procure large amounts of weapons at the fastest rate, particularly heavy artillery and tanks." To be sure, Goering was prone to exaggerate, but certainly Germany was making much better use of its time than Britain, where Hore-Belisha and Gort were still struggling to convince Chamberlain that their country needed any army at all.

4

The accelerated pace of German armament was realized in London, but there is no available evidence that there was any knowledge of Hitler's secret directives. In the light of post-Versailles history, of course, Danzig and Memel were predictable targets of German aggrandizement.

But if there was no intelligence of these matters, there soon were reports of other and even more alarming German designs. In mid-December, Ivone Kirkpatrick was recalled from Berlin to serve under Strang in the Foreign Office. He reported having been told by a retired German official closely acquainted with the now-retired General Beck that Hitler, enraged against Britain, had decided to attack her in March, starting with a surprise air raid on London.

Chamberlain took the report seriously enough to summon an emergency meeting of ministers and staff the following morning, December 17. The Prime Minister declared that Hitler's "next move" was more likely to be eastward, but thought it possible "that they had this plan so as to give us a knock if we showed signs of interfering with Hitler's eastern ambitions." The service departments and Sir John Anderson were directed to report on the steps which might be taken to improve Britain's defensive position in March, and on December 22 the CID directed the acceleration of air raid precautions and provision of antiaircraft defenses.

In fact Hitler had no such plan and Kirkpatrick's story may have been a plant. The episode was important, however, because for the first time since Munich Chamberlain was genuinely worried about the possibility of imminent war. This boded well for expanded rearmament, as Pownall (who was present at these meetings) recorded in his diary:

Again a "flap" that will be very useful to us, it is bound to loosen the purse strings a little and to ease the dreadful constipation caused by our financial system. On these waves of fear we get propelled a little further forward each time, sinking into the lazy hollows of the waves in between times. If we have enough of these crises we may even be able to get a properly equipped field force without the Chancellor, Sam Hoare and such like being aware of it.

Pownall did not have long to wait for the next "crisis." Chamberlain, Halifax, and their party returned in mid-January from their visit to Rome, to confront a basketfull of secret intelligence reports,* many of which indicated that (contrary to the Prime Minister's prior impression) Hitler might well decide to attack first in the west rather than the east, and some of which pointed to the Netherlands as the initial victim. Thus began what became known, in circles privy to secret intelligence, as the "Holland scare" of January 1939. On January 18 the Cabinet, apprized of this new threat, referred the matter to the Foreign Policy Committee for a prompt evaluation and report.

The committee met on the twenty-third, with the benefit of analyses by Cadogan, Vansittart, Strang, Jebb, and Kirkpatrick. A covering memorandum by Halifax admonished the members not to take the individual reports too seriously, but emphasized their collective thrust as pointing toward a German attack in the west in order to head off Anglo-French rearmament. Cadogan stressed the danger to Britain of a German occupation of Holland:

> It has always been held that the independence of the Low Countries is a vital interest to this country, and in these days of air and submarine warfare this seems to be more than ever true, and I should have thought that we should be bound immediately to do all that lay in our power to prevent or hinder it. . . . Once in command of Holland and the Dutch coast, Germany would aspire to dictate terms to us, under threat, regarding the colonies, and she might at the same time bribe Poland and perhaps other countries with promises of colonial loot.

Strang's paper portrayed the difficult military and political situation which would arise if Germany attacked Holland but not France or Belgium: "An attack on Holland would not, of course, bring any obligations into play, since neither the United Kingdom nor France nor Belgium are pledged to assist Holland. But Great Britain has a traditional interest in the integrity of the Low Countries, and it is for her rather than for France to take action for their defence." He observed that there had been no discussions with the "secretive" Dutch General Staff, and that the British Minister at The Hague, Sir G. N. M. Bland, had suggested an effort to open the door to interstaff talks.

Halifax opened the committee meeting with a warning that the information in the intelligence reports came from sources sufficiently credible so that "it could not be ignored and we must proceed as if it were true." He urged that "we should communicate our views to President Roosevelt and also tell him what

---

* Many of these reports emanated from the Secret Intelligence Service, otherwise designated M.I.6., the head of which was always referred to by those in the know as "C" after the first chief of the service, Admiral Cummings. In 1938 the chief was Admiral Sinclair.

action we proposed to take"—a proposal which, had he heard it, would certainly have given Anthony Eden grim satisfaction.

Oliver Stanley referred to a suggestion in Cadogan's memorandum that, if Germany "picked a quarrel" with Holland, Britain should "be ready at once to propose some form of arbitration," and suggested that Roosevelt be asked "whether he would agree if the necessity arose to appoint an arbitrator." Chamberlain and Hoare threw cold water on this idea, and the Prime Minister raised the question whether the United States should be told that Britain would intervene if Holland were invaded. Cadogan observed that, if Britain failed to step in, France and Belgium would also stay on the sidelines, whereas they would probably agree to join in if Britain would also. Halifax remarked a "growing feeling" in France that Britain would limit herself to the air and sea, "leaving it to the French to fight on the land," prompting Chamberlain to declare that a large British Expeditionary Force was out of the question in any event.

Hoare proposed that the Government should issue a statement declaring the intergrity of The Netherlands a "vital British interest." No conclusion was reached; the discussion grew diffuse, and the conferees passed on to other subjects, having decided nothing except to inform the Dominions and draft a message to Roosevelt.

The Chiefs of Staff met on January 23 and 24 to prepare advisory papers for the Cabinet on "the strategical importance of Holland to ourselves, and what steps we could take, if any, to assist her to defend herself." Newall, counseled by Slessor, strongly opposed any public declaration of support for Holland, on the ground that the evidence of Germany's aggressive intentions was questionable, and a statement might "give the German Government another excuse for working up resentment against us."*

The Chiefs' paper on *whether* to intervene declared: "On purely strategical grounds . . . if our preparations were reasonably complete we should have no doubt in advising that the integrity of Holland constitutes so vital a strategical interest to this country that we should intervene in the event of aggression by Germany on Holland." Despite this, the Chiefs declared themselves unable "to submit a definite recommendation in favor of intervention until we have considered what action we could take in present circumstances."

Their second document was directed to that question. It concluded that the Dutch could only slightly delay the German forces; that if Belgium and France remained neutral, Britain could do nothing that would "materially delay the German advance"; and that if Belgium and France fought, they nevertheless would send no troops to Holland, and so the B.E.F. should be sent to France rather than Holland. In short, nothing could be done to save the Netherlands from German occupation. The dilemma was total, for "we could not afford strategically to let Holland and her colonies go," but "If we were compelled to enter

* Slessor had reminded Newall of the "May crisis," when false reports of German troop movements had triggered British warnings that "aroused great resentment in Germany, and there is reason to believe that it was an important factor in making up Hitler's mind to resort to extreme measures in September."

such a war in the near future we should be confronted with a position more serious than the Empire has ever faced before." Nevertheless:

> . . . failure to intervene would have such moral and other repercussions as would seriously undermine our position in the eyes of the Dominions and the world in general. We might thus be deprived of support in a subsequent struggle. . . . In our view it is hardly an exaggeration to say that failure to take up such a challenge would place Germany in a predominant position in Europe and correspondingly lower our prestige throughout the world. We have as we see it, no choice but to regard it as a direct challenge to our security.

This came very close to saying that Britain was virtually at Germany's mercy, and made gloomy reading for the Cabinet meeting on January 25. Opening the discussion, Halifax undertook to reassure his colleagues that "there is no ground for extreme pessimism, or for a belief that we shall, in the near future, inevitably be the victims of a German attack." He then gave a summary of the intelligence information, reported that the letter to Roosevelt authorized by the Foreign Policy Committee had already been sent, and read some extracts.* In conclusion, Halifax laid before the Cabinet several questions. Was the integrity of the Netherlands a "vital interest of this country"? What, if any, communication should be had with the French, Belgian, and Dutch governments? Should any public declaration of Britain's interest in Holland's integrity be made?

None of these questions was decided. Chamberlain allowed that the intelligence reports could not be ignored, but he was "a long way from accepting all this information." There was no need for concern about Hitler's speech on the thirtieth, as Dirksen had given assurances that it was directed to economic and trade matters. Chamberlain agreed that, if Germany attacked Holland, Britain must intervene, but there was no reason to give a commitment unrequested by the Dutch which "in certain circumstances might be embarrassing." Maugham inanely suggested telling Hitler that Britain would now accept the disarmament proposals he had made in 1936, after the Rhineland re-entry. There was general agreement that all possible acceleration of defense preparations had already been effected, and the whole problem was passed back to the Foreign Policy Committee, with an injunction against any public statement until they had studied the last report from the Chiefs of Staff.

The service ministers and chiefs of staff were also present when the committee met the next day. Halifax opened by "warmly assenting" to the conclusions of the Chiefs, and said it was now a question of what practical steps to take and whether to announce the British attitude toward aggression against Holland. Newall at once reminded Halifax that the Chiefs "had refrained from giving any precise answer to the question whether we ought to intervene."

Taking the cue, Chamberlain referred to a passage in the Chiefs' report suggesting that the Dutch, realizing the hopelessness of resistance, "might think

---

* Much of the letter, dated January 24, 1939, was adapted from Cadogan's memorandum for the Foreign Policy Committee. It mentioned the arbitration idea but did not suggest that the President undertake to choose the arbitrators. The final paragraph suggested that, if the President were disposed to make any public announcement, it be done before January 30, when Hitler was to address the Reichstag. On the twenty-ninth Hull informed the British chargé that the President would not reply.

it safer to bow to *force majeure,* to avoid warlike action, and to acquiesce, even unwillingly, in German domination"—the plain implication being that in such an event Britain could do nothing and would be in an embarassing position if she had previously committed herself to intervention. Kingsley Wood and Stanhope thought this a possible eventuality, while Halifax, Inskip, and MacDonald held that the Dutch would certainly fight. Chamberlain cut short the speculation and declared that the committee would have to act on the assumption that the Dutch would resist a German invasion. What then?

Halifax answered firmly that Britain would have to intervene, for the reasons given by the Chiefs, and Chamberlain, Simon, and MacDonald expressed agreement. The Prime Minister then said that, if a public statement were to be made, it should be in the Commons when it reconvened on February 2. Kingsley Wood (no doubt persuaded by Newall) opposed making any statement; no decision was reached. The committee finally agreed that, if the Netherlands suffered and resisted a German attack, Britain must go to war with Germany; that Halifax should at once open diplomatic discussions with France and Holland on the matter, and the Dutch should be sounded out informally; and that Anglo-French staff conversations should be initiated, covering "all likely fields of operation" in the event that both Germany and Italy were enemy belligerents.

Halifax immediately set things in motion in Paris, Brussels, and The Hague, and on February 1 he reported results to the Cabinet. Brussels was determined to remain neutral and not serve again as a battleground for Europe, but the Belgians would defend themselves if attacked. The Hague was noncommittal and would do all possible to avoid war, but Bland (who had been at The Hague for only a few months) had given his opinion that, if suddenly attacked by Germany, "the Dutch would fight literally to the last ditch." The French Government agreed that an attack on Holland should be a *casus belli,* and suggested that this should also apply to Switzerland.

While these diplomatic exchanges were in process, the immediate tension over Holland started to ease. Hitler's Reichstag speech on the thirtieth was, as Dirksen had predicted, chiefly concerned with economic matters. The Fuehrer once again denounced Churchill, Eden, and Duff Cooper (adding Harold Ickes, who was flattered by his inclusion), and blamed most of the world's ills on the Jews. But he thanked Chamberlain for assisting in the Munich settlement, labeled the colonial question "in no sense a problem which would cause a war," and declared that he "looked forward to a long period of peace."

Halifax warned the Cabinet that Hitler's speech gave no excuse for relaxation, but there were no further signs that he was about to attack in the west, and Holland ceased to be the focus of apprehension. In fact the Fuehrer was harboring no such designs, and the "Holland scare" proved to be just that and no more.

But whereas Kirkpatrick's bombing story in December gave rearmament only a slight nudge, the "Holland scare" gave it a mighty push, of which the Army was the principle beneficiary. On December 21, largely owing to Newall's opposition, Gort had been unable to push through the Chiefs of Staff the Army's request for full equipment for the two-division field force. Even at the beginning of the "Holland scare" (January 18) Newall was still opposed to making any commitment to send troops to France; he told his fellow-Chiefs that the needs of the Navy and Air Force were so great that the country's industry could not also meet the Army's demands.

A week later, with the scare at its peak, Newall saw the light, and the Chiefs finally approved the "Role of the Army" recommendations which they had been holding since mid-December. As Pownall describes this meeting and the CID meeting the next day (the twenty-sixth):

> The C.O.S. also took the "Role of the Army" and, I am delighted to say, backed up all our recommendations. The C.A.S. [Newall] was a very doubtful factor at first, but came round well in the end, I fancy not so much because he really believes in it—or likes it—as because Backhouse [Chief of the Naval Staff, successor to Chatfield] came down so strongly on our side. The Cabinet are to take it at a special meeting next week and I have considerable hope that in their present frame of mind, it will go through—which would be a real triumph.
>
> The current frame of mind was well illustrated at the C.I.D. on Thursday [the twenty-sixth] when Hore-Belisha was strongly supported in his demands for a Ministry of Supply by Ernest Brown, Kingsley Wood and Stanley.* The urge is partly political . . . but there are good arguments as well. They really think we are close to a war, and in war we must have the Ministry, so set it up now if only to clear the ground and start the machinery ticking over. . . .

The much-debated Ministry of Supply was still several months away, and at the special Cabinet on February 2 the "Role of the Army" scored only a partial victory. Relaxation from the "Holland scare," Pownall grumbled, "did not serve well our 'Role of the Army' paper" in the Cabinet. Hore-Belisha had shrewdly framed his request as not for enlargement of the Army, but for acceleration in equipping existing units, not merely for "defensive" warfare, but with sophisticated modern weaponry for waging "offensive" warfare by European major power standards.

Chamberlain nevertheless characterized the request as "rather a new conception." To be sure, "an unanswerable case could be made out for increased armaments in every area, if the financial aspect of the proposals was ignored. But finance could not be ignored . . ." It was the same old song from the same old singer, and Simon shortly made it a duet, stressing that £81 million was about equal to the entire Army estimate of £82 million for 1937–38. Fortunately, Halifax came to Hore-Belisha's rescue, observing that the present situation was "wholly abnormal" and, with an acridity unusual for him, that he would rather be bankrupt in peace than beaten in war. But in the upshot Hore-Belisha got only £16 million for training equipment for the Territorial Army, while consideration of the major items was postponed.

This recession, however, proved short-lived in spite of the fact that the Holland scare was dying of malnutrition. On February 10, Hore-Belisha met

---

* According to Hore-Belisha's diary, also by Halifax.

with Chamberlain, Simon, and Lord Chatfield (who had replaced Inskip*), and persuaded them to allow £13 million to equip the two regular infantry divisions for "continental" warfare. Pownall, whose diary is generally replete with scathing references to Hore-Belisha,† now waxed rapturous over the War Minister's "gallant" fight "for the Field Force, indeed for the Army as a whole."

Hore-Belisha did even better on February 22, when the Cabinet approved the Army's major demands, to the tune of £64.6 million. Pownall hailed "A historic week from my own, and the Army, point of view." The Prime Minister himself made the presentation, declaring that "there was no alternative to the course proposed," and explaining the reasons for his change of heart:

> Hitherto the Cabinet had not been asked to agree to any commitment that [the two regular] divisions would be sent to the Continent. The situation, however, had been changed by the events of the previous Autumn, and France now had to face the possibility of meeting a far stronger German force. There was also a feeling in France that we should not be playing an adequate part unless we made contribution on land . . . Not only did this involve a higher scale of equipment and reserves for the forces to be dispatched to the Continent, but we must also take steps to ensure that the first echelon could be dispatched as quickly as possible.

Of course, these circumstances had been apparent since the previous October, yet up to this time fiscal factors had overcome Chamberlain's own intuitive distrust of the French Army. What finally swung him must have been continuing pressure from Halifax and the service chiefs, and a realization that even if Hitler did not attack Holland now he could do so at any time, and that neither France, cut off by neutral Belgium, nor Britain, impotent on the ground, could do anything to stop the Luftwaffe from thus halving the distance between its airfields and the heart of England.

Authorization for a well-armed expeditionary force of modest size was not the only beneficial consequence of the Holland scare. It also gave the necessary impetus for long overdue staff talks with the French, and hastened the advent of a Ministry of Supply. On the diplomatic front February also saw final recognition in London and Paris that they were mutually committed to the defense, not only of their two countries, but of the small nations bordering Germany on the west and southwest—the Netherlands, Belgium, and Switzerland.

These developments were not the result of the moves that Hitler was actually

---

* In January, Chamberlain had carried out a minor Cabinet reorganization. Inskip took the Dominions Office (Malcolm MacDonald remained at the Colonial Office) and the troublesome Winterton was dropped and replaced as Chancellor of the Duchy of Lancaster by Morrison, who acted as Chatfield's deputy and spokesman in the Commons, and who was succeeded at Agriculture and Fisheries by a newcomer, Sir Reginald Dorman Smith, past president of the Farmers Union and, according to Pownall, a strong supporter of the Army. Chatfield's selection did not meet with universal approval; his ability was generally acknowledged, but Harvey expressed the view of some that "professionals do not make good Cabinet Ministers," and criticized Chatfield as "the great defeatist, besides being very reactionary in sympathies—pro-Italian, pro-Franco."

† For a more charitable assessment of Hore-Belisha as Secretary of State for War, see the work by Pownall's then deputy, Major General Sir John Kennedy, *The Business of War* (1958), pp. 4–6, 131.

planning, for they remained unknown in London and Paris. Thus it came about that Britain's first moves to regain the power to make war on the European continent were the immediate consequence not of what Hitler had done or intended to do to other countries, but of false reports of imminent peril to Britain herself.

Munich had, to be sure, laid the bed of circumstance which brought about these things, but it did not teach Chamberlain the lesson he needed. Even as he finally yielded to the Army's pleas, he was writing (on February 19, 1939) to his sisters in a vein which showed no loss of faith in his own indispensability to the preservation of peace:

> I myself, am going about with a lighter heart than I have had for many a long day. All the information I get seems to point in the direction of peace and I repeat once more that I believe we have at last got on top of the dictators. Of course that doesn't mean I want to bully them . . .
>
> I think we ought to be able to establish excellent relations with Franco . . . and then, if the Italians are not in too bad a temper we might get Franco-Italian conversations going and if they were reasonably amicable we might advance towards disarmament. At any rate that's how I see things working round, and if I were given three or four more years I believe I really might retire with a quiet mind . . .

5

During the week preceding the Holland scare Chamberlain, in company with Halifax, Cadogan, and lesser lights from Downing Street and the Foreign Office, made his last foreign journey of appeasement. His hesitation early in December, following the anti-French outburst in the Italian Chamber, was dispelled by Lord Perth's warning that Mussolini "would regard the cancellation of the visit as a personal insult and this is a thing he never forgets or forgives." Furthermore, news of the impending visit had already leaked to the press.

Halifax explained to the Cabinet on December 21 that it was hoped to improve relations with the Duce, but that "the central fact of the visit was that a visit of the Prime Minister to Italy would go far to influence Italian public opinion in the right direction." Spain and French-Italian relations were likely to be the main subjects of discussion, and "our main principle should be 'nothing for nothing.'" There would be "no concession to Signor Mussolini unless he would help us to obtain the *détente* which it was the object of our policy to attain."

The Prime Minister struck a different note. He "did not object to the Foreign Secretary's phrase 'nothing for nothing,' but its complement was 'something for something.'" Chamberlain was "undertaking the visit with the definite purpose of securing Signor Mussolini's good offices in Berlin" and in the hope that the Duce "could be persuaded to prevent Herr Hitler from carrying out some 'mad dog' act."

The British party left by train on January 10 and stopped that evening in Paris for a brief meeting with Daladier, Bonnet, and Léger. The Premier "made it quite clear that the French Government would not make any concessions at all to Italy," and the British gave reassurance that they would give Mussolini no encouragement in this regard. They reached Rome the following afternoon, and after due formalities Chamberlain and Halifax met with Mussolini and Ciano at the Palazzo Venezia.

There was much affability, but small accomplishment, as the conversation glanced lightly over Spain, disarmament, the Anglo-Italian Agreement, and Jewish refugees. Mussolini complained about French policy in Spain, and Chamberlain gave voice to his disappointment at Berlin's post-Munich attitude and actions. No problem was really probed, and the conferees adjourned for the evening festivities.

Mussolini and Ciano were not impressed. They smirked openly behind the Englishmen's backs, and after the state dinner the Duce confided to his son-in-law: "These men are not made of the same stuff as Francis Drake and the other magnificent adventurers who created the Empire. They are, after all, the tired sons of a long line of rich men. And they will lose the Empire."

Cadogan, for quite other reasons, was not satisfied with the progress of the talks, and the following morning told the Prime Minister that "we must . . . get Musso on subject of Hitler and latter's intentions. We must take away from here some assurance that Musso will try to restrain Hitler, and leave behind us here the idea that, if Hitler is *not* restrained, there'll be a blow-up. P.M. I think quite ready for this but must, of course, choose his moment."

The moment came, but the Duce would not play. The leading four met again that afternoon and, after Mussolini had reiterated that there could be no progress in French-Italian relations "until after the Spanish affair was settled," he inquired "whether there was any point which the British Minister wished to raise." Chamberlain took the plunge, acknowledging that the point was "of some delicacy" and setting forth in detail his disappointment and alarm over German actions which were "giving rise to great deal of anxiety and doubt, not only in his mind but all over Europe." He stressed the pace of German rearmament and the rumors of impending German military moves, and concluded: "What he would like to know was whether the Duce could give him any assurances that could do something to mitigate his anxiety on this very important matter."

Mussolini pondered, and replied slowly, but gave not an inch. German rearmament was "only for defensive purposes and Hitler desired a long period of peace"; the rumors were the work of "propagandists"; a German attack in the west was "absolutely out of the question"; as to the scope and pace of German rearmament, Hitler had to take account of possible anti-German coalitions and warmongers like Léon Blum. Frustrated, Chamberlain turned to disarmament and the promised guarantee to Czechoslovakia, and after a desultory interchange the leaders finally settled the momentous problem of a procedure for fixing the boundary between Ethiopa and British Somaliland.

With that the formal discussions ended, but Chamberlain returned to the charge in a private conversation with Mussolini after dinner that evening. The Prime Minister was wholly ineffective; he complained about German press attacks on "the fighting qualities of democracies" (apparently in an effort to carry out Cadogan's advice), and the conversation ended in an argument about control of the press, in which the journalist-dictator outtalked the merchant-minister.

The British took much comfort from the enthusiasm with which Chamberlain was greeted by the Italian crowds; Halifax and Harvey thought it "certainly proved that the Italian people are on our side." But the Fascist leaders were unimpressed. Reflecting on the discussions, Ciano noted "the deep preoccupation of the English with their confrontation with Germany," and wrote further: "German rearmament weighs on them like a cloak of lead. They would make any sacrifice to see the future clearly. . . . The English don't want to fight. They will try to give way as slowly as possible, but they don't want to fight. Mussolini defended Germany with great loyalty, and was air-tight [*ermetico*] on the Fuehrer's future projects. The talks with the English are finished: nothing of consequence." And he quoted approvingly the British journalist who wrote that "the game ended nothing to nothing."

Overall, the talks reflected an unsuccessful effort by Mussolini to weaken British support for the French, and an equally unsuccessful attempt by Chamberlain to loosen the bond between Duce and Fuehrer. The Prime Minister's task was hopeless from the start, in part owing to circumstances of which he was unaware at the time.

As the Italians had departed from the Munich conference, Ribbentrop had handed Ciano the draft of a project for transforming the tripartite Anti-Comintern Pact into an outright military alliance. Such a step had been proposed to Ribbentrop in July 1938 by General Hiroshi Oshima, then the military attaché in Berlin, and was much favored by the "military" group in the Japanese Government. Ribbentrop and Oshima worked out a draft during the summer of 1938, and the general idea of a military alliance with the Axis powers was approved by the Japanese Cabinet in August.

Late in October, Ribbentrop came to Rome, and on the twenty-eighth he discussed the project with Mussolini and Ciano, telling them that Hitler thought it "a useful and prudent step" as a counterbalance to the Franco-Soviet pact and the close relations between France and Britain. The Duce agreed that "this alliance ought to be drawn up," but declared that the Italian people were not yet ready for such a step and declined to commit himself to "the moment at which the Pact ought to be made."

On New Year's Day of 1939, Mussolini informed Ciano that he was now prepared to enter into the alliance, and that he wanted the signing to take place during the last ten days of January. Ciano promptly informed Ribbentrop, explaining that:

> The real reasons which have led the Duce to accept your proposal at this point are as follows:
> 1. The existence—now proved—of a military pact between France and Great Britain;*
> 2. The acceptance of the possibility of war in reponsible French circles;

---

* There was as yet no such pact in a formal sense, but the Holland scare was shortly to produce its equivalent.

3. The military preparations of the United States which are intended to furnish men and above all materials to the Western democracies in case of necessity.

Such being the case, the Duce considers that it is now necessary for the Anti-Communist triangle to become a system. . . .

On January 10 Ribbentrop handed to Attolico a letter to Ciano stating that "an exact draft of the pact and of an additional secret protocol" had been given to Oshima (who had meanwhile been appointed ambassador) and Attolico. Ribbentrop's letter expressed the hope that agreement would quickly be reached, proposed that the document be signed on January 28, and invited Ciano to visit Berlin for that purpose. It must have reached Ciano at about the time the British arrived in Rome.

The fact that Berlin, Tokyo, and Rome were discussing a strengthening of the Anti-Comintern Pact had for some weeks been known to the British Government, both from reports of their ambassador to Japan, Sir Robert Craigie, and from secret sources. But London knew nothing of Mussolini's decision of January 1 or of Ribbentrop's proposal to carry out the project on January 28. Had matters developed as Mussolini and Hitler were planning, Chamberlain's visit to Rome would have been followed barely two weeks later by the announcement of a military alliance of Germany, Italy, and Japan.* The timing could hardly have been better arranged for the purpose of making fools of the British.

Blissfully ignorant of what his hosts had in mind, Chamberlain departed Rome at noon on January 14, happy with the popular reaction and the Duce's friendly farewell. The British colony was again in attendance, and as the train started to move, they burst into "For He's a Jolly Good Fellow," causing a bemused Duce to ask Dino Grandi: "What is this canzonetta?"

Writing to his sister on the fifteenth, Chamberlain declared: "I have achieved all I expected to get, and more, and I am satisfied that the journey has definitely strengthened the chances of peace." In Cabinet on the eighteenth he was more cautious and spoke at length about the "heartfelt, spontaneous" welcome he had been given "in Rome society" and "by the Italian people," the exhibitions he had witnessed, and the personality of Mussolini. The Prime Minister then dealt rather cursorily with the business conversations and, concerning his previously disclosed "purpose of securing Signor Mussolini's good offices in Berlin", said:

". . . that he was convinced that Signor Mussolini and Herr Hitler could not be very sympathetic to each other, and that, although they had some interests in common, their interests were not identical. Further, he rather doubted whether Signor Mussolini was aware of Herr Hitler's plans. Accordingly he had on several occasions given Mussolini a chance to express his real feelings of Herr Hitler. He had never taken the opportunity offered him, but had remained absolutely loyal to Herr Hitler . . . at the time he had been

* By coincidence, the Italian and Japanese governments simultaneously reversed their roles. On January 4 the Konoye cabinet resigned, and there was sharp division of opinion within the new Hiranuma cabinet with respect to the scope of the proposed pact, in particular whether it should be directed exclusively against Communist Russia or, as Hitler and Mussolini wanted, be general in its application. The first indications of Japanese hesitation reached Berlin on January 13. The Tripartite Pact was not signed until September 27, 1940.

somewhat disappointed at this attitude, but on reflection he thought that it reflected credit on Signor Mussolini's character.

Disillusionment came swiftly. Already on January 17 the London *News Chronicle* had published a report that, shortly before the British visit, Ciano had told the Japanese Ambassador that Italy was ready to sign a tripartite alliance, while Japan was hanging back. At the Foreign Policy Committee meeting on the twenty-third, Halifax mentioned the probability that the Anti-Comintern Pact might be transformed "into a formal alliance against any third power, not necessarily Russia." And on the twenty-fifth the Foreign Secretary told the Cabinet that "two days ago we received information from an absolutely certain source" that Italy had agreed to a German proposal for such a move, but that Japan was undecided.

On February 15 the Cabinet listened to a reassuring report from Craigie that the Tokyo government had rejected the Italo-German plan. But what London did not know was that on February 8 Mussolini, irked at the Japanese delays, told Ciano that Germany and Italy should conclude an alliance "solely to confront the Anglo-French joint forces, but without any anti-English or anti-American flavor." It was the germ of what would become the Italo-German "Pact of Steel" the following May.

6

In Germany, there was little conspicuous activity during the first two months of 1939 as Hitler, moving leisurely between Berlin, Munich, the Berghof and occasionally other places, confined his official activities largely to party and other domestic matters. There was, however, a portent in January when Hjalmar Schacht made a last effort to exercise his influence as President of the Reichsbank by submitting to Hitler a memorandum calling for curtailment of the enormous armament expenditures in order to avert a disastrous inflation. The result was his immediate dismissal from the Reichsbank, where he was replaced by the Nazi functionary Walther Funk.*

Beyond public view, Hitler kept up the grinding pressure on Prague. Furthermore, Poland was beginning to feel the pinch. In January, Colonel Beck came to the Berghof and was told by an overtly friendly Fuehrer that "Danzig was a German city" and "sooner or later it must return to the Reich." Beck departed with pessimistic forebodings, but on January 30, Hitler, in the Reichstag, declared that "the friendship between Germany and Poland has been one of the reassuring factors in the political life of Europe," and in the European diplomatic corridors there was little anxiety.

The first really ominous move in Berlin was the rejection, at the end of February, of the Anglo-French effort to implement the promised guarantee to Czechoslovakia. As we have seen, this too remained a diplomatic secret; Coulondre saw handwriting on the wall, but the egregious breach of faith made

---

* Schacht (widely regarded abroad as a German "moderate") retained the empty title Reichsminister without Portfolio, but he had lost all influence and ceased to play any effective part in Reich officialdom.

little impression in London, probably because nobody there was very keen about a guarantee, promised or not.

Hitler's rejection of the guarantee would have surprised Coulondre less had he known that on February 12 the Fuehrer had received Vojtech Tuka, a leading Slovak separatist spokesman, and after a rambling monologue had closed the interview by saying "it would be a comfort to him to know that Slovakia was independent." In fact, for some time two Nazi agents (Wilhelm Keppler and Ernst Woermann) experienced in the art had been stimulating and supporting the Slovakian separatist movement. By March the fruit was ripe, and on the thirteenth the Slovakian leader, Josef Tiso, was summoned to Berlin. The Fuehrer was by now the Lord of Central Europe, and his edict was brief and blunt:

> It was not a question of days but of hours. If Slovakia wished to make herself independent, Hitler would support this endeavor and guarantee it. If she hesitated and did not wish to dissolve the connection with Prague, he would leave the destiny of Slovakia to the mercy of events, for which he was no longer responsible.

For the Slovaks, it was Hobson's choice. On March 14, the Slovakian diet in Bratislava declared its independence. Hungarian troops, by prearrangement between Hitler and Horthy, occupied Ruthenia, the eastern tip of Czechoslovakia.

While the Prague regime was being done to death, its aged President, Dr. Emil Hácha, was brought to Berlin to officiate at the funeral of his own state. After hours of harassment at the hands of Hitler, assisted by Goering, Ribbentrop, and Keitel, Hácha put his signature to a document incorporating Bohemia and Moravia in the Third Reich as a "protectorate."

Even before Hácha succumbed, German troops were within the protectorate-to-be. For the Wehrmacht, the occupation was no more than an exercise, and the only enemy the wintry weather. It was simply a matter of assembling and equipping the troops of the commands bordering Bohemia and Moravia for the short march into the rump state. General Johannes Blaskowitz, the new army group commander in Dresden, occupied Bohemia, and List took Moravia. Planes from Kesselring's, Sperrle's, and Loehr's air fleets demonstrated, and then settled on the Czech airfields.

This was the last of the Wehrmacht's *Blumenkriege,* but this time the flowers were lacking as well as the bullets. Silence and despair greeted Blaskowitz as his troops marched into Prague. Hitler was nervous about his own personal safety, and consulted Rommel, who was again in command of the escort battalion. The nerveless Rommel, however, advised his Fuehrer to "get into an open car and drive through the streets to the Hradschin without an escort."

The Fuehrer acted on Rommel's suggestion, to the astonishment and grudging admiration of friendly and hostile observers alike. From the Hradschin he issued on March 16, 1939, a formal decree establishing the protectorate. Autonomy in name was coupled with complete German control in fact. Neurath was taken out of cold storage and appointed "Reich Protector." As in the case of Austria, Himmler promptly moved in; this time his chosen representative was Konrad Henlein's former deputy, Karl Hermann Frank.

In Slovakia, domestic autonomy was not as completely crushed, but German military, diplomatic, and economic domination was assured. Under the "Treaty of Protection" of March 23, 1939, in return for a German guarantee to protect Slovakian independence and territory, Germany secured unlimited rights to garrison troops and build military installations. Slovakian military and diplomatic activities were to be conducted "in close agreement" with Germany. A confidential protocol to the treaty laid the basis for extensive economic controls in line with German needs.

In "justification" of the final destruction of Czechoslovakia, German diplomacy reached a new level of cynical mendacity. Weizsaecker promptly instructed all German diplomats abroad to declare that the action had been taken "with the full agreement of the Czechoslovakian government." A few days later, when Coulondre came to protest the blatant violation of the Munich accord, Weizsaecker insultingly refused "to enter into any discussion of this matter" because, "Legally regarded, there was an agreement between the Führer and the Czechoslovakian President. The Czech President had come to Berlin according to his own desire and had immediately stated . . . that he wanted to place the fate of his country in the hands of the Führer." Weizsaecker scornfully suggested that the French Government should not "be more Catholic than the Pope and mix into affairs which rightly were settled between Berlin and Prague."

Indeed, Hitler had succeeded in making everyone but himself look ridiculous. At Munich, his internal opponents such as Beck and Adam were discredited because the Anglo-French opposition which they predicted failed to materialize. Instead, the English and French were bluffed into abandoning a position in support of the Czechs which they might have successfully maintained, in return for empty promises that Germany had no further territorial demands in Europe. They were left morally committed to guarantee a Czech state which was no longer militarily defensible or politically viable. The events of March 15, 1939, laid bare the utter worthlessness of the bargain they had made.

The German march into Czechoslovakia could hardly have come at a more awkward moment for the British Government. On March 8, Halifax told the Cabinet that Ashton-Gwatkin, who had recently visited Germany and spoken with Goering, Ribbentrop, and Funk, had found "a very friendly atmosphere" and "had gained the impression that no immediate adventures of a large type were contemplated." The following day Chamberlain, without informing Halifax or anyone at the Foreign Office, gave a "background" interview to the press in which he took an upbeat view of the international situation, suggesting that with the end of the Spanish Civil War in sight France and Italy might resolve their problems, that much might be hoped from a visit to Berlin by Oliver Stanley scheduled for March 17, and that a disarmament conference might meet before the end of the year. To Halifax's annoyance, the newspaper gave good play to these optimistic expressions on the tenth. That evening Hoare spoke in his London constituency and, at Chamberlain's suggestion, described the "golden age" of peace and prosperity that co-operation among the leaders of Britain, France, Germany, and Italy might bring.

Until that time the Government apparently had no warning of Hitler's impending move. But even as Hoare spoke, the Foreign Office received a message from Henderson relaying consular and military attaché reports that suggested the imminent possibility of a German coup.* Then on the eleventh General Sir Vernon Kell, the chief of the counterintelligence service, handed Cadogan reports that Germany would go into Czechoslovakia "in the next 48 hours." Confirmatory secret intelligence information came in during the next two days, and on the fourteenth Cadogan noted reports that the occupation would take place that night, with the comment "probably true."

Halifax conferred with the senior Foreign Office staff, and all agreed that: "Nothing can be done to stop Germany." From Paris came word from Phipps that Bonnet thought "the less we interfere in this crisis the better." That evening Halifax sent, via Henderson, a note to the German Government deploring "any action in Central Europe which would cause a setback to the growth of . . . confidence on which all improvement in the economic situation depends. . . ." —crass indeed, to pick out financial values as those mainly involved in the destruction of Czechoslovakia!

On March 15, the Cabinet held its regular morning meeting; Parliament was to assemble that afternoon. In both, the Prime Minister's main purpose was to escape from the "moral guarantee of Czechoslovakia," which, Inskip had told the Commons after Munich, was already in effect. In Cabinet he declared that "the fundamental fact was that the State whose frontiers we had undertaken to guarantee . . . had now broken up." But what had broken it up? Chamberlain had an answer: "It might, no doubt, be true that the disruption of Czechoslovakia had been largely engineered by Germany, but our guarantee was not a guarantee against the exercise of moral pressure." That was an odd way to describe the subversion and threats which the Nazis had used.

Halifax said that he wanted to "steer a middle course between pious and futile lectures and . . . the undesirability of leaving public opinion in any doubt as to our attitude to Germany's action in this matter." In pursuit of that aim, the Cabinet agreed to "postpone" Oliver Stanley's trip to Berlin, but rejected Halifax's proposal to recall Nevile Henderson for consultation as going too far. Chamberlain and Halifax then left to work on the Prime Minister's statement to be made in the Commons that afternoon.

As related at the end of the previous chapter, in the Commons Chamberlain relied chiefly on the Slovakian Diet's declaration of independence as the basis for his conclusion that the British Government was no longer bound by the guarantee which Inskip had acknowledged. He announced the postponement of Stanley's trip, described the German action as a violation of the "spirit" of the Munich Agreement, and noted the "regrettable circumstance that the Germans had for the first time departed from the policy of "only incorporating in the Reich neighboring masses of people of German race," by now occupying "territory inhabited by people with whom they have no racial connection."

These criticisms, however, were considerably softened by Chamberlain's re-

---

* On February 18, Henderson had reported his "definitive impression . . . that Herr Hitler does not contemplate any adventures at the moment and that all stories and rumours to the contrary are completely without real foundation."

CHAPTER 32–6

fusal "to associate myself today" with "charges of breach of faith bandied about. . . ." Furthermore, he concluded his statement by saying that although he did "bitterly regret what has now occurred," the country should not "on that account be deflected from our course," and that: "The aim of this Government is now, as it always has been, to substitute the method of discussion for the method of force in the settlement of differences." That passage, added by Chamberlain to the statement he had worked out with Halifax, Cadogan, and Wilson, sounded like a declaration that appeasement would continue. Cadogan, by now far from appeasement-minded, so construed it and in his diary noted: "Fatal!"

Two days later, giving a previously scheduled address in his native Birmingham, Chamberlain discarded a speech on domestic economic problems and delivered himself of sensationally different views on what had occurred. Angrily he recounted Hitler's assurances on which he had relied: "This is the last territorial claim which I have to make in Europe. I shall not be interested in the Czech State any more and I can guarantee it. We don't want any Czechs any more." Then, rhetorically:

How can these events this week be reconciled with those assurances which I have read out to you? . . . Who can fail to feel his heart go out in sympathy to the proud and brave people who have so suddenly been subjected to this invasion, whose liberties are curtailed, whose national independence has gone? What has become of this declaration of "No further territorial ambition"? What has become of the assurance "We don't want Czechs in the Reich"? . . . Is this the last attack upon a small state, or is it to be followed by others? Is this, in fact, a step in the direction of an attempt to dominate the world by force?

Chamberlain did not answer the questions, but declared that they would require "grave and serious consideration," and that his government would "review the position with that sense of responsibility which its gravity demands." His tone plainly implied that new policies were likely. What had caused such a change in forty-eight hours?

In a letter to his sister on the nineteenth, Chamberlain wrote: "As soon as I had time to think I saw that it was impossible to deal with Hitler after he had thrown all his own assurances to the winds." Not much time had been needed, for on the sixteenth, at lunch with Halifax and R. A. Butler, the Prime Minister had said: "I have decided that I cannot trust the Nazi leaders again."

Perhaps the stormy public reaction to Hitler's move, both at home and abroad, impressed him.* But he had great confidence in his own judgment, his appeasement policy had been based in large part on his belief that Hitler would fulfill his undertakings, and it seems most probable that the revolution in his outlook was due to his painful awakening to the enormity of his miscalculation, and the extent to which he and his country had been gulled. Since the basis of

---

* On March 16, Liddell Hart noted in his diary the "wave of hysteria" in the press. Even Sir Nevile Henderson, archchampion of appeasement, advised Halifax on the sixteenth that Britain should "consider what attitude to adopt toward a Government which has shown itself incapable of observing an agreement not six months old and which is apparently set on domination by force of the whole of the Danube basin."

the appeasement policy had been destroyed, as Chamberlain saw it, a new one had to be framed.

At a Cabinet meeting on March 18, Chamberlain drew the conclusions his Birmingham speech had implied:

> The Prime Minister said that up till a week ago we had proceeded on the assumption that we should be able to continue with our policy of getting on to better terms with the Dictator powers, and that although those powers had aims, these aims were limited. . . .
>
> The Prime Minister said he had now come definitely to the conclusion that Herr Hitler's attitude made it impossible to continue to negotiate on the old basis with the Nazi regime. . . . No reliance could be placed on any of the assurances given by the Nazi leaders. . . .
>
> The Prime Minister said that it was on the basis of this conclusion, and after consultation with the Foreign Secretary, and others of his colleagues who were immediately available, that he had made his speech at Birmingham. . . .
>
> The Prime Minister said that he regarded his speech at Birmingham as a challenge to Germany on the issue whether or not Germany intended to dominate Europe by force. It followed that if Germany took another step in the direction of dominating Europe, she would be accepting the challenge. . . . He agreed, therefore, with the Foreign Secretary's view that if Germany was to proceed with this course after warning had been given, we had no alternative but to take on the challenge. . . .

The Cabinet "warmly approved" the Birmingham speech. "Appeasement" had ceased to be the British Government's declared policy. But what would replace it, and would the new one perpetuate any of the content of the now discredited word?

7

Whether "appeasement" was really dead or was still lurking about in disguise, there seemed to be no doubt that its leading product, the Munich Agreement, was dead as dead could be.* Zones, International Commission borders, population transfers, and international guarantees had all been swept away by Hitler's march into Prague, and the corpse of the country that the agreement had purported to protect lay in plain view, sprawled across Central Europe.

The title and theme of this work is "Munich," and if the agreement died on March 15, 1938, why should not this narrative now come to the end which those who have read this far may already have thought long overdue? Fortunately, we have only a few more weeks to go, but this is not quite the moment to stop. History is a two-way street; if what happens earlier helps to explain what comes later, the reverse is also true. And by coincidence, the episode which triggered the new British policy occurred the day after the German coup, and the outlines of that policy emerged at the same Cabinet meeting on March 18 at which Chamberlain acknowledged the bankruptcy of "appeasement."

---

* And so it not only "seemed to be" but was in fact, until after the Second World War, when disputes of nationality and property raised question whether the Munich Agreement was a valid international treaty.

On March 16 the Rumanian Minister to Britain, Virgil Tilea, visited Sir Orme Sargent, Assistant Under-Secretary at the Foreign Office, and declared: "His Government, from secret and other sources, has good reason to believe that within the next few months the German Government would reduce Hungary to vassalage and then proceed to disintegrate Roumania in the same way as they had disintegrated Czechoslovakia, with the ultimate object of establishing a German protectorate over the whole country." Tilea went on to say that he was speaking personally rather than officially, and asked whether the British Government would consider loaning Rumania £ 10 million to purchase war materials.

The next day Tilea saw Halifax and Cadogan (and reporters from *The Times* and the *Daily Telegraph* as well) and added to his account that the German Government had asked Bucharest to give Germany a monopoly of Rumanian exports (including, of course, oil from the Ploesti fields), and accept, in Germany's interest, certain internal economic restrictions. Tilea described the request as in the nature of an ultimatum, which Rumania had refused, but he stressed the "extreme urgency" of a "precise indication" of the British position "in the event of Roumania becoming victim of German aggression."

With a haste which can be explained only by nerves made jumpy by Hitler's latest move, that evening Halifax, Cadogan, and Sargent, without first checking with the British Legation in Bucharest, sent telegrams to Paris, Moscow, Warsaw, Ankara, Athens, and Belgrade recounting Tilea's story and asking the British representatives in those capitals what would be the attitude of the governments to which they were accredited in the circumstances so described. The minister in Bucharest, Sir Reginald Hoare, was also informed, and the following morning he telephoned to London a request (disregarded) that the telegrams to the other capitals be canceled.

On the heels of this message came another, in which Sir Reginald explained that he had found Tilea's tale "utterly improbable," and that the Rumanian Foreign Minister, Grigore Gafencu, had denied that there was a word of truth in the story. Economic negotiations between Rumania and Germany were indeed in progress, but they "were proceeding on completely normal lines as between equals." From Warsaw, Ambassador Kennard reported that Beck was highly skeptical of Tilea's account.

Confronted with the denial from Bucharest, Tilea stuck to his story, which was thought sufficiently alarming so that Chamberlain was summoned from Birmingham and a special Cabinet meeting was called late that afternoon, Saturday, March 18. Halifax reported the conflicting statements of Gafencu and Tilea; he thought the situation was probably not so "immediately threatening" as Tilea had suggested, but that the Cabinet ought to consider what attitude the Government should take if the danger arose in the future. Halifax's own view was that "if Germany committed an act of naked aggression on Roumania, it would be very difficult for this country not to take all the action in her power to rally resistance against that aggression and to take part in that resistance herself."

Chatfield then reported that hasty consultations with the Chiefs of Staff and service ministers had yielded an informal consensus that German domination of

Rumania would have "very serious consequences." Rumanian oil and agricultural produce would greatly improve Germany's strategic position "since she would be able almost to neutralize the efforts of the British Navy to blockade her in time of war." Furthermore, "there would be nothing to prevent Germany from marching straight through to the Mediterranean, more especially since she could rely on Bulgarian friendship." However, as in the recent case of Czechoslovakia, there was nothing Britain could do to prevent the Germans from overrunning Rumania. Actions by Poland and Russia could change this situation, and "the provisional view of the Chiefs of Staff would be that, if Poland and Russia would be prepared to help us, we should join with them in resisting German aggression." If those countries were unwilling, "the only plan which appeared feasible was that we should obtain the support of Greece and Turkey."

These ideas were a reworking of the "Grand Alliance" which Churchill had unsuccessfully proposed a year earlier, after *Anschluss*. It was in the context of Halifax's and Chatfield's statements that Chamberlain then made the disavowal of appeasement already quoted, and then went on to say: "A German attempt to dominate Roumania was, therefore, more than a question whether Germany would thereby improve her strategical position; it raised the whole question whether Germany intended to obtain domination over the whole of South Eastern Europe." The next move "was to ascertain what friends we had who would join us in resisting aggression." Before doing this, he "wished to ascertain whether the Cabinet agreed generally with the change of policy he had outlined."

Simon, Halifax, Maugham, Inskip, MacDonald, Kingsley Wood, Stanley, Stanhope, Colville, Morrison, Hore-Belisha, and Brown all expressed agreement. There was no opposition, though Maugham and Kingsley Wood stressed the need of another six to nine months of peace to strengthen the country's forces.

Chamberlain concluded the meeting by declaring that "the real point at issue was whether we could obtain sufficient assurances from other countries to justify us in a public pronouncement that we should resist any further act of aggression on the part of Germany," and then adding that "Poland was very likely the key to the situation, and he suggested that our communication to Poland should probably go somewhat further than our communications to other countries." His singling out of Poland was, no doubt, a reflection of views he expressed a week later in a letter to his sister:

I must confess to the most profound distrust of Russia. I have no belief whatever in her ability to maintain an effective offensive, even if she wanted to. And I distrust her motives, which seem to me to have little connection with our ideas of liberty, and to be concerned only with getting everyone else by the ears. Moreover, she is both hated and suspected by many of the smaller States, notably by Poland, Roumania and Finland.

The "Rumania scare" soon proved as insubstantial as the "Holland scare." The German-Rumanian economic negotiations were conducted for the Reich by

Goering's agent Helmuth Wohlthat, a hard bargainer well informed on the political aspects of his assignment. Some of the terms he proposed were unwelcome to Bucharest, and he drove his hosts hard to reach an agreement quickly. But neither the published nor the secret provisions of the treaty of March 23, 1939, contained coercive or preclusive provisions, and there is no evidence that Hitler at the time had the slightest intention of using military force against Rumania. However, realization in London that there was no imminent danger to Rumania appears to have left unaffected the fundamental policy change which Tilea's grossly exaggerated report had triggered.*

The answers received from the capitals to which Halifax had sent inquiries on the seventeenth were unhelpful. All were noncommittal; Belgrade and Athens turned the question back on London, and Moscow characteristically proposed an international conference of Britain, France, Poland, Rumania, and the U.S.S.R. to map "common action." These countries, together with Yugoslavia, Turkey, and Greece, were those which the Cabinet, on the eighteenth, had authorized Halifax to approach "with a view to obtaining assurance from them that they would join with us in resisting any act of German aggression aimed at obtaining domination of South-Eastern Europe."

The Soviet conference idea had little appeal for Chamberlain and Halifax, who also concluded that an approach to all the countries listed by the Cabinet would be unduly time-consuming. On the twentieth Halifax reported to the Cabinet that "the essential point was to secure the early consent of France, Russia and Poland to some pronouncement which could be made public," and presented a draft pursuant to which the four governments would agree "to consult together in the event of any action being taken which appeared to constitute a threat" to the "security and political independence of European States."

Halifax acknowledged that "a pledge to consult . . . was not a very heroic decision," but explained that "it was very important to take some action quickly" and that the statement "would have an immense political significance." Chamberlain declared that the purpose of consultation would be to "decide what military action" should be taken. Germany should be stopped "by attacking her on two fronts" (which a combination of two Western European and two Eastern European powers could do), and that the concept was not "to save a particular victim" but "to pull down the bully."

There ensued a long discussion of the declaration's wording, after which Chamberlain solicited his colleagues' views on the wisdom of his writing a "private letter to Mussolini" pointing out that Hitler was now including non-Germans in the Reich, and asking the Duce to exercise some restraint on his fellow-dictator. Halifax thought that if any letter were written to Mussolini it ought rather to warn him against putting his claims against France "in a provocative manner." It was plain that these two themes did not combine harmoniously, but the Cabinet authorized the Prime Minister to send a letter, the wording to be agreed between him and Halifax. The result was in line with the Prime Minister's notions. The letter reached the addressee just after that gentleman had told his

---

* Tilea, whose sin was regarded in Bucharest as overzealousness, was temporarily recalled at about the time the treaty was signed.

son-in-law that they should expedite their plan for the annexation of Albania. Ciano recorded: "Mussolini will answer after the Albanian coup:* the letter confirms his intention to go ahead with it, as he finds in it another proof of the democracies' inertia."

On March 21, Bonnet accompanied President Lebrun on a state visit to London and conferred that afternoon with Halifax and Strang. The burden of Bonnet's remarks was that Russian help would be of little value against Germany if Poland and Rumania remained neutral, and it was therefore vital to bring them, and especially Poland, into the Anglo-French plan. Halifax agreed and observed (contrary to his views during the Czech crisis) that "the primary question would not be: can we give direct assistance to Poland or Roumania? but: can we conduct a successful war against Germany?"

The following day Chamberlain, as well as Cadogan, Phipps, and Corbin, joined in the meeting with Bonnet, who at once announced that his country was ready to sign the proposed four-power declaration. But by this time it was clear that Poland would not, both from distaste of such a public association with the Soviet Union,† and reluctance to step openly into the anti-German camp. The declaration thus dropped out of the discussion, which chiefly concerned how best to ensure Polish assistance if Germany attacked Rumania. Halifax warned of the danger that Russia might feel "that we were pushing her to one side," and it was agreed that Moscow should be approached once the Polish question had been settled. Thus, despite Bucharest's repudiation of Tilea, Rumania remained the focus of concern although, as events soon proved, it was Poland that was immediately in danger.

While Bonnet and the British were conferring, a seasick Fuehrer was on the battle cruiser *Deutschland* in the Baltic en route to Memel. During the preceding week strong diplomatic pressure on Lithuania had been exerted from Berlin, resulting in a treaty signed March 22, by which Lithuania ceded the port and its hinterland to the Reich. The fifty thousand inhabitants of the city were mostly German, and the territory was contiguous to the northern tip of East Prussia and had been part of it until after Versailles, when the Lithuanians seized it. The German move had long been expected; of course, it was accomplished by threats of military action, but the annexation did not appear to go beyond the incorporation of ethnic Germans. Anyhow, after letting Czechoslovakia disintegrate it would have seemed bizarre for the democracies to go to war over Memel, particularly since much larger matters were threatening, and the episode aroused little concern in London or Paris.

At the other end of Europe, the Spanish Civil War dragged to its miserable close, as the last Loyalist-held cities—Valencia, Alicante, Almería, Cartagena— were occupied by Franco's forces. The collapse of the Republican cause had for some months appeared inevitable and caused no new crisis. However, the re-

---

* In fact the Duce answered on April 1, before the Albanian move. He echoed Hitler's anticipation of "a long period of peace" but declined to "take the initiative before Italy's rights have been recognized."

† The Soviet Government was disappointed that their conference proposal was not taken up, but late on the twenty-second Litvinov told the British Ambassador that, if France and Poland signed the declaration, his government would do likewise.

moval of what Mussolini had described as the main obstacle to French-Italian amity did not do much to alleviate the tension, as the Duce, in a public speech on March 26, spoke of the democracies, and Italy's colonial demands on France, in terms which Cadogan found "pretty offensive," and which triggered groans and catcalls from his audience at the mention of Britain or France.

Far more significant than these events which made headlines were the secret diplomatic discussions in Berlin, London, and Warsaw, whereby Poland became the focus of power politics. German domination of Slovakia had done to Poland what *Anschluss* had done to Czechoslovakia, for now the northern, western, and southern Polish borders lay exposed to German attack. Through the winter German pressure for Danzig and a "corridor across the Corridor" had been persistent but courteous and nonthreatening; now spring brought a chilly wind from Berlin.

On March 21, Ribbentrop summoned Ambassador Lipski and renewed the Danzig and corridor demands, coupling them with complaints about the Polish press and anti-German demonstrations. The failure of the Poles to evince a "positive reaction" to the Danzig question "had made an unfavorable impression on the Führer" who now "felt nothing but amazement over Poland's strange attitude on a number of questions." It would be a very good idea, Ribbentrop declared, for Beck to pay a visit to discuss these matters with the Fuehrer, who might otherwise "form the impression that Poland simply was not willing."

After a trip to Warsaw to report and receive Beck's instructions, Lipski called on Ribbentrop on the twenty-sixth and presented a memorandum which, in substance, was a polite refusal of the German demands, and an indication that Beck would not visit Berlin until "the questions had been suitably prepared from the diplomatic angle beforehand." Ribbentrop replied that the Polish response "could not be regarded by the Führer as satisfactory," and warned that "if things went on this way a serious situation might arise." The next day Ribbentrop took advantage of German press reports of anti-German riots in Bromberg* to summon and berate Lipski, saying in conclusion "that he could no longer understand the Polish Government," and that:

> An evasive answer had been given to the generous proposal which Germany had made to Poland. . . . Relations between the two countries were therefore deteriorating sharply.

These hostile rumblings did not greatly surprise Beck, who, since his visit to the Berghof in January, had been expecting this kind of trouble. Later that month, feeling a growing need for allies, he had quietly approached the British, and early in March it was arranged that he would visit London during the first week of April—a meeting which now, in view of the German moves in late March, assumed great significance.

The Lipski-Ribbentrop confrontations coincided with the London inquiries and proposals generated by the supposed threat to Rumania. Halifax's four-power declaration was out of tune with Polish policy for reasons already noted,

---

* A city (Bydgoszcz in Polish) in western Poland with a large German population.

but it triggered a counterproposition from Warsaw, described in instructions sent by Beck on March 23 to Count Edward Raczyński, the Ambassador in London. As he put the proposal to Halifax the next day, it amounted to a secret bilateral convention between Britain and Poland, under which the two countries would mutually undertake to act in accordance with the terms of the Halifax declaration. The effect of this would be that, if Germany took action which threatened Poland's independence, Britain would be bound to consult with Poland with a view to taking joint action to counter the threat. Raczyński explained that the confidential bilateral nature of the compact was necessary to avoid open association with Russia and minimize the possibility of provoking Germany.

Beck was a secretive man who played his diplomatic cards close to the chest, and he gave the British no information about the Lipski-Ribbentrop talks. Consequently, Chamberlain and Halifax remained under the belief that Rumania rather than Poland was the most threatened eastern country, and therefore the bilateral aspect of Beck's proposal did not appeal to them. Nor did they like the secrecy element, which would be embarrassing in Parliament and vis-á-vis the French.

Beck's message did, however, start the British thinking of something beyond a declaration and more like a defensive alliance. Halifax and the Foreign Office staff spent March 25 and 26 working up the outlines of a new policy, the keystone of which was that any aggressive move by Germany would involve her in a two-front war.* Since Poland would not associate herself with the Soviet Union and there was no Russo-German frontier, Halifax concluded, according to Harvey, that "adherence of Poland is essential to any effective scheme to hold up Germany in event of aggression," and that "we cannot have Russia in the forefront of the picture."

In the evening of the twenty-sixth Halifax, Butler, and Cadogan went to Downing Street with their plan, and the Prime Minister "approved in principle." The following afternoon it was presented to the Foreign Policy Committee, in the form of the instructional messages Halifax proposed to send to Paris, Warsaw, and Bucharest. The core of the plan was an Anglo-French commitment to come to the support of Poland or Rumania if either were attacked by Germany and resisted. In the case of Rumania, the commitment was contingent on Poland's also coming to her assistance, and Poland was to give a reciprocal undertaking to support Britain and France if they were attacked by Germany or went to war in order to resist German attacks on Yugoslavia or any Western European country. Kennard in Warsaw and Hoare in Bucharest were told to take no action until Phipps had secured the French Government's agreement, so

* Finding himself working on plans for a defensive agreement with Poland led Cadogan, after all his imprecations on Vansittart, to reflect on the turn events had taken, and record: "I must say it is turning out—at present—as Van predicted and as I never believed it would. If we want to try to stem the German expansion, I believe we must try to build a dam *now*. . . . If we are set on this course, we must set about it quickly and firmly. It *might* act as a deterrent to avert war, though I confess I think the chances of that are rather slight. But on the whole, it is probably the right thing to do."

that the French representatives in Warsaw and Bucharest could join in presenting the plan to the Polish and Rumanian governments.

Chamberlain described the program to his colleagues on the basis that
Rumania seemed, "on the whole, likely to be the next victim of German aggression," and that her occupation by Germany would be especially serious because
it would vitiate a naval blockade, which was Germany's greatest fear. Chatfield
doubted that Rumania was next on Hitler's list, or that Britain and France
could do anything to prevent the Germans from overrunning both Rumania and
Poland. "Soviet Russia would act as a greater deterrent so far as Germany was
concerned," Chatfield thought, and on this he was strongly supported by Hoare,
Morrison, and Stanley. But the awkward fact remained that Poland and
Rumania simply would not play on the team with Russia, and the best that
Hoare could get was Chamberlain's halfhearted agreement to consider a separate bilateral agreement with Russia after Poland had reacted to the present
program. Halifax acknowledged the force of Chatfield's points, but replied that:

> We were faced with the dilemma of doing nothing, or entering into a devas-
> tating war. If we did nothing this in itself would mean a great accession to
> Germany's strength and a great loss to ourselves of sympathy and support in
> the United States, in the Balkan countries, and in other parts of the world. In
> those circumstances if we had to choose between two great evils he favored
> our going to war.

Chatfield hastened to agree to this, which was the same argument that Duff
Cooper had made, even more forcefully but unsuccessfully, before Munich.
Nobody gave him a credit line, but all swung into support of the new policy and
approved sending the telegrams, after Chamberlain had told them that full Cabinet clearance was unnecessary.

If all had gone as then expected, further action would have awaited the response from the other capitals and, in all probability, discussion with Beck, who
was to arrive in London on April 3. But on March 28 came the fourth and last
of the false reports of imminent German action that triggered important changes
in British policy.

The bearer of alarming tidings this time was Ian Colvin, Berlin correspondent
of the London *News Chronicle*. In January, Colvin had been told by "a reliable
source" that "a victualling contractor to the German army had then received instructions to provide the same amount of rations as he had supplied in September 1938, and to have them ready by March 28th, 1939," for delivery "in an
area of Pomerania that formed a rough wedge pointing to the railway junction
of Bromberg in the Polish corridor." On March 27 the German press carried reports of anti-German excesses in Bromberg, which Colvin thought resembled the
charges against the Czechs in the Sudetenland prior to Munich. He put all this
to Mason-Mac, who "agreed that a rapid move to cut the Polish corridor might
be intended, though he had no positive information," and advised Colvin to
take the information to London in person.

Colvin flew to London on the twenty-eighth, and through Sir Reginald Leeper
(head of the Foreign Office News Department) arranged to see Cadogan,

Simon, and Halifax on the twenty-ninth. Late that afternoon Halifax took Colvin to Downing Street, and Colvin told his story to the Prime Minister in the presence of Halifax, Cadogan, Leeper, and Dunglass. Harvey was told that Colvin made a "great impression," and that must have been the case, for Cadogan recorded that Halifax remained with Chamberlain after the meeting and then came to the Foreign Office with the information that the Prime Minister had "agreed to the idea of an *immediate* declaration in support of Poland, to counter a quick putsch by Hitler." Halifax, Butler, Cadogan, and others stayed until the small hours in the morning of the thirtieth, drafting the declaration and the dispatches to Paris and Warsaw which its issuance would entail.*

A special Cabinet meeting was called the next morning to consider these documents and the new situation to which they were addressed. Halifax explained that the reason for the meeting was that "information received on the previous day appeared to disclose a possible German intention to execute a *coup de main* against Poland," and summarized what Colvin had reported. The proposal he wished the Cabinet to consider was "that we should make a clear declaration of our intention to support Poland if Poland was attacked by Germany," primarily for the purpose of deterring Hitler from taking such action.

Carefully Halifax listed objections to such a commitment: it would give Beck "what he wanted without obtaining any reciprocal undertaking from him"; it might upset the prospects of direct agreement between Germany and Poland; it might provoke Germany to take the very action that was sought to be prevented; it was drastic action to take "on the meagre information available to us." For all these reasons, Halifax did not propose to issue the declaration at once, but to have its text approved by the Cabinet, the leaders of the Opposition, and the French, so that it could "be published at a moment's notice, if the situation should require it."

The Prime Minister, acknowledging that "the action now proposed was a serious step and was the actual crossing of the stream," supported the proposal:

> It had already been pointed out, as a result of the German action against Czechoslovakia, instead of the Czech army being on our side, Czech resources were now available to Germany. It would be a very serious matter if Poland, instead of being a potential ally, also became added to the resources of Germany. If, therefore, we took no action, there was a risk that, in a short time, we should find that Poland had been over-run and that we had missed an opportunity. On the other hand, if we uttered a warning such as was now proposed, we should be commited to intervention if Germany persisted in aggression.

There followed a long discussion, in which Chatfield took the leading part. Referring to a report submitted by the Chiefs of Staff, he declared that they had come "to a fairly definite conclusion that, if we have to fight Germany, it would be better to do so with Poland as an ally, rather than to allow Poland to be absorbed and dominated by Germany without making any effort to help her."

---

* Meanwhile, the French Government had agreed to the proposals formulated on the twenty-seventh, and Kennard and Hoare were instructed to lay them before the Polish and Rumanian governments.

Even though Poland might be overrun, Germany would suffer heavy casualties and the Germans would have to leave considerable forces there. On the other hand, the Chiefs had "no evidence that either the Germans or the Italians intend to make any major move," and doubted that an attack on the Polish Corridor was imminent, though something might be planned for Danzig.

No one directly opposed the plan, though Kingsley Wood and Lord Zetland expressed grave doubts. But the language of the draft statement and telegrams caused prolonged discussion, in the course of which Chatfield pointed out a flaw in Halifax's proposed timing: if they waited for further information, the attack might occur before the statement had been issued, in which case it would be useless as a deterrent. He proposed instead the prompt issuance of a "more general statement . . . which would give more timely warning," and this was agreed to, with the further suggestion that the statement be handled by a parliamentary question-and-answer on the thirty-first. In conclusion, the Foreign Policy Committee was authorized to draft the statement and send the telegrams to Warsaw and Paris.

The draft was settled, and both Warsaw and Paris promptly agreed to the procedure. Opposition leaders were "much disturbed" at the evident exclusion of Russia from the new arrangement, and not wholly mollified by the Prime Minister's assurance that "the absence of any reference to Russia . . . was based on expediency and not on any ideological ground." British intelligence had uncovered nothing that confirmed the likelihood of a German military move, and the question to be asked and answered in Parliament was modified: "To ask the Prime Minister whether he could make any statement on the European situation." The Cabinet approved the whole procedure, and that afternoon, March 31, 1939, Neville Chamberlain answered the question:

> . . . His Majesty's Government have no official confirmation of the rumours of any projected attack on Poland and they must not, therefore, be taken as true. . . .
>
> As the House is aware, certain consultations are now proceeding with other Governments. In order to make perfectly clear the position of His Majesty's Government in the meantime before these consultations are concluded, I now have to inform the House that during that period, in the event of any action which clearly threatened Polish independence, and which the Polish Government accordingly considered it vital to resist with their national forces, His Majesty's Government would feel themselves bound at once to lend the Polish Government all support in their power. They have given the Polish Government an assurance to this effect.
>
> I may add that the French Government have authorized me to make it plain that they stand on the same position in this matter as do His Majesty's Government.

The British had crossed the Rubicon. It would be too much to say that Ian Colvin built the bridge, for in all probability a comparable commitment to Poland would have been made following Beck's visit. But the timing, setting, and unilateral character of the guarantee were, indeed, the product of Colvin's story, even though by the time Chamberlain announced the undertaking, the journalist's warning had lost much of its force.

Colvin's appearance at the Foreign Office coincided with the Lipski-Ribben-trop interviews and with Hitler's first thoughts about military steps against Poland. Of these things Colvin knew nothing, and his real contribution was that he got the British ministers thinking primarily in terms of Poland rather than Rumania, which was a much more accurate assessment of the direction of Hitler's next move. But at the time there was as yet no German plan for an attack against Poland, much less any deployment of forces with which to carry it out.

Hitler returned from Memel to Berlin on March 24 and went to Munich the following day. Before leaving Berlin he gave information and instructions to Brauchitsch on many aspects of the international situation, recorded in a memorandum by the general's adjutant, Major Siewert. With regard to Poland, he wrote:

> The Führer does not wish . . . to solve the Danzig problem forcefully. He does not wish thus to drive Poland into England's arms. . . . For the time being, the Führer does not intend to solve the Polish question. However, it should now be worked on. A solution in the near future would have to be based on especially favorable political conditions. In that case Poland shall be knocked out so completely that it will not be a political factor for the next decades. . . .

This was minatory but not immediate. The "work" on the "Polish problem" was commenced early in April, pursuant to a directive to the Wehrmacht signed by Hitler on the eleventh, which gave the cover name "Case White" to a plan "to destroy the Polish armed forces." It specified September 1, 1939, as the date by which preparations were to be completed, and that proved to be the day the Second World War began.

Neither Colvin nor the British Government had any knowledge of these directives and plans. In default of sure information on Hitler's intentions, London had to do the best it could with reports such as Colvin's and, given the tension of the times, it is not surprising that the Government thought it prudent to act on the basis that the pictured dangers were real.

Far more important and difficult to appraise is the rapidity with which the British Government reversed its basic European policy. In September, Chamberlain had exercised every means to make it possible for the French to avoid fulfillment of their guarantee to Czechoslovakia. Six months later, he and Halifax, without any request from Warsaw or Paris, breathed new life into the Franco-Polish alliance and themselves assumed parallel obligations. What accounted for this 180-degree turn? And why was it so readily followed by their Cabinet colleagues and the Parliament?

Some weeks later (May 22) Cadogan summarized the reasons as he saw them:

> The principal object of our guarantee to Poland was to deter Germany from any further acts of aggression, and by obtaining a reciprocal guarantee from Poland to ensure that, if war came, Germany would have to fight on two fronts. . . . Germany is unable at the moment to embark on a war on two fronts. If she were free to expand eastward and to obtain control of the re-

sources of Central and Eastern Europe, she might then be strong enough to turn upon the Western countries with overwhelming strength.

Halifax, in his memoirs, said much the same. If it was Hitler's intention to dominate Europe:

> . . . it might still be possible to deter him from its execution if, as we had failed to do in 1914, we made it unmistakably clear that the particular acts of aggression which he was believed to have in mind would result in a general war. And if . . . Hitler was not to be restrained, it was better that the nations under threat should stand and fight together than that they should await German attack one by one. That was in two sentences the justification for the decision to give guarantees.

Chamberlain's and Chatfield's comments in Cabinet, quoted above, were to the same general effect. It all amounted to the double proposition that the certain prospect of a general war might deter Hitler and keep the peace and, if not, Britain and France would have allies in the east who would involve Germany in a two-front war.

That was very well as far as it went, but all these reasons were operative in 1938 and were disregarded. Indeed, they were then even stronger, for Czechoslovakia was a much more desirable eastern ally than Poland. The Czechs had fewer divisions, but they were better armed, the country had natural defenses, extensive fortifications, and a strong armaments industry, and Russia was her ally instead of, as the Poles viewed her, an enemy.

Halifax, again in his memoirs, explained that after the events of March 15th "it was no longer possible to hope that Hitler's purposes and ambitions were limited by any boundaries of race, and the lust of continental or world mastery seemed to stand out in stark relief. Here indeed was the simple explanation a few weeks later of the guarantee given to Poland." That amounts to saying that, if the British leaders had known in September 1938 what they learned in March 1939, they would have acted otherwise on the earlier date—in other words, that they acted wrongly in 1938 because of insufficient information.*

All in all, this comes fairly close to the mark. Essentially, it was a case of "once bitten, twice shy." The records do not show that any of the British ministers or top civil servants invoked the name of Eyre Crowe or quoted his famous memorandum of 1907 on the "balance of power," but they were following his teaching. In these terms, the rebirth of German military power, *provided it did not go too far,* was a harmless and even desirable counterweight to French dominance of the Europe of Versailles. In the mid-thirties it became apparent that the German development might well go too far, but Britain and France lacked the will to cut her back by force. In 1938 the gravity of the German peril became apparent, but their own weakness led most of the British leaders to look for reasons to avoid a military confrontation; Chamberlain found them in a be-

---

* Halifax does not, however, confess error for Munich, but his argument that Czechoslovakia was not "a defensible proposition" was stronger as applied to Poland. He also comments on the Dominions' attitude at the time of Munich, but that amounts only to saying that their governments were no better able to assess what Hitler was confronting them with than was the British Government. Hoare, in his memoirs, gives much the same explanation as does Halifax.

lief that Hitler would observe the limits which he himself had announced, and the Chiefs of Staff on the ground that delay would work to Britain's military advantage. The destruction of Czechoslovakia on March 15 convinced Chamberlain and the public that Hitler would not observe those limits, and the Chiefs of Staff that a delay which enabled him to extend his sway over more of Central and Eastern Europe would work to Britain's military disadvantage.

This analysis led to the conclusion that any further German move should be met by force, but not necessarily to a guarantee of support for Poland. The announced purpose of the guarantee was deterrence, and it failed. Another purpose, less openly acknowledged, was to encourage the Poles to refuse any German demands which would seriously weaken them, and to resist an attack. The Poles did so, but very probably would have fought even had there been no guarantee. From the British standpoint, its main value was internal and psychological. From then on everyone knew or assumed that war between Germany and Poland meant war between Britain and Germany. This was a useful stimulant to rearmament, though the pace remained far below a war tempo.

The wisdom of the guarantee to Poland has been much criticized. Liddell Hart, for example, called it "foolish, futile, and provocative" and "an ill-considered gesture." But the gist of his complaint was not so much that Poland had been guaranteed as that Russia had been excluded, and that remains, in retrospect, the vital flaw in British policy at the time.

The Chiefs of Staff were sound in their endeavor to commit Germany to a two-front war, but obviously an alliance with Rumania or Lithuania would not accomplish that in any meaningful way. Poland was at best marginal, and the Chiefs of Staff badly overestimated her staying capacity against the Wehrmacht. Furthermore, she would probably fight anyhow, and the alliance with her was an obstacle to enlisting the Russians. But as the Prime Minister told the Cabinet on April 4, he had "very considerable distrust of Russia, and no confidence that we should obtain active and constant support from that country," and therefore "Poland was the key to the situation, and an alliance with Poland would ensure that Germany would be engaged in a war on two fronts."

Right or wrong, the guarantee to Poland was generally approved by the leading political figures, although Lloyd George voiced the doubts entertained by Liddell Hart. For the Labour Party, Arthur Greenwood congratulated Chamberlain on his "momentous" move, which would "give pause to those who sought to impose their will on others by show of the mailed fist." The Liberal leader, Sir Archibald Sinclair, echoed those sentiments, and Winston Churchill, while urging the desirability of Russian support, expressed "the most complete agreement with the Prime Minister on the matter" and declared that the guarantee gave "the most solid reassurances of peace."

8

After March 31 the road to war was downhill all the way. Colonel Beck proved a very tough negotiator; he readily agreed to reciprocate Britain's guarantee but would not join the British in guaranteeing Rumania or western countries such as Belgium and Holland, nor would he express any interest even in buying weaponry from the Soviet Union. The communiqué issued upon Beck's departure from London on April 6 recited that the two countries were "prepared to enter into an agreement of a permanent and reciprocal character" to replace the oral understanding, but no formal treaty was signed until late August, on the eve of war. The same day, in Berlin, Weizsaecker summoned Lipski and told him that "the most recent trend of Polish policy was altogether incomprehensible . . . we had suddenly heard strange sabre-rattling in Warsaw." The Fuehrer's "offer to Poland" (to guarantee the Polish-German borders in return for a German extraterritorial road and rail connection with East Prussia and the annexation of Danzig) "was one which would not be repeated," and "the future would show whether Poland had been well-advised in her attitude."

The next day, Good Friday, April 7, Italian troops invaded and overran Albania, adding another jewel to the rather shabby collection in Victor Emmanuel's crown. It was a flagrant violation of the provisions of the Anglo-Italian Agreement respecting maintenance of the territorial *status quo* in the Mediterranean area, and Cadogan at once concluded "that this proves Musso a gangster as Czechs proved Hitler." The Prime Minister, still clinging to his hopes for Mussolini, saw the matter otherwise. According to R. A. Butler's account:

> On the Good Friday of 1939, which Mussolini chose for invasion of Albania, I hurried up from the country and at once called at No. 10 for instructions. I was led into a small room upstairs, overlooking a garden, which the Prime Minister used as a study. The window was partly open, showing a table for birdfood suspended outside. Neville seemed irritated at my intrusion and expressed surprise that I was perturbed. He said, "I feel sure Mussolini has not decided to go against us." When I started to talk about the general threat to the Balkans, he dismissed me with the words, "Don't be silly. Go home to bed," and continued to feed the birds. . . .

In line with this "cool" attitude, Chamberlain refrained from any such criticism as he had leveled against Hitler at Birmingham, and Italy was not formally charged with violating the Anglo-Italian treaty. But Albania, and subsequent reports (unfounded) that the Italians were about to attack the Greek island of Corfu, put the guarantee machinery again in operation, this time with Greece and Turkey as the intended beneficiaries.

In the case of Greece, the primary purpose was to warn Mussolini that an attack on that country would involve him in war with Britain and France. The Turkish situation was more complex. There was no sign that she was imminently threatened by either Germany or Italy, but Turkey was militarily strong and would be a valuable ally not only in the Mediterranean, but also as the guardian of access through the Dardanelles to the Black Sea coasts of Russia, Rumania, and Bulgaria.

The Turkish Government was friendly but indicated that they did not want a guarantee and preferred a less formal declaration of common purpose.* The

---

* On May 12, 1939, Britain and Turkey issued a "Declaration of Mutual Assistance" providing that "in the event of an act of aggression leading to war in the Mediterranean area they would be prepared to cooperate effectively and to lend each other all aid and assistance in their power" and that they would also consult together "to ensure the establishment of security in the Balkans." On June 23, 1939, France and Turkey signed a similar declaration.

Greeks accepted with gratitude, and on April 11 the British Foreign Policy Committee approved the text of the announcement which Chamberlain would make in Parliament on the thirteenth.

However, on the tenth Tilea, accompanied by the Secretary-General of the Rumanian Foreign Ministry, M. Cretzianu, called on Halifax and Cadogan, pressing their government's request for an immediate, unilateral guarantee. They got little encouragement, as Halifax wished to maintain the pressure on Warsaw to join in guaranteeing Rumania. But on the twelfth Corbin came to Cadogan with the draft of the statement that the Quai d'Orsay proposed to issue, embodying guarantees to both Greece and Rumania. It was plainly desirable that the British and French statements should be of like scope, and Daladier was strongly of the opinion that guarantees to Poland and Greece would raise the implication that Rumania would be left to shift for herself, and invite attack by Germany or Hungary. For once, the British found the French arguments compelling, and on the thirteenth both governments announced their respective unilateral guarantees to Greece and Rumania, for the purpose of avoiding "disturbance by force or threats of force of the *status quo* in the Mediterranean and the Balkan Peninsula."

While handing out the guarantees, the British Government had taken several other steps, which were, probably, even less to Adolf Hitler's liking. When Bonnet was in London in March, Chamberlain had read him a stiff lecture on the shortcomings of the French air arm. Bonnet took it politely, but the next day riposted by urging upon Halifax the necessity of Britain's adopting military service conscription. Because of the Labour Party's intransigent opposition, this was regarded in government circles as "politically impossible." But the pressure was increasing for some move that would show that Britain "meant business," and on March 29, accepting Hore-Belisha's spur-of-the-moment suggestion, Chamberlain announced in the Commons that the Territorial Army would be doubled in size.*

Albania gave rearmament another push, and Hore-Belisha spoke out publicly for both conscription and the establishment of a Ministry of Supply. On April 20 (Hitler's birthday) the Prime Minister finally yielded, and announced in the Commons that a Ministry of Supply would be established, and headed by Leslie Burgin, the then Minister of Transport—a selection which, like Inskip's, was not acclaimed. On the same day Chamberlain agreed to conscription and, after tense discussions with the union leaders, on April 26 he announced in Commons the introduction of legislation for compulsory military service for all men between the ages of twenty and twenty-one.

Two days later, in the course of a long address to the Reichstag, Hitler gave answer to these developments, with harsh words and news for the two principal offenders, Britain and Poland. The former was now carrying out "the policy of encirclement" and thereby "the basis for the [Anglo-German] naval treaty has been removed." A formal note denouncing the treaty was on its way to the British Government. As for Poland, the mutual Anglo-Polish guarantees were "con-

---

* More accurately, it would be raised from its peacetime strength (130,000) to its wartime strength (170,000), and then doubled.

tradictory to the agreement which I made with Marshal Pilsudski." Accordingly a memorandum had been sent to the Polish Government denouncing the nonaggression declaration of 1934.

Secret military preparations for the attack against Poland were already under way when Hitler spoke. During May the leading staff officers were drawing tactical plans, and on the twenty-third Hitler called a meeting of the service commanders-in-chief and their chiefs of staff, together with Keitel, Warlimont, and the OKW adjutants, to "indoctrinate" them politically, announce his decision "to attack Poland at the first suitable opportunity," and warn them that there would be "no repetition of the Czech affair" and "there will be war."

Meanwhile Mussolini, whose nose had been put out of joint by the German occupation of Bohemia and Moravia, had been recovering from his pique with the help of the Albanian conquest, pallid as it was. Japan was still holding back from the Tripartite Pact project, and early in May, while Ribbentrop and Ciano were conferring in Milan, the Duce suddenly decided that an alliance between the two Axis countries should be signed promptly. Hitler gave his approval, and on May 7, at the conclusion of the Ribbentrop-Ciano meeting, the communiqué announced that it had been "decided finally to define, in a formal manner, the relations between the two States of the Axis in a political and military pact." The resulting "Treaty of Friendship and Alliance" (commonly known as the "Pact of Steel") was signed by Ribbentrop and Ciano in Berlin on May 22. Its principal provision bound each of the contracting parties, in the event that the other became "involved in hostilities with another Power or Powers," to "come immediately to its side as ally and support it with all its military forces on land, sea, and in the air."

The Pact of Steel wrote finis to Chamberlain's efforts to weaken the Italo-German relation, but it came as no surprise, and the British leaders were busy with other diplomatic problems, of which the largest, by far, was what to do about Soviet Russia. On April 18 in Moscow, Litvinov handed to the British Ambassador, Sir William Seeds, an official proposal for an Anglo-Franco-Russian alliance binding the three countries to "render mutually all manner of assistance, including that of a military nature, in case of aggression in Europe" against any one of them, or against "Eastern European States situated between the Baltic and Black Seas and Bordering on U.S.S.R.," and not to negotiate or conclude peace "with aggressors separately from one another and without common consent of the three Powers."

This was a real blockbuster, full of domestic political as well as diplomatic and military problems. It was considered the following day by the Foreign Policy Committee, with the benefit of a memorandum by Cadogan, which described the Soviet proposal as "extremely inconvenient," minimized the help which Russia could give, listed several objections to the plan and declared that "from the practical point of view, there was every argument against accepting the Russian proposal." But then it was observed that "there is great difficulty in rejecting the Soviet offer," because "the left in this country may be counted on" to exploit a rejection, and there was a "very remote" risk that the result might be to turn Moscow toward an agreement with Berlin. However, the memorandum concluded that "on balance" the Soviet offers should be rejected as likely to "alienate our friends and reinforce the propaganda of our enemies without bringing in exchange any real material contribution to the strength of our Front."

Cadogan's advice was congenial to the Prime Minister (Halifax was absent) and most of the committee members. Only Hoare and Chatfield were at all receptive to the Soviet project, and the former successfully insisted that the Chiefs of Staff furnish a report on "the military value of Russian assistance" before any decision was reached. In the meantime, the French (who had also received the proposal) were to be asked not to reply until there had been consultation, and the whole matter was to be held secret.

For the Chamberlain government, the situation was indeed "very awkward." An outright rejection of the Soviet proposal, once it became known, would call down upon them the wrath not only of the Labour and Liberal opposition, but also of Churchill, Eden, and the other Conservative dissidents. It soon became apparent that the French were favorably disposed toward using the Soviet plan, at least as the basis for further discussion. But the Polish and Rumanian objections reinforced the intense dislike and distrust of Moscow which Chamberlain, Halifax, Simon, Inskip, Wilson, Cadogan and others shared, and which no doubt helped to inflate their notions of Poland's importance and durability as keystone of the second front.

The Chiefs of Staff report on April 24 was a reasonably objective summary of the Russian military pluses and minuses, but its conclusion played into Chamberlain's hands by declaring, no doubt accurately, that "the positive assistance, whether it be in the shape of military support, or of supplying war material, which Russia could afford to Roumania, Poland, or Turkey is not so great as might be supposed generally." This rather submerged the following observation that "Russian cooperation would be invaluable in that Germany would be unable to draw upon Russia's immense reserves of food and raw materials and should succumb more quickly to our economic stranglehold."

The following day the Foreign Policy Committee, in a brief meeting, unanimously agreed not to accept either the Soviet proposal or a proposed French counterproposal. But how to put the matter to Moscow remained a difficult question. On the twenty-ninth Halifax was obliged to apologize to Ambassador Maisky for the delay in replying to the Soviet proposal, and before the problem was resolved, on May 3, Litvinov was relieved as Commissar for Foreign Affairs by Vyacheslav Molotov.

To anxious inquiries, both Molotov and Maisky assured the British that the change of face involved no change of policy, and that the Soviet proposals of April 18 were still in effect. But the replacement of the cosmopolitan Litvinov by the brusque, stubborn Molotov, who spoke only Russian, certainly brought a change of atmosphere, as Seeds discovered when he finally, on May 8, submitted the British reply, rejecting the alliance as incompatible with Poland's attitude and renewing the "suggestion" that Moscow issue a unilateral statement promising assistance in the event that France and Britain became "involved in hostilities" in support of their guarantee obligations.

So began a process of proposal and counterproposal which was to last for over three months, well into August. By May 22, when Halifax and Maisky conferred in Geneva, it became clear to the British that the Soviet Government would not accept the "suggested" unilateral pronouncement. Meanwhile the Chiefs of Staff had reconsidered the problem and on May 16 advised Chatfield that: "A full-blown guarantee of mutual assistance between Great Britain and France and the Soviet Union offers certain advantages. It would present a solid front of formidable proportions against aggression. . . . If we fail to achieve any agreement with the Soviet, it might be regarded as a diplomatic defeat which would have serious military repercussion, in that it would have the immediate effect of encouraging Germany to further acts of aggression and of ultimately throwing the U.S.S.R. into her arms. . . . Furthermore, if Russia remained neutral, it would leave her in a dominating position at the end of hostilities."

Chamberlain, according to Cadogan, was "annoyed" at the Chiefs and in the Foreign Policy Committee argued against their conclusions, eliciting from Chatfield the response that the Chiefs were "very anxious that Russia should not under any circumstances become allied with Germany. Such an eventuality would create a most dangerous situation for us." Four days later, the Prime Minister was threatening privately to "resign rather than sign an alliance with the Soviet." But Halifax and Cadogan were beginning to change their minds, and by May 23, Chamberlain had yielded, most reluctantly, to proceed with negotiations on the basis of an Anglo-Franco-Soviet alliance.

And negotiate they did, with much acrimony on each side. As Cadogan viewed the process: "The Russians are impossible. We give them all they want, with both hands, and they merely slap them. Molotov is an ignorant and suspicious peasant." Ambassador Maisky, *per contra,* remained convinced that Chamberlain, dominated by the "Cliveden set," wanted the negotiations to fail and kept them going only to quiet the political opposition.

In any event, the British and French were too slow and too late. Since mid-April, German and Soviet diplomats had been probing occasionally, cautiously, and suspiciously to see whether there was any possibility of an advantageous *rapprochement* between the two countries, despite the propaganda war they had been waging since Hitler took power. At the end of May, Berlin decided to take the initiative in establishing closer contact, the first fruits of which were not gathered until mid-July, when long-suspended trade negotiations between the two countries were resumed. By August 3, Ambassador von der Schulenburg, after a meeting with Molotov, was able to inform Berlin that the Soviet Government was "increasingly prepared for improvement in German-Soviet relations, although the old mistrust of Germany persists." Ten days later Molotov sent word that the Soviet Government was "interested in a discussion" of several subjects, including a trade agreement and "the Polish question," and would like it to be held in Moscow.

From this point on, things moved very rapidly. Ribbentrop replied the same day (August 14) that he himself was prepared to make a "short visit to Moscow in order, in the name of the Führer, to set forth the Führer's views to Herr Stalin." Molotov reacted favorably, especially to the idea of a nonaggression

pact, but observed that a visit by Ribbentrop would require "adequate preparation." On the nineteenth, Molotov agreed to receive Ribbentrop on August 26 or
27, but this was not soon enough for Hitler's purposes, as the attack against
Poland was scheduled for the last week of August. The Fuehrer himself now
took a hand in the negotiations and on August 20 sent a personal message to
Stalin asking that Ribbentrop be received on the twenty-second or "at the latest" on the twenty-third, and Stalin promptly agreed to the later date.

The Treaty of Non-Aggression was signed by Molotov and Ribbentrop, in the
presence of Stalin, on August 23, 1939. It contained a provision that, if either
country should "become the object of belligerent action by a third party," the
other country "shall in no manner lend its support to this third power"—thus
ruling out any Russian aid to Britain or France if they went to war with Germany in fulfillment of their guarantees. There was also a secret protocol establishing Russia's and Germany's "respective spheres of influence in Eastern
Europe," which provided the basis for the division of Poland between Germany
and Russia a month later.

On August 25, the formal treaties between Poland and Britain and France
were finally signed, and the news caused Hitler to postpone the attack for a few
days in the hope of buying off the British with new promises. The effort failed, and
early in the morning of September 1, 1939, German troops crossed the Polish
border at all points of attack. Two days later Britain and France honored their
guarantees and declared war against Germany.

And so, eleven months after Munich and five after the Anglo-French guarantees of Poland, "peace for our time" ran out.

CHAPTER 33

An Assessment of Munich

1

On November 24, 1938, Malcolm MacDonald, Minister of Colonies, addressed the House of Commons on the situation in Palestine, where Arab and Jew were at each other's throats. For him Palestine was not "a faraway country" inhabited by "people of whom we know nothing"—on the contrary, the minister could not "remember a time when he was not told stories about Nazareth and Galilee, about Jerusalem and Bethlehem, where was born the Prince of Peace."

Winston Churchill, in a mood of impishness verging on truculence, remarked audibly: "I always thought he was born in Birmingham." Later, confronting Neville Chamberlain, he declared: "You were given the choice between war and dishonour. You chose dishonour and you will have war."*

It was the most epigrammatic and perhaps savage contemporaneous critique of Munich. Clio's files do not disclose what reply, if any, the Prime Minister made, but Chatfield, Newall, Slessor, Pownall, and other service chiefs would have probably said: "It was not dishonorable because it was necessary for the security of Britain. It is true that we got war, but we got it eleven months later, when Britain was far better armed for defense of the Island." Numerous ministers and other civil officials, politicians, and publicists would have echoed agreement, and their followers do so to this day.

Considering the unanimity with which "Munich" and "appeasement" have been accepted as legitimate symbols of feckless, cowardly, and counterproductive yielding, it is noteworthy that the substance behind the symbols still remains a matter of vigorous dispute. Some, but by no means all, of the judgments which have been expressed are jejune, superficial, ill-informed, or distorted by the tug of personal involvement. Others who have spoken, presumably well informed, have nevertheless been very cautious or even noncommittal.

Stanley Baldwin, for example, was critical of Chamberlain's "peace with honour" outburst, and declared that he would have handled the crisis "very

* Churchill first used this diction on September 11, 1938, in a personal letter to his wealthy friend Lord Moyne (William Edward Guinness), declining an invitation for a Caribbean cruise on the lord's yacht: "Alas, a cloud of uncertainty overhangs all plans at the present time . . . Owing to the neglect of our defences . . . we seem to be very near the bleak choice between War and Shame. My feeling is that we shall choose Shame, and then have War thrown in a little later on even more adverse terms than at present." In various forms, Churchill subsequently repeated the remark.

differently." But he left no record of what he would have done. Anthony Eden's judgment is ambivalently phrased: "I have never blamed the British and French Governments for not supporting Czechoslovakia to the point of war, though I think it would have been to their nations' advantage to have done so."

Ambiguity and ambivalence may be legitimate weapons of diplomats and politicians, but should not be the tools of historians. *Caution,* however, is another matter, and is essential to any considered assessment of Munich, if for no other reason than that, retrospectively, the lens of *hindsight* can so distort one's vision of the world which the Men of Munich viewed. That, of course, is a difficulty intrinsic to the historical process in general, but in this instance it is much aggravated by the claims made for Munich by Chamberlain and others at the time, and the rapidity with which they were discredited. "Peace with honour" rang hollow the moment it was uttered, and "peace for our time," less than a year later, exploded in the most cataclysmic war of modern times. How could those men have been so blind? So cynical? So cowardly? Above all, so unctuous?

That, indeed, is precisely why "Munich" and "appeasement" won their places in the vocabulary of strategy and diplomacy. But, of course, it is not at all that simple. If we are to venture an analysis of Munich in terms of "good and bad" or "right and wrong," we much first separate the tangled issues which envelop the controversy.

In the first place, when we identify the focus of the dispute by the word "Munich," do we mean the events of September 1938 which led directly to the conference in that city? Or do we mean the course of world politics during the six or eight preceding years which created the situation in which the "interested" nations found themselves in that month? Many would hold that, *given* the circumstances of September 1938, the British, French, and Czech governments were wise to give way. Fewer would undertake to defend the policies of those countries which permitted these circumstances to arise.

Secondly, what are the values which, arguably, Munich preserved or promoted? Most commonly today the value asserted is the military security of Western democracy. Britain, the lynchpin of any effort to "stop" Hitler by military means, was incapable of self-defense, let alone aid to her allies, in 1938, and had to buy more time to rearm. In the French phrase, the necessary strategy was *reculer pour mieux sauter*. This is not, of course, an argument that Munich was intrinsically "good," but that the alternatives were worse, and therefore Munich was "right" as a necessary expedient.

There are other defenses of Munich, however, which are substantive. One is, essentially, that peace is better than war, and Munich postponed the war. The fact that the peace was brief is irrelevant; the failure could not be certainly foreseen, and the effort to defuse the European powder keg had to be made. The second is that the Sudetenland rightly "belonged to" Germany, and that the Munich cession accomplished this good result by peaceful means. These arguments are seldom advanced today but have been forcefully stated from time to time.

2

I will begin by considering the last argument described above, because it was used by the Germans as the foundation of the demands which led to the Munich crisis. The principal contemporaneous spokesman for this view was, of course, Adolf Hitler himself, although he did not formulate it categorically until the meeting with Chamberlain at the Berghof. Since the Fuehrer laid no claim to objectivity and was using the Sudetenland as an avenue to his larger objective of destroying Czechoslovakia, a more suitable proponent should be found.

Fortunately one is ready to hand in the person of the eminent historian A. J. P. Taylor. It is not always easy to tell when Mr. Taylor's tongue is in his cheek, which makes reading him especially good fun. But in this instance, the context and tone leave little room for doubt that he meant every word:

> British policy over Czechoslovakia originated in the belief that Germany had a moral right to the Sudeten German territory, on grounds of national principle; and it drew the further corollary that this victory for self-determination would provide a stabler, more permanent peace in Europe. The British government were not driven to acknowledge the dismemberment of Czechoslovakia solely from fear of war. They deliberately set out to impose this cession of territory on the Czechs before the threat of war raised its head. The settlement at Munich was a triumph for British policy, which had worked precisely to this end; not a triumph for Hitler, who had started with no such clear intention. Nor was it merely a triumph for selfish or cynical British statesmen, indifferent to the fate of far off peoples or calculating that Hitler might be launched into war against Soviet Russia. It was a triumph for all that was best and most enlightened in British life; a triumph for those who had preached equal justice between peoples; a triumph for those who had courageously denounced the harshness and short-sightedness of Versailles. . . . With skill and persistence, Chamberlain brought first the French, and then the Czechs, to follow the moral line.

The members of the British Government who supported Chamberlain did not all share the same reasons for approving Munich, but the purpose most generally shared among them was certainly not concern for the principle of national self-determination. Dissatisfied national minorities were a dime a dozen in Europe in 1938—Germans in Czechoslovakia, Poland, and the Italian Tyrol; Hungarians in Czechoslovakia, Yugoslavia, and Rumania; Poles in Germany and Czechoslovakia; White Russians and Ukrainians in Poland and Czechoslovakia. There is no evidence of British concern for these other groups, and the reason for singling out the *Sudetendeutsche* was that, unlike the others (except, in a backhanded way in the last few days, the Poles and Hungarians in Czechoslovakia), they had the backing of Hitler and the Wehrmacht. It was not "moral right" but military might that called the turn.*

---

* I do not know what Mr. Taylor had in mind in stating that the British Government "deliberately set out to impose this cession of territory on the Czechs before the threat of war raised its head," for which he states no basis. The British and French never pressed Prague to agree to more than the Henleinists were asking and, as Mr. Taylor correctly observes, Beneš met their demands on September 4. To be sure, Chamberlain had decided after *Anschluss* that Britain would not go to war to preserve Czechoslovakia's territorial in-

Unquestionably "self-determination" played a part in the formulation of British policy. Probably some members of the Government sincerely felt its weight, and certainly others found it a convenient cover of self-righteousness. Furthermore, and like the "back yard" feeling at the time of the Rhineland remilitarization, "self-determination" was a significant obstacle to rousing a war-like spirit in Britain. But the Government's virtual abandonment of Czechoslovakia after Munich, and its indifference to the International Commission's custodianship of the principle, show the shallowness of the Government's dedication to "moral right."

But suppose we look not at what the British Government did, but what, in line with Mr. Taylor's thesis, it *should* have done in the name of "equal justice between peoples"—i.e., follow the principle of self-determination by forcing cession of the Sudetenland to the Reich. There are several flaws in this prescription. Mr. Taylor exalts ancestry and language to the exclusion of all else, quite disregarding the political and social gulf between Nazi Germany and democratic Czechoslovakia, which many residents of the Sudetenland must have accounted far more important than the "national" issue. Vienna after *Anschluss* had been a public demonstration of the consequences of Nazi conquest.

Furthermore, there never was any "self-determination," but only a decision by Germany backed by threats. The Henleinists shouted loud and waved big banners, but no one ever asked the residents of the disputed areas, in a secure and peaceful poll, what they wanted.

Finally, Taylor's prescription takes no account of the dynamics of the situation. One does not give back a gun even to the owner, if it appears probable that he will shortly use it to shoot the giver. Daladier and Churchill and Duff Cooper accurately foresaw precisely that result from the Sudetenland cession.

3

The other of what I have called the "substantive" defenses is that the cession of the Sudetenland was a necessary step toward the prospect of a stable Europe and an enduring peace. As Hoare later wrote, Chamberlain "was right to make the effort to save the world from a great catastrophe."

This view was a natural outgrowth of Chamberlain's long-standing wish to reach an understanding with the Germans, Nazi or not—to "sit down at a table and run through all their complaints and claims with a pencil." It likewise harmonized with the opinion stated by Cadogan after *Anschluss,* and echoed repeatedly by Halifax, that Britain should not "choose any course of action that might plunge Europe into war now to avert what might be a war later on."

All this came to full flower in Chamberlain's mind while formulating Plan Z, as reflected in the letter to his sister Ida on September 11 in which he wrote of the probability that if the plan "came off," it would "go far beyond the present crisis" and furnish "the opportunity for bringing about a complete change in the

tegrity, and it may safely be assumed that his close associates knew of and shared this view. But that is far short of deciding "to impose this cession of territory on the Czechs." There is no substantial evidence of such a policy until *The Times* leader of September 7 (if that is regarded as government utterance despite its disavowal) or, more plausibly, the Cabinet meeting of September 14 just before Chamberlain took off for the Berghof meeting.

international situation." Such was the reach of his hope, and soon the rosy prospect served also as a tool for the persuasion of his colleagues. Right after Godesberg he urged the Cabinet to accept the Hitler ultimatum on the ground that "it would be a great tragedy if we lost this opportunity of reaching an understanding with Germany on all points of difference between the two countries." Thereafter, the combination of apparent success at Munich and popular acclaim both in Germany and England gave the Prime Minister the impression that his hopes for a general settlement would be realized.

Quite naturally, the speedy collapse of the "Munich peace" caused the defenders of the agreement to shift their ground, and Chamberlain himself, before his death in 1940, sought justification in the argument of military necessity for buying time. But the fact that Munich as a peace producer failed the pragmatic test is not a sufficient answer to the point that it should have been attempted.

There was an important corollary to the peace argument, which was that a war among the Western European powers would so weaken them that Soviet Bolshevism would emerge the real winner and spread over Europe.* Indeed, Maisky and others have charged that the British and French governments sacrificed Czechoslovakia with the deliberate purpose of turning Hitler eastward and precipitating a Russo-German war.

Although individual British ministers and officials occasionally made remarks indicating that they would not be displeased by such a conflict, the records lend virtually no support to the idea that such motives played a part in the decision-making. What is clear beyond dispute, however, is that the fear that even a victorious war against Germany would open the way to a westward flow of Soviet power strongly predisposed a number of the British leaders against risking a military solution. Inskip and Zetland both took this line in Cabinet on September 17, and the strong anti-Russian sentiments voiced by Chamberlain, Cadogan, and others at the time of the guarantee to Poland must have likewise affected their judgments during the Munich crisis.

There can be no quarrel with the preference for peaceful rather than violent resolutions of problems, nor with the opposition of democratic governments to the spread of communist dictatorship. But exaltation of peace and democracy does not, without more, illuminate the path to their preservation. How good were the prospects, as viewed in 1938, that cession of the Sudetenland to Germany would ensure, or at least promote, peaceful behavior on Hitler's part thereafter? If the effort failed, how much would have been lost by ceding the Sudetenland rather than facing war in support and with the aid of Prague?

The weight of the "peace" argument is thus dependent on the resolution of other diplomatic or military questions. If, as most of Britain's and many of France's leaders believed, their countries' military situations were desperate in

---

* As we have seen, it was also argued that war was futile because Czechoslovakia would in any event be overrun, and even after an Allied victory would not regain her Versailles borders. But this prediction was used chiefly to bludgeon Prague. It would have been preposterous for Britain to support France in a war to fulfill France's treaty obligation to protect Czechoslovakia's territorial integrity, and at the same time declare that after victory the victors would do precisely what they had shed blood to prevent.

1938 and would be substantially better in a year or two, that was an end of the matter, unless "honor" was to be exalted above national survival. Their only course was to purchase delay, and if by great good fortune it developed into a stable international situation, so much the better. If the military consequences of delay were not so clear, a reasonable or even a slight prospect of a stable peace might justify concessions, if not too costly, to a strong and determined claimant. But if time was running against them, then the chances of peace by propitiation must be strong indeed to warrant yielding.

And so the analysis reverts to the issue as posed by Churchill's thrust at Chamberlain. He and Duff Cooper (and a few others) thought the chances of peace by concession minimal, and that the trial by battle should be confronted at once, if Hitler forced the issue. But most of the civilian officials and nearly all the military leaders thought otherwise on both scores. Can a sound verdict, in retrospect, be rendered?

4

Even allowing for the warping effect of hindsight, it is a safe conclusion that the chances of securing a stable European peace by ceding the Sudetenland were remote, both in fact and as viewed at the time by those involved in decision-making. Even Chamberlain, until the eve of the Munich conference, repeatedly revealed his doubts of such a prospect, in his private letters as well as in ministerial conclave. Believing as he did that the French Army was much less than its image, and well aware of Britain's unpreparedness, he fully shared the view that even if war were inevitable it should be postponed if at all possible. It was not until the excitement of Plan Z, the naïve belief that he had established a "personal influence" over Hitler, and the acclaim of the German crowds had inflated his hopes of emerging as the peacemaker of Europe, that he succumbed to the disastrous conviction that Munich had made war less likely, and therefore the rearmament program did not need to be expanded.

Very few of Chamberlain's colleagues shared his optimism, fluctuating and uncertain as it was. The Halifax-Cadogan opposition to having war immediately rather than the prospect of one later was, at bottom, no more than a hope that something might turn up to avert a later one, and Cadogan in his diary acknowledged "the Micawber strain." In Cabinet on September 17 (after Berchtesgaden) Halifax and Colville drew some comfort from Chamberlain's optimism, but at the crucial meeting on September 25 (after Godesberg), when Halifax parted company with the Prime Minister, he spoke of the necessity of destroying Nazism, which would be a threat to peace as long as it lasted. Only MacDonald and Ernest Brown showed any interest in Chamberlain's hope for a peaceful future once the Sudeten crisis was surmounted, and MacDonald was careful to say that he did not fully share Chamberlain's optimism.

The others who supported Chamberlain's recommendation that the Godesberg terms be accepted invoked the ground that Czechoslovakia could not be protected from German occupation (Maugham, Elliot, Inskip, Kingsley Wood), that even a victorious war would be the ruination of Britain and Western civilization (Inskip, Zetland, Simon), or that Britain's ability to wage war would be improved by delay (Hoare, Burgin, Morrison). Hailsham forcefully repudiated the idea that Hitler would be pacified by annexation of the Sudetenland, and four other members (Duff Cooper, De La Warr, Oliver Stanley, and Winterton) agreed and also thought that if war were to come, delay would be disadvantageous to the western allies. Daladier and Gamelin were of the same opinion but lacked the force to act on the basis of their convictions. Beneš and most of the Czech leaders saw the issue the same way, and surely would have fought had the French backed them firmly. The British Chiefs of Staff and their participating subordinates were all of the view that war was coming, that Britain would be better able to cope with it a year or more hence, and that buying time at the cost even of Czechoslovakia was not only desirable but essential.

In summary, Munich was not, except in Chamberlain's autointoxicated phase, the product of a hope for an enduring European peace. Rather it was the result of a feckless procrastination on the part of some, and of a sincere conviction on the part of others, that the Allies could fight better in the future even with the loss of Czechoslovakia, than they could with her aid in September 1938.

An assessment of Munich in the given circumstances of that month therefore turns on the question of how well founded the "sincere conviction" was. Before essaying the very difficult task of seeing the issue of war now or later through the eyes of those who made the decision, let us take advantage of hindsight and suppose that they then knew all that we know now about the strengths and intentions of the nations directly concerned.

5

A major difficulty with the discussion of most historical hypotheticals is that they are almost infinitely variable. In the case at hand, much might depend on when, between *Anschluss* and September, the Allies had decided to support Czechoslovakia.

If everything had gone as it did in fact until Prague's rejection of the Godesberg terms on September 25, at which point London and Paris had decided that Hitler was impossible, made no further approaches, and ordered full mobilization and war readiness, it would have been almost but not quite too late for the Fuehrer to hold back. *Probably* there would have been war, with only the Germans, the Czechs, and the British fleet mobilized and the Allies unable to take any action in support of Czechoslovakia for some days. But Hitler might have backed off and settled for the Anglo-French terms. These envisaged a cession which would have stripped the Czechs of most of their fortifications. The psychology of such a solution would have been much less favorable for Berlin, but Czechoslovakia would have been nearly defenseless and, before long, would probably have disintegrated and been overrun as it was in March 1939.

Quite different results might have flowed from an Anglo-French decision after *Anschluss*—or even in August when the German mobilization became apparent —that they could not afford to lose Czechoslovakia as an ally and therefore had to commence preparing for war. Hitler might then have postponed Green indefinitely or, if he pressed on, have been obliged either to divide his forces or risk an immediate French attack against Adam's weak screening forces. Decisive action of this sort would likewise have made effective Russian aid much more probable.

But for present purposes, let us take the worst case from the Allied standpoint: the actualities until late September, at which time negotiations broke down, Green was launched, and Britain and France went to war against Germany with the same degree of determination that they exhibited in 1939. Would they have been better or worse off in 1938 than they were in 1939?

Neville Chamberlain's answer, in a private letter written on May 25, 1940, as the Dunkirk evacuation loomed, was categorical: "Whatever the outcome, it is clear as daylight that, if we had had to fight in 1938, the result would have been far worse." He, like many of those who after the fact expressed the same opinion, had a personal stake in it, but it would be wrong to stress this circumstance, for virtually everyone who played a part in the consultations had a personal stake in the verity of what he then counseled. Eminent historians, presumably more dispassionate, such as Sir John Wheeler-Bennett and Captain Stephen Roskill, have held the same opinion.

Some factors, I believe, may be taken as virtually certain. The Chiefs of Staff were desperately worried about war against a German-Italian-Japanese alliance. But Italy did not go to war in 1939, or in 1940 until France was on the brink of defeat, and there is no reason to believe that she would have joined forces with Germany in 1938. Japan did not strike until 1941, and then with the United States as her prime target; there is no reason to think she would have acted otherwise had the European war begun in 1938. In that year Spain was still embroiled in civil strife; Franco was fearful of French or British intervention and would have been more neutral than he was during the war. To summarize, in 1938 Britain and France would have confronted no more foes than in 1939.

For allies, in 1939, they had Poland only. In 1938 they would have had Czechoslovakia, less populous but far better armed and more defensible than Poland. The Soviet Union, which in 1939 joined in the partition of Poland and subsequently sent supplies to Germany, in 1938 would have supported Prague —how effectively would have depended in part on the determination and energy shown by Britain and France. Poland was hostile to Czechoslovakia but, as Jozef Beck later wrote, could not join Germany against the western democracies, and an invasion of Czechoslovakia would have exposed her to attack by Russia. In terms of the balance of forces, and the second front which the Chiefs of Staff ardently desired in 1939, Britain and France would have been far better off in 1938.

In naval strength, the Anglo-French Allies far outmatched Germany and Italy in both years. In August 1938, Raeder told Hitler that only one pocket battle cruiser and six submarines were ready for action. Perhaps this was an understatement, intended to dissuade Hitler from ventures beyond the Reich's reach, but the German strength could have been tripled and still have been minuscule compared to the fleets of the other great powers. In 1939 the heavy battle cruisers *Scharnhorst* and *Gneisenau,* two pocket battle cruisers, and two heavy and five light cruisers were ready for action, as well as twenty-six submarines capable of service in the Atlantic, with many more in training. The British fleet had also been augmented, but certainly its superiority, especially in submarines, was substantially greater in 1938 than 1939.

For offensive purposes, the Royal Navy's weight could be brought to bear only by blockade, and the greater Germany's access to material resources in Central and Eastern Europe, the less effective the blockade. "In so far as sea power is concerned," wrote H. A. Smith* in December 1938, "an analysis of the consequences of the Munich Agreement compels us to draw the inference that the ability of Great Britain to exercise a decisive influence in time of war by her command of the sea has been materially weakened."

He was right; the consequence in 1939 of yielding in 1938 was that Germany had not only the material and industrial resources of Czechoslovakia (including the Skoda munitions plants), but also a clear road to economic domination of southeast Europe, including Rumania with her oil resources. Furthermore, the switch in Soviet policy consequent upon Munich gave Germany trade access to Russian supplies, whereas in 1938 Soviet policy, in the Balkans as well as at home, would have been exerted in support of the British blockade.

In October 1938 the British Army was almost useless for European war purposes—lacking the equipment to fulfill its air defense responsibilities at home and able to send only two poorly equipped infantry divisions to the continent. By September 1939 it had made some progress, especially in antiaircraft defense, but the creation of a viable expeditionary force had been held up for half of the intervening time by Chamberlain's obstinate unwillingness, until February 1939, to acknowledge the necessity of any European field force at all. When war came, the British were nevertheless able to deploy four infantry divisions in France within a few weeks, and there were ten when the Germans finally struck, in May 1940.

The French Army in 1939 had not been, and considering France's population limits could not be, much enlarged over the hundred divisions it could have fielded after full mobilization in 1938. It had considerably more modern equipment in 1939 (its tank strength rose from about 1,350 to 2,250), but the deficiencies in heavy tanks and antiaircraft artillery had not been corrected, and the Army as a whole remained muscle-bound in structure and leadership.

These modest advances in Anglo-French strength on the ground paled in comparison to the strides made by the German Army. The standing army was not greatly enlarged (forty-seven to fifty-one divisions), but the armor was nearly doubled. Mass production of the heavier tanks (Marks III and IV) from the prototypes of 1936 got under way in 1938, and 335 Czech tanks made a useful increment. To the three panzer divisions of 1938, three more were added in 1939, and after the defeat of Poland the four light divisions were converted to panzer divisions, using Czech equipment.

In the summer of 1939 the reserve components were greatly enlarged by calling up twenty-nine divisions of combat-age men and twenty-two of overage *Landwehr* troops. Including these last, Germany in September 1939 had about

* Professor of international law at the University of London, in "The Munich Settlement and the Problem of Sea Power," in *The New Commonwealth Quarterly*, vol. IV, no. 3, p. 287 (December 1938).

a hundred divisions, thus equaling the French in unit strength. It might fairly be concluded that Germany entered the war with some seventy divisions fit for first-line use, and about thirty suitable for static defense in the West Wall, guarding neutral borders, protecting lines of communication, and performing other secondary missions. The result was that on the western front, where in 1938 Adam had five regular and four reserve divisions, in 1939 Leeb (commanding the western front army group) had twelve regular and ten reserve divisions as well as fifteen *Landwehr* divisions.

Leeb's forces were not as large as those the French could deploy against them, but his army group was far superior to the measly screening force that Adam had been saddled with, and of course the Wall itself was by 1939 much stronger. Fifty-two divisions were committed against Poland, as compared to thirty-seven against Czechoslovakia in 1938. All in all, it is clear that, in terms of strength on the ground, the situation was far more favorable to Britain and France in 1938 than in 1939.

The question of comparative air power in the two years is more complicated. Owing to the change-over from the earlier types to those used during the war, the Luftwaffe's tally of operational aircraft did not rise rapidly in 1937 and 1938. But in quality and performance potential, it was certainly greatly improved in 1939 over 1938. Virtually all the combat units were equipped with the Messerschmitts, Stukas, Heinkels, and Dorniers that (with the Junkers 88s and Focke-Wulfs that came later) were the backbone of the Luftwaffe during the war. The year of training had been put to good use, and in the spring of 1939 the Condor Legion returned from Spain and swelled the ranks of combat-experienced flyers.

In 1938 the French had but the shell of an air force, and in 1939 not much more. In Britain the story was quite different. Thanks to Swinton's energy and foresight, aircraft production grew rapidly; in 1939 it was approaching and in April 1940 surpassed the German rate.

Despite this progress, the RAF's *offensive* power was not much greater in 1939, largely due to Chamberlain's opposition to the bomber program because of its cost. The four-engined heavies were not operationally available until 1941, and the Wellingtons, Blenheims, and other medium bombers lacked the range and load to do Germany serious damage. Nor had significant progress been made in the development of tactical air units to support the ground forces.

Defensively, however, the picture was altogether brighter in 1939 than 1938. One thing of which the Cabinet had been thoroughly convinced by the Chiefs of Staff was the danger of a "knockout blow" by the Luftwaffe, and the one military lesson that Chamberlain learned from the Munich crisis was that, despite his own rosy hopes of a general settlement, Britain ought to buy more insurance against this hazard. So the Army got additional funds for antiaircraft guns and other defenses, and the RAF's fighter program was enlarged and accelerated. By September 1939 a majority of the fighter squadrons were equipped with Hurricanes and Spitfires, the radar stations (only three of which were operational at the time of Munich) covered most of southern and eastern England, and the antiaircraft forces were greatly expanded.

The upshot of this reckoning is that only in the defense of Britain against German air attack was the western Allies' situation more advantageous in 1939 than 1938. In every other important military respect, they would have been better off had they fought in support of Czechoslovakia in 1938 instead of throwing her to the wolves.

Still, it may be and is argued that the improved defense against air attack was an *absolutely* necessary prerequisite to Britain's engaging in war. The probability that Germany could, for one or more years after 1938, increase her military capacities faster than Britain and France was recognized by some of the military leaders at the time of Munich. They nonetheless rejected it as a sufficient reason for going to war. The reason—advanced by Slessor, Ismay, and others—was that there was an *absolute* rather than a comparative level of strength which Britain must first attain.

Assuming that in September 1938 there was a substantial and imminent possibility that Germany could and would attempt a "knockout blow," this argument might well be compelling. But, as we have seen, Germany could not accomplish, and her leaders did not intend to attempt, any such thing. Hitler's purpose was to isolate Czechoslovakia and annihilate her without confronting Britain and France, and therefore he had no intention of bringing the British into the fray by attacking them.

Operating from German bases, the Luftwaffe had neither the range nor the clout to do much. Furthermore, its major strength was committed to the attack on Czechoslovakia, and it would have been out of the question for the Luftwaffe, after operations there which must have been at least somewhat costly, to regroup for an assault against Britain before the bad weather of late fall and winter set in. Nor would the Army, after a Czech campaign, with three battered panzer divisions instead of the six available in 1939, have soon ventured a full confrontation with the west, which was the only way to win for the Luftwaffe airfields on the Channel coast. Furthermore, Poland and Russia, allies of France, would overhang Germany's eastern frontiers.

The "knockout blow," short of at least a year, was no more than a bad dream if Britain and France had engaged Hitler in 1938.

Which of these factors and circumstances were unknown, or less surely known, in London and Paris at the time of Munich? The behavior of Italy and Japan could not be surely foreseen, but there were no signs of Italian mobilization or other preparations for war, and Japan was heavily engaged in China. It was expected that Italy, as in 1914, would wait to see how the tide was running before committing herself. Furthermore, the hazard of this hostile triple alliance was an enduring circumstance, and if Britain continued to draw back from a confrontation with one through fear of what the two others might do, the consequence would be an indefinite sequence of retreats, leaving her each time in a poorer position than before. It was to avoid a repetition of this consequence that Britain declared war against Germany in 1939, with no assurance that Italy and Japan would remain neutral.

The comparative strengths of the British, French, and German forces were well known in Paris and London both in 1938 and 1939. The German dispositions against Czechoslovakia were also perceived with substantial accuracy, as was the fact that Adam had only a handful of divisions on the western front. It was likewise known that most of the Luftwaffe was deployed on fields near the Czech frontiers. Of course, it was not known that Helmuth Felmy's assessment of the German operational potential against Britain was so negative, but the performance of the German aircraft types and the operational obstacles they would confront in attacking Britain from German bases were no secret. It must be accounted a major failure of British air intelligence *judgment* that the estimates of German bombing probabilities and potential were so extravagant. The Luftwaffe's threat to Paris and northern France, however, was real, and undoubtedly strongly influenced the French Government to follow the British down the appeasement path, little as Daladier believed that it would yield more than a breathing spell.

In summary, while many details, interesting and some of them important, have become known since the war, most of the factors upon which the foregoing assessment is based were known at the time of Munich. The contribution of hindsight is not so great as to give one much pause about concluding that the British and French governments *should have* realized, as a number of their members did, that they could confront Germany more advantageously *with* Czechoslovakia in 1938 than without her during the next several years.

6

There is, however, one important question to which London and Paris did not have the answer in 1938, and about which we are still poorly informed today. How strong were the Czech forces, and how long would they have contained a substantial part of the Wehrmacht? The reasons that we are still largely in the dark are that the French made little effort and the British virtually none to get the answer to these questions at the time, and that no answer has emerged since the war from Prague's own surviving records. The French maintained a military mission in Prague headed by the very pro-Czech General Eugène Faucher,* but the French Government never authorized Gamelin to engage in staff discussions with the Czechs. The British had a competent military attaché but, as we have seen, Chamberlain was not concerned about the question because his policy was to bring about a nonmilitary solution of the crisis.

The fortifications were, of course, the object of special curiosity on the part of the Germans and were closely scrutinized, as Keitel's memoirs indicate:

> The Czech border fortifications, which had been built on the model of the French Maginot Line under the supervision of French construction engineers, aroused the greatest interest, not only among us soldiers, but with Hitler. We were truly surprised by the strength of the larger forts and artillery emplacements. In the presence of the Führer there were firing tests with our types of

---

* In protest against his government's Munich policy, Faucher announced his resignation from the French Army and offered his services to the Czechs. On September 22, 1938, Faucher had reported to Daladier the scorn manifested by Czech officers at the French "betrayal." This so enraged his superiors that on September 28 Gamelin sent Faucher a stern reprimand: "I impose on you the censure of the Chief of the General Staff and urge you to continue to do your duty as a French general."

artillery. The penetration of our 88-millimeter anti-aircraft guns was amazing, for they went right through the standard emplacement by direct fire at 2000 meters . . .

It is not clear what Keitel meant by the "standard" (*normalen*) fortifications, and, as we have seen, there were four "standard" categories, ranging from the light machine-gun emplacement to the huge "fortifications group." Possibly because the Fuehrer was often on the scene and no one wanted the tests to turn out badly for the German artillery, precise reports of the tests and their results were not circulated widely.* The heaviest Czech fortifications (along the Moravian frontier) were built according to French designs, and on September 28, Gamelin informed the Quai d'Orsay that either they should remain in Czech territory or be destroyed (neither was accomplished), as otherwise "their possession would give Germany precious information about our fortification system." Plainly these forts were placed as they were (before *Anschluss*) to prevent the Germans from cutting the country in two at the narrow waist between Moravia and Slovakia, and enable the Czech forces to stage a fighting retreat eastward into Slovakia.

General Otto-Wilhelm Förster, writing in 1960, described the Czech fortifications as "very strong" in comparison to those of Poland, but remarked that they covered nearly a thousand miles of German frontier, and that "even if the 30 available [Czech] divisions had all been deployed in the border works, they would have been unable to prevent a breakthrough." The "misproportion" between the spread of the fortifications and the size of the Czech Army, and the Czechs' reliance on the aid of allies, Förster described as "basic errors" on the part of the Czech leadership. Strategically, this critique is naïve. Czechoslovakia could not possibly have held out single-handed against Germany, and the whole purpose of the fortifications and, indeed, of the Czech forces as a whole (over and above what they needed for defense against the Poles and Hungarians) was to delay and inflict losses upon the Germans, in the hope of ultimately decisive aid from powerful allies.

Certainly the Czechs could better accomplish these objectives with than without the fortifications, and the question was: how long would be the time and how heavy the German losses? The French-style fortifications lay opposite Rundstedt's Second Army front, and it was behind them at Freudenthal that Student's airborne force was to have been landed in the hope of taking them in the rear and assisting the breakthrough. General von Choltitz later wrote that, after careful study of the structure and layout of the fortifications, he and his colleagues concluded that, even if the defenders had fought with determination, "the support that we [the airborne force] would have given the main body of the German army debouching from Silesia would have effected a breach in the strong line of blockhouses." But how soon, Choltitz did not say, and his opinion is self-serving and speculative at best.

Major Kenneth Strong, touring the Sudetenland with a German staff officer as

---

* Presumably the technical reports were in the files of the ordnance division of the Army General Staff, the fate of which I have so far been unable to trace.

escort, reported: "As we drove through the line of Czech fortifications at Freudenthal the Staff Officer with me remarked that the German Staff had been surprised at the completeness and extent of the Czech fortifications. They were more formidable than they expected—an opinion I have heard from more than one German officer."* He added, however, that it was the man behind them that mattered, and the Czech moral [sic] would never have been equal to the task of holding them."† The speaker had seen the fortifications, but the basis for his assessment of Czech morale does not appear.

To the west opposite Bock's Eighth Army, where the defenses were lighter, Colonel Röhricht studied his chosen breakthrough point and concluded that the rolling terrain would have given his troops enough cover from the Czech bunkers' field of fire to get behind them. Further west near Teplice, Guderian found the fortifications "not as strong as we had expected," but was greatly relieved "that we did not have to capture them in bloody battle."

Apart from these personal reports, there are scattered references to the fortifications in the contemporaneous army records. There were test shootings, but the results are not recorded.‡ In Reichenau's sector, XIII Corps reported that the Czech forts were not made of the "best material" and that their own good training and heavy artillery would have produced a breakthrough in a single day. But the operations officer of the VII Corps, Lieutenant Colonel Emil Vogel, who inspected bunkers near Hintring, recorded that they "seemed very solid, and our troops would have suffered heavy losses in an attack."

After a survey the intelligence section of the Army General Staff recorded that the state of the Czech fortifications on the Silesian front was "very diverse," and that on the Austrian front some sectors were "ready" and others not. Considering their geographical extent, the multinational make-up of the Czechoslovak forces, and the variety of terrain, that description is plausible, and one can only conclude that in some sectors the defenders would have held out for some time and inflicted heavy losses on the attackers, while in others the Germans would have broken through easily and either cut off substantial bodies of Czech troops or forced them rapidly eastward into Slovakia.

Of course the fortifications were by no means the only factor. The Czechs would not, at the onset, have been greatly outnumbered on the ground, but they were greatly inferior in air power. They had a considerable quantity of good tanks—good enough so that in 1940 the Germans used them to equip three

---

* Ian Colvin later wrote: "When they returned from Bohemia, the German reserve officers told me that they had found the Czech fortifications impressive and impregnable to our arms. We could have gone around them, perhaps, but not reduce them. As it is, we have left engineers to fill them with earth and rubble."

† Strong's escort officer added that "now they had seen the Czech fortifications they knew exactly what the Maginot line was like, as these former, according to their information, were modelled on it."

‡ For example, on October 7, Leeb ordered that two Czech bunkers be selected as targets for experimental shooting, and on the tenth that the press and public should be excluded and the results reported through his headquarters. Brauchitsch and Förster visited Leeb on the fourteenth and probably witnessed the tests. On the eighteenth, again at Leeb's direction, the 1st Mountain Division shot at a bunker near Hintring with machine guns, mountain artillery, an antitank gun, and a field howitzer.

panzer divisions. The Czech Army as a whole appears to have been spotty in equipment and leadership, but Faucher and the perhaps more objective British military attaché, Colonel Stronge, both reported that it was well prepared and would give a good account of itself.*

7

Strictly military and diplomatic factors are not the only considerations in an assessment of Munich. It has often and forcefully been argued that the state of public opinion and sentiment in Britain was such that the country would not have marshaled its resources or fought with determination in 1938, and that this became possible only after Hitler's destruction of the Prague government in the spring of 1939. The same point is not often made about France, largely because French morale was thought to be nearly as poor in 1939 as 1938.

Proponents of this view point to Britain's long years of disarmament and peace; to the unanimous counsel against war given by the military leaders; to the overwhelming support given Chamberlain by his Cabinet and party colleagues; to the explosion of heartfelt gratitude and even adulation touched off by the Munich Agreement. These features of the situation cannot be disregarded, and lend substance to the view that, for Britain, war in 1938 would have been politically and psychologically too soon.

Nevertheless, I believe that these circumstances must be considered in conjunction with others, if one is to attempt a picture of what the British mood would have been in the event of war. The pronounced shift in public opinion during and after the Godesberg meeting, resulting from Hitler's rejection of Chamberlain's proposals and from publication of Hitler's terms, showed that the British *could* be aroused to a high pitch of indignation; the subsequent general approval of Munich was given under the misapprehension that the Prime Minister had secured good terms for Czechoslovakia and good prospect of peace with Germany.

Let us suppose that, after Godesberg, Chamberlain had told Britain and the Empire that the Prague government had accepted proposals which would yield all German-majority areas and most of the Czech nation's natural and constructed defenses to the Reich; that Hitler had reneged on the Berchtesgaden understanding and rejected these terms; that his word was not to be trusted and he probably nourished further plans of aggrandizement; that the loss of Czechoslovakia's military capacity, especially after the Rhineland and *Anschluss,* would gravely affect Britain's security; and that unless Germany were checked Britain would confront a new and more sinister Napoleon—

---

* Thirty years after Munich, Generals Krejčí and Syrový (the latter had been imprisoned from 1945 to 1960 under a treason conviction for selling arms to the Germans in his official capacity after the 1939 occupation) and several younger Czech officers published short articles describing the military situation at the time of Munich. *The Reporter,* vol. 3, no. 3, pp. I–XV (Prague, October 9, 1968). They yield little new information; Krejčí wrote that the Germans got from the Czechs some 1,600 aircraft, 550 antitank guns, 2,175 artillery pieces, 43,000 machine guns, and 469 tanks and armored cars.
For a generally negative assessment of the Czech forces, see Hauner, *Zari 1938: Kapitulovat ci Bujovat* in the Prague periodical *Svedectvi,* no. 49 (1975).

would not the island and the Dominions have understood and acted upon his warning? If the Prime Minister in his radio address to the nation late in September had trumpeted a fanfare instead of intoning a dirge, could he not have awakened his country to its peril? No doubt it would have gone to war grimly rather than ardently, but that was also the case in 1939.

Furthermore, it should have been apparent that Germany would not have been able to hurt Britain very badly for at least a year. The time the services wanted to buy could have been theirs without sacrificing the aid that Czech arms would provide. To make the most of that time, Britain most needed a sharp jab with the needle of danger. Munich itself should have done that, but Chamberlain did not feel the prick, and the result was a disastrous setback to the development of the offensive forces that were so necessary if Germany was to be held away from the Channel coast, where the possibility of a "knockout blow" would become real.

General "Tiny" Ironside, who in 1938 had opposed war because of fear that the Luftwaffe would blow Britain to bits, in May 1940, as the German Army was cutting through the Allied front, lamented to Eden that: "N.C. had not decided on a continental army until April last year. . . ." War would have been a needle thrust that Chamberlain would surely have felt, and Britain would have rearmed faster than it did after Munich had postponed the evil day.

8

The perils of attempting a description of what would have happened, even in the early stages of a war in 1938, are surely obvious. But the British and French should not have ventured a confrontation that year without reckoning the probable consequences. What should they have foreseen, and how would the war have developed?

Spain and probably Italy and Japan would have remained neutral. Russia would have massed troops on her western frontiers (the Baltic States, Poland, and Rumania), raised the charge of German aggression at Geneva, perhaps sent a liaison mission and some air and technical support to Czechoslovakia, and waited to see whether or not Britain and France meant business. Hungary would have held back, awaiting developments. The Poles would have been in a real bind; if Prague had promptly ceded Teschen, they would have remained neutral but, in a long war, would have eventually joined the western powers, voluntarily or in consequence of a German attack.

If vigorously led, the French could have improvised a striking force that could have cut through Adam's screen and invaded the Rhineland, including much of the Ruhr, thereby at worst relieving pressure on the Czechs and destroying a vital part of Germany's industrial resources, and at best precipitating Hitler's overthrow. But Gamelin was not the man for such an hour, and the British, petrified at such rashness, would have tried to restrain any such move. A slow and cautious French advance would have helped the Czechs a little, but not much. The British might have attempted a few air raids (as they did in 1939), but would have accomplished little. Since the bulk of the Luftwaffe was committed against Czechoslovakia, there would have been no German attempt at a "knockout blow" and probably nothing but a few reconnaissance flights over Britain.

At Munich, a few hours before the agreement was signed, Bodenschatz button-holed Stehlin and told him that the Luftwaffe would have carried out a crushing (*foudroyante,* Stehlin's word) operation against the Czechs, with low level attacks on their airfields and military objectives near the front, and dive-bomber assaults on "small targets" of importance (probably the fortifications and ammunition dumps). He continued:

> We have of course taken into account the effect of the Czechoslovak anti-aircraft defences. Our general staff knows that they are strong and have even estimated that, in such an operation, the losses could amount to half of the aircraft employed. Nevertheless we are sure that in assessing at this proportion the size of these losses, all the targets would be destroyed, and the ground forces could, for their part, attack under the most favorable and decisive conditions. The losses could be made up without delay from our plentiful reserves.

No doubt much of this was said for effect, but the expectation of heavy losses was probably both sincere and well founded. Indeed, it is unlikely that the Luftwaffe would have been able to bring off its attack *foudroyante* because of the bad weather. All the accounts of those going into the Sudetenland with the German troops confirm the cloudy, wet weather, and the war diaries of VII Corps and Leeb's headquarters recorded six days of rain and eight of fog from September 30 to October 11.

The post-Munich reports from Sperrle's and Kesselring's air fleet headquarters reflected the difficulties their airmen would have confronted. Sperrle's observed that the Czechs had been alerted by the German deployment and had moved their air units from their regular bases to satellite fields. This would have dulled the edge of a sudden German assault, though ultimately attacks on the Czech transport and supply systems would have crippled their air force. But the bad weather would have sharply curtailed German air operations, since the commitment of big formations would have entailed intolerable operational losses. Only small attacks with highly trained crews would have been possible, and these might not have been decisive. Kesselring's staff reported that the Czech Air Force could have caused serious difficulties by attacking the German airfields in Silesia and the transportation network south of Breslau.

The air reserves of which Bodenschatz boasted were virtually nonexistent. The OKL Chief of Supply reported that the Luftwaffe was woefully short of both repair facilities and aircraft reserves, and probably could not have fought for more than four weeks. The weather would have affected the ground forces too; on October 3, VII Corps' war diary recorded that the heavy early fog of the past few days would have given their infantry cover in approaching the fortifications, but would have hampered both the artillery and the air force in supporting the assault.

Considering the bad weather, the lack of training of most of the German air crews, the quality of the Czech artillery, and the close quarters at which much of the fighting would have taken place, it is altogether probable not only that

Bodenschatz's predictions of heavy losses would have proved accurate, but also that the Luftwaffe's bombs would have killed a lot of German as well as Czech soldiers. All this would have prolonged Czech resistance and multiplied German losses.

But the German weight would soon have told, and within a matter of weeks the Czechs would have been fighting desperately to hold open the narrowing passage to Slovakia, so that the surviving formations from Bohemia and Moravia could pass through to regroup and establish a front. Whether or not that would have been possible would have depended upon the extent of the German losses, the degree of pressure on the Germans in the west, the actions of Poland and Russia, and whether France and Britain showed themselves determined to fight it out to a finish.

No doubt Hitler would have made peace overtures, as he did after conquering Poland. For Britain and France to accept them would have meant their total elimination from Europe east of the Rhine and the Alps, and domination of the entire subcontinent by Germany. If, as is probable, Hitler's peace bid was rejected, a period of stagnation must have ensued, for the Wehrmacht would not have been strong enough to attack in the west in the late fall of 1938, and probably not in 1939, especially with the Russian and perhaps the Polish threat overhanging the eastern front.

Further than this it is idle to venture a judgment. But one can safely say that the possibility of establishing an Allied front in France that would hold would have been far better than it was when the war actually began—both because France and especially Britain would have had more time to strengthen the front, and because Germany could not have denuded her eastern frontiers and concentrated virtually all her forces in the west, as she was able to do after the Nazi-Soviet pact and the destruction of Poland.*

9

The foregoing considerations were insufficient to sway the decisions of the Allied statesmen and generals in September 1938, and today many historians defend Munich as, in A. J. P. Taylor's phrase, "the best that could be done in almost impossible circumstances."† What were these circumstances? The question has been answered, both at the time and since, by describing Munich as the unavoidable consequence of prior mistakes. Sir John Wheeler-Bennett has made the classic statement of this view:

> Let us say of the Munich Agreement that it was inescapable; that, faced with the lack of preparedness in Britain's armaments and defences, with the lack of unity at home and in the Commonwealth, with the collapse of French morale, and with the uncertainty of Russia's capacity to fight, Mr. Chamberlain had no alternative to do other than he did; let us pay tribute to his

---

* In this hypothetical analysis I have taken no account of the "Halder plot" and its possible effect on the German military and political situation. It is, I believe, too speculative a factor to be included in a conservative assessment.

† In his introduction to H. Montgomery Hyde, *Neville Chamberlain* (1976), p. x. This assessment appears to reflect a considerable tempering of the views expressed in his own *The Origins of the Second World War* (1962), discussed earlier in this chapter.

persistence in carrying out a policy which he honestly believed to be right. Let us accept and admit all these things. . . . But, because of these sins of omission between 1933 and 1937, Britain was forced to other sins of commission in 1938; because she was too weak to do otherwise, she was compelled to condone chicanery, aggression and injustice and to become an accessory to these outrages. There is nothing for pride or congratulation in the story of this whole period. . . .*

What were the "sins of omission between 1933 and 1937"? The deficiencies in rearmament and lack of unity mentioned by Wheeler-Bennett were interlocking factors; had there been greater unity there would have been more rearmament. There is very general agreement that British rearmament was too little and too late, and Britain's political leadership bears the responsibility both for the insufficiency of the program and for the failure adequately to enlighten the public on the nature and gravity of the dangers Britain faced.

Wheeler-Bennett joined with Churchill and others in placing the responsibility on Baldwin rather than Chamberlain: "The blame for the delay in British rearmament lies not so much at Mr. Chamberlain's door as at those of Mr. Baldwin and Mr. MacDonald, and the credit for the fact that Britain began to rearm even in 1936 is due in great measure to their Chancellor of the Exchequer [Chamberlain]." While none of the three† prime ministers who held office between 1923 and 1940 deserves any accolades on this score, the official records now available do not support that judgment.

The good and bad points of Baldwin's rearmament record have been examined in Chapter 10, and the reader need only be reminded that MacDonald and Baldwin initiated the first system for survey of Britain's needs through the DRC and DPRC, from whose deliberations emerged the first rearmament program; that a five-division initial Army expeditionary force was agreed upon; that the RAF program was substantially enlarged and much of the basic Second World War weaponry—Spitfires, Hurricanes, four-engined bombers, and radar defenses—was designed and put under construction; that Swinton, Inskip, and Duff Cooper were brought into the service ministries. In the rearmament field, Baldwin's major sins were his failure to galvanize the public, his illness in the summer of 1936, and his preoccupation with the royal abdication after his return from convalescence. Indubitably this caused nearly a year of leaderless drift at a critical time.

Should Baldwin have resigned in June 1936, when his health failed? Had he done so, Neville Chamberlain would have come to power almost a year sooner (how he would have dealt with the King and Mrs. Simpson is only collaterally relevant). No doubt he would speedily have brought order out of chaos and reestablished systematic procedures for the review and determination of rearmament questions, as he did when he became Prime Minister in the spring of 1937. But would rearmament have benefited from his advent?

* The passage quoted was composed in 1948. In the Foreword to the 1962 reprinting of his book, Sir John wrote that intervening disclosures had confirmed it as a "true assessment of what happened at Munich."

† Ramsay MacDonald's period of real responsibility for rearmament was too brief to warrant comparative assessment.

Consider the Chamberlain record in rearmament in the eight years from November 1931, when he became (for the second time) Chancellor of the Exchequer, to the outbreak of war in 1939. In March 1932, when the Chiefs of Staff strongly urged cancellation of the "ten-year rule," Chamberlain opposed them. In May 1934, while Chamberlain was boasting in his diary that he had "practically taken charge of the defence requirements of the country," the DRC's first report on defense needs came before the Cabinet committees for review. Chamberlain opposed both the DRC's recommendation for expansion of the fleet to meet the Japanese menace and for a five-division Army continental expeditionary force. In June he reinforced the second point in a personal memorandum which described the Army's proposed expenditures as so large "as to give rise to the most alarmist ideas of future intentions or commitments." He supported an increase in the RAF's home defense squadrons,* but in November 1934, when definite information on German air rearmament became available, he unsuccessfully opposed an Air Ministry proposal for acceleration of aircraft production. A year later the DRC renewed its recommendation of an Army field force for continental employment. Early in 1936, Chamberlain joined with Lord Weir in opposition to the plan, and it was Baldwin who proposed the compromise that salvaged something for the Army. In December 1936 the War Office renewed its pleas for modern equipment for the Territorial Army, and won Inskip's qualified support, but once again Chamberlain, questioning the assumption that Britain must be prepared to fight on the continent, stood in the way.

Such was Chamberlain's rearmament record as Chancellor of the Exchequer, and his accession as Prime Minister, with the compliant Simon at the Treasury, cemented his power to give effect to his opinions. It is certainly true, as a recent and able student of the subject, Dr. Robert P. Shay, Jr., has written, that Chamberlain brought "order to the rearmament program." But the "order" was achieved by means of the £1500-million five-year rationing plan, with priorities within that limit to be settled among the services in the light of the Inskip report. Inskip himself was dutiful but doubtful of the wisdom or practicability of a fixed ceiling, and of course the system broke down under the successive blows of *Anschluss,* Munich, the war scares, and the destruction of the Prague government. But the rationing concept was a sea anchor on rearmament at the most critical prewar period.† Its immediate result was to suppress, for over a year, virtually all progress toward an Army force capable of continental warfare, postponement for at least a year of the two-ocean naval standard, reduction in the appropriations for antiaircraft artillery and other ground defenses against air attack, and even curtailment of what the Air Ministry regarded as an already inadequate aircraft production program. Finally, Chamberlain returned from Munich dazzled by

---

* As in later years, the one area in which Chamberlain was less miserly with rearmament funds was the defense of Britain against air attack.

† I cannot follow Dr. Shay's conclusion that the Chamberlain reorganization made British rearmament "more efficient and effective," in the light of his immediately preceding statement that it resulted "in the development of programs that were not adequate to meet the nation's defence requirements." Perhaps he overlooked Swinton's reply when Simon advised him to get along with a "smaller, more efficient" air force, that efficiency was no substitute for effectiveness.

spurious prospects of peace, with the consequence that, except for air defense, there was virtually no expansion or even acceleration of rearmament until the spring of 1939.

Baldwin's failings in rearmament were primarily due to his own tendency to procrastinate, and to physical debilitation. Chamberlain's conduct of affairs was considered, energetic, and uncompromising. In weighing Churchill's comparison of the two men, it is well to remember that he had been Baldwin's Chancellor of the Exchequer in the twenties, and that Baldwin did not take him back to the Cabinet in the thirties, while Chamberlain restored Churchill to office in 1939.

Churchill's verdict in 1937 that "when the government were at length convinced of the urgent need to rearm no one was more active than Mr. Chamberlain" is literally accurate, for "active" indeed he was. But his activity was too often directed to the rejection or reduction of programs which the service ministers and Chiefs of Staff thought necessary, and his success in imposing those limits was based on misjudgments which had disastrous results. Energetic and dedicated to the public good as he was, Chamberlain must be held primarily responsible for the parlous state of British arms in 1938 and 1939.

10

Was Britain's slowness in rearming an all-sufficient determinant of Munich, or could military action have been taken at some earlier time to bring Hitler down or clip his wings, so as to end at least the apparent and proximate German threat to peace? No doubt from a purely military standpoint the Reich could easily have been brought to heel by the western democracies between 1933 and 1935; some think it was still the case at the time of the Rhineland remilitarization, but others contend that by then it would have taken a major war to overcome the Wehrmacht. Practically speaking, the issue is not purely military, and its ambit included Italy as well as Germany.

When Hitler's intent to rearm became manifest, no doubt the French Government secretly considered forceful preventive action, and Hitler, as noted in Chapter 6, remarked that "real" French statesmen would do just that. But except for Britain the Versailles victors, especially France, had so bad a record on the promised international disarmament that the moral and political case for such action would have been hopelessly weak. Indeed, at least until the Roehm massacres and the assassination of Dollfuss in mid-1934, a French invasion to suppress German violations of Versailles would have been almost the only thing that would have made Adolf Hitler the object of sympathy in the democracies. The same factors were still operative, though perhaps less compellingly, in March 1935, when German rearmament was officially acknowledged.

In fact, the first (and perhaps best) opportunity for Allied military action directly concerned Italy rather than Germany, and arose from the Italian invasion of Ethiopia in October 1935. Closing the Suez Canal and oil sanctions— perhaps either of them—would have cut off the Italian forces in Ethiopia and stopped them in their tracks. Chatfield and his fellow-admirals were certain that, if Mussolini were stung into hostile action in the Mediterranean, Britain single-handed could defeat the Italians. It is very doubtful that the Fascist regime could have survived such a blow.

Furthermore, acting pursuant to the League's decision and in support of collective security, the Royal Navy would have been on the side of the angels. But that was just where neither Chatfield nor the First Lord, Sir Bolton Eyres-Monsell, wanted to be, for neither of them believed in collective security or the League. A few weeks before the Italians attacked, Chatfield wrote to his fellow-admiral W. W. Fisher:

> I have mixed feelings about a war. The bumptiousness of Italy is so great that it may be worth fighting her now to re-assert our dominance over an inferior race. But against that a hostile Italy is a real menace to our imperial communications and defence system. We have relied on practically abandoning the Mediterranean if we send our Fleet East. For that reason I do not want to go to extreme measures and hope the Geneva Pacifists will fail to get unanimity and the League will break up.

This was a politically primitive and psychologically obtuse analysis. Combined with Hoare's equally purblind policy of lip service to sanctions and negotiation with Mussolini, the disastrous result was that the League powers hit Italy hard enough to make the Duce very angry, but not hard enough to stop him from conquering Ethiopia.

Thus Chatfield proved his prediction that collective security would never work by combining with Hoare to murder it. Italy emerged from the affair not as a defeated country painfully aware that Britain and the League meant business, but as a proud victor over not merely Ethiopia but the effete western democracies as well. Nazi Germany, diplomatically isolated after Stresa, merely by neutrality during the Ethiopian affair reawakened Mussolini's interest in an entente with the Reich, and the Duce gave Hitler a green light for the Rhineland remilitarization—a move that Hitler would probably not have ventured had the British and French acted decisively against Italy. Thus was laid the basis for the Axis, without which there would have been no *Anschluss,* and therefore no Munich, in 1938.

Chatfield and Hoare were the main agents of this disaster, but of course Baldwin bore the ultimate responsibility. It was a blow to his prestige and self-confidence from which he never fully recovered, and which no doubt contributed to his physical breakdown a few months later. Except for the Rhineland crisis, when there was no significant division of opinion within the British Government, and the abdication, Baldwin never again played a leading part in major policy decisions.

In the Ethiopian matter France discouraged Britain, and in the Rhineland crisis Britain discouraged France, from doing what needed to be done to protect their mutual interests in European security. Both morally and pragmatically, the two problems were very different. Whether Ethiopia was independent or part of the Italian Empire was, in itself, quite irrelevant to the balance of power in Europe, whereas the demilitarized Rhineland was one of its keystones. But while Germany's claim to freedom of action in the Rhineland was flawed in a treaty sense, otherwise it was very plausible; Italy, in contrast, had no legal or moral grounds for the annexation of Ethiopia.

The British public understood the moral ("Jerry can do what he likes in his own back yard") but not the pragmatic point. The latter was more complicated, and the Government made no effort to explain its importance, because they did not want to intervene, or to see France intervene. Baldwin was adamantly opposed to taking any action because of Britain's unpreparedness and his fear that a defeated Germany might "go Bolshevik," and the Chiefs of Staff gave their opinion that war with Germany would be a "disaster." Militarily, it was a gross misjudgment; to be sure Britain was ill-prepared, but Germany in 1936 was in no shape to take on France, and Poland and Czechoslovakia had made it clear that they would give France full support.

But what about the moral issue: would it have been "right" for Britain and France to use force to keep the Rhineland demilitarized? Like the comparable question with the Sudetenland, this was a matter of timing and dynamics. In a Locarno world, moving toward a détente, the Rhineland restrictions would have been an unjustifiable anomaly. But by 1936 the likelihood of German aggrandizement was plain enough so that long-standing safeguards should not have been eliminated unless new ones were substituted. If the Rhineland demilitarization had been preserved, Chamberlain could not have said in 1938 that Britain and France could do nothing to protect Czechoslovakia against a German occupation. Therefore, it would have been no sin to use force to preserve this gage, and Britain, by restraining the French, lost the last good opportunity to preserve a European balance of power and hold Hitler in check without seriously risking a major war.*

11

If I have focused the foregoing analysis on Britain, it is because the major decisions during the crucial 1935 to 1938 years were made in London. But Baldwin, Chamberlain, and their colleagues had to deal with the world around them, and primary responsibility for the collapse of European security lay elsewhere.

The most important factor in the causal sequence was the ossification of French military doctrine and practice, in consequence of which France's once-powerful air force withered away, and her army degenerated into a lumbering, inflexible defensive force. Thus the Pétain of Verdun became the Pétain of Sedan, and his name rightly serves as the symbol of France's military decline. His age may mitigate Pétain's guilt, but it likewise underlines the responsibility of the politicians and generals who allowed his palsied hands to freeze on the levers of military policy.

France suffered as much as Britain from the consequences of Ethiopia, but her responsibility for the fiasco was of a different nature. Laval's policy was entirely logical, given his belief that Stresa was more important than Geneva. He

---

* Austria in March 1938 presented no comparable opportunity. She had small means of self-defense and no treaty allies. Italy had been regarded as her guarantor, and French hopes to preserve Austrian independence were based on the Gamelin-Badoglio plans, which the Axis relegated to the wastebasket.

and Gamelin had just concluded an arrangement with Mussolini and Badoglio which in effect gave the Duce a free hand in Ethiopia, in conjunction with a military alliance in support of Austrian independence. Laval thought its preservation a greater protection to France than collective security via the League. But Laval, like Hoare, completely misjudged public opinion, and the "deal," which was more his than Hoare's, blew up in his face. It was altogether fitting that Pétain and Laval became the twin pillars of Vichy France, for no others did as much as they to bring about the disaster of which Vichy was the product.

The decline of French diplomacy during the between-war years is somewhat puzzling, because (in contrast to the military leadership) France was well served by her professional diplomats. Léger and Bargeton at the Quai d'Orsay were perceptive and articulate, while ambassadors such as François-Poncet, Corbin, Coulondre, and Noël clearly outmatched most of their British and American colleagues.* But French diplomacy lacked continuity, perhaps because of the frequent gyrations of French politics. This may go some way to explain the rickety system of alliances which Bargeton analyzed so critically in his memorandum of June 30, 1936, wherein he pointed out that France's Eastern European allies were not allied with each other, and that among the three most important, Poland was at swords' points with Soviet Russia and unfriendly to Czechoslovakia.

This had the consequence that France could not count on the aid of more than one ally except against a danger which threatened more than one. Remilitarization of the Rhineland was a menace to all of them and furnished the only occasion when France could have counted surely on the support of both Poland and Czechoslovakia, the only two who could act immediately against Germany. Even given the sluggishness of the French Army organization, the triple assault would have been quite too much for the newborn Wehrmacht to cope with, and Britain's assistance would have been unnecessary. Gamelin's estimates of German strength were so fantastic, and his later statement that he was not informed of Poland's support so incredible, that one might well suspect him of deliberately undercutting Léger and the several ministers who wanted to take military counteraction. Certainly he, as well as Pétain and Laval, must be accounted a major architect of the situation that produced Munich.

And what of Poland? In the fall of 1969, A. J. P. Taylor lectured at Churchill College in Cambridge. Without a note and speaking with great and apparently extemporaneous fluency, he concluded by comparing the wartime fates of Czechoslovakia, which suffered comparatively little physical damage, and Poland, where Warsaw was flattened and there was general devastation, and asking

---

* It is remarkable that both British and American diplomatic representation in the major European capitals during the pre-Munich years was so poor. Henderson, Phipps, and Perth were all professionals, presumably trained to report dispassionately, but Henderson and Phipps were extremely tendentious, and all three were defeatist-appeasers—the main difference among them being that Henderson and Perth truckled to their hosts, while Phipps laid down the law to his. Of the Americans, Dodd was a sturdy anti-Nazi but no diplomat, while his successor, Wilson, was a competent professional. Wilson, Bullitt, and Kennedy were all of the peace-at-any-price school of thought, and the last two functioned more as floating presidential spokesmen than as State Department agents. Of Joseph E. Davies as Ambassador in Moscow, the less said the better.

rhetorically whether this did not show that the Czechs were wise to yield in 1938, and the Poles fools to fight in 1939.*

However, one good question deserves another. Were the Poles fools not to fight in 1938 in alliance with Czechoslovakia, instead of assisting in her destruction? In the early stages of the war they could have helped each other far more than France could have helped either of them. With the two countries in defensive alliance Hitler probably would not have launched Green; if he had, British and French pressure on Prague would have been much lessened, the Czechs would not have given in, and the prospect of a two-country eastern front might even have stimulated Gamelin to do something drastic in the Rhineland.

The Poles well knew that the Russians coveted their eastern and the Germans their western marches, and that their ostensibly good relations with the Reich were only an *amitié de convenance*. Squeezed between the hostile giants, in the long run Poland depended for her security on support from the west, and for the short run Czechoslovakia was the only neighboring power that could give her effective aid against Germany. Blind or indifferent to all this, the Polish "colonels" allowed old grudges and Teschen† to prevail over common sense, and chose to walk the tightrope between Berlin and Moscow. As in France, there were many who bore responsibility for these disastrous policies, but surely Jozef Beck's name leads all the rest.

12

"Unfortunately, as a deterrent to a serious historical investigation of the Czech crisis, the 'lessons of Munich' linger on," wrote Keith Robbins in a thoughtful study of the subject. He continued:

> Whatever contemporary practice, contemporary theory has erected "anti-appeasement" into a general law of foreign policy. The stale legends of political polemic still serve as substitutes for serious thought. Yet the only great lesson of Munich, the most difficult to learn, is that there are no great lessons. Historians, useless in predicting the future, achieve something if they prevent others doing so.

While at first blush Dr. Robbins appears to be saying that Munich *in particular* teaches us no "great lessons," the last-quoted sentence indicates that his point is that history *in general* teaches no such lessons, which he appears to equate with "predicting the future." Compassion forbids that in the closing pages of this long book I should inflict on the reader a theory of history, but I must observe that the quoted paragraph, while containing a useful warning, can only be accepted subject to much qualification.

There is no need to labor the point that history, in its broad sense, is the basis

---

* The first limb of this comparison is sounder than the second, for even if Poland had given way she might have soon become the battlefield for Germany and Russia, and a favorite playground for Heinrich Himmler.

† I do not mean to say that the Poles were solely to blame for the mutually suicidal bad relations between the two countries. Beneš made the mistake of relying *too* much on the west. Voluntary cession of Teschen would have cost little and, especially if coupled with the early cession to the Reich of heavily German border districts such as Asch and Eger, would greatly have strengthened Czechoslovakia's diplomatic posture vis-à-vis Germany.

of all prediction, since the past is all we know. It has always seemed to me that the unending argument about the classification of history as art, or science, or neither is unprofitable, since most if not all art and science are the products of history. Despite Henry Ford's "history is bunk" dictum, he could no more have designed the Model T without the aid of history than Michelangelo could have shaped the *Pietà*. Prediction, like creation, is an extrapolation of the past, and in fields where the variables are manageable in number, it is often highly accurate.

But in political-diplomatic-military history, which is the kind with which Dr. Robbins and I are treating, the variables are virtually infinite, and prediction correspondingly difficult if not impossible. His caution against deriving from Munich a general principle of intransigence is well taken, for it has indeed become a feature of our political rhetoric to characterize any concession as appeasement in the manner of Munich.

That is intellectually stultifying, for of course it may often be the better part of wisdom to yield, or "run away and live to fight another day." But the decision whether or not to give way must be faced, and that inevitably involves prediction.

Historians, in their capacity as such, may be no better able to predict the future than other men. However, they do provide a resource of information that those charged with the responsibility of decision are bound to use, and men's fates often turn on the skill with which the decision-makers read the record. The study of Cannae and Agincourt may not tell Wellington how to deploy his troops at Waterloo, nor the Marne cast any direct light on the issues in the SALT talks. But major political and military questions are almost always a compound of innumerable and imponderable pluses and minuses, pros and cons, maybes and probablys. Those responsible for such decisions, when called on to explain, commonly give varying and often inconsistent reasons, and it is probable that in many if not all cases they are unable to explain to themselves exactly how they struck the balance. The weight given to particular factors is bound to be determined not so much by measurement as by mood, predilection, and memory of facts, events, and stories that have stuck in the mind.

Great events, especially those that are intrinsically dramatic and have a signally fortunate or unfortunate outcome, inevitably become symbols of an attitude, a quality, a failing. Munich has thus become a symbol of decisions to yield, wrongly reached because of fear and selfishness. It was a particularly unlovely episode because great powers broke their promises and yielded up a small nation to the mercies of a regime openly preaching racial hatred and bent on conquest. "Democratic Czechoslovakia was, in the last resort, a victim of democracy," writes Dr. Robbins, and he quotes T. S. Eliot, who had experienced "a feeling of humiliation" and was shaken by the event "in a way from which one does not recover" because Munich raised a doubt "of the validity of civilization." Alexander Solzhenitsyn, in his 1972 Nobel Prize lecture, invoked the symbol of Munich in a fierce indictment of our times:

> The spirit of Munich is not a thing of the past, it was more than a short episode. I would even venture to say that the spirit of Munich is predominant in

the twentieth century. The entire civilized world trembled as snarling bar-barism suddenly re-emerged and moved into the attack. It found it had noth-ing to fight with but smiles and concessions. The spirit of Munich is an ill-ness of the willpower of rich people. It is the everyday state of those who have given in to the desire for well-being at any price, to material prosperity as the main aim of life on this earth. Such people—and there are many of them in the world today—choose to be passive and to retreat, just so their normal lives may last a little bit longer, just so the move into austerity may not happen *today*. And as for tomorrow, it'll be all right, you'll see . . . (But it won't be all right! The price you have to pay for your cowardice will be all the worse. Courage and victory come to us only when we resign ourselves to making sacrifices.)

Adolf Hitler made the Munich crisis, and Neville Chamberlain resolved it by the sacrifice of Czechoslovakia. But in so doing, he acted for the men and women of Britain as he divined their wishes, and at the time he read them aright. They wanted "their normal lives" to "last a little bit longer."

It is not for us to criticize them; so do most of us today, despite looming perils such as poverty, pollution, resource depletion, terrorism, and nuclear war-heads. Munich does not tell us how to overcome these hazards, but it is a potent and historically valid symbol of the dangers of not facing up to unpleasant reali-ties. That is not a new lesson, but it is a great one, and it is the lesson of Munich.

ORDER OF BATTLE

GERMAN AIR AND GROUND FORCES

SEPTEMBER 1938

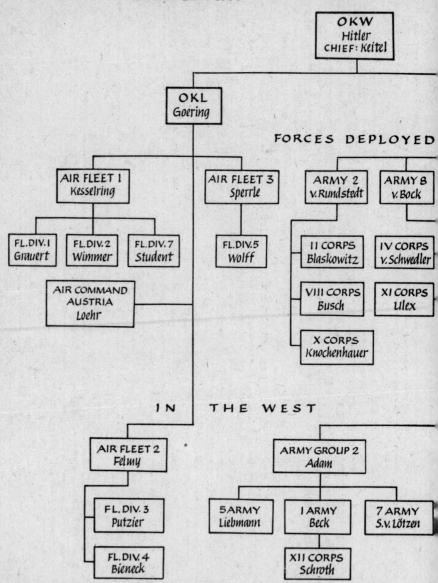

The I Corps headquarters would have become the Third Army.

The XIV and XV Corps were probably inactive; their divisions (motorized and light) were distributed among the corps facing Czechoslovakia. General von Wietersheim, Commander of XIV Corps, became chief of staff to Adam, and General Hoth, Commander of XV Corps, took over the 18th Division from Manstein, who became chief of staff to Leeb. None of the "Halder plot" accounts indicates that Witzleben or Brockdorff left Berlin, so it may be assumed that neither the III Corps headquarters nor

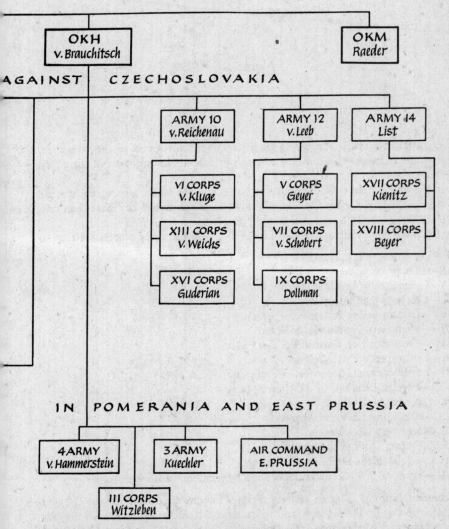

OKH
v. Brauchitsch

OKM
Raeder

AGAINST CZECHOSLOVAKIA

ARMY 10
v. Reichenau

ARMY 12
v. Leeb

ARMY 14
List

VI CORPS
v. Kluge

V CORPS
Geyer

XVII CORPS
Kienitz

XIII CORPS
v. Weichs

VII CORPS
v. Schobert

XVIII CORPS
Beyer

XVI CORPS
Guderian

IX CORPS
Dollman

IN POMERANIA AND EAST PRUSSIA

4 ARMY
v. Hammerstein

3 ARMY
Kuechler

AIR COMMAND
E. PRUSSIA

III CORPS
Witzleben

the 23rd Division was committed against Czechoslovakia.

According to the plans as of September 18, the Second Army would have had eight infantry divisions, one armored and one light division; the Eighth Army four infantry divisions; the Tenth Army three infantry and three motorized infantry divisions, one armored and one light division; the Twelfth Army seven infantry divisions and one mountain division; and the Fourteenth Army one infantry, one motorized infantry, one armored, and one light division, and two mountain divisions.

Notes

The bracketed numbers [ ] preceding each paragraph correspond to the numbered sections of the chapters. The italicized numbers in parentheses are those of the pages in this book to which the notes refer.

When the source is an authored book, the Notes give the author's name, and the alphabetical Bibliography gives the title of the work. If the author has more than one work listed there, a short title is also given in the Notes.

The following abbreviations are used for the major documentary sources utilized:

AIR—Air Ministry documents
CAB—Cabinet documents
CID—Committee of Imperial Defence documents
COS—Chiefs of Staff documents
DBFP—Documents on British Foreign Policy
DDF—Documents Diplomatiques Français
DGFP—Documents on German Foreign Policy
DIA—Documents on International Affairs
ESF—Les Evénements Survenus en France de 1933 à 1945
FRUS—Foreign Relations of the United States
NA—National Archives
NCA—Nazi Conspiracy and Aggression
ND—Nuremberg Documents
PREM—Prime Minister documents
TMWC—Trial of the Major War Criminals
TWC—Trials of War Criminals before the Nuremberg Military Tribunals

Documents from the German military archives may be cited either by the German file designation or by the category and roll numbers from the microfilms in the National Archives in Washington, D.C. Documents from the Public Records Office in London are cited by file designations—PREM, CAB, etc.

INTRODUCTION

(*xi*) John Barlow Martin, *Adlai Stevenson of Illinois* (Doubleday, 1976) 677; *Adlai Stevenson and the World* (Doubleday, 1977) 741. (*xii*) Kennedy 186; Maugham Ch. 19; A. J. P. Taylor 189.

CHAPTER 1

[1] This chapter is based largely on documents in DBFP, DGFP, and FRUS, as well as on François-Poncet, Cadogan, and Ciano. (*4–5*) Bullitt 260.

[2] There are many accounts, some by eyewitnesses, of the scene in the House of Commons, Sept. 28, 1938, e.g., Churchill 316–17; Nicolson 368–71; Eden, *Reckoning* 33–35.

[3] (*11*) Masaryk at Foreign Office: Wheeler-Bennett, *Munich* 170–71 (citing no source, apparently based on personal information). (*12*) House of Commons, Feb. 21, 1938, pp. 63, 154; Maisky: DBFP-3d-II No. 1221.

CHAPTER 2

[1] (*14–15*) DBFP-3d-II No. 1227; Douglas-Home 65; Strang 144; Wheeler-Bennett 104–09; Eubank 128–32; Noguères 124–25.

[2] (*15–18*) Bonnet, *De Washington;* François-Poncet, *Fateful Years;* Gamelin; Stehlin; and personal interviews with Léger, Rochat, and Clapier. (*16*) Radio speech: Werth, *France and Munich* 309.

[3] (*18–20*) Ciano; Anfuso.

[4] (*20–21*) TMWC, testimony of Goering and Neurath; TWC, testimony of Erich Kordt and P. O. Schmidt; memoirs of Kordt, Ribbentrop, Schmidt, and Weizsaecker. (*20*) Weizsaecker agenda: DGFP-D-2 No. 1169 and p. 1005 fn. 10.

[5] (*21–23*) Anfuso; Ciano, *Diary;* Donat. (*22†*) Anfuso 72–75.

[6] (*23*) Attolico: Stehlin 99; Shirer, *Berlin Diary* Sept. 28, 1938.

CHAPTER 3

The descriptive material in this chapter is based on accounts of the conference by Anfuso; Ciano, *Diary;* Donat; Douglas-Home; François-Poncet; Henderson; Kirkpatrick; Kordt; Ribbentrop; Schmidt; Stehlin; and Weizsaecker, as well as the testimony of Goering, IX TMWC 293; and Kordt; Schmidt; and Weizsaecker; TWC Case No. 11. Daladier's account in *Candide* (September 1961) adds some detail but is unreliable on his own conduct.

The semiofficial records of the conference by Schmidt and Kordt are in DGFP-D-II Nos. 670 and 674, and by Sir Horace Wilson in DBFP-3d-II No. 1227.

[1] (*24–25*) Standard travel guides and Dresler, *Das Braune Haus* (Munich) 1939.

[2] (*29*) Ribbentrop's disputed presence: personal interviews with Léger and Douglas-Home, and letter from Sir Horace Wilson, Jan. 21, 1970.

[3] (*31*) Daladier-Bullitt: FRUS 1938 v. I p. 711.

[4] (*34*) French journalist: Georges Blun of *Le Journal,* quoted in Noguères 269. (*34–35*) Hitler-Mussolini lunch: Donat; Anfuso 82.

[5] (*36–37*) List of points: PREM 1/266 No. 40; see also DGFP-D-IV No. 1 and DBFP-3d-II No. 1225.

[6] (*37–38*) Beneš, *Pameti* (340–41); Masařík's official report is reprinted in English in Ripka 224–27 and in German in Král No. 245. My text is supplemented from Masařík's letter to me of Mar. 26, 1974.

[7] (*42*) Chamberlain letter to sister: Feiling 363–64, 366–68. (*43*) Bullitt: FRUS 1938 v. I p. 711. (*46*) Anfuso 82–83.

[10] *(54)* Shirer, *Berlin Diary* 144–48. *(55)* Daladier-Lacroix: DDF-2e-XI No. 480. *(54–57)* Czech decision to accept Munich terms: Ripka, *passim;* Korbel 128–43; *New Documents* Nos. 57–60.

CHAPTER 4

[1] *(58–59)* French return: Daladier, *Candide;* François-Poncet, *Fateful Years;* Stehlin; Werth; see also Noguères 300–3.

[2] *(59)* Italian return: Anfuso; Ciano, *Diary;* Arnaldo Cortesi in New York *Times* Oct. 1, 1938.

[3] *(59–66)* Chamberlain-Hitler and British return: Strang; Douglas-Home; Schmidt; Feiling 376; Schmidt's record: DBFP-3d-II No. 1228. *(63)* Birchall: New York *Times* Oct. 1, 1938; Gunther, *Inside Europe* (1938 ed.) xx; Shirer, *Berlin Diary;* Daladier: FRUS 1938 v. I pp. 711–12. *(64–66)* Halifax; Duff Cooper; Douglas-Home; Wheeler-Bennett, *King George VI* 356.

CHAPTER 5

For general background I have used, among other books, Paul Birdsall's *Versailles Twenty Years After* and J. M. Keynes' famous indictment, *The Economic Consequences of the Peace.*

[1] *(69)* Wilson's Armistice Day announcement: Birdsall 22. The jingle is from the First World War song "Goodbye Maw, Goodbye Paw." The treaty arms limitations are discussed in Taylor, *Sword and Swastika* 21–28 and 42–45.

[5] *(76)* The anti-Keynes revisionists include Birdsall and Etienne Mantoux, whose *The Carthaginian Peace or the Economic Consequences of Mr. Keynes* is a cogent if not wholly convincing riposte.

CHAPTER 6

General sources: Bullock; Carsten; Craig; Hitler; O'Neill; Papen; Robertson; Taylor, *Sword and Swastika;* Waite; Weinberg, *Foreign Policy;* Wheeler-Bennett, *Nemesis* and *Wooden Titan;* also Hitler's speeches and press interviews from collections edited by Baynes (English) and Domarus (German).

[8] *(95)* Hitler to Reichenau: *Vierteljahreshefte für Zeitgeschichte* 1959 p. 429; Hitler's speech at Hammerstein's home: *id.* 1955 p. 434; to Army and stormtrooper leaders: General von Weichs' unpublished memoirs.

[10] *(98–100)* Foerster; Geyr von Schweppenburg; Hossbach; see also Braubach, *Der Einmarsch Deutscher Truppen in die entmilitarisierte Zone am Rhein im März 1936* (Köln 1956); Robertson, *Zur Wiederbesetzung des Rheinlandes 1936,* 10 Vierteljahreshefte für Zeitgeschichte 178 (1962).

[11] *(101*)* DGFP-C-III pp. 1109–10. *(101)* *Schulung:* NC 139-C; Beck's reaction: Foerster 30–31.

CHAPTER 7

General sources: Baer; Beaufre; Brogan; François-Poncet, *Fateful Years;* Gamelin; Griffiths; Micaud; Pertinax; Reynaud; Rowe; Shirer, *Collapse;* Warner;

Werth, *Destiny;* also essays by F. W. Fox and R. D. Challener in E. M. Earle, edit., *Problems of the Third and Fourth Republics;* DDF and ESF.

[3] (*108*) Weygand, *Foch* (1947) 337.

[4] (*109*) Shirer, *Collapse* 184. (*110*) *ibid.*

[10] (*126*) Laval: Gamelin II 178–80; Laval-Goering: Rochat's memorandum, printed as an annex to Baraduc, *Tout ce qu'on vous a caché* (Paris 1949) 301–11.

[11] (*128–34*) Dobler: testimony in ESF II 407 *et seq.*, Gamelin II 193–217.

[12] (*136*) At Gamelin's home: DDF-2d-I No. 334. (*138*) At Sarraut's home: ESF testimonies.

CHAPTER 8

General sources: Aloisi; Anfuso; Baer; *Ciano's Diplomatic Papers;* Del Boca; Fermi; Kirkpatrick, *Mussolini;* Macartney and Cremona; Seldes; Wiskemann; essays by H. Stuart Hughes and Felix Gilbert in Craig, edit., *The Diplomats;* DBFP, DDF, DGFP.

[7] (*158**) DBFP-2d-VI Nos. 530–33 (July 26, 1934).

[9] (*165*) DGFP-C-IV Nos. 579, 598, 602.

CHAPTER 9

General sources, Soviet Union: Dirksen; Eudin and Slusser; Fischer (both); Hilger and Meyer; Ulam; essays by Laue and Roberts in Craig and Gilbert, edits.; DBFP, DDF, DGFP.

[3] (*177*) DGFP-C-I Nos. 284, 460, and II No. 47.

[4] (*181*) Schulenburg-Litvinov Nov. 1933: DGFP-C-IV No. 407.

[7] General sources, Poland: Debicki; Jedrzejewicz; Lipski; Lukasiewicz; Noël; Roos; Szembek; H. L. Roberts' essay in Craig and Gilbert, edits.

[8] (*187†*) DBFP-2d-IV No. 298 and V No. 43.

[9–10] General sources, Balkans: Stephen A. Fischer-Galati, *The New Rumania* (Cambridge, 1967); Milan Hodža, *Federation in Central Europe* (London, 1942); John A. Lukacs, *The Great Powers and Eastern Europe* (1953); Hugh Seton-Watson, *Eastern Europe Between the Wars* (1945); Felix J. Vondracek, *The Foreign Policy of Czechoslovakia, 1918–1935* (1937).

CHAPTER 10

General Sources: Avon, *Facing the Dictators;* Churchill, *While England Slept;* Divine; Londonderry, *Wings;* McElwee; Middlemas and Barnes; Mowat; Muggeridge; Nicolson, *Diaries* and *King George the Fifth;* Postan; Richards; Rowse; Shay; Templewood; Neville Thompson; Watt, *Naval Agreement.*

[1] (*197–99*) Oxford debate: Hollis, *The Oxford Union* (London 1965) 184–93; interview with Dr. Frank Hardie; contemporaneous news accounts.

[2] (*199*) Crowe memorandum: Ashton-Gwatkin, *The British Foreign Service* (1949) 82–83. (*200*) Martin 21. (*201*) Grenadier's bones: Middlemas and Barnes 356.

[3] *(202)* Churchill, 220–21. *(203–4)* Middlemas and Barnes 317–41; Gilbert and Gott 68–79, 82–91, 101–5, 128–30, 289–92, 312–13.

[4] *(206–9)* Lapse of the Ten-Year Rule: CAB 19/32, 23/70, 24/229, 53/4; CID 1082-B and 1087-B; Roskill, *Hankey* II pp. 537–38; Shay 22–27.

[5] *(211)* CID Nov. 9, 1933: CAB 2/6, CID 1112-B. *(212)* DRC Feb. 28, 1934: CAB 4/23, CID 1147-B. *(213)* COS 335, Mar. 5, 1934.

[6] *(218)* DRC May 17, 1935: Weir papers, D.C.(M.) *(32)* 143. *(218†)* AIR 8/186.

[7] *(219–24)* General sources: Churchill 137–42; Dönitz, *Memoirs* (1959) 9–11; Hinsley 4–9; Papp; Raeder 166–67; Schmidt 32–36; Templewood 135–48; Watt, *Anglo-German Naval Agreement*. *(221)* CAB 23/82 June 19, 1935. *(224)* Litvinov-Bullitt: FRUS 1935 I p. 168, June 28, 1935.

[8] *(224–33)* General source: Marder. *(225*)* Vansittart, *Lessons of My Life* (1943); Hardie 47. *(227)* DPRC July 1, 1935; CID 1187-B. *(227*)* Vansittart, *The Mist Procession* 45. *(227)* Baldwin to Hoare: Jones, Jan. 7, 1936. *(228–31)* Chatfield 88; DRC 37; CAB 23/82, 83, 84. *(231)* Vansittart-Corbin: CAB 24/257. *(231*)* Middlemas and Barnes 881; Hardie 166. *(233*)* Vansittart, *The Mist Procession* 522–23, 545.

[9] *(233–34)* Hankey-Fisher-Vansittart: CAB 21/540. *(234–35)* Air Staff reports: AIR 8/186/7, 12. *(235)* DRC reports July 24 and Nov. 21, 1935: DRC 25, 37, in CAB 24/257, 259. *(236–38)* DPRC discussions: Weir papers. *(238–39)* White Paper: Cmd. 5107.

[10] *(240)* Phipps: CAB 24/257, 259; CID 1206-B, 1210-B, 1211-B. *(241)* Vansittart and Cabinet: CAB 24/260, CAB 23/83. *(243)* Jones-Toynbee: Jones Mar. 8, 1936; Toynbee 281. *(244–45)* CAB 23/83. *(246)* German attachés: Geyr von Schweppenburg 63. *(246–47)* Service memoranda: AIR 9/69/100 and AIR 9/73. *(247†)* Collier App. XXVI pp. 494–95. *(248)* German air staff report: Völker 74 and note 137; COS April 1, 1936, CID 1224-B.

[11] *(249)* Rowse 54. *(250)* "lunatics": Jones Apr. 30, 1936; Kennedy 143. *(251†)* Schmidt 112. *(252)* *Times* and Versailles: Rowse 7.

Chapter 11

General sources: Adlon; Aga Khan; Anfuso; J. R. M. Butler; Colvin, *None So Blind;* Dirksen; Martha Dodd; William E. Dodd; Fromm; Henderson; Jones; Londonderry, *Ourselves;* Meissner; Schmidt; Shirer, *Berlin Diary;* Stehlin.

[1] *(255–59)* Taylor, *Sword and Swastika* 99–117. *(256)* Milward, *The German Economy at War* (1965), based on Table A. 21 in S. Andic and J. Venerke, *The Growth of Government Expenditure in Germany Since the Unification (1964)*. *(256)* U-boats: Dönitz 28–32; Raeder 194–95. *(258)* Völker, *Deutsche Luftwaffe* 101–3.

[2] *(260–61)* Japan: DGFP-D-I *passim*.

[5] *(269)* Liu, *A Military History of Modern China* (1956).

Chapter 12

General sources: Avon, *Facing the Dictators;* Bolín; Cattell, both works; Ciano, *Papers* and *Diary;* Dahms; Markes; Oliveira; Raeder, 220–30; Thomas; Toynbee and Boulter, *Survey of International Affairs 1937,* II; DDF, DBFP, DGFP.

[3]   (*280–84*) Sources on Condor Legion: Beumelberg, *Kampf um Spanien* (Oldenburg 1939); Bley, *Das Buch der Spanienflieger* (Leipzig 1936); *Deutsche Kämpfe in Spanien* (Berlin, issued by Condor Legion, 1939); Dwinger, *Spanische Silhouetten* (Jena 1937); Hoyos, *Pedros y Pablos—Fliegen, Erleben, Kämpfen in Spanien* (Munich 1939); Kuhl, *Deutsche Flieger über Spanien 1936–1939;* Lent, *Wir kämpften für Spanien* (Oldenburg 1939); Sperrle, *Condor Legion,* Völkischer Beobachter, May 31, 1939; K. G. von Stackelberg, *Legion Condor* (Berlin 1939). On the Spanish Nationalist Air Force: Kindelan, *Mis Cuadernos di Guerra* (Madrid 1947); Larios, *Combat over Spain—Memoirs of a Nationalist Fighter Pilot* (Macmillan 1966). (*282*) Warlimont's description of his mission: United Nations Security Council, *Report of the Subcommittee on the Spanish Question* (June 1946) 13. (*283*) First use in Spain of Messerschmitts and Heinkels: Green, *Augsburg Eagle—the Story of the Messerschmitt 109* (Doubleday 1971); Price, *German Air Force Bombers of World War Two,* I (Doubleday 1968); Windrow, *German Air Force Fighters of World War Two,* I (Doubleday, 2nd ed. 1971).

[4]   (*284†*) DGFP-D-3 No. 151, Dec. 11, 1936. (*285**) Cattell, *Soviet Diplomacy* 4; DGFP-D-III No. 489.

[5]   (*286*) Guernica: Galland, *Die Ersten und die Letzten* 42–43; Morgan-Witts and Thomas, *The Day Guernica Died* (Hodder & Stoughton, 1975); G. L. Stern, *The Tree of Gernika* (London 1938), which describes the campaign against Bilbao from the Basque side and gives a detailed account of the bombings of Durango and Guernica.

CHAPTER 13

General sources: Foerster; Hossbach; Jodl diary; Keitel; Taylor, *Sword and Swastika* 136–45.

[1]   (*294–95*) Goering, Farben: Taylor 95–99, 121–26; ND NI-051. (*295*) Blomberg order Mar. 1937: ND NI-623. (*296–97*) Blomberg directive: ND C-175. (*296**) The three directives described: NDs C-139, C-140, C-159. (*297–98*) OKW-OKH dispute: Jodl diary, ND 1780-PS; Keitel, *Memoirs* 35–37, *Verbrecher* 93–114, 123–42; Manstein, 280–95.

[2]   (*299*) Hossbach memorandum: ND 386-PS; better translation, DGFP-D-I No. 19; Blomberg memorandum of Nov. 5, 1937: NA T-77, Roll 237, fr. 978604. (*301–2*) Ensuing discussion: Hossbach 138, 217–20.

[3]   (*302*) I TMWC 189–92. (*302–4*) Provenance and authenticity: Bussman, *Zur Entstehung und Überlieferung der Hossbach-Niederschrift,* in *Vierteljahreshefte für Zeitgeschichte* (October 1968); D. S. Detwiler, *The Origins of the Second World War,* unpublished paper read at several historical association meetings in 1965–66; Hossbach; H. G. Seraphim, *Nachkriegsprozesse und zeitgeschichtliche Forschung,* in Festschrift für Herbert Kraus entitled *Mensch und Staat in Recht und Geschichte* (Kitzingen 1954) 436, 444–46. (*303†*) Transcript of Blomberg interrogation Sept. 5, 1945. (*303–4*) Nuremberg defendants on Hossbach: Goering, IX TMWC 306–07; Raeder, XIV TMWC 34–36, and *My Life* 267; Neurath, XVI TMWC 639–41. (*304*) Bullock 370; A. J. P. Taylor 122. (*305**) Goering statement: NCA Supp. B. pp. 1089, 1101. (*306*) Beck's critique: Foerster. (*306**) Blomberg memorandum is from German naval files and was kindly furnished to me by David Irving. (*306–7*) Supplemental directive: ND 175-C, in XXXIV TMWC 745–47, lacking the appendices for "Green," which are in DGFP D-II 635–38.

CHAPTER 14

[1] (*308–12*) Halifax visit: Avon, *Facing the Dictators* 576–85; Halifax 184–91; Churchill, *Gathering Storm* 249; Schmidt 75–78; DGFP-D-I; Halifax papers in "Hickleton Collection" at York. (*311*) Schmidt transcript: DGFP-D-I No. 31.

[2] (*312–13*) Goering vs. Schacht: Taylor, *Sword and Swastika* 122–74; Schacht, *Confessions* 335–45; NDs EC-244, 248, 251, 255, 256. (*314*) Wehrmacht and police: ND D-665, a leaflet distributed to the troops in 1941. (*314–15*) Fritsch-Himmler: ND 1780-PS (Jodl) March 1937.

[3] Blomberg-Fritsch crisis, general sources: Foerster; Förtsch; Hossbach; Keitel 35–53; Kielmansegg; Manstein 296–319; Röhricht 111–19; Taylor, *Sword and Swastika* 127–74; ND 1780-PS. Dates of various events referred to in the text have been fixed, in some instances, with the aid of a calendar of Keitel's appointments kept by his adjutant, Captain Wolf Eberhard.

[7] (*327*) Hitler on Feb. 5, 1938: Manstein 115–17, 233, quoting recollections of Generals Hoth and Liebmann; Weichs's unpublished memoirs. (*328*) Relation between Hossbach conference and dismissals of Blomberg and Fritsch: Kielmansegg, *Die militärpolitische Tragweite der Hossbach-Besprechung*, in *Vierteljahreshefte* (1960) 268–75. (*329**) Henderson 107; Blomberg's Nuremberg interrogation Sept. 5, 1945.

CHAPTER 15

General sources: Brook-Shepherd, *The Anschluss* (1963); Eichstädt, *Von Dollfuss vs. Hitler;* von Hartlieb, *Parole: das Reich;* Karl Itzinger, *Tagebuch vom 10. Feb. bis 13. März 1938* (1938); Manstein 320–32; Papen; Puax, *Mort et Transfiguration d'Autriche* (1966); Selby; Schuschnigg, *Austrian Requiem* (1947) and *The Brutal Takeover* (1971); Wagner and Tomkowitz, *Ein Volk, ein Reich, Ein Führer—The Nazi Annexation of Austria 1938* (1971); Zernatto, *Die Wahrheit über Österreich* (1939). Nuremberg testimony (TMWC) of participants: Glaise-Horstenau, XVI 113 *et seq.;* Goering, IX 293 *et seq.;* Jodl, XV 354, 457 *et seq.;* Keitel, X 503 *et seq.;* Neurath, XVI 642 *et seq.;* Papen, XVI 299 *et seq.;* Ribbentrop, X 244 *et seq.;* Guido Schmidt, XVI 149 *et seq.;* Seyss-Inquart XV 614 *et seq.;* see also *Der Hochverratsprozess gegen Dr. Guido Schmidt* (Austrian State Press, Vienna 1947) with testimony of Glaise-Horstenau, Goering, Jansa, Liebitzky, Miklas, Müllmann, Papen, Schuschnigg, Guido Schmidt, and Seyss-Inquart.

[1] (*331–32*) Hitler July 26, 1934: ND 2799-PS. (*332**) Sauerbruch, *Das war mein Leben* (1951) 515. (*333–34*) Schuschnigg, *Requiem* 98–99. (*334*) Agreement text: DGFP-D-I Nos. 152, 153.

[2] (*334*) Protocol: DGFP-D-I No. 182. (*335*) Venice meeting: Ciano's *Papers* 108–15; Schuschnigg, *Austrian Requiem* 109–11. (*336*) German financial support: DGFP-D-I Nos. 192, 202. (*337*) Hitler's authorization to Keppler: DGFP-D-I No. 241 and ND NG-2934. (*338*) Papen December scolding: DGFP-D-I No. 275.

[4] (*344*) Keppler's testimony: XII TWC 761–64. Draft protocol: DGFP-D-I No. 294. (*345*) Signed protocol: *Id*. No. 295.

[5] (*346*) Deceptive military measures: NDs. 1775- and 1780-PS. (*348–50*) Hitler meetings with Keppler and others: DGFP-D-I Nos. 318, 328; Keppler meetings with Schuschnigg, Schmidt, and Seyss-Inquart: *Id*. Nos. 333–35 and XII TWC 767–68; Schuschnigg, *Brutal Takeover* 249–51. (*350**) DGFP-D-I No. 336.

[6] (351) Miklas approval of plebiscite: Schuschnigg, *Brutal Takeover* 236; Miklas testimony at Guido Schmidt trial 260, but compare Wagner and Tomkowitz 15–16.

[7] (354*) XX TMWC 568; NA T-78 Roll 24. (354†) Manstein 322. (353–56) Military assembly orders: Manstein 320–32; Guderian 49–57; NDs. C-102, -103, -175, -182; Goering, Keitel, Jodl testimony and memoirs cited *above;* Weichs's unpublished memoirs.

[8] (358–67) Events of Mar. 11–12, general sources: In addition to those already cited, Friedrich Rainier testimony, XVI TMWC 123 *et seq.;* ND 812-PS; Eichstädt. (360) Goering's telephone calls: ND 2949-PS. Affidavits of Brauchitsch, Weichs, Milch, Günther Altenburg, and Wilhelm von Grolmann submitted in behalf of Keppler as Documents 13, 67, 96, 8, and 7 (respectively) at his Nuremberg trial, TWC XII-XIV. (365*) Transcript of Nuremberg Case No. 11, U.S. v. Weizsaecker, p. 12868.

[9] (367–69) Entry of German troops: General von Bock's official report of July 18, 1938, *Der Einsatz der 8. Armee im März 1938 zur Wiedervereinigung Österreichs mit dem Deutschen Reich,* T79 Roll 14; Guderian 49–56.

[11] (370) Ribbentrop memorandum: DGFP-D-I No. 146. (372) Hitler decree of Mar. 15, 1938: ND 2936-PS. (372*) Gannon 154–59. (373) "Clean-up" of Austrian officers: Schuschnigg, *Brutal Takeover* 284–86.

[12] (373) Schmidt circular telegram: *Brutal Takeover* 318–19. (374–75) Schuschnigg's thoughts: *Id.* 140, 197, and *Austrian Requiem* 14.

CHAPTER 16

[1] (377–80) Relevant documents in DGFP-D-II, which is entirely devoted to the Sudeten-Munich crisis and covers the period from Oct. 1937 to Sept. 30, 1938.

[2] (381) Mussolini comments: Ciano, *Papers* 151–52. Mackensen letter: DGFP-D-I No. 745. (382*) Schmundt file on "Green": ND 388-PS. (383) Weizsaecker analysis: DGFP-D-I No. 755.

[3] (383–86) Hitler trip to Italy, general sources: Anfuso 55–65; Ciano, *Diary,* entries Jan. 7 and 20, Apr. 5, and May 2–10, 1938; Schmidt 80–84; Speer 109–10; Weizsaecker 129–30; DGFP-D-I Nos. 756–62.

[4] (386) 1937 plan: ND 3798-PS, a statement signed at Nuremberg in 1945 by Brauchitsch, Halder, Manstein, Warlimont, and Westphal. (386–87) OKH and OKW leadership memoranda: Keitel, *Verbrecher* 143–66; ND L-211. (387) Viebahn: Keitel, *Memoirs* 60–61; my interview with Viebahn on Jan. 27, 1948. (387–88) ND 388-PS item 2. (389) Kirkpatrick: DGFP-D-II No. 151. (389–90) May 20 "Green" draft: ND 388-PS item 5.

[5] (390 et seq.) "May crisis": Relevant documents in DBFP-3d-I and DGFP-D-II; Stehlin 79–81; Frantisek Moravec (chief of Czech military intelligence), *Master of Spies* (1975) 109–11. (391) Thuringian war game: Völker, *Dokumente und Dokumentarfotos* item 186. (392) Czech assessment: DBFP-3d-I No. 349. (393) Schmundt telegram from Berghof: ND 388-PS item 8. (394–95) Directive May 30, 1938: *Id.* item 11. Wiedemann affidavit: ND 3037-PS; Kordt, *Wahn und Wirklichkeit* 110; Beck's notes: Foerster 88–90.

CHAPTER 17

The major sources are the messages from and to the British, German, and French legations in Prague for the period, contained respectively in DBFP-3d-I and II,

DGFP-D-II, DDF-3d-VIII-XI. In addition to the sources on Czechoslovakia listed in the notes to Chapter 9, see Beneš; J. W. Brügel, *Tschechen und Deutsche 1918–1938* (Munich 1967); V. Kràl, *Das Abkommen von München 1938;* E. Moravec, *Das Ende der Benesch-Republik* (Prague 1942); *New Documents;* E. Nittner.

[1] (*399*) Stronge: DBFP-3d-I No. 120. Purchase of Russian bombers: DGFP-D-II Nos. 141, 146. (*399**) The German memorandum (H21/306) is on microfilm T-78 Roll 642 in the National Archives. (*399*) Faucher comment: Ripka 415. (*400*) Litvinov: *New Documents,* No. 14. (*401*) Prague's minorities proposals: DBFP-3d-I No. 150. (*402*) Sudeten June demands: *Id.* App. III. (*403**) *Id.* No. 482.

[2] (*404*) K. H. Frank guidelines: DGFP-D-I No. 366. (*405*) Ribbentrop instructions: *Id.* No. 369. (*405–10*) Ashton-Gwatkin notes and letters to Strang on Henlein talks, etc.: DBFP-3d-I App. II. (*409*) Runciman report: *Ibid.* (*409**) Ripka 23.

CHAPTER 18

Rumania, Yugoslavia, and Hungary, general sources in addition to those cited in Chapter 9: Faber du Faur (German military attaché in Belgrade), *Macht und Ohnmacht* (1953) 213–30; J. B. Hoptner, *Yugoslavia in Crisis 1934–1941* (1962); Robert Machray, *The Struggle for the Danube and the Little Entente 1929–1938* (1938); D. N. Ristic, *Yugoslavia's Revolution of 1941* (1966).

[1] (*411*) Bratislava 1936: Hoptner 52–53; Beneš 30; FRUS 1936-I 368–70. (*412*) Ciano, *Papers* 98–105. (*412–13*) Beneš-Stoyadinovitch; Beneš 32. (*413–14*) Hitler-Stoyadinovitch: DGFP-D-V No. 163. (*414*) Petrescu-Comnene: *Id.* No. 171. (*415–18*) Hungarian efforts to weaken the Little Entente: DGFP-D-II and V. (*415*) Kiel: Weizsaecker 138–39; ND 1780-PS. (*416*) Yugoslav General Staff warning: Hoptner 114–15. (*416–17*) Hungarian-Italian-Yugoslav negotiations: Ciano, *Papers* and *Diary;* ND NG-2390. (*417*) Sinaia and Bled: DIA I pp. 281–84.

[2] Additional sources on Poland: Beck; Cienciala, *Poland and the Western Powers 1938–1939* (1968); Cienciala, *Poland and the Munich Crisis 1938—A Reappraisal,* III East European Quarterly (1969) 201–19, 239–47; Mackiewicz, *Colonel Beck and His Policy* (London 1944). (*421*) Beck in Rome: Beck; Ciano, *Diary.* (*423*) Neurath-Lipski: DGFP-D-V No. 13.

[3] (*425*) Cudahy and Biddle: FRUS 1937 and 1938. (*425–29*) Discussion of Polish-Czech alliance: Beneš 35; Gamelin II pp. 225–38; Ripka 426–29; DDF-2d-III-Nos. 214, 301, 308, 326. (*427*) Beck justification: Beck 171.

CHAPTER 19

Additional general sources: Alliluyeva; Beloff; Bohlen; Budurowycz; Carr; Coulondre; Davies; Erickson; Fainsod, *Smolensk Under Soviet Rule* (1958); Fischer, *Russia's Road;* Foster, *Soviet Policy and the Munich Crisis* (Stanford University Microfilm 1951); *Geschichte des Grossen Vaterländischen Krieges der Sowjetunion,* Bänden I, VI (Berlin 1962–68); Gorbatov, *Years off My Life* (1964); Kennan, *Russia and the West* and *Memoirs; Letters of an Old Bolshevik* (Rand Press, N.Y. 1937); "Litvinov"; Maisky, *Spanish Notebooks* (1966) and *Who Helped Hitler?;* McSherry, *Stalin, Hitler and Europe* (1968); *New Documents;* Slusser; *Soviet Documents;* Teske; Wolin and Slusser.

[1] (*430†*) Professor Carr's reassessment was confirmed in personal correspondence with me in 1973. The Soviet ex-diplomat whom he believes to be the au-

thor is Grigori Bessedovsky, former Soviet counselor in Paris and other embassies. (*431*) Beloff II, p. 26. (*432*) Kennan, *Russia and the West* 255; *Memoirs* 64; Bullitt 118; "Litvinov" 187; Alliluyeva 138. (*433*) Death of Stalin's first wife: Alliluyeva 108–36; "Litvinov" 212–17; *Letters of an Old Bolshevik* 37–53. (*434*) Description of Yezhof: "Litvinov" 241, 259. (*435*) Köstring: Teske 196–97, Mar. 28, 1938. (*435**) Fischer, *Russia's Road* 292; Kennan, *Russia and the West* 255. (*435†*) *Geschichte des Grossen Vaterländischen Krieges* I p. 77. (*436–37*) Military purge: DDF-2d-IV No. 420, V No. 434, VI Nos. 54, 144, 162; Davies, Mar. 23, 1937; Erickson, 401 *et seq.;* Loy Henderson dispatches in FRUS-The Soviet Union 1933–1939; "Litvinov" 178 *et seq.* (*436**) Tukachevsky as violin maker: Professor Albert Parry, letter to New York *Times*, June 9, 1937. (*437*) scope of military purge: *Geschichte* VI p. 150. (*438*) The Jewish factor is noted by Coulondre in DDF-2d-IV No. 412, and Henderson in FRUS, Sept. 1, 1936.

[2]   (*439*) Alliluyeva 30, 75; Davies, June 8, 1938. (*439–40*) Foreign assessment of trials: Davies, Feb. 17, 1937 and Mar. 17, 1938; Köstring, Mar. 28, 1938; Kennan, *Memoirs* 82–84; Bohlen 42–47; DGFP-D-II No. 222; FRUS-Soviet Union, June 23, 1937. (*440*) Coulondre 90; Köstring June 21, 1937, and pp. 96–102. (*440*) Coulondre 82, 112; Firebrace DBFP-3d-I No. 148, Apr. 8, 1938; Bullitt 236; Red Army statistics: *Geschichte* VI p. 150. (*441*) Isolation: Köstring 188. Consulates: DGFP-D-I Nos. 614, 615, 620. (*442*) Bullitt: FRUS-Soviet Union Dec. 24, 1933, and Jan. 4, 1934; *For the President* 60 *et seq.;* Hilger and Meyer 276; DDF-2d-VI No. 327, Aug. 10, 1937.

[3]   (*442–45*) Russia and the Spanish Civil War, general sources: *Geschichte* I p. 131; Maisky, *Spanish Notebooks* 65 *et seq.;* Slusser 219–20; *Soviet Documents* III; DDF-2d-IV, V, VI. (*443*) Simon: DDF-2d-II No. 141. (*445*) Coulondre and Corbin: DDF-2d-IV No. 153; V Nos. 16, 83; VI No. 76; Fischer, *Russia's Road* 273. Stalin speech, *Soviet Documents* III. (*446*) Soviet approaches to Germany: Hilger and Meyer 269–71, 277–79; Köstring 125–26, 165. (*446*) Tukachevsky and French: Gamelin II 195–96; DDF-2d-III No. 343, Oct. 13, 1936. (*447*) Coulondre-Léger: DDF-2d-III No. 506. (*447*) "Short Course": Slusser 223–26.

[4]   (*448*) Litvinov and Potemkin meetings: Davies, Mar. 14, 1938, and FRUS 1938 I p. 41; DBFP-3d-I Nos. 85, 92; Nittner No. 97. (*449*) Bomber sale and Kulik visit: *New Documents* Nos. 6 and 9; Nittner No. 105. Kremlin conference: *New Documents* No. 7. (*449–50*) Litvinov at Geneva: Bonnet, *De Washington* 125; Nittner No. 113. (*450*) Litvinov-Suritz question: Nittner No. 116; Coulondre 152–53. (*451*) Maisky-Halifax: DBFP-3d-II No. 637; Litvinov-Schulenburg: DGFP-D-II Nos. 380, 381, 396; Payart-Potemkin: *New Documents* No. 25; Litvinov telegram: *Id.* No. 26; Maisky-Churchill: *Who Helped Hitler* 78–81, 294–96. (*451–52*) Coulondre 157–58; Bonnet, *De Washington* 199–208.

[5]   (*452*) Rumanian transit: Shirer, *Collapse* 347–48; Foster 99 *et seq.;* Churchill, *Gathering Storm* 305. (*453*) Kennan, *Russia and the West* 323–24. (*453–54*) Bullitt: FRUS 1936-I pp. 200, 212. (*454*) Gamelin II p. 230. Gerodias: DDF-2d-IV No. 457. (*454†*) *Geschichte* I pp. 168, 176. (*455*) Krantz-Vientzov: "Litvinov" 270. (*456*) Beck 157.

CHAPTER 20

Additional general sources: Bonnet, *De Washington* and *Dans la Tourmente* (1971); Bullitt; Colton; Cot (both); Jacomet; Lefranc, *Histoire du Front Populaire*

(1965); Anatol de Monzie, *Ci-Devant* (Flammarion, 1941); *L'Oeuvre de Léon Blum*, vols. 4-1, 4-2 (Paris 1964-65); Paul-Boncour; Paxton, *Vichy France* (1972); Werth, *France and Munich.*

[1] (*457–58*) Léger's views: FRUS 1936-I 267–68, 308–9; my interviews with Léger in Aug. 1969. (*459*) Georges-Abrial-Bargeton: DDF-2e-III No. 113; Chiefs of Staff meeting: *Id.* No. 138. (*460*) Förster: DGFP-C-V No. 273.

[2] (*462*) Blum and preventive war: ESF-I p. 127. "Co-ordination" decree: Gamelin II pp. 251–52. (*462–63*) Note and Permanent Committee meeting: DDF-2e-II Nos. 357, 369. (*463*) Army armament program: Gamelin I pp. 220–22, 261–62, and II pp. 243–46; ESF Rapport, Part II, p. 177–81. (*464*) Cot, *Triumph* 311, 400–1; Bargeton: DDF-2e-II No. 372. (*465*) Lifting sanctions: *Id.* Nos. 233, 265, 311, 328, 335; Paul-Boncour 48–53; *L'Oeuvre* 4-1 pp. 357–581.

[3] (*466–68*) Blum, London and return: ESF-I pp. 215–19; Cot (both); Lefranc, Annex 17 (Blumel memorandum) pp. 400–66; DDF-2e-IV No. 133. (*469*) Darlan-Chatfield: DDF-2e-III No. 87; Clerk admonition: *Id.* No. 108. (*470*) Luna Park Speech: *L'Oeuvre* 4-1 pp. 387–96. (*471*) Auriol: Colton 258–59.

[4] (*472–76*) Belgian neutrality: Documents in DDF-2e-II, III, IV, and V give a sufficient account of French policy. (*474*) Secret Franco-Belgian conversations: Blum in ESF-I pp. 130–32.

[5] (*476*) Gamelin II 239; Welczeck DGFP-C-V No. 499. (*477*) "Spanish ulcer": Brogan 713. (*478*) Paxton 247–48; Bullitt 173.

[6] (*478*) Chautemps and Delbos: FRUS 1937-I pp. 117–18 and 149. (*480–81*) Schacht-Blum: DDF-2e-III No. 213, and V No. 470; Schacht, *Confessions* 348–49. (*481*) Beck: Gamelin II pp. 282–83. Udet and Milch: DDF-2e-VII No. 43: Bonnet, *De Washington* 48. (*481**) Bullitt on Phipps: FRUS 1937-I pp. 84–85. (*481†*) F.D.R., Jr.: Bullitt vii, xli–xlii, 223–24.

[7] (*482*) London talks: DDF-2e-VII Nos. 287, 291. (*483*) Chamberlain-Chautemps on French Air Force: Bonnet, *De Washington* 49–50. (*483–85*) Delbos tour: DDF-2e-VII Nos. 207, 319, 324, 327, 349, 365; Werth, *France and Munich* 21–31. (*484*) Rumania: Paul-Boncour III pp. 60–62; Gamelin p. 279.

[8] (*485*) Weygand, ESF-I p. 240. (*486*) Jacomet and Martignon; ESF-I pp. 187–213, and VII, pp. 2139–62. (*487–90*) French Air Force: Cot, ESF-I pp. 263–86; La Chambre ESF-II pp. 295–96; Cot, *Triumph* 274–335. (*490*) Vuillemin views, 26 Sept. 1938: ESF-II p. 313.

[9] (*491*) Jacomet: ESF, *Rapport* II pp. 292–96. (*491*) German tanks: F. M. von Senger und Etterlin, *Die Deutschen Panzer 1926–1945* (1968) 19–65; W. J. Spielberger, *Die Deutschen Panzerkampfwagen III und IV mit ihren Abarten 1935–1945*, 11–12, 44–49. (*491†*) Guderian 94, 472–73; Gamelin I 150–55, 260–63, and II 187; Thoma in Liddell Hart, *German Generals Talk* (1948) 94. (*492*) DDF-2e-III No. 9. (*493†*) DDF-2e-V No. 151 (*494*) Army "Instructions": Reynaud 219–23; German tanks in Spain: FRUS 1937-I pp. 46, 68, 247. Daladier to CPDN: DDF-2e-V No. 450; Blum-De Gaulle: *L'Oeuvre* V pp. 113–15; ESF-I p. 223; De Gaulle 24–26; Reynaud 223–33.

[10] (*497*) Chautemps, Delbos, and Chamber debate: I DIA 1938, pp. 207–14; Werth, *France and Munich* 44–61. (*497–98*) Pessimism on Austria: FRUS 1937-I pp. 85, 153, 188 and 1938-I p. 28. (*498**) Bullitt 251. (*498–99*) Gamelin-Daladier: Gamelin II, 312–16. (*499*) Daladier on Austria crisis: ESF-I, 26–27.

[11] (*499–503*) Second Blum government: Blum and Paul-Boncour in ESF-I pp. 252–55, and III 281–83; Paul-Boncour III, 76–79; Colton, 292–305. (*499**) Jeanneney, *Françoise De Wendei en Republique* (1976), 486, 499, 547, 551, 575, 580.

(500) CPDN, Mar. 15, 1938: Gamelin II, 321–31. *(502–3)* Blum government and Britain: DBFP-3d-I Nos. 62, 81–83, 106–9, 112. *(503)* Ambassadors' meeting: Noël, 195–97.

CHAPTER 21

[1] *(504–5)* Daladier: There is no good biography. For a qualified apologia, see S. B. Butterworth; generally, Pertinax, *passim;* Daladier, *In Defense of France* (1939), introductory "profile" by Yvon Lapaquellerie, himself the author of a short biography, Eduard Daladier (Bern, 1939). *(505)* Gamelin on Daladier: *Servir* II 221–22, 249–50, 333; Selection of Bonnet: Daladier and Paul-Boncour in ESF-9 p. 2888, and 3 p. 804; Paul-Boncour III, 86–102.

[2] *(507)* Gamelin II 318–19. *(508)* Anglo-French meeting: DBFP-3d-I No. 164. *(510)* Bullitt: FRUS 1938-I pp. 493–95.

[3] *(511)* Rejection of Gamelin program: *Servir* II 335–37; Pertinax 35. *(511*)* DDF-2e-II No. 375. *(511)* Abortive Italian approaches: Ciano, *Diary;* Bonnet, *De Washington* 144–48. *(512)* Spanish border: FRUS 1938-I 192–93, 216, 232. *(512–15)* Franco-Soviet military relations: Gamelin II, 285–87; Blum in ESF-I, 128–29; Villelume in ESF-IX 2742–44; DDF-2e-III No. 343, IV No. 457, V Nos. 299, 429, 480, VI No. 35, VII No. 436; Coulondre 13, 20, 142–43, 157. *(513)* Delbos-Vinogradov: Szembek, Dec. 9, 1937. *(514)* Chamberlain-Chutemps: FRUS 1938-I, 24. *(514–15)* Litvinov-*Le Temps:* DDF-2e-VI No. 390. *(515)* Coulondre 141–46, 150–54.

[4] *(516)* Gamelin on Bonnet: *Servir* II, 333. *(516†)* Bullitt 206. *(517)* Belgium: Gamelin II 334. *(517–18)* Lukasiewicz 81–104. *(518)* Bullitt in Warsaw: Szembek; Bullitt, 256–57. *(519)* Halifax and Phipps: DBFP-3d-I Nos. 256–57, 271. *(522*)* Noël 198–203.

[5] *(523)* Halifax luncheon: ESF-I pp. 31, 255; French advise to receive Runciman: *New Documents* Nos. 21, 23. *(524)* Mandel-Osusky: Král No. 147. *(524–25)* Military preparations: Gamelin II, 340–44. *(525)* Pointe de Grave: Bonnet, *De Washington* 205–12; Werth, *France and Munich* 235–36; *The Moffat Papers* (1956), Sept. 2, 1938. *(526*)* ESF-III p. 805. *(526–27)* Military preparations and conferences: Gamelin II 344–48, III 471 *et seq.* *(529)* French Press: Micaud; Werth, *France and Munich* 225–56. Effect of press on Daladier: ESF-I 33. *(529)* Cabinet meeting: Monzie, Sept. 4, 19, 25, 1938.

CHAPTER 22

Additional general sources: Cadogan; Colvin; Eden, *The Reckoning;* Hardie, Middlemas, *The Strategy of Appeasement;* Roskill, *Hankey: Man of Secrets.*

[2] Britain and the Spanish Civil War, general sources: Kleine, *The Policy of Simmering—A Study of British Policy during the Spanish Civil War 1936–1939* (Geneva 1961); Watkins, *Britain Divided: The Effect of the Spanish Civil War on British Political Opinion* (London 1963). *(536–37)* Labour Party and Spain: Hugh Dalton, *Memoirs* II. *(537*)* Thomas 634–39. *(537)* Baldwin: Jones, July 27, 1936; Barcelona: Chatfield 92; Eden, *Facing the Dictators* 449. *(537–38)* Clerk-Delbos and Chatfield-Darlan: Carlton, *Eden, Blum, and the Origins of Non-Intervention,* 6 Journal of Contemporary History 40 (1971); Liddell Hart, *Memoirs* 134. *(539–40)* COS Report: CAB 23/85, CP 234 (6). *(540–41)* Halifax: *Fulness of Days* 192.

[3] (*542**) Davidson, *Memoirs of a Conservative* (R. R. Jones edit. 1969) 417. (*543*) Meeting of ministers: Eden, *Facing the Dictators* 464–65; Templewood 256–57. (*543–44*) CAB 23/86 and 87. (*544–46*) Rejection of Eden proposal: Eden 487–91; CAB 23/87. (*546**) DDF-2e-IV No. 302. Jan. 14, 1937. (*547*) Eden's views: Harvey; CAB 23/88, Mar. 24, 1937. (*547–48*) Belgium: generally, British Cabinet minutes and Corbin's reports in DDF. (*548*) Baldwin and "madmen": Eden, *Facing the Dictators* 501.

[4] (*549–55*) On Neville Chamberlain: Extracts from his diary and letters in Feiling, Hyde, and Macleod; passages in memoirs of his associates, including Amery, Baldwin, Butler, Churchill, Douglas-Home; Eden; Halifax, Hoare, and Strang. (*549*) Wilson: quoted in Middlemas 46. (*550*) Harvey 243; Duff Cooper and Sinclair: quoted in Pyper, *Chamberlain and His Critics* (1962) 111–12. (*552**) Davidson, *Memoirs* 417–18. (*552*) Eden: Harvey Mar. 5, 1937; FRUS 1937-I Mar. 11, 1937. (*553*) Lady Astor: Jones May 30, 1937. (*555*) Maisky's "pencil" story was told by him in a BBC broadcast in 1961, entitled *The Origins of the Second World War*.

[5] (*555–71*) Chamberlain-Eden conflict: in addition to general sources listed above: Amery III 235; Ciano, *Papers* 157–58 and *Diary* Jan. 1 and Feb. 1, 2, 4, 7, 8, 15–22, 1938; Halifax 193–96; Pownall 132, 135; Roskill, *Hankey* III 298–305. (*562*) J. P. L. Thomas' diary, so far as I know, is available only through the extracts quoted in Eden's memoirs. (*564†*) Ciano, *Diary* Dec. 25, 1937 and Feb. 15, 1938. (*565**) Sir Joseph Ball: Macleod 216–20. (*569*) Eden-Delbos on Russia: DDF-2e-V No. 429. Eden rejection of French proposals: DDF-2e-VI Nos. 249, 482, 465; VII Nos. 28, 137, 198. (*570*) Italian reaction: Ciano, *Diary* Feb. 21, 1938. Henderson letter: Eden, *The Reckoning* 6. François-Poncet: DGFP-D-I No. 220. (*570–71*) Chautemps: FRUS 1938-I 24. Eden-Bingham: FRUS 1937-I 58.

[6] (*574–78*) Hitler-Henderson, Halifax-Ribbentrop: DBFP-D-I Nos. 138–51, March 1938.

[7] (*580–81*) Phipps and Paul-Boncour: Phipps papers, library of Churchill College, Cambridge. (*582*) Text of the agreement: DIA 1938-I, 141–56. (*584, 585*) Kennedy reports: FRUS 1938-I.

CHAPTER 23

[1] (*588*) Ismay 80; Pownall. (*589*) AIR 9/69 folio 104; Webster and Frankland I 89. (*589**) Reader 243–44. (*589*) Inskip reminder: AIR 9/76 folio 4. This and subsequent references to Cabinet discussions are from CAB 23/83 to 88. (*590–92*) Austen Chamberlain-Churchill deputation: Middlemas and Barnes 946–48, 989; Churchill, *Gathering Storm* 228–31, 681; Roskill, *Hankey* 232–33, 250; Pownall 116; AIR 9/8 folio 60. (*592*) RAF Navy convoy disagreement: CID 1276-B, Nov. 11, 1936. (*593*) Swinton: CID 1265-B. Joint Planning Report: Roskill, *Hankey* 236. (*594*) COS report, Jan. 28, 1937 and Brown memorandum: Colvin, *Chamberlain*. (*597*) Two-ocean standard: *Hankey* 286–88. (*597**) *Id.* 280. (*598*) White Paper: Cmd. 5374. (*599**) Hopkins: *Hankey* 315.

[2] (*599–603*) British Army, general sources: Liddell Hart; Minney. (*599*) Selection of Hore-Belisha: Feiling 317. (*601*) Hart, *Europe in Arms* 117–18, 130.

[3] (*603–7*) The alphabetically designated "schemes" are given tabular comparison in Slessor 184; Webster and Frankland IV 103–4; AIR 8/238, piece 2. (*603*) Air Staff 1937 estimates: AIR 8/204; Webster and Frankland I 71. (*605*) Fleet Air Arm and convoys: Reader 269–81; Slessor 186–94; CAB 23/89/32–33; Roskill, *Hankey*

251; COS 535 (JP), COS 640, CAB 2/7; CID 1368-B. Radar chain approval: Richards I 25. *(606)* Slessor 158. Scheme J: CAB 24/273, D.P.(P) 12. Hankey-Inskip: CAB 21/626. Eden, *Facing the Dictators* 552–58.

[4] *(607)* Priorities: Roskill, *Hankey* 290–91. Inskip memorandum, Dec. 9, 1937: Webster and Frankland, IV 96–98; Air Staff response: I 77. *(609)* Inskip report: CAB 24/273. CP 316*(37)*. *(612)* Dec. 22 COS: 227th meeting. *(613)* Duff Cooper 215–17; Newall "standstill": Webster and Frankland I 77–78. Inskip report Feb. 16, 1938: CAB 24/244, CP 24 (38). *(613–14)* Hore-Belisha memorandum: CP 26 *(38)*; Liddell Hart *Memoirs II* 88–101; Minney 89–90; Pownall Jan. 13 to Feb. 14, 1938. *(615)* White Paper: Cmd. 5682.

CHAPTER 24

[2] *(619)* Hart memoranda: *Defence of Britain* 63–74; *Memoirs* II 104–5; Pownall Mar. 14, 1938. *(621)* Newton: DBFP-3d-I No. 86, Mar. 5, 1938; Foreign Office studies: C1865/132/18. *(626)* Foreign Policy Committee: CAB 27/623. *(628)* Feiling 347–48; Middlemas 188. *(629)* COS 698, CAB 27/627 and CAB 53/27.

[3] *(633*)* Dawson: Wrench XXXI. *(634–35)* France and Russia: DBFP-3d-I Nos. 106–10, 112, 116. *(635)* 333 Parl. Debates 1399 *et seq.* *(636)* Press reaction: Middlemas 206–7. Harvey Mar. 25, 1938; Duff Cooper 218; Cadogan Mar. 26, 1938.

[4] *(637–38)* Army rearmament: Hart, *Memoirs* 118; Minney 108; Pownall; CAB 23/93; CAB 24/276. *(638–40)* Navy: Duff Cooper 219–22; CAB 23/94; CAB 24/278. *(640)* Swinton-Inskip on Scheme K: C.P. 86 (38); CAB 23/93. *(641)* Newall note Apr. 5, 1938: AIR 8/237 piece 24; Slessor 152. *(641–42)* CAB 23/93. *(642)* Labour: AIR 8/238. *(643–44)* Swinton dismissal: Balfour 99–110; Churchill 231–32; Colvin, *Chamberlain* 126; Reader 289–93; Roskill, letter to me, July 30, 1974, and *Hankey* 320, 355; Swinton, *I Remember* 146–50; Winterton 227–36. *(645)* Labour deputation: Dalton II 170.

[5] *(645)* Swinton: AIR 8/237 piece 43. *(646)* "Western Air" plans: Webster and Frankland I 90–99, IV 99–102. *(646–47)* Slessor 205–6, 214. *(647–48)* Slessor-Douglas-Dowding: AIR 2/2948; Webster and Frankland 101–2. *(648)* Joint Planning Staff memorandum: COS 554, Jan. 7, 1937, and CAB 2/6. Bomb tonnage 1941 and 1943: Collier 494–95, 503–5; Webster and Frankland IV 455–57. *(649)* Air Staff and Ludlow-Hewitt: AIR 9/69 folio 111; AIR 2/4474 piece Ia; AIR 9/90 piece XIII. *(649–50)* MacDonald: Nicolson, *Diaries* Mar. 29, 1938. *(649*)* Slessor 12–15, 151. *(650)* Fisher: FRUS 1938-I p. 55. Cadogan Mar. 6, Apr. 25, May 21–22, 1938. Ironside Sept. 16 and 22, 1938

[6] *(651)* COS opposition to Anglo-French staff talks: Harvey 89; Middlemas 218 *et seq.;* Pownall 142–43; COS 680, CID 1394-B, Feb. 4, 1938; CAB 23/93; Apr. 6, 13, 27, 1938; CAB 24/273, Apr. 11–12, 1938; AIR 2/273/1. *(652–53)* Anglo-French meeting: DBFP-3d-I No. 164 (record); CAB 27/276 (Halifax on Madagascar); CAB 23/93 (May 4, 1938); Feiling 353. *(653–54)* Henderson-Woermann-Ribbentrop: DBFP-3d-I Nos. 172, 180, 187, 193, 198, 206; DGFP-D-II Nos. 149, 154; Cadogan 75–76. *(654)* Henlein visit: DBFP-3d-I No. 219, App. III; Nicolson, May 13; CAB 23/93, May 18, 1938; FRUS 1938-I p. 498. *(654–55)* May crisis: Duff Cooper 220–21; Feiling 354; Harvey 142–44; Middlemas 234–41; Pownall 146–47; CAB 23/93; DBFP-3d-I Nos. 232, 238, 240, 249, 250, 254, 287. *(656–57)* Aftermath, Strang trip: DBFP-3d-I Nos. 299, 326, 347, 349, 354, 421, 429, and II

No. 601; CAB 27/623 (June 1) and 27/624 (June 16); DGFP-D-II No. 237 (June 3, Henlein and Lorenz). (*657–58*) Runciman mission: CAB 23/94 (June 22, July 6 and 27); PREM 1/265 (June 22); DBFP-3d-I Nos. 495, 508. (*658*) Chamberlain's optimism: Middlemas 256–57; FRUS 1938-I (July 6). (*658–59*) Wiedemann: Cadogan 87–88; Harvey 161–64; Middlemas 265; Wiedemann, *Der Mann, der Feldherr werden wollte* (1964) 158–67; CAB 23/94 (July 20); DBFP-3d-I No. 510; DGFP-D-VII p. 628. (*660*) Chamberlain's distrust of French Army: interview with Sir Alec Douglas-Home, July 10, 1974. Dirksen: DGFP-D-II Nos. 266, 290. "Rotten Americans": Harvey 148.

[7] (*660–61*) Mason-Mac: Pownall 150–51. Staff talks: COS 727, CAB 24/277. Strang-Henderson: DBFP-3d-I No. 530, II No. 553. (*661*) "Prohibited areas" and Mason-Mac: DBFP-3d-II Nos. 562–64, 575, 580. (*662*) Henderson "no risk" comment: *Id.* No. 337; Halifax message imbroglio: *Id.* Nos. 608, 614, 620, 661; DGFP-D-II Nos. 347, 348, 354, 356, 365. (*662–63*) Koerber: DBFP-3d-II No. 595. (*663*) "Herr X": *Id.* No. 658. Kleist: *Id.* App. IV. (*663*) Danger signals: *Id.* Nos. 649 (Attolico), 675 (Toussaint), 667, 670, 682, 709 (Bucharest and Belgrade), 692 (Mason-Mac). Kordt-Wilson: DGFP-D-II No. 382. (*664*) Martin 255–56. (*664–67*) Ministers' meeting: Colvin, *Chamberlain* 140; Duff Cooper 224; Harvey 169–70; Inskip diary; Minney 138; Middlemas 280; Templewood 299–300; CAB 23/94; FRUS 1938-I p. 560. (*666†*) Boothby letter: PREM 1/265.

[8] (*668*) Wilson memoranda on Plan Z: PREM 1/266. (*669*) Chamberlain to sister: Feiling 357. (*669**) Weir letter: PREM 1/265. (*669*) Churchill plan: *Ibid.* 293. (*669–70*) Halifax draft and Wilson reaction: PREM 1/265. (*670*) Kordt: Cadogan 95; Colvin, *Chamberlain* 147; Middlemas 321–22. (*670–71*) *Times* leader: Wrench 370–72. Reactions: Churchill 296; Duff Cooper 226; Eden, *Reckoning* 24; Harvey 171; Nicolson 358; Middlemas 320; DGFP-D-II No. 443. (*672*) Labour at Blackpool: Dalton 174–75. Eden—Halifax: *Reckoning* 25–26; Harvey 175–76. (*672–73*) Message to Hitler and Henderson opposition: Cadogan 96; Harvey 172–73; DBFP-3d-II Nos. 815, 818, 819, 823, 825. (*673‡*) DBFP-3d-No. 482. (*674*) Press conference: DBFP-3d-II App. III. Chamberlain letter: Feiling 360; Middlemas 327. (*674–75*) Wilson-Henderson: PREM 1/266. (*675–76*) Letter to Runciman: *Ibid.* Cabinet Sept. 12 and 14: CAB 23/95. (*677*) Wilson draft message to Hitler: PREM 1/266. (*677*) Big Four meetings: CAB 27/646/I-II-III. (*677–78*) Big Four—service meeting, Sept. 13: CAB 16/189, CZ3. (*618*) Wilson-Simon notes: PREM 1/266. (*678–79*) Message and Hitler invitation: DBFP-3d-II Nos. 862, 873, 878; DBFP-D-II Nos. 469, 480. (*678–79*) Letters to the King: Wheeler-Bennett, *King George VI* 344–46. (*680*) Masefield poem: *The Times*, Sept. 16, 1938; Feiling 365.

CHAPTER 25

Additional general sources: Buchheit, *Ludwig Beck* (Munich 1964) and *Soldatentum und Rebellion* (1961); Engel; Förster; Groscurth; Irving; and the unpublished memoirs of Generals Wilhelm Adam and Maximilian von Weichs, deposited at the Institut für Zeitgeschichte in Munich.

[1] (*681–83*) Beck memoranda: Foerster 81–118; long extracts in English translation in O'Neill 152–58. (*682–83*) Keitel reaction: *Memoirs* 63–64. (*683*) General staff exercise: Röhricht, 119–23; Lossberg, *Im Wehrmachtsführungsstab* (1949) 18; Warlimont 15–16; ND EC-368.

[2] (*684*) Butler-Kordt: DGFP-D-I Nos. 128, 750. (*685*) Daladier-Welczek: DGFP-D-II No. 194.

[3] (*685*) German fortifications policy 1933–38: Förster 41–45; NA T-78 Roll

300 frame 6251273. *(685–87)* Fortifications 1938: Förster 45–50; Adam; Engel; Förtsch 176–77; NA T-78 Roll 300 frames 6251277, 6251289, 6251300. *(688–89)* Hitler on fortification: ND 1802-PS, reprinted in Förster 123–48.

[4] *(690)* Goering, Karinhall, and Krauch: ND R-140; VII TWC 878–929. *(692)* Generals Aug. 4, 1938: Adam; Förtsch 171–73; Weichs. *(694)* Guderian 32–33, 462. *(695–96)* Manstein's letter is among the Beck documents (*Nachlass*) at the Institut für Zeitgeschichte; see also Manstein 335–36.

[5] *(698–99)* Beck false appearance as Chief of Staff: *Times*, Sept. 15, 1938. Jüterbog meeting: Förtsch 173–74; Eberhard, Aug. 15, 1938. *(699*)* Gannon 209; Colvin, *Vansittart in Office* 250.

[6] *(699)* Draft June 18: ND 388-PS item 14. *(700)* "Normal" and "special" case: VII Corps war diary, T-79 Roll 16 frame 338. *(701–2)* "Concealed mobilization": Keitel, *Memoirs* 66; Röhricht 131–36. *(701–2)* Mason-Mac and Stronge reports: DBFP-3d-II Nos. 564, 575, 579, 593, 628, 692, 770, 820, 821, 831.

[7] *(702–3)* Hitler criticism: Engel. *(703)* Dispute over RAD withdrawal: Gkdo. 2 Ia 97/38; OKW 130/38 WFA/L II. *(703–6)* Hitler tour: Adam; Jodl. *(705)* Chevallerie record: DGFP-D-VII pp. 640–43.

[8] *(706)* Composition of German Army 1938: Müller-Hillebrand, *Das Heer 1933–1945*, I. *(706–9)* Army order of battle: ND 388-PS items 16b, 27; Eberhards' notes, appendix; various unit histories. *(708–12)* Luftwaffe deployment: Maas, *Die Spitzengliederung der Luftwaffe—Aufbauzeit bis zum Kriegsbeginn* (Munich 1956); NA T-79 Roll 24, T-84 Roll 67; Völker, Dokumente 84–86. *(712)* Kesselring directive: Völker, Dokumente 154–55. *(713)* Airborne operation: Choltitz, *Soldat unter Soldaten* 48–49. *(713)* Raeder-Hitler: Groscurth, Aug. 29, 1938.

[9] *(714–15)* Weizsaecker-Ribbentrop: DGFP-D-II Nos. 259, 288, 303, 304, 332, 374, 409. *(715–18)* "Halder plot": Bor, *Gespräche mit Halder* (1950) 120–23; Buchheit, *Beck* 175–81, and *Soldatentum* 180–91; Gisevius 283–325; Schacht, *Confessions* 355–57, and *Account Settled* 118–25; Adam; my interrogation of Halder, Dec. 12–13, 1947.

[10] *(719)* Hitler-Mussolini: DGFP-D-II No. 223. *(719–20)* Vuillemin visit: Heinkel, *Stormy Life* (1956) 180–81; Irving 63: Stehlin 86–93. *(720)* Jodl memorandum: ND 388-PS No. 17a. *(721)* Hitler-Bürger and Henlein: Groscurth, Sept. 2 and 4, 1938. *(721–27)* Hitler and the generals debate operational plans: ND 388-PS Nos. 18, 19; Engel's, Groscurth's, and Jodl's diary entries; Keitel, *Memoirs* 67–70; Adam and Weichs. *(725†)* Irving 62–63.

[11] *(727)* Hitler-Mussolini: DGFP-D-II No. 415; Ciano, *Diary*, Sept. 2, 3, 6, and 7, 1938. *(728)* Krosigk memorandum: ND EC-419. *(728)* Troup-Siemens: DGFP-D-II No. 451; DBFP-3d-II No. 836. Kordt-Kennedy: DGFP-D-II No. 460. *(728–29)* Franco-German contacts: *Id.* Nos. 423, 426, 439, 456; Gamelin II 342–44. *(730)* Ribbentrop to Prague: DGFP-D-II No. 475.

[12] *(730)* Hitler's movements and meetings after the Nuremberg Party Rally are based on the Bormann and Wünsche diary entries. For the German handling of Chamberlain's message, see DBFP-3d-II Nos. 862, 873, 878; DGFP-D-II Nos. 469, 480.

CHAPTER 26

[1] *(733)* Departure from Heston: Cadogan, Sept. 15, 1938; Kordt, DGFP-D-II No. 486; Sir Horace Wilson's memorandum, in the Thomas Jones papers, Aberyst-

wyth, Wales. (*733*) Flight: Wheeler-Bennett, *Munich* 108. (*733–34*) Wilson notes: PREM 1/266. (*736**) PREM 1/266A.

[3] (*737–38*) Arrival at Munich and trip to Berchtesgaden: Price, *Years of Reckoning* 254 *et seq.;* Feiling; Schmidt. (*739–43*) Schmidt record: DGFP-D-II No. 487; Chamberlain records: DBFP-3d-II Nos. 895, 896.

[4] (*744–45*) Return trip: Above sources and *Id.* No. 897.

[5] (*746*) Price; Wünsche and Bormann diaries; Groscurth and Jodl diaries; DGFP-D-II Nos. 490, 500.

[6] (*746*) Return to Heston: Kordt *Id.* No. 521. (*747–48*) Big Four meetings: CAB 27/646. (*748–51*) Cabinet Sept. 17; Cadogan; Duff Cooper; Harvey; Inskip; Minney; Feiling; CAB 23/95. (*752*) Labour deputation: Dalton 176–83. Kennedy FRUS 1938-I 609–12.

CHAPTER 27

[1] (*754–56*) Lindbergh to 1936: Wayne S. Cole, *Charles A. Lindbergh and the Battle Against American Intervention in World War II,* II (1974); Kenneth S. Davis, *The Hero: Charles A. Lindbergh* (1959); Anne Morrow Lindbergh; Leonard S. Moseley, *Lindbergh* (1976); Walter S. Ross, *The Last Hero: Charles A. Lindbergh* (1964).

[2] (*756–59*) First visit to Germany: Truman Smith; Heinkel, *Stormy Life* 164–67. (*758*) Fromm, *Blood and Banquets* (1942) 223–25. (*759*) Nicolson, *Diaries* 272, 283. (*760–62*) Second visit to Germany: Truman Smith. (*763*) Nicolson, *Diaries* 343. The published portions of Lindbergh's own notes, entitled *The Wartime Journals of Charles A. Lindbergh,* begin with the entry for Mar. 11, 1938, and are a useful additional source.

[3] (*765*) Phipps and Fraser on Lindbergh: DBFP-3d-I Nos. 855 and 1012.

[4] Joseph P. Kennedy: David E. Koskoff, *Joseph P. Kennedy—A Life and Times* (1974); Richard J. Whalen, *The Founding Father* (1964). (*767–69*) Kennedy-Dirksen: DGFP-D-I pp. 713, 721, 725, and II 368; Koskoff 143–44. (*769–70*) Kennedy-Chamberlain and Halifax: FRUS 1938-I 560, 565; DBFP-3d-II No. 744. (*770*) F.D.R. on Aberdeen draft: J. B. Blum, *From the Morgenthau Diaries* (1959) 518. (*771**) Ione Robinson, *A Wall to Paint On* (1946) 311. (*771*) Kennedy-Halifax: DBFP-3d-II Nos. 824, 836; FRUS 1938-I 585, 587. Selzam: DGFP-D-II 743. (*771*) FDR: Ickes 467–68.

[5] (*772–75*) Dominions, general sources: Nicholas Mansergh, *The Commonwealth Experience* (1969) Chapt. 10, and *Survey of British Commonwealth Affairs* (1952) Chapts. 3–9; Massey 229–32, 257–67; Ovendale, *"Appeasement" and the English-Speaking World* (1975); D. C. Watt, *The Influence of the Commonwealth on British Foreign Policy: The Munich Crisis,* in *Personalities and Policies* (1965) 159–74, also published (slightly altered) as *Der Einfluss der Dominions auf die Britische Aussenpolitik vor Munich 1938* in vol. 8 Vierteljahreshefte für Zeitgeschichte (1960) 64–74. (*772–73*) Hertzog references: Oswald Pirow, *James Barry Munnik Hertzog* 276; C. M. Van den Heever, *General J. B. M. Hertzog* (1945) 266–67, 271, 275. (*774*) Hertzog draft resolution: Selections *from the Smuts Papers* (J. Van der Poel, edit.) VI 138 n. 3. (*775*) Nicolson, *Diaries* 360.

CHAPTER 28

[1] (*776*) Lukasiewicz 127. Halifax-Phipps: DBFP-3d-II Nos. 907, 908. (*776–77*) Phipps letter: Churchill College, Cambridge, archives. Daladier-Vuillemin-

Gamelin: ESF I pp, 33–34; Gamelin II 344–49. (*777–78*) Beneš-Nečas, Beneš-Lacroix: ESF, *loc. cit. supra*, and 256; Beneš, *Pameti* 245; Colton 315–16; Bonnet, *De Washington* 237–38; Daladier archives, 2 DA 1 dossier 3 Chapt. VII, and 2 DA 2 dossier 7. Hodža-Newton: DBFP-3d-II Nos. 888, 902, 813. (*778*) French home front: Werth, *France and Munich* 225–32, 257–63; Micaud 161–70.

[2] (*778–82*) Anglo-French meeting: DBFP-3d-II No. 928; Harvey 185–86; Cadogan 100–1; Bonnet 238–43. (*782–83*) Message to Prague: DBFP-3d-II No. 937. (*783–84*) CAB 23/95; Colvin, *Chamberlain* 159–60; Inskip; Middlemas 354–56; Minney 142. (*784**) Daladier 2 DA 2 dossier 1: "Contraire à la décision du Conseil des Ministres," written on Bonnet's memorandum describing his interview, after the Cabinet meeting, with Osusky.

[3] (*785*) Osusky report: Nittner No. 143. (*785*) Newton reports: DBFP-3d-II Nos. 951, 952, 961. (*785–86*) Ripka 69–104. Masaryk-Eden: Kral No. 197. Churchill in Paris: 302–3. Léger-Osusky: Kral No. 204. (*786*) Beneš-Alexandrovsky-Gottwald: *New Documents* Nos. 36, 37, 38. (*786†*) King George: Cadogan Sept. 19, 1938; Harvey 187, 189; Wheeler-Bennett, *King George VI* 350. (*787*) Washington plea: FRUS 1938-I, 626. Runciman and Phipps: Harvey, Sept. 19 and 21. (*787*) Czech arbitration proposal: DBFP-3d-II Nos. 979, 981. Halifax rejoinder: *Id.* No. 991. (*788–90*) Paris-Prague on French attitude: Beneš, *Pameti* 245; Lacroix, ESF Rapport II pp. 266 *et seq.* and DDF-2e-XI No. 232; Bonnet, *De Washington* 246–53, and DDF-2e-XI No. 249; Pierre Comert, ESF VII 2178; Werth, *France and Munich* 267–69; Ripka 86–93; Wheeler-Bennett, *Munich* 120–26. (*790–91*) Beneš, *Pameti* 267–68; L. K. Fierabend, *Vladach Druhe Republiky* 172 (Universum Press, New York, 1961); Moravec, *Master of Spies* 116. References to telephone conversations by Beneš-Masaryk and Beneš-Osusky are based on the German intercepts in F.O. 371/21742, explained in Chapter 29. (*792–93*) Newton messages: DBFP-3d-II Nos. 992, 993, 996, 998, 1002. Cadogan call to Masaryk: *Id.* No. 1000. Bonnet-Lacroix letter: Kral No. 208 (source given as Krofta archives). Czech acceptance: DIA 1938, vol. 2, p. 217.

CHAPTER 29

[1] (*795*) Sargent: PREM 1/266A item 16. (*796–97*) Inner circle meetings: CAB 27/646. (*796*) Poles and Hungarians: DBFP-3d-III Nos. 1–20 inclusive; Lukasiewicz 127–33. Hore-Belisha and Gort: PREM 1/266A items 17, 18; Minney 143. (*797–98*) Runciman: DIA 1938 vol. 2 p. 218; Kral No. 211; Harvey 187. (*798*) Cabinet Sept. 21: CAB 23/95 No. 41; Harvey 191: Middlemas 362; Duff Cooper 231–32; Minney 143. (*798–99*) Halifax-Newton: DBFP-3d-II No. 1003. Beneš' appeal: PREM 1/266A item 20. Syrový speech: Ripka 108–10. (*799*) Paris-Midi: Werth, *France and Munich* 269.

[2] (*800*) Engel and OKW instructions: Jodl. 7th Division: *Mit dem VII Korps im Sudetenland*, Anlage 67, WK VII Roll 44, N.A. French reconnaissance: Stehlin 91–92. Freikorps: DGFP-D-II Nos. 550, 558, 561; DBFP-3d-II No. 1013; Jodl. (*801*) German memoranda: DGFP-D-II No. 536; ND 388-PS item 29. (*801–2*) Goering-Lipski and Stojay: Lipski 401–5; DGFP-D-II No. 506. Weizsacker-Lipski: *Id.* No. 508. (*802*) Hitler and the Hungarians: DGFP-D-II No. 554; Hitler-Lipski: Lipski 405–12. (*804*) *Forschungsamt* intercepts: F.O. 371/21/742, Public Records Office. (*805*) Shirer, *Rise and Fall* 391.

[3] (*805*) Heston: DGFP-D-II No. 570. (*805–6*) Arrival Cologne and Godesberg: Dirksen 121–22; Henderson 156–57; Kirkpatrick 112–14. (*806–8*) Schmidt

record: DGFP-D-II No. 562; Kirkpatrick record: DBFP-3d-II No. 1033. (*808*) Keitel instructions: Jodl. (*808*) Wilson calls to London: CAB 27/646 No. 11, and PREM 1/266A No. 22. (*808–10*) Chamberlain-Hitler correspondence: DBFP-3d-II Nos. 1048, 1053, 1057.

[4]   (*810*) Inner group Sept. 22 and 23: CAB 27/646. (*813**) PREM 1/266A No. 22.

[5]   (*814–16*) Schmidt record: DGFP-D-II No. 583; Kirkpatrick record: DBFP-3d-II No. 1073. (*816*) Ribbentrop testimony: X IMT 253. (*816*) Hitler demands: many sources, e.g., DGFP-D-II No. 584. (*818*) Mason-Mac's mission: Evan Butler 80–83.

[6]   (*819*) "It is up to the Czechs now": Wheeler-Bennett, *Munich* 139, quoting *The Times,* Sept. 24, 1938. Heston: DIA 1938 vol. 2 p. 224. (*819*) Inner group: CAB 27/646. (*821*) Cabinet meeting: CAB 23/95. (*824–25*) Halifax-Chamberlain notes: originals are in the "Hickleton papers" at York; at the time I examined them, in the City Library. (*827–28*) Beneš-Masaryk: F.O. 371/21742. Delivery times of Hitler ultimatum in Prague: DBFP-D-II Nos. 1080, 1152; Mason-Mac trip: Evan Butler 80–83; Colvin, *Vansittart in Office* 260. (*828*) Lacroix-Beneš: DDF-2e-XI No. 350. (*829**) Beneš, *Pameti.* (*829–30*) Masaryk note: DBFP-D-II No. 1092. (*829†*). Strang memorandum: *Id.* No. 1095.

CHAPTER 30

[1]   (*832–34*) Chiefs of Staff appreciation: CAB 24/278, CAB 53/41. (*832**) Joint Planning Staff paper: CAB 55/13. (*834*) Ismay memorandum: CAB 21/544. (*835**) Hart, *Memoirs* II 164–65, 170. (*835*) Ironside 61, 62, 64. Slessor 151. Newall: CAB 53/41. (*835–36*) COS replies Sept. 23 and 24: COS 770, COS 773, both in CAB 53/41. (*836*) Fraser letter: DBFP-D-II No. 1012. (*837**) Pownall 158–60. (*837*) Kingsley Wood prediction: II Hart, *Memoirs* 170. Balfour 108–11.

[2]   (*838*) High Commissioners' minutes: PREM 1/242; see also Massey 258–60. (*838*) MacDonald in Cabinet: CAB 43/38 210.

[3]   (*839*) Fraser: DBFP-3d-II Nos. 1012, 1034. (*839*) Phipps: *Id.* Nos. 1075, 1078, 1083. (*840, 840**) Cadogan-Phipps: *Id.* Nos. 1094, 1099. (*840–43*) Butler-De La Warr, Litvinov: DBFP-3d-II Nos. 1043, 1071. (*841*) Litvinov speeches: DIA vol. 2 pp. 224, 233. Channon Mar. 11, June 4, Sept. 4, 9, 10, 15, 21, 1938. (*841*) Maisky 82–83. (*843*) Soviet *démarche* to Warsaw: DGFP-D-II No. 579; Krejci's concern: letter to Beneš, Sept. 25, 1938, printed in Kral, No. 222. (*843**) *New Documents* No. 53; New York *Times* Sept. 26, 1938, p. 2. (*844–45*) Ciano, *Papers* 232–37, and *Diary* Aug. 20 to Sept. 26, 1938; DBFP-3d-II Nos. 754, 863, 887; DGFP-D-2 Nos. 384, 415, 494, 495, 509, 510. (*844–45*) Mussolini's speeches: DIA 1938 vol. 2 pp. 239–43.

[4]   (*846*) American policy in the Far East: FRUS 1938-III. (*846**) *Id.* pp. 296, 298; DBFP-3d-VIII Nos. 95, 102. (*846–48*) F.D.R.-Lindsay: DBFP-3d-VIII 627, 630; *Secret Diary of Harold Ickes* II 467–70; Blum, *From the Morgenthau Diaries* 519. (*848–52*) Charles Lindbergh, *Wartime Journals,* and Anne Lindbergh, *The Flower and the Nettle.* Letter to Kennedy: Truman Smith; FRUS 1938-I 72–73. Slessor 216–31. (*851*) Ione Robinson 315; Rowse 80; Wrench 377. (*851*) Cliveden: Jones 409–12. (*852**) Dalton 92–93.

[5]   (*853*) Masaryk coded telegram: Berber, *Europäische Politik 1933–38 im Spiegel der Prager Akten* (Essen 1941) 128, No. 174. (*853*) Leo Amery III 275.

(*853**) Czech Government communiqué: Ripka 163–67. (*853*) Chamberlain's reassurances: DGFP-D-II Nos. 605, 610.

[6] (*854–55*) France after Godesberg: Werth, *France and Munich* 223–314. Phipps DBFP-3d-II No. 1099. (*854*) Daladier-Gamelin: ESF-I p. 34; Daladier archives 2 DA 1 Dr 2, 3, and 2 DA 3 Dr 2. Geffrier: DDF-2e-X No. 317; Stehlin 83–86, 94. Gamelin-Fraser: DBFP-3d-III No. 1075. (*855–57*) Record of Anglo-French meeting: DBFP-3d-II No. 1093. (*855**) *Id.* No. 1089. (*857*) Midnight Cabinet: CAB 23/95 No. 44; Duff Cooper, Hoare, Minney; Cadogan. (*858**) General Maurice trip: CAB 23/95 n. 228; DGFP-D-II Nos. 599, 626. (*858–59*) Chamberlain-Daladier: CAB 23/95 pp. 248–49; Chamberlain-Gamelin, *Id.* 258–59; *Servir* II 350–52. (*859–60*) Gamelin and ministers: CAB 21/595; Slessor, personal notes. (*861**) Hart papers, Sept. 26, 1938. (*861*) Second Anglo-French meeting: DBFP-3d-II No. 1096. (*862–63*) CID Meeting: CAB 16/189, CZ8; Duff Cooper, Minney, Slessor 224. (*863*) F.O. release: DIA vol. 2 p. 261; DBFP-3d-II No. 1111 n. 1; Gilbert, 984–85.

[7] (*863–64*) Hitler Sept. 24–25, 1938: Jodl. (*864*) IX Corps: T79, Roll 211 frs. 751–53. OKH orders: T79 Roll 24 frs. 492–98, 625–26; T79 Roll 25 fr. 208. (*864*) Manstein's arrival: T79 Roll 24 fr. 94. (*865*) Withdrawal: KTBs 7th Division and VII Corps, T79 Roll 16. (*865–66*) Felmy reports to Goering: Irving 64–65; T. Taylor, *Breaking Wave* 105–7; Völker 158–60. (*866–67*) Halder plot: Schall-Riancour, *Aufstand und Gehorsam* 245–52, 248–50. (*867*) Troops at disposal of Witzleben and Brockdorff: *Das deutsche Heer 1939* 95, 99. (*867*) Beck as ostensible Chief of Staff: DBFP-3d-II No. 943. Olbricht-Röhricht: Röhricht 138–40.

[8] (*870*) Masaryk-Beneš: F.O. 371/21/742; Chamberlain notes and Wilson draft: PREM 1/266 No. 34. Czech reply: DBFP-3d-II No. 1112. Chamberlain-Hitler: *Id.* No. 1097. (*870–71*) Chamberlain's full "confidence" note is quoted in Wilson's memorandum in the library of the University of Wales. (*871–72*) First Hitler-Wilson meeting: Kirkpatrick record: DBFP-3d-II No. 1118 (*872–73*) Hitler speech: DIA 1938 vol. 2 pp. 249–60; Shirer, *Berlin Diary* 141–42. Wilson-Chamberlain: PREM 1/266 No. 35; DBFP-3d-II No. 1121. (*873–74*) Press release: DIA 1938 vol. 2 pp. 260–61. (*874–75*) Second Hitler-Wilson meeting: Schmidt's record DGFP-D-II No. 634; Kirkpatrick's DBFP-3d-II No. 1129.

[9] (*875*) Order Sept. 27 to assault units: VII Corps War Diary, 17:50 and 20:30 hours; Wkr. VII Roll 49; XIII Corps T314, Roll 525. (*875*) Western front: Adam; ND 388-PS item 31. (*876*) Ciano, *Diary*. (*876*) Hitler-F.D.R. DIA 1938 vol. 2 p. 264. (*878*) Hitler letter to Chamberlain: DBFP-3d-II No. 1144; DGFP-D-II No. 635. (*878**) Beneš, *Pameti*.

[10] (*878–81*) France Sept. 26–27, 1938: Werth, *France and Munich*, 273–314; Micaud 168–75; Bonnet, *De Washington* 272–85; Gamelin II 353–57; DBFP-3d-II Nos. 1120, 1132, 1137, 1139, 1143, 1150, 1151; FRUS 1398-I 674.

[11] (*881–83*) Ministers' meetings: CAB 27/646 Nos. 14 and 15. (*882*) Mason-Mac's message: DBFP-3d-II No. 1113. (*882–83*) Dominions: PREM 1/242 and Massey. (*883*) "Time-table": DBFP-3d-II Nos. 1136, 1137, 1138, 1140; Cadogan. (*884–85*) Chamberlain broadcast: DIA 1938 vol. 2 pp. 270–71. (*886–87*) Pownall Appendix II. (*887–88*) Cabinet Sept. 27, 1938: CAB 23/95 No. 46. (*888**) FRUS 1398-I p. 681. (*888*) Newton-Beneš: DBFP-3d-II No. 1149. (*888–89*) Stronge *contra* Mason-Mac: *Id.* No. 1148; Stronge in *The Times*, Aug. 1967; Strong 34; Butler 83–84.

[12] (*889–90*) F.D.R.'s second peace appeal: Blum, *From the Morgenthau Diaries* 520; Ickes II 478–79; *Memoirs of Cordell Hull* I 593; Alsop and Kintner,

American White Paper 10–11; Bullitt 293–96; FRUS 1938-I 669, 675–76, 678–80, 686–88; DIA 1938 266–67. (*890*) Wheeler-Bennett, *King George VI* 352. (*890–91*) Chamberlain to Hitler and Mussolini: DBFP-3d-II 1158, 1159, 1165. Perth to Foreign Office and reply: *Id.* 1125, 1161, 1166; Ciano, *Diary.* (*892**) PREM 1/242. (*892*) French proposals: François-Poncet 266–67; DBFP-3d-II Nos. 1151, 1157, 1162, 1163, 1193; DGFP-D-II No. 656. (*892†*) Léger and Halifax qualifications: DBFP-3d-II Nos. 1169, 1177. (*893–95*) Attolico chronological account: FRUS 1938-I pp. 727–29; Kordt, *Wahn und Wirklichkeit* 124. (*894*) Henderson-Hitler: DBFP-3d-II Nos. 1180–82. (*895*) OKH orders Sept. 28, 1938: ND 388-PS Items 34–37. (*895–96*) Kordt-Schulenburg: Kordt testimony at Nuremberg, Case No. 11, Tr. 7385. Gisevius 325–26.

[13] (*897*) Orders to stop the assault units: Wkr. VII roll 49; T79 Roll 45; T314 Roll 525. Röhricht 139–40.

CHAPTER 31

[1] (*899*) Kirkpatrick-Jebb: PREM 1/266. (*899–900*) This and subsequent Cabinet references in this chapter are to CAB 23/96 Nos. 49, 50, 55–58. (*900–1*) Last two "inner group" meetings: CAB 27/646, items XVI and XVII. (*901*) White Paper: Misc. No. 8 (1938) Cmd. 5848. (*901–3*) Speech extracts: DIA 1938 vol. 2 pp. 292–303. (*903–4*) Daladier in Chamber: *Id.* 307–14; Werth, *France and Munich* 323–32.

[2] (*904 et seq.*) Minutes of the nine meetings of the International Commission are in DGFP-D-IV, Chapt. 1; see also descriptions in François-Poncet, Henderson, Stehlin, Weizsaecker.

[3] (*906*) Henderson report: DBFP-3d-III No. 79. (*906*) Hitler arrival in Berlin: New York *Times* Oct. 2, 1938. (*907*) Hitler meeting Oct. 2: DGFP-D-IV No. 12 (*907–10*) Fracas over Oct. 10 line: Cadogan Oct. 5; François-Poncet, *Fateful Years* 274–75; DBFP-3d-III Nos. 125, 127, 134, 140; DGFP-D-IV Nos. 24, 25, 30–33, 41; Gannon 197.

[4] (*910*) Advance of German troops into Sudetenland: Choltitz 45–46; Gedye, *Betrayal in Central Europe* 477–86; Groscurth 130–56, 327–56; Guderian 57–59; Röhricht 140; Shirer, *Berlin Diary* 148; Strong 35–39; Weichs; war diaries of Leeb HQ (H. Gr. z.b. V), VII Corps, and 7th Division, NA T-79 Roll 16 N.A.; DBFP-3d-III Nos. 104, 118, 191. (*911†*) Anne Lindbergh 184. (*912–14*) Refugees: Crane, *Mr. Carr of State* (N.Y. 1960) 350; Ripka 252; Werth, *France and Munich* 344–45; DBFP-3d-III Nos. 2, 9 and notes, 231, 235, 260. (*914*) Anglo-French loan: DBFP-3d-III Nos. 251, 398, 415, 512, and IV Nos. 1, 7, 12, 14, 15, 25, 68, 105. Hitler's, anti-Semitic pressures: DGFP-D-IV Nos. 55, 61, 67, 158, 159.

[5] (*914–15*) Henderson-Weizsaecker: DBFP-3d-III No. 179. Plebiscites: DGFP-D-IV Nos. 53, 56. (*915*) Hitler-Chalkovsky: *Id.* Nos. 55, 61. (*915–17*) Final Czech-German border: *Id. Nos.* 108, 110, 113–17, 121, 125; DBFP-3d-III Nos. 261, 266; CAB 23/95 No. 56. Czech-German "protocol" and map: Misc. No. 11 (1938) Cmd. 5908.

[6] (*917–18*) Hungarian claims and Vienna award: Ciano, *Papers* 238–41 and *Diary* Oct. 3–Nov. 4, 1938; DGFP-D-IV Nos. 82–84, 86–99.

[7] (*918–19*) Chalkovsky request for guarantee: DBFP-3d-III No. 252. Halifax memorandum: CAB 24/480. (*919–20*) Anglo-French meeting: DBFP-3d-III No. 325. (*921*) Instructions to Newton: *Id. No.* 408, 423. (*921–22*) Ribbentrop-Bonnet-Léger: DGFP-D-IV No. 370. (*922*) Ribbentrop-Coulondre: *Id.* No. 373; Magistrati

Id. No. 154. Reply: *Id.* No. 175. (*922**) DGFP-D-IV No. 178. (*922*) Coulondre report: DIA 1939–1946 vol. I pp. 43–44.

[8] (*923*) Vansittart: Middlemas 406, citing "the Vansittart papers." (*924*) Ogilvie-Forbes: DBFP-3d-III No. 397. (*924*) Bonnet at Périgueux: Werth 345.

CHAPTER 32

[1] (*926*) Halifax 199–200. Stanley, De La Warr: PREM 1/266. Swinton, *Sixty Years* 120, and letter quoted in Colvin, *Chamberlain* 168. (*926 et seq.*) Cabinet minutes for this chapter are CAB 23/95 (Oct. 3), 23/96 (Oct. 19–Dec. 21, 1938), 23/97 and 23/98 (Jan. 1939 *et seq.*). (*927*) Chamberlain Oct. 22 and comment on Eden: Middlemas 414–15, 418–19. (*928**) Foreign Office papers are summarized in Middlemas 430–32. (*928 et seq.*) CID papers in October and early November: CAB 24/279–80. (*929*) Scheme M: Collier 63–70; Slessor 174–85. (*929*) Army: Middlemas 426–27; Minney 158–60; Pownall. (*931**) AIR 8/1235 No. 1. (*932–33*) Anglo-French talks: DBFP-3d-III No. 325.

[2] (*934*) Saarbrücken. DIA 1938 pp. 337–40; Hitler questions and OKW answers: ND 388–PS No. 48. (*935*) Directive Oct. 21: ND C-136. Weimar: Guderian 60. (*936*) Lipski 453–54; Kennedy-Halifax: FRUS 1938-I pp. 85–86. (*937–38*) Grynszpan-Rath background: Lipski 461–62. (*937*) Dirksen: DGFP-D-IV Nos. 260, 269; Foreign Policy Committee: CAB 27/624 No. 32. (*938**) Gilbert 1010, note 1. (*939*) François-Poncet in Rome: *Au Palais Farnése* 14–26; Chamberlain-Perth: DBFP-3d-III No. 432. (*939–40*) Ribbentrop in Paris: Bonnet, *De Munich à la Guerre;* Coulondre, Noguères 341–47.

[3] (*941–42*) Woermann Oct. 7: DGFP-D-IV No. 45. (*942*) Goering-Durcansky: *Id.* No. 68. Directive Dec. 17: ND C-138. (*942*) Danzig directive: ND C-137. (*943*) Goering Oct. 14: ND 1301-PS.

[4] (*943*) Kirkpatrick, *Inner Circle* 136–39; Cadogan Dec. 15; Harvey Dec. 17; Pownall Dec. 16, 1938. (*944–47*) Holland scare: Cadogan Jan. 17, 23, 25, 1939; Pownall Jan. 20 and Feb. 13, 1939, CAB 23/97 Nos. 1–3; CAB 27/624 Nos. 35–37; CAB 24/267, FP (36) 74, 75–77; CAB 24/282, C.P. 3, 6, 20 (39); AIR 8/235 No. II; DBFP-3d-IV Nos. 18, 20, 27, 30, 39, 41, 44, 45, 48, 57, 72. (*948–50*) "Role of the Army" recommendations: CAB 23/97 Nos. 3–8; Pownall Dec. 12, 1938, Jan. 2, 23, 30, and Feb. 6, 13, 20, 1939; CAB 53/10, Dec. 20, 1938, and Jan. 18, 1939. Chamberlain letter: Gilbert 1041.

[5] (*950–54*) Trip to Rome: Ciano, *Diario* I, Jan. 11–14, 1939; Feiling 393; Shirer *Berlin Diary* 156–57; DBFP-3d-III Nos. 477, 495, 496, 500, 502; CAB 23/96 Dec. 21, 1938, 23/97 Jan. 18, 1939. (*952–54*) Strengthening of Anti-Comintern Pact: Ciano, *Papers* 242–46, 258; *Diary* Sept. 30, Oct. 27–28, 1938; *Diario* Jan. 1, 2, 7, Feb. 5, 8, 1939; T. Taylor, *Breaking Wave* 31–32. (*953–54*) British knowledge: DBFP-3d-VIII Nos. 194, 197, 254, 308, 433, 457, 491; CAB 27/624 Jan. 23, 1939; CAB 23/97 Jan. 25, 1939, 23/98 Feb. 15, 1939.

[6] (*955*) German occupation of Bohemia-Moravia: T. Taylor, *Sword and Swastika* 234–38; DGFP-D-IV No. 168. (*955*) Young, *Rommel the Desert Fox* (1950) 42. (*956–57*) British lack of warning: Cadogan, Mar. 11–15; Colvin, *Chamberlain* 184–85; Feiling 396–97; Harvey 260–61; CAB 23/97 Mar. 8; DBFP-3d-IV Nos. 197, 234. (*757–59*) British reaction: Butler 77; Hart, *Memoirs* 219; DIA 1939–45 vol. I p. 66; CAB 23/98 Mar. 15, 18; DBFP-3d-IV No. 247.

[7] (*960–62*) Tilea scare: DBFP-3d-IV Nos. 298, 390, 397, 398. (*962*) Wohlthat and German-Rumanian treaty: DGFP-D-IV Nos. 78, 131; Replies

to inquiry of Mar. 17, 1939: DBFP-3d-IV No. 496. Four-power proposal and letter to Mussolini: CAB 23/98 Mar. 20; DBFP-3d-IV No. 596. (*963*) Bonnet in London: *Id.* Nos. 458, 484, 507. Memel: T. Taylor, *Sword and Swastika* 234. (*964*) Mussolini Mar. 26: Ciano, *Diario* 66. Lipski DGFP-D-VI Nos. 61, 101, 108. (*964–65*) Beck-Raczyński-Halifax: Beck 187–89; DBFP-3d-IV No. 518. (*965*) Polish-Rumanian proposal: Cadogan Mar. 25–27; Harvey Mar. 25–27; CAB 27/624 Mar. 27. (*966–69*) Colvin story: Colvin, *Chamberlain Cabinet* 194–98, *None so Blind* 298–311; Cadogan, Mar. 29; Harvey Mar. 29, 30; CAB 23/98 Mar. 30, 31. (*969*) Hitler plans: ND R-100, C-120. (*969–71*) Reasons for Polish guarantee: Cadogan 166; Halifax 204–5; Hart, *Memoirs* 214–22; Templewood 347–52; CAB 23/98 Apr. 4, 1939.

[8] (*971–72*) Beck negotiations: DBFP-3d-IV Nos. 1, 2, 10, 11, 16. Lipski-Weizsaecker: Lipski 528; DGFP-D-VI No. 169. Albania: Lord Butler 79; Cadogan Apr. 7. (*973*) Rumanian-Greek guarantees: Cadogan Apr. 11–13, 1939; DBFP-3d-V Nos. 37, 49, 49, 53, 57, 58. (*972**) DIA 1939-45 vol. 1 pp. 202–4. (*973*) Increase in Territorial Army and conscription: Minney 185–203. (*973–74*) Hitler speech: DIA 1939–45 vol. 1 pp. 214–56. Hitler May 23: ND L-79. (*974*) Pact of Steel: Ciano, *Papers* 282–87; *Diario* May 6–7, 21; DIA 1939-45 vol. I pp. 163–72. (*974–76*) Anglo-French and German negotiations with Soviet Russia: Cadogan Apr. 19–Aug. 24, 1939 *passim;* Colvin, *Chamberlain* 199–216; Halifax 206–7; Hilger and Meyer 288–314; Maisky 116–205; Templewood 341–71; DBFP-3d-V Nos. 241, 247, 250, 277, 282, 305, 316, 344, 351, 359, 401, 421; *Nazi-Soviet Relations 1939–41* (U. S. State Dept. 1948) 1–78; CAB 27/624 Apr. 19 *et seq.;* CAB 27/627 Apr. 24, 1938.

Chapter 33

[1] (*978*) Churchill Nov. 24, 1938: Kay Halle, *Irrepressible Churchill* (1966) 139. (*978**) Letter to Moyne: Gilbert 972. (*978–79*) Baldwin: Middlemas and Barnes 1046. Eden: *The Reckoning* 35.

[2] (*980–81*) A. J. P. Taylor 189.

[5] (*985*) Chamberlain May 25, 1940: Feiling 446.

[6] (*991**) Colvin, *Vansittart in Office* 274.

[7] (*993*) Ironside: Eden, *The Reckoning,* May 19, 1940.

[8] (*994*) Bodenschatz: Stehlin 106–9; Sperrle's and Kesselring's reports: Murray 425–39.

[9] (*995–96*) Wheeler-Bennett, *Munich* 433–34. (*997*) Shay 285.

[10] (*998–99*) Chatfield: Marder 1342.

[11] (*1001*) A. J. P. Taylor's lecture: I was present.

[12] (*1002*) Robbins 4–5. (*1003–4*) Alexander Solzhenitsyn, *Nobel Prize Lecture* (Stenvalley Press, London 1972) 39.

Sources and Acknowledgments

Contemporaneous and subsequent documentation on Munich is extensive, and literature collaterally or incidentally relevant is quite beyond the bounds of individual coverage. Since I have endeavored to describe Munich in the context of Europe as a whole, taking some account also of the Dominions, the United States, and the Far East, my sources cover as wide a range as time and my limited linguistic talents have permitted. There remains, however, a serious gap, as yet unclosed in this or any other account: the diplomatic and military records of Czechoslovakia, the Soviet Union, and Poland. The two collections published in Prague in 1958 (*New Documents*) and 1968 (Král) are selective, and the authenticity and accuracy of the translated texts are unconfirmed. I am not aware that any Western historian has been given substantial access to these sources.

The single most important source for this book is the diplomatic documents for the period of Britain, France, Germany, and the United States. Apart from the published series of selected documents (DBFP, DDF, DGFP, and FRUS), historians have access, with varying limitations, to the British, German, and United States files, but not to the French.

The British, French, and German volumes thus far published suffer from gaps in the mid-thirties. The DBFP Second Series (vols. I–XVI) ends in July 1936 (after the Ethiopian and Rhineland crises), and the Third Series commences with *Anschluss* early in March 1938. The DDF *Première Série* (Tomes I–VI) runs from July 1932 to July 26, 1934, while the *Deuxième Série* (Tomes I–XI) thus far published begins January 1, 1936, and ends October 2, 1938. The DGFP (published jointly by the State Department and the Foreign Office) commences with Series C (*The Third Reich*—First Phase, Vols. I–V), covering January 30, 1933, to October 31, 1936, and continues with Series D (vols. I–XIII), arranged by subjects rather than chronologically, and running generally from September 1937 to December 1941, though a few subjects (e.g., Austria and Spain) are carried back to July 1936.

A wide range of British military documents and Cabinet records is available through the Public Records Office. German military records captured at the end of the Second World War were extensively microfilmed and are available at the National Archives. The published Nuremberg documents were originally collected for legal rather than historical purposes and are correspondingly variable in coverage, but the testimony and documents alike are a valuable source on many subjects. In addition to official publications, there are institutional compilations such as those of the Royal Institute of International Affairs, and private collections of less certain reliability.

For French policy during the prewar years, an essential source is the record of the postwar parliamentary inquiry, published as *Les Evénements Survenus en France de 1933 à 1945*, containing extensive testimony by Daladier, Bonnet, Blum, Gamelin, and other important figures of the period. Despite the witnesses' natural efforts to portray themselves favorably, the record gives much detail not otherwise available. The first two volumes constitute the report (*Rapport*) itself, and the succeeding ones the transcript of testimony (*Témoinages*).

Another major document source comprises the various records of the Nuremberg trials. The testimony and documents received at the first trial, before the International Military Tribunal, are in the "Blue Book" series of volumes entitled "Trial of the Major War Criminals." The testimony and documents received at the twelve ensuing Nuremberg trials are in the "Green Book" series entitled "Trials of War Criminals before the Nuremberg Military Tribunals." Individual Nuremberg documents, whether or not received in evidence, are identified by series and number, e.g., 100-PS, C-200, etc. They include the personal diary kept by Colonel (later General) Alfred Jodl, Chief of the Operations Section of the Armed Forces High Command (OKW), which is of great historical value for the periods it covers, including most of 1937 and 1938.

The papers retained by individuals, who played a part in these events, that I have found useful are those of Halifax ("Hickleton Papers," at York), Phipps and Weir (Churchill College, Cambridge University) and Daladier (Fondation Nationale des Sciences Politiques, Paris). Daladier's papers contain his notes and drafts for an autobiography which he did not complete.

I have not had access to the papers of Winston Churchill or (more importantly for purposes of this book) of Neville Chamberlain; in both cases these are in the hands of official biographers. In the fifth volume of the authorized Churchill biography, Martin Gilbert has made use of the Churchill papers in his able coverage of the Munich period, and has included previously unpublished Chamberlain letters. The unpublished memoirs of Generals Adam and von Weichs and the Beck papers, at the Institut für Zeitgeschichte in Munich, are of substantial value for the period immediately preceding Munich. Less important but also useful is the diary-calendar of Captain Wolf Eberhard, adjutant to Keitel, which was made available to me by David Irving.

More than twenty years before I began work on this book, and while involved with the Nuremberg trials, I had occasion to question Generals Adam, Halder, Hossbach, Viebahn, and Wietersheim with respect to matters pertinent to Munich, and I have made use herein of the notes of those interviews. While working on the book, I have interviewed numerous persons directly or tangentially involved, including five who were present at the Munich conference, of whom the most important and informative was the late Alexis Léger, at least equally well known as the poet St. John Perse. The four others were Léger's immediate subordinate Charles Rochat, Daladier's *chef de cabinet* Marcel Clapier, Chamberlain's former parliamentary secretary Sir Alec Douglas-Home (Lord Dunglass at the time), and Paul Stehlin, former assistant attaché for air at the French Embassy in Berlin. Others with whom I have had helpful interviews or correspondence include Sir John Slessor, Robert Wright, Dr. Frank Hardie, Dr. Hubert Masarik, and the late Sir Horace Wilson.

More than a decade has passed since I began work on this book; the long span is due primarily to the circumstance that historical writing is not my livelihood, and secondarily to the enormous proliferation of documentary sources, especially the opening of the Public Records Office to Munich historians by the substitution of a thirty year rule, barring public access to official records, for the former fifty-year rule, which occurred during this time. My editors, Kenneth McCormick and Walter Bradbury, have been forbearing, understanding, and supportive in accepting the many delays, as in every other way. My dear friend and former editor, the late Joseph Barnes, advised me to make this effort and gave me good counsel during its early stages.

I feel deep gratitude to Churchill College, of Cambridge University, for granting me an overseas fellowship which made possible my one period of uninterrupted work on the book. Particularly I am indebted to Captain Stephen Roskill, who has given full support, valuable criticism, and warm friendship throughout the undertaking. So too has Peter Calvocoressi, not the least of whose contributions was enabling me to secure Rosemary Righter as collaborator in research at the Public Records Office.

I give thanks also to Robert Wolff and John Mendelssohn of the National Archives, Dr. Herbert Krausnick and the staffs of the Institut für Zeitgeschichte and of the Bundesarchiv in Koblenz, and Detmar Finke of the U. S. Army Historical Division; to David Irving and William L. Shirer for generously leading me to sources that I would not otherwise have tapped, to Edward H. Carr for aid on the Soviet material, to Norman Kogan for like assistance in the Italian field, to Hedi Lanham for frequent linguistic assistance, to Dr. Jan Stepan for access to rare Czech sources, to Susan Donald for research assistance, to Virginia Woods and the Columbia Law School Secretariat for indefatigable and expert transmutation of hen-tracks into typescript, to my wife, Toby Golick, for careful editing, and to the many others who have given me a helping hand.

* * *

Since the ensuing Bibliography is intended for use in conjunction with the Notes, I have put everything of more than minor importance which bears an author's name (published or unpublished, book or article) into a single alphabetical list. Official and institutional works are listed separately beginning on the first page of the Bibliography.

Bibliography

I. Official and Institutional

British "White Papers" on Munich crisis and Agreement: Misc. Nos. 7, 8, and 11 (1938), respectively Cmd. 5847, 5848, and 5908.

Documents on British Foreign Policy 1919–1939, Second and Third Series, H.M.S.O.

Documents Diplomatiques Francais 1932–1939, First and Second Series. Ministère des Affaires Etrangères, Imprimerie Nationale.

Documents on German Foreign Policy 1918–1945, Series C (1933–37) and D (1937–45). U. S. Department of State, Government Printing Office.

Documents on International Affairs. Edited by the Royal Institute of International Affairs under the direction of Arnold J. Toynbee. Oxford University Press.

Les Evénements Survenus en France de 1933 à 1945. Assemblée Nationale, Session de 1947. *Rapport* (2 vols.) and *Témoignages et Documents* (9 vols.).

Foreign Relations of the United States. U.S. Department of State, Annual, Government Printing Office.

Nazi Conspiracy and Aggression, Vols. I–VIII, Supps. A and B. Office of United States Chief of Counsel for Prosecution of Axis Criminality. Government Printing Office.

New Documents on the History of Munich. Ministries for Foreign Affairs of the U.S.S.R. and Czechoslovakia. Prague: Orbis, 1958.

Oberkommando des Heeres: Heeres Personalamt, *Stellenbesetzung des Heeres 1938*. Bad Nauheim: Podzun Verlag, 1953.

Soviet Documents on Foreign Policy, vol. III, 1939–41. Edited by Jane Degras. U. S. Department of State, 1953, Government Printing Office.

Trial of the Major War Criminals Before the International Military Tribunal. 42 vols. Allied Control Authority for Germany. Nuremberg, 1947–49.

Trials of War Criminals Before the Nuremberg Military Tribunals Under Control Council Law, No. 10. 15 vols. U. S. Department of the Army. Government Printing Office.

II. Individually Authored

ADAM, WILHELM: *Erinnerungen.* Unpublished. Deposited with Institut für Zeitgeschichte, Munich.

ADLON, HEDDA: *Hotel Adlon.* Trans. N. Denny. London: Barrie, 1958.

AGA KHAN: *World Enough and Time.* New York: Simon & Schuster, 1954.

ALLILUYEVA, SVETLANA: *Twenty Letters to a Friend.* Trans. Priscilla J. McMillan. New York: Harper & Row, 1967.

ALOISI, POMPEO: *Journal.* Fr. trans. R. Vaussard. Paris: Plon, 1957.

AMERY, LEO S.: *My Political Life.* 3 vols. London: Hutchinson, 1953.

ANDREAS-FRIEDRICH, RUTH: *Berlin Underground 1938–1945*. Trans. Barrows Mussey. New York: Henry Holt, 1947.

ANFUSO, FILIPPO: *Da Palazzo Venezia al Lago da Garda 1936–1945*. IIIe Edizione. Capelli, 1957.

ATTLEE, CLEMENT R.: *As It Happened*. London: Heinemann, 1954.

AVON, EARL OF (Anthony Eden): *Facing the Dictators*. Boston: Houghton Mifflin, 1962.

————: *The Reckoning*. Houghton Mifflin, 1965.

BAER, GEORGE W.: *The Coming of the Italian-Ethiopian War*. Harvard University Press, 1967.

BALFOUR, HAROLD: *Wings over Westminster*. London: Hutchinson, 1973.

BEAUFRE, ANDRE: *The Fall of France*. Trans. Desmond Flower. London: Cassell, 1967.

BECK, JÓZEF: *Final Report*. New York: Speller, 1957. Originally published as *Dernier Rapport: politique polonaise 1926–1939*. Neuchatel: Editions de Baconnerie, 1951.

BELOFF, MAX: *The Foreign Policy of Soviet Russia 1929–1941*, 2 vols. London: Oxford University Press, 1947–49.

BENEŠ, EDUARD: *Memoirs*. Trans. G. Lias. Boston: Houghton Mifflin, 1954.

————: *Pameti-Mnichovsky Dny*. Prague: Svoboda, 1968.

BOHLEN, CHARLES: *Witness to History 1929–1969*. New York: Norton, 1973.

BOLÍN, LUIS: *Spain—The Vital Years*. London: Cassell, 1967.

BONNET, GEORGES: *De Munich à la Guerre*. Paris: Plon, 1967.

————: *De Washington au Quai d'Orsay*. Editions du Cheval Ailé: Geneva, 1946.

BROGAN, DENIS W.: *The Development of Modern France 1870–1939*. London: Hamish Hamilton, 1967.

BUDUROWYCZ, BOHDAN BASIL: *Polish-Soviet Relations 1932–1939*. New York: Columbia University Press, 1963.

BULLITT, ORVILLE H., Ed.: *For the President: Personal and Secret—Correspondence Between Franklin D. Roosevelt and William C. Bullitt*. Boston: Houghton Mifflin, 1972.

BULLOCK, ALAN: *Hitler*, revised ed. New York: Harper and Row, 1962.

BUTLER, EWAN: *Mason-Mac: The Life of Lieutenant-General Sir Noel Mason-Macfarlane*. London: Macmillan, 1972.

BUTLER, J. R. M.: *Lord Lothian, Philip Kerr, 1882–1940*. London: Macmillan, 1960.

BUTLER OF SAFRON WALDEN, RICHARD AUSTEN BUTLER, BARON: *The Art of the Possible*. London: Hamish Hamilton, 1971.

BUTTERWORTH, SUSAN B.: *Daladier and the Munich Crisis: A Reappraisal*. 9 Journal of Contemporary History, No. 3 (1974), p. 191.

CADOGAN, SIR ALEXANDER: *The Diaries of Sir Alexander Cadogan*. Edited by David Dilks. New York: G. P. Putnam's Sons, 1972.

CARLTON, DAVID: *Eden, Blum, and the Origins of Non-Intervention*. 6 Journal of Contemporary History, No. 3 (1971), p. 40.

CARR, EDWARD H.: *German-Soviet Relations Between the Two World Wars 1919–1938*. Baltimore: Johns Hopkins Press, 1951.

CARSTEN, FRANCIS L.: *Reichswehr and Politics 1918–1933*. Oxford: Clarendon Press, 1966.

CATTELL, DAVID T.: *Communism and the Spanish Civil War*. Berkeley: University of California Press, 1955.

————: *Soviet Diplomacy and the Spanish Civil War*. Berkeley: University of California Press, 1957.

CELOVSKY, BORIS: *Das Münchener Abkommen 1938*. Stuttgart: Deutsche Verlags-Anstalt, 1958.

CHANNON, SIR HENRY: *Chips: the Diaries of Sir Henry Channon*. Edited by Robert Rhodes James. London: Weidenfeld & Nicolson, 1967.

CHATFIELD, ADMIRAL OF THE FLEET LORD *Autobiography: It Might Happen Again*. Vol. II, The Navy and Defense. London: Heinemann, 1947.

CHOLTITZ, GENERAL VON: *De Sebastopol à Paris*. Trans. from German. Editions J'ai Lu. Aubanel, 1964. Originally published as *Soldat unter Soldaten*. Zurich: Europa, 1951.

CHURCHILL, WINSTON: *The Gathering Storm*. Boston: Houghton Mifflin, 1948.

CIANO, GALEAZZO: *Ciano's Diplomatic Papers*. Edited by Malcolm Muggeridge. London: Odhams, 1948.

————: *Diario*. Milano: Rizzoli, 1946.

————: *Diary 1937–38*. London: Methuen, 1952.

COLE, WAYNE S.: *Charles A. Lindbergh and the Battle Against American Intervention in World War II*. New York: Harcourt Brace Jovanovich, 1974.

COLLIER, BASIL: *The Defence of the United Kingdom*. H.M.S.O., 1957.

COLTON, JOEL G.: *Léon Blum*. New York: Knopf, 1966.

COLVIN, IAN: *Vansittart in Office*. London: Gollancz, 1965.

————: *The Chamberlain Cabinet*. London: Gollancz, 1971.

————: *None So Blind*. New York: Harcourt, 1965.

COOPER, ALFRED DUFF: *Old Men Forget*. New York: Dutton, 1954.

COT, PIERRE: *L'Armée de l'air 1936–1938*. Paris: Editions Grasset, 1939.

————: *Le Procès de la république*. 2 vols. New York: La Maison Française, 1944. Published in English as *Triumph of Treason*. Chicago: Ziff-Davis, 1944.

COULONDRE, ROBERT: *De Staline à Hitler: Souvenirs de deux ambassades 1936–1939*. Paris: Machette, 1950.

CRAIG, GORDON: *The Politics of the Prussian Army 1640–1945*. Oxford: Clarendon, 1955.

CRAIG, GORDON, and GILBERT, FELIX, edits.: *The Diplomats 1919–1939*. Princeton University Press, 1953.

CRANE, KATHERINE: *Mr. Carr of State*. New York: St. Martin's Press, 1960.

DAHMS, HELLMUTH G.: *Der Spanische Bürgerkrieg in Augenberichten*. Tübingen: Wunderlich, 1962.

DALTON, HUGH: *Memoirs, 1931–1945: The Fateful Years*. London: Muller, 1957.

DAVIES, JOSEPH E.: *Mission to Moscow*. New York: Simon & Schuster, 1941.

DAVIS, KENNETH S.: *Charles A. Lindbergh and the American Dream*. New York: Doubleday, 1959.

DEBICKI, ROMAN: *Foreign Policy of Poland 1919–1939*. New York: Praeger, 1962.

DE GAULLE, CHARLES: *War Memoirs: The Call to Honor 1941–1942*. New York: Viking Press, 1955.

DEL BOCA, A.: *The Ethiopian War 1935–1941*. University of Chicago Press, 1969.

DELFINER, HENRY: *Vienna Broadcasts to Slovakia 1938–1939*. Boulder, Colorado, *East European Quarterly*, distributed by Columbia University Press, 1974.

DETWILER, D. S.: *The Origins of the Second World War*. Unpublished lecture, 1965.

DIRKSEN, HERBERT VON: *Moscow, Tokyo, London*. London: Hutchinson, 1966.

DIVINE, DAVID: *The Broken Wing*. London: Hutchinson, 1966.

DODD, MARTHA: *Through Embassy Eyes*. New York: Harcourt Brace, 1939.

DODD, WILLIAM E.: *Ambassador Dodd's Diary*. New York: Harcourt Brace, 1941.

DOLEŽAL, JIŘI, and KŘEN, JAN: *Czechoslovakia's Fight: Documentation on the Resistance Movement of the Czechoslovak People 1938–1945*. Prague: Publishing House of the Czechoslovak Academy of Sciences, 1964.

DOMARUS, MAX: *Hitler: Reden und Proklamationen 1932–1945*. Neustadt an der Aisch: Schmidt, 1962–63.

DONAT, PETERPAUL VON: *Das Münchener Abkommen vom 29. September 1938*. Deutsches Adelsblatt, No. 6, 1971.

DÖNITZ, KARL: *Memoirs: Ten Years and Twenty Days*. Cleveland: World, 1959. Published in German, *Zehn Jahre und zwanzig Tage*. Bonn: Athenaeum, 1958.

DOUGLAS-HOME, ALEC: *The Way the Wind Blows: An Autobiography*. New York: Quadrangle/New York Times Book Co., 1976.

DUFF COOPER, ALFRED, see COOPER, ALFRED DUFF.

DZIEWANOWSKI, M. K.: *Poland in the Twentieth Century*. New York: Columbia University Press, 1977.

EDEN, SIR ANTHONY, see AVON, EARL OF.

ENGEL, GERHARD: *Heeres-Adjutant bei Hitler 1938–1943*. Stuttgart: Deutsche Verlags-Anstalt, 1974.

ERICKSON, JOHN: *The Soviet High Command*. London: MacMillan, 1962.

EUBANK, KEITH: *Munich*. Norman: University of Oklahoma Press, 1963.

EUDIN, X. J., and SLUSSER, ROBERT N.: *Soviet Foreign Policy 1928–1934*. Pennsylvania State University Press, 1967.

FEILING, KEITH: *The Life of Neville Chamberlain*. London: MacMillan, 1947.

FERMI, LAURA: *Mussolini*. University of Chicago Press, 1961.

FISCHER, LOUIS: *Russia's Road from Peace to War*. New York: Harper and Row, 1969.

————: *The Soviets in World Affairs 1917–1929*. Princeton University Press, 1951.

FOERSTER, WOLFGANG: *Ein General Kämpft gegen Den Krieg*. Münchener Dom Verlag, 1949.

FÖRSTER, OTTO-WILHELM: *Das Befestigungswesen*. Neckargemünd: Vowinckel, 1960.

FÖRTSCH, HERMANN: *Schuld und Verhängnis*. Stuttgart: Deutsche Verlags-Anstalt, 1951.

FRANÇOIS-PONCET, ANDRÉ: *Au Palais Farnèse: Souvenirs d'une ambassade à Rome 1938–1940*. Paris: Libraire Arthème Fayard, 1961.

————: *The Fateful Years: Memoirs of a French Ambassador in Berlin 1931–1938*. New York: Harcourt Brace, 1949. Originally published in French. Paris: Flammarion, 1946.

FROMM, BELLA: *Blood and Banquets: A Berlin Social Diary*. New York: Harpers, 1942.

GAFENCU, GRIGORE: *The Last Days of Europe*. Trans. by Fletcher Allen. London: Muller, 1947.

GALLAND, ADOLF: *The First and the Last—The Rise and Fall of the German Fighter Forces 1938–1945*. New York: Henry Holt, 1954. Originally published, *Die Ersten und die Letzten*. Darmstadt: Franz Schneckluth, 1953.

GAMELIN, GENERAL MAURICE GUSTAVE: *Servir*. 3 vols. Paris: Plon, 1946.

GANNON, FRANK REID: *The British Press and Germany*. Oxford: Clarendon, 1971.

GEYR VON SCHWEPPENBURG, LEO: *The Critical Years*. London: Allen Wingate, 1952.

GILBERT, MARTIN: *Winston S. Churchill*, vol. V *The Prophet of Truth 1922–1939*. Boston: Houghton Mifflin, 1976.

GILBERT, MARTIN, and GOTT, RICHARD: *The Appeasers*. Boston: Houghton Mifflin, 1963.

GISEVIUS, HANS B.: *To the Bitter End*. New York: Houghton Mifflin, 1963.

GLADWYN, LORD: *Memoirs*. New York: Weybright & Talley, 1972.

GÖRLITZ, WALTER: *History of the German General Staff 1657–1945*. New York: Praeger, 1953.

GRIFFITHS, RICHARD M.: *Pétain*. Garden City: Doubleday, 1972.

GROSCURTH, HELMUTH: *Tagebücher eines Abwehroffiziers 1938–1940*. Edited by Helmut Krausnick and Harold Deutsch. Stuttgart: Deutsche Verlags-Anstalt, 1970.

GUDERIAN, GENERAL HEINZ: *Panzer Leader*. Trans. by Constantine Fitzgibbon. London: Michael Joseph, 1952.

HALIFAX, EARL OF: *Fulness of Days*. London: Collins, 1957.

HARDIE, FRANK: *The Abyssinian Crisis*. Hamden: Archon, 1974.

HART, BASIL H. LIDDELL: *The German Generals Talk*. New York: William Morrow, 1948.

————: *The Memoirs of Captain Liddell Hart*. Vol. II. London: Cassell, 1965.

HARVEY, OLIVER: *The Diplomatic Diaries of Oliver Harvey 1937–1940*. Edited by John Harvey. London: Collins, 1970.

HENDERSON, SIR NEVILE: *Failure of a Mission: Berlin 1937–1939*. New York: G. P. Putnam's Sons, 1940.

HILGER, GUSTAV, and MEYER, ALFRED: *The Incompatible Allies: German-Soviet Relations 1918–1941*. New York: Macmillan, 1953.

HINSLEY, F. H.: *Hitler's Strategy*. Cambridge University Press, 1951.

HITLER, ADOLF: *Hitler's Secret Book*. New York: Grove Press, 1951.

HODŽA, MILAN: *Federation in Central Europe*. London: Jerrolds, 1942.

HOARE, SIR SAMUEL, see TEMPLEWOOD, VISCOUNT.

HOFFMANN, PETER: *The History of the German Resistance 1933–1945*. Trans. by Richard Barry. Cambridge: MIT Press, 1977.

HORTHY, NICHOLAS: *Memoirs*. New York: Speller, 1957.

HOSSBACH, FRIEDRICH: *Zwischen Wehrmacht und Hitler*. Wolfenbütteler Verlagsanstalt, 1949.

HOWARD, MICHAEL: *The Continental Commitment*. London: Temple Smith, 1972.

HYDE, H. MONTGOMERY: *Neville Chamberlain*. London: Weidenfeld & Nicolson, 1976.

ICKES, HAROLD L.: *The Secret Diary of Harold L. Ickes*. Vol. II. New York: Simon & Schuster, 1954.

INSKIP, SIR THOMAS: *Diary*. Unpublished. Deposited in Library of Churchill College, Cambridge University.

IRONSIDE, WILLIAM EDMUND: *The Ironside Diaries 1937–1940*. Edit. Col. Roderick McLeod and Denis Kelly. London: Constable, 1962.

IRVING, DAVID: *The Rise and Fall of the Luftwaffe: The Life of Field Marshall Erhard Milch*. London: Weidenfeld & Nicolson, 1973.

ISMAY, GENERAL LORD: *The Memoirs of Lord Ismay*. New York: Viking, 1960.

JACOMET, ROBERT: *L'Armement de la France 1936–1939*. Paris: Editions Lajeunesse, 1945.

JAMES, ADMIRAL SIR WILLIAM: *The Sky Was Always Blue*. London: Methuen, 1951.

JEDRZEJEWICZ, WACLAW: *The Polish Plan for a "Preventive War" Against Germany in 1933*.

JONES, THOMAS, C. H.: *A Diary with Letters 1931–1950*. Oxford University Press, 1954.

KEILIG, WOLF: *Das Deutsche Heer 1939–1945.* Loose-leaf. Bad Nauheim: Podzun Verlag, 1957 *et seq.*

KEITEL, WILHELM: *The Memoirs of Field Marshal Keitel.* Edit. Walter Görlitz. Trans. David Irving. London: Kimber, 1965. Published in German, *Verbrecher oder Offizier.* Göttingen: Musterschmidt, 1961.

KENNAN, GEORGE: *Memoirs 1925–1950.* Boston: Little, Brown, 1967.

———: *Russia and the West under Lenin and Stalin.* Boston: Little, Brown, 1961.

KENNEDY, JOHN F.: *Why England Slept.* New York: Wilfred Funk, 1964. Originally published 1940.

KESSELRING, ALBERT: *A Soldier's Record.* Trans. Lyton Hudson. New York: William Morrow, 1953. Originally published in German, *Soldat bis zum letzten Tag.* Bonn: Athenaeum, 1953.

KIELMANSEGG, GRAF: *Der Fritsch Prozess 1938.* Hamburg: Hoffman und Campe Verlag, 1949.

KIRKPATRICK, IVONE: *The Inner Circle.* London: Macmillan, 1959.

———: *Mussolini, A Study of Power.* New York: Hawthorn Books, 1964.

KORBEL, JOSEF: *Twentieth Century Czechoslovakia.* New York: Columbia University Press, 1977.

KORDT, ERICH: *Nicht aus den Akten.* Stuttgart: Union Deutsche Verlagsgesellschaft, 1950.

———: *Wahn und Wirklichkeit.* Stuttgart: Union Deutsche Verlagsgesellschaft, 1948.

KOSKOFF, DAVID E.: *Joseph P. Kennedy, A Life and Times.* New Jersey: Prentice-Hall, 1974.

KRÄL, VACLAV, edit.: *Das Abkommen von München 1938: Tschechoslovakische Dokumente 1937–1939.* Prague: Academia, 1968.

LAGARDELLE, HUBERT: *Mission à Rome Mussolini.* Paris: Plon, 1955.

LAROCHE, JULES: *La Pologne de Pilsudski: Souvenirs d'une ambassade 1926–1935.* Paris: Flammarion, 1953.

LINDBERGH, ANNE MORROW: *The Flower and the Nettle: Diaries and Letters of Anne Morrow Lindbergh 1936–1939.* New York: Harcourt Brace Jovanovich, 1976.

LINDBERGH, CHARLES A.: *The Wartime Journals of Charles A. Lindbergh.* New York: Harcourt, 1970.

LIPSKI, JÓZEF: *Diplomat in Berlin 1933–1939.* Edited by Waclaw Jedzrejewicz. New York: Columbia University Press, 1968.

"LITVINOV, MAKSIM MAKSIMOVICH": *Notes for a Journal.* New York: William Morrow, 1955.

LONDONDERRY, MARQUIS OF: *Ourselves and Germany.* London: Robert Hale, 1938.

———: *Wings of Destiny.* London: Macmillan, 1943.

LUKASIEWICZ, JULIUS: *Diplomat in Paris.* Edit. Waclaw Jedzrejewicz. New York: Columbia University Press, 1970.

MACARTNEY, MAXWELL, and CREMONA, PAUL: *Italy's Foreign and Colonial Policy 1914–1937.* Oxford University Press: 1938.

MACLEOD, IAIN: *Neville Chamberlain.* London: Muller, 1961.

MACMILLAN, HAROLD: *Winds of Change 1914–1939.* London: Macmillan, 1966.

MADGE, CHARLES, and HARRISON, TOM: *Britain by Mass-Observation.* London: Penguin, 1939.

MAISKY, IVAN: *Who Helped Hitler?* Trans. Andrew Rothstein. London: Hutchinson, 1964.

MANSTEIN, ERICH VON: *Aus einem Soldatenleben 1887–1939*. Bonn: Athenaeum, 1958.

MARDER, ARTHUR: *The Royal Navy and the Ethiopian Crisis of 1935–1936*. LXXV *The American Historical Review*, No. 5 (1970), p. 1327.

MARKHAM, DAVID ROGER: *The Foreign Office and the Search for Peace*. Unpublished Cornell thesis, May 1973.

MARTIN, KINGSLEY: *Editor*. London: Hutchinson, 1968.

MASSEY, VINCENT: *What's Past Is Prologue*. Toronto: Macmillan Company of Canada, 1963.

MAUGHAM, VISCOUNT: *The Truth About the Munich Crisis*. London: Heinemann, 1944.

MCELWEE, WILLIAM: *Britain's Locust Years*. London: Faber & Faber, 1962.

MEISSNER, OTTO: *Staatssekretär unter Ebert, Hindenburg, Hitler*. Hamburg: Hoffman und Campe, 1950.

MICAUD, CHARLES A.: *The French Right and Nazi Germany 1933–1939*. New York: Octagon Books, 1964.

MIDDLEMAS, KEITH: *The Strategy of Appeasement*. London: Weidenfeld & Nicolson, 1972.

MIDDLEMAS, KEITH, and BARNES, JOHN: *Baldwin*. London: Weidenfeld & Nicolson, 1969.

MINNEY, R. J.: *The Private Papers of Hore-Belisha*. London: Collins, 1960.

MOFFAT, JAY PIERREPONT: *The Moffat Papers*. N. H. Hooker edit. Harvard University Press, 1956.

MOWAT, CHARLES LOCH: *Britain Between the Wars*. University of Chicago Press, 1955.

MUGGERIDGE, MALCOLM: *The Thirties*. London: H. Hamilton, 1940.

MURRAY, WILLIAMSON: *The Change in the European Balance of Power 1938–1939*. Unpublished doctoral thesis, 1975: Yale University Library.

NICOLSON, SIR HAROLD GEORGE: *Diaries and Letters, 1930–1962*. 3 vols. Nigel Nicolson edit. London: Collins, 1966.

———: *King George the Fifth*. London: Constable, 1952.

NITTNER, ERNEST, Ed.: *Dokumente zur Sudetendeutschen Frage 1916–1967*. Munich: Ackermann-Gemeinde, 1967.

NOËL, LEON: *L'Agression allemande contre la Pologne*. Paris: Flammarion, 1946.

NOGUÈRES, HENRI: *Munich*. Trans. Patrick O'Brien. New York. McGraw-Hill, 1965.

OFFNER, ARNOLD A.: *American Appeasement: United States Foreign Policy and Germany 1933–1938*. Harvard University Press, 1969.

OLVEIRA, A. RAMOS: *Politics, Economics, and Men of Modern Spain: 1808–1946*. London: Gollancz, 1946.

O'NEILL, ROBERT J.: *The German Army and the Nazi Party 1933–1939*. London: Cassell, 1966.

OVENDALE, R.: *Appeasement and the English-Speaking World*. Cardiff: University of Wales Press, 1975.

PAPEN, FRANZ VON: *Memoirs*. Trans. Brian Connell. London: André Deutsch, 1953.

PAPP, MICHAEL J.: *The Anglo-German Naval Agreement of 1935*. Unpublished dissertation, 1969: University of Connecticut.

PAUL-BONCOUR, JOSEPH: *Entre deux guerres*. Paris: Plon, 1946.

PERTINAX (ANDRÉ GERAUD): *The Gravediggers of France*. Garden City: Doubleday, 1944.

POSTAN, M. M.: *British War Production*. London: H.M.S.O., 1952.

POWNALL, LIEUTENANT GENERAL SIR HENRY: *Chief of Staff*. Vol. I, 1933–40. Edit. Brian Bond. London: L. Cooper, 1972.

PRICE, G. WARD: *Year of Reckoning*. London: Cassell, 1939.

PYPER, C. A.: *Chamberlain and His Critics: A Statesman Vindicated*. London: 1962.

RAEDER, ERICH: *My Life*. Trans. Henry W. Drexel. Annapolis: U. S. Naval Institute, 1960.

RAUSCHNING, HERMANN: *The Revolution of Nihilism*. New York: Alliance Book Corp., Longmans, Green, 1939.

———: *The Voice of Destruction*. New York: G. P. Putnam's Sons, 1940.

READER, WILLIAM JOSEPH: *Architect of Air Power; the Life of the First Viscount Weir of Eastwood, 1877–1959*. London: Collins, 1968.

REYNAUD, PAUL: *Au Coeur de la Mêlée*. Paris: Flammarion, 1951.

RIBBENTROP, JOACHIM VON: *The Ribbentrop Memoirs*. Trans. Oliver Watson. London: Weidenfeld & Nicolson, 1954.

RICHARDS, DENIS: *Royal Air Force 1939–45*. Vol I. The Fight at Odds. London: H.M.S.O., 1953.

RIPKA, DR. HUBERT: *Munich: Before and After*. Trans. Sindelkova and Young. New York: Howard Fertig, 1969.

RITCHIE, CHARLES: *The Siren Years: Undiplomatic Diaries 1937–1945*. London: Macmillan, 1974.

ROBBINS, KEITH: *Munich 1938*. London: Cassell, 1968.

ROBERTSON, E. M.: *Hitler's Pre-War Policy and Military Plans*. New York: Citadel, 1963.

ROBINSON, IONE: *A Wall to Paint On*. New York: Dutton, 1946.

RÖHRICHT, EDGAR: *Pflicht und Gewissen*. Stuttgart: Kohlhammer, 1965.

ROOS, HANS: *A History of Modern Poland*. Trans. J. R. Foster. London: Eyre & Spottiswoode, 1966.

ROSKILL, STEPHEN: *Hankey: Man of Secrets*. Vol. III. 1931–63. London: Collins, 1974.

———: *Naval Policy Between the Wars*. 2 vols. London: Collins, 1968 and 1976.

———: *The War at Sea*. London: H.M.S.O., 1954.

ROTHSTEIN, ARNOLD: *The Munich Conspiracy*. London: Lawrence & Wishart, 1958.

ROWE, VIVIAN: *The Great Wall of France*. London: G. P. Putnam's Sons, 1959.

ROWSE, ALFRED LESLEY. *Appeasement: A Study in Political Decline*. New York: Norton, 1961.

SCHACHT, HJALMAR H. G.: *Account Settled*. Trans. Edward Fitzgerald. London: Weidenfeld & Nicolson, 1949.

———: *Confessions of the "Old Wizard."* Trans. D. Pyke. Boston: Houghton Mifflin, 1956.

SCHMIDT, PAUL OTTO: *Hitler's Interpreter*. London: Macmillan, 1951.

SCHUSCHNIGG, KURT VON: *Austrian Requiem*. Trans. Franz von Hildebrand. New York: G. P. Putnam's Sons, 1947.

———: *The Brutal Takeover*. Trans. Richard Perry. London: Weidenfeld & Nicolson. 1971.

SELBY, SIR WILFRED: *Diplomatic Twilight: 1930–1940*. London: John Murray, 1953.

SELDES, GEORGE: *Sawdust Caesar*. New York and London: Harper & Bros., 1935.

SHAY, ROBERT PAUL, JR.: *British Rearmament in the Thirties: Politics and Profits*. Princeton University Press, 1977.

SHIRER, WILLIAM L.: *Berlin Diary*. New York: Alfred H. Knopf, 1941.

———: *The Collapse of the Third Republic*. New York: Simon & Schuster, 1969.

———: *The Rise and Fall of the Third Reich*. New York: Simon & Schuster, 1960.

SIMON, RT. HON. VISCOUNT: *Retrospect*. London: Hutchinson, 1952.

SLESSOR, SIR JOHN: *The Central Blue*. London: Cassell, 1956.

SLUSSER, ROBERT: *The Role of the Foreign Ministry*, pp. 197–239 in *Russian Foreign Policy: Essays in Historical Perspective*, edit. I. J. Lederer. New Haven: Yale University Press, 1962.

SMITH, COLONEL TRUMAN: Air Intelligence Activities: Office of the American Military Attaché, American Embassy, Berlin, Germany. Unpublished. Deposited in Yale University Library.

SPEER, ALBERT: *Inside the Third Reich*. Trans. Richard and Clara Winston. London: Weidenfeld & Nicolson, 1970.

STEHLIN, PAUL: *Témoignages à l'histoire*. Paris: Laffont, 1964.

STRANG, LORD: *Home and Abroad*. London: André Deutsch, 1964.

STRONG, MAJOR GENERAL SIR KENNETH: *Intelligence at the Top*. London: Cassell, 1968.

SWINTON, EARL OF, with MARGACH, J. D.: *Sixty Years of Power*. London: Hutchinson, 1966.

SWINTON, VISCOUNT: *I Remember*. London: Hutchinson.

SZEMBEK, COMTE JAN: *Journal 1933–1939*. Trans. Rzewuska et Zalinski. Paris: Plon, 1952.

TAYLOR, A. J. P.: *The Origins of the Second World War*. New York: Atheneum, 1962.

TAYLOR, TELFORD: *The Breaking Wave*. New York: Simon & Schuster, 1967.

———: *Sword and Swastika*. New York: Simon & Schuster, 1952.

TEMPLEWOOD, VISCOUNT (Sir Samuel Hoare): *Nine Troubled Years*. London: Collins, 1954.

TESKE, HERMANN: *General Ernst Köstring: der Militärische Mittler zwischen dem Deutschen Reich und der Sowjet-Union 1921–1941*. Frankfurt/Main: S. Mittler & Sohn, 1965.

THOMAS, HUGH: *The Spanish Civil War*. New York: Harper's, 1961.

THOMPSON, LAURENCE: *The Greatest Treason: The Untold Story of Munich*. New York: William Morrow, 1968.

THOMPSON, NEVILLE: *The Anti-Appeasers*. Oxford: Clarendon Press, 1971.

TIMES, THE: *History of the Times*. Vols. IV and IVA, 1912–1948. London: Macmillan, 1952.

TOYNBEE, ARNOLD J.: *Acquaintances*. Oxford University Press, 1967.

ULAM, ADAM B.: *Expansion and Coexistence: The History of Soviet Foreign Policy 1917–1967*. New York: Praeger, 1968.

VANSITTART, LORD: *The Mist Procession*. London: Hutchinson, 1958.

VÖLKER, KARL HEINZ: *Die Deutsche Luftwaffe 1933–1939*. Stuttgart: Deutsche Verlags-Anstalt, 1967.

———: *Dokumente und Dokumentarfotos zur Geschichte der Deutschen Luftwaffe 1919–1939*. Stuttgart: Deutsche Verlags-Anstalt, 1968.

WAITE, ROBERT G. L.: *Vanguard of Nazism—The Free Corps Movement in Postwar Germany 1918–1923*. Harvard University Press, 1952.

WALLACE, WILLIAM V.: *New Documents on the History of Munich*, 35 *International Affairs*, 1954.

WARLIMONT, WALTER: *Inside Hitler's Headquarters, 1939–45.* New York: Praeger, 1964.

WARNER, GEOFFREY: *Pierre Laval and the Eclipse of France.* New York: Macmillan, 1969.

WATKINS, K. W.: *Britain Divided: The Effect of the Spanish Civil War on British Political Opinion.* London, New York: Thomas Nelson & Sons, 1963.

WATT, D. C.: *The Anglo-German Naval Agreement of 1935: An Interim Judgement.* 25 Journal of Modern History (1954), pp. 155–75.

———: *German Plans for the Reoccupation of the Rhineland.* 1 Journal of Contemporary History No. 4 (1960), p. 193.

———: *Personalities and Policies.* University of Notre Dame Press, 1965.

WEBSTER, SIR CHARLES: *Munich Reconsidered: A Survey of British Policy.* 37 International Affairs (London, 1961), p. 137.

WEBSTER, CHARLES, and FRANKLAND, NOBLE: *The Strategic Air Offensive Against Germany: 1939–1945.* Vols. I and IV. London: H.M.S.O., 1961.

WEICHS, MAXIMILIAN VON: *Erinnerungen.* Unpublished. Deposited with Institut für Zeitgeschichte, Munich,

WEINBERG, GERHARD: *The Foreign Policy of Hitler's Germany.* University of Chicago Press, 1970.

———: *Secret Hitler-Benes Negotiations in 1936–37.* 19 Journal of Central European Affairs (1960), p. 366.

WEIZSAECKER, ERNST VON: *Memoirs.* Chicago: Regnery, 1951.

WERTH, ALEXANDER: *The Destiny of France.* London: Hamish Hamilton, 1937.

———: *France and Munich.* London: Hamish Hamilton, 1939. Reprint New York: Howard Fertig, 1969.

WHALEN, RICHARD J.: *The Founding Father: The Story of Joseph P. Kennedy.* New York: New American Library, 1964.

WHEELER-BENNETT, SIR JOHN: *King George VI, His Life and Reign.* New York: St. Martin's Press. 1958.

———: *Munich: Prologue to Tragedy.* New York: Duell, Sloane & Pearce, 1948.

———: *The Nemesis of Power.* 2d ed. New York: St. Martin's Press. 1964.

———: *Wooden Titan.* New York: William Morrow, 1936.

WILSON, HUGH R., JR.: *A Career Diplomat: The Third Chapter: The Third Reich.* New York: Vantage Press, 1960.

WINTERTON, EARL: *Orders of the Day.* London: Cassell, 1953.

WISKEMANN, ELIZABETH: *Fascism in Italy: Its Development and Influence.* 1st ed. New York: St. Martin's Press, 1969.

———: *The Rome-Berlin Axis.* London: Collins, 1966.

WOLIN, SIMON, and SLUSSER, ROBERT: *The Soviet Secret Police.* New York: Praeger, 1957.

WRENCH, JOHN EVELYN: *Geoffrey Dawson and Our Times.* London: Hutchinson, 1955.

WRIGHT, QUINCY: *The Munich Settlement and International Law.* 33 American Journal of International Law. (Washington, 1939), p. 12.

YOUNG, G. M.: *Stanley Baldwin.* London: Rupert Hart-Davis, 1952.

Index

A

Abdication (Edward VIII), 541–42, 552, 996
Abetz, Otto, 125
Action Française, 114, 116, 140
Adam, Gen. Sir Ronald, 886
Adam, Gen. Wilhelm, 686–89, 833, 837, 867
  Hitler's fortifications tour, 702–6
  mobilization, 875–76
Adams, Vyvyan, 923
Aeroclub, 758
Africa, Italy's claims, 149–50
  See also British Somaliland; Ethiopian War; South Africa
Aga Khan, 265, 298
Aggression
  Italy in Ethiopia, 163, 229
  League of Nations proceedings, 3
Agincourt, 1003
Agnew, Spiro, 199
Airborne troops, 911
  Case Green, 712–13
  See also Case Green; Student, Gen. Kurt
Aircraft
  Blenheim, 606–987
  Dornier, 605, 648, 976, 987
  Focke-Wulf, 760, 987
  Heinkel, 283–84, 605, 648, 713, 720, 757–59, 760, 987
  Helicopters, 760
  Hurricanes, 218, 605, 763, 987, 996
  Junkers, 713, 757–58, 987
  Messerschmitt, 283, 757, 760, 987
  Spitfire, 218, 605, 763, 987, 996
  Storch, 760
  Stuka, 713, 758, 987
  Wellington, 987
Air Forces
  Czechoslovakia, 991–94
    Case Green, 712
  French, 464, 839, 856, 932, 973, 987
    Chamberlain's comment, 483
    foreign purchase plan, 488–89
    Lindbergh's German comparisons, 764–65
    Luftwaffe compared, 463
    obsolescence, 487–90
  Italian, 152
  Soviet
    Hitler-Chamberlain discussion, 61–62
    Lindbergh's assessment, 851
  See also Aircraft; Luftwaffe; Royal Air Force
Air mail, 756
Albania
  Italian annexation, 385, 963, 972, 974
  Treaty of London, 143
"Albert" (code word), 713
Albord, Tony, 137n.
Albornoz, Alvaro de, 470
Alcira, 564
Alexander I, King, 182
Alexandrovsky, Sergei, 449, 786, 791
  Moscow on Munich Agreement, 55–56
Alliluyeva, Nadezhda
  suicide, 433
Aloisi, Pompeo, 153
  Ethiopian War, 160–64
Alphonso XIII, King, 272
Altenburg, Guenther, 366
American-Russian Chamber of Commerce, 449
Amery, Leopold, 66, 590, 619, 853, 903, 923
  on Neville Chamberlain, 549, 551
Anderson, Sir John, 927, 938, 943
Andreas-Friedrich, Ruth, 877n.
Anfuso, Filippo
  Hitler meeting, 168
  Hitler-Mussolini
    journey to Munich, 21–22
    meeting, 156–58
Anglo-French-Belgian Conference, 466
Anglo-French-Russian alliance, 974–76
Anglo-German post-Munich Agreement, 60–62
  reactions, 63
Anglo-German Fellowship, 733

Anglo-German Naval Agreement (1935), 60, 62, 97, 100, 123, 168, 220–24, 651
  blame for placed, 223
  denounced, 973
  ratios and provisions, 220–24
  reactions, 223–24
  See also Submarines
Anschluss, 565, 616, 981, 984, 997, 999
  Austrian attitudes, 333
  Beneš's plan to prevent, 193
  day described, 370–71
  Hitler's directives, 355–56, 363
  Hitler's Reichstag speech, 347
  Italy
    blow to foreign policy, 18
    effects, 381–82
  Jansa, Alfred, 345
  Nazi program for, 96, 155–58, 331–33
  plebiscite, 373
  public opinion, 831
  reactions
    British, 370–71, 374, 577–79, 617–18, 634
    Dominion, 773
    French, 374
    Gamelin's, 498
    Litvinov's, 447–48, 621
    Polish, 421–22
  Schuschnigg-Hitler meeting, 341–46
    ten imposed measures, 344–45
  Spain linked, 619–20
  Stresa Front's relation, 331, 334
Antiaircraft defenses, 617–18
  Czechoslovakia, 994
Anti-Comintern Pact. *See* Comintern
Anti-Semitism
  Austrian Jews at *Anschluss,* 372
  Blum's Jewishness, 477
  Kennedy, Joseph P., 768
  Polish-German similarities, 919
  post-Munich Nazi behavior, 66
  Sudeten occupation, 912–14
  See also Crystal Night
Antonescu, Victor, 195
Apell, Gen. Georg von, 703
Appeasement
  bankruptcy acknowledged, 959
  Chamberlain, Neville, speech, 959
    foreign policy post-Munich, 930
    Italian trip, 950–52
    results in Rome and Berlin, 586–87
  decline, 940–41
  Dominion policies, 772–75
  Flandin, Pierre, 497, 507, 516
  French Cabinet, 529–30

French right wing, 128
  Henderson, Sir Nevile, 653, 914, 958n.
  Hertzog, Gen. J. B. M., 772–74
  Massey, Vincent, 773
  Maugham, Lord, 652
  Monzie, Anatole de, 524
  Munich as meaning, xi, 978
  Phipps, Sir Eric, 776
  Schuschnigg's policy, 374–75
  Stanley Baldwin, 249–50
  Wood, Sir Kingsley, 644, 652
Arbeitszimmer, 25, 29
Arbitration
  German-Czech treaty, 787–88
Arc de Triomphe, 940
Arditi, 145–46
Armaments
  Belgian rearmament, 474
  French rearmament, 485–502
  German rearmament, 96–97
    British estimates of, 216–17
    pace redoubled, 943
  British rearmament
    assessment, 995–96
    Baldwin-Churchill arms debates, 213, 216–18
    Chamberlain's record, 997–98
    Churchill's views, 211–14
    Conservative deputation to Baldwin, 590–91
    Defense Requirements Committee reports, 212–14, 235–36
    Holland scare, 947–50
    1930s, 209–14
    post-Munich views, 926–28
    Ten-Year Rule, 201, 203, 208–9, 590, 997
  Halifax-Hitler meeting, 309–10
  Hossbach Conference, 302
  Popular Front armament program, 463–64
  See also Geneva Disarmament Conference
Army
  Czechoslovakia, 992
    Foch, Marshal Ferdinand, 192
    Mason-Mac's assessment, 882, 885–86, 887, 888–89
  France
    analyzed, 111–13
    armaments program, 463–64
    assessed, 96
    doctrinal deficiencies, 492–93, 1000–1
    favorable situation, 490–91
    manual of instructions, 108–9, 121, 494
    offensive capabilities, 777

postwar years analyzed, 107–9
reserves called, 854
Spanish Civil War's effect, 494–95 (*see also* Spanish Civil War)
strength on German frontier, 859
three great military figures, 108
Germany
    combat readiness, 864–65
    Czech border deployment, 836–37 (*see also Couverture*)
    mobilization, 875–76
    weapons procurement, 943
    See also Wehrmacht
Great Britain, 996
    assessed, 986
    British Legion, 901
    Chamberlain's policies, 592–96
    Chiefs of Staff report, 833 (*see also* Chiefs of Staff)
    Continental force, 602–3, 637–38, 930–32
    costs, 929, 948–49
    Defence Plans (Policy) Committee, 596–97
    Regulars, 592, 594–96
    "role," 600–3, 613–15, 637, 929–30, 948–49
    Territorial Army, 593–96, 948, 997
    war preparation, 862–63
    Weir's (W. D.) views, 236–37
Soviet Union
    purges, 435–39, 440 (*see also* Purges)
    Reichswehr relations, 95, 175–77, 435, 447 (*see also* Wehrmacht)
    western front deployment, 843n.
Arranz, Capt. Francisco, 272
Artillery, French, 491n.
Asch-Eger incident, 800–1, 810–11
    occupation as blunder, 896, 910
    timetable for occupation, 882
    See also Sudetenland
Ashton-Gwatkin, Frank, 15, 46, 745, 827, 956
    Runciman mission, 403–10 (*see also* Runciman mission)
Astor family, 760, 763, 851–52, 872
    Lady Nancy Astor, 553
    William Astor, 938n.
Atholl, Duchess of, 619
Attlee, Clement, 583
    British rearmament, 213
Attolico, Bernardo, 20–21, 23, 164, 663, 844, 908, 953
    war postponement, 893–95
Aube, L', 16

August 1914, 854
August Wilhelm, Prince, 81
Auriol, Vincent, 461, 471
Australia, 772–75
    war attitudes, 838n. (*see also* Dominions)
Austria
    annexation plans, 96, 152–53, 155–58, 166–67
    condition described (1934), 332
    Fatherland Front, 332, 341
    flag incident, 336
    German march-in
        described, 367–69
        goals, 367–68
        Mussolini's reactions, 365–66, 376
    German *rapprochement* urged, 166–67
    Goering-Mussolini meeting, 266
    Hitler-Halifax meeting, 309
        Eden's reaction, 311–12
    Hitler's strategy, 349
    Hossbach Conference, 300 (*see also* Hossbach Conference)
    Italian support, 333–34
    Little Entente, 161 (*see also* Little Entente)
    Nazi Party *Putsch*, 96, 158
    Ostmark, 371
    plebiscite (first), 576
        German demands following, 360–61
        Hitler's first directive, 355–56
        "Otto," 353–55
        wording, 351–52
    plebiscite (second), 373
    Spanish Civil War related, 293 (*see also* Spanish Civil War)
    treaties
        German, 334–37
        St. Germain, 72
    Wehrmacht amalgamates military, 371, 372–73
Austro-Hungarian Empire, 72–73
Autobahnen, 686, 687
Auwi, 81n.
Auxiliary Territorial Service, 881
Avanti, 145

                            B

Backhouse, Adm. Sir Roger, 882
Badini, Major, 905
Badoglio, Marshal Pietro
    Ethiopian War, 163–64
    Gamelin-Badoglio plan, 122, 462–63

Balabanoff, Angelica, 145
Balance of power, 885, 970
Balbo, Italo, 147
  Italian Air Force, 152
Baldwin, Stanley, 117, 756, 851, 978, 998
  air warfare fears, 211
  anti-Americanism, 208
  assessment, 996
  Baldwin-Churchill arms debates, 213,
    216–18
  Chamberlain contrasted, 550–51
  Conservatives on defense policy, 590–91
  Edward VIII's abdication, 541–42 (see
    also Abdication; Simpson, Mrs.
    Wallis)
  ex-minister's criticism, 535
  Fund for Jewish refugees, 941n.
  Hitler-Baldwin meeting proposed, 262
  Peace Society speech, 252, 590–91
  physical condition, 535–36
  prime ministership's analyzed, 202–4,
    249–53
  Rhine as Britain's frontier, 214
    Hitler's reaction, 216
  Rhineland remilitarization, 131, 139, 245
    (see also Rhineland remilitarization)
  Spanish Civil War, 537 (see also Spanish
    Civil War)
  Winston Churchill on, 202
Balfour, Capt. Harold, 615, 644, 837, 933n.
Ball, Sir Joseph, 568, 569
Barcelona bombings, 565, 581–82, 794 (see
    also Guernica; Spanish Civil War)
Bargeton, Paul, 459
  France's Eastern European treaties,
    464–65, 1001
Barroso, Maj. Antonio, 466
Barthelemy, Joseph, 507, 516
Barthou, Louis, 118–20, 465
  Eastern Locarno proposed, 119–20, 188
  ministry summarized, 119
Baruch, Bernard, 851
Bastianini, Giuseppe, 167
Bastico, Gen. Ettore, 266, 287
Battle of Britain, 647
Beatty, Adm. Lord, 203
  on air power, 206
Beaumont-Nesbitt, Brig. F. G., 859
  Rhineland remilitarization, 132
Beck, Col. Jozef, 917, 954, 964–66, 985
  Anglo-Polish guarantees, 971–72
  assessment, 1002
  biography, 187
  Czech relations, 189, 427–28
  Italian's impression of, 421

Rhineland remilitarization, 129 (see also
    Rhineland remilitarization)
  Sudeten question, 422
  transit of arms question, 428
Beck, Gen. Ludwig, 85, 867
  characterized, 694–96
  Hossbach Conference, 306 (see also
    Hossbach Conference)
  interservice jealousies, 297–98
  resignation, 698–99
  senior generals' conference, 692–94
  surprise attack plan on Czechoslovakia,
    101
Becker, Gen. Karl, 690
Beer Hall Putsch, 25, 79, 152, 315
Beigbeder, Col. Juan, 273
Béla Kun, 171
Belgium
  flamand-wallon schism, 472, 475
  neutrality, 472–76, 547–48, 854
  Pétain's notions of border defenses, 110,
    120–21
  Rhineland remilitarization, 135, 137 (see
    also Rhineland remilitarization)
  Versailles' seventh and eighth points, 70
Belhague, Gen., 195
Bell, Lawrence, 760
Beloff, Max, 198, 431
Beneš, Eduard, 735, 808
  Anglo-French plan, 784–94
  Czech nationalism, 72–73
  foreign policy, 397–98
  fourth plan on Sudetens, 407–8
  Godesberg memorandum reaction,
    827–30 (see also Godesberg
    memorandum)
  Little Entente undermined, 411–13, 417
  Munich Agreement accepted, 55–57
  Nazi abuse of, 4
  Polish memorandum, 425–26
  resignation, 910
  Rhineland remilitarization, 129 (see also
    Rhineland remilitarization)
  Runciman mission, 403–10 (see also
    Runciman mission)
  Runciman's views of, 747–48, 779
  Sudeten cession, 777–78
Bergen, Gen. E. M. van der, 473, 475
Berghof, 696
  described, 738
Beria, Lavrenti, 437
Berle, Adolf, 890
Berlin Kriegsakademie, 75, 98
Bernhardt, Johannes, 272, 281
Berti, Gen. Francesco, 291

Berzin, Gen. Ian, 445
Bethlen, Count Stephan, 416
Bidault, Georges, 16
Biddle, Anthony J. Drexel
  Polish-Czech question, 425
Bingham, Robert, 537–38, 552
Birchall, Frederick, 63
Birmingham speech, 958 (see also
    Chamberlain, Neville; Speeches)
Bismarck, Prince von, 421
Black, Senator Hugo, 756
Bland, Sir G. N. M., 944
Blaskowitz, Gen. Johannes, 258, 955
Blenheim, 606 (see also Aircraft)
Blockade (Roosevelt plan), 847–48
Blomberg, Axel von, 758
Blomberg, Field Marshal Werner von, 87
  as Defense Minister, 90
  colonial question, 311
  Directive (1937–38), 296–98
  German military attitudes, 258–59
  Hossbach Conference reactions, 301–2
    (see also Hossbach Conference)
  marriage and resignation, 315–18
    Hitler's motives, 327–30
  Schulung (secret order), 101
  Waffen-SS-Wehrmacht conflict, 313–15
  Wehrmacht's Commander-in-Chief, 98
Blondel, Jules, 511, 892
Blood Purge, 93–94
Blum, Léon, 16, 116–17, 529, 777, 794, 840
  Franco-Russian army staff talks, 512–13
  nonintervention. See Non-Intervention
    Agreement
  Popular Front, 460–61, 478, 499–502
    (see also Popular Front)
  Rhineland remilitarization, 140 (see also
    Rhineland remilitarization)
  Stalin compared on Spain, 470
Blumenkriege, 369, 375, 910, 955
Bock, Gen. Fedor von, 912
  "Otto," 355
Bockelberg, Gen. Alfred von Vollard, 175
Bodenschatz, Gen. Karl, 712, 719, 757, 994
Bodleian Library, 197n.
Boehme, Gen. Franz
  Anschluss government, 345
Bohle, Ernst, 272
Bohlin, Charles
  Davies as a diplomat, 439
Bolín, Luis, 273, 275
Bomber aircraft
  British production, 606
  German, 760
  Hitler-Chamberlain ban-the-bomber talks,

61–62
  See also Air Forces; Aircraft; Barcelona
    bombing; Guernica; Luftwaffe;
    Royal Air Force
Bonnet, Georges, 118, 478–79, 765, 776,
    785, 787, 789, 811, 854, 855, 859,
    879–80, 924, 950, 957
  Anglo-French plan, 778–84
  Bullitt's Pointe de Grave speech, 525
  Czech boundary guarantees, 920–21
  Daladier's reasons for choosing, 505–6
  financial retrenchment, 478–79
  Franco-German declaration, 939–40
  Gamelin's opinion of, 615–17
  May crisis, 517–20 (see also May crisis)
  on French war with Germany, 5
  Polish-Czech relations, 427
  Russians intentions toward Czechs,
    449–50
  stability, 530
Bono, Gen. Emilio de, 123, 147
Bonzo, Col. Count Valfre di, 2
  Sudeten annexation proposed, 7
Borah, Senator William E., 767
Bormann, Martin, 99n., 706, 730, 866
Boston Evening American, 770, 771
Boundaries. See Munich—the Agreement;
    German-Czech Frontier Committee
Bourget, Le, 755, 764
Braeuer, Dr. Curt, 526
Brand, Lord Robert, 851
Brauchitsch, Gen. Walther von, 723–25
  Case Green exercise, 681–84
  Fritsch scandal, 319–20
  mechanized forces, 493
  senior generals' conference, 692–94
  Wehrmacht reorganization, 322–23,
    324–30, 386–87
Bredow, Gen. Ferdinand von, 93
Briand, Aristide, 104, 105–7
  Locarno Pact, 83
  See also Kellogg-Briand Pact
Bridgeman, William, 203
Bridges, Sir Edward, 747, 779, 855
Brinon, Count Fernand de, 510n.
British Daily Mail, 746
British Empire. See Dominions
British Guiana, 938
British Legion, 901
British Somaliland
  Ethiopian borders, 951
Brockdorff-Ahlefeldt, Gen. Walter Graf
    von, 717, 866–67
Brocket, Lord, 733
Brogan, D. W., 103, 106, 477

Bromberg (Poland)
  anti-German riots, 964, 966
Brook-Shepherd, Gordon, 367
Brown, Ernest, 618, 642
  on Neville Chamberlain, 549
Brown, Sir Harold, 594
Brown, Sir John, 600
Brown House, 25
Bruce, Stanley, 772, 838, 882–83
Brückner, Wilhelm, 366
Brüning, Heinrich
  dismissal, 86–87
  Weimar Chancellor, 83, 84, 85
Brünn (Czechoslovakia), 914–15
Bucard, Maurice, 114
Budenny, Semyon, 172
Buerckel, Josef
  Austrian Nazi Party matters, 372
Bukharin, Nikolai, 433
Bulgaria
  Yugoslavian friendship treaty, 411–12
Bullitt, William C., 431, 763, 764, 881, 889,
  1001n.
  biography, 481
  Chamberlain's Berchtesgaden trip, 534
  conference proposals, 4–5, 518–19, 869
  Léger on Rhineland remilitarization, 458
  May crisis, 518–19 (see also May crisis)
  Polish-Czech relations, 427
  Pointe de Grave speech, 525
  Russian purges, 440
Bullock, Alan
  Hossbach Conference, 304
Bull of Vaucluse, 16, 504 (see also
    Daladier, Edouard)
Bülow, Bernhard von, 176
Bürger, Friedrich, 721, 727
  Sudeten German Party, 378
Burgin, Leslie, 784, 973
Busch, Gen., 693–94
Butler, R. A., 571, 684, 812, 840–43, 863,
  924, 972
  Chamberlain-Baldwin contrasted, 550–51
Bydgoszcz (Poland), 964

C

Cabinet meetings
  Czechoslovakia
    Anglo-French plan, 784–86, 790–91
  France
    Anglo-French plan, 784
    "cascade of cabinets," 106, 107, 506
    Godesberg memorandum rejected,
      854–55
    mobilization considerations, 529–30,
      880–81
    Rhineland remilitarization, 134–36 (see
      also Rhineland remilitarization)
  Great Britain (Baldwin)
    Defence White Paper, 238–39, 589, 598
  Great Britain (Chamberlain), 887–88
    Anglo-French plan, 783–84
    Belgian neutrality, 547–48
    Big Four, 671–73, 677
    Birmingham speech, 959
    Chamberlain's French commitment
      plan, 857–58
    Colvin scare, 967–68
    Czech crisis, 664–67
    Czech destruction, 957
    Defence Programmes and Acceleration,
      930–31
    final Czech frontiers, 917
    Godesberg agenda, 796–97
    Godesberg reactions, 819–26 (see also
      Godesberg memorandum)
    Holland scare, 946
    National Unity government
      recommended, 926–27
    rationing concept, 597–99, 614
    refugees, 901
    Rhineland remilitarization, 244–46 (see
      also Rhineland remilitarization)
    role of the Army, 948
    Rumanian scare, 960–61
    Spanish Civil War, 543–47 (see also
      Spanish Civil War)
  Japanese, 953n.
  United States
    Czech crisis, 889–90
Cadman Committee on RAF, 643
Cadogan, Sir Alexander, 7, 10, 520, 560,
  650, 779, 792, 794, 795, 810, 827,
  839n., 855–56, 875, 881–82, 919, 936,
  944, 950–51, 965, 972, 982
  British policy reversals, 969–70
  Czech question memoranda, 621–25
  Godesberg memo reactions, 819–21, 823,
    824 (see also Godesberg
    memorandum)
  Runciman mission, 403 (see also
    Runciman mission)
  timetable for Sudeten occupation, 882–83,
    884, 888
Caecilienhof, 757
Caillaux, Joseph, 521, 839, 880
Camm, Sidney, 218
Campbell, Roland, 520

Campinchi, César, 501
Canada, 772–74 (see also Dominions)
Canaris, Adm. Wilhelm, 715
  Spanish Civil War, 275, 282 (see also
    Spanish Civil War)
Carls, Vice-Adm. Rolf, 274
Carpatho-Ruthenia, 918
Carr, Wilbur, 869
Carrel, Alexis, 755
Case Green
  Anglo-French reactions prior, 728–29
  Army
    composition and deployment, 706–9
    criticized, 722–25
  basic theory, 896
  Beck's objections, 681–84, 690–91
  Chiefs of Staff and Hitler meeting,
    696–99
  directives, 700, 864
  justification and timing, 720–21
  Luftwaffe's role and deployment, 709–13
  Mannstein's letter to Beck, 694–95, 700–1
  Navy, 713
  politico-military problems, 699–702,
    729–30
  preparations, 746, 808
  senior generals' conference, 692–94
  See also Czechoslovakia; Halder plot;
    Hitler, Adolf; Wehrmacht
Case White, 969
Casey, Richard G., 772, 773
Casus foederis, 190
Cecil, Lord Robert, 200
  Peace Ballot, 226
Cerny, Josef, 790
Cerruti, Vittorio, 156, 164
Chalkovsky, Frantisek, 910, 915, 918–19,
    921
Chamberlain, Austen, 105
  Conservatives on armaments, 590–91
  Locarno Pact, 83
  Mussolini friendship, 150, 557
  Ten-Year Rule, 208–9
Chamberlain, Lady Ivy
  Anglo-Italian agreement, 562–63, 564,
    566, 569
Chamberlain, Neville, 767, 917
  acclamations
    London, 14, 64–65
    Munich, 60
  Albanian annexation, 972
  Anglo-French meetings, 509–10, 778–84,
    855–62
    Chamberlain's plan, 857–58
  Anglo-German agreement with Hitler,

    60–63
  anti-Americanism, 560, 660, 848
  armaments
    Conservative Party, 590–92
    record assessed, 997–98
    See also Armaments
  Baldwin contrasted, 550–51
  biography, 549–55
  Birmingham speech, 958
  broadcast to nation, 884–85
  Cabinet, 555 (see also Cabinet meetings)
  character and motives, xii–xiv
  conference proposals
    formal proposal to Hitler, 9–10
    House of Commons comments, 10–11
    two meetings with Hitler, 7 (see also
      Hitler meetings, below)
  Czech question, 628–29
  Daladier contrasted, 16
  Defence Requirements Committee reports,
    212–14, 237–38
  Eden, Anthony
    agreements, 560, 569
    differences, 558–59, 561–68
  Edward VIII-Simpson affair, 551–52 (see
    also Abdication; Edward VIII;
    Simpson, Mrs. Wallis)
  entourage en route to Munich, 15
  Exchequer, Chancellor of the, 209
    armaments budgets, 213–14, 588–89
  fishing, 44, 660, 744
  five power conference proposal, 890–92
  foreign policy, 555–56
  François-Poncet's impressions of, 25
  Franco-Soviet military pact, 514
  French Air Force, 483 (see also Air
    Forces—French)
  Grandi-Eden-Chamberlain meetings,
    566–67
  Hitler meetings (first), 532–33
    cabinet meetings following, 747–51
    Chamberlain's views, 749–50
    conversation, 739–43
    Hitler's reactions, 743–44
    Labour opposition's views, 752
    sources for discussion, 734–37
    view of mission, 733–34
  Hitler meetings (second), 806–10, 814–17
    Dominion reactions, 837–38
    Godesberg memorandum, 817–18
    inner Cabinet meeting, 810–14
    See also Godesberg memorandum
  Hitler's impressions of, 35, 935–36
  Hitler's letter to, 877–78
  Hitler's Sportspalast speech, 873–74

impressions of Mussolini, 42
Italian sanctions, 465
Lady Margot Oxford's opinion of, 66
letters to sisters, 950
  Czech crisis, 674
  Hitler as a person, 743
  Hitler meeting (first), 738–39, 743
  Ida, 628–29
  May crisis, 655 (*see also* May crisis)
  Plan Z, 669, 981
  Russia, distrust of, 961
Litvinov's conference on *Anschluss,* 449
Masaryk's (Jan) views of, 853
May crisis, 655 (*see also* May crisis)
"midsummer of madness" speech, 552, 554
Munich Conference
  first meeting, 30–34
  relations with Mussolini, 44–45
Munich defense, 901–3
Mussolini meeting, 950–52, 953–54
no-commitment speech, 634–37
"people of whom we know nothing," 8, 884, 978
physical condition, 14
Plan Z, 668–69, 671–72, 674–80
  message to Hitler, 678
rationing concept for military, 597–99, 614
self-image, 553
Ten-Year Rule, 209
various impressions of, 549–55
See also Cabinet meetings; Daladier, Edouard; Great Britain; Hitler, Adolf; Mussolini, Benito
Chamber of Deputies (French)
  Munich Agreement debate and vote, 903–4
Chambrun, Count Charles de, 154
Channon, Sir Henry, 570n., 841
Charles, Sir Noel, 844–45
Chatfield, Adm. Lord, 469, 966–67, 978, 999
  Anglo-German Naval Agreement, 223
  (*see also* Anglo-German Naval Agreement)
  Ethiopian War, 228
Chautemps, Camille, 114, 461, 467
  political sketch, 478–79
  Popular Front government, 478–79, 496–99
Cheka, 691
Chevallerie, Col. Kurt von der, 705
Chiang Kai-shek, 81, 269
  Soviet aid, 442

Chicherin, Georgi, 173
Chiefs of Staff (Great Britain)
  Anglo-French staff talks, 651–52
  Czech question, 629–33
  Holland scare, 945–46
  Poland, 967–68
  Pownall's last "appreciation," 886–87
  Soviet alliance proposal, 975–76
China
  China incident, 206–7
  Soviet nonaggression treaty, 442
Chinese Eastern Railway, 442
Cholitz, Gen. von, 990
Churchill, Randolph
  King and Country debate, 199
Churchill, Winston, 560, 669, 786, 862, 863n., 882, 923, 934–35, 947, 971, 978, 998
  Anglo-German Naval Agreement, 224
  (*see also* Anglo-German Naval Agreement)
  Baldwin-Churchill arms debates, 213, 216–18
  Beneš and Czech question, 793
  British rearmament, 211–13
  Chamberlain's reaction, 213–14
  Chamberlain's no-commitment speech, 635–36
  Conservatives on armaments, 590–91
  Grand Alliance speech, 619, 832
  Litvinov's Czech question proposal, 451
  Munich Agreement, xi, 65, 903
  on Stanley Baldwin, 202
  on Neville Chamberlain, 550
  policies assessed, 983
  Royal Navy budget cuts, 203–4
  Russian aid to Czechs, 452–53
  Spanish Civil War, 538 (*see also* Spanish Civil War)
  Swinton's dismissal, 643
Churchill College, 1001
Ciano, Count Galeazzo, 10, 844, 876, 890–91
  Albanian annexation, 963
  Anglo-German post-Munich Agreement, 63
  anti-French policy speech, 939
  Chamberlain-Mussolini meeting, 951–52
  Daladier described, 44
  Foreign Affairs ministry assumed, 167–68
  Hitler described, 168–69
  Hitler-Mussolini journey to Munich, 21–23
  Hungarian claims in Czechoslovakia, 918
  Munich Conference, first meeting, 30–34

Mussolini, impressions, 19–20, 41, 43, 59
Neurath-Ciano Protocol, 261
Pact of Steel, 974
Ribbentrop's draft treaty, 385–86
Stoyadinovitch, impressions, 412, 416
Tripartite pact proposal, 952–53
Citrine, Walter, 752
Clapier, Marcel, 18, 505
Clemenceau, Georges, 107
Rhineland policy, 70
Versailles author, 103–4
Clerk, Sir George, 465, 469
Britain's Spanish posture, 537
Rhineland remilitarization, 135 (see also
Rhineland remilitarization)
Cleverly, Oscar S., 15
Clichy riot, 477
Cliveden, 760, 763, 851 (see also Astor
family)
Coalition Twenty, 791–92
Code words
"Albert," 713
"Harvest Festival," 897
"Starflight," 713
Collective security
Chamberlain, Neville, 554, 497
Chatfield-Hoare views, 999
genesis in Soviet Union, 442, 445, 447
Léger after Rhineland remilitarization,
457–58
New Zealand, 773
Paul-Boncour, Joseph, 500
Colonies
British proposals to Germany, 571–75
Hitler-Halifax meeting, 310–11
Blomberg's views, 311
Lothian-Goering-Hitler meetings, 263–64
Versailles Treaty, 71
Colson, Gen., 728
Colvin, Ian, 828, 991n.
Colvin scare, 966–69
Comintern, 173
Anti-Comintern Pact, 3, 260–61, 298
Tripartite Pact proposed, 952–54
Japan's views on, 846n.
United Front phase, 179–82
Commons. See House of Commons
Commonwealth. See Dominions
Communism
French right wing's fear, 127–28
gains (1930), 84
Neurath-Ciano Protocol, 261
Stalin's "Short Course," 447
See also Soviet Union
Condor Legion, 283–84, 987 (see also

Luftwaffe; Spanish Civil War)
Conscription, 973
Continental Commitment, 602–3 (see also
Army—Great Britain)
Conwell-Evans, T. P.
Lloyd-George and Hitler meeting, 262–63
Coolidge, Pres. Calvin, 755
Europe's war debts, 113
Cooper, Alfred Duff, 555, 666, 756, 783,
798, 811, 813, 837, 857–58, 862, 890,
927, 934, 947, 982, 996
Chamberlain-Hitler meeting, 749–50
Godesberg memorandum reaction, 823,
825, 826
Munich Agreement reactions, 64–66
New Naval Standard, 638–40
on Neville Chamberlain, 550
rationing concept, 639
resignation, 900, 903
Rhineland remilitarization, 245 (see also
Rhineland remilitarization)
Territorial and Regular armies, 593–96
(see also Army—Great Britain)
Corbin, Charles, 465, 778, 855, 1001
Rhineland remilitarization, 135 (see also
Rhineland remilitarization)
Corfu, 972
Italian occupation, 149
Cot, Pierre, 461
Czech aid, 463
French Air Force, 464, 487–89
Coty, François, 114
Coulondre, Robert, 431, 922, 939, 954–55,
1001
Franco-Czech-Soviet general staff talks,
515
Russian purges, 440
Courtney, Air Marshal Christopher, 604
Couverture, 136n., 524–25, 836, 860
reinforced, 527
Craigie, Sir Robert, 846n., 953–54
Cramm, Baron Gottfried von, 319
Cranborne, Vincent, 568
Cretzianu, M., 973
Crichton, J. R. D., 198
Cristea, Miron, 414
Croix de Feu, 114–16
Croix de Guerre, 905
Crowe, Eyre, 885, 970
England's foreign policy, 199–200
Crussol, Marquise de, 505
Crystal Night, 913, 939
British reaction, 937–38
See also Anti-Semitism
Cudahy, John, 425

Cummings, Adm., 944n.
Cunningham, Vice-Adm. A. B., 941
Curzon, Lord and Lady, 185
  Mussolini friendship, 562
Czechoslovakia
  airfields' value, 500–1
  Anglo-French plan, 778–84
    Coalition Twenty, 791–92
    reaction and acceptance, 784–94
  Anglo-French talks, 509–10
  Anschluss, effect of, 377, 381
  basis of security, 397
  boundaries drawn, 73–74
  Case Green. *See* Case Green
  excluded from Munich Conference, 11–12
  France
    aid from, 500
    Popular Front aid, 463 (*see also*
      Popular Front)
  German-Czech Frontier Committee, 915
  German mobilization, 660–62
  Great Britain's policy memoranda,
    621–25
  Hitler-Halifax meeting, 309–10, 312
    Eden's reactions, 311–12
  Hitler's concerns about Mussolini, 382–83
  Hossbach Conference. *See* Hossbach
    Conference
  Hungarian claims, 795, 796–98, 801–2,
    807–8, 917–18 (*see also* Minority
    populations)
  Lindbergh's visit, 764
  Masaryk-Beneš regimes characterized, 192
  May crisis. *See* May crisis
  military defenses, 398–99
  mobilization, 813, 814–15
  morale, Mason-Mac's views, 882, 885–86,
    887, 888–89
  Munich Agreement accepted, 54–57
  Munich Conference, 30–34
    "observers," 37–38
  Polish claims, 795, 796–98, 801–3, 807–8,
    917–18 (*see also* Minority
    populations; Teschen)
  "protectorate," 955
  Slovakia, 193
    Hungarian claims, 795, 796–98
    German protection treaty, 956
    independence declared, 955–56
    independence movement, 941–42
  Soviet aid, conditions and feasability,
    449–56
  Sudeten complaints, 378 (*see also*
    Sudetenland)
  surprise attack planning in Germany,

  101n.
  Teschen attack, 184 (*see also* Teschen)
  transit of arms question, 515
  treaties, 2–3
    French mutual defense, 111, 192–93,
      782
    French repudiation, 789, 792
    German arbitration, 787–88
    Soviet Mutual Assistance, 99, 100–2,
      179, 196, 378, 449–50, 841–42
  Wehrmacht directive for liquidation, 935,
    936, 941–42
  See also Beneš, Eduard; Case Green;
    Masaryk, Jan; Sudetenland;
    Wehrmacht

D

Daily Express, 198–99
Daily Herald, 732
Daily Telegraph, 909n., 960
Daimler-Benz aircraft factory, 760
Daladier, Edouard, 776–78, 789, 811, 812,
  880, 950
  Anglo-French meetings, 509–10, 778–84,
    854–62
  Anglo-French plan, 778–84
  biography, 504–5
  Blum's cabinet, 461–62
  "Bull of Vaucluse," 504
  Chamberlain contrasted, 16
  Chamberlain's Berchtesgaden trip, 533–34
  Ciano's impressions of, 44
  Czechoslovakia
    aid to, 494–95
    ambivalence toward, 521–22
    Anglo-French talks, 509–10
    boundary guarantees, 920
  Gamelin's relations with, 505
  Hitler's impressions of, 34–35
  impressions of Hitler, 28, 31
  Munich Agreement defended, 903–4
  Munich Conference
    Czech boundary proposal, 39–40
    entourage en route to, 17–18
    French version, 31
    homecoming celebrations, 58–59
    luncheon recess described, 35–36
    proposals for, 7
    relations with Hermann Goering, 25,
      35–36, 43–44
    second meeting attitudes, 43–44
  nonintervention, 511–12 (*see also*
    Non-Intervention Agreement)

passive posture pre-Munich, 15, 18
Premier, first term, 113–14
radio address on Munich Conference, 16
Stehlin's impressions of, 47 (see also
    Stehlin, Capt. Paul)
See also Chamberlain, Neville; France;
    Hitler, Adolf; Mussolini, Benito
Dalton, Hugh, 536, 645, 752, 852n., 903
D'Annunzio, Gabriele, 146
Danzig, 802, 954, 968, 972
    German occupation prepared, 942–43
    German-Polish relations, 419–23
    Hitler-Halifax meeting, 309
    post-Munich German plans, 936
    Ribbentrop-Lipski confrontation, 964
    statute of 1920, 420–23
    See also Polish Corridor
Daranyi, Kalman, 415
Dardanelles, 972
Darlan, Adm. Jean François, 469
Davies, Joseph E., 431, 1001n.
    characterized, 439
Dawes Plan, 83, 105
Dawson, Geoffrey, 805, 838
    Anschluss, 577
    The Times on Hoare-Laval agreement,
        232 (see also Times, The; Hoare, Sir
        Samuel)
Day of the Diplomats, 895
Debeney, General, 110
Defence White Paper, 238–39, 589, 598,
    615
De Gaulle, Charles, 489, 494–96
    military doctrine, 492–93
De La Warr, Earl, 667, 750, 786, 825,
    840–41, 863, 923, 926–27
Delbos, Yvon, 118, 461, 464
    Eastern Europe visit, 482–85
    nonintervention plan, 468–71 (see also
        Non-Intervention Agreement; Spanish
        Civil War)
Denikin, Anton, 171
Dentz, Gen. Henri, 836–37, 839
Depression in Germany, 83
Deschanel, Pres. Paul, 104
Deutsche Lufthansa
    and Luftwaffe, 257 (see also Luftwaffe)
Deutschland, 912n., 963
Dieckhoff, Dr. Hans, 274, 769
Dietrich, Otto, 312, 365
    Hitler-Schuschnigg meeting, 343
Digby, Kenelin, 197
Diplomacy
    Davies, Joseph E., 439, 1001n.
    Day of the Diplomats, 895

French decline, 1001
Hungarian, 411–18
Kennedy, Joseph P., 766–72
Poland, 183–86
Directive Green. See Case Green
Dirksen, Herbert von, 743, 806
    Kennedy, Joseph P., contacts, 767–69
    Russo-German relations, 174–78
Disarmament. See Armaments
Disraeli, Benjamin, 64n.
Dmowski, Roman, 183
Dobler, Jean
    Rhineland remilitarization, 128–34 (see
        also Rhineland remilitarization)
Dodd, Mrs., 758–59
Dodd, William E., 264–65, 1001n.
Dodecanese Islands, 149
    Treaty of London, 143–44
Doenitz, Capt. Karl, 257
Dollfuss, Engelbert, 96, 158, 998
    consequences of his murder, 331
    See also Austria
Dominions
    Commissioners' views on Czech crisis,
        883
    Godesberg meeting, reactions, 837–38
    Rhineland remilitarization, 772
    spokesmen for, 772
    war position, 862
Donat, Lt. Col. Peterpaul
    Munich Conference
        first meeting memoirs, 34–35
        Hitler-Mussolini journey to, 21–23
Dornberg, F. von, 738, 806
Dornier aircraft, 605, 648, 976, 987 (see
    also Aircraft)
Douglas, Sholto, 647–48
Douglas-Home, Sir Alec, 15
    Anglo-German post-Munich Agreement,
        60–63
    Chamberlain's homecoming described,
        64–65
Douhet, Giulio, 112, 205, 648 (see also
    Trenchard-Weir doctrine)
Doumergue, Pres. Gaston
    radio broadcasts (1930s), 115
Dowding, Sir Hugh, 647
Dragon Rapide, 273
Drake, Francis, 951
Dreyer, Adm. Sir Frederick
    Ten-Year Rule, 208–9
Drummond, Sir Eric, 155, 158, 556
Dual Monarchy. See Austro-Hungarian
    Empire; Hungary; Little Entente
Duclos, Jacques, 140

Duff Cooper, Alfred. *See* Cooper, Alfred Duff
Dunglass, Lord. *See* Douglas-Home, Sir Alec
Dunkirk, 985
Durand-Viel, Adm., 459–60
  Rhineland remilitarization, 136–37
Durcansky, Ferdinand, 942
Duval, Gen. Maurice, 494
Duvivier, Gen., 475

E

Eagle's Nest, 743, 745, 746
Earl of Perth. *See* Drummond, Sir Eric
Eastern Locarno. *See* Locarno Pact
Eau de Cologne, 805
Ebert, Friedrich
  death, 81
  Weimar presidency, 78
Echo de Paris, 126, 467
Eden, Anthony, 6, 125, 786, 823, 827, 841n., 923, 927, 934–35, 947, 978
  Chamberlain, Neville
    agreements, 560, 569
    differences, 558–59, 561–68
  Ethiopian War, 162–63 (*see also* Ethiopian War)
  Grandi-Eden-Chamberlain meeting, 566–67
  Halifax-Hitler meeting, reaction, 311–12
  Hitler, impressions, 215, 217
  Minister for League of Nations Affairs, 218–19
  Moscow visit, 179
  Munich Agreement, objections, 66, 901, 903
  Mussolini warned on Ethiopia, 225–26
  on Neville Chamberlain, 552
  Polish anti-German visit, 188
  resignation, 568–71
  Rhineland remilitarization, 131, 135, 240–49 (*see also* Rhineland remilitarization)
Edward VIII, abdication, 541–42, 552, 996 (*see also* Simpson, Mrs. Wallis)
Eger. *See* Asch-Eger incident
Egypt, 833
Eire, 772
Eisenhower, Dwight, 591n.
Eisenlohr, Ernst, 378–80, 389, 400
  Sudeten Germans, 401
Eliot, T. S., 1003
Elles, Sir Hugh, 601

Elliot, Walter, 679, 926
Endymion, 564
Engel, Capt., 800
Epoque, 778
Epp, Gen. von, 738, 744
Erntedank (Harvest Festival), 897
Estienne, J. B. E.
  on tank warfare, 108–9 (*see also* Tanks)
Ethiopia
  British Somaliland borders, 951
Ethiopian War
  allied inaction assessed, 998–1000
  Great Britain, 161–62, 224–33
    Hoare-Laval agreement, 231–32
    results of policy, 233
  Italy, 98–99, 122, 123–25, 160–64, 224–33
  sanctions
    lifted, 465
    proposed, 163–64, 230, 232–33
      Litvinov's comment, 181
Europe in Arms (Hart), 601
Evacuation, 589
Eyres-Monsell, Sir Bolton, 999
  Anglo-German Naval Agreement, 222–23
  Ten-Year Rule, 209

F

Fabricius, Wilhelm, 418
Facta, Luigi, 147–48
Falange, 272
Falkenhausen, Gen. Alexander von
  and Chiang Kai-shek, 269
Farben (I. G.) Chemicals, 690
  military importance, 295
Farinacci, Roberto, 147
Fascism
  early leaders, 147
  French, 114
  meaning, 145
  rise to power, 146–48
Fatherland Front, 332, 341
Faucher, Gen. Eugène, 777, 989, 992
  Sudeten German question, 399–400
Faupel, Wilhelm, 282
Faymonville, Col., 436
Felmy, Gen. Helmuth, 709, 865, 866n., 989
Féquant, Gen., 488
Ferdinand, Prince Louis, 758
Fierlinger, Zdenek, 448, 515
Fiesler-Storch liaison aircraft, 760 (*see also* Aircraft)
Figaro, Le, 778

Fighter aircraft
  British, 763
    parity, 607–8
  German, 760
  See also Aircraft; Luftwaffe; Royal Air
    Force
First World War
  France devastated, 103
  Great Britain in, 200
Fischböck, Dr. Hans
  in Anschluss government, 344, 345
Fischer, Louis, 172
  Stalin's Spanish policy, 445
Fisher, Adm. W. W., 999
Fisher, Sir Warren, 562, 643, 650
  British rearmament policies, 233–34
  Ethiopian War, 227
Fiume
  annexation to Italy, 149
  D'Annunzio, Gabriele, 146
Flandin, Pierre-Etienne, 497, 839, 879, 906
  national unity government, 115–16
  Rhineland remilitarization, 130–31, 134,
    136, 241–49 (see also Rhineland
    remilitarization)
  prise de gages proposal, 137–38
Flemish
  flamand-wallon schism, 472, 475
Flower wars, 369, 375, 910, 955
Foch, Marshal Ferdinand, 107–8
  Czech Army, 192
  Rhineland policy, 70
Focke-Wulf aircraft, 760, 987 (see also
    Aircraft)
Force majeure, 788, 947
Ford, Henry, 1003
Foreign policy
  appeasement post-Munich, 930
  Czechoslovakia, 397–98
  Great Britain
    disarmament as cornerstone, 210–14
    Ethiopia. See Ethiopian War
    Eyre Crowe on, 199–200
    Foreign Policy Committee. See Foreign
      Policy Committee
    four moves to avert Czech crisis, 664
    Germany, two elements, 234
    Japanese concerns, 205–9
    reversal, 969–70
  Italy, 149–51
    Chamber of Deputies, 939
  Soviet Union
    first year, 170–71
    France, distrust of, 446–47
    German relations sought, 446

Litvinov as symbol, 441
  "Munich issue" drawn, 456
  primary and secondary aims, 172
  purges, effects, 439–41
  Russo-German understandings, 174
  United States, 846
Foreign Policy Committee (Great Britain),
    773
  aide-mémoire to French, 633
  Anglo-German relations, 937–38
  Anti-Comintern Pact, 954
  Czech boundary guarantees, 919
  Czech question, 626–28
  Holland scare, 944–47
  Polish defensive alliance, 965
  Polish guarantees, 968
  Soviet alliance proposal, 974–76
  See also Foreign policy; Great Britain
Forlì (Italy), 145
Forster, Dirk, 460
Forster, Gen. Otto-Wilhelm, 685, 990
Fortifications
  concepts contrasted, 685
  Czechoslovakia, 17, 22–23, 989–92
  Eastern, 943
  five enemies of, 689
  West Wall, 22n., 759–60
    assessment, 987
    civilian labor, 703, 705
    defenses, 685–90
    Gamelin's estimates of, 854, 860
    Hitler's tour of, 702–6
    Manstein's letter to Beck, 694–95,
      700–1
    post-Munich, 934
  See also Maginot Line
Foster, Charles R., 452
Four Power Pact, 119, 153–55
Four Seasons Hotel (Munich), 18, 58
Four Year Plan, 321
Fourteen Points. See Versailles Treaty
France
  Anglo-French general staff talks, 508–9,
    651–52, 833
  Anglo-French plan, 778–84
    Czech reaction and acceptance, 784–94
  Bank of France
    democratized, 462
    franc devalued, 476–77
  Belgian neutrality, 472–76
  Cartel des Gauches, 105
  "cascade of cabinets," 106, 107, 506
  Conference proposals, 6–7
    Daladier's efforts, 7
  couverture, 136n., 524–25, 527, 836, 860

Ethiopian War, 124–25, 160–64 (*see also*
    Ethiopian War)
First World War
    devastation, 103
five countries closely tied, 517–20
Foreign Affairs Ministers (1930s), 118
    Barthou's policies, 118–20
forty-hour work week, 486, 490–91 (*see*
    also Popular Front)
Four Power Pact, 119, 153–55
Franco-German declaration, 939–40
Germany
    rapprochement, 480–81
    reparations percentage, 104
Hossbach Conference, 300–2 (*see also*
    Hossbach Conference)
Italian *rapprochement*, 122
late 1920s characterized, 106
left coalitions of 1930s, 116–17
May crisis, 392–95, 517–20 (*see also* May
    crisis)
Military High Commission, 125
    Rhineland remilitarization, 131
Munich Agreement vote, 903–4
Munich issues, position memo, 17
Nazi-Fascist organizations, 114–16
1930s described, 113–17
political figures post-World War I, 104
right wing's pro-Hitler stance, 127–28
royal visit (British), 22
Soviet Union
    alliance proposal, 974–76
    Army staff talks, 512–14 (*see also*
        Army)
Spanish Civil War. *See* Spanish Civil War
strikes. *See* Popular Front
Sudeten crisis. *See* Sudetenland
treaties
    Anglo-Polish, 977
    Czech Mutual Defense, 111, 192–93,
        782
        repudiation, 789, 792
    Eastern Europe treaties evaluated,
        464–65
    London, 143–44
    obligations, 2–3
    Polish Mutual Defense, 111, 450, 969
    Rumanian Mutual Defense, 111
    Soviet Mutual Assistance, 99, 121, 127,
        165, 174, 179, 418, 734
        major weakness, 454
        Rhineland remilitarization, 130
    Versailles, views, 70, 76
war debts, 113
War Ministers (1930s), 118

Pétain's influence, 120–21
"white" years, 103, 111
Yugoslavian Mutual Defense Pact, 111,
    413
See also Daladier, Edouard
Francisme, Le, 114
Franco, Gen. Francisco, 272–293 passim
    Italian-Spanish relations, 291
    Spanish neutrality, 868–69
François-Poncet, André, 483, 905, 907, 908,
    1001
    Chamberlain, impressions, 25
    Great Powers conference proposed, 6
    Hitler meetings, 126, 892–94, 935, 939
    Munich Conference described, 39 (*see*
        also Munich—the Conference)
    Mussolini, impressions, 39
    Rhineland remilitarization fears, 99 (*see*
        also Rhineland remilitarization)
Frank, Hans, 167
Frank, Karl Hermann, 378, 955
    Runciman mission, 404, 409 (*see also*
        Runciman mission)
Franzoni, Francesco, 55
Fraser, Col., 765, 836, 839
Freeman, Air Marshal Sir Wilfred, 850
Freikorps. *See* Sudetenland
Frente Popular, 470
Fritsch, Gen. von
    Hossbach Conference, 301–3 (*see also*
        Hossbach Conference)
    interservice jealousies, 297–98
    scandal and resignation, 318–20
        Hitler's motives, 327–30
    trial tribunal, 354
    Waffen SS-Wehrmacht conflicts, 313–15
Fromm, Bella, 758
Front National, 477
Front Populaire, 116
Fuehrerbau described, 25, 28
Fuller, Col. Horace H., 494, 764
Fuller, Gen. J. F. C., 492
    on French military, 113
Funk, Walther, 313, 954

G

Gafencu, Grigore, 960
Galland, Lt. Adolf
    Guernica and Condor Legion, 286–87
Gamelin, Gen. Gustave, 17, 118, 840, 880
    Anschluss, military consequences, 498
    assessment of, 1001
    Badoglio-Gamelin plan, 122, 462–63

Belgian General Staff contacts, 474–76
Bonnet, opinions of, 516–17
  Daladier's relations with, 505
  French war capability, 854, 859–61
  Laval's German policy, 126
  military assessed post-Rhineland, 462–63
  Polish-Czech relations, 425–26
Rhineland remilitarization
  German strength analyzed, 138–39,
    141–42
  mobilization possibilities, 134, 136–37,
    459
  position criticized, 141–42, 459–60
Soviet military contacts, 513–14
Gandhi, Mohandas, 201
Gare de l'Est (Paris), 854
Gasnier-Duparc, Alphonse, 461
Gasparri, Cardinal Piero, 151
Gauche, Col. Ferdinand Georges, 524, 839
Gaus, Friedrich, 743, 806
Gedye, G. E. R., 912n.–13
Geffrier, Col. Hubert-Marie-Joseph, 719,
  854n.
Geneva Disarmament Conference
  Germany withdraws, 94, 154–55, 210
  Lord Robert Cecil as architect, 210
Gentlemen's Agreement, 544
George VI, King, 734, 772, 881, 890
  Chamberlain's homecoming, 64
  French visit, 522
Georges, Gen. Joseph, 459
Géraud, André. See Pertinax
German-Czech Frontier Committee, 915
German reparations
  Anglo-French squabbles, 104
  Dawes Plan, 83, 105
  French efforts to squeeze out, 78–79,
    105–15
  Hoover moratorium, 84, 113
  Lausanne Conference, 113, 176
  total obligation, 104
  Young Plan of 1930, 83, 84, 106–7
Germania, 912
Germany
  American public opinion, 769 (see also
    Public opinion)
  Anglo-German Naval Agreement, 220–24
    (see also Anglo-German Naval
    Agreement)
  Anti-Comintern Pact, 3 (see also
    Comintern)
  Army. See Army; Wehrmacht
  Austrian annexation, 96, 152–53, 155–58,
    166–67 (see also Austria; Anschluss)
  depression, 83

Four Power Pact (1933), 119, 153–55
Franco-German declaration, 939–40
French rapprochement, 480–81
General Staff dissolved, 75, 80
inflation, 78–79
Italian-German relations, 155–56, 158–60,
  164–69
League of Nations
  admission, 83
  withdrawal, 94, 154–55
  See also League of Nations
Lindbergh's impressions of, 759, 760–62
Luftwaffe. See Luftwaffe
mobilization on Czech borders, 660–62
rearmament program, 96–98 (see also
  Armaments)
Reichstag
  elections (1932), 87–88
  Nazis and Communists in, 84
Reichswehr. See Wehrmacht
Rhineland remilitarization. See Rhineland
  remilitarization
Russo-German understandings, 174
Secret Cabinet Council, 324, 327
Spain. See Spanish Civil War
trade agreements with Russia, 175, 178,
  976 (see also Trade agreements)
treaties
  Anglo-German Naval Agreement, 973
    (see also Anglo-German Naval
    Agreement)
  Austro-German, 334–37
  Czech arbitration, 787–88
  German-Italian-Japanese agreement,
    268–71 (see also Tripartite Pact)
  Italian Pact of Steel, 974
  Lithuanian, 963
  Polish nonaggression, 95–96, 188, 418,
    974
  Rapallo with Russia, 80
  Rumanian, 962
  Slovakian, 956
  Soviet nonaggression, 977
  Versailles
    military provisions, 74–76, 103
    treaty views, 70, 76
    See also Versailles Treaty
Wehrmacht. See Wehrmacht
Youth, 315
See also Hitler, Adolf; May crisis;
  Weimar Republic
Gerodias, Gen. Paul Henri, 454
Gessler, Otto, 82, 83
Gibraltar, 846
Gilbert, Prentiss, 267

Giral, José, 466
  and Léon Blum, 276
Gisevius, Hans, 715, 718, 866–67, 895
Glaise-Horstenau, Edmund von, 334
  Austrian plebiscite (first), 352, 357–58
  German demands following, 360–61
Gliders, 911 (see also Airborne troops)
Globocznik, Odilo, 357
Gneisenau, 985
Gneisenau, August von, 75
Goded, Gen. Manuel, 272
Godesberg memorandum, 7–8
  boundaries accepted, 907–10
  Czech rejection of, 852–54
  Hitler-Chamberlain meeting, 806–10,
    814–17
  memo set out, 817–18
  Munich Agreement compared, 64, 900–3
  reactions to
    Czechoslovakia, 827–30
    Dominions, 837–38
    France, 839–40
    Great Britain, 819–26
    Italy, 843–45
    Poland, 843
    Soviet Union, 840–43
    Spain, 845–46
    United States, 846
Goebbels, Dr. Joseph, 92, 806, 866, 872,
  906, 937
Goerdeler, Dr. Carl, 715
Goering, Hermann, 757–58, 866, 906
  Anschluss explained to Czechs, 379
  arms production, 690
  Army derided, 725–26 (see also
    Army—Germany)
  Austrian plebiscite (first)
    countermeasures, 353
    German demands following, 360–62
  Blomberg's marriage, 315–18
  Czechs derided, 4
  Daladier, relations with, 25, 35–36
  Four Year Plan, 321
  Halifax meeting, 311
  Hitler-Papen conference, 90
  Hungarian-Polish claims in
    Czechoslovakia, 801–2
  Lindbergh's impression of, 761
  London visit proposed, 658–59
  Munich agenda drawn, 20, 32
  Schacht-Goering conflict, 312–13
  Slovakian independence, 942
  war atmosphere speeches, 294–95
  Wehrmacht leadership reorganization, 387
  western fortifications, 687 (see also

Fortifications)
  See also Luftwaffe
Goga, Octavian, 414
Goicoechia, Antonio, 273
Goltz, Count Rudiger von der, 319
Gorbatov, Gen. A. V., 437n.
Gorlitz, Walter, 302
Gort, Gen. Lord, 601, 797, 859, 861, 886
Gottwald, Klement, 56, 454, 786
Graham, David, 197
Graham, Sir Ronald, 150, 155
Grand Alliance, 619, 621, 623, 625, 628,
  630, 632, 832, 961 (see also
  Churchill, Winston)
Grand Hotel (Berchtesgaden), 743
Grandi, Dino, 147, 556, 953
  Foreign Affairs Ministry, 151–52
  Grandi-Eden-Chamberlain meeting,
    566–67
Graziani, Gen. Rodolfo, 161–64
Great Britain
  Air Ministry reformed, 643–44 (see also
    Royal Air Force)
  Anglo-French plan, 778–84
    Czech reaction and acceptance, 784–94
    ultimatum to Czechs, 788
  anti-Americanism, 207–8 (see also
    Baldwin, Stanley; Chamberlain,
    Neville)
  Chiefs of Staff. See Chiefs of Staff
  conference proposals, 5–6, 530–31, 853,
    870, 890–92
  Czech crisis, four moves to avert, 664
  Defense Policy and Requirements
    Committee
    "no war policy" report, 227, 235
  defense priorities, 607, 609
  Defence Requirements Committee
    collective security views, 230, 235 (see
      also Collective security)
    report, 212–14, 235–36
  Ethiopian War, 124–25, 161–62 (see also
    Ethiopian War)
  Foreign office
    Central European policy, 936
    post-Munich views, 928
  Foreign Policy Committee. See Foreign
    Policy Committee
  Four Power Pact (1933), 119, 153–55
  French military staff contacts, 508–9
  Henleinists, 400–2 (see also
    Sudetenland-Henleinists)
  Italy
    French reaction to policy, 578, 580–81
    Gentlemen's Agreement, 544, 582, 583

Chamberlain-Eden split, 565–67
Labour Party/Popular Front compared,
　536–37
May crisis, 392–95, 519–20 (see also May
　crisis)
　military budget, 607–15 (see also
　　Army—Great Britain)
Munich Agreement opposition, 65–66
　(see also Munich—the Agreement;
　Munich—the Conference)
Mussolini's comments on, 19
1920s concerns, 201
no-commitment policy, 633–37
Peace Ballot, 226
Rhineland remilitarized. See Rhineland
　remilitarization
Royal Air Force. See Royal Air Force
Runciman mission, 403–10 (see also
　Runciman mission)
Sudetenland. See Sudetenland
Ten-Year Rule, 201, 590
　abolition of, 208–9 (see also
　　Armaments—British)
treaties
　Anglo-German Naval Agreement,
　　220–24, 973 (see also Anglo-German
　　Naval Agreement)
　Franco-Polish, 977
　Italian Accord, 381–82, 511, 582–83,
　　843, 939, 972
　London, 143–44
　Polish defensive alliance, 965
　See also Versailles Treaty
War Office reform, 599–603
See also Chamberlain, Neville; Churchill,
　Winston; King and Country debate
Greece, British guarantee of, 972–73
Green. See Case Green
Greenwood, Arthur, 451, 971
Greenwood, A. W. J., 198
Grew, Joseph, 846n.
Grey, Sir Edward, 143n., 875
Grigg, Sir Edward, 590
Grille (yacht), 730
Gringoire, 140
Groener, Wilhelm
　anti-Nazi decree, 84–85
　as Defense Minister, 83
　resignation, 86
　storm troopers banned, 86, (see also
　　Storm troopers)
Grohe, Joseph, 805
Gronau, Wolfgang von, 758
Groscurth, Maj. Helmuth, 911–12
Gruhn, Fräulein Erna

　marriage to Blomberg, 315–18, 328
Grynszpan, Herschel, 937
Grzybowski, Waclaw, 419
Guderian, Gen. Heinz, 492, 910, 935
　Austrian occupation, 367 (see also
　　Anschluss; Austria)
　on Gen. Beck, 694
　"Otto," 355
　tank warfare, 256
Guernica (Spain), 61, 286–87, 794
Guertner, Franz, 319
Guillaumat, Gen. Adolphe, 110
Guinness, William Edward, 978n.
Gunther, John, 63

H

Hague, The, 889
　four-party conference site proposed, 5
　Holland scare, 947
Haile Selassie, Emperor, 160–64 (see also
　Ethiopian War)
Hailsham, Lord, 750–51, 825
Halder, Gen. Franz, 325, 690, 722–24
Halder plot, 715–18, 866–68, 943, 995n.,
　1005
　plot abandoned, 895–96
Halifax, Edward Lord, 14–15, 555, 664–67,
　669–70, 733, 751, 763, 767, 770, 786,
　795, 799, 808, 810, 812–13, 831,
　840–43, 855, 859, 913, 917, 950, 952,
　956–57
　Anglo-French plan, 779–84
　Austrian question, 370–71
　British foreign policy reversed, 970 (see
　　also Foreign policy; Foreign Policy
　　Committee)
　Chamberlain-Baldwin contrasted, 551
　concerted Anglo-French action urged,
　　885–86
　Czech boundary guarantees, 919–20
　Czech-Henlein question, 400–2
　Czech rejection of Godesberg
　　memorandum, 852–53
　Godesberg memorandum position, 823–25
　　(see also Godesberg memorandum)
　Germany, visit to
　　Goering meeting, 311
　　Hitler meeting, 309–10
　Holland scare, 947–49
　International Hunting Exposition, 558–59
　Munich defended, 902–3
　Non-Intervention Committee's value,

540–41 (*see also* Non-Intervention Agreement)
press statement, 863
Roosevelt plan, 848
Runciman mission, 403–10, 522–23 (*see also* Runciman mission)
Russia's exclusion from Munich Conference, 12
timetable for Sudeten occupation, 882–83, 884, 888
Hamburger Fremdenblatt, 906
Hammerstein-Equord, Gen. Kurt von, 83
Hanesse, Col. Friedrich-Karl, 757, 758, 760
Hankey, Sir Maurice, 205, 469, 606, 626–27
British rearmament policies, 233–34
Hansen, Gen. Erik, 725
Hardie, Frank, 197
Hart, Basil Liddell, 492, 600–3, 613–15, 861n.
mechanized field forces, 638
Polish guarantees, 971
Spain, 619–20
See also Hore-Belisha, Leslie
Hartmann, Col. Otto, 177
Harvest Festival, 897 (*see also* Code words)
Harvey, Oliver, 552, 784, 787, 795
on Neville Chamberlain, 550
Hase, Col. Paul von, 718, 866
Hassell, Ulrich von, 99, 155, 165
Hauptmann, Bruno Richard, 756
Haus der Deutschen Kunst, 697
Havock, 557
Hébrard, Col., 475
Heiderich, M., 907n.
Heinkel aircraft, 605, 648, 713, 720, 757–59, 760, 987
in Spanish Civil War (*see also* Aircraft; Spanish Civil War)
Helicopters, 760 (*see also* Aircraft)
Helldorf, Count Wolf Graf von, 692, 718, 866, 895
Blomberg's marriage, 316
Hencke, Andor, 405
Henderson, Arthur, 210, 619
Hitler meeting, 215
Henderson, Loy, 438
Henderson, Sir Nevile, 2, 265, 570, 653–54, 661–62, 685, 728, 730, 737, 744, 787, 805, 808, 815, 853, 883, 892–93, 903, 906, 908, 914–15, 957, 1001n.
May crisis, 390–92 (*see also* May crisis)
Plan Z, 668, 672–80
Ribbentrop confrontations, 654

Runciman mission, 404 (*see also* Runciman mission)
Wilson mission to Hitler, 871–72, 875
Henlein, Konrad. *See* Sudetenland
Henleinists. *See* Sudetenland
Henry, Jules, 778, 855
Henschel aircraft, 713, 760
Herbert, Sidney, 903
Herrick, Myron, 755
Herriot, Edouard, 105, 114, 461, 467, 840
war debts to U.S., 113
Herter, Albert, 854
Hertzog, Gen. J. B. M., 772–74
Hess, Myra, 535
Hess, Rudolf, 274, 866
Hesse, Prince Philip of, 727, 844
as Hitler's courier to Rome, 358, 365–66
Hewel, Walter, 743
Heye, Wilhelm, 82, 83, 85
Hierl, Konstantin, 687–89
Hilger, Gustav, 431, 442
Himmler, Heinrich, 806, 866, 906, 910, 955
Austrian occupation, 368 (*see also* Anschluss; Austria)
Slovakian independence, 942
Waffen SS-Wehrmacht conflicts, 313–15
Hindenburg, Oskar von, 82
Hitler-Papen conference, 90
Hindenburg, Field Marshal Paul von Beneckendorff und von
Army's imperial traditions retained, 79 (*See also* Army—Germany; Wehrmacht)
second term campaign, 86
Weimar presidency, 81–82
History, discussed, 1002–3
Hitler, Adolf
accolades post-Munich, 906
Anglo-German agreement, 60–63
anti-Hitler conspiracy (1944), 91n.
Arbeitszimmer, 25, 29
Army's anti-Nazi trial, 84–85
Austria
Braunau-am-Inn speech, 369–70 (*see also* Speeches)
march-in directive, 355–57
strategy, 349
Vienna speech, 372
Austrian plebiscite (first)
letter to Mussolini, 358–60
Blomberg scandal, 315–18, 327–30
British impressions of, 215–17
British visitors (1936), 262 (*see also* Olympic Games)
Chamberlain meeting (first)

conversation, 739–43
expectations, 737
Hitler's reaction, 743–44
Chamberlain meeting (second), 806–10
Godesberg memorandum, 817–18 (see also Godesberg memorandum)
Chamberlain's misjudgment of, 555
chancellorship denied, 88
Chiefs of Staff meeting, 696–99
Czech political and military possibilities, 387–88
Czech-Soviet pact, reactions, 100–2
Daladier's impressions of, 28, 31
"eastern space" aspirations, 95, 100–1
fortifications, 685–90, 702–6
François-Poncet meetings, 126, 892–94, 935, 939
French right wing's support, 127–28
Fritsch scandal, 318–20, 327–30
Fuehrer and Supreme Commander
first foreign policy moves, 94
Red Army contacts stopped, 95
Godesberg memorandum. See Godesberg memorandum
Halder plot. See Halder plot
Halifax meeting, 309–10
Hossbach Conference, 299–302 (see also Hossbach Conference)
Italian Pact of Steel, 385
Léger, impressions, 45
letter to Neville Chamberlain, 877–78
Lloyd George meeting, 262–63
Marquess of Lothian, 263–64
May crisis, 390–95 (see also May crisis)
Mein Kampf, 84
eastern space theme, 95, 100–1
Mussolini in, 152
Russia in, 175–76
Munich apartment described, 34
Munich Conference
comments at first meeting, 31–33
Czech boundaries, 39–40
German delegation to, 17
journey to with Mussolini, 21–23
lunch with Mussolini, 34–35 (see also Munich—the Conference)
preconference attitudes, 2, 12
Chamberlain meetings, 7
Godesberg memorandum, 7–8 (see also Godesberg memorandum)
relations with Mussolini, 42–43
Mussolini compared, 157
Mussolini meetings, 156–58, 267–68, 383–86
Nuremberg Party Rally (1938), 404, 408

(see also Speeches)
Papen conference, 89–90
Rhine industrialists, 90, 91, 92
rise to power analyzed, 91–92
Roosevelt's peace appeal, 876 (see also Roosevelt, Pres. Franklin D.)
Schuschnigg meeting, 341–46, 565 (see also Anschluss; Austria)
Spain. See Spanish Civil War
Speeches
Braunau-am-Inn, 369–70
Nuremberg, 408, 528–29, 726, 727
Reichstag, 347, 378, 947
Saarbrücken, 934
Sportspalast, 872–74, 881, 897
Vienna, 372
Weimar, 935
See also Speeches
Sudeten crisis summed up, 896–97 (see also Sudentenland)
war postponement, 892–94
Wehrmacht Commander-in-Chief directives, 355–56, 363
Wehrmacht's role, 314
Weimar
campaign (1932), 86
chancellorship, 90–94
Hlinka, Andrej, 193
Hoare, Sir Reginald, 960, 965
Hoare, Sir Samuel, 555, 562, 597, 673, 779, 810, 813, 819, 821, 826, 855, 956, 981
British position on Spain, 545–46 (see also Spanish Civil War)
double policy, 228
Foreign Office Minister, 218–19
Hoare-Laval Ethiopian plan, 125, 163–64, 231–32, 535, 1001
Sudeten Germans, 401
Hodža, Dr. Milan, 194, 788–89
Hoepner, Gen. Erich, 718, 866
Hoesch, Leopold von, 215
Hofer, Andreas, 352
Hogg, Quentin
King and Country debate, 197–99
Hohenlohe, Princess, 658
Hohenlohe, Prince Max von
Runciman-Henlein meeting, 405
Holland scare, 944–50, 961
Hoover, Herbert, 623, 756
Hoover moratorium, 84, 113
Hopkins, Harry, 889
Hora, Josef, 57
Hore-Belisha, Leslie, 555, 763, 783, 797,

822–23, 825, 837, 859, 862, 881, 948–49
Liddell Hart's views on Spain, 619–20
shortcomings, 637–38
War Office reform, 599–603
See also Hart, Basil Liddell
Horthy, Adm. Nicholas, 262, 906, 955
Hossbach, Col. Friedrich. *See* Hossbach Conference memorandum
Hossbach Conference memorandum, 299–302
authenticity and accuracy, 302–3
Beck's (Gen. Ludwig) reactions, 306
conference itself, 299–302
historical significance, 304–5
Nuremberg trial's use of, 302–4
Hotta, Masaaki, 269
House of Commons (Great Britain)
Munich Agreement vote, 903
Hoyos, Lt. Max Graf, 281
Hueber, Dr. Franz, 362
Hugenberg, Alfred, 86, 176
Hugger-mugger defined, 29n.
Hughes, William, 774
Hull, Cordell, 769, 770, 869, 889–90
Humanité, L', 140, 778
Hungary
claims in Czechoslovakia, 41–42, 66, 795, 796–98, 801–2, 807–8, 917–18
Little Entente negotiations, 417 (*see also* Little Entente)
revisionist diplomacy, 418
Ruthenia occupied, 955
Treaty of Friendship, 150
Treaty of Trianon, 72–73
Yugoslavia, Hungarian fears of, 415–17
See also Little Entente; Minority populations
Hunt, David W. S., 198
Hurricane (aircraft), 218, 605, 763, 987, 996 (*see also* Aircraft; Fighter aircraft; Royal Air Force)
Hus, John, 830
Husárek, Gen., 907n.

I

Ibarruri, Dolores, 470
Ibero-American Institute, 282
Ickes, Harold, 847n., 947, 989
Imredy, Bela, 415, 802, 906
India, 772
Inflation, German, 78–79
Information, 778

Innitzer, Theodor Cardinal
Anschluss, 372
Austrian plebiscite (first), 357
Inskip, Sir Thomas, 555, 763, 783, 810–12, 819, 823, 825, 834–35, 857, 859, 882, 918–19, 925, 928–29, 996, 997
British arms, 588
Defence Ministry, 239–40
military budgets, 607–15
rationing concept, 599, 614
RAF parity with Luftwaffe, 607–8 (*see also* Royal Air Force)
Intelligence
British Service, 944n.
German bombing probabilities, 989
Holland scare, 944–46
telephone interceptions, 804, 853, 870n., 872
Wehrmacht's Czech march-in, 957
International Boundary Commission, 882
International Brigades, 277, 443 (*see also* Spanish Civil War)
International Commission for execution of Munich Agreement. *See* Munich—the Agreement; Munich—the Conference
International Hunting Exposition, 558–59
International Labour Organization, 71
Ironside, Gen. W. E., 650 835, 993
Isle of Wight, 751
Ismay, Gen. Hastings, 588, 834, 859
Isolationism, 518, 766–67
Dominion policy, 775
Istrian Peninsula, 143–44
Italy
Albanian annexation, 963, 972, 974
Anti-Comintern Pact, 3 (*see also* Comintern)
Austria, support for, 333–34
Austro-Italian Tyrol
German minorities in, 18–19, 72, 96 (*see also* Minority populations)
Hitler-Mussolini meeting, 386
Treaty of London, 143–44
Versailles treaty, ninth point, 71
British Chiefs of Staff report, 832, 836
Ethiopia. *See* Ethiopian War
French attitudes toward, 6, 9, 121–22, 161
Gentlemen's Agreement, 544, 582, 583
German-Italian relations, 155–56, 158–60, 164–69
neutrality, question of, 993
Spain. *See* Spanish Civil War
Sudeten crisis. *See* Sudetenland
treaties

Anglo-Italian Agreement, 381–82, 511, 582–83, 843, 939, 972
Four Power Pact (1933), 119, 153–55
German-Italian-Japanese agreement, 268–71 (*see also* Tripartite Pact)
German Pact of Steel, 974
Hungarian Friendship, 150
Lausanne, 149
Yugoslav nonaggression pact, 195

J

Jacomet, Robert, 485–87
Jansa, Alfred, 345
Japan
  Anti-Comintern Pact, 3, 260–61 (*see also* Comintern)
  British Chiefs of Staff report, 832, 836
  China incident, 206–7
  Comintern, 846n. (*see also* Comintern)
  German-Italian-Japanese agreement, 268–71 (*see also* Tripartite Pact)
  neutrality in West, 993
  Sino-Japanese conflict, 175
  Soviet fears of, 442
Jeanneney, Jules, 467
Jebb, Gladwyn, 899
  Czech question memo, 621–22
Jeschonnek, Lt. Col. Hans, 683–84
Jeunesse Patriotes, 114
Jews. *See* Anti-Semitism; Crystal Night
Joad, C. E. M.
  King and Country debate, 197–99
Jodl, Gen. Alfred, 681, 726, 737, 865n., 875, 934
  Case Green, 389–90, 394–95 (*see also* Case Green)
  Chiefs of Staff meeting with Hitler, 697–98
  war of the future, 387
  Wehrmacht reorganization, 323, 324–30 passim
Joffre, Marshal, 108
Johnson, Herschel, 849
Jones, Thomas, 535, 763
  Baldwin-Hitler meeting proposed, 262
  Chamberlain and foreign affairs, 553
  Lindbergh's effect on, 851–52
  Rhineland remilitarization, 243 (*see also* Rhineland remilitarization)
Jordan, W. J., 772, 838
Joseph, Archduke of Liechtenstein, 906
Jour, Le, 140
Journalistic opinion

Anglo-French plan, 794
Anglo-German post-Munich Agreement, 63
Chamberlain-Hitler meeting (first), 732
Chamberlain's no-commitment speech, 636
Crystal Night, 937 (*see also* Crystal Night)
Ethiopian War, 164
Franco-Czech treaty, 507, 516, 529
French aid to Spanish Republic, 467
German press on Churchill, Eden, Duff Cooper, 937
Godesberg boundaries, 909
Hitler's views of, 310
King and Country debate, 198–99
Luftwaffe, 97 (*see also* Luftwaffe)
May crisis, 393–95 (*see also* May crisis)
Munich meeting announced, 16
Poles on Rhineland remilitarization, 190
Rhineland remilitarization, 140, 243 (*see also* Rhineland remilitarization)
Soviet and Nazi papers, 176
Sudeten cession, 778
Wehrmacht reorganization, 324
See also Dawson, Geoffrey; Shirer, William; *Times, The*
Juárez, Benito, 145
Jubaland, cession to Italy, 149
Judas Iscariot, 771
Junkers aircraft, 52, 713, 757–58, 987 (*see also* Aircraft)

K

Kagan, S. B., 443–44
Kaiser Wilhelm II, 71
Kamenev, Lev, 433
Kanya, Kalman, 802
  and Hungarian diplomacy, 415–18
  Ballplatz mentality, 416
Kapp-Lüttwitz Putsch, 78n.
Karinhall plan, 690
Karlsbad demands, 388, 402, 507, 844 (*see also* Sudetenland—Henlein, Konrad)
Keitel, Gen. Wilhelm, 682–83, 722–23, 743, 806, 808, 863–64, 876, 906, 910, 934
  Blomberg's marriage, 315–18
  Czech fortifications, 989–90 (*see also* Fortifications)
  May crisis, 390–95 (*see also* May crisis)
  Wehrmacht reorganization, 321, 324, 326 (*see also* Wehrmacht)

Kell, Gen. Sir Venron, 957
Kellogg-Briand Pact, 106, 869
Kennan, George
  Davies (Joseph E.) as diplomat, 439
  Kirov murder, 432
Kennard, Sir Howard, 421, 960, 965
  Polish-Czech relations, 427
Kennedy, John Fitzgerald
  Munich Agreement described, xii
  on Stanley Baldwin, 250
Kennedy, Joseph P., 650, 728, 763, 764,
    765, 936, 1001n.
  bombing of British shipping, 584–85
  Chamberlain-Hitler meeting (first), 752
  diplomatic-political career, 766–72
  Dirksen contacts, 767–69
  Lindbergh's effect on, 768–69, 848–50,
    851n.
Keppler, Wilhelm, 955
  Austrian Party matters, 337–38, 348–50
  Goering's instructions on Austria, 362,
    365
  See also Anschluss; Austria
Kerillis, Henri de, 140, 467, 778
Kerr, Philip. See Lothian, Marquess of
Kesselring, Gen. Albert, 712–13, 994
Keyes, Adm. Sir Roger, 851, 903
Keynes, John Maynard
  on Versailles Treaty, 76, 200 (see also
    Versailles Treaty)
King, Mackenzie, 773
King and Country debate, 197–99
Kirkpatrick, Sir Ivone, 805, 899, 943
  German-Czech relations, 389
  Godesberg translator, 806–10, 814–17
    (see also Schmidt, Paul)
  Hitler described, 34
  Munich Agreement signing described, 48
  Wilson mission to Hitler, 872
Kirov, Sergei
  murder's effect, 432–33
Kitzinger, Gen. Karl, 690, 705, 725
Klausner, Hubert, 349
Kleist-Schmenzin, Gen. Ewald von, 326,
    663
Klenze, Leo von, 24–25
Klockner, Peter, 175
Knock-out blow, 236n., 589, 608, 644, 835,
    933, 993, 987–88, 994 (see also
    Luftwaffe)
Knox, Sir Harry, 601
Köchling, Col. Friedrich, 745
Koenig, Capt. Theodore, 756
Koerber, Viktor von, 662
Kolchak, Alexander, 171

Königsplatz (Munich) described, 24–25
Konoye, Prince, 906
Kordt, Erich, 23, 746, 893, 895
Kordt, Theodor, 663, 670–71, 715, 728,
    732, 746, 805, 853
Köstring, Gen. Ernst, 431
  Soviet military ability, 430
Krauch, Carl, 295, 690
Krejcí, Gen. Ludvik, 521, 786, 790, 843
  Munich concession objections, 37–38
Kressenstein, Gen. Franz Kress von, 326
Krestinsky, Nikolai, 176–77
  show trial, 434–35 (see also Purges; Show
    trials)
Kriegk, Otto, 906
Krofta, Kamil, 37, 194, 777, 788, 910
  Czech submission to Munich Agreement,
    56
  Rhineland remilitarization, 135 (see also
    Rhineland remilitarization)
  Sudeten question, 388 (see also
    Sudetenland)
Krosigk, Count Schwerin von, 728
Krupp, 75, 80, 175, 935
  donations to Nazis, 90
Küchler, Gen. Georg von, 707
Kuhlenthal, Maj. Gen. Erich, 274, 494, 728
Kuhn, Ferdinand, 63
Kulik, Marshal G. I., 449
Kundt, Dr. Erich
  Sudeten German Party, 402
Kurhotel Petersberg, 805

L

La Chambre, Guy, 495, 764–65, 854
  French Air Force, 489–90 (see also Air
    Forces—French)
  Lindbergh's effect on, 777 (see also
    Lindbergh, Col. Charles A.)
Labor supply, 642, 703, 705
Laboulaye, Lefebvre, 176
Lacroix, Victor de, 55, 785, 788, 789, 790
  Polish-Czech relations, 427
L'Action Française, 778
Lambeth Walk, 37
Lammers, Dr. Hans, 662
Lanark speech, 664, 669 (see also
    Speeches)
Land warfare. See Army; Wehrmacht
Landwehr troops, 986–87
Langenheim, Adolf, 272
Lansbury, George, 204, 264
Lantsheere, Viscount de, 472

Laroche, Jules, 188n., 472
Lateran Agreements, 151
Lausanne Conference (1932), 113, 176, 507
Laval, Pierre, 107, 840
  German policy, 125–28
  Hoare-Laval Ethiopian plan, 125,
    163–64, 231–32, 535, 1001
  Italian *rapprochement*, 122
  Italy's Ethiopian War, 123–25, 160–64
  Moscow visit, 179
  Pétain's relations with, 126–27
  policies assessed, 1000–1
  Rhineland remilitarization, 130 (*see also*
    Rhineland remilitarization)
League of Nations
  aggression proceedings, 3 (*see also*
    Aggression)
  Ethiopian War. *See* Ethiopian War
  Germany
    admitted, 83
    censured for rearmament, 99
    excluded, 71
    withdrawn, 94, 154–55
  Italy's resignation from, 270–71, 480
  Lytton report, 207
  Rhineland remilitarization. *See* Rhineland
    remilitarization
  Soviet Union's admission, 120, 159, 179
  See also Geneva Disarmament
    Conference; Versailles Treaty
Lebensraum, 95, 698, 936
  Hossbach Conference, 299–302
  Ukraine, 4
  See also Hitler, Adolf—*Mein Kampf*
Lebrun, Pres. Albert, 789, 963
Lee, Col. Raymond L., 764
Leeb, Gen. Wilhelm Ritter von, 326, 910
Leeper, Sir Reginald 966
Léger, Alexis, 778, 811, 812, 855, 859,
    903n., 921, 940, 950, 1001
  biography, 118
  composition of Munich delegations, 17
  four-power conference, 677
  Hitler's impressions of, 45
  Jozef Beck's opinions of, 189
  nonintervention plan, 468–71 (*see also*
    Non-Intervention Agreement)
  Rhineland remilitarization, 135, 457–58
    see also Rhineland remilitarization)
Légion d'Honneur, 905
Leibstandarte Adolf Hitler, 355, 805, 912
Leipzig, 556
Lenin, Nikolai, 172
Leopold, Capt. Josef
  Austrian Legion, 332–39

Papen-Leopold feud, 337
  replaced, 348–49
Leopold III, King
  Belgian neutrality, 547–48
  on Rhineland remilitarization, 473
Liardet, C. F., 600
Liberté, 879
Liebitzky, Col. Emil, 352
Liebmann, Gen. Curt, 698
  Berlin Kriegsakademie commandant, 98
Lilienthal Congress, 760
Limes. *See* Fortifications
Lindbergh, Anne Morrow, 755, 849
  impressions of Reichenau, 911n.
Lindbergh, Col. Charles A., 857n., 872
  Berlin visit, 262
  biography, 754–56
  effects on
    Bonnet, Georges, 765
    Bullitt and La Chambre, 764–65
    Dirksen, 768
    French, 776–77, 839
    Great Britain, 848–52
    Kennedy, Joseph P., 768, 769
    Nicolson, Harold, 759
  England criticized, 763
  French-German aircraft compared, 764–65
    (*see also* Air Forces; Aircraft)
  influence summed up, 852
  "Lone Eagle," 754, 755
  Luftwaffe's power, xiii, 849–52 (*see also*
    Knock-out blow; Luftwaffe)
  Soviet Union, visit to, 764
  See also Luftwaffe; Royal Air Force
Lindbergh, Jon, 756
Lindemann, F. A., 219
Lindsay, Sir Ronald, 660
  Roosevelt meeting, 846–48
Lippmann, Walter
  on Stanley Baldwin, 219
Lipski, Jozef, 802–3, 964, 972
  minorities declaration with Germany,
    419–20, 421
Lisicky, Karel, 37, 38n.
Lithuania
  German treaty, 963
  Polish border incident, 422
  Polish relations, 185
  See also Memel
Little Entente, 161
  Beneš's role, 193
  decline, 194–96, 397, 411–18, 514
  primary purpose, 182
  Sinaia Council, 417
Litvinov, Maxim, 173, 786, 812

Anglo-Franco-Russian alliance, 974–76
Anglo-German Naval Agreement, 224
 (see also Anglo-German Naval
 Agreement)
Anschluss, 447–48, 621
international conference proposed, 634–35
political stature assessed, 441
Russo-German rapprochement, 514–15
Soviet Union's exclusion from Munich, 1
Sudeten Germans, 400 (see also
 Sudetenland)
U.S. recognition of Soviet Union, 179
Yezhov characterized, 434, 437
Lloyd, Lord George, 590–91
Lloyd George, David, 560, 852, 971
 Britain's Ethiopian War policy, 233 (see
 also Ethiopian War)
 Hitler meeting, 262–63
 Litvinov's Czech question proposal, 451
 Rhineland plan reaction, 70
 Ten-Year Rule, 201 (see also Ten-Year
 Rule)
Locarno Pact, 3, 82–83, 105–6, 111
 Austen Chamberlain as architect, 200–1
 chief sponsors, 83
 "eastern Locarno" proposed, 119–20, 188
 Franco-Polish alliance weakened, 187
 Rhineland
 military provisions, 98–99
 remilitarization convocation, 137, 248
 (see also Rhineland remilitarization)
 Russo-French pact as breach 99–100
Loetzen, Gen. Hans Seutter von, 707
London evacuation plans, 589
London Daily Mail, 97
London Daily Telegraph, 198
London Economic Conference, 176
Lone Eagle. See Lindbergh, Col. Charles A.
Lords. See House of Lords
Lorenz, Werner, 808
Lossberg, Maj. Bernhard von, 908
Lothian, Marquess of
 Hitler meeting, 263–64
Lotschberg. See Lossberg, Maj. Bernhard
 von
Low Countries. See Holland
Luca di Tena, Marqués, 273, 275
Luce, Henry and Clare, 763
Ludendorff, Gen. Erich, 79
 Beer Hall Putsch, 79, 315
Ludin, Hans, 85n.
Ludlow-Hewitt, Sir Edgar, 646, 649
Ludwig I and Königsplatz (Munich), 24–25
Luftwaffe
 assessment of strength, 987–89

basic aircraft types, 258
bomber force capacities, 649
British Chiefs of Staff report, 834
British estimates of, 216–18, 234–35, 590,
 593, 606 641 648–50
 British compared, 604
Case Green
 aircraft used, 713
 code words, 713 (see also Code words)
 deployment, 709–13
 primary goal, 712
Condor Legion, 283–84, 987
Czech airfields occupied, 955
Daladier-Stehlin conversation, 47
effectiveness, German assessment, 865–66
fivefold increase ordered, 943
French Air Force compared, 463
Goering's power, 257
groundwork for creation, 97
growth, 257–58
Guernica, 286–87 (see also Guernica)
Italian airfields used, 160
knock-out blow, 236n., 589, 608, 644,
 835, 933, 987–88, 993, 994
Lindbergh, Col. Charles A.
 assessment, xiii, 849–52
 French production compared, 764–65
 report, 761–62
 visits, 757–59, 760–64
major mission, 257–58
mission in Czech campaign, 390
order of battle, 1005–7
Paris question, 527
strategy
 main aim, 236n.
 RAF contrasted, 607–8
strength during Rhineland
 remilitarization, 248
Vuillemin, Gen. Joseph
 aircraft production, 524
 visit, 719–20
weather's effect, 993
See also Air Forces; Aircraft; Bomber
 aircraft; Fighter aircraft; Lindbergh,
 Col. Charles A.; Royal Air Force
Lukasiewicz, Juliusz, 191, 476, 517–18, 776
 Soviet attitude to Poland, 419
Lunacharsky, Anatoli, 174
Lupescu, Magda, 195
Lüttwitz, Gen. Walther von
 Kapp-Lüttwitz Putsch, 78
Lutz, Gen. Oswald, 177, 326, 492
 tank warfare, 256 (see also Tanks)
Lutze, Viktor, 906
Luxembourg

French occupation proposed, 138
Lyons, J. A., 862
Lytton Report, 207

M

MacDonald, Malcolm, 579, 649, 773, 775, 810, 813, 819, 823, 825, 838, 858, 862, 882, 883, 927, 978, 996
MacDonald, Ramsay, 105, 202, 215, 555, 759
Mackensen, Hans Georg von, 379, 869
Macmillan, Harold, 66, 903
Magaz, Marqués de, 868–69
Maginot Line, 109–11, 637, 651, 759, 856, 860, 989–90, 991n.
  André Maginot sketched, 109–10
  British Chiefs of Staff on, 631
  extension to sea, 602, 611
  Hastroff fortress sold, 111n.
  war strength achieved, 854
  See also Fortifications
Magistrati, Count Massimo, 907n., 922
Maisky, Ivan, 181, 441, 841, 975, 982
  Chamberlain and Axis leaders, 555
  nonintervention's failure, 443–44 (see also Non-Intervention Agreement)
Malkin, Sir William, 15, 805, 814
  Czech boundaries guaranteed, 41–42
Manchester Guardian, 125, 636
Manchurian incident (1931), 175, 206–7
Mancini, Gen. Mario Roatta, 285
Mandel, Georges, 54, 524, 786
Maniu, Iuliu, 195
Maniu, Dr. Julius, 414
Manstein, Gen. Erich von, 298, 325, 695–96, 700–1, 864
  "Otto," 354–55
Manual of Instructions (French Army), 108–9, 121, 494
Margerie, Roland de, 778, 855
Martin, Glenn, 760
Martin, Kingsley, 200, 664, 671, 851
Marx, Wilhelm, 81
Masařík, Hubert
  Munich Agreement disclosed, 48–49, 54
  objections to conference results, 46
  "observer" at Munich, 37–38
  reception at Munich described, 38
Masaryk, Jan, 654, 785, 786, 792, 798, 804, 823, 826, 831
  Godesberg memorandum reaction, 827–30, 852–53 (see also Godesberg memorandum)

refugees, 900–1 (see also Refugees)
Runciman report, 827 (see also Runciman mission)
Masaryk, Thomas, 192, 827, 830
  Czech nationalism, 72–73
Masefield, John, 680
Mason-Macfarlane, Col. Frank, 660–61, 882, 966
  Case Green reports, 701–2
  Czech morale, 882, 885–86, 887, 888–89
  May crisis, 391 (see also May crisis)
  Prague trip, 818, 828
Massey, Raymond, 772
Massey, Vincent, 772, 775, 838 (see also Dominions)
Massigli, René, 524
Massow, Col. von, 758
Mastny, Vojtech, 904, 908
  Czech-German relations, 378
  Munich Agreement disclosed, 48–49, 54
  "observer" at Munich, 37–38
Matignon Agreement, 461
Matin, Le, 140, 778
Matteotti, Giacomo, 151
Maude, Angus, 198
Maugham, Lord Chancellor, 652, 783
  Munich Agreement comment, xii
Maurice, Sir Frederick, 858n.
Maurin, Gen. Joseph-Léon-Marie, 130–31
Maurras, Charles, 116n., 140
May crisis, 390–95
  British Cabinet reaction, 654–55
  international reactions, 517–20
  See also Czechoslovakia
Mayer, Col. Emile, 494
Mecklenburg, Duke Adolf Friedrich, 758
Médaille Militaire, 905
Medhurst, Wing Commander C. E. H., 234–35
Mein Kampf. See Hitler, Adolf
Meissner, Otto, 82, 90
Memel, occupation directives, 936, 942 (see also Lithuania)
Menelik, Emperor, 160
Menthan, M., 907n.
Menzhinsky, Rudolph, 435
Menzies, Robert, 774
Messerschmitt aircraft, 757, 760, 987 (see also Aircraft; Fighter aircraft; Luftwaffe)
Micaud, Charles, 529
Michelangelo, 1003
Miklas, Wilhelm, 367
  Austrian President, 334
  resignation, 371

Schuschnigg's resignation, 361–62
Milch, Erhard, 257, 757–58
Military doctrine, French, 492–93, 1000–1
Millerand, Alexandre, 104
Milne, Gen. Sir George, 208–9
Ministry of Supply, 593, 929–30, 948
    establishment of, 973
Minorca, 649
    Anglo-French occupation proposed, 480
Minority populations
    Czech-Hungarian issues, 417
    Germans
        Polish Silesia, 187, 419–20, 980
        South Tyrol, 18–19, 72, 96, 980
        Sudetenland, 2, 73–74, 399–403, 980
            (see also Sudetenland)
    Hungarians and Poles in Slovakia, 3,
        41–42, 72–74, 980
    Hungarians in Rumania and Yugoslavia,
        417, 980
    minorities declaration, German-Polish,
        419–20
    Poles in Teschen, 184, 419–20, 422, 980
        (see also Teschen)
    Ruthenians and Rumanians in Hungary,
        72
    Slovaks in Hungary, 417
    See also Austria; Czechoslovakia;
        Hungary; Italy; Sudetenland; Teschen
Mitchell, R. T., 218
Mobilization
    British Chiefs of Staff memo, 835–36
    Czechoslovakia, 813, 814–15
    French Cabinet, 529–30
    German Army, 875–76
    twenty-four-hour delay of German, 91
Model, Gen. Walter, 702
Mola, Emilio, 272
Molotov, Vyacheslav, 975–77
    Soviet-German relations, 181
Monnet, Georges, 461
Montez, Lola, 24
Montgomery-Massingberd, Field Marshal
        Sir Archibald, 237
Monzie, Anatole de, 524
Moravec, Col. Frantisek, 449, 790
Moreau, Lt. Rudolf Freiherr von, 281
Morell, Dr. Theodor, 34
Morgan, J. P. & Company, 755, 769
Morgenthau, Henry, 770, 847n., 869, 889
Morris, Dave, 472
Morrison, Herbert, 752
    Munich Agreement reaction, 65
Morrow, Anne. See Lindbergh, Anne

Morrow
Morrow, Dwight, 755, 849n.
Mošcicki, Ignacy, 186
Mosley, Oswald, 199
Most-favored nation, 71
Mostler, Jean, 521
Moyne, Lord, 978n.
Muff, Gen. Wolfgang, 346, 362
Mühlmann, Dr. Kajetan, 344
Muirhead, Lt. Col. A. J., 643
Müller, Hermann, 83
Munich
    lesson, 1004
    pejorative use, examples, xi, 1003–4
    See also Munich—the Agreement;
        Munich—the Conference
Munich—the Agreement
    boundary guarantee annex, 918–22
        British follow-up criticized, 922–25
        Halifax memorandum, 919–21
    Chamberlain-Halifax on enforcement of,
        917
    Czech acceptance of, 54–57
    defenses of, 979
        Bolshevism over Europe, 982
        buying time, 982, 984–89
        Taylor, A. J. P., 980—81
    disclosure of terms to Czechs, 48–49, 54
    French Chamber of Deputies acceptance
        of, 59, 903–4
    fulfillment, possibility of, 66
    Godesberg memorandum compared, 64,
        900–3
    Great Britain's acceptance of, 65–66, 903
    inescapability of, 995–96
    International Commission for execution
        of, 899–903
        composition, 55, 899, 902, 904–5
        defects, 904
        final frontiers, 916–17
        first meeting, 905–6
        German-Czech Frontier Committee,
            915
        Godesberg boundaries accepted, 907–10
        military subcommittee, 905
        plebiscites, 914–15
        seat, 905
        subcommittees, 907
    odd features summarized, xiii
    set out, 50–53
    two prime features, 902, 922
    viewpoints summarized, xi–xiv
Munich—the Conference
    Agreement set out, 50–53
    Agreement signing described, 48

Arbeitszimmer described, 29
"atmosphere" described, 42–44
Czechoslovakia
  disclosure of agreement, 48–49, 54
  "observers" designated, 37–38
  reception at Munich, 38
"directly interested" countries, 2–3, 9
excluded parties, 1
  Czechoslovakia, 11–12
  Soviet Union, 12
first meeting
  discussion outline, 30
  French version, 31
  luncheon recess activities, 34–37
  participants, 28–29
International Commission for execution
    of the agreement, 37, 46 (*see also*
    Munich—the Agreement)
issues
  French views, 17
  German demands, 20
proposals
  French, 6, 530–31, 889
  Great Britain, 5–6, 530–31, 853, 870,
    890–92
  United States, 4–5, 847–48, 869,
    889–90
reactions to realization
  Czechoslovakia, 11–12
  Italy, 18–20
  London, 10–11
  Paris, 16
  Soviet Union, 12
second meeting
  Daladier's Czech boundary proposal,
    39–40
  firsthand recollections, 39
  François-Poncet's description, 39
  Polish and Hungarian claims, 41–42
  state dinner described, 45–46
signposts toward, 641
who was who, 26–27
Munich-Prien airfield, 760
Mushakoji, Count Kintomo, 260–61,
  269–70
Mussolini, Benito
  Albanian annexation, 963
  Anglo-German post-Munich agreement,
    63
  Austria
    German march-in reactions, 365–66,
      376
    independence supported, 96
    plebiscite (first), 352
  Britain and British policy, 19

Chamberlain meeting, 950–52
Chamberlain's impressions of, 42
Chamberlain's misjudgment of, 555
Ciano's impressions of, 19–20, 41, 43, 59
early years, 145
English relationships, 150
foreign policy, 149–51 (*see also* Foreign
  policy)
Four Power Pact (1933), 119, 153–55
François-Poncet's impressions of, 39
German Pact of Steel, 385
Hitler compared, 157
Hitler meetings, 156–58, 267–68, 383–86
in *Mein Kampf*, 152
internal affairs, 151–52
Italian intervention, possibility of, 876
  (*see also* Non-Intervention
  Agreement; Spanish Civil War)
journalistic activities, 145, 844
journey to Munich with Hitler, 21–23
linguistic abilities, 19
mediator of Sudeten crisis, 10, 19
mobilization delay, 891, 893–94
Munich, the Conference
  first meeting, 30–34
  homecoming celebrations, 59
  lunch with Hitler, 34–35
  Polish and Hungarian claims pressed,
    41–42
  relations with Chamberlain, 44–45
  relations with Hitler, 42–43
Night of the Long Knives, reaction, 158
personal style, 149
rise to power, 146–48
Spain. *See* Spanish Civil War
Mussolini, Vittorio, on bombing, 163

N

Nachtausgabe, 906
Nadolny, Rudolph, 178
Napoleon, Treaty of Tilsit, 75
Nationalist Party (South Africa), 774
National Labour Council, 752
National Labour Executive, 672
National minorities. *See* Minority
  populations
National Register of Occupational Skills,
  938
National Socialist German Workers Party.
  See Nazi Party
Navies
  France
    Popular Front years, 486–87

Rhineland remilitarization, 139 (*see also* Rhineland remilitarization)

Germany, 940–41, 943
  Anglo-French compared, 985–86
  British Chiefs of Staff report, 836 (*see also* Chiefs of Staff)
  Case Green, 713 (*see also* Case Green)
  program, 256–57
  Spanish Civil War losses, 288–89 (*see also* Spanish Civil War)

Great Britain
  Chiefs of Staff report, 832–33, 836 (*see also* Chiefs of Staff)
  Churchill's budget cuts, 203–4
  fleet mobilization proposed, 677–78, 679–80
  German compared, 985–86
  mobilization, 881–82
  New Naval Standard, 638–40
  1930s posture, 204–5
  post-Munich, 929, 931
  Spanish Civil War, 538 (*see also* Spanish Civil War)
  two-ocean Navy, 596–97, 609–10, 638–40, 997

See also Air Forces; Army; Singapore; Wehrmacht

Nazi Party
  Austrian Nazis, 96, 158
    Austrian Legion, 332
  establishment, 24–25, 79, 84
  financial problems, 88, 90
  growth, 84
  Harzburg rally (1931), 86
  losses in 1932 election, 88
  seizure of power, 92
  storm troopers. *See* Storm troopers
  Sudeten Nazis, 193–94 (*see also* Sudetenland)
  See also Hitler, Adolf; Germany; Nuremberg Party Rally; Speeches

Nebe, Arthur, 718
Nečas, Jaromir, 777
Netherlands. *See* Holland
Neurath, Baron Constantin von, 955
  Ciano meeting, 168
  Danzig question, 423 (*see also* Danzig; Polish Corridor)
  Hossbach Conference
    Nuremberg testimony, 304
    reactions, 301–2
  minorities declaration with Poland, 419–20
  Munich agenda drawn, 20, 32
  Neurath-Ciano protocol, 261
Neutrality Act (1935, 1937), 518, 848

Newall, Basil, 641, 835, 859, 861, 945, 978
Newall, Sir John, 605
New Guinea, 773
News Chronicle, 954, 966
Newspapers. *See* Journalistic opinions
New Statesman, 636, 664, 671
New Statesman and Nation, 200
Newton, Basil, 520, 785, 787, 788, 789, 790, 808, 820, 883, 913, 918, 921
  conference proposals, 5–6
  Czech question, 621
New York *Times*, The, 63, 853
New Zealand, 772–73 (*see also* Dominions)
Nicolson, Harold, 6, 66, 649, 732, 756, 759, 763, 775, 903
  Madrid government, 538
  Rhineland remilitarization, 244 (*see also* Rhineland remilitarization)
Niebelschütz, Gen. Günther von, 326
Niemöller, Reverend Martin, 35, 575
Night of the Long Knives, 93–94
  Mussolini's reaction, 158
Nikolaiev, Leonid, 432
Nobel Peace Prize
  Briand and Stresemann, 106
Noël, Léon, 1001
  Czech aid, 503
  Franco-Polish relations, 189–92
  Polish attitudes to, 424
Noel-Baker, Philip, 469
Non-Intervention Agreement, 277, 280–81, 442, 477
  British position, 538–41
  Daladier, 511–12
  French reassessment, 500
  naval patrols, 28–29
  Popular Front program, 468–71
  relaxed nonintervention, 471
  See also Spanish Civil War
Nonpartisan League, 754
Nuremberg Party Rally, 669, 677, 706, 722, 771, 844 (*see also* Hitler, Adolf; Nazi Party)
Nuremberg speech, 528–29, 726, 727 (*see also* Speeches)
Nuremberg trials
  Hossbach Conference memorandum, 302–4
Nyon Conference, 557–58

O

Ogilvie-Forbes, Sir George, 907n., 913, 916–17, 924

Ohnesorge, Wilhelm, 726
Oil-fields (Ploesti), 918, 960
Oil sanctions. *See* Ethiopian War
Olbricht, Gen. Friedrich, 718, 866, 868, 897
Olmütz, 914–15
Olympic Games (1936), 259–60
Opinion testing. *See* Public opinion
Orlov, Alexander, 445
Oshima, Gen. Hiroshi, 952–53
Oster, Lt. Col. Hans, 715, 866, 895
Ostmark. *See* Austria
Osusky, Stefan, 500, 515, 519
"Otto," 353–55 (*see also Anschluss;*
    Austria)
Ovey, Sir Edmond, 174
Oxford, Lady Margot
  on Neville Chamberlain, 66
Oxford Magazine, 198
Oxford Union
  King and Country debate, 197–99, 204

P

Pact of Steel, 385, 954, 974
Paderewski, Ignace Jan, 184
Painlevé, Paul, 110
Palairet, Sir Michael, 575, 576–77
Palazzo Chigi (Rome), 891
Palestine, 660, 833, 978
Panay, 846
Papen, Franz von
  Austrian Ambassador, 96
  chancellorship, resignation, 89
  Gold Medal, 372
  Hitler conference, 89–90
  Hitler-Mussolini meeting proposed, 156
  Leopold-Papen feud, 337
  Minister to Austria
    fired and rehired, 340
    reasons for appointment, 331–32
  Reichstag prorogued, 88–89
  Russian fears of, 175–76
  Weimar Chancellor, 87–89
Pareto, Vilfredo, 145
Pariani, Gen. Alberto, 693, 876
Paris, exodus from, 878
Paris-Midi, 778, 799
Paris Peace Conference, 73 (*see also*
    Versailles Treaty)
Paris-Soir, 778
Parity. *See* Royal Air Force; Submarines
Pasionaria, La, 470
Passchendaele (Belgium), 595
Paul, Prince, Regent of Yugoslavia, 841n.

Paul-Boncour, Joseph, 118, 484, 500
  British fears of, 580–81
  Czech aid, 494–95, 500–3
  Czech policy, 506
Pax Germanica-Britannica, 822
Paxton, Nicholas, 478
Payart, Jean, 451
Peace Ballot, 226
"Peace for our Time," 674, 900, 941, 977
  dissents from, 926
Peace Society, Baldwin's speech, 252
"Peace with honour," 900, 923, 978–79
Perth, Lord, 890–92, 1001n.
Pertinax (André Géraud)
  French arms to Spain, 466–67
  Gamelin, 511
  Pétain-Goering relations, 126
  Runciman mission, 523
  Soviet alliance, 128
Pétain, Marshal Philippe, 840
  Belgium and northern defenses, 110,
      120–21
  Inspector General of Aerial Defense,
      112–13
  Laval's relations with, 126–27
  military doctrine, effect on France, 108
  policies assessed, 1000
  postwar years characterized, 108
  Vichy France, 108, 125
  war ministry summarized, 120–21
Petit Parisien, 778
Petlura, Ataman Semyon, 171, 184
Petrescu-Comnene, Nicolas, 414
Phillips, William, 890
Phipps, Sir Eric, 6, 497, 787, 854, 879–80,
      883, 957, 965, 1001n.
  Bonnet, Georges, 507
  Czech aid, 502
  French bluffing, 530
  French defeatist attitude, 839–40
  French intentions on Czechoslovakia,
      527–28
  Hitler meeting, 215
  Lindbergh report, 776–77 (*see also*
      Lindbergh, Col. Charles A.;
      Luftwaffe)
  May crisis, 519–20 (*see also* May crisis)
  Rhineland remilitarization, 240–41 (*see
      also* Rhineland remilitarization)
Piatakov, Yuri, 434
Pilsudski, Marshal Józef, 974
  biography, 186–87
  Russian war (1920), 183–85 (*see also*
      Poland)

Pirow, Oswald, 774, 941n.
Plan Z, 668–69, 671–72, 674–80, 734–35,
    981, 982 (see also Chamberlain,
    Neville)
"Plate-glass window" strategy, 132
Plebiscites
  Austria, 373, 576 (see also
      Austria, plebiscites
  International Commission consideration,
      914–15
  Saarland, 97, 128
  Sudetenland (proposals), 735–37, 801,
      804, 807–8, 844–45
    French opposition, 779–80
    Godesberg meeting, 807–08
    See also Sudetenland
Plessen, Baron Johann von, 280
  Mussolini's political realism, 376
Ploesti oil-fields, 918, 960
Pogrell, Gen. Günther von, 326
Poincaré, Raymond, 104–5, 106
Poitou, 18, 58
Poland
  Case White directive, 969
  claims in Czechoslovakia, 41–42, 66, 795,
      796–98, 801–3, 807–8, 917–18
  Danzig. See Danzig
  diplomacy between wars, 183–86
  Enabling Act (1933), 187
  foreign policy
    Czechoslovakia, 424–27
    equilibrium, 418–19
    France, 423–24
  independence gained, 183–84
  Lithuanian border incident, 422
  Lithuanian relations, 185
  May crisis, 517–18 (see also May crisis)
  Pilsudski-Beck era, 186–92
  Poles in Central and Eastern Europe,
      72–73 (see also Minority populations)
  policies assessed, 1001–2
  Sudeten crisis. See Sudetenland; Teschen
  Teschen attack, 184 (see also Teschen)
  transit of arms question, 418, 428,
      450–52, 526
  treaties
    Anglo-French, 977
    British defensive alliance, 965
    French mutual defense, 111, 450, 969
    German nonaggression, 95–96, 188,
        418, 974
    Riga, 185

    Rumanian mutual assistance, 185
    Russian nonaggression, 187, 418, 843
    Versailles Treaty, Thirteenth Point, 71
        (see also Versailles Treaty)
  war with Soviet Union, 171–72, 184–85
  (see also Beck, Col. Jozef; Danzig;
      Pilsudski, Marshal Józef; Polish
      Corridor)
Polish Corridor, 695, 802, 847, 936, 968,
    972
  Austen Chamberlain on, 201
  German officers on, 95
  Hitler-Mussolini meeting, 386
  Lipski-Ribbentrop confrontation, 964
  See also Danzig
Polls. See Public opinion
Pomerania, 966
Pontine Marshes, reclamation, 413
Popolo d'Italia, 145, 844
Populaire, Le, 16, 140, 778, 794
Popular Front (France)
  armament program, 485–502
  Blum resigns, 478
  British Labour compared, 536–37
  Chautemps government, 478–79, 496–99
  composition, 460–61
  Czech aid, 463, 500
  diplomatic weakness, 464–65, 476
  forty-hour work week, 486, 490–91
    suspended, 524
  New Deal compared, 461–62
  Spanish Civil War, 466–72 (see also
      Spanish Civil War)
  strikes, 486, 490
  See also Blum, Léon; France
Potemkin, Vladimir, 441, 512, 786, 843
Pownall, Maj. Gen. Henry, 588, 603, 637,
    662, 667, 928, 948–49, 978
  "appreciation," 886–87
  on London air raid scare, 943–44
Pravda, 173, 176, 177
Press. See Journalistic opinions
Price, Ward, 97, 746
Primo de Rivera, Don Miguel, 272
Prince Paul, Regent, 194–95
Prise de gages, 137–38
Propaganda march (Berlin), 877
Public opinion
  Anglo-French plan, 832
  Anschluss, 831
  Berlin propaganda march, 877
  British fleet mobilization, 54n.
  French, against war, 839–40

Great Britain, post-Godesberg, 992–93
  polls, 831–32
Pujo, Maurice, 459–60
Purges (Soviet Union)
  Central Purging Commission, 432
  effects, 439–41
  Europe's reaction, 440
  French reaction, 513–14
  officer corps, 435–39, 440
  reasons, 438–39
  Red Army, 435–39, 440
  Wehrmacht reorganization compared,
    438–39
  See also Stalin, Joseph; Yezhov, Nicolai
Putna, Gen. Vitovt, 436

Q

Queen Elizabeth, 881
Queipo de Llano, Gonzalo, 273–74

R

Raczyński, Count Edward, 965
Radar development, 219, 605, 647, 987, 996
Radek, Karl, 433–34, 436
  Pravda editor, 176
Radio speeches
  Chamberlain on Sudeten crisis, 8
  Daladier on forty-hour work week, 524
  Daladier on Munich Conference, 16
  Doumergue, Pres. Gaston, in France, 115
  Schuschnigg to Austrians, 352–53
Raeder, Adm. Erich, 220, 222
Rakovsky, Christian, 434
Ramsay, Sir Alexander, 642
Raschick, Gen. Erich, 912
Rasin, Ladislav, 56
Rassemblement Populaire, 116
Rath, Ernst von, 937
Rationing plan, 597–99, 614
  assessed, 997
  criticized, 639
Raumer, Dr. Hermann von, 269
Red Army. *See* Army, Soviet Union
Refugees, 900–1
  Baldwin Fund for Jewish Refugees, 941n.
  German Jews, 938
  Sudeten Czechs and Jews, 912–14
Regular Army. *See* Army, Great Britain
Reichenau, Gen. Walter von, 95, 663, 746,
    910–11
  Anne Lindbergh's impressions of, 911n.
  Austrian plebiscite (first), 353 (*see also*

Austria; Plebiscites)
  senior generals' conference, 693
  surprise attack on Czechoslovakia, 101n.
  Wehrmacht reorganization, 322–23, 329
Reichsbank
  Schacht's dismissal, 954
Reichstag. *See* Germany
Reichswehr. *See* Wehrmacht
Reidinger, Gen., 475
Reinhardt, Hans, 258
Reinhardt, Gen. Walter, 79n.
Religion
  Hitler's attitudes, 157
  Mussolini's attitudes, 157
Renondeau, Gen., 893
Reparations. *See* German reparations
République, La, 529, 530
Repulse, 667
Réquin, Edouard, 521
Resigned Nationalists, 529
Reynaud, Paul, 54, 489, 492, 786, 840
Rheinhotel Dreeson, 805
Rheinmetall, 75
Rhineland
  demilitarization, 75–76, 103, 112, 1000
  French plans for, 70
  occupation terminated, 83
Rhineland remilitarization, 98–100
  Franco-Soviet treaty as provoking, 130,
    241
  inaction assessed, 998–99
  Litvinov's remarks, 187
  Locarno convocation, 137
  reactions
    Anglo-French, 100, 128–34
    Belgian, 472–73
    Dominions, 772
    Eastern European, 135, 142
    French
      Cabinet, 134–36
      Communist, 140
      Gamelin, 458–60
      Léger, 457–58
      military leaders, 141–42
    Great Britain, 100, 131–32, 240–49
      Cabinet, 244–46
      Chiefs of Staff, 246–47, 589
      shadow cabinet, 243
    Poland, 190, 423
  strategic significance, 241
Rhine River
  as British frontier, 214, 216
Ribbentrop, Joachim von, 125, 714–15, 737,
    743, 787, 805, 806, 808, 814, 815,
    816, 844, 876, 908, 964
  Anglo-German Naval Agreement, 260–61

(*see also* Anglo-German Naval
    Agreement)
Anti-Comintern Pact, 260–61 (*see also*
    Comintern)
Ciano's draft treaty, 385–86
Czech boundary guarantees, 921
Franco-German declaration, 939–40
German-Italian-Japanese agreement,
    268–71 (*see also* Tripartite Pact)
Great Powers conference, 6
Henderson confrontation, 654
Henlein's Czech policy, 405 (*see also*
    Sudetenland—Henlein, Konrad)
Hitler-Papen conference, 90
Hitler-Schuschnigg meeting, 343
Hungarian claims in Czechoslovakia, 918
Pact of Steel, 974
Soviet-German nonaggression treaty, 977
Tripartite Pact proposed, 952–53 (*see
    also* Tripartite Pact)
Wilson mission to Hitler, 871
Richthofen, Herbert Count von, 907, 915
Richthofen Squadron, 757
Riegele, Olga, 719
Ríos, Fernando de los, 467
Ripka, Hubert, 785, 793
    on Czech nationalist attitudes, 400
Ritchie, Charles, 773
Roatta, Gen. Mario, 282, 285
Robbins, Dr. Keith, 1002–3
Roberts, Frank, 779, 855
Robinson, Ione, 851
Rochat, Charles, 17–18, 126, 483, 778, 855
Roche, Emile, 529
    four-power conference, 530–31
Rockefeller, John, 768
Rockets (V-2), 300
Rocque, Col. François de la
    Croix de Feu, 114–16
Roehm, Ernst
    blood purge affair, 92–93, 158, 805, 998
Röhricht, Lt. Col. Edgar, 683, 868, 897, 991
Rome-Berlin Axis, 3, 143, 160
    Hitler-Mussolini meeting, 265–68
    term coined, 169
    Treaty of London as leading to, 143
Rommel, Col. Erwin, 910–11, 955
Roosevelt, Pres. Franklin D., 756, 769–71
    Bullitt's Pointe de Grave speech, 525–26
    conference proposals, 889–90
        Bullitt's letter, 4–5, 518–19
        open message to Hitler, 8–9
    Hitler-Chamberlain talks, 771
    Holland scare, 944–46
    Kennedy's (Joseph P.) appointment, 766
    peace appeal, 869

Hitler's reaction, 876
    quarantine speech, 561
        British reaction, 561, 563–64, 569
    Sudeten crisis proposals, 846–48
Roosevelt, Franklin D., Jr., 481n.
Rosenberg, Alfred, 215
Rosenberg, Marcel, 443–45
Rosengoltz, Arkady, 434
Roskill, Capt. Stephen, 985
Rothermere, Lord, 906
Rowse, Alfred Leslie, 851
    on Stanley Baldwin, 249, 251
Royal Air Force, 996
    Air Staff views, 835
    bombing questions, 645–50
    Cadman Committee, 643
    Defence Requirements Committee
        reports, 212–14, 235–36
    Defence White Paper, 238–39
    fighter production post-Munich, 931–33
    fighters' abilities, 647–48
    German compared, 216, 235
    Luftwaffe strategy contrasted, 607–8
    Manchester and Halifax bombers, 931,
        932n.
    modernization plans, 214, 216–19
    naval control of fleet air arm, 604
    offensive-defensive power assessed,
        987–88
    parity defined, 607–8, 611, 615
    parity pledge, 603
    posture (1919–33), 206
    priority order for defense, 607, 609
    radar, 219, 605 (*see also* Radar
        development)
    "schemes" for growth, 603–8, 610, 618,
        640–42, 645
    "schemes" post-Munich, 929, 931–32
    Spitfires and Hurricanes, 218, 605 (*see
        also* Aircraft)
    three commands established, 239
    Trenchard-Weir doctrine, 645, 648
    war preparation, 863
    Weir's (W. D.) views, 236–38
    See also Air Forces; Aircraft; Bomber
        aircraft; Fighter aircraft; Lindbergh,
        Col. Charles A.; Luftwaffe
Rumania
    British guarantees, 973
    Iron Guard, 195
    Little Entente, 195, 414–15 (*see also*
        Little Entente)
    National Peasant Party, 414
    Rumanian scare, 960–62
    reactions, 962
    Sudeten Germans, 418

transit of arms questions, 418, 428, 449–52, 453, 484, 515, 526
treaties
French mutual defense, 111
German, 962
Polish mutual assistance, 185
Runciman, Walter Lord, 237, 786, 787, 927
arbitrator of Czech question, 6–7, 734–35, 736
Runciman mission
Daladier's reaction, 522–23, 531
launched, 657–58
origins, 656
report, 747–49, 797–98
Masaryk's reaction, 827
See also Sudetenland
Rundstedt, Gen. Gerd von, 717, 911, 990
Wehrmacht reorganization, 322
Russia
Treaty of London, 143–44 (see also Soviet Union)
Ruthenia, 918
Hungarian claims in, 795–98
Hungarian occupation of, 955
See also Minority populations
Rykov, Alexei, 433

S

Saarland plebiscite, 97, 128
Saarland Theatre, 934
St. Wenceslas, 830
Salata, Francesco, 352
Salengro suicide, 477
Salisbury, Marquess of, 590–91
SALT talks, 1003
Sander, Gen. See Sperrle, Gen. Hugo
Sandler, Rickard, 427
Sanjurjo, Sacanell, 273, 274
Sargent, Sir Orme, 621–22, 795, 960
Sarraut, Albert, 130–31
Schacht, Hjalmar H. G., 86, 715, 866–67, 954
Goering-Schacht conflict, 312–13
Scharnhorst, 985
Scharnhorst, Gerhard von, 75
Scheele, Maj. Alexander von, 276, 281
Schilhausky, Gen. Sigmund, 362, 375
Schleicher, Kurt von
as Chancellor, 89–91
as Oskar von Hindenburg's friend, 82
chancellor-making, 83–84
characterized, 87
murdered, 93

Schlepegrell, A. F. K., 198
Schmidt, Guido, 334, 337, 346, 373
Hitler-Schuschnigg meeting, 341
Schmidt, Paul Otto, 738, 893, 940n.
Anglo-German agreement, interpreter, 60–63
Hitler-Chamberlain meeting (first), 739–43
interpreting problems, 45
Munich Conference
Hitler-Mussolini journey to, 21
notes of first meeting, 30–32
Wilson mission to Hitler, 871, 875
Schmitz, Richard, 367
Schmundt, Col. Rudolf, 45, 683–84
Hitler's observation of Mussolini, 382–83
Wehrmacht reorganization, 322
Schneider-Creusot (munitions manufacturers), 486
Schniewind, Rear Adm. Otto, 941
Schobert, Gen. Eugen von, 864n., 872, 875n.
Austrian occupation, 369
Austrian plebiscite (first), 353
"Otto," 355
Schoerner, Lt. Col. Ferdinand, 368
Schroder, Baron Kurt von, 89
Schulenburg, Gen. von der, 325
Schulenburg, Friedrich Graf von der, 430
Schulenburg, Count Fritz von der, 895
Schulenburg, Count Werner von der, 178, 976
Schuschnigg, Kurt von
Austrian-German rapprochement, 166–67
Austrian plebiscite (first), 351–52
canceled, 358 (see also Plebiscites)
biographical sketch, 332
Bundestag speech, 348 (see also Speeches)
conduct analyzed, 373–76
Goering-Mussolini meeting, 266
Hitler meeting on Anschluss, 341–46
resignation speech, 362–63 (see also Speeches)
Seyss-Inquart negotiations, 338–39
"three main enemies" speech, 335
Schwedler, Gen. Viktor von, 325
Schweisguth, Gen. Victor, 473, 512–14
Sebekovsky, Dr. Wilhelm, 406
Second World War
beginnings outlined, 67
commencement, 977
Secret Cabinet Council (Germany), 324 327
Seeckt, Hans von

Hitler's Weimar presidency campaign, 86
military advice to Chiang Kai-shek, 269
Reichswehr command described, 79–81
Reichswehr-Red Army contacts, 80, 95
resignation forced, 81
Seeds, Sir William, 974
Self-determination, 980–81
non-ethnic Russians, 170
Sudetendeutsche, 2, 752–53, 779 (see also
Sudetenland)
Semenov, Gen., 512–13
Seyss-Inquart, Artur
Austrian National Opposition, 336–39
Austrian plebiscite (first), 352, 357–58
German demands following, 360–61
Braunau-am-Inn speech, 369 (see also
Speeches)
chancellorship accomplished, 366
Interior Minister, Austria, 346
Miklas's objection to, 362–63
Schuschnigg negotiations, 338–39
Shadow factories, 605, 610, 611, 640 (see
also Armaments—British)
Shakhty trial, 431 (see also Purges; Show
trials)
Shaw, George Bernard, 763
Shay, Dr. Robert P., Jr., 997
Shirer, William, 54
André Maginot's line, 109–10
Anglo-German post-Munich agreement,
63
Anschluss plebiscite, 373 (see also
Plebiscites)
Anti-Comintern Pact, 261
Austrian crisis, 366
French armored divisions, 492
French "cascade of cabinets," 106–7
German people on Rhineland
remilitarization, 255
Hitler at Godesberg, 805
Hitler's Sportspalast speech, 873 (see also
Speeches)
Hossbach Conference, 302
Olympic Games (1936), 259–60
post-Munich observations, 906
Sudeten crisis, 23
transit of arms problem, 452
Show trials, 431–35 (see also Purges)
Siegfried Line. See Fortifications
Siemens, Capt. Leopold, 728
Siewert, Major, 969
Sikorsky, Igor, 760
Simon, Sir John, 209, 555, 611, 613, 664,
728, 779, 783, 784, 796, 810, 812,

819, 821, 823, 825, 855, 856–57, 858,
881, 900, 930–31
Hitler, impressions of, 217
Lanark speech, 664, 669 (see also
Speeches)
on Neville Chamberlain, 549
rationing concept, 598–99, 614
Simpson, Mrs. Wallis, 541–42, 552, 756,
996 (see also Edward VIII)
Sinclair, Admiral, 944n.
Sinclair, Sir Archibald, 619, 971
on Neville Chamberlain, 550
Singapore, 210, 213–14
Anglo-German Naval Treaty's effect on,
224
Sinn Fein, 201
Sino-Japanese conflict, 175
Skorzeny, Otto, 367
Slavic populations, 72–74 (see also
Minority populations)
Slavik, Dr. Juraj, 424–25
Slessor, Group Capt. John, 604–5, 835, 850,
859, 861, 945, 978
bomber-fighter strategy, 646–47
Slovakia. See Czechoslovakia
Smigly-Rydz, Gen. Edward, 189, 880
Beneš's memo to Poland, 426
French loan negotiated, 190–91
Smith, H. A., 986
Smith, Sir Reginald Dorman, 949n.
Smith, Maj. Truman, 756–57, 760
Smuts, Gen. Jan, 774
on Versailles Treaty revision, 76–77 (see
also Versailles Treaty)
Social Democrats
Comintern reaction to, 179–80
Sokolnikov, Gregori, 434
Soldat Inconnu, 940
Solidarité Française, 114
Solzhenitsyn, Alexander, 1003–4
Sosnkowski, Gen. Kazimierz, 422
South Africa, 772–74
Union policy resolution, 774 (see also
Dominions)
Soviet Union
Anglo-French plan, 786, 791
Anschluss reactions, 447–48
British Chiefs of Staff report, 832
civil war, 171–72
Czech aid, conditions, 449–52
feasibility, 452–56
transit of arms question, 418, 428,
449–52
Decree on Peace, 170
Eastern European attitudes toward, 182

excluded from Munich, 1, 12
foreign intervention, 170–72
French Army staff talks, 512–14 (see also Army)
Hitler-Mussolini meeting, 157–59
League of Nations admission, 120, 159, 179 (see also League of Nations)
Lindbergh's visit, 764 (see also Lindbergh, Col. Charles A.; Luftwaffe)
New Economic Policy, 172
officer corps slaughtered, 435–39, 440 (see also Purges; Show trials)
Papen, Franz von, 175–76
Polish war, 171–72, 184–85
Purges. See Purges
reaction to Munich Agreement requested, 55–56
show trials, 433–35
  causes, 431–32 (see also Purges)
  Shakhty trial, 431
Spanish Civil War, 442–47 (see also Spanish Civil War)
Sudeten crisis. See Sudetenland
trade agreements
  Germany, 175, 178
  Italy, 178
transit of arms question, 418, 428, 484, 515, 526
treaties, 2–4
  Berlin, 174
  Brest-Litovsk, 170–71
  Czech mutual assistance, 99, 100–2, 179, 196, 378, 449–50, 734, 841–42
  French mutual assistance, 99, 121, 127, 130, 165, 179, 418, 436, 734
  major weakness, 454
  German nonaggression, 977
  nonaggression (1932), 174–75
  Polish nonaggression, 187, 418, 843
  Rapallo, 80, 174
  Riga, 172, 185
  Sino-Soviet nonaggression, 442
United States recognizes, 179
"White," Russians, 171–72
Spaak, Paul Henri, 472–73
Spain, neutrality, 868–69, 993
Spanish Civil War, 142
  Anschluss linked, 293, 619–20
  France
    Blum and Stalin compared, 470
    Blum's position, 276–77, 280
    Blum's second government, 500–2
    Popular Front responses, 466–72, 477

Germany
  aircraft supplied, 274–76, 283–84
  casualties, 283
  Condor Legion established, 283–84
  Guernica, responsibility for, 286–87
  Hitler-Mussolini relations, 290–91
  naval losses, 288–89
  objectives, 275, 292–93, 301
  Great Britain
    cabinet divisions, 543–47
    Chiefs of Staff report, 539–40
    Eden's cabinet paper, 545–46
    Navy's position, 538
    shipping attacked, 584–85
  Guernica, 61, 286–87, 794
  Hitler-Chamberlain discussions, 61
  Italy
    aircraft supplied, 273, 275
    Black Shirt Militia, 284–85
    casualties, 285
    Corpo Truppe Volontarie, 285, 290
    divisions in, 266
    Mussolini's stake, 290–91
    submarines, 289–90 (see also Submarines)
  massacres, 537 (see also Barcelona bombings; Guernica)
  Neurath-Ciano talks, 168
  Non-Intervention Committee, 277–78, 282 (see also Non-Intervention Agreement)
  Republican collapse, 963–64
  Soviet Union
    Blum and Stalin compared, 470
    military aid, 283, 285, 444
    "nonintervention," 280, 442–47
    shipments attacked, 289–90
    volunteers, 537n.
  See also Air Forces; Luftwaffe; Navy
Sparticists, 171
Speeches
  Baldwin, Stanley, Peace Society, 252, 590–91
  Bullitt, William, Pointe de Grave, 525–26
  Chamberlain, Neville, 884–85
    Birmingham, 958
    "midsummer of madness," 552, 554
    no-commitment, 634–37
  Ciano, Galeazzo, anti-French policy, 939
  Goering, Hermann, war atmosphere, 294–95
  Hitler, Adolf
    Braunau-am-Inn, 369–70
    Nuremberg, 528–29, 726, 727

Reichstag, 347, 348, 947
  Saarbrücken, 934
  Sportspalast, 872–74, 881, 897
  Vienna, 372
  Weimar, 935
Roosevelt, Pres. Franklin D.
  Quarantine, 561, 563–64, 569
Schuschnigg, Kurt von
  Bundestag, 348
  resignation, 362–63
  three main enemies, 335
Seyss-Inquart, Artur
  Braunau-am-Inn, 369
Simon, Sir John, at Lanark, 664, 669
  See also Radio speeches
Speich, Gen. Richard, 688
Sperrle, Gen. Hugo, 712, 994
  Luftwaffe in Spain, 282–83 (see also
    Luftwaffe; Spanish Civil War)
Spinasse, Charles, 479
Spirit of St. Louis, 755
Spitfires (Aircraft), 218, 605, 763, 987, 996
  (see also Aircraft; Royal Air Force)
Sportspalast speech, 872–73, 897
  British reaction, 881
  Chamberlain's reaction, 873–74
Stalin, Joseph
  Blum compared in Spain, 470
  Short Course in Communist Party
    History, 447
  wife's suicide, 433
Stanhope, Lord, 927, 940
Stanley, Oliver, 555, 627, 667, 676, 751, 784,
  822, 824, 834, 923, 926, 945, 956–57
Stapf, Col. Otto, 355
Starace, Achille, 59
Starflight, 713
Starhemberg, Prince Ernst von, 332
Stauffenberg, Claus von, 91
Stavisky, Serge, 114
Steel-Maitland, K. R. F., 197
Stehlin, Capt. Paul, 18, 712, 719, 905, 994
  German air support techniques, 258
  impressions of Daladier, 47
  International Commission meeting
    described, 907
  May crisis, 391 (see also May crisis)
  western fortifications, 854n.
Stein, Gertrude, 735
Stemmermann, Col. Wilhelm, 355
Stephanian, Georges, 111n.
Stevenson, Adlai, xi, 117
Stieff, Lt. Helmut, 91n.
Stimson, Henry L.
  Chinese "open door," 207–8

Stockinger, Fritz, 352
Stohrer, Ambassador, 868n.
Stojay, Dome. See Sztojay, Dome
Stoke Poges, 766
Storch (aircraft), 760 (see also Aircraft)
Storm troopers
  banned, 86
  Fritsch scandal, 319
  Night of the Long Knives, 93–94
    Mussolini's reaction, 158
  radical wing, 93
  Waffen SS-Wehrmacht conflict, 313–15
Stoyadinovitch, Dr. Milan, 194–95, 270
  Ciano's impressions of, 412, 416
  Italy's policies in Prague, 381
  See also Yugoslavia
Strachey, John, 197
Strachey, Lytton, 198
Strang, Sir William, 733, 779, 805, 814,
  819, 855, 919, 924
  Anglo-German post-Munich Agreement,
    59–60, 62
  atmosphere at Munich, 42
  conference proposals, 5–6
  Czech question memo, 621–24
  on Neville Chamberlain, 549
  See also Chamberlain, Neville;
    Munich—the Agreement;
    Munich—the Conference
Strasser, Gregor, 89
Straus, Jesse I., 135, 457
Stresa Conference (1932), 506
Stresa Front, 123, 125, 127, 159–60, 164–65
  Anglo-German Naval Agreement's effect
    on, 222
  Anschluss, 331, 334
  Ethiopian War, 225 (see also Ethiopian
    War)
Stresemann, Gustav, 82–83
  "fulfillment," 105
Strong, Kenneth, 889n., 905, 911, 990–91
  May crisis, 391 (see also May crisis)
Stronge, Lt. Col. H. C. T., 6, 663, 702, 785,
  992
  Czech fortifications, 399 (see also
    Fortifications)
  Czech morale, 888–89
Student, Gen. Kurt, 712–13, 911, 990 (see
  also Airborne troops)
Stuka (aircraft), 713, 758, 987 (see also
  Aircraft; Luftwaffe)
Stülpnagel, Gen. Karl-Heinrich von, 718,
  723
Stumpf, General, 865
Submarines, 486–87

Anglo-German Naval Agreement, 221–22
  (*see also* Anglo-German Naval
  Agreement)
German construction, 256–57 (*see also*
  Navies—Germany)
German parity begun, 940–41
Spanish Civil War, 289–90, 557, 564–65
  (*see also* Spanish Civil War)
Sudetenland
  Anglo-French plan, 778–84
  Czech reaction and acceptance, 784–94
  public opinion, 832 (*see also* Public
    opinion)
  Roosevelt's reaction, 846–48
annexation proposals, 6–7
  Hitler's demands, 7–8
Asch-Eger incident, 800–1, 810–11
Beneš-Hodža plan, 407–8
British press concessions, 652–54
cession to Germany, 803
  Beneš's proposal, 777–78
  journalistic opinion, 778 (*see also*
    Journalistic opinion)
  Runciman report, 797–98
  Times, The, 528
  transfer, 795, 796, 798
creation of, 73–74
crisis summed up, 896–97
Dominions' reaction to crisis, 773–75
Freikorps, 745, 796, 798–99, 828, 895
  Asch-Eger incident, 800–1, 810–11,
    812, 819
  creation as blunder, 896
  SS reinforced, 864
German moral rights to, 980–81
Godesberg meeting. *See* Godesberg
  memorandum
Halifax-Cadogan timetable, 882–83, 884,
  888
Henlein, Konrad, 194, 377–78, 380, 721,
  727, 745, 906, 955
  Karlsbad demands, 388, 402, 507, 844
  London visit, 654
  Reich Commissioner, 912
  seven-point program, 405–6
Henleinists, 196, 399–403, 905
  Asch-Eger incident, 800–1, 810–11
  occupation behavior, 910
Hitler-Chamberlain meeting (first),
  739–43
Nazi party within, 193–94
occupation, 910–14
plebiscite proposals, 735–37, 801, 804,
  807–8, 844–45
  French opposition, 779–80

See also Plebiscites
Polish price for neutrality, 422–23
riots, 677
Runciman mission, 403–10
Sudeten German Party
  complaints against Czechs, 378
  motivations and demands, 399–403
  policy, 380
self-determination proposed. *See*
  Self-determination
See also Czechoslovakia; Hitler, Adolf;
  Minority populations; Wehrmacht
Suez Canal, 813, 998
  and Ethiopian war, 124–25, 161–62,
    224–25 (*see also* Ethiopian War)
Surits, Jakob, 178, 450
Suvich, Fulvio, 153
Svehla, Antonin, 193
Swinton, Lord, 555, 603–4, 837, 926, 996
  biography, 643–44
  RAF, schemes for growth, 640–42
Syrový, Gen. Jan, 57, 786, 790, 799, 880,
  910
Szembek, Count Jean, 189
Sztojay, Dome, 415, 801

T

Talleyrand, Charles Maurice de, 502
Tanks, 694, 932
  Czechoslovakia, 991–92
  Estienne's predictions, 108–9
  French, 986
    Army thinking, 492–93 (*see also*
      Army—France)
  German, 986
    advances, 256
Tardieu, André, 107
Tatarescu, George, 414, 484
Tavs, Dr. Leopold, 339
Taylor, A.J.P., 995
  Czech-Polish wartime fates compared,
    1001–2
  German moral rights to Sudetenland,
    980–81
  Hossbach Conference, 304–5
  Munich Agreement described, xii
Tegetthoff, Wilhelm von, 343
Temps, Le, 778
  Franco-Czech treaty, 507
Ten-Year Rule, 201, 203, 209, 590, 997
  (*see also* Armaments—British)
Teplitz-Schönau, 828

Territorial Army. *See* Army—Great Britain
Teschen, 796, 802–3, 843, 861, 880, 993, 1002
  cession, 917–18
  Czech attack on, 184
  German-Polish relations, 422 (*see also* Danzig; Polish Corridor)
  Holland scare, 947
Te Water, Charles, 772, 838, 883 (*see also* Dominions)
Third Communist International. *See* Comintern
Thomas, James P. L., 559, 562, 563, 568
Thorez, Maurice, 116, 140, 180
Tilea, Virgil, 960, 973
Times, The, 600, 636, 643, 670–71, 685, 728, 805, 838, 851n., 853, 889, 960
  cession of Sudetenland, 528
  Hoare-Laval agreement, 232
  See also Dawson, Geoffrey; Journalistic opinion
Tirpitz, Grand Adm. von, 81
Tiso, Josef, 193, 956
Titulescu, Nicholas, 135, 194
Tizard, Sir Henry, 219
Todt, Dr. Fritz, 686–89, 703–5, 876 (*see also* Fortifications—West Wall)
Toscanini, Arturo, 351
Toussaint, Gen. Rudolf, 2, 453, 663
  May crisis, 391 (*see also* May crisis)
  Sudeten annexation proposed, 6
Toynbee, Arnold, 243
Trade agreements
  German-Russian, 175, 178, 976
  Russo-Italian, 178
Training, German air crews, 993–94
Translators. *See* Kirkpatrick, Ivone; Schmidt, Paul Otto
Treaties
  Anglo-German Naval Agreement, 220–24
    denounced, 973
    See also Anglo-German Naval Agreement
  Anglo-Italian Agreement, 381–82, 511, 543, 544, 582–83, 939
  Anti-Comintern Pact, 260–61 (*see also* Comintern)
  Austro-German agreement, 334–37
  Brest-Litovsk, 170–71
  Czech-Soviet mutual assistance, 99, 100–2, 179, 196, 378, 418, 449–50, 841–42, 734
  European alliances post-World War I, 2–3
  Four Power Pact (1933), 119, 153–55

  Franco-Czech, 111, 192–93, 782
    French repudiation, 789, 792
  Franco-Polish, 111, 450, 969
  Franco-Soviet mutual assistance, 99, 121, 127, 130, 165, 174, 179, 418, 734
    major weakness, 454
  Franco-Yugoslav, 111, 413
  German-Czech arbitration, 787–88
  German-Italian-Japanese agreement, 268–71 (*see also* Tripartite Pact)
  German-Polish mutual nonaggression, 95–96, 188, 418
    denounced, 974
  German-Slovakian, 956
  German-Soviet nonaggression, 977
  Hungarian-Italian friendship, 150
  Lausanne, 149
  Lithuania-Germany, 963
  London (1915), 143–44
  Pact of Steel, 974
  Polish-British-French, 977
  Polish-Rumanian mutual assistance, 185
  Rapallo, 80, 174, 187
  Riga, 172, 185
  Rumanian-German, 962
  Russo-Polish nonaggression, 187, 418, 843
  St. Germain, 72–73
  Sino-Soviet nonaggression, 442
  Tilsit, 75
  Trianon, 72–73, 193
  Tripartite Pact, 261, 952–54
  Triple Alliance, 143
  Versailles. *See* Versailles Treaty
  Washington (1922), 204–5
  Yugoslav-Bulgarian friendship, 411–12
  Yugoslav-Italian nonaggression, 195
Trenchard, Sir Hugh, 201
  Royal Air Force, 206
  See also Trenchard-Weir doctrine
Trenchard-Weir doctrine, 236, 608, 645, 648 (*see also* Douhet, Giulio)
Trentino, 143–44
Tresckow, Gen. Henning von, 91n.
Tripartite Pact, 261, 952–54
Troost, Paul Ludwig, 25
Trotsky, Leon, 170
Troup, Rear Adm. J. A. G., 728
Troyanovsky, Alexander, 449
Tuka, Vojtech, 955
Tukachevsky, Gen. Mikhail, 172, 175, 177
  career and purge described, 435–37
  See also Purges
Turkey, British guarantees, 972–73
  Italy's claims, 144, 149

U

Udet, Ernst, 257, 720, 757–58, 760 (*see also* Lindbergh, Col. Charles A.; Luftwaffe; Vuillemin, Gen. Joseph)
Ukraine and *Lebensraum,* 4
Ulyanov, Vladimir Ilyich. *See* Lenin, Nikolai
Union of South Africa. *See* South Africa
Union policy resolution, 774
United Party, 774
United States
    conference proposals, 4–5
    public opinion on Germany, 769 (*see also* Public opinion)
    Soviet Union recognized, 179
Usaramo, 276

V

Valle, Gen. Giuseppe, 876
Vanaman, Maj. Arthur, 760
Vansittart, Sir Robert, 162, 169, 779, 810, 813, 819, 855, 887, 965n.
    Britain's Japanese policy, 208
    British rearmament policies, 233–34 (*see also* Armaments—British)
    Ethiopian War, 227, 231 (*see also* Ethiopian War)
    Franco-Soviet military pact, 514
    German expansion, 621–22
    Germanophobia, 241
    International Commission proceedings, 923
Vayo, Alvarez del, 538
Ventzov, General, 512
Versailles Treaty
    armament provisions, 74–76
    English reaction to, 200
    Fourteen Points described and criticized, 70–71
    French and German views of, 69–70, 76
    Italian memories of, 144
    John Maynard Keynes's judgment on, 76
    Military Inter-Allied Commission of Control, 75
    signing of, 69
    territorial provision, 72–74
    U.S. responsibility for infirmities, 69–70
    verdict on, 76
    war guilt clause, 71
    See also League of Nations; Treaties
Vichy regime, 108, 125, 127, 1001
    Riom trial, 471
    See also Laval, Pierre; Pétain, Marshal Philippe
Victor Emmanuel, King
    Emperor of Ethiopia, 164
    Fascists' rise to power, 147–48
    Hitler-Mussolini discussions, 35
    Mussolini's homecoming post-Munich, 59
Viebahn, Gen. Max von, 325
Vier Jahreszeiten Hotel, 18, 58
Vilna. *See* Lithuania
Vinci-Gigliucci, Count Luigi, 160
Vishinsky, Andrei
    show trials, 431 (*see also* Purges; Show trials)
Vladivostok, 171
Völkischer Beobachter, 324
Voroshilov, Marshal Klimenti, 177, 435
    and Yezhov, 437 (*see also* Purges)
Vuillemin, Gen. Joseph, 489–90, 524, 728, 765
    Luftwaffe visit, 719–20
    See also Air Forces—French; Luftwaffe

W

Wagner, Winifred, 702
Wagner-Jauregg, Dr., 341
Waldenfels, Baron von, 897
Walloons
    flamand-wallon schism, 472, 475
Wangenheim, Lt. von, 317
War
    Cadogan, Sir Alexander, 625
    Chamberlain's feelings, 553–54
    Jodl's writings, 387
    Kennedy, Joseph P., 767
War criminals, 71
War guilt clause. *See* Versailles Treaty
Warlimont, Lt. Col. Walter, 282, 746, 905, 907
Washington Treaty (1922)
    capital ship ratios, 204–5
Watergate, 923
Watson-Watt, Robert A., 219
We, 755
Weather
    effect on Luftwaffe, 993
Wehrmacht
    Army
        anti-Nazi trial, 84–85
        composition, 706–7
        deployment, Case Green, 707–9
        See also Army—Germany
    Austrian military amalgamated, 371–73

Blomberg-Fritsch scandals, 3▮▮▮,
   327–30
British Chiefs of Staff report, 833
Case Green
   Hitler on prospects, 387–88
   Jodl's new draft, 389–90, 394–95
   outlined, 386
   See also Case Green
Case White directive, 969
Chiefs of Staff and Hitler meeting,
   696–99
Czech liquidation directives, 935, 936,
   941–42
Czech march-in, 955
growth, 255–59
Hitler as Commander-in-Chief, 321–22
Hitler on role of, 314
interservice rivalries, 296–98
May crisis, 390–95 (*see also* May crisis)
military attitudes summarized, 258–59
Navy
   Case Green, 713
   program, 256–57
   See also Navies—Germany
occupation zones, 899
order of battle, 1005–7
Reichswehr becomes, 98
Reichswehr-Red Army contacts, 95,
   175–77, 435, 446
reorganization, 321–30, 386–87
   Red Army purges compared, 438–39
senior generals' conference, 692–94
Sudeten occupation, 910 (*see also*
   Sudetenland)
tank warfare advances, 256
Waffen SS conflict, 313–15
Weichs, Gen. Maximilian von, 725, 912n.
   "Otto," 335
Weimar
   Hitler's anti-British speech, 935–36 (*see*
     also Speeches)
Weimar Republic
   chancellors
     Adolf Hitler, 90–94
     Franz von Papen, 87–89
     Heinrich Brüning, 83, 84
     Hermann Müller, 83
     Kurt von Schleicher, 89–91
   creation, 78
   early chancellors, 79
   presidencies
     Friedrich, Ebert, 78–81
     Hindenburg, 81–82
Weir, William Douglas

RAF rearmament, 236–38 (*see also*
   Trenchar-Weir doctrine)
Weizsaecker, Ernst von, 714–15, 743, 802,
   806, 808, 814, 816, 853, 868–69,
   892–93, 904–8, 913–14, 956, 972
   German aims in Spain, 293–94, 301 (*see*
     also Spanish Civil War)
   Munich agenda drawn, 20, 32
Welczeck, Count Johannes von, 476, 481,
   685
Welles, Sumner, 561, 889–90
Wellington, Duke of, 1003
   on Spain, 39
Werth, Alexander, 854
   August in France, 524
   Daladier's homecoming after Munich, 59
   France's February (1934) days, 115
   Franco-Soviet treaty, 127
   French people, 529
   Laval's German policy, 125
   Paris exodus, 878
Western Air Defense Zone, 687, 705, 709,
   725
West Wall. *See* Fortifications
Wever, Gen. Walther, 236n.
Weygand, Gen. Maxime, 104, 118
   Spanish Civil War, 494
   War Council composition, 108
Wheeler-Bennett, Sir John, 733, 985,
   995–96
   Hossbach Conference, 302
   Munich Agreement, xiv
White Paper
   Munich Agreement, 901
   omissions, 883
Widkum, Frau von, 758
Wiedemann, Capt. Fritz, 394, 658–59
Wietersheim, Gen. von, 697–98
Wilberg, Gen. Helmuth, 280
Wilmot, John, 204
Wilson, Edwin, 457, 1001n.
Wilson, Sir Horace, 607, 668, 670, 685,
   733–34, 743, 779, 804–5, 815, 819,
   834, 855, 882
   Berlin mission, 858, 862, 865, 870–75,
     877, 883, 897
   foreign policy role, 561–62
   Munich Conference
     memoirs, 30–33
     second meeting agenda drawn, 36–37
   on Neville Chamberlain, 549
Wilson, Pres. Woodrow
   armistice announcement, 69
   Rhineland plan reaction, 70
Winchell, Walter, 850

Windsor, Duke of, 298
  Hitler meeting, 265
  See also Edward VIII; Simpson, Mrs.
    Wallis
Winterton, Earl, 750–51, 783
Wise, Rabbi Stephen
  Munich Agreement described, xii
Wiskemann, Elizabeth, 397
Witzleben, Gen. Erwin von, 692, 717–18,
    866–67, 895, 943 (see also Halder
    plot)
Woermann, Dr. Ernst, 570, 653, 869, 941,
    955
Wohlthat, Helmuth, 962
Wood, Kingsley, 14, 644–45, 652, 667, 676,
    813, 832, 834, 850, 859, 929, 931,
    932n., 947, 968
World press. See Journalistic opinions
World War I. See First World War
World War II. See Second World War
Wrangel, Baron Piotr, 104, 171–72

Y

Yagoda, Genrikh, 433
Yague, Col. Blanco, 273
Yegorov, Marshal, 513
Yezhov, Nicolai, 432

Cent.   15_ ᵧₒ .ɩnmission (see also
    Purge..)
  Litvinov's characterization, 434, 437
Young Plan (1930), 83, 84, 106–7
Yudenitch, Nikolai, 171
Yugoslavia
  Bulgarian friendship treaty, 411–12
  French mutual defense pact, 111, 413
  independence, 72–73
  Italian nonaggression pact, 195
  Little Entente, 194–95, 411–18
  Stoyadinovitch's diplomacy, 411–14

Z

Zeebrugge naval raid, 851
Zeeland, Paul van, 137, 474
Zehner, Gen. Wilhelm
  murdered, 373
Zeitzler, Lt. Col. Kurt, 389
Zeligowski, Gen. 186
Zernatto, Guido, 341, 357
  escape, 366–67
  Fatherland Front, 341
  Hitler-Schuschnigg meeting, 346
Zetland, Lord, 568, 968
Zinoviev, Grigori, 173, 433
  letter of, 201

About the Author

Telford Taylor is a lawyer who served in Army intelligence during the Second World War and thereafter, as a brigadier general, represented the United States at the Nuremberg war crimes trials. Since then he has pursued a dual career as lawyer and writer. As a journalist he covered the Eichmann trial in Jerusalem for the London *Spectator,* and the 1972 "Christmas Bombing" of North Vietnam for NBC television and the New York *Times*. He has contributed articles to *Life, Saturday Evening Post, Harper's,* the New York *Times Magazine,* and many other periodicals, and published several books, including the widely acclaimed *Nuremberg and Vietnam: An American Tragedy*. In addition to practicing law, Mr. Taylor has taught at the Yale and Harvard law schools, and currently teaches at the Columbia and Benjamin Cardozo law schools. He resides in New York City.